THE
PEOPLE'S
PENSION

THE STRUGGLE TO DEFEND SOCIAL SECURITY SINCE REAGAN

ERIC LAURSEN

PRESS
EDINBURGH • OAKLAND • BALTIMORE

Advance Praise for *The People's Pension*:

"Laursen has given us a comprehensive account of the three decade long war against Social Security, beginning with its origins in the bowels of the Reagan administration. This is a fascinating history that progressives must learn, not only to protect Social Security but also to understand the dynamics behind an effective long-term strategy. It is remarkable that such a popular and successful program could actually have its survival called into question."
—Dean Baker, author of *Taking Economics Seriously*

"Defenders of Social Security owe Eric Laursen a great debt. In *The People's Pension* he has given us as thorough, illuminating—and disturbing—a look at the decades-long ideological attack on this all-important program as we are ever likely to get."
—Michael Hiltzik, author of *The New Deal: A Modern History*

"This magnificent history documents the hydra-headed campaign to cut and kill Social Security, conducted over decades by rightwing bankers, foundations, economists and politicians. It is a mark of Roosevelt's genius that he foresaw these endless battles, and built a System that could withstand so much propaganda for so long, while transforming life for the elderly in America. This book is utterly urgent as the war now comes to climax in an act of epic betrayal."
—James K. Galbraith, author of *The Predator State: How Conservatives Abandoned the Free Market and Why Liberals Should Too*

"Eric Lauren's *The People's Pension* is a wonderful book. He demonstrates that Social Security and other 'entitlements' were not benefits granted working people by a benevolent elite. Rather they were gains won through popular struggle by mass movements. Ever since, they have been protected by popular sentiment and support. How this happened, and how Social Security could be made even more radically democratic, is the subject of this fascinating book."
—Wayne Price, author of *The Abolition of the State*

"A magnificent and long-awaited volume that should mark a fundamental change in public thinking about the very nature of public goods."
—David Graeber, author of *Debt: The First 5,000 Years*

To the memory of
Lois Sherwin Laursen
July 13, 1927–July 4, 2004

The People's Pension: The Struggle to Defend Social Security Since Reagan
© 2012 Eric Laursen
This edition © 2012 AK Press (Oakland, Edinburgh, Baltimore)

ISBN-13: 978-1-84935-101-0 | Ebook ISBN: 978-1-84935-108-9
Library of Congress Control Number: 2012933068

AK Press   AK Press
674-A 23rd Street   PO Box 12766
Oakland, CA 94612   Edinburgh EH8 9YE
USA   Scotland
www.akpress.org   www.akuk.com
akpress@akpress.org   ak@akedin.demon.co.uk

The above addresses would be delighted to provide you with the latest AK
Press distribution catalog, which features the several thousand books, pamphlets, zines, audio and video products, and stylish apparel published and/
or distributed by AK Press. Alternatively, visit our web site for the complete
catalog, latest news, and secure ordering.

Visit us at www.akpress.org and www.revolutionbythebook.akpress.org.

Printed in the U.S. on acid-free, recycled paper
Indexed by Chris Dodge
Interior layout by Magpie Killjoy, birdsbeforethestorm.net

Cover photo, "Thousands of Irate Senior Citizens Protesting at Capitol," ©
Bettmann/CORBIS. Used by permission.

CONTENTS

IMAGE CREDITS

ACKNOWLEDG-MENTS

Pensions and retirement benefits are nobody's idea of a glamorous subject—unless, of course, you are counting on them to pull you through your elder years. Which would be more than ninety-five percent of the American people.

I first began writing about pensions in the mid-1990s, when I edited *Plan Sponsor*, a monthly magazine for pension executives. Inevitably, I had to familiarize myself with Social Security, since it forms the base retirement benefit for all private-sector American workers as well as many public employees. As these pages make clear, the Social Security debate reached its second great height during those years. I quickly became fascinated. My first and greatest debt, then, is to Charlie Ruffel, founder and former CEO of Asset International, which publishes *Plan Sponsor*, and who is now a partner at Kudu Advisors. Journalist, entrepreneur, raconteur, colleague, and friend for more than twenty-five years, Charlie allowed me to take on this daunting subject with no intellectual or partisan preconceptions or preconditions. I hope he enjoys the result.

Two economists and writers, James K. Galbraith and Dean Baker, have encouraged and supported this book, practically from the start and in countless ways. I am most grateful for their advice, feedback, and friendship throughout this long but rewarding process.

The People's Pension is informed by interviews and correspondence with hundreds of people. The two most extraordinary individuals who took the time to help me have since died: Robert M. Ball and Robert J. Myers were practically synonymous with the history of Social Security almost from its beginning. They shaped its development even after retrenchment set in during the mid-1970s. Both provided me with information and perspectives that no one else could have offered. For anyone with an active interest in and regard for Social Security, Bob Ball and Bob Myers are greatly missed. Others who provided valuable help and are no longer with us are Edward Gramlich, former Rep. J.J. Pickle, John Trout, and Sam Beard. I regret that they will not see the results of our discussions.

Early on, I received valuable advice, perspectives, and suggestions from individuals including Martin Mayer, Al Ehrbar, Edward Berkowitz, Terry Devine, and Michelle Varnhagen. Three individuals were particularly important: Dallas Salisbury, for his deep knowledge and understanding of the retirement benefits field; William Arnone, for his keen political analysis and experience as a pension advocate; and Moshe Adler, for his economic insight. I am especially grateful for Moshe's help in developing my own perspective on the economics of social insurance and retirement benefits, not to mention our long friendship. For innumerable tips, suggestions, and assistance early in the process, I am happy to thank Karen Ferguson at the Pension Rights Center and Virginia Reno, Catherine Hill, and others at the National Academy of Social Insurance.

Daniel Béland, a fine scholar of social policy, generously offered me his thoughts and perspective on the period covered in this book. Other friends and comrades whose advice and viewpoints helped me include David Graeber, Anne Kornhauser, Jeremy Varon, and especially, Merton C. Bernstein, who probably knows as much about Social Security as anyone alive.

Sources and interviewees who were especially generous with their time and effort include Nancy Altman, Steven J. Entin, Teresa Ghilarducci, Roger Hickey, Eric Kingson, David Langer, John Mueller, Jane Bryant Quinn, Hans Riemer, Bruce Schobel, William Shipman, Rep. Jan Schakowsky, and Lawrence Thompson. I would also like to single out for their help Andrew Biggs, Alan Blinder, Peter Diamond, Peter Ferrara, Stephen Goss, Robert Greenstein, Laurence Kotlikoff, former Sen. Bob Kerrey, Phillip Longman, Tom Mattzie, Alicia Munnell, Peter Orszag, Peter G. Peterson, Robert Reischauer, Stanford Ross, Roger Sanjek, Donna Shalala, Gene Sperling, and Lisa Witter.

I am especially grateful for the time and care that former Rep. Bill Archer applied to recalling for me his role in the Social Security debate during the second Clinton administration, and to David Lindeman and Sylvester J. Schieber for their recollections and their analysis of the politics of Social Security. Finally, I am grateful for the news, opinions, passion, and good humor of the members of GoogleGroups' Social Insurance email list.

While most other sources are cited in the notes, others who contributed are not, but deserve to be mentioned here as their comments were especially helpful: Nancy Alexander, Michael Astrue, Nancy Birdsall, Donna Butts, Sharon Daly, David Ellerman, Sandy Fisk, Richard Fontenrose, Mike Foudy, Steven

Hanke, Kenneth J. Kies, Steve Kofahl, Jeffrey Liebman, Derrick Max, Olivia Mitchell, Guy Molyneaux, Eileen Parlow, Jill Quadagno, Witold Skwierczynski, David Smick, Lawrence H. Summers, Ruy Teixeira, and David Wilcox.

I am extremely grateful to Blue Mountain Center and The Mesa Refuge, which gave me the opportunity to write portions of this book in beautiful surroundings and among wonderful groups of writers and artists who provided some of its first substantial critical reaction. I would also like to thank the New York Public Library for giving me space in the Wertheim Room to do research in the library's holdings. Most especially, I am grateful to the Social Security Administration for access to the tremendous collection housed in the Historian's Office—and for the generous help of historian Larry DeWitt, the best friend of every student of this subject.

This book was supported entirely by my income as a freelance writer and editor. Freelancing can be lonely work, and I have benefited hugely from the friendship and common-sense advice of Christopher Cardinale and the rest of the Autonolistas of New York City. In overt as well as more subtle ways, this book has also benefited from my own simultaneous political activism. I am especially grateful to all my comrades in the New York City Direct Action Network, the New York Metro Alliance of Anarchists, No Blood for Oil, and the New York City chapter of the War Resisters League.

DePauw University (thanks to Keith Nightenhelser); Middlebury College (Linus Owens); The New Space, New York City (Seth Weiss); and the New America Foundation provided opportunities to bring some of my ideas and findings before live audiences. Friends and colleagues who have listened, commented, and put up with this project include Meryl Altman, Mary Baine Campbell, Kate Crane, John Dearborn, Richard and Margery Dearborn, Jeremy Feldman, Brooke Lehman, Joe Markulin and Lynne LeBrasseur, Bram Moreinis, Chuck Morse, Jesse Nahan, Ian and Melissa O'Brien, Sanchia Playfair, Fionn Reilly, Nick Romanenko and Debbie Goodsite, Tina Ruyter, Ben Shephard, Paul Smart and Fawn Potash, Seth Tobocman, Tom Vinciguerra, and—especially—David Wyner. I regret that the estimable Dan Rosenblatt and the inimitable Michael Shenker are no longer alive to read *The People's Pension*.

Anyone interested in delving further—if you dare!—can visit my blog, at HTTP://PEOPLESPENSION.INFOSHOP.ORG/BLOGS-MU/. I am grateful to Chuck Munson for helping me create and manage the blog, along with his continuing great work at INFOSHOP.ORG.

AK Press, my publisher, has been consistently enthusiastic, helpful, professional, and committed to this book since first getting wind of it. Zach Blue, Kate Khatib, and Lorna Vetters have worked hard every step of the way to make this book as good as it can be. Please support brave and tireless independent publishers like AK Press.

This book would never have come about without the love, support, patience, and faith of three people. My father, Robert Laursen, grew up during the Great Depression. He lived through the Dust Bowl. He remembers the Townsend Clubs, Share Our Wealth, and much of the mass movement that stirred Social Security into being. This book was written, in part, to suggest that that spirit still lives. Tom Laursen, my brother, has been my best friend and exemplar from the day he came home from the hospital. I hope he will enjoy the product of what was, for me, an intensely rewarding, engrossing, and often fun journey.

The third person is Mary V. Dearborn—scholar, biographer, gardener, passionate reader, and my life companion. Not a word of this book left our home without her reading and, if necessary, critiquing it. She was there to celebrate, commiserate, and comment, every step of the process. I hope that *The People's Pension* rewards her love and faith.

PROLOGUE

I. "Everything? Everything."

"To preserve the benefits of what is called civilized life,
and to remedy, at the same time, the evils it has produced,
ought to be considered as one of the first objects of reformed
legislation."

—*Thomas Paine*[1]

"Sir, is everything on the table for this?"

"Everything is on the table. That's how this thing is going to work."

When Barack Obama briefly answered a reporter's question at the end of a February 18, 2010, White House press conference, everyone in the small world known as "Washington"—lawmakers, their staffs, lobbyists, policy wonks, executive-branch officeholders—knew what the president meant by "everything."

He had just signed an executive order creating the National Commission on Fiscal Responsibility and Reform, and introduced its co-chairs. The objective of the new panel, he said, was to "produce clear recommendations on how to cover the costs of all federal programs by 2015, and to meaningfully improve our long-term fiscal picture." America was afflicted with "chronic deficits" and a rapidly rising national debt burden. "Without action," Obama said, "the accumulated weight … will hobble our economy, it will cloud our future, and it will saddle every child in America with an intolerable burden."

If "everything" was "on the table," that would include government-sponsored health care programs, especially Medicare* and Medicaid. It would include the defense budget, which was bulging to support an open-ended U.S. commitment to two Middle East military occupations. It probably would include restructuring the tax code.

But to most people paying attention that day, "everything" mostly meant Social Security, the nation's old-age income support program.

In its search for savings, the president's commission "could begin with Social Security, which oddly enough has gone from being the 'third rail of American politics' to the low-hanging fruit," suggested Robert Bixby, director of the Concord Coalition, a group that had been campaigning for deficit reduction for close to twenty years.

Social Security would contribute not at all to reducing the deficit over the next five years—and even longer. Meeting the program's long-term obligations would be nowhere near as difficult, either, as reducing the soaring cost of health care in the U.S. But finding a way to cut Social Security benefits "would be a confidence builder with our foreign lenders," argued Pete Peterson, the eminent Wall Street banker whose crusade against deficits went back nearly thirty years.[2]

Sixteen months later, the president's commission handed in its report, calling for long-term cutbacks that would reduce Social Security to a shadow of the powerful anti-poverty program it had become. The right-wing populist "Tea Party" movement had helped sweep a Republican majority into control of the House of Representatives, knocking the Obama administration off balance and setting up a series of humiliating capitulations by the White House on spending cuts and taxes. When Republican leaders demanded another round of drastic cuts in exchange for raising the limit on borrowing by the federal government—essentially, holding hostage the government's ability to function from day to day—Obama decided it was time to offer them "something big."

If the GOP would agree to some tax increases, Obama was prepared to raise the age at which older workers qualified for Medicare, and cut Medicare benefits for more affluent recipients. He would also cut Social Security—a little at first, more and more over time—by changing the formula used to calculate benefits. Within a dozen years, current retirees—millions of them

---

* Medicare, like Social Security, was targeted for cutbacks, phase-out, and even privatization during the period this book covers. However, the issues Medicare faced were more closely tied to the problems of the U.S. health care system generally and were significantly different from those facing Social Security. Therefore, I have chosen in this book to focus on Social Security's political history since 1980, except where the connection with Medicare is especially close.

living on just the right side of the poverty line—would feel the pinch. Within decades, the real value of Social Security would decline such that it would be ineffective at keeping future generations of retirees out of poverty. Both the Medicare and Social Security proposals had been recommended by the president's commission.

Politically, Social Security "reform" would amount to an earthquake. Social Security has historically been by far the largest income support program in the U.S. and a necessity for the 95% of American workers who participate in the above-ground economy. Some 54 million people were receiving benefits in 2010, including 37 million retirees and their dependents, 6 million survivors of deceased workers, and 10 million disabled workers and their households. In total, they collected $713 billion from the program. About 157 million people paid a total of $781 billion in payroll taxes to support those benefits.[3]

Republican opposition to Social Security was well known, stretching back to the beginning of the program. If Obama—a Democratic president—was really ready to consider significant reductions in benefits, however, he would be cutting himself off from his party's New Deal/Great Society legacy, the edifice of public-welfare benefits that the federal government constructed between the Great Depression and the Reagan Revolution to address the social disruptions of a mass, industrial society. No wonder, then, that progressive Democrats—many of whom had been defending Social Security from attack for decades—greeted Obama's offer to Republican leaders as a monstrous

Pres. Obama signs the executive order creating the National Commission on Fiscal Responsibility and Reform, February 18, 2010. Standing, from left: Vice President Joe Biden, co-chairs Erskine Bowles and Alan Simpson.

betrayal. "We are facing the greatest threat EVER to the future of the New Deal and Great Society programs. And now, sadly, it's a bipartisan threat," warned Maya Rockeymoore, a well-known Washington social policy analyst, in an email to Social Security supporters.

Some of the most powerful elements of the Democratic Party, it seemed, were now ready to combine forces to upend more than seven decades of public commitment to the elderly. "We've got to educate the American people at the same time we educate the President of the United States," John Conyers, the civil rights veteran, longtime House member from Detroit, and founder of the Congressional Black Caucus, told reporters. "The Republicans, [House] Speaker [John] Boehner or Majority Leader [Eric] Cantor *did not* call for Social Security cuts in the budget deal. *The President of the United States called for that.*" Conyers added, "My response to [Obama] is *to mass thousands of people in front of the White House to protest this.*"

The coalition of labor organizations and advocacy groups that had been defending Social Security, some of them for decades—the Campaign for America's Future, the Alliance of Retired Americans, the National Committee to Preserve Social Security and Medicare, MoveOn.org, and others—threw themselves into a series of campaigns using all the tools of public pressure: rallies, letter- and email-writing, radio and television ads, calls to Congress and the White House. Polls proclaimed, as they almost always did, working Americans' devotion to Social Security and their opposition to any attempt to cut it as a way to shrink the deficit.

The defenders won—temporarily, at least. When Obama and Republican lawmakers at last sealed a deal to raise the debt ceiling at the end of July, the first round of spending cuts—Obama obtained not one dime of higher tax revenues—spared Social Security. However, the deal also created a joint congressional committee charged with lining up a second round of deficit reduction, which Congress would then be obliged to vote on with no changes. The committee would be free to consider Social Security cuts along with anything else it pleased.

If the program survived, it would be thanks to the broad public support it had always commanded. But not entirely. A Democratic president had made an offer to cut Social Security to a House Republican leadership filled with people who had criticized and even condemned the program for years. The Republicans had decided not to take up Obama's offer, for two reasons: First, they were dead set against any tax increases. Second, the president wasn't offering enough. Not for the first time, many friends of Social Security asked themselves which was the greatest threat to the program: a Republican president bent on restructuring it out of existence, or a Democratic president ready to do the same, only more gradually—and with the built-in goodwill, going back to Social Security's origins in the New Deal era, to cushion the attempt politically.

"The reality is that liberals should be sending Eric Cantor a fruit basket," wrote the *Washington Post*'s Ezra Klein. "It's increasingly clear that he has … saved them from a deal they'd hate."

* * *

The story that unfolds in the following chapters—a story of thirty years of American political life—is populated with episodes like this one: of deals made and not made, of ideological grandstanding and self-righteousness, of spin control aimed at inoculating politicians from the public response to their own ruthlessness. The scenario plays itself out over and over: Republicans and center-right Democrats search for common ground that can offer them a way to cut Social Security without having to pay the political price. They encounter fierce opposition from liberal or progressive Democrats—and, for the most part, lose. But for how long? Each time, the movement against Social Security acquires new financial backers, new political champions, and an ever more urgent tone.

Caught in the middle is a program set up to provide a basic income for retirees, the disabled, and their dependents. For over seventy years, it has been a fundamental element of American workers' lives.

Social Security, along with its later offspring, Medicare, also formed the glue that, for much of that period, held together the New Deal coalition—a loose political alliance including organized labor, southern farmers, African-Americans, Latinos, and women. A sizable chunk of the middle class knew they owed their prosperity to the opportunities afforded them by government programs, from Social Security to the GI Bill to subsidized home loans. That coalition had helped the Democratic Party dominate Congress and largely set the public policy agenda, even when Republicans occupied the White House, during the half-century starting August 14, 1935—the sweltering summer day, just a few months short of seventy-five years before Obama's press conference, when Franklin Delano Roosevelt signed the Social Security Act into law.

Even after the New Deal alliance began to splinter, Social Security remained the country's most popular social program, the Democrats' ace in the hole at election time, and a constant temptation and peril for Republicans. All along, the program's supporters insisted that because Social Security was funded by its own dedicated tax—the payroll tax, which nearly every worker in the above-ground economy paid out of his or her paycheck—it wasn't like other social spending, and shouldn't be part of any discussion of how to balance the rest of the government's books. Social Security wasn't just another federal program, either. It was social insurance: a collective possession of all American workers, who earned their old-age, disability, and survivors' benefits by paying for those of the preceding generation.

The story of how that consensus gradually broke down starts with another effort to put "everything on the table" in the name of deficit cutting. When Reagan administration officials in 1981 proposed drastic cutbacks in early-retirement benefits under Social Security, which they said were necessary to reduce the overall federal deficit, they ran into a political firestorm. Republicans lost heavily in the next year's midterm congressional elections, Reagan was forced to accept a compromise plan to bolster Social Security's funding, and the country's most popular conservative leader backed off any attempt to change the program for the rest of his presidency.

Thirty years later, Washington was quite a different place. Instead of a unique, semi-independent social insurance system, politicians of the right and center-right saw Social Security as just another item on the government's balance sheet—eminently vulnerable if not easily cuttable. To adopt this viewpoint was actually considered a sign of seriousness as a statesperson, and of independence from special interests like the Gray Lobby and organized labor. Social Security had to be cut because it was the hub of a collection of "entitlements"—programs that automatically paid benefits unless Congress enacted laws to stop them. These entitlements increasingly outran "discretionary" spending—everything from the military budget to national parks, which lawmakers needed to approve each year in its budget.

Decades of tax cuts, wage stagnation, and rising imbalance between entitlements and discretionary spending had swollen the federal deficit to the point where it was expected to hit $1.5 trillion in 2011. That would equal 9.8% of gross domestic product (the statistic used to represent the whole U.S. economy)—close to a sixty-five-year high, according to the Congressional Budget Office. Deficits would decline for the rest of the decade as the economy—presumably—recovered. But it would shoot up after 2021 as expenses associated with the baby boom generation's retirement kicked in.* Social Security would play a large role in this drama. Together with Medicare and Medicaid, it would make up nearly 70% of all mandatory federal spending in 2011, growing to 80% by 2021. Social Security benefits alone would equal 4.8% of GDP in 2011, rising to 5.3% by 2021.[4]

What was to be done? Strict free-market conservatives argued that the only way to fend off fiscal Armageddon was to privatize the entitlements, fully or partially. Workers should have the right to shift a portion of their payroll taxes into private investment accounts, in exchange for a cut in benefits. Center-right Democrats were reluctant to go that far, but many envisioned letting workers set up government-sponsored investment accounts separate from Social Security, balanced out by benefit cuts. The result in both cases would be the same: steadily lower Social Security payments, relieving long-term pressure on the federal budget and gradually shifting the responsibility for retirement income, disability, and survivors' support from the program to individual workers and their households. Congress would reduce the burden of benefits by lowering them for higher-income individuals; cutting the formula, based on growth in wages, that the Social Security Administration used to adjust benefits each year; and gradually raising the retirement age.

---

* The Administration on Aging of the Department of Health and Human Services defines the baby boomers as Americans born between 1946 and 1964. Most businesses that sell to this population, as well as non-profits that offer them services, and academic institutions and think tanks that study them, use a roughly similar time frame.

The beauty of this was that one could argue for benefit cuts that would gradually shrink Social Security to the point of insignificance or perhaps oblivion, and justify doing so by pointing out that this was necessary to keep the program from going broke. To save Social Security, in other words, it was necessary to destroy it.

Republicans and center-right Democrats had been gradually coalescing around this scenario for several years—ever since President George W. Bush had disastrously attempted to sell a scheme to partially privatize Social Security to Congress and the public in 2005. Five years later, with the economy still recovering from its worst slump since the Great Depression, the deficit was reaching its highest level since the Second World War and the struggle to bring it down had taken on the aura of a moral crusade. Cutting Social Security benefits would be essential to the task.

Soon after Obama signed his commission into being, one of the commission's co-chairs, Erskine Bowles, gave a speech in which he said that in pursuit of smaller deficits, "We're going to mess with Medicare, Medicaid, and Social Security because if you take those off the table, you can't get there. If we don't make those choices, America is going to be a second-rate power and I don't mean in fifty years. I mean in my lifetime."

Legislating for Social Security had always been a bipartisan project, because in the end, Republican lawmakers, no less than their Democratic counterparts, wanted to be seen as supporting the people who depended on it. But the meaning of bipartisanship had changed. In the decades when Social Security was growing and evolving to meet the changing needs of American workers—from 1935 to roughly the mid-1970s—Democratic congressional leaders could always rely on a solid group of GOP lawmakers who would work with them to improve and expand benefits. By 2010, the dynamic had reversed: Republican leaders nurturing ambitions to cut Social Security—or to enact other deficit-cutting measures—allied themselves with a small but influential caucus of center-right Democratic deficit hawks.

Three sides, not two, now disputed the future of Social Security. Winding down the program and replacing it with private investment accounts—"choice," in conservative parlance—was now a fundamental Republican principle. That created a pivotal role for the Democratic center-right, which included such figures as Pat Moynihan, Joe Lieberman, and—at times—Bill Clinton as well as the Federal Reserve chair and the Treasury secretary of whichever party was in power. These deficit hawks had no popular constituency other than the major banks and bond investors that funded their electoral campaigns. Controlling inflation and maintaining the value of their enormous Treasury bond holdings was of paramount importance to these interests. But the deficit hawks also commanded great respect from the elite Washington press corps, which they used to argue for a virtuous-sounding politics of austerity: running budget surpluses, cutting the national debt, and keeping inflation down. They were also determined to rein in programs like Social Security, which they feared would become more costly in succeeding decades and thus require the government to borrow more and, perhaps, raise taxes.

Republicans could only hope to phase out Social Security by allying themselves with this largely Democratic center-right. The mainstream media accepted the deficit hawks' pose as "post-partisan" good citizens, and so provided necessary cover for the more ideologically transparent Republicans, who otherwise would seem to be attacking Social Security for purely political reasons. As a result, Social Security was often safer from attack during periods when a Republican was president and these Democratic centrists were less likely to make common cause with the other party.

Left out of this dynamic were progressive Democrats, most prominent among them Senate Majority Leader Harry Reid and Speaker of the House Nancy Pelosi, who continued to defend Social Security. To the annoyance of the Republicans and the deficit hawk faction, they denounced the dismantling of the New Deal legacy, undermining, in the view of their opponents, a virtuous effort to rein in federal deficits by "demagoguing" the sensitive issue of retirement benefits.

But very few in Washington believed that if Social Security was restructured as part of a deficit-cutting package, the savings from cutting the program wouldn't be used to make room for something else—say, continuing the low tax rates for high-income Americans that the Bush administration had enacted. "These politicians see Social Security as a piggy bank that can be used to pay for their failed economic policies," Rep. Barbara Lee of California observed.[5]

Progressives argued that most of the $1.5 trillion deficit expected for the fiscal year 2011* was caused by three factors:

- The massive tax reductions the Bush administration had pushed through Congress earlier in the decade;

- The cost of maintaining a huge U.S. military presence in the Middle East, including mounting bills for veterans' benefits; and

- The impact of the economic slump that began in 2008, including the cost of bailing out large banks and other financial institutions.

To cover the cost, total federal debt held by the public would have to rise to $10.4 trillion by the end of 2011. That would equal 69.4% of GDP, according to the CBO, the highest proportion since 1950. If the economy didn't turn around and tax revenues didn't improve, those numbers could get much worse.

But, as progressives had been arguing for years, far from aggravating the deficit dilemma, Social Security helped to moderate it. That's because the

---

* According to federal government practice, "fiscal year 2011" covers the period from October 1, 2010, to September 30, 2011.

proceeds of workers' payroll tax contributions went into two trust funds that were invested in U.S. Treasury bonds—$2.4 trillion worth in 2009–10. The proceeds from those Treasury bond purchases could then be used by the government, along with its other tax revenues, to pay for everything from aircraft carriers to highway repair to AIDS research. For the past twenty years, in other words, the Social Security trust funds had been "masking" a portion of the federal deficit by loaning money to the Treasury to cover its everyday expenses.

That was projected to end in 2036, by which date some 70 million baby boomers would have retired, nearly doubling the elderly population and draining the trust funds. Since, by law, Social Security isn't allowed to borrow money, it would then have to get by on just what its payroll tax collections brought in each year. Congress could make up the difference, but only if it wanted to. If not, the Social Security Administration (SSA) estimated the program could continue paying only a little less than 80% of normal benefits.

That would certainly be a problem, progressives argued, but not as serious a one as the program's critics claimed. The ratio of workers to retirees was expected to decline from 3-to-1 to 2-to-1 by 1990. It had already dropped from 18-to-1 in 1950 to 4-to-1 in 1965 without precipitating a disaster—even though government spending on education, social services, and the Cold War was expanding fast at the same time. That's because worker productivity, and average wages, continued to go up—increasing the payroll tax revenues that support Social Security.

Besides, cutting benefits wasn't the only way, or the best way, to deal with an aging population.[6] First of all, the 2037 end-date for the trust fund surplus was an actuarial projection, not prophecy—and one that had shifted back and forth quite a bit in recent decades. There were plenty of ways to push it further into the future. One was to raise the payroll tax—gradually, and at a lower rate than the cost of living. That's how Congress had kept the program solvent in its first four decades, without overburdening workers or their employers. Another solution that most progressives supported was to raise the cap on the percentage of annual income subject to payroll tax—currently $106,000. That would mean that 90% of all earned income in the U.S. would be taxed to pay for Social Security, instead of 86%, and solvency would be assured for the better part of another seventy-five years.

Aging workers and a coming surge in the elderly population weren't the only reasons Social Security was expected to have problems. Two other factors were very important—and cutting benefits wouldn't do a thing to address them. One was stagnating wages; except for a few years in the late 1990s, wages had grown hardly at all since 1973. Blue-collar workers and those at the bottom of the ladder were especially hard hit, since Congress failed to raise the minimum wage at all from the late 1970s to the mid-1990s, while passing a series of trade deals and other legislation that opened the U.S. economy to competition from poorer countries. Low wage growth meant that payroll tax receipts weren't keeping up with the projected growth in benefits once the baby boomers were no longer working.

At the same time, health care costs had been rising swiftly for two decades. These were boosting the cost of Medicare and other government-sponsored health programs. Already, part of seniors' Social Security checks was deducted to pay Medicare expenses. Much of the rest, which in the past they had used to cover expenses like food, housing, and transportation, was now being eaten up in out-of-pocket medical expenses.

A return to faster wage growth, along with a moderation in health care cost inflation, could eliminate nearly 60% of the deficit Social Security was expected to face over the next seventy-five years, according to one estimate.[7] Rather than looking for political gambits to persuade voters to accept the slow phase-out of their retirement benefits, progressives argued, Washington would do better to pursue economic policies geared to raise wages and control health care costs—which would help Americans in plenty of other ways too, of course. One of these would be to lower the deficit, since health care costs were the biggest driver of the government's budget shortfall, and higher wages would mean higher income tax as well as payroll tax revenues.

The U.S. was indeed running high deficits, progressives acknowledged. But that was normal in a recession, and attacking the deficit while the economy recovered would only slow down the recovery—which could take years anyway. Social Security actually helped speed recovery by keeping millions of elderly and disabled Americans from sliding into poverty, further burdening their families, communities, and government. It wasn't far-fetched to assert, as progressives often did, that doctrinaire conservatives found the deficit useful as an excuse to destroy programs that they opposed on doctrinal grounds, or simply out of self-interest.

"My goal is to cut government in half in twenty-five years," Grover Norquist, the conservative ideologue and head of Americans for Tax Reform, once famously said, "to get it down to the size where we can drown it in the bathtub." Conservatives argued, often with great conviction, that Social Security made working people lazy and irresponsible as well as dependent on government, thereby weakening the traditional family structure and dissuading people from saving on their own for retirement. Government should get out of the way, they said, and leave these matters to the people—to restore not just fiscal responsibility but the nation's moral fiber.

That was the more fundamental reason why some believed workers' payroll taxes should be diverted from Social Security into private investment accounts. Americans' low rate of personal savings would go up, fueling a powerful private-sector economic expansion, building more wealth. Right-wing ideologues at the Cato Institute, the Heritage Foundation, and other conservative hotbeds envisioned a new, long-lasting equilibrium—a "virtuous cycle"—that would restore the ethic of self-reliance that government handouts had, supposedly, eroded. Class conflict would end because workers' fortunes in old age would be closely tied to their success as investors. Granted, more workers—those who could never accumulate a large enough nest egg—might end their lives in poverty. Yet in this vision, the U.S. would become, at last, a capitalist nation in every respect—the "ownership society."

But Social Security and the deficit were a Washington obsession for other reasons as well. Conservatives resented the lingering power of labor unions, which had played a major role in Social Security's evolution during its decades of growth and—as we shall see—were surprisingly successful at defending it even after American politics lurched to the right.

The economics profession had also drifted rightward over the past forty years. Its leading practitioners had had great success convincing lawmakers—especially the centrists who tend to wield the balance of power in Congress—that raising taxes was something to be avoided at all costs. That left spending cuts, increasing lawmakers' focus on "untouchables" like Social Security. Foreign policy was another factor. Generals, defense contractors, and pundits who believed in projecting U.S. power globally feared that programs like Social Security were ruining the country and taking away resources needed to maintain the American empire overseas. Wall Street, which exercised growing ascendancy over economic policy-making, was also very interested in promoting privatization of Social Security, which it envisioned opening up a vast new stream of revenue from managing private investment accounts carved out of the program.

It wasn't only ideology, then, that occasionally coaxed paroxysms of frustration from the coalition of privatizers and deficit hawks who attempted to join hands against Social Security when progressives insisted on opposing their moral crusade. In the months after Obama's deficit commission began meeting, editorialists and op-ed writers in the *New York Times* and *Washington Post* repeatedly denounced liberal opponents of its work as "denialists" who were indulging in "strident," "maddening" opposition to changes that "reasonable people" and "a consensus of economists" agreed were necessary.[8]

Economists were actually far from agreed on this. Some pointed out that the Social Security debate had become so focused on long-term fiscal projections that it ignored the other side of the equation: the people who funded the program and depended on it. The one thing all sides agreed upon was that the U.S. would be considerably older in the future. Were these elderly also human beings, perhaps with something positive to offer society, or merely a mathematical inconvenience? Curiously, Republicans and Democratic deficit hawks seldom addressed the question of what the impact would be on the elderly if Social Security was severely cut, or what should then be done with them, other than to repeat platitudes about the virtue of private investment and the miracle of compound interest.

Even progressives seemed to prefer discussing the baby boomers' retirement in fiscal rather than practical terms. But how would the millions of new seniors, many of whom had never held even a middle-income job, be housed? Would they have appropriate and adequate medical care? If society wanted them to work longer, would workplaces need to be made more accommodating to them, and laws against age discrimination better enforced? Arguably, Washington's fixation on Social Security's supposed fiscal problems was keeping U.S. lawmakers from grappling with these urgent matters.

Alan Simpson, now co-chair of the president's commission, had made a dubious career denouncing AARP and other groups that advocated for the elderly, lampooning seniors as greedy oldsters ensconced in gated retirement communities, unwilling to sacrifice benefits they didn't need so that the country could meet its other obligations—like educating the next generation. The facts were quite different. Social Security pays modest benefits—and it's less generous than the pensions that most other industrialized nations provide. The average monthly benefit in January 2010 was $1,166, or about $14,000 a year. A widowed mother with two children would receive an average $2,404, or about $28,850 annually. The 2010 federal poverty guideline for a family of three was $18,310 a year.[9]

At exactly the same time Washington was turning against Social Security, the economic supports that kept elderly Americans out of poverty were disappearing, leaving them more, not less, dependent on the program's modest payments. As of 2008, two-thirds of seniors relied on Social Security for half or more of their income. The proportion tilted even higher for people of color, women, the unmarried, and people who worked all of their careers at low-wage jobs. More than one in four seniors had little or no income besides Social Security.

Perhaps that was why poll after poll found that Americans, much to the annoyance of the anti-deficit coalition, solidly opposed cutting the program or raising the retirement age. Social Security was always more than a safety net or an income support program—and certainly much more than a "welfare" scheme. It represented a compact between generations, and a collective promise that American workers made to each other. To understand its uniqueness, and how it could survive decades of sophisticated political attacks from the right and the center-right, we'll first have to take a fresh look at the origins of Social Security—the economic landscape it grew out of and the hopes and aspirations of the masses of working people who called it into existence.

II. From Mutual Aid to Social Insurance

"If there is no struggle there is no progress.... This struggle
may be a moral one; or it may be a physical one; or it
may be both moral and physical; but it must be a struggle.
Power concedes nothing without a demand. It never did,
and it never will."

—*Frederick Douglass*[10]

National old-age insurance has been a controversial idea since it first took shape in Germany in the late-19th century. It took the U.S. political class a generation to debate, test at the state level, and ultimately enact a national Social Security program in 1935. Even after the program came into being in America, conservative financial interests accepted it only grudgingly.

A former Social Security commissioner once defined "social insurance" as "simply an agreement among the citizens that one section of the population will receive certain benefits and another segment will pay for such benefits. The government may administer and enforce compliance with a social insurance system, but in the final analysis it's paid by—and is for the benefit of—the people of the nation. The government is simply the intermediary that carries out the wishes of the people."[11] Benefits covered by social insurance programs typically include unemployment, health care, survivorship, and retirement.

The Anglo-American revolutionary Thomas Paine proposed a rudimentary system of economic security in his 1797 pamphlet, *Agrarian Justice*. Paine's program was based on a fund created through an inheritance tax. This fund would make a one-time award of £15 to each citizen upon reaching twenty-one, to get a start in life, and £10 annually to every citizen fifty or over. Paine was careful to specify that each payment "is justice and not charity"—something each member of the community had a right to receive.[12]

Paine's idea didn't catch on. But something similar was soon gestating in Europe, in the minds of such figures as the French anarchist Pierre-Joseph Proudhon, who didn't envision government being involved, and German socialist Ferdinand Lassalle, who did. Both saw social insurance as a way to take localized or occupationally-based mutual aid networks that had existed for hundreds of years and expand them to the national level. Social insurance could be any type of program that workers paid for themselves through a dedicated tax or premium and that had eligibility requirements and benefits defined by law. As such, it would help bring about a transformation of society along cooperative lines—a fact that conservative U.S. politicians loved to point out when they wanted to tag it as a socialistic import from abroad.* To them, it smacked of collective values rather than the extreme self-reliance that an increasingly dominant business elite was teaching Americans to believe was their tradition.

Better to promote household thrift, American commercial and financial leaders argued, not least because it promised to put workers' extra earnings directly into the hands of bankers and businesspeople. Compulsory programs

---

* Racial prejudice poisoned much of the deliberation that led to the passage of the Social Security Act of 1935. This included thinly veiled attacks on the "Americanism" of foreign-born advocates of social insurance, often shading over into antisemitism (J. Lee Kreader, "Isaac Max Rubinow: Pioneering Specialist in Social Insurance," unpublished undated doctoral dissertation, University of Chicago; see esp. pp. 506, 517, 550, 583).

to support the elderly were "un-American and socialistic and unmistakably earmarked as an entering wedge of communist propaganda," the Pennsylvania Chamber of Commerce declared in 1924.[13] A generation of American reformers nevertheless went to work promoting social insurance as a way to bring some social justice to the modern capitalist economy. Borrowing from the models that other industrialized nations were adopting, they succeeded in getting workers' compensation programs adopted in several states and almost pushed through a universal health care plan in California in 1916.

But it took a series of financial collapses—1907, 1920, and of course 1929—to build popular support for some kind of guaranteed income in old age. Changes in workers' preferred lifestyles played a role as well. Starting in the Victorian era, Americans turned away from the traditional family model of household welfare, in which the elderly lived with their working offspring and the third, younger generation lived at home as well until they married, contributing to the family fund with their earnings.* Instead, the American household came to picture itself as a "nuclear" family, with parents and underage children living together, and the elderly living independently if possible. In 1900, more than 60% of all over-sixty-five persons lived with their children; by 1962, the proportion was down to 25%, and by 1975 to 14%. Additionally, the practice of taking in boarders, which used to be the primary source of income for older persons living by themselves, was increasingly frowned upon in early 20th century America. Workers were clearly looking for another way to manage old age that was less burdensome to those of working age.

But in 1929, despite the rapid economic expansion of the past decade, the very concept of retirement was new, and few private employers offered pensions to rank-and-file workers—this despite the fact that more and more Americans were now working most of their lives in an industrial workplace that spit them out in favor of younger bodies once their physical capabilities started to fail. As for the labor movement, while some leaders talked of collective pension provision, few unions yet extended retirement benefits to their members. The gap was filled by a patchwork of fraternal and mutual aid societies offering health insurance and death benefits to dues-paying members; private insurance companies peddling annuity contracts; and charities and community-run poor houses and shelters.[14]

"I can remember the terror that existed with regard to those county poor farms," recalls Rep. John Dingell Jr., the longtime House member from Michigan whose father was a sponsor of the Social Security Act while serving in the same seat his son would later occupy.[15]

The early years of the Great Depression made clear this combination of resources wasn't adequate. Unemployment by 1933 reached nearly 25%

---

* This wasn't strictly a matter of necessity in a rapidly industrializing society, as some historians have concluded, but of preference. See Carole Haber and Brian Grattan, *Old Age and the Search for Security: An American Social History* (Bloomington and Indianapolis: Indiana University Press, 1994), pp. 37–47.

nationwide, but the plight of the elderly, who had been finding it harder to get work for nearly two decades, was catastrophic. During the supposedly prosperous 1920s some 22% of the aged were living below the "danger line" of $300 a year, and the Depression destroyed the wealth of many more. A study by the Committee on Economic Security, which Roosevelt appointed in 1934 to draft the Social Security Act, found that nearly 50% of the sixty-five-and-over population in Connecticut, New York, and Wisconsin had less than subsistence income and a third of those in Connecticut had no income whatsoever. By 1937, unemployment for men sixty and over topped 50%.[16] This was a crisis not just for the elderly but for their families, many in desperate financial straits themselves.*

A national old-age pension system took shape not just out of desperate need, however, but because that need arose during a period of enormous popular upheaval and radical social experimentation. The first half of the 1930s was punctuated by general strikes and the resurgence of organized labor, campaigns against housing evictions and price gouging, and greater openness by much of the public to radical social and political ideas.

A variety of plans to provide a uniform base for each elderly U.S. citizen nationwide were floated in the early 1930s. One of the most popular, developed by an aged and jobless California physician named Francis E. Townsend, mushroomed into a mass organization with a national membership of 3.5 million— the first large-scale movement of the elderly in the U.S. An astonishing 20–25 million people are estimated to have signed Townsend petitions.[17] The doctor's original proposal, echoing Paine, would have provided citizens over sixty, who hadn't committed a felony, with a monthly pension of $200, which they would be required to spend within thirty days. It would be paid for by a 2% tax on the gross dollar value of every commercial and financial transaction.[18]

"Responsible" economists found such schemes appalling. America's political and policy-making elites were not—still are not—ready for a guaranteed income based entirely on age, with no regard for work history. But Townsend's plan clearly addressed a desperate need. By the end of 1934, 28 states had enacted mandatory pension systems providing benefits to some 236,000 people.[19] One of these was New York state, under then-Governor Franklin D. Roosevelt.

---

* H.L. Mencken, covering the 1936 convention of the Townsend Clubs for the *Baltimore Sun*, noted this: "I soon found, circulating among them, that a large part of the strength of the movement lay among persons who were not old themselves, but were burdened by the support of aged parents. One such convert that I encountered told me that he had to maintain not only his father and mother, but also the father and mother of his wife. He said that the costs of discharging this filial duty kept him broke, and I could well believe him" (H.L. Mencken, *Thirty-five Years of Newspaper Work*, Fred Hobson, Vincent Fitzpatrick, Bradford Jacobs, eds., Baltimore: The Johns Hopkins University Press, 1994, pp. 280–81). Leo McCarey's *Make Way for Tomorrow* (1937) is a classic Depression-era film treatment of a financially constrained family struggling to support elderly parents who have run out of resources.

Once in the White House, Roosevelt appointed the Committee on Economic Security, in part, to develop blueprints for social insurance schemes. By 1935 it had produced a plan for a "Social Security" system. This provided an old-age pension for retired workers, paid for by a dedicated payroll tax of 2% split evenly between workers and their employers with no direct contribution from the government itself. These revenues would be paid into a government-administered trust fund that would earn a fixed 3% interest on its assets.

The Roosevelt administration billed the Social Security Act of 1935 as a prudent alternative to the "preposterous" plans emerging from groups like the Townsendites—a way to marginalize those groups while stealing some of their thunder. The individual would "earn" benefits through work, not claim them merely because he or she was old. Public-sector jobs were excluded, as were self-employed persons. That left most women out of the program, since so many of them were concentrated in teaching or government clerical jobs or in domestic service. Agricultural and domestic workers were explicitly excluded, effectively eliminating most of the African-American population.* In all, more than 50% of future retirees were excluded under the Act.

The result was a program geared to the needs of the most politically significant constituency: white, male industrial workers. Forty-two million of them were enrolled by 1940, cementing them, incidentally, as a loyal constituency of Roosevelt's Democratic Party. Crucially, funding for Social Security would come from a tax on payrolls, not from a broader-based tax that would hit business directly.

The new law was a meager beginning for the reformers who had fought for decades to introduce a social insurance system to America and for the mass movement that had demanded government action after 1929. Yet business bridled—especially life insurers, who feared the new old-age benefit would decimate their annuity sales. The Republican Party attacked the new law in the next year's presidential election, arguing that it unduly raised the cost of employment. When Roosevelt was reelected in a landslide, the business

---

*   How and why this came about is a fascinating and complex matter. Daniel Béland shows that southern lawmakers as a group made no special effort to exclude blacks. Rather, the Roosevelt administration opposed including most agricultural and other non-payroll workers in Social Security's original old age insurance program to keep the program from becoming too complicated to administer. Another scholar, Mary Poole, points out that some members of the administration were nevertheless afraid of provoking opposition from southerners, while the academic experts who designed Social Security were anxious to keep it focused on benefiting urban, mostly white male industrial workers (Béland, *Social Security: History and Politics from the New Deal to the Privatization Debate*, Lawrence: University Press of Kansas, 2005, pp. 88–89; Poole, *The Segregated Origins of Social Security*, Chapel Hill: University of North Carolina Press, 2006). The result was that most African-Americans were shunted into "relief" programs and didn't receive Social Security coverage for another twenty years.

community tried another tack, challenging the Social Security Act's constitutionality. Again, failure: the Supreme Court in May 1937 ruled in favor of the Act, citing specifically the general welfare provisions of the Constitution.

Labor got behind the new Social Security system too, the American Federation of Labor (AFL) helping to circulate literature in support of the program during the 1936 election. Clearly, by the mid-1930s the mainstream American labor movement's leaders, such as AFL President William Green and Congress of Industrial Organization President John L. Lewis, were rethinking their relationship with government. That process would continue during the Second World War, when organized labor became a partner in the war effort, developed a larger organizational infrastructure in Washington, and got used to working through bureaucracies.

Over the next four decades, Republican lawmakers mounted several unsuccessful efforts to cut benefits or replace Social Security with a needs-based, "welfare"-type system that would command less broad-based support and would thus be more vulnerable to budget discipline. In 1964, Republican presidential candidate Barry Goldwater actually suggested, in a statement that didn't become part of the party's platform, that workers be allowed to invest some part of their payroll taxes separately. The Democrats roundly denounced him, and his casual suggestion helped send his campaign down in a landslide.

Pres. Franklin Delano Roosevelt signs the Social Security Act, August 14, 1935. Standing behind Roosevelt is Secretary of Labor Frances Perkins, who chaired the President's Committee on Economic Security. As such, she was one of the primary architects of Social Security in its earliest form.

But for the most part, opposition to Social Security was muted. The program helped carry forward the evolution of American society from the extended-family household model. Contrary to some expectations, it didn't stifle the development of private-employer pension schemes or discourage sales of the insurance industry's annuity products, both of which grew briskly in the decades ahead. Plus, Social Security was still young and relatively inexpensive. In Goldwater's day, Social Security didn't yet represent a significant segment of the federal budget and in any case was taking in more than enough money to sustain itself year to year, given that many more workers were contributing to it than were taking benefits.

Meanwhile, the program was expanding. In 1950, Social Security covered barely half the U.S. workforce; twenty-five years later, almost all workers participated. This expansion was the fruit of twenty-five Social Security bills that Congress passed between 1935 and 1973, including four key sets of amendments to the original Act. The most important changes:

- In 1939, the size of benefits was increased, the date when they would start paying out was shifted from 1942 to 1940, and benefits for dependents were added. The benefits formula was changed to one based on average monthly wages instead of the total amount of wages, helping those who may have worked only a short time in covered employment. Crucially, a financing mechanism was set up that included a formal trust fund but in effect gave each generation of active workers the task of funding the benefits of the current crop of retirees—what was known as a "pay-as-you-go" system.*

- In 1950, the size of benefits was increased again. This was the first time they were boosted to compensate for a rise in the cost of living. Many self-employed, agricultural, and domestic workers were added to the rolls.[20]

- In 1956, a new Disability Insurance program came into being, with its own trust fund financed by another chunk of payroll tax, and

---

* Roosevelt and his Treasury secretary, Henry Morgenthau, originally favored a "funded" system that would build up a large reserve to pay for future generations' benefits, and this was established in the 1935 Act. But some influential economists argued that this would hinder recovery from the Depression by retarding consumer spending. And conservative critics warned that a large trust fund would wind up either being spent on new liberal programs or invested in the private securities markets, creating a big, government-owned segment of the economy that they equated with socialism. To end such squabbles, the 1939 Amendments cut back the trust fund drastically and authorized use of general revenues—that is, revenues from income taxes—to fill out benefits coverage if payroll tax receipts fell short. Washington wouldn't try again to create a large trust fund "surplus" until 1983.

women were allowed to retire early, at age sixty-two, in exchange for accepting a lower benefit.

- In 1957, members of the armed forces were added into the program.

- In 1961, the early retirement option was extended to men.

- In 1972, Congress approved a 20% boost in benefits, thereafter permanently indexing benefits increases to adjustments in the cost of living index. This followed a succession of cost-of-living boosts that Congress had made a quasi-ritual of passing every two years.

- Also in 1972, Congress consolidated a plethora of state- and local-level programs to aid the poor, as well as federal grants-in-aid to assist certain categories of needy persons—the blind, children of the disabled, and the elderly—into a new program administered by the Social Security Administration, dubbed Supplemental Security Income. For retirees who spent most of their working lives in low-wage jobs, SSI represented a basic "welfare" benefit if their Social Security check wasn't enough to get them out of poverty. That made it, effectively, the fourth "leg" of the "three-legged stool" of retirement benefits, alongside Social Security, employer-sponsored pension plans, and personal savings.

The cost-of-living adjustments, starting in 1950, were by far the most important changes, because they enabled Social Security to keep pace with inflation much better than most other sources of retiree income. Without them, Social Security would have dwindled to an insignificant program replacing only a very small portion of workers' pre-retirement pay. At the same time, the expansion of Social Security taught lawmakers a powerful lesson: politically, you couldn't go wrong creating new benefits for the elderly or augmenting existing ones. In the decades following World War II, government at all levels vastly expanded the network of services for retirees, ranging from subsidies for those living in poverty to funding for medical research on aging, to nutritional and home care programs—and, in 1965, Medicare.

The net result was that, by the early 1970s, more and more of elderly Americans' income was coming from Social Security payments. At the same time, those payments, along with other government programs, were having an unprecedented effect on seniors' standard of living. The overall percentage of Americans over sixty-five living in poverty shrank from 35.2% to 14.6% between 1959 and 1982; well over half of that improvement came between 1966 and 1973 alone. Social Security and Medicare drove this change. Over the same thirty-three-year period, combined social insurance payments to the elderly rose from $39.1 billion a year to $194.6 billion.[21]

From a modest income-augmentation scheme in 1940, Social Security had by 1980 evolved into the most successful antipoverty program in U.S. history, according to some estimates. In the beginning, it had covered a narrow base of mostly white, male industrial workers; only about 60% of the labor force was included until 1950. Thirty years later, its constituency made up 96% of the working population. Elderly women and people of color were now among the groups relying most on Social Security. Without Social Security benefits, the poverty rate among the African-American elderly, by 1997, would have been 59.9% instead of 29.1%, while 52.6% of women would have been poor instead of 14.7%.[22] Social Security was also the most important factor in reducing poverty among children. In 2002, more than 3 million received benefits under the program. Social Security paid enough money to families with children to reduce the aggregate child poverty gap by 21%—more than any other government program.[23]

But the evolution of Social Security had even more wide-reaching implications. Poor people aren't just isolated individuals. They have families, friends, and connections in their communities. Alleviating poverty among the elderly—and among the disabled, widows, and orphans—also relieves pressure on family members and others who make up their support system. These people, as we've seen, were among the strongest supporters of a guaranteed old-age income system during the Depression years.

Social Security transformed American society by making it easier for working people to join and maintain themselves in the middle class. It also freed them to invest long-term in homes, businesses, and education for their children by moderating a major source of uncertainty in their lives—how they would support themselves in old age. The faith that the labor movement's leaders had decided to place in a government-sponsored retirement scheme in the days of the New Deal was borne out—the program had become part of the fabric of everyday life.

Social Security's political foundation seemed practically unassailable. Basing benefits on wages and focusing the system around workers didn't create the universal support program that visionaries like Townsend had demanded. But the pay-as-you-go nature of Social Security, with current workers essentially funding benefits for those who went before them, gave it the character of a solemn compact between the generations, one that bound children more closely to parents. The "insurance" part of the social insurance equation, the mechanism by which "premiums" in the form of payroll taxes go to fill up a common pool known as a "trust fund," lent it the form of a contractual relationship that government was obliged to honor just as an insurer must honor its policies. Overall, Roosevelt's creation assumed the shape of a delicate balancing act between market-based capitalism and a cooperative, intergenerational transfer system.*

---

* "Now, Miss Perkins, wouldn't you agree that there is a teeny-weeny bit of socialism in your program?" Senator Thomas P. Gore of Oklahoma queried

Social Security's ideological opponents never really gave up the fight, however. For one thing, they pointed out, the program was becoming more expensive. Payroll taxes rose through the period of Social Security's expansion from the original 2% of payroll to 12.4% (plus another 3.3% for Medicare) by 1990, still evenly split between employer and employee. And while the program more than paid for itself through each year's payroll tax contributions, it was assuming a more conspicuous profile on the federal balance sheet. By 1982, all payments to the elderly, survivors, and the disabled totaled $156 billion a year, or 21% of combined federal outlays,* up from 12.6% in 1960.[24] As a result, Social Security's first four decades continued to see sporadic efforts by congressional lawmakers to curtail the program.

* * *

One way to think about politics is that it's the way communities work together, or delegate authority, to address problems or execute projects that people choose to handle collectively. It's how communities take charge of their individual and collective desires and plot strategies for achieving them. It's also how they decide which problems to set aside for individuals or subsets of the community to handle. The creation of Social Security in 1935 wasn't so much an economic decision as a political act, born when a movement boasting millions of members demanded that the State take responsibility to fashion a system of old-age benefits.

The program itself was never merely a relief measure. In fact, monthly benefit payments under the original Social Security Act at first weren't scheduled to begin until 1942.** Social Security's roots and rationale went back decades, to the European anarchist and socialist pioneers who extracted the idea of social insurance from the practice of mutual aid and to reformers who created the first U.S. workers' compensation laws during the Progressive Era. The Social Security program that grew out of the New Deal embodied the tension between the desire to create a society founded on the principle of mutual aid and another set of priorities, the same ones that had already motivated other industrialized countries to establish social insurance programs.

The national pension systems that had superseded independent mutual aid associations in most industrialized countries by World War II were designed,

Labor Secretary Frances Perkins during Senate Finance Committee hearings, February 1935. Cited in Arthur J. Altmeyer, *The Formative Years of Social Security* (Madison: The University of Wisconsin Press, 1966), p. 38.

* Combining all payments made by the federal government, regardless of whether they come from general revenues or Social Security and Medicare trust fund assets.

** To address this problem, Title I of the Social Security Act set up Old Age Assistance, a separate program making direct payments to impoverished seniors. OAA benefits were awarded based on need, and funded from general revenues rather than payroll taxes.

in part, to deflate the radical segment of the labor movement and integrate working households more fully into the emerging state-capitalist order. In a statement attached to the 1881 legislation that created the first government-run insurance program against workplace accidents, German Chancellor Otto von Bismarck wrote,

> That the State ... should interest itself to a greater degree than hitherto in those of its members who need assistance, is not only a duty of humanity and Christianity ... but a duty of state-preserving policy. These classes must ... be led to regard the state not as an institution contrived for the protection of the better classes of society, but as one serving their own needs and interests. The apprehension that a socialistic element might be introduced into legislation if this end were followed should not check us.[25]

Crucially, Bismarck's system of social insurance required a person to work and earn the money—that is, the right—to participate. This was quite different from the anarchist conception of mutual aid, which extended to everyone who belonged to a particular community by virtue of their humanity. Every state-sponsored social insurance system that succeeded and built on Bismarck's model had this same, conservative feature. The revolutionary aspect of mutual aid—the promise of a new, cooperative way of life that could provide working people with some control over their economic destiny—drained away. Instead, social insurance emerged as a device for mitigating the worst aspects of capitalist society—a way to partially balance out the effect of laws and policies restricting trade unions, subsidizing corporate profits in certain industries, and protecting financial institutions from their own mistakes, for example.

But even some of the pioneers of state-run social insurance had hoped the spirit of mutual aid would persist and even thrive within the new programs.

W.J. Braithwaite, one of the creators of the U.K.'s first national unemployment and health insurance legislation in 1908, argued unsuccessfully that the new system should be run on "mutual, local, autonomous, self-governing lines in such a way that it 'could be run from a third floor office in the Strand'"— that is, without a large national bureaucracy. William Beveridge, one of the authors of the postwar British welfare state, including its old-age insurance provisions and the National Health Service, had a similar inclination. He wished that "human society may become a friendly society" organized as "an affiliated order of branches, some small, each with its own life in freedom, each linked to the rest by common purpose and by bonds to serve that purpose."[26]

These musings weren't just exercises in nostalgia. Industrialized society not only became more complex in the 20th century, it became more violent and dangerous as the power of the State and capital grew rapidly and with little restraint. Social insurance, with its roots in mutual aid, was one way to counteract the dislocation and alienation of modern life and perhaps make society less prone to explosions of violent hatred. I.M. Rubinow, one of the pioneers of social insurance in the U.S., hoped that "the present quest for security" embodied in the Social Security Act "is but the first symptom of a radical turn in mass psychology ... the growth of a new set of social and spiritual values."[27]

Speaking in 1935, when the Nazis were busily rebuilding the German war machine, Rubinow saw a "sense of economic insecurity" behind the threat of fascism. "Back of the paranoiac, religious, biologic and historical vagaries of the National Socialist philosophy" and its exploitation of antisemitism and other "group antagonisms," he detected the insecurity of a country in which economic security had broken down.

"Only when free from the harassing, inhibiting influences of fears, worries, uncertainties, can the human intellect function at its best, or at least normally," Rubinow said. "Only upon the foundation of fact and sense of economic security can there be built a normal social structure of a peaceful society."[28] From this point of view, Social Security, national health care, and unemployment insurance were never just methods of paying for and delivering services. They were the key to unlocking reserves of human potential and neutralizing the racial and other group hatreds that the modern world had unleashed.

The Democratic Party leaders of the New Deal era accepted enough of this vision to recognize social insurance as an organic force that should develop to meet the evolving needs of its participants. It could, and would, change over time. In 1940, with the possibility of war looming, Roosevelt had created a National Resources Planning Board to develop proposals "for the avoidance of a depression after the defense period," including expanded Social Security. Suspicious congressional Republicans scuttled the project. In his 1944 State of the Union address, however, the president went on to propose "a second bill of rights" for the U.S. that would include "adequate protection from the economic fears of old age, sickness, accident, and unemployment."

The rationale behind this proposal had everything to do with the fifteen years of depression and war the country had just endured. "True economic freedom cannot exist without economic security and independence," Roosevelt said. "People who are hungry ... are the stuff of which dictatorships are made."[29] With the president's death a year later and the election of a Republican Congress in 1946, however, nothing came of his bill-of-rights initiative.

In 1948, Harry Truman found himself struggling to retain the presidency against a Republican Party still in command on Capitol Hill. Among many other things, the "terrible 80th Congress," as he called it, had overridden his veto to narrow the definition of "employees" qualified for Social Security coverage and exclude newspaper and magazine vendors from the program. Truman won back his office in a dramatic upset. In his next message to Congress, now controlled by the Democrats, he called for changes that eventually became the 1950 Amendments to the Social Security Act—the biggest expansion of the program since its creation.

Before Social Security could become operative in the late 1930s, workers and employers had to sign up. These posters were part of the effort to inform and, effectively, sell the new program to the public. They also illustrate the different faces Social Security could assume for different audiences. The poster at left invokes the mass movement and impulse

MORE SECURITY FOR THE AMERICAN FAMILY

WHEN AN INSURED WORKER DIES, LEAVING DEPENDENT CHILDREN AND A WIDOW, BOTH MOTHER AND CHILDREN RECEIVE MONTHLY BENEFITS UNTIL THE LATTER REACH 18.

E.S. 45a

FOR INFORMATION WRITE OR CALL AT THE NEAREST FIELD OFFICE OF THE
SOCIAL SECURITY BOARD

toward collective solidarity that compelled the Roosevelt administration to push a collectively funded, national retirement income program through Congress. On right, a more conventionally reassuring pitch that Social Security reinforces the middle-class family.

The 1950 Amendments were also the next step on a path Truman believed he saw clearly, taking the U.S. away from welfare, with its humiliating means tests, and toward a society built on social insurance. "Public assistance was designed as a backstop, a second line of defense, eventually to be replaced by social insurance benefits," he said in his message.[30] Charity and public assistance would be replaced by a state-run form of mutual aid. In Truman's vision, "the dole" would be completely superseded by a societal commitment to a guaranteed, adequate standard of living.

This dovetailed with changes taking place in other industrialized countries during the postwar era, where the basic elements of a secure and minimally comfortable existence were coming to be regarded as fundamental human rights. One of the signature events of the period was the 1948 drafting by a UN commission, chaired by Eleanor Roosevelt, of the Universal Declaration of Human Rights, which enshrined the rights of the elderly, disabled, and survivors to "social security."

Conservatives denounced the declaration's Covenant on Economic, Social and Cultural Rights—the section enforcing its language on social security—as "socialistic."[31] The U.S. only signed it in 1979, and even then it was never sent to the Senate for ratification. And while Social Security did evolve into a much broader, more generous program, social insurance never fully replaced welfare. Nor did the "adequate protection" that Roosevelt spoke of ever became a statutory objective of Social Security.

Organizationally, too, what the American people got was something else. A fundamental paradox of Social Security is that while it was perhaps the most populist program the federal government ever created, welcoming all American workers as participants regardless of need, crucial decisions about it were always made by a remarkably small group of policymakers. Congressional committee chairs, actuaries, and a few influential outside policy strategists managed the evolution of the program, always in near-total isolation from the public.

The Social Security Administration itself, which evolved to more or less its present form by the late 1940s, was roughly similar to other federal agencies. Its commissioner was a presidential appointee and its other trustees included the Secretaries of the Treasury, Labor, and Health and Human Services. The two "public" members who served on the board of trustees after 1983 were also appointed by the president, not popularly elected by the program's participants.

This was consistent with the overall domestic policy-making structure that emerged from the New Deal, which in fact wasn't populist at all. Leaders like FDR concluded that "the economic and social condition of a complex society must be centrally organized and administered by intellectuals."[32] It was the heyday of the technocrat.

As mainstream historians, such as Arthur M. Schlesinger, Jr. and Richard Hofstadter, saw the U.S. in the industrial era, two impulses were fighting for control of the country's destiny. One carried the future in its hands and the other, with any luck, didn't. On one side was "the trend toward management, toward bureaucracy, toward bigness everywhere"[33] that the New Deal was trying to tame and harness for the good of the nation. On the other was populism, which sometimes favored legitimate reforms but could also produce a Huey Long or a Joe McCarthy—a populism that liberals saw as rural, racist, and paranoid.

The Townsend movement, backing as it did the "unreasonable" idea of a guaranteed income for the elderly, clearly tapped into this mass side of culture. In fact, Social Security very possibly wouldn't have come about except for the constant pressure applied by the Townsendites—and Long, whose "Share Our Wealth" campaign was even more radical than the doctor's. Once the program was in place, however, the best thing was obviously to put it in the hands of qualified experts, far from the influence of anyone lacking respectable academic and professional credentials.

Social Security had begun a long process of running away from its own radicalism. It was a good thing, Hofstadter wrote in 1955, that Americans had been "not only mechanized and urbanized and bureaucratized but internationalized as well," since now their "domestic life is largely determined by the demands of foreign policy and national defense."[34] Domestic policy matters, in other words, would now rest safely in the hands of a self-selecting, presumably rational elite, just as did—presumably—military and foreign affairs.

John F. Kennedy, in a May 1962 press conference, gave a quasi-official stamp to this trend when he noted, "Most of us are conditioned for many years to have a political viewpoint—Republican or Democrat, liberal, conservative or moderate," whereas the most serious public concerns were now "technical problems, administrative problems" that "do not lend themselves to the great sort of passionate movements which have stirred this country so often in the past."[35]

Not everyone thought politics really was being replaced by technocracy— or even that it should be. Paul Goodman, anarchist and author of *Growing Up Absurd* (1960), a bestselling critique of American education, argued in 1965 that the New Deal and the Great Society had spawned a "large stable of mandarins to raise the tone, use correct scientific method, and invent rationalization." But these enlightened bureaucrats weren't addressing the core problem. "Instead of tackling the political puzzle of how to maintain democracy in a complex technology and among urban masses, it multiplies professional-client and patron-client relationships."[36]

To many good liberals, dazzled by Lyndon Johnson's early legislative successes—the Voting Rights Act, Medicare—Goodman's concerns sounded too much like the complaints of the anti-government Goldwaterites to be taken seriously. But with "the reduction of the citizen to a consumer of expertise,"[37] there was no room and no obvious continuing role for the populist movement that had fought for programs like Social Security. The Social Security Administration created under Roosevelt was a bureaucracy, although a vigorous, imaginative, and highly efficient one. Even though their payroll taxes were earmarked to support Social Security as a self-sustaining institution, working households lost any clear sense of ownership over the program. The role of

Social Security began to suffer from the perception that it was an elite institution, not part of the everyday glue that binds society.

Even some of the people who created the program's bureaucratic structure noticed and were worried by this trend. Wilbur Cohen, one of the architects not only of Social Security but also of Medicare, and who came to be known in Washington as "Mr. Social Security," was one of these.

"There has been a noticeable unwillingness on the part of those persons studying or formulating social insurance policy to find out what the consumer thinks," Cohen told a conference on aging in 1959, "because of the fear that it would be subject to criticism that this democratic approach would be 'unscientific' and would result in a benefit level which would bankrupt the country and put the Townsend plan to shame. But what evidence we have on this matter," Cohen continued, "indicates that such 'conventional wisdom' is not rooted in fact. Survey experts report that the average American is more 'reality conscious' than he is given credit for and that his level of desirable economic well-being is usually below the effective capacity of our expanding economy."[38] There was no reason to think that if the public took a more direct role in determining policy for Social Security, they would somehow wreck it.

Cohen's concerns didn't register. Social Security policy continued to be made by technocrats and the few lawmakers who worked closely with them.

Why had Social Security become politically vulnerable by the time Ronald Reagan entered the White House? Conservatives argue that the New Deal and the welfare state were products of a liberalism that had failed in a multitude of ways. The American people, accordingly, turned back to a philosophy of individualism and economic freedom. Certainly, the decline of the labor movement, Social Security's most powerful political champion in the postwar years, helped weaken its support in Washington.

Political philosopher Michael Sandel argues that the structures set up to run the New Deal and Great Society programs didn't "rest on a sense of national community adequate to its purpose.... [The New Deal] managed to create a strong national government but failed to cultivate a shared national identity.... The liberalism of the procedural republic proved an inadequate substitute for the strong sense of citizenship that the welfare state requires."[39] Built on the philosophical foundation of mutual aid, Social Security had the potential to revitalize the idea of citizenship. Instead, it became a new bureaucracy.

The decisional distance between Social Security, its political champions, and the people it was supposed to serve grew larger as the decades wore on. Women joined the workforce in masses, more and more people were spending their entire working lives in low-wage jobs, advanced education was less affordable for surviving children—these changes and more presented new challenges to the program. Yet while the Democratic leadership stood fast against any radical restructuring, after the mid-1970s it made little effort to propose improvements or new directions for Social Security that would help it keep pace. Moreover, by the 1980s, the technocratic elite that Hofstadter expected to continue guiding the country was itself splintering and in some cases turning to the right in the wake of racial and civil unrest, Vietnam, and a brutal economic transformation.

What would save Social Security time and again during the period we'll be revisiting, however, were the vestiges of the mass movement that had propelled it into being. Social Security was the product of a long, difficult popular struggle, not the bipartisan, consensus-based politics that Washington likes to practice. Since 1980, each time it has been threatened with drastic cutbacks or privatization, grassroots coalitions of workers and retirees, with union labor, women, and people of color prominent among them, have turned out to oppose the changes. As we'll see, without an active popular base ready to confront, annoy, and vote out of office politicians who aren't loyal to the program, Social Security would have been on the road to disappearance barely a year after our story begins—and on many occasions since then.

Public programs like Old-Age, Survivors', and Disability Insurance can't survive or maintain that degree of loyalty while standing still, however. They must evolve to meet the needs of successive waves of constituents, or they attenuate, lose their mass appeal, and die. As Social Security became more and more firmly linked in the public mind to an interminable and unresolvable debate over the "solvency" of the trust funds, it stopped evolving. Along the way, the notion of social insurance as a *right* was lost, replaced by the more selfish-sounding concept of the "entitlement."

The war against Social Security is now in its fourth decade. The program still hasn't been slashed or radically restructured—grassroots opposition keeps getting in the way. But without any continuing direct role in running the program, its popular base has to be reassembled and re-energized each time the program is threatened. The movement against Social Security, meanwhile, is patient, well funded, and ideologically sure of itself.

* * *

We begin with Ronald Reagan's election in 1980. Reagan first attacked Social Security and the fundamental idea of social insurance during the early 1960s, as part of his duties as a spokesperson for General Electric. At the time, few other mainstream Republican politicians were willing or inclined to do so. In a speech that he delivered over and over again, he referred to Social Security as an intrusion on liberty. He essentially repeated this in addresses supporting Barry Goldwater's presidential candidacy in 1964—speeches that helped launch Reagan's national political career. He also campaigned hard against Medicare, branding it as socialized medicine.

Reagan continued to oppose Social Security in his high-profile weekly radio addresses throughout the 1970s, advocating conversion of the program into a system of individual investment accounts.[40] This helped sink him in his first race for the White House, in 1976. Incumbent Gerald Ford reportedly

characterized the idea as "something dragged out of the sky."[41] He took the
Florida primary from Reagan with a campaign pledge to "preserve the integrity
and solvency of the Social Security system." Ford's chief of staff, Dick Cheney,
was in charge of the campaign messaging.

Reagan was in some respects the most radical American politician of his
day. Few other important members of the U.S. political class were then willing
to suggest publicly that the New Deal principle of social insurance be ripped
out, root and branch. But he was also a master at deflecting attention from his
most controversial views, coaxing voters to focus on his genial personality and
rhetorical style rather than the substance of what he was saying. In his 1980
campaign he only briefly mentioned making Social Security voluntary. And he
denied he wanted to do anything other than improve Medicare—the gist of
his famous "There you go again" rejoinder to President Carter during one of
their television debates. He remained fundamentally opposed to any kind of
social insurance, however. When he became president in January 1981, a new
offensive against Social Security was about to begin.

PART I

Social Security and the Reagan Revolution

(1981–83)

CHAPTER I
A NEW DEAL

"The next few years will see a massive battle of conserva-
tives and liberals to determine who governs the nation for
the next three decades—and we've got a head start of years
on them."
                                    —*Richard Viguerie, 1981*[1]

The war against Social Security didn't start with a privatization proposal. It began when the program found itself squeezed between two conflicting goals of the new Reagan administration: cutting taxes and cutting the deficit.

The 1980 election was a stunning Republican victory in nearly every way, the party's most successful since 1952. Not only did Reagan roundly defeat Carter, but conservatives seized effective control of Congress. Reagan's party captured 53 Senate seats for a slim majority and picked up 34 seats in the House, raising their delegation to 192 versus 242 Democrats and one independent. But the Democratic delegation was transformed as well. Forty conservative, mostly southern, members quickly organized themselves into the Democratic Conservative Forum, soon nicknamed the "Boll Weevils," and demanded better committee assignments and more influence from Speaker Tip O'Neill. They also sent clear signals that they would be willing to work with the Reagan White House.

Reagan's political advisors sensed that the American voter had genuinely rejected the traditional Democratic leadership. In the past decade, the country had fallen into a seemingly intractable funk engendered by a series of crises: the end of the over-stimulated Vietnam War economy, two severe oil crises, the collapse of the international currency management system and the decline of the dollar, and inflation that pushed into the double digits.

One consequence was that Social Security benefits payments, which had been indexed to inflation early in the decade, exploded, and the program began to run deficits for the first time in its history. Meanwhile, unemployment was stubbornly high through much of the decade, wage growth and productivity were down, and nothing the philosophically different Ford and Carter administrations did seemed to relieve the problems. The result bewildered most economists, who tagged it "stagflation."

Reagan had promised to end this cycle. He also promised to balance the budget by eliminating government "waste." But he hadn't specified where he expected to find the savings. He didn't have an economic plan, either. If the new administration wanted to enact a conservative New Deal, it would have to act fast. By late February, when he was scheduled to deliver his State of the Union address, and in the first few weeks thereafter, when the president traditionally sent the budget to Congress, Reagan would have to develop a fully thought-out economic package that he could sell on Capitol Hill. He had less than four months to go.

The Reagan team began hearing from a loose team of conservative ideologues who thought they had the answer: an economist from the University

President Reagan passes a jar of jellybeans to budget director David Stockman, February 11, 1981. A few months later, Stockman sold Reagan on a bold—and disastrous— attempt to slash Social Security benefits and hobble the program's growth.

of California at San Diego named Arthur Laffer; a *Wall Street Journal* editorial writer named Jude Wanniski; Rep. David Stockman, a second-term House member from Indiana; and their senior partner, Rep. Jack Kemp, former pro football star and five-term House member from western New York State. For several years these crusaders had been refining and promoting supply-side economics, a stripped-down version of classical free-market theory and a kind of shock therapy that advocated the aggressive use of tax cuts and business incentives to encourage economic growth and job creation.

Government spending designed to stimulate demand was a waste of money, the supply-siders argued, because it drew too much credit and capital away from the private sector. Once the tax cuts they advocated were in place, boosting the supply of capital available to investors and entrepreneurs, demand would surely follow. Inflation would subside too, because the new growth would increase the supply of goods and services available. Longer-term, the supply-siders also favored a hard-money policy that would permanently wipe out inflation by moving the globe toward a single currency standard: preferably the dollar and preferably backed by gold.

Of the four revolutionaries behind this stern prescription, only one, a buccaneering journalist, wasn't drawing a public salary, and only one was a trained economist. Each had his own ideas about which part of supply-sideism was most important, and this would become increasingly apparent as they began to collect real power in their hands. "Laffer and Wanniski … sometimes argued that tax cuts would pay for themselves," Stockman later wrote. "They implied the Treasury would take in more taxes after the cuts than before. I never bought that literally and didn't think they did, either. I put it down to salesmanship."[2]

Stockman himself was a precocious young go-getter, one of the many drawn to Washington out of college or graduate school by the prospect of being near the center of power. But he was an unusually earnest example of the type, having bounced from neo-Marxist anti-Vietnam War activist to Harvard Divinity School student to speech writer for another midwesterner, Rep. John Anderson, a fiscally conservative Republican from Illinois. Along the way, Stockman had picked up a reputation as a *wunderkind*. He had also become a passionate ultra-free marketeer who naturally gravitated toward Kemp after he was himself elected to Congress in 1976.

But he also understood that a course of their brand of economic policy was liable to balloon the federal deficit, at least in the early years. Mustering enough cuts in government operations to prevent that "would have hurt millions of people in the short run," Stockman realized. "It required abruptly severing the umbilical cords of dependency that ran from Washington to every nook and cranny of the nation. It required the ruthless dispensation of short-run pain in the name of long-term gain."

Written the better part of a decade later, after Stockman's own whirlwind career in Washington was over, his words still convey the moralistic fervor and appetite for risk—other people's—that animated the supply-side revolutionaries at the end of the Carter years. To achieve the tax cuts necessary to make the supply-side game plan succeed, jobs programs would have to be "zeroed out," educational subsidies cut, and the whole "political maintenance system" represented by "federal social welfare outlays" drastically reduced. Standards for public assistance would have to be calculated according to "exacting, abstract principles—not human hard-luck stories." Morality, for Stockman, was defined by economic performance. For example, there would no longer be any "right to draw more from the Social Security fund than retirees had actually contributed, which was a lot less than most were currently getting."[3]

Politically, however, the supply-siders knew their opportunity had come. As soon as the election was over, Kemp and Stockman campaigned to get Stockman a position in the Reagan Cabinet. They succeeded, partly on the strength of a memo by Stockman entitled "On the Danger of a GOP Economic Dunkirk," which Kemp brought along to a review of economic policy with the president-elect and his advisors in Los Angeles in mid-November. "My résumé," as he later called it,[4] laid out the usual supply-side arguments but emphasized the need for spending cuts to balance out the tax cuts. Otherwise, the new administration's economic package "will generate pervasive expectations of a continuing 'Reagan inflation,'" keeping interest rates high, deadening the housing market, and keeping industry from investing in new production. In other words, more stagflation.[5]

Reagan had used the phrase "safety net" many times during his campaign, as a sort of mantra to banish the accusations by Carter that he intended to shred Social Security, Medicare, and other important social programs. The phrase was more pregnant with meaning than many listeners may have realized, however. The aim of Social Security's old-age benefits, for example, was not merely to provide a lifeline for elderly people threatened with destitution, but to guarantee an income adequate to keep the worker living in dignity after retirement. The difference in real life between a handout to keep body and soul together, and a minimal yet reliable reward for a lifetime of work, was inestimable.

Reagan was never asked about his choice of words and once in office, his aides were happy to create the impression that budget cutting would come from eliminating waste, however vaguely defined. Only a few weeks after the election, however, Stockman's memo was suggesting that the new president attack the very thing he had apparently pledged to leave alone.

Recommending that Reagan declare an economic state of emergency and push through a sweeping rescue package as part of a Rooseveltian first hundred days in office, Stockman prescribed cuts to be "equally weighted between out-year spending and entitlement authority reductions and cash outlay savings." Included among the possible "entitlement authority reductions": $260 billion from Social Security. Thus he called for "the legislative committees to address a carefully tailored package of initial entitlement reductions."[6]

Stockman's prescription might be alarming to Democratic lawmakers and tens of millions of older workers and retirees, but it reassured some of the more traditionalist members of the president's inner circle, including James Baker III, chief of staff-designate and former campaign manager for George H.W. Bush, who Reagan had made his vice presidential nominee after defeating Bush in the primaries. Bush had once called Reagan's tax-cut prescriptions "voodoo economics." But that was in the past, and Baker was an adept operative who appeared more concerned to protect the president from political missteps than to push any specific economic strategy. Other new members of the team included two economists, Herb Stein and Paul McCracken, both of whom had headed the Council of Economic Advisors under Nixon: traditionalists with no time for radical supply-side prescriptions.

O'Neill decided not to use his prerogative as Speaker of the House to bottle up the president's agenda in committees, instead promising to allow final floor votes by summer on both his tax and his spending measures. One reason was that the Democratic caucus itself was much more conservative than it had been the last time a Republican occupied the White House. Carter himself had passed a groundbreaking capital gains tax cut in 1978, and Reagan's tax cut proposals, although more sweeping, looked to many conservative House Democrats like something they would have to support. Knowing that his hold over them was tenuous at best, O'Neill "was looking for the opposition to make errors," aide Kirk O'Donnell later said of his boss.[7]

The Reagan team rushed to take advantage. Stockman in particular seized on the very magnitude of the deficit to sell the president on the necessity of cutting government vastly more than Reagan had thought he would have to during his campaign. At a two-hour meeting with the president-elect in January, Stockman told him the budget would have to be cut by around $40 billion.

"Do you have any idea what $40 billion means?" the budget director asked journalist William Greider a short time later. "It means I've got to cut the highway program. It means I've got to cut milk-price supports. And Social Security student benefits…" and on and on. Reagan agreed in principle, seemingly prepared to stretch to the breaking point the definition of the "safety net" he had promised to protect during his campaign. Over the next few weeks, as Reagan officially entered office, Stockman began his search for the $40 billion. The cuts needed to reach that magic number had to be vetted by the president and his advisors: Baker, presidential counsel Ed Meese, and key Cabinet secretaries.

Up to a point, this could be done without violating conventional wisdom in Washington. During the Ford and Carter administrations, economic thinking had moved significantly to the right. Both of Reagan's immediate predecessors had boosted military spending, and Carter's last two budgets were designed to lower the deficit—although he had proposed to do it the conventional way, relying mainly on tax hikes. So it was no surprise when Stockman's boss pulled defense spending firmly off the table, or that the budget director proposed to stamp out tax loopholes such as tax-exempt industrial development bonds, home-mortgage deductions, the oil-depletion allowance, and other features of the tax code that benefited business. Stockman veered further to the right with a menu of proposed cuts to social welfare programs, centered around such measures as tightening food stamp eligibility, cutting federal aid to education, and "zeroing out" programs like the Comprehensive Employment and Job Training Act, which he considered to be pure pork.[8]

One of the principal sites of Stockman's budget demolition, however, was much more sensitive: Social Security. Two elements of the program looked especially cuttable. One was the student benefit. Since 1965, children of deceased workers had been able to continue receiving Social Security survivors' benefits until age twenty-two if they stayed in school. This helped keep some 772,000 students in college, but it cost $2.4 billion a year. The other target was the minimum monthly benefit, which was designed to reduce paperwork and protect low-income workers who might not have received an adequate income under the regular Social Security formula. It provided payments mostly running $122 per month to some 2 million persons—retirees and surviving spouses—at a total cost of about $1.3 billion a year.

The minimum benefit was controversial, however, because many people who received it hadn't worked very long under Social Security. For example, about 15% of recipients were what Republican opponents referred to as "double dippers," meaning they had only worked a short time in private-sector jobs covered by Social Security and the rest of their careers in government jobs for which they received a pension. It wasn't fair, critics had been saying for some years, that these people should receive a minimum benefit for which they had no need.

Stockman's Office of Management and Budget (OMB) team worked at breakneck speed to build agreement within the new administration on a package of cuts. Reagan aimed to propose a series of revisions to the 1982 budget that Carter had submitted in the final weeks of his presidency, and to push resolutions through the House and Senate that would lock these in place.

On February 18, the president went before a joint session of Congress with what he called his "Program for Economic Recovery." It called for an across-the-board tax cut of about 30%, with the lowest rates reduced from 14% to 10% and the top rates from 70% to 50%. The tax cuts would be phased in over three years and so were later christened the "10-10-10 scheme." Counterbalancing them would be $41.4 billion in spending reductions for the 1982 fiscal year, $16 billion of these from programs that primarily aided the poor. As a first step, Reagan proposed eighty-three major cuts that would shrink spending by $34.8 billion, most of them amounting to only a few hundred million to 1 or 2 billion dollars each: what Stockman referred to as "cats and dogs." Eliminating the minimum Social Security benefit would yield at least $1 billion, while ending the college benefit would knock out $700 million. Tightening requirements for receiving Social Security's Disability Insurance benefits would eliminate a further $550 million.

Reagan followed up that first request with a second, on March 10, which completed his budget proposals, bringing the total to a net $41.4 billion. Again, the package weighed heavily on social and regulatory programs: the Occupational Safety and Health Administration, much reviled by business, would lose 9,000 of its 70,000 inspectors, for example.

But what made Reagan's critics take notice was the vagueness of his long-range plans to balance the budget. To compensate for the tax cut, the Reagan blueprint assumed that inflation would go up—even though the administration was supposedly committed to reducing inflation.[9] But even with that, another $29.8 billion of cuts would have to materialize for fiscal 1983, and $44.2 billion more in 1984. Stockman wouldn't suggest more than vaguely where these reductions, soon derided as the "magic asterisk," might come from. That was exactly the idea, according to an OMB aide, who told a journalist that the budget outline "was carefully crafted so that no one could identify precisely any of the programs likely to come under the knife."[10] But without more concrete details, Wall Street in particular would have a hard time believing that an end to the cycle of federal deficits was near.

But the Reagan magic was working. In April, after recovering from an assassination attempt and riding a new wave of personal popularity, the president used his first public statement to push for passage of his budget cuts. These were now embodied in a bill cosponsored in the House by Phil Gramm of Texas, one of the most conservative of the House Democrats, and Republican Delbert Latta of Ohio. Gramm-Latta reflected the administration's proposals almost entirely, having been written at least in part by Gramm's friend Stockman.[11] It passed the House on May 7 by a lopsided vote of 253 to 176, with 63 Democrats joining a unanimous Republican minority. Five days later, a substantially similar measure passed the Senate, seventy-eight to twenty, including twenty-seven Democrats but with two Republicans opposed.

The two votes marked the first time Congress had ever voted to cut back or eliminate any part of Social Security. As such, they ended an unprecedented, nearly half-century-long period that embraced the establishment and expansion of social insurance and social welfare programs in the U.S. That said, they didn't even remotely approach the heart of the system. Eliminating the minimum benefit and payments to college-age students affected a combined 2.7 million beneficiaries out of a total of 35 million slated to receive checks in 1982.[12] And neither of these ideas was new, both having been considered by the Ford and Carter administrations when they were struggling with budget deficits in the 1970s. Still, nothing like it had ever happened. Social Security, the heart of the New Deal, was no longer an impregnable citadel. The lack of interest by even Democratic lawmakers in debating the proposed cuts in the early months of Reagan's first term was remarkable—even more so considering the outrage that would erupt in the months to follow.

In fact, lawmakers and many Washington watchers in the spring of 1981 were wondering why the White House wasn't more concerned about Social

Security as it plotted to remake government. "President Reagan's delay on Social Security has been understandable so far," the *New York Times* editorialized on May 10. "But his own Administration estimates that the cost of Social Security is now rising by $45,000 a *minute*. These days, the time for reflection does not come cheap."

Two days later, his big victory with Gramm-Latta still fresh, Reagan would take on Social Security—and confront the first real defeat of his short time in office.

* * *

By 1981, the financial health of the Social Security system had been an issue for almost six years. The trouble started with the program's last big expansion: the 20%, one-time benefits increase and annual cost-of-living-adjustments that Congress enacted in 1972. Congress had been boosting benefits semi-regularly to keep up with the cost of living for more than a decade. More than anything else, these increases were responsible for the sharp drop in poverty among the elderly. The Nixon administration decided to support the new legislation for two reasons: as economic stimulus during an election year, and to strip the Democrats of the political advantage they always seemed to gain from the successive rounds of increases.

Things didn't go quite as planned. The same year the automatic Cost-of-Living-Adjustments (COLAs) began, 1975, the Social Security trustees surprised many when they reported a looming fiscal crisis. Payouts were exceeding deficits by $1.5 billion on revenues of $50 billion. The trustees predicted that "without legislation to provide additional financing," both the Social Security retirement and disability funds "will be exhausted soon after 1979."

Longer term, the prospect looked even worse. The 1975 Quadrennial Advisory Council on Social Security warned that the retirement of the baby boom generation of workers, decades in the future, would place intolerable strains on the program's finances. Fleshing out this analysis, the Senate Finance Committee staff calculated that payroll taxes would have to rise some 20% by 2010 and another 40% by 2050 to keep Social Security solvent.[13]

In reality, the program hadn't suddenly slid into decrepitude. A quirk in the structure of the new automatic COLA, combined with a severe economic slump, had created a short- to medium-term financing crisis. Other government programs were suffering too. But Social Security's problems looked worse on paper, partly because the trustees made solvency projections seventy-five years into the future. Estimating the program's future based on a suddenly deteriorating set of economic indicators was bound to make it look like a monstrous strain on the taxpayer.

Social Security's troubles, nevertheless, were real. The U.S. faced multiple economic crises in the mid-1970s, all of which hit the program hard. The spiraling cost of the Vietnam War, followed quickly by the oil and gas shortages and price shocks of 1973, caused inflation to skyrocket from a band of 2.2% to 4.5% in the late 1960s to a new range of 5.5% to 11% from 1968 to 1976. Productivity growth, which had increased steadily in the lush decades following World War II, declined to a feeble 1.1% between 1972 and 1978. One result was a strangling of new investment by business and a gradual but severe decline in the stock market that would take a long time to ease. By December 1974, when the benchmark Dow Jones Industrial Average bottomed out, it was worth only a little more than one-third—adjusted for inflation—of its 1965 peak. Seventeen years later, and after a fairly successful run in the 1980s, the Dow was still below its value in 1929, adjusted for inflation.

Of more immediate importance for Social Security, unemployment rose to 9%: by far the highest level since the war. Wages were entering a period of stagnation that would last for twenty years, declining 0.6% over the decade of the 1970s alone. With a shrinking workforce and shrinking corporate profits—except in the energy sector—narrowing the available tax base, the federal budget deficit ballooned from $2 billion in 1974 to $31 billion in 1978.

For Social Security, steeper inflation meant that each year's COLA must rise faster to preserve the purchasing power of beneficiaries' checks. Retiree benefit payments soared from $31.1 billion in fiscal 1971 to $71.3 billion in 1977.[14] But the program was also losing money because of unemployment and declining or stagnating wages. Sluggish wages and more workers out of jobs meant less money coming into the system to pay current beneficiaries. As economists and policymakers discovered, it also meant more people applying for disability as a way to shore up their income during the bad times. A record number of new applicants—592,000—filed in 1975, and between 1969 and 1979 disability expenditures rose from $2.5 billion a year to $13.7 billion.[15]

Economists were puzzled. Recession, in the American experience, had usually been accompanied by price collapse, not inflation. What if the traditional tools for restarting the economy—lower interest rates and stimulative government spending, including the "cushion" provided by Social Security, Medicare, and welfare payments—only caused inflation to ratchet up? The supply-siders' policy prescriptions were meant to address all of these problems at once. But few economists in the Ford and then Carter administrations expected stagflation to last very long. And the 1972 Social Security amendments, which had put the automatic COLAs in place, were written before the new economic picture had fully developed.

That year, the Social Security Administration's actuaries projected inflation to grow by 15% between 1973 and 1977, versus 12% wage growth, for 3% net inflation. The actual result was a shocking 41% inflation and 1% wage growth.[16] The 1972 amendments called for an automatic benefits increase whenever the Consumer Price Index rose 3% or more. That figure was chosen based on the assumption that wages would rise about 2.25% faster than prices—more or less in keeping with the country's experience over many decades. Between 1973 and 1977, however, the usual relationship between the two reversed itself and prices exceeded wages by 0.5%. Retirees, the disabled, and survivors began to receive COLAs that pushed up long-term benefits payments much faster than expected.

Traditionally, when Congress had made cost-of-living adjustments in Social Security benefits, it had "coupled" them so that they applied to both active and retired workers. That meant when retirees received a boost, active workers got a boost in their future benefits as well. So active workers actually received two cost-of-living boosts at the same time for their future benefits: one from the rise in the wages they received from their employers and one from the Social Security program itself. Congress kept this practice in place when it instituted automatic COLAs in 1972.

"Coupling" remained acceptable as long as inflation was relatively under control. But once it took off, the Social Security actuaries' projections began to show "windfall" payments to disabled workers and middle-aged survivors of deceased workers and, over the next few decades, huge, inordinate benefits hikes for future retirees. The trustees' long-range assumptions suddenly flew off the chart.

This put Social Security in a new and politically precarious spot. Until the economic crises of the 1970s, the program had almost always taken in more money than it paid out. For some years, in fact, Washington had been using it to mask the rising deficits in the overall federal budget. In 1967, at the height of the Vietnam War, a presidential commission recommended that Social Security's budget, which had always been kept separate, be incorporated into the unified federal budget. President Johnson agreed and the immediate result was a 1969 budget that scored a very slight surplus instead of a deficit. But by the middle of the next decade, Social Security had become a drain. Every year from 1975 until 1982, in fact, it would add to the deficit.[17]

Not all of this was the program's fault. Changes in America's wage-earning economy had altered the landscape for a program that based both revenues and benefit payments on wages. At least since the early 1960s, tax-advantaged fringe benefits like health care and private pensions had been eroding the portion of income on which workers paid payroll taxes. By the early 1990s the Social Security tax base—the portion of income upon which payroll taxes were levied—was down 10%, amounting to tens of billions of dollars a year in lost revenues. Implicitly, the federal government was permitting a system to develop that favored private pensions and benefits over Social Security. But this development wasn't easy to see in the mid-1970s, and with the program no longer playing a helpful fiscal role, attacking it became a lot less politically risky.

Social Security's traditional champions on Capitol Hill and within the Social Security Administration drew up a menu of changes to address deficiencies in the benefit structure. For instance, workers who spent their entire careers in minimum wage or near-minimum wage jobs found themselves with only meager income from Social Security once they reached retirement age. Women lost benefits when they took time off to raise families during what might have been their best earning years. The 1975 Advisory Council had entertained proposals to address these disadvantages.

But with Social Security seemingly in a fiscal crisis, Washington didn't want to tackle these problems. High officials in government instead began to speak of drastically cutting back payments, with the minimum monthly benefit coming under particular attack. Caspar Weinberger, President Ford's Secretary of Health, Education and Welfare—the department that oversaw Social Security—wondered in a memo to his boss "whether the so-called minimum benefit is tantamount to welfare under Social Security."[18] Stanford G. Ross, Social Security commissioner in the Carter administration, summed up the new official outlook: "The optimistic expansionist philosophy that underlay Social Security planning since World War II has now changed to one of guarded hope that the best of the past can be preserved while the considerable needs of the future are addressed." The next decade, he predicted, would see "painful adjustments in which finances and benefits will have to be closely scrutinized and balanced."[19]

That America with an unlimited economic future was giving way to an austere new "zero-sum society," was one of the most frequently heard political/economic judgments of the decade. A well-connected Republican running for a House seat in Texas in 1978, for instance, told an audience at the Midland Country Club that Social Security "will be bust in ten years unless there are some changes." The solution, said thirty-two-year-old George W. Bush, would be to give people "the chance to invest the money the way they feel."[20]

Others, less extreme, at least agreed about the need to cut back benefits and give workers more opportunities to save on their own. In his 1975 State of the Union address, President Ford suggested imposing a 5% ceiling on Social Security benefit increases, although he could get no support for such a measure. But when Jimmy Carter entered the White House two years later, he had a Congress of his own party behind him and was prepared to act.

While the Democrats had seemed poised, post-Watergate, to dominate Washington again, the party was moving in a new direction ideologically. Carter, the former Georgia governor, was elected as an outsider, willing to question Washington orthodoxy and averse to being seen as just another "tax-and-spend Democrat." He had also campaigned as an opponent of any increase in payroll taxes.

Four months after entering office in 1977, President Carter unveiled a set of restructuring proposals for Social Security. One of these would completely remove the "earnings test"—the ceiling on earnings subject to the employer's half of the payroll tax. Another would increase the portion paid by employees. The president asked for an acceleration of payroll tax rate hikes that were already scheduled and higher taxes for self-employed persons. As a stopgap to tide the program over until these revenue-boosting measures kicked in, he also proposed that some general revenues—from federal income taxes—be transferred into the Social Security trust funds.

Republican lawmakers fought Carter on lifting the ceiling on employers' contribution to payroll taxes and pushed their own proposal to raise the amount of earnings that retirees could make before their monthly benefits were reduced. By December, however, the legislative process was complete and Carter signed the Social Security amendments of 1977 into law five days before Christmas.

The measure gave him most of what he had requested. It increased payroll tax rates for Social Security and Medicare very slightly in 1979 and 1980 and more significantly thereafter. The ultimate tax rate for the two programs together would be 7.65% each for workers and their employers, to be achieved in 1990, instead of the 7.45% previously scheduled for 2011. The bill didn't remove the earnings ceiling but increased it to $22,900 in 1979, $25,900 in 1980, and $29,700 in 1981, with automatic increases thereafter so that benefits would stay abreast of wage increases and help retirees' standard of living keep up with current workers'.

That was on the revenue-raising side. As for benefits, the 1977 Amendments changed the formula for workers who reached age sixty-two or became disabled in 1979 or later and for dependents of workers who died during that period. "Coupling" was ended, and initial benefits for future retirees from then on would be indexed strictly to the growth in their own wages, not to current retirees' COLAs as well.[21] The new formula was calculated to lower Social Security payouts by reducing the income replacement rate by 5% from where it was previously projected to be in 1979, correcting the indexing "mistake" of 1972.[22] To please the Republican minority, the bill also lowered the age at which the earnings test no longer applied, from seventy-two to seventy, beginning in 1982: a change that would benefit mainly upper-income retirees.

At the bill signing, Carter waxed enthusiastic, saying that the 1977 Amendments "will guarantee that from 1980 to the year 2030, the Social Security funds will be sound" and praised the new law as "the most important Social Security legislation since the program was established." At least two points made the new law less than an outstanding success, however.

First was the creation of the "notch babies." Congress had decided not to penalize those retirees—roughly, those who were born between 1911 and 1916—who had begun receiving benefits indexed to the Consumer Price Index under the 1972 law. Instead, under the new rules, the next cohort of retirees—those born between 1917 and 1922—would have their benefits reduced an average of 20% compared with the previous one, although gradually, over five years. The cohort following them would see an immediate reduction.

The result was that retirees who were born, say, in the first days of 1917 could end up enjoying a much lower initial benefit from Social Security than others fortunate enough to have been born only a few days earlier: but on the right side of New Year's. The notch babies' dilemma very much depended on where the eye of the beholder was directed. It wasn't so much that the 1917–22 cohort were being penalized as that the previous cohort were getting a break.

And while some 6 million people could be identified as notch babies, the only ones who incurred the "penalty" were those who worked well past age sixty-two at high earnings levels.[23]

Nevertheless, what could be called, in Washington terms, an entrepreneurial opportunity had been created. Lobbyists and direct-mail entrepreneurs who noticed the notch baby phenomenon in the bill created a cottage industry over the next two decades, soliciting money from the 1917–1922 cohort of retirees to press Washington for redress of the "wrong" that had been done them.[24]

More urgently, the 1977 amendments were built on another set of forecasts that went wrong. Government economists, it seems, had still not yet stopped the wild economic swings of the 1970s. Carter's claim that Social Security was "sound" for another fifty years depended on predictions by the program's trustees that inflation would rise a cumulative 28.2% from 1977 to 1982, while real wages would increase 12.9% and the unemployment rate would hover around 5.9%. In reality, inflation more than doubled the trustees' estimate, reaching 60%; real wages declined 6.9%; and the unemployment rate hit a cumulative 6.7%.[25] Meanwhile, the beneficiary population was expanding fast: from 16.8 million recipients in 1962 to 31.9 million in 1982. Retiree payouts, as a result, continued to balloon, from $71.3 billion in fiscal 1977 to $135.3 billion in fiscal 1982.[26]

There was probably no way the Carter administration or the economists and actuaries at Social Security could have predicted the dire effects of the second oil shock of 1979. While their economic forecasts may have been optimistic, these were based on historical trends, just as they always had been. "Everything went along really rather nicely until the body blow that OPEC delivered to the economy, which made everybody's forecast look optimistic," Henry Aaron, an assistant secretary at the Department of Health, Education and Welfare (HEW) at the time, said later. "It wasn't only the Administration's problem, it was the problem of private forecasters as well."[27]

Nor did anyone know when Carter appointed Paul Volcker as head of the Federal Reserve Board in August 1979 that he would pursue a stringent deflationary policy that would boost interest rates and squeeze capital out of the markets, sending the economy into a deeper recession. That further depressed payroll tax receipts, upsetting Social Security's fiscal position even more. Very quickly it became clear that the 1977 Social Security amendments had only bought a bit more time for the program and that at some point early in the following decade, another fix would be needed.

The administration wasn't averse to tackling the problem again. Carter had been elected as a "new" Democrat, fiscally responsible and critical of "welfare" programs. In late 1978, barely a year after the president had declared Social Security "sound," his HEW secretary, Joseph Califano, proposed a menu of changes—all benefits cuts—that he said would save some $600 million in costs. These included eliminating the $255 lump-sum burial benefit, tightening disability criteria, and repealing the minimum monthly benefit.

Califano, a veteran of the Johnson administration, shared some of his former boss's forceful style. "If you lean on people enough, you get what you want," says one official whose path he crossed on numerous occasions.[28] But Califano's proposals quickly ran into opposition from traditional champions of Social Security on Capitol Hill and even within the administration itself. On December 22, Califano met with three of the most venerated figures connected with the program to hear their objections.

Wilbur Cohen, sixty-five, long nicknamed "Mr. Social Security," was a legendary civil servant who had been HEW secretary under Johnson. Robert M. Ball, sixty-four, had served the SSA in various capacities for years, including as commissioner from 1962 to 1973, under both Democratic and Republican presidents—the longest stint of anyone to head the agency. Both had been instrumental in the creation of Medicare and nearly every improvement in Social Security itself practically since its inception. Rounding out the trio was Nelson Cruikshank, seventy-six, then serving as Carter's advisor on aging but known in Washington previously as the longtime head of the AFL-CIO's influential Social Security policy office.

Formerly among the most powerful figures in shaping the future of Social Security, two of the three were now on the outside but still influential and determined to have their way. Cohen said he was ashamed of Califano and his colleagues. "You'll destroy the Social Security program by what you're doing," he said. "You're trying to dismantle it."[29]

Six days later, the three met with Carter. They denounced the proposed HEW cuts as "horrendous." The president listened, but at the end of the meeting, surprised them. According to Cohen, he "bent over his chair and said in a questioning but affirmative quiet manner, 'But Social Security is not sacrosanct.'" It's likely that no sitting president since the program was created had ever said such a thing, and Carter's statement left Cohen feeling "emotionally exhausted," he later said.[30]

Cohen, Ball, and Cruikshank were shaken but not defeated. They pulled together a coalition of political allies called Save Our Social Security (SOS) to lobby against the cuts. AFL-CIO President Lane Kirkland, United Auto Workers President Douglas Fraser, former House Speaker John McCormack, and former Eisenhower HEW Secretary Arthur Flemming all took prominent roles. SOS went public with a bang when Cohen denounced Califano as the worst secretary in the history of HEW. Cruikshank, despite his post in the Carter White House, testified before the House Select Committee on Aging, calling the HEW proposals "a breach of faith between the government and millions of Social Security contributors."[31]

This trio of policymaking veterans found a crucial ally in what was becoming known as the Gray Lobby. Retired Americans came into their own as a conscious political group in the 1960s. From the start, their numbers gave them a loud voice. By the end of the 1970s, Americans older than sixty for the first time outnumbered those under ten and those between eleven and nineteen years of age. But Social Security itself helped create the opportunity for more seniors' activism, according to political scientist Andrea Louise Campbell. Poor people are generally the least likely to participate in the political process, and Social Security lifted millions of seniors out of poverty, giving them a relatively secure life in old age.[32] As benefits improved, seniors became less dependent on their children and on charity. More elderly of modest means were able to live independently and devote more of their time to community activities and, if they so chose, to political work. At the same time, they came to believe that they could do something about the deficiencies and injustices that remained in their lives.

Seniors were rapidly becoming one of the country's most dependable and powerful groups of voters. Previously, they had always voted at lower rates than the middle-aged population, the thirty-five to forty-five-year-olds. In the 1980s they reached parity with this group. Between the 1950s and the mid-1990s, however, their participation rate in presidential elections would increase from 73% to 84%, while the middle-aged group held steady at 77% to 78%. Seniors were contributing more to political campaigns as well. Between 1952 and 2000, the proportion of retirees who made contributions would steadily rise from a mere 3% to 14%, while the middle-aged group's political giving would peak at 13.9% in 1976, then fall back to 8.6% in 1996. And seniors went from being the age group least likely to volunteer for political campaigns in the 1950s to parity with the middle-aged group, which was formerly the most likely to do so.[33]

When the first White House Conference on Aging was called in 1961, seniors were tacitly added to Washington's roster of so-called "special interest groups," along with labor, racial minorities, women, white southerners, and the business and financial establishment. The first of a once-a-decade series of events, the 1961 conference had 3,000 attendees representing almost 300 organizations. A quick glance at the legislative victories that seniors won in the years that followed demonstrates the power they could wield.

In 1965, Medicare was signed into law. That same year the Older Americans Act was passed. It created within HEW the Administration on Aging (AoA), charged with coordinating federal and state programs for the aged. It also funded a host of state-level programs, from nutrition to in-home services to special services targeted at minority and low-income seniors. AoA offices also provided handy local pressure points for senior advocacy groups. Congress greatly expanded AoA programs in 1973, and the House established a Select Committee on Aging in 1974, the same year the Employee Retirement Income Security Act (ERISA) was passed to strengthen private-sector pension protection.[34]

An even bigger landmark was passage of the Age Discrimination in Employment Act in 1967. This initiated a twenty-year succession of amendments that finally outlawed mandatory retirement in the U.S. Not coincidentally, the term "ageism" was coined in 1968 by gerontologist and psychiatrist Robert N. Butler and swiftly came into common use.[35]

As did the slogan "Gray Power."

Bill Arnone, a longtime advocate for Social Security who got his first exposure to elder issues while running a senior center in the Bronx in the 1970s, witnessed the transformation. "I saw what it was like for many people living just on Social Security," he recalls. "Middle class people became poor in retirement." Arnone helped create one of the first senior action groups at the center. One of their first projects was to send groups of seniors to pharmacies in the area to compare drug prices, then use the local press to publicize the discrepancies. Then they started comparing interest rates offered by their banks.

"I realized this is a powerhouse," says Arnone. "These were people with knowledge and with time on their hands. Given the opportunity, they knew how to organize and get things done."[36]

This new wave of activism crystallized in an explosion of new seniors' groups with distinct political agendas, including the Gray Panthers, the National Senior Citizens Law Center, the Older Women's League, and the National Caucus and Center on the Black Aged. Earlier groups like the American Association of Retired Persons and the labor-funded National Council of Senior Citizens became more politically active as well. The 1971 White House Conference on Aging served as a chance for the Gray Lobby to highlight some of its priorities. Soon, lawmakers began paying closer attention to seniors' demands. The 1972 Social Security amendments, indexing benefits against inflation, were one product.

When SOS was formed, many of the more politically charged elder advocacy groups jumped on board the effort to defend Social Security, giving a strong grassroots base to what could have been merely a letterhead for Ball, Cohen, and their Washington allies. These eminences were well aware of the power the seniors' movement brought to the fight: Cruikshank's position as White House advisor on aging was created in part to reassure elderly voters that the Carter administration was listening to their needs.

A business-backed organization, the National Alliance of Senior Citizens, had established itself in 1974 as a right-leaning alternative to the other elder groups, most of which had a more liberal orientation. But the alliance failed to make much of an impression. By far the most visible of the new senior groups, in fact, was the farthest left: the Gray Panthers. Formed in Philadelphia in 1972 by Maggie Kuhn, a visionary retired social researcher with the United Presbyterian Church, the Panthers' organizers included a number of veterans of the labor struggles of the 1930s, among them some former members of the Communist Party USA.

The Panthers' philosophy, however, was anti-authoritarian and closer in some respects to that of the anarchist and syndicalist movements that nurtured the concepts of mutual aid and social insurance in the late-19th and early-20th centuries. Initially the Panthers were a decentralized group that delegated power to its local networks and developed a shared leadership arrangement instead of a hierarchical structure. Some of the local networks included clinics and other resources for self-help. The Panthers adopted a broad social and political agenda that included nationalizing transportation and the oil industry, opposing nuclear energy and "the concentration of corporate power." From the outset they sought to attract younger members, ensuring a future for the movement after the current generation of organizers was gone.[37]

One of their central demands was that Social Security be improved and strengthened, not cut. Like the Townsend Clubs during the Depression, the Panthers positioned their demands as part of a crusade for social justice. Like other groups that emerged in the 1960s to practice what became known as identity politics, the Panthers understood that they needed to establish a degree of autonomy and control over their lives if they wanted to achieve respect and influence. In advocating health care reform, for example, they insisted that patients must be able to exercise direct control over the programs set up to serve them. The Washington policymaking nexus barely had the conceptual ability to understand this sort of politics.

The Panthers, for their part, only slowly got accustomed to working Capitol Hill and never commanded the numbers that other seniors' groups did. While the AARP boasted upwards of 30 million members, the Panthers counted only 5,000 to 6,000 at their height. But these were hardcore, committed activists who knew how to stage a public spectacle and were unafraid to embarrass elected officials into taking a stand on issues important to the elderly.

The Panthers were "gadflies to keep the older, more established … organizations going toward ever more radical goals," Kuhn said.[38] They quickly gained a reputation as possibly the most uncompromising defenders of Social Security.

These, ironically, were some of the grassroots activists who would prove most valuable to Ball and Cohen, who had spent their careers trying to turn the program into a respectable technocracy removed from the passions of street-level activism. The elderly had already shown their muscle in Washington with the passage of the 1978 Age Discrimination in Employment Act, which banned mandatory retirement at age seventy, and when they lined up with SOS against Califano's attempt to cut Social Security, the Carter White House had to honor their opposition. The proposals never found a lawmaker to sponsor them and Califano himself was fired in 1979. Thanks in part to the organizing already done by the AARP, the NCSC, the Gray Panthers, and others, SOS would soon count 125 separate groups into its coalition.[39]

Ball and Cohen had won by allying themselves with a rising political movement of the elderly. This marked the beginning of a pattern. Time and again over the next thirty years, whenever Social Security was under attack, grassroots organizers would step in to rescue or provide crucial aid to the insiders who were working the levers behind the scenes to defend it. But inside the Washington establishment, Ball and Cohen were perceived as out of step. Califano complained that Cohen and other traditional defenders of Social Security had lost touch and didn't understand that they were now living in a time when painful decisions would have to be made about scarce resources. No program, not even this one, could be considered sacred.

Califano himself failed to see the distinction between, on one hand, changing the formula for calculating benefits and raising payroll taxes, and on the other, actually eliminating elements of the program itself. Congress had changed the benefits formula and raised taxes numerous times without any repercussions. In fact, in a poll taken during the debates over what became the 1977 amendments, 56% of respondents said they approved of higher taxes if it would improve the fiscal health of Social Security.[40] But eliminating the minimum benefit and even the burial payment meant removing organs from the body of the program: the first step on what Cohen and others regarded as a slippery slope to eventual dismantlement of Social Security.

Carter did manage to push through one more significant measure related to Social Security, however: A study of disability costs by the SSA's Office of Assessment in 1979 found in a random sample that in more than 20% of cases, recipients were either ineligible or receiving more money than they were entitled to. Concerned about the explosion of new disability payouts, in 1980 Carter asked from Congress and received a measure requiring the SSA to regularly review the eligibility of all recipients who weren't permanently disabled.

The review wasn't scheduled to start until 1982 and wasn't expected to be much of a money-saver: a mere $10 million over four years, in fact.[41] But it underscored the fact that by the time Carter left office, Washington policymaking on Social Security had already entered a new era of austerity.

CHAPTER 2

"A DESPICABLE THING"

"Should any political party attempt to abolish Social Security, unemployment insurance, and eliminate labor laws and farm programs, you would not hear of that party again in our political history. There is a tiny splinter group, of course, that believes you can do these things. Among them are H.L. Hunt and a few other Texas millionaires, and an occasional politician or business man from other areas. Their number is negligible and they are stupid."
                              —*Pres. Dwight D. Eisenhower[1]*

The editorial writers at the *New York Times* who chastised Reagan for failing to address Social Security's problems in the first months of his term were perhaps unaware that he had begun an attack on one component of the program, Disability Insurance, before he even took office. In December 1980, the congressional General Accounting Office presented to his transition team a report suggesting that as many as 584,000 of Disability Insurance's 2.9 million recipients might be ineligible, and were costing the government $2 billion a year. This was music to the ears of the Reagan team, who were scrambling for ways to make good on the president-elect's claim that the budget could be balanced simply by cutting government "waste" and fraud.

They quickly developed a plan to prioritize the disability review by launching it in spring 1981 instead of on January 1, 1982, as scheduled. They also prepared new estimates of how much could be saved, projecting $3.45 billion in six years: more than thirty-three times what the Social Security Administration had estimated under Carter. The SSA had always done eligibility reviews, but previously conducted only a small number each year—less than 4% of total cases—and generally only when the agency suspected a recipient could probably return to work. But like other parts of the executive branch, the SSA was being given an additional job under Reagan: budget cutting.

"What had been conceived by Congress in 1980 was deliberate invigoration of a review procedure that had been too feeble to have much effect," writes Social Security historian Martha Derthick. "What was set in motion in 1981 was more like a purge."[2]

But Reagan wasn't eager to take on Social Security directly. Chief of Staff James Baker, concerned it was one of the new president's big points of vulnerability, felt that part of his job was to distance the president from any suggestion that he might be preparing to slash the program. Even Stockman wanted to keep Social Security off the agenda during the budget cutting negotiations that led up to passage of Gramm-Latta, because he was unsure of his leverage with lawmakers on such as sensitive issue. Of course, he was counting on bringing it into play during round two. "The $44 billion we had plugged into the March 10 budget under the line 'Future savings to be identified,'" he revealed later, "was nothing more than a euphemism for 'We're going to go after Social Security.'"[3]

For the moment, then, the program was off the table. In March, when a group of mostly Republican senators led by Budget Committee chair Pete Domenici of New Mexico and majority leader Howard Baker of Tennessee began to publicly discuss saving $6 billion by cutting COLAs for Social Security and federal pensions, the president went to Baker's office in the Capitol to discuss it. The meeting included the entire Senate Republican leadership plus the Budget Committee members. It stands as testimony to how far the Republicans had come in believing they could get their way—even on the most popular social program in the country—that "nearly to a man," the senators insisted that balancing the budget "was impossible without curtailing the entitlement COLAs," as Stockman, who was there, later recalled.

"Fellas, I promised I wouldn't touch Social Security," Reagan responded. "We just can't get suckered into it. The other side's just waiting to pounce. So let's put this one behind us and get on with budget cutting." Howard Baker replied, "Mr. President, we hear you loud and clear."[4] Later that day, Democratic Sen. Ernest Hollings of South Carolina, the ranking minority member of the Budget Committee and the penny-pinching champion of the COLA cutback idea, who earlier had told Domenici he could get five of the ten Democrats on the Budget Committee to vote for COLA cuts,[5] said, "It looks like I can't get but one vote."[6] Hollings did bring such a measure to the floor of the Senate on April 1, which he said would save $2.6 billion in fiscal 1982, and was defeated, eighty-six to twelve, with lawmakers from both parties citing opposition to any changes in the COLA formula.

Stockman chalked up the senators' eagerness to carve up Social Security, if it weren't for Reagan's opposition, to a desire to use the savings to protect programs of their own. But within a few weeks, and while Gramm-Latta was still being debated, he changed his mind and decided to put together a more drastic Social Security proposal. What pushed him to do so was action in the House Social Security Subcommittee, whose chair, Democrat J.J. "Jake" Pickle of Texas, introduced a bill to stabilize the program's finances.

* * *

Because the Carter administration had failed in its 1979 effort to fix Social Security's fiscal problems entirely through benefit cuts, coming up with a solution was one of the biggest challenges facing Congress in the first year of the Reagan era. More money was going out in benefit payments than was coming in through payroll taxes: $15 billion vs. $10 billion a year. The trust fund for old-age and survivors' benefits was nearly empty, forcing it to borrow from the trust funds for Disability Insurance and Medicare to make payments.[7]

The centerpiece of Pickle's plan to restore balance was a gradual increase in the retirement age from sixty-five to sixty-eight, which wouldn't take effect until 2000–12. It also included a permanent shift in the date when COLAs kicked in, to October 3 from July 3, beginning in 1982. Since regular COLAs produce cumulatively larger benefits, a three month delay would result in permanently lower benefits. That would produce annual savings of $1 billion in fiscal 1983, $1.1 billion in fiscal 1984, and slightly larger savings each year thereafter, helping tide the program over the expected difficult decade. Pickle also called for funding half of Medicare from income tax rather than payroll tax, freeing up more payroll tax revenues to bolster the old-age insurance fund. Lastly, he proposed changes similar to the ones Reagan had made, eliminating the minimum benefit and the student benefit.

The subcommittee quickly approved all of Pickle's proposals except the COLA shift, which Democratic Rep. Richard A. Gephardt of Missouri called "too much political dynamite" since the president was on record opposing such a move.[8] But the Pickle bill had the effect of putting the Democrats out in front on an issue that was arguably much more immediately important to most voters than Reagan's tax and spending cuts: saving Social Security.

Pickle's bill was of a piece with the incremental approach to Social Security reform that the Carter White House had pursued with the 1977 Amendments, adjusting the rules here and there to find savings but leaving the basic structure of the program alone. This was how most Republican lawmakers expected a deal to be made as well. In early March, Rep. Barber Conable of New York, the ranking Republican member of the Social Security Subcommittee, had introduced another bill to improve the program's finances incrementally by requiring all 2.8 million federal employees to join Social Security, adding their payroll tax receipts to the pot.

All this put Stockman in an awkward position. The OMB director didn't want merely to stabilize Social Security: he wanted to milk it for far greater savings in the unified budget by drastically cutting benefits. If Pickle's bill, now before the Ways and Means Committee, acquired momentum in the House, it could make any Social Security proposals the administration came up with much harder to put across.

On April 10, Stockman "set in motion a plan to get more savings." What was to follow, he later wrote, was no less than "a frontal assault on the very inner fortress of the American welfare state—the giant Social Security system, on which one seventh of the nation's populace depended for its well-being."[9] Coming up with an alternative to Pickle's bill wasn't just a matter of extending the White House's budget-cutting exercise. Stockman was determined to go farther than either party had ever gone in overhauling Social Security.

As a supply-side revolutionary, this was what he had come to Washington to do. During his first term in the House in 1975, he had contributed an article entitled "The Social Pork Barrel" to the *Public Interest*, a neoconservative magazine that was one of the first to give Wanniski and Laffer a forum for their economic ideas. The article, which attracted considerable attention for Stockman, was a blistering attack on "the prevailing liberal faith in meeting unfulfilled 'human needs' by means of social welfare programs," denouncing nearly all such programs as corrupt giveaways to political constituencies. He particularly attacked the social insurance concept as a "mythology" that encouraged the government to hand out benefits through Social Security and Medicare to middle-class workers who could do without them instead of concentrating on low-income populations that really needed the help.[10]

This argument reflected one of the core complaints that conservatives had been making about Social Security ever since the program was enacted. When attacked as heartless scrooges, prepared to let older Americans starve or become a burden on their families, they often argued that they had no problem with the concept of a needs-based welfare system distributing benefits to workers in real distress. What they objected to was a program that provided benefits to everyone based on what they had earned, not on their actual needs. A program such as this, they feared, could acquire a life of its own and become politically impossible to cut even if it became too expensive.

The conservatives were essentially right. When Franklin Roosevelt's staff were developing the Social Security Act in 1935, some cautioned against creating a separate payroll tax, since it would hit lower income workers harder than the middle and upper classes. FDR famously replied, "we put those payroll contributions there so as to give the contributors a legal, moral, and political right to collect their pensions and their unemployment benefits. With those taxes in there, no damn politician can ever scrap my social security program."[11] He was well aware that he was creating a program that would be uniquely difficult to get rid of—and he wanted it that way.

Pickle's challenge energized Stockman philosophically, and the day after the Democratic bill hit Ways and Means, a meeting was called—in the Roosevelt Room—to find an alternative. The meeting included Stockman; Martin Anderson, head of the Office of Policy Development; Health and Human Service's (HHS) Secretary Richard Schweicker; and Richard Darman, chief legislative strategist. They quickly agreed to "save" Social Security through benefit cuts—$75 billion to $100 billion in cuts over the next five years—rather than higher payroll taxes. When Schweiker proposed Conable's idea of pulling federal government workers into the payroll tax pool, Stockman replied, "Our job is to shrink the Social Security monster. Not indenture millions more workers to a system that's already unsound."[12]

By the end of the meeting, Stockman says, he had prevailed, and HHS staff began developing a series of options to balance Social Security's books by reducing the "redistributionist elements" of the system. But he didn't trust HHS, or the Social Security Administration, to develop a plan on their own. And so all their suggestions were fed through Stockman's OMB staff, who gave the director a crash course on the fine points of the system.

"We were on an exceedingly fast track owing to the drumbeat from the Hill for an administration plan," Stockman wrote later, and the next month saw a furious effort to boil down a coherent set of options to give the president. Reagan met with Stockman, Anderson, and Schweicker on Monday, May 11 for one hour, by which time Stockman had decided that cutting benefits for workers who retired at sixty-two instead of sixty-five was going to be the centerpiece of his proposal. It fit his philosophic dislike of benefits that he felt weren't based on genuine needs. Also, early retirement benefits hadn't been included in the original Social Security Act. That fit the Republican picture of a program expanding out of control, which struck a chord with Reagan.

"I've been warning since 1964 that Social Security was heading for bankruptcy, and this is one of the reasons why," the president said. The group agreed to propose increasing the penalty for retirement at sixty-two to a 45% benefit cut, from the current 20%—a figure that SSA Deputy Commissioner Robert Myers later said Stockman's team arrived at because it would save them the particular amount of money they needed for budget purposes, even though it "had nothing to do with actuarial soundness or fairness."[13] This would become a familiar pattern as the decade wore on.

"The President pronounced himself enthusiastic about the final package and approved it all on the spot," Stockman recalled. "It was one of the rare instances in which this ever happened."[14] One participant in the meeting, Myers, who had previously served for decades as Social Security's chief actuary, says that at one point during the session he "happened to look up at the wall where a portrait of Franklin D. Roosevelt was hanging. I couldn't help but think that he had to be spinning in his grave at what we were trying to do to Social Security."[15]

At a full meeting of the White House Legislative Strategy Group that afternoon, however, James Baker predictably worried that calling for Social Security cuts would put the president in political hot water. Rather than Reagan himself announcing it, he said Schweiker would do so as HHS secretary. That way, if it met a hostile response, the White House could claim it wasn't the president's initiative. The fact that the proposal got by Baker may have been, in part, because Schweiker, a former senator, and Stockman, a former House member, argued that they knew what they were doing in peddling such a package to Congress.[16] Also, Gramm-Latta had just passed, encouraging the Reaganauts to believe they were in control of the legislative machinery.

Stockman would later claim that the entire plan had been hatched in secret until the moment he and his colleagues brought it to the president. Eugene Steuerle, who represented the Treasury Department at some of the meetings that led up to the May 11 decision, contended that it got through partly because any experienced civil servants who might have opposed it were excluded from the deliberations by Reagan administration "newcomers." "Many of the most talented individuals in the executive branch, including top analysts from the Social Security Administration," were prevented "from attending these meetings," Steuerle wrote. "Valuable information was thereby excluded through inadequate use of staff," which in turn was largely because the "newcomers" were so distrustful of the bureaucracy.[17]

But Stockman and other administration officials were already putting out the word several days before the May 11 meeting with the president that Social Security cuts would be on the table soon, and were even expanding on the philosophy behind the cuts. On May 6, Treasury Secretary Donald Regan told the *Washington Post* that the administration was looking at COLA reductions and "a penalty for early retirement" as ways to accomplish the goal. Social Security was originally intended only to be a "backup" for workers' private savings, he said, but it had expanded beyond offering simple "subsistence."

As for the president's pledge not to touch the "safety net," Regan said it had applied only to the current year—not subsequent years—and that the president "did not put himself in cement forever" on Social Security.[18]

The same day, in an address to the American Newspaper Publishers Association convention in Chicago, Stockman warned that despite the White House's looming victory with Gramm-Latta, "hand-to-hand combat" over the budget would take place during the next few months in what he termed a "once-in-a-generation debate."

That debate, Stockman said, would center on the "false premises" that were leading to big increases in federal spending every year. The administration's goal would be to reverse a fifty-year trend toward a "vast, unwieldy, and mindless" government bureaucracy. In particular, Stockman said the White House and Congress would have to work this year on a program to prevent Social Security insolvency in two years. "All aspects of the program should be considered," the *Washington Post* reported Stockman saying, "including the benefit structure, unearned benefits, early retirement, and cost-of-living escalators"—in short, the same elements Reagan had put off-limits two months earlier, plus the ones OMB was now preparing to put on the table.

Next day, Senate minority leader Robert Byrd of West Virginia received a letter from Regan and Stockman on behalf of the president, saying that the administration was getting ready to propose further Social Security cuts that would "reduce current-law outlays" by some $8 billion a year.

Senate Republicans, too, sensed that the White House was pulling away from its opposition to scaling down the program. What prompted Byrd to request the letter was an effort by Sen. Donald Riegle, Michigan Democrat, to turn back a sudden revival of the very bill the president had asked the Republican leadership not to pursue just two months earlier. The Senate Budget Committee proposal, which also aimed to save nearly $8 billion a year, included a major change in how COLAs were calculated. Instead of being pegged to consumer price increases, they would rise in tandem with either prices or wages, whichever rose less. The bill also proposed a three-month delay in COLA adjustments.

Riegle protested that these seemingly technical adjustments represented a "sweeping change" to Social Security and "broken promises" to some 45 million elderly beneficiaries. "Just to save some money," Democrat Lawton Chiles of Florida mocked, "we're going to take it out of your hides." "That's political garbage," retorted Hollings, who noted triumphantly that the administration will "have a hard difficult time making those cuts" needed to meet its budget targets unless it went along with the Budget Committee bill.

On May 8, the bill made it to the floor and passed, forty-nine to forty-two. Coming a day after the House passed Gramm-Latta, it represented the second time in two days that a house of Congress voted to cut Social Security. Collectively, the cuts on the table on Capitol Hill now amounted to some $10.2 billion a year.

Thus, when Schweiker stepped before the television cameras at a news conference four days later to announce "his" package of Social Security proposals, he and Stockman had reason to feel that Congress was primed to accept it and that the media largely wouldn't question it. Under the proposals, a person retiring at sixty-two would receive 55% of full benefits rather than the current 80%. Schweiker also outlined a three-month COLA delay, much like the one the Senate had just passed; a longer waiting period to receive disability benefits; and an echo of the change, just accepted by the House as part of the Gramm-Latta budget resolution, to eliminate "windfall" benefits to government workers who had worked a short time in private-sector jobs. As a sweetener, the earnings test for Social Security recipients over sixty-five would be phased out over three years.

The entire package would cut outlays by $9 billion in 1982, up to some $24 billion annually by 1986, for a 10% drop from current levels. By 2055, the last year of the Social Security trustees' projections, actuarial calculations showed that the reduction would increase to about 25%, if current trends remained steady. That would be enough to push millions of Social Security recipients over the poverty line.

Pickle and Ways and Means Chair Dan Rostenkowski initially tried to play down any controversy, thinking their duty was to work quietly with the Republicans toward a solution to Social Security's funding problems. But the speaker was another matter. Tip O'Neill was a New Deal stalwart for whom cutting the COLA was nearly unthinkable. He was also an extraordinarily crafty politician. Guessing that the Reaganauts had overreached, he instantly decided to go public. "I have a statement on Social Security," he said at a press conference the next day, focusing on the early retirement cut. "A lot of people approaching that age have either already retired on pensions or have made irreversible plans to retire very soon. These people have been promised substantial Social Security benefits at age 62. I consider it a breach of faith to renege on that promise. For the first time since 1935 people would suffer because they trusted in the Social Security system."

"Are you saying that is a serious political mistake?" a reporter asked.

"I'm not talking about politics," O'Neill replied. "I'm talking about decency. It is a rotten thing to do. It is a despicable thing."[19]

That was the curtain raiser to a week of outrage that united and invigorated the Democratic opposition for the first time since November. Leading lawmakers including Sens. Edward Kennedy and Daniel Patrick Moynihan, the latter a one-time academic mentor of Stockman's, denounced the early retirement cut. Just about every major Democratic constituency was quickly heard from. Rep. Patricia Schroeder, Colorado Democrat, said it would "worsen the already precarious situation of women nearing their retirement years." AFL-CIO President Lane Kirkland said it would punish workers forced by ill health or disability to leave the workforce early. Wilbur Cohen called the proposal "a calamity, a tragedy and a catastrophe."

One Republican senator, William Campbell of Colorado, may have come closest to the heart of the matter, calling Schweiker's announcement "a masterpiece of bad timing."[20] The most damaging part of the Social Security proposals, the one that provoked the most outrage, was the date of the early retirement benefits cut: January 1, 1982. This meant that someone planning to retire in less than nine months and expecting to receive $650 a month would only be receiving $450, Stockman noted.

What had gone wrong? Stockman would later explain that, at the May 11 meeting with the president, the assembled officials hadn't had time to pin a date on the change. "HHS technicians," the Social Security loyalists within the agency who he suspected were against him, had "presumably" inserted the date before Schweiker opened his press conference.[21]

Wherever the date came from, Republican lawmakers were soon flooded with phone calls demanding to know if they supported the administration's "despicable" plan. In turn, they complained to the White House that none of the principal Republican leaders on Social Security—Barber Conable; Senate Finance Committee chair Bob Dole; John Heinz, chair of the Senate Special Committee on the Aging—had been consulted before Schweiker's announcement.

This wasn't entirely justified. Dole and members of the Senate Budget Committee had themselves been looking for ways to cut Social Security using many of the tools the president was now proposing. Lawrence Kudlow, Stockman's chief economist at OMB, initially defended the package by saying explicitly that the cuts reflected "what amounts to an agreement by both Congress and the administration to lower the safety net" on key spending programs the president pledged to leave intact.[22] And of course, less than a week earlier, the entire Senate had voted to carve almost $8 billion a year out of the program.

Unlike their congressional partymates, however, the Reaganauts had more in mind than just some revenue-raising cuts. The severity of the proposal Schweiker had unveiled made it plain that the White House wanted to redesign the program, ultimately reducing it to something akin to welfare. "They're taking advantage of a temporary financing problem to make major permanent cutbacks in the long-range role of Social Security," said Bob Ball.

The Democrats' outrage seemed to translate instantly into public opposition. A *Washington Post*-ABC News poll, taken days after the issue ignited, found that 59% of respondents were against reducing benefits for early retirees and 66% were against reducing initial benefits for any group. More embarrassing still, given the administration's priorities, was a poll by the National Federation of Independent Business that found that two-thirds of the public would rather see taxes raised than Social Security benefits cut.

With numbers such as these at their fingertips, the Democrats turned their attention to capitalizing at the ballot box. When Democrat Steny H. Hoyer won a special election to the House from Maryland later that month, party chair Charles T. Manatt called it "rejection of the Reagan Social Security cutbacks."

The blowup had an immediate impact on the larger budget talks, in which House and Senate conferees were trying to reconcile their just-passed measures. Three days after Schweiker's press conference, they agreed on a $695.4 billion budget for the next fiscal year. The controversy gave the House delegates sufficient leverage to demand that the final bill drop all references to Social Security cuts: either the administration's proposals or those the Senate had approved earlier.

Soon the Republicans were backpedaling further. At the annual Tidewater Conference for Republican officeholders on May 15, the attendees voted informally to assure "those who are now concerned that no particular age group or segment of our population will sustain an unfair burden" from any plan to ease Social Security's financial situation.

The same day, Schweiker said on television that the administration wouldn't stand rigidly by its proposals and "would certainly strongly consider working out a bipartisan bill" on Social Security. Dole said on *Face the Nation* that Reagan's proposals would face "a lot of compromises" and that "those who will turn sixty-two in the next few years probably don't have very much to worry about." And he pointedly complained of not having been consulted by the White House before Schweiker unveiled the package of proposals.

Stockman wasn't happy. He had wanted the party to stand and defend its position and he wanted Reagan, with his personal warmth, to take command. "I had argued that we had to fight tooth and nail to get the President out front," Stockman later wrote, "even have him give a nationwide speech on TV in order to calm the political uprising. It was crucial. The package we had devised would save $50 billion over 1982–86, nearly a third of our budget gap for those years. We couldn't afford *not* to fight." But the president's advisors, led by James Baker, had already decided, "*No presidential involvement.*"[23] Reagan himself, in his autobiography, would later express bitterness at his defeat, which he wrongly maintained was "a plan to cut millions of dollars in waste and fraud from Social Security," not a benefits cut.[24] But he listened to Baker and went along.

As if to validate its concerns, the Senate on May 20 passed a bipartisan resolution, 96-0, against any proposal that would "precipitously and unfairly penalize early retirees" or reduce benefits more than "necessary to achieve a financially sound system and the well-being of all retired Americans." The momentum was so solidly in one direction that the Senate first had to vote down by the narrowest of margins, 49-48, a more harshly worded Democratic resolution that actually attracted two Republican votes. The resolution had no binding effect, of course, but the White House could see that it would have to back off, at least temporarily.

The next day Schweicker reiterated that the administration's Social Security stance was "negotiable." Meanwhile, a conciliatory letter to congressional leaders arrived from Reagan himself, saying his goal was simply to save Social Security from "bankruptcy" and that he would support any "bipartisan" alternative that would do so.

Opening up further, Schweicker said a few days later that the White House was prepared to negotiate with Pickle, whose own proposal Stockman had been so eager to preempt just a couple of weeks earlier. On the table could be COLA changes, which Reagan had earlier rejected, and another round of borrowing by the Old Age and Survivors' Insurance trust fund from the Disability and Hospital Insurance trust funds. As for the controversial early retirement benefits cuts, Schweicker said the White House would consider phasing them in more slowly but wanted to do so before 1990, because the trust funds needed the money.

* * *

It's easy to exaggerate the defeat Reagan suffered with the failure of his and Stockman's "frontal assault" on "the American welfare state." Even as the

Democrats—and then the Senate Republicans—made Reagan's team pay in public for their political naïveté, the same coalition of conservative lawmakers that had served the president so far continued to do so as if nothing had gone wrong. The same day the Senate voted 96-0 on its Social Security resolution, the House voted, 244-155, to adopt a 1982 budget resolution that gave Reagan most of what he wanted.

Throughout the summer Reagan continued to rack up legislative victories. In June, the House passed a huge budget bill fleshing out the cuts mandated in the joint budget resolution. Stockman and his staff had pasted it together overnight and it was full of technical errors, but elimination of the minimum Social Security benefit was still there, buried so deep that many lawmakers may not have known they were voting for it.[25] House and Senate conferees preserved the change, agreeing to end the minimum benefit as of March 1982 even as the Ways and Means Committee was searching for support to keep it in place for current retirees.

In late June, Reagan proposed a further package of budget cuts totaling $20 billion over the next three years. After turning back a Democratic substitute, the House passed "Gramm-Latta II," which actually upped the cuts to $35 billion. In each case, the coalition of Republicans and Democratic Boll Weevils, not Speaker O'Neill, determined the outcome. And in each case, the Social Security reductions Reagan had requested earlier, eliminating the minimum benefit and students' benefits, stayed in the package.

Finally, in late July came the showdown on Reagan's tax-cut package, the centerpiece of the supply-side program, which had by then been whittled down in negotiations to 25% over three years across all tax brackets. The $750 billion package won comfortably in both House and Senate on July 29. The supply-siders' scenario for economic recovery would now have its chance.

Reagan's ill-considered assault on early retirement benefits hadn't made it easier for Democrats to oppose the president's overall progress on Capitol Hill, but it had reinvigorated the grassroots movement to defend Social Security that had been born when Califano attempted to float his package of benefits cuts in 1978.

Save Our Social Security declared war on the Reagan cuts at a May 27 press conference. United Auto Workers President Douglas Fraser said, "It is wrong to wring tens of billions of dollars out of retiree benefits so that they may be applied to other parts of the federal budget." Organizers were careful that reporters understood that SOS represented ninety national organizations with more than 40 million members combined. Most were unions or labor-funded groups. But the opposition was spreading. The same day as the SOS press conference, another meeting took place in which the House Select Committee on Aging, the Congressional Black Caucus, and the National Caucus on the Black Aged denounced Reagan's plans to cut Social Security and other programs. "Being old, black and poor, there are three strikes against you," said Tennessee Democratic Rep. Harold Ford.[26]

The coalition's biggest asset, aside from the support of grassroots elder activists, was Bob Ball. Ball's career in the Social Security Administration dated back almost to its inception. Washington widely—and accurately—regarded him as a great administrator and one of the key architects of Social Security's growth over the decades. He was one of the designers of Medicare and had engineered the last great improvement in Social Security: the 1972 Amendments that boosted benefits 20% and indexed them to the cost of living.

Perhaps more important, Ball was a consummately skillful political strategist and operator. A calm, well-spoken man with a distinguished mien and impressive shock of white hair, he probably acquired his disarming "mixture of solemnity, high purpose, and humor" from his father, a Methodist minister.[27] But "his strategic sense always put him a few moves ahead of his competitors," Ball's biographer, Edward Berkowitz, says.[28] While he was known to be a liberal Democrat, he had worked well with the Eisenhower and even the first Nixon administrations, and had always taken care to include Republicans within the SSA's top ranks.[29] He probably understood more deeply the subtle balancing act that made social insurance programs work politically than any of their enemies and all but a few of their friends.

Ball had retired from the SSA in early 1973, when it became clear that Nixon wanted to appoint a commissioner of his own choosing for his second term, but he remained influential behind the scenes, primarily as an advisor to the Democratic side. He was a fluent writer who turned out a stream of position papers, op-eds, and policy statements from the office he maintained in Washington at the Institute of Medicine and, later, the National Academy of Social Insurance. He maintained his contacts on Capitol Hill and built new ones assiduously. Over the years he had also developed an impressive Rolodex filled with the names of reporters and editors at major national publications, TV, and radio. Whenever he had a legislative or regulatory agenda or point of view to push, he worked these contacts assiduously.[30]

Ball headed SOS's advisory committee, which after the early retirement debacle, began to develop a rhetorical and legislative strategy against Reagan. It began with a careful look at what the president and Congress were really trying to do with Social Security. Reagan—and conservative Democrats like Pickle, with his proposal to raise the retirement age—were using very long-run, seventy-five-year projections to build a case for drastically scaling back the program, Ball argued, when in fact the problem was temporary. The real trouble, he said, was that until the baby boomers were fully integrated into the workforce around the end of the decade, boosting payroll tax receipts, Social Security would face financing problems. Inflation was already starting to ease and if real wages began to rise again, the program should be assured of good health as long as anyone could reasonably foresee.

Instead of cutting benefits, Ball argued, the solution to the shortfalls was an accounting maneuver. Simply extend the Carter administration's practice of shifting assets from the relatively healthy Disability and Hospital Insurance trust funds into the Old Age and Survivors fund. That, and perhaps some minor trims in benefits while moving up the payroll tax increases already ordered by the 1977 Amendments, should tide the program over until the baby boomers were all working.

As for the seventy-five-year projections, which included the years when the baby boomers would start to retire and withdraw payments, how well the system would be able to sustain the drain would depend on the size of the labor force decades hence, said Ball. "But the size of the labor force that far off depends on impossible-to-predict factors such as the fertility rate, immigration rates, the extent to which older people continue to work as against taking benefits, labor force participation rates for women—so it is plausible that the 1990 rate [of taxation] will be adequate, but equally plausible that more money will be needed in 2020."[31]

Making too much of the seventy-five-year projections, in other words, smacked of an ideological agenda geared to dismantle Social Security, not save it. But the immediate challenge was one particular element of Reagan's tax-cut package. Now that the early retirement cuts had been defeated, at least for current retirees, Ball concluded that the Democrats and SOS should call for preserving the minimum benefit—at least for those already receiving it.

Given a choice, Ball and many other longtime Social Security practitioners would have preferred to let this particular feature of the program die. While the minimum benefit dated back to the 1935 Social Security Act itself, it didn't fit well with the social insurance philosophy. It wasn't directly linked to what workers paid into the system and therefore wasn't really an "earned" benefit. Also, the 1972 Amendments had included a new benefit called the "special minimum" for workers who had contributed to Social Security for at least ten years, making the minimum benefit somewhat redundant.

Ball's main objection to the action by Reagan and Congress on this issue was that it extended to current retirees. As with the proposed early retirement cuts, it had the advantage of raising money to balance the White House's budget right away. But that was precisely what the Democrats objected to: that the administration was balancing the books on the backs of those most in need.

Ball established working relationships with a small number of key lawmakers who he urged to complain that the president was exaggerating Social Security's long-run problems and to make an issue of elimination of the minimum benefit. Senate Democrats Moynihan of New York and Russell Long of Louisiana and, in the House, Tip O'Neill and Democratic Rep. Richard Bolling of Missouri, who chaired the Rules Committee, were his closest partners.

In late July, as the House and Senate passed their versions of the budget reconciliation act, the House approved a nonbinding resolution to "ensure that Social Security benefits are not reduced for those currently receiving them." By this time, SOS and other organizations had mobilized their membership around the minimum benefit and lawmakers were sensing they might pay a political price for cutting it. While the vote was taking place, a rally on the

Capitol's west steps, organized by the National Council of Senior Citizens, listened to O'Neill and Kennedy, among others, denounce Reagan's Social Security proposals. "Congress—When My Security Goes, You Go," one sign read.

Inside, Democrats and Republicans traded charges. "These are unearned benefits to non-needy citizens," said Gramm. "We're not talking about a group of merry widows who clip coupons by day and waltz by night," said Pat Schroeder.[32]

The House Rules Committee shortly thereafter allowed Bolling to hold up the reconciliation bill long enough to reach a deal that would allow the House to also pass a bill restoring the minimum benefit. That meant that when Reagan achieved his great victory in late July with the final reconciliation bill, making his tax cuts the law, Social Security was, in effect, still on the table because the House bill on the minimum benefit was still awaiting action in the Senate.

Reagan and his advisors knew this was a potentially serious problem and in a newspaper interview, the president seemed to concede a little ground. While he wouldn't agree to a blanket restoration of the minimum benefit, the president might be willing to discuss a rules change that would allow some of the recipients to qualify for welfare, SSI, or some other program that would give them back some of the lost income. "What we want to do," he said, "is to get rid of those people" for whom the $122 minimum payment "is not a necessity, and then take care of those other people in some way that does not raid the Social Security fund."[33]

Philosophically, such a tradeoff had no appeal for Ball and his allies because it would have furthered the goal that Stockman and other conservatives had long put forth for Social Security: to convert as much of it as possible from an all-inclusive social insurance system into a poverty program, eminently cuttable, politically vulnerable. On a more immediate level, the administration soon found itself the victim of its own numbers regarding the minimum benefit, which were more dire than it had expected. Some 3 million would be affected by the cut, out of whom the vast majority either would be eligible for other types of benefits or already received substantial retirement income from other sources, deputy commissioner Bob Myers told Pickle's subcommittee in September. But according to Pickle, the numbers also indicated that some 400,000 of those eligible for other benefits probably wouldn't apply.[34]

Meanwhile, with Social Security still a live issue because of the House bill, Domenici's Senate Budget Committee was considering its earlier plan to close the budget gap by limiting COLAs for Social Security and other government retirement programs. This time, the formula would hold COLAs to 3-percentage-points less than each year's CPI increase. Stockman, too, was loudly urging Reagan and his inner circle to get behind another round of budget cutting: a "September offensive" that would include domestic program cuts, defense cuts, and another shot at restructuring Social Security. A major part of Stockman's plan was to delay all COLAs—for Social Security, federal employees' pensions, and every other inflation-indexed program—until October 1, 1982.

Reagan initially agreed, and even drafted a speech appealing to the nation to support restructuring Social Security, arguing that younger voters would be concerned that their elders were getting overly generous benefits that they themselves would never enjoy. But in a meeting with Baker and Bob Michel, the Senate and House Republican leaders, the president heard their candid opinion that they couldn't sell Stockman's cuts to lawmakers. What was to be done? Reagan asked. Social Security was facing a budgetary crisis. Baker suggested a classic Washington gambit: appoint a commission to look into it.

At a meeting on September 13, the president told Stockman the only thing he would consider was a three-month delay in COLA increases.[35] The Republicans' one hope to make significant changes in Social Security before Reagan's honeymoon period ended was now Pickle, who continued to insist to fellow Democrats that they had a "moral obligation" to work with their rivals on the issue.

O'Neill put a stop to that on September 17, at a meeting in his office with Pickle and Bolling. After listening to the Social Security Subcommittee chair, Bolling said, "Jake, we are all proud of your work. But I want to say one thing. As long as I am chairman of the Rules Committee there won't be any Social Security legislation in this Congress." Afterward, O'Neill told the press that the Democrats wouldn't cooperate with efforts to cut Social Security and that Pickle's subcommittee "does not intend to go forward at the present time."[36]

A short time later, both House and Senate Republicans told the White House that they had no more political cover to support any Social Security changes. The Senate Democratic Caucus then pushed the subject of cuts even further off the table with a resolution opposing Reagan's proposals, instead calling upon Congress to "protect the soundness of the Social Security system" by authorizing the trust funds to borrow from one another, as Ball was proposing. On September 24, the Senate Finance Committee essentially agreed, unanimously voting to reverse the elimination of the minimum benefit for those already receiving it. It also agreed to allocate some payroll tax revenues into Social Security's Old-Age and Survivors' Insurance Trust Fund (OASI) that would normally have gone into the Disability Insurance and Hospital Insurance trust funds, thus staving off bankruptcy for OASI for at least a year. Anticipating more trouble in 1982, it also authorized OASI to borrow some further monies from the Disability Insurance fund.

The same day, in a letter to O'Neill and a television address, Reagan conceded the minimum benefit cut and proposed that the president and both parties create a bipartisan commission to draft a permanent plan to shore up Social Security's finances. The full Senate voted to reverse the minimum benefit elimination and authorize interfund borrowing, and a House-Senate conference committee sealed the deal in December. But the borrowing authority would last only until December 31, 1982, creating a deadline for the commission, the White House, and the Democratic leadership to agree on a long-range plan.

CHAPTER 3

THE "THIRD RAIL" OF AMERICAN POLITICS

In an appearance before the House Budget Committee, Stockman added a new item in his deficit analysis: "Inaction on Social Security." Cuts in the program had been the lynchpin of Stockman's drive to balance the budget in the first year of Reagan's term. Without them, he predicted federal deficits of $60 billion in each of the next three years. And without success at long-term budget cutting, Stockman told Greider, supply-side economics had no substance but was "really new clothes for the unpopular doctrine of the old Republican orthodoxy," Greider wrote. "So the supply-side formula was the only way to get a tax policy that was really 'trickle down.' Supply-side is trickle-down theory."[1]

That fall, Greider published a long article in *The Atlantic* based on his interviews with Stockman. The OMB director made scathing comments about the chaotic nature of the budget process he had led in the spring. And he denounced, much as he had in his *Public Interest* article six years earlier, the feeding frenzy of

Capitol Hill lawmakers fighting for goodies for their constituents at the expense of the budget. Only this time, his eloquence wasn't appreciated. Democrats were outraged, Republicans flushed with embarrassment, and Stockman himself offered to resign. The president asked him to stay on, but the revolution he had most wanted to bring about in Washington was scrapped.

In an interview with the *New York Times* in October, Ball reviewed the success of his and the Democrats' strategy to upend Reagan on Social Security. "We feel the Social Security bill is a victory, but it's a battle and not the war," he said. "The reason President Reagan wants a commission to study Social Security for a year or more is to get the issue out of the 1982 congressional elections. He'll be back after that."[2]

Ball knew that Reagan retained his personal hold over voters, despite the defeat he had suffered. According to a series of *Washington Post*-ABC News polls, his approval rating among voters over sixty—those most loyal to Social Security—dropped from 70% to 50% after the May press conference at which Schweiker announced the early retirement and other cuts. By October, after he had announced the bipartisan commission, Reagan was back up to 59% approval with this age group.

Most importantly, the Reagan tax cuts would now start to do some of the president's budget work for him. Stockman had told Greider that one of the most important reasons for supporting the cuts was that they would "put a tightening noose around the size of government."[3] This would make Social Security a tempting target for budget-cutting for years to come. In that sense, supply-side economics—the Reagan version—was a glass half full after all.

* * *

When Ball spoke with the *Times*, the Democratic leadership's primary concern was how to turn their victory on Social Security to electoral advantage. Ironically, this was because of Stockman. If he hadn't insisted on pushing Social Security cuts to the forefront in the first year of Reagan's presidency, the Democrats would have had little to campaign on in 1982, because they had either cooperated in or effectively decided not to fight most of the president's other major budgetary and tax measures. Three factors made their one clear victory of the year possible: O'Neill's sharp political instincts in picking a fight over cuts in early retirement benefits, Ball's belief that opposing the minimum benefit cut for current recipients could build broad opposition, and a strong grassroots effort to rally voters and activists around those issues.

The Democrats were helped by the fact that some of the Social Security cuts that had seemed like mere abstractions a few months earlier were now hitting recipients directly. By December, high school guidance counselors across the country were informing seniors with deceased parents that they wouldn't be receiving the $259 a month they had previously expected if they went to college. Some 40,000 lost benefits for the 1982 school year. Another 734,000 already in college would see their benefits cut back by 55% in 1982 and then more gradually until the program ended in 1985. Individual notifications of the cuts weren't scheduled to go out from the Social Security Administration until the spring, so it fell to school officials to explain the change to students already making their plans for the coming school year.

"What bothered me," a counselor said in a *Washington Post* story about the benefits cuts, "was telling the kids and seeing the expressions of helplessness, hopelessness and anger, as they realize they were caught in this. Some cases are especially sad, like kids with both parents dead, who planned to use their Social Security checks to continue their education as well as feed and clothe themselves."[4]

The economy, meanwhile, wasn't following the supply-siders' glide path to sustained, robust growth that the Reaganauts had expected once their tax cut package was in place. Stockman had projected 5.2% growth in GNP in 1982, the year the Reagan tax cuts kicked in. But the Fed, overreacting to a slight economic upturn in 1981, tightened interest rates still further that fall. The result was the most severe economic collapse since the Depression. GNP fell 2.2%. Some 17,000 businesses failed, the second highest number since 1933. Nine million workers lost their jobs, pushing the unemployment rate up to 9.4% in May, the highest since the Depression. Even for Americans less affected, the hard times were difficult to ignore, as homelessness grew and sick, elderly, and poor people without roofs over their heads became a common sight in cities across the country.

All of which gave the Democrats' protests about fairness an even more impressive ring. Reagan had pushed almost every major element of his economic program through Congress, and for working people, conditions had only gotten worse. The tax cuts were real and the deficit was getting worse. But little or nothing was trickling down to the people who most needed it.

This picture only began to materialize fully in the first months of 1982 as it became clear that the economy was moving in the wrong direction and would become a powerful issue in the fall elections. By that time, Social Security was already proving to be one of the Democrats' strongest weapons against the Republicans. The White House followed its legislative missteps during the spring and summer of 1981 with another series of embarrassments in the fall.

In December, Bob Myers suddenly resigned as deputy Social Security commissioner. One of the program's revered elders along with Bob Ball and Wilbur Cohen, Myers had served as the SSA's chief actuary from 1947 to 1970. Unlike them, he was a Republican who had always chafed at what he regarded as the Democratic bias of the SSA staff and their constant efforts to expand the agency's empire. In 1969, he had advised the undersecretary of HEW to fire Ball and campaigned to take over the commissioner's job himself. A year later, after accusing the agency's leadership of pursuing an "expansionist" agenda behind the Nixon administration's back, he resigned.

Myers had remained a well-known consultant and authority on public pensions, however. When the Reagan team was preparing to enter office, they chose him for a close-to-the-top post in the SSA partly as a statement that they intended to take a narrow view of the institution's goals but also to reassure Social Security's supporters that the new direction would be undertaken by experienced hands with a deep knowledge of the agency and its programs.

But Myers had watched all year as the White House and OMB consistently made the major decisions for Social Security, with the agency itself left only to do the scut work of compiling figures and researching proposals. He also object-ed to the administration's decision to end the minimum benefit for current as well as future retirees: a "lousy" policy he then had to defend before Rep. Claude Pepper's House Select Committee on Aging. And he disagreed strongly with the administration's "bone-headed" attempt to slash early retirement benefits.

Yet when Baker and Meese created a "report card" for the first year of the Reagan administration, "they bravely gave their boss the grade which they thought he deserved: an A-plus" on Social Security, Myers later noted wryly. "The White House is probably the only place outside of George Orwell El-ementary School where somebody can louse up that badly and still claim a place on the honor roll."[5]

By December Myers had had enough and submitted his letter of resigna-tion to Schweicker, including a series of scathing judgments on the legislative development process in the executive branch. OMB "develops policy without regard to the social and economic aspects of Social Security," he wrote, "and

More than 5,000 seniors gather in downtown Detroit on July 30, 1982 for a "Save Our Social Security" rally protesting Reagan's efforts to cut Social Security.

even the political aspects. This was well exemplified by the disastrous results that occurred from the proposal to eliminate the minimum benefit for all persons currently on the rolls and also from the proposal to sharply increase the early-retirement reduction factor."[6]

Myers's resignation made headlines and prompted more criticism of the administration from Democrats. Moynihan called the deputy commissioner a man of "integrity and experience" whose departure made it "painfully clear that policymaking in the Social Security Administration has been thoroughly politicized."[7]

Democratic politicians and progressives of various stripes were tying their specific issues to Social Security at every opportunity. Supporters of the Equal Rights Amendment, faced with an uphill battle to find three more of the required thirty-eight state legislatures to ratify the measure by a June 30 deadline, released a television commercial in January that showcased the inequities of Social Security's treatment of women. It displayed a tombstone marked "George Baker," indicating that he had died some years earlier. A voiceover said, "When George Baker died, his widow was left with almost nothing. Under the law, she was not his equal partner, but his dependent. Her credit died with him. She wasn't old enough for Social Security and she barely made enough to live on." Then the camera revealed the tombstone of Edna Baker, who died in 1981. The voiceover: "Three weeks ago, Edna Baker finally became George's equal."

The commercial concluded with National Organization for Women President Eleanor Smeal, standing at the foot of the grave, saying, "No woman should have to wait that long."

While the commercial was airing, the SSA was pressuring the Postal Service to investigate an increasingly familiar gambit. A Democratic fundraising letter, which Republicans said looked too much like an official government mailing, had gone out. Sent out by the Democratic National Committee and signed by Pepper, the acknowledged champion of senior citizens in Washington, it was stuffed into an envelope with "Important Social Security Notice Enclosed" printed on its front. The letter started with the message, "Social Security is no longer secure" from Reagan administration cuts. Some 3.5 million copies of the mailing went out; it reaped $600,000 for the party, according to the DNC.

But the most controversial ad of the 1982 election cycle proved to be a Republican spot that appeared in early July and featured a folksy-looking postal delivery person with a big white mustache delivering Social Security checks "with the 7.4% cost-of-living raise that President Reagan promised." "I'm probably one of the most popular people in town today," he chuckled, before adding: "President Reagan has made a beginning. For gosh sakes, let's give him a chance."

The spot was produced by Carroll A. Campbell, Jr., a South Carolina House Republican and Reagan loyalist, dipping into the RNC's $10 million ad budget, and was timed to hit TV screens just after the annual COLA increase kicked in on July 1.

Of course, the COLAs weren't something that Reagan had promised. They were automatic and dated back to the Nixon administration. And leading

Republican lawmakers had been trying to cut or cap the COLAs for over a year at the time the commercial ran. Reagan himself had pushed for a three-month delay in the adjustments. O'Neill lashed out at the TV spot as a "lie to the American people" and reminded reporters that COLAs had stayed intact that summer "because we in Congress refused to go along with" plans to reduce them.

The ad also raised complaints from the Postal Service to match the uproar about the earlier Democratic mailing. The agency said the use of the mail carrier was "an apparent violation" of the Hatch Act, which prohibited federal employees from engaging in partisan political activity. At the same time, the National Association of Letter Carriers wrote to the RNC complaining that the commercial "deliberately misleads the American public on the attitudes of letter carriers toward President Reagan."

Rather than confine themselves to complaining, however, the Democrats lashed back with their own commercial, a thirty-second spot showing a pair of scissors cutting into a Social Security card. "The Republicans all say they believe in Social Security—a sacred contract with the American people," a voiceover intoned. "That's what they say. Look at what they do."

"In 1981, they tried to cut cost-of-living increases by $60 billion over ten years. In 1982 they said, 'Either increase Social Security taxes or cut $40 billion to help balance the budget.' When are they going to stop? Not until it hurts."

The voice concluded, "It isn't fair. It's Republican."

How hard a political ad hits depends most of all on who sees it, however, and in this department the Republicans held the advantage. The DNC had so little money to throw at television stations that they had to demand that stations show their commercial free of charge, as a way to provide equal time on the issue, or refuse to carry the Republican ad. Only a few state Democratic organizations in Ohio, California, and Florida had the money to bankroll the commercial right away, although party leaders said they hoped to raise more.

Republicans, meanwhile, were building up a $6 million to $7 million war chest earmarked to fund a television ad campaign that would run throughout the fall. In August, surveys by Richard Wirthlin, the White House pollster, showed that the Republican ad with the mail carrier had had an effect, as 20% more respondents thought that Reagan had raised Social Security benefits and 8% fewer thought he had cut them. The RNC decided to run the ad again in nineteen major markets, Postal Service complaints notwithstanding.

Republicans continued to have problems with the president's statements about Social Security, however. At a press conference in late March, Reagan declared, "We haven't touched Social Security." O'Neill rushed to call the statement "completely inaccurate," noting that the administration had eliminated the minimum benefit, student benefits, and aid for burial expenses. White House aides were forced to acknowledge that the president had created some "misleading impressions."[8]

No matter how much money they showered on the issue, however, the Republicans had a hard time convincing the public that they were friends of Social

Security. A *Washington Post*-ABC News poll released in the spring showed that 51% of respondents sixty-five and older believed that Reagan would cut Social Security if he could, despite his statements to the contrary.

* * *

The National Commission on Social Security Reform—the president's "bipartisan" commission, chaired by Alan Greenspan—met throughout the year, wrangling over ways to bridge the members' differences. What kept the issue before the public as the midterm elections approached, however, was again the battle of next year's budget. Reagan's budget for fiscal 1983, released in February 1982, left Social Security alone except for a move to deny 100% of disability benefits to partially disabled veterans. And it attempted to bolster revenues flowing into the program by adding participants in the separate retirement system for railroad workers into Social Security.

Stockman later admitted that he "out-and-out cooked the books, inventing $15 million of utterly phony cuts" to get the deficit below the $100 billion deficit level."[9] But the resulting proposals were a flop with lawmakers of both parties, who immediately began hammering out their own alternatives. The more conservative Senate Democrats favored working closely with Republicans. Hollings, the biggest fiscal conservative, laid out a plan to freeze defense spending, freeze federal pay, partially roll back the Reagan tax cut—and eliminate COLAs for Social Security and other retirement programs. Majority leader Howard Baker called Hollings's proposals "interesting and worthwhile," but in the House, O'Neill said shortly, "I just don't particularly care for the Hollings plan."[10]

Once again, however, the Republicans were determined to put Social Security in play—despite the embarrassments they had suffered in 1981 and even though the White House had agreed to leave any decisions about the program to the Greenspan commission. Before February was over, Domenici had unveiled a budget plan that included $60 billion of savings over three years by eliminating 1983 COLAs for all entitlement programs including Social Security. All told, Domenici claimed his plan would save $320 billion over three years, compared to $240 billion for Reagan's. The only other alternative, he predicted, would be inaction on the deficit, which would then total up to $200 billion over three years. "Political leaders do all a disservice by pretending that we can swallow $100 billion [per year] deficits as though they were aspirin tablets," he groused.[11]

Amazingly, the White House decided to work with Domenici. Testifying before a House Budget Committee task force on entitlements three days later, Stockman said that freezing COLAs "may be warranted … as a temporary expedient" to help reduce budget deficits. He didn't mention Social Security, but he didn't rule it out of such a package, either.[12] But James Baker and the president's other aides were determined that their boss not go first with any controversial proposals. O'Neill, meanwhile, said that Reagan "must come forward with some specifics" if he wanted a compromise.[13]

By late April, three distinct proposals to cut Social Security COLAs were under discussion on Capitol Hill—a combined Hollings-Domenici plan, an option offered by Stockman, and a Congressional Budget Office plan—all of which aimed to solve the program's financial problems and alleviate the federal deficit strictly through benefit reductions. Any of the three would be devastating to a large number of beneficiaries, according to a study by the House Committee on Aging. Retirees expecting to receive $657 monthly by 1990 with COLA increases would only receive between $507 (with Domenici-Hollings) and $554 (under the CBO scheme). At least 1.2 million elderly would land in poverty by 1990.[14]

Talks between White House emissaries and the House Democratic leadership broke down at a last-ditch meeting on April 28, whereupon Reagan threw in his lot with the Senate Republicans. Hours after the Budget Committee formally rejected his budget, 20-0, on May 5, the White House agreed to a compromise plan that included $77 billion in deficit reductions for fiscal 1983. The plan, which passed on an 11-9 vote with all Democratic members opposed, leaned hard on $40 billion in unspecified savings from Social Security. The first $6 billion would come in 1983, and $17 billion each in the two following years: nearly a 10% cut in total.

The next two weeks witnessed a dizzying round of meetings, private discussions, and public castigation that ended with the White House backing away from its agreement with Domenici, who admitted on May 17 that he lacked the votes to push his bill through; the next day, the Budget Committee officially dropped it.[15] The Senate Republican leadership shortly followed suit. "We've run the Republicans off on the issue of Social Security," Riegle declared. Byrd, the courtly southerner, congratulated the GOP on "coming around to our point of view."

The Senate on May 21 approved a $784 billion budget for fiscal 1983 that would raise taxes and cut defense and domestic spending, leaving a nearly $116 billion federal deficit—and leaving Social Security untouched. A similar bill passed the House in June. That was the end of any discussion of Social Security cuts for the rest of 1982.

The Republican budget surrender prompted a private observation by Kirk O'Donnell, the O'Neill aide, that would reverberate through the years. To a number of acquaintances among the Washington press corps, O'Donnell dropped the comment that Social Security was "the third rail of American politics. Touch it, you're dead." No doubt a deliberate election-year attempt to create a mystique around the program while the Democrats were beating up mercilessly on their opponents over this one issue, the "third rail" quote appeared without attribution over and over in the press while the budget battle was raging, generally credited to "one Democrat" or "an aide to Speaker O'Neill."

An article in the *Boston Globe* that month explained where the analogy came from. "One Democratic aide who used to have nightmares about the subways he rode as a child likens Social Security to the third rail of American politics," it said. "Anyone who touches it gets electrocuted."[16] Whether it arose from O'Donnell's childhood memories or a bout of campaign strategizing in the speaker's office, the image of Social Security as the deadly "third rail" would become one of the most parroted American political metaphors of the next quarter-century and, at times, a prophecy.

* * *

As the election approached, the accusations back and forth about Social Security reached a crescendo. Partly to blame was the Reagan White House, where the president, his more pragmatic advisors, and the ideologues in his administration still couldn't get their message straight. In July, Reagan led a White House-organized rally for the proposed Balanced Budget Amendment, which he called a "people's crusade," on the steps of the Capitol. In his speech, he suggested that Congress would have to make "tough choices to control so-called 'uncontrollables'"—seemingly a reference to Social Security.

That summer Reagan picked a new chair for his Council of Economic Advisors: Martin Feldstein, a Harvard economist who had provoked controversy several years earlier with a theory that Social Security drags down private saving. While often a critic of the supply-siders, Feldstein was also an advocate of trimming Social Security benefits for middle- and upper-income recipients: the usual conservative solution of turning the program into pure welfare. The appointment, along with recent statements by Stockman that the government would have to make more domestic spending cuts in 1983, indicated strongly that Social Security would again be on the cutting board.

An earlier decision was coming back to haunt Reagan as well. Speeding up the Carter-ordered national review of disability cases, which the incoming president's team had latched onto as a money-saving measure even before he took office, was instead turning into a political disaster and a tragedy for thousands of beneficiaries. By September 1982, the review of some 2.7 million cases[17] had resulted in the SSA dropping 157,980 persons from the disability rolls, many of them by mistake. The Senate Finance Committee, which was monitoring the process, found that administrative judges had ruled in favor of recipients in 67% of appeals. And whatever savings the reviews achieved were offset by a huge volume of complaints.

By the second full year of the process, the SSA was decreasing the number of reviews it expected to send to the states. Then in September, after complaints from groups representing the disabled and from lawmakers of both parties, the administration ordered a partial halt to the reviews. But the White House still would make no changes in the standards that had resulted in the high termination rates. The problem would fester for another eighteen months, adding to the Reaganauts' reputation for ruthless treatment of the unfortunate.

All of these self-inflicted wounds, but principally Reagan's short-lived embrace of Domenici's $40 billion Social Security cut, made it clear that whatever expediencies the political situation forced upon him, the president's real purpose was to use the program as a source of budget cuts whenever he got the chance. The magnitude of the president's tax cuts and his record defense budget had created a great deal of the pressure to keep the deficit at levels that were vaguely acceptable to Wall Street's bond traders.

But as the election loomed, the Republicans' clumsy attempts at benefits cuts were more attractive campaign fodder. "What have we accomplished?" O'Neill asked in an interview in October. "We've saved Social Security."[18]

The party pushed this theme relentlessly through election day. In California, Gov. Jerry Brown picked up a short-lived advantage over his opponent in a Senate race, San Diego Mayor Pete Wilson, by calling Wilson to account for remarks in favor of making Social Security voluntary. In New Jersey, Frank Lautenberg, running for another Senate seat against longtime Rep. Millicent Fenwick, slammed her for voting twice to eliminate the minimum benefit. Claude Pepper, Social Security's loudest Capitol Hill supporter, was the Democrats' hottest ticket on the campaign trail, stumping for seventy Democratic candidates in twenty-five states that fall.

"Claude Pepper is the sexiest man in America," said DNC political director Ann Lewis. "We get more requests for him than for Robert Redford, Paul Newman and Warren Beatty combined. A visit by Claude Pepper is the biggest favor we can do for a Democratic candidate."[19] The DNC even issued a position paper calling for reforming Social Security to give women a "fair share" of retirement benefits, although it left the exact changes unspecified.

Sticking with O'Neill's theme of fairness, the DNC unveiled a set of six commercials calling attention to various Republican attacks on social programs, including one that showed an elephant staggering through a china shop, smashing everything around it. In a closeup, the elephant's hoof crushes a plate labeled "Social Security."

The Republicans handed their opponents one final gift in October when the *Washington Post* obtained and published a copy of a fundraising letter in which the Republican Congressional Committee asked recipients to indicate their favorite method of balancing Social Security's books. The first: "Making Social Security Voluntary"; the second: "Split Off the Welfare Aspects of Social Security," presumably by applying a needs-based test to recipients; the third: "Adjust the Financing of Social Security Without Making Any Fundamental Change in Its Structure," which would include, for example, cutting COLAs, raising the retirement age, or tightening eligibility requirements. Most of the "ballots received back favored the first two solutions," an RCC spokesperson said.

Any of the three would have drastically altered the nature of the program. More proof, O'Neill commented, that "Republicans are plotting to destroy Social Security."[20]

In a final gambit, the Republicans late that same month revamped their earlier commercial featuring the mail carrier, running it in areas with high concentrations of the elderly. "Well, I'm still delivering those Social Security checks," he said this time.

It helped not a bit. While the Republicans actually picked up one seat in the Senate, bringing their majority to fifty-four, in the House they lost twenty-six seats, giving the speaker a working majority no longer jeopardized by the conservative Boll Weevils. That meant solid House opposition to any more domestic program cuts. As the president and his aides sat down for their first discussions of the next, 1984 budget shortly after the election, senior Republicans like Sens. Dole, Domenici, and Mark Hatfield of Oregon were publicly calling upon him not to submit a proposal that would end—in Domenici's words—in a "bloodbath."[21]

Democratic leaders regarded the November 1982 election as a watershed in the Reagan era: the drawing of a line beyond which, in most major areas, ideologues like Stockman could not step. The Democrats now had an opportunity to chip away at, if not reverse, the tax cut and some of the president's domestic initiatives.

The Democrats had won the election, but on Social Security, they were losing the war for the hearts and minds of the policymaking establishment and the elite Washington press corps. The abandonment of Domenici's effort to secure $40 billion in savings from the program in fiscal 1983 had added another $51 billion to the deficit, he figured, and already in the spring and summer the air was starting to fill with complaints—not just from Republicans—about the Democrats' "irresponsibility" and tendency to "play politics" on this important problem. It was a strange accusation to make against an opposition party attempting to hold back the damage from a budget-busting tax cut and a massive defense spending increase, but it stuck surprisingly well.

Already in August, *Washington Post* columnist David Broder remarked on how "the Democrats demagogue the Social Security issue while continuing to pretend that the refusal to discipline the growth of entitlement spending is unconnected to the severe cutbacks in programs that provide a lifeline for the jobless and the poor." Why the growth of Social Security, which had its own dedicated tax revenues and trust funds, was to blame, Broder did not explain.[22] But by December, he was calling for a bipartisan effort to slow down the growth of Social Security and other entitlements and berating "dogmatic Democrats" who were "digging in their heels" against any cutbacks.[23]

Wall Street was beginning to zero in on Social Security too. While most important figures on the Street had confined their criticism of Washington, since Reagan's election, to concerns about the deficit, some were willing to get specific. As early as May, five former Treasury secretaries, joined by Pete Peterson, Commerce secretary under Nixon and now chairman of investment banking firm Lehman Brothers Kuhn Loeb, urged the president and Congress to slash defense and nondefense spending alike to rein in the deficit. They specifically called for a one-year freeze on Social Security, Medicare, and federal retirement benefits. A month later they released a similar statement, this time in the company of the heads of most major Wall Street firms including Merrill Lynch, Shearson/American Express, Salomon Brothers, Paine Webber, Morgan Stanley, Drexel Burnham Lambert, Goldman Sachs, Kidder Peabody, and E.F. Hutton, plus the presidents of the New York and American stock exchanges.

The financial barons made no mention of any need for the White House to compromise on the tax cut. But once the election was over and with the federal government's finances causing still more alarm in Washington and on Wall Street than joblessness and the social safety net, the Democrats were under increasing pressure to deal. Shortly, they would do so.

CHAPTER 4

"WAITING FOR THE COMMISSION"

"Social Security does not develop in a vacuum. It exists because of the real needs and interests of people and organizations, filtered through existing political mechanisms."
—*Stanford G. Ross, Commissioner of Social Security, 1978–79[1]*

Two days after the November 1982 election rewrote the map of Congress, Bob Dole, serving as a member of the president's Social Security commission, took a political potshot. The Senate majority leader called upon the commission not to make any recommendations until House Speaker O'Neill drafted his own plan to save the program. Dole charged the Democrats with using Social Security as a bludgeon against the Republicans during the election. By his reckoning, as many as ten of the twenty-six seats the Democrats picked up in the House may have resulted from their campaigning on Social Security. Rather than being "trapped by partisan Democrats" into sticking their own necks out at the commission's next meeting, Dole said Republicans should let their accusers make the first move.

O'Neill rejected the idea. Reform proposals had to come from the commission, after which the House Ways and Means Committee would look at them—just as with any other piece of Social Security legislation. The same day the frustrated Dole made his statement, however, the trustees used the authority Congress had granted them in the fall to borrow $581,252,000 from the Disability Insurance trust fund to tide the OASI fund over until a long-term solution to its financial problems could be hammered out. All told, OASI would borrow $17.5 billion that year from the Disability and Hospital Insurance trust funds.[2]

Time to reach a deal was running out: or so it seemed. Congress could choose to authorize another round of borrowing. But unless the economy began to improve, this Band-Aid approach would eventually deplete the other trust funds, and Congress would have to consider covering beneficiaries' Social Security payments out of general income-tax revenues. Not everyone agreed this was inevitable. Ball, for example, argued that the Disability and Hospital Insurance funds were overloaded with assets and that interfund borrowing could keep the OASI fund solvent until at least 1989, when the troublesome period would be over.[3] Gambling that he was right would be risky for Democratic lawmakers, however. Since the Reagan tax cut was already slashing general revenues, if the program's financial picture didn't improve, Social Security would have to fight for funding with other federal spending—just as if the Reaganauts had planned it that way.

The National Commission on Social Security Reform (the "Greenspan commission"). Seated, left to right: Bob Myers, executive staff director; Rep. Claude Pepper (D-FL); Martha Keys; Chairman Alan Greenspan; Mary Falvey Fuller; Rep. Bill Archer (R-TX); Lane Kirkland. Standing, left to right: Robert Beck; Robert Ball; Alexander Trowbridge; Rep. Barber Conable (R-NY); Sen. John Heinz (R-PA); Sen. Pat Moynihan (D-NY); Sen. Bob Dole (R-KS); Joe Waggonner, Jr.

But the election had left the White House in no mood for brinkmanship either. Greenspan, the commission chair, responded to Dole by saying blandly that the panel's next meetings would go forward as scheduled and that he hoped it would finish its work by the end of the year, as planned.

* * *

Few experienced people in Washington expected much of the Greenspan commission, as it quickly became known. Such bodies were generally a convenient way for the president to sweep a big, divisive issue under the carpet for a long or short period of time, after which its recommendations could generally be ignored. Ball liked to claim that Reagan only decided to refer Social Security to a commission so he could get through the midterm elections without having to address the issue again.[4]

But the latest installment of Washington's budget soap opera had forced the president to deviate from that strategy. Because Social Security was authorized to borrow from the Disability Insurance and Hospital Insurance trust funds only through December 1982, another method of keeping the program fully funded would have to be found by that time. Accordingly, Reagan, as well as the House and Senate leaderships, chose a sufficiently high-powered group of members for the commission—seven members of Congress, including the Senate majority leader, Claude Pepper, and Bob Ball—that they might actually feel secure making a deal. "It would be extraordinarily influential," thought Ball himself, who had a lot of experience with such bodies.[5]

What was the basic structure of the program that the commission was trying to fix?

Critics like Stockman weren't entirely wrong when they complained that Social Security had changed profoundly from the modest program that had originally emerged out of the politics of the New Deal. It had fulfilled most if by no means all the demands of the mass movement that pushed for creation of a universal old-age income support system during the depths of the Depression. In this sense it was a reasonably true expression of the people's desires and needs. The Social Security Administration in 1983 actually ran three separate programs:

Old-Age and Survivors Insurance, the original program: The Social Security Act created old-age benefits only for private-sector, non-agricultural workers. Amendments passed in 1939 added benefits for surviving spouses and for children of workers who died before they reached retirement age. OASI was the resulting program, later expanded to include virtually every category of worker. In fiscal 1982, it paid out $134.7 billion in benefits to 35.5 million recipients.[6]

Disability Insurance, added in 1956: DI was first limited to workers aged fifty and over and by 1960 it insured everyone who contributed to Social Security for an extended period. In fiscal 1982, it paid out $17.4 billion in benefits to 4.1 million recipients.[7]

Collectively, OASI and DI are sometimes known as *Old-Age, Survivors, and Disability Insurance* (OASDI). In 1982, a board of four trustees, all presidential appointees, oversaw the two programs. They were the Secretary of the Treasury, who was also managing trustee of the trust funds; the Secretary of Health and Human Services, whose department in the early 1980s included the SSA; the Secretary of Labor; and the Commissioner of Social Security, who ran the SSA.

A third program under the SSA's jurisdiction was *Supplemental Security Insurance*. Created in 1972, SSI wasn't a retirement or disability program, although it served some of the same people as OASI and DI. It was an attempt to rationalize a multitude of local- and state-based poverty programs, as well as the grants-in-aid to the states that the federal government made to assist certain categories of needy persons including the blind, children of the disabled, and the elderly whose Social Security benefits didn't provide an adequate income. SSI was administered by the SSA instead of by the states, but the states still set many of the eligibility requirements. In 1982, it paid out $16.2 billion in benefits to 3.9 million recipients.[8]

SSI proved a great burden to the SSA in the 1970s, requiring a huge investment in new computer systems, personnel, and more local offices. The transition didn't go smoothly, and the SSA's reputation as one of the federal government's best-run agencies suffered as a result.[9] But the benefits provided under SSI continued to be paid for out of state funds and general revenues, not out of payroll taxes, and so SSI wasn't part of the debate over the future of Social Security itself.

Until 1977, SSA administered a fourth program as well: *Medicare*. The old-age medical insurance program was created in 1965, and it consisted of two separate packages of benefits. *Hospital Insurance* (HI), also known as Medicare Part A, covered hospitalization, skilled nursing facilities, and other inpatient services, and was funded out of payroll taxes. *Supplementary Medical Insurance* (SMI), otherwise known as Medicare Part B, covered doctors' visits, medical equipment, and other outpatient services and was funded, like SSI, out of general revenues and, later, from premiums charged to beneficiaries. In 1977, the Carter administration shifted Medicare out of the SSA and into a new Health Care Financing Administration, but the funding structure remained the same.

Except for SSI and SMI, that funding structure was what the programs created under the auspices of Social Security had in common—along with the fact that they were all grouped under the wing of the Department of Health and Human Services. The U.S. is the only country in the world that finances its national old-age pensions through a separate tax paid into a dedicated trust fund (see Fig. 1). By 1982, those contributions, known as payroll taxes, equaled 13.4% of each American worker's gross pay up to $32,400 a year. Workers and their employers made $148 billion in OASI and DI and $31 billion in HI contributions.[10] Here's how that 13.4%, with employer and employee each paying the same amount, broke down:

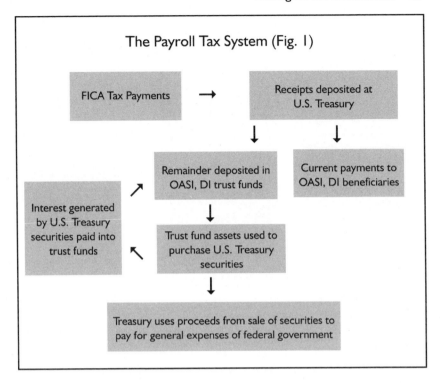

The Payroll Tax System (Fig. 1)

- OASI: 4.575%

- DI: 0.825%

- HI: 1.3%

Because employer and employee each paid the same percentage, workers in fact only contributed 6.7% in payroll taxes through their paychecks: the "FICA" (Federal Insurance Contributions Act) line that deducts federal insurance contributions from gross pay. Self-employed persons instead paid "SECA" (Self-Employment Contributions Act) taxes as part of their quarterly tax payments. For OASI, these were set generally at about 75% of the combined employer-employee rate for workers with "regular" jobs and 50% for HI.[11] However, payroll tax rates were scheduled to rise under the 1977 Amendments to 15.3% of gross income in 1990, with worker and employer each contributing 7.65%.

What happened to those contributions? All were deposited in three trust funds, each attached to one of the three programs: OASI, DI, and HI (see Fig. 2, p. 84). By law, FICA and SECA taxes were used only to pay benefits and administer the trust funds. When money was left over, it was invested in a special-issue class of Treasury bonds. Interest on these bonds formed an additional stream of revenue for the OASI and DI trust funds, which in 1982 came to $2.1 billion.[12] The

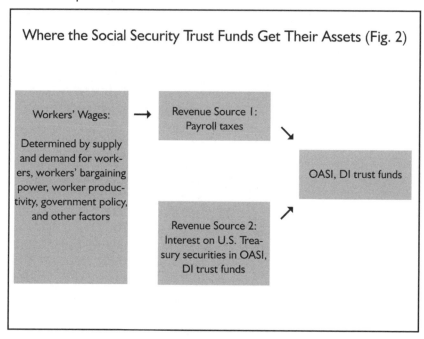

Where the Social Security Trust Funds Get Their Assets (Fig. 2)

Workers' Wages:

Determined by supply and demand for workers, workers' bargaining power, worker productivity, government policy, and other factors

Revenue Source 1: Payroll taxes

OASI, DI trust funds

Revenue Source 2: Interest on U.S. Treasury securities in OASI, DI trust funds

government could use the money it received for the bonds to help pay for other government activities, just as it did with the monies it brought in through income tax payments, service charges, and other revenue sources. But the money it borrowed from OASI and DI would have to be paid back when the bonds matured.

Until 1982, however, those extra payroll tax revenues were generally very small. Since the early days of Social Security, policymakers had endeavored to keep payroll taxes just slightly higher than the level needed to meet each year's obligations. Otherwise, they risked building up a large trust fund that could then become a political football. And of course in recent years, as inflation jacked up benefits payments while a listless economy depressed payroll tax revenues, the problem had usually been how to meet each year's obligations, not what to do with excess revenues.

Social Security and Medicare Part A were, in other words, pay-as-you-go systems. Despite the dedicated payroll tax and the trust fund mechanism, that was about the same way most national pension schemes in other industrialized countries were funded as well. The problem, of course, was what to do when birth rates fell, the number of workers declined, and benefits payments flowing out of the system started to regularly exceed revenues coming in. Actuaries had known all along that this would happen. Workers who had started their working careers before Social Security was enacted would die off. Later, the huge baby boom generation would retire and begin drawing down benefits. If benefits outstripped the assets in the Social Security trust funds, then by law, benefits would automatically be reduced to an affordable amount, unless

Congress either raised payroll taxes or figured out a combination of payroll tax hikes and smaller benefit cuts.

In the mid-1960s, the Social Security trustees began making more detailed forecasts of major changes in the program's cash flow.

Each year thereafter, the agency's Office of the Actuary drew up a range of projections for the next seventy-five years: Low-Cost, High-Cost, and Intermediate-Cost. The Social Security trustees then reviewed and approved those projections and published the results in their annual report. Over time, the Intermediate estimate came to be treated as the "most likely" scenario and received a great deal of play in the press when the numbers were published every April.

A series of technical panels, also in the mid-1960s, had fixed on seventy-five years as the projected time period, since that was the average anticipated lifespan of an American at the time.[13] It made sense, says Stephen C. Goss, who joined the SSA's Office of the Actuary in 1973 and in the mid-1990s became deputy chief actuary, because seventy-five years was "long enough to cover the remaining lifetimes of essentially all people currently engaged in Social Security either as contributors or beneficiaries. It's also sufficient to show the full evolution of any proposal we can put a price tag on. Also, our ability to make projections over any longer period is probably worthy of being questioned."[14] The seventy-five-year rule-of-thumb was never enshrined in law, but nevertheless became a standard measure for the Social Security trustees.

The trouble was that even seventy-five years was much farther in the future than anyone could hope to predict with a high degree of accuracy. That's why the trustees decided to publish a range of projections in their annual report, rather than a single one. Each year the report included a disclaimer that the seventy-five-year estimates were not meant to dictate policy but only to give an indication of Social Security's fiscal direction at that moment in time and only if nothing—not workforce trends, not wage trends, not immigration or birthrates or anything else—changed in the future.

Another problem was that the seventy-five-year projections tended to obscure an important reality about the program: that it was backed by the full faith and credit of the federal government. Retirement benefits offered by the government are different from those extended by private-sector employers. Private pensions that pay guaranteed benefits are always a gamble because the company sponsoring the plan might endure a severe downturn or even go bankrupt and not be able to pay its obligations. In that case, employees and retirees just have to take their place in the queue along with all the other creditors and most likely settle for pennies on the dollar. That's why, traditionally, private pension plans are advance-funded with assets projected to cover the plan's obligations thirty years into the future: roughly, the length of time a "lifetime" employee would work for the company.

The federal government isn't likely to go out of business, because it has one big advantage over private businesses: the power to tax. If a bad economic cycle reduces the revenues it collects, Washington can always raise tax rates to compensate. Even if the decision isn't politically easy or popular, people still have to pay. In this sense, it was a distortion to claim, as some critics did, that Social Security would go "bankrupt" at some point in the future, because the government could always raise the money to cover its obligations. It could also decide to cut future benefits along with boosting taxes. In any case, the financial markets, which factor possibilities such as these into their investment decisions, had never seemed to regard any of this as a looming threat. The United States of America was still considered one of the best financial risks in the world, as demonstrated by the favorable, low interest rates it pays on its Treasury bonds.

Nevertheless, the seventy-five-year solvency estimates in the trustees' annual report provided leverage for groups that wanted to insist on radical, "long-term" solutions to Social Security's problems, not just quick fixes. Although the Reaganauts didn't specifically mention the seventy-five-year projections when they proposed drastic cuts in the program in April 1981, they did invoke the need to find long-term solutions.

One of the issues facing the Greenspan commission, then, was the extent to which it wanted to address the program's long-term health, instead of concentrating on the more immediate problem of how to keep Social Security solvent for the rest of the decade.

Resolving that problem would be tricky. The president, reflecting the views of his allies in the business world, had ruled out any new payroll tax boost, but the 1977 Amendments already called for increases over the next several years, so perhaps the timing of those increases could be hastened. Democrats were set against any benefits reductions: unless, of course, the White House agreed first. That opened another possible avenue for negotiations. With that in mind, the commission members reviewed the structure of benefits under Social Security: how the SSA actually calculates the payments that individuals receive as retirees, as survivors, and when they are disabled.

The complex formula in place by the early 1980s covered both old-age and disability benefits and was built around three variables: how long an individual had worked, how much she had earned, and at what age she left the labor force (see Fig. 3). First, the SSA determined the worker's thirty-five highest earning years and indexed her earnings in those years to the average growth in wages up to the year she turned sixty. Next, those wage-indexed earnings were averaged and divided by twelve months to come up with an average monthly amount. The result was meant to express the worker's lifetime earnings in terms of today's wage levels and was called the Average Indexed Monthly Earnings (AIME).

The second step was to take the AIME and calculate the worker's actual monthly benefit payment. For workers who became eligible to receive benefits in 1982, for example, Social Security paid 90% of the first $230 of AIME, 32% of AIME between $230 and $1,158, and 15% of AIME over $1,388.[15] The dollar amounts to which each percentage was applied changed every year based on shifts in average wages.* The result was the cost-of-living-adjusted

* These were the "bend points" whose creation in the 1977 Amendments

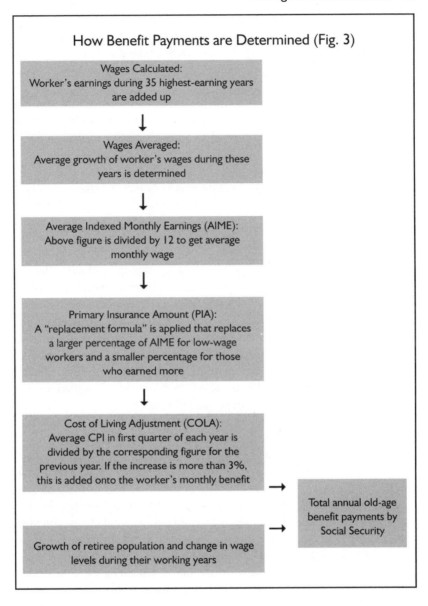

How Benefit Payments are Determined (Fig. 3)

Wages Calculated:
Worker's earnings during 35 highest-earning years
are added up

↓

Wages Averaged:
Average growth of worker's wages during these
years is determined

↓

Average Indexed Monthly Earnings (AIME):
Above figure is divided by 12 to get average
monthly wage

↓

Primary Insurance Amount (PIA):
A "replacement formula" is applied that replaces
a larger percentage of AIME for low-wage
workers and a smaller percentage for those
who earned more

↓

Cost of Living Adjustment (COLA):
Average CPI in first quarter of each year is
divided by the corresponding figure for the
previous year. If the increase is more than 3%,
this is added onto the worker's monthly benefit

→

Total annual old-age
benefit payments by
Social Security

→

Growth of retiree population and change in wage
levels during their working years

Primary Insurance Amount (PIA). The formula ensured that lower-wage work-ers received proportionately more from their Social Security contributions than middle- or high-income workers.

The most crucial of these successive calculations, however, was the first: each individual's retirement benefit was based on the average growth in *wag-es*—not *prices*. Since wages generally grow faster than prices, the net result generated so much anguish for the so-called "notch babies," whose plight we discussed in Chapter 1.

was to guarantee the worker not just that she wouldn't lose purchasing power to inflation during her years, or even decades, of retirement, but that her standard of living wouldn't deteriorate either. She would still be able to afford the same level of housing, food, and other amenities at eighty-five as she did at sixty-five.

Thanks to various benefits increases up through the early 1970s and, crucially, the automatic COLA created in 1972, the PIA generally replaced about 56% of income for low-wage earners, 35% for high-income earners, and 42% for those in between. But no matter your income level while working, if you were a retiree in 1982, your monthly Social Security check wasn't taxed. You received your benefits payment, based on your PIA, free and clear.

Workers could also choose to retire earlier or later than the normal retirement age (NRA), which in 1982 was age sixty-five for all workers. If you retired anywhere between sixty-two and sixty-five years of age, your benefit was reduced five-ninths of one percent for each month before NRA. If you decided to put off retirement after you reached sixty-five, you received a 3% deferred retirement credit (DRC) for each year you continued to work up until age seventy, when Social Security would start to pay you whether you wanted the money or not. Since 3% is less than the actuarial equivalent of what your benefits would be had you retired at sixty-five, the net result was that you would receive, on average, lower lifetime benefits than if you had stopped working at the normal retirement age. The point of these provisions was to encourage people not to retire early but also not to stay in the workforce past sixty-five— taking jobs away, presumably, from younger workers.[16]

Retirees could keep working after they started to receive their Social Security checks, but at the time the Greenspan commission was meeting, there were penalties for doing so. When the program was set up, Congress established a dollar amount above which workers' benefits were trimmed $1 for every $2 they earned. But it raised the limit periodically thereafter, so that in 1982 the limit was quite generous. A retiree receiving average benefits could earn up to $8,160 a year while a retiree receiving maximum benefits could receive $17,628 combined from Social Security and other earnings before losing any benefits. No further benefits increases were awarded based on income above $27,096 per year.

What about survivors' benefits? These varied depending on your circumstances. If you were over sixty-two and your spouse was also of retirement age, you were eligible to receive 50% of your late husband or wife's PIA; that amount was reduced 25% if you weren't yet sixty-five. However, if you and your spouse both worked and his or her earnings were higher than yours, you got more: 71.5% of your spouse's PIA starting at age sixty, plus a supplement at sixty-two. A "young widow" who was below age sixty received an additional benefit for each child he or she might have under the age of sixteen. That benefit was equal to 50% of the deceased worker's PIA. Until 1981, it continued until the child reached twenty-one if he or she stayed in school; then, as we've seen, the law changed to stop it at eighteen. The result was that for many households, even those with relatively high incomes, Social Security paid benefits that could go significantly higher than the PIA.

Workers with long employment histories at very low wages were eligible for one more benefit: a "special minimum" created in 1972 that ranged in 1982 from less than $20 a month for workers with eleven years of service in very low-wage jobs to a few hundred dollars for those who spent their entire careers in such employment. These payments, which still fell below both the poverty level, and the average benefit amount under Social Security,[17] were kept in place even after the elimination of the more broadly applied minimum benefit in 1981.

* * *

How adequate, generous, and fair was the system that Reagan's commissioners were examining? The best way to answer this is in relative terms, since every society has a different standard. By 1982, Social Security benefits increases and COLAs, plus the advent of Medicare, had reduced poverty among the elderly in America to 14.6%. But that still left almost one in seven aged Americans in need, a relatively high rate compared to other large industrialized countries—and many of those were women or minorities, due to the continuing discrimination they suffered in employment. By contrast, other industrialized nations based their retirement systems less strictly around what the worker had contributed to the system and more on individual need.

Social Security—and particularly OASI, the old-age and survivors' program—was not overgenerous, at least by these countries' standards. The PIA replaced over half of average earnings only for workers who had earned low wages throughout most of their careers, whereas Japan and most European countries replaced over half for the bulk of retirees. Social Security required individuals to continue working until sixty-two to receive any benefit under OASI and until sixty-five to receive a full benefit. Most other industrialized countries started retirement benefits at an earlier age.

It's not surprising, then, that when Democrats looked for points to attack in the Republicans' plans to cut Social Security in 1981, they found plenty. What seemed like reasonable cuts that merely eliminated "unearned" benefits, looked altogether different when the actual impact on the retiree was considered.

The minimum benefit was "unearned," Republicans argued; therefore, it should be abolished. But it stood as a bulwark against extreme poverty for many people who had worked for years at low-income jobs, including many who were already receiving it. Early retirement benefits were not contemplated in the original Social Security legislation, said critics like Stockman, who were formulating a standard for social programs similar to the strict-construction argument conservative legal scholars applied to the Constitution. Therefore, these benefits ought not to be exempt from cutting. Liberals countered that individuals who did physically taxing or even disabling work shouldn't be forced to take a severe cut in benefits just because they were no longer able to continue at their long-term jobs and weren't employable for many others.

A more difficult issue of fairness centered on the payroll tax itself, which, unlike income taxes, had a regressive slant. The poor paid more than the rich to support a system that benefited workers in every financial bracket. In 1982, workers paid into the payroll tax system only up to $32,400 a year. Those who earned more—in many cases, much more—thus were obliged to contribute only about the same as an ordinary middle-income person. Of course, lower-income retirees got back more each year from Social Security relative to the payroll taxes they contributed, because those who earned high incomes received only as much in benefits—in 1982—as someone who earned $32,400 a year when they worked. But at the same time, Social Security benefits weren't subject to income tax, which would have made the entire tax system more progressive overall.

Conservatives, while no friends of progressive taxation—Reagan advisor Ed Meese referred to the income tax as "immoral" at a press briefing in May 1982—liked to point to the regressive nature of payroll taxes as proof that workers got a bad deal from Social Security. Ball, Wilbur Cohen, and others who had played a role in developing the program had hoped at some point to add some general revenues from income taxes to Social Security's funding sources, making the entire system more progressive. But because Social Security's fundamental fiscal premise was that retirees' benefits should be tied at least roughly to the amount they contributed, this idea was politically risky, laying the program open to conservative attacks that it was "welfare," not social insurance.*

* * *

These were some of the key issues the commission had been considering since its first meeting came to order in February 1982. But the deep-seated differences between the fifteen members, led by Alan Greenspan, a former Council of Economic Advisors chair under Ford, had come to a head almost immediately. Thereafter, and especially after the midterm election season heated up, nothing much in the way of constructive discussion took place, although Ball, who had been appointed to the panel by O'Neill and was known to be the speaker's eyes and ears in its deliberations, was busy drawing up lists of changes that could be combined to plug Social Security's long-term funding gap. It didn't help that the members had decided early on that whatever package they agreed to must have unanimous support—otherwise lawmakers of both parties would reject it.

---

* Civil rights leaders A. Philip Randolph and Bayard Rustin's famous 1966 "Freedom Budget" proposal called for vastly increasing OASI payments as a step toward eventually providing an adequate income to anyone unable to work. They proposed to fund the higher payments "with greatly enlarged Federal contributions." Despite support from such diverse figures as John Kenneth Galbraith and Stokely Carmichael, no Washington lawmakers took it up.

In August, the commission spent a whole meeting considering a radical idea: cutting back benefits and allowing workers to put some of their payroll taxes into personal accounts. Michael Boskin, a Stanford University economist and Reagan advisor on Social Security, made a presentation in favor of a scheme to gradually phase out and privatize Social Security. Traditional Social Security, he pointed out, would offer "a very bad yield to younger workers and those who are not yet in the labor force when they retire in the next century."[18]

The idea appealed to the commission's conservatives, but they chose not to pursue it, principally because they were operating under too tight a deadline. "With the time that's ours, we're not going to have any real opportunity to evaluate that plan, as good as it might well be," one commissioner, former Rep. Joe Waggonner of Louisiana, a conservative Democrat, said in response to Boskin's testimony.* Greenspan said more or less the same thing to Ball later.

For the first time, albeit unsuccessfully, the idea of privatizing Social Security had been broached before a presidential Social Security commission. But with a fiscal crisis looming, the basis for a deal would have to be some combination of incremental changes—benefits reductions and revenue increases—that would together balance the books. Despite the fact that the conservatives had a majority on the panel, time and perhaps political caution prevented them from taking the initiative and instead they handed it to the program's defenders.

Greenspan himself briefly considered another radical change, this one brought to him by Stephen J. Entin, deputy assistant secretary of the Treasury for economic policy. Stockman's disastrous package of Social Security cuts the year before had included a change in how the COLA was calculated; instead of being tied to growth in wages, he wanted it to be determined by the change either in wages or prices, whichever was lesser. Instead of tinkering with the COLA, Entin's idea was to index the benefits formula—the AIME and the three brackets or "bend points" in the PIA calculations that determine initial benefits—to wages. This would cause retirees' checks to grow more slowly, although they would still keep pace with inflation. Entin's colleague, Aldona Robbins, had calculated that the switch would save Social Security some $3 trillion in present value over time, covering most of the unfunded future liability—much more than under Stockman's scheme.

A Republican political appointee who came in with the Reagan administration, Entin had studied the Social Security problem while previously serving on the Joint Economic Committee of the Congress. At Treasury, he played a role in preparing the trustees' annual report and so had watched the underfunding problem develop. Switching to price indexing "would have fixed the

---

* Another problem, recalls Sylvester Schieber, a former SSA economist whose in-progress book on Social Security was being used by commission staff and some commission members as background material for their discussions of private accounts, was that Boskin's presentation was "unconvincing" (interview with Sylvester Schieber, June 1, 2007).

problem for good," Entin said later.[19] "If this had been done, we wouldn't be talking about Social Security today," Robbins said years later.[20]

Strictly speaking, this was correct. If COLAs had been keyed to changes in prices rather than wages when the program was first put in place, the real purchasing power of OASI benefits that retirees received in 1983 would have been exactly the same as when the first retirees received their checks in 1940. The vast improvement in living standards that occurred in the postwar decades—Americans born in 1940 witnessed an 875% increase in living standards during their working lives[21]—would have completely bypassed Social Security recipients. If OASI benefits were to shift completely to price indexing, within a few decades they would dwindle to insignificance.

Greenspan was intrigued by price indexing as a way to solve Social Security's funding problem once and for all, Entin says, but was dissuaded from pressing the idea by the commission staff.[22]

The election offered Ball a way to break the logjam. Among his other skills, Ball was a master operator in settings like the Greenspan commission. "He was a superb negotiator who had the knack of getting people to put aside their differences and find common ground," says his biographer.[23] Others would say that behind the tall, white-haired man's gentlemanly and somewhat pastoral

Bob Ball with Tip O'Neill in January 1983, when Ball was representing the Speaker in negotiations with the White House over Social Security. Ball, a key architect of Social Security for decades, remained an influential behind-the-scenes figure for decades after stepping down as commissioner of the Social Security Administration in 1973.

demeanor lurked a determined infighter who knew how to make a consensus process turn his way.

Says Thomas Bethell, Ball's longtime friend and frequent co-author, "Bob's modus operandi was to be ready with a coherent, comprehensive proposal and to talk about its virtues until he wore his critics out. He had infinite patience, and liked nothing better than to explain the advantages of his proposals as often and as exhaustively as necessary."[24] Ball could frustrate allies as well as opponents. David Lindeman, an economist who knew Ball for years in government, recalls a former colleague who "once observed that Bob would have made a truly great diplomat. But I'm sure he would have driven the Secretary of State under whom he served slightly crazy."[25] Inevitably, some who crossed paths with Ball when he served on the 1979 Social Security Advisory Council took to referring to him behind his back as the "Silver Fox."[26]

Ball understood that he and Greenspan were actually on the same side. Greenspan's job was to rescue his boss, Reagan, from the consequences of his attack on Social Security by putting the issue to bed with as little fuss as possible. O'Neill, through Ball, also wanted to resolve the issue quickly, keeping Social Security funded through the rest of the decade. Neither the president nor the speaker wanted to attempt a long-term "permanent" solution—probably not politically doable at this point—to how to fund the program.

Just before the commission's next meeting, Ball agreed with Greenspan and Bob Myers, who was serving as the panel's executive director, running its staff, and effectively in charge of its number-crunching operation, on how to quantify the size of the Social Security deficit—something all had to understand the same way before serious negotiations could begin.

They decided to use the actuaries' most pessimistic estimates for the short-term period through the end of the decade, and the intermediate set of figures for the longer, seventy-five-year period. That meant the short-term deficit would be pegged at between $150 billion and $200 billion, which Ball felt was a sufficiently stringent standard that no surprise deficit was likely to materialize before the end of the decade.[27] The long-term figure would be a larger one, equivalent to 1.82% of payroll. In other words, the long-term fiscal gap could be filled by immediately raising payroll taxes by that much. Greenspan persuaded the Republican members to go along with this definition of the goal they were all working toward and Ball got the Democrats to agree—although they stated publicly that they continued to believe the pessimistic assumptions overstated the problem.[28]

That set the stage for a three-day commission meeting in Alexandria with both sides trading proposals and counterproposals before the largest audience that had yet come to witness one of its sessions: about 400 reporters, congressional aides, think tankers, and other Beltway denizens. On Friday, November 12, the Democrats unveiled a menu of changes:

- Advancing the tax increase scheduled for 1990 to 1984, which would close $132 billion of the gap;

- Increasing the payroll tax on self-employed workers, reaping another $18 billion;

- Bringing all nonprofit workers into the system, for another $7 billion;

- Covering all newly hired state and local workers, adding $13 billion; and

- Covering all federal employees with less than five years' experience, for $21 billion.

All told, the package came to $198 billion, the vast majority of it from revenue-raising measures. But the proposal was dangerous for some of the members, especially AFL-CIO President Lane Kirkland, who was quickly skewered by some of his union constituents—especially government employees, who didn't want to be forced into Social Security. Accordingly, the Democrats insisted they wouldn't take the package to O'Neill until the president signaled he would embrace it.

The next day, the Democrats sweetened the package for the Republicans by adding a three-month COLA delay, which would save the program another $25 billion. The conservatives' favorite idea, raising the age for receipt of full benefits, was still not part of the offer, but the Democrats seemed to have gone about as far as they could. Their package was now on the table.

Greenspan relayed the offer to the White House through James Baker, who answered back that it was still too heavy on new taxes. The $132 billion achieved by moving up the 1990 tax increase reportedly was too much for the president. In fact, Reagan, who was engrossed in the details of getting his MX missile program through the new Congress, seemed to have forgotten what had compelled him to assemble the commission in the first place. "Up to November, he was still talking about voluntary Social Security as an option," an aide said.

The commission held another meeting on December 10. It lasted fifteen minutes. Appearing on the Sunday morning Washington chat shows shortly afterward, Greenspan and Dole both indicated that the next move would be up to the party leaders, not the commission itself. "We are now at a point," Greenspan declared, applying his customary patina of nonspecificity, "where I think it probably requires a judgment and agreement at the next level." Dole was more direct: "Unless the president signs off and the speaker signs off on any recommendations, I don't care what the commission does. We're just wasting our time."[29] Yet when Reagan was asked, nine days after that meeting, what he planned to do about Social Security, he replied simply, "We're waiting for the commission."[30]

CHAPTER 5

THE COMPROMISE
OF 1983

While Reagan may have thought he could still push any questions regarding Social Security over to his commission, events were compelling him to come to the table. The administration had abandoned the supply-side argument that its tax cuts could stimulate the economy enough to reduce the deficit; OMB was now estimating the shortfall would rise to $185 billion in 1984. An internal administration estimate projected that even if the economy recovered, the U.S. would be running $150 billion-a-year deficits throughout the second half of the decade. Meanwhile, Reagan himself was insisting that his income tax cuts and his military spending plans were non-negotiable. Any savings would have to come from domestic spending. Some White House insiders were already assuming that the president's next budget would be rejected just as his last had been.[1]

Something would have to give; many in Washington were predicting it would be taxes. Since the House Democratic leadership was now in a better position to oppose domestic program cuts, only a tax increase would ensure that Reagan could still meet his military spending goals. But the guess was that any increase would have to come from areas other than the ones the president had cut in his first two budgets—income and capital gains taxes—so as not to damage his standing with

his constituency among the affluent. That left payroll taxes, which fell disproportionately on lower- and middle-income Americans. With all pretense of bringing
deficits under control abandoned, a payroll tax increase could help to mask part
of the budget shortfall if it was large enough to generate surpluses.

The White House, which had just signaled its rejection of a deal to move
forward the scheduled 1990 increases, now began—very quietly—to backtrack.

First, Stockman brought the president a set of proposals to close the Social
Security gap, developed by Alexander Trowbridge, president of the National
Association of Manufacturers, who was one of the White House appointees on
the Greenspan commission. Trowbridge thought he could sell these to Ball and
Dole. The four principal ingredients were $80 billion in revenues from moving
forward the 1990 tax increases, $50 billion from a six-month COLA delay, $32
billion from including federal employees in the Social Security system, and, to
address the longer-run fiscal problem, raising the age for payment of full benefits to sixty-seven. Reagan agreed, and also signaled that his aides could open
up secret negotiations with the liberals on the commission.[2]

The White House now had a negotiating package to counter the Democratic commission members'. The Reaganites' first move was to set up a meeting
between legislative strategist Richard Darman and Ball for December 17. The
two quickly agreed that finding a middle ground was now a matter of juggling
the numbers: how much in tax cuts and how much in benefit cuts?

Reagan still thought the tax increases the Democrats wanted were too high,
Darman said. But of course, Ball reminded him, the line between what defined
a tax increase as opposed to a benefits cut could be massaged. For instance, the
Democrats' idea of taxing some Social Security payments could be considered
either a new tax, or a benefits cut for the wealthy. Darman thought that idea
might appeal to Reagan, who preferred to see Social Security as a means-tested program for the poor—cuttable, like all "welfare" schemes—rather than a
broad-based social insurance program.[3]

Clearly, an agreement was achievable, and the president signaled that talks
were still on six days later, when he signed a one-sentence executive order extending the commission's life through January 15.[4] Shortly afterward, Reagan
for the first time publicly reversed his position against any payroll tax boost.
Asked at a press conference about the possibility of moving up the scheduled
increases, he replied, "There is a limit with regard to how far you can go on the
tax, and the limit is caused by the fact that a big proportion of our working
people today are paying a greater tax in Social Security than they are in income
tax." But, he added, "We will look at that."

Stockman, the one-time revolutionary, was now playing the role of pragmatist,
working to bring enough Democrats to the table to make a deal.[5] The first meeting,
at James Baker's home, took place on January 5. Because the purpose was to get the
commission's agreement, the attendees, who would soon start calling themselves
the Gang of Nine, included only two Democrats—Ball and Moynihan—along
with three Republican members of the Greenspan commission—Greenspan,

Dole, and Rep. Barber Conable, ranking Republican member of the House Social Security Subcommittee. The White House representatives were Stockman,
Darman, Baker, and congressional liaison Kenneth Duberstein.

"Only two people really mattered—Ball and Stockman. They represented
the speaker and the president," one participant said later. "Most of the negotiations eventually involved just those two representatives, sitting across from
each other at the table."

Most of the Gang of Nine package was in place by Friday, January 14. The
major elements were:

- A six-month permanent delay in the COLA, shifting the date when
  the adjustments took effect from the beginning of Washington's fiscal
  year on July 1 to the beginning of the calendar year on January 1, saving $40 billion through decade's end;

- Acceleration of the scheduled payroll tax increases, from 5.4% per
  worker to 5.7% in 1984 and then to 6.06% in 1986, reaping another
  $40 billion;

- Coverage of new federal employees as of December 31, 1984 ($20
  billion);

- An increase in payroll taxes for the self-employed ($18 billion); and

- Payments in lieu of subsistence for military personnel ($18 billion).

Gaining White House acceptance depended a great deal on whether the
biggest benefit cuts and the biggest tax increases offset each other. With the
first two of these items, the Gang of Nine achieved that goal. The package also
included new benefits for surviving and divorced spouses, worth about $500
million, fought for by the commission's two female members, Rep. Martha
Keys of Kansas, a Democrat, and Mary Falvey Fuller, a California business executive who had served on the Reagan transition team. (Tellingly, the women
are reported to have moved the topic along during the first Gang of Nine
meeting, when most of the male negotiators were preoccupied with watching a
football game.) And it recommended removal of Social Security from the unified federal budget. Another commissioner, Sen. John Heinz of Pennsylvania,
chair of the Senate Special Aging Committee, thought this would make the
program less of a tool in budget policy disputes in the future by freeing it from
the budget committees' oversight.

The package still added up to only about $140 billion over the remain-
der of the decade and less than half the seventy-five-year target of 1.8% of
payroll. How to bridge that final gap? The answer was Ball's idea of taxing
Social Security benefits for upper income recipients: the same one he had

raised with Darman a few weeks earlier. Now Ball calculated that this change would raise $36 billion in short-term revenue and over a third of what was needed over the seventy-five-year period. To maintain the 50-50 split between tax increase and benefits cuts, the negotiators agreed to classify half of this change as a tax increase and half as a benefits cut. The addition brought the package to $168 billion over the rest of the decade, or 1.2% of payroll over seventy-five years.

Each side made some political concessions. The White House negotiators agreed to create a partial credit for the first year of the tax increase, which the Democrats said would be the price of Kirkland's support. The Democrats agreed to institute the six-month COLA delay immediately rather than phasing it in. Nothing in the package would change the basic structure of Social Security.

But it was still about one-third short of the changes needed to bring the program into seventy-five-year balance. The Republicans favored raising the age for full benefits payment, the Democrats raising payroll taxes a bit more. Sensing that they couldn't resolve this final issue in a way that Congress wouldn't pull apart, the negotiators decided to leave it up to the lawmakers and submit the Gang of Nine package "as is."

After holding their last meeting the morning of Saturday, January 15, the negotiators fanned out to obtain approval from the key commission members. Ball called Kirkland and outlined the package. The AFL-CIO leader said he would accept the six-month COLA delay if Claude Pepper would go along. Pepper agreed, thinking it was the best deal he could get, and that it would ensure O'Neill's acceptance. The president told his White House negotiators that he would accept the deal if the speaker would.

That same afternoon the commission reconvened, just hours before its mandate was set to expire. Once O'Neill and Rostenkowski were reached—in Palm Springs, where they were playing in the Bob Hope Desert Classic—and their agreement obtained, the rest of the job was easy. The compromise package passed, 12-3, with only the three most conservative members—Waggonner; Sen. William Armstrong of Colorado, who chaired the Senate Social Security Subcommittee; and Rep. Bill Archer, a member of the House Social Security Subcommittee—voting against. This wasn't the unanimous approval Greenspan had hoped for, and on top of it, commission members wrote eleven dissenting opinions objecting to various aspects of the plan, but it would have to do. Reagan quickly issued a statement that "the American people will welcome this demonstration of bipartisan cooperation" while O'Neill promised to put the commission's proposal at the top of the new Congress's agenda.

* * *

The House majority and minority leaders also issued statements of support. That sent a not-so-subtle message to members to get in line behind the proposals while also providing them with political cover if their constituents complained. Indeed, few major bills in congressional history outside of war resolutions have entered the legislative cockpit with as much support from such a wide range of influentials. "It was veto-proof, fail-safe—this was gone," Robert Rubin, then an HHS assistant secretary, later remembered. "The skids were really greased on this baby."[6]

In late January, Rostenkowski announced his proposed schedule for legislation based on the commission plan: Ways and Means hearings starting February 1, passage of a House bill by early March, passage of a Senate bill by mid-March, and final enactment by March 25. It was a blistering pace that would have been considered laughable for any other major project.

The commission members were the chief salespeople for the bill, and the rhetoric they favored in testimony to Congress was next to apocalyptic. The Social Security crunch was threatening to undermine America's stature as a global power, possibly weakening its ability to borrow, by giving the impression Washington couldn't govern. Ball sounded a similar theme before the Senate Finance Committee. Passing the bill was "a matter of restoring confidence in the financing of the program," he said. Consequently, lawmakers must "design a plan that would result in the Board of Trustees saying officially that the program was in full actuarial balance both in the short- and long-term."[7]

Why the rush? "It had to pass," one Republican said about the bill going into the Ways and Means mark-up in March. "The alternative [was] chaos. For better or worse, this package [was] going to stumble through." This greatly overstated the matter. Congress could always authorize more interfund borrowing or borrow general revenues from Treasury and delay more difficult measures. One senator, Republican Paula Hawkins of Florida, suggested the government issue specially earmarked Social Security bonds to float the program until Treasury could repay the money.

But the White House and the House Democratic leadership had each decided that it was politically expedient to put the issue of Social Security behind them. For Reagan, it remained a drain on his popularity, as polls showed that public disapproval of his performance on Social Security remained in the embarrassing range of 70% to 75% even after the commission completed its work. Accordingly, O'Neill and the other Democratic leaders realized they would probably reap most of the political benefit for "solving" Social Security's problems.

Rostenkowski opened his Ways and Means hearings on February 1, as promised, giving prospective players just two weeks to prepare. There was opposition. A new coalition called the Fund for Assuring an Independent Retirement (FAIR), composed of some 6 million active and retired federal workers, was opposed to having their new coworkers folded into Social Security.

Most business groups heeded pleas from the White House to get in line behind the deal—except for one, the National Federation of Independent Business, which feared the impact of higher payroll taxes on employers during a recession. Seniors' groups were split. The National Council of Senior Citizens and SOS, dominated respectively by organized labor and SSA veterans—including

Ball—who were versed in the Washington political world and its habits of compromise, supported the proposal.

Other groups, representing the insurgent Gray Power movement, rejected it. The Gray Panthers had been suspicious of the Greenspan commission from the start; their feisty leader, Maggie Kuhn, had even been thrown out of one of the commission's public meetings. The AARP found the tax increases and benefits cuts to be too harsh. The AARP dubbed the whole plan "a lousy agreement." It was especially on guard against any increase in the eligibility age for full benefits or change in the COLA formula, which lawmakers might still adopt to close the remainder of the long-term funding gap.[8] "We'll fight anything we don't like to the bitter end—pull out all the stops," the AARP's chief lobbyist, James Hacking, promised.[9]

Claude Pepper was a pivotal figure as Congress started to dissect the commission package. He was the acknowledged champion of senior citizens in Washington, chaired the House Rules Committee, and had voted in favor of the commission's report as a member. He could reconcile liberal House members to provisions that cut benefits, like the COLA delay. He was also a useful *bête noir* to dangle in front of Senate Republicans, whose leaders could admonish them not to tamper with the deal lest Pepper lead a revolt in the House. In fact, the closest the package came to foundering may have been the very beginning of the legislative process, when AARP leaders met with Pepper. They came to complain that the six-month COLA delay was actually a permanent benefit cut, since the extra money would never be recouped for beneficiaries.

Pepper, claiming he didn't realize this, called Ball and said he was backing out of the deal. Ball quickly consulted with aides from O'Neill's office plus

Gray Panthers protest congressional deliberations aimed at "saving" Social Security by cutting benefits. Legendary Panther founder Maggie Kuhn, left, had earlier been thrown out of one of the Greenspan commission's public meetings.

Kirkland and Cohen, then went to Pepper's office to talk to him and engage others to plead with him by phone. Bolling, now a Boston College professor, seemed to make the biggest impression by flattering the Floridian, reviewing the many ways in which he had contributed to Social Security. Finally, Pepper gave in, announcing to the AARP that the COLA delay was the only way to get a good agreement.

The real sticking point, of course, was how to fill the one-third gap in the program's long-term funding that the commission had left up in the air. Congress had two routes to choose between. Pepper proposed a payroll tax increase to take effect in 2015—plenty of time for Congress to change its mind if there was no need. Pickle, still, was intent on raising the age at which workers could retire and collect full benefits. Rostenkowski and O'Neill decided to let both lawmakers make their proposals on the House floor.

When the showdown came on the final House bill, Rostenkowski, to keep the bill moving, asked for a "closed rule," meaning that only two amendments could be offered: Pickle's and Pepper's. Pepper, as Rules Committee chair, agreed. Pickle went first, arguing for a gradual increase in the eligibility age to sixty-seven, against strong opposition from labor and most of the House Democratic leadership. But he stunned the chamber by winning on a 228-202 vote, because Rostenkowsi made it known that he supported Pickle[10] and because Republican members and more conservative Democrats were able to briefly revive their alliance of the previous two years.

Pepper followed up with a teary, thirty-minute speech in which he pleaded with his colleagues not to sacrifice some portion of the elderly to poverty just to squeeze a few more dollars to solve a problem too far in the future to calculate. The speech received a standing ovation, but Pepper's 2015 tax increase proposal went down, 132-296. It had been partly a tactical error on Pepper's part to let Pickle make his plea first, but the outcome was also a lesson that the new, stronger Democratic majority in the House was still not as unified as it had been before Reagan. Pepper couldn't support the final bill now, but it passed on March 9 anyway, by a sound 282-148 margin. Ball, who fiercely opposed the age eligibility hike, later blamed the outcome on Tip O'Neill for not paying attention, and AFL-CIO lobbyists who he said were so focused on preventing extension of Social Security coverage to federal employees "that they let the retirement age issue get away from them."[11]

Senate passage of the bill was far easier, because the major issues had been dealt with in the House and the leadership of both parties in the Senate were determined to enforce discipline. S.1, as the Senate bill was designated, passed on the 23rd, and, less than twelve hours later, a House-Senate conference committee met to reconcile their two bills.

The House conferees succeeded in removing Social Security from the unified budget starting in 1992. The Senate argued succesfully for moving up the date when the COLA "stabilizer" would come into effect. The House had adopted the Gang of Nine's provision for switching the basis of the COLA formula to the lesser of the CPI or the rate of wage increase if the trust fund reserves slipped below 20% of estimated annual expenditures, with the change to take effect in 1988. To give Dole a victory, Rostenkowski agreed to advance that date to 1984, although with a slightly less stringent trigger of 15% for the years 1984–88 and 20% for 1989 and thereafter.[12] That way, the lower standard would only apply to the next few years when Social Security's finances were expected to remain somewhat precarious.

The stabilizer was no minor matter. In a bad year, it could prompt a benefits payout cut of $55 billion, the SSA actuaries calculated when they got around to examining the final legislation. But the congressional leadership were working so fast now that no one—most importantly, Claude Pepper—knew about this until the stabilizer had become law.

Both House and Senate met Rostenkowski's deadline. At 10 p.m. on March 24, the same day the House-Senate conference committee met and struck a deal, the House passed the committee's report, 243-102, with Pepper casting a yea. At 1 a.m. on March 25, with Republican majority leader Howard Baker appealing to the chamber to "get on with the business of fixing Social Security," the Senate did the same.

In a strenuously bipartisan ceremony, Reagan signs the Social Security amendments, April 20, 1983. Standing behind him are eight key players in the negotiations that produced the bill. Left to right: Sen. Bob Dole (D-KS), Rep. J.J. Pickle (D-TX), Rep. Claude Pepper (D-FL), House Minority Leader Bob Michel (R-IL), Sen. Pat Moynihan (D-NY), Tip O'Neill (D-MA), and Sen. Howard Baker (D-TN).

* * *

The president signed the Social Security amendments of 1983 on April 20 in a media-saturated ceremony on the South Lawn of the White House. Bargaining continued right up until the last minute. To get O'Neill and other Democratic leaders to attend, the administration had to agree to let O'Neill speak before the signing. Reagan himself reiterated what everyone knew: "None of us here today would pretend that this bill is perfect. Each of us had to compromise in one way or another. But the essence of bipartisanship is to give a little in order to get a lot."

To do his part in the wheeling and dealing, Reagan had had to persuade himself to look at the tax provisions of the 1983 Amendments very differently than he would have two years before. Some Social Security benefits would now be subject to taxation, undeniably contradicting the administration's avowed policy of not burdening the taxpayer any further. Reagan squared the circle by convincing himself that the new taxes weren't really new taxes at all, but a decrease in benefits: in other words, a spending cut.[13] And that was the line that administration staffers stuck to in explaining the 1983 Amendments to the public.

The White House, in its somewhat Jekyll-and-Hydish manner, still couldn't get its signals straight on Social Security, however. "By working together in our best bipartisan tradition," the president said at a news conference the day after the 1983 Amendments left Congress, "we have passed reform legislation that brings us much closer to insuring the integrity of the Social Security System." But that afternoon, in a meeting with teenagers, the president once again called the payroll tax system into question.

"I'm not sure that the benefits that you will receive when you come to the point of retiring from the work force will justify the amount of that tax," he said. "I don't think there would be anything wrong if we had some solid studies made as to whether we could improve that program for all of you so that it would be more fair for you and for the younger workers in the work force."

A White House spokesperson said the president was "just expressing his thoughts in answer to a student's question," and that no such study was planned.[14] And by this time, few Democrats wanted to make an issue of whether the administration had bargained with the Greenspan commission in good faith. Both the president and his legislative team and the Democratic congressional leaders knew that the new law would probably be the last major revision of Social Security for a generation. With inflation down and the economy at last recovering, the elements that had spawned the Social Security crisis in the mid-1970s and then undermined the effort to solve it with the 1977 Amendments were gone. Without them, the unique opportunity to remake the program, too, was gone.

The 1983 Amendments marked the final act as well of a two-year drama in which the White House had tried to initiate the winding down of Social Security and instead ended up endorsing a plan that largely cemented the existing tax-and-benefits structure in place. Despite David Stockman's best efforts, the Democrats had succeeded, and not for the last time, in decoupling the problem of funding Social Security from the far bigger problem of the overall federal budget deficit. They were happy to leave it at that, and Republican leaders—most of them, for now—didn't want to rock the boat again right away.

In the backslapping that accompanied passage of the 1983 Amendments, which brought $169 billion in new savings and revenues over five years, the celebration of bipartisanship—rather than the bill itself—often seemed to be the real point. "The passage of this bill through Congress over the last two months is as remarkable as it is monumental," Rostenkowski exulted after the House approved the conference report. "In the face of crisis we have shown that we can rise above partisan differences." "The system does work," O'Neill said at the signing ceremony. "This is a happy day for America."

Since then, political scientists and historians of Washington policymaking, who tend to credit process, expertise, and professionalism over self-interest wherever they can find these qualities, have enshrined the 1983 Amendments as a classic case study of how "the system works."[15] Paul Light, who wrote a detailed account of the Greenspan commission, called the Amendments "a legislative miracle."[16] But the principal reasons the process that began with the Greenspan commission ended up in a sweeping new law were twofold: First, the commission had agreed early in its existence not to challenge the fundamental structure of Social Security, explicitly rejecting in its final report any proposal to make the program voluntary or to cut benefits for better-off workers. Narrowing the discussion made it easier for the members to find common ground.

Second, both Republicans and Democrats saw immediate political advantages in making it so.

The president bought himself one very important thing with the new Social Security law: a smaller deficit. Since Social Security would remain part of the unified federal budget until 1992, the 1983 Amendments netted Reagan a $169 billion reduction in the deficit between 1984 and 1989. Given that he faced another tough budget battle at the very time Congress was negotiating its adoption of the Greenspan commission's proposals, this was immensely important. The fate of the third leg of Reagan's three-year income tax cut, the heart of the supply-side economic plan that Stockman had crafted for him, depended on his ability to find savings—or revenue—elsewhere. So did his plans to continue the military buildup. Thanks to the Social Security debate, he found much of what he needed by raising the payroll tax.

The 1983 Amendments did indeed show that the system worked, in the sense that politicians could assemble outside of public view, make some fairly ruthless tradeoffs, and hide them behind a cloak of "bipartisanship" when a real or imagined deadline for action imposed itself. The language of the new law, and of the debate that preceded it, was full of terms of art meant to obfuscate the hard facts of tax increases ("tax acceleration") and benefits cuts ("permanent delays" in COLAs). "It was a way to disguise the pain, a way to help the public accept the cuts," Light comments. "If there was a lesson here for other redistributive policies, it was to confuse, not to educate."[17]

Amidst this cloud of euphemism, the biggest restructuring of Social Security in more than forty years became law. The major money-raising and money-saving changes were:

- Add nonprofit and new federal employees into the Social Security system;

- Prohibit any further withdrawals from the program by state and local government employees;

- Tax the benefits of high-income earners;

- Delay the next COLA adjustment by six months and make the resulting change in the annual effective date permanent;

- Accelerate already-scheduled increases in the payroll tax rate;

- Revise SECA taxes for the self-employed so that they would make payroll tax contributions equal to the total paid by employers and employees;

- Credit the OASI trust fund in a lump sum with catch-up contributions by the federal government for military service wage credits;

- Gradually increase the eligibility age for payment of full benefits to sixty-seven;

- Credit uncashed benefit checks to the trust funds; and

- Create an automatic stabilizer in the form of a switch to the lesser of the CPI or the wage rate for computing COLAs in case trust fund reserves fell too low.

On the surface, the 1983 Amendments were much like the package the Carter administration pushed through six years earlier—a combination of tax hikes and benefit cuts. In reality, they were very different. The 1983 Amendments were the first Social Security "fix" to not include a payroll tax boost—only a move forward in the date that some already-scheduled payroll tax increases were to take effect. And even counting these, the entire package was weighted two to one in favor of benefit cuts. That was thanks to the hike in the eligibility age for full benefits, which represented a cut in lifetime benefits for most workers.

The legislation also contained a couple of small but significant revenue-reducing measures, however. One, included at Reagan's insistence, was a change to the deferred retirement credit, boosting it from 3% to 8% by adding 0.5% a year from 1990 until 2009. The president's goal was to increase the likelihood that a person who delayed receiving Social Security until seventy-two would get the same amount or more than a person who stopped working at sixty-five in average lifetime benefits. This represented the first attempt by the federal government to encourage older people to stay in the workforce as long as they could: the first sign that the coming retirement of the baby boomers was causing Washington to change its policy on aging.

The other important revenue-reducing change was a package of four measures designed to make Social Security fairer to women in old-age. Keys and Fuller had argued for an earnings sharing system that would combine a husband's and wife's earnings for the purpose of calculating their Social Security payments. The idea was to improve benefits for women, who generally only received 50% of their retired husband's benefit after he died. But when this was rejected, they settled for a package of smaller changes to benefit women, plus further study of the earnings sharing idea. All this made its way through the legislative process unscathed, because the adjustments were calculated to eat up only a very small fraction of payroll. They were:

- Continued benefits after remarriage for disabled widows, widowers, and divorced spouses;

- Indexation of widows' and widowers' benefits based on the greater of wages or CPI;

- An increase in the benefit rate for disabled widows and widowers aged between fifty and fifty-nine to 71.5% of the primary benefit; and

- Permission for divorced spouses aged sixty-two or over to receive benefits when the ex-husband or wife is eligible.

The HHS secretary was directed to prepare a report on earnings sharing, to be submitted within two years.

* * *

Thus far in Social Security's history, new legislative packages had always included benefit improvements for some important constituency. In 1983, as ever, it had seemed a matter of course. But for traditional defenders as well as critics of Social Security, the primary fact about the amendments was that they didn't change the basic structure of benefits. The program took in money the same way as before and paid it out according to the same formula.

The amendments did change the program's long-term finances in fateful ways, however. The most important of these—although many of the key players may not have realized at the time they were doing it—was a vast expansion of the OASI and DI trust funds. Social Security in 1983, like most national pension schemes, was effectively a pay-as-you-go system. The 1977 Amendments began to move that model in a different direction by jacking up payroll taxes. The 1983 Amendments pushed forward the date of the tax hikes and augmented them with a series of benefits cuts and a later age at which workers could start to receive full benefits.

An additional $169 billion were now expected to pour into the once merely symbolic trust funds from 1984 to 1989. While payroll taxes were technically dedicated exclusively to financing Social Security and Medicare, the Treasury borrowing mechanism meant that in fact Washington could use them for other purposes as well—such as to make up for rising deficits in the overall budget. What if budget deficits persisted into the next decade—and Social Security continued to enjoy surpluses?

No one on the Greenspan commission or in Congress—at least publicly— anticipated such a thing in 1983. Most expected wages to begin rising again as the economy recovered, boosting income tax receipts and lowering the deficit. There's evidence, too, that neither the commission nor anyone in Congress ever performed an actuarial study that would have revealed just how huge a boost the Social Security trust funds would get from changes like the higher eligibility age. What they didn't know, then, was that the trust funds wouldn't just become temporary relief from Washington's deficit pressures, but a way of life.

Social Security, then, was about to evolve quickly from a pure pay-as-you-go system to a "partially funded" system, in a vast new accounting scheme that was perfect for the coming era of large national deficits. Nothing operated any differently than before. Money coming into Social Security would still be used to pay current benefits: anything left over would still be loaned to Treasury in exchange for bonds. It was just that vastly more money would now be loaned to Treasury.

If this scheme made it easier for Reagan to fund his military projects and offset his income tax cuts, it made sense for the Democrats too, because a smaller bottom-line federal deficit—or the appearance of one—removed some of the president's leverage for cutting domestic spending. Even as the 1983 amendments were being finalized, the White House was pushing a budget that would implement the final year of the Reagan tax cuts and pay for it with, among other things, housing, Medicaid, and food stamp cuts; a freeze on civil service and military pay increases; and, possibly, a six-month delay in COLA increases for federal retirees—all hitting Democratic constituencies hardest. The 1983 Amendments put O'Neill and the other party leaders in Congress in a stronger position to resist those cuts.

The problem was that the new law achieved this at a large cost to beneficiaries—and for some more than others. Payroll taxes were more regressive than income taxes. Many of the policy experts who had steered the evolution of Social Security up through the 1970s had hoped that at some point income tax revenues could be added to supplement the payroll tax system, because this would make the system less regressive. Instead, the 1983 Amendments locked Social Security into a funding system entirely based on payroll taxes.

Even before, it was clear that the tax code was becoming more favorable to upper-income households and less favorable to lower-income ones. Drawing on the results of a Congressional Budget Office study in February 1982 of the impact of the Reagan budget cuts and tax reductions, the *Washington Post* concluded, "The middle class has a net gain from the budget and tax cuts, although the gains are, except for those in the upper ranges of the middle class, largely eliminated by the effects of bracket creep, inflation, Social Security tax hikes and the recession." And an analysis by the staff of the Greenspan commission showed, for example, that raising the eligibility age for full benefits to sixty-seven would result in a substantial lifetime benefit cut of 12.5% for younger workers: those who would bear the brunt of the upcoming payroll tax increases.[18]

The quarter-century that began with Reagan's election would see a vast wealth transfer from middle and working class Americans into the hands of the wealthy. Two separate but related events in the first two Reagan years brought this about: the slashing of income taxes for upper-income households and the boost in payroll taxes for other workers.

This shift represented a huge opportunity cost to those workers. Reversing the Social Security deficits of the late 1970s and early 1980s, the federal government would collect $4.5 billion more in payroll taxes in 1983 than it needed to pay out benefits: an extra 2.7¢ per dollar. By 1990, that would snowball to $1.20 for every dollar needed to pay benefits. All told, from 1984 to 2002 the Social Security trust funds would collect—and then loan to the U.S. Treasury—$1.7 trillion from payroll taxes for an average of $16,000 per household. By then, three of four households would be paying more in payroll taxes than they would be in income taxes.[19]

Arguably, the Treasury needed that additional $1.7 trillion to cover the ongoing costs of government during an era of huge federal deficits. It also bolstered Washington's standing in the credit markets, because instead of having to borrow that $1.7 trillion by selling Treasury bonds, at whatever rate of interest the market saw fit to charge, it could borrow the extra money from the Social Security trust funds, at a rate it was comfortable paying. But by obtaining the extra money through payroll taxes instead of the more progressive income tax system—a change for which there was no strictly economic rationale—Congress and the White House collaborated on altering the tax system to weigh more heavily on the poor and middle class.

The rationale was three-fold. First, that the coming baby boom retirement bulge made it necessary to prefund their disability and retirement benefits by piling up big trust funds for OASI and DI. Second, borrowing from the Social Security trust funds was a better deal for the taxpayer than borrowing in the Treasury market, which was capricious and could be expensive. Third, by prefunding, Social Security could "solve" its financial problems for the next seventy-five years, answering the Reagan White House's demand that the program's finances be stabilized for the long term.

It's been suggested that the Greenspan commission and the principal lawmakers who pushed through the 1983 Amendments hadn't any intention of moving away from pay-as-you-go and creating large OASI and DI trust funds. That's principally because in calculating the effect of its proposals on Social Security's future balances, the commission used the "average cost" method of accounting, which assumes benefits will be paid out of taxes rather than from trust fund assets. The growth of the trust funds may have been an "unwitting byproduct" of the process, in this view.[20]

But much of the commission's—and Congress's—work was done in a hurry, and individuals who served as commission staff members and as congressional aides remember otherwise. The issue of building up trust fund assets was discussed within the commission—Myers argued against it but was overruled*— while key lawmakers including Rostenkowski, Pickle, and Rep. Byron Dorgan of North Dakota, a member of the Ways and Means Committee, were aware that they were significantly increasing the revenue stream into Social Security—far more than was needed to get it over its short-term funding hurdle in the 1980s.[21]

Why would a group of relatively liberal Democrats agree to extend a relatively regressive system of funding for Social Security? Because their primary concern wasn't whether the program would encounter real fiscal problems in future decades—it was too soon to know for sure—but maintaining public confidence in the program.

In January, as the Gang of Nine talks were moving toward a conclusion, Moynihan noted in an op-ed that there had been "what [financial columnist] Sylvia Porter has called 'a scare campaign of vicious proportions' to convince the American people that Social Security was a fraud, and that they would never get their benefits." Moynihan wrote that as he left the negotiations at Blair House on the 15th, a cab driver told him it was a waste of time to try to "save" the program, since it had all "been given away as foreign aid. He—age 59—was sure he would never get any of his promised benefits."[22]

Moynihan, Ball, and the rest of the Democratic leadership made a political decision to turn the trust funds from a technical accounting device into a real repository of wealth for Social Security in order to solidify the promise that those benefits would be paid and extend it far into the future. This, they hoped, would help restore the public's faith in the program. No other industrialized country felt the need to build up a reserve of this sort. But politics in the U.S. was moving to the right more quickly than in most others, and Ball, particularly, sensed that the war against Social Security would be fought around such technicalities. Meanwhile, trust fund financing would help dampen fears about the program's future.

---

*   "Bob Ball said to Bob Myers: 'I want people to see that there are ample trust fund reserves to pay promised benefits' … and Bob Myers concurred" (Merton C. Bernstein to author, May 9, 2011). Bernstein was present at the meeting between Ball and Myers where this was discussed.

When the SSA trustees scored the 1983 Amendments, they concluded that the new law would keep Social Security solvent until 2058—meaning that, other factors remaining the same, it could continue to pay full benefits until that year using only payroll tax revenues and the interest on the bonds deposited in the trust funds. Surely that was a reasonable standard of success?

Perhaps it seemed so. But the creation of an enormous reserve in the Social Security trust funds raised new questions about the program's funding that would loom larger over the next two decades. In reality, the huge trust funds meant everything and nothing: everything in the sense that they bolstered the promise of payment of benefits, and nothing in that someday Congress would still have to exchange the bonds they contained for real money to pay those benefits. Whether it could do so or not would depend on the success of the enterprise in which it was "investing" those excess payroll tax revenues: the one represented by the Treasury bonds sitting in the trust funds. That enterprise was the federal government and, by extension, the U.S. economy, whose success in turn generated the tax revenues that underwrote Social Security benefits.

Would federal spending on education, defense, health and social services, research and development, and other areas help to produce a vigorous, productive population and an expanding economy? And would Washington make the right decisions about how to allocate the revenues that resulted, including those going to pay elder benefits? Perhaps the most unfortunate consequence of creating large OASI and DI trust funds was that their existence obscured the real measures of Social Security's success. Instead of its ability to provide an adequate retirement income to working Americans, the criteria would seem to be the payroll tax system's capacity to generate trust fund assets over a seventy-five-year period.

Would Washington have the money? If the economy grew at a healthy clip and, more importantly, if wages kept pace, the answer would be yes. If wages stagnated, as they had been doing for nearly ten years by the time the 1983 Amendments were passed, Congress would have two options: either find the money by cutting other federal spending, or raise it by increasing taxes.

In the many, many thousands of pages and thousands of hours of debate over Social Security in the decades following the 1983 Amendments, perhaps the least-asked question was what the economic consequences would be if the program stopped paying all or most of its promised benefits. Increasingly, as the trust funds' "solvency" came to dominate the discussion, Social Security's critics would put across the premise that the program was strictly a liability to the taxpayer—despite the fact that it represented a valuable asset to millions of households.

Social Security's critics quickly developed and repeat a series of arguments founded on this premise—arguments that would change very little throughout the three decades covered in this book. The genesis of a new movement to do away with Social Security in its traditional form was starting to become visible. Reagan, with the vital help of David Stockman, had showed the way.

PART II

The Movement against Social Security Is Born

(1983–94)

CHAPTER 6

MAKING THE CASE

The 1982 midterm election campaigns were roaring into their final weeks when a short item appeared in the *Washington Post* about a White House policy advisor who had just published a book. Peter J. Ferrara's book wasn't precisely new but a shorter version of one he had published two years earlier entitled *Social Security: The Inherent Contradiction.* The first book brought out by the Cato Institute, a little-known libertarian think tank that had recently moved to Washington from San Francisco, it was more than merely an attempt to rationalize cuts in a domestic program disapproved of by the administration.

Instead, as the title implied, Ferrara offered a top-to-bottom dissection of the very idea behind Social Security as well as the economic basis of the program. The last chapter laid out a roadmap for how Social Security could be replaced by a system of individual savings accounts.

The fact that a White House aide had developed such a radical scheme inflicted an additional bit of discomfort on the Republicans. But the *Post* story only amounted to a one-day blow-up, according to Ferrara. The White House quickly pointed out that the views expressed in his book weren't the administration's, and that he had written it before he joined the staff. If any-one's political judgment was to be questioned, it was Cato's. The obscure think tank's timing in unveiling a popularized version of Ferrara's original book—long, technical, and tedious—wasn't considered astute if Cato's goal was to win friends in Washington.

But Ed Crane, the ex-financial consultant who was Cato's founder, had something else in mind. Opponents of Social Security had never gotten very far denouncing the program or looking for ways to cut or shrink it. Ferrara offered instead to replace it with something better: private accounts. Cato saw a chance to reorient the whole Social Security debate around a concept that couldn't seem more American: the right to "own" one's retirement nest egg.

Ferrara had actually hit upon his proposal while attending Harvard Law School in the late 1970s. At the time he was working as a research assistant at a Boston consulting firm, where he helped a group of economists, including Stockman's then-mentor Arthur Laffer, to devise an econometric model test-ing the impact of supply-side tax cuts. He then began writing a paper laying out the private-account concept, which quickly morphed into a 600-plus-page manuscript. This he submitted to Cato, where Crane seized on it as an opportunity to inject his young think tank into a potentially huge na-tional debate.[1] When it was published in 1980, *Social Security: The Inherent Contradiction* quickly became a live topic among ideological conservatives in Washington.

But it failed to gain much attention in the Reagan White House. The ad-ministration's clumsy attempts to cut the program left it with little room to maneuver. The leaders of the Greenspan commission tacitly agreed not to in-clude among the possibilities they discussed any such radical notions as slicing Social Security into millions of private investment accounts. Tucked into its final report to the president was the following statement:

> The National Commission considered, but rejected, propos-als to make the Social Security program a voluntary one, or to transform it into a program under which benefits are a product exclusively of the contributions paid, or to convert it into a fully-funded program, or to change it to a program under which benefits are conditioned on the showing of financial need.[2]

"One of the most important things that the commission did was what it didn't do," Bob Myers later commented.

Proponents of more radical change were furious. In late February, midway between the unveiling of the Greenspan commission's final report and passage of the 1983 Amendments, the Senate Finance Committee heard a scathing attack on the report from A. Haeworth Robertson, a former life insurance executive who had been chief actuary of the SSA in the Ford administration. Robertson called the work by the bipartisan panel "extremely disappointing," first, for leaving Congress to figure out how to close the last third of OASDI's $200 billion, 1983–89 fiscal gap, and second, for what he implied was a kind of intellectual dishonesty.

While "the pressures imposed by the size of the [program's] fiscal problems had diverted [the commissioners'] attention from … a comprehensive study" of Social Security reform, he wrote, "the Commission was appointed in December 1981, when the financial problems were well known and well documented, so the Commission had more than adequate time for a thorough study." Greenspan and his colleagues were a threat to public confidence in Social Security, Robertson charged, because they had done nothing to address whether the program still suited the needs of people under forty-five: 80% of the nonretired population.

By the late 1980s, he predicted, the program's troubles would become worse, and discontent with the tax increases scheduled for the next several years would become acute. "The first children of the post-World War II baby boom will be approaching age fifty, and they will not take kindly to a suggestion that they work another five years or so beyond their planned retirement date of 65. 'Why didn't you tell me sooner?' they will ask." With this in mind, Robertson warned, "The strife and turmoil of the late 1980s and early 1990s will make today's problems with Social Security look like an afternoon picnic."[3]

Pete Peterson, the statesmanesque Wall Street executive who the previous year had organized a coalition of his counterparts plus five former Treasury secretaries to demand that Washington attack the deficit with a round of big budget cuts, had another big complaint. This he expressed to a more liberal-intellectual audience in the *New York Review of Books* just after the Greenspan commission wrapped up its work. While the panel "deserves praise" for "coming up with a series of politically workable proposals," he castigated it for having "made a deliberate decision not to deal at all with the HI problem": the accelerating costs of the Medicare Hospital Insurance program.

Leaving HI out of the equation, the commission's proposals eliminated two-thirds of Social Security's projected seventy-five-year deficit, based on the trustees' intermediate actuarial assumptions. But, Peterson pointed out, if HI was added in and the SSA trustees' pessimistic assumptions were substituted, the commission's suggestions would eliminate only one-fifteenth of the deficit.[4] While this wasn't an apples-to-apples comparison, Peterson seemed to be pointing out a huge problem that Greenspan and his colleagues had ignored.

Some ideologically sympathetic observers were not surprised. In fact, they had been criticizing Social Security's effect on the political process for decades. In a democratic political system, something like the 1983 compromise was almost inevitable, Edgar K. Browning, a University of Virginia economist, had declared in a 1975 paper.[5] "Majority voting leads to an overexpansion in the size of a social insurance system because of the short run effects of a change in the tax rate, which are concentrated increasingly on those who are older when a change is made," he wrote. Some younger voters might become aware that they are paying so much to support their parents' and grandparents' generation that the system will capsize before they get a chance to enjoy their own benefits. But "the same young people who would like to see reductions in social insurance today will become staunch supporters of increases when they are older."

Carolyn Weaver, an economist at Virginia Polytechnic Institute and State University, shared Browning's doubts about democracy. She traced the problem back to the Social Security amendments of 1939, which made the program a pay-as-you-go rather than a prefunded system. Instead of each generation footing its own bill, Weaver concluded sourly,[6] "the rate of return on Social Security payments would come to be determined after 1939 by the relatively unconstrained operation of majority rule." At the same time, "the incentive and ability of taxpayers to monitor the ensuing growth and evolution of the program would be dulled by the broad dispersion and misunderstood incidence of tax costs, and by the Social Security Administration's monopoly of information" on the program.

The SSA and other old-age programs had engendered a new category of professionals, many employed by government, to care for and minister to the needs of the elderly. Were these people virtuous public servants? Or were they nest-feathering bureaucrats, doling out taxpayer-sponsored services to people, many of whom could just as well pay for them on their own?

"The programs have served … to finance the work of large numbers of professionals, providers, and advocates," Robert B. Hudson, an assistant professor of politics and social welfare at Brandeis University, complained in 1978. "It is these groups, more than the elderly themselves, that have been the motivating force behind these programs. As with all in-kind programs, it is these groups which consume the actual appropriations while the formally targeted population receives what those appropriations happen to buy."[7]

Social Security critics also cited the influence of advocacy groups representing the elderly. "The power of the Gray Lobby is overwhelming," said one.[8] From being a class of people who needed to be defended from want, abuse, and indignity, the elderly had allegedly become a political juggernaut willing to sacrifice the needs of their children at every turn.

Most studies actually suggested that older Americans weren't monolithic voters. For example, 54% of those sixty and older in a *New York Times*/CBS News exit poll in 1980 said they voted for Ronald Reagan—about the same proportion as any other age group—even though several major seniors' groups had endorsed Jimmy Carter. And the "Gray Lobby" was always careful how far it extended itself and for what. But it seemed obvious that the AARP, the National Council of Senior Citizens, and the Gray Panthers could apply huge pressure to lawmakers when they felt the interests of the elderly were threatened, for example against Califano in 1978 and against Reagan's proposed Social Security cuts three years later.

Was there any way for fiscally prudent people who understood the problem to short-circuit the Gray Lobby? To circumvent the "unconstrained operation of majority rule" and begin rolling back Social Security?

The first step would be to break the SSA's information monopoly, the second to develop a campaign capable of delivering a different and possibly more effective message to the public. As soon as Social Security began to experience funding pressures during the 1970s economic downturn, several prominent Washington think tanks began churning out reports, analyses, and recommendations for change, making Social Security perhaps the biggest quasi-academic growth industry since the U.S. war in Vietnam at its height. "It's sometimes hard to keep up with everybody," a high official at the SSA told historian Martha Derthick in 1977. "It's like the economists discovered money."[9]

Most of the money was coming from a string of right-wing policy shops including Cato, the Heritage Foundation, and the American Enterprise Institute. These organizations in turn were funded by a group of conservative endowments and family trusts including the John M. Olin Foundation; the Charles G. Koch and Claude R. Lambe Foundation (chief backers of the Cato Institute); the Adolph Coors Foundation; and the Smith Richardson, Bradley, Richard Mellon Scaife, and Scaife Family foundations. Olin, headed by William E. Simon, who had been Treasury secretary in the Ford administration, was especially active in supporting think tanks that bolstered conservative ideology in the economic sphere, including Heritage, Stanford University's Hoover Institution (headed by Simon's predecessor at Treasury, George P. Schulz), the American Enterprise Institute, and Cato.

Established by businesspeople and their families, who had amassed huge fortunes but in many cases were no longer actively involved in running businesses, the conservative foundations were much more ideologically centered than the actual corporate leadership of the time—less inclined to compromise, more intent on moving society in an ideologically consistent direction. Well endowed and highly focused, they represented a new force in American politics in the 1970s and perhaps the most powerful attempt at ideological warfare the country had ever seen.[10] Between 1986 and 2005, they were to make $2.6 million worth of grants for research and propaganda with Social Security privatization as a specific objective, along with countless others that included privatization as a goal.[11]

Programs like Social Security, Aid to Families with Dependent Children, and Medicare were integral parts of what the right-wing brain-trusters identified as the liberal "permanent government." What was needed was a cadre of researchers and analysts who could crack the code in each of these areas of knowledge, and develop a thorough conservative perspective and set of recommendations for change.

Many of the policy analysts and researchers who populated the right-wing think tanks considered themselves to be fugitives from academia, and especially from elite universities that marginalized them for being too conservative, both culturally and politically. The think tanks supplied a modest sort of untenured support system, giving these figures the time and space to flesh out conservative positions on every conceivable aspect of public policy.

Ferrara, a lonely conservative at what so many thought of as the far-left Harvard, was fairly typical of these young, ambitious, alienated, and ideologically driven outsiders. His career reads like a right-wing *Pilgrim's Progress* through a succession of subsidized think tank positions: associate professor of law at George Mason University, general counsel and chief economist at Americans for Tax Reform, senior fellow at Cato, senior fellow at Heritage, senior fellow at the National Center for Policy Analysis, director of the International Center for Law and Economics, director of the Free Enterprise Fund's Social Security Project, senior policy advisor on Social Security and Medicare at the Institute for Policy Innovation, and so on. As a result, the think tanks themselves have often been characterized as a kind of alternate academy, a counterweight to supposedly ultra-liberal Harvard, Berkeley, Yale, and MIT.

They were actually quite different. By the early 1980s, the "strategic philanthropists" had already funded a number of educational institutions that together formed that alternative academy. George Mason University, Boston University, Claremont McKenna College, Hillsdale College, and university affiliates like Stanford's Hoover Institution all focused their educational mission in the direction their conservative donors prescribed. Cato, Heritage, AEI, and the other think tanks fulfilled another role.

Some of the ideological and organizing drivers behind the new neoconservatism, such as Irving Kristol, publisher of *The Public Interest*, were ex-Marxist-Leninists who retained from their former allegiance a profound respect for the power that ideas possess when developed and disseminated in a directed, programmatic way. Functionally, they never strayed far from Trotsky's concept of permanent revolution, of politics as "a type of warfare in which ideology is an essential weapon."[12]

Accordingly, Cato, Heritage, and the American Enterprise Institute were less like a conservative recasting of the American elite university than they were the successors to the Red Professors' Institute and the Communist Academy, think tanks that the Communist Party established in the newborn Soviet Union in the 1920s. These "ideology factories" were set up to flesh out, expound, and justify theoretically each new policy and policy shift emanating from the Kremlin.[13]

For the politicized right wing of the American business establishment in the 1970s and 1980s, the think tanks served the same function, focusing tightly on issues of prime concern to those who funded them. Susan George, a scholar and journalist and close observer of the neoconservative trend, characterized these intellectual entrepreneurs as the "Gramscian Right," underscoring the similarities between their strategy and the arguments of Antonio Gramsci, the unconventional Italian Marxist who contended in the 1920s that culture, not the economy, was the battleground the followers of Marx and Lenin needed to command to defeat capitalism. By achieving "cultural hegemony"—victory in the realm of ideas—socialism would have no need of violence to achieve social transformation.[14]

The New Right of the 1970s grasped this basic idea, funded it generously, and created a highly efficient network to harness it for action. Unlike an academic institution, moreover, the think tanks could focus their resources on a particular issue, quickly developing both a comprehensive position and a promotional campaign to sell it. They cultivated a sober and scholarly profile that helped them get their ideas exposed in mainstream but sympathetic publications like the *Wall Street Journal, Business Week, Fortune,* and *Forbes*—and even on public television, when they were willing to sponsor the programming.* Ferrara's book and a subsequent stream of articles and books on Social Security that issued from his pen were exactly the kind of work the conservative policy shops were set up to do.

The think tanks played no role in the Greenspan commission process. Business itself, in fact, was completely unsuccessful at lobbying for changes to the final compromise package and even suffered the strange humiliation of being lectured to by the Reagan White House on the necessity to get in line behind the president. Most corporate executives still didn't see Social Security "reform" as a major objective anyway. Even Wall Street, which would benefit most from the gradual disappearance of government-sponsored old-age insurance, wasn't prepared to build a new business model around millions of individual accounts for which it had neither the data-processing capacity nor the sales organization to cultivate profitably. Business, in the early 1980s, wasn't what the conservative think tanks represented. It was, in fact, one of the constituencies they would have to win over.

In the months following the celebratory signing of the 1983 Amendments, two Heritage Foundation analysts, Stuart Butler and Peter Germanis, wrote a paper for Cato laying out a plan for how "would-be reformers" could build a successful long-run campaign to prevent any further squalid compromises. It appeared in the *Cato Journal* that fall under the provocative title, "Achieving a 'Leninist' Strategy." Unlike Haeworth Robertson, Butler and Germanis doubted that the next Social Security crisis would arise for some time, so they argued for building a movement to work actively at altering the political landscape for change: not simply trusting that the arguments for privatization would eventually prove too powerful for most people to ignore. "As Lenin well knew," they wrote, "to be a successful revolutionary, one must also be patient and consistently plan for real reform."

The strategy was twofold. First, recognize that Social Security had the support of a firm coalition, including unions, retirees, community activists, and federal bureaucrats, which the conservative critics must divide, casting doubt on its picture of reality. Second, build a coalition around a coherent agenda, like Peter Ferrara's, for restructuring the program.

---

*   Milton and Rose Friedman's series *Free to Choose,* backed by $4 million from the Olin, Scaife, *Reader's Digest,* and other conservative foundations, was a hit on PBS the year of Reagan's election; the book drawn from it was a bestseller (John J. Miller, "Eight Books that Changed America," *Philanthropy,* July 1, 2002).

"That coalition," Butler and Germanis wrote, "should consist not only of those who will reap benefits from the IRA-based private system Ferrara has proposed but also the banks, insurance companies, and other institutions that will gain from providing such plans to the public."[15] The money to bankroll a sustainable campaign, in other words, must come from the financial services industry, since its wallet was the one that a privatized system would ultimately fatten.

Along the way, Butler and Germanis counseled, the "Leninists" of the right must avoid some political traps while exploiting opportunities. Don't adopt a plan that would cut existing retirees' benefits. Expand the existing system of individual retirement accounts, encouraging workers to use them more extensively and, ultimately, think of them—not Social Security—as their main bulwark in retirement. Bring the banking and financial services industries into this process, both as lobbyists and public educators.

Above all, be flexible. Don't commit to a rigid blueprint when much can be achieved gradually, for example by pushing for more liberal IRA rules. Social Security must be treated as a political, not an economic problem, the Heritage analysts stressed. Leninists, or any other group of aspiring revolutionaries, don't succeed by winning a theoretical debate but by offering an attractive political package to each of the constituencies involved.

* * *

Social Security's conservative critics had already been at work for well over a decade when Butler and Germanis laid out their "Leninist strategy," critiquing the program and developing proposals to revamp, abolish, or phase it out.

Social Security's original sin, in the eyes of conservatives like Ferrara, was the way it combined an income support program—"welfare"—for the impoverished aged with a universal, contributory pension scheme for all workers. While a modest government benefit for those "residual" ex-workers who were living below the poverty line was perhaps marginally acceptable, a universal scheme geared to maintain a certain level of income for everyone wasn't. "Many critics of the present system believe, as Marx and Lenin did of capitalism, that the system's days are numbered because of its contradictory objectives of attempting to provide both welfare and insurance," Butler and Germanis wrote in their Cato strategy piece.

Why should an "unearned" benefit be extended to affluent people who had no need of it? Why should all workers be forced to participate in such a program when they might be able to earn a better return on their payroll tax dollar from some other investment? And why should retirees be guaranteed an income that kept up with the wages of people who were still working, rather than saving for retirement? Couched this way, any indexing of benefits beyond what someone would have received in the past was unearned and fiscally unsound.

The first of these three arguments was heard from the moment Social Security was instituted. In fact, the program was able to go into operation only after a constitutional challenge on these grounds in 1937. In *Helvering v. Davis*, attorneys for a stockholder of the Edison Electric Illuminating Company argued that the government was robbing their client of part of his equity by forcing Edison to pay payroll taxes for its employees. They argued that a payroll tax wasn't one of the kinds of taxes enumerated in the Constitution; therefore, Congress had no power to impose one. The tax couldn't be justified either under the rationale that it was needed for the government to provide for the general welfare, because this power was reserved for the states. The government argued that Helvering's lawyers were defining the power to tax in such a limited way that it would make any kind of social spending impossible.

The court ruled 7-2 against Helvering. Justice Benjamin Cardozo, in his majority opinion, agreed with the government about taxation and argued that the federal government had an obligation to provide for general welfare when a problem—like the massive unemployment of the 1930s—was national in scope. That included the obligation to protect workers from the fear of destitution in their old age.[16]

But the feature of the program that conservatives found philosophically most objectionable was the same one that provided it with a thick coat of political armor. If it had been strictly an income support for the impoverished—as welfare for the indigent aged, essentially—it would have been vulnerable to the same attacks as all other "welfare" programs in the age of Nixon and Reagan: first, that it encouraged a "culture of dependency" and therefore harmed the very people it was designed to help; second, that it was too expensive to maintain in an era of budget constraints.

But since it was a universal program, Social Security by the 1970s was almost as essential for much of the middle class as it was for the poor. Since it was an *earned* benefit, it removed the stigma of "the dole" from the benefits paid to elderly people who would otherwise be poor—an important factor in a society that frowned on individuals who were less than self-reliant. That gave it a base of political support unique among government-run social programs.

Conservatives understood this, adding to their determination to de-hybridize Social Security. "The historical evolution of Social Security may simply be the natural outgrowth of institutional weaknesses embedded in the early program," wrote Weaver, "so that truly effective reform will require excision of these central weaknesses."[17] Separating the pension and the welfare aspects of the program "is the essential first step after which further reform can follow," Ferrara declared more simply.[18]

By the late 1960s, conservatives were turning out plans to do so. James M. Buchanan, professor of economics at the University of Virginia and a future Nobel Prize winner, published a paper in 1968 in which he proposed scrapping the payroll tax and the Social Security program altogether, replacing them with required savings in the form of social insurance bonds that would pay the equivalent of either the interest rate on long-term U.S. Treasuries or the rate of growth in GNP, whichever was higher.[19]

An even more drastic scheme to force Social Security out of the government's hands came from the redoubtable conservative economist Milton Friedman in 1972.[20] Friedman, the embodiment of the neoclassical Chicago school, proposed to abolish the payroll tax and halt any further accumulation of benefits. The income subsidy portion of the program would be replaced by a tax credit that would increase in value the lower a person's income. Those whose tax bills were lower than the value of the credit would receive a check from the government—essentially, a negative income tax.

* * *

Economists—especially conservative ones—paid a great deal of attention to these proposals to "rationalize" Social Security. But the discussion reached new prominence in 1974 when Martin Feldstein, a Harvard professor who ran the influential National Bureau of Economic Research, published a paper arguing that the program had directly caused a massive decline in personal savings.[21]

Some economists had suspected for a long time that workers saved less because of the income they anticipated from Social Security, but none had ever been able to prove the point or pin a reasonable cost estimate to it. Based on his own econometric study covering the years 1929–1971, Feldstein concluded that a worker—one who earns, say, $20,000 a year—and who previously planned to save a certain amount each year—say, $2,000—would only end up saving $200 a year, since payroll taxes strip $1,800 from her paycheck. Feldstein estimated that this "lost" saving—lost because the federal government doesn't save payroll tax revenues but spends them and replaces them with Treasury bonds—came to $2 trillion in 1971, reducing total private household wealth from $5 trillion to $3 trillion.

"Social security wealth" was the term Feldstein coined to describe the value workers believed they were piling up through the program, consisting of the present value of their net benefits minus the present value of the contributions they still had to make before they retired. The "asset substitution effect" is what he called the tendency to save less in anticipation of Social Security income in retirement.

Feldstein's findings and assertions provoked an enormous controversy in academic circles, later referred to as "Martygate." The implications were huge. If Social Security really reduced private saving by some 40%, that meant 40% less money was entering the economy for growth-generating capital investment, employment, and improvements in economic efficiency. Ignoring the possibility that some of the items for which the federal government spends those payroll tax revenues—roads, schools, scientific research, infrastructure maintenance—may add value to the economy as well, Feldstein provided a powerful new way to argue that Social Security erodes the country's well-being. His findings, amplified in later papers, also seemed to give credence to conservative arguments: that the program was morally wrong, corrupting workers who might otherwise be virtuous, frugal savers with the false promise of benefits the government wasn't really putting funds aside to cover.

But Feldstein's findings had some major logical flaws, as Selig D. Lesnoy and Dean R. Leimer, two researchers in the SSA's Office of Policy, pointed out in a 1985 paper reviewing the controversy.[22] First, more and more workers in the 1970s were retiring early. Some economists asserted that these workers were actually motivated to save more to make up for the lower benefits they would lose in their early years of retirement, at least partially balancing out Feldstein's asset substitution effect.[23]

Second, Feldstein assumed that effectively all saving is for retirement. But what about money that parents set aside for their children's college education, or the savings they may need to tap to support an aged or chronically ill relative? And what if they want to leave a bequest to their children or other persons? If the worker earmarks a large percentage of her savings for these or other purposes, the amount affected by the asset substitution effect is reduced.

Third, finding a direct connection between Social Security and saving rates depends on individuals having as clear and carefully considered a view as possible of what their future will hold: what their lifetime earnings might be, what tax brackets they are likely to inhabit at different stages of their careers, and what expenses in the way of family members, debts, and possessions they are likely to accumulate. Conservative economists liked to think of individual workers as "rational actors" who could be assumed to know all these things. But others were skeptical. If the American workforce wasn't a collection of 100 million-plus rational actors, how could one be sure that they understood clearly enough what Social Security would pay out to them, to know as well how much less they needed to accumulate in their savings accounts?

Some researchers—social scientists rather than economists—were finding that the program actually encouraged saving, in part because Social Security made it easier for workers to calculate how much more they would need to maintain their current lifestyle after retirement.[24] A focus-group study by pollster Daniel Yankelovich several years later found that when people were shown the amount of money they would need to support themselves in old age, their response was to resign themselves to work until they died. But when they saw how much of that amount would be covered by Social Security, they began to look for practical steps to save the balance.[25]

An important piece of circumstantial evidence in favor of this conclusion was the fact that employer-based pension plans had flourished rather than withered in the decades after the government started interfering in the pension business. The annuities industry, which had fiercely opposed Social Security for fear the program would ruin its business, didn't fold up and die after Social Security came into operation, but grew as well.* Also not jibing with Feldstein's

---

* "The Social Security Act has greatly stimulated interest in pension plans in general—a fact surprising to many. Insurance companies are swamped with requests for information from companies which heretofore have not considered

conclusions was the fact that in Western European countries, which offered far more generous national pensions than Social Security, workers had much higher private saving rates.

The fourth and last problem with the idea that Social Security reduces private saving, Lesnoy and Leimer pointed out, was that it misunderstood the economics of old age that existed in the days before the New Deal. Back then, many if not most elderly ex-workers relied not on personal saving but on their children for support. That being the case, doing away with Social Security would most likely not lead to a corresponding increase in private saving, because many workers, knowing they could never reach whatever number they needed to support themselves, would simply plan to do so the traditional way: by moving in with their offspring.

Numbers, however, have a way of obscuring such vexed issues, and Feldstein's studies initially had a powerful impact on researchers' notions about the economic impact of Social Security. Other papers written over the next few years used the same "social security wealth" measurement that Feldstein had concocted. Some of these found a much smaller negative effect on saving, or else yielded statistically insignificant results, but none fundamentally challenged his methods or conclusions.

That changed in 1980, when Lesnoy and Leimer reexamined the evidence[26] and found that Feldstein had made a serious computer programming error that overstated the growth of social security wealth—and the damage to private saving—by 37%. When they tried to replicate his construction of social security wealth, they arrived at numbers for the postwar period—when Social Security was in full effect—that were strangely different from the ones for the prewar years.

The postwar coefficient for social security wealth turned out to be negative, not positive, meaning that the growth of Social Security actually corresponded to an increase in saving, not a reduction. The findings "do not prove that social security has had effect on saving," Lesnoy and Leimer concluded. "They do show, however, that the historical evidence does not provide statistically significant support for the hypothesis that personal saving is affected by social security."

Feldstein acknowledged the computer error, reran his numbers, and published the results that same year.[27] Again he came up with a positive coefficient for social security wealth, but many economists considered the number too small to be statistically significant. And this time, the coefficient for the postwar period was not only negative, but strongly negative: so much so that it indicated private saving would be negative without Social Security. Once again, Leimer and Lesnoy concluded that Feldstein's time series evidence was too weak to support the assertion that Social Security reduces personal saving.

retirement plans. Insurance men liken this pension-consciousness fostered by the government to the encouragement to life insurance given by the government during the world war" (*Forbes*, December 15, 1936).

The story of the Social Security debate is about, among other things, a search for statistical certainty in a field that defies any such thing: human behavior. Most proposals to restructure or privatize the program have been founded on some basic perception that human behavior—birth rates, investment patterns, work habits—has become knowable, thanks to some methodology or set of numbers that didn't previously exist. Feldstein's attempt to pin down the effect of Social Security on saving rates was just one example of such a dashed hope. While his assertion that the program reduces savings wasn't necessarily wrong, Leimer and Lesnoy wrote, "no one knows how individuals form their expectations of future benefits, and therefore a range of alternative perceptions must be explored."

* * *

It wasn't until 1980, however, that anyone knew Feldstein hadn't discovered something fundamentally damaging about Social Security.* By then, his conclusions had become thoroughly absorbed into the conservative critique of Social Security, bolstering the basic assertion that the program exercised an immoral influence on American workers. From a thrifty nation of savers, conservatives argued successfully, the U.S. was turning into a nation of credit-card-happy consumers, besotted with instant gratification.

There was always more myth than reality to this picture, however, especially for less well-off households. In the 1950s, supposedly the heyday of thrift in the U.S., over half of all personal saving was in the hands of the affluent minority while more than two-thirds of American households had no savings at all. This at a time when the payroll tax rate was still quite low.[28] Virtue, which in mainstream economic terms equals thrift, is much easier to achieve with a bit of spare disposable income.

But Feldstein's findings helped induce an outpouring of new proposals, including one of his own, to "reform" the system and restore economic virtue.[29] The scheme that attracted the most attention was launched by Peter F. Drucker, the revered management guru and conservative political-economic seer, in an influential 1976 book, *The Pension Fund Revolution*. His plan: to convert Social Security from a social insurance program, which guaranteed a minimally acceptable standard of living for all retirees, into a "welfare agency for the uninsurables." The one-quarter or so of workers who were disabled, handicapped, poorly paid, or otherwise not able to get jobs that would help them build up an adequate retirement nest-egg would receive minimum allowances similar to welfare, paid for out of general federal revenues, not payroll

---

*   Many writers carried on as if Feldstein's conclusions had earned their place in the body of accepted knowledge. When Peter F. Drucker reissued his influential 1976 book, *The Pension Revolution*, in 1996, for example, he felt no need to revise the statement that workers' belief that Social Security constitutes "real" savings "tends quite understandably to cut down sharply on the economy's propensity to save."

taxes. Social Security would be shrunk into a "reinsurance" fund to back up the private pension system.[30]

Arthur Laffer, already deep in planning with David Stockman, Jack Kemp, and Jude Wanniski on how to reform the U.S. economy, offered his own suggestion a year later.[31] Together with David Ranson, a consultant with the economic research firm H.C. Wainwright and Co. in Boston, he developed a plan to convert Social Security into a fully funded system, with a trust fund invested in negotiable government bonds. Workers would be allowed to opt out of Social Security if they could show that they had other means to provide for their retirement.

Laffer's goal wasn't to reform but to unwind Social Security—but only after fiscal soundness was achieved. Carolyn Weaver suggested something quite similar around the same time as well: "Once [the program was] funded, the need would be eliminated to coerce others to remain within the system simply as a means of protecting one's own expected income," she wrote.[32]

Some of the data crunching for Laffer and Ranson's proposal was done by Ferrara, who was still at Harvard Law and working part-time at Wainwright. Soon he was writing his own book on Social Security, its troubles, and possible solutions to them. But the plan he developed in *Social Security: The Inherent Contradiction* was actually a synthesis of elements that had appeared in all of the plans developed over the past dozen years. Ferrara's book is still the most thorough discussion of the subject from a conservative point of view. It rehearses almost every major argument for doing away with Social Security. The basics of nearly all the schemes to replace the current system of financing the program that would become commonplace in the 1990s appear for the first time in Ferrara's book.

He began by separating out the major features of the payroll tax system. Workers would henceforth buy disability coverage, as well as the hospital insurance currently provided through Medicare, from private insurers. That left the OASI portion of Social Security, with both its pension and its welfare aspects.

Ferrara would guarantee existing benefit levels for persons already retired or nearing retirement, but with some cost-reducing changes. Among other things, he would alter the benefits formula so that retirees would receive payments based strictly on what they had paid into the program, adjusted for inflation, not on their earnings history. The retirement age would also be raised gradually from sixty-five to sixty-eight. This would reduce the amount of benefits each worker received over her life in retirement: at first by very little, but more and more significantly over time. If anyone required additional funds to maintain a minimally acceptable lifestyle, they could apply to a new, needs-based program under SSI. The payroll tax would be abolished and payments to retirees would instead come from general income tax revenues.

How about for younger workers? In return for being relieved of their payroll tax obligations, they would have to save a certain percentage of their incomes for retirement—possibly an amount equal to what they would have paid in payroll taxes. The guidelines for this "saving" would be loose, in keeping with Cato's faith in the economic wisdom of the autonomous individual. Anything from an individual retirement account to a diversified investment portfolio of stocks, bonds, or mortgages to a simple savings account would be acceptable. The resulting investments would be tax-exempt, just like IRAs, 401(k)s, and other individual retirement saving vehicles.

Workers above a certain age could choose to participate in this system as well or to stay under the "traditional" Social Security structure. If they opted to stay put, they would receive Social Security bonds equal in value to their past payments into the program, adjusted for inflation. Once they retired, they could redeem the bonds and use the proceeds to support themselves. At some point, Ferrara envisioned eliminating the requirement that workers either save and invest a portion of their incomes or take the Social Security bonds, reasoning that the market for retirement investments would have matured and workers would have become familiar enough with it that they could guide themselves.

The big practical issue, Ferrara recognized, would be the transition costs: how to support current and soon-to-be retirees while current workers transitioned to a market-based system? Implementing his changes would cost the Treasury $62 billion in the first year alone, he calculated.

The answer was unclear. Congress could raise taxes to generate the extra money. Or it could delay making the new system of retirement savings tax-exempt. Or it could delay the kind of sweeping tax cuts for which Reagan was already campaigning. Other gambits were those old conservative hobbyhorses, cutting "wasteful or marginal programs in the federal budget" and freezing all existing programs. Finally, Ferrara turned to a suggestion that Roger MacBride, the Libertarian Party candidate for president, had made in 1976: sell some of the federal government's assets, such as land it owned in the western states.

Because these measures would reduce the cost of his Social Security phase-out scheme over its first few years, the introduction of such a plan would be less politically risky. But in the long run, Ferrara wasn't all that worried: "The increased economic activity resulting from removal of the payroll tax burden will also increase general revenues," he wrote, in lines that could easily have come from Laffer. "Meanwhile, the liabilities that have to be met will be shrinking every year after the first five years. Eventually, these two trends will converge, and the deficit will be completely eliminated."[33]

Ferrara saw his proposal not just as a way to resolve the contradictions and dangers of traditional Social Security, but as the centerpiece of a monumental effort to return America to the path of economic virtue. Adopting his plan for Social Security would correct any number of social and economic injustices, he argued, making it the right thing to do even if Social Security wasn't in long-term trouble. The arguments he mustered would be heard again and again as the Social Security debate matured over the next two decades.

Abolishing payroll taxes would "go a long way toward resolving the capital shortage problems currently facing the economy," Ferrara wrote—this despite the fact that many economists ascribed these shortages simply to high interest rates. It would free up capital to reduce unemployment. It would inspire the financial sector to develop new products for insurance and retirement protection, tailored more exactly to workers' individual needs. This would especially help poor people and people of color, whose life expectancies made it less likely that they would get full value for their payroll tax contributions. And it would give Americans "greater individual liberty and greater freedom to control their own lives and their own incomes."

Most importantly, Ferrara claimed his Social Security proposal would result in "more widespread ownership of America's business and industry. Every individual will be accumulating a trust fund that will represent his ownership interest in the country's productive assets." Workers, he wrote, "would have simply become full-fledged capitalists in their own right.... There will also be less opportunity for political demagogues to manipulate antibusiness sentiment."[34]

Ferrara's book provided more than just a synthesis of the most fashionable Social Security phase-out proposals on the table while he was writing. He had sketched a vision with the potential to captivate the leadership of the American business class. That vision included labor peace, less upward pressure on wages, a vast new pool of investible capital, and, for Wall Street, a major market for new lines of financial services products it could sell to a vast audience of small investors. That's because Ferrara's plan wasn't, strictly speaking, a scheme to dismantle Social Security.

Instead, he proposed changing the law in ways that would compel workers to funnel their payroll tax contributions into a preselected menu of private investments. Rather than spending the extra money on current needs or consumer indulgences, workers would be channeled into a particular set of investment vehicles, packaged as a private-sector alternative to Social Security. Far from wanting to abolish the program, Ferrara proposed harnessing its bureaucratic power to promote free-market ends. This "directed" approach to restructuring had a built-in advantage over simply wiping out the program, since ending the payroll tax wouldn't mean much to Wall Street unless it had some assurance that the resulting flood of money would be directed to that address. Ferrara was proposing a way to ensure this.

Ferrara's plan also suggested a new, populist approach to selling workers on the end of Social Security as they knew it. Most existing proposals had emphasized the need to rationalize the program and end what critics saw as an overgenerous benefits structure. Ferrara agreed, but he recognized the importance of offering workers something in return. Private investment accounts, which could be shown to produce higher returns than Social Security itself—if not make the possessor rich—were the carrot that must accompany the inevitable stick of lower—or no—COLAs.

Ferrara's book was the first to identify Social Security restructuring as something more than a matter of fixing a fiscally troubled government program. He and his sponsors at Cato wanted to turn Social Security into a vehicle for achieving an ideological transformation of society, an opportunity to promote a different vision of America from the "socialistic" New Deal. It was thus the most perfect expression of the prospect that bewitched conservatives at the dawn of the Reagan era. But the quick demise of Stockman's attempt to cut Social Security and the success of the 1983 Amendments made it clear that Cato was running ahead of lawmakers. Convincing Washington would take cautious and careful preparation of the grounds, carried out in a manner that appeared as nonideological as possible. Making the job easier was a decade-long series of economic upheavals that were making Social Security more politically vulnerable than it had been in forty years.

CHAPTER 7

"GENERATIONAL EQUITY"

"Nothing amuses me more than the easy manner with
which everybody settles the abundance of those who have a
great deal less than themselves."
> —*Jane Austen,* Mansfield Park

Until the mid-1970s, Washington lawmakers had been improving and expanding old-age benefits for decades. Since the days almost forty years earlier when business leaders had gone to the Supreme Court trying to stop Social Security, programs for the elderly had been one of the easiest sells on Capitol Hill. Besides the straight entitlements—OASI, DI, and Medicare—retired Americans had come to enjoy government aid for nutrition, transportation, mental health, home repair and energy assistance, housing, and many other needs. No one suggested this was unfair, or even that the elderly should live within their means. The old already had done so, and given back to society through their labor and their progeny. Now, according to the commonly accepted belief, it was society that owed them.

This analysis, built on the assumption that the economic fortunes of workers and retirees rose in tandem, not at each other's expense, stopped seeming so obvious in the 1970s. In that decade, middle class families endured a severe economic and cultural upheaval that made the 1960s seem calm in comparison. High inflation eroded much of their savings, and rising prices for energy and other essentials plus skyrocketing interest rates made them feel that many of the certainties of postwar life were now on shaky ground.

A series of recessions slowed down and even reversed average real-wage growth, which shrank by 0.9% from 1973 to 1982, and was expected to be sluggish, at best, in the 1980s for reasons that many economists figured would be permanent. These included high energy prices, a downturn in the global economy that was eroding the world's appetite for American goods, an already perceivable shift from high-paying manufacturing jobs to lower-paying service-industry jobs, and less available credit. The benchmark prime lending rate—the rate bankers charge to borrowers they consider most creditworthy—exploded from the single digits to 15% in 1979, and even touched 20% briefly the following year.[1]

Plus, the economy seemed to be changing fundamentally, in unexplained and disturbing ways. Upward mobility, one of the fundamental economic promises of American life, was giving way to a very unfamiliar period of stagnation. Earl Wysong, a sociologist at Indiana University, conducted a study comparing the incomes of 2,749 father-and-son pairs from 1979 to 1998. He found that almost 70% of the sons remained either at the same economic level as their fathers in 1979 or were faring worse.[2]

The assumption that economic growth was the answer to most of the nation's problems—poverty, inequality, even racism—no longer seemed valid. Previously, each economic expansion had narrowed the gap between the largest incomes and those at the bottom, alleviating poverty, at least marginally, and introducing more people into the middle class. Starting with the recession of 1969–70, however, the gap started to grow steadily, regardless of whether or not the economy was expanding. The middle class itself was being squeezed. Between 1969 and 1989, as the economy lurched from oil shock to inflation to wildly high interest rates to recovery, the income share of the middle quintile of total family income actually fell.[3]

People of color were hit hardest. The last ones to be picked up by the rising tide of a rapidly expanding economy in the second half of the 1960s, they were also the first ones let go when business turned sluggish a few years later. But it was white, middle-class and blue-collar families who felt most angry and, in some ways, betrayed.

Conservatives grabbed onto these signs of distress to argue that America was entering a new era of austerity. The affluent, liberal welfare state of the 1960s was simply going to have to stop overpromising services and benefits, like Social Security, to people who weren't actually needy. Social solidarity across generations and income categories was going to have to be abandoned because we could no longer afford it. The nation's retirement system was a prime example. Social Security was out of control, paying wildly generous benefits to nonworkers and suddenly creating a burden on the federal budget after decades of paying its own way.

As the middle class looked about for some group to blame for what was happening to their future, conservatives pointed out to them two possible culprits: high taxes and "dependent" populations like the elderly.

In California and Massachusetts, white, middle-class voters joined in a tax revolt initially focused on rising property tax rates. The media made an instant star of Howard Jarvis, the leader of the Proposition 13 initiative to rein in property taxes in California in 1978, and his crusade caught on in state after state.* This "sagebrush rebellion" taught politicians a couple of important lessons: tax cuts buy votes, and once a tax cut is on the books, to attempt to reverse it is politically very dangerous.

At the same time, middle- and working-class families were noticing that while their income and prospects wilted in a prolonged recession, the elderly weren't feeling the effects so acutely. Thanks to more than a decade of steadily rising benefit levels, climaxed in 1972 by permanent indexing to the CPI, retirees were protected from the worst of the downturn. They even reaped a windfall from the mistake in the indexing formula that was put in place that year and only corrected in 1977.

The perverse result was that while economic stagnation was continuing so long that it threatened to wipe out the gains that workers had made during the prosperous 1960s—average real wages rose only 0.6% from 1960 to 1982— the elderly watched their well-being grow. Total benefits from Social Security, including those paid to survivors and the disabled, rose at three times the rate of GNP in those same years. Seemingly adding insult to injury, payroll tax rates climbed from 2.3% of GNP to 5.9%, underscoring the extent to which the young seemed to be paying for the improved lifestyle of the old.

That didn't explain *why* rising income for the old necessarily implied stagnating wages for the young. Did the needs of active workers really have to be sacrificed to raise benefits for the retired? Was social welfare really a zero-sum game? Furthermore, a look at where the elderly were starting from during that twenty-two-year period suggested that the shift wasn't so unfair.

The portion of aged Americans living in poverty had dropped from 35.2% to 15.7%—quite a falling off, but still high compared with most other industrialized countries. Young families benefited, too, because for the first time many were able to proceed with starting new families and households without having to take care of parents or other aging relatives. But the figures at least did provide a skin-deep case for arguing that Social Security was a bad deal for the young.[4]

---

* Jarvis himself hoped that his followers would soon turn their guns on Social Security, which he described as "a fake ... not actuarially sound at all." He wanted to see it replaced by a privatized system in which "each worker pays for himself" (Howard Jarvis with Robert Peck, *I'm Mad as Hell: The Exclusive Story of the Tax Revolt and Its Leader* (New York: Times Books, 1979, pp. 298–99).

* * *

Another set of figures provided a spur to the Social Security debate and would help furnish the program's critics with scary numbers for years to come. Until the Reagan presidency, the annual reports produced by the Social Security trustees had never provided startling reading. The document focused on the year-to-year mechanics of the program—inflows and outflows, schedules of interest payments on the trust fund assets—and while it included some long-range solvency projections, these were few and not given much prominence.

A small group of officials who came together at the Treasury Department under Reagan decided it was time to revamp the assortment of figures in the annual report—along with how they were presented. Norman B. Ture, a longtime Capitol Hill tax expert who had become a passionate advocate of supply-side economics, was named undersecretary of the Treasury for tax and economic affairs by the new president. His deputy was Steve Entin, who had previously served as a staff member of the Joint Economic Committee of the Congress. There he worked with Aldona Robbins, an economist who had moved to the Economics Affairs office from the Labor Department in 1979.

Entin and Robbins had both had exposure to Social Security policy making in their previous jobs. The secretaries of Treasury, Labor, and HHS are all ex officio trustees of Social Security. One of Robbins's duties had been to serve as the Labor secretary's point person on the annual report, working with the SSA staff that prepared it, and reporting to and advising the secretary on the results. When she moved over to Treasury, she assumed the same role there.

Ture's main preoccupation during his nearly two years at Treasury was getting the Reagan tax cuts passed. He resigned in protest when some elements of them were repealed in 1982. But he was a great believer in teasing out the economic impacts of federal tax policies, and when he took a closer look at the Social Security trustees' report, he concluded that it didn't go nearly far enough in analyzing these. Entin and Robbins, working with their counterparts at Labor and HHS, began looking for ways to improve it.[5]

Their work wasn't necessarily the product of pure conservative economic zeal, however. Robbins and Entin had first become aware of Social Security as a public policy issue during the mid-1970s and early 1980s, when the program really was in immediate crisis and the trustees' projections, with their short-term focus, were little help to lawmakers or officials who were trying to figure out what was wrong. "So I'm there in 1981, two or three years after the last fix, and we're back in the soup again," Robbins remembers. "I suspect that more than anything else formed my view of the program."[6]

Above all, they wanted to make the long-range, seventy-five-year projections more transparent. Even before the 1983 Amendments improved their financing, the trust funds were calculated to be in balance over the next seventy-five years. It was the next five to ten years that were the troublesome period. Except for these, however, Entin and Robbins noticed that the trust funds' best years were concentrated in the early part of the period, followed by deficits later on. The annual report provided tables tracking changes in the trust funds' solvency, as well as a breakdown of where they stood at the end of each twenty-five-year period within the seventy-five-year time frame. So Entin and Robbins asked the SSA actuaries to calculate each of those twenty-five-year periods all by itself, to make plain that the trust funds might be entering dangerous territory again in the later years.

To show more plainly how differing economic assumptions can produce different results for the program, they also created an additional set of estimates. Instead of Optimistic, Intermediate, and Pessimistic alternatives, the annual report would now include two sets of what used to be Intermediate projections: Alternatives II-A and II-B. Both made the same demographic assumptions—birthrate, mortality rate, immigration—but II-B assumed lower real-wage growth, employment, and inflation, producing an overall more pessimistic set of estimates.

Just as importantly, Entin and Robbins beefed up the Highlights section at the beginning of the annual report and the section on Actuarial Cost Projections to include more discussion and analysis of these numbers.[7] The result, Robbins says, was a report painting a picture of Social Security not as an isolated entity but as part of a larger economic "ecosystem." "We tried to get the tables to where they showed what people really got from the system and that to pay for a specific benefit, if there's not enough, then it has to be paid for from somewhere else."

The revamped annual report changed the way lawmakers and Washington policyheads looked at Social Security. "Once you have something in an official document, it gives legitimacy to it," Robbins says. "You have people in the press looking at it, or pulling out a table. So the tables started affecting the debate at a policy level fairly quickly."

The revamped report could also be a bit misleading. "It's difficult to get people to focus on the fact that the seventy-five-year number is not a shortfall for this year, but over that whole period," says Stephen C. Goss, who was then working in the SSA's Office of the Actuary. "It's more reasonable to express the deficit in relative terms—as a percentage of GDP, not an absolute number—and the trustees' report does express it that way. But if you're a consumer of the reports, they give you a wide range of figures to select from, including those large absolute numbers, which are easy to misinterpret."[8]

What Robbins and Entin had done wasn't an isolated effort. A major new ingredient in Washington policymaking in the 1970s and 1980s was an expanded economic forecasting capability. During the Nixon administration, the White House budget director's office was enlarged into the Office of Management and Budget, while Congress created the Congressional Budget Office. The SSA was one of many offices in the executive branch that beefed up their analytic staffs as well. At the same time, lawmakers and the president were asking these agencies to extend their cost projections further into the future.

If the numbers were there, it seemed, someone would inevitably use them. Lyndon Johnson famously commented that if Congress had been able to project the cost of Medicare further than two years, the program never would have been passed. Washington's new legion of economic analysts effectively placed a fresh hurdle in front of any policy initiative other than defense—and any expansion of existing programs like Social Security. Not only did the program have to prove that it was in the public interest, it had to show that it wouldn't add significantly to the future cost of government. Otherwise, it would amount to "robbing" future generations unable to speak in their own interest.

Entin and Robbins continued working with the SSA staff to tweak the trustees' assumptions. Some of these changes doubtless improved the numbers—for instance, correcting the age distribution for immigrants that went into each set of assumptions and adding a table projecting inflation-adjusted benefits for recipients. The report continued to warn that its seventy-five-year projections were "not precise forecasts" but "inherently uncertain ... indications of how the trust funds would operate under present law if the assumed economic and demographic conditions actually were to materialize."[9] But they shaped a document that laid much greater emphasis on the furthest-off years in the projections: the shakiest part of the actuarial data and the part that tended to paint the gloomiest picture of Social Security's prospects.

After leaving Treasury in 1987, Entin joined his former boss Norman Ture's think tank, the Institute for Research on the Economics of Taxation, later becoming its executive director. Robbins left in 1985 and started an economic consulting firm, Fiscal Associates, with her husband, Gary. She and Entin continued to write as well as offer congressional testimony about Social Security, always emphasizing the program's clear course for disaster, and both advocated allowing workers to carve private retirement accounts out of their payroll taxes.

* * *

The new picture the annual reports presented of Social Security added the appearance of an official seal of approval to conservative economists' arguments against the program. But it wasn't enough to build a popular case for reining in elder benefits. That would rest on something more primal: a new critique of the program's "fairness." The focal point of what became known as the "generational equity" argument against Social Security was a notion of fairness that seemed to put traditional analyses based on class, race, and gender in the background and thus provide a common way for liberals and conservatives to understand the country's economic problems. It started with the assertion that the elderly didn't really need all the benefits being heaped upon them.

Once one of the poorest demographic categories in the country, the elderly were now one of the wealthiest. Many retirees in the 1970s had only paid payroll tax for part of their career, but were receiving benefits calculated as though their wages had been taxed all along. Others, retirees and workers nearing retirement, had started work when benefits were much lower; their checks would reflect only the current, higher rate.

The wellspring of the generational equity argument was a study—more of a "thought experiment," she would later say—that Barbara Boyle Torrey, a thirty-year-old researcher in OMB's fiscal analysis branch, made in 1975 on the effect of demographic change on the federal budget. "Nobody actually asked for it," Torrey says. "I just did it because I thought somebody should." She calculated that 40% of budget outlays were for age-specific entitlements. Later, in the final year of the Carter administration, OMB officials were intrigued by Torrey's work and asked her to conduct another, more formal study. This was included as a section of Jimmy Carter's federal budget for fiscal year 1980, portions of which appeared shortly thereafter in the *Washington Post* and then in scholarly publications.[10]

Brandeis's Robert Hudson was one of the first to pick up the argument. "If—on an aggregate basis—[the elderly] are now less disadvantaged and wish to be perceived as such, the question of why they should continue to receive special policy treatment immediately arises," he wrote in an article for *The Gerontologist* in 1978. Spending on OASI benefits totaled $71 billion in 1977 and was expected to top $120 billion in 1983, he noted, citing OMB. Total outlays for the aging, survivors, and retirees were $122 billion in 1977 and were projected to reach $148 billion, or 29.6% of the federal budget, just two years later.

Arrayed against all the other needs of government, Hudson perceived a zero-sum game. "The question here is simply 'whose' pot should be raised? The feeling is widespread in government circles and elsewhere that spending for health and welfare functions generally is already excessive and within the health and welfare community, it is widely—if not openly—acknowledged that 'the elderly' get too much."[11]

Hudson cited no authorities for this "widely acknowledged" view, but others in and out of more partisan government positions were beginning to speak his language. Joe Califano, locked in the first, unsuccessful struggle within the executive branch to cut Social Security, delivered an address the same year in which he predicted that unless it was reined in, real spending on behalf of the elderly would triple by 2010.[12] Robert Samuelson, a widely published economic columnist, complained that such "uncontrollable" expenditures were destroying Congress's ability to govern.[13]

By the early 1980s, the revolt against the old had spread from conservatives like Samuelson to relatively liberal economists and pundits as well. Lester Thurow, professor at the Massachusetts Institute of Technology, published a best-seller the year Reagan was elected, the title of which, *The Zero-Sum Society*, provided the catch phrase for a new way of viewing America's economic future. Thurow's thesis was that Americans no longer lived in a country where perpetual economic growth was either possible or desirable. Therefore, solving the various problems the nation faccd— energy crisis, environmental destruction, unemployment, discrimination—required taking from some groups within the society and giving to others. "The problem with zero-sum games," he wrote, "is that the essence of problem solving is loss allocation."[14]

On the surface, all of this sounded like the position of a reasonable liberal: "Our society has reached a point where it must start to make explicit equity decisions if it is to advance."[15] Thurow used his thesis to argue for a guaranteed job program, and also that the system of taxes and transfer payments should be aimed at redistributing income to meet a set goal of "equitable distribution of economic resources."[16] But those transfer payments include Social Security and Medicare. To subject OASI, for example, to the kind of rigorous test Thurow suggested would be to scrap the idea of social insurance in favor of a new principle of "equity."

But who would decide what was equitable and whether there was any room for exceptions? Thurow soon was found complaining in the pages of *New York Times Sunday Magazine* that America is making "the elderly rich while the average tax-paying worker is becoming poorer."[17]

All this seemed to paint a very dramatic picture. But whether America really was a zero-sum society wasn't so clear. For example, a 1994 study of public benefits policy in the U.S. and seventeen other industrialized nations by University of Colorado economist Fred C. Pampel, found little or no tradeoff between the amount of money governments spent on the elderly and their expenditures on children. In fact, countries that spent liberally on the one group tended to spend generously on the other as well.

The key variable in determining how much a nation spent on either children or the elderly wasn't the average age of the population, Pampel found, but its political and social structures.[18] Did the country have a strong union movement with a class-conscious identity? Did it have vigorous left-wing political parties with a strong ideological commitment to social insurance? The answer was yes for many nations of western Europe, which were taking a much slower and more deliberate approach to pension reform than Social Security's critics were calling for in the U.S.

America, by contrast, had a greatly weakened labor movement and a Democratic Party that had never identified itself as "left"—indeed, it was now moving rightward. The country also had a long cultural tradition of masking and denying the social and economic significance of class in general. Generational equity fit right into this pattern, because it seemed not a matter pitting rich versus poor—or, by extension, Republican versus Democrat—but a nonpartisan issue that should be of concern to everyone: to conservatives worried about fiscal sustainability, to liberals concerned about the potential crowding out of other important social programs, to moderates anxious that the problem might ignite conflict between the generations.

The need to solve the problems posed by Social Security and Medicare, from this perspective, was the perfect issue for politicians wishing to build an image as "bipartisan" policymakers. But what did "generational equity" really mean? What was implied in—and what was left out of—an analysis that started by questioning how and why government allocated resources to one age cohort instead of another?

* * *

The basic complaint voiced by Hudson, Samuelson, and a host of critics over the next decade was that Social Security had grown too fast and was overtaxing the young in order to pay overgenerous benefits to the old—benefits the young would never enjoy, since, by the time they retired, the program would either have gone bankrupt or begun devouring the rest of the federal budget because there were too few active workers to support it anymore. By 2035, if Medicare Hospital Insurance was thrown in, the system would "absorb fully 44% of each worker's taxable payroll just to break even," Pete Peterson wrote in a widely read, two-part series in the *New York Review of Books*.[19]

Critics like Peterson argued that a toxic stew of political forces—a beaten down and deprived population of current workers, bureaucrats with vested interests in resisting program cutbacks, and a powerful and seemingly ruthless Gray Lobby—had combined to produce a situation in which promised benefits were running way ahead of the contributions actually going into the Social Security system. One generation was borrowing from another and leaving it with a massive pile of bills to pay into the future. Paying these bills would absorb all the resources the country might otherwise invest in education, job training, infrastructure—all the projects and programs that enable a society to prosper and grow.

Here, the revamped numbers in the Social Security trustees' annual report became useful. According to the "pessimistic" projections in the 1982 report, OASI would rack up a $63.4 billion deficit by 1995, $2.5 trillion by 2025, and a staggering $21.65 trillion by 2050. Disability Insurance would add another $148 billion on top of that in the final year. Together, OASI and DI would absorb 70% of all federal spending, assuming that federal spending retained a constant share of GNP.

"The entire system, already sinking into deficit by the beginning of the century, will simply disappear from sight in a pool of red ink," Peterson concluded.

The pessimistic scenario wasn't even the most likely one. Given that these projections had proved overoptimistic since the early 1970s, chances were the future would look even worse should the sluggish economic conditions of the 1970s continue. For instance, the pessimistic projections showed unemployment running 7.3% from 1982 through 2000—not much worse than the uninspiring 6.9% rate that actually prevailed from 1973 to 1982. But the projections also called for average real-wage growth to swing back to a positive 0.4%

from 1982 to 2000, even though it posted a 1.6% drop during the previous decade. This would seem to indicate that either unemployment would move higher or the quality of employment—compensation, especially—would deteriorate. Either way, there would be less payroll for the Social Security system to collect in contributions, leading to even larger deficits.

In spite of which, it was argued, Social Security benefits weren't even a very good deal anymore. Three New York Fed researchers, James R. Capra, Peter D. Skaperdas, and Roger M. Kubarcych, provided an example in an article for the bank's *Quarterly Journal.* A new retiree in January 1982 who had earned average wages from 1937 through 1981 would have made lifetime payroll tax contributions of $7,209. She would qualify for a $535-per-month payment if she were single, and $803 if she had a nonworking spouse also aged sixty-five or older. That meant that, if single, after only thirteen months of retirement her benefits would more than cover her contributions to the system; if married, after nine months. The ratio of the present value of expected benefits to the total contributions this worker made to Social Security, plus interest, would be 2.7:1. In other words, she would reap benefits equaling almost three times what she had paid into the system.

For workers who retired between 1982 and 2030, the picture would be quite different. Their ratio of the present value of benefits to contributions would level off at 1.25—less than half the return their elders would receive. And this would only be possible if benefits were cut and payroll taxes raised to keep the system solvent.[20]

Calculations such as these appeared in article after article in both the scholarly and popular presses during the 1980s, as the generational equity debate gained momentum, but Social Security's critics didn't neglect the class-based side of the picture either. The program had morphed into a system of "welfare

Pete Peterson as Secretary of Commerce in the Nixon administration. A decade later, Peterson, now a member of the Wall Street elite, was launching his sideline as a fierce and influential critic of federal deficits, debt, and Social Security and Medicare.

for the well-to-do," with only 9% of total payments going to persons earning $10,000 or less while some 30% went to recipients earning twice that figure—and the other 30% to the elderly with incomes in the top fifth.[21]

Whatever rabble-rousing outrage was implicit in those statistics disappeared as soon as critics like Peterson started proposing solutions. One of their favorite themes was the need for "Baby Boomers to recover the ethos of thrift"[22] if they were to survive the inevitable collapse. Peterson recommended switching to a system of consumption taxes, including a tax on gasoline, as a way to encourage saving. He also called for a one-year COLA freeze, taxation of some recipients' OASI benefits, raising the retirement age, and adding civil servants into the system. After the COLA freeze was over, he would hold any future increases to 60% of the CPI—or, alternatively, index benefits to average wages minus 1.5%. He would reduce the PIA benefit formula at the upper end, lowering the income replacement rate for retired people "with a record of high earnings." And he wanted to tax everybody for any benefits they received "in excess of contributions" to the system—a change that would effectively slash benefits for many recipients.

Generational equity critics like Peterson spoke a different language than the libertarian insurgents at the Cato Institute and the other right-wing think tanks. They knew how to make their dire prescriptions appeal to a more liberal audience, with invocations of the harm that the fiscal irresponsibility of present-day retirees was doing to children and the poor.

"The excessive Social Security and public pension benefits that flow today to the relatively well-off are, literally, stealing capital from tomorrow's citizens and making cuts in government programs to the poor irresistible," Peterson wrote. "There is nothing liberal or humanitarian about pretending that the unaffordable can be afforded," he scolded his critics. "One should hope that liberalism implies some boldness, some vision, some willingness to devise new solutions."[23]

* * *

Peterson's series in the *New York Review of Books*, where he first laid out many of these arguments, did more than any other piece of writing to put the story of Social Security as generational crime into wide circulation within both the U.S. political class and the mainstream corporate media. His obsession with "entitlement reform" runs like a thread through nearly the entire period we're exploring. Peterson himself was and remains, as well, an all-American paradox.

A Midwestern son of Greek immigrants who was typically described as "patrician" and one-half of "one of the East Coast's quintessential power couples," he rose to become CEO of Bell & Howell Corporation before joining the Nixon administration as assistant for international economic affairs and, later, Secretary of Commerce. But like another aspiring East Coast power broker in a Republican White House—Henry Kissinger—Peterson spent much of his time in the capital cultivating liberal establishment figures such as *Washington Post* publisher Katherine Graham and columnists Art Buchwald and Joseph Kraft.*

Afterward, he moved to New York and became CEO of Lehman Brothers Kuhn Loeb, an old-line Wall Street investment bank. After a bitter management dispute that resulted in Peterson's ouster and the sale of the firm in 1983, he became chairman of the Council on Foreign Relations, a prestigious post at the hub of the Washington policy consensus. At about the same time, he cofounded the Blackstone Group, a boutique investment firm. Thanks in part to Peterson's legendary network of business and social contacts, Blackstone quickly made him very rich.

Peterson's many influential friends found him unpretentious—"you don't notice money on him," TV journalist Peter Jennings observed in a magazine profile—although they sometimes adopted the manner of courtiers in speaking of him. ("It's a brain that is very powerful," Stephen Schwarzman, the other cofounder of Blackstone, said of the contents of his partner's cranium. "It's different than normal people.") And he clearly believed passionately in generational justice and the evils of long-run deficits.

But a low-key, man-of-the-people image can be as difficult to maintain for a person who has enjoyed wealth for a long time as is a clear sense of the perils that less fortunate people face in their lives. Thus Peterson, the crusader against "windfalls for the well-off," posed for a profile in *Vanity Fair* on a beach in the Hamptons with his wife and poodle and described a supermarket in that enclave of the super-rich where he sometimes went shopping as "a good place to get reacquainted with your roots."[24]

Social Security first showed up on Peterson's radar in the early months of Reagan's presidency, when he was still at Lehman. The head of the Women's Economic Roundtable asked him to deliver a speech on the new president's first budget. Peterson remembers that he was then trying to buy the roundtable chair's house in the Hamptons, but that she was being "ambiguous" about the deal. He told her he would pay her asking price and also give the speech. She agreed, on the condition that he "really take it seriously."[25]

Peterson made a thorough examination of the Reagan budget and was "quite stunned" by the effects of the tax cuts as well as what he regarded as the "exaggerated promises" of supply-side economics. He also looked at some projections further into the future. In the course of his studies, "it became obvious that entitlements were where the massive growth was going to be"—and that Washington wasn't making much effort to curb the trend. He began testing his

---

*   Hillary Mills, "Pete and Joan," *Vanity Fair*, August 1993. When the Watergate scandal was beginning to reach the White House, Peterson was one of the few administration officials who kept lines of communication open to the *Post*, even warning its editors of Nixon's fury at the paper (Ben Bradlee, *A Good Life: Newspapering and Other Adventures*, New York: Simon & Schuster, 1995, p. 331).

ideas about Social Security, not long afterward, in dinner-table conversations with Jason Epstein, editorial director of Random House, whom he had met through his third wife, television executive Joan Ganz Cooney.

Around Epstein's kitchen table in exclusive Sag Harbor, Long Island, joined by a disparate group of influentials including TV producer Don Hewitt, real estate magnate and publisher Mort Zuckerman, and Robert Silvers, editor of the mainstream-liberal *New York Review of Books*, Peterson began expounding on such subjects as Americans' failure to adjust their expectations to a declining GNP. The *New York Review* series, which would receive a huge response and which conservative columnist George F. Will quickly labeled "the most important journalism of 1982," was arranged by Epstein with his friend Silvers.

Generational equity may have been one of the ways Peterson evolved to bridge the Republican, old-line business establishment, from which he emerged into Washington in the Nixon era and the mainstream-liberal, New York-centered world in which he apparently preferred to spend his time. This perhaps helps explain the philosophical differences between his approach to restructuring Social Security and those adopted by libertarian conservatives like Ferrara, who had no such social-cultural pretensions.

But the plan Peterson sketched in the *New York Review of Books,* calling it "the Salvation of Social Security," was extremely harsh. In fact, it ended in substantially the same place as the one Ferrara detailed for Cato.[26] Ferrara proposed abolishing payroll taxes so that workers could put the money instead into individual accounts. Peterson would leave payroll taxes in place, but he and other generational equity advocates ruled out any future hikes in payroll tax—even those already scheduled for 1985 and 1990.

Both proposed raising the retirement age at least three years. The biggest impact on the budget from either of their proposals, however, would have come from their slowing the growth of benefits. Ferrara wanted to reduce benefits for anyone choosing to stay within Social Security rather than investing their money privately, by basing those benefits strictly on what they had paid in payroll taxes and not on their earnings history. Peterson's idea was to tax all benefits in excess of contributions or else downgrade wage-based COLAs by 1.5%.

Either way, the point was to eliminate the "windfall" benefits Peterson and Ferrara felt older Americans were unfairly, if not immorally, skimming from the payroll taxes of young workers. The system would thus be forced to live within its means, with each generation of workers receiving back only what they had paid into it. The result, under both Ferrara's and Peterson's plans, would be a drastic drop in benefits payments. Over decades, this would reduce the value of the basic Social Security benefit to insignificance, since it wouldn't keep pace with current workers' standard of living.

Meanwhile, middle- and upper-income earners, taking advantage of the expanded rules for private retirement saving, would come to depend less on Social Security, eroding its political base. The program as it had been known for more than forty years would wither away, leaving workers to fend for themselves using either Ferrara's individual accounts or the liberalized savings rules that Peterson envisioned—or, if they had no money available for saving, to rely on SSI. Ferrara's proposals formed the basis for what became known as the "Free Lunch" position on Social Security restructuring, and Peterson's for the "Pain Caucus." But the end result from either was much the same. It could be called, loosely, privatization.

* * *

"We have all of us sufficient fortitude to bear the misfortunes of others."
　　　　　　　　　　—François, Duc de la Rochefoucauld

Unlike the tax revolt, the generational equity offensive wasn't a heavily bankrolled, voter-level campaign that sought to put laws on the books in a matter of months. Pete Peterson was no Howard Jarvis, let alone Ronald Reagan, and no figure connected with the idea ever made the cover of *Time* magazine. Generational equity, at least in the 1980s, was an argument aimed at the liberal intelligentsia with the objective of sowing doubts about the premises behind orthodox New Deal liberalism itself—about the economy, about the economic relationship between generations, about where the threat to programs for the poor was really coming from.

But the two crusades were more closely entwined than their differing styles would suggest. Alicia Munnell, chief economist at the Federal Reserve Bank of Boston, pointed out in a reply to Peterson's *New York Review of Books* series that Social Security's deficit by 1982 only totaled $20 billion compared to $500 billion in total federal budget deficits, making it an extremely small contributor to the government's fiscal problems.[27] To that, Peterson responded by invoking Howard Jarvis.

"We have recently seen a major taxpayer revolt across this country," he shot back. "The result ... was to make income-tax increases politically impossible and an across-the-board income tax cut virtually inevitable. Thus I think it likely that current unified budget deficits can to some degree be attributed to Social Security even though the funds themselves have historically been in balance."[28] According to this reasoning, even if Social Security was doing no harm to the budget, if Reagan's tax cuts made it look like it was, then it was.

Like many journalistic big-thinkers, the generational equity advocates reached their conclusions by grabbing hold of one narrow set of circumstances and assuming the trend they reflected would continue forever—or at least, that the nation was best off assuming so. Peterson acknowledged the trouble with this practice in his *New York Review* series, but forged ahead with it anyway. "If productivity stays roughly the same," he wrote "—if the trend of recent years continues (but does not get worse)—the average worker in 2020 will produce

$22,800 in goods and services, just about what he does today. The country, for the first time in its history, will have stood still for a span of forty years."

On the other hand, if "productivity were now to start growing again at the 2.5 percent rate which prevailed from 1948 to 1967, the average worker in 2020 would produce $57,500 in goods and services, an increase of about 160 percent. In that case, our grandchildren would look back on us as relative paupers."

But Peterson chose to believe that something had changed decisively in the 1970s and that only radical measures could prevent disaster. With regard to Social Security, "it would be far more sensible," he wrote, "to take a prudent course for now and, if events turn out better than expected, to increase benefits or lower taxes at some later date." If anything, the trustees' pessimistic estimates might be too sanguine, Peterson suggested, hinting that "the optimism of the advocate" was prompting the SSA and its analytic staff to produce numbers that painted a rosy picture of the program.

Hindsight tells us that the inflation and recessions of the 1970s and early 1980s were caused by the two oil price shocks, along with budget and currency crises triggered partly by American overspending on the Vietnam War. These factors resulted in high inflation, high unemployment, and stagnating wages, which damaged the funding system for Social Security—along with many other things. For the first time in memory, inflation was rising faster than wages, which meant that money was flowing into the program more slowly and out of it much faster. The long recession discouraged capital investment and discouraged businesses from using all their productive capacity.

In the 1980s, this "perfect storm" ended when inflation subsided and energy prices collapsed. The "era of cheap energy" made quite a comeback, contrary to Peterson's prediction. And the Fed finally decided to let interest rates float down to more reasonable levels. At that point, and possibly with some help from the Reagan tax cuts, the economy began to recover, employment rose, and capital and credit became available again to business, although real wages continued to languish. By the mid-1990s, productivity was rising, too. After having to borrow from the HI and DI funds in 1982, OASI's funding situation started to even out and, after a few years, to improve greatly. None of this was brought about by drastic surgery.

Alicia Munnell's reply to Peterson's *New York Review* series divided the next eight decades into three periods and analyzed the chances of his dire predictions coming true for each. She checked with two private economic forecasters, Chase Econometrics and Data Resources, Inc., whose conclusions presumably wouldn't be affected by "the optimism of the advocate." They estimated that from 1983 to 1989, the period with which the Greenspan commission was most concerned, the Social Security deficit would fall in between the trustees' optimistic and intermediate estimates of $75 billion to $200 billion. The 1983 Amendments were scored to close a gap of $200 billion, thus eliminating the problem.

The next period, 1990 to 2014, would be a kind of "golden age" for Social Security as the baby boomers moved fully into the labor force and the first generations of retirees who collected benefits under the system passed on, taking their "windfalls" with them. If wages rose a mere 1.5% during that period, as the trustees' intermediate projections stated, Social Security would rapidly build up a trust-fund surplus.

The third period, 2015 to 2060, Munnell acknowledged, would be "characterized by rapidly rising costs as the baby-boom generation start to retire" and "the growth of the labor force slows markedly." In other words, the baby boomers weren't having children fast enough to maintain the current ratio of workers to retirees. But not everyone's predictions foretold disaster. According to the pessimistic scenario Peterson favored, fertility levels in the U.S. would fall from 1.83 in 1980 to 1.7 in 2005. But estimates by another government agency, the Census Bureau, were for fertility rates to hold steady, increasing to 1.96 in 2000 and then falling to 1.9 in 2050—but never dropping as low as 1.7. Since future payroll tax revenues are very sensitive to changes in fertility rates, this was a significant difference.

Munnell also pointed out that while the population would be aging, the total dependency ratio—nonworking adults over sixty-five, plus children under twenty—didn't look bad going forward. The SSA projected the total dependency ratio in 2035 to be lower than it was in the 1960s. While medical costs, in particular, were making it more expensive to care for seniors, the expected drop in total dependency was significant: from 36% in 1982 to 30% in the first decade of the new century, versus 40% in the 1960s. And that was actually understated for the 1960s, when many women were still stay-at-homers.[29]

Rosemary Rinder, a private-sector economist, in another reply to Peterson, questioned whether the kind of extremely long-range projections he was making—Social Security plus HI absorbing 44% of taxable payroll by 2035—were even worth taking seriously, given the five decades during which any number of things could happen to alter the outcome.

"If we were to attempt to solve now all the dire problems that are likely to emerge over the next fifty years, we would be in trouble indeed!" she wrote. One problem was that these estimates generally are based on projections of where the economy, or Social Security, will be in a given number of years if present trends continue exactly as they are, or shift only slightly in a few predictable ways. As a result, the total picture that emerges isn't usually a very coherent one. Looking at the federal budget, for example, the projections for each individual item may add up to several times the total that's projected for the budget as a whole. That's because they are projections, not predictions. A future Congress would have to decide which items to trim to make more resources available for others.

So it was with the projections Peterson used to arrive at his 44% figure. Munnell noticed that this broke down into 24% from OASI and DI and

20% from HI, meaning that health care costs for the elderly would equal old-age benefits, survivors' benefits, and disability benefits combined. That merely underscored the fact that something had to be done about the rising cost of the entire American health care system, not just Medicare itself, Munnell observed.

As for whether Social Security was a "good deal"or not, that couldn't be determined by the simple rate-of-return analyses that the three New York Fed economists ran, liberals contended. For instance, Social Security frees children of at least part of the responsibility for taking care of elderly or disabled family members. It provides benefits to widows and widowers and to surviving children of workers who die before they are of age. Unlike private pensions, it provides fully portable coverage, and unlike most private annuity contracts, it's indexed to inflation. "To realize all of Social Security's benefits privately, one would have to buy disability coverage, life insurance, and find a fully indexed private pension plan," economic journalist Robert Kuttner noted. "Few could afford it."[30]

Generational equity advocates caricatured Social Security in other ways as well, the liberal opposition pointed out. Perhaps most harmful was their picture of retirees as a new affluent class, receiving windfall benefits that they hadn't earned. In a scholarly piece published while the generational equity argument was raging, Brandeis University law professor Robert Binstock noted that a retired couple with a near-poverty-line income in 1981 would see all of their money outside of what they spent for food and lodging swallowed up by medical costs. "Over 4 million older persons are below [the poverty] line," Binstock wrote, "and several million more are clustered just above it."[31] Social Security and Medicare, clearly, weren't a ticket to affluence, but a lifeline out of destitution.

The reason many elderly had become better off over the past twenty years was, in fact, because of the improvements in Social Security payouts, plus the creation of Medicare: especially since the 1972 Amendments indexed OASI to inflation. These were the very changes that Peterson now lampooned as "Panglossian excesses, economic accident, or just plain electioneering." But without them, many more elderly would be living in poverty, and Peterson would no longer have been able to argue that they represented a new pampered class. Of the people Binstock cited, who was to say that many of them weren't middle-class retirees or disabled persons who had had the hard luck to see their homes or their mutual fund portfolios plummet in value in the 1970s, and were now relying largely on Social Security to get by?

Payroll taxes are regressive, collecting more from the struggling than from the affluent, Kuttner acknowledged in a 1986 article in the *New Republic*, but this was offset by the redistributive way in which the system paid out benefits. A lifelong minimum-wage earner would receive a pension from OASI equal to 60% of her last paycheck, while a worker who earned $32,400—the top rate in 1982—would receive only 27% of that.[32] Looking at it a little differently,

Rinder found that Social Security payments were skewed mostly on the upper end of the income scale: 30% of benefits went to the top 20% of households and only 2.5% to the wealthiest 5%. That still left room for improvement, but it didn't make OASI "welfare for the rich."*

If Congress decided it wanted to make the program more progressive, there were ways to do so: It could eliminate the tax on wages that Social Security recipients earned, Kuttner suggested, but only for retirees making less than $20,000 a year, while higher-income earners would have to keep paying the tax. Or, Rinder offered, Congress could eliminate the ceiling on payroll taxes so that higher earners would have to pay the tax on their entire incomes—a change that would also go a long way toward resolving any long-range fiscal problems for the program.

In any case, the system of private retirement investment with which a wide range of Social Security critics proposed to replace the program was likely to make the overall U.S. old-age pension system *more* regressive, not less, for two reasons. First, the significant portion of workers who had too little in their accounts to support themselves in retirement might well end up being cared for by their families instead. This new "tax" would be rendered invisible by the fact that it stayed within the family rather than going to the government. But it would probably fall disproportionately on the working poor.

Second, private pensions and retirement accounts received large subsidies from Washington in the form of tax exemptions and deferrals. Yet only half the working population were covered by these employer-based benefits in the early 1980s, a figure that hadn't grown significantly in decades, and most beneficiaries—especially of individual retirement accounts as opposed to employer-sponsored plans—were higher-earning workers.

One of the liberals' key arguments concerned Social Security's political, not financial, capital. Programs for the poor make poor programs, they said, citing an old social workers' saying. Programs based on needs rather than earned benefits tend to get short shrift in American society. Welfare, unemployment compensation, food stamps, Medicaid, and other such means-tested offerings are looked down on because individuals have to supplicate for them: unpleasant for the individual and unwelcome to the politicians and interest groups claiming to speak for taxpayers. Yet conservative policy designers prefer them to earned benefits like Social Security, because they provide more leeway for cuts or even elimination.

"Demands for means tests are invariably accompanied by protestations of genuine humane concern," Kuttner observed. "But when the moment comes

---

* Virtually all the income redistribution in Social Security come from the Survivors' Insurance and Disability Insurance portions of the program. Because the more affluent tend to live longer than do lower-income workers, they tend to collect more old-age benefits from Social Security, canceling out the redistributive effects of the Primary Insurance Amount (PIA) formula (email from Henry J. Aaron, Brookings Institution, September 27, 2011).

to provide the funding, the right invariably produces a Stockman-like character to explain that, unfortunately, the money is not available."[33]

"This is stunning," Peterson responded—essentially, a case of "bribing the elderly well-off to get on the political bandwagon."[34] But the past decade, Peterson's favorite political-economic benchmark, showed just how vulnerable means-tested programs were. While the tax advantages extended to employer-based pension and retirement plans were sacred, for example, benefits provided through Aid to Families with Dependent Children fell 25% behind inflation in the decade up to 1982. Home mortgage deductions, mainly benefiting the middle class and above, were untouchable, while means-tested public housing programs were always on the chopping block. Why would anyone hoping to preserve Social Security in any form want to move it into the means-tested category?

Or, for that matter, place it behind military spending in importance? While not technically an entitlement, solid vested interests—the "Iron Triangle" of the Pentagon, Congress, and arms makers—were pushing military budget increases that could be expected to continue into the indefinite future. Peterson noted in his *New York Review* series that defense accounted for 28% of the current federal budget and Social Security for 26%, but, he concluded blandly, "it is unlikely that cuts much larger than $25 billion in 1985 can actually be achieved" in military spending. While he protested in the strongest ethical terms against the political expedient of "bribing the elderly well-off," he was willing to accept the untouchable status of the Reagan military buildup as a fact of life.

The generational equity advocates' stated core argument wasn't that entitlements like Social Security were overgenerous or a form of bribery, however. Their big worry, they asserted, was that, in a "society of scarcity," automatic benefits were crowding out investment, research and development, and all the other spending that produces a bigger and more prosperous economy in the future.

"To increase our savings rate, we must lower our consumption rate," Peterson declared. "This is an inexorable law: There is no way to increase the one without decreasing the other." As a result, each generation must take out of the "pot" that was Social Security no more than it put in. Peterson's proposals for reducing COLAs and taxing benefits were designed to quickly move America into line with this rule.

Almost invariably, when Social Security defenders asked what would happen to the millions of people who depended on the program for all or most of their retirement income if it was slashed or phased out, critics like Peterson offered what seemed at first glance like a bulletproof answer: These unfortunate people would have nothing if Social Security wasn't restructured, since the program would "inexorably" go bankrupt. So cutting Social Security, ironically, was the best means of helping those who depended on it—even though it would heap more responsibility on their shoulders, not less. To this point, Peterson and his allies could only paint optimistic pictures of the prosperity that would flow from higher rates of personal saving and investment.

Yet a glance at recent history would have revealed that Americans' savings rates were high during the postwar boom—just when they were happily creating a broad-based consumer culture unlike anything the world had yet seen. That saving slowed down in the 1970s was understandable; the recession was making it difficult if not impossible for American workers to put anything aside. A sudden burst of self-indulgent overconsumption by a "nation of spendthrifts" was probably not the reason.

Beyond this circumstantial evidence, the idea that Social Security's deficits were eating into capital investment depended on what balance sheet you used. The New York Fed analysts who Peterson cited used a strict standard: what did you pay in taxes and what did you get back as monthly checks?

Looking at the first cohorts of Social Security recipients, the "windfall generations," they indeed appeared to have been fortunate. But there's more than one way to define what they put into the system. Starting families, keeping them together, and helping to maintain their communities through the "perfect storm" of the Depression years, often while caring for aged and infirm relatives, represented a contribution to the economy that had "earned" them their pension from Social Security. The same could be said for people who sacrificed family members during the Second World War.

People of color who never earned a fair wage because of race discrimination, too, and likewise women whose careers suffered because of their gender, possibly ended their working lives feeling they were still owed something for their economic contribution. None of these people could necessarily demonstrate any special "need" for a larger benefit based on either their present circumstances or whatever definition of the term suited Congress's current budget requirements—although a worker who lost all of her savings following the 1929 stock market crash, for example, might be able to do so. But many could make a good case that they had earned something more than what they had already received: in other words, that their benefits were only a fair return for their economic efforts.

Not surprisingly, then, Americans remained overwhelmingly supportive of Social Security, despite their propensity since 1968 to elect presidents who campaigned against big government. The 1977 Amendments had imposed the biggest payroll tax hikes in American history, as Reagan liked to remind his audiences, in order to save Social Security, and no one is known to have lost their seat in Congress as a result. Five years later, polls showed that 90% of Americans under age fifty-four—for whom retirement was still a long ways off, in other words—opposed major changes in the system.[35] A year after that, with the 1983 Amendments, Congress voted to advance the date of the payroll tax hikes they had approved in 1977, and again there was no outcry.

Against this apparent contentment, the arguments of Peterson and other generational equity critics seemed to collapse into a series of double standards. No one was "entitled" to a Social Security windfall, and these must be stopped, yet uncontrolled military spending could continue because stopping it was politically too difficult. OASI benefits that rewarded middle- and upper-income workers as well as the poor were unacceptable, yet tax breaks for private pension and retirement saving, which benefited mainly the well-off, were apparently all right. And while Peterson based much of his argument against excessive old-age benefits on the notion that they were crowding out resources needed for children and the poor, he never actually proposed any increase in the latter.

Yet over and over, the champions of generational equity insisted that theirs wasn't a partisan issue. "The rescue of Social Security is not a liberal or a conservative cause; it will depend on combining a realistic understanding of fiscal deficits with a humane sense of social fairness," Peterson wrote. Continuing the present system would result in "a full-fledged rebellion of young workers, crushed by taxes, against the entire notion of supporting the elderly at a decent level of income."

In a book titled *Megatraumas*, about long-run issues facing America, published in 1985, Colorado Gov. Richard Lamm wrote, "Social Security has taken an unacceptably large portion of the worker's paycheck and has certainly accounted for the intergenerational antagonism that has been so plaguing this country for the last fifteen years."[36] Vietnam, civil rights, women's rights, and all the other popular issues that had separated young from old in 1960s America were merely sideshows, Lamm, a rising star in the Democratic party, seemed to be saying. The real cause of the rift was Social Security. But if this was the case, why weren't the students mounting the barricades over this issue?

To explain the apparent disinterest of the young, generational equity advocates invoked the concept of "sunk costs." The basic idea was that households continued to support Social Security even though it was demonstrably a bad deal for them because they'd decided to write off their earlier years of contributions and think only about what their future contributions will buy them.[37] Presumably, a few more years or decades were needed before the inequity became intolerable. *Après* the baby boomers, perhaps, *le déluge*.

CHAPTER 8

THE WAR AGAINST THE GEEZERS

The generational equity argument was heavily impregnated with conservative ideology. But this wasn't easy to see at the time, especially coming off the real funding crises Social Security had survived in 1977 and 1983. Jane Bryant Quinn, who wrote a widely read consumer finance column for *Newsweek*, in 1983 called Social Security "a classic pyramid" in which "right from the start, each recipient has been promised more money out of the system than the value of what he and his employer put in."*

But it was in the years following the 1983 Amendments that the movement against Social Security—the ideological backlash against the program

---

* Jane Bryant Quinn, "Social-Security Stopgap," *Newsweek*, Feb. 14, 1983. Years later, she said, "Looking back at my younger self, I'd change that. I didn't start digging deeply until they started talking about private accounts. But at the time, it looked like there was a serious problem" (interview with Quinn, Feb. 19, 2009).

and against the idea of social insurance—took hold of Americans' cultural consciousness. If Peterson and his *confrères* lacked the intellectual goods to nail their argument, they nevertheless used it to develop something almost as seductive: a sweeping moral indictment of America as a profligate society, devouring its young and borrowing recklessly to enjoy supersized, unearned benefits today. In so doing, they defined an ideological position that over the next two decades would become orthodoxy for the center-right of both major political parties and, increasingly, for the Washington press corps and much of the rest of the American opinion-making elite.

Liberals like Alicia Munnell and Bob Kuttner, anxious to reassure the public that the "Social Security hysteria" was just that and the system was working fine, were less immediately convincing, no matter how good their arguments. Americans of all social classes had just lived through a decade of profound economic dislocations. Their intuition about most major issues tended to be that something *was* wrong. The generational equity advocates were offering to explain to them what that was; their opponents weren't.

Elderly advocacy groups like AARP laid themselves open to this kind of attack, Binstock argued, because of their own success at portraying the aged as a monolithic group that shared the same basic characteristics: needy, deserving, and helpless. This "compassionate ageism" was easy to turn on its head when less sympathetic voices wanted to portray the old as rich, selfish, and powerful. Because the public had been conditioned to view the elderly as all one thing, it wasn't so hard to shift the characteristics of that one thing from a sympathetic to a harsh light.[1]

Because the generational critics presented their argument in moral terms, their analysis of the economic future was also easier to understand superficially for journalists and ambitious politicians. It was loaded with powerful catch phrases—"generational warfare," "welfare for the rich," "justice between generations"—but at the same time carried an aura of intellectual seriousness and high public spiritedness. Who could resist an analysis that not only indicted the old for their greed, but excoriated the young—then coming to be known as the "Me Generation"—for following in their footsteps?

Key figures in popularizing this kind of thinking were two wealthy ideological entrepreneurs, Marty Peretz and Charles Peters, who, through their respective publishing ventures, became intellectual godparents to what would later be tagged the New Democrats. Peretz, a former assistant professor at Harvard, purchased *The New Republic* (*TNR*) in 1974 and used it to push the Democratic Party to the right. Peters, editor and publisher of a silk-stocking political journal called the *Washington Monthly*, which he founded in 1968, also built a degree of influence in the capital by questioning traditional liberal positions in ways that weren't traditionally conservative.

Neither *TNR* nor the *Washington Monthly* had mass readerships, but they were closely read in the Beltway and thus were powerful career portals. Peretz and Peters recruited as writers mostly Ivy League college graduates, ambitious young men—and few if any women—to whom they offered a modest salary and two years to write groundbreaking stories that would launch them on careers in journalism, government, or the think-tank community. Along the way, they would help to flesh out and popularize their mentors' notions about the crisis of liberalism, especially the problems with the welfare state.

TNR and *Washington Monthly* alumni—the latter dubbed "Charlie's Angels" after the well-favored women on the TV series—would become some of the leading überjournalists—pundits and media framers of public issues—of the next two decades and beyond. Those who would take a special interest in Social Security and especially in promoting the generational equity argument included Charles Krauthammer, Michael Kinsley, Mickey Kaus, and James Fallows.

Phillip Longman, a *Washington Monthly* freelancer—lacking a trust fund, he recalls, he couldn't afford to work for Peters full-time—helped to kick generational equity into wide discussion in the capital with a cover story, "Taking America to the Cleaners," subtitled "What the Old Are Doing to the Young," in November 1982. The piece came about when Peters interested Longman in the research Barbara Torrey had conducted for OMB and that was later published in the *National Journal*.[2]

Longman's piece was noteworthy for foregrounding the concerns of younger workers. "If ever there was a generation that had reason to take to the streets, it is this one," he wrote.[3] But his was only one of a spate of prominently placed articles pushing the generational equity argument that appeared that fall, just as the negotiations leading to the 1983 Amendments were coming to a head. The New York Fed published in its *Quarterly Review* the much-quoted paper by Capra, Skaperdas, and Kubarcych in which they summarized their findings—that Social Security was a bad deal for younger workers.

In November, Fallows penned a piece for the *Atlantic* in which he concluded that "the original genius of Social Security was precisely that it did treat everyone the same.... As a political ideal, this is most attractive. But in Social Security, as in Medicare, it may simply have become too costly to maintain."[4] In December came Peterson's two-part *New York Review* series, which he wrote with help from Neil Howe, a young Yale graduate and aspiring pundit who had recently worked for the right-wing Smith-Richardson Foundation.

The latter received so much response that Bob Silvers decided to devote most of another issue, in March, to replies by Munnell and Rinder and a rebuttal to their arguments by Peterson. The issue was unprecedented for the *New York Review* for the sheer space devoted to a technical exchange about an arcane subject, and the fifty-three footnotes between the three pieces may have set a record for a mainstream American magazine. Peterson's rebuttal, which mainly reiterated his earlier arguments, was almost twice as long as Munnell's piece.

Kuttner had already published an article defending Social Security in the *New Republic* in which he noted the effect the generational equity argument was starting to have. "It's hard to pick up a newspaper or magazine these days," he wrote, "without encountering an imaginative headline like ... A COLLAPSING SYSTEM (*Chicago Tribune*) or—my favorite—THE MONSTER

THAT'S EATING OUR FUTURE (*Forbes*)."[5] Kuttner's arguments were quickly answered by letters from Fallows, Peterson, and Longman; the latter accusing him of "'trickle-down' liberalism" for condoning Social Security payments to anyone other than the poor.[6]

With regard to Social Security, and so much else, conservatives had perfected the ability not just to argue the issue but to frame it. Often, the trick was to find a previously obscure word or phrase and invest it with new and more culturally resonant meaning. Some time around the end of the 1970s, a category of budget items that the OMB had previously referred to as "relatively uncontrollable" expenditures acquired a new euphemistic tag: entitlements.

The term had actually been around for nearly forty years as a technical description that distinguished a benefit that an individual "earned" by making direct contributions from one that Congress simply awarded as part of the annual appropriations process. OASI, DI, and HI payments are entitlements because the formulas that determine how much is paid out each year, and to whom, are written into law. But the term "entitlement" was very seldom used outside bureaucratic circles.

No one knows exactly when "entitlement" became the catchall term for programs like Social Security, Medicare, and unemployment insurance. Barbara Torrey guesses that it might have been prompted by the fact that "uncontrollable" is "not too precise a term."[7] Norman Ornstein, a scholar at the American Enterprise Institute, once suggested that Reagan began referring to entitlements in the first year of his presidency because he no longer wanted to refer to the Social Security "safety net," as he had done during his election campaign. "One Reagan adviser has suggested that Mr. Reagan was tired of getting beaten up every time he mentioned Social Security, and wanted a broader and more neutral term to use," Ornstein noted.[8]

Whether Reagan regarded the word as "neutral" or not, "entitlements"— usually described as "out-of-control"—quickly acquired a pejorative aura that helped sell conservative economic views. In 1980, *Business Week* published a special issue—almost a manifesto—calling for a "new social contract" between business, labor, and government, which would facilitate the "reindustrialization of America." A list of "attitudes" that supposedly undermined economic growth included "the notion of entitlement, a new definition of equality that called upon government to level economic and social disparities, an adversary stance toward government and business, and changed motivations toward work."[9]

* * *

Editors love "man bites dog" stories—big-picture stories that draw a neat yet counterintuitive picture of reality—because they're attention getting and require minimal digestive effort in exchange for an apparent nugget of wisdom. Successful journalists quickly develop a knack for teasing out such yarns, with the caveat that they stay within what advertisers consider the limits of conventional opinion.

Generational equity was one of the biggest and best stories of the man-bites-dog genre, irreverently poking holes in "myths" about the aged and about a once-sacred government program yet offering no evident challenge to capitalism, the State, or acceptable public behavior. Calling Social Security an entitlement—as in "sense of"—set the public's moralistic streak to quivering and helped cast a hint of possible illegitimacy over the program. It caught on quickly with the press as well.

A bestseller in 1981 that propelled its author into the new president's inner circle was George Gilder's *Wealth and Poverty*. Gilder had thus far been known mainly for a series of diatribes against feminism, but in *Wealth and Poverty* he threw out a string of provocative ideas attacking the social safety net for, he claimed, aggravating the very problems it was intended to alleviate. "Social security payments may discourage concern for the aged and dissolve the links between generations,"[10] Gilder wrote—a moralistic critique echoed by many other right-wing pundits. Who was at fault for the supposedly imminent collapse of Social Security? It wasn't the young who were greedy, unappreciative, and materialistic, it turns out. It was their parents and grandparents. Who knew?

Critics of the generational equity argument never seemed to have the same open door to the major media, in part because their positions didn't have this deliciously counterintuitive element. "We have to tell the younger people that Social Security is not a fight between generations—it's a family affair," said Cy Brickfield, executive director of AARP.[11] But unlike well-connected advocates such as Peterson, even a powerful and well-endowed organization like AARP had trouble getting its message across outside its—admittedly large—membership. AARP's stature could actually be a handicap, in fact, since the other side could easily suggest it was merely protecting the perks of its "interest group."

Meanwhile, Longman wrote another reiteration of the generational accounting argument, "Justice Between Generations," for the June 1985 issue of the *Atlantic*. It became a frequent handout for Social Security critics and was translated into several languages once their arguments began penetrating other countries in the 1990s.[12] Two years later he published a book, *Born to Pay*, that expanded his previous articles into an exploration of the history of Americans and debt in the 20th century. In it, he hailed Peterson as "the great Jeremiah of the Social Security debate."[13]

Peterson contributed a long article to the *Atlantic* in 1987 denouncing the Reagan deficits and arguing that the U.S. wouldn't reclaim its place as a first-class economic power until it sharply reduced programs for the elderly.[14] The piece was given a National Magazine Award as best public interest article of the year. In the next year, in a book entitled *On Borrowed Time*, he stated firmly that excessive Social Security disbursements were "a direct cause of our federal deficit"[15]—even though the program was again piling up surpluses, in effect helping to hold down the overall deficit.

An apogee may have been reached when the *New Republic* ran a cover story, in March 1988, entitled "Talkin' 'Bout My Generation," echoing The Who's 1964 hit with its refrain, "Hope I die before I get old." The cover was emblazoned with the headline "Greedy Geezers" and a cartoon of an advancing phalanx of malevolent looking oldsters armed with golf clubs and gardening tools, suggesting a geriatric version of *Night of the Living Dead*.

The "Greedy Geezers" cover was a true artifact of the decade, a geriatric counterpart to welfare queens, crack babies, and other alleged perverse spawn of the welfare state. Inside, the article rehearsed the by now familiar generational justice arguments, but upped the ante slightly, speculating, "With the increasing

The notorious "Greedy Geezers" cover. Respected center-right publications like the New Republic *helped make anti-Social Security arguments that stigmatized the elderly politically acceptable in the late 1980s.*

number of people living beyond 85, we may even have to decide that today's costly medical technologies, such as transplants, should not be provided to truly elderly people." How the authorities were to define "truly elderly," the author didn't say.

* * *

The idea of "generations" is one of American cultural mythology's most familiar and powerful sources of metaphor and quick popular understanding. Thomas Jefferson may have been the first to calculate the boundaries of a typical generation; he set it at eighteen years and eight months exactly. The Virginian may also have fathered the idea of generational equity, arguing that the government should never take out loans that couldn't be paid off within nineteen years, lest they become a burden on the next generation.[16]

Generations became a preoccupation of both the liberal and conservative wings of the Washington establishment during the early years of the Depression, crystallizing as fear of the old, their potential political power, and their demands on the State, and grouping them with such other unreliables as radical unionists, hobos, and the 1932 Bonus Army of impoverished veterans. Roosevelt's original Social Security program was in part a response to the agitations of the Townsend Clubs. Political leaders, academics, and social welfare professionals safely ensconced in the establishment lumped Townsend together with Huey Long, Fr. Charles Coughlin, and even Adolf Hitler as the kind of disruptive populist demagogue who could bring down American democracy if he wasn't stopped.*

Prefiguring the later warnings of generational warfare, Frank G. Dickinson, a University of Illinois economist, charged that Townsend and his followers were fomenting a new kind of class war that would pit workers and employers against senior citizens and the politicians who catered to them. "Townsend-ism," he declared in 1941, "may be as important in the next fifty years as were the doctrines of Karl Marx during the last half-century." In some cities, the response by the government and private foundations that funded social work was a string of recreational old-age clubs that not-so-covertly attempted to wean the elderly away from the doctor's politically charged gatherings. Some worried policy wonks called for limiting or even eliminating retirement in order to keep the idle elders from organizing in a politically unacceptable manner.[17]

The Townsend movement faded in the 1950s, along with similar groups it helped spawn, after the first of several major boosts in Social Security old-age

---

*   In fairness, Townsend himself gave his critics some reasons to be concerned. He ran his network of clubs in an autocratic manner. In 1936 he collaborated with Coughlin and the racist and antisemitic evangelist Gerald L.K. Smith, who had briefly taken over Long's movement after the Kingfish's death, on an abortive attempt to launch a new populist political party. But Townsend soon repudiated Smith. See Abraham Holtzman, *The Townsend Movement: A Political Study* (New York: Bookman Associates, 1963).

benefits. But the concern lingered over the next three decades that unless America returned to the "traditional" family structure and, presumably, started to have more children, senior citizens might unite to create a populist "gerontocracy" that would enslave the rest of the nation.

An effective, organized movement on behalf of the elderly reappeared in the 1960s and 1970s, when groups like the Gray Panthers and the National Council of Senior Citizens won some notable legislative victories. But their style of action—street-level protests, decentralized organizing in the case of the Panthers, occasional targeting of politicians who didn't agree with them—contained an echo of the tactics the Townsend movement had cultivated forty years before. That alarmed many liberals as well as conservatives: the latter because it seemed to reach beyond the political framework that business could easily control and the former because it smacked too much of the unconventional, countercultural politics from which they were trying to distance themselves.

As the generational equity argument seeped into the media mainstream, then, a "blame the old" thread repeatedly surfaced. Business magazines such as *Fortune* and *Forbes* were the first mainstream venues to latch onto the generational equity argument, picking up the theme from articles in a few scholarly publications and running with it consistently throughout the decade.* But it was popular, general interest magazines aimed at educated, conspicuously literate audiences, including *Time*, the *Atlantic*, the *New Republic*, and the *New York Times Sunday Magazine*, that moved the issue into common discourse.

Time, for example, ran a cover story in January 1983, when the negotiations leading up to the 1983 Amendments were in full gear, headlined "The Social Security Crisis" and sporting a subhead highlighting "The Growing Burden on the Young." The cover featured an illustration of a hapless teenager supporting three levels of elders—parents, assorted baby boomers, and the elderly—on his sagging shoulders. Inside, the article misrepresented the "modest old-age program that Franklin Roosevelt signed into law in 1935" as "only a supplement designed to ensure that no one suffers extreme privation," when in fact the program had always been intended to guarantee a minimal but adequate standard of living.

The article chastised the Democratic members of the Greenspan commission for denying there was a serious financial problem with Social Security because two of them, Pat Moynihan and Claude Pepper, had pointed out—correctly—that the current shortfall would reverse itself as the boomers' incomes picked up in the late 1980s. The authors quoted, without offering any opposing point of view, a financial consultant who declared that Social Security was "institutionalized pickpocketing" of the young by the old, and predicted, "For

---

*   Examples: Jerry Flint, "The Old Folks," *Forbes*, February 18, 1980 ("The myth is that they're sunk in poverty. The reality is that they're living well. The trouble is there are too many of them—God bless 'em."); Paul Craig Roberts, "Social Security Has Become a Giant Pyramid Scheme," *Business Week*, October 10, 1988 ("The Greenspan Commission 'reforms' simply stick future generations with the bill for monstrous deficits.").

every old person eating dog food today four will be eating it when *we're* old" if the program wasn't restructured.[18]

Ideas were being tossed around that sounded suspiciously like something out of Jonathan Swift, or perhaps the 1973 dystopian film *Soylent Green*. In 1984, Dick Lamm shocked a meeting of Colorado's Health Lawyers Association by telling seniors, "You've got a duty to die and get out of the way. Let the other society, our kids, build a reasonable life." Waxing poetic, he described the dying elderly as "leaves falling off a tree and forming humus for the other plants to grow up."*

Those who refused to die on command would be feeding new racial tensions, according to some alleged experts. The population due to retire a few years into the 21st century would be largely white, whereas the working population would be increasingly nonwhite, David Hayes-Bautista, a professor of medicine at the University of California, Los Angeles, pointed out: "The elderly will be seen as an Anglo problem, pediatric health as a Mexican problem."[19]

In a similarly creepy mode that the *New Republic*'s "Greedy Geezers" feature would shortly pick up on, the conservative bioethicist Daniel Callahan suggested it was time to introduce the concept of a "natural lifespan," beyond which the use of expensive medical procedures should be limited.[20] The technologies he proposed denying to people above a certain age included mechanical ventilation, artificial resuscitation, antibiotics, and artificial nutrition and hydration. Callahan's book, *Setting Limits*, was respectfully reviewed in the *New York Times*, the *Washington Post*, the *Wall Street Journal*, and a wide assortment of national magazines and scholarly journals.[21]

Such talk echoed, queasily, the long period of anxiety about European birthrates in the decades leading up to the Second World War; Germany and France both experienced plunging birthrates during the early years of the 20th century. A host of politicians and presumed experts placed the blame on contraception, government-run welfare programs, and a decline in the authority of the family.[22]

"The striving of the past to fulfill all tasks of national welfare principally through public agencies and institutions has proven itself to be a fateful error," since it was expensive and undermined the impulse to self-help, the Nazi-controlled Prussian Ministry of the Interior stated in a June 1933 decree, presaging language Gilder would use to attack "welfare" forty-eight years later. The result was a spate of laws in prewar Germany and France, as well as others including Italy and Belgium, to subsidize and otherwise encourage large families.

Lamm, Callahan, and Hayes-Bautista hardly constituted the vanguard of an American neo-fascist movement. No doubt they would have argued that they were merely looking for a way to tackle the birthrate "crisis" that would neutralize the desire for more extreme measures. But some of the ideas and proposals coming out of the movement against Social Security, especially those

---

* "Gov. Lamm asserts elderly, if very ill, have 'duty to die'" (*New York Times*, March 29, 1984). Afterward, the American Life Society called for Lamm's resignation. He replied, "I am in contempt of their request. If politicians can't discuss sensitive issues, we're all lost." ("Dust-to-dust fuss," *New York Times*, April 1, 1984).

related to birthrates, partook of the same primal fears about cultural decline. Nazi Germany was obsessed with the prospect of being overrun by Jews, Slavs, and other "inferior" races that presumably were multiplying much faster; forty to fifty years later, both Americans and Europeans were consumed with fear that they would be overrun by fertile, dark-skinned immigrants from, respectively, Latin America and the Middle East.

In the U.S., anxiety about the supposed failure of the baby boomers to reproduce fast enough to support the next wave of retirees stood side-by-side with fears that immigrants were having too many children, turning any social services they accessed into tax-devouring machines. One group of families— the native-born—presumably should be encouraged to bear children because theirs wouldn't be a drag on the economy, while the other group—the foreign-born and people of color—should be denied services so as not to bring more "unproductive" individuals into the loop. But the generational equity critics were careful not to broach such matters directly.

The immediate effect of their more radical suggestions—denial of life-saving services to the elderly, a Social Security surcharge for the childless—was to suck the air out of any discussion of the very thing the generational critics allegedly were most concerned about: the country's ability to grow economically again. "Few people are discussing how many workers it takes to finance an aircraft carrier, a tobacco subsidy, a renal dialysis unit, or an investment tax credit," Robert Binstock observed in a 1983 scholarly article entitled "The Aged as Scapegoat." "By pitting the generations against each other, scapegoating the aged once again diverts our attention from other issues of significance to American society."[23]

Much of the power of print—and, later, the Internet—is concentrated in its headlines, captions, and visuals, not in the text, and generational equity lent itself to some of the most florid expressions ever of what was generally a dry topic. A 1988 *Forbes* piece on government overspending on the elderly was titled, "Consuming Our Children."[24] A 1982 *Fortune* piece depicted a collection of elderly people crowded into a rollercoaster car, about to crash into a barrier marked "2015—DEFICIT!"[25] Five years later, a photo accompanying a long piece on generational equity in the same magazine, showing a group of elderly people outdoors, was captioned, "At 77, these retirees can relax …. But who will pay for the baby-boomers' jacuzzis?"[26]

Thus the popular press created an instantly understandable iconography and slogan bank around the idea of generational indulgence and injustice. But why was the presumably more intellectually sophisticated wing of the mainstream media so willing to carry wood for the movement against Social Security?

There were two reasons. The first was that the Washington press corps's collective inclinations always tended to align with what they regarded as the consensus among their sources. When such a consensus didn't exist, they did their best to cobble one together. In the highly partisan atmosphere of the 1980s, generational equity looked like the kind of issue that could define a new consensus. The second reason was structural: most major media outlets effectively split their coverage of issues like aging. In every medium—print, radio, television, and later, the Internet—stories about poverty, social welfare, and problems facing households tended to be prepared by a different set of writers, reporters, and editors than the ones who handled stories about government, finance, and business. Journalists have a strong tendency to take on the ideological coloration of the people they write about. Since the Washington reporters who covered Social Security tended to do so from the top down, they seldom came into contact with the people who the program served—and seldom factored them in their stories.

A groundbreaking 1998 survey for Fairness and Accuracy in Reporting of 444 Washington journalists by David Croteau, a professor at Virginia Commonwealth University, found that 56% saw the need to "reform entitlement programs by slowing the rate of increase in spending for programs like Medicare and Social Security" as "one of the top few" priorities of government. Of those surveyed, 19% considered it the highest agenda item. A poll taken at about the same time found that only 35% of the public counted it as one of their top priorities. Conversely, 59% of the public identified the need to "protect Medicare and Social Security against major cuts" as a top priority, compared with only 39% of Washington journalists.[27]

Charlie Peters was doing his best to perpetuate the trend. By the early 1980s, publications like the *New Republic* and the *Atlantic* were seeded with graduates of his finishing school in maverick middle-of-the-road journalism who brought with them Peters's ideas about what was wrong with welfare and entitlements. Pete Peterson was another pivotal figure. His own writings attracted attention, but his vast connections in media, business, and politics served to extend his pet issue beyond its natural base in academia and the think tanks.

Part of Peterson's early career was spent at the McCann-Erickson advertising agency. By the early 1980s, he and his wife's media connections included TV producers and personalities such as Barbara Walters, Diane Sawyer, Mike Wallace, Peter Jennings, and Roone Arledge, gossip columnist Liz Smith, and *New York Times* publisher Arthur Sulzberger, Jr. Peterson was adept at crossbreeding these friends with his government and business contacts, making, for example, Jim Hoge, former publisher of the *New York Daily News*, editor of the Council on Foreign Relations' policy journal, *Foreign Affairs*, and *New York Times* columnist Leslie Gelb president of the council.[28]

He brought his influence to bear on Social Security as well. Mort Zuckerman attended some of Peterson's kitchen-table discussions with Jason Epstein and afterward brought Peterson together with the editor of a publication he owned, the *Atlantic Monthly*. Leslie Stahl, whom Peterson had cultivated in the early 1980s when she anchored *Face the Nation*, turned out to be helpful a few years later when she prepared a segment for *60 Minutes* on the deficit and budget cuts. Peterson followed the project closely. "If I didn't follow up on something I'd get a little note saying it was good but you really should have asked X," Stahl later told *Vanity Fair*. "He began to educate me."

With his corporate pedigree and connections across a wide portion of the political spectrum, Peterson also provided an aura of high respectability if not noblesse oblige to a movement with quite radical aims. Unlike Cato's Ed Crane, he didn't talk like an ideologue, and unlike the rumpled Peter Ferrara, he was right at home at swanky parties. Other business executives would play a similar role as the movement gained ground in the next decade, but in the 1980s, Peterson was the major force in planting the generational equity argument in the media's everyday discourse.

Despite the boom time that was beginning for business and financial media in the early to mid-1980s, most journalists found hardcore economics boring. But generational equity was different. Boiled down, it told a simple story of good and bad behavior, with a stark lesson at the end: recover the thrift ethic or accept a declining standard of living; stop pampering the elderly or the next generation will pay. Clearly, this was much bigger than the average business-page story, whether it proved valid or not.

And the financial media were ready for it. Formerly staid publications like the *Wall Street Journal*, *Forbes*, *Fortune*, and *Business Week* were abandoning the stuffy prose, for which they had formerly been known, in favor of a breathless style adapted from the entertainment and trend-watching pages of general interest newspapers and magazines. General interest publications expanded their coverage of business and financial news and gave it more prominence.

In American journalism, most economic issues are covered by the business desk, where the reporters tend to rely on analysts employed by brokerage and investment banking firms for perspective on the direction of the economy and a quick interpretation of issues like Social Security and retirement. The technical nature of this subject matter gave Wall Street bankers like Peterson a presumed advantage over other interested parties like unions, community activists, and non-mainstream economists.[29] Sometimes, just the impression that a prominent financier like Pete Peterson might have a better grasp of the true nature of an economic issue was enough for the media to assume that he did.

In at least one other respect, the time was exactly right for generational equity to become trendy. The bitter aftermath of Vietnam and Watergate, followed by the fights between Reagan and O'Neill, the Reaganauts and the traditional Democrats, had left much of the old Washington political consensus in tatters. Generational equity was the type of issue that suggested a way to rebuild the center and create a new bipartisan policy consensus for "responsible government" in Washington. Particularly after the defeat of Walter Mondale's presidential campaign, Longman suggests, many Democrats gave up on the traditional liberal "interest group politics" he represented and began looking for something else.

"We drove the paleoliberals crazy because we interfered with their standard class analysis of how the system worked," Longman later said with some satisfaction.[30] At the same time, he and Peterson and their co-crusaders scolded the Reaganauts for mortgaging the country's future and ripping apart programs and services for the needy. The working class was invisible in this analysis and racial discrimination was either irrelevant or a minor part of a much bigger problem. This appealed to mainstream journalists and pundits uncomfortable with issues of class and race, but also, Longman thinks, to another rising constituency much discussed in the 1980s.

"The term 'yuppie' was just coming about," he said, "and they had little regard for the labor movement, for example. Labor had turned hostile to young people, and they were concerned about their retirement. Many fewer of them were members of unions. But as baby boomers, they had a deep sense of cultural identity. People took their politics for granted. They were victims. And they were getting into real positions of power but were not beholden to the whole Democratic line." The dashed hopes of the 1970s seemed to provide the answer: a new kind of activism, its target the greed of the elderly.

Often, it was hard to tell whether the überjournalists who came to prominence in the post-1960s decades were describing a real cultural-economic shift or merely a plausible story concept to which they'd ingeniously fit the facts. It's true that baby boomers lived different lives from their parents', but as the social safety net eroded, their lives were becoming more precarious, not less, and thus more dependent on the benefits that remained, such as Social Security. AARP, which Longman believed wouldn't "capture the hearts and minds of the [yuppie] generation" because it was "rooted in the old labor movement," was actually signing up more members at earlier ages as the decade wore on.

One group of baby boomers to whom Longman's scenario applied quite nicely, however, were the überjournalists themselves. Charlie's Angels and the rest of the generation of "name" magazine writers who carried the generational equity story to the public were ambitious, well-educated, competitive free agents. They chose peripatetic careers, often shifting back and forth from government to consulting to think tanks and back to journalism again. They did indeed lead lives very different from those of the retirees who benefited from New Deal–era old-age social programs and protections, which must have seemed at once too costly and too modest for their own ambitions. Very quickly an organization appeared that allowed them to team up with allies on Capitol Hill and carry the message from print and TV into government.

* * *

Americans for Generational Equity (AGE) was founded in 1985, but the impulse behind it grew out of the Republican massacre in the 1982 congressional elections. "Claude Pepper was riding high, the seniors groups were scaring everybody, and it felt to me, as someone who cared very much about budget deficits, that we were shortchanging our future," says Paul Hewitt, then a young Republican Senate staffer. "So I thought of founding something to speak out for younger generations."[31]

Hewitt at the time was staff director of the Subcommittee on Intergovernmental Relations, which he describes as being effectively a think tank for its chairman, Sen. David Durenberger, a fast-rising Minnesotan with an image as a reformer. Hewitt started drawing up a charter for a new group to represent younger voters and brought it to his boss, who liked the idea. "I said, 'You can be the chairman.' It wasn't long before we became notorious." Durenberger and Hewitt talked up the idea, and by the time he left the Senate staff to become AGE's executive director, Hewitt had already been asked to debate the AARP's Cy Brickfield about old-age benefits.

AGE wasn't a think tank or a traditional lobbying organization, but a "public opinion lobby," Hewitt says, which "brought together a lot of good research that other people did" in order to sell a specific idea to the section of the public that could turn that idea into policy. AGE's goal, said Durenberger, was "to promote the concept of generational equity among America's political, intellectual and financial leaders.... The more America's leaders talk about and think in terms of generational equity, the more effective AGE will be in its education program, and the better chance we will have of making the difference on crucial legislative issues."[32]

Organizationally, the group started small, in "a squalid basement apartment, with cans of Raid by each of our desks to squirt at the roaches, and a couple of PCs," says Longman, who Hewitt recruited as research director after someone gave him a copy of Longman's *Washington Monthly* cover story.[33] The small, underpaid staff's activities fell into three basic areas: churning out articles and press releases, holding conferences, and making its principals available to the press.

All that didn't take a lot of money, but it helped that AGE rallied a prestigious and scrupulously bipartisan group of collaborators who were already sold on the idea of generational equity. Democratic Rep. Jim Moody of Wisconsin was Durenberger's co-chair; Republican Sen. Jim Jones, Budget Committee chair, became its president; and Democratic Rep. Tim Penny of Minnesota eventually took over from Moody. Its advisory board included Donald McNaughton, former chairman of Prudential Insurance; Donald Kennedy, president of Stanford University; and of course Pete Peterson. On a slightly less exalted level, the board also numbered among its members former SSA chief actuary A. Haeworth Robertson; Michael Boskin, the Stanford economist and Reagan advisor; Larry Kotlikoff, a young professor at the University of California–Los Angeles who had served as senior economist to Reagan's Council of Economic Advisors in 1981–82 and was beginning to work up a formal method of "generational accounting"; demographer Samuel Preston; and representatives of conservative think tanks including Heritage and the American Enterprise Institute.

AGE made a concerted effort to bring together every available voice of any prominence in the war against deficits and old-age benefits. "What fascinated me," says Dallas Salisbury, president of the Employee Benefit Research Institute, who attended AGE conferences in the 1980s, "was the degree to which they melded people from ideologically different worlds: very liberal Democrats and very progressive Rockefeller Republicans—Durenberger—and Social Security advisors—Robertson—all in one room for relatively distinct reasons."

To the extent they found common ground, Salisbury says, "they were advocating at an absolute minimum a return to pay-as-you-go. And the way to rationalize pay-as-you-go was voluntary or mandatory private accounts."[34] Not fully folded into this agenda, however, were the Cato Institute and Peter Ferrara. "At AGE, we never talked about private accounts except to criticize them," Longman recalls.

The restructuring scenarios that Ferrara and Peterson, for example, had drawn up were clearly aimed at the same final result: the phasing out of Social Security. But AGE's sponsors were more focused than Cato at this stage on persuading lawmakers to adopt generational equity on a wide range of domestic spending issues, not just Social Security. And so they were careful not to wrap their banner around any one big idea for remaking the program, such as private accounts.

Longman, for example, in his *Atlantic* "Justice Between Generations" piece, published while he was at AGE, carefully restricted himself to a few very general, sketchy suggestions, such as changing the tax code to encourage individual saving, raising the retirement age, and subsidizing families to encourage more children.

The formula worked, and AGE was a hit with journalists from the start. "We had to do very little," Hewitt says. "People flocked to us." Seemingly, "the more AARP got mad, the more the media would come knocking. We'd get 20 to 30 press calls a week." Hewitt and Longman already had the generational equity argument well worked out in their minds before AGE was even established, and they became adept at debating advocates for the elderly and delivering the timely soundbite that fed off the other side's outrage.

Hewitt made an appearance on *Face the Nation* early in AGE's run during which he declared, "We're not granny-bashers!" Some reporters picked up on this over-the-top description, which served to make AGE seem colorful and iconoclastic, not threatening. Longman recalls a TV appearance with a retiree who accused the young publicist of attacking his benefits check. "It's not about your check, it's my check," Longman retorted, turning aside the assumption that AGE would want to cut benefits for anyone already retired.

At its inception, AGE had a small budget, a few corporate sponsors, and about 100 members. Durenberger was the answer to this problem. As a member of the Senate Ethics Committee he had a Mr. Clean image, but as chair of the Finance Committee's Health Subcommittee, he had easy access to some well-heeled companies in the health care field, one of whose favorite topics, Medicare, was also one of AGE's.

By the end of its first year in operation, AGE had an $88,000 budget and 600 members. By 1987, its revenues were $367,316 and it had a total of eighty-five organizations on its donor list. Its board included such corporate powerhouses as Exxon, BF Goodrich, General Dynamics, American Cyanamid, US Steel, General Motors, Chrysler, and Ford Motor Company. Durenberger, by now one of the Senate's leading recipients of money from political action committees, "did heavy fundraising" for the group, says Hewitt.

With the money pouring in aiding its media outreach effort, AGE became so well accepted an authority on generational issues that some prominent publications seemingly stopped talking to anyone else when they wanted to address the topic. A long feature on "The War Between the Generations" by *Fortune*'s Lee Smith in 1987 included quotes from ten sources, six of whom were associated in one way or another with AGE, while the rest sported views well in line with the group's positions. The article itself read as if it could have been drafted by Longman or Hewitt.[35]

By 1988 AGE's profile was so high that Jim Jones was able to claim that in the two weeks following the October stock market crash, AGE was contacted for interviews or background information by NBC, CBS, PBS, the *New York Times*, the *Wall Street Journal, Newsweek, Time, U.S. News and World Report, Fortune*, the *Chicago Tribune*, and the *Des Moines Register*.[36]

Conferences, up to three a year, were another way that AGE spread its message to the influential audience it was targeting. Topics included the baby boomers' retirement, Medicare reform, deficits and demographics, and downward mobility in America. At the Medicare conference, Dick Lamm delivered a more carefully worded version of his message that the elderly should be denied "some forms of medical intervention" in the "interests of doing the greatest good for the greatest number."[37]

Very quickly, AGE's thinking was turning up in the words of leading lawmakers. "The decision we've made as a country is the children come last," Republican Sen. John Danforth of Missouri told an audience of trustees from children's hospitals in 1987.[38] California Democratic Rep. Anthony Beilenson saw things the same way. Because "retired persons as a class are not worse off than other groups of Americans," he wrote in an op-ed, Social Security should be included in any deficit reduction calculations.[39]

Why did AGE catch on so readily? One reason was that Democratic lawmakers with no firm liberal views were being pulled to the right by conservatives' new political dominance and refusal to compromise. Any Democrat who wanted to get his or her name on legislation and thus make a reputation in Washington was severely tempted to step across the aisle rather than stick close to traditional party principles. Consistently, the Washington media praised them for doing so.

Soon after AGE was born, this tendency found a name. "We were working very hard to recreate a center with AGE," says Hewitt. "Some thought of us as 'radical centrists.'" That tag could easily describe some of the ambitious young baby-boomer politicians whose names were associated with AGE and generational equity to various degrees. Lawton Chiles, the Florida Democrat who was Durenberger's best friend in the Senate, and Rep. Dick Gephardt, a rising young Missouri Democrat, were typical of these middle-of-the-road mavericks. So was Dick Lamm, whose pronouncements about the duties of the elderly provided the dose of outrageousness essential to any group of radicals, even of the center.

A roughly characteristic profile of the "radical center" politician of the 1980s would include rigid fiscal conservatism combined with some libertarian views on social-cultural issues and perhaps a dash of environmentalism to appeal to the young. A slightly less interventionist foreign policy stance often figured in, too. Durenberger himself, for example, despite his orthodox economic views, clashed with CIA director William Casey over funding of the Contras in Nicaragua. One important characteristic the radical centrists shared with conservatives, however, was a dedication to denying that poverty reduction actually required an investment by government.

"Healing" was also very important, rhetorically, to the radical centrists, however. The views of many politicians who fit the epithet had been affected by the imagery and thematics of the Kennedy presidency. They were concerned, after Vietnam and the other events of the 1960s that destroyed what had once seemed like a national consensus culture, with finding some formula for restoring it. Many advocated various Peace Corps–like national service programs as a way to implement the kinds of lofty national projects—educating the children of the inner city, ending illiteracy and malnutrition—that they felt would help reunify America.

AGE's message, which conveniently glided over class, racial, and gender issues that might scramble the neat generational split, fit with these ideas because it offered yet another way for competitive young politicians to paper over, if not solve, the difficult issues that had dominated America since the 1960s.

But the radical center's actual influence on public policy was lopsided. While AGE paid lip service to the idea of public spending to improve education and combat poverty, it never came out in favor of any definite program that could risk upsetting its backers, who were almost exclusively corporate. Instead, it used its influence to put a chill on any new spending for the elderly or for programs that might benefit them, meanwhile broadcasting the advantages of private-sector alternatives.

Longman, for example, called for "increasingly generous provisions for individual retirement accounts" and abolition or reduction of taxes on savings and capital gains. IRAs had, in fact, been around since 1974, but their popularity exploded in 1982, when Congress changed the rules to allow taxpayers to deposit money in them all the way up to April 15, instead of December 31, and still receive a break on their taxes. If they asked for an extension, they could make a contribution all the way until August 15, in fact. A *New York Times/CBS News Poll* taken just before the April tax filing deadline indicated that Americans had put as much as $30 billion in IRAs so far during the 1982 tax year, vastly exceeding earlier Treasury Department estimates.

Mainly the older and better-off—those who tended to need the least help toward their retirement—were taking advantage of IRAs, however; 28% of families earning more than $40,000 a year had opened an account, the poll found, the figure dropping to 17% for those earning $30,000 to $40,000, and 10% for those earning $20,000 to $29,999. The figures dropped steadily for younger workers as well. And while workers who lacked a pension plan were presumably most in need of a retirement savings account of some kind, the poll found that those already participating in a pension plan were more likely to open an IRA.

Was this because lower-income workers couldn't afford to open an IRA? Or only because they needed to be educated to understand the advantages of private retirement accounts? Whatever the answer—and this debate would go on for decades—the fact that IRAs weren't taking the lower end of the income scale by storm suggested they wouldn't help sell a privatized Social Security system to the unconverted. Before the decade was over, however, AGE's role in sparking such discussion was finished.

* * *

After a tough reelection campaign in 1988, Durenberger, always the group's principal rainmaker, came under investigation by the Senate Ethics Committee for a host of alleged ethics breaches and rules violations, some of which prompted the committee to subpoena AGE's financial records. In December 1989, he resigned as co-chair. Hewitt and Longman had both left by this point, and Neil Howe—who had collaborated with Pete Peterson on his latest anti-Social Security book—replaced Longman as research director. But without Dureneberger's name and fundraising energy, the organization wound down.

Hewitt left Washington for a time, to return as executive director of the anti-tax National Taxpayers Union Foundation, but wouldn't resume direct work on Social Security-related issues for some years. Longman also left Washington but found it harder to put AGE's confrontations with the Gray Lobby behind him. In 1987 he was recruited to work for Buddy McKay, a rising Republican House member from Florida who was impressed by the generational equity analysis even though he represented a district with a large senior vote. "He had seen my *Atlantic Monthly* piece and he paid me to hang out and write speeches," Longman says.

When Longman's book on the politics of aging, *Born to Pay*, was published that same year, *West 57th Street*, a prime-time CBS newsmagazine program, did a segment on him in Miami Beach. "I said nobody should have to lose their job because they were 65, and nobody should get a check just because they're 65," he recalls. McKay's office received a barrage of phone calls complaining about Longman, and McKay soon had to fire his new brain-truster. The ever-supportive *Washington Monthly* wrote a piece about the targeting of its former contributor by the senior lobby, as did the *Wall Street Journal*, but Longman moved on and, like Hewitt, didn't return to the Social Security debate for several years.

AGE's demise was no great loss for the movement against Social Security, however, because by then it had accomplished a great part of its mission. At the end of the 1980s, the generational equity analysis was firmly implanted in America's political discourse, where it would remain. A search of the Nexis database in 1997 yielded more than 1,000 references to "generational equity" and "generational conflict,"[40] testimony to how well-ensconced these concepts had become.

CHAPTER 9

THE ANTI-
DEFICIT
OBSESSION

"Values or preferences are the black hole of capitalism.
They are what the system exists to serve, but there are no
capitalistic theories of good or bad preferences, no capi-
talistic theories of how values arise, and no capitalistic
theories of how values should be altered or controlled....
To ignore the social aspects of humankind is to design a
world for a human species that does not exist."
　　　　　—Lester Thurow, The Future of Capitalism[1]

Between Reagan's naming of the Greenspan commission in fall 1981 and the
passage of the 1983 Amendments nearly a year and a half later, the economic
picture of the U.S. changed. So did the financial profile of Social Security.

Inflation was dropping, and would continue to do so, mostly, for the rest of the decade. Interest rates, too, were falling, although they remained in double digits and it would be close to ten more years before they reached the low levels that had been considered normal before the economic shocks of the 1970s. The economy itself was beginning to recover, stimulated by the Reagan tax cuts and nurtured by the fall in interest rates.

By 1986, moreover, energy prices were clearly dropping, possibly for an extended period. Some factors still kept the outlook less than rosy, however. Wages were still stagnant and would remain so for years to come. And government budget deficits remained stubbornly high. Without wages going up, neither would tax revenues, thus keeping Washington in the red.

But the 1983 Amendments had a powerful and lasting effect on budget politics. Suddenly, a program that not long before had appeared to be dragging the federal government further into deficit was shoring up its balance sheet. Of the $30 billion in deficit reduction measures the Reagan administration had asked Congress for in February, $12 billion was embodied in the Amendments: especially, the six-month COLA delay. Each year after that, Social Security revenues swelled because of the way the 1983 Amendments advanced the dates of the payroll tax increases scheduled in the 1977 Amendments. New money poured into the Treasury, seemingly making deficit reduction less urgent for Congress.

Social Security's critics lost one of their biggest rhetorical weapons, too, because the trustees' long-term estimates of the program's health no longer looked overly optimistic. Whereas in 1983 OASI had to borrow $17.5 billion from the Disability and Hospital Insurance trust funds to keep the checks flowing to retirees, in April 1984, the trustees' annual report stated that OASI and Disability Insurance should be able to pay all benefits on time "well into the next century." The situation was so positive that the "stabilizer" that Congress had included in the 1983 Amendments, which would automatically switch to the lesser of the CPI or the wage rate for computing COLAs if trust fund reserves fell too low, would probably be unnecessary that year. The good news reflected both the improving economy and the changes embodied in the 1983 Amendments, the trustees said.

Why, then, did a group called the Association of Informed Senior Citizens, in 1984, find it necessary to release a fundraising letter that stated, "We will be battling to preserve Social Security and Medicare—two programs facing serious threats to their continued existence"? The fabled Gray Lobby didn't celebrate its victory, fold up its operations, and leave town after the 1983 Amendments were passed. In fact, it seemed to be just as embattled the following year—and the one after that—as it had when Stockman was threatening to start Social Security on a slow road to oblivion.

The cause, indirectly, was the deficit, which hit $200 billion in 1983, putting it at a postwar high of 6% of GDP, and was expected to drop only slightly to $185 billion in 1984. For 1989, the administration was projecting something back in the neighborhood of $200 billion. Given that prospect, and their desire to rein in the red ink as much as possible through budget cuts rather than tax increases, Republican leaders in Congress naturally looked for savings in the same place they had looked before: Social Security.

One reason AGE encountered such a warm reception was that it answered these lawmakers' quest for a solution to the deficit dilemma that fit with their inclination to keep domestic spending lean and taxes low. Cutting Social Security benefits instead, and specifically the annual COLAs, was the obvious alternative.

The most conspicuous voice for placing Social Security cuts at the forefront of the deficit war was a former member of the Greenspan commission: Bob Dole. Less than six months after Reagan signed the 1983 Amendments, Dole's Senate Finance Committee was studying a plan to cut $150 billion out of the deficit within three years, divided evenly between tax increases and spending cuts. The latter included $32 billion from reducing COLAs for Social Security and other retirement programs.

The White House gave the idea little support and Tip O'Neill gave it none at all, but a hard core of Republicans plus a few Senate Democrats promised to forge ahead. John Glenn of Ohio, seeking the Democratic presidential nomination, insisted in a position paper that controlling the deficit "means controlling the rapid growth of entitlement programs with more reasonable cost-of-living adjustments (COLAs)"[2] while Democrat David L. Boren of Oklahoma insisted, "The stakes for the economy are too high for us to quit."[3]

Quit they would not. Unless one belonged to the more progressive wing of the Democratic Party, denouncing the deficit was good politics. It provided an automatic rationale for Republicans to demand cuts in domestic programs, and Democrats to oppose Republican tax cuts. It also earned points for politicians with the elite Washington press corps, which had been won over by influential deficit hawks like Pete Peterson. In the decade and a half that followed passage of the Reagan tax cuts, bringing down the deficit became a near-obsession for lawmakers, pundits and the mainstream media, arm-chair moralists, and the mainstream of the economics profession. It became the litmus test of serious and responsible thinking on domestic policy.

This was to some extent understandable, since the U.S. had never before run deficits the size of the ones that appeared in the 1980s, except during wartime. Arguably, they held the economy back to some degree by encouraging the Federal Reserve and the bond market to keep interest rates relatively high throughout the decade. Many highly qualified economists questioned whether the deficit was really that destructive and whether the measures needed to eliminate it—such as, in the long run, radically reducing Social Security—were worth the price. But they had very little access to the higher policymaking circles or the Washington media.

* * *

The obsession of the American political class with cutting entitlements to reduce the deficit grew out of the series of financial crises that wrenched the country starting in the late 1960s. Combined with high inflation and the end of the managed currency regime that the industrialized countries had put in place after the Second World War, these created a riskier financial environment than anyone had known since the 1930s. That meant, not surprisingly, that financial institutions were imposing higher interest rates. Those interest rates in turn were more volatile and unpredictable than before.

From 1900 through 1984, real interest rates—the "nominal" rate on high-quality corporate bonds, minus inflation—averaged 1.5%. That figure actually declined in the period after the Second World War, to 1.34%. But in 1983–84, real interest rates averaged a frightening 8.2%.[4] And while they dropped in the course of the decade, they continued to whipsaw back and forth.

That threw a great deal of new power in the lap of the Federal Reserve, the one institution that could manage interest rate movements. Under Paul Volcker and then Alan Greenspan, the Fed became politically untouchable, operating almost completely independent of Congress and the White House, and its focus narrowed to virtually a single policy goal: preventing any further attack of inflation.

This was partly because the Fed is controlled by banks, whose profits from their vast portfolios of loans and debt securities—investments that pay a fixed return—suffer when inflation rises even a little. But it was also the result of two other factors: First, the tripling of the outstanding national debt under the Reagan and Bush administrations made the owners, underwriters, and managers of that debt—especially Wall Street—vastly more influential. The opinion of the bond market became a more and more decisive factor in the formation of U.S. economic policy. In general, bond investors preferred to keep interest rates relatively high and the national debt low, even if that meant slower economic growth.

Second, in the face of this, the president and Congress arrived at a de facto agreement to leave monetary policy and all responsibility for monitoring and controlling inflation up to the Fed. U.S. economic policy increasingly reflected the narrow views of bankers and the Wall Street bond dealers, which, like banks, make money by lending money to governments and businesses and tend to look at the world in much the same way.* Their views boiled down to three main beliefs.

The first was that a strong economy can be, and often is, a bad thing. Too vigorous economic activity leads to "overheating," which leads to a runaway boom featuring order backlogs and escalating prices—in other words, inflation. At the same time it pushes unemployment close to zero, which employers

---

*   The dividing line between the business of banks and the business of bond dealers actually began to blur in the 1980s and 1990s, as new mechanisms appeared for "securitizing" loans: packaging bank loans and selling them as securities in the bond market.

don't like because it leads to demands for higher wages. These in turn can lead to inflation, which bankers frown on. As the new economic order took hold, so did a theory that there existed a natural, "nonaccelerating inflation rate of unemployment" (NAIRU): the rate at which each additional worker hired would cause inflation to accelerate and eventually slip out of control.

The search for the NAIRU became a favorite parlor game of economists and, for some, a good route to academic and government appointments. Meanwhile, whenever the economy threatened to become too lively and jobs too easy to obtain, the Fed would come under pressure to once again raise its prime lending rate, pushing other interest rates up as well, to stop the overheating. The solution, in other words, was higher unemployment and lower wages.

The second part of the bankers' world view had actually been codified as early as 1929 in a paper issued by the British Treasury, titled "Memorandum on Certain Proposals Relating to Unemployment," after which it became known—sometimes sneeringly—as the "Treasury View." Economists who embraced this outlook believed that the most desirable policy is always for the government to balance its expenditures with its income: in other words, not tolerate any fiscal deficit.

Written in response to opposition politicians who were calling for the British government to initiate a program of public works spending in order to revive a sluggish economy, the Treasury paper argued that this would merely crowd out other investment and wouldn't increase total employment. Why? Because at any given time there's only a certain amount of savings available in the economy to be invested. If government spending sops it all up, then nothing's left for the private sector and business will stagnate.

A third belief, a corollary of sorts to the Treasury View, was what might be called the personal saving imperative. Every economy needs to grow in order to provide for the changing needs of each generation of workers. But if that growth can't come from government spending, since the government, according to the Treasury View, is supposed to keep its books as close as possible to balanced, then it must come from somewhere else. The nation shouldn't depend on foreign investment to finance growth because foreigners could decide at any time to pull their money out. So growth would have to be fueled by money that individual workers stash in their personal savings accounts and private investments.

Accordingly, Washington should do everything possible to rechannel workers' money away from taxes and "false savings" like Social Security payroll tax contributions into "real" savings and investments in the private sector. Personal saving was such a central economic virtue, in other words, that it must be encouraged even if lower consumption and lower taxes—and lower tax revenues—were the price paid to achieve it. Martin Feldstein may not have been able to prove that Social Security crowded out personal saving, but a lot of powerful people made this an assumption because it bolstered the conventional wisdom taking hold in Washington and on Wall Street.

In the 1970s and, increasingly, in the 1980s, the NAIRU religion, the Treasury View, and the personal savings imperative congealed into a new consensus that abhorred inflation, valorized private saving, and tacitly accepted that a long period of wage stagnation was necessary to make America competitive again. There was nothing surprising about this. Inflation represents a real threat to bankers' and bondholders' profits. Given the insular nature of Wall Street culture, it was only natural that the bankers and their political allies would assume that what was a threat to them was dangerous to the whole country—and would construct an elaborate series of intellectual justifications around their position. Their sheer economic clout and political influence helped them to crowd out any other perspective.

Pete Peterson played an influential role in getting the Washington community to accept the new economic consensus. By the time the Greenspan commission had completed its work, it already dominated the punditocracy, thanks in part to the influence of Charlie's Angels. By then the consensus view was also in the process of being embraced by the leadership of both parties in Congress, whether or not they were fully conscious that this was what they were doing. This had two huge implications for the Social Security debate.

First, if economic "overheating" and rising wages were a danger to a really healthy economy, then how would a "healthy" economy be able to support the Social Security system? Social Security depends on rising payroll tax contributions to fund current and future benefits. An unofficial national policy of holding down wages would directly threaten the program's long-term health.

Second, an obsessive focus on deficit reduction would place enormous pressure on elected officials to look at policymaking as a financial zero-sum game. If spending goes up for one program, it must go down for another. "Entitlements"—especially Social Security and Medicare, because they're the biggest—would become the focus of ever more anger and resentment on the part of policymakers who subscribed to the Treasury View: anger that was already boiling over in the mid-1980s in the rhetoric of generational equity proponents like AGE. Automatic COLAs, particularly, would come under attack because Congress and the president couldn't change them without risking dire political consequences.

Another consequence of the new Washington economic consensus was that a plethora of tax breaks in the form of long-term retirement savings vehicles, like IRAs and 401(k) plans, poured out of Congress. This not only decreased the government's tax revenues, contributing to the deficit, but widened the Social Security debate into an argument about retirement policy in general. Should the core of that policy really be a program that taxes workers' wages and "invests" them in building more government? Or should it encourage private savings, which the new orthodoxy held was the only acceptable way to capitalize future economic growth? If the latter, then Social Security represented just the sort of crowding out of private investment that the Treasury View warned against.

The new economic consensus meant that the direction of Washington policymaking would henceforth be to undermine Social Security in three important ways: by eroding its revenue base, attacking COLAs, and building a parallel system of private retirement accounts that could someday supplant it.

* * *

Plenty of economists outside the Wall Street-Beltway axis had serious concerns about the new consensus, even if hardly anyone listened to them.

The first problem was with the NAIRU. No one has ever succeeded in pinning down what the natural, non-accelerating inflation rate of unemployment really is. The theory presupposes a perfect market where the real value of everything is transparent. But markets are affected by too many outside forces—monopolies in some business sectors, differences in the information available or affordable to various groups of businesses and consumers—for a NAIRU to be identifiable, even if it does exist.[5]

The Treasury View, too, has little concrete experience to back it up. Jumping ahead of our story by a few years, in 1993 the Clinton administration and Congress agreed upon a massive deficit-cutting package. The Fed's response was to double short-term interest rates. Long-term rates kept going up for another two years, contradicting the notion that lower government deficits lead to lower interest rates. Within just three months, the rise in short-term rates had added $100 billion to the deficit, wiping out some 20% of the deficit-cutting progress Washington had achieved in 1993.[6]

The basic concepts behind the Treasury View also have problems. The best, least painful means of reducing the deficit is for the economy to grow and wages to rise. This boosts tax revenues from individuals and businesses even if the rate of taxation—the percentage of sales or of workers' wages that the government takes—stays the same. But if the economy isn't expanding, there are only two ways left to lower the deficit: raise tax rates and cut government spending. Either one tends to depress the economy. And if raising taxes or cutting spending doesn't very quickly result in lower interest rates, and if those interest rates aren't low enough to overcome stagnant wages and sluggish business and consumer spending, then the gamble has failed. The economy goes deeper into its funk.

The relationship between deficits and inflation was itself hard to pin down—if one even existed. Most large industrial economies were experiencing budget deficits in the 1980s, and the U.S. was by no means the worst offender. Despite the accumulating red ink, America actually had to pay investors less to hold its Treasury bonds in 1986 than it did in 1980. So did Germany and Canada, whose deficits sopped up an even larger percentage of GDP than did Washington's. Deficits weren't leading to more inflation, either. Inflation rates were actually falling during the 1980s.

The one fact that nearly all economists agreed upon was that business's own investment in the economy was declining. That meant less capital goods—factories, machines, tools, office buildings, housing—going into production or being re-placed. And that meant less production and less need for workers to generate it. Net private fixed investment averaged 5.4% of net national product during the twelve-year period ending in 1992, well below the average 8% from 1959 to 1979.

But again, other industrialized countries suffering worse deficits weren't ex-periencing the same decline in production. What set the U.S. apart was not rel-ative fiscal irresponsibility, but that Washington wasn't using the public sector to take up the slack. Instead, government investment in public infrastructure, education, training, research and development, and other growth-promoting investment was shrinking.[7]

Whether deficits had any relationship at all to the rate of saving and invest-ment, the "crowding out" that the Treasury View described was dubious as well. Peter L. Bernstein, a respected and conservative economic consultant who studied the problem, saw no connection. Compared to other large industrial economies, he found that America had experienced the largest relative rise in consumption during the first half of the 1980s but the smallest relative increase in its total national debt.

"The relationship between deficits and saving rates appears to be essentially random," he concluded.[8] In fact, gross investment in the 1980s was actually a bit higher as a percentage of GDP than it had been during the booming 1960s.[9]

At the other end of the ideological spectrum, Robert Eisner, professor of economics at Northwestern University and past president of the Ameri-can Economic Association, pointed out that reducing government deficits and increasing personal savings, as Washington policy peddlers and pundits agreed was necessary, could also lead to less consumption, which could cause a business slowdown. There was no way around it. Less government spending meant less spending power for somebody in the economy, which meant less inducement for business to step up production and hire more workers.

Shrinking Social Security and Medicare, for example, could retard econom-ic recovery because it translated into less disposable income for seniors, not to mention less investment in housing, medical technology innovation, and other such useful projects. Even if a lower federal deficit succeeded in reducing interest rates, would this outweigh the effect of lower business sales? That was "very much in doubt," Eisner concluded.[10] In fact, he suggested, the econom-ic slowdown that could result from a vigorous deficit-fighting campaign—complete with tax hikes and cuts in federal spending—might be severe enough to completely wipe out whatever short-term deficit reduction was achieved.[11]

Economists as different in their approaches as Eisner and Bernstein also agreed that the best way to bring down the deficit was to apply public policies that encouraged growth in economic productivity. These in turn would raise incomes, which would raise tax revenue, which would gradually reduce the budget shortfall, with or without a drop in government spending. For proof, they could point to the fact that the over-sixty-five population tripled in the five-decade period that began in 1950. But living standards rose to unheard-of levels, and the size of the U.S. economy doubled in those years. Clearly, a productive economy could take care of the needs of an aging population.

Bernstein and Eisner disagreed about plenty. Bernstein, not to mention Arthur Laffer and the other supply-side enthusiasts, saw tax reduction as the only brand of growth stimulation that government could legitimately engage in, and then only if it firmly refrained from toying with the supply of money.

Eisner and other liberal economists held no such taboos. Tax reduction was one way to goose the economy, but not necessarily the best, most lasting, or most equitable. Much of the money that no longer went to Washington might simply be spent, or stored up in affluent citizens' savings accounts. The point was to plow it into activities that would create a lastingly more valuable economy. Government could achieve that result simply by applying it to such traditional purposes as education, infrastructure like roads and bridges, and technological research and development. That was what happened when, for example, Social Security's payroll tax revenues were lent to the Treasury instead of being squirreled away in private savings.

Either way, it seemed clear to many economists outside the Washington consensus that the crusade against inflation and the deficit would only dampen economic growth and discourage any relief from the wage stagnation the U.S. had fallen into during the mid-1970s. Another result would be slumping payroll taxes and continuing financial trouble for Social Security. The only clear beneficiaries would be banks and the bond market, since low—or no—deficits, low inflation, and high personal savings boosted the volume and value of their assets. But since the Fed now had undisputed control of the government's inflation policy, and given that the Fed was largely controlled by the major commercial banks, the new consensus was the most professionally advantageous point of view for an economist to take.

Often, it took a moralistic turn. In a 1989 speech, coming in the wake of a stock market meltdown in October 1987, Richard Darman, now Treasury Secretary, attacked what he called Americans' "self-indulgent theft from the future." "In our public policy—as, to some degree, in our private behavior—we consume today as if there were no tomorrow," he said. "We attend too little to the issues of investment necessary to make tomorrow brighter." Darman was addressing several audiences at once: a spendthrift government and corporations that rewarded financial manipulators during the Wall Street merger-and-acquisition boom of the 1980s. But he was arguing more generally against what he termed Americans' "pervasive cultural short-sightedness."[12]

In the early 1980s, Darman's indictment was already being refined into a cultural critique of the average American household. Instead of saving, it was going into debt to finance present consumption, piling up IOUs instead of capital to invest in the future. Without a doubt, the numbers proved that saving was declining and consumer credit was exploding in the 1980s. But economists outside the consensus had little trouble explaining why without resorting to moral condemnation. Wages had stagnated and the cost of essentials like housing, health care, and education were escalating, making it less possible for Americans—if they wanted to live a middle-class lifestyle—to save.

But in an economic policy environment that focused obsessively on removing any incentive for wages to rise above the hypothetical NAIRU, this kind of analysis only made Washington—and the banking community that supplied the credit—uncomfortable, and was generally ignored. Instead, lawmakers and pundits tended to wag their fingers at the American consumer and call for a cultural shift that would wean households away from profligacy and win them back to the habit of thrift. The result, supposedly, would be greater personal financial security, including less reliance on Social Security and Medicare, and more funds for the private sector to invest in productive—nongovernment—development.

* * *

"Long run is a misleading guide to current affairs. In the long run we are all dead."
—*John Maynard Keynes* [13]

Surely there was nothing wrong, generally, with encouraging Americans to save and invest? Maybe there was. The British economist John Maynard Keynes had pointed out the trouble during the depths of the Depression. He called it the "paradox of thrift."

What's good for the individual or the household isn't necessarily good for the whole economy, Keynes cautioned. For example, it's obviously worthwhile for individuals and households to save and invest more of their money, because they're more likely to have the nest egg they need for old age. But when everyone in the society saves more, especially during a recession, then aggregate demand falls, production slows down, wages and incomes fall—and aggregate savings decline. The exercise becomes destructive.

At one time, Keynes's insight was commonplace economic teaching. Paul Samuelson enshrined it in *Economics: An Introductory Analysis*, the textbook that was the standard for legions of students of the discipline from the time the first edition appeared in 1947. "High consumption and high investment ... go hand in hand rather than competing," Samuelson wrote in the 1955 edition. To encourage, or even to force, all households to save all the time, wouldn't be good for the overall economy. "What is true for the individual—that extra thriftiness means increased savings and wealth—may then become completely untrue for the community as a whole."

The same principle applied to Social Security and employer-sponsored pension funds as to households. Piling up assets to fund its workers' retirement was clearly a good thing for Exxon, for example. But Exxon, big as it was, employed only a sliver of the U.S. workforce. Social Security embraced 95%-plus of all workers. Collecting too large a portion of their paychecks to fund their benefits in advance would leave them with too little to meet their own, and their children's, present needs.

Even during periods of rapid economic growth, there can be too much saving. If there's no shortage of investment capital—as we've seen, gross investment was actually higher in the U.S. in the 1980s than in the 1960s and the financial sector was booming—then massive new saving by ordinary American workers would likely be a case of good money chasing after bad. Much of it would go into unwise ventures that were doomed to fail, or into the increasingly exotic forms of speculation practiced in the derivatives markets.

None other than Karl Marx predicted the outcome more than eighty years before Richard Darman was born: the emergence of a "rentier society," in which the financial sector becomes increasingly unmoored from the part of the economy that actually produces goods and services for the people.[14]

As we've seen, bankers and the bond market often would rather have a weak economy and low wages than a healthy economy and rising wages, if forced to choose. And so when a large percentage of workers become shareholders and bondholders, either directly or indirectly, they find themselves wrestling with two competing sets of interests: their jobs and the affordability of their households versus the value of their investments in a casino-like securities marketplace. As Wall Street historian Doug Henwood comments, "It seems odd that workers should be asked to trade a few extra percentage points return on their pension fund, on which they may draw some decades in the future, for 30 to 40 years of falling wages and rising employment insecurity."[15]

Thrift would turn workers not into capitalists, as some free-market enthusiasts liked to argue, but into speculators in financial assets that have little healthy impact on the "real" economy. But there was a deeper problem with the new consensus's promise that saving and investment would provide workers with a secure retirement in a growing economy.

According to Keynes, money put aside for the future could actually undermine the future economy if it wasn't used to create products and services that would be needed in the future. "Insofar as our social and business organization separates financial provision for the future from physical provision for the future so that efforts to secure the former do not necessarily carry the latter with them," he wrote, "financial prudence will be liable to destroy effective demand and thus impair well-being."[16]

The "physical provision" we can establish today to serve our children's needs is very limited. We can put up houses, factories, office buildings, and schools, construct roads and bridges and airports, laboratories and farm equipment. We can develop food products, medicines, and clothing that will last for years without deteriorating. But even these things require storage and maintenance every day in the future just as they do in the present. Most of our needs would still have to be provided in the here-and-now.

"The world lives from hand to mouth," George Bernard Shaw wrote, with his customary attention to everyday detail. "A drawingroom poker will last a lifetime; but we cannot live by eating drawingroom pokers.... Even our clothes will not last very long if we work hard in them; and there is the washing."[17] The French Situationist Raoul Vaneigem put it somewhat more dogmatically a few decades later: "A solidly constructed present is the only necessity—the rest will take care of itself.... In collective as well as in individual history, the cult of the past and the cult of the future are equally reactionary."[18]

Applying the same principle to Social Security, economist Christopher J. Niggle of the University of Redlands in California noted that, while the problem of funding the program would change qualitatively if it was privatized, "the real burden on future workers would remain the same. Increasing prefunding of pension systems is not equivalent to survivalists storing up canned goods or squirrels nuts. The only way to support the aged at higher levels or to reduce the real burden of a given level of support is by increasing the productivity of labor through time."[19]

How are we to know what the next generation's economic needs will be? Which of the assets we leave to them will they really want to use and maintain? What will they spend their savings (and ours) on, and what will they be trying to achieve by doing so? Every year in their annual report, the Social Security trustees tried to quantify how much actual money would be needed to cover the needs of the next three generations of retirees. That required a lot of complicated estimates involving the ebb and flow of birth rates, wage rates, and changes in the basket of goods and services American households had purchased in the past, plus some educated guesses about how these would change in the future. But in a free-market society, the economic imperative to constantly create new needs is strong, making it nearly impossible to predict what sorts of needs will emerge twenty, thirty, or fifty years from now, when the present generation of workers are retired and the next ones paying into Social Security and Medicare to support them.

What's the effect of an economy fueled by such a process? "Our demonstrated ability to generate new wants has eliminated the possibility ... of ever being able to satiate everyone's wants," Lester Thurow wrote in *The Zero-Sum Society*. "Since the problem of unsatiated wants is always with us, the problem of specifying economic equity is always with us."[20] That problem of "economic equity" would include equity between generations as well as between classes, income groups, and any other preferred division of society. And like them, it was unsolvable so long as the process of creating new needs continued.

Moshe Adler, a Columbia University economist, provided a real-life example. The auto industry produced vehicles that were always quite different in many details from the ones it had turned out a few years earlier. Airbags, by the early 1990s, were standard, but navigation systems were becoming typical, CD players had become standard long ago, and other improvements were coming along all the time. Plus, in the era of the SUV, cars were bigger and bulkier than ever. Government economic measures told us that fitting all these enhancements into one new vehicle added to the country's productivity, making the economy more vigorous. Yet the number of vehicles produced hadn't changed: each new model was merely a bit more luxurious than the last. More resources and perhaps more labor were going into each new car, but the auto industry's ability to satisfy the public's—and that includes seniors'—need for cars hadn't changed.

The same would go for any good or service needed by the nation's growing population of elderly, from cars to dentures to insurance policies for long-term health care. The needs of the elderly can't be met simply through economic growth or greater productivity per worker. We have to know what that economic growth and higher productivity are being used for. We would have to have an industrial policy that focused on producing goods and services that the elderly need, but more cheaply, efficiently, and affordably than at present.

"The only financial rearranging that could ease the workers' burden without cutting retirees' benefits would be a program that focused investment of Social Security taxes in activities that would increase the quantity of goods available for consumption," Adler wrote. "Otherwise, investment in stocks can change neither the demographics of retirement nor the economy's productivity.[21]

The argument for replacing Social Security with private savings, whether by converting the program into private accounts or reducing benefits so that workers must rely more on their own savings, is based on a series of fallacies. Higher rates of saving and investment don't necessarily mean that more of the nation's resources will go into productive growth. Much if not most of it will go into a casino—the stock market—that speculates on the direction of various parts of the economy. Higher rates of saving and investment can actually retard future economic growth, especially if they necessitate cutbacks today in vital investments like education, health care, and infrastructure.

But most important, higher rates of saving and investment tell us nothing about where that money will be invested. Will some of it be used to create inexpensive but high-quality housing for seniors? To provide better but also more efficient long-term care services for them? Will it subsidize the labor of family members who choose to care for aged relatives themselves, rather than institutionalize them? Will it be used to encourage families to have more children, relieving some of the demographic burden on the next generation of workers obliged to support a larger population of elderly? Or the opposite? And even if the answer to all these questions was yes, would the benefits accrue to seniors at every income level, or mainly those at the top?

Keynes ridiculed the conventional view that society should always push for more saving and investment as an exaggerated form of "purposiveness," meaning that "we are more concerned with the remote future results of our actions than with their own quality or their immediate effects on our environment. The 'purposive' man ... does not love his cat, but his cat's kittens; nor, in truth, the kittens, but only the kittens' kittens, and so on forward forever to the end of cat-dom." The "purposive" person might imagine she has gained "a spurious and delusive immortality" through her actions. But she hasn't really made her community any richer or more vigorous in the long run.[22]

Eisner argued that the only investment a society could really make for the time when more of its population would be aged was the kind that society traditionally makes collectively. "The only way ... we can help now to provide for the needs of future retirees," he wrote, "is to accumulate real capital, and most of that will have to be in the human capital of education, training and health, and in our social infrastructure, both largely provided by government."[23] For example, America at the tail end of the 20th century faced a shortage of geriatric doctors and nurses who could provide qualified care to the elderly.[24] Was there any guarantee that some of that increased retirement savings would be spent on expanded geriatric services, or would this be crowded out by other, more profitable investments that create new needs? And would only the most affluent elderly then receive proper geriatric care?

Without knowing the answers to the above questions, we can't be sure whether cutting benefits and forcing people to rely more on private savings really would boost personal savings—and leave the elderly better off, as Social Security's critics asserted. Not knowing where and how those savings would be invested, we can't know whether it will give each generation of workers more resources for their old age, relieving the burden on their children and grandchildren, or instead just make daily life a more expensive, more resource-intensive experience.

The same would go for any scheme, like the one Congress adopted with the 1983 Amendments, that raises taxes in advance to build up a trust fund to finance Social Security benefits. "With no reason to believe that more investment would reduce the burden of providing for retirement, no justification exists for raising the Social Security tax rate before benefits paid out actually exceed taxes collected," Adler concluded.[25]

"What is called saving is only making bargains for the future," Shaw wrote.[26] But unless society has some mechanism for making binding collective decisions about what future needs it's going to invest in today, it stands little chance of providing ahead of time for its older members. In a free-market economy, those decisions are made by businesses that create and sell goods and services to the people. They will decide on the basis of how the next innovation will be welcomed rather than, say, what's needed to balance the needs of older and younger citizens.

In such a system, if Social Security really were headed for a crisis because the U.S. population was aging and would at some point have too few workers to sustain it, the country wouldn't be able to save and invest its way around the problem. "Thus for all practical purposes, and at an aggregate level, funded pension schemes operate [the same] as pay-as-you-go schemes," wrote Colin Gillion, director of the International Labour Office, a UN affiliate that had been advising governments on pension plan design for decades.

"To increase the share flowing to pensioners means that the share flowing to active persons must be reduced."[27]

The notion that American workers can somehow save and invest their way out from under a looming demographic crisis of too many retirees is a myth, a magic-bullet solution in which everything can be made all right without any redistribution between generations or from the more affluent to the less so. As Nicholas Barr, a British economist and expert on the welfare state, wrote, "The economic function of a pension scheme is to transfer consumption over time. But, ruling out the case when current output is stored in holes in people's gardens, this is not possible for society as a whole; the consumption of pensioners as a group is produced by the next generation of workers."[28]

Nothing, not even turning Social Security into a system of private investment accounts, would change this. As the population ages, spending on the elderly must increase, unless they are to be given up to destitution. The only question is whether this is to be done collectively or by individual households, and which method is most equitable. "Under most privatization schemes, Social Security is still a government program—only outsourced," notes David Lindeman, a former U.S. Treasury and SSA official who has consulted on pension design in many countries. Private accounts may or may not produce better returns for some workers, but they don't relieve society of the need to provide a minimally comfortable and dignified retirement for each citizen, no matter how her investments pan out.

"If the state is going to require someone to participate in its programs, it has to provide them some kind of guarantee," says Lindeman, invoking the American philosopher John Rawls's theory of justice as fairness. Even without an explicit guarantee, the political reality is that workers who participate in a government-mandated private account system will demand that the State come to their aid if, some time in the future, that system lets them down.[29]

It would take a radical restructuring of the responsibilities of the American governmental system to change this, Richard Posner, a legal scholar and U.S. Appeals Court judge, pointed out in *Aging and Old Age* (1995). Government, and the voters to whom it answers, can't be forced to tailor their spending to some hypothetical generational-equity master budget. Neither can workers be forced to save for retirement when they're young.

Therefore, "it is not apparent what public or private means exist for preventing the elderly from shifting these burdens [the cost of medical and home care, for example] to taxpayers and family members," Posner wrote. Even if Social Security were drastically curtailed today, wouldn't the millions of new retirees simply use their votes to reverse the action decades from now, when they realize their benefits aren't worth as much as they had expected? One way to avoid this, Posner hypothesized, might be to strip the elderly of some of their voting power and give each child a vote, half of which could be exercised by each parent, as a way to shift the balance more in the direction of young families.

But would this really be the right thing to do? Posner invoked what he called "multiple-selves analysis" to examine the logic behind generational arrangements like Social Security and Medicare. Young, middle-aged, and elderly people have such different views of themselves in some respects, he argued, that it makes sense to regard them almost as separate individuals at each stage of life. People nearing retirement tend not to feel "cheated" by Social Security even if it can be shown that the retirement benefits they will soon be receiving are worth less than the payroll taxes they contributed during their working careers. By this time they view their payroll taxes as "sunk costs," no longer part of the financial equation, and focus instead on the benefits they're about to get. Likewise, younger people may not place much value on the benefits that Social Security and Medicare pay to the elderly because they can't yet envision themselves needing that kind of support.

Perhaps, Posner suggested, the "excessive" voting power the elderly exercise serves a purpose, enabling them "to act as proxies for our otherwise unrepresented future elderly selves."[30]

Troublingly, the new economic consensus had nothing to say to these realities other than to insist that workers trust the intuition of the market. No other insight had a place in the consensus that Washington and Wall Street were settling into during the 1980s. Meanwhile, responsible elected officials and their advisors behaved more and more as if the needs of the living were of little import. Instead, they hunkered down to the task of stopping deficit spending from "crowding out" private saving and investment and stealing from a future of which they had no sure knowledge.

CHAPTER 10

THE STRUGGLE FOR AUSTERITY

"The budget is the skeleton of the state stripped of all misleading ideologies."

—*Rudolf Goldscheid*[1]

The deficit, in the dozen years after the 1983 Amendments passed, would be the Great White Whale of establishment Washington, and Congress something like the crew of the *Pequod*, doomed to slay it or die trying. Even with the famously damaged right arm, Dole, the Second World War veteran, still made only a so-so casting choice as Captain Ahab. With his stiff and formal manner, he lacked the inner fire for the part. But again and again, along with Senate allies Pete Domenici, Alan Simpson, and Slade Gorton and, occasionally, Dan Rostenkowski in the House, he would have at the Sea-Beast, seemingly blind to the number of crew members lost in the repeated attempts.

Driven by economic orthodoxy and the demands of the bond market, the lawmakers held in highest esteem in Washington returned again and again to Social Security and its COLAs as the ultimate solution to the deficit problem. In explaining this near-obsession, lawmakers and those who reported on their doings would resort more than a few times to the worn-out anecdote about bankrobber Willie Sutton's reason for always going back to banks for the answer to his financial troubles: "Because that's where the money is."

A Congress led by anti-entitlement crusaders was bound to have an increasingly uneasy relationship with the Reagan White House, which was understandably less eager to take on Social Security following the 1983 Amendments. It was the beginning of a pattern that would persist for the rest of his time in office, his successor's, and the first term of the following presidency, making the dozen years after the 1983 deal a protracted struggle to achieve fiscal austerity.

In 1982 and 1983, Reagan had gone so far as to accept tax increases on corporations and on gasoline, respectively, which had lopped a significant amount off the deficit. But the $925 billion budget he submitted to Congress in February 1984 as the blueprint for the next fiscal year contained only a few domestic spending cuts.

Despite a few miscues by the president, who still couldn't help every now and again declaring that Social Security faced a "day of reckoning" and would have to be "revamped" after the election, Reagan was returned to office with a landslide 58.1% of the vote over Democrat Walter Mondale on November 6.* Control of Congress was unchanged, although Republicans picked up sixteen seats in the House and the Democrats added two in the Senate. The overall result seemed to reinforce the conclusion that the Republicans had successfully inoculated themselves on Social Security.

Reagan, at first, stuck by a campaign pledge not to touch the program— or at least, not to reduce benefits for persons now receiving them. When he submitted his own $973.7 billion budget on February 3, it included no Social Security cuts. But for the first time in his presidency, he faced a barrage of criticism from the business and political establishment: a remarkable show of force that stretched from Wall Street to Congress to leading business lobby groups. Reporters credited Dole, just elected Senate majority leader, for engineering much of the pressure on Capitol Hill, with assists from Domenici, still Budget Committee chair, and Alan Simpson of Wyoming.

In April, Reagan essentially agreed to an austere Budget Committee blueprint, abandoning his campaign pledge and agreeing with Senate negotiators on a complicated COLA reduction formula that reportedly was developed in the White House itself. Beneficiaries would get a 2% increase whatever the inflation rate, plus, if the CPI topped 4%, an amount tracking the excess over that figure. If inflation hit 4% for the next three years, the COLA would thus be cut in half, to 2%. Over three years, the savings would be about the same as for a one-year COLA freeze: $21 billion.

A bruising, six-week period of negotiations followed, culminating in a late-night meeting between the president and congressional negotiators on July 9,

***

* By far the biggest vote-getter among the third-party candidates was Libertarian David Bergland, whose platform called for winding down Social Security by divvying up the surplus among all participants.

when Reagan reversed himself, tentatively agreeing to remove Social Security cuts from the final deal in return for allowing military spending to grow with inflation. That effectively hung out to dry the majority leader and the bipartisan group of senators he had lined up behind the bill. Afterward, many Republicans and many ardent budget hawks of both parties were furious with the president for what they regarded as an unprincipled betrayal.

Another way to look at it, however, was that Reagan and his advisors had merely experienced another of their timely fits of political realism. Despite their anger, the Republican Senate leadership went back and negotiated a budget that reflected the deal sketched out in the negotiators' nighttime meeting with Reagan.

Rather than dampening Washington's deficit-cutting ardor, the defeat of the COLA cuts pushed political leaders to look again for ways to demonstrate their commitment to fiscal austerity. That fall, Phil Gramm, now a senator, and his fellow Republican Warren Rudman of New Hampshire drew up a budget amendment that set a series of targets for eliminating the deficit in five years. It worked off a formula for predetermining a set of budget cuts that the president could impose if Congress didn't meet its target each year. Half would come from entitlements, including Social Security, and half from discretionary spending, including defense. But Gramm and Rudman quickly changed their proposal to exclude Social Security in order to garner more support.

The law that Reagan signed into effect on December 12, the 1985 Balanced Budget and Emergency Deficit Control Act, better known as Gramm-Rudman-Hollings after its three leading Senate co-sponsors, set the trigger for automatic cuts at $36 billion. But the new law still posed a significant potential threat to Social Security and Medicare. Given the pressure they promised to apply to all other areas of the budget, including old-age benefits outside of Social Security, advocates for the elderly feared that the program itself would inevitably come under attack.

* * *

Lawmakers made some modest progress with the deficit in May 1986, when House-Senate conferees serendipitously added the final touch to the 1983 Amendments by approving legislation for a new Federal Employees' Retirement System (FERS). The deal, which the White House had a hand in crafting, would raise the minimum retirement age for government workers from fifty-five to fifty-seven and end COLAs on benefits paid to retirees under age sixty-two. It was expected to save $2 billion a year by 1991.

Under the arrangement, federal employees who were hired beginning in 1984 would all be Social Security contributors, as well as participating in the new FERS plan with reduced benefits, and have the option of contributing to personal accounts run by a new entity called the Federal Employees' Thrift Savings Plan (TSP). Some supporters of Social Security phase-out saw the

TSP, which could potentially count millions of federal government employees among its participants, as a way to demonstrate that a very large-scale retirement program based on individual investment accounts was financially viable and could become an important factor in retirement planning.

But as a deficit reduction tool, the new structure wasn't expected to deliver much payoff right away. Congress would have to lop another $50 billion to $75 billion off the deficit by October 1 to get it down to the next Gramm-Rudman milestone, $144 billion for fiscal-year 1987.

The stage was set for one of Washington's proudest acts of bipartisanship, the Tax Reform Act of 1986. It was a schizophrenic creation that carried tax policy in several directions at once. Born out of Reagan's campaign pledges to simplify the tax code and his backers' intense desire to drive top tax rates relentlessly down, it also became a vehicle for eliminating some abusive tax shelters and removing some of the financial burden facing the working poor. Despite the high regard that later cloaked it, almost nobody was completely happy with it at the time, especially the radical centrists and libertarians who wanted to promote private-sector alternatives to Social Security.

In the final conference bill that emerged in mid-August, the top individual tax rate dropped from 50% to 28% and the top corporate rate from 46% to 34%. To balance out those moves, it simplified the code by taxing all types of income—wages, capital gains, dividends, rent—at the same rate, eliminating a lot of the incentive to search for loopholes with which to game the system. Social Security was affected in four ways, all indirect but some potentially very important.

Most important, the new law hugely augmented the Earned Income Tax Credit (EITC), which had been created in 1975 to supplement the earnings of low- and moderate-income families with children and was already well on its way to becoming the federal government's largest means-tested cash assistance program. The new tax rules both raised the maximum EITC and indexed it to inflation, essentially removing from the tax rolls 6 million workers living under the poverty line. The impact was greater the larger the household.

Hatched by the House Democrats but embraced by Reagan, the EITC expansion constituted "the most important anti-poverty legislation in more than a decade," the *Wall Street Journal's* Alan Murray concluded, with justification, although it was partially offset by a provision making unemployment insurance payments fully taxable.[2]

For Social Security, the net result was mostly beneficial, but not entirely. With income taxes disappearing for many impoverished individuals, payroll taxes continued to represent a larger and larger portion of what they paid the federal government. On the other hand, by making income taxes less onerous for the working poor, the new law also made the overall system less regressive for them. And it compensated for the shift, in part, by increasing the Alternative Minimum Tax for upper-income taxpayers whose deductions would otherwise have enabled them to pay very little or no tax at all.

The biggest disappointment to conservatives, and particularly to critics of Social Security, was a sharp reduction in tax preferences for individual retirement accounts. The final bill eliminated the deduction for IRA contributions by taxpayers with adjusted gross income—before their IRA deductions—of more than $35,000, or $50,000 for couples, and who were covered by employer-sponsored pension plans. The bill also slashed the contributions that workers were allowed to make annually to their tax-deferred 401(k) savings plans from $30,000 to $7,000.

To get the flatter income tax structure they desired, then, Republicans had to sacrifice some of their other long-term goals, such as moving workers toward greater reliance on private saving for retirement and less on benefits like Social Security.

For the mainstream media, however, including the *Washington Post* and the *New York Times*, with their perennial desire to reassure the public that the System worked, the new tax law was one of the Reagan administration's great achievements and, like the 1983 Amendments, a sterling example of what bipartisanship could achieve. For the first time, it gave Washington a legitimate claim to have cut the deficit. It raised $20 billion in new revenues in its first year. That, and a strong economy in 1987, caused the shortfall to drop from $221 billion to $150 billion, providing a bit of relief from the demands of the deficit hawks.[3]

By the time the president signed it into law, however, the 1986 midterm election campaigns were in full swing and both the Republicans and Democrats were scrambling to take credit for this major piece of legislation. Social Security gave the Democrats the edge, just as it had in 1982. Thanks largely to their second attempt in four years to cut COLAs, the Republicans lost control of the Senate, shedding eight seats along with five in the House. Many of the lawmakers who had joined Dole in his leap into the void on behalf of fiscal probity were paying the price.

But the budget deficit, despite the Tax Reform Act, was still expected to hit $137.5 billion in fiscal 1988, $29.5 billion over the Gramm-Rudman target. At a White House meeting on November 6, 1987, two weeks before the trigger date for mandatory spending cuts kicked in, Domenici pleaded with the president to back a solution based on limiting Social Security COLAs. Democratic Reps. Leon Panetta and William Gray, the House Budget Committee chair, were supporting the idea of a three-month postponement of COLA increases for all programs, including Social Security, as was Oregon's Bob Packwood in the Senate. A few days later, for the second time in two years, Reagan reportedly told Republican congressional leaders he would accept some form of COLA reduction as part of a deficit-reduction package. But the next day the White House backed off, denying he had done so.[4] What followed was an agonizing three weeks of negotiations aimed at meeting the magic $23 billion mark, mostly focused on the possibility of a COLA cut.

Save Our Social Security conducted a weekend poll that found 76% of voters opposed to any cut in the COLA scheduled for January 1. Meanwhile, the National Committee to Preserve Social Security and Medicare, an advocacy group that James Roosevelt, FDR's son, had founded in 1982, collected 1 million signatures on a petition against cutting COLAs and delivered them to each of their respective congressional offices. Three days before the Gramm-Rudman deadline, Rep. Tom Foley of Washington, the new House majority leader, said flatly, "It's off the table."

Conservatives and radical centrists attached to the idea of restructuring Social Security were most disappointed because the latest deficit-cutting exercise was effectively Ronald Reagan's last chance to throw his popularity and leverage over lawmakers into the cause. And he had "blinked."

* * *

The early months of the 1988 presidential election were dominated by candidates who focused on deficit reduction and some form of radical restructuring of Social Security. By the time the primaries were over, however, these candidates had all been eliminated and the emerging Democratic and Republican nominees either opposed cutbacks or were extremely cagey about the idea.

For the first time, Social Security privatization had a voice on the presidential campaign trail—in fact, two. Pete du Pont, yachtsman and scion of one of America's wealthiest family business dynasties, former Delaware governor and U.S. representative, in late 1986 unveiled a plan for "Financial Security Accounts," to which workers could contribute an amount equal to their Social Security payroll tax contributions each year. They would also receive an income tax reduction to go along with it. Once they retired, though, their Social Security benefits would be reduced as well. Pat Robertson, the televangelist whose presidential candidacy was pulling large numbers of Christian fundamentalists into national political consciousness, had been advocating private accounts since at least 1981.

But with Robertson, it could get strange. "By the year 2000," he explained in an appearance on PBS's *Firing Line*, "we will have aborted 40 million children in this country. Their work product by the year 2020 will amount to $1.4 trillion, the taxes from them would amount to $330 billion, and they could ensure the fiscal stability of the Social Security system." Afterward, even conservative columnist Charles Krauthammer was stunned. "As an argument against abortion (of which there are many)," he wrote, "this reasoning is loony enough. Coming through Robertson's fixed Jonathan Winters grin, it causes a chill."[5]

By the time the Republican convention rolled around that summer, however, du Pont and Robertson were gone and the nominee was the person the party leadership had anointed more or less from the beginning: Vice President George H.W. Bush.

The Democratic Party had been agonizing over its position on Social Security, and much else, since Reagan trounced Mondale in 1984. Three months later, the radical center created an organizational identity of its own when a group of conservative and centrist Democrats, mostly southerners, including Rep. Al Gore, Jr. of Tennessee; former Gov. Charles Robb of Virginia; and Robert Strauss, fundraiser and former Democratic National Committee chair, founded the Democratic Leadership Council (DLC). The real leader of the group was Al From, departing executive director of the House Democratic Caucus, who worried that the party was losing its appeal to middle-class American voters and had to revamp its positions to regain its base. From the start, balancing the budget and scaling back Social Security were among the DLC's highest profile issues.

It never was able to claim a mass movement. The group's chronicler, Kenneth S. Baer, calls the New Democrats and their flagship organization "a faction of elites," an affinity group of politicians out to convince the public that their policy positions were correct even though the Democratic Party continued to be dominated by the "interest groups" the DLC despised: labor, teachers, and public employees, among others. The dilemma they would face, on Social Security as well as other issues, would be "to change a public philosophy without the benefit of a realigning event and without a mass or activist base."[6]

After its first year, however, the DLC began to attract major sponsorship from corporations, Wall Street banks, and affluent individual donors. By the end of the decade, it was pulling in $2.2 million a year.[7] In 1988, it created its own version of right-wing ideology factories like the Heritage Foundation when it founded the Progressive Policy Institute (PPI), whose godfather was hedge fund baron Michael Steinhardt. The PPI started life with a bankroll of $1.2 million and a non-partisan, non-profit status that kept it officially separate from the DLC.[8]

One prominent DLC member was former Arizona Gov. Bruce Babbitt, the first Democrat to lay the groundwork for a 1988 presidential run. As early as the summer of 1986, he was traveling Iowa to make himself known. Billing himself as a truth-teller, Babbitt made Social Security one of his key issues. He advocated requiring upper-income Americans to pay higher taxes on their benefits from the program—for individuals, on everything they earn over $25,000, and for couples, on everything over $32,000—money he would invest in programs aimed at the poor.

But the candidate who seemed to have the approval of the party leadership was Massachusetts Gov. Michael Dukakis, a stranger to the DLC. Dukakis avoided Social Security for the most part during the primaries. While he called for fiscal responsibility, with a suggestion of a freeze in military spending, he didn't rule out new taxes, even after he took the nomination.

Both Bush and Dukakis, in fact, stressed the need for budget discipline. Even on points where they seemed to disagree, few government insiders expected the differences to extend into practice. Robert Strauss, DLC member and co-chair of the new National Economic Commission (NEC) that Dole had engineered to look for ways to eliminate the deficit, discounted the fact that Bush was swearing adamantly that he wouldn't raise taxes as president. "I know George Bush," Strauss said, "and I know he knows better."[9]

* * *

As soon as Dukakis went down in defeat on November 8, sunk by Reagan's coattails and Bush's faithful clinging to the outgoing president's public positions, his rival was overwhelmed with admonitions to do the right thing. A pattern seemed to be forming under Gramm-Rudman whereby Congress and the White House played a game of chicken until the date approached that would trigger automatic cuts, at which point the key players would finally sit down to talk.

At the end of the following October, after months of frustrating budget haggles, the administration was forced to move up its borrowing schedule so that Social Security checks could continue to go out on time. But nothing gelled until just before the Thanksgiving holiday, when the White House and Congress finally agreed on a deficit-cutting bill that relied, as many lawmakers had expected it would from the start, on $8 billion in thinly disguised tax increases.

Knocked out of the bill was a provision to liberalize the earnings limit for Social Security recipients that had earlier made its way back in. Also eliminated was a proposal to make the SSA a separate agency, which ran into solid opposition from the White House and HHS. Tacked on when the reconciliation bill was nearing completion, however, was another obscure change, one that Rostenkowski had volunteered during the summer. Retirement account income would now be added into the income calculation for payroll tax assessment. Under the formula Congress adopted, that meant the tax would now be levied on the first $51,300 each worker earned instead of the previous $50,400. That pulled in another $400 million a year in extra revenues. It also added about $60 a year to the Social Security taxes of 8.5 million high-income individuals.

The Pain Caucus had for the first time, if only modestly, got their way. Upper-income recipients would have to pay more for their Social Security. But the new Bush administration was encountering pressure not just from the deficit hawks but from a group of upstart conservative Republicans led by House minority whip Newt Gingrich. Ardent supply-siders, they opposed such backdoor measures even to relieve the deficit, and pushed instead for a large tax cut as their preferred way to revive the economy. In December 1989, they found an unlikely ally in Pat Moynihan.

Just before jetting off on a trip to Africa, Moynihan made headlines when he called a press conference to announce that he would shortly propose a drastic cutback in payroll taxes. Moynihan attacked the "thievery" of the Bush administration in using the Social Security surplus, now $52 billion, to partially obscure the federal deficit from view. But he also criticized the regressive nature of the payroll tax, which he said "the elevator man and the man who owns the building" pay at the same rate.

Moynihan was calling for cancellation of the last phase of the payroll tax hikes mandated by the 1983 Amendments, from 7.51% to 7.65%, which was scheduled to go into effect January 1, then dropping it to 6.55% in 1991, and for the existing surplus to be used to help pay off the national debt. The result would be a $62 billion tax cut over two years. He also renewed his call for legislation to prohibit the use of the Social Security trust fund assets to calculate the overall federal deficit. The net effect would be elimination of the big trust fund that the 1983 Amendments had aimed to build up to pay for the baby boomers' retirement, making Social Security once again a pure pay-as-you-go program.

The reaction was just the kind of befuddlement and scrambling of normal political boundaries that Moynihan had delighted in provoking throughout his political career. The Heritage Foundation, Cato, the National Taxpayers Union, and the U.S. Chamber of Commerce all praised his proposals.[10] Democratic leaders feared that removing $62 billion from the federal budget books would require raising an enormous amount of revenue immediately to meet the Gramm-Rudman targets—probably through a tax increase for which they would be blamed.

No one felt more embarrassment over the Moynihan proposal than the president, however. After avoiding the issue in public for days, the administration finally let Chief of Staff John Sununu speak about it on *Face the Nation* on January 7. First, he accused Moynihan of attempting to "undo" what the senator himself had accomplished as a member of the Greenspan commission. Second, he suggested that cutting payroll taxes might force the government to cut Social Security benefits as well—at what point, he didn't say.

In March, Moynihan; his former aide Mike McCurry, now press secretary of the Democratic National Committee; and Ron Brown, DNC chair, managed to get the DNC to endorse the payroll tax cut. McCurry also worked to get the DLC to back it. But by April, Democratic congressional leaders including Rostenkowki and Senators Lloyd Bentsen and Bill Bradley were signaling plainly that they had had enough. In early May, Moynihan's proposal was voted down in the Senate Budget Committee. Moynihan would keep pushing his idea for the rest of the year, but it was now essentially dead.

* * *

Bush was still determined to push through a capital gains tax cut, which he insisted was vital to knocking the economy out of the doldrums. But his window of opportunity was narrowing, because the deficit was again on the rise.

In late January Bush sent Congress a $1.2 trillion budget that would reduce the deficit by $37 billion, including $13.9 billion in new revenues and federal fees. On Capitol Hill, Ways and Means chief Rostenkowski had even greater ambitions. In March, he countered with a budget that would reduce the deficit by $55 billion through a combination of increased taxes, especially on high-bracket payers, and reduced federal spending—including a one-year suspension of Social Security COLAs that he calculated would yield $60 billion in savings over three years.

Generational equity advocates rejoiced that COLAs were back on the chopping block—and that a Democrat had put them there. "Social Security's Days as a Sacred Cow Are Numbered," proclaimed a headline in *Business*

Week, under which reporter Howard Gleckman denounced, in typical zero-sum fashion, the vise-like grip seniors had achieved over federal spending.

By early May, the House had passed Rostenkowski's bill and the Senate had its own proposed budget together, this one calling for steeper domestic and military spending cuts than the House or the president's plan. Complicating matters, however, was the fact that 1990 was the year that foes of the earnings limits on Social Security recipients had decided to make a concerted push to get the restriction repealed entirely. Illinois Republican Rep. Dennis Hastert found 226 co-sponsors for a repeal bill for people over 65, 8 more than the House rules said was needed to bring a measure out of committee and onto the floor for a vote. But Rostenkowski wouldn't let the legislation out of Ways and Means.

His motivation was simple. Repeal of the earnings limit would eliminate $26 billion in tax revenue over three years, crippling the deficit reduction plan he was trying to achieve. And on the face of it, his critics had some clear and highly populist complaints about earnings rules. In 1990, the limits were $9,360 for seniors between age sixty-five and sixty-nine; over that amount, for every $3 a retiree earned, she lost $1 in Social Security benefits. For those aged sixty-two to sixty-six, the limit was $6,840, over which the retiree lost $1 in benefits for every $2 she earned. The earnings tax expired at age seventy.

But how onerous was the earnings limit, really? "Contrary to calculated myth," wrote Rep. Andy Jacobs, the Indiana Democrat who headed the Subcommittee on Social Security, "there is nothing in the Social Security law that prohibits a senior citizen from working full time. There is and always has been something in the Social Security law that prohibits a senior citizen from working full time and pretending to be retired." The real beneficiaries of repeal, Jacobs wrote in a letter to the *Wall Street Journal*, would be "those senior professional and business people who have already chosen continued six-figure incomes instead of, say, $12,000 Social Security benefits," and who "would suddenly hit a big Social Security Lotto—without ever having purchased a ticket."[11]

Even without repeal of the earnings limit, however, the revenue numbers looked grim enough to make deficit cutting especially difficult in 1990. Accordingly, Social Security and other entitlements remained in the negotiators' sights. One possibility, not of recent vintage, that House and Senate negotiators were reportedly discussing was to lower or eliminate the current income thresholds above which benefits were subject to tax: $25,000 for single taxpayers and $32,000 for couples. Another was to keep the current thresholds but raise the taxable percentage of benefits from 50% to as much as 85%. Repeal of the earnings limit quickly went into the reject bin. Despite heavy conservative support for the measure, it was just too costly.

Finally, in late October, just days before the midterm elections, Congress was able to pass a bill constructed around a $41 billion deficit reduction. Bush had still not obtained the reduction he wanted in the capital gains tax rate, which the new law held at 28%. The Alternative Minimum Tax that wealthy individuals paid, already boosted to 21% as part of the 1986 tax reform, was raised again to 24%. The limit on income subject to the Medicare payroll tax was raised even further than in the previous bill, from a $53,400 income to $125,000. Even with that, the impact on most middle-class households was modest. A family that earned $36,000 would end up with $290 less, for example, a reduction of 8/10th of a percent of its income.[12]

Over five years, however, the bill was expected to yield almost $100 billion in savings from a Medicare tax hike that was henceforth indexed to wage increases. The rest of the savings came from other programs—not including Social Security benefits, which were untouched.

The deficit hawks, once again, were bitter at Washington's failure to rein in the big entitlement. "The great untold story of this year's budget debate is that it represents yet another step in turning the national government into a gigantic machine for taxing workers to support retirees," *Washington Post* and *Newsweek* columnist Robert J. Samuelson fulminated.[13]

But one Democratic lawmaker felt moved to answered back to the geezer-bashing in general and Samuelson's column in particular.

"I am distressed by the growing insistence of writers in *The Post* to pit the young against the old in our national budget debate," wrote Rep. Mary Rose Oakar, an Ohio Democrat. "Thirty-one percent of Americans over 65 live on less than $10,000 per year," she pointed out. "An even greater number are near poor. Two-thirds of these citizens are women, most of whom live alone. Only 20 percent of women over 65 have any source of income other than an average $511 per month Social Security check."

The vaunted Gray Lobby had failed to protect Medicare, which had been cut by $30 billion over the past nine years, Oakar pointed out. Defending Social Security against COLA cuts wasn't the same as asking for an increase in benefits: only for those benefits not to be eroded. And while spending on children lagged, Oakar noted, "The children of our nation have suffered, not at the hands of their elders but at the hands of Reagan/Bush economic priorities and a 100 percent growth in defense spending."[14]

* * *

Getting nowhere with Social Security meant that to achieve deficit reduction, the president was forced to renounce his "Read my lips" pledge and sign a budget that raised income taxes, increased the Medicare contribution, boosted the Alternative Minimum Tax—and enraged the Republican Young Turks. It didn't do much to halt the deficit's rise, either. In January, estimates of the budget shortfall for the current fiscal year were up $50 billion, to somewhere between $300 billion and $350 billion—not counting another $30 billion projected to pay for deploying U.S. troops in the Persian Gulf in case a crisis over Iraq's invasion and occupation of Kuwait turned into a full-scale war. By fall 1991, however, the "Bush recession" was starting to abate, although only technically. Most working Americans could still feel the effects. Right-wing

TV commentator Pat Buchanan announced an upstart challenge to Bush's renomination in December, proposing a cut in Social Security taxes as well as capital gains taxes along with his signature pleas for an end to immigration and a return to "Judeo-Christian values."[15]

Once again, however, the candidates attracting the most media attention in the early months of primaries were those with strong reputations as deficit hawks. Amongst the Democrats, former Massachusetts Sen. Paul Tsongas and Nebraska Sen. Bob Kerrey were both promoting entitlement reform. Gov. Bill Clinton of Arkansas, who had served as chair of the Democratic Leadership Council the previous two years and was a vocal supporter of overhauling welfare, at first appeared to be cut from the same cloth. Tsongas called his supporters "economic patriots" and agitated, like Bush, for a capital gains tax cut to encourage long-term investment.

Clinton had been conspicuously groomed as the DLC's standard-bearer in the race, and he promised, initially, to be just the kind of candidate the radical centrists had hoped for. His presidency would mean "no more something for nothing," he said.[16] But then Tsongas won in New Hampshire and went on to victories in Utah, Maryland, and Washington, making him the frontrunner, along with Clinton. Going into the March 10 Florida primary, Clinton picked the most obvious weapon to hand, attacking Tsongas for proposing a higher gas tax—and for teaming up with Dole on his 1985 vote to freeze COLAs for Social Security.

Tsongas retorted by calling Clinton a "pander bear" and informing him, "You're not going to pander your way into the White House as long as I'm around. What the Democratic Party needs and what America needs is more courageous lions and less pander bears in the zoo." The analogy didn't catch on with voters, but Clinton's television commercials exposing the unpleasant side of the "courageous lions"—especially for Social Security, in a state with a large elderly population—helped win him the Florida primary.[17]

The wild card in the race was H. Ross Perot, a supersalesperson from Texas who had made a fortune in the 1960s selling computer database services to federal agencies, including the SSA, as founder of Electronic Data Systems. The Perot campaign's early success in the polls and at getting its candidate on the ballot was fueled by disgust at traditional politics and the failure of establishment politicians to address people's real concerns. But Perot's platform, which he seemed to be improvising as he went along, was anything but populist.

Perot made deficit-cutting the centerpiece of his appeal, calling the budget shortfall "arterial bleeding" and inveighing against the nation's habit of robbing its own children to pay for entitlements. Part of his solution was to cut $20 billion annually from the federal budget by taking Medicare and Social Security benefits away from the wealthy. Yet by some calculations, to achieve that kind of savings, the definition of "wealthy" would have to be stretched to embrace anyone with income above $60,000 a year.

The elderly—those who didn't count themselves among the affluent—were going to be one of the pivotal constituencies in the race, and the Clinton and Bush campaigns in particular were falling over themselves trying not to offend them. The outcome of the race would depend on which candidate could convince retirees he was capable of resisting the increasingly insistent demands of bankers, the bond market, and "responsible" lawmakers and pundits that entitlements would have to be sacrificed to deficit cutting.

In August, Perot revealed the details of his economic plan in hopes that it would influence the debate between Bush and Clinton. Instead of taxing 50% of benefits for retirees earning $25,000 a year—$32,000 for couples—they would be taxed on a sliding scale rising to 85% of benefits for high-income households. The change would raise an estimated $30 billion in revenues over five years, Perot's team said.

The Bush campaign, preparing for the Republican convention in Houston, wasn't jumping into the tax-the-affluent conga line, instead calling for cuts in all entitlements except Social Security. Clinton, meanwhile, accused Bush every chance he got of secretly planning to slash Social Security.

By early November, the economic policy divide between the candidates boiled down to the differences between Bush's cautious package of health care tax credits and Clinton's more ambitious plan to create a national health care system. This he was selling, in part, as a way to cut overall entitlement spending by folding Medicaid into the new program. Mostly, though, what the Washington press corps saw were two candidates who had flunked the test of "seriousness" by failing to address the deficit—and, especially, entitlements.

Something had to be done to make the people see reason, and Rudman, together with Tsongas and Pete Peterson, spent the summer formulating a campaign to educate them about the deficit. Launched in September in the like-named Massachusetts town, as the Bush-Clinton race was hitting its most intense phase, the Concord Coalition came wrapped in a marketing pitch that connected deficit-fighting with patriotism and the American Revolutionary tradition of communities pulling together to meet a common threat. Its founders also emphasized the present generation of workers' obligation to the future. "Every newborn baby starts out with a debt of over $50,000, because he or she will owe that much more in taxes than he or she will ever receive in government benefits," Rudman and Tsongas proclaimed in the Concord Coalition's initial statement.

Armed with a well-heeled group of patrons, the coalition began signing members up for $25 minimum, for which they received a newsletter, suggestions for organizing activities, and research reports. The group claimed to have received over 50,000 calls on its toll-free number after just a month in operation and was targeting 250,000 sign-ups within a year. The idea was for each new member to spawn others, with the goal of influencing elections if not running candidates of its own. Kitty Kurth, a former Tsongas campaign director in Illinois who was the Concord Coalition's national field director, told the *Washington Post* that it

wanted to set up organizations in every congressional district. "We want to create the social climate so politicians feel comfortable making choices," she said.[18]

* * *

Clinton took 43% of the popular vote on November 3 against 37.4% for
Bush and 18.9% for Perot. While some observers concluded that Bush would
have won if Perot hadn't siphoned votes away from him, proving that was difficult. Both Clinton and Perot had centered their campaigns on Bush's neglect of
the economy. Of the two, Clinton was probably in better touch with the voters'
feelings, since he was less inclined to hammer on the need for deficit-cutting,
which ultimately was the major theme of Perot's campaign.

The "pandering" for which Tsongas had reviled him during the primaries
really amounted only to a mild acknowledgment that Americans were still suffering from an economic recession and, more fundamentally, the "Great Stagnation" in real wages that had begun nearly twenty years earlier.* Moynihan in
1990 worried over reports that the latest figure on real median family income
was actually $458 lower annually than in 1973.** The absence of wage growth
was the most serious problem facing Social Security, since it directly retarded
payroll tax collections. But in all the anxious talk about entitlements by Tsongas and his Concord Coalition colleagues, this point rarely came up.

Clinton's picks for his cabinet and other key posts were split between critics
and defenders of entitlements. But the former seemed to be snapping up more
and better of the openings. The new budget director was Leon Panetta, who had
been one of forty-one House Democrats supporting the abortive effort to slash
COLAs for Social Security and other federal programs in 1985. Alice Rivlin, his
deputy, was a former CBO director and also a well-known advocate of balanced
budgets. Accordingly, once he was elected, a battle broke out for the economic
soul of Bill Clinton in which the numbers favored the deficit hawks.

Clinton and his staff looked seriously at cutting Social Security COLAs, going
so far as to sound out four Republicans in the Senate and several in the House.
None would even discuss it.[19] They even asked Moynihan to look into a New
Democrat proposal to raise the retirement age, which the senator regarded as po-
litically dangerous.[20] Senate majority leader George Mitchell killed the idea at an
Oval Office meeting a week after Clinton's inauguration. "This is wrong," he said.
It would hurt people who couldn't afford the delay or the increasingly lower ben-
efits they could expect once the COLA resumed. And it wouldn't pass the Senate.

When Clinton unveiled his ambitious economic plan in February, however, it included a tax increase from 50% to 85% on Social Security benefits

---

*   The phrase was actually coined in 2010 by Edward Luce, bureau chief of the
    Financial Times ("The Crisis of Middle-Class America," *Financial Times*, July
    30, 2010).
** Steven R.Weisman, ed., *Daniel Patrick Moynihan: A Portrait in Letters of an
    American Visionary* (New York: PublicAffairs, 2010), p. 524.

above $25,000 for an individual and $32,000 for a married couple, estimated to raise a substantial $21 billion in new revenues over four years and $32 billion over five. The president's menu of initiatives to invest in people and infrastructure—a major theme of his campaign—came in at a modest $11 billion in fiscal 1994, offset by cuts in military spending. Net result: a reduction of $145 billion in the fiscal 1997 deficit.

Sold as a way to boost collections from those who could most afford it, the tax increase on Social Security benefits caused difficulties for the White House by calling attention to the complicated nature of the benefit tax itself—and to the fact that it was affecting more and more not-so-affluent workers. Created as one of the 1983 Amendments' revenue-raising gambits, the tax for each individual or couple was determined by first taking 50% of the Social Security benefit itself and adding it to the taxpayer's other income. Half of the benefit, or half of the excess over $25,000—again, $32,000 for a couple—whichever was less, would then be subject to income tax.

Clinton proposed to continue using 50% of the taxpayer's Social Security benefit to calculate her income level. But instead of paying taxes on half of that benefit or half of the excess over $25,000, she would pay it on 85%. The same rate would apply to couples, but with a $32,000 excess threshold. Most experts who studied the White House economic package concluded that the benefits tax boost was its most regressive provision. Accounting firm Price Waterhouse estimated that 70% of the burden would fall on seniors with less than $100,000 in income. Hardest hit would be retirees who continued to work. They could end up with a marginal tax rate of as much as 90% when the benefits tax boost was added to the earnings penalty for Social Security recipients.

These beneficiaries tended to be among the more affluent. The real problem was that inflation was exposing more people to the benefits tax each year. Only 10% of recipients paid taxes on their Social Security income when the tax first went into effect in 1984. By 1993, 22% were paying, and by 1998, the Congressional Joint Committee on Taxation estimated the figure would be 30%. Clearly, the tax was moving downstream, and would soon affect many people who could ill afford for it to be applied to 85% of their benefits.[21]

Within weeks, conservative advocacy groups were in full gear. But instead of preaching the need to encourage seniors to work, they took a leaf from the Democrats' own book by attempting to generate alarm amongst retirees. AARP and the National Committee to Preserve Social Security and Medicare joined in, creating an odd alliance. One proposal that wilted in the face of this opposition, sponsored by two Republican and two Democratic senators, would have cut the deficit by some $542 billion over five years—instead of Clinton's $496 billion—by replacing most of his tax cuts with program reductions including limits on Social Security COLAs above $600 a month.

If there were more "efficient" ways to turn Social Security into a means-tested program, however, the president seemed to have picked the one that was most politically astute. On May 27, Clinton's tax package squeaked through the House by a 219-213 vote, with all Republicans and 38 Democrats voting against it. The Social Security provision came through intact.

The fight to get the tax package through the Senate was equally tough, coming down to a scramble for one last vote. The search focused on Bob Kerrey, Clinton's unsuccessful opponent in the New Hampshire primary. Kerrey had objected to the economic plan earlier, saying it didn't sufficiently attack entitlements, but he had voted to send it to the conference committee anyway. On August 5, however, the day the House was scheduled to vote on the final bill, he called the president to say he was voting against it and that nothing would change his mind.

The Clintonites won Kerrey over by including one of the senator's own ideas in the bill: a bipartisan commission to recommend spending cuts, chaired by Kerrey himself. This would give him a pulpit from which he could argue for serious reductions to Social Security and other entitlements and perhaps issue recommendations to that effect. Clinton agreed to create the commission, but not to Kerrey's other demand: that its recommendations automatically become part of the president's next budget.

At 7 p.m. on August 6, Kerrey announced he was switching and would vote for the economic plan. But he first delivered a long, moralistic speech to the Senate on the entitlement theme. "My heart aches with the conclusion that I will vote yes for a bill that challenges America too little," he orated. "Get back on the high road, Mr. President.... Our fiscal problems exist because of rapid, uncontrolled growth in the programs that primarily benefit the middle class." The bill squeaked through the Senate, on a tie-breaking vote by Vice President Al Gore.[22] The Social Security benefits tax boost, in the narrower version approved by the Senate, was still included.

Some 4 million to 5 million relatively affluent seniors were slated to pay higher Social Security taxes as a result of the Clinton economic package. More would do so in later years, since the new tax threshold wasn't inflation-indexed. No federal tax-and-spending plan is all of a piece, however, and the Clinton package retained a couple of significant progressive elements. The most important was a steep increase in the Earned Income Tax Credit, putting the EITC on the way to becoming the most important anti-poverty measure since the Great Society era.[23] Clinton's insistence on raising taxes on Social Security benefits only for the most affluent could also been seen as a progressive move. Only about 22% of Social Security recipients paid any income tax at all on their benefits in 1995 and only one in eight paid tax on 50% or more of their benefits.[24]

But the economic package's sharp focus on deficit-cutting virtually guaranteed that Social Security would be targeted again in the search for budget reductions, especially given Clinton's promise to Kerrey to revisit entitlements.

CHAPTER 11

BOB KERREY
GETS HIS PULPIT

As the midterm congressional elections loomed, some lawmakers again started looking for more fundamental ways to restructure Social Security. In April, the trustees shocked Congress with their latest annual report. It projected that the trust funds would run out of money in 2029: seven years earlier than the previous year's estimate. Later that month, Dan Rostenkowski introduced a comprehensive bill aimed at balancing Social Security's books. The main provisions were a payroll tax boost for both employers and employees from 6.2% to 8.15% over thirty-eight years, beginning in 2020; moving up from 2027 to 2016 the date by which the eligibility age for full retirement benefits was scheduled to rise to sixty-seven; and a COLA reduction beginning in 2003.

The revised COLA formula would lower an average earner's take by 8.4% over fifty years and a high earner's by 20.2%. An average earner was defined as earning $20,090 a year and a high earner $60,600. Wouldn't that depress the purchasing power of future retirees? No, Rostenkowski said confidently, because wage growth over the next seventy-five years would more than offset not just inflation but the increased payroll taxes: ignoring, it seemed, the fact that real wage levels in the U.S. had been stagnant for the past two decades.

Rostenkowski also proposed requiring all state and local government workers hired after December 31 to pay Social Security taxes and participate in the program. He said his bill would restore confidence in the program and enable it to pay benefits for the next seventy-five years at least.[1]

The Ways and Means chair's bill wasn't given much chance of passing in an election year: especially after he was indicted in June for financial misconduct, a charge that led to his defeat for reelection in the fall, after which he was convicted and imprisoned. Neither did a bill proffered in July by two conservative House Democrats, Tim Penny and Marjorie Margolies-Mezvinsky. Their plan called for raising the retirement age to seventy by 2013, limiting COLA raises for all but the poor, and stopping the Social Security surpluses from being used to show a lower federal deficit.

Whatever their prospects, fiscally conservative Democrats were jumping at the chance to encourage a full-blown entitlements debate. Penny's and Margolies-Mezvinsky's bill arrived in the hopper at about the same time as one sponsored by Texas Democrat Charlie Stenholm, which would cap overall entitlement spending, limiting annual increases for Medicare, food stamps, and Social Security to an amount that would offset inflation and any increase in the number of eligible recipients.

Over time, since health care and housing costs, for example, were running ahead of inflation, the result would be a drastic decline in the value of these benefits. And the decline wouldn't be gradual. According to one congressional estimate, Stenholm's proposal would slash all entitlement spending by $150 billion in the first five years. Congress would have the choice of either cutting entitlement programs to keep spending under the cap, or raising the cap. If it failed to act, the programs would be cut automatically across the board.

Caps and automatic spending cuts were the necessary "hammer" that would compel Congress and the White House to make tough budget choices, Stenholm said. Since Washington had been able to stick with caps on discretionary spending in some other programs, he argued, "Congress has shown it can perform when we have to."[2]

But the House rejected both bills and instead passed a measure that would require review of federal programs each year if spending was higher than expected. The bill explicitly excluded Social Security from the annual reviews. It passed 316-107, attracting some Republican supporters along the way: but not before some GOP lawmakers took the opportunity to accuse the Democratic sponsors of plotting to raise payroll taxes to pay for other benefits. "The lesson is, as always, don't touch Social Security," a House Democratic leadership aide told the *Washington Times*. The whole debate, the aide said, was "mostly to protect Social Security votes."[3]

Rostenkowski, Stenholm, and their colleagues had sought to stimulate debate on COLA cuts and other such devices even though they hadn't much chance of winning other lawmakers to their side in an election year. But they continued to hope for some kind of bipartisan convergence almost until Election Day. In early October, the House voted on a rule sponsored by Democratic Rep. Bill Orton of Utah with the support of the party leadership that would launch debate on a series of nonbinding resolutions to limit entitlements by means-testing them for middle- and upper-income people.

The rule went down to defeat, 339 to 83, with most Democrats rushing to join Republicans in opposition. Even the latter were incredulous that their opponents would jeopardize their ace-in-the-hole, Social Security, during a tight midterm election. "We are talking about a sense of Congress, which means you go out there and get shot and you don't even get any chance of rewards," since no actual spending cuts would be involved, said Florida Rep. Porter Goss.[4]

By this time, however, the president's Bipartisan Commission on Entitlement and Tax Reform—or the Kerrey commission, as it quickly became known, with Rostenkowski himself as a member—had already spent months discussing a wide range of entitlement measures. Bob Kerrey said later that he hadn't insisted on a quid pro quo the previous year, when he agreed to vote for the president's economic package and Clinton in turn announced that he would appoint a commission on entitlements.[5] Rather, the Nebraskan had only said he would serve as chair if the president wanted him to. In any case, Clinton named the thirty-two-member panel in early February, vowing it would "grapple with real issues of entitlement reforms, not caps or gimmicks that defer hard choices, but specific and constructive proposals."

But Kerrey, who had been tutored on budget policy by two of the most fiscally conservative members of the Senate, Domenici and the Georgia Democrat Sam Nunn, was a passionate believer in the urgency of cutting middle-class entitlements. He and Sen. John Danforth, the Missouri Republican who was his vice-chair, set as their objective holding the federal budget deficit to its current share of GDP—2.3%—through 2030. They proposed to accomplish this entirely through cuts in entitlements and some tax increases. That left out a vast swath of government expenditures, most noticeably the defense budget, meaning that the poor and aged would disproportionately bear the burden of this exercise in fiscal austerity.

Not on the commission's agenda at all were any unintended ill effects of cutting entitlements, such as lost economic activity generated by poorer seniors or increased expenses that their families might face to support them. "The underlying theme," writes Jill Quadagno, a Florida State University sociologist who was on the Kerrey commission staff, "was that programs of social provision were budgetary problems to be resolved by budgetary mechanisms, and the relevant measures for judging their merit were fiscal responsibility and cost containment."[6] With this narrow definition guiding it, much of what the commission did or didn't conclude in its reports was preordained, regardless of who served on the panel and what their political proclivities were.

The commission was scheduled to turn in its final report and recommendations in early December, so its conclusions wouldn't become an issue in 1994 electoral campaigns. The chair and vice-chair set a ground rule early on that 60% of the members must agree for any recommendation to "pass," effectively preventing the Democratic commissioners from passing a report over the heads of the Republicans. But the Kerrey-Danforth commission would be directed in a far more top-down manner than the Greenspan commission. Kerrey and Danforth appointed the staff and directed their work. The commission itself only met three times.

To frame the issue and strengthen their case with the public—and their fellow commissioners—the chair and vice-chair first produced an Interim Report. The slickly produced publication, released August 8, was as much as 50% graphics and only 50% loosely spaced text, diced into easy-to-read soundbites. Pete Peterson, a commission member, and the Concord Coalition had a great deal of input with the staff, says Eric Kingson, a Social Security scholar then at Boston College who served as a staff member on both the Greenspan and Kerrey commissions. But Kingson and Quadagno weren't allowed to introduce much of any data or perspective from the opposite viewpoint. Peterson's latest attack on entitlement spending, *Facing Up*,[7] was "a bible to some of the staff members," Quadagno remembers.

The report itself consisted of seven "findings," which boiled down to balancing "entitlement promises"—Social Security and Medicare—with "the funds available to pay for them" and raising national savings "substantially." Unless this was done, the report concluded, payroll taxes would have to rise from the current 12.4% level to more than 16.5% by 2030 to make up the difference. It arrived at these figures by meshing a number of economic projections drawn from previously issued government documents, including from the CBO, the White House's annual Budget Outlook report, and the Social Security and Medicare trustees' reports. But it presented its nightmare vision not as projection but as unalterable fact: what was bound to happen unless Congress took active steps to change the laws and improve its behavior. The result was more a position paper than a balanced assessment of the evidence.

There were three problems with the report's findings. First, they ignored other, equally valid numbers that would have provided a very different perspective on the magnitude of the entitlements "problem." Second, they isolated the statistics on the growth of entitlements and the decline in saving from the wider picture of the federal budget and the U.S. economy, implying that there were no other possible culprits behind the rising deficits. Third, they drew a dubious connection between the growth rates of Medicare and Medicaid to give an exaggerated forecast of the growth in health care entitlements.

Nevertheless, newspapers across the country ran front-page articles, and network news programs assembled major segments on the upcoming fiscal crisis brought about by out-of-control entitlement spending. One participant who tried to keep track says he noted the report being cited "thousands of times."[8] Its dramatic line graphs quickly popped up in congressional budget debates as well. On the other hand, seniors' groups launched some 350,000 postcards at the commission protesting its attack on Social Security.[9] At a commission meeting in September—the first following the release of the Interim Report—a packed chamber in the Capitol heard speakers representing government employees, retired military personnel, older women, and the disabled urge the panel not to go after their programs.

* * *

Later that month, Senate majority leader George Mitchell declared dead for that session of Congress a massive national health care measure that the White House had been working on for more than a year. The reverberations from the Health Security Act's defeat would continue for years as health care financial reform became toxic in Washington and the Clinton administration ceased pursuing such ambitious schemes. But the Republicans weren't content to let their rivals hang themselves.

The younger, more ideological members who rallied to minority whip Newt Gingrich were determined to turn the upcoming election into a referendum on a radical new program of sweeping tax cuts. Three days before Mitchell buried the Clinton health plan, Gingrich and Dick Armey unveiled the "Contract with America," which they described as "a detailed agenda for national renewal, a written commitment with no fine print."

Signed by all but two incumbent House Republicans and all of the party's candidates for Democratic seats, the purpose of the Contract was to "transform the way Congress works." Over the first 100 days of the next Congress, Gingrich and his allies vowed to deliver eight bills to the House floor that would bring about "the end of government that is too big, too intrusive, and too easy with the public's money."

The Contract consisted of two parts: a series of eight changes in the House rules and ten bills ranging from tax cuts to welfare restrictions and new savings accounts. Politically, however, the shrewdest aspect of the Contract may have been the way it approached Social Security. The year before, Republicans had attempted to win points with the elderly by attacking Clinton's tax boost for higher-income retirees. Sensing an opportunity to deflect the inevitable Democratic charge that they were planning to gut Social Security, Gingrich and Armey took up this issue again. Unmentioned in the Contract was anything like slowing the growth of benefits or carving private accounts out of the system, ideas that Gingrich himself had been among the first to put in legislative form in the 1980s.

But how would they pay for their tax cuts and the proposed $60 billion increase in defense spending, not to mention comply with the Balanced Budget Amendment they intended to pass? "If they say they're not doing Social Security, then you're talking about scalding Medicare and agriculture," among other things, OMB director Leon Panetta said at a briefing for reporters the day before the Republican pledge was officially unveiled.

Congressional Democrats followed up with a $750,000 television advertising campaign attacking the Contract with America as a threat to Social Security. But as election day approached, this didn't seem to be enough to forestall what looked to be big Republican gains in Congress. In a *Wall Street Journal/ NBC News* telephone survey of registered voters, 40% said they preferred the Republican candidate for Congress in their district versus 37% for the Democrat. On Social Security, voters trusted Democrats best, 32% to 27%. But the Republicans came out ahead on two hot issues: crime and taxes. Arguably, too, the administration had disenchanted its own supporters with its failure to produce either tax relief for the middle class or health care reform.

The "Republican Revolution" at the voting booth on November 8 changed the balance of power in American politics more firmly than any election in sixty years. Some 9 million votes shifted into the Republican camp that fall—a record. The Democrats lost 54 seats in the House, leaving them with 204 against a Republican majority of 230. In the Senate, the Republicans picked up nine seats, giving them a four-member majority—comfortable, although not the sixty-seat supermajority they would need to override a Clinton veto.

The president would still have a lot of room to maneuver on Capitol Hill, but for the first time since Harry Truman, a comparatively liberal president would be forced to work with a resolutely conservative Congress, euphoric and brimming with ideas for remaking the federal government's economic role. "Social Security, essentially a check writing operation, should go to the Treasury," the *Wall Street Journal's* George Melloan suggested.[10]

Gingrich and his allies had been too shrewd to mention any such thing in the Contract with America, however, and the Democrats were ready to jump on any attempt to do so. "Of all the dead issues," a White House aide said of Social Security cuts, "that's the deadest."[11]

So, it seemed, was Bob Kerrey's project to remake Social Security. A week before the Kerrey-Danforth commission was to hold its last meeting, the chair and vice-chair went public with their own package of entitlement cuts and tax hikes. The Kerrey-Danforth plan would meet its goal of holding the federal budget deficit to 2.3% of GDP through 2030, the authors declared. Only 10% of the savings would come from higher taxes, the rest through spending cuts. The principal Social Security-related items included:

- Gradually raising to seventy the eligibility age for Medicare and for full Social Security benefits;

- Creating an "affluence test": essentially, a higher tax on the benefits of wealthy retirees;

- Indexing the "bend points" in Social Security's benefits schedule for inflation, defined by the CPI, instead of for average wage growth;

- Adjusting the CPI to "better reflect inflation"—i.e., to reflect a more conservative view of the growth of inflation;

- Reducing the growth of benefits for mid- to upper-income workers by adding a third bend point to the benefits calculation formula;

- Adding all state and local government workers into Social Security;

- Cutting other entitlements, including SSI, Food Stamps, and AFDC, by 10% in 2000 and limiting their growth thereafter; and

- Reducing the payroll tax by 1.5 percentage points and requiring workers to "invest that money for their family's health and retirement needs."

For the first time, a plan by two sitting U.S. senators would appropriate part of workers' payroll taxes to fund personal savings accounts and reduce Social Security benefits accordingly—and allow workers to opt out of Medicare to boot.

The benefit cuts it envisioned—from raising the retirement age, rejiggering the bend points, and adjusting the CPI—would be massive, averaging 43% per recipient, according to one later analysis.[12] Switching the basis for indexation of the bend points alone would have resulted in huge cuts. In the U.K., where the Thatcher government had done the same thing in 1980, the effect was so drastic that a 1996 study projected the country's public pension burden would decline from 4.3% of GDP in 2000 to 3.4% in 2050. This, despite the fact that Britain had an older population than the U.S.[13] Britain was on its way to offering the stingiest state-sponsored pension in Western Europe, equivalent to a nearly 50% cut over thirty to forty years.[14]

Yet, "the Chairman's mark had no distributional analysis" of the plan's effects on different populations, another commission member, Democratic Rep. John Dingell of Michigan, complained a short time later in his statement for the final commission report, although they could have supplied one.

At the commission's last meeting, after having worked the phones with some members he thought he could persuade, Kerrey acknowledged that his plan couldn't achieve the twenty-vote supermajority needed for the panel to recommend it to Congress. Thus ended the only effort Washington has yet made to balance its long-term budget, solely or almost solely through cuts in entitlements.

Plenty of people were relieved. "It's a good resolution," said Bob Ball, who had been keeping tabs through a commission staffer, when he heard it had thrown in the towel. "They did no harm."

Kerrey and Danforth nevertheless had achieved a great deal. Carving private accounts out of Social Security, a course of action that the Greenspan commission had refused even to discuss a decade earlier, was now enshrined in the final report of another prestigious government panel. "Policymaking is … about bringing public attention to a problem and giving shape to the way that problem is defined," commission staffer Kingson later concluded. "Judged in this way, I believe the Commission succeeded."[15]

CHAPTER 12

TAX CUTS AND MAGIC BULLETS

As they settled into their new leadership position in Congress in January 1995, the Republicans found themselves dealing with a more complex political environment than they had previously acknowledged. They also faced a Democratic president far more at home working the tricky interface between ideology and lawmaking than he had been upon entering office.

The centerpiece of the Republicans' legislative agenda was a constitutional amendment requiring a balanced federal budget. It quickly passed the House, 300-132, with 72 Democrats voting in favor. The same day, January 26, Clinton, in his State of the Union speech, made his famous pronouncement that "the era of big government is over." He went on to tout his soon-to-be-unveiled budget proposal—and in so doing, made clear that he was drawing a line in the sand. "My budget cuts a lot," he said, "but it protects education, veterans, Social Security, and Medicare. You should, and I hope you will." That implied opposition to the Balanced Budget Amendment, which didn't exempt Social Security.

The president's budget, dead on arrival, called for $60 billion in middle-class tax cuts along with slashing the deficit by $60 billion by cutting a total of $130 billion over five years from domestic spending outside Medicare and Social Security. The Republicans were calling for nearly $200 billion in spending cuts to help finance the $570 billion in tax cuts outlined in the Contract with America—and this before they even began to lay out a plan for balancing the budget by 2002.

Clinton's strategy was to portray his opponents as fiscally reckless and ready to sacrifice Social Security and Medicare to a tax-cut program skewed to benefit the affluent, while he was ready to embrace tax cuts—but only if they would help the people who really needed them. "The president has decided that the wisest course is to let Republicans grapple with their grand and conflicting promises, while he sits back and watches," The Economist observed.[1]

On March 2, Dole let the Balanced Budget Amendment go to a vote in the Senate. It lost, 65-35. "The tragedy is, this is the crown jewel of the Contract With America," said Phil Gramm. Dole and the other party leaders vowed to exact vengeance in the 1996 election,[2] but the public seemed to approve of the result. While 54% of respondents to a Wall Street Journal/NBC poll said they wanted Congress to set the national agenda, versus 33% favoring the president, 64% said the Democrats were right to oppose a balanced budget amendment that didn't specifically exempt Social Security.

* * *

Gingrich insisted that the amendment's defeat would make no difference. Congress would forge ahead with its plan to bring the budget into balance by 2002. In mid-March, Ways and Means passed a Republican bill cutting taxes by $630 billion over ten years. Along with a $500-a-child credit for families earning up to $200,000 a year, repeal of the Alternative Minimum Tax for corporations, capital-gains tax reductions for individuals and corporations, and a more liberal equipment write-off for small businesses, the bill fulfilled a Republican campaign pledge by repealing Clinton's 1993 Social Security benefits tax hike for high earners. Passage by the full House followed a few weeks later.

As the budget bill neared completion in June, however, the Republican leadership thought they had found another way to use Social Security as a weapon to force the White House to go along with their tax-cutting plans— one that didn't require them to explicitly endorse cuts in government benefits. In an interview with Time, Gingrich threatened that if Clinton didn't sign the bill, Congress would force a shutdown of all but essential government services, including the mailout of Social Security checks.

"He can run the parts of government that are left, or he can run no government," the speaker said. "Which of the two of us do you think worries more about the government not showing up?"[3]

Before the Republicans could go on to pass their promised tax cuts, however, each chamber would have to create its own detailed package of spending reductions and the CBO would need to certify that they would balance the budget in seven years. Then the Republicans would face the strong possibility of a Clinton veto. They responded by pushing through a complicated measure that would effectively hike Medicare payments, resulting in $270 billion in savings from the program over seven years.

Since October 1, the federal government had been operating under a continuing resolution (CR) that kept funds flowing into the departments until new budgets were signed. The CR was due to expire in mid-November. On November 13, the president held a last-ditch meeting with Republican leaders. House majority leader Dick Armey—"a big man who always wore cowboy boots and seemed to be in a constant state of agitation," as Clinton later described him—berated the president for scaring his elderly mother-in-law with statements on television about the Medicare cuts.

The meeting led nowhere.[4] The president vetoed the bill. That day, 770,000 federal employees went home on furloughs and large portions of the government shut down, just as Gingrich had hinted months before. The SSA had to furlough more than 85% of its employees.[5] Applications for Social Security stopped going out while national parks closed and veterans' benefits went unmailed. Treasury Secretary Bob Rubin borrowed $61 billion so Washington could keep making national debt payments and keep the most vital services functioning.

Gingrich and Armey had assumed the public would blame Clinton for this embarrassment, but the polls contradicted them. A *Business Week*/Harris sampling in November asked respondents if they believed along with the president that "Republicans' proposed reforms aren't being driven by a different vision of the role of the federal government" but by a desire for domestic program cuts "to pay for a big tax cut that will go to people who don't need it." Fully 62% agreed.

Almost as soon as the shutdown began, Gingrich was backpedaling. Within twenty-four hours, he offered to push through some bills to fund such popular functions as processing Social Security applications. Here, however, the congressional leaders couldn't seem to get their signals straight. Senate Republicans wouldn't go along with these temporary measures, preferring to make a stopgap deal with Clinton that would end the shutdown.

One big deadline was looming for both sides: December 1, when the next round of Social Security payments were scheduled to go out to 42 million recipients. Dreading the certain fury were checks not to hit the mail, the White House and congressional leaders reached a handshake deal shortly before the end of the month to work together for a balanced budget in seven years, whereupon Congress passed another CR temporarily restoring funding to the government. The checks went out.

But when the mid-December expiration of the new CR came without a deal, the Republicans decided to let the government shut down again. This time some 500,000 federal employees were allowed to work for free until a deal could be struck. Social Security payments kept going out, although veterans' benefits and other payments halted. The shutdown lasted through the holidays, ending on January 2 when Dole, Gingrich, and Armey acknowledged defeat and made a deal to send additional "clean" CRs to Clinton that restored most government services without any Republican pet measures attached.

The second partial federal government shutdown in two months had damaged the Republican insurgents far more than it had the White House. Clinton, in his weekly radio address on January 3, noted that many vital programs were already out of money or close to it, including Medicaid. Programs that helped the elderly were heavily affected. In Dallas, the veterans' hospital was unable to pay its suppliers. In Omaha, the Eastern Nebraska Office on Aging, which delivered some 1,300 meals a day to elderly shut-ins, said it was likely to close 34 senior centers. And in San Francisco, the Social Security office was unable to process requests for new Social Security numbers and replacement cards even though it was still taking care of claims and mailing out benefit checks on schedule.

None of this was helping Gingrich and his allies to make their case that they could run the country better than the president. Why, after a year in control of Congress, had so many of the Republicans' big plans come to nothing?

The principal problem was that the Republicans had picked the wrong time to attempt to move their agenda forward. Republicans preferred to think that Americans' attachment to Social Security, Medicare, Medicaid, the EITC, and other low- and middle-income economic lifelines was a habit they could be weaned away from. But the party now in control of Congress missed the fact that the elderly, and their children, had good reason to be afraid that they were losing ground in the mid-1990s. Half a dozen years of a sluggish economy had started to erode many of the income gains the elderly had made since the 1960s, when Social Security benefits became more generous and Medicare was established.

Gingrich's revolutionaries were playing with fire, and it showed in the negative polls that dogged their tax and spending initiatives throughout the year they had expected to upend Washington.

* * *

New Democrats who castigated the president for not leaping to support the Republicans' budget-balancing measures may have been unaware of the extent to which the White House was searching for a compromise. For a time during the summer and fall of 1995, Clinton's economic advisors thought they had found the magic bullet: the consumer price index (CPI), the yardstick that determines, among other things, the annual rate of increase in Social Security benefits.

The problem that vexed critics of Social Security, as Butler and Germanis had noted a decade earlier in their "Leninist" paper for Cato, was that the only politically feasible way to cut benefits was to hold current retirees and near-retirees harmless. But that would mean slashing benefits for future generations so deeply as to reduce the program to insignificance.

The CPI, the standard measure of inflation in the U.S. economy, seemed to offer a way out of this dilemma. Produced and updated monthly by the Bureau of Labor Statistics (BLS), it quantifies the cost of a representative basket of some 80,000 goods and services consumed by urban Americans. Surveys of an additional 40,000 landlords and tenants and 20,000 homeowners blend housing costs into the mix. Rural Americans are excluded because their urban counterparts make up about 80% of the total population.

The BLS's job is to determine whether the monetary value of each item in the basket has changed from month to month and whether any of the current menu of items should be moved out while others are moved in. A lower CPI is what the Federal Reserve seeks to achieve through its efforts to regulate the money supply in the U.S.; a higher CPI means higher Social Security payments and generally greater pressure on Washington to cut spending so as not to aggravate inflation.[6]

If the CPI could be found to overstate inflation, correcting it would lift a great deal of pressure from both the Fed and the White House. The economy would appear to be doing better—maybe for a considerable period of time—and workers to have more purchasing power. The Fed could achieve the same monetary policy goals with, arguably, much less severe interest rate adjustments. The president's budget advisors would have more leeway to cut taxes, increase other domestic spending or leave it untouched, because the rate of increase in Social Security payments would be smaller and—since tax brackets are also adjusted for inflation—tax collections would increase. Reductions in current retirees' benefits, otherwise politically unthinkable, could be disguised as technical adjustments in the CPI.

In 1995, the advantages were obvious. Smaller Social Security payments would mean more money left in the trust funds to help cover the federal deficit. That meant the seven-year budget gap could be closed with less painful measures than the Republicans were proposing, bringing a budget compromise that much closer.

Conservative economists had been calling for downward revision of the CPI for years, in part because this would tend to cast a more positive light on workers' economic situation during the nearly decade-and-a-half since the Reagan tax cuts took effect. It would also furnish a seemingly blameless way to advocate Social Security cuts. In 1994, the CBO calculated that a .5% cut in the CPI would shave $25 billion a year from Social Security payments over five years. As far back as the early 1980s, when he chaired Reagan's Council of Economic Advisors, Martin Feldstein proposed indexing benefits under the program at a rate set somewhat below the CPI.[7] This would gradually lower the rate of increase, resulting over time in benefits that rose much more slowly than inflation.

Feldstein's idea didn't catch on, but economists over the following decade began developing arguments to justify a "downward adjustment" in the CPI. Four major points cropped up repeatedly:

- The CPI doesn't account for changes in behavior—for example, when a rise in the price of one product prompts people to consume more of another one instead. If they're consuming less beef, shouldn't beef be weighted less heavily in the BLS's "basket"? How about when consumers substitute generic for brand-name drugs or shop more often at bargain stores like Wal-Mart?

- The CPI has a hard time capturing improvements in the quality of a product over time. Arguably, these improvements are the equivalent of a drop in the product's price.

- The BLS performs the consumption surveys that establish the "basket" only every ten years or so—a lifetime in the cycle of product introductions and substitutions—although it does rotate some items in and out of the sample each month.[8]

- Price increases mask some wider improvements that work in the consumer's favor. For example, the CPI captures increases in the cost of automobiles—but doesn't account for the improvements in quality of life when car companies produce cars that pollute less.[9]

A 1994 *Business Week* article noted, for example, that the CPI had personal computers representing less than 1% of household purchases: possibly too low a figure, but understandable given that it had been more than ten years since the last complete "scrubbing" of the index. That year, Congress gave the Labor Department $50 million for research and development work on the CPI: among other things, to recalculate the "basket."[10]

By the time the Kerrey-Danforth commission was wrapping up its work, the notion that the CPI was "overstated" had become close to conventional wisdom in Washington circles. So Kerrey and Danforth's own set of proposals included adjusting the CPI to "better reflect inflation."[11]

In January 1995, while lawmakers and the White House were digesting Kerrey's final report, Alan Greenspan lent his considerable public stature to the cause, testifying before the House and Senate Budget Committees that the CPI may overstate inflation by "perhaps .5%–1.5% per year." Lowering the index 1% over the next five years could save the government $150 billion in payouts to Social Security recipients and others receiving COLAs from federal programs, he calculated.[12]

Gingrich and other Republican leaders, delighted that the Fed chair had bolstered the legitimacy of the idea, went into a flurry of activity on CPI during their first couple of months in control of Congress. Noting that the BLS review of the index wasn't scheduled to be completed until 1998, the House Appropriations Committee voted on March 2 to include non-binding language in its package of fiscal 1995 spending rescissions stating that the "BLS must redouble and accelerate its efforts to produce a more accurate CPI."

Prepared by Illinois Republican John Edward Porter, the text originally went on to say that the committee "will review these efforts in making decisions on [the bureau's] funding for fiscal 1996." Another committee member, Democrat David Obey of Wisconsin, accused the Republicans of attempting to "intimidate" the BLS, whereupon they removed the additional language. Gingrich and his staff had worked closely with Porter and committee chair Bob Livingston of Louisiana on the resolution, despite the party leadership's unspoken decision not to bring up Social Security directly that year. At one point, Gingrich reportedly threatened that the BLS would be "zeroed out in 30 days" if it didn't make the CPI changes.[13]

Neither was the president biting. At least not at first. Noting that the CPI was already under review, Clinton said bluntly, "I would have to be absolutely persuaded that there was a rock-solid case on the merits because, otherwise, it's just going to look like a bunch of politicians tried to keep their promises by cutting people's Social Security and raising people's taxes."[14]

In June, Congress named its own five-member commission of economists, headed by former Bush aide Michael Boskin, to investigate the CPI. To call the panel stacked would have been an understatement. Every member had previously testified before Congress that the index substantially overstated inflation.[15]

Complicating the debate for both parties, but most vexingly for the Republicans, was the fact that estimates of how much or how little the CPI may have been overstated seemed to be built on quicksand. Greenspan had told Congress that the index exaggerated inflation by .5% to 1.5% a year. The CBO found a much narrower bias: .2% to .8%. Researchers at the Dallas Fed concluded that while "a figure of less than 1 percent ... strikes us as a plausible estimate of the overall [upward] bias" in the CPI, "the true figure may be a lot larger or a lot smaller; at present, we simply do not know."[16]

Others questioned whether applying the same index to the entire U.S. population, in all its diversity, really made sense. A BLS study, issued after the CPI controversy had ended but reflecting concerns that were already in the air, found that price increases for the elderly might exceed the CPI by .2% to .3% per year since their consumption patterns were quite different from the working population's. Economist Trudi J. Renwick, who specialized in poverty studies, found that the CPI had understated the cost of living for a household at or below the poverty line by 50% to 100% since 1993.[17]

Getting it right wasn't easy, given all the variables involved. Politicians, however, were going ahead as if the BLS existed to make their case. The multi-year budget resolution that House Republicans passed in April was built on the assumption that the CPI would rise less rapidly. There was only one problem: modeling the impact of a CPI shift on current and future retirees was relatively easy—and the numbers yielded were ugly. When David Certner, an economist at AARP, analyzed the effect of CPI changes on elder benefits, he found that it wasn't dismissable. A mere .5% reduction, for example, would cost the average Social Security recipient $2,700 over ten years, or $7 a month: a modest but noticeable amount for retired persons whose other income, if they had any, wasn't indexed to inflation.[18]

Another expert, Bruce Schobel, vice president and actuary at New York Life Insurance Company and formerly an actuary with the SSA, found the losses could be even greater the more years were added in. For *Money* magazine, Schobel calculated the impact of shaving a percentage point from the CPI. Using the inflation rates projected in the Social Security trustees' 1996 annual report, he found that for a couple receiving a combined $18,720 a year, their cumulative loss after ten years would be $9,858. By 2010, they would be out $25,786— and this at a time when their medical costs would likely be rising fast.[19]

Congressional zeal to balance the budget—or at least, appear to do so— trumped such considerations. In September, the Boskin panel released an interim report finding that the index overstated inflation by between .7% and 2%, ending with an "interim best estimate" that the overstatement was about 1%. That spurred members of the Senate Finance Committee to introduce a proposal calling for the CPI to be adjusted down. The adjustment would generate deficit reductions of as much as $281 billion over seven years, they noted, including over $101 billion from Social Security. That would considerably ease the task of balancing the budget and decrease pressure on other programs such as Medicare, which the committee was still trying to cut.

This time the Republican members had a powerful Democratic ally, Pat Moynihan. Always searching, in his inimitable way, for a position that would confound the usual ideological lines between the parties, Moynihan saw the CPI adjustment as a way to pull off a statesmanesque masterstroke. This despite his longtime political identification as a defender of Social Security, which had led him to emphatically reject a one-year COLA freeze when Clinton suggested it two years before.[20]

"Here is a real bipartisan opportunity," he said now. "I hope we don't miss an historic moment." When Dole made some statements encouraging discussion, Moynihan reportedly was on the phone like a shot to Council of Economic Advisors chair Joseph Stiglitz. "Get the President to call Bob Dole— fast!" he urged. Sen. William Roth of Delaware, who had taken over as Finance Committee chair after Bob Packwood resigned over sexual harassment charges, also backed the "notion" of adjusting the CPI.[21]

As usual, no one was willing to take a major step without knowing in advance the White House's response. But the president's aides surprised some in Congress by not rejecting the idea as Clinton had done in the spring. The administration was "discussing it internally," said Gene Sperling, head of the National Economic Council. "We are open to reviewing this further."[22]

That fall, the arguments for and against—but mostly for—a downward adjustment of the CPI flew thick and fast, peppering academic journals, popular business magazines, and the bulletins of the Beltway economic think tanks. What kept the debate alive in the capital, however, was the increasingly plain fact that the great bipartisan crusade for budget balancing couldn't succeed without a magic bullet. "Without a change to the CPI," declared the *Wall Street Journal's* David Wessel, "which could reduce projected Social Security spending and raise tax receipts as much as $140 billion over seven years, the two sides may fail to achieve their balanced budget goal." The alternative, passing legislation that would explicitly call for setting Social Security benefits by some amount less than the CPI, was too politically risky for either party to contemplate.

Seemingly every political figure with nothing directly to lose was pushing the same argument. The executive committee of the National Governors' Association, which included both conservatives like Republican John Engler of Michigan and liberals like Howard Dean, Democrat of Vermont, issued a resolution urging Congress to "adopt a CPI that accurately reflects the real rate of inflation."[23]

In December, the BLS panel, appointed the year before to examine the CPI, came out with its report, and the bureau announced a series of changes to the index formula based on its recommendations. The alterations would shave between one- and three-tenths of a percentage point, beginning in 1997. White House economists said the rejiggering would save some $32 billion in Social Security payments over seven years and announced that the new formula would be factored into the president's next budget. "That won't suffice," Wessel at the *Wall Street Journal* wrote. More aggressive changes were needed if the CPI was to play its assigned role in budget balancing.

Boskin's panel provided the required answer in January when it released another interim report, concluding that the CPI overstates inflation by 1% or even 2%. Moynihan, the commission's political godfather, hailed the findings in a *Washington Post* op-ed, noting, "If we were to do no more than declare that henceforth the cost of living adjustment will be the CPI minus one percentage point, we would save $634 billion over the next ten years."[24] In May, Bob Kerrey offered an amendment to a Senate budget resolution that would have adjusted the CPI downward. It was rejected, 63-36.

Curiously, the wind by now had largely gone out of the revisionistas' sails. Not everyone in Washington thought a downward reformulation was such a good idea. Some conservatives, like Republican Rep. Christopher Cox of California, didn't want to see the tax revenue increases that Boskin's CPI changes would trigger, even if they helped to balance the budget. Rep. David McIntosh, Republican of Indiana, went so far as to call the reformulation "a hidden tax increase on the middle class."[25] On the Democratic-leaning side, AARP and the AFL-CIO both lined up against a CPI revision for their own rather different reasons. And minority leader Dick Gephardt of Missouri was vocally opposing the move in the House.

This was crucial. CPI revision, like anything else affecting either Social Security or taxes, required political cover—or, in Washingtonspeak, the willingness of both parties to jump off the cliff arm-in-arm. As the presidential election year of 1996 got under way, Gephardt's stubborn refusal to pull the

House Democrats into line made it less and less likely that the White House would publicly endorse a change. Earlier, after months of urging by Moynihan as well as careful internal consideration, the administration had come close to endorsing a downward CPI revision beyond the one the BLS had already decided to make. But at a contentious White House meeting at which Clinton and Moynihan tried to argue him around to supporting the change, Gephardt stood his ground and refused. Soon afterward, sensing that CPI revision wasn't the political masterstroke he had taken it for, Moynihan lost interest and stopped pressing the issue.[26]

The Boskin panel was still working away, however. It released its final report in early December, concluding that the CPI overstated inflation by a substantial 1.1% annually. Its recommendations for how to deal with the "problem" were geared to hardwire this analysis into the government's future policy orientation and focus both Congress and the BLS on efforts to rejigger the index downward. Along with some suggestions of how to improve the bureau's data gathering, it recommended that the BLS make ongoing top-to-bottom revisions of the CPI instead of just once a decade and that it create and transition to a new index that would better reflect consumers' substitution of cheaper goods for more expensive ones. Congress should take the index partially out of the agency's hands by creating a rotating "independent committee or commission" that could "advise" the BLS on the "appropriate interpretation" of its own statistics.

The commission also advised Congress and the president that they "must decide whether they wish to continue the widespread overindexing of various federal spending programs and features of the tax code." If not, they must "pass legislation adjusting indexing provisions accordingly."[27]

Treasury Secretary Rubin left the door open for a deal on the issue, telling *Meet the Press*, "I don't think that we should rule out a change in the CPI if, based on technical analysis, there is a broad-based agreement that the CPI can be changed in such a way as to better and more accurately reflect inflation." But any deal would have to be bipartisan, and without Gephardt on board, that wasn't possible. By this time, too, Clinton had been reelected, the deficit numbers were improving, and Democrats were, in general, less convinced that balancing the budget was something that had to be done in as short a time as five years.

* * *

Outside the halls of Congress, the notion didn't die easily that the government could take a short cut to a balanced budget by way of CPI manipulation. Journalists and think-tank denizens continued to speak of a CPI "overstatement" as if the notion was accepted by all informed people.[28] Two things are striking about this: first, how little inclined the revisionistas were to look at the effects of a CPI change on seniors and other vulnerable populations, even though these could be quite severe; second, how speculative the arguments for CPI revision were and how studiously its advocates ignored equally valid positions on the other side. All in the hope that they had found a magic bullet—or, at least, "a fig leaf" to cover efforts to slow the growth of Social Security and Medicare, as one Boskin commissioner, Harvard economist Zvi Griliches, admitted to *Money*.[29]

The problem, some economists wrote at the time—although the mainstream press largely ignored them—was that the revisionistas' arguments were based primarily on anecdote. For example, the high-tech goods included in the basket: The Boskin commission "cites VCRs, televisions, microwave ovens and PCs as hallmark examples," noted Jim Klumpner, chief minority economist of the U.S. Senate Budget Committee, in an article for the journal of the National Association of Business Economists. However, "non-auto consumer durables account for only 4.2 percent of the expenditure weights in the CPI. House furnishings, which can hardly be said to show rapid increases in quality, account for 3.5 percent of spending, leaving only 0.7 percent of monthly expenditures for the whiz-bang stuff. This very low weight stems not from low prices for these items but from the fact that they are infrequently purchased."[30]

The revisionistas also argued that the index understated the effect of large discount "box stores" on prices. But, as economist Dean Baker pointed out, for all their power in the consumer economy, Wal-Mart and other discount chains could sell, at best, only 15% of total goods: mainly clothing, appliances, and household furniture. And even if the box stores dropped prices in these categories fully 10%, Baker calculated, the effect on the CPI would be just .015% a year. Boskin attached a .2% figure to the "bias" from ignoring discount stores.

Whatever the degree of overstatement, there was also evidence that the CPI understated some ingredients in the inflation mix—though Boskin and other revisionistas ignored these factors. For instance, the CPI didn't count most increases in insurance premiums for individual health plans or hikes in deductibles and copayments for plans that employers purchase. Crime was another factor, Baker noted. The CPI didn't reflect the extra money people needed to spend to live in a safe neighborhood or the cost of joining a private gym because public facilities were closed or had been allowed to deteriorate.

Some observers criticized the revisionistas on more fundamental grounds. One of Boskin's major arguments for the CPI being overstated was that it didn't account for substitutions—for example, of chicken for beef when beef became too expensive. But was the one really equivalent to the other? The argument seemed to imply a double standard, one for the haves and one for the have-nots. On the other side of the coin were the revisionistas' "improvements" and "innovations"—changes in style or additions of bells and whistles that made products more expensive but that many consumers may not even have wanted. "The Boskin Commission would treat owning Windows 6.0 as an increase in my well-being," economic journalist Jeff Madrick pointed out, "especially since prices dropped. But I consider it an additional cost of simply standing still."[31]

Adjusting the CPI downward would have changed more than just the future trajectory of Social Security benefits and the federal budget: it would have changed the past. Amazingly, the Philadelphia Fed's 1995 paper on the issue found that "if the CPI is revised down 1 percent annually, the post-1975 decline in real wages disappears."[32] That would be good news for conservatives eager to prove that the last twenty years of increasingly conservative economic policy were a success, but it would contradict the perceived experience of millions of Americans who were feeling the policy's effects.

A revised CPI that rewrote the last twenty years of economic history would have had an even more powerful effect if the analysis was extended an additional two decades. "If incomes have grown much faster in order to reach their current level, it means that families were much poorer, say, thirty years ago, than we generally realized," Baker noted. "According to my calculations, more than half of the nation's families may have been below the current poverty level as recently as 1962."

Looking further into the future, the people could be on their way to unheard-of prosperity. "Applying some estimates of the size of the bias in the CPI to the Social Security Administration's wage projections implies that the average annual wage will exceed $80,000 by 2030 (in 1996 dollars)," said Baker.[33] That, in a final irony, would obviate the need for cuts in Social Security, because incomes would be rising rapidly enough to ensure that a shortfall never occured.

The Boskin commission failed to prove that the impact of upward pressure on the CPI was very substantial, Baker concluded, however much lawmakers of both parties wanted to believe it. Whatever "bias" did exist, he predicted, "will be reduced further in the near future as BLS implements changes in procedures based on research findings." Boskin's drastic measures were unnecessary.

But the last word on the CPI-as-budget-balancer had, perhaps, been spoken more than a year before Boskin's final report came out and had less to do with the nitty-gritty of the debate than with the objectives of the revisionistas themselves. The pundit in this case wasn't a liberal like Baker, but Herb Stein, the much-quoted economist who had headed the Council of Economic Advisors under Nixon and was now ensconced at the American Enterprise Institute. Stating what should have been obvious, Stein noted that the CPI is merely an inflation gauge, not an index of the "true" cost of living that can tell us precisely how "well off" we are.

Theoretically, other and better yardsticks might yet be created that could determine more precisely how fast or slow Social Security benefits should rise. But until then, defects in the CPI shouldn't be made a pretext for lowering those benefits. That decision, Stein said, should be made straightforwardly, based on whether or not Congress felt—politically—they should be lower.[34] There was, in other words, no magic bullet.

PART III

Selling Privatization

(1994–96)

CHAPTER 13

"JUST ABOUT UNANIMOUS"

A lot had changed for the movement against Social Security. In April 1994, while the Kerrey-Danforth commission was still meeting, a new Advisory Council on Social Security held its first session. Unlike such bodies in the past, this one included members who were open enemies of the program, determined to use the occasion to press major changes on it. In November, voters elected a new Congress whose leaders were ideologically predisposed against Social Security and other entitlements. The following May, the first major legislation to drastically cut benefits in exchange for those private-account carve-outs was introduced in Congress. A spate of similar bills was about to follow.

Suddenly, Social Security privatization seemed not just possible but, perhaps, the lynchpin of the political strategy the conservative movement had been following since the late 1960s. That strategy aimed at making white working-class voters the drivers of a new, long-term Republican ascendancy.

During the 1980s and early 1990s, the dominant voices in the movement against Social Security were the deficit hawks, personified by Pete Peterson, with his dour demeanor and gloomy exhortations to fiscal austerity. They had succeeded in winning over to their views much of the Washington elite—including the upper reaches of the national media; affluent, serious-minded donors; and politicians concerned with burnishing their reputations as statespeople—but they held little appeal for the average middle-class voter or the young but upwardly mobile, who saw in their relentless deficit-cutting prescriptions only pain and not much gain for themselves.

What the conservative movement needed, and what it achieved in the 1990s, was a vast widening of the *kulturkampf* against Social Security. The hoped-for end result of this populist effort would be a grassroots movement demanding that the people's elected officials save them from baby-bust bankruptcy by giving their payroll taxes back to them in the form of private investment accounts. In the new decade, the anti-Social Security forces would learn to present a sunnier side of themselves, attempting to catch the fancy of the nation's "new" middle class, who counted—or aspired to count—much more of their net worth in the form of mutual funds and securities holdings than in wages and salaries.

When pollster and political consultant Frank Luntz memoed Republican lawmakers shortly before the new Republican Congress was seated, he challenged them to "create 'The New America,' the post-welfare state vision as powerful to Americans as the New Deal was 60 years ago."

To accomplish it, Luntz wrote, would take "precision and repetition." "Only … when you've described an irresistible future to the American public—will the nation support you and your agenda unconditionally." Just as important, he stressed, was to talk about the challenges the Republicans wanted Americans to embrace: "irresponsible debt, runaway spending, destructive welfare and an anti-saving tax code." They must discuss them "in moral—as well as economic—terms." The voters must see these issues as a matter of "wrong values," not just bad policy.[1]

"A movement is stirring to reshape the nation's most untouchable federal program: Social Security," the *Wall Street Journal* announced in May. "With bankruptcy looming fairly early in the next century, the debate over changes boils down to two questions: How soon and how much?"[2] The *National Journal* alerted its readers six months later that "conservatives in both parties, libertarians and business interests are gearing up for the mother of all entitlement battles: a fundamental overhaul of Social Security."[3]

* * *

The first step in creating a new piece of conventional wisdom is simple: assert that it's true. If you can do this in a major media outlet, the battle is nearly half-won.

Despite losing ground to cable television and the Internet, *Time* remained one of the top-selling magazines in the U.S. in the mid-1990s. When it chose to feature a major policy issue on its cover, often what followed inside would be the general public's first relatively in-depth discussion of the topic. *Time's* coverage could still, when it chose to address a serious subject in serious language, play a big part in molding the way the public approached that topic.

The cover story of the March 20, 1995 issue was headlined "Social Insecurity" and its cover copy was even starker: "The Case for Killing Social Security." The piece announced its thesis up front: "Though it's anathema to most politicians to say so, among the scholars and policy analysts who study the budget charts and chew their nails in suspense as the baby boomers inch toward later life, the verdict is just about unanimous: as Social Security nears its 60th birthday, it is ripe for retirement."

Summarizing the thinking of the "scholars and policy analysts" they relied upon, the story's authors, George J. Church and Richard Lacayo, concluded that most Americans "would be better assured of a financially secure old age by a two-tier system." That system would include a guaranteed safety net "for those who really need it"—in other words, a means-tested, welfare-type system—plus a second part "funded through mandatory private savings."

The authorities cited in the article were a collection of the program's most prominent critics, including Sens. Alan Simpson and Bob Kerrey; Milton Friedman; Dan Mitchell, a Heritage Foundation analyst; and Pete Peterson. Only two unequivocal critics of privatization were cited in the article. One, Richard Trumka of the United Mine Workers, was there to point out that raising the retirement age might not be fair to older blue-collar workers, many of whom had jobs that were too physically demanding to allow them to keep working past sixty-five. The other, John Rother, legislative director of the AARP, was on hand to admit that in the future, benefits might have to be lowered and payroll taxes raised somewhat to keep Social Security solvent. But the authors didn't explore the implications of Trumka's point any further and included none of Rother's or the AARP's detailed thinking about the program.

"Just about unanimous" was perhaps the key phrase in *Time's* take on Social Security, however, assuring the magazine's readers that the experts basically agreed that the new, private accounts-based model was the way it had to be and that anyone who disagreed or sidestepped the issue was somehow dishonest or behind the curve. Arguing for ending COLAs, for example, the article asked, "Why should Social Security pensioners alone be fully protected" when private-sector pensions were not? "Political clout, and no other reason."

This made no sense, other than to set up an antagonism that didn't exist. With private-sector pensions declining, polls showed that working people were more than thankful they at least had Social Security to count on. Having access to defenders of the program like Trumka and Rother, the magazine could easily have set this straight.

But if *Time* in this case did a poor job of reporting the different sides of a major public policy debate, it succeeded in packaging for easy public consumption an important new piece of conventional wisdom. The beauty of the new master narrative about Social Security was that it dovetailed perfectly with the widely accepted conservative rhetoric framing the collapse of the Soviet empire after the fall of the Berlin Wall in 1989—that it was one more element in the unstoppable triumph of the new neoliberal economic consensus.

In the domestic counterpart to that triumph, class conflict would come to an end when Social Security privatization engendered a new culture of saving and investment. "More Americans may well assume attitudes formerly confined to a thin stratum of creditors at the top," Ron Chernow, a journalist and author of a popular history, *The House of Morgan*, wrote in 1993 in the *Wall Street Journal*. Since more and more Americans would come to see themselves as investors, or creditors, rather than debtors, "The see-saw battle that has historically raged between debtors, who favor inflation, and creditors, who like hard money, will tilt more toward the latter."[4]

Cato, Heritage, and other boosters launched a series of arguments that painted Social Security privatization as the free lunch to end all free lunches: a kind of financial cornucopia that required absolutely no redistribution of wealth from haves to have-nots. Women would benefit because a personal nest egg is better, more secure, and more consistent with the needs of the modern family, which was more likely to be headed by a woman than in the past. African-Americans would be better off, because they suffered worse mortality rates than white people. Private accounts would be with the black worker and her heirs even if she died too early to collect much—or any—of her earned benefits.

Best of all, younger workers wouldn't have to depend on a Social Security system that, by some people's perspective, robbed them of a great deal of money in payroll taxes but paid out a relatively meager benefit. Even the baby boomers, contemplating their own retirement early in the next century, could feel better that they wouldn't be enjoying their leisure years at the expense of their children and grandchildren. As for the government itself, while it would be giving up a huge chunk of the payroll taxes that helped cover its chronic deficits, it would also be sloughing off a huge obligation in later years—and probably expanding its net revenues in the near term as well, since the economic boom sparked by the new private accounts would boost its tax receipts.

There were, of course, other, less drastic ways to address the retirement-related worries of each of these groups. What made the privatization argument so powerful was that it promised to solve all of those headaches at once. This encircled it with an aura of 360-degree optimism that could be quite seductive. And while it had its critics—many, in fact—by early 1995 it was creating a sense that significant change was inevitable for Social Security, and sooner rather than later.

Even some of the program's most stalwart supporters suddenly were softening their language and speaking as if they would soon have to negotiate with the other side. "We sense our members are willing to accept some modifications," a spokesperson for the National Committee to Preserve Social Security and Medicare said, cryptically. "The time is now," said Moynihan, still busily engaged in his campaign to reshape the CPI. "The Republicans and Democrats are both at fault, in my judgment, in saying that certain things are off the table." He declined, however, to be specific about what those "certain things" might be.

* * *

Introduction of a full-fledged privatization plan in Congress was the breakthrough that legitimized all of these currents and anointed them as a major political trend. Until 1995, even lawmakers who supported the idea were too timid to put their names to a bill. Bob Kerrey and Alan Simpson were always among the least cautious, however, and they broke the ice in May when they introduced an ambitious package of eight bills proposing a complete overhaul of Social Security.

The legislation combined Kerrey and Danforth's proposals from their entitlement commission's final report in January with some new elements, notably allowing workers to partially withdraw from Social Security if they wanted to. It also proposed permanent changes to the CPI and new rules for federal budgeting aimed at keeping entitlements from ever again growing to be such a significant portion of Washington spending.

The savings, its sponsors predicted, would be nearly $1 trillion over the next decade. As the first major legislation in almost fifty years to propose cutting Social Security down to size, the Kerrey-Simpson package called for:

- Reducing federal civil service pensions;

- Reducing military pensions;

- Setting up a commission to study and recommend ways to make the CPI more "accurate." To ensure that the job got done, all adjustments based on the CPI—such as for OASI and DI benefits—would be automatically reduced by a half percentage point until the panel submitted its report;

- Permanent COLA reduction for Social Security as well as civil service and military pension recipients who placed in the 30th percentile— those, in other words, who had earned the most money in their working careers. Instead, they would get a flat dollar amount equal to the COLA received by those at the lowest end of the 30th percentile;

- A requirement that Congress and the White House compute thirty-year projections of the impact of their budgets. The president would also have to include a generational accounting calculation, measuring lifetime net tax rates, in the administration's budget each year;

- Gradually raising the retirement age to seventy. After 2030, the normal retirement age and the age of eligibility for early retirement benefits would go up by one month every two years;

- An option for workers to divert 2% of their 6.2% payroll tax into "I.R.A.-type" personal investment accounts, in exchange for a reduction in the benefit they would receive from Social Security; and

- Investment of Social Security trust fund assets in corporate stock rather than Treasury bonds.

The Kerrey-Simpson plan would not only reduce benefits all round; it went a great distance toward fulfilling the two major criteria that privatization advocates had long insisted were necessary to "reform" any social insurance system: separating out the saving and the poverty-reduction aspects of the program, and means-testing the latter. "Social insurance in which one generation of retirees consumes the next generation's taxes will simply not hold up," the two senators wrote in an op-ed piece. The purpose of their proposals was to "transform what is now a consumption-based system into a system that encourages savings and investment."[5]

Kerrey-Simpson wasn't the first privatization measure to be introduced in Congress—Gingrich had preceded them with one, nine years earlier—but it was the first that sparked serious discussion. No one gave it an immediate chance of enactment, but it easily passed the first test that any bill must if it is ever to become viable. The Senate Finance Committee scheduled hearings on the proposal. "A preliminary, closed-door airing before the committee, according to committee members, drew few objections," the *Wall Street Journal* reported.[6] Moynihan was a member of the Finance panel. Meanwhile, another Democrat, Rep. Bill Orton of Utah, was getting ready to introduce a House version of the Kerrey-Simpson package.

To balance out the pain their plan would otherwise cause the next generation of retirees, the two senators held out the vision of a new "culture of saving" in America. The eight bills were "a first step toward enabling people in the workforce to acquire the wealth they need to satisfy their retirement requirements," Kerrey said.

The Kerrey-Simpson plan promised to give people who had once depended on government real financial independence, perhaps for the first time in their lives—perhaps for the first time in their families' history. OASDI, by contrast, "puts them in a position where their retirement income is dependent on Congress's willingness to keep the law the way it is. That doesn't provide social security, that provides social insecurity."[7]

In one interview, Kerrey spoke about the seemingly limitless possibilities for expanding upon his initial set of ideas if they were accepted. "I would prefer to let individuals with income up to $10,000 a year put as much a full 12% into their own retirement savings," he said. "We would have a sliding scale, down to 2% for people making $60,000. I would be able to say to an audience that they might make only $10,000 to $15,000 a year over the course of their entire working lives, yet they would be millionaires when they retired."

How anyone making only $10,000 annually would be able to put 12% of his or her income off-limits for any purpose, let alone retirement, Kerrey didn't say, and it's doubtful that many people believed such wild forecasting. But the presentation he chose to give his scheme was a new departure for Social Security critics. Rather than stressing the need for sacrifice and fiscal austerity—although these elements were also part of his proposals, and had been the centerpiece of his fiscal philosophy for years—Kerrey determinedly emphasized the positive.

Any objection that his scheme might somehow be robbing Peter to pay Paul, Kerrey flicked away with missionary zeal. Suppose employers cut back on their offerings of 401(k) plans, since workers would now have an independent means of saving for retirement? "Once employees discover the power of compound interest and making small contributions over a long period of time," he declared, "they're going to want to do more" and their employers will rise to the occasion.

Would other lawmakers follow Kerrey and Simpson's lead? Dallas Salisbury, president of the Employee Benefit Research Institute and a shrewd Washington observer, didn't like the senators' chances in the immediate future. Despite the collapse of the Clinton health care proposals, Medicare still faced the more urgent fiscal problems, he noted. Social Security's troubles wouldn't become immediate until some time between 2005 and 2013, giving Congress plenty of time to address them. What Kerrey and Simpson had achieved, however, was to make the issue less radioactive in Congress, especially for Democrats.[8]

"It no longer means political death to suggest alterations in Social Security," *Pension Management*, a newsweekly for pension plan executives, proclaimed. Following Kerrey-Simpson, also in 1995, Gingrich encouraged Rep. Jim Kolbe, an Arizona Republican, and Rep. Charlie Stenholm, a Texas Democrat—both regarded as centrist budget hawks—to form a Public Pension Reform Caucus in the House. Its first event, a dinner lecture on the privatization of Chile's public pension system, drew almost forty lawmakers.

Kolbe's goal was "to have people talking about it, thinking about it," he said, "and to prove to members that you can talk about this without dying."[9] By the end of the year, Steve Forbes, the billionaire publisher and a supply-side disciple of Jude Wanniski, had declared his candidacy for the Republican presidential nomination, calling for younger workers to be allowed to put their payroll tax contributions into individual accounts instead of the Social Security trust funds.

CHAPTER 14

PRIVATIZATION REPACKAGED

Magazines like *Time* and politicians like Simpson and Kerrey would have had a much harder time making Social Security privatization a hot topic if it hadn't dovetailed with a major new marketing push by the financial services industry to persuade working households to become investors. The mid-1990s saw an outpouring of books, articles, op-eds, advertising and promotional material, websites, and television and radio commentary urging Americans to save and invest more for what they "knew" would be a future without Social Security. The return of virtue, thrift, the family, bourgeois values, the centrality of property, what have you, wasn't merely something to be desired anymore, so the story line ran. It was an inevitability.

Don't count on the politicians "saving" Social Security yet again once the young get the message, *U.S. News & World Report* cautioned in early 1995: "Social Security has been called the 'third rail' of American politics—fatal to those who touch it. But for younger workers, it might be called the fright at the end of the tunnel."[1] As for the boomers, *Wall Street Journal* columnist Tim Ferguson warned that they would feel "seduced and abandoned" if they didn't do something about their "insidious failure" to save and invest for retirement as if Social Security didn't exist.

Medical Economics, a financial magazine for physicians, was advising its well-heeled readers to get real about a retirement program on a slippery slope. "Even if you're only a decade or so away from retirement, you can't be sure how much Social Security will supplement your retirement plan," it warned. "What if you haven't yet turned 50? Forget Social Security, retirement advisers say. 'Just put as much as you can into your retirement plan,' recommends Roy Huntsman, president of Medical & Dental Management in Gainesville, Florida. 'Consider any Social Security payment you get a bonus.'"[2]

Niche-market professionals weren't the only ones receiving tailored messages about the program's demise, which were becoming a common piece of boilerplate in articles on personal finance and investment. A 1996 *Good Housekeeping* piece urged readers to look elsewhere for retirement security. "The Social Security Administration projects its trust fund will run out of money around the year 2030," the venerable women's magazine warned. "If it survives in some form, it won't provide the same generous benefits it once did; currently benefits amount to about one-third of an average worker's wages and are likely to decrease. Those doing well financially may not even qualify for benefits."

This was misleading. COLAs would keep OASI benefits at the same replacement rate unless Congress decided to reduce or eliminate them. And virtually every worker would continue to qualify for benefits—unless Congress decided to means-test them. The article also gave Peter Ferrara space to label Social Security "a rip-off for young workers" and tout his plan to let workers carve private investment accounts out of their payroll taxes. "Private savings accounts that make it possible to invest in a variety of financial instruments can produce much higher returns than Social Security," *Good Housekeeping* noted helpfully, but failed to provide space for any opposing point of view.

At least one self-appointed baby boomer advocate took up the cry, urging his cohorts to demand that seniors tighten their belts lest there be nothing left in the till when their children started to retire. The American Association of Boomers was founded in 1989 by Karen Meredith, a Dallas-area CPA, and four years later claimed a list of 26,000 persons nationwide who paid $10 a year to call themselves members—not to mention a catchy toll-free phone number, 1-800-BOOMERS. That hardly compared with the 34 million on the AARP's rolls, but the "strident but credible" Meredith, as the *Boston Globe* described her, was good at getting herself quoted—almost invariably to lambaste Social Security for undermining her generation.

"You won't get any payback from Social Security," she said in a typical conversation with a reporter. "It's a generational pyramid scheme, and it's about to collapse."[3] In 1993, she announced that her organization was going to sue the SSA for disseminating misleading financial information to the public by omitting mention of that imminent event from its publications.

There really was no trust fund, she would explain, and no cash surplus to pay for the benefits the boomers were expecting to collect, starting in the next couple of decades.

This message, repeated endlessly and often in virtually the same stock phrases by self-appointed experts like Meredith and the journalists who used her, and others like her, as sources, was simple. The baby boomers had better start saving—and fast—or they wouldn't be able to maintain their precious lifestyles in retirement. They might even turn their own children against them.

Where were they to go for advice? One of the financial press's favorite hot trends of the decade was investment clubs, a way for the less-affluent to pool their resources and make larger investments, presumably for greater profit. Investment clubs had been around for many years but had fallen out of fashion when the stock market cooled in the early 1970s. They made a comeback in the bull market of the 1990s, however; the number of clubs grew from 3,200 clubs in 1980 to 13,600 in 1995 with over 200,000 members, according to the National Association of Investors Corporation, an umbrella group.

Easily the most famous was the Beardstown Ladies, sixteen mostly elderly women from Illinois who were reported to have earned fabulous returns on their investment pool. In January 1994, *The Beardstown Ladies' Common-Sense Investment Guide* was published and sold over 100,000 hardback copies within four months. It was followed the next year by *The Beardstown Ladies' Stitch-in-Time Guide to Growing Your Nest Egg: Step-by-Step Planning for a Comfortable Financial Future*. The press loved the Ladies, who seemed to have transferred the humble, tenacious, no-nonsense attributes of the country sewing bee to the world of personal investment.

"Call it prudence or panic," reported *Publishers Weekly*, "but bookstore customers are buying more personal finance titles these days, a testament to the current consumer fascination with money. The reasons are no mystery.... In the 1990s, falling interest rates prompted savers to pull their money out of bank accounts and CDs in search of higher yields. Add to that the unique anxieties of the nervous '90s—corporate downsizing, pension fund imbroglios and widespread fears about Social Security—and you have a recipe for a far more entrepreneurial attitude toward personal finance."[4]

Workers who were more comfortable with the tools of the New Economy than with printed matter could find the help they needed too. In a report on newly issued multimedia products in May 1995, *U.S. News & World Report* mentioned—alongside the digital *All-Movie Guide* and the *Microsoft Wine Guide*—the *Quicken Financial Planner*, available for $40 in a Windows version only. "Custom retirement planning allows dozens of what-if scenarios so you can calculate what you need to save if, for example, Social Security goes bust," *U.S. News* noted helpfully.

* * *

Clearly, the long fade-out of Social Security would allow a new world to unfold, one in which working people could embrace all this newly available knowledge and use it to build wealth, not just survive. By turning the "false" savings in the Social Security trust funds into "real" investments in individual accounts, it also promised to solve another problem that obsessed Washington, the media, and the financial services industry.

According to figures derived from the National Income and Product Accounts by Sylvester Schieber of The Wyatt Company, a management consulting firm with a strong corporate pension practice, and John Shoven, holder of an economics chair at Stanford University that was funded by the head of the Charles Schwab discount brokerage firm, 1980 was approximately the starting point of a sharp national downturn in saving. Personal and business saving, plus government surpluses or minus government deficits, had averaged a stable 7% of GDP from 1951 to 1980, Schieber and Shoven found.

Since then, it had collapsed to less than 1%, they said. Personal saving, which had generally topped 5% before 1980, afterward was consistently below 4%.[5] Another study, by Merrill Lynch, calculated that the average middle-aged baby boomer earning $100,000 a year would need $653,000 in current dollars to retire "in comfort"—but that workers in this category had saved only 31% of the necessary amount. "Savings rates will have to triple," a 1995 *Wall Street Journal* article about the study concluded.

Mainstream economists worried about the long-run impact of the savings decline. Either the U.S. would be starved for investment capital and unable to maintain the long-term economic growth needed to support its population, or it would become ever more dependent on foreign capital to finance that growth. That couldn't be healthy, since international investors might decide eventually to park their assets someplace where growth prospects were greater: perhaps in China or one of the other rapidly expanding economies of East Asia.

Who was to blame for this dire situation? The same *Journal* article pinned the ribbon firmly on the most obvious target: the people. "Boomers are still dreaming big, materialistic dreams," reporter Bernard Wysocki, Jr., wrote, citing Marilyn Steinmetz, a financial planner in West Hartford, Connecticut, about the prevailing ethos: "They want everything. They had it all. They still want it all. And they want it now." Wysocki rattled off case after case of boomers living beyond their means, seemingly either blind to the dangers of debt or too terrified to do anything about it. One man, a thirty-eight-year-old laid-off Unisys engineer with a suburban Connecticut home and a Long Island beach condominium, neither of which he could afford anymore, was quoted as saying, "I can't think about the long-range future. I'd love to have a better car—a 911 Porsche Turbo."[6]

The reasons for the decline in saving probably had less to do with boomers' appetite for Porsches and beach houses than with fundamental shifts in the economy since the 1960s. The cost of education, housing, and health care—the three most important material underpinnings of the American middle class—were rising in the 1980s and accelerated in the following decade. And while the income of the top 1% of the population was shooting up, average income during that same period was stagnating.*

"No student of economics would deny the educational, character-building value of thrift," social insurance pioneer I.M. Rubinow wrote, dryly, in 1913. "But the assertion that, in the case of the wage-earning class, individual saving may solve the problem of poverty, necessarily supposes the existence of a surplus in the budget of the average wage-earner's family."[7]

Eighty years later, this remained a dubious supposition. Between 1947 and 1969—the height of a financial golden era—the income of a family in the 20th percentile of the Current Population Reports almost doubled. Between 1969 and 1991, however, the income of 20th percentile families actually fell slightly. The poverty rate was also following a new pattern, rising faster during recessions and falling more slowly during economic recoveries than it had during the postwar period.[8]

In the 1990s, real wages were entering their third decade of stagnation; automation and computerization enabled employers to produce the same output if not higher with fewer workers; and the nation's large-scale manufacturing sector continued to hollow out. In one especially scarifying period, from January 1993 to March 1994, twenty-nine U.S. companies announced the termination of at least 5,000 jobs each—major employers including General Motors, Procter & Gamble, RJR Nabisco, IBM, McDonnell Douglas, General Electric, DuPont, Phillip Morris, and Lockheed.[9] Once, jobs with these companies had represented long-term economic security to millions of people, and, in turn, an automatic step onto the fabled American ladder of upward mobility. Those days seemed to be over, and with them the financial calculations of thousands of middle- and lower middle-income families—not to mention many others whose livelihoods depended on theirs.

That left far less leeway for American households, nearly half of which were now headed by baby boomers, to put money aside, especially since those boasting two parents plus children were less able to avoid any one of the three big sets of expenses—housing, education, health care—than other demographics. At the same time, the value of real estate was rising fast, encouraging many workers to believe that buying a home was the best way for them to save.

While this huge change in American life wasn't under-reported, few journalists seemed to connect it to the decline in saving. Instead, the news in the mid-1990s was full of simple, moralistic analyses warning of the consequences of America's improvidence. "Americans should be saving like crazy," the *New York Times*'s Sylvia Nasar complained in September 1998, "or they will wind up working a lot longer than they expected because they failed to save enough

---

*   The benchmark studies on average income decline, and the reappearance of a vast gulf between top-percentile and average incomes in the U.S. since the 1970s are by Thomas Piketty and Emmanuel Saez, including "The Evolution of Top Incomes: A Historical and International Perspective," *AEA Papers and Proceedings*, Vol. 96, No. 2, May 2006.

for retirement.... Everyone agrees that middle-class, middle-aged Americans ought to be more worried about the future than they appear to be."

Nowhere in her article did Nasar note the rising cost of maintaining a middle-class household. Nor did most reports in the media on the decline in saving connect it with other problems converging around middle-class households, such as the rising cost of long-term care for the elderly.

One very conventional response to this state of affairs was that it didn't matter. Washington simply wasn't doing enough to encourage saving, many analysts said. Lloyd Bentsen, shortly after closing out his tenure as Treasury secretary during the first two years of the Clinton administration, blamed the collapse of personal savings rates for America's transformation from a creditor to a debtor economy, increasingly reliant on foreign investment. The answer was to expand the tax deductions available to savers. "From 1981 to 1986," he noted in a *Wall Street Journal* op-ed, "contributions to IRAs were fully deductible for all Americans, and IRAs accounted for one-third of the nation's net savings. After 1987, when Congress severely limited the deductibility of IRAs, the amount saved in IRAs dropped precipitously."

Karen Ferguson, director of the Pension Rights Center, a Washington-based nonprofit working on behalf of pension plan participants, responded to Bentsen's article in a letter to the editor, noting that the reason more of the 47 million American workers without pension plans weren't contributing to IRAs was because "in most cases ... they can't afford to put money aside today for retirement far in the future." According to census data, the median income of individuals without IRAs or employer-sponsored savings or pensions was $15,000; that of persons who had these assets was $44,500. "Expanded IRAs for this higher-income group will give costly tax breaks to people who are already saving for retirement": not to those who were struggling to do so, Ferguson pointed out.

Arguably, the decline in personal saving was a reason to preserve Social Security's old-age income guarantee, not gut it. And encouraging, or forcing, low- or even average-wage workers to save more without first giving them a raise could actually be dangerous to an economy dependent on consumer spending, some economists pointed out. As consumption declined, so would economic growth. But Congress, impressed by the rhetoric of the crusade to restore thrift to America and unimpressed by the credentials of a bunch of unfashionable Keynesian economists, ignored such arguments. Instead, it embarked on a series of efforts to fill perceived gaps in the availability of retirement savings vehicles to different groups of individuals.

Workers already had a bewildering tangle of these to choose from, each offering slightly different tax breaks. An older generation of money purchase, thrift, and stock bonus plans was gradually being replaced by IRAs, Keough plans, and 401(k)s, while some employers offered 457 plans (for public employees), 403(b)s (for nonprofits and hospitals), and 401(a)s (for teachers). IRAs came in four different varieties. In 1978, Congress created Simplified

Employee Pension Plans (SEPs) for small businesses, which companies were offering to as many as 1.7 million workers by 1992. The 1986 tax reform created Salary Reduction SEPs (SARSEPs), which allowed employees to have a portion of their pay directly deposited in their SEP accounts. But SARSEPs never enjoyed much popularity.[10]

Remains of the Alfred P. Murrah Federal Building in downtown Oklahoma City, shortly after the April 19, 1995 bomb attack. The Murrah Building contained a Social Security Administration district office. Victims included sixteen SSA employees and twenty-four visitors to the office. The bombers had vague ties to the militia movement, some of whom denounced Social Security.

So, in the Small Business Job Protection Act of 1996, Congress replaced SARSEPs with the Savings Incentive Match Plan for Employees (SIMPLE), in both IRA and 401(k) versions, which differed from the SARSEP in that they weren't subject to nondiscrimination rules, which key the level of contributions that higher paid employees can make to the level of contributions from lower paid workers. The following year, Congress created the Roth IRA, which flipped the traditional structure of the tax advantage for retirement savings accounts. Whereas IRAs, 401(k)s, and most other such vehicles allowed workers to contribute tax-free but required them to pay taxes on any money they withdrew from their accounts, Roth IRAs required them to pay taxes on their contributions up-front, after which they or their heirs could make withdrawals tax-free after retirement.

The result was a jumble of overlapping structures liable to give a migraine to any hard-working person forced to study all of them carefully. If the funds involved were just money the affluent would have saved anyway, even without the tax breaks, as a number of studies indicated, then U.S. taxpayers weren't getting their money's worth. One way to correct this might be for the government to offer matching grants to low-income families that wanted to save. That idea had been around at least since the Carter administration, but was not much discussed in the years when Social Security privatization was becoming sexy.

The mainstream media wasn't inclined to dwell on such problems either. Instead, media were treated to a sub-apocalyptic vision of war between the thrifty few and the profligate multitudes, with rarely a reference made to their respective income levels. Those virtuous souls who found a way to save, despite the costlier world they lived in, might become the victims of either government greed or the desperation of the spendthrift masses, suggested the *New York Times*'s Peter Passell.

"At one extreme," he wrote in July 1996, "Washington might resolve the conflict between the boomers' expectations and the nation's fiscal realities" by reneging on its Social Security and Medicare promises. "It might start by limiting benefits or raising taxes and financial penalties on those who have saved significant amounts." Or, the boomers "may gang up on the next generation of workers, heavily increasing taxes to sustain Social Security and Medicare."

"It's the retirees in the middle who are most vulnerable" to this "soak-the-prudent" approach, Syl Schieber, the Wyatt consultant, told Passell: "the people with incomes between $50,000 and $100,000." That led Schieber and Shoven to one unavoidable conclusion: Social Security must be privatized. A paper they published in 1996 laid out a partial-privatization plan under which workers could build Personal Security Accounts with a portion of their payroll taxes. Such a plan "would generate significant net savings for the economy for the long run and even more in the first thirty years or more of the program due to its maturity," Schieber and Shoven claimed. By 2043, the account balances "would likely be several $trillion [*sic*]" in 1996 dollars.

As the idea of Social Security as savings vehicle began to take hold, so did speculation about what it could mean for the financial firms that, presumably, would sell investments to the new "owners" of capital. The short answer was that it would enable them to vastly expand what was already a huge business selling investment products to "portable" pension plans like IRAs and 401(k)s.

By 1992, some $1.4 trillion was invested in these vehicles, which workers could take with them from job to job or—for a penalty—cash out. Wall Street by then was deeply engrossed in publicizing the urgent need for Americans to rediscover thrift. Otherwise, "retirees could face indigence on a scale previously unseen in the U.S.," a 1991 Merrill Lynch study proclaimed. Appearing at about the same time was a brochure advertising mutual fund and insurance products from MFS Financial Services, its cover emblazoned, "The Shocking News About Your Retirement."[11]

Baby boomers "are concerned about getting guidance about taking risks" with their assets, Jane King, a financial planner in Wellesley, Massachusetts, told *American Demographics*. "They know they have to take risks because no one else is going to take care of them." "Soothing those fears," a 1994 feature in the magazine concluded, "will create loyal, affluent customers for financial-services firms."[12]

A month after the Kerrey-Danforth commission's final report was published, an article in the *Wall Street Journal* reported on "what could be the biggest bonanza in the history of the mutual-fund industry": Social Security. The *Journal* noted that some members of the president's Social Security Advisory Council favored allowing workers to put some of their payroll tax contributions in private accounts. Simultaneously, the article reported what seemed to be a snowballing of support for privatization amongst not only mutual fund providers but mainline Wall Street firms—and from both, a feeling that the change was no longer a matter of if, but when. "There's an inevitability to this," said James Riepe, managing director of mutual fund giant T. Rowe Price. "This is a movement that will be the next tax rollback."

"Hundreds of billions of dollars could shower into fund companies and brokerage firms, the same way money gushed from pension plans into mutual funds when employers began installing retirement savings plans" like 401(k)s, the *Journal* predicted. If only two-percentage-points of workers' payroll taxes went into the private accounts, the total flowing into portfolio managers' hands could be $60 billion a year, said Robert Pozen, general counsel and managing director at Fidelity Investments, the mutual fund industry titan. Two months after the *Journal* article appeared, Pozen said he favored a two-tiered system in which people had the option of placing a chunk of their Social Security contributions with the mutual fund industry, and he intended to proselytize for such a change. "Right now we're at the beginning of the political debate," he said. "I think it's critical that the industry play a very active role in the political process."

"It's about managing money," Ann Combs, a principal at William M. Mercer, a leading pension consulting firm, commented. The current crop of individual retirement accounts "pale in comparison" to private Social Security accounts, she said.[13]

Financial services trade organizations reported to be studying the potential of Social Security privatization included the Investment Company Institute (representing mutual funds), the Securities Industry Association (brokerage firms), the American Council on Life Insurers, and the American Bankers Association. Schieber, the pension consultant at the Wyatt Company—which had recently become Watson Wyatt Worldwide—was publishing a steady stream of papers in support of privatization. Bill Shipman, principal of State Street Global Advisors, a unit of State Street Bank & Trust, a powerful custody bank, was moonlighting as co-chair of a new Cato Institute initiative called the Project on Social Security Privatization.

"Obviously, there's a lot of self-interest in there," John Brennan, president of another mutual fund giant, the Vanguard Group, said coyly of all this hustle and bustle. Significantly, Shipman's co-chair was José Pinera, a Harvard-trained economist who had created and executed a plan to privatize Chile's national pension system in 1980. A decade and a half later, the Chilean system of private retirement accounts had become a profitable venture for a small number of big financial services companies hired to provide portfolio management and administration of the accounts, among them Fidelity, Salomon Brothers, and Aetna Life & Casualty. The firms' experience in Chile encouraged them to think they could handle the burden of another $60 billion directed into their hands out of U.S. payroll taxes as well.[14]

The corporate media seemed to agree. The sensational April 1995 *Time* cover story touting Social Security privatization included a sidebar bluntly titled, "How Chile Got It Right." Holman W. Jenkins, Jr., a *Wall Street Journal* columnist and fierce spokesperson for the corporate viewpoint, projected a dazzling vision of the future in an April 1998 column celebrating the mega-merger of banking giant Citicorp and insurance behemoth Travelers, headlined, "Meet Your New Commissioners of Social Security." The new financial powerhouse, which brought together commercial banking and insurance for the first time since the two businesses were split apart by the Glass-Steagall Act in 1934, represented a new model, Jenkins argued: the "private welfare agency."

"Social Security and Medicare," Jenkins noted scornfully, "are destined to become poorhouses for those who failed to provide comfortably for themselves." The new Citigroup, with its array of financial products and its army of salespeople, could take their place.

CHAPTER 15

WALL STREET ENLISTS

Privatization advocates recognized that getting Wall Street's full-hearted support would be important, if not crucial, to their success. The 1989 edition of the Heritage Foundation's conservative policy blueprint, *Mandate for Leadership*, argued in language that reads almost like a sales pitch to the captains of Wall Street that Social Security "displaces a private array of services offered in a competitive market with a highly politicized government monopoly—in effect, socializing a large part of the nation's financial industry."

Political influence-peddling by corporate America rose during the 1970s and 1980s to levels not seen since the Gilded Age. Virtually every major public company established a political action committee and lobbying office in Washington. Generous corporate contributions transformed sleepy pressure groups like the National Association of Manufacturers and the U.S. Chamber of Commerce into formidable influence peddlers.[1] Curiously, however, until well into the 1990s the financial sector was reluctant to throw its money and influence behind the Social Security privatization movement.

Wall Street's change of mind was the by-product of a crisis it underwent in the 1970s, out of which it remade and redirected itself during the first dozen or so years after Ronald Reagan's election catalyzed the anti-Social Security forces. The industry evolved, painfully, away from a clubby business largely played out between large corporations, the institutions that bought and sold their securities, and the investment banking giants that orchestrated the deals. The "white shoe" era gave way to a new, more fiercely competitive business model that depended not so much on gigantic underwritings as on trading profits and fees generated for managing money.

This transition played out within the anti-Social Security forces as well. Wall Street's old school included financiers like Pete Peterson and Felix Rohatyn, whose opposition to the program was part-and-parcel of their belief in balanced budgets, low or no deficits, and reining in entitlements. The "privatization" movement of the 1990s, on the other hand, was championed and bankrolled by representatives of the "new" Wall Street: high-volume trading and money management operations like Merrill Lynch and State Street.

* * *

Despite their pivotal role in the U.S. economy, the broker-dealer, investment banking, and insurance companies that made up Wall Street in 1970 still inhabited an inbred world—"the Club"—in which collusion and cooperation between supposedly competing firms was at least as important a part of everyday life as were the distinct personality types and (white) ethnic identities of many of the firms themselves. Furthest from the minds of the bankers, traders, and salespeople who ran the Street was the thought that they could possibly fulfill the enormous administrative and management responsibilities that would fall to them if Social Security were privatized and the payroll contributions of 89 million workers dumped in their laps.

Change began with the traumatic year between May 1969 and May 1970, when the Dow Jones Industrial Average lost nearly one-third of its value. Volume surged, only the orders were all sells. Prolonged unprofitability led to a rash of failures as some 160 New York Stock Exchange member firms went out of business.[2] Another jolt came four years later—May Day, 1975—when the SEC abolished the system of fixed-commission rates for securities transactions. Fixed commissions had meant that any investor of any size, from a multi-billion-dollar insurance company to a retired postal worker in Duluth, paid exactly the same price to buy or sell the same share of stock.

Now, for the first time since the Depression, broker-dealers could charge investors whatever they pleased; the market would set the price. For big institutions like pension funds and endowments, this was good news. Commissions plunged from an average $0.26 a share in 1975 to $0.08 a share in 1986. Volume of shares traded surged from 7.13 billion to 65.74 billion in 1992.

Brokerage firms prospered again, their revenues rising from $8.9 billion in 1977 to $90 billion in 1992.

But with "the Club" replaced by a state of wide-open competition, the days of guaranteed profits were over. This forced surviving firms to raise money in order to straighten out their balance sheets and remain competitive. Much of the new capital went into new trading and clearing systems to handle the higher transaction volumes.

Hoping to increase the chances that they would earn back their investment in these new and rebuilt systems, investment banks and broker-dealers sought out or created new businesses—or fresh variations on old ones—that could command higher commissions, or fees, than the relatively simple transactional services they had traditionally sold. Luckily for them, the convulsive changes that the international system of foreign exchange and capital flows had been undergoing since the mid-1960s created a huge demand for products that could help investors, businesses, and governments to hedge, manage, or even exploit the seemingly chronic instability of the post-Bretton Woods financial world.

Accordingly, the investment banks began hiring "rocket scientists"—techies with a background in mathematics, physics, and computer programming. Their job was to create new financial instruments and trading strategies enabling clients to "hedge" their positions in inventory, raw materials, and anything they might need to purchase that suffered from price swings. Marrying these new strategies to the hardware and software that ran their trading desks required major new technology spending.

"Selling software on Wall Street has become the Bloomingdale's of the '90s," *Wall Street & Technology* magazine reported in February 1994.

One small corner of the Street—money management—was becoming "increasingly the driving force behind the rest of finance," *The Economist* reported.[3] In the 1980s and 1990s, as the stock market finally recovered from its previous-decade's funk, pension investment blew up into a multi-trillion-dollar industry. From controlling "only" $891 million in assets in 1980, pension funds for corporate and public employees commanded $2.5 trillion worth in 1990.[4] Creative money managers—along with managers who were merely creative at selling their strategies—became major profit centers for investment banks and brokerage firms. This, despite the general perception that the vast majority of managers were having a hard time beating the market.*

A little to one side, another phenomenon was remaking financial services. A provision of the 1978 federal budget law had created 401(k) plans: individual investment accounts funded by deductions from workers' paychecks, which they weren't allowed to access without a stiff penalty until retirement. After the

---

* Dyan Machan, "Monkey Business," *Forbes*, October 25, 1993. According to a 1992 Brookings Institution study, the average professional investment manager underperformed the benchmark Standard & Poor's 500 index by 2.6% over seven years.

1986 tax reform restricted the use of IRAs, advisors' attention focused more intensely on 401(k)s and the product took off.

Mutual funds, which already had large marketing and sales operations, were the big beneficiaries, since that's where most 401(k) investment dollars went. From $15 billion in assets in 1979, the year after the 401(k) emerged, mutual fund assets burgeoned to $1.5 trillion by 1992.

The flood of new business meant that the fund providers, too, were spending millions on technology. To make their product consumer-friendly, mutual fund companies needed to offer such features as voice response systems and the capability to update fund valuations daily. Administering the vast numbers of new accounts and the dizzying transaction volume they generated compelled Fidelity, Vanguard, T. Rowe Price, Massachusetts Financial Services, Putnam, and other giants to make huge new investments in PC-to-mainframe interfaces, networking tools, and advanced record-keeping software, plus the back-office staff to run them.

By the early 1990s, then, the financial services industry was burdened with an enormous, and continuing, investment in the infrastructure needed to process a wide assortment of financial transactions. Generating the fees to cover those ever-rising costs was of paramount importance—especially because, ever since 1975, those fees were deregulated and large investors could demand low, low prices. The wider margins that firms could charge small investors were looking more alluring.

* * *

Social Security had also been transformed in these years. The number of workers paying into the OASI and DI trust funds grew 33%, to 132 million, between 1970 and 1992. Thanks in large part to the payroll tax hikes mandated under the 1977 and 1983 Amendments, however, the assets in the trust funds had expanded almost eleven times, from $28.2 billion to $319.2 billion.

The view was quite different to Wall Street executives than it was twenty-two years earlier. Some educated guesses placed total managed assets in the hands of the financial services firms at around $14 trillion worldwide, including around $8 trillion in the U.S.[5] Financial executives now felt they had the capacity to handle the blizzard of buys, sells, and administrative notifications of infinite kinds that would be required for them to take over the assets pouring into Social Security as well. To some moguls, Social Security looked like the golden goose that would sustain the financial services industry through the next levels of its relentless expansion.

Wall Street didn't want to compete with Washington for workers' retirement savings, however. It wanted to enlist the federal government as a collaborator.

"Privatization" was, and remains, the term most widely used to describe what the movement against Social Security wanted to achieve in the 1990s, but a more accurate description of Wall Street's goals would be outsourcing or contracting out. Privatization could be easily achieved, after all, by simply phasing out payroll taxes, reducing or canceling OASI and DI, and letting workers use the extra pocket money to provide for their old age—or not—in any way they saw fit. Reducing benefits "represents a de facto privatization for people not yet retired," wrote two MetLife executives, William Poortvliet and Thomas Laine, in 1995, "since individuals will be encouraged to increase their retirement savings or seek increases in employer-provided pensions."[6]

Far from leaving government out of the process, however, Wall Street was counting on the government to provide the rules, administrative processes, and incentives needed to direct workers' forced savings their way. In a sense, "privatization" could better be described as a form of regulatory aid to private financial providers than as an effort to truly privatize retirement provision. Consequently, most of the proposals to restructure Social Security that Congress considered starting in the mid-1990s would retain the payroll tax system—except that instead of routing contributions into the Treasury, the money would be funneled by the government directly to Wall Street.

The effect would be to contract out an enormous pool of wealth into the hands of a preselected group of financial managers, with little or no leakage. Additionally, once the participants retired, many of the proposals to restructure the system mandated that they place at least part of their accumulated balances in annuities—investment contracts paying out a stream of income over time. A set of "qualified" annuities would be proffered, again minimizing leakage of assets from the financial services sector.

The objective, then, wasn't to get government out of the business of managing or directing workers' money or controlling how they planned for old age. It was for Wall Street to burrow *into* government, into the apparatus of the State itself, in order to redirect the flow of retirement capital into the hands of the banks, brokerage and mutual fund houses, and insurance companies. A rough analogy could be drawn with the U.S. health care system. Pharmaceutical companies, managed care providers, and insurance companies earned enormous chunks of their revenues providing services to Medicare, Medicaid, Disability Insurance, and SSI. Now financial services companies could benefit, through individual Social Security accounts.

Much of the rhetoric behind the movement against Social Security continued to have a libertarian flavor, especially when mouthed by the Cato Institute. But in practical terms, private providers would be earning a steady and dependable stream of fees, channeled to them by government.

* * *

Accordingly, when Cato in 1995 launched the Project on Social Security Privatization, a major push to sell the idea to the public, it received enthusiastic support from Wall Street. Announced less than six months after Kerrey and Simpson introduced their privatization bill, the new initiative quickly scored a coup by snagging the domain name www.SOCIALSECURITY.ORG for its website—one of the first devoted to a single political issue. (The SSA had to make do with www.SOCSEC.GOV.)

"It was the number one priority item we were doing," says Michael Tanner, director of health and welfare studies at Cato, who helped organize the project from the start. "It was also set up differently from any other issue we had taken on, with co-chairs from outside the organization, a much more independent budget and ability to function."[7]

As co-chairs of the privatization project, Cato chose José Pinera, the former Chilean minister of Labor and Social Security who had presided over privatization of his country's national retirement system in the early 1980s, and Bill Shipman, a principal with State Street Global Advisors, the money management arm of State Street Bank. Members of the "working group" Cato assembled for a first meeting of the privatization project in September 1995 included representatives of the American Bankers Association, the American Council on Life Insurers, American Express, insurer American International Group, Enron Corporation, IBM, the Investment Company Institute (ICI), Kemper Corporation (insurance and financial products), insurer Travelers Inc., and the Progress & Freedom Foundation.[8]

Cato raised a $2 billion war chest[9] and recruited a dedicated policy analyst for the privatization campaign, Andrew Biggs, from another conservative think tank, the Congressional Institute. By early 1997, the campaign was launched with a stream of full-page newspaper columns and radio advertisements. R. Kent Weaver, an analyst with the Brookings Institution, calculated that in 1992, Cato got more newspaper citations per dollar spent than all but two of twenty-one Washington-based think tanks he studied.[10] To help attract the non-policymaker audience, the website included a "Social Security Calculator" that allowed the worker to measure her guaranteed Social Security benefit against what she might earn if she could invest the money privately.

On K Street, the anti-Social Security campaign was preparing to turn itself into a more active and organized lobbying effort. Anne Canfield, a former congressional aide who had lately worked for the Privatization Project, announced she would be heading up the Retirement Security Coalition, which aimed to pull together a comparable group of well-heeled donors. The new group would be run out of the offices of McClure, Gerard & Neuenschwander, a leading lobby shop.[11]

State Street, in particular, wasn't coy about its reasons for supporting a project advocating the transfer of billions in payroll taxes to an industry in which it was a major player. "With 130 million people in the labor force, you could be staring at 130 million new accounts," said Shipman. State Street was already getting set for them, added Marshall Carter, the bank's CEO and chair: "We're preparing ourselves across the whole product line, from [our] small mutual fund family to our institutional family of products."[12]

State Street quickly became one of the most conspicuous corporate advocates of the privatization cause, for example, taking out a sixteen-page paid supplement on Social Security in the November–December 1996 issue of the prestigious policy journal *Foreign Affairs*. That same year, Shipman and Carter brought out a book entitled *Promises to Keep: Saving Social Security's Dream*. In a mailing of the book to journalists, State Street included a letter from a senior vice president noting that "Marsh and Bill" derive their "knowledge and experience" from a financial institution "that holds some *$2.6 trillion* of investors' assets in custody and directly manages more than *$270 billion*."

State Street also joined foundations like the Bradlee, Olin, and Kaplan funds in sponsoring think tank research on privatization. By January 1997, it could take credit for a $20,000 grant to the Progressive Policy Institute, another $20,000 to the Employee Benefit Research Institute to evaluate privatization proposals, and $25,000 to the Shorenstein Center on the Press, Politics, and Public Policy for research on the media's role in the debate.[13]

As a sugar daddy to the privatization movement, however, State Street was getting a run for its money from PaineWebber, the big investment banking and brokerage firm whose CEO and chair, Donald Marron, spoke and wrote widely in favor of "reform." Meanwhile, Pete Peterson's investment banking and private equity firm, the Blackstone Group, was quickly growing into a major Wall Street presence. This helped to enlarge Peterson's profile as head of the Concord Coalition, which continued to promote his campaign for fiscal austerity and a gradual end to entitlements. By 1997, Concord had a nearly $3 million annual budget and a claimed membership of 170,000. Heritage and the American Enterprise Institute were also benefiting as they focused more of their attention on Social Security.[14]

Besides funding think tanks and pressure groups, Wall Street performed another important service to the privatization movement by increasing its access to Congress. Political campaign giving by securities and investment firms quadrupled from $11.5 million during the 1990 election cycle, to $46.6 million in 1996, helping the industry climb from sixth to third place in total campaign donations, according to the Center for Responsive Politics. Meanwhile, the industry's preference switched decisively to the Republican side, with GOP candidates receiving 58% of securities and investment firms' contributions in 1996, versus 41% in 1990.

The Street took care, however, to reward Democrats it considered to be on the right side of the Social Security debate. Bob Kerrey, for example, was the keynote speaker at the ICI's spring 1996 membership conference, and two days later reportedly received $2,000 from the group's political action committee.[15]

But Social Security privatization became an issue even for top executives of big companies with no financial wares of their own to sell. Why? The short answer was that they believed in it. A survey of 347 chief financial officers of major companies, conducted in 1997 by Watson Wyatt Worldwide, found that 78% supported establishment of private Social Security accounts with workers controlling the investments. Another 73% supported reducing COLAs, the survey found.

There was a more practical matter, too. Conservative economists had argued for years, to the point where their views were widely accepted in the profession, that employers and employees don't "really" split the payroll tax load between them, because the bosses can simply lower wages by the amount of payroll tax they owe.[16] Nevertheless, corporations seemed to care greatly about increases in payroll tax, which they always opposed. If Social Security really was in danger of going under, the government would boost payroll taxes again rather than face workers' wrath, they feared. The National Association of Manufacturers (NAM), in 1994, set up a Social Security task force headed by Chrysler's chief Washington lobbyist to watch this issue.[17]

The following year, the ICI, the NAM, the U.S. Chamber of Commerce, the Securities Industry Association, the American Council of Life Insurers, and two lobbying groups for companies that sponsor defined-benefit pension plans—the ERISA Industry Committee and the Association of Private Pension and Welfare Plans—bankrolled the Retirement Savings Network to push their interests on retirement issues. One matter the network planned to address was Social Security. By then, many of its members already had their own task forces in place to study privatization.

The sudden emergence of powerful contributors from the financial services industry who wanted to restructure Social Security helps explain the attention and support that the Kerrey-Simpson bill and, shortly, other privatization proposals gained in Congress in the mid-1990s. The ICI, for example, was an early endorser of Kerrey-Simpson. But Wall Street's proselytizing was also directed at the public through marketing, advertising, and press outreach for its growing inventory of personal investment products.

A full-page magazine ad by Scudder Investment Services, a no-load mutual fund company, featured an appealing image of a dog and the following urgent question: "Social Security may be history by the time I retire. Doesn't seem fair. Okay. So how can I be smart about this?" Interspersed among this text, and ignoring the many assumptions required to get from the first to the last, were a series of options for what the reader could do with her "year-end bonus," among them: "All-terrain vehicle." "250 MHZ multiprocessor." "Home theater system." "Flying lessons." The choices finally dwindled down to: "Chinese take-out." "Return the video." "Oh, right. Feed the dog."

The message, of course, was that it was time for American workers to face facts. Social Security was going broke. Every possible penny needed to be saved or invested if the worker was to have the means to pay even for the necessities in retirement. Pouring these modest savings down the drain in the form of payroll taxes was just not acceptable anymore.

CHAPTER 16

"WHAT'S IN IT FOR ME?"

*"One of the small but rewarding vocations of a free society
is the provision of needed conclusions, properly supported
by statistics and moral indignation, for those in a position
to pay."*

—*John Kenneth Galbraith*[1]

By 1995, the focus of the propaganda war on Social Security was changing. Alongside the generalized appeals to the citizenry to save their skins before the program crashed in ruins, Wall Street and the conservative think tanks were now prompting them to ask themselves another question: "What's in it for me?" Privatization might do more than just fund your old age. It might make you rich.

After stagnating for several years, the Standard & Poor's 500, the benchmark U.S. stock index, began moving northward again in late 1991. Then, in early 1995, it began a steep ascent that saw it more than double in less than three years, passing the 1,000 mark for the first time, in February 1998. By the time this unprecedented boom ran its course at the end of 2001, the S&P would pass 1,300.

A great deal, if not most, of this record run was due to a boom in high technology stocks. The boom reflected the delayed impact of computers and high-speed interconnectivity on American business and consumers, but also a surge in speculation that the SEC and the Federal Reserve did nothing to check. The composite index for the NASDAQ, the electronic stock market on which many new high-tech companies first sold their shares, jumped from 1,000 in 1995 to more than 5,100 in 2000.

For proponents of Social Security privatization, the stock surge represented a powerful new opportunity to argue that the market, not the government, was where workers were most likely to achieve old-age financial security. And maybe even wealth. Privatization offered current workers the chance to take back what Washington, under FDR, had snatched away.

Two important groups were conspicuously held up as test cases of Social Security's alleged unfairness: African-Americans and women. The Heritage Foundation, in January 1998, made waves with a report that claimed Social Security was shortchanging African-Americans.[2] Because they had generally shorter life expectancies than other ethnic groups, black Americans were likely to collect less benefits—or no benefits at all, Heritage analysts William Beach and Gareth Davis concluded. Social Security taxes also "impede the intergenerational accumulation of capital among African-Americans," the report said, because when the worker dies, her OASI benefits go with her. Social Security was thus partly to blame for black families' failure to become more affluent from one generation to the next.

Heritage backed up its claims with some fairly alarming numbers. A low-income African-American male, age thirty-eight or younger, "is likely to pay more into the Social Security system than he can ever expect to receive in benefits after inflation and taxes. Staying in the current system will likely cost him up to $160,000 in lifetime income in 1997 dollars." Even black females, who tended to live longer, could expect to generate "at least $93,000 more in retirement income (in after-tax 1997 dollars)" if they invested their payroll tax contributions in a low risk/low yield Treasury portfolio.

No surprise, then, that the Heritage report drew attention even before its official release date. Six days earlier, *Wall Street Journal* columnist Alan Murray argued that the new, financially sophisticated American worker was waking up to the reality that Social Security was "a bum deal." Among the "surprising and disturbing" conclusions in the forthcoming Heritage report were the "low rates of return for African-Americans." Mark Sanford, a Republican House member from South Carolina and privatization advocate, was already using Heritage's findings in speeches before black audiences in his home district, Murray reported. "'People can't believe there is that kind of unfairness in the system,' he says. 'Black audiences are horrified.'"

Less than two weeks after the Heritage report first appeared, however, Steve Goss, the SSA's deputy chief actuary, let much of the air out of its balloon with a memo to chief actuary Harry Ballantyne that responded to the think tank's revelations.[3] Goss's research found that Heritage had employed some of its data to contradictory ends. While it used the fact that many African-American workers collect no old-age benefits from Social Security because they die before retirement age, it failed to allow for this fact in calculating the amount of payroll taxes they paid into the program. African-American workers make fully six years fewer payroll tax payments than Heritage's model predicted, according to the actuary.

Another flaw was that the conservative think tank looked only at retirement benefits, failing to include any analysis of the return to African-Americans from the other two important parts of the program: disability and survivors' benefits. Because black workers are more likely to die before retirement age, the CBPP found, nearly half of African-Americans who received Social Security were disabled or survivors of deceased workers, compared with 28% of whites.

Beyond this, Heritage seemed oblivious to the fact that its African-American analysis had raised an uncomfortable issue that had nothing to do with Social Security: If blacks have a shorter life expectancy than whites, what should the government do about it? One solution would be to correct the conditions related to health care, economic status, and access to quality education that contributed to the shortfall. By instead using those conditions as leverage to argue for private Social Security accounts, Heritage gave the appearance of accepting lower life expectancy for blacks and attempting to tailor public policy to the assumption that it would continue indefinitely. "Beware of the race card," the Century Foundation warned readers of the Beach-Davis report.[4]

However specious the reasoning might have been, Heritage succeeded in making this argument a popular talking point among conservative champions of privatization. Despite the borderline racism of its underpinnings, it would crop up repeatedly over the next several years.[5] Meanwhile, privatization proponents were developing a separate set of arguments aimed at another audience: women.

"Privatization of Social Security in fact would offer tangible financial benefits to women," the Cato Institute argued in a 1998 paper. In fact, privatization could solve all the inequities women faced under Social Security in one fell swoop. Cato analysts Ekaterina Shirley and Peter Spiegler endorsed a plan that would maintain the current total payroll tax rate of 12.4% but allocate 70% of that contribution to an individual investment account, the remainder going toward survivors' coverage and disability insurance.

Total contributions by a married couple would be added up and split 50-50 before being deposited in each partner's account, so each would benefit equally from their collective efforts. This would also free elderly women from having to rely on their husbands' financial decisions by ensuring they had some retirement assets of their own. For lower income wage earners, including women, the government would provide a matching contribution to their accounts.

Critics of privatization had reason to doubt that this arrangement would offer "tangible financial benefits" to women. John Williamson, a Boston College sociologist, pointed out that privatization would create two classes of women within the Social Security system: those in high-wage jobs could count on a comparable benefit or even one a bit better than what they could expect under the existing program, the rest would likely receive less. More elderly women would be living on the margins of poverty, since women are more likely than men to be low-wage workers—and thus, risk-averse with their investments. They would also be less able to afford good investment advice.[6]

Nevertheless, the notion that Social Security was unfair to women joined the soundbite about African-Americans as a commonly repeated nugget of conventional wisdom. One reason was that it dovetailed with the perspective on social reform that Pete Peterson and others had by now been propagating for years. Instead of working to improve the prospects of disadvantaged groups through education, household assistance, and enforcement of non-discrimination laws—to say nothing of the investment needed to end wage stagnation for all working people—government must retool its programs for a permanently diminished economic future. While Social Security's critics liked to build utopian visions around private investment accounts, their proposals really just sugar coated the basic message that in future, working people would be on their own.

* * *

Social Secur-uh-tee
Has run out
For you and me
             —*The Circle Jerks, "When the Shit Hits the*
                                              Fan" (1983)

While women and African-Americans served as demonstration cases, the privatization movement pinned its highest hopes on the post-Baby Boomers—twenty- to thirty-year-olds born after about 1964—appealing to them more directly and aggressively than to any other demographic. By the mid-1990s this generation had become a pop-culture phenomenon and a subject of intense interest for any and every merchant selling a product that could possibly be described by the adjective "lifestyle." Like the boomers before them, they quickly acquired a nickname: Generation X.

Everyone wanted to sell Gen X something, from CDs to computers to clothes to exciting new careers in high tech, multimedia, biomedicine, investment banking, and real estate development. One "product" being pitched especially hard was a secure retirement. One tool the salespeople found useful was to encourage the assumption that Social Security wouldn't be there when the Xers retired.

The bottom line: every Xer for him- or herself. In July 1998, the *Bank Investment Marketing Ultimate Sales Guide* noted a survey in which "only 2% of the Generation X sample claimed they expect most of their retirement money to come from Social Security. If offered the opportunity, this group would opt out of Social Security and choose to invest on their own."[7] Gen X "will be a planner's dream," Jennifer Jarratt, vice president of Coates and Jarratt (described as "a Washington, D.C.-based futurist organization"), told the *Journal of Financial Planning* in December 1997.[8] Accordingly, much of the advertising that flooded the media for financial services in the mid- to late 1990s was geared toward Gen Xers and their perceived irreverent style.

The political implications of Wall Street's courtship of the young quickly found expression in the corporate media. "Generation X appears, on the whole, well suited to handle the demands of self-directed investing of a portion of Social Security," concluded a long feature article in the November 1998 issue of the *Washington Monthly*, now going on twenty years with its own crusade against the program. "They are, as a group, far more committed to saving for themselves, far more financially sophisticated, far more self-reliant, and far more capable of handling the information tasks of personal financial management in the future than were past generations." The article's authors were Eric B. Schnurer and Linda Colvin Rhodes, public sector policy and management consultants with ties to the Democratic Leadership Council. The DLC had by now come out in favor of restructuring Social Security through benefits reduction and personal accounts.

So the Xers had the talent and the temperament for privatized Social Security. But how to mobilize them as a force in the political debate? As the mainstream media and publications catering to the financial services industry kept parroting, Gen X were hip, savvy, individualistic, and disinclined to be overtly led along by their elders. What was needed to make them understand where their best interests lay was a political pressure group of their own that could offer the Xers their own "I'm mad as hell!" moment. Interested parties of an older vintage were, of course, ready to fund it. And a cadre of aspiring young policy entrepreneurs were ready to create the ideological content. Or to borrow and update it, largely from the script written in the 1980s by Pete Peterson and Americans for Generational Equity.

The first Gen X advocacy group to make a big splash, Lead...or Leave, was founded by Jon Cowan and Rob Nelson, two young Washington denizens who had previously been, respectively, press secretary to Rep. Mel Levine, a conservative Democrat from Los Angeles, and a consultant at Malchow & Company, a political campaign advisory firm.

Lead...or Leave earned some press mentions during the 1992 campaigns with a not especially successful attempt to get congressional candidates to pledge not to run again if the fiscal 1996 budget deficit ended up being more than half the size of the 1992 deficit. Only 100 signed, of whom just 17 got elected, and Bill Clinton dismissed the pledge as a "gimmick." But Cowan and Nelson caught the attention of Paul Tsongas, who signed the pledge, and Ross Perot, who did likewise and also plugged their fledgling group in some of his speeches. Perot handed them $42,000 with which to build an organization. They obtained nearly as large an amount from Peterson and launched on a crusade to convince Xers that the deficit was "our generation's Vietnam."[9]

In February 1993, they appeared on the cover of *U.S. News & World Report* sporting a vaguely outlaw biker look and topped by a banner reading, "The Twentysomething Rebellion." Cowan, a blustery sort, made a reputation for himself with cheeky stunts such as including condoms in a mailing whose message was the need to "practice safe politics" by attacking the deficit: a misstep that caused one conservative backer to quit. He dismissed any potential problems with such tactics, saying, "Sometimes you have to be a butthead to get things done."

Then suddenly, in spring 1995, Lead…or Leave ceased operations. As it turned out, much of their "organizing" within the Gen X community had been smoke and mirrors: What they called "the largest grassroots college/twentysomething organization in the country," with over 1 million members and chapters at 115 colleges and in every state, actually had no paying members and manufactured that figure by counting every student at colleges "where it had at least one local, unelected representative," according to a report in the *American Prospect*.

By that time, however, another Xer advocacy group with deeper leadership—if not membership—and virtually the same policy positions had arisen to fill the gap. Third Millennium was born during a well-publicized meeting in March 1993 at Hickory Hill, Virginia, in the former home of Sen. Robert Kennedy, and hosted by the late presidential candidate's son Douglas, a freelance writer. Two dozen young, aspiring leaders attended, representing "an ideological cross-section of twenty- and thirty-somethings," according to a semi-official account. They decided to write a manifesto laying out their concerns: topped by "the national debt and entitlement reform."

Another group of Gen X spokespeople, meanwhile, were trying to get off the ground in New York. Richard Thau, just a few years out of college and an editor at the trade publication *Magazine Week*, and his friend Michael Collins, an advertising salesperson for *Spy* magazine, had discussed setting up "a younger person's version of the AARP."[10] This organization would have a dues-paying membership, take positions on issues of concern to members, and use size to leverage discounts for products and services that they valued. Thau and Collins thought of calling it the National Organization for Generation X, or NOG-X.

Through a mutual acquaintance, the two groups met in May at an Au Bon Pain café in Manhattan. Attendees included Kennedy and three other Hickory Hill participants. Jonathan Karl and Don Mathis were staffers at Freedom House, an advocacy group for political freedom abroad that had started as a liberal organization in the 1940s but had since become tightly associated with the more right-wing elements of the U.S. foreign policy establishment. Deroy Murdock was a conservative political commentator with the Scripps Howard News Service who had worked on the 1980 and 1984 Reagan campaigns.

The two groups decided to blend their efforts, naming themselves Third Millennium: Advocates for the Future. On July 14 they released a thirty-two-page manifesto, titled the "Third Millennium Declaration." By this time their core group also included Robert Lukefahr, a staffer with the Madison Center for Educational Affairs, a right-wing organization that, in its words, recruited "promising Ph.D. candidates and undergraduate leaders" on college campuses and funded campus newspapers with a conservative bent, such as the some-times racist *Dartmouth Review*. Jon Cowan and Rob Nelson also reportedly contributed to the manifesto.[11]

With a few exceptions, the participants were graduates of name universities who had gravitated to Washington in search of careers in politics and policymaking. There, they had absorbed the anti-entitlement, deficit hawkish politics that had become requisite for anyone wishing to build a respectable mainstream career on Capitol Hill and its environs. Second, they had all read one or more of the books and pamphlets that Neil Howe and Bill Strauss had written over the past five years.

Howe, Pete Peterson's frequent literary collaborator, and Strauss, an older Washington hand who had previously served in the Ford White House and as counsel to two Senate subcommittees, were setting themselves up as experts on the mindsets of different generations of Americans. In 1991, they published *Generations*, which interpreted U.S. history as a succession of generational bi-ographies, with Gen X being the thirteenth. The book snagged a great deal of attention in Washington circles, including, reportedly, a photo op on Bill Clin-ton's Oval Office desk. Among other things, it predicted that in the 2010s, the boomers, in an act of dramatic self-sacrifice, would "snap the chains of ever-rising benefits" from Social Security and Medicare in order "to avoid raising the burden on younger generations.… In a turnabout from the … entitlement ethic, Boomers will derive self-esteem from knowing they are not receiving rewards from the community."[12]

Two years later, Howe and Strauss returned with *13ᵗʰ Gen: Abort, Retry, Ignore, Fail?* This time they were pitching their product not to Washington wonks, but to Xers themselves. Leading with a hip, hot-pink-on-black-and-white cover design and generously illustrated with cartoons and drawings, the book's text was a near sick-making avalanche of pop cultural references and trend-checks calculated to titillate its audience while kindling a kind of cynical outrage—all in service of a carefully directed generational rebellion. "LISTEN UP DUDES!" Howe and Strauss trumpeted. "Where earlier twentieth century generations could comfortably look forward to outpacing mom and dad, you'll be lucky just to keep up."

To drive home the point, *13th Gen* included a succession of cartoons of which the following is typical: A pair of smirking "geezers" drop their Lincoln off at the country club and saunter in while tossing the keys to the valet, an impoverished looking Xer, with the remark, "Thanks Sonny, and don't forget our senior citizen discount …"[13]

Howe and Strauss, both in their forties, were the intellectual godfathers of Third Millennium. Strauss himself was present at the Hickory Hill gathering and Thau credited *13ᵗʰ Gen* as "a kind of script that [Third Millennium] is trying to live up to."[14] The pair also wrote a pamphlet for Lead…or Leave titled "Deficits in Your Face," that featured some of the group's most incendiary prose. "Older Americans are waging a generational war against YOU," it warned. "Like Vietnam, it's going to take the youth of America to stop it."

"The Third Millennium Declaration" itself closely echoed Howe and Strauss's hipster lingo, right down to the baby boomer cultural references. "Like Wile E. Coyote waiting for a 20-ton Acme anvil to fall on his head," the declaration read, "our generation labors in the expanding shadow of a monstrous national debt." Its startlingly austere recommendations included allowing no new net federal spending, limiting entitlement spending, and funding only "programs that work." Social Security, it judged, "is a generational scam."

Shortly after it was issued, Strauss compared the "Third Millennium Declaration" to Students for a Democratic Society's Port Huron Statement, the landmark aspirational document of 1960s-era student activism. "I am optimistic that when we look back at the history of the '90s and the youth movement, this will be an important document," he told *Time*.

The media seemed primed to believe it. When Third Millennium unveiled its call to arms on July 14, 1993 at the National Press Club, major outlets that either covered the event or picked up the story in succeeding weeks included NBC's *Today Show*, *Time*, *U.S. News & World Report*, the *Washington Times*, *New York Newsday*, and the *San Francisco Chronicle*.[15] Douglas Kennedy and Jonathan Karl, the co-chairs, were frequent interview subjects over the next few months as the media warmed to the high concept of politically committed "slackers" whose position papers read like hip liberals' but were Reaganite in substance.

By January, Third Millennium had a one-room office in New York in the same suite as the League of Women Voters, and Thau was its first paid employee, with the title of executive director. If it was to evolve into a grassroots organization with a substantial membership empowered to make decisions, however, Third Millennium had a long road to travel. Its leaders had thought more carefully about the difficulties of doing so than Cowan and Nelson, and sensibly, they were guarded as to whether this was even a serious goal. The group garnered some 2,000 members fairly quickly, each paying $9 for the privilege of belonging, but it was already clear to Thau that mustering them into a political force wasn't going to be easy.

"We had plans to get them to call their congresspersons—things like that," Thau recalled years later. "Then we tried to band people together into local chapters. But what could they do locally that was not national in focus?" Searching for a distinction, he says, "Third Millennium was a think tank whereas Lead…or Leave was an action tank."

Not having enough funding to support a team of research fellows who could do the sort of quasi-academic studies that think tanks typically turn out, Third Millennium actually was a hybrid "tank," much like Americans for Generational Equity before it. It eschewed any attempt to give the semblance of a mass organization, but never specifically denied it was one, or could be one some day. Instead, it concentrated on polling, publicizing research generated by other organizations that supported its views, and making itself available to the press and lawmakers for oracular statements on issues that concerned America's younger voters. Third Millennium avoided showboating stunts of the kind Lead…or Leave had favored, preferring to come across as serious policy advocates, in part by highlighting its connections with established groups like the Concord Coalition.

Its reward was healthier financial backing than Lead…or Leave. One early supporter was Lawrence A. Benenson, a retired publisher and investor "with a visceral hatred of debt," says Thau.[16] Other donors in Third Millennium's first five years included the inevitable Pete Peterson—"a constant donor," says Thau, writing checks from $3,000 to $10,000 in size—along with the Prudential Foundation, controlled by the big financial services company of the same name; Merrill Lynch; and an anti-deficit alliance that included the Business Roundtable and the U.S. Chamber of Commerce.[17]

What made Third Millennium especially valuable to such backers was, paradoxically, its aura of nonpartisanship, or "postpartisanship," in its own, carefully chosen terminology. And while the group's backing came overwhelmingly from the conservative end of the eleemosynary field, Thau also went to great pains to dispel any suspicion that its agenda was controlled by Wall Street.

"The conspiracy and the cabal is not happening," he told USA Today in 1997. "The Wall Street money is not there, despite my efforts and other's efforts to get some. We're all bitching and moaning to each other that Wall Street should be doing more, and it's not." Years later, Thau would recall that the deficit, rather than Social Security, was the theme Third Millennium intended to ride when it first came together. But Social Security was the issue that gave the group its biggest and most memorable PR coup.

* * *

Backed by a $25,000 dollop from the Smith Richardson Foundation, Third Millennium decided in 1994 to commission a poll of young adults about their opinions and attitudes on Social Security. Mindful of their postpartisan stance, they retained as pollsters Frank Luntz, who had helped hone the Contract with America and test it in polls, and Mark Siegel, former executive director of the Democratic National Committee and a well-known lobbyist and speechwriter. As the Third Millennium board drafted the survey, Deroy Murdock focused on one crucial query: Do you think Social Security will exist when you retire?

Instead of simply asking that straightforward question, Murdock suggested, why not set it up to compare Social Security's credibility with that of something crazy? Like what? Thau asked. Like, for example, the tooth fairy. Or UFOs. "I said, 'Stop right there!'" Thau remembers.

Asked whether they believed UFOs exist, 46% of Americans surveyed between ages eighteen and thirty-four said yes. Asked if they expected Social Security to exist when they retire, only 28% said yes.

"If we had done nothing else, that was our signal achievement," Thau says proudly "—perhaps more important to the culture and the Social Security discussion than anything else we did." The "UFO factoid" rippled through the corporate media after Third Millennium announced the poll findings at a press conference in September and, in part thanks to Luntz's success at talking it up, quickly became a staple of Capitol Hill chitchat that fall and winter. A Nexis search of U.S. newspapers and wires alone from 1994 to 1999 yields 483 mentions, making it one of the most often cited statistics of the decade. The poll instantly made Third Millennium a visible, go-to opinion source whenever something significant happened involving Social Security, such as the introduction of the Kerrey-Simpson bill.

"Last year, we discovered more young people believe UFOs exist than believe Social Security will exist by the time they retire," Thau told the *St. Louis Post-Dispatch* on that particular occasion. "Now we hope our peers will believe in something else: Kerrey-Simpson is a politically feasible plan to bring our future back to Earth." When Cato launched the Project on Social Security Privatization in 1995, the backgrounder it prepared for the media led off by citing the factoid.

Third Millennium's message was clear: No one should take for granted that younger Americans would continue to willingly pay into a system they didn't believe would give anything back to them. The UFO poll had "shattered the myth" that Social Security is an "intergenerational contract no one wants to see touched," Murdock wrote in an op-ed for the conservative *Washington Times*. "Americans, especially the young, increasingly eye Social Security with suspicion and would reward officials bold enough to let them take control of their own retirement assets. Visionary leaders in Washington ought to advance a plan to employ economic liberty as a catalyst for private capital formation and long-term growth."[18]

Soon, Thau remembers with amusement, PaineWebber was using "the factoid" to sell 401(k) accounts—it was just one of a host of sales organizations that thought it could serve as a way to get inside Gen X's head.

Every time the "factoid" seemed ready to fade away, it came back, in the kind of feedback loop between the Beltway and the national media and back again that is such a feature of Washington political culture. In February 1995, at a Senate committee hearing to reconfirm Shirley Chater as Social Security commissioner, Alan Simpson confronted her with the UFO poll. Next month, the incident led off *Time*'s "Social Insecurity" feature, with its alarming cover image of a torn-up Social Security card and the words, "The Case for Killing Social Security." "Whatever the merits of their judgment on extraterrestrials," the lead paragraph announced, "on Social Security the new workers have it exactly right. Given enough time, reality bites."

While there was nothing phony about the results of the Third Millennium poll, the way the group presented them was slightly disingenuous. Lawrence Jacobs and Robert Shapiro, two political scientists who studied public and media attitudes toward Social Security in the 1990s, pointed out that the "factoid" didn't report the results of a single question in the survey, but of two separate ones. The fifth question in the poll asked respondents about their confidence in Social Security, the fourteenth whether they believed in UFOs.[19] Respondents didn't know their answers would be combined to create an artificial comparison.

If they had, the results might have been different. They were three years later, when the Employee Benefit Research Institute asked 1,000 young adults between 18 and 34 years old, "Which do you have greater confidence in ... receiving Social Security benefits after retirement or that alien life from outer space exists?" This time, 63% said they had more confidence in Social Security, versus 33% who placed their faith in alien life.[20]

A somewhat narrower survey, of eighteen- to twenty-nine-year-olds, taken less than four years after Third Millennium's, found that fully 94% still believed Social Security was "essential" to retirement. And while most believed they could do better managing the money from their payroll tax contributions themselves, 90% wanted to receive Social Security anyway, "just in case."[21]

When push came to shove, then, it was unclear which way Gen X would turn. Perhaps the youngsters would resign themselves to never receiving a dime of what they paid in. Or perhaps, given the combined pressure of their student loans and the high cost of health care, housing, and graduate education, they would give up and demand that Washington figure out a solution that would get them their Social Security somehow.

Then there was the question of whether Gen X were inclined to demand anything at all. One reason financiers like Pete Peterson and conservative endowments like Smith Richardson smiled upon Third Millennium was that they thought it could persuade younger voters to pressure lawmakers to shrink Social Security and remake it as a private investment vehicle—or at least convince those lawmakers that they could do so.

But if Gen X didn't turn out, the politicians would cease wooing. Here, the evidence was mixed. Younger people did indeed vote for Ross Perot in large numbers in 1992, but this was just as likely because of his stand against the NAFTA trade treaty—an extremely unpopular deal that Washington coalesced around anyway—as for his anti-deficit fumings. A 1993 survey by the National Opinion Research Center found that people aged eighteen to twenty-nine were almost twice as likely to be members of political organizations than those aged forty to sixty-four. And eighteen- to twenty-four-year-olds were becoming a larger part of the electorate, increasing their share from 29% to 37% between the 1988 and 1992 elections, according to the Committee for the Study of the American Electorate. But they still had the lowest turnout in that year of any age group.

"The basic truth," William Schneider, a political analyst at the American Enterprise Institute, said bluntly, "has been that young people and poor people don't vote."[22] Seemingly to prove his point, Christian Klein, a law student, tried in 1995 to launch the first Gen X political action committee. PAC 20/20 was the centerpiece of a major, and typically alarmist, feature on Social Security in the *New York Times Sunday Magazine.* The piece was by Elizabeth Kolbert, a *Times* political reporter who had never written about pension or retirement issues before but had followed Bob Kerrey when he ran for president briefly in 1992. The group didn't last the year, however. It held a couple of fundraisers, taking in $4,000: only enough to cover the cost of the events. Klein dissolved the group when he passed the bar and took a job with a New York law firm.[23]

Given the sheer size of Gen X—its potential to turn out voters, that is— Third Millennium nevertheless remained an alluring presence in Washington and in the media for the rest of the decade. Between September 1994 and early 1998, representatives of the group testified before Congress fourteen times, always emphasizing its twin demands for a balanced budget and entitlement reform. By 1997 its staff included four full-time employees and a consultant. Thau and the group's new chairperson, Heather Lamm, Dick Lamm's daughter and a Kerrey commission staffer who had since moved into a job at the Concord Coalition, were familiar figures on TV and in the print media.

The group was issuing reports and getting included in educational forums on budget balancing and entitlement reform with members of Congress who had a hankering after both, including Jim Kolbe and Charlie Stenholm and Sens. John Warner and Rod Grams. It even organized a program, dubbed "Third Millennium 30," that placed thirty inner-city high school students in weekly seminars, which introduced them "to nationally-recognized thinkers and writers addressing long-term issues facing the United States."[24]

By this time, Third Millennium wasn't alone. Its success at attracting media attention had convinced a further gaggle of young, aspiring policy entrepreneurs to set themselves up as Gen X advocates. Besides the short-lived PAC 20/20, there was the Fund for a New Generation, created in 1997 by Adam Dubitsky, a conservative public relations executive who had formerly worked for Frank Luntz. Dubitsky's firm counted AT&T, *Wall Street Journal* editorial board member Amity Shlaes—a fierce anti-tax, anti-entitlement polemicist— and the union-busting National Right to Work Foundation among its clients.

Despite these stolidly establishment connections, the Fund for a New Generation adopted much the same in-your-face tactics as Lead...or Leave to promote an agenda closely focused on what Dubitsky called "free market Social Security reform." In September 1997, when President Clinton and his family were vacationing in the affluent resort of Martha's Vineyard, Fund for a New

Generation took out a full-page ad in the local *Vineyard Gazette* urging him to restructure the program by allowing workers to carve out personal accounts.[25]

Dubitsky's creation didn't last long, but another new group, the National Association of Twentysomethings, quickly popped up, hoping to turn it into a Gen X equivalent of the AARP—much like the concept Thau had discarded to join in the launch of Third Millennium. Ten months after its inception, the group still had only 700 members.[26]

Even at the time, it took very little reporting to reveal that the "mass" support for organizations attempting to harness the generational outrage of the Xers was a mile wide and about an inch deep. In retrospect, the reason they never commanded a broad following is fairly obvious. Despite their efforts to dress up the movement against Social Security with trendy, media-genic stunts, the message from Third Millennium and its kind was unrelentingly sour and disheartening, more Pain Caucus than Free Lunch Caucus in inspiration. While they supported private accounts, they were much more intent on painting a gloomy, Petersonesque picture of a desolate future than in touting the wonders of the ownership society. Most young voters found their vision less than attractive.

But for the remainder of the decade, the media were bewitched by the prospect of a new kind of activism built around generational rather than ethnic or class differences. Often Boomers or Xers themselves, the journalists who cottoned on to this narrative were already conditioned to rationalize social change according to a generational pattern. Howe and Strauss had made this analysis seem almost scientifically compelling with the success of *Generations* in 1991. Much of the time, then, journalists didn't feel they needed evidence of numbers to confirm that they had spotted a trend. Confronted with savvy, twentysomething policy entrepreneurs like Cowen and Nelson, Thau and Dubitsky, their gut was all they needed to tell them it was so.

CHAPTER 17
SCARY NUMBERS

*"If you want to be a popular speaker, you need to feed the
paranoia of your audience."*
                                        —*Uwe Reinhardt*[1]

At a time when lawmakers, policyheads, and the mainstream media were obsessing over the notion of generations, a new method of assessing the government's long-term fiscal health called "generational accounting" was sure to draw attention. Its creator was Larry Kotlikoff, a Boston University economist and Elizabeth Kolbert's source for scary numbers. He had first introduced the methodology in a 1989 paper for the National Bureau of Economic Research and in 1992 expanded it into a book titled *Generational Accounting: Knowing Who Pays, and When, for What We Spend.*

The new methodology gave substance to the idea of generational equity that critics like Dave Durenberger had been talking up for years. Now, seemingly, it was possible to create separate "accounts" for each individual worker or household that could be picked apart to discover which generations were paying for which. Much as Social Security's critics wanted this to be true, generational accounting ran into controversy almost from the start, but it sparked an intense debate over how much each generation "costs" the ones that come next. And it gave the enemies of Social Security another weapon, however imperfect, with which to attack the program.

* * *

Kotlikoff and his frequent co-authors—Alan Auerbach, a professor of economics and law at the University of Pennsylvania, and Jagadeesh Gokhale, an economist with the Federal Reserve Bank of Cleveland—estimated the present value of the total payments an individual would make to the federal, state, and local governments over his or her lifetime, depending on the year that individual was born and assuming that current tax rates and other rules stay the same.* Based on computations that Kotlikoff, Auerbach, and Gokhale developed and published in an NBER (National Bureau of Economic Research) working paper, generational accounting, they claimed, could make inferences not only for those currently alive but for future generations as well.

What their model yielded was sensational, immediately attracting a great deal of attention. "Throughout the rest of their lives young and middle-aged generations can expect, on balance, and on a present value basis, to pay more money to the government than they receive," Kotlikoff said in his book. "Older generations can expect, on balance, to receive more money from the government than they will pay."[2]

The situation would only get worse. When unborn generations of Americans arrive on the scene, "their lifetime net tax bills will be at least a 21 percent larger share of their lifetime incomes than is the case for those just born."[3] Generational accounts are a zero-sum game, Kotlikoff wrote. What was needed to prevent this disastrous burden being dumped on our offspring, therefore, was some combination of tax hikes and cuts in government spending. The longer this was put off, the higher the bill would rise. A ten-year delay of belt-tightening would raise the bill for future generations 35%; a twenty-year delay would bump it up by 57%.[4]

Frightening though its conclusions might be, generational accounting was a more honest means of adding up the government's obligations than the conventional methods used to measure the federal deficit and national debt, Kotlikoff claimed, because it wasn't confused by labels. No matter what the government chose to call its revenues and expenditures to make the books look good in a given set of years—taxes, transfers, loans, repayment of principal, whatever—the truth, under generational accounting, couldn't be masked. Conventional deficit accounting, on the other hand, is "smoke and mirrors." Henceforth, Kotlikoff argued audaciously, "we must abandon the use of it in favor of generational accounts for purposes of making fiscal policy."[5]

---

*   They defined "generational accounts" as follows: "A set of values, one for each existing and future generation, with the property that their combined present value adds up to the present value of government consumption less initial government wealth" (Alan J. Auerbach, Jagadeesh Gokhale, Laurence J. Kotlikoff, "Generational Accounting: A Meaningful Way to Evaluate Fiscal Policy," *Journal of Economic Perspectives*, Vol. 8, No. 1, Winter 1994).

Beyond that, all Americans needed to "become generationally conscious—to realize that preserving the economic welfare of our children, grandchildren, and so forth, even at our own sacrifice, is a goal worthy of our great and generous nation."[6] By sacrifice, Kotlikoff meant higher taxes and less government spending now so that we didn't soak the grandkids down the road. The alternative: monstrous tax hikes leading to severe capital shortages; panicked selling of Treasury bonds jacking up interest rates, further depressing the climate for investment; and hyperinflation as Washington turned on the printing presses to keep paying Social Security and other benefits. In short: economic meltdown.

For such a momentous discovery, the method behind generational accounting was actually rather simple, at least for a trained economist with a fast computer and suitable software. It took off from the insight that if you looked at government's payments and receipts as flows over time, you got a much more accurate, less manipulable picture than the yearly "snapshot" the government's deficit number provided. And because of the projections that the Social Security and Medicare trustees provided annually, most of the data needed to calculate these flows was already available.

The first step was to project the average taxes that each generation would pay, and the transfers they would receive from government during each year that at least some members of the generation would be alive, then subtract the second number from the first.[7] In the next step, the resulting total was converted into a present value: the amount of money this generation would need to have on hand to invest today in order to pay off everything it owed the government for the rest of its time on earth.

Determining this present value required choosing an "assumed discount rate": the rate at which today's money could reasonably be expected to appreciate in value between now and the time the last member of the generation under discussion breathed his or her last. Another assumption, of course, was how many of this generation's members would be alive in each successive year. Kotlikoff adopted the same assumptions the Social Security trustees used, both for discount rate and longevity. The computer did the rest of the work.

Generational accounting was very much a product of its era. Like Pete Peterson, Kotlikoff was calling for a great national project of self-sacrifice: a new age of austerity dedicated to keeping future generations out of hock. Behind him was the firm position he held within the economic establishment. Kotlikoff had studied economics with Martin Feldstein at Harvard and then become a research associate with Feldstein's National Bureau of Economic Research, where he collaborated on papers with other economists who would later have a lot to say about Social Security, including Michael Boskin and John Shoven. His early research took off from work that Feldstein had done on the size and potential effects of unfunded government liabilities, especially Social Security.

One night during a vacation in the early 1980s, when he couldn't sleep, Kotlikoff says, he suddenly got the fundamental insight that "there's nothing in economic theory to define government debt. I realized that all these numbers are some kind of hogwash—extremely arbitrary—a factor of the way we label government receipts and payments. We needed to go back to economic theory and have a look at each generation's lifetime budget constraint, whose movement is the same regardless of labels."[8]

"Economic theory," for Kotlikoff, was the neoclassical or neoliberal tradition that had inspired everyone from Milton Friedman to Ronald Reagan. In this world, individuals and households by and large have knowledge of and plan reasonably for their economic futures, despite the unpredictable ups and downs of life in a free-market economy. Neoliberal theory also posits a zero-sum world in which "letting one set of Americans off the hook in meeting the government's bills means putting some other set of today's or tomorrow's Americans on the hook."[9]

This view meshed perfectly with that of the generational equity warriors of the 1980s, although Kotlikoff says he had no contact with them or with AGE at the time. But the key to reforming Social Security—and every other ingredient in Washington's budget pie—was first to get the practice of generational accounting accepted. In 1981, while serving as a senior economist on Reagan's Council of Economic Advisors, Kotlikoff managed to include a critique of the standard definition of the federal government's debt in the Economic Report to the President.

Ten years later, Richard Darman, a dyed-in-the-wool deficit hawk who had spent two years at the Wall Street firm Shearson Lehman Brothers after holding several sub-Cabinet-level positions in the Reagan administration, was head of the Office of Management and Budget (OMB) under George H.W. Bush. According to Barry Anderson, then the senior career officer at the bureau, generational accounting intrigued Darman as a way to counter some lawmakers who were proposing that the federal government adopt a separate capital budget. Commonly used in the private sector, a capital budget would highlight items like education, research and development, and infrastructure improvements that contribute to the long-term productive capacity of the country and its people. A capital budget would make it more difficult to justify cuts in these areas—hence Darman's hostility to the idea.

Darman and Anderson had both heard of Kotlikoff's work and decided to include a generational accounting exercise, along with a capital budget analysis and several other "analytical perspectives" on the federal government's finances, as a short appendix to the fiscal-year 1993 budget. When Anderson called Kotlikoff and told him that OMB wanted to include a "brief description" of generational accounting in the budget, Kotlikoff was "ecstatic," Anderson remembers. "He looked at it as a massive endorsement of generational accounts. But what we were really interested in was to diminish the case for capital budgets."[10]

When the budget appeared, just as the Clinton team was moving into the White House, the generational analysis—just a few pages at the back-end of a lengthy document—captured a great deal of press attention. Sylvia Nasar, a conservative economics writer for the *New York Times*, devoted a column to what had been, until now, an obscure academic theory.[11] Baby boomers born in 1950, she wrote, relying on the budget figures, could expect to pay $200,000 more in taxes than they collected in benefits over their lifetimes. And unless limits were placed on entitlements and other government spending, their grandchildren could find themselves paying 71% of their incomes to Uncle Sam in taxes.

What was to be done? "The generational imbalance between the newly born and future Americans could be largely eliminated by imposing a cap on mandatory spending (excluding Social Security) from 1993 to 2004 or by an appropriate tax surtax," the analysis in the budget document concluded. "Both policies significantly increase net taxes—the taxes paid less transfers received—by current Americans." Those would be the boomers and their children, who would pay as much as 40% more in order to keep future generations' taxes down to a mere 50%. Darman, at the time, was still pleading for some attention to be paid to limiting the growth of Social Security. The generational analysis suggested what the price tag might be, assuming one accepted Kotlikoff's zero-sum worldview and if the program was left to operate by its current rules.

The 71% lifetime tax rate was the figure that provided the best soundbite, and it appeared over and over in the early months of 1993, as Clinton prepared his own economic plan and Republican lawmakers touted a balanced budget amendment. Mainstream business and economics writers and many editorial columns repeated the message they had absorbed from the appendix to the Bush budget: spending must be cut and taxes must be raised on today's workers in order to lower taxes for tomorrow's.

"By increasing taxes on his generational peers, Clinton is lightening the load on Chelsea and her friends—somewhat," wrote Alex Beam, a *Boston Globe* columnist, referring to the president's daughter in one fairly representative piece published in March. That was the only way to deal with the oldsters, who "are sucking down an ever-increasing array of benefits, such as Social Security and Medicare, beaten out of Congress by their powerful lobbyists."[12] Buying into the vision, to some extent, was Clinton himself, who said in February that unless the federal debt was cut, "we will be condemning our children and our children's children to a lesser life than we enjoyed."[13]

Thanks to the platform the OMB had provided, Kotlikoff and his colleagues took their place alongside Third Millennium in the collection of forces that was reviving discussion of the economic gap between the generations in the mid-1990s. What they wanted most, however, was to legitimize generational accounting as a federal budget tool, banishing conventional deficit accounting to the scrap heap. In this, they were unsuccessful. By the time the new Clinton administration was preparing the fiscal 1994 budget, the drumbeat for a capital budget had largely died down and the motivation to again include an appendix of alternative fiscal analyses had dissipated too.

* * *

While generational accounting may have been a victim of politics, it also made enemies within the economic community. If one bought Kotlikoff's point of view, it seemed, no government—and perhaps no one—should ever make an open-ended commitment to provide any service to anyone, because some set of numbers could always be produced to show it was untenable. But that wasn't how life was actually lived. "People in real life make long-term commitments like buying a house, sometimes even with an adjustable-rate mortgage," wrote economic historians Joseph White and Aaron Wildavsky. "They have children, plan to send them to college; they will figure out later what to sacrifice to that end. The government, with heavy public support, committed itself to social security.... Some problems come with the territory."[14]

Brookings Institution budget scholar Henry Aaron cautioned that Kotlikoff's methodology was far too sensitive to changes in its discount rate assumption and to shifts in demographic and other trends to be useful in setting public policy. It attracted great attention in Washington, however, because the details touched so closely on current efforts to fight the deficit and especially the developing arguments for cutting back Social Security.

Generational accounting ignored the economic gaps within generations, critics charged, using average tax and benefits rates to paint a smooth picture of a landscape that actually had a lot of striations. And in totaling up what each generation paid and what it received from Social Security and Medicare, for example, it ignored the insurance aspect of the programs, as if protection from the possibility of destitution in old age or, for children, following the death of a working parent, had no value.[15]

But the critique that counted the most was a lengthy study requested by the chair of the Senate Finance Subcommittee on Long-Term Growth, Debt and Deficits and issued by the Congressional Budget Office (CBO) in November 1995. At the time, CBO was headed by June Ellenoff O'Neill, a conservative economist and critic of Social Security. O'Neill says Kotlikoff lobbied her extensively while her bureau was preparing its report.[16]

What it produced didn't please him, however. The agency concluded that generational accounts shouldn't become a regular part of its annual budget outlook presentation, mainly because "they depend on calculations that are ... empirically ambiguous." Therefore, "they lie in the realm of analysis, not accounting."[17]

Kotlikoff and his colleagues used 6% as their discount rate for determining the present value of the benefits taxpayers receive from government, including the risk that they might not receive some or all of those benefits. But people of different ages—say, a thirty-year-old and a seventy-year-old—value their benefits differently, not to mention the risk that goes with them, the CBO pointed out.* Kotlikoff and his colleagues said they chose 6% because it was

---

* Economist Peter Diamond of the Massachusetts Institute of Technology noted in a later critique that since most working people don't hold either government or private debt or stock, it makes no sense to assign a discount rate to them that presumes they would be making a comparison between the risk "roughly halfway between the real historical returns on government bonds and private sector capital."[18] That's not good enough, the CBO said. Government transfer payments aren't necessarily riskier than government debt, or even stock in public companies.[19]

Besides, the generational accounts were extraordinarily sensitive to the discount rate. Over a 200-year period, for instance, a $33 investment today at a 9% discount rate would be worth $1 billion, pointed out economist Dean Baker of the liberal-leaning Economic Policy Institute, while at a 2% rate, it would take a $19,053,101 investment today to yield that same $1 billion. That translates into a 166% tax burden on labor income at the 9% rate, versus "just" 37% at the 2% discount rate.[20]

Another problem the CBO spotted was that Kotlikoff and his co-creators based their calculations of lifetime net tax rates on only one source of workers' income: labor. Many if not most could expect to receive a great deal of their lifetime income from homeownership, from capital gains on investments, or from gifts or inheritances. In fact, while current net tax rates amounted to 30% of labor income for all workers, the CBO found that they only made up 24% of total income.[21]

Perhaps the biggest problems with generational accounting had to do with the very dicey practice of making economic and demographic forecasts so far into the future. The generational accountants' predictions of monstrously higher taxes in the future were based on "uncertain forecasts well into the 21st century of what will be happening to population, productivity and health costs," wrote economist Robert Eisner in a November 1994 letter responding to a Kotlikoff op-ed in the *Wall Street Journal*. Kotlikoff's prescription—higher taxes now—"might just stifle the economy and slow our long-term growth," Eisner pointed out, "thus raising future tax burdens."

All just to forestall a future problem that was far from certain.

The objective of generational accounting was to reveal who would pay for the bulk of the tax burden that would loom so large if these disasters did strike. But even here, Kotlikoff and his colleagues may have stumbled. Baker, in his report for the EPI, noted that in the table of net tax rates they assembled for OMB, each year's lifetime rate rose fairly gradually—from 35% for those born in 1960, for example, to 36.3% for those born in 1992—then abruptly shot up to 82% for "future generations."[22] The implication was that, if maintaining Social Security and Medicare benefits in the future required raising taxes, the burden would fall entirely on future generations and none of it on those boomers, Gen Xers, and even Gen Yers already living.

This might be useful for illustrating the magnitude of the burden, but it wasn't very realistic. If a tax hike really was needed, would Congress wait until

that these assets will lose value and, say, the risk that Social Security benefits won't be paid. Only for more affluent people would this be appropriate (Peter Diamond, "Generational accounts and generational balance: an assessment," *National Tax Journal*, December 1996).

every last member of the previous generations had passed on to impose it?

Another issue CBO found the generational accountants had skirted was how much of that burden each generation ought to pay—in other words, how much each one could reasonably be expected to cover. To figure this out would require a much fuller accounting of the benefits each generation received from government than Kotlikoff and his colleagues provided. Their calculus only looked at taxes paid and benefits directly received from government: Social Security, Medicare, Medicaid, SSI, food stamps, and welfare, for instance.

But what about the benefit each person derived from sanitation, police, public transportation, roads and bridges, and all the other services U.S. residents enjoyed in common? And what about the additions to that capital stock that each generation leaves for the ones that follow? Eisner asked. Arguably, each generation is responsible for leaving the nation better off—richer, better endowed with infrastructure and other resources—than the ones that came before. Which would mean incurring some costs that would have to be passed on, partially, to the next generation.

Generational accounting erred in balancing all taxes paid by each generation against only one group of benefits that generation received back, omitting a host of others. Practically everything the government does affects the resources of future generations, but generational accounting seemed to leave most of it out of the calculation.

Kotlikoff acknowledged as much in his 1992 book: "Obviously, a full assessment of generational policy requires an understanding of which generations are the beneficiaries as well as which are the financiers of government spending," he wrote. That didn't make his formula any less valuable, he added, because it's "irrelevant for assessing much of what occurred in the 1950s [when the vast increase in Social Security and other generational transfers began] and virtually everything that has occurred since." As a result, "these policy changes involve either no change or very minor changes in government spending."[23]

Not so, said the CBO. Government spending of almost any kind has "spillover" effects that can benefit so many different groups as to make nearly impossible the kind of neat separation Kotlikoff wanted to achieve between his narrow tax-and-benefit assessment and all the rest of government spending.

"For example, education directly benefits children, but other generations benefit indirectly because the children will be literate when they enter society," the CBO report noted.[24] Just as Kotlikoff complained that leaving long-term payments from Social Security and Medicare out of Washington's annual deficit calculations painted an unreasonably narrow picture of the government's impact on the life of the individual, so did generational accounting's omission of education and other services from its own fiscal portrait.

At the root of the problem with generational accounting, it seemed, was the uncomfortable fact that government and private-sector economic activities, and their impact, were so thoroughly intertwined that separating them produced no very useful result. "What counts," Eisner wrote, "is not net taxes but total net benefits received from government.... What counts even more is the total real benefits that each generation receives from the economy."[25]

Looked at this way, the deficit itself, and the long-term national debt it engendered, presented not so awful a prospect either. According to the generational accounting view, the problem with financing the deficit by issuing more debt—rather than taxing everyone more, as Kotlikoff thought was inevitable—was that it would spook the bond markets. That would jack up interest rates high enough to stifle investment and ruin the economy. This was the same view held by deficit hawks like Richard Darman and Alice Rivlin, which is why generational accounting had intrigued them enough to want to attach it to the president's budget.

But not every reputable economist held this view. Eisner, like Alexander Hamilton in the early days of the republic, saw the debt as an "asset of the American public," which held the bulk of it. The debt was money citizens loaned to the government to provide services they needed, which in turn would help grow the economy and enable the government to pay back the debt to future generations of Americans.

Economists who had closely studied the effect of deficits on interest rates found either that there was very little or that the evidence was inconclusive. As for whether deficit spending really does "crowd out" private investment, a 1993 study by Steven M. Fazzari of the Economic Policy Institute looked at 5,000 companies over 20 years and found that the impact is "likely to be small." The U.S. built up an enormous national debt during World War II, Dean Baker pointed out, equal to 111% of GDP: more than twice the mid-1990s ratio of 52%. But Americans didn't have to shoulder an enormous tax burden to pay it off because the average real interest rate on the debt was -2.6% over the twenty-nine-year period from 1946 to 1975, not the 6% rate that generational accounting used for long-range estimates.

Why a negative rate of interest? Because inflation, even though it was moderate for most of those years, was slightly higher on average than the interest on the debt, causing payments on the debt to lose 40% of their value. While Kotlikoff and his colleagues argued that the expansion of Social Security and the creation of Medicare in the 1960s rewarded current generations with benefits that later generations would have to pay for, the CBO report concluded that inflation went a long way toward evening this out: "Unexpected inflation reduces the real value of government debt and shifts costs from future generations to current holders of the debt."[26]

Because of this, and because each generation tends to enrich the economy it bequeaths to its descendants, each generation doesn't have to return exactly what it put in for the economy to avoid a crash landing in the long run. Kotlikoff's assumption of a zero-sum game was mistaken.

In fact, society already had an institution for redistributing wealth between generations, Baker pointed out: the family. While it's hardly a perfect mechanism in this respect, taking the responsibility for equalizing the benefits of wealth between parents and children out of the family's hands and placing it in the government's would be a controversial move at best—and an ironic one for ostensibly conservative lawmakers to advocate.

Despite the attacks, generational accounting continued to provide a popular set of arguments—plus a lot of scary numbers—for advocates of Social Security privatization. "In a 'wakeup call' study for Merrill Lynch," *Fortune* reported in 1994, "economists Alan Auerbach of Penn and Laurence Kotlikoff of Boston University calculate that Americans not yet born would have to pay nearly all their labor income in taxes. Strong medicine will be required, they say—like a 12% cut in Social Security and health benefits and a 12% rise in income and excise taxes. Immediately. A few lonely Congressmen are trying to kick the dogs. Wish them luck—the longer the wait, the sharper the bite will be."[27]

CHAPTER 18

THE "INTER-GENERATIONAL CHAIN LETTER"

"This is Washington, where nobody ever gets to the second paragraph."

—*Howard Gleckman[1]*

Years after generational accounting first became a topic of conversation in Washington, and with a different President Bush in the White House, Larry Kotlikoff would argue that "reversing the Bush II income tax cuts, eliminating the Medicare drug benefit, or cutting back on military spending are political nonstarters. The only real hope lies in reforming the Social Security and Medicare programs."[2] Was this an admission that focusing on the two big entitlements wasn't the only mathematically feasible way, according to his model, to end the generational imbalance—just the most politically expedient? And just what was a "political nonstarter": something the voters would reject, or something Washington legislators couldn't consider for fear of offending some important sources of funds and, perhaps, future employment?

The answers to these questions weren't forthcoming in the mid- to late 1990s, when full or partial-privatization was being peddled as an inevitable component of any plan to rescue Social Security from catastrophe. Kotlikoff was often an interview subject in the press and a frequent visitor to Capitol Hill, thanks to his breathtaking estimates of future tax burdens if entitlement programs weren't scaled back and his sometimes outrageous rhetoric ("This is not a conservative issue, it's an issue of older people ripping off younger people and extending the scam knowing it was going on," he once told this writer).[3] Between 1992 and 2000 he testified eleven times before House and Senate committees and subcommittees, including three times before panels on Social Security and aging. In 1998, together with Harvard economist Jeffrey Sachs, he produced his own privatization plan.

Kotlikoff and other Social Security critics seemed to have a sort of passkey to the corporate media, judging from a brief scan of leading headlines from some major publications in just the first half of one year—1995:

- "Social Security's Future: Congress Fakes the Ledger" (*New York Times*, column by Martin Mayer, January 30, 1995)

- "We Are a Nation in Deep Denial" (*Newsweek*, March 13, 1995)

- "The Case for Killing Social Security" (*Time* cover story, March 20, 1995)

- "Congress Warned of Peril to Medicare Fund" (*Washington Post*, April 3, 1995)

- "Social Security: Apocalypse Soon—Or Sooner" (*Business Week*, May 1, 1995)[4]

Bob Ball had often said that Social Security would only be in real danger if it lost public confidence. If its defenders were to prevent this, they would need a strong and well-regarded voice in the media's conversation about the program. But groups that had traditionally championed Social Security, such as the AFL-CIO and AARP, found most reporters from mainstream—corporate-owned— print and broadcast media had become innately unsympathetic to their position.

When the labor federation and the National Council of Senior Citizens, which it funded, worked with AARP on a series of press briefings on the subject, "some felt that dinosaurs had walked into the room," Gerald Shea, assistant on government affairs to the president of the AFL-CIO, said of journalists' attitude. "What strikes me about these conversations is that journalists took it personally that they couldn't keep their own money," he told the *Nation*.[5]

"The media have closed off discussion," complained Dean Baker. "They think everyone agrees Social Security is a basket case and has to be overhauled." The presuppositions were often worse in big media hubs like Washington, DC and New York than in smaller urban centers and rural areas where editorial boards were farther from the reach of powerful advocacy groups and the dazzle of their high-profile figureheads. A February 1996 article by the not-unsympathetic Robert Pear of the *New York Times*—extensively quoting Baker defending Social Security's fiscal soundness—ran complete in the *Pittsburgh Post-Gazette* but was published minus any of Baker's quotes in the *Times* itself.

Why the evident bias? The answer has to do with the way in which elite opinion is generated and disseminated. For the most part, members of the Washington press corps and the upper-echelon business journalists who cover economics, the financial markets, and government fiscal policy don't aim to be one-sided. But they prefer to have the facts interpreted for them by people of stature, whether in government, think tanks, or the academic world. In part that's because these people tend to come from the same educational and social backgrounds as do the most prominent journalists. Over time, both groups come to inhabit the same social circles in Washington or lower Manhattan, engendering a mutual familiarity and confidence. On economic and financial matters and fiscal policy, for example, the most prominent reporters turn to economists employed by Wall Street firms or those with prestigious academic credentials. It's then an easy step to assuming that the consensus opinion among these eminences represents a sensible middle ground, when in truth it may only be conventional wisdom. Some prominent reporters and columnists eventually make a career out of translating conclusions and viewpoints that capture what appears to be the best of elite opinion in Washington or New York into language that can persuade popular audiences as well.

The emerging Washington consensus on Social Security was an example of this process. Plenty of reputable economists and public policy analysts didn't agree that the program was in trouble or that it was a danger to the nation's fiscal future, but they tended to inhabit a world far enough to the side of mainstream opinion as to make the journalistic elite tune them out.

In the realm of economics, for instance, one of the most prestigious institutions in the U.S. is the National Bureau of Economic Research (NBER), a think tank run by one of Social Security's longtime critics, Martin Feldstein—"Marty" to everyone of stature in the profession. As a finishing school for mainstream economists, the NBER was instrumental, during the decades following the 1960s, in moving the entire profession to the right. Feldstein's protégés included not just Kotlikoff but Lawrence Summers, who became Bob Rubin's right hand in the Clinton administration.

The NBER also encouraged a shift in economics in a more quantitative direction, which welcomed the challenge of designing more sophisticated long-term projections for such matters as Social Security's fiscal solvency. The new approach promised to make economics more of a hard science and less of a humanistic debating circle like philosophy and political science. But most of the highly influential scholarship emerging from the NBER—the work that attracted the most media attention—was very conservative.

Between 1979 and 1995, the NBER published more than sixty papers authored or co-authored by Larry Kotlikoff, including those that launched and gave initial validation to the concept of generational accounting. Michael Boskin had his byline on thirty NBER working papers between 1975 and 1989, when he left Stanford to become CEA chair in the Bush administration. Half of his topics were related to Social Security, saving, and other aspects of retirement—one of these was on Feldstein's pet topic of Social Security and savings rates.

Feldstein himself authored or co-authored 130 NBER papers between 1977 and 1995 on a wide range of topics, but at least 30 focused on Social Security, savings, and retirement. Overall, the bureau published more than 150 working papers on Social Security between 1975 and 1995, the vast majority of them by conservative economists including Olivia Mitchell, Andrew Samwick, Laurence Lindsey, John Shoven, Sylvester Schieber, Alan Auerbach, Mark Warshawsky, R. Glenn Hubbard, Douglas Puffert, and Zvi Bodie. By contrast, Peter Diamond, a critic of privatization who became a NBER research associate in 1991, published only one paper on Social Security with the bureau during his first five years of affiliation.

The National Academy of Social Insurance (NASI) in March 1995 published a study by Lawrence R. Jacobs and Robert Y. Shapiro—associate professors at the University of Minnesota and Columbia University, respectively—of seventeen years of reporting on Social Security.[6] The study looked at a sample of the largest media outlets, covering some 18,392 Associated Press stories that ran from 1977 through the middle of 1994, plus 7,218 stories from the *New York Times*, the *Los Angeles Times*, the *Washington Post*, *USAToday* and *USAWeekend*, *Time*, *Fortune*, ABC News, and CNN that appeared between 1992 and mid-1994.

Some of the findings were interesting but not surprising. The press tended to equate a story's newsworthiness with the degree to which it suggests "change in people's lives, controversy and partisan conflict." And so the NASI found that Social Security coverage tended to peak in times of crisis: in 1981–83, when the trust funds were nearing exhaustion, the Reagan White House was proposing cuts, and the Greenspan commission was laying the groundwork for the 1983 Amendments; in 1985, when Congress again considered cuts; in 1990, when the Moynihan proposal to return the program to pay-as-you-go status was exciting attention; and 1993–94, when private accounts were becoming widely discussed. Other important but less negative events, like the buildup of a substantial Social Security trust fund and the elevation of the SSA to independent agency status in 1994, barely registered.

None of this would be very alarming if coverage of the issues and events was balanced. What was startling, however, was the clear bias in the overall reporting. "Reports on Social Security's problems and the need for reform was [*sic*] nearly double the coverage given to statements favoring the status quo and maintaining the existing program," the NASI study found for the entirety of AP's coverage from 1977 to 1994. Analyzing 1992–94 coverage paragraph by paragraph, the report found support for benefit reductions ranged from 63% of instances in the newspapers to an overwhelming 81% for the magazines.

Who were the media's sources? "The Republicans were more regularly used as sources than Democrats by an almost 2-to-1 margin," the NASI discovered. This was true regardless of which party controlled the White House: a factor that tends to make a big difference in coverage of most issues. The press cited Democratic lawmakers who favored changing Social Security almost twice as often as Democrats who opposed it, even though the latter outnumbered the former.

Groups like AARP, which opposed cutting or privatizing the program, received "far less coverage" than "pro-change sources." In fact, "interest groups like the AARP were the only major sources who consistently defended Social Security benefits"—creating the impression that policymakers were uniting behind the need for "change" and that support for the program was confined to "interest groups" that, for selfish reasons, were opposed to "reform."

Jacobs and Shapiro declined to speculate on how deliberate all this was, but their study makes clear that by the mid-1990s, the belief that Social Security was troubled and ought to be restructured was deeply ingrained among the relatively small but powerful tribe who make up the mainstream national media.

Asked about the *Washington Post*, which was by then beating the drum regularly against Social Security and Medicare, Martha Phillips, executive director of the Peterson-funded Concord Coalition, explained, "When we first started up, they weren't singing our tune. We sat down and explained why we felt so strongly about the [deficit reduction] program. [The *Post* has] just been reformed on this since then. They are saying entitlements have to be part of the solution. It's like they're reading right out of our playbook."[7]

* * *

In fairness to the media who covered it, the Social Security debate in the mid-1990s was more complex than it had been when Pete Peterson first kicked it into mainstream discourse a dozen years earlier. Every aspect of the program was coming under the microscope now, from the nature of the trust fund assets to the numbers used by the trustees to project its future viability. The critics were adopting harsher and more sensational language to attack Social Security and brand it a rip-off.

The one rhetorical device Americans heard more than any other was the "Ponzi scheme" charge. The epithet was first applied in a 1967 *Newsweek* column by none other than Paul Samuelson, the eminent economist and author of the benchmark college textbook in his field. "The beauty about social insurance," he wrote, "is that it is *actuarially* unsound. Everyone who reaches retirement age is given benefit privileges that far exceed anything he has paid in. And exceed his payments by more than ten times as much (or five times, counting in employer payments)!" The mechanism worked, according to Samuelson, because "there are always more youths than old folks in a growing population.... A growing nation is the greatest Ponzi scheme ever contrived. And that is a fact, not a paradox."

Samuelson wasn't implying that the program was a criminal enterprise. He was only making the point that it was a system of generational transfers, with each wave of recipients deriving their benefits from the contributions of the current generation of active workers. And it was true that most of what the IRS collected every year in payroll taxes went directly to pay for the benefits of current retirees. Only what was left over went into the OASDI trust funds.

How was this different from a Ponzi scheme? A precise answer requires a bit of history. In 1919, Charles Ponzi, an Italian immigrant, set up a company called Financial Exchange of Boston that promised a 50% return to investors within forty-five days. His strategy, he said, was to purchase international postage stamps in countries with low exchange rates and resell them in countries where the exchange rate was high. Within six months he had 20,000 investors and $10 million in capital. Ponzi paid off the first waves of investors with the money chipped in by the next wave, and so on. Daily cash flow was a then-impressive $250,000 or so at the operation's height. But when the *Boston Globe* caught on that there were no real revenues coming into the company, just an endless recycling of investors' cash, and published an exposé, Ponzi was arrested, convicted of fraud, and deported. He died a pauper in Brazil.

A Ponzi scheme relies on successive waves of believers to maintain the flow of funds until there are either no more potential participants or the scam is detected, good faith that fueled it thereupon drying up. Social Security "is akin to an inter-generational chain letter," John Shoven once said. "If today's system could stay in place, today's adults would get $11 trillion more from Social Security than what they will pay in from now on."[8]

But the analogy doesn't hold. First, there's nothing illegal or unethical about paying benefits out of newly contributed funds and borrowing to meet future obligations. Businesses as well as governments do it all the time. Second, Ponzi's scam was a black box—investors took his word that an investment strategy was at work generating returns, but didn't know the details. The mechanism that funds Social Security, on the other hand, is transparent and fully disclosed in an annual report. Third, "real" Ponzi schemes don't last long. Charles Ponzi's racket was designed to generate returns extraordinarily rapidly. The returns were the fruit of an investment strategy that couldn't be verified by anyone but Ponzi himself and that eventually turned out to be nonexistent. Even Bernard L. Madoff's notorious operation, which masqueraded as a money management firm and accumulated assets clear through the most heated years of the Social Security debate, only lasted a bit more than twenty years—mainly due to a network of feeder funds that gave it continuing access to new groups of clients—before a market slump sunk it in a wave of withdrawals. Social Security has a quite different profile: benefits accumulate slowly, over a lifetime of participation.

Fourth, Ponzi schemes aren't invested in anything except more investors. Social Security, through the Treasury bonds contained in the trust funds, is invested in the federal government and its stewardship of the U.S. economy. Expectations of future benefits from Social Security are essentially a bet on the future growth of federal revenues, from payroll taxes and any other receipts Congress may decide to use to fund the program in years to come. This, in turn, is a bet on Washington's ability—through its expenditures on vital services such as infrastructure, research, education, and public health—to keep the economy growing and becoming more productive over time, which, in turn, helps keep those tax revenues rising. Unlike Ponzi's scam, none of this is secret; it's all completely transparent.

"Any attempt to measure the solvency of the Social Security and Medicare trust funds outside the context of the rest of the budget provides an inadequate perspective on their financial status," the CBO said in a 2000 report. "The ability of the government to meet its obligations to Social Security and Medicare beneficiaries depends on the government's overall fiscal conditions."

Its track record on this was easy to check. Over the past 200 years, federal revenues had grown to the point where the United States government was one of the largest enterprises of any kind in the world, with one of the best credit ratings. Looked at this way, Social Security payroll taxes were a good and safe investment. Ponzi's scam, which pledged investors an unheard-of 50% return over just forty-five days and then in perpetuity, had little or nothing in common with a program that promised to pay a modest benefit to each generation out of payroll taxes paid in over decades by current workers, their children, and their children's children. The one was based on chutzpah and flimflam. The other was based on reasonably plausible estimates of how GDP, population, and other factors would affect tax receipts over time.

If workers' payroll taxes were going into a Ponzi scheme, it would be just as proper to suggest that so were the assets that any investor, from an ordinary American worker to the Bank of Japan, used to buy Treasury bonds. However, the real point of the Ponzi scheme analogy wasn't to accuse Social Security's creators of a literal crime or scam. It was to convict them of having granted a huge, unfair "windfall" to the first generations of retirees under the program. "Policymakers have been able to give away $11.4 trillion in unearned benefits to the windfall generations," Schieber and Shoven wrote in 1999. "Now they are going to have to start taking some of it back from those born after 1937."[9]

But how outrageous was this, really? Another way to look at what Schieber and Shoven denounced as a "giveaway" was that it merely institutionalized a benefits system that had already existed informally. Previous generations of workers and their families had taken care of their elderly and infirm relatives out of their own pockets; Social Security merely translated this system into a funded government program with a far wider base of support, without changing its intergenerational nature. If the first generations of retirees under the program had received no benefits, they would have been deprived of support they had earned by caring for their own aged parents and bringing up their children who were now paying payroll taxes.

Besides, as Larry Thompson, principal deputy commissioner of the SSA, pointed out, it's hard to imagine how any national pension scheme—public or private—could gain political acceptance in the first place if the initial cohorts of retirees received very little from the program.[10] As for the debt those first generations passed on to their successors, another name for it was Treasury bonds—which the vast majority of investors would regard as an addition to their personal wealth rather than a burden.

Slashing benefits and partially replacing them with private accounts wouldn't eliminate society's obligation to care for the elderly or make that any cheaper or more manageable. Working households would merely return to the system they had lived under before Social Security was created, supporting their aged and infirm family members out of their own pockets. The cost would be the same whichever of these two systems was in place, except that in transitioning to the new one, workers would have to pay double: to support their parents' retirement as well as save for their own. If the investments that workers chose for their private accounts failed to pan out, however, they would have fewer assets to cover those costs.

* * *

Privatization still had one major advantage over the present system, the critics maintained: it created ownership. Despite its rich use of terminology borrowed from the insurance industry, Social Security wasn't an insurance policy, and workers' payroll taxes weren't premiums that bought them the legal right to a benefit such that it could never be taken away or altered by some whim of Congress. The problem with this particular entitlement, curiously, was that it wasn't really an entitlement at all.

In *Helvering v. Davis*, the 1937 case that established the legality of the payroll tax system, the Supreme Court ruled that Social Security wasn't an insurance program. In a 1960 case, *Nestor v. Flemming*, the Court went further, deciding that the program was actually two legally unrelated things: a welfare program and a taxation scheme. Payroll tax, in other words, was just a tax like any other. It didn't "earn" the worker the right to old age, survivor's, or disability benefits.

While the benefits formula linked the two, this didn't need to be the case. Any time it wanted, the government could adopt a different formula completely unrelated to contributions.[11] In fact, Congress had changed the rules on

Social Security beneficiaries many times in the past: with the 1977 and 1983 Amendments, and later when it cut benefits for former federal government workers who go back to work elsewhere after they retire and begin earning OASI benefits in their new jobs.

Admittedly, beneficiaries didn't have the same kind of rights to Social Security as, say, a private investor had over her IRA, mutual funds, or stock and bond portfolios.* But was OASI really so much less secure a promise than an insurance policy purchased in the private sector? Private insurers can, and do, change the rules governing their policies almost at will: including and excluding certain classes of people, changing the parameters of coverage and the premiums charged, all without any input from policyholders.

Payroll taxpayers, on the other hand, have some ability to stop unwanted changes to Social Security because they can vote out of office any lawmaker they regard as a threat to their benefits. And the Treasury bonds that Social Security purchases with workers' payroll taxes at least have the advantage of being sound investments. Insurance companies have almost total discretion as to how they use their policyholders' payments, sometimes exposing them to very reckless and ill-judged investment strategies: as AIG demonstrated during the 2008 collapse of the home mortgage market.

The criticism of Social Security's lack of property rights merely underscored the fundamental difference between social insurance and the private variety. The one is a collective agreement between all members of society to cover certain needs: a form of mutual aid. The other is a contract between a private provider and a customer in which the provider always has the upper hand. The bottom line for Social Security's defenders was that social insurance was still the best mechanism for meeting a societal obligation like a minimally adequate old-age income.

* * *

When all else failed, critics of Social Security had another, more crudely powerful argument to muster: that the trust funds backing it up weren't "real." The money the government collected in payroll taxes either went to pay current retirees' benefits or was commingled with general revenues at the Treasury and used to pay for other, unrelated government activities. All that was left in the OASI and DI trust funds, the critics argued, were those Treasury bonds—mere IOUs, pieces of paper representing a promise to pay.

Legally, however, those "IOUs" came with the exact same rights as the trillions in Treasury securities sold to the public and traded every day around the

---

* It's an odd contradiction that some of Social Security's critics argue against the program on the ground that it gives politicians too much power over workers' retirement while also complaining that its entitlement status gives too little room to congressional budget cutters to realize their virtuous intentions. See, for example, Sylvester J. Schieber and John B. Shoven, *The Real Deal: The History and Future of Social Security* (New Haven: Yale University Press, 1999).

world. "If the Treasuries are mere IOUs and subject to embezzlement," wrote pension actuary David Langer, "then the mutual funds that carry Treasury securities should, of course, label them as risky, instead of promoting them as the safest of investments, and demand higher interest rates from the Treasury."[12] Nothing of the sort was happening, despite the warnings of Social Security's critics, and investors continued to treat Treasuries as the gold standard.

Perhaps those investors knew something the critics didn't. One possibility was that the Treasury bond market built in an assumption that Washington would figure out how to solve such problems when the time came without either creating a panic among beneficiaries or damaging its long-standing economic prospects. After all, Congress had done this once before, with the 1983 Amendments. "It can be argued," Vincent Truglia, a managing director of the bond rating agency Moody's Investors Services, wrote in 2000, "that the United States 'defaulted' on its social security obligations once it changed the tax laws on social security payments in the 1980s."[13]

Yet no one panicked then, and participants absorbed the long-range changes incorporated in the 1983 Amendments, such as a later retirement age, without much complaint. The U.S. political system was pretty well set up to make long-range adjustments in a vital program like Social Security as long as they were modest and could be phased in gradually. This didn't satisfy the program's critics, however, because they had settled upon the belief that radical changes had to be made, and the sooner, the better.

If benefits remained unchanged—in other words, if the trustees remained committed to making sure retirees' standard of living didn't slip below the current level—they would have to raise the Social Security payroll tax 0.05% a year for both employer and employee for thirty-six years beginning in 2010, Dean Baker calculated, for a total of 3.6%. But this would actually represent a slower rate of growth than in the past: payroll taxes rose by that much in just thirteen years, from 1977 to 1990, for example. Chances were that future taxpayers could handle it, too. By the end of that thirty-six-year period, workers' wages, according to the Social Security trustees, would be 45% higher than in 1998.[14] The economy would probably not capsize either. Over the next seventy-five years, former Clinton national economic advisor Laura Tyson wrote in 2000, Social Security's revenue shortfall would amount to just 2% of total payrolls, or less than 1% of GDP.

Nor was Social Security an appreciably larger burden on the taxpayer than many other government programs. As a percentage of GDP, that seventy-five-year shortfall would be about comparable to the size of the ten-year escalation in military spending that began under Gerald Ford in 1976 and accelerated vastly under Reagan.[15] If such a massive shifting of resources could be engineered in just one decade, surely there was time to absorb something comparable over seventy-five years—if need be.

This missed the point, according to a popular counterargument. Social Security is an entitlement that goes on forever, whereas Congress can increase or decrease military spending as it pleases. The 1976–85 military escalation "paid off" with the winning of the Cold War, in some people's estimation, and a subsequent "peace dividend" of lower military budgets. Social Security, by contrast, would always be in danger of going out of balance, no matter how many times it was fixed.[16]

Yet there was an economic payoff from the provision of old-age, survivors', and disability insurance: a smaller economic burden on the family; a more affluent, higher-consuming elderly population; and better odds that children would become productive workers. Whether this was as economically valuable an outcome as the collapse of the Eastern Bloc was, of course, a matter of opinion.

* * *

When it comes to winning an economic argument in Washington, however, numbers matter. And Social Security's critics had a lock on the numbers: specifically, the projections that appeared every year in the program's annual report. These were prepared by the SSA's Office of the Actuary but were reviewed and signed off by the trustees themselves. The 1983 Amendments, as we've seen, mandated three sets of projections—low cost, high cost, and intermediate—each covering the succeeding seventy-five years, of which the intermediate projections were the ones taken most seriously by lawmakers, the Washington establishment, and the media.

Actuaries are among the most influential groups of quantitative analysts in America and perhaps the least familiar to the general public. A bit like an accountant with a crystal ball, an actuary evaluates the likelihood—the risk—of future events and quantifies the cost of the undesirable ones. Actuarial estimates are the life-blood of the insurance business. In the last quarter of the 20th century, they also came to play a bigger and more central role in the securities industry as Wall Street began creating an array of options, futures, and other "derivative" instruments that played on risk expectations. Earlier, actuarial science was integral to the development of old-age and other social insurance programs. Isaac M. Rubinow, one of the pioneers who fought for workers' compensation and old-age insurance in the decades before the Social Security Act, was also a founder of the Actuarial Society of America.

But "actuarial science" is inexact. The farther into the future actuaries peer, the more their prognostications resemble the odds that bookmakers draw up and the less like truly informed estimates. Not taking into consideration the possibility of a major war or depression is bad enough. But actuaries can commit a major blunder just by getting a projected average interest rate or GDP growth rate wrong by a fraction of a percentage point. The result can be a vast over- or underestimate of the future costs of a program like Social Security.

The problem with the seventy-five-year projections was obvious. No one could reasonably expect to know what sorts of twists and turns the economy, workers' wages, and therefore the revenues flowing into the trust funds would experience over such a long period. When the Social Security Act was passed in 1935, for example, the U.S. had such unforeseeable events in its future as a second World War; the baby boom; an unprecedented, generation-long surge in economic growth; the Cold War; the oil shocks of the 1970s; and the Reagan tax cuts. None could have been predicted by FDR or his advisors.* "The most accurate prediction that can be made about such a forecast is probably that it will be wrong," a SSA economic researcher once wrote.[17]

The intermediate projections, despite their higher level of public acceptance, weren't necessarily any "better" than the high-cost or low-cost projections, either. They just happened to nestle in between the other two. For periods of years in the 1970s and 1980s, the high-cost projections were consistently more accurate than the others; for periods of years in the 1990s, the low-cost projections proved more reliable.

The rate of GDP growth is another crucial factor in the Social Security projections, because there's generally a close connection between economic growth, wage growth, and payroll tax receipts. But the trustees' GDP projections haven't been terribly accurate either. David Langer, a respected pension actuary and student of Social Security, found that the future GDP they chose in their annual reports from 1979 through 1998 ranged from 3% to a depression-level 1.5%, whereas actual long-term average GDP from 1960 through 1998 was 3.3%. [18]

The trustees clearly envisioned a bleak future, not just for Social Security but for the entire U.S. economy. Prudence, or even a healthy dose of pessimism, in predicting the future of an enormous benefits machine like Social Security of course makes sense. But the kind of numbers the trustees were generating appeared to make a case, on the surface at least, for either drastic cutbacks in the program or hefty payroll tax hikes or both. They worked off assumptions very different from those used by other, equally respected government economists. While the trustees in 1997 predicted GDP growth of 2% for that year, for example, the CBO predicted 3.4%. For every year in the next ten, the trustees foresaw 2% growth, over and over, while the CBO projected growth largely ranged from 2.1% to 2.4%.[19]

A year later, the trustees had become even more pessimistic, predicting average 1.8% GDP growth over the next twenty years and not much more than

---

*   Republican politicians, too, were happy to make this point when it suited them. When New Jersey Gov. Christine Todd Whitman was attacked for proposing to reduce the state's funding of its public-employee pension program in 1996, clouding prospects for beneficiaries over a much shorter period than seventy-five years, she answered back, "Sure, you can say 5 years, 10 years, 15 years, maybe the world is going to come to an end, and something bad might happen.... But you know, everything might not come to an end and it might be good" (Lisa Belkin, "Keeping to the Center Lane," *New York Times Sunday Magazine*, May 5, 1996).

1% for much of the period thereafter. How bad would that be? The U.S. would be stuck at the lowest rate of economic growth of any sustained period in its history. America would be a nation in steep economic decline.

If that were the case, the program's defenders often said, Social Security would be far from the biggest concern facing the American people. The nation's attention would likely be focused on how to revive a semi-comatose economy, not how to cut back the disposable income of the elderly. Better yet, many of Social Security's defenders said, why not concentrate on stimulating growth now, as the best way to ensure that the trustees' gloomy scenario wouldn't come true?

For instance, according to Langer, if that less-than-2% GDP growth rate was nudged up to a more realistic 2.9% over the next seventy-five years, the trust funds' deficit would fall from 2.19% of payrolls to 0.71%. The trustees' 1999 report had GDP growth at a shocking 0.4% in 2050 and 0.3% in 2060.[20] A 2.9% GDP growth rate wasn't overly optimistic, either, Langer pointed out, since it was still significantly lower than the 3.2% the economy had experienced since 1930—through depression, recession, stagflation, and several grinding wars.[21]

Not surprisingly, then, the trustees' estimates contained some strange elements. They projected little or no rise in immigration, even though the country would likely be experiencing a labor shortage due to the retirement of the baby boomers. This was because current immigration rates were historically very high: 3.8 persons per thousand in the U.S. were from another country during the period 1991–97, versus 2.1 in the 1960s, for example. For 1998 and 1999, total immigration, including undocumented persons, was 795,000. The trustees, in their 2000 annual report, projected future immigration at 900,000 annually on average over the next seventy-five years.

But was it reasonable to expect the high immigration rates of the 1990s to pick up by only one-eighth, just when the need for labor would be accelerating? Not only does each new arrival add to the current workforce, but since immigrants tend to have higher birthrates than native-born Americans, the effect is multiplied in succeeding decades.[22]

What if the workforce really was going to decline? That might not be such a disaster either. Normally, a declining labor force means growth in wages. This in turn would encourage employers to find more efficient and productive ways to use their workers, which in turn would spur economic growth. So a slowdown in the number of workers entering the job market need not lead to an economic depression. But even these compensating factors didn't make it into the trustees' forecasts. Far from being intermediate, "these projections are genuinely a worst-case scenario," Dean Baker wrote.[23]

How this happened was hard to pin down, because the trustees didn't make the Office of the Actuary's preliminary findings—the raw numbers on which the trustees based their report—available to the public. But some observers were willing to make educated guesses. Langer liked to point to two guidelines of the Actuarial Standards Board, the oversight body for professionals in the business of making economic and demographic projects for insurers, pension funds, and others with long-term liabilities.

Actuarial Standard of Practice (ASOP) No. 27 said that actuaries must use "appropriate recent and long-term historical economic data in making their forecasts." ASOP No. 32 was more specific: "The actuary should consider the actual past experience of the social insurance program, over both short- and long-term periods, also taking into account relevant factors that may create material differences in future experience." If the actuary comes to a conclusion that differs greatly from recent experience, "the report should discuss [the factors] that led to the choice of the assumptions used."[24] In other words, if actuaries decide to weight other factors more heavily than past performance, they must explain why.

The trustees appeared to have been violating these guidelines, increasingly, for at least a decade, Langer charged. Their projections for trust fund solvency were so drastically pessimistic that they seemed to take history into account hardly at all, only economic and demographic trends drawn from the very recent past. That would be the two decades when wages were stagnating and payroll tax revenues, as a result, were consistently depressed. The result would of course be unrealistically bleak long-term projections.

Rep. Jerry Nadler of New York, a Democrat, sent a letter in 1999 asking the Government Accountability Office (GAO) to look into Langer's charges, especially his assertion that the Social Security trustees weren't complying with standard actuarial practices. The GAO hired PricewaterhouseCoopers (PwC), the big accounting firm, to do a study (cost: $500,000). PwC's report came back stating that the actuarial projections in the trustees' report that year were based on generally accepted actuarial standards and that there were "no material defects" in the economic and demographic assumptions behind them.

The firm's 101-page, highly technical document evaluated the methodologies the trustees used to arrive at their projections, from wage growth to retirement rates to disability instance and future GDP, and pronounced them all sound. But it offered no proof that the trustees actually observed those methodologies, nor any explanation for why the results differed so profoundly from past experience.

This didn't satisfy Langer, who noted, for example, that the GAO and PwC accepted assumptions about the increase in total hours worked that were based entirely on workers in the eighteen-to- sixty-four age bracket. What if one result of the predicted imbalance between workers and retirees was that older workers stayed longer in the labor force, or returned to work? And could immigration and productivity gains really be expected to have next to no impact? Evidently, that was what the trustees believed. According to their 1999 report, GDP would rise only 1.5% per year on average for the next seventy-five. Of that, 1.3% would be due to productivity increases—historically, a very low rate. The remaining, barely visible 0.2% would represent a rise in total hours worked. This in spite of the increased burden that caring for a larger population of elderly, for example, would impose.

To many Social Security critics, it made perfect sense to give more weight to recent years in judging the impact of demographics and the economy on the program. "The further back in history you look the less resemblance the economy of that day has to today's economy and, presumably, to that of the future," the Cato Institute's Andrew Biggs wrote.[25] The trouble with this argument was that the shorter the period of time one used to formulate an estimate of future economic performance, the more difficult it became to detect where and how a period of fluke behavior might skew the projections.

Stephen Goss says the trustees had to move to a more "dynamic scoring mechanism" in the 1970s, after Congress made COLAs for Social Security recipients an automatic annual event. And he dismisses complaints about the tendency of the trustees' numbers to veer back and forth between overly optimistic and gravely pessimistic. "One thing that we don't pretend to try and get right is near-term cycles," he says. "But historical paths have followed very closely what we've assumed over the past 20 years."[26]

The trustees assumed long-term real-wage growth in 1983 of 1.5%, for example. In 2010, that had dwindled to 1.2%. But this begs the question of how seriously the trustees' estimates are to be taken when wage growth in that vicinity over a much longer period would be economically disastrous. Surely something would have to change?

Langer's opinion was unequivocal. The trustees were "politically motivated to produce an alarming financial picture of the Social Security program to worry the public into accepting the benefit cutbacks and privatization that have been promoted by those who would benefit from them."[27] The sensitivity of actuarial estimates to the slightest change makes them highly vulnerable to manipulation, Langer noted, especially over a period of seventy-five years and three generations into the future.

Baker, too, complained of "verbal or accounting trickery" and "manipulating" of official numbers in the trustees' reports.[28] But when pinned down, he took a milder position. "Baker suspects the trustees selected assumptions for the 1999 report that would show some solvency progress, but not so much as to jeopardize their plan for keeping Social Security reform on the table," the *Christian Science Monitor* reported that year, when Congress was deeply engrossed in schemes to restructure the program.

The trustees, as a group, were nothing if not partisan. All were political appointees. Their most influential member, the Treasury secretary, was traditionally the most fiscally conservative person in the Cabinet, regardless of the party in power. Together, they had absolute control of the picture their annual report broadcast about Social Security, and suspicions as to how they managed that responsibility weren't confined to the left. Haeworth Robertson, who was the SSA's chief actuary from 1975 to 1978, when the projections were overoptimistic year after year, later said that he encountered White House pressure when he submitted a bleak set of estimates in 1977. The secretaries of Labor and the Treasury, as Social Security trustees, refused to approve his numbers until they were revised upward.[29]

But, in the mid-1990s, all the trustees were Democrats, presumably well disposed toward Social Security. The trend toward more pessimistic trust fund projections began under Bush, yet it had continued undisturbed into the Clinton years. Moreover, not only the GAO study but a Technical Panel on Assumptions and Methods, appointed in 1999 by the Social Security Advisory Board, found the trustees' actuarial estimates to be sound—perhaps even a little more optimistic than warranted.

Neither Langer nor Baker could produce a smoking gun to prove the trustees deliberately distorted the Office of the Actuary's findings to produce overly pessimistic estimates, but they and other critics highlighted an uncomfortable truth about the art of the actuary, and econometrics in general: their inherently subjective nature. If the CBO, with an equally respected collection of technical experts, and well-regarded professionals like Eisner and Langer could come up with very different conclusions about the future direction of Social Security, then why should the trustees' numbers be accepted so much more readily?

One reason, of course, is that the trustees were fiduciaries, public officials appointed by the president and confirmed by Congress, with a legal obligation to carry out their duties responsibly and impartially. David Langer for all his professional attainments, could say whatever he wanted without fear of being brought to book if he was wrong.

Another reason was that the U.S. political and economic mainstream did, in fact, accept the trustees' numbers as the basis for public debate on Social Security. The parties agreeing on this ranged from stalwart defenders of the program like Bob Ball and Henry Aaron to critics like Cato's Andrew Biggs and the AEI's Carolyn Weaver to the major media somewhere in between. PricewaterhouseCoopers, presumably, fell within this spectrum too. This didn't prove the trustees were unimpeachable, only that the assumptions backing their actuarial projections produced numbers that none of the most influential parties felt it necessary to criticize. This was quite an accomplishment at a time when Social Security was becoming a high-profile political issue.

It shouldn't be too surprising, however, when we look back at the past two decades of history accumulated around the trustees and their actuarial forecasts. In the 1970s, when Social Security first lurched into crisis, the trustees' numbers again and again underestimated the fiscal gap the program faced in the near future. The trustees themselves faced a severe loss of credibility they didn't want to repeat.

The 1977 Amendments corrected the over-indexing problem, and the 1983 Amendments made Social Security solvent decades into the future. But by then, the federal budget deficit had become a Washington obsession and both Republican and Democratic leaders, for different reasons, were anxious to emphasize the long-range problem rather than downplay it. By the end of the decade, the trustees' projections were trending more and more in a pessimistic direction. Whether or not this group of political appointees consciously cooked the books may be unanswerable. What constitutes an acceptable actuarial standard is partly subjective, which means that a wide range of assumptions are justifiable.

What's probable is that each group of trustees, being political appointees, were motivated to produce numbers that at least didn't dash the expectations of the people to whom they owed their office. The art of the actuary gave them plenty of room to do so without overstepping accepted practices, at least by very much. So, as each decade gave way to the next, those expectations trended more fiscally conservative. This doesn't mean the trustees' numbers were incorrect or dishonest—whatever that means when it comes to forecasting decades into the future. But it doesn't mean they were correct, either. They were, at least partly, a product of the political climate of the time. And the future, as The Clash liked to say, is unwritten.

CHAPTER 19

MODEST
PROPOSALS

The guts of the arguments for and against Social Security remained invisible to the public in the first half of the 1990s, because the debate didn't satisfy the media's thirst for the sensational. What remained visible were the anti-Social Security movement's most crudely powerful assertions about the program: That it was a scam. A Ponzi scheme. Bankrupt.

"Those who support the generational equity framing tend to focus on the mass media as the arena in which to present their message," John B. Williamson and Diane M. Watts-Roy, two Boston College sociologists, wrote in 1999, when the two sets of arguments were pretty well established. "That arena is supportive of flamboyance, simplification, polarization, and the related styles that emphasize the crisis nature of social problems and issues. Much of the response from the [defenders of the existing Social Security program] is presented in professional journals and academic books."

Over the years, conservatives had acquired a far better comprehension than liberals of how to use the power of the corporate media. As far back as 1954, historian Richard Hofstadter noted how mass communication had "made politics a form of entertainment" and thus, "more than ever before, an arena in which private emotions and personal problems can be readily projected. Mass communications have made it possible to keep the mass man in an almost constant state of mobilization."[1]

By the mid-1990s, conservatives had learned how to keep their core audience in an "almost constant state of mobilization" on any number of hot-button issues, from abortion to crime to their crusade to bring down the Clinton presidency. Social Security seemed, at least superficially, to be ripe for the same treatment. Findings of an imminent "crisis," whether clear-cut or not, are typical of the kind of alarmism that makes headlines and leads off the evening news: the public affairs equivalent of watching car wrecks pile up in a Hollywood blockbuster. "Private emotions and personal problems" are galvanized when Social Security is presented as a "rip-off," and lack of "action" on the issue as the result of a conspiracy of silence amongst do-nothing Washington politicians.

The result, as Hofstadter noted, wasn't really political discourse, but entertainment. By the mid-1990s, the Social Security "crisis" was more than just a matter of discussion amongst the denizens of Washington policy shops, a few lawmakers, and the media bigfeet. It was a full-fledged pop culture phenomenon, with all the attendant wackiness and carnivalesque capers.

In February 1997, *George*, a spiffy new mass-circulation magazine that was attempting to be *Vanity Fair* for addicts of inside-the-Beltway doings, published a special section entitled "Future Crisis: Social Security."[2] It included not a single voice in opposition to the view that the program was in crisis. But it featured a sidebar by Pete Peterson, pleading for the current generation not to hand a huge bill for Social Security and Medicare to Generations X and Y ("C'mon, boomers, all that youthful indulgence will have to mean some extra laps around the track").

The centerpiece of *George*'s coverage wasn't a piece of reportage but a futuristic tale by a cult science fiction writer named Harry Turtledove, menacingly titled "Elder Skelter." In it, after having "cut everything else [in the federal budget] to the bone and further, but not entitlements," there's no money left for Washington to send peacekeeping troops to end a war between Canada and the Republic of Quebec. Elderly demonstrators outside the White House are demanding repeal of a recently passed balanced budget amendment and Social Security spending caps. Young counter-demonstrators are carrying signs reading, "We didn't earn it so you can spend it!" One despondent Cabinet secretary laments, "Too many old folks are voting their monthly checks and their hospital bills. Maybe they could have done something about it back in the '80s or the '90s, but they didn't and it's too late now."

As a kind of doomsday porn, Turtledove's short story was only outdone by a cover piece that ran in the *Weekly World News* in 1995. The supermarket tabloid had been astonishing shoppers for years with such revelations as who fathered the Loch Ness monster's baby, the adventures of Bat Boy (half-bat, half-human, sometime resident of a cave in West Virginia), and a never-ending series of alien abductions, to the point where it had acquired a vigorous hipster following. Readers on July 11 were greeted by the sinister image of a "masked whistleblower" in a black leather cowl with a zipper over the mouth.

"Secret Plot To End Social Security!" the headline screamed, while readers were beckoned inside by the promise, "Gov't informant reveals *EXACT DATE* your benefits will stop!" The "whistleblower's" picture was accompanied, naturally, by a shredded Social Security card.

Not all of the popular media picked up the narrative quite so sensationally. A *New Yorker* cartoon from 1996 showed a tastefully dressed dad glancing away from his newspaper to tell his son, "By the way, Sam, as someday you'll be paying for my entitlements, I'd like to thank you in advance." Running in everything from the supermarket tabs to the top-drawer *New Yorker*, the story of Social Security's impending doom truly had become a sign of the times akin to the proliferation of SUVs and suburban McMansion developments.

As such, it was attracting a new breed of advocates, neither credentialed economists nor think-tank wonks but consultants, policy entrepreneurs, and a few lawmakers, who knew how to infuse the debate with a bit of P.T. Barnum.

The mid-1990s escalation in concern over the long-term cost of Social Security inspired the imaginative Weekly World News. *Other, more prestigious publications were nearly as credulous.*

Pat Moynihan, with his statesmanesque preening while campaigning for a return to pay-as-you-go funding in 1991, may have started the trend, but just a few years later it had attracted several new practitioners.

Perhaps the most extreme was Alexei Bayer, a Russian-born political risk analyst who was welcomed in a variety of mainstream op-ed pages. Bayer published an article in the *New York Times* Sunday business section in 1997 warning darkly about the increasing political dominance of the elderly and offering a remarkable solution. "The elderly are growing richer and more numerous," he wrote, "and unless something is done to curb their expanding political power, programs to benefit them may yet become untouchable." Unless action could be taken, "a mass of Baby Boomers will soon start joining their ranks. In American democracy, money and numbers spell power."

What to do? "A drastic solution," Bayer noted, "would be to put an upper limit on the voting age." Not that he would advocate such a thing. "Depriving the elderly of their right to vote would not be democratic, and it wouldn't sit comfortably with today's political ideals." What might not prove too offensive to those ideals, however, would be to extend the right to vote "to encompass all Americans. A legally designated parent or guardian of a minor should have the right to cast a vote on his or her behalf until the age of 18." Since parents make plenty of economic and social decisions on behalf of their children, they should also have the right to make political decisions on their behalf.[3]

Bayer's scheme eerily recalled the founding days of the republic, when the Constitution allotted a fifth of a vote to slaveholders for each slave they owned—under the rationale that the slaveholder made economic, social, and political decisions on behalf of his human chattel as well. Bayer's article provoked a flurry of negative replies to the *Times*, and no one appears to have pressed his modest proposal any further.

Meanwhile, Sam Beard was angling for a bigger role in the push for privatization. Scion of a wealthy family descended from 19th century railroad baron James J. Hill, Beard was founder of the National Development Council (NDC), a non-profit that helped funnel investment capital into community development projects. A registered Democrat and enthusiastic centrist, Beard liked to talk of his past connections to such disparate figures as Sens. Robert Kennedy and Robert Taft, Jr., and Jacqueline Kennedy Onassis, the latter two having played a role in the NDC.

In 1996, after "more than three years in extensive research and consultation with the leading Social Security and pension experts," Beard popped into the debate with a book entitled *Restoring Hope in America: The Social Security Solution*. The book echoed the by-now familiar theme that Social Security ought to become the cradle of a new society in which everyone was a capitalist: a nation of J.P. Morgans and Bill Gateses where the rising tide would at last truly lift all boats.[4]

Beard duly disparaged America's high rates of personal and state indebtedness, as well as "out of control government spending." A "Battle of the

Generations" was posited. Projections of coming bankruptcy for OASI were trotted out along with the dark suggestion that "government bureaucrats may prefer that this information remain obscure." The Kerrey commission was singled out for "courageous leadership." Mini-profiles of average Americans, not saving enough and nervous about their future in retirement, leavened the projections of how much workers could earn from private accounts, over and above the amounts existing Social Security promised. In language better suited to a huckster than a do-gooder, Beard proposed to ignite an "economic revolution" and create 100 million millionaires in America by the end of 2000.

His bipartisan posture notwithstanding, the scenario he proposed was the same one that had percolated up from conservative economic circles decades earlier. Beard would split the "welfare" and "savings" elements of the program apart by whittling down the existing program into a reduced "Tier 1" benefit and adding as "Tier 2" a mandatory funded, personal investment and retirement account. To run the private accounts, an "independent public-private entity—the Grow America Corporation"—would be established, its nine- to eleven-member board appointed by the president and confirmed by the Senate. Grow America would certify private-sector investment firms to run the accounts, leaving the actual selection of the provider to the participant.

Paying for the transition wouldn't require new taxes, Beard asserted. Instead, he proposed to create and float a new class of government debt: "Liberty Bonds," which more affluent individuals could purchase in exchange for their expected Social Security income. "Liberty Bonds will appeal to Americans' sense of fairness and pride," Beard suggested. And they would save the government close to $100 billion a year by 2025—time enough, theoretically, for the bounty from the private accounts to start kicking in. The result, Beard prophesied, would be a new "democratization of capital ownership" and the salvation of our children's standard of living, not to mention America's economic supremacy, because, he noted, in "the twenty-first century, capital accumulation will be a determining factor in world leadership."

Nothing that Beard proposed differed in any important way from the Kerrey-Simpson bill or the ideas Peter Ferrara had laid out for the Cato Institute more than a decade and a half earlier. Beard's analysis of Social Security's fiscal problems was more or less the same as the one Peterson had been circulating for years. What was new was Beard's tone of earnest, eleemosynary goodwill combined with glib promises of instant wealth.

New, also, was a canny refusal to poor-mouth the existing Social Security system, as Ferrara and many other critics had done in prior years. "America has created a sacred compact through Social Security," Beard wrote. But "business as usual won't work," he warned. His two-tier proposal was a way to "save" the program and extend its promise to create not just old-age security, but wealth. His was a stance calculated to appeal not just to people's greed or their resentment at government, but seemingly to their deeper concerns about the system and the promises it had made.

At the back of his book, Beard included a form that readers could tear out and mail to him care of a new entity called Save Social Security—soon to be superseded by another, more catchily named Beard organization, Economic Security 2000. Beard clearly expected to play a large public role over the next several years.

Some well-heeled backers were hoping he would. To launch Economic Security 2000, Beard received funding from Peter Lewis, a Cleveland millionaire; Teresa Heinz, widow of Pennsylvania Sen. John Heinz, the Republican deficit hawk; Bob Galvin, executive committee chairman of Motorola; and Richard Fisher, retired CEO of Morgan Stanley. Within a few years, Economic Security 2000 would claim a $1.7 million annual budget, active volunteers in every major city, and a team of full-time coordinators to match.[5]

* * *

Given the punchiness—the sheer entertainment value—of the privatization movement's rhetoric,* not to mention its ample funding and access to media, Social Security's defenders had their work cut out for them. There was no shortage of critical voices writing consistently about the shortcomings of the doomsday scenario and defending the program against claims that it was a rip-off. Arguably, their expert credentials were just as good as their rivals'.

One problem was that their position acknowledged that shoring up Social Security's finances while protecting the people who depended on it would require some redistribution of wealth—something that privatization was designed to stave off. Second, their position acknowledged that finding airtight long-range economic solutions to complex challenges such as long-term demographic shifts might be neither possible nor desirable.

Neither of these acknowledged problems was simple, easy, or comfortable to assert in the mainstream media. All too readily, the Social Security proponent came across as a class-warfare radical, an economic ostrich, or both. And so most widely quoted defenders of Social Security shied away from addressing the fundamental economic issues surrounding the program. Instead, they focused on the potential harm privatization could do to the elderly and the lack of proof that Social Security really was in "crisis."

That was a fine short-term political strategy. But it didn't convince most journalists that the program's defenders had as penetrating an economic analysis as its critics did.

Another challenge was the Social Security critics' practice of offhandedly denigrating their opponents to the point of willing them out of existence. "Virtually all serious students of the issues conclude that the nation's demographic structure and the resulting commitments in current law to federal entitlements

---

*   "Hey, shouting 'Bankruptcy' pays off, politically," finance columnist Jane Bryant Quinn noted acerbically a few years later. "Only bores complain" ("Social Security's Fixable 'Crisis,'" *Washington Post*, July 17, 2000).

will continue to outstrip the economy," Syl Schieber and John Shoven wrote with finality in 1999.[6] This was not true. But such assertions leeched easily into the assumptions of the journalists who covered them as news.

For Social Security's defenders, funding was a more basic problem, as it was for any progressive policy position. Between 1990 and 1993, four neoconservative publications—*National Review*, the *Public Interest*, the *New Criterion*, and the *American Spectator*—received a total of $2.7 million in funding from various conservative foundations. These magazines had a limited audience, but they served as a springboard for conservative ideas into the mainstream press. Four large magazines of a progressive bent and with comparable or larger circulation—*The Nation*, *The Progressive*, *In These Times*, and *Mother Jones*—received only a tenth of that funding during the same period.[7] A similar comparison could be made of well-endowed conservative think tanks and their more liberal rivals.

Another problem was perceived credibility. Bob Ball and Bob Myers, the most eminent defenders of the program, were seen as part of the Social Security "establishment" and therefore as representing the vested interests of the SSA bureaucracy. Any diminution of OASI, Disability Insurance, or SSI would lessen their prestige and that of their successors in the agency. Therefore, they could be pigeonholed as knee-jerk opponents of change, whatever the merits or changing circumstances might recommend. Ironically, it wasn't their many disagreements over the years that made them questionable, but the one point on which they did agree—namely, that Social Security shouldn't be privatized.

Robert Eisner was a highly honored academic economist, but he was also a plain spoken, unreconstructed Keynesian and therefore easily dismissable by financial journalists who were taught to believe that Keynesian economics had been discredited in the 1970s. Economists like Dean Baker and public policy scholars like Teresa Ghilarducci of the University of Notre Dame were serious analysts who raised important questions about the Social Security critics' line. But Baker had no academic affiliation, instead working for an organization—the Economic Policy Institute—that received much of its funding from organized labor and therefore could be viewed as biased in favor of the program as it was. And Ghilarducci occasionally consulted for the AFL-CIO, making her, too, clearly suspect.

Of course, the same could be said about the scholars and economists on the other side of the issue. Economists like Michael Boskin, Richard Darman, John Cogan, and John Shoven were denizens of Stanford University's Hoover Institution on War, Revolution and Peace, a neoconservative hotbed nurtured by generous funding from corporations as well as longtime right-wing donors like the Scaife family. Other critics of Social Security were similarly tainted by their patrons' ideological predilections. Peter Ferrara, for instance, was a creature of the Cato Institute, Syl Schieber the employee of a private consulting firm that could profit from Social Security privatization.

Neither side in the Social Security debate, then, was even remotely free of ideology. Yet the program's critics enjoyed a certain exemption from the skepticism this would normally cast over their views. One reason was the position several of the key critics occupied in the mainstream of the economics profession. However ideologically biased Boskin and Shoven, for example, might be, their work bore the imprimatur of the NBER—for many, the Good Housekeeping Seal of Approval, ensuring that their work wasn't quirky or questionable. Baker, by contrast, was not an academic economist.

Eisner, Munnell, and Diamond were. But while their peers held them in high regard, they didn't have quite the cachet of their opponents. Diamond had seven NBER working papers to his credit by 1995, for example, but Munnell and Eisner had none.

Additionally, Social Security's defenders didn't have an institution comparable to the NBER to confer an aura of authoritativeness on their work. In the pre-Reagan era, the SSA itself housed an Office of Planning and Evaluation that was a nexus for creative thinking about Social Security. Much of the conceptual and planning work that led to the creation of Medicare, for example, took place there. Republicans considered it to be part of the "permanent government": the liberal bureaucracy they made it their mission to root out during the Reagan years. Accordingly, the Office of Planning and Evaluation was downsized and then phased out. The SSA never again had a strong capability to assess the evolving needs of Social Security participants and develop proposals to address them, even though its people were the best placed to do so.

Some progressive-leaning think tanks partially took up the role. Besides the EPI, the New York-based Twentieth Century Fund and the somewhat more centrist Center on Budget and Policy Priorities consistently criticized the position papers flowing out of Cato, Heritage, AEI, and the like and took issue with privatization proposals popping up in Congress. And Bob Ball in 1986 organized a group of progressive economists and policy analysts to create the National Academy of Social Insurance, to help rejuvenate the vision behind Social Security and Medicare.

The NASI quickly became a respected member of the Washington think-tank community and produced much valuable research, not to mention accurate information, otherwise scarce, about how Social Security and Medicare really work. However, the academy never played the role Ball had hoped it would. He complained that the NASI was "afraid to take strong stands for social insurance principles because that wouldn't represent the views of all the members."[8] By the mid-1990s, those members included enemies of Social Security such as Carolyn Weaver and Haeworth Robertson.

Another problem, especially from the mainstream media's point of view, was the very analysis the critics of Social Security's critics put forward, which always had a defensive air. Economists like Diamond and Baker and public policy scholars like Kingson and Quadagno attacked the arguments against the program on every front, and in so doing, developed a credible alternative view of what Social Security's future could, or likely would, look like. But it was difficult to find that view expressed concisely in one place, either in their scholarly writings or in their rare incursions into the corporate media, except as elements of an argument against the program's enemies.

Kingson and Williamson worried that the pro-Social Security side lacked a concise, overarching message. Fundamentally, the program stood for a few simple and understandable principles, which were virtually unchanged since Bismarck had adapted them from mutual aid to implement State-based social insurance more than 100 years earlier:

- In a highly complex, interdependent society, individuals have needs that can only be met by other individuals and social institutions;

- This creates a collective responsibility, promoting social cohesiveness in a culturally diverse nation; and

- Every generation owes something to those that came before, who gifted it with customs, education, and skills that help it to make its way in the world.*

But there was nothing forward-looking in these statements, and in any case, they too often got lost in a sea of rebuttal, the content of which was dictated not by the defenders of Social Security but by the critics they were struggling to answer. Social Security's critics offered a stirring vision of a new "ownership society" in which everyone had a chance to strike it rich through private accounts. Aside from criticizing the critics, where was the inspiring picture of the future coming from Social Security's defenders?

What the program's defenders needed to emphasize, Kingson and Williamson wrote in 1998, was that the debate wasn't really about demographics, fiscal projections, or the definition of Social Security "insolvency." It was a struggle between "two very different value systems: the community-enhancing values of the program's defenders versus [the] libertarian values of its critics."[9]

In other words, the debate was "fundamentally about our sense of responsibility to each other; about the basic protection that each American should be assured of for themselves and their families" against old age, disability, and survivorship. Others recognized this as well. Jeff Nygaard of the Social Security Project of Minnesota called for a long-term, grassroots effort to reestablish the

---

* "We all stand on the shoulders of generations that came before," Bob Ball wrote. "They built the schools and established the ideals of an educated society. They wrote the books, developed the scientific ways of thinking, passed on ethical and spiritual values, discovered this country, developed it, won (and protected) its freedom, held it together, cleared its forests, built its railroads and factories and invented new technology" (quoted in John M. Cornman, Eric Kingson & Donna Butts, "Should We Be Our Neighbor's Keeper?" *Church & Society*, May/June 2005).

program's founding principles. "We need to formulate a positive proposal that states what we want in a system of Social Security, based on clearly articulated values," he wrote. "Without such a proposal, it is unreasonable to expect anything other than cutbacks in the program; the only question will be how many and how large."[10]

One problem, then, was an apparent lack of vision. Another was that the program's defenders didn't form the kind of intensive, tight-knit community their opponents did.

Journalist David Brock has written of his personal experience being nurtured in the web of conservative think tanks, publications, informal groups for study and deliberation, and staff positions with sympathetic lawmakers that did so much to remake the American political establishment. By keeping its members in close, self-reinforcing proximity to each other, one of its achievements was to foster the development of a remarkably consistent storyline about complex issues such as Social Security.[11]

Within the movement against Social Security there were disagreements, principally between the Free Lunch Caucus and the Pain Caucus, but these differences were of emphasis, not of methods or basic objectives. The result is that the "story" about Social Security that comes through in countless academic papers; promotional pieces and advertising; magazine, newspaper, and network television features; and public statements on the campaign trail and in the halls of Congress is more or less the same. We've already seen its elements repeated many times, but it's helpful to remind ourselves of how simple, compact, and powerful it was:

- Social Security is unquestionably going bankrupt, victim of fundamental flaws in its structure, an aging population, and overgenerous benefits;

- If Social Security isn't to bankrupt the next generation along with it, the solution must be some combination of benefits cuts and higher contributions; and

- Social Security is a bad deal for the young. The above solutions don't do much to help them. To correct this, they must be allowed to divert some portion of their payroll taxes, at least, into personal investment accounts. This will accomplish two other, necessary things: raising the nation's woeful savings rate and injecting much-needed investment capital into the American economy.

Each of these arguments was based on a quicksand of dubious assumptions and misused actuarial projections. But nothing in privatization opponents' arsenal could match the sheer rhetorical punch of these three simple declarative statements, which people in all walks of American life heard repeatedly, in one form or another, year after year.

Serious differences between the propagators of this basic analysis—especially, what to do about the transition costs, which would complicate any attempt to fund private accounts out of carve-outs from payroll tax revenues—were seldom discussed outside Capitol Hill meeting rooms and Washington working breakfasts and lunches and in conferences and formal gatherings of the faithful. And they rarely got aired in the corporate media, in part because it was understood that they weren't helpful in selling the vision and in part because the media itself generally found them too arcane.

The result was that, for the public, the argument against Social Security came infused with a sense of inevitability, and its opponents' reasoning with the odor of an anxious attempt to hold back the future.

* * *

Social Security's critics weren't remiss in attacking their opponents more directly—in particular one of Social Security's strongest defenders: the Gray Lobby.

AARP was widely regarded, not completely accurately, as the chief promoter of Gray Power and thus the chief institutional obstacle to Social Security change. In fact, the most effective groups in the battle for the rights of the elderly over the past three decades had been grassroots organizations like the labor-backed National Council of Senior Citizens and the far more militant and radical Gray Panthers. But AARP, with its 32 million members and its sprawling new headquarters building at Sixth and E Streets, in the heart of downtown Washington, had greater symbolic value.

Alan Simpson, fresh from his service on the Kerrey commission, decided to take on AARP in the early months of the Gingrich Congress. The group was one of several nonprofits—the National Rifle Association was another—that depended for a great deal of its revenue on royalties, including income from discounted insurance and prescription drug deals for members. It also received grants—competitively bid—to run a number of federal programs for the aged. After a great deal of struggle finding Democrats to work with him, Simpson managed to get a provision aimed at AARP into a Lobby Reform Bill that passed Congress and received the president's signature in December 1996. It made any registered 501(c)4 nonprofit organization—any nonprofit in the social welfare field—that lobbies, ineligible to receive federal grants.[12]

AARP didn't oppose the measure, however. "Its impact was purely a structural/legal matter," says John Rother, the group's leader on policy and strategy. AARP found it could meet the new standard simply by moving its federal grant-driven activities into a non-lobbying, non-profit entity or charity. Accordingly, it transferred its federal projects to its existing charitable arm, the AARP Foundation. "We adapted to the new law, but we haven't changed the fundamental nature of our mission or how we work to achieve it," says Rother.[13] The National Council of Senior Citizens did the same, creating the National Council of Senior Citizens Education and Research Center to house its grant work. Conservative critics of welfare for lobbyists would continue to search, mostly fruitlessly, for ways to stop this sort of thing.

The assault on AARP wasn't entirely a failure, however. Sensing that the tide of public opinion might be shifting, its leadership began pulling back from more strenuous opposition and instead began to advocate for restructuring Social Security over the next several years, adopting a tacit policy of refusing to take a position on specific proposals.

Horace Deets, AARP's executive director, pointedly declined to oppose partial-privatization of the program in an April 1998 appearance on *Face the Nation*. Chances that AARP would ever become a full-fledged ally of privatization were next to zero, of course. But if conservative critics of Social Security couldn't cripple AARP, they could still do the next best thing: create a rival.

Three groups, by this time, were trying to forge a mass-based rival to AARP on Social Security: the Seniors Coalition, founded in 1989; United Seniors Association, formed in 1991; and 60 Plus, which opened its offices in 1992. All three were incubated by Richard Viguerie, the powerful Virginia-based Republican direct-mail guru. Viguerie had received his political baptism working on the 1964 Goldwater presidential campaign and later played a role in bringing several important anti-abortion and Christian right groups to visibility.

The idea was that Republican leaders could use the conservative seniors' groups to demonstrate that their policies had support among the elderly; the groups in turn could use the lawmakers' attention as a way to legitimize themselves. All three were classic examples of "astroturfing"—ostensibly spontaneous, grassroots political advocacy efforts that actually generated their "mass support" through direct mail and phone banks rather than on-the-ground organizing. Astroturfing had been used by private companies, foreign governments, unions, religious organizations, and other interests that wanted to disguise their sponsorship of a particular cause. But as data collection capacity grew ever bigger, some list entrepreneurs began midwifing astroturf groups themselves—in part, it was charged, to generate new customers for their lists.

The Seniors Coalition and United Seniors worked unsuccessfully with 60 Plus to defeat the boost in taxes on Social Security benefits that Clinton included in his first economic bill. When Congress took up abolition of the earnings limit for Social Security recipients, that provided an opportunity for the three groups to augment their popular base by underscoring their support for measures that helped seniors. And all three were on board when the new Republican Congress made its failed run at a Balanced Budget Amendment.

Not surprisingly, the three groups also found time to attack their big rival directly. "AARP: Association Against Retired Persons" was the slogan on a bumper sticker distributed by 60 Plus. The trouble was, the three groups couldn't claim a very solid base to begin with, and nowhere near the size of the giant at Sixth and E. At an April 1995 rally on the Capitol steps to pump up support for the Republican Congress's first budget, leaders of the Seniors Coalition, United Seniors, and 60 Plus stood with congressional leaders. "With us in charge, we've given them a voice, and appropriately so," House Majority Whip J. Dennis Hastert of Illinois said later in an interview. But even though the Seniors Coalition offered to pay the way for some of its members to come to Washington for the event, the *National Journal* counted only about fifteen seniors in the crowd. The rest were reporters or aides.[14]

One reason for the conservative seniors groups' relative lack of success was financial pressures. The fees they paid to Viguerie made it impossible to make full use even of the dues they collected. But this wasn't the whole story. Viguerie was a skilled and successful movement builder who had used similar techniques to help transform other conservative organizations from astroturf entities into something resembling large, active membership organizations. Try as they might, however, advocates of Social Security privatization found that their message received a better welcome from the country's policy-making elite than from the country itself. Another approach was needed. Even as their attempts at "grassroots" organizing stumbled along, the master narrative they were selling to the elite was evolving in a new direction.

CHAPTER 20

CHILE'S PENSION REVOLUTION

America's conservative polemicists and policy entrepreneurs discovered a new poster child in the 1980s: Chilean dictator Augusto Pinochet. Leader of the junta that had engineered a bloody coup against socialist president Salvador Allende in 1973, Pinochet then went on to wage a savage clandestine war against his country's leftists. But he also spent much time trying to stimulate Chile's crisis-ridden economy. Privatizing Chile's national old-age pension system was at the core of the economic program he finally settled on, after several sharp bumps in the road.

Chile was hit hard by the price collapse of copper and many other commodities in the 1970s, and during Pinochet's early years in power, the situation mainly deteriorated. From a 4.3% unemployment rate in 1973, the nation's workforce slumped to 22% jobless a decade later. Chile was running a huge budget deficit, and inflation was galloping, while wages failed to keep up. Initial efforts to revive growth through currency devaluation and removal of price controls failed to pan out. Two years after the coup, Pinochet's government turned to a cadre of U.S.- trained economists known as the "Chicago Boys" who were urging a more drastic solution.

José Pinera, an engaging young economist who had earned his Ph.D. at Harvard under Kenneth Arrow, an economist sharing Milton Friedman's free-market positions, became labor minister in 1978. The country's pay-as-you-go pension system* was, by then, essentially bankrupt, victim of both inflation and a decades-old social compact according to which the government paid generous social benefits but had never taxed personal incomes adequately to pay for them. Pinera proposed replacing the program with a privately funded system.

Adopted by the Pinochet government in 1981, this new system was something dramatically different from virtually any existing national pension program: a government-administered and regulated marketplace of private investment accounts. Chile replaced guaranteed, universal state pensions for most retired workers with a small, means-tested minimum benefit. In addition, workers could opt to deposit at least 10% of their wages—the size of the old payroll tax—each month in private investment accounts (PRAs). Employers, who had contributed to the old system, no longer had to do so.

Legally, the accounts were private property, earmarked to fund each worker's retirement. In reality, however, the contributions were funneled into a set of government-approved and regulated private Pension Fund Administration (AFP) companies, each of which invested in a diversified, low-risk investment portfolio. Each PRA holder was required to make an additional 2% contribution to purchase disability and survivor's insurance. Since the remaining minimum old-age benefit was so small, 95% of current workers elected to join the AFP system. All new entrants to the work force were required to join the new system.

Once aboard, they were free to switch between the various AFPs, setting up competition for which provider could supply the highest returns and best service. Every three months, participants received a statement telling them how much was in their accounts and how well their investments had performed. Later, many AFPs put computers in their offices, allowing customers to project how large a benefit they would receive at retirement and how much more, if any, they should contribute with each paycheck if they wanted to augment that figure. "Once he gets the answer, he simply asks his employer to withdraw that new percentage from his salary," Pinera noted.[1]

Upon retirement, the worker could either purchase an annuity from a private insurer, take phased withdrawals from her AFP account, or some combination of the two. The annuity must guarantee a monthly income for life and be indexed to inflation. And if there was any money left over from the phased withdrawals after the retiree died, the balance would go to her heirs.

The new retirement system also retained a safety net. Those who had worked at least twenty years but hadn't accumulated a benefit at least equal to what the law defined as a "minimum pension" by the time they reached retirement age,

---

*   Chile was the first country in the Western Hemisphere to establish a comprehensive social security program providing coverage for old-age, survivors, and disability benefits (Barbara E. Kritzer, "Privatizing Social Security: the Chilean Experience," *Social Security Bulletin*, September 1996).

were entitled to receive a minimum benefit out of general government revenue once their PRAs had been depleted.

By March 1995, five years after Pinochet stepped down and the country began its transition back to democracy, Chile had twenty-one approved AFPs managing assets worth $23 billion, or half of the country's GDP, for 6 million workers. The government boasted that the average retiree with a PRA was receiving a pension equal to 70% of average annual income while for those whose investments didn't pan out, a means-tested safety net was still in place.[2] By 1990, total government expenditures had dropped from 34.3% of GDP in 1984 to just 21.9%, half of that decline owing to the transition away from the old pension system with its more generous guaranteed benefits.

Perhaps most important for critics of social insurance systems, the injection of billions of dollars of workers' assets into the Chilean markets "has been the

José Pinera, architect of the private accounts-based revamping of Chile's national pension system under the Pinochet regime. He later became co-chair of the Cato Institute's Social Security Privatization Project and a global ambassador for pension privatization.

single most important structural change that has contributed to the doubling of the growth rate of the economy in the 1985–1997 period," as Pinera later asserted. Turning Chilean workers—and their paychecks—into a legion of investors would speed the birth of a new market economy, modeled after the U.S. It would also encourage the dissolution of a separate working-class consciousness, Pinera prophesied, as Chileans became instead "a Nation of Owners."[3]

This was a powerful vision, and one that began to attract attention in elite circles in the U.S. even before the PRA system went into effect. In November 1980, with the ink drying on the new social security laws and their effective date still six months away, conservative pundit William F. Buckley, Jr., lunched with Pinera in Santiago, heard the story of the new, market-driven pension system, and was enchanted. Two weeks later, he devoted his syndicated column to it.

Less than two months later, Pinera received another American visitor, George P. Shultz, Bechtel president, former Treasury secretary, and one of the key figures on President-elect Reagan's transition team. Shultz, who had taught at University of Chicago Business School when Friedman was the star of its economics department, was also interested to hear about the PRA program. On January 25, he followed up this meeting with a letter to Pinera that concluded, "I look forward to getting from you the English-language statement about your new and creative Social Security system."[4] Whatever one thought of Milton Friedman's economics, the reach of his personal influence among conservative influentials was impressive.

One important aspect of the PRA program that Buckley's column had failed to mention, however, was transition costs. Pinera boasted his creation "solves the typical problem of pay-as-you-go systems with respect to labor demographics: in an aging population the number of workers per retiree decreases. Under the PRA system, the working population does not pay taxes to finance the retired population." No generational conflict, no prospect of eventual bankruptcy for the system. But the Chilean state still had to pay the benefits of current retirees under the old pay-as-you-go arrangement. And it couldn't start out millions of mid-career workers from scratch: it had to credit their accounts somehow for the years they had already been employed.

The answer was to deposit a "recognition bond" in each worker's new PRA reflecting the rights she had earned under the old pension system. The bonds were indexed to inflation, earned a 4% real interest rate, and matured when the worker reached legal retirement age. They were also tradeable on the secondary markets, like other Chilean government bonds. In other words, the government gave each worker a sum of money to start off with, backed by the tax-payers—i.e., the workers themselves.[5] In addition, when the new system was inaugurated, all employers were required to increase their workers' pay 18% to ensure the deductions going into their PRAs wouldn't leave them strapped.

All this was very costly—especially launching the recognition bonds. Chile could pay for it because, thanks to drastic government spending cuts imposed a few years earlier, plus a recovering copper market, the country was running a budget surplus equal to a hefty 5.5% of GDP—large enough to cover most of the transition bill.[6] Workers, for their part, got PRA accounts that looked nothing like the diversified investment portfolios that most individual savers would expect. The PRAs couldn't hold stocks, either of Chilean or foreign companies. Investment in Chilean corporate bonds was limited, too. Instead, workers held the recognition bonds, plus other government bonds as well as bank debt, including mortgage-backed securities. Effectively, workers were being asked to place a big bet on the government and on a narrow group of reprivatized banks that had fallen into the hands of two speculators, Javier Vial and Manuel Cruzat.

Vial and Cruzat used capital from foreign loans as well as PRA investments to buy up Chilean manufacturers and other newly privatized companies, creating two very shaky conglomerates that collapsed when another economic downturn commenced in 1982. With them ended a real estate and consumption boom that had given the country the illusion of prosperity for a few years. Many local financial operators went bankrupt, leaving more and more of the AFPs in the hands of North American titans like Citibank and Bankers Trust Company. Chile experienced its worst economic downturn since the 1930s, with GDP dropping 14% and unemployment reaching 30% in 1983: more than six times the rate during the worst days of the reviled Allende. By the time military rule ended in 1990, real wages were 40% below where they had stood when the junta took over.[7]

Beset by public unrest, the regime dismissed the austere prescriptions of the Chicago Boys and rushed to stabilize the situation. It devalued the overpriced peso, took over many large businesses, and assumed $16 billion of foreign loans that Vial, Cruzat, and other speculators had taken on during the fat years.[8] Many of the AFPs fell back into government hands, too, after which they were sold off to U.S. companies.

The copper industry remained government property even after Pinochet reprivatized many of the failed businesses—often into the hands of the AFPs, which ended up purchasing up to 35% of the equity of, for example, the Santiago subway system and Chile's national telecom network.[9] Copper revenues covered much of the cost of the bailout and, in many years, supplied more than half of the nation's export earnings. Another source of funds, of course, was the AFPs, which continued to buy government debt and stuff it into workers' PRAs.

By the end of the Pinochet era, then, Chile's economic profile wasn't all that different from the one the general had inherited. Natural resources exports still accounted for the lion's share of growth, supplemented by a vibrant agricultural sector that had benefited from a land reform program begun, ironically, under Allende. The PRA pension system, ostensibly privatized, still held 44% of its assets in government bonds, 33.5% in bank debt and bank-guaranteed mortgage bonds, and a mere 11.3% in publicly traded stock.[10] Pre-dictatorship, workers depended on the government for their pensions; post-dictatorship, they still depended largely on government, the only difference being that this relationship was now embodied in treasury bonds sitting in their PRAs.

In fairness, Chile continued to tweak the PRA system throughout the military period, widening the circle of permitted investments, introducing tighter regulation of financial institutions and markets, and keeping the AFP business separate from banking and insurance companies to prevent conflicts of interest. Workers' investment choices were limited to securities that were appropriate to each stage in their careers—riskier in the early years, less risky as they approached retirement—somewhat reining in the possibility of reckless behavior.

The system had a nagging drawback, however: it cost the worker a lot of money. Because the investment choices were so tightly constrained, the AFPs had a hard time differentiating their products. So they launched massive, expensive marketing campaigns, including TV advertisements and the dispatch of an army of salespeople to buttonhole workers, often in and around their workplaces, to place their PRA with one or another AFP. Often, the sales reps mobilized were young, female, and clad in short skirts.

All of this was unprecedented in a relatively small market like Chile. Rolling up all the expenses associated with the program—collection, maintenance, and fund management; annuity charges for retirees; disability and survivors' insurance—two researchers, Peter Diamond and Salvador Valdés-Prieto, placed its average total cost at $89.10 a year per worker in 1991. In the U.S., by contrast, Social Security cost an average $15.10 a year. Administrative costs alone swallowed up about 13% of Chilean workers' contributions, whereas corresponding costs for Social Security claimed less than 1% of Americans' payroll taxes.[11] A later study found that the average worker entering the privatized system after 1990 would have received negative returns through 1998 while the average worker contributing since 1982 would have had better results investing her account in ninety-day bank certificates of deposit.[12]

"Chilean costs are close to those of very expensive government-managed systems," Diamond and Valdes-Prieto found—for example, the Zambia Provident Fund, or the 401(k) market in the U.S., with its high marketing and administrative costs. Meanwhile, the government offset the cost of launching the new system partly by eroding the benefits paid to retirees under the old, pay-as-you-go system. In 1985, in the midst of the economic collapse, it slapped a COLA freeze on retirees. After the downturn eased, it partially made up what they had lost, but also allowed inflation to reduce the minimum pensions under the old system—upon which the poorest retirees depended.[13]

There were other problems. Under the old system, which had a complicated structure, the big chunk of the population who worked in low-wage jobs or the large informal sector received either very low benefits or none at all. Because the new system included only people who held formal employment, and because their accumulated benefits depended on how much they were able to contribute to their PRAs, it did nothing to correct this. By the late 1980s, thanks to a combination of high unemployment, weak enforcement of labor laws, and widespread casual labor, only 56% of workers and their families were participating in the PRA scheme.[14]

For women, the figure was 45%, and therein lay another major problem with the new system: there was nothing redistributive about it. Unless she spent nearly her whole working life in low-paying employment, and thus qualified for a minimal benefit from the government—for "welfare," in the American sense—the worker's old-age income depended entirely on what she was able to contribute to her PRA. The more you earned, and the more years you could contribute, the more you got. As most everywhere else, women in Chile worked fewer years than men and for lower pay, seriously disadvantaging them under the new system.

"The new private pension system thus reinforces the gender inequalities generated in the labor market," one study concluded. It also "punishes maternity: women pay higher costs for bearing children if it leads them to interrupt their participation in the labor market, to stop making contributions, or to lose productivity and income." The commission the AFPs charged for managing the assets in the PRAs was fixed; no income-based discounts were offered. Therefore, they hit women and low-income men harder than more affluent males.

Thanks to the inability of these workers to accumulate an adequate benefit through their PRAs, one economist calculated that the government—that is, the taxpayer—would still be paying out some $60 billion a year, or 3% of GDP, in minimum pension benefits. While this was far below what the State had expected to owe under the old system, it still represented a major expenditure.[15]

* * *

Very little about these headaches surfaced in U.S. press coverage of the Chilean experiment. It helped that the Chicago Boys proved an adept group of self-promoters once international attention was focused on their work. As early as 1988, Pinera was wooing an American audience with an appearance on his friend Buckley's PBS TV show, *Firing Line*. "The key to the hour is Mr. Pinera's persuasive charm," the *Firing Line* program notes stated. "He describes his hopes for his country's political and economic future with eager confidence, and it is easy to see how he convinced a government that must have been dubious at best to try something new and daring."

By the mid-1990s, when Pinera, defeated in a run for the Chilean presidency, announced he was joining the new Cato Project on Social Security Privatization in Washington, a large swath of elite opinion, including many Democrats, had seemingly agreed that the "Chilean miracle" was an extremely compelling model for restructuring Social Security. The evident success of a personal account-based "solution" to the problems of a mature old-age pension system became perhaps the most powerful weapon in the privatization movement's arsenal.

"Even though most (North) American politicians would rather talk about *any* other issue than this one, it's a reform that will have to be considered as our fragile social-security system slides toward financial and demographic catastrophe," *Newsweek*'s Joe Klein wrote confidently in December 1994.[16]

The quotable Pinera was adept even at deflecting misgivings about his rather grim employer. Asked about the paradox that the brutal Pinochet regime had given him the room to conduct his pension experiment, he responded, "Pinochet has a great nose. He smelled the future. He could have sold out to the vested interests—as most generals do—and retired with $50 million in a Swiss bank account, but he was more interested in a place in history."*

Nothing was more crucial to putting across the privatization argument, however, than the fact that other nations were thinking about adopting Chile's example. In 1988, Margaret Thatcher's U.K. government allowed workers to redirect their contributions from the state's supplementary earnings-related pension program into personal pension accounts. In 1994, a new, conservative government in Italy cited the PRA system as the model that country must adopt to overcome its own projected old-age crisis. "Recently, several Latin American nations, including Mexico, Peru, Colombia and Argentina, have adopted variations of the Chilean pension system," the *Wall Street Journal* reported that same year.[17]

By the early 1990s, Pinochet and his advisors, just out of office, seemed to have captured something of a mood shift among policy elites—not just in Latin America, but in Western Europe—that paralleled the rise of the movement against Social Security in the U.S. and, in turn, would help to reinforce it. Soon, the new governments of post-Soviet Eastern Europe would experience the same shift. Worried to varying degrees about aging populations and sluggish economic growth, all were searching anxiously for a set of solutions that would put these problems to rest.

The World Bank in 1994 published a report titled *Averting the Old Age Crisis*, which promoted the PRA program as not only a path to pension reform but a blueprint for transforming an entire economy. In this highly influential book,[18] the Bank, whose lending operations wielded extraordinary power over the cash-strapped states of Latin America and the former Soviet bloc, codified the Chilean system into what it called the "three-pillar" model of pension reform. The three "pillars" followed precisely the model that the Social Security privatization movement was pushing for in the U.S.:

- A means-tested, "publicly managed system with mandatory participation," intended only to reduce poverty among the elderly;

---

*   It came to light several years later that Pinochet had indeed secreted quite a few millions in discreet Alpine banks. But in the 1990s, he was successfully burnishing a reputation for personal integrity that aided his advisors' public relations success.

- A privately managed, mandatory savings system; and

- Voluntary savings.

The Bank gave *Averting the Old Age Crisis* a tremendous publicity build-up, and its impact in developing countries was huge. Its genius—as a marketing tool, at any rate—was to cast pension privatization as the catalyst for a "virtuous cycle" of rapid economic growth and development: private pension accounts lead to larger and deeper securities markets, which increase economic growth, which further build up pension funds, and so on.

Critics found this scenario unconvincing. Pensions can't create large, robust securities markets. The markets must exist first. Other developing countries, including India, had kickstarted their economies without either enormous pension accumulations or enormous stock markets. And unless the markets had a strong legal underpinning and were well regulated, the result of pumping them full of pension assets would likely be fraud and collapse.

But Eastern European finance ministers, desperate for a way out of their post-Soviet fiscal nightmares, read *Averting the Old Age Crisis* avidly and embraced the teams of World Bank advisors who arrived to help them apply the book's template in their own countries. By 2000, the Bank had extended seventy credit programs to thirty-six countries either wholly or in part to finance pension reform. The portion specifically aimed at pension restructuring came to $3.4 billion.[19] A dozen years after the PRA system was inaugurated, the vision behind it seemed on the verge of sweeping the globe.

* * *

Washington lawmakers and policy entrepreneurs spent a great deal of time during the 1990s poring, selectively, over the transformations happening around the world. At times it seemed that Chile, or the abstraction of the Chilean program sketched in *Averting the Old Age Crisis, was* the world. The feedback effect from this superficial view of overseas pension politics had a powerful effect on the Social Security debate in the U.S.

Bruce Bartlett, a former Jack Kemp aide and Bush administration Treasury official turned newspaper columnist, brandished the Chilean example in November 1994, after Virginia Senate candidate Oliver North suggested letting younger workers opt out of Social Security. When the ex-Iran-Contra conspirator's opponent, Democrat Charles Robb, called this a "dangerous proposal" because it would slash payroll taxes supporting current benefits, Bartlett hit back with a column in the *Roanoke Times & World.*

"Chile, Peru, Colombia, Argentina and Bolivia have already moved to shift some or all of their Social Security systems into the private sector," Bartlett noted. "And a recent World Bank report, 'Averting the Old Age Crisis,' recommends that other countries move in the same direction as quickly as possible...."

North should be congratulated, not condemned, for raising this issue." Nevertheless, Robb won the Senate seat.

Undeterred, Bartlett kept the World Bank study close at hand as he continued to inveigh against Social Security. "The World Bank now urges developing countries to adopt Chilean-style pension systems," he noted in a column published as the 1996 presidential race was heating up. "While the American Association of Retired Persons will no doubt fight to the death to stop privatization, in the long run its position is untenable."

Speaking to a special Senate committee on aging in September 1996, Estelle James, a World Bank economist and the principal author of *Averting the Old Age Crisis,* presented the Bank's arguments at length. After running through the multitudinous sins of pay-as-you-go pension systems—overpromising of benefits, lost opportunities for "real" saving, excess benefits for the middle class, an unsustainable burden for younger generations—she got down to discussing the Bank's "framework for reform." Then she painted an ominous picture of the dilemmas younger workers would face if Social Security wasn't reformed.

"Are they worried about the availability of jobs?" she asked. "Are they optimistic about wage growth? How will they feel if their net disposable income and therefore their standard of living increases little over their working lives, as contribution rates demanded by [pay-as-you-go] pension, health and social insurance systems rise? Relatedly, how will they feel when they realize that they are getting back a low, perhaps even a negative, return on their lifetime contributions?"

James's final message: act now as the Bank recommends. "The sooner [Americans] start building the second pillar, the less painful the transition can be."

In what seemed like no time flat, it had become almost reflexive for Social Security's critics to make similar debatable assertions, bolstering them with a quick reference to Chile. In April 1998, none other than Jeffrey Sachs, the Harvard economist who had become the public face of economic shock therapy for former Communist states, teamed up with the apostle of generational accounting, Larry Kotlikoff, to offer yet another blueprint for privatization. "Social Security is in deep water," they wrote in an op-ed for the *Los Angeles Times.* "We need to fix it for good, from the ground up." Their plan, they claimed, had been "endorsed by 75 of the nation's leading economists" and would "fix the system for good."

Sachs and Kotlikoff weren't advocating partial-privatization, in which some portion of payroll taxes would be diverted into mandatory personal accounts. They wanted it all moved to those accounts. And they added a generational accounting twist to the model by stipulating separate investment pools for each new "class" of retirees. But they also proposed guaranteeing current retirees' benefits. To cover the transition costs, they threw out a few suggestions. Some of these were politically near-impossible: cutting corporate welfare, reducing "excessive defense and other federal purchases." Another, "fixing" the consumer price index, would cut current retirees' benefits, even though Kotlikoff and Sachs had said they wouldn't do this. Two others, "raising 'sin' taxes and imposing a targeted retail sales tax," would heap a huge new burden on lower-income workers.

The centerpiece of their plan, however, was those private accounts. And to the skeptics, they had an easy answer: similar reforms that had "been adopted by a growing number of countries around the world, including Chile and Britain."

PART IV

Mating Dance

(1996–99)

CHAPTER 21

THE PENSION REVOLUTION COMES HOME

"PRIVATIZE SOCIAL SECURITY? NOBODY'S LAUGHING NOW" shouted a *Business Week* headline in early February 1996. "Conservatives long have dreamed about privatizing Social Security," said the article that followed. Irony of ironies, just such a prospect was "about to land on Washington's center stage—launched not by the GOP, but by a panel appointed by the Clinton Administration. The panel's explosive findings portend a battle that will make the fight over Medicare cuts look like a tea party."

The panel was the White House-appointed Advisory Council on Social Security, which had been meeting since the spring of 1994. After months of infighting that brought out deep ideological splits among its members, the council had announced in December 1995 that it was too divided to consense around a single set of policy recommendations. It would miss its deadline to turn in its recommendations that month and instead would write up a report offering three very different proposals for restructuring—all of which, however, recommended investing some portion of Social Security's revenues in the stock market.

Sensing a watershed, Washington roused itself to attention. In his article a couple of months later for the *Wall Street Journal*, Peter Ferrara started out with a whirlwind account of the Chilean miracle, then noted, "This spring the usually staid and moribund Advisory Commission [*sic*] on Social Security will pleasantly surprise the nation with a recommendation by five of the 13 commissioners [*sic*] advocating an option for workers to shift almost all of their share of the Social Security payroll tax to private alternatives."

This was, for Social Security critics, an exciting moment. Free-market pension populism seemed to be sweeping the world, forcing the liberal elites up out of their bureaucratic slough. "Grass-roots sentiment is now shifting strongly in favor of what was anathema just a few years ago: privatization of the system," Ferrara wrote. "Perhaps more surprisingly, every day brings more establishment and institutional support for the idea."[1] To true-believing conservatives, the success of a group of enterprise-minded Advisory Council members at thrusting their ideas to the forefront of a Clinton-staffed policy panel was an event akin to the fall of the Soviet Union.

And almost as hard to believe. Olivia Mitchell, the influential head of the Pension Research Center at the University of Pennsylvania's Wharton School, who served on one of the council's technical panels, said she "thought there was absolutely no chance of any sort of privatization option being on the table" when the council started its work in 1994. What changed, she added diplomatically, was that "for the first time people started realizing the current system is insolvent and it will probably take something dramatic to restore confidence in the retirement income system."[2]

In the course of a few months at the end of 1995 and the beginning of 1996, while much of the political class was still preoccupied with welfare reform and the ugly aftermath of the federal government shutdown, the Advisory Council put Social Security at the top of the capital's policy agenda. What sent a thrill through the likes of Mitchell and Ferrara was the possibility that all the factors undermining Social Security for many years now—domestic deficit politics, the stock market boom, the careful cultivation of fears about the program's solvency, feedback from overseas pension privatizations—were at last coming together to create a magic moment when change could happen.

* * *

Unlike the Kerrey-Danforth commission, the 1994–96 Advisory Council wasn't put together as part of a political deal. The president was required by law to call one every four years to review the state of the program and recommend changes. In the early decades, if the president accepted those changes, the full weight of the executive branch would accompany the effort to enact them into law.

After 1970, however, and especially after OASI and Disability Insurance benefits were indexed to inflation, Social Security became a more politically sensitive subject, and advisory councils a place not to advance ideas for improving the program but to bury them. According to many people who participated in the process, the Clinton administration wasn't enthusiastic about having to appoint a new council in 1994 and exercised very little political control over how it was put together. George Stephanopoulos, Clinton's senior advisor on policy and strategy, was delegated as White House point person, but the officials charged with organizing the council and choosing its membership were HHS Secretary Donna Shalala and Social Security Commissioner Shirley Chater. They delegated the day-to-day work to Larry Thompson, principal deputy commissioner and effectively Chater's second-in-command.

Thompson had worked nearly his entire career in the federal government as an economist and policy analyst. In the 1970s he had served as an assistant secretary of the Department of Health, Education and Welfare, specializing in Social Security policy, then was executive director of the 1979 Social Security Advisory Council. Commissioner Stan Ross brought him into SSA to revitalize the agency's research and policy development effort as head of the Office of Policy. Thompson moved on to positions at the GAO during the Reagan administration before Shalala brought him back as principal deputy commissioner of SSA in 1993.

Thompson was inclined to encourage a wide intellectual debate about Social Security. He tended to believe that another payroll tax hike, like the one in the 1983 Amendments, wouldn't be politically doable. And Thompson was willing to allow discussion of individual accounts, which he felt had become a prominent enough topic that it couldn't be kept off the agenda.

Working closely with him was David Lindeman, an old friend from HHS who was finishing up a stint at the Pension Benefits Guaranty Corporation, the federal government's private pension insurer. Lindeman already had a new job lined up at the World Bank, but agreed to join SSA temporarily, as a consultant on reduced pension before the new position began: time enough to complete the Advisory Council's report, which it was scheduled to turn in by December 1995. Lindeman brought the same ecumenical approach to choosing the panel as did Thompson.

Accordingly, the charter that Shalala approved for the council was more open-ended and ambitious than usual. Subjects it was charged with addressing included "financing issues," not very carefully defined; the "relative equity/adequacy" of benefits, especially for women; and "the relative roles of the public and private sectors in the provision of retirement income." Previous advisory councils that had succeeded in putting new issues into the public agenda had usually worked with carefully defined mandates. This time, the charter read like a quick sketch of topics for a debating society.

"The Advisory Council was the creature of me and Larry, whether we care to admit it or not," Lindeman later said wryly. "We were trying to create a group not in the old mold, but to see if we could create a real consensus about where Social Security should move. In the end, there wasn't a consensus."[3]

The "old mold" had been to carefully select a panel of experts evenly divided between Democrat and Republican, management and labor, but all fundamentally supporters of Social Security. This went back to the early days of the program, when the Roosevelt administration had tried hard to make it a bipartisan project and when union leaders and executives of large corporations had played a major role in developing it. The thirteen-member panel would typically include a chair—generally someone seen as ideologically even-handed—plus three representatives each from labor and business and others representing such constituencies as older persons, women, and the self-employed. The AFL-CIO traditionally had a strong voice in choosing the labor representatives, and the National Association of Manufacturers in choosing the business advocates.

Thompson and Lindeman came up with quite a different mix. Labor, as usual, got three union officials aboard, but the group that could be described as representing business got four. Two of these were corporate executives: Marc Twinney, retired pension director of Ford Motor Company, and Joan Bok, chairman of New England Electric System. But the other two, Syl Schieber and Ann Combs, were actually employed by pension consulting firms: he by Watson Wyatt Worldwide and she by William M. Mercer. This was a significant change. The corporate members had traditionally played a low-key role on advisory councils. But pension consulting firms, whose mandate was to help companies run their retiree benefit programs more cheaply and who could be expected to benefit from privatization, would tend to push in a more conservative direction.

Combs was on the Advisory Council because its charter emphasized issues affecting women and low-wage workers. Areas it was supposed to look into included "relative equity/adequacy provided for persons at various income levels, in various family situations, and various age cohorts, taking into account such factors as the increased labor participation of women, lower marriage rates, increased likelihood of divorce, and higher poverty rates among women." Lindeman says he and Thompson approached Combs as a women's representative, since she had spoken up for women as a member of the Greenspan commission a dozen years before. They recruited Edith Fierst, an attorney in private practice, as another voice for women from the Democratic side.

Schieber was a much riskier appointment. Lindeman and Thompson both knew him from the days when all three had worked at HHS; they respected his professional abilities and knowledge of Social Security. "I encouraged the National Association of Manufacturers to nominate him because I thought it would be nice if we had someone of his analytic caliber," says Lindeman. And since his and Thompson's intention was in part to encourage discussion of private accounts, Schieber's prominent advocacy of individual investment as part of a restructured Social Security didn't handicap him in their eyes.

Two Advisory Council members lobbied for their seats. One was Carolyn Weaver, who used her connection with Dole to obtain a spot. Along with

Schieber, her presence meant that at least two members were sure to push hard for private accounts. Unlike Schieber, she had spent most of her professional career as a think-tank denizen, largely at the Hoover Institution and the American Enterprise Institute, and according to some who knew her, had grown unused to working with people whose viewpoints didn't line up with hers.

Her polar opposite in this and many other respects was Bob Ball. His experience on advisory councils went back to the 1947 panel, for which he had been staff director, and included membership on three others plus the Greenspan commission. Even though his views differed from Thompson's, Ball wrote later, "they really didn't know how to turn me down when I made it clear that I would like to be on it."

Something had alerted Ball's keen political sense that the new Advisory Council was going to be an important one. "I felt I needed to be on the Council to have my point of view strongly represented," he wrote.[4] Ball's thinking had changed since the days of the Greenpsan commission, however. He was increasingly concerned that the movement against Social Security had convinced Americans that the program was a bad deal. "Every time I read about these programs, they'd treat them like a near-term train wreck," he later recalled. "I wanted to say, 'Relax.' So although I didn't think the programs were menaced at the time, we could make some recommendations that'd be effective and would boost the confidence factor."[5] Ball hoped the Advisory Council could provide some reassurance in this way.[6]

Two members had no connection with any of the groups that traditionally claimed a place on advisory councils. One was Fidel Vargas, a former policy analyst to the mayor of Los Angeles, now serving as mayor of Baldwin Park, a Los Angeles suburb. A Republican with no previous experience with Social Security, he was selected, in part, for his Hispanic background, but soon came to see himself as the Gen X representative as well.

The other was Thomas Jones, vice chairman, president, and chief operating officer of TIAA-CREF, the big independent pension system for teachers and other school employees. Another financial services industry figure, Jones was chosen to speak for older workers trying to build up nest eggs for retirement. He and Vargas were the only non-white members of the Advisory Council.

To chair the panel, Thompson and Lindeman originally wanted Charles L. Schultze, who chaired the Council of Economic Advisers during the Carter administration. But Schultze was rejected by AFL-CIO President Lane Kirkland, who hadn't forgiven him for not supporting wage and price controls during the inflation surge of the late 1970s. They then turned to Edward Gramlich, a well-known economist and dean of the School of Public Policy at the University of Michigan, who had briefly served as acting director of the CBO during the 1980s.

Ned Gramlich had no policy or administrative experience with Social Security, but Thompson and Lindeman had known him since the early 1970s, when all three had served in the Office of Economic Opportunity.[7] They guessed, correctly, that Gramlich didn't support private-account carve-outs. Also like Thompson, Gramlich was concerned that raising payroll taxes would be politically impossible in the future and that some way would therefore have to be found to make up for the inevitable benefit cuts, possibly by creating add-on accounts not funded out of payroll tax contributions.

Instead of a fairly narrow group of insiders who could be expected to easily reach consensus on some very specific issues, Thompson and Lindeman had created a kind of "Noah's Ark," Gramlich later commented.[8] "Ball was not enthusiastic about people like Syl and Ann," Lindeman recalls. "He wanted the insurance executives he'd known in the past."[9] His ideological opposite numbers saw an opportunity. "I think there was a sense we could challenge some of the historical structure of the system," Schieber recalls.[10]

The 1994 Advisory Council got off the ground in June with no fanfare. Substantive discussions didn't begin until February and March, 1995, after the fall elections had brought the new Republican Congress to power. This lent urgency to the proceedings, since a real political change of direction seemed possible in Washington. Right away, two things were clear to Gramlich[11]—that the council would have to concentrate entirely on the financing issues, and that higher payroll tax contributions were out of the question.

Once again, a high-level panel was going to ignore the other questions mentioned in its charter—about changing family structures and adequacy of benefits for women and low-wage workers. In mid-November, Edith Fierst had presented a memo to the council outlining seven steps to improve benefits for elderly women, all of which would have modest or no impact on Social Security's long-term funding. This proposal wasn't taken up.[12]

At eighty-one, Ball retained his political mastery. Understanding that the first comprehensive plan to hit the table could set the agenda for the final product, at the April meeting he unveiled eight proposals that together would more than

Leaders of the three factions on the 1994–96 Social Security Advisory Council, from left: Bob Ball, Ned Gramlich, and Sylvester Schieber. The council's failure to agree on a unified plan to restructure the program pushed the Social Security wars into a new and more partisan phase.

eliminate the program's seventy-five-year shortfall, currently projected at 2.17% of payroll. All were incremental changes except one: investing one-third of the trust fund assets in the stock market. This was a huge shift for Ball, who had argued against such an idea for years. Now, however, stock market investment looked like a good way to raise the public's confidence in the system and check-mate the arguments for private accounts. "I am trying to illustrate that it can be done without great big benefit cuts or increases in contributions," Ball said.[13]

Weaver was chagrined. She had virtually demanded at the March meeting that the council discuss whether to recommend a fundamental, from-the-ground-up restructuring of Social Security before considering any incremental changes that would preserve the existing program. Ball was clearly trying to squash such a discussion.

Schieber countered with a sketchy counterproposal that included four principal elements: raising the normal retirement age two months per year, beginning in 2000, until it reached 68 in 2017; raising the early retirement age in step with the normal age; replacing the current benefit calculation system, which was tilted in favor of lower-income workers, with a flat benefit set at whatever level would rebalance the system, phased in over twenty years; and allowing workers to "buy back" the early retirement benefits they lost in the form of contributions to voluntary private accounts.[14]

Schieber deliberately made his proposal extreme, so the council members would have to think about the priorities they wanted to set if Social Security was fundamentally redesigned. Ball complained that to accept Schieber's approach was to judge Social Security on rates of return alone: as though it were a simple investment fund rather than a system of social insurance.[15]

The differences of opinion multiplied in May, when Gramlich opened the meeting with his own proposal that seemed to combine elements of both the Ball and Schieber plans. Like Schieber, he would begin by replacing the program's current benefit formula with a flat rate. Added on top of this would be a second benefit equal to 15% of average wages earned over the worker's career. Putting the two pieces together, low-wage workers would get about the same amount of Social Security income as they currently received, and those with higher incomes would face 20% to 30% reductions. Early retirement would rise to sixty-five by 2027 and the normal retirement age to sixty-eight by 2018. Future retirees would not get spousal benefits. The government would invest 25% of the trust fund assets in stocks. And workers would be allowed to "buy" higher benefits by contributing another 1% to 4% of earnings to private accounts.

The basic differences between the three proposals were simple. Ball would make minor adjustments but leave the essential structure of Social Security intact, while investing some of the trust fund assets to boost returns. Schieber would slash benefits and allow workers to place some of their payroll tax contributions in private investment accounts. Gramlich would cut benefits, although less severely and with more affluent workers bearing the brunt; invest some trust fund assets; and allow workers to set up private accounts by making additional contributions. Politically, Ball's plan could be described as progressive; Schieber's as conservative; and Gramlich's as center-right. What they had in common was that all three made do without raising payroll taxes. With the Gingrich Congress in power, taxes were politically out of favor.

At first, the press had more or less ignored the Advisory Council's deliberations. That changed when it emerged that some members were looking at ambitious proposals to restructure Social Security, and the emergence of three distinct sets of proposals brought their deep ideological divisions—verging on the personal—out in the open. "I had hoped we might agree on how to solve 80 percent of the problem, but my hopes are fading," said Ann Combs. Ball said he was "still hopeful" that eight or nine council members could agree on enough incremental changes to balance Social Security's financial prospects for decades to come, but "we're certainly not going to have a unanimous report, or a consensus one."

Weaver and Schieber couldn't put their plan to replace the existing "construct" on the table until the council's December meeting, which was supposed to be its last. They had to do all their own research and development work because by then Lindeman had left and the council was effectively without a staff. Ball and Gramlich also modified their proposals.

Ball's revised proposal, which became known as Maintain Benefits (MB), boosted the amount of saving to be achieved from a change in how the Bureau of Labor Statistics calculated inflation. Retirees would pay taxes on all the benefits they received from Social Security. The MB plan also called for setting a 1% increase in employer and employee payroll tax contributions beginning in 2050 "as a fail-safe provision." And the federal government would invest 37.5% of the trust funds in a passively managed domestic stock portfolio, which he projected would boost returns from the 2.2% to 3.8% per year.

That last was Ball's attempt to out-maneuver the privatization movement's argument about the allegedly poor returns that Social Security earned on workers' payroll taxes. "If Social Security invests a significant amount in stock," he predicted, generating higher returns without putting individual workers at risk, then "the complaint disappears."[16]

Under Schieber's Personal Savings Account (PSA) proposal, workers ten or fewer years from retirement would receive Social Security benefits under the current formula. He was also making his personal accounts mandatory. Workers under fifty-five would be required to contribute 5-percentage-points of the current employer-employee contribution of 12.4% to fund the new accounts. The second half of the package would be a flat benefit, valued at around $360 a month in current dollars but with the exact figure dependent on how many years the worker participated in the new system. The normal retirement age would rise from sixty-five to sixty-eight by 2017, and the early retirement age from sixty-two to sixty-five.

How to pay for all this? Preliminary estimates by the SSA's actuaries put the cost at up to 2% of GDP a year for sixty years. Schieber called for Congress to impose a 1.52% supplemental payroll tax on workers—in plain language, to raise taxes—for the next seventy-five years and to issue $1.9 trillion of new government bonds, which he took to calling "Liberty Bonds." This was staggeringly expensive. Even those least ideologically in sympathy with him allowed that Syl Schieber, of all the champions of privatization, was the least inclined to cook up overly optimistic numbers or otherwise bend the logic of his own analysis for political purposes.[17]

Left unexplained, though, was how anyone could keep Congress from using all those new funds from the payroll tax supplement and the Liberty Bonds to do what they had been doing for years with the Social Security trust funds: underwrite a larger and larger federal budget deficit. Even if a mechanism was legislated to bar them from doing so, future Congresses could, of course, reverse it. Rigorous devotion to a particular kind of analysis didn't, perhaps, carry over into good political strategy.

Gramlich's proposal, which came to be known as the Individual Accounts (IA) plan, expanded the number of years used to calculate Social Security benefits from thirty-five to thirty-eight. It would raise the normal age of eligibility for full benefits from sixty-five to sixty-seven by 2011 and gradually lower the benefits schedule over time, with higher earners taking the biggest hit. Like Schieber, Gramlich had also decided to make his personal accounts mandatory, adding another 1.6% of covered payroll to fund them. In a huge divergence from the way Social Security had always been managed, employers wouldn't share this burden. And unlike the PSA plan, retirees couldn't do as they pleased with the proceeds. The government would convert them into annuities.[18]

The Advisory Council listened to presentations of all three proposals at what was supposed to be its final meeting, in December 1995. Many of the members were furious with each other by this time. "We didn't see the proposal by Carolyn and Syl's group until days before the final meeting," Gerald Shea of the AFL-CIO later said. "So the entire discussion of this idea of radically restructured Social Security was in one three-hour meeting."[19]

A straw poll turned up six votes for Ball's MB plan, five for Schieber's PSA, and two for Gramlich's IA. Ball's supporters were Jones, who had given him the idea to invest part of the trust fund assets; Fierst; and the three labor representatives. Gramlich could muster only one supporter for his plan, fellow Michigander Marc Twinney, the retired Ford pension director. Schieber and Weaver rallied the rest to their PSA scheme: Combs, Vargas, and Joan Bok of New England Electric.

The members were supposed to have a final report complete by January 15, 1996. Its preparation became an agonizingly drawn out process, however. As the details leaked, the three opposing sides realized their work was being thrown into the court of public opinion, so they hastened to broadcast their messages.

Ball blasted the PSA scheme as "a terrible plan. It costs a lot and the average worker is worse off."[20] Weaver countered in a long May article for the ultra-free market magazine *Reason* that "proposals that once were ignored or denounced as efforts to 'smash and destroy' Social Security" were now "possibly the only real means of saving" it.

But press coverage over the next several months concentrated mostly on the PSA plan as a kind of bellwether for change, a new element in the Washington zeitgeist. It couldn't be a complete coincidence that publisher Steve Forbes, now running for the Republican presidential nomination and enjoying much attention for a flat tax proposal developed by his advisor Jude Wanniski, also proposed to privatize Social Security. It helped, too, that the stock market was sailing atop a massive bull run. And, as the *Boston Globe* noted, "A number of Latin American countries—Chile is the most prominent—have already replaced their social security systems with a private savings plan."

Ignoring the fact that the likes of Schieber, Weaver, and Bob Kerrey were hardly well inclined toward the program, *New York Times* business reporter Peter Passell commented, "For the first time in the 60-year history of Social Security, some of its friends are asking for fundamental changes before the system cracks under the weight of promises that would be inconceivably expensive to honor."

Bob Ball's hopes to end such talk, clearly, weren't being realized.

The council's most crucial audience—the president—kept himself rigorously neutral, however. In July, Clinton told MSNBC, "If you privatize the whole thing, you would really put people who are not sophisticated investors and didn't have a lot of money on their own at serious risk." He said any recommendation to partially privatize Social Security would have to be studied carefully, and that any fix would need to be a bipartisan effort.[21]

The Republican Congress was eager to give at least one of the council's factions greater visibility. In March, the Senate Finance Committee's Social Security and Family Policy Subcommittee heard testimony from Schieber—a hefty, exhaustive written analysis of his and the MB and IA plans—Olivia Mitchell; Howard Young, a University of Michigan professor who was chairing its Technical Panel on Assumptions and Methods; and Brookings's Henry Aaron. Weaver addressed the subcommittee as well in May.

Wall Street was lobbying Advisory Council members now. Jones later told the *Washington Post* that representatives of the Investment Company Institute had asked him why he didn't support the PSA proposal. "They made the point that Option 3 [PSA] offered my company—TIAA-CREF—the greatest potential for new business," Jones said. "My response was that I was appointed as a public member of the advisory council, not as a representative of a company or an industry. I also told them that if the amount of overcharging and underperformance that is common in the mutual fund business was any measure, I was not optimistic about the free market taking care of things."[22]

Henry Aaron of Brookings, too, tried to provide some balance with a long op-ed in the *Washington Post* on July 21 analyzing Social Security's "problems." "Taxes will have to be increased, benefits cut, or both," he acknowledged. "But … the total projected increase in the cost of Social Security, measured as a share of gross domestic product, is less than the decline in defense spending since

1990. Can a problem that does not become immediate for a third of a century be a 'crisis'? In a pig's eye."

Aaron then turned, scathingly, to Social Security's critics and their posture of extreme civic virtue. Far from being a political untouchable that took courage to challenge, he noted that the program had been the subject of legislation that cut benefits three times in the past two decades: in 1977, 1983, and 1993. Yet "chest-thumping members of Congress and febrile journalists brag of their own courage in daring to call for cutbacks in Social Security. With macho fanfare, they call on all to watch them grab this 'third rail'—and somehow not one of them fries. The truth is that talking about scaling back Social Security is politically chic."[23]

What with three proposals jockeying for position and the increasingly public views of many of its members, the Advisory Council was having trouble writing its final report in such a way as to satisfy all factions. The January deadline stretched into March and the council had to apply for new funds to finish its work. Further delays piled up. In August, Schieber claimed to have "heard rumors that neither party wants this out before the election." Gramlich denied that either the Dole or Clinton campaigns had asked him to hold it up, but noted that "there are some risks to having a report like this come out in the heat of a political campaign."[24]

* * *

Budget politics and the looming release of the Advisory Council's final report made Social Security a constant presence during the 1996 presidential campaign, even if the two front runners tried hard not to say much about it. But Republicans were looking for a fresh approach, and another GOP candidate thought he saw the key to it in Social Security.

Steve Forbes was the media hit of the campaign season's early days. Talking up his pet proposal to replace the current income tax system with a 17% flat tax on wages, hosting *Saturday Night Live*, he came across as a charmingly wonkish WASP with too much money to be anything other than purely disinterested—Ross Perot in tasseled loafers, perhaps. His second favorite subject, closely tied to the first, was Social Security.

The program is "going bust both morally and financially," he proclaimed. It was a Ponzi scheme and should be replaced by a "market-based retirement system." Charmingly vague on the details, the millionaire publisher proposed placing "part or all of a young person's payroll taxes into a personal savings account" while leaving unstated what the rest would be used for—presumably, to fund a drastically reduced "safety net" version of the existing program. Current retirees and workers nearing retirement could continue to enjoy the current system.

Transition costs? "Not a problem," Forbes reassured. The surpluses currently residing in the trust funds—about $500 billion—could be converted into "real bonds" and the proceeds used to finance the changeover. The bonds could then be amortized using the additional tax revenues pouring in thanks to the economic overdrive achieved after the injection of workers' private-account investments into the stock market.[25]

Forbes's ambitious scheme was another idea out of the supply-side playbook that his advisor Jude Wanniski had been pushing ever since his days as sidekick to Jack Kemp in the 1970s. It made Forbes the first serious presidential candidate to propose Social Security privatization since Pete du Pont and Pat Robertson had earned George H.W. Bush's incredulity by doing so in the 1988 Republican primaries, although two other early Republican contenders, Phil Gramm and ex-Kentucky Gov. Lamar Alexander, hinted that they might consider something of the sort. But the idea still inspired equal parts encouragement and skepticism.

"The more that's discussed about the idea, the more popular it will become," predicted Third Millennium's Richard Thau. "Young people are impressed with [Forbes's] ideas." Henry Aaron, the acerbic Social Security analyst at Brookings, wasn't. "For Forbes to add his embrace to a plan that would enormously benefit the well-to-do seems a gift beyond the wildest dreams of Democratic political strategists," he sniffed.[26]

But in some journalistic circles, that's exactly what made Forbes such an attractive maverick. "The ideas Forbes is offering on the stump are quietly being debated by the advisory council that reports to Congress later this year on Social Security's future," Time pointed out. "Depending on how much he stresses it, Forbes could take credit for making Social Security an issue that actually gets addressed in 1997 rather than punted, Washington-style, beyond the next few elections."

The $25 million Forbes spent on his campaign, and the widespread media coverage he achieved, won him few actual votes, and by March he was out of the race. Soon the Republican contest reduced itself to religious conservative and sometime economic populist Pat Buchanan, who didn't support Social Security privatization, and the party establishment's choice, Bob Dole.

Clinton and Dole both came close to tipping their hand. In February, the Senate majority leader mused to a Time reporter about the "possibility [of] something that lets people, say, below 45, maybe opt out of Social Security. But it won't be easy." Clinton, in a July interview on MSNBC, said, "If you gave people a choice, I think that's something that could be tested." From that rather vague suggestion, press reports had it that the president was interested in creating a limited test program in which some people would be allowed to invest part of their payroll taxes.

Neither candidate would budge any farther. Instead, both proposed tax cuts—Dole's was considerably larger—and took credit for a recently materialized drop in the deficit, even though entitlement spending was likely to balloon the budget shortfall once more in coming decades.

Republican leaders in Congress were at last throwing off the reticence about Social Security they had adopted during their drive for control of Capitol Hill two years earlier. In the House, majority leader Dick Armey announced that changing Social Security would be on the table "after liberals have taken their beating" in the November elections. At that point, "we can have reasonable, responsible, forward-looking, long-term policy discussions even about sacred-cow subjects like Social Security."[27]

But Dole was unwilling to join the chorus. He and Clinton both clung to the old caution to avoid the third rail. And rather than a goad, they found the Advisory Council to be a welcome defense. With a report expected soon from a blue-ribbon panel, neither had any reason to stake out a position in advance. Dole, particularly, had a lot to lose if he were tied too closely to his former aide Carolyn Weaver's privatization proposal.

"It would be awkward if someone was successful in connecting [Dole] to Carolyn Weaver's plan," Larry Thompson, who had chosen Weaver for her council seat and had since departed SSA to join the Urban Institute, blandly commented in September.[28] Weaver had, in fact, offered Dole sub rosa advice on Social Security earlier in the campaign. After seeing a TV ad by her old boss prior to the Iowa caucuses that savaged Steve Forbes for his privatization proposal, she fired off a memo to Dole campaign staff, reminding them that some leading conservative economists favored privatization.[29] It was then that Dole tossed out his hint about the possibility of younger workers opting out. But he went no further.

The Washington press corps played all of this the same way in story after story. Avoiding the issue on the campaign trail wouldn't save the candidates from having to reckon with Social Security's certain fate once one of them began the next presidential term. "Whether there's a Republican or Democrat in the White House, they'll be forced to make changes in Social Security," Bob Kerrey prophesied. "The world has changed a lot since 1935." Kerrey, as was his way, could be threatening on the subject. Asked by *Mother Jones* how he would respond to progressive Democrats who tried to upend his Social Security privatization bill after the election, the former Navy SEAL vowed, "I'll kick the shit out of any liberal who tries that."

* * *

It was the Democrats, for the most part, who administered beatings in November. Clinton handily won reelection and the Democrats picked up eight seats in the House, although they lost two in the Senate. Nearly 8 million fewer people cast ballots for president than had done so in 1992, supplying some ammunition for those who claimed voters were disillusioned by Washington politics. Whether this was because they were upset with the candidates for not supporting a sweeping revamp of Social Security wasn't apparent, however.

What had long since become a written-by-committee nightmare finally came to an end on Monday, January 6, when the Advisory Council's report was released. Conflict within Ball's faction was one major cause of delay.

The three labor representatives had misgivings about his and Jones's proposal to invest part of the trust fund assets. As a result, they had to revise their plan substantially. Instead of outright recommending investment in stocks, they called for "further study and examination" of the idea. To neutralize the arguments against—that turning part of the trust funds into a government-run stock portfolio would create conflicts of interest and invite political tampering—Ball's crew suggested a number of actions, including setting up an independent investment policy board and "barring the voting of Social Security-held stocks by law." Meanwhile, they urged that Congress pass the other changes they recommended, such as lengthening the number of years for calculating benefits, "within the next year or two."[30]

Ironically, and despite all the bickering, there were some important similarities between the three proposals. All three called for including new state and federal employees under Social Security. Both the IA and PSA plans would accelerate the rise in the retirement age for receiving benefits. And all three called for somehow investing Social Security funds in stocks. What if Treasury—not to mention Congress—missed all those lost dollars, and felt it had to bring billions of dollars of new government bonds to market to replace them, adding to the nation's public indebtedness? None of the three council proposals addressed this sticky point.

But by putting their faith in the stock market, all three factions—even Ball's—signed on to a principle that wasn't part of the philosophy that originally underpinned Social Security. The program "should provide benefits to each generation of workers that bear a reasonable relationship to total taxes paid, plus interest," the entire council said in its joint statement. Social Security should be judged as either a good or a bad deal for each successive generation based on whether it produces "a greater return on accumulated funds than low-yielding Government bonds"— a purely investment-driven standard. Apparently, the insurance that Social Security provided to retired and disabled people and to survivors was no longer as important.

Another major change in approach, outlined in the second volume of the council's report, would become extremely important to the Social Security debate in the next decade. This involved actuarial standards. Since 1983, seventy-five years had been the trustees' official standard for assessing whether the program was in good long-run fiscal health.

But the members' joint statement invoked something far more rigorous as well. They urged that "instead of just arriving at actuarial balance for 75 years," any legislative action by Congress should "in addition assure that the ratio of fund assets to annual expenditures ... be stable over the final years of the forecast horizon." In other words, Social Security should attempt to keep its books in order not just for the overall seventy-five years but for the last twenty-five years of that period—years when it was expected to again be paying out more money than it brought in.

The point was to avoid a situation like the one following the 1983 Amendments, which balanced the program's books for the next seventy-five years, but with more money projected to be going out than coming in during the last years of that period. As a result, in each succeeding year, the next seventy-five-year period showed a smaller surplus. Ensuring the surplus was growing, not shrinking, at the end of seventy-five years would require more sacrifice, whether through higher taxes or lower benefits.

Stephen Goss, then deputy chief actuary at the SSA and later chief actuary, called this "sustainable solvency," and it quickly became the accepted standard in the Social Security debate, although it had no legal status as such. "Essentially, every plan we've scored since then has emphasized sustainable solvency," Goss said more than a decade later. "They didn't call it that at the time, but somehow it evolved during the Advisory Council that everybody realized this is what they ought to be doing."[31]

Schieber believes that getting this principle accepted by the council was one of his and Weaver's most important achievements. "We were adamant that we must consider options that would balance the books not just for seventy-five years," he said, "but would leave the program stable at the end."[32] Even Ball tried to meet the standard, proposing a 1.6% payroll tax hike fifty years in the future, just in case a problem developed. Gramlich and Schieber proposed to cut benefits drastically. But all three factions committed to meeting a much more rigorous standard for solvency than any major advisory commission had adopted in the past.

Could the council have united behind a single plan if events had played out differently? It's unlikely. To create a stronger impression that they had "won," Schieber and Weaver encouraged journalists and lawmakers to look upon their proposal and Gramlich's as moving in essentially the same direction. There was a major difference between the IA and the PSA plans, however.

Schieber and Weaver emphasized over and over that the main objective of Social Security must be redirected from guaranteeing income to encouraging self-reliance. "We believe that it is important to turn our Social Security system into a major engine of real saving for workers so they can both secure their own retirement income needs while also making a contribution to the future growth of the national economy," Schieber told the Senate Labor and Human Resources Committee's Subcommittee on Aging in July, 1996.

Gramlich agreed it was necessary to increase national saving, but he was unwilling to do so by carving out a portion of current payroll taxes. In an interview the year before he died, Gramlich said, "The private-sector system of defined benefit pension plans in this country is on the verge of collapse. So I believe more strongly than before that we need a defined-benefit backstop in place of what the private sector can't and won't do. I'm a lot more religious about this. It's the wrong way to go to invest Social Security in private accounts."

"I was playing for the history books," he said, "and I felt they were playing to their constituencies. So it didn't bother me that [the council] went in three directions." He felt his plan for cutting benefits and creating add-on private accounts would accomplish two important things: "fix the fiscal problem and get people to save more." He quickly realized his scheme wouldn't get a majority on the council, "but in the broader arena it would. I haven't given up on that view," he said. "The world will come around."[33]

Weaver suggested that a compromise might have been possible if Ball had been willing to give a little. "Take Bob's proposal and raise retirement age and that probably would have gotten a majority vote," she said during the August 1995 meeting. But by that time, Schieber was working on his own proposal and he and Weaver were showing every sign that they would stick by it. Weaver herself noted that to accumulate a "meaningful" level of assets, contributions to private Social Security accounts would have to be set at 3–5-percentage-points of payroll tax. Weaver and Schieber opted for the larger of the two figures, suggesting strongly to Ball that they were more interested in creating their version of an ideal privatization plan than in leaving the door open to a compromise.[34]

In any case, no one on either side was making much effort to negotiate, either by forcing a vote on details of the three plans or by working between meetings, Shea observed.[35] Instead, they promoted their proposals energetically to the press, lawmakers, and anyone else who would listen, creating ever more entrenched positions.

* * *

Because of the repeated delays, the world had been grappling with the council's work for well over a year when its report finally came off the press. If anything, the series of blown deadlines had intensified interest, which built to a crescendo by January 1997 and continued for months afterward.

A problem not expected to become critical for decades into the future became one of the top domestic legislative items before Congress and the president as Clinton's second term was about to begin. In an article headlined "Barn Door Open On Privatization Of Social Security," the *Christian Science Monitor* proclaimed, "Nineteen ninety-seven may be remembered as the year Washington began a serious debate on one of the most fundamental issues of United States public policy: the federal government's role in ensuring retirement financial security."

From her seat on the Advisory Council, Ann Combs pointed out, helpfully, that rescuing Social Security "would be something Clinton could do as his legacy. Most presidents in their second term worry about their place in history. This would be a perfect issue for Clinton, a Nixon-to-China kind of thing."[36] The Nixon metaphor reverberated around the Beltway in the weeks after the report was released until it became wearying.[37]

Powerful groups were massing on either side of the issue. In October 1996, before the report was released and before the presidential election, the National Association of Manufacturers announced that it was launching a national campaign to pressure the next president and Congress to deal with what it termed the "financial and political crisis" facing Social Security. The day the Advisory

Council report was officially released, Gloria Johnson, president of the Coalition of Labor Union Women and one of the labor representatives on the panel, followed up with a more specific threat: "We will begin today to form a powerful coalition to dispatch this twin-headed monster supported by Wall Street and its right-wing 'think tanks' so we can get on with the business of stabilizing Social Security with thoughtfulness and restraint," she announced. "The coalition won't be hard to build because individual retirement accounts give everyone something to loathe."[38]

Unions had more or less stayed out of the Social Security war that had been building over the past several years. Elated by the effectiveness of a $35 million radio and TV blitz they had launched against Republican candidates during the elections just held, they were ready to wade in again.

Change now seemed inevitable. "It used to be said that no politician could propose big changes to the system and survive," the *Economist* noted in December. "Now all support some kind of reform to it." Even though one of its proposals would have left the investment decisions to the government, Cato's Michael Tanner was within bounds to claim that the Advisory Council report represented "an important breakthrough in the debate over Social Security reform" because the council produced "a consensus that private capital markets can provide a better return on investment than can the government."[39] And so, following the release of the report in January, it made sense for at least one editorial, in the *Colorado Springs Gazette Telegraph*, to proclaim, "A 'third rail' no more."

Whether the electricity had really drained out of the Social Security debate was unclear. But talking about change on Capitol Hill certainly became easier after the Advisory Council's report was out. While most witnesses invited to testify before Congress about Social Security in 1994 could be described as supporting the program as currently configured, the balance of power soon was reversing itself. By 1999, witnesses who favored carving out private accounts outnumbered those opposed by two to one.[40]

The Advisory Council had a lot to do with this. The mere presence of private accounts in the council's report served as a kind of coming out, its debut in the ranks of serious—that is, politically doable—policy proposals. The report "gave a legitimacy to the discussion of individual accounts that had never been there before," Schieber recalled later.[41] Ball, he said, seemed to understand this. At the Advisory Council's penultimate meeting, the grand old man of Social Security "looked at me and said, 'Well, Syl, you should be happy.' I said, 'Why is that?' He said, 'You got everything you wanted here.'"[42]

In the months after it became clear in what direction the Advisory Council's work was heading, a stream of wealthy and powerful financial-sector figures—including Lazard Freres eminence Felix Rohatyn, and Robert Pozen, general counsel at mutual fund giant Fidelity Investments—had come out publicly in favor of private accounts. Joining them was Pete Peterson.

Thus far, the corporate godfather of the movement against Social Security had been skeptical of the laissez-fair approach of libertarian voices like Cato.

Rather than pushing private accounts, Peterson had called simply for Social Security to be cut back. Now, he was joining the bandwagon. "I have concluded—reluctantly—that a fully funded, privately managed, and portable system of personal retirement accounts should be mandatory," he wrote in the *Atlantic Monthly*. "The system I envision would initially supplement Social Security—and over time might increasingly substitute for it."

The financial, insurance, and real estate industries made $59.8 million in soft-dollar contributions and contributions to political action committees during the 1995–96 election cycle, the Center for Responsive Politics (CRP) reported in December, a figure that did not include giving by individuals. Social Security "is definitely a big priority for Wall Street in the next Congress," said the CRP's Nancy Watzman.

Many firms remained cautious about being too up front with their ambitions, however, trying hard to downplay the bounty that privatization could bestow on their businesses. Schieber, whose consulting firm, now called Watson Wyatt Worldwide, formed an alliance with State Street to service pension clients while he served on the Advisory Council, also played down the profits financial services firms could make.

"The idea that the stock market will get pushed up because people are buying stock with Social Security money is just nonsense," Donald Straszheim, chief economist at Merrill Lynch, told AP, because private accounts would be phased in over time. The most commonly heard figure was some $60 billion a year—a large number, but not when stacked up against the $8.3 trillion already held in stocks, or the $10.1 trillion in government and corporate bonds at year-end 1995.

But most privatization plans envisaged mutual funds being the primary recipients of the new payroll tax investments. And $60 billion would be quite an addition to the $200 billion-plus of new money that flowed into stock mutual funds in 1996. Some estimates went much higher.[43] Lehman Brothers analyzed the Schieber-Weaver PSA plan in September 1996 and estimated that it would unleash a flow of payroll taxes into the stock market possibly exceeding the entire $123 billion that flowed into stock and bond funds in 1995.[44]

Thomas Jones, himself a top financial services executive as well as an Advisory Council member, noted that by comparison, "there was no money for Wall Street" in his and Ball's MB proposal: only some $10 million in the first year for managing the trust fund investments they envisioned.[45]

What seemed like a bonanza to some was simply alarming to defenders of traditional Social Security, however—none more so than labor. At a news conference after release of the Advisory Council report, AFL-CIO Secretary-Treasurer Rich Trumka insisted, "No to privatizing Social Security.... No to Wall Street greed."[46]

These, however, were by far the least commonly quoted voices and opinions in the early days of 1997, when privatization seemed to be gathering irresistible momentum. The cumulative picture emerging from press coverage of the response to the Advisory Council report was of a three-part consensus solidifying among the American political and business elites: that Social Security must be radically restructured; that its new form must contribute directly to a larger public policy agenda of boosting household savings as a means of encouraging economic growth; and that private accounts and lower old-age benefits were how it would play a role in that agenda.

In reality, there was no such consensus. Months before the Advisory Council issued its split report, the entire project was an "orphan," recalls Lindeman, as the administration lost any interest in supporting it with more resources. Gramlich, its leader, spent those final months negotiating with the White House for a seat on the Federal Reserve Board, which he would receive the following April, and was losing focus on his council work. Understandable, perhaps, considering how poisonous the atmosphere had become.

"At the start, our meetings were not adversarial. There was a lot of joking around," he later recalled. "We never came to blows, but at the end they were pretty wrenching." Gramlich was staying at the home of his son's family in Silver Spring when he came down for council sessions. "By the end, I'd go to a one-day meeting and it was all I could do when it was over to take my granddaughter for a long walk." He would credit her in a subsequent book on Social Security: "She was important for my mental peace of mind."

For proponents of private accounts, however, the release of the Advisory Council's report signaled that now was the time to start making plans.

It was also time to start lobbying the president. What was Bill Clinton going to do? All through the election cycle, he had been sidestepping questions about how he would "save" Social Security. To launch the discussion properly, both parties needed the political cover that only the president could provide: the Republicans to avoid being fingered once again for attempting to gut the program and the Democrats so as not to be accused of reneging on their promises to protect it. But that was asking the White House to take a big chance.

CHAPTER 22

"SAVE SOCIAL SECURITY FIRST"

When Bill Clinton's second term began, the question of how to tame the federal budget deficit and, to a lesser extent, the overall federal debt had dominated public policymaking for over fifteen years. The movement against Social Security had been patiently building its case all through that time. But the program was running a substantial surplus, and Congress couldn't afford to lose the payroll tax revenues by shifting them into private investment accounts.

Then on May 1, as the White House and the congressional Republican leadership were struggling yet again to agree on a budget that would keep the government within the Gramm-Rudman-Hollings guidelines, the CBO announced that the five-year deficit estimates it had released in January were overstated by a substantial $225 billion. The extra money came largely from an upward revision in the government's expected tax revenues. The federal government would actually enjoy a $70 billion budget surplus in the next fiscal year, its first in three decades. The CBO was projecting a $4 trillion surplus over the next fifteen years.

Overnight, Washington politics was transformed. Shortly afterward, Congress and the White House announced a tentative budget agreement that projected a modest federal surplus of $32 billion by 2002.

The administration seemed to grasp quickly what the shift from deficit to surplus implied. Gene Sperling, director of the president's National Economic Council, and John Kasich, the Ohio Republican chair of the House Budget Committee, quietly began holding meetings to work out a final budget deal that incorporated the new deficit figures.[1] Soon they were cobbling together a package using the extra revenues that would add a few items from both Republicans' and Democrats' 1997 wish lists without pushing the whole thing back into the red—provided, of course, that the economy continued to cooperate.

For Republicans, the package would include $91 billion in tax cuts over five years—the first such reduction since the early Reagan era—paid for by $115 billion of savings from Medicare, with a capital gains tax cut as the centerpiece. For Democrats there was a $24 billion, five-year plan to provide health insurance for 3–5 million children who would otherwise have been without it, plus a series of targeted tax cuts centered on education. Both could please their constituencies with a new, targeted tax credit of $500 per child. And both could feel virtuous for having agreed to achieve a balanced budget at least by 2002.

Once the president put his signature to the Balanced Budget Act of 1997 on August 5, a consensus quickly materialized among Washington's power centers that addressing the Social Security and Medicare "crises" must come next. "Having probably achieved a balanced budget," the respected former CBO director Robert D. Reischauer proclaimed in the *Washington Post*, "it is time to shift the focus of the policy debate to balancing the non-Social Security budget and restructuring Social Security and Medicare for the long term." Lawmakers mustn't place the nation at risk of facing a future of mass poverty and generational ruin, Reischauer wrote, where either "retirees are scrimping by on inadequate social insurance benefits" or "workers are unduly burdened supporting the aged."

While many economists disputed that such a future was really imminent, voices like Reischauer's were the only ones Washington seemed to hear. Shortly before the budget law was signed, Kasich and Sperling both assured the public that it would reinforce efforts to "shore up" the two big entitlements. In negotiating the deal, the administration was "most concerned about … not having an overall tax cut that was going to have exploding costs in the second ten years," Sperling told PBS. "We don't want to be draining money away from the Treasury when we need that to shore up long-term Medicare and Social Security."

"Gene Sperling and I are both committed as baby boomers—to not only fixing Medicare on a long-term basis but also beginning to solve the problems related to Medicaid and Social Security," Kasich chimed in.

* * *

In reality, the Balanced Budget Act contained nothing to make restructuring of Social Security and Medicare a natural next step for Washington. But along with the Advisory Council's report, it provided a convenient rationale for a wide range of influential organizations and individuals who were eager to open up a debate about the "entitlements."

The president, apparently, was one of these. Clinton had been paying closer attention to Social Security during the months leading up to release of the Advisory Council report. Despite largely avoiding the subject during his reelection campaign, this most adaptable of presidents nevertheless ordered up a set of talking points on Social Security from Sperling and Laura Tyson, Sperling's predecessor as National Economic Council director. The main points:

- Reiterate that Social Security is "one of our most successful programs" and is essential to keeping seniors out of poverty;

- Oppose privatization;

- Call for a "non-political, bipartisan review" by a presidential commission to consider the program's "long-term viability"; and

- Oppose Steve Forbes's privatization proposal.[2]

Two months later, however, Clinton appeared a bit more open-minded. After reading Pete Peterson's latest attack on Social Security in the *Atlantic Monthly*, he dashed off a note to Tyson asking to what extent she agreed with Peterson's views on entitlements and the danger they might pose to economic growth.[3]

At the height of his political career, after symbolically beating the Gingrich Congress to win reelection, Clinton had campaigned carefully on a modest slate of minimal reforms such as more public school teachers, gun control, and evening hours for high school basketball courts. By all reports, however, he still wanted a victory on a signature issue that would define his presidency and wipe away the hint of scandal and unfulfilled promise that had dogged him.

Social Security, with its maze of technical detail and slippery political surface, appealed to a president who liked to think of himself as a policy wonk and delighted in impressing visiting Capitol Hill denizens with his command of seemingly abstruse topics. "It was a perfect Clinton triangulation," says Cato's Michael Tanner, providing the president an opportunity to develop a compromise proposal and force Democrats to go along, lest they be viewed as standing in the way of reform. Republicans, too, would have to accept a compromise brokered by the president for fear of otherwise being tarred as privatizers.

Some of them suspected the president was ready to deal. Shortly after the November election, Clinton had received a call from Bill Archer, the Republican Ways and Means chair who, like the president, was planning to retire after 2000, to talk about how they might work together. Clinton asked Archer to meet with him at the White House during the week between Christmas and New Year's.

They spent twenty to thirty minutes of a one-hour meeting talking about Social Security, Archer recalls. "He expressed a desire to solve the Social Security problem and we agreed to work on it." Clinton mentioned at least two possible items to place on the table: COLA reductions and raising the retirement age. He also said he was prepared to "take the heat for Republicans" on these matters. Not much came of that first meeting, however, except an agreement to continue discussions. For one thing, while the meeting had been private, AARP soon found out and "put a big chill on it," Archer says—this despite the fact that the group had earlier told Archer they would go along with these changes if the president would.[4] The debate that eventually produced the Balanced Budget Act intervened as well.

Clinton's chief of staff, Erskine Bowles, had stayed on for the second term in part because of the prospect of deals on Social Security and Medicare. While the president was talking to Archer and working through the budget bill, Bowles contacted Gingrich about Social Security as well. Bowles told Gingrich that if they could agree on a restructuring plan, the president was willing to champion it and would try to get the congressional Democrats to go along. The Democrats wouldn't use it as an issue in the 1998 elections. Gingrich agreed to a basic scenario under which the Republicans would give up on passing a large tax cut in exchange for incorporating private investments in Social Security. This left much to flesh out, including the crucial issues of whether private investment would be through the trust funds or through private accounts and, if the latter, whether they would be carve-outs or add-ons. But there was at least a platform to begin discussions.

"The balanced budget bill was act I," Gingrich later told historian Steven M. Gillon. "This was act II.... We were going to have a very workmanlike, very intense, remarkably creative two or three years."[5]

By the time the budget bill passed, however, the president's interest in Social Security reform was common knowledge among Washington policymakers. His aides were soon talking up the issue in public. "We want people to read in their history books in 2052 that Clinton preserved the Social Security system," press secretary Mike McCurry boasted.[6]

While many of the hardcore Republican insurgents still despised him, others—including Gingrich and Lott, the House and Senate leaders—couldn't resist the president's pull. Arguably, the passion with which his opponents hated him merely enhanced the fascination that had grown up around the rather solitary figure in the Oval Office. To his fans and secretly, perhaps, to many of his enemies, the president was the contemporary equivalent of a picaresque hero: Tom Jones, as portrayed by Albert Finney in the film version of the 18th century novel, a vast distraction who could perhaps be harnessed for practical purposes if he could only keep his mind on serious matters.

In September, the White House began holding meetings of top administration officials, economists, and political advisors to coordinate policy on issues related to the surplus, with an eye to developing a set of initiatives for the president to unveil in the State of the Union speech. The meetings took place under a tight veil of secrecy. White House employees carried cards listing the day's events; and in case a lost card fell into a reporter's hands, the gatherings were identified only as "Special Purpose Meetings."

Sperling and Deputy Treasury Secretary Larry Summers orchestrated the sessions, which continued for four months and veered in several different directions before the principals arrived at an approach Clinton could accept. Along the way, Sperling and his staff relayed memos to the president summarizing not just the options they were discussing but what the best political timing might be if any of them were to be placed on the table.[7] Sperling, a former aide of New York Gov. Mario Cuomo who had joined Clinton's team during the 1992 campaign, "was brilliant, rarely slept, and worked like a demon," Clinton later wrote.[8]

Early on, White House officials were agreed on opposing a large Republican tax cut and that Social Security would be their rationale for doing so. But could they set the whole surplus off-limits when some social programs were in desperate need—and Clinton himself had publicly expressed interest in expanding Medicare for early retirees?

In a series of memos to the president, Sperling's team explored the timing of the administration's Social Security initiative and how it would be organized, complete with exhaustive analyses of the political risks and rewards of each approach. There wasn't time for the White House to simply issue its own set of proposals, perhaps in the president's next State of the Union address, Sperling warned, since they would only become a punching bag in the 1998 midterm elections. Sperling also argued against setting up another blue-ribbon commission, fearful that it might become bogged down and not produce its recommendations in a timely manner. It could give the public a bad case of "commission-itis," he warned, after the slow-motion debacle of the Advisory Council.

The president still had to decide what his objective was in taking on Social Security. Was it simply to eliminate the seventy-five-year funding imbalance? Or was it to achieve sustainable solvency, as the Advisory Council had defined it? And should raising Americans' personal savings be one of the goals?[9]

Answering these questions would depend to some extent on who the administration's partners were. Bowles continued working behind the scenes to make Gingrich a co-owner of the project. At last, a secret meeting was scheduled between the president and the speaker for Wednesday, October 28. The House Democrats, who would be most likely to express alarm at a possible sellout, weren't told about the meeting. Neither was Al Gore, who was planning his race for the presidency and developing positions on issues like Social Security. By this time, Clinton and his staff suspected, correctly, that to secure union support, Gore would have to renounce his position as a leader of the New Democrats by opposing any form of privatization.

Setting up the meeting was a careful exercise in accommodating agendas and personalities, similar to the delicately arranged meetings Reagan and Tip O'Neill had held over Social Security more than a dozen years earlier. Both leaders were taking gambles. Gingrich had to worry that any effort to cooperate with the president might undermine his authority with conservative House members, a small group of whom had recently tried to unseat him for being too cooperative with the other party. Clinton also was on thin ice with House Democrats and especially Gephardt, who was planning his own presidential run in 2000.

The meeting took place in the White House Treaty Room, where Gingrich could gaze upon Clinton's collection of biographies of world leaders. Attending were the president, the speaker, Bowles, congressional liaison John Hilley, and Gingrich chief of staff Arne Christenson.[10]

An agreement took shape that the president would announce a plan to "save" Social Security in his 1998 State of the Union address. Gingrich would make positive comments and assign Ways and Means to make recommendations as to the details. Both would attempt to keep the issue from coming to a head before the November election, and Clinton would use the interval to build public support by talking up the need for reform. That campaign—the "National Dialogue on Social Security," it was eventually named—would culminate in a White House conference after the election, following which the lame-duck Congress would vote on the bipartisan measure that had, presumably, come together by then. The working assumption of the new allies was that Congress contained enough centrists from both parties to outvote their left and right wings if they could arrive at a middle-ground proposal.

In the weeks that followed, Clinton and Gingrich aides decided to add Medicare into their long-range cooperative plans. The idea was to set up a bipartisan commission on Medicare reform, charge it with developing a plan to put the program on a financially sustainable footing by March 1999, and then push that proposal through Congress before the 2000 presidential campaign cycle squelched any further such opportunity.

In January, the Social Security initiative began in earnest when Archer asked Ken Kies, a tax lawyer who had just joined the accounting firm PricewaterhouseCoopers after serving as chief of staff of the congressional Joint Committee on Taxation, to head up negotiations with the White House for the Republican side. Sperling would be his principal interlocutor. "We had figured out how to get things done," Bowles recalled later. "We were all feeling very confident."

* * *

Clinton took a Social Security briefing book with him on his vacation to the Virgin Islands at New Year's and upon his return, came down in favor of

reserving all of the surplus. One of the most influential voices in the deliberations reportedly was Gore. Many White House staffers expected the vice president to favor something less than the 100% option so that he would have more
budget leeway to propose new initiatives during his race for president. Instead,
he surprised the room by supporting the president's position.

By early January, the deal struck in the Treaty Room seemed to be working.
Clinton and Gingrich both said they wanted to take on Social Security sometime between the 1998 and 2000 elections. Also that month, the president and
speaker put together the membership of the National Bipartisan Commission
on the Future of Medicare, to be chaired by Sen. John Breaux, a conservative
Democrat from Louisiana.[11]

But Republican lawmakers were already hinting that they would be reluctant to stick their necks out on an issue that had always been troublesome for
them unless Clinton was prepared to do so as well. "The question of whether
anything is going to grow is one of political leadership," said New Hampshire
Republican Sen. Judd Gregg.[12]

"Leadership" was a buzzword Republicans would resort to often over the
next two years, and not only in reference to Social Security. On January 21,
1998, news of Clinton's affair with Monica Lewinsky, a former White House
intern, hit the press, triggering the long crisis that would end in his impeachment and trial before the Senate. As the date of Clinton's State of the Union
address approached, the question of whether the president had lied in his de-
position, in a lawsuit against him, by denying he had had a sexual relationship
with Lewinsky was coming to overshadow his public policy agenda.

"It was game over," Bowles later recalled thinking. Gingrich knew the plans
he had made with Clinton, on Social Security and much else, were probably
dead. "I knew that for him to survive he had to go to the left because the only
way he could survive was to keep his left wing furious with us," he told Steve
Gillon. "I knew it was over."[13]

That wasn't the view of the negotiators working behind the scenes for Clinton, Gingrich, and Bill Archer. Ken Kies says the talks continued without missing a beat, expanding to include outreach to members of Congress such as Bob
Kerrey and even to the mutual fund industry. Clinton's advisors pursued more
public discussions with lawmakers about a Social Security deal as well. Keeping
all options open, Clinton's advisors told some reporters the president had also
not rejected carve-outs.

On January 27, hours after First Lady Hillary Rodham Clinton said in a
broadcast interview that a "vast right-wing conspiracy" was behind the charges
against her husband, a tired-looking president delivered his State of the Union
speech. Prominently placed in his litany of accomplishments was the projection that soon "the federal deficit, once so incomprehensibly large that it had
11 zeroes, will be simply zero." OMB's latest figures indicated a $200 billion
surplus over the next five years, up from the $32 billion projected in the Bal-
anced Budget Act. In fact, Clinton said he expected to submit the first balanced

U.S. budget in three decades for the very next fiscal year, with $20 billion to $30 billion in "spare change."[14]

What should the nation do with its surplus? Clinton asked. "I have a simple, four-word answer: Save Social Security first." Clinton had coined the phrase while standing in the Capitol theater room shortly before delivering the speech, rejecting his writers' formulation, "Save the surplus for Social Security," as too wordy.[15]

The Democrats roared with approval; even Gingrich, perhaps realizing the parameters of the fight now looming, stood up and applauded. The president then proposed that "we reserve 100% of the surplus—that's every penny of any surplus—until we have taken all the necessary measures to strengthen the Social Security system for the 21st century." The White House would devote the next year to a "national dialogue" on Social Security consisting of town meetings across the country and culminating in a White House conference in December. After that, "one year from now, I will convene the leaders of Congress to craft historic, bipartisan legislation to achieve a landmark for our generation: a Social Security system that is strong in the 21st century." Co-sponsoring the town meetings, it was later announced, would be the Concord Coalition and AARP, regarded as being on opposite sides of the privatization issue but in agreement that the program needed to be fixed.

The speech, watched by more than 53 million people, was a much-needed success for the president, whose approval ratings bounced from the high fifties to the high sixties overnight.[16] It also included more than a little sleight of hand. Clinton had not once mentioned his personal crisis, smoothly carrying off the long speech as if Lewinsky and special prosecutor Kenneth Starr didn't exist. And the president hadn't offered any details of how he would "strengthen" Social Security.

Senate Budget Committee chair Pete Domenici called "Save Social Security First," not incorrectly, a stalking horse for a drive to pay down the federal debt. Clinton was asking Congress not only to keep its hands off the surplus, but to endorse an alternative strategy for achieving economic growth.

That impression carried over to the fiscal-1999 budget that Clinton unveiled a week later. The $1.7 trillion measure showed that "you can have a smaller government, but a more progressive one," the president said in announcing a budget that would include a $21 billion child care initiative, over $7.3 billion in new education spending, new proposals to expand Medicare, and other items—all paid for by $25 billion in tax loophole closings and an anticipated $65 billion over ten years from settlement of a lawsuit against the tobacco industry. At the end of the presentation, Gore handed Clinton a magic marker; the president turned to a chart and filled in "0" under the box for "1999 deficit."

Staying within the budget would allow surpluses to build up to a projected $218.8 billion over the next five years, which the government could then apply to shrinking the federal debt. The theory, whose champions included Treasury

Secretary Robert Rubin; his deputy, Larry Summers; and, outside the administration, former CBO head Reischauer, asserted that shrinking the federal debt would lower the federal government's debt payments, leaving room for other types of spending, helping to reduce interest rates, and leaving more money available for private saving and investment.

Soon to be dubbed "Rubinomics," this optimistic game plan was something that Rubin had been lobbying for the Clinton White House to make official policy for some time. In 1996, he had gone so far as to ask Pete Peterson to pull together a group of prominent business leaders to urge the president not to give up on balancing the budget—an effort he later told Peterson was very helpful in getting Clinton on board.[17]

Rubinomics was a direct descendant of the "Treasury View" that originated in 1920s Britain and had been nudging its way into Washington's economic thinking since the 1970s. It made sense to the fiscally conservative because the U.S. economy, after a twenty-year funk, was at last moving into a high-growth period that would last for several more years. Labor productivity rose from a sluggish 1.4% on average between 1972 and 1995 to a healthy 2.5% from 1996 through 1999.[18] The opportunity had arrived, it seemed, to put something aside for the next string of lean years.

Suddenly, the government's fiscal objective was not just to lower deficits but to shrink the entire outstanding federal debt.

This could be ensured simply by depositing the entire surplus projected over the next five years in the Social Security trust funds. These assets would be lent temporarily to the government to retire debt, which would allow them to collect additional interest when the government paid the money back. That would extend the life of the trust funds by as long as a decade, or until roughly 2042, according to White House numbers, even if Washington made no structural changes in the system. It would also limit both Democrats' and Republicans' ability to use the surplus to fund new projects or initiate tax cuts. The whole thing sounded so ingenious that when Sperling explained it to Greenspan, the Fed chair said, "Let me be clear: You've found a way to make debt reduction sexy."[19]

Dissenting voices came from both ends of the political spectrum. To Republican lawmakers, debt paydown represented a poor substitute for the tax cuts that the party's top contributors expected them to deliver. Conservative critics such as *Washington Post* columnist James K. Glassman noted that merely keeping the budget balanced would cut the national debt's size relative to GDP from 50% to about 25% by 2026: about the same share it had represented in the 1960s. So the goal could be accomplished without giving up on the prospect of broad tax cuts. Glassman also pointed out that the debt itself, in the form of Treasury bonds, is owed not just to financial institutions but to private individuals who use the proceeds to generate economic activity. Eliminating debt owed by government also eliminates a large amount of assets held by the public.

On the other side, liberals like former Clinton Labor Secretary Robert Reich complained bitterly that Rubinomics was yet another excuse for Washington not to make the new investments in education, health care, social services, and infrastructure that America needed after nearly two decades of Carter-Reagan-Bush starvation of domestic programs. "It's not that these basic goals are anathema to us," said Reich. "It's just that every time we approach the point where they seem attainable, we decide that we can't afford them quite yet."

Like the bond market during Clinton's first term in office, Social Security and debt reduction had become the grand rationale for the deficit-cutting obsession. "As soon as Social Security is deemed to be out of danger," Reich predicted, "the tax cutters will compete for floor space with the debt cutters. The conversation over the public good thus has been reduced to this cramped debate."[20]

Many liberal Democrats were inclined to go along with Clinton's proposal at least for the time being, however, since it reduced the chances of a Republican across-the-board tax cut. Besides, giving priority to Social Security appeared to play tremendously well outside the capital. According to a *Wall Street Journal*-NBC News poll taken shortly before the president's speech, 77% of the public felt that overhauling Social Security should be "an absolute priority this year," against 19% in favor of a delay. Clinton's advisors could also congratulate themselves that by not making any too-specific proposals, the president was "keeping the debate substantive and not too politicized."[21]

The further liberals looked down the road, however, the more danger "Save Social Security First" seemed to pose. It meant that a Democratic administration was admitting that Social Security had to be "saved"—an open invitation for the pro-privatization forces to flood Washington with their own proposals. Early in the fall discussions that preceded the State of the Union address, some Clinton advisors had suggested instead simply putting the president on record against a tax cut, on the grounds that it would endanger Social Security. In the end, Clinton decided on the more positive-sounding message he delivered, ensuring, for better or worse, that the program would become a political focal point for the fall elections. And by not advancing any specific ideas for a Social Security overhaul, the president, for the time being, held himself above the fray.

Sensing that the debate was live, lawmakers of both parties unveiled proposals to "save" Social Security. Shortly before the State of the Union speech, two senators, Ted Kennedy of Massachusetts and Republican John Ashcroft, weighed in with proposals centered on reducing payroll taxes.

Kennedy, in an effort to show that incremental changes could correct the system's problems, went public with a suggestion that the cap on wages subject to payroll tax be removed. The 6.2% that employer and employee each paid would then apply to wages and salaries, however high they might go, not just up to the current $68,400 limit. Kennedy would then use the extra revenue to lower payroll taxes to 5.3% each for employer and employee.

Ashcroft called for a simpler change. Noting that payroll taxes were one of the least progressive parts of the U.S. tax system, he proposed making them deductible from income taxes. But he provided no hint of how he would recoup the income tax revenues lost. And critics quickly pointed out that by using an income tax deduction rather than a straight payroll tax cut, Ashcroft wasn't making the system much more progressive, since most of the breaks would go to high-income earners.

Neither Kennedy's nor Ashcroft's ideas took hold on Capitol Hill. Meanwhile, the one-year campaign to build support for Social Security reform that Clinton and Gingrich had discussed was expanding in scope. In November, Congress had passed, and Clinton signed into law, the Savings Are Vital to Everyone's Retirement (SAVER) Act of 1997, which specified that the president convene three national summits on retirement savings, the first to be held in June 1998.

While basically symbolic, the SAVER campaign placed a series of media events, replete with some of the highest elected officials in the land, on the 1998 political calendar. Coupled with the president's National Dialogue on Social Security, SAVER encouraged lawmakers to meld the two issues in their minds.

* * *

Following the State of the Union speech, the first detailed proposal along the lines that Kasich prescribed came from two Democrats. On March 12, Pat Moynihan joined forces with Bob Kerrey to introduce the latest chapter in Moynihan's long and mercurial involvement with Social Security, unveiling a bill they said would preserve the program's basic benefits while solving its fiscal problems and offering something else besides: a wealth-building vehicle. "The fellow who worked at Bethlehem Steel for 40 years would not just have a pension, an annuity, but could leave substantial amounts of money to his children," Moynihan declared, adding that his plan "responds to the energy that the privatizers have had, without losing your basic annuity."

Moynihan framed his apostasy as a grand compromise between the privatizers' desire to substitute private initiative for guaranteed benefits and the unreconstructed New Dealer's desire to keep Social Security as it was. As a child of the Depression, the scheme he was now outlining proposed to complete Roosevelt's work—as he interpreted it—by cutting payroll taxes and allowing workers to either pocket the money or place it in personal accounts. Either way, the assets that workers accumulated wouldn't evaporate when they died, but could be passed on to their heirs. Since Social Security was the biggest wealth-building engine most workers had, Moynihan and Kerrey reasoned, it only made sense to allow people to put some of those assets to work for their heirs, not just themselves.

This was a complete reversal of the stand Moynihan had himself taken less than a year before. "Once the great majority of citizens found that they would do better in the private investment part of this new system, support for the redistributive aspects of Social Security would quickly erode," he had written in the *New York Times* in January 1997.[22] Arguably, that was no less true a year later. Only now, he appeared to have decided that significant cuts in Social Security were inevitable and that private accounts could help make up the difference—if not more.

David Podoff, Moynihan's longtime economic aide on the Senate Finance Committee, recalls that the senator started hatching the idea in July 1997, after a meeting with Rubin and Bowles. He had already been thinking about ways to heal the rift exposed by the Advisory Council, and when the two Clinton aides asked him if he had any ideas for what to do about Social Security, he went to work.[23]

Under Moynihan-Kerrey, the 12.4% payroll tax would decline to 11.4% over the next two years, then to 10.4% from 2001 to 2004. It would then start climbing again, to 11.4% from 2025 to 2029, then to 12.4% from 2030 to 2044, and finally to 13.4% for the next sixteen years. Gradually, the trust funds would dissolve and Social Security would once again be a pay-as-you-go system, as it had been before 1983, its annual intake from payroll taxes closely approximating the benefits paid out.

To pay for the cuts, Moynihan-Kerrey would raise the cap on wages subject to payroll tax from the current $68,400 per year to $97,500 by 2003, rather than the scheduled $82,800, and increase the normal retirement age to sixty-seven by 2016, to sixty-eight in 2023, and then to seventy in 2073. The pool of Social Security participants would widen to include all newly hired state and local employees: another 5 million workers. Moynihan-Kerrey also revived the New York senator's 1995 crusade against "overstatements" in the CPI, shaving an estimated 1% from the annual Social Security adjustments.

Finally, in 2001, workers could start setting up "voluntary investment accounts" financed with the difference in payroll tax cut proceeds, or take that money as a 1% increase in taxable wages. Either way, the assets they accumulated would be theirs to keep, to spend, or to pass on to their heirs.

At least until his engagement in the CPI debate in 1995, Moynihan had always been sensitive to the pain that Social Security cuts would inflict on its most vulnerable members. Now, he seemed happy to pass off some very serious cuts as "corrections" and computational "adjustments." Perhaps the biggest cuts under his and Kerrey's plan would come from raising the retirement age. What about those who were no longer fit to work into their late sixties? Moynihan-Kerrey provided for further study of the impact on those workers. According to Podoff, Moynihan rationalized that "if the overwhelming majority of the population are able to work to seventy, we shouldn't build a system around the exceptions."[24]

Progressive Democrats were scandalized by Moynihan's sudden assault on Social Security. Henry Aaron at Brookings called it "the My Lai approach to Social Security reform," since Moynihan was calling for Congress to "burn the system down in our attempt to save it." That bit of Vietnam hyperbole brought down attacks, and Aaron quickly apologized. But he continued to point out the sheer cost of administering millions of private accounts, exacerbated by private-sector providers' inevitable marketing expenses.[25]

A further problem was that by allowing a worker's heirs to "inherit" anything left over in her account after she died, Moynihan-Kerrey blurred the conceptual line between personal Social Security accounts and any other type of tax-advantaged savings account. If it could be passed on to someone else who wouldn't necessarily use it to save for retirement, then a great deal of money would "leak" out of the nation's retirement system, after which it could be used for any ordinary expense. The fundamental objective of Social Security, to offer protection against destitution in old age, would be lost.

Privatization advocates were delighted by Moynihan's conversion, however. "This is, by far, the most important development in advancing privatization thus far," Bill Beach of the Heritage Foundation said.[26]

The senator's personal prestige suggested that a certain number of his Democratic colleagues might follow his lead. "Messrs. Kerrey and Moynihan have … done a favor to Republicans, liberating them to talk about Social Security," declared the *Wall Street Journal's* Washington columnist, Paul A. Gigot. "And the senators are helping President Clinton by giving him at least some chance at a legacy other than scandal."

CHAPTER 23

THE DEBATE HITS THE ROAD

Moynihan unveiled his restructuring proposal less than a month before the first summit of the president's National Dialogue on Social Security was scheduled to start in Kansas City. Over the next several weeks, all ears were awaiting the president's reaction.

Clinton began by going down the list of options for a restructuring. He all but ruled out a payroll tax hike and declared his opposition to any change that would involve "totally privatizing the system." And while he appeared to endorse—at least for purposes of discussion—raising the limit on earnings subject to payroll tax, he argued against an idea popular with some privatizers: means-testing Social Security. Doing so would erode upper-income taxpayers' commitment to the system, he said, because "they'd just be writing 6 percent of their income for something they'd never see."

Hoping to establish parameters for the debate, Clinton offered "Five Principles for Reforming Social Security":

- Reform should strengthen and protect Social Security for the 21st century;

- Reform should maintain the universality and fairness of Social Security;

- Social Security must provide a benefit people can count on;

- Social Security must continue to provide financial security for disabled and low-income beneficiaries; and

- Social Security must maintain America's fiscal discipline.

On the surface, nothing in these five points ruled out any of the current crop of partial-privatization proposals, all of which would continue to provide a guaranteed benefit of some size and none of which sought to cut disability benefits. But buried in the language—along with the emphasis on "fairness" and the need to "protect" the system—opponents of privatization already spotted some reasons to believe Clinton would ultimately not back even partial privatization. And by including the seemingly unrelated issue of "America's fiscal discipline" in his set of non-negotiable points, Clinton appeared to be ruling out any plan that would erode the budget surplus—a stand that would become crucial as the current budget battle heated up.

The panelists in Kansas City also included Kerrey, who argued for his and Moynihan's plan, and Republican Sen. Rick Santorum of Pennsylvania, pushing the fashionable argument that privatization would be good for "the poor and minorities."

"The lure of privatization has turned a no-win political debate about how much to cut benefits and how much to raise taxes into an exercise with interesting possibilities," Peter Passell of the *New York Times* commented. "That fact alone makes a major overhaul of Social Security more likely in the next few years." In fact, Moynihan-Kerrey was about to be joined by another bipartisan bill to transform Social Security.

* * *

In the early 1990s, the Center for Strategic and International Studies (CSIS), a conservative think tank known mainly for defense studies, started to move into domestic issues as well. Its first such foray was to sponsor a "Strengthening America" commission co-chaired by Democrat Sam Nunn and Republican Pete Domenici, which came up with an attention-getting plan that called for excluding all saving and investment from taxation.

In late 1996, CSIS decided to follow up with an initiative to solve the retirement dilemma.[1] The following February, CSIS announced the creation of the National Commission on Retirement Policy (NCRP), to be co-chaired by three Democrats and three Republicans: John Breaux of Louisiana, Charlie Stenholm, and former Glaxo chairman Charles B. Sanders from the

Democratic side, and Judd Gregg, Rep. Jim Kolbe of Arizona, and PaineWebber chief executive Donald B. Marron from the Republican.

The rest of the NCRP's twenty-two-member panel was also evenly divided between the two parties. CSIS claimed it deliberately avoided picking extremists who would resist compromise on any major points. In reality, however, the only "extremists" excluded were those who opposed private-account carveouts, of whom the commission contained not a single one. Estelle James, the World Bank's leading proselytizer for pension privatization, was a member. Besides Marron, the commission also included two other financial services industry executives, one of them the president and CEO of Fidelity Investments. Two members headed business-backed research institutes. Mark Weinberger, the NCRP's legal counsel, had served as the Kerrey-Danforth commission's executive director and was now a high-powered corporate lobbyist whose law firm, Washington Counsel, advised clients including Aetna, Anheuser-Busch, General Electric, and AT&T on tax law.

Nevertheless, CSIS took pains to frame the NCPR not just as a sort of unprejudiced arbitrator in the Social Security debate, but as a quasi-official body whose product would have more significance than the usual think tank report. The name suggested as much, as did CSIS's ostentatious press release announcing its formation: "CSIS and Congress Announce The National Commission on Retirement Policy." The commission also announced that it would be holding hearings not just in Washington—where some would take place in meeting rooms in the Capitol—but in "roundtables, conferences and town hall meetings ... around the country," mostly in the lawmakers' home bases. Its intention, the NCRP proclaimed portentously, was to consult with "all affected constituencies, special interests, and the American public in a national debate" on Social Security.

With an overall budget of around $700,000 funded by PaineWebber (a major donor to Breaux, Stenholm, and Gregg's reelection campaigns), Fidelity, Aetna, several Fortune 500 companies, and the J.M. Kaplan Fund,[2] the NCRP became CSIS's top-priority project.[3] In January 1998 the panel put out its first publication, a preliminary report titled "Can America Afford to Retire?" Replete with concise, bullet-pointed presentations and colorful diagrams, the report painted a dire picture of an aging nation slowly going bankrupt, with no hint of a single mitigating factor.

Some progressive lawmakers and writers attacked the report as a propaganda piece, but press coverage was almost uniformly respectful. Then, in May, the commission released its final report. By this time it was already known in Washington that the congressional co-chairs of the NCRP would be introducing legislation based on the plan it outlined, which would thus become the highest visibility proposal yet to restructure Social Security.

Mark Schoeff, Jr., then CSIS's media director, describes a "feeding frenzy" the day before the report was to be released, with at least seventy calls from Capitol Hill offices alone and "the phone ringing off the hook" the rest of the day with press inquiries. CSIS had planned to give the *New York Times* a first-day exclusive, but a leak allowed the *Wall Street Journal* to get a one-day jump on the story detailing the report. The anger with which at least one prominent columnist reacted to the botched strategy suggests the seriousness with which the press took the project.[4]

That was reflected in the coverage itself. The *Times*[5] and the *Journal* both reported the commission's findings as if they signaled a significant change in the direction of public policy. Both stories waited until the third paragraph to mention that the "bipartisan panel" wasn't a government-appointed body, and neither mentioned that any of its members held previously known views on Social Security. Instead, the *Journal* emphasized the prominence of several of the members, and the *Times* the likelihood that it would "wield considerable influence at the White House and on Capitol Hill"—although the only authorities cited to prove this were members of the panel.

Neither publication bothered to include perspectives from anyone opposed to the panel's proposals or even the basic premise of its arguments. CSIS counted at least eighty-five news stories and editorials in newspapers, wire services, cable, broadcast, and radio news by the end of May alone. And while some cited critics of the proposals—Democratic Rep. Jerrold Nadler of New York told the *Washington Post* that Social Security's problems weren't so severe as to warrant "this kind of drastic action"—virtually none gave the critics any room to argue the specifics of the recommendations or offer counterproposals.

The press response was a tremendous public-relations victory for the privatization camp and ensured that when a version of the NCRP plan was introduced in Congress it would carry a strong aura of reasonableness and moderation.

Under the "21st Century Retirement Security Plan," as it was titled, individuals would be required to place 2% of their 6.2% payroll tax into separate investment accounts, although they could then choose from a menu of investments options. The plan also prescribed how the system would be set up. Initially, workers' contributions would accumulate in a government-run, pooled fund, while Washington set up the administrative machinery to handle 160 million separate accounts. After several years, workers would be credited with the gains from this pooled fund and could then allocate their assets to either an equity or a bond fund. Other investment options would be added later, and workers would be allowed to contribute an additional $2,000 annually to their accounts.

Like Moynihan-Kerrey, the NCRP proposed to raise the retirement age to seventy—but by 2029, not 2073. The early retirement age would rise to sixty-five by 2017. This and other "adjustments" would reduce first-year benefits for a worker born in the 1980s by about 30%. These changes would help to offset the heavy cost of setting up the individual accounts at the same time that Social Security continued to pay current-level benefits to current retirees. Reducing those costs further would be cutbacks in benefits for more affluent retirees. But the taxable income threshold wouldn't increase. The 21st Century plan would also, similarly, include all new state and local government workers in Social Security.

The NCRP recognized that some workers, perhaps 30%, would lose benefits under this scheme, either because of the higher retirement age or bad choices with their investment allocations. To compensate for this, the plan would create a minimum benefit starting at 60% of the poverty line for workers with at least twenty years on the job, increasing to 100% for those with at least forty years. Social Security recipients could also continue working without any reduction in benefits. However, implementing the plan would require no new taxes, the NCRP report said.

The commission made another recommendation on an issue that Moynihan-Kerrey hadn't addressed. What would happen after the worker retired? The NCRP's proposal was the first to incorporate annuities into a Social Security restructuring scheme. "On retirement," it said, "individuals would be required to annuitize that portion of their [individual account] balances." The government would preselect the insurance companies that workers could choose from in a competitive bidding process, as well as offer an alternative, "government-provided standard option."[6]

Critics pointed out that even if 160 million individual Social Security accounts were opened up to the annuities market, the problem of adverse selection would remain. Insurers would still offer significantly better rates and more attractive payout packages to workers from more affluent backgrounds and whose profiles suggested healthier lives in retirement. Just as they feared about the individual accounts themselves, critics predicted a system that forced tens of millions of retirees into the private annuity market would create winners and losers where previously everyone had been guaranteed a base income. Critics also found the NCRS's claim that its plan could be carried through without raising taxes or requiring new revenues beyond current-level payroll taxes less than credible.

Like Moynihan-Kerrey, however, the NCRP proposal pushed privatization a step closer to plausible enactment. By requiring partial annuitization, it appeared to address one of privatization's big remaining conceptual question marks. By means-testing benefits, it seemed to make the system more "progressive"—even though affluent workers wouldn't be required to pay any more than before. By including a series of recommendations to make private retirement accounts, such as 401(k)s, more portable and simplify pension rules for employers, it presented Social Security restructuring as an element of an overall plan to increase private saving—a popular theme during the year of the SAVER summits.

And with the signatures of four prominent members of Congress from both parties, it seemed to signal a boost in legislative momentum behind an overhaul of Social Security. Kolbe and Stenholm quickly introduced their House bill, modeled faithfully on the NCRP plan, with a companion measure sponsored by Gregg and Breaux in the Senate. In the weeks following, Capitol Hill saw more and more activity around Social Security. Senate Finance Committee chair William V. Roth, Jr., of Deleware, introduced a bill to create personal accounts funded with a portion of the $39 billion budget surplus, then announced hearings on public and private retirement saving, starting the week of June 15 and extending into fall. Early in June, the House Social Security Subcommittee held a hearing explicitly focused on ways to implement individual accounts.

* * *

Later in the month, some Republican supporters began taking the privatization message on the road in a series of out-of-town hearings. Rick Santorum, a member of the Senate Special Committee on Aging, hosted one such "field hearing" on June 30 at St. Joseph University in the Philadelphia suburb of Bala Cynwyd, on "Preserving America's Future Today." Its purpose was "to explore public sentiments on Social Security and to review solutions."

The two panels of witnesses included some community members, but the "experts" recruited for the events were almost entirely advocates of privatization, including Carl Helstrom, a member of Third Millennium; Sam Beard of Economic Security 2000; Cato's Michael Tanner; and Marshall E. Blum, a professor at the Wharton School.

A few days before Beard appeared on Santorum's panel, Economic Security 2000 held its 4,000[th] event, in Baltimore. The group had developed a strategy of approaching younger voters at "hip" events like rock concerts and in accessible settings like teach-ins, where its workers—usually also young—would pitch the need for Social Security "reform" and then urge their listeners to sign petitions for Congress to let them invest part of their payroll taxes in private accounts. Economic Security 2000 also had logged appearances on over 500 radio talk shows and published op-eds in more than 200 newspapers. Perhaps most importantly, it boasted having met with over seventy editorial boards, bringing the privatization message directly to the people who set the agenda on what to cover and how.

Other groups were stepping up their efforts. Cato reportedly was pushing its donors to contribute $100 million to fund a new advertising campaign around the benefits of privatization.[7] In the fall, business lobbyists came together to launch a new advocacy group, the Alliance for Worker Retirement Security. Backed by the National Association of Manufacturers (NAM), the U.S. Chamber of Commerce, the Business Roundtable, the National Federation of Independent Business, the National Retail Federation, and other powerful groups, and headed by former Cato staffer Leanne Abdnor, the alliance had a 1999 budget of $500,000 and announced its intention to launch an educational effort targeting factory workers, who traditionally prized their Social Security benefits.

One propaganda piece, a four-color brochure produced early on by the NAM, denounced the Social Security system as "corrupt," and recommended private accounts as the solution.[8] Over the next few months, organizations backed by the same constellation of Wall Street and business interests would continue the PR barrage. A highlight came in February 1999, when mutual fund giant Oppenheimer teamed up with Third Millennium to release a survey updating the UFO factoid of a few years prior. It found that 50% of Americans believed a Super Bowl bet was a better investment than Social Security.[9]

In the face of such well-funded opponents, Social Security's traditional defenders felt acutely frustrated. "There are already 15 privatization proposals out there, and it is getting to be dangerous and persuasive," said Bob Ball. Tim Fuller, executive director of the Gray Panthers, said bluntly, "We've been sandbagged."

What was more curious, however, was the anti-privatization side's silence. By the time Santorum was packing for his road trip to Philadelphia, efforts to mount a counterattack added up to just one informal meeting a few months earlier. Some initiatives were pending in Congress. Jerry Nadler introduced a nonbinding "sense of the Congress" resolution in June calling individual accounts a "hastily conceived and radical" idea that would require "significant reductions in guaranteed benefits" and proclaiming, among other things, that "any solution must be equitable to people of all ages." Nadler's office billed the resolution as "the first step in a major campaign to turn back efforts to replace Social Security with individual accounts." The resolution garnered ninety-three cosponsors: all Democrats except for Vermont Independent Bernard Sanders.

Along with Ted Kennedy in the Senate, Rep. Earl Pomeroy, a North Dakota Democrat and former state insurance commissioner, was planning to submit a bill structured around Bob Ball's proposal to invest a portion of the trust funds in the stock market. AFL-CIO officials said they were contemplating a $30 million fall campaign against privatization, telling the *Wall Street Journal* they expected an "11th-hour advertising blitz" to be more effective than a "protracted debate."

But the *Journal* pronounced the big labor federation "AWOL" on Social Security and most close media observers noted the lack of activity too.

The beginnings of a counterattack were glimmering, however. Its center of energy was the Campaign for America's Future, a four-year-old progressive pressure group. The CAF had been formed in reaction to the seemingly commanding position the New Democrat agenda had achieved in the first Clinton administration. Its goal was to stop the rightward drift of U.S. politics by formulating an agenda that could help Democrats rebuild the old New Deal coalition.

* * *

The co-directors of the Campaign for America's Future (CAF) were two long-time Washington policy coordinators, Robert L. Borosage and Roger

Hickey. Borosage had advised Jesse Jackson during his 1988 presidential race and had more recently run the Campaign for National Priorities, which he founded in 1989 to push Congress to redirect post–Cold War federal spending from the military to pressing domestic needs. Hickey was a founder of the Economic Policy Institute, a labor-oriented think tank. The CAF's leaders had close ties to the "new labor" team of John Sweeney, the incoming president of the AFL-CIO, and the federation became the group's most prominent backer.

During the last months of the Social Security Advisory Council, Hickey began looking for reporters who might want to present the argument against private accounts. He netted a strong cover story in *Mother Jones* magazine, but little else. After the council report was unveiled, Hickey felt what was needed was a way to alert a larger circle of groups, which depended on Social Security in one way or another, that the program was in danger.

That could be the gateway to something more ambitious. "It helped us create an ongoing program that would unite a lot of single-issue groups around a fundamental economic battle," says Hickey. Labor had helped midwife the program into existence and had strongly supported it since its inception. Social Security was critical to women and communities of color as well as the disabled. The privatization threat could pull these groups back together.

By including liberal think tanks and polling organizations and tapping organized labor's ability to bring labor activists into the streets, CAF could begin to approximate the force that conservative policy entrepreneurs had been bringing to such broad-stroke issues as tax cuts, family values, abortion, guns, and school choice since the 1970s. More important, it could impel progressives to relearn the ability to build a mass movement around a political issue: a skill many of them had forgotten in the decades when the Democrats had dominated Capitol Hill.

Roger Hickey, co-director of the Campaign for America's Future. The CAF, and Hickey in particular, were instrumental in building an effective progressive alliance against Social Security cuts during the second Clinton administration. They remained vital to the defense of the program thereafter.

In late 1997, the CAF launched the Social Security Information Project (SSIP) to develop a coherent intellectual argument against privatization, line up coalition partners, and create a mechanism for recruitment and messaging. Hickey was the project's pivot, its most active proselytizer, and the person most responsible for pulling together the newly conceived alliance. As its sole staffer, policy analyst, and webmaster he hired Tom Matzzie, a recent Notre Dame graduate who had earlier interned in Washington. Matzzie quickly set up a website for the SSIP and began scouring actuarial reports for data the CAF could use to counter the privatizers' arguments.

The SSIP's most effective tool, however, was an email listserv, also engineered by Matzzie. It quickly included hundreds of labor leaders, economists, policy analysts, journalists, Democratic party activists, women's groups, ethnic political alliances, and traditional Social Security supporters such as advocates for the disabled and the elderly. One of the first email lists used to build a campaign around a political issue, the SSIP listserv carried a steady stream of news articles, releases, and economic analyses, including summaries by Hickey and Matzzie of how each piece of news affected the direction of the debate.[10]

"Our goal was to drive a wedge, if not between Clinton and the Democratic Leadership Council, then between the rest of the party and the DLC," Matzzie recalls.[11] "We were trying to politicize the issue," adds Hans Riemer, a policy analyst and organizer who had founded the 2030 Center, a public policy group for young people and a counterweight to Third Millennium. "The Concord Coalition and all these other groups pushing for some drastic downscaling of Social Security were putting across a message that this is not about politics, it's about solutions, tackling big problems. Very high-minded and technical: in fact, you won't understand it. [Instead,] we were trying to say that it's about real people, about politics."[12]

When he set up 2030 in the early months of 1997, Riemer, twenty-four, was attempting to insert another wedge, this one between younger voters and conservative advocacy groups that claimed to speak for them, especially on Social Security. The new group set about creating working alliances with established student groups such as the United States Student Association as well as some public interest research groups that Third Millennium had written off as too liberal.

In this fashion, 2030 began to fund and build an alliance to counter the portrait of Gen X that Third Millennium had been able to paint through the media. Beyond this, there wasn't much difference organizationally between the two. 2030 had no mass membership, instead initiating polls and research projects and looking for opportunities to get its views into the press. While it had to overcome some presumption in favor of Third Millennium's position, Riemer says plenty of reporters responded to the notion of a "Gen-X rift" over Social Security.

Gradually over the next few months, Hickey and Matzzie made progress, helped also by Riemer. Traveling the country, they began putting together a cadre of young activists with an interest in public policy, who caught the urgency of defending Social Security. In Seattle, Riemer met Lisa Witter, a legislative aide to a city council member who was interested in women's rights, housing, and health services issues. He asked her if she could represent 2030 when Social Security came up in local media or public discussions. Several members of Witter's family wouldn't have been able to get by without survivors' benefits at various points in their lives and she was captivated by the idea of educating the public that Social Security was an important benefit for a wider group of people than just the elderly.

"Within six months I became an expert on Social Security," she recalls. In 1999, she moved to Washington and went to work for the National Council of Women's Organizations, where she set up conferences and developed public education campaigns around Social Security.[13]

On a walk back from a meeting with AFL-CIO officials, Hickey and Mattzzie conceived the New Century Alliance for Social Security, which would include not just the organizations that had been focusing on Social Security in recent years, such as the National Committee to Preserve Social Security and Medicare, the Gray Panthers, and the National Council of Senior Citizens, but others whose members benefited from the program but hadn't engaged with the issue thus far.

In meetings over the summer and fall, they quickly persuaded dozens of groups to sign on—including Jesse Jackson's Rainbow/PUSH Coalition, the National Association for the Advancement of Colored People, and the National Organization for Women. Riemer had written a plank on Social Security for the national platform of the U.S. Students Association three years earlier. This gave him entrée to ask the group to join the new coalition.*

Some members of the New Century Alliance had already become concerned about the privatization movement's PR successes and were mobilizing their memberships. At the Institute for Women's Policy Research, Witter made a concerted outreach effort to other women's groups. The CAF wanted to announce the New Century Alliance's formation before the White House summit on December 8 and 9, which was to cap the year-long National Dialogue on Social Security. When few important groups could act quickly enough, Hickey and Mattzzie persuaded some of their key leaders to sign on as individuals.

Hickey wanted to make sure all of these organizations became active on the issue rather than riding on the CAF's coattails. He obtained a large, two-year commitment from the John D. and Catherine MacArthur Foundation that funded the SSIP's activities—including Mattzzie's salary—and provided separate grants up to $200,000 for other groups in the coalition, including the National Urban League, the National Council of La Raza, the National Council of Women's Organizations, and the Institute for Women's Policy Research. The money started flowing in early 1998.[14]

---

* Interview with Hans Riemer, June 26, 2003. Earlier, his contacts with student groups had helped him alert activists to attend Santorum's "field hearings" on Social Security, most of which were not well publicized and were held at small colleges outside the large cities.

As the alliance started to take shape, participants from the various organizations drafted a statement of principles focusing tightly on one key point: that private accounts carved out of payroll taxes would mean cutting Social Security benefits. "Congress and the President should work to strengthen the finances of Social Security for future generations," it declared. "'Privatization' proposals to shift a portion of Social Security taxes to private investment accounts would inevitably require large cuts in Social Security's defined benefits and make retirement income overly dependent on the risks of the stock and bond markets."

At its core, the statement insisted that Social Security remain a social insurance program, guaranteeing benefits "that provide a decent income and are adjusted to keep up with inflation for as long as you live," rather than become a personal investment vehicle. It warned against raising the retirement age to balance the program's books, terming this "the equivalent of a benefit cut," and called for strengthening Social Security's protections for women. Most emphatically, it said private accounts "should not be substituted for Social Security's current defined benefits."

In a reminder to the president, the statement concluded, "We should save Social Security first, instead of using budget surpluses to pay for tax cuts."

* * *

The SSIP, meanwhile, was making rapid progress. Within a few months, its members included religious groups such as Catholic Charities USA and the United Church of Christ, the usual collection of liberal think tanks and economists, a wide range of labor leaders, and even John Mueller, a former Jack Kemp aide who was now working with Gary Bauer, the religious-right leader and head of the Family Research Council. Bauer was considering running for the Republican presidential nomination on a family-values platform and had taken the position that privatizing Social Security would be bad for families. USAction, a loose confederation of local progressive citizens' groups, was helping to provide forums for CAF-connected policy experts to talk about Social Security, including as a response to statements coming out of the White House's National Dialogue road show.

Other groups on the progressive end of the spectrum now recognized defending Social Security as a great opportunity to rebuild their own base of support and reinvigorate their mission. The Gray Panthers, for example, had seen their membership decline from some 250,000 to around 20,000–25,000 active members over the past ten years. The group's new executive director, Tim Fuller, was looking for an issue the Panthers could use as a starting point for rebuilding. Social Security made sense because the Panthers had a long history of involvement with it. So they worked with the CAF while launching their own "Lift the Cap" campaign at rallies and seniors' events around the country, arguing that much of the Social Security trust funds' long-term fiscal shortfall could be eliminated if Congress raised the cap on the amount of income subject to payroll tax.[15]

Social Security also struck a chord with members of the United Church of Christ, recalls Pat Conover, then legislative director of the church's Justice and Witness Ministries. After sending out a Social Security action packet, "we got a lot of response," with 20% answering in some form, and many volunteering to take the church's analysis to unions and other organizations to which they belonged. "Even though the national church is generally more engaged in children's issues, the church is a very graying population, and the people in the pews are very interested in elderly issues," said Conover.[16]

Another reason for the success of the SSIP was that it lost no time in mobilizing the anti-privatization side's intellectual capital to issue a barrage of studies, polls, and white papers. These gradually found their way into the op-ed pages and, in so doing, finally started to provide a counterweight to the dominant vocabulary of crisis.

One of the first people the CAF met with after launching the SSIP was Bob Greenstein, executive director of the Center on Budget and Policy Priorities (CBPP), a respected center-left think tank. The year before, the CBPP's board had identified Social Security as an issue it wanted to focus on, and subsequently, it received a grant that enabled it to set up a unit on Social Security with two dedicated economists. So the CBPP quickly became the new Social Security alliance's chief source of intellectual arguments and analysis against privatization.

While the NCRP's plan for restructuring Social Security had scored a hit in May with the press and lawmakers, it also proved an excellent recruiting tool for privatization opponents in the summer and fall. "It was a boon," says Matzzie, "because it provided us with a way to show how the privatizers were going to cut benefits. It became an organizing device for us."[17] One of the first op-eds the CAF bylined on Social Security was a piece by Borosage in the *Arizona Republic* that noted how the NCRP had asked the SSA actuaries to estimate workers' projected returns under their proposal. When the actuaries responded that workers would do better under the current system, since the costs of transitioning to a system of millions of private accounts would outweigh the investment gains, the commission buried the results.

The CAF was finding that the most effective way to instill doubts about the wisdom of privatization was to mention that it would probably include raising the retirement age. Focus groups the CAF convened, and polls the AFL-CIO conducted that fall, showed that "it stopped the conversation when you told them that changing Social Security would raise their retirement age," Matzzie recalls.[18]

This in turn helped the New Century Alliance build a core argument against privatization, calculated to appeal to as many of its potential coalition partners as possible—particularly economists such as the CBPP's Greenstein and Henry J. Aaron of the Brookings Institution, who supported the program but accepted in principle the assertion that there was a Social Security "crisis" that Washington should resolve sooner rather than later. At the same time, the alliance refused to step into the quicksand by proposing its own "solution" to the crisis.

By the end of 1997 the new coalition against privatization was starting to make itself felt—even in the White House, where the Clinton team was planning how the president would introduce the topic in his 1998 State of the Union speech. Memos from that period show Sperling and Summers, for instance, taking into account whether certain approaches—for instance, allocating some of the budget surplus for the Social Security trust funds and some for private accounts—might "alienate the Ball camp or split the Democrats."[19]

Not everyone who signed on to the New Century Alliance was happy with its strategy. Some, like the Gray Panthers and the church coalition for which Pat Conover of the United Church of Christ became the unofficial spokesperson, would have preferred a more aggressive approach that questioned the assertion that Social Security was "in crisis" at all. Conover wanted to push an argument questioning the Social Security trustees' economic and workforce growth projections, which he felt were too pessimistic.

"My colleagues mostly regarded it as a good idea to do this, but the Hickey coalition didn't push it," he says. "Instead, they pushed the details of the damage that the various privatization schemes would do and the costs of privatization."[20]

Tim Fuller of the Gray Panthers was drawn to another set of analyses that also questioned the trustees' assumptions as being unrealistically pessimistic. Dean Baker and Mark Weisbrot of the Economic Policy Institute suggested a three-point plan to reform the system, which wouldn't involve tax increases or benefits cuts.

- Committing a portion of the federal government's projected budget surpluses to the trust fund or indexing payroll taxes to increases in life expectancy;

- Fully incorporating the impact of recent changes in the CPI into the trust funds' projections; and

- Raising the cap on wages subject to the payroll tax.[21]

Fuller adopted the last point for the Panthers' "Raise the Cap" campaign; the group produced some powerful information pieces that didn't shy away from raising the class-based issues at the root of the Social Security debate. "An elite 5% of American wage earners makes more than $72,600," one piece pointed out. "They do not pay any additional FICA taxes on money earned above this amount—this is known as the 'cap.' They pay FICA taxes on less than 100% of their income." But Fuller couldn't get the strategists at the CAF to adopt the Panthers' approach.

"I thought, and still think, we would come to regret supporting the characterization that Social Security is in serious financial danger and trying to turn it on [the privatizers'] heads," Conover recalled six years later.

But the CAF had a coalition to hold together, and rather than stake out a more detailed position, "our imperative was to keep everybody working together toward that end," Hickey says. And it couldn't ignore its own polling. "People were seriously concerned that Social Security had financial problems, and merely dismissing this as an accounting problem probably was not the way to go."[22]

The polling also showed overwhelming opposition to benefits cuts, and Hickey and his colleagues held their position firmly even when some of their more moderate allies suggested in the months ahead that they should be willing to compromise. The alliance carefully avoided using the word "crisis" in its propaganda and public speaking, lest it validate the opposition's arguments.

CHAPTER 24

DEMOCRATIC BACKLASH

By mid-summer of 1998, Social Security was competing for the White House's attention with something more tantalizing. Coverage of the Starr commission's inquiry into the president's relationship with Monica Lewinsky dominated the media. The proliferation of twenty-four-hour news channels meant the scandal was "on" seemingly all the time. With an election pending and a twenty-two-seat Republican margin in the House, Democrats began looking for an issue that would connect easily and powerfully with their constituents—and perhaps distract voters from the accusations of presidential perjury. Social Security appeared to be it.

Focusing on their strongest constituencies, Democratic strategists took note of polls suggesting their positions played best among women and the elderly. Both groups favored Democrats by more than ten points, according to an Associated Press poll, and both tended to place Social Security high on their priority lists. So did most Americans, in fact, according to a Pew Research Center poll: when offered a choice between tax cuts and Social Security reform as budget and policy priorities, three-quarters of Americans picked Social Security.

The polls also strengthened a new perspective that progressive Democrats had gradually been forming about their party's political future. Fostered by the CAF and liberal think tanks, including the Economic Policy Institute and the Century Foundation, this view held that the Democrats' natural constituency was among working-class voters who relied on "entitlements" like Social Security, Medicare, and public education. Downscale voters with household incomes under $50,000 a year and without college degrees formed the critical swing group that moved from Bush to Clinton in 1992—attracted, in part, by his pledge to remake the health care system—and then helped Clinton resurrect his fortunes in 1996, argued progressives like pollster Stan Greenberg. Defending programs under attack, such as Social Security and Medicare, rather than competing with Republicans on how best to "reform" them, had to be the Democrats' standard position if they were to continue making gains toward recovering a majority in Congress.

Congressional Democrats and some of their allies in the less-conservative think tanks were starting to come together around the bill that Ted Kennedy and Pomeroy were working up, which was built on the idea of investing part of the Social Security trust fund in stocks as a way to boost returns on the assets. This would be a better alternative to the private accounts that Moynihan was proposing, argued Brookings's Henry Aaron, because a single investment portfolio would be easier and cheaper to administer than millions of individual accounts, it would not be keyed to a single worker's retirement schedule and therefore would be easier to invest effectively, and it would not expose individual workers to the hazards of the markets.

By summer, the new position was being articulated in a series of op-eds, policy forums, and publications. Bob Ball coauthored a policy primer for the Century Foundation titled *Straight Talk about Social Security*, which laid out a Chinese menu of three possible changes to the system, most of them not dissimilar to those he had offered on the Advisory Council. But there were a few surprises:

- Adopting the BLS's proposed revisions in the COLA formula to provide a more "accurate" inflation adjustment;

- Lengthening the averaging period—the number of working years used to figure Social Security retirement benefits—from thirty-five to thirty-eight years; and

- Increasing the normal retirement age, indexing it to life expectancy once it reached sixty-seven in 2022 as specified in current law.

As usual with Ball, he wasn't recommending any one or more of his proposed changes—the idea was for Congress to pick from a menu of reasonable, incremental adjustments. In his conclusion, however, he raised another possibility, although in such gingerly fashion that he seemed almost embarrassed to do so. "Really quite modest changes" were needed to balance Social Security's books for years to come, he wrote. However, "it is possible, of course, that no consensus will emerge from bipartisan consideration of possible Social Security changes." In that case, he suggested, pursuing a partial fix, extending the date of trust fund "exhaustion" from 2030 to 2050, would likely be more acceptable to a majority of Congress than to attempt more ambitious changes.

This made sense, given that the traditional seventy-five-year projections were just that: projections, not prophecy. Yet no Democratic politician would straightforwardly assert that his or her goal was anything less than "sustainable solvency" over the full seventy-five years. By tacitly accepting the seventy-five-year fiscal horizon, preferably with rising trust fund assets at the end of that period, as the litmus test for success fully fixing Social Security, the system's traditional champions had constrained themselves to fight on the privatizers' own turf. Anyone who attempted to argue for a restructuring that didn't meet the most stringent standard for guaranteeing Social Security's "sustainability" would henceforth be seen as "not serious about reform" and their proposals as not worth considering.*

Divisions were beginning to appear in the privatization camp as well, however. Martin Feldstein, who had been working with Ken Kies on the secret Clinton-Gingrich-Archer collaboration, produced one restructuring proposal that grabbed a great deal of attention. His plan would use some $1 trillion of general revenues over ten years to cover the cost of setting up private accounts, to be funded by a mandatory contribution of 2% of workers' earnings. Feldstein proposed retaining a reduced version of the traditional Social Security benefit. And once a worker retired, she would only be allowed to keep 25% of the assets accumulated in her private account. The rest would be "clawed back" into Social Security to boost her "traditional" benefit. In return, the worker would receive an annuity, three-quarters of which would finance her basic Social Security benefit with the rest constituting a "bonus" for successful investing. If there wasn't enough left to pay the traditional OASI benefit, perhaps due to a market downturn, the government would make up the rest.

Feldstein's aim with this peculiar payout arrangement, which reflected some of the ideas Kies was discussing with White House staff, was to hold down the cost of transition to a privatized program. That made it popular with lawmakers who were uncomfortable with the sacrifices the NCRP plan

---

* While he argued for a "medium-term fix" as a last resort, Ball wanted to retain the seventy-five-year, long-range estimates: as an expression of the intent to maintain Social Security as a self-supporting system, as a yardstick for assessing the cost of proposed changes, and to give lawmakers an early alert that action was needed on any looming problems. But he didn't explain why seventy-five years was the optimal benchmark period, and noted that this was a longer yardstick than almost any other country used for its national retirement system (Robert M. Ball and Thomas N. Bethell, *Straight Talk About Social Security*, A Century Foundation/Twentieth Century Fund Report, 1998, pp. 36–37).

called for. But it made many Republicans uneasy. It would be less than a system of "true" personal accounts—recipients couldn't pass any remaining assets on to their heirs—while the government wouldn't be divesting itself of any "entitlement" obligations. Such guarantees might make the plan more saleable to rank-and-file workers, but they wouldn't achieve the true goals of the privatization movement.

Amongst pro-privatization lawmakers, the Pain Caucus—those who insisted Social Security couldn't be "reformed" without cutting benefits heavily—generally supported the NCRP plan, while the Free Lunch Caucus—Cato and other groups arguing that private accounts would be so successful as to make only modest benefit cuts necessary, at most—favored something like Feldstein's framework. But it would be an exaggeration to call this a split, and through the summer and fall, privatization advocates searched hard for ways to make their arguments appeal to a broader spectrum of workers.

* * *

By summer 1998, thanks in large part to the progressive coalition's work, the Democratic leaders in both chambers, Tom Daschle and Dick Gephardt,

embraced the strategy of "nationalizing" the midterm election around Social Security. By early July, Daschle wanted to make the flagship role of Social Security official "sooner rather than later," the *Wall Street Journal* reported.[1]

Many Republican leaders, meanwhile, were worried and angry. Some strategists advised their candidates to mute their views on Social Security during the campaign and to refuse to become engaged in a national debate by countering Democrats' criticisms. "Shut up about it, don't make it easy for them," counseled William McInturff, the Republican pollster.

The NCRP plan, put into legislative form by the Kolbe-Stenholm and Gregg-Breaux bills, was becoming an easy target for Democrats. Their critique centered primarily on the bills' provision raising the retirement age to seventy in 2029, then indexing it to life expectancy, which would cause a further projected rise to seventy-two-and-a-half after seventy-five years. Less than two days after Kolbe and Stenholm introduced their legislation, a Government Accounting Office (GAO) report on current private-account proposals, prepared for hearings before the Senate Special Committee on Aging, leaked to the press. An article in the *Los Angeles Times* highlighted the report's warnings that boosting the date of retirement would cause hardship for many workers.

"Blue-collar workers are more likely to have musculoskeletal problems, respiratory diseases, diabetes and emotional disorders than are white-collar workers," the GAO found. "For example, blue-collar workers are 58% more likely to have arthritis, 42% more likely to have chronic lung diseases and 25% more likely to have emotional disorders." One reason Americans had been retiring earlier for decades was that many of these blue-collar workers were physically unable—not just unwilling—to work beyond age sixty-two, if not sixty-five. For older workers who want to keep working and are physically able to do so, "it is unclear whether employers will be willing to retain or hire them because of negative perceptions about costs and productivity."[2]

To then raise the age at which one could begin to collect full Social Security benefits to seventy would compel many of those who most needed it to spend several years living off their savings—if any—before they could begin collecting benefits.

Some economists drew attention also to the fiscal justification for upping the retirement age and to the benefits workers would lose. Gary Burtless of the Brookings Institution testified to the Committee on Aging that a one-year extension of the retirement age would be equivalent to about a 7% cut in total lifetime Social Security benefits for an average worker. With Kolbe-Stenholm and Gregg-Breaux promising to raise the retirement age even further by indexing it to life expectancy, the total cut in guaranteed benefits for the children of Gen X would come to nearly 40%, the Congressional Research Service estimated. The 2030 Center slammed the bills for attempting to balance Social Security's books on the backs of Gen X and its progeny, and questioned whether private investment accounts could make up the difference, let alone leave younger workers ahead of the game.

* * *

On July 27, Clinton declared himself "open to the idea that if we can get a higher rate of return in some fashion than we have been getting in the past, while being fair to everybody," then investing some of the trust funds in the stock market might be acceptable. That same day, Monica Lewinsky was meeting with Kenneth Starr's prosecutors in New York and signing an immunity agreement to provide information on her affair with the president. In mid-August the sex scandal entered a new phase when Clinton and then, for the second time, Lewinsky testified to the grand jury. Shortly after Labor Day, Starr turned over his report and supporting materials to the House Judiciary Committee, which promptly began releasing them both to the public. By the end of September the committee was considering a resolution for an impeachment inquiry.

As the prospect of impeachment loomed, the November election assumed a new character. Issues such as Social Security and how to dispose of the impending budget surplus receded, and the press, public, and politicians began to see the election as a referendum on Bill Clinton.

The prospect of the president being forced to step down wasn't one that privatization advocates necessarily relished. Cato's Michael Tanner told the *Wall Street Journal's* Glenn Burkins, "If the president survives, I think it actually improves the prospects" for revamping Social Security. "I think this is a president who badly wants a legacy aside from Monica. Social Security reform certainly would be that. I think it's one of the few areas where he could make his mark on history." Others agreed that Clinton's status, and his decision as to whether he still wanted to pursue the issue or not, would determine what could be achieved in 1999.

"You tell me what's going to happen to the president, and I'll tell you what's going to happen to Social Security," said Martha Phillips, executive director of the Concord Coalition.[3]

In early fall, Archer unveiled a bill to set aside 90% of the $1.6 trillion federal surplus now projected over the next decade for use in a Social Security restructuring effort. The other 10% would help pay for an $80 billion tax cut package, including breaks for married couples, a new annual exclusion for savings and dividend income, another for estate taxes, and a new 100% deduction for self-employed people's health insurance costs. Thus, Archer and his colleagues could claim that the cuts would encourage saving and investment. But the most striking thing about the package was that it relied on the surplus to finance the tax breaks, despite the fact that until 2006, each yearly surplus was projected to come entirely from Social Security.

Archer defended the cut on the grounds that, "If we don't cut taxes, does anyone really think the politicians won't waste your money and spend the surplus?"[4] But this drove a wedge between him and the president, who insisted on preserving the entire surplus until a bipartisan overhaul could be approved. And that left the Republicans' proposal to preserve only 90% of it less than reassuring. As soon as Ways and Means passed Archer's bill in mid-September, the White House pounced. Chief of Staff Erskine Bowles wrote to Archer that Clinton would veto any bill that didn't preserve the entire Social Security surplus.[5]

Blundering House Republicans had handed their rivals a potent weapon. The Clinton sex scandals were reaching their peak—the House Judiciary Committee had just released the first 445 pages of Starr report background materials to the public—and the Democrats were desperate for anything their candidates could use to counterattack as the election approached. Since the Advisory Council report, numerous Republican lawmakers had gone public with their support for private accounts in some form. Many were on record as co-sponsors of Kolbe-Stenholm or Gregg-Breaux.

"The 1998 election was a simple choice," as Clinton himself formulated it later. "Democrats wanted to save Social Security first."[6] In Ohio, Rep. Ted Strickland, running for reelection against a Republican lieutenant governor, proclaimed in a television ad, "Nancy Hollister wants to raid Social Security to the tune of $80 billion. And Nancy Hollister wants to gamble your retirement on Wall Street."

In Kansas, Dennis Moore, running to unseat a first-term Republican representative, put a TV commercial into heavy rotation in which he said, "I'll vote to use the entire budget surplus to save Social Security. Vince Snowbarger opposes this plan, and he actually said we should, quote, phase it out." His opponent shot back with an ad in which elder statesperson Bob Dole accused "liberal Democrat Dennis Moore and the big labor unions bankrolling his campaign" of "spending hundreds of thousands of dollars distorting Republican Congressman Vince Snowbarger's record on Social Security."

Yet Snowbarger had indeed said during his first campaign in 1996 that Social Security should be phased out "maybe not completely," with younger workers encouraged "to buy their own retirement plans."[7] Not only that, but the 1998 platform of the Kansas Republican Party itself included as one of its planks the following: "the eventual privatization of Social Security."[8]

Other Republican candidates fell into similar caught-with-the-goods traps. In Ohio, an aide to Hollister told reporters firmly that "Nancy's against privatization." Strickland's staff responded by brandishing a mailing in which the lieutenant governor said she "supports allowing workers to invest a portion of their payroll taxes in private accounts, which they manage."

In fact, most congressional races in 1998 didn't involve Social Security to any great extent. Local issues dominated, along with the stands that many lawmakers—especially Republicans—were taking on the prospect of the president's impeachment. But the election gave the New Century Alliance another valuable opportunity to disseminate educational and propaganda pieces against privatization, and press Democratic candidates to declare themselves on the issue.[9]

As election day neared and Washington remained gridlocked on the bud-get—on October 1, Congress had to pass a temporary measure to continue funding the federal government—the lack of progress also favored the adminis-tration. The press made much of the fact that a government shutdown, like the one the first Gingrich Congress had precipitated in 1995, again loomed—even though the Republican leadership clearly wasn't going to precipitate another such occurrence. To prevent it, budget negotiations moved from Capitol Hill to the White House, culminating in a series of semi-secret meetings between the president, the speaker, and the Senate majority leader.

By that time, Archer's bill, with its $80 billion tax cut largely carved out of the Social Security surplus, had passed the House but died for lack of votes in the Senate, marking the first time any spending bill had ever gone down to defeat due to its effect on Social Security. In early October, the House and Senate replaced it with, respectively, a $9.2 billion and an $8.6 billion package, both stretched out over nine years. The result was a major win for the White House, putting Gingrich and Lott firmly in the position of supplicants in their negotiations with the president.

Clinton got what he wanted, signing the combined spending bill on Octo-ber 22. Instead of estate tax and marriage penalty relief, the tax cuts in the final $520 billion bill that passed both chambers consisted largely of an extension of a research and development credit for businesses and an assistance program for workers harmed by lower U.S. tariffs. Republicans anxious about reelec-tion settled for a raft of spending measures calculated to appeal to voters in their districts, from $4 million for a Jewish History Center in New York (Sen. Alfonse D'Amato) to loans for expansion of fish processing plants in Alaska (Sen. Ted Stevens).

What the bill didn't do—curiously, given the solemn promises both sides had made—was preserve the Social Security surplus. Roughly a quarter of the surplus would be swallowed by new spending initiatives in the form of a $21 billion emergency spending bill designed to get around the Gramm-Rudman limits. The 1999 "emergency" budget was ticketed at roughly three times the size of the last five such measures, noted columnist Robert J. Samuelson, and stretched the definition perhaps farther than ever to cover such items as peace-keeping forces for Bosnia and the Y2K computer problem.

What mattered both on Capitol Hill and in the national press, however, was the defeat of the Republican tax cuts, which blew apart the well-oiled image of the Gingrich-era Republican Congress, less than two weeks before a bitterly fought election was to take place. Meanwhile, the White House's budget victory, and the prominent role it assigned to Social Security, struck a chord with some campaigning Democrats, who picked up the message and ran with it. The party ran Social Security-related ads in Texas, Kentucky, and Oregon, among other states. The AFL-CIO targeted fourteen House districts. The Committee to Preserve Social Security and Medicare donated $650,000 to 262, mostly Democratic, candidates.[10]

The AFL-CIO announced plans to mount TV and radio ads in twenty se-lected congressional districts, mostly against House Republicans who had spo-ken in favor of privatization or had sponsored bills to that end. Sixty trained activists were taking the drive to labor stalwarts in those districts. Meanwhile, in ten two-day-long "train-the-trainers" sessions at the George Meany Center in suburban Washington, the federation's legislative field staff was prepping hundreds of activist union members on how to educate their colleagues on the issues around Social Security privatization. In turn, they trained members at the state-federation and local levels, eventually getting the AFL-CIO's basic argu-ments out to many thousands of union members. Some large member unions created their own infrastructure in support of Social Security. The American Federation of Teachers, for example, had some twenty-five national staffers working full time to educate members on the issue by the end of 1998.[11]

Opponents at the National Association of Manufacturers assailed the feder-ation as being out of touch with its own members and scaring voters with false claims that private accounts would endanger their benefits. In the meantime, Cato struggled to raise Social Security as an issue in the fall campaigns, pressing congressional candidates to add private accounts into their platforms. But few were in the mood to expose themselves to Democratic attacks.

A Hart-Teeter *Wall Street Journal*/NBC poll taken days before the election showed that since April, support for individual accounts carved out of payroll taxes had slipped from 52% to 43%. Significantly, the question was phrased to pose the possibility that private accounts could either yield a better return or leave people with too little money for retirement.

Republican strategists insisted the "scare tactics" wouldn't work and fought back with their own ad blitz in seventy-three markets as part of a last-minute, $25-million effort that insisted on the need to both save Social Security and cut taxes. But Clinton and the Democrats had forced them into a rear-guard action. And while they could campaign on the need for tax cuts, they had nothing to show for the effort to achieve them.

CHAPTER 25

"SO SURREAL YOU WOULDN'T BELIEVE IT"

When the ballots were counted on November 3, the Republicans held on to their fifty-five-seat majority in the Senate. But they lost five seats in the House, narrowing their control from 228 seats against 206 Democrats and 1 Independent, to 223 seats against 211 and 1. And while none of the most prominent champions of privatization from either party—Kolbe, Stenholm, Archer, Shaw in the House; Gregg, Breaux, Domenici in the Senate—lost their seat, the Campaign for America's Future noted that many Republicans were forced to hedge their support for the concept in the face of Democratic attacks, using terms such as "personalization" or "personal accounts" to describe what they supported.

Social Security clearly played a large role in some races. All ninety incumbents who had signed Nadler's resolution against individual accounts won re-election (three didn't run again). In at least one case, Peter Fitzgerald's defeat of

Illinois Sen. Carol Moseley-Braun, the Republican challenger strongly opposed privatization in a televised debate. And one incumbent Republican House member who was co-sponsor of a privatization bill, Nick Smith of Michigan, had to disavow the bill—"It's just an idea. I'm not an advocate for any one solution"—and distance himself from the cause in order to defeat a Democratic challenger who attacked him on privatization.

Backing up the lesson from a different direction, Rep. Scotty Baesler, running for an open Kentucky Senate seat against Republican Jim Bunning, who as House Social Security subcommittee chair had entertained a succession of witnesses in favor of privatization, failed to attack Bunning on Social Security—and lost.

Once again the Republicans failed to win a filibuster-proof sixty seats in the Senate, severely limiting their ability to challenge the president. And the party's favorite issue, taxes, hadn't inspired voters to support them. National exit polls showed that only 11% of the electorate considered taxes their biggest concern, noted Grover Norquist of Americans for Tax Reform.[1] Given that the Democrats had portrayed them as wanting to sacrifice Social Security for tax cuts, Republicans appeared to have greatly misdiagnosed the voters' mood.

The first consequence of their setback was the fall of Gingrich. Having twice overreached pursuing the Contract with America agenda, once in 1995 and again with the 1999 budget, and no longer commanding the loyalty or even the liking of many influential House members, much of the blame for the election failure went to him. The following Friday, after learning that some thirty House Republicans wouldn't vote for him, and that Robert Livingston of Louisiana had said he would run for speaker as well, Gingrich announced he would leave his post and resign from Congress entirely. At the end of the year, he would announce that his new fundraising group, the Friends of Newt Gingrich Political Action Committee, would be focused on passing legislation to free up Social Security funds and allow individuals to invest their contributions in the market.

Livingston secured support for his speakership, then announced that tax cuts wouldn't be the new Republican House's first legislative project, as Gingrich had stated. Instead, it would be to save Social Security.

As the House Judiciary hearings on the Starr commission's report ground on through November, then, both parties seemed to be coalescing around the position the beleaguered president had taken in January: save Social Security first. Clinton Chief of Staff John Podesta, who had taken over from Bowles just before the election, met with congressional Democratic leaders the week of November 16 to explore the possibility of cobbling together a unified party position. "We are going to mount a fairly vigorous effort to try to get some consensus and move forward on this issue," said Gephardt's office.[2]

The polls suggested that a time had come when the Democrats could introduce a Social Security plan of their own without too much risk. A nationwide poll conducted by International Communications Research for the Institute for America's Future shortly after the election found that 44% of voters trusted the Democrats to "save Social Security without unfairly cutting benefits or raising the retirement age" versus 27% who preferred the Republicans. Even among eighteen- to thirty-four-year-olds, widely considered to be the most enthusiastic about private accounts, 50.9% trusted the Democrats most and only 13.3% the Republicans.[3]

At the White House, aides like Sperling realized there were other factors involved; the president's party was becoming polarized on the issue. "Middle ground for Democrats has not emerged," an analysis for an economic advisors' meeting the day after the election concluded. "Democrats are either for trust fund investments in equity which would leave the government with a significant share of the stock market or relatively harsh Individual Accounts with significant cuts in the traditional program (e.g., Kerrey, Moynihan, Breaux, Stenholm). We must help bring Democrats to middle ground."[4]

Clinton was eager to appear magnanimous and willing to work with Republicans, but he was also reluctant to make life too easy for them. Besides, impeachment was robbing the president and his staff of their ability to focus on larger matters. On the day the House floor debate on impeachment began, Podesta called a White House senior staff meeting at which he asked Sperling for a progress report on "our bipartisan Social Security process. The room erupted in laughter," presidential speechwriter Michael Waldman later recalled.[5]

Less than a week before the White House Conference on Social Security was to begin, another reason for caution cropped up. On December 3, the New Century Alliance held its debut event, unveiling its Statement of Principles for Social Security's Future at a Washington press conference that included over 170 members of groups that had signed on to the alliance. The event was the culmination of the CAF's six-month recruitment drive. AFL-CIO President John Sweeney announced the largest member mobilization around a single political issue in the federation's history. The presence of high-profile figures such as Jesse Jackson, then counseling the president about his crisis over the Starr investigation, ensured heavy media coverage.[6] Jackson's appearance also lent a sharper edge to the alliance's rhetoric than Hickey and his aides had generally indulged in thus far.

In his speech, Jackson said privatization is "a bogus solution to an inflated crisis," concocted by a group of "hucksters" out to dismantle Social Security for their own profit. "We don't ask arsonists to help fight fires. We don't ask the fox to help design the chicken coop." Jackson also ridiculed Republican leaders' "family values" rhetoric, given their support of Social Security privatization, singling out former Education Secretary William Bennett and former Christian Coalition leader Ralph Reed.[7]

The one individual the alliance members most wanted to reach, of course, was in the White House, planning how to counter the House Republican leaders' drive to impeach him. Clinton had never shown much interest in the

CAF's efforts to revive the progressive wing of the Democratic Party. Neither he nor Gore ever spoke at any event sponsored by the CAF or any of the co-alitions associated with it and they never invited CAF officials to the White House during the period they were considering a deal on Social Security.

But the administration had been intrigued by CAF-connected polling about the program, and the results were beginning to influence the thinking of the president's aides: especially the findings about young people, who they knew the Republicans would try to appeal to in the 2000 election. Neither could Clinton and Gore ignore the AFL-CIO and its 13 million members and their families. Leaving the New Century Alliance press conference early to meet with Clinton again, Jackson took a copy of the Statement of Principles to give to his friend.[8]

* * *

For the better part of the year, however, the administration had been pursuing a very different course, by way of the secret talks between White House aides and Ken Kies, the negotiator appointed by Gingrich and Archer to craft a bipartisan plan to restructure Social Security. By early December, the two sides had come very close to an agreement. Later dubbed by Kies the Social Security Guarantee Plan, the proposal called for setting up mandatory private savings accounts for every American worker. The federal government would fund these accounts with annual contributions equal to 2% of the OASI wage base. Workers' payroll tax contributions would continue to go into Social Security as before; there would be no "carve-outs" to fund the private accounts. When the worker was ready to retire, the SSA would calculate a monthly stream of payments based on the balance in her private account. If the amount was less than her expected OASI benefit, Social Security would make up the difference. If the amount exceeded her OASI entitlement, she could keep the extra for herself.

Kies says the proposal reflected a fundamental point of agreement between Clinton, Gingrich, and Archer that the only way to "save" Social Security for the long run without resorting to the politically difficult "four uglies"—raising payroll taxes, benefit cuts, means testing, or raising the retirement age—would be to increase the yield on the program's assets. Instead of paying for it entirely through payroll taxes and interest on the trust fund assets, the federal government would be transferring the funding of much of Social Security to general revenues, in the form of contributions to the private accounts. According to one actuarial estimate, Kies says the Guarantee Plan would have saved the government $22 trillion in real dollars over 75 years—sufficient for lawmakers to consider lowering payroll taxes.

Gingrich, for one, was enchanted. The speaker talked up the secret deal with some of his Republican colleagues, and even had laminated cards printed up to help sell it to them. Under the deal the speaker was working on, the cards said, the following were all true: everyone would get their promised Social Security benefits; nobody would have their taxes raised; and everyone would have the opportunity to earn some upside on their personal accounts. The prospect seemed almost too good to be true.

Which, indeed, it may have been. Despite the absence of carve-outs, a study released the following year by the Center on Budget and Policy Priorities, after the plan became public, found that it suffered from many of the same deficiencies as outright privatization. First, there were transition costs—the massive borrowing needed to fund the private accounts. This would cost the Treasury some $300 billion to $600 billion a year from 2016 to 2042. That would put a major strain on the federal budget, causing deficits already projected to reappear during that period to balloon.

Coincidentally, the 2% of the OASI wage base that would fund the accounts was just a shade less than Social Security's projected seventy-five-year shortfall of 2.07%. If solvency was the concern, why not simply transfer the sums to the trust funds instead? The accounts might not be the windfall their proponents expected, either. Investment providers would be able to charge their administrative and marketing costs against the assets, pocketing some $34 billion a year by 2030 and more thereafter, the Social Security actuaries estimated. Only affluent households would likely enjoy much upside from the accounts, according to the CBPP, since only they would accumulate enough assets to exceed their projected income from Social Security. That in turn would undermine better-off Americans' support for Social Security, since their entire contributions to the program would, effectively, be used to fund other people's benefits.

Yet Kies recalls no pushback from White House negotiators in "detailed" talks about the Guarantee Plan in fall 1998. Mostly, they focused on the details. The administration wanted to add a Social Security benefit enhancement for lower-wage workers to the package, while Gingrich and the Republicans wanted retirees to be able to pass on any unused portion of their private account assets to their heirs. Both sides believed they had a window of opportunity, says Kies, and felt they had a workable formula to seize it.

When the White House conference opened on December 8, however, the atmosphere was dramatically different from what it had been when the event was being planned in February. The conference convened just as Clinton's lawyers were appearing on Capitol Hill to present his defense in the impeachment hearings.

"I'm sitting there at the table with all these lawmakers and thinking, Salvador Dalí would have liked this," remembers the Urban Institute's Robert Reischauer, who along with Martin Feldstein served as a technical consultant at seminars with sixty members of Congress and administration officials on the second day at Blair House. "This was so surreal you wouldn't believe it, because the first thing these Republicans were going to do after Christmas was to raise the impeachment issue."

Other factors contributed to the air of unreality. Members of women's groups, which were distinctly underrepresented in the "conversation," stood in the entrance, handing out cards decorated with hearts reading, "Keep the Heart in Social Security."[9] Yet most attendees were impressed by the harmony and profuse expressions of willingness to cooperate on both sides. Reischauer, for one, believed this was entirely genuine—and, knowing politicians' ability to compartmentalize their concerns, strangely understandable.[10]

Republican leaders at the summit toned down their demands that the president show his hand as Clinton listened to a rundown of the proposals that had appeared in Congress earlier in the year. Looking for signs that the president was open to working with them, they were pleased to hear him say on the first day that he wanted "to open honest debate and to build consensus, not to shoot down ideas."

Sperling helpfully said White House officials would work with congressional staffers to put briefing books together for all members of Congress, describing the options and noting the pros and cons of each—and meetings actually began less than a week later between Sperling, NEC legislative affairs director Lawrence Stein, and Senate Finance and House Ways and Means staffers. Clinton and his people made every effort to appear open and unbiased about Social Security. Pointedly, however, aides said the president made no statement about the core issue: whether private accounts or a pool of trust fund assets should be the chosen vehicles for investment.

On the second day, walking together from Blair House to the White House, Clinton observed to Archer that "we would have to draw on the earning capacity of the private sector if we're ever going to make this work." Archer took this as a reference to the proposal he was then formulating, with which Clinton was familiar and which included private accounts funded by tax credits.[11]

To the press afterward, Republican leaders noticeably dropped the assaults that some had earlier made on Clinton's ability to negotiate in good faith. "It was a productive discussion that creates some momentum for us to move ahead," Kolbe said. "There was no heel-digging, and a desire to discuss the subject openly and positively," Gregg noted. In what must have pleased the White House, he answered a reporter that a House vote to impeach the president, followed by a trial, would reduce "significantly" the chances of a Social Security deal.[12]

Archer, who remained the White House's chief interlocutor amongst congressional Republicans, decided to take the initiative. "It was amazing when we first sat down and put our cards on the table how close together we were on how to fix Social Security," Ken Kies later recalled of the meeting with Sperling's team. "I don't have any doubt there was a potential deal there." To show that negotiation was possible, Archer produced a set of four basic principles for restructuring Social Security, which he had been working on since his first, post-election meeting with Clinton and which resembled the five principles the president had been reiterating for most of the year:

- No increase in taxes;

- Preserving the social safety net for elderly and disabled persons;

- Treating current and future retirees fairly, especially women; and

- Creating "new options" to help younger workers realize a higher return on Social Security.

Clearly meant to signal to Clinton that a private accounts-based plan could
be structured in a way that would give him political cover, Archer's list embodied many Republican lawmakers' calculation that the beleaguered president
would once again "triangulate" and make a deal with them. Democratic leaders were quick to warn that they wouldn't go that far. Gephardt, the avowed
opponent of any change that smacked of privatization, had also attended the
White House conference and said he could support private accounts only if
they didn't take money away from the established system, telling the *New York
Times* he would have "grave concerns" if funds for the accounts came out of
payroll taxes.

* * *

If Gephardt sounded less cooperative, it was in part because the November election results had encouraged Democrats to believe they had more to
gain—perhaps even recapturing Congress in 2000—by standing fast on core
issues such as Social Security. Shortly before the White House conference, Jesse
Jackson threatened to speak out as quickly against a Democrat who supported
privatization as he would against a Republican, the *New York Times* reported.
The net result was to marginalize legislators such as Kerrey and Moynihan, who
had hoped to move their party in the opposite direction.

Pro-privatization forces had already taken a page from their opponents' own
playbook, and less than two weeks after the New Century Alliance announced
its existence, held their own press conference to declare a new Campaign to
Save and Strengthen Social Security. The group's membership consisted mainly
of the organizations that had formed the Alliance for Worker Retirement Security, a pro-privatization advocacy group founded by the National Association
of Manufacturers a couple of months prior, along with Economic Security
2000, Third Millennium, and a few of the usual free-market Republican advocacy groups such as Norquist's Americans for Tax Reform and the National
Taxpayers Union. Its three guiding principles included "permitting workers to
invest a portion of their FICA contributions into individually controlled and
owned Personal Retirement Accounts."

Other prominent supporters of privatization did their part to heat up the
debate. The Democratic Leadership Council (DLC) naturally felt threatened

by the New Century Alliance's debut and rallied its own forces at a conference later in December. "I am a Democrat because I believe in the dignity, not the density, of every American," said Bob Kerrey, defending private accounts against the argument that workers couldn't be expected to serve as money managers for their payroll tax dollars.[13]

Proponents of private accounts had already launched some of their efforts to raise popular support for their cause before the election, using some of the same language as Clinton himself. In September, Economic Security 2000 and Third Millennium had announced "The Billion Byte March," co-chaired by the 100% No Load Mutual Fund Council and billed as "the first e-mail 'March on Washington' using Cyberspace."[14]

By visiting a special website, WWW.MARCH.ORG, you could send a message to your member of Congress, senator, or the president to "Save Social Security and Create Individually Owned Savings Accounts Invested in the Private Sector." The "march" was scheduled for December, with a goal of getting "millions" of Americans to contact their elected officials before the next Congress took its seats.

Then, after being outed by publisher Larry Flynt, on December 18, House Speaker-elect Robert Livingston admitted to having had an extramarital affair. He resigned from Congress, throwing the post-Gingrich Republican leadership into turmoil. Next day, the House, after thirteen-and-a-half hours of debate over two days, approved two articles of impeachment, charging the president with lying under oath to a federal grand jury and obstructing justice. One of those voting to impeach was Gingrich. His last vote as a member of Congress was against the president with whom he had tried to create a roadmap for overhauling Social Security. With a showdown on the presidential scandals finally approaching and the Republicans determined to go all the way with a Senate trial, some White House aides said the task of "reforming" the program had become "all but impossible."[15]

CHAPTER 26

THE UNBRIDGEABLE GULF

In the weeks following Livingston's resignation, most policy discussion in winter-bound Washington slowed down or went behind closed doors as all attention focused on arrangements for the upcoming impeachment trial. The administration confined its public Social Security efforts to a photo-op press conference at which it announced that the SSA had fixed all of its computers ahead of the new year, ensuring the "Y2K bug" wouldn't delay delivery of retirees' benefits checks.

Behind the scenes, however, Clinton was preparing his State of the Union speech, which, aside from underscoring his focus on substantive policy at a time when he was standing trial for "high crimes and misdemeanors," he now intended as a springboard for his own plan to restructure Social Security. By all accounts, Sperling belied his Washington reputation as a slick political player with little academic background in economics, holding long meetings replete with grinding technical discussions, then taking his findings to the president, the vice president, and Rubin for decisions that brought politics more fully into consideration.

Those findings included exhaustive analyses of every known option, including outright privatization. Some sources who saw them later were more than a little surprised how much serious discussion the privatizers' various plans received. But Sperling insists that he merely believed it was his job to analyze everything and explain it to Clinton before the president made a decision. No one on his economic team wanted carve-outs or would recommend them, he maintains.[1]

They did want to find some way to include private accounts in the president's proposal. But now that the president himself was in peril, the Guarantee Plan that Sperling and Kies had been working on behind the scenes for so many months was no longer at the top of the administration's list.

Ever hedging his bets, Clinton, during the months of secret negotiations that led to the Guarantee Plan, had put a group of aides to work under Sperling and Larry Summers, to evaluate other ideas for restructuring Social Security. Bob Ball was reportedly holding frequent meetings with Sperling and others at the White House, in which he argued against adopting any proposal that would ultimately transform Social Security into a politically vulnerable welfare program.[2] Instead, he wanted the administration to consider his idea to invest some portion of the trust funds directly in the stock market.[3]

Podesta, meanwhile, was holding frequent meetings with Democratic congressional leaders including Gephardt, Daschle, and other strong supporters of traditional Social Security like Rep. Robert Matsui of California, focusing on how the administration would address the idea of individual accounts. Slowly it became clear that the balance of power was shifting. While Clinton and Sperling had gone out of their way the year before to get the input of Cato and other privatization advocates, now they were meeting more often with advocates for the opposite side, such as Ball, as well as administration figures who emphatically rejected privatization, such as Social Security Commissioner Ken Apfel.[4]

Hoping more than anything to stake out his plan as a sensible, middle-of-the-road proposal in the face of Republican extremism, Clinton decided to include far more detail in his State of the Union speech than his aides at first thought wise.

By mid-January, it was understood in Washington that the "middle-ground" proposal Clinton was preparing would feature voluntary, supplemental accounts that the government would help fund with matching contributions or tax incentives. This was quite different from the Guarantee Plan, but Kies says he received no heads-up from his erstwhile White House negotiating partners about the change of direction.

The idea nevertheless allowed the president to come out in favor of something rather than simply reject carve-outs.[5] It was also a genuine bid to spur a compromise, Sperling says. The president would keep his Democrats happy by leaving the basic Social Security funding mechanism untouched. Yet

Republicans could declare victory too, since they would have individual accounts—and the expectation that if workers liked their new nest eggs well enough, in the future they might prefer them and support true privatization.[6]

Clinton had reason to think that he was skating on thinner ice with Democrats than with Republicans. On January 12, forty Democratic and one Independent House member signed a letter to the president saying that Social Security privatization poses "unacceptable risks" and urging him to "reject any Social Security individual account privatization plan offered in the coming year." That same week, Rep. Dennis Kucinich of Ohio called a conference for the 21st on the privatization threat, for congressional staff and the community, with twenty-five other representatives signed on as co-sponsors.

On the Republican side, Dennis Hastert of Illinois, who was elected speaker after Livingston withdrew, put it about that he was holding the H.R.1 designation—the first bill of the new Congress—as an enticement for the White House to submit a Social Security bill. And Senate Finance Committee chair William V. Roth, Jr., of Delaware, creator of the Roth IRA, was talking up a similar new savings vehicle, organized outside the Social Security system but to be funded over five years by drawing down half the federal budget surplus. "I'm hopeful that we're seeing the beginning of a consensus that could be very helpful," Roth told the *New York Times*.

Clinton delivered his address on the evening of January 19. That same day, his legal team began its arguments in his defense before the Senate—a presentation that would take three days. With the Lewinsky scandal and the possibility of being forced from office hanging over him, the president needed the public to perceive him as being firmly in control, his attention focused on substantive issues. The best way to do this was to deliver a speech laced with bold initiatives, challenging the Republicans to demonstrate a similar focus.

"We must help all Americans, from their first day on the job, to save, to invest, to create wealth," Clinton told the assembled lawmakers, federal government officials, and television cameras—all wondering how this consummate performer would fare under the greatest pressure of his career.

Clinton's plan was exactly what both parties had come to expect over the past month. He proposed turning over about 62% of the anticipated federal budget surplus, or some $2.7 trillion, to the Social Security trust funds. Between 75% and 80% of that money would continue to be used in the traditional way, loaned to the federal government for general-revenue purposes in the form of Treasury bonds. But in the new, deficit-less era, the Treasury would use that money only to pay down the federal debt. Theoretically, that would keep interest rates low, making benefits easier to fund once the baby boomer wave of retirements began.

The rest of the surplus, about $650 billion, would be invested in the stock market, where Clinton estimated it would earn an average annual return of 6.75%, versus 3% for the Treasury bonds. White House officials explained in the days following Clinton's speech that a private firm would manage the portfolio, investing it in a broad index of stocks. The extra money from the surplus, along with the higher returns on the stock portfolio, would extend Social Security's fiscal solvency under the trustees' intermediate assumptions until 2055 from the current projection of 2032: a medium-term fix, just as Bob Ball had recommended. Accordingly, the administration called upon Congress to join in "a bipartisan effort to make the hard-headed but sensible and achievable choices needed to save Social Security until at least 2075."

At the same time, the president proposed a voluntary, subsidized savings program, separate from Social Security, called Universal Savings Accounts (USAs), which would receive some $500 billion in matching government funds over the next fifteen years. The largest grants would go to the lowest-income workers and the smallest grants—or none at all—to the highest. One possible framework that White House aides cited would be for the government to give a base-line $100 to each worker earning up to $45,000 a year, then match 50% of his or her own contributions up to a maximum $600.

There was more on the social insurance front. After a succession of measures boosting the limits, Clinton promised to back Republican efforts to entirely abolish the "outdated and confusing earnings test," which limited Social Security recipients' outside earnings to about $15,500 a year. He declared himself committed to improving the status of widows under Social Security by raising the percentage of benefits they received after a spouse's death to 75% from a range of 50% to 66%. In another move designed to help women who spent years outside the workforce, Clinton proposed a $250-per-child tax credit for parents who stayed home to raise infants. Similarly, he offered $1,000 in tax credits to families with long-term care needs, another initiative that would help people who might otherwise not be able to keep working and accumulate Social Security benefits.

Republicans would quickly complain that this constituted less than the full opening proposal they sought from the president. What Clinton described "looked like it was put together with a stapler," Cato's Tanner complained. "For something they'd been working on for a year, it made no sense."[7] Leaving a big hole in the long-range plan and calling on Congress to fill it was asking too much of a deeply divided group of lawmakers. But the central item of the Clinton plan reflected a fiscally conservative approach that Republican leaders would soon find hard to resist, much as it discomfited them.

"The best way to keep Social Security a rock-solid guarantee is not to make drastic cuts in benefits; not to raise payroll taxes; and not to drain resources from Social Security in the name of saving it," the president said in his speech. Instead, the answer was to continue putting the federal government's fiscal house in order, helping to keep interest rates low and thus making capital investment easier for American business. The resulting economic growth would raise tax revenues and thus help to buoy Social Security when the boomers started to pull down big benefit checks.*

* The basic idea was actually at least ten years old. It was the principal recommendation of "Can America Afford to Grow Old? Paying for Social Security,"

One way to look at Clinton's proposal was that he had mixed Rubinomics into the concept his aides had worked on with Gingrich, Archer, and Kies: retaining the separate private accounts, but using the federal surplus mostly to make Social Security itself more secure, with only a fraction going to fund the accounts. It was, in other words, a classic Clinton triangulation.

Tanner questioned the idea that a forced march to pay down the federal debt would have much effect on interest rates and complained that shifting money into the trust funds was a gimmick—an attempt to "make the problem go away with creative bookkeeping." Unless Rubin was right about interest rates, the Clinton plan wouldn't actually increase the government's ability to meet its Social Security obligations over the next couple of decades.

The Rubinomics debate would continue for the next two years as the surplus kept piling up. Meanwhile, however, the long, policy-heavy State of the Union speech gave Clinton a tremendous personal boost. Polls released the next day by the three major broadcast TV networks showed his job approval ratings ranging from 66% to 76%, and three to five points higher after the speech. Three-fourths of people who watched the speech, polled in a CNN/USA Today/Gallup survey, said they thought the president's proposals would save Social Security. Democrats especially took heart from an ABC poll that produced a two-to-one margin agreeing with the statement that saving Social Security was more important than tax cuts—this despite a proposal for a 10% across-the-board income tax cut that Republican leaders unfurled in their response to the State of the Union message.

Republican lawmakers concentrated most of their public criticism on the proposal to invest trust fund assets in the stock market. "No. No. A thousand times, no," Archer declared in a statement issued the morning of the speech, as details leaked around Capitol Hill. "If you thought a government takeover of health care was bad, just wait until the government becomes an owner of America's private-sector companies."[8]

Over in the president's camp, Rubin argued that an independent board appointed by the Social Security trustees could eliminate the threat of political interference with the trust fund investments. "The Federal Reserve Bank is independent, and it has maintained its independence over many decades, much to the benefit of this country," he told NBC's *Today Show*. "I think what we need to do is provide a similar independence for this function."* He also

---

a 1989 Brookings Institution study by economists Henry Aaron, Barry Bosworth, and Gary Burtless. The study also recommended investment of some trust fund assets—but not in stocks.

* "GOP Willing to Save Most of Surplus," *The Buffalo News*, January 21, 1999. Other Democratic observers pointed out that the Fed's own pension plan, which invests directly in the stock market, had never been under pressure to adopt a socially responsive investment stance and—more to the point—had never been accused of slanting its asset allocation in a politically motivated way.

emphasized that since only a fraction of the trust funds would be invested, the new strategy wouldn't put the system in danger during down markets.

Rubin's primary input in the later stages of crafting the president's Social Security message had been to minimize the amount of trust fund assets that would be invested in the stock market, so as to limit what he knew would be Republican condemnation of the idea. One yardstick he reportedly made much of was the percentage—10%—of the market owned by state and local pension funds. Trust fund purchases should amount to less than half that, Rubin counseled. Thus, the roughly $650 billion figure Clinton settled on would represent only about 4% of the market.

The congressional Democratic leadership was happy that the Clinton plan placed the White House firmly in the anti-privatization camp, but some lawmakers had concerns about any form of government subsidy for the stock market. In a perhaps prophetic assessment, Kucinich, described scoffingly as "spokesman for a couple dozen liberal Democrats," told *Washington Post* columnist David Broder that he objected to the USA accounts even though they wouldn't be funded out of payroll taxes, because in effect they would use workers' savings to help prop up what might be a dangerously overvalued stock market.

"He's headed in the right direction," Kucinich said of Clinton, "but I hate to see him take a detour down Wall Street."[9] At a gathering of progressive Democrats the week before Clinton's speech, when some of the details were already known, he expressed deeper concerns: that by agreeing to invest some of the trust fund assets, the president "has created an opening and a vehicle for privatizers to radically dismantle Social Security."[10] Economists Paul Davidson and James Galbraith warned that the president's debt paydown scheme would rob public services vital to keeping the economy growing: public schools, universities, environmental protection, transportation, housing, health care, libraries, parks, and other amenities.[11]

These larger worries aside, the White House projections had overestimated the returns on investment of trust fund assets, economists Edith Rasell and Jeff Faux noted in a paper for the Economic Policy Institute—ironically, in much the same way that pro-privatization lawmakers had been overstating the benefits of individual accounts. Clinton was projecting an overall 6.75% stock market return over the next seventy-five years, just slightly less than the return over the previous three-quarters of a century. Yet the Social Security trustees were predicting slower economic growth in the future, pegging stock market returns at only about 3.75% for the upcoming period.

More seriously, Rasell and Faux warned that with a burgeoning stock portfolio within the Social Security system, "a rising stock market will tend to become a more important objective of economic policy than keeping the unemployment rate low, for example." In an era when Wall Street tended to welcome falling employment as good news, it was doubtful the interests of stock market investors and the average citizen would match up very closely.

The progressive critics shared a sense that, while he hadn't truly touched the third rail, Clinton had nevertheless shown willingness—perhaps too much— to deal with the Republicans on their own rhetorical turf when it came to Social Security. They weren't wrong about this. According to Sperling, the White House didn't see the president's Social Security plan as simply a way to block GOP tax initiatives but as a genuine attempt to find middle ground with its opponents. "The Democrats said this was brilliant, because it blocks the Republicans," he recalls. "What they didn't understand was how sincere we were about working together."[12]

But the White House didn't envision the president moving any further in the direction of carving private accounts out of Social Security, which quickly turned out to be the Republicans' unequivocal demand. Some Republican leaders still hoped for a compromise, however, and took pains not to be perceived as unduly obsessed with prosecuting the president. They chose to see the speech, especially the USA accounts proposal, as a small move in their direction.

"There is a bipartisan commitment in Congress that real Social Security reform must create more IRAs, not IOUs," said Armey, a strong supporter of private accounts who had voted for impeachment. "The president seems ready to join us on that principle." As the *Wall Street Journal* pointed out, "by endorsing the concept of individual accounts and stock-market investments, Mr. Clinton has essentially begun negotiations with Republicans and Democrats who favor such ideas."

The deeper problem with Clinton's Social Security plans for Republicans was the sheer size of the revenues he proposed to wall off. Over fifteen years—an eternity in Washington time—the president's Social Security and Medicare packages would leave only about $650 billion of the projected surplus for other, discretionary uses—such as tax cuts. The Republicans countered Clinton's speech by proposing a 10% across-the-board income tax cut that would cost some $776 billion over ten years. But they placed themselves at a disadvantage right away.

Nearly as soon as the president put his speech back in his pocket and exited the House chamber, they agreed to his basic proposal that 62% of the surplus be walled off until the two parties could resolve the question of Social Security's future. This meant that without explicitly agreeing to it, they had accepted—at least for the time being—the basic component of Rubinomics: using the surplus to pay down the federal debt. The White House had succeeded in making this synonymous with "saving" Social Security first.

With the ground rules set this way, a major tax cut would be very hard to achieve. So would an individual accounts program based on payroll tax carve-outs, since at least on paper these would deprive the trust funds of revenues needed for debt pay-down. Again and again in the next few months, the Republicans' efforts to pass a significant tax cut would butt up against intractable opposition from the White House and congressional Democrats.

Nevertheless, both parties were now officially committed to finding a way to restructure Social Security. Implicitly, both accepted the proposition that the system was in trouble and needed saving soon if the price tag was not to rise steeply in coming years. A few Democratic lawmakers implicitly acknowledged that Congress was trying to solve a nonexistent problem, but that politically, Clinton, Rubin, and the privatizers had left them no choice. While the Clinton plan was acceptable to him, Jerry Nadler told the *Village Voice* that he believed "there is probably no problem" with Social Security. But since the right had convinced the public otherwise, "What you have to do is to appear to be solving this problem which isn't really a major problem."

* * *

The most pressing matter for progressives was to make sure the president moved no further in the Republicans' direction. In the weeks before the State of the Union address, the AFL-CIO and the New Century Alliance developed an action plan calling for community summits in more than fifty cities between February 11 and 22. These would feature labor leaders and other organizations including the NAACP, women's and religious groups. Events would include home-office meetings with members of Congress and a "radio talk show push" in seventy-five communities, in which local "citizen leaders" would angle for invitations to appear on the popular programs. April would be "Save Social Security" Month, centering on public rallies and press conferences during the spring congressional recess.[13]

The AFL-CIO aimed to keep the possibility of a Clintonian triangulation from solidifying. By early February, state-level versions of the New Century Alliance had formed in California and Texas while a labor-organized coalition had come together in New Hampshire to criticize Judd Gregg for his comments in the *Concord Monitor* that Clinton's Social Security proposal was an "accounting trick" that "has about as much credibility as a late night drinking party." At a meeting for organizers in Miami Beach, the AFL-CIO gave out hundreds of "Save Social Security" postcards to send to Congress, urging lawmakers not to privatize the system. And it bankrolled the CAF with $500,000 to coordinate lobbying by groups opposing privatization.

The federation took a far tougher line with Wall Street, the mutual fund industry, and some pension funds within its own unions. Union leafleting at workplaces to rally opposition to Social Security changes was being answered by hand-outs and bulletin-board postings by executives belonging to the National Association of Manufacturers, which was investing more than $500,000 in radio and television ads to convert its member-companies' workers: exceeding the amount the NAM spent on lobbying on Capitol Hill itself.[14] But the bulk of the money carrying the privatization movement forward was coming from the financial services industry.

In January, knowing they could be entering a very expensive war, top officials at the AFL-CIO, the American Federation of State, County and Municipal Employees (AFSCME), and other unions conducted a letter-writing campaign to nine leading Wall Street firms, asking them to detail their position on Social Security restructuring. The firms included FMR Corp. (Fidelity Investments' parent), J.P. Morgan & Co., State Street Global Advisors, Merrill Lynch, Morgan Stanley Dean Witter, American Express Co., Chase Manhattan Corp., Citigroup, and Bankers Trust New York Corp. As an AFSCME official described it, the letter said, "It disturbs us that your firm or its officials may be helping to underwrite pro-privatization organizations and campaigns and we would like to know directly from you if this is the case so that we can correctly inform our local leaders and membership."[15]

Union officials denied they intended any threat, but the AFL-CIO's corporate affairs director pointedly noted that all of these firms did big business with union pension funds, which collectively represented $371 billion of assets. State Street Global, for one, handled $4.5 billion for union funds.[16]

State Street had stuck its neck out as perhaps the most vocal proponent of Social Security privatization in the financial services sector, but by early 1999 it seemed to be shrinking back. According to a widely read newsletter, a Washington lobbyist who opposed carve-outs said that State Street CEO Marsh Carter told him at the December White House conference, "If you want State Street's position on Social Security, talk to me. Bill Shipman is not representing State Street's current position." Shipman, still connected with the Cato Project on Social Security Privatization, denied this, and a State Street spokesperson indicated that the bank's position hadn't changed.[17]

Carter made the break more complete a few days later. In an interview with the *Boston Herald*, he praised Clinton's Social Security proposals, including the trust-fund investments and add-on individual accounts. Asked if he had the same concerns as Republican lawmakers that this would lead to corruption and politicized investment, Carter said, "I don't have the same concerns others have."[18] A few days later, Carter met with Sperling for a friendly discussion of the idea of investing a portion of the trust funds directly in the stock market.[19]

Critics of the Clinton proposals got their biggest boost, meanwhile, from Alan Greenspan. Already the previous July, the Fed chair had warned that direct government investment in the stock market would pose "very far-reaching dangers for the free American economy and the free American society." Appearing at a Senate Budget Committee hearing a week after the State of the Union speech, he said that "even with Herculean efforts, I doubt it would be feasible to insulate, over the long run, the trust funds from political pressures." Pressed by committee chair Domenici, he added that unless the government could protect the surpluses—that is, pay down the debt—curbing elected officials' urge to spend on old or new projects or beef up benefits, he would prefer to see a tax cut.

Such was Greenspan's political heft that "he in effect killed [the president's] proposal absolutely cold dead in the marketplace," Archer, who was pleased, later recalled.[20] The White House felt the impact right away. "I'm running and briefing everyone who could walk and chew gum" about the president's plan, Sperling recalls, "but when Greenspan criticized investing in the stock market, everyone who'd supported [Clinton] jumped off the bandwagon."[21]

Republicans picked up on another theme, which the press quickly labeled "double counting." In a flurry of press releases and op-eds, Republican leaders and conservative economists accused the president of using an accounting trick to balance Social Security's books. *Newsweek* columnist Allan Sloan fired the first volley less than a week after the speech, noting that the $2.8 trillion Clinton proposed to inject into the Social Security trust funds consisted of roughly $500 billion of general revenues—"cold, hard cash"—and the trust funds' own projected surplus of $2.3 trillion. In effect, Sloan wrote, Clinton was proposing to spend "$6.8 trillion of a $4.5 trillion surplus."

Feldstein slammed Clinton's plan as "the biggest and most creative budget sham I've ever seen."[22] Dominici observed that Clinton "appears to double count the Social Security surpluses," extending the trust funds' fiscal solvency "without doing anything," while Gregg more forthrightly accused the president of playing an "accounting trick."[23]

The attacks somewhat puzzled White House advisors like Sperling, who says that preserving budget discipline "became my personal mission" during the secret White House policy discussions that culminated in the president's speech.[24] Republican proposals to use the surplus to create private accounts would also be a form of double counting.[25] What Sloan called the president's "high-stakes new math" was actually the same procedure that every administration, Democrat and Republican, had used to balance the budget since the Vietnam War—borrowing from the Social Security trust funds to pay for the day-to-day operations of government, then paying off the loans in order to cover benefits.

Feldstein, in fact, had chaired the Council of Economic Advisors when the Reagan administration used the trust fund surplus to temper the budgetary effects of sweeping tax cuts that expanded the federal debt to a peacetime high of 5% of GDP. The only difference was that Clinton proposed to use the funds not to cut taxes but to pay down the federal debt.

Several of the Social Security proposals Republicans had introduced the previous year also depended on using the surplus, including the portion coming from payroll taxes, to create individual accounts. Now, Republican congressional leaders were getting ready to propose their own economic package, including another large tax cut. By accusing the president of playing accounting tricks, they were effectively conditioning the public to believe that the only legitimate use of the surplus was to remove it from the table by cutting taxes, creating individual investment accounts, or a combination of the two.

* * *

The next step was for Clinton to incorporate his proposals into his fiscal 2000 budget. From projected revenues of $1.88 trillion, the president proposed spending $1.767 trillion, leaving a surplus of $117 billion. The USA accounts alone would absorb $33 billion a year, eating up 11% of the projected fifteen-year surplus, deputy Treasury secretary Larry Summers estimated. Beyond this, the budget contained only a few, carefully targeted tax cuts totaling $32.6 billion over five years, including for inner-city investment, child care and higher education expenses, increased fuel efficiency, and retirement saving through 401(k)s.

Clinton hoped this package would help solidify his credentials as a prudent tax cutter and friend of middle-class savers. Republicans instead, as expected, called for an across-the-board income tax cut. Kasich quickly suggested this could be as high as 10%–20%, a 10% cut returning $511 to a single taxpayer earning $30,000 a year and $600 to a couple earning $40,000 combined.

Two weeks later, in an interview with the *New York Times*, Rep. E. Clay Shaw, Jr., who chaired the Ways and Means Committee's Social Security Subcommittee, began outlining the other half of the Republicans' response to Clinton—their Social Security proposal. As expected, it would use the surplus to fund individual accounts. It would also set a guaranteed minimum benefit for all retirees, even if their accounts didn't perform up to a certain level. And the private accounts would be voluntary, so that workers who didn't want to risk their money in the stock market could instead stay in the current system. Shaw offered only this broad outline, leaving for later such details as whether workers who stayed in the current program would see a reduction in their benefits, who would administer and manage the individual accounts and under what guidelines.

Both sides nevertheless remained eager to demonstrate their willingness to work together. On February 24, as Washington's obsession with the presidential scandals began to subside, Archer announced that Ways and Means would consider a joint budget resolution expressing bipartisan support for shoring up Social Security, one point of agreement being that 62% of the projected budget surplus should be set aside for the purpose. Two days later, Clinton met with Lott, Hastert, and Armey for an hour in the Oval Office. Emerging, they announced that they were prepared to work together, and the first order of business was Social Security. Hastert, who had lately told Fox News that the president's idea of investing part of the trust fund surplus in stocks was a "nonstarter," now declared that the Republicans had agreed in principle to "put a lock" on 62% of the federal budget surplus starting that year.[26]

The next day, Clinton began a brief fundraising and vacation swing through the western states, declaring, "There now seems to be broad agreement among leaders and rank-and-file members in both parties of Congress to set aside the lion's share of the surplus to save Social Security." Closely attached to the president as he visited Tucson was Kolbe, who had voted for the articles of impeachment in the fall but who now praised Clinton's leadership on Social Security. Asked if he still thought Clinton unfit for office, Kolbe responded, "The impeachment's over. Let's talk about Social Security here."[27]

In their eagerness to emphasize common ground, some Republican leaders began to reverse the rhetoric they had used just weeks earlier to describe Clinton's proposals. Archer now called the president's plan to invest trust fund assets in the stock market "a breakthrough" and stated that, while he would prefer to see the money placed in individual accounts, he didn't "intend to let this important difference stop us from making progress."[28] To reinforce their support for preserving the surplus, House and Senate Republican leaders appeared at a news conference where they symbolically slammed shut a giant steel safe.

Already there was a fly in the ointment, however. In his Oval Office meeting with Republican leaders, Clinton had pressed them to boost their commitment to shoring up the nation's two biggest benefit programs by devoting another 15% of the deficit to funding Medicare. Skeptical Republicans believed this was merely a ploy to make even less of the surplus available for tax cuts—especially after Gephardt told reporters that congressional Democrats wouldn't agree to any long-range restructuring of Social Security unless Medicare received its 15% of the surplus. The glimmerings of an impasse were coming into view as Clinton admitted, "We don't yet have that kind of agreement."

But the element of Clinton's Social Security plan that looked shakiest as winter wore on was investment of the trust fund assets, now coming under attack from left and right. The day after the president's Oval Office meeting with Republicans, the AFL-CIO released a blistering, incisive attack on the proposal, complaining in a letter to Gephardt that it would "introduce unwise market risk" into the system. It also raised an important issue about the practicality of privatization.

The Republican proposals for Social Security introduced the previous year along with Clinton's plan all built off the trustees' economic growth projections. If those numbers weren't a reliable guide to the future—a 1.5% rate of growth would be half the growth rate of the previous seventy-five years, a period that had included the Great Depression, the AFL-CIO noted—then restructuring the system using assumptions drawn from them might not be such a good idea.

Pro-privatization lawmakers and economists never satisfactorily answered this point, which Dean Baker, for one, had been raising for several years. But even if future returns were just as bad as Baker predicted, surely a forty-year return of, say, 3.74% on one's personal account was better than the 2% that baby boomers who stayed in the present OASI program could expect?

The answer was yes: if returns on the stocks themselves were the sole determining factor. But this provoked another sticky debate, about the cost of farming out management of private Social Security accounts to financial services firms. Nothing is free in the free market, including returns on investments. Everyone who manages money—from mutual fund companies that cater to the masses to high-end money managers serving the wealthy—charges for their services. The price tag includes management fees that pay for the expertise of the portfolio managers themselves and administrative fees charged for account maintenance and transaction processing. Baked into these are the costs of marketing and advertising the provider's services. Together, these can be quite high. Ironically, the smallest customers often pay the highest fees per dollar under management, since they have the least leverage to negotiate lower fees.

Standard neoclassical economics dismisses all this. "Fierce competition in sophisticated markets has driven down costs in these businesses. There is no reason why the same should not be true for pensions," *The Economist* declared flatly in June.

Actually, financial services have always been different from any other "sophisticated" market. Financial firms sell an intellectual service—the ability to perform better in the investment markets than other providers—which doesn't boil down to natural or unnatural advantages in production, delivery, or other manufacturing-related costs. For intellectual capital that's perceived to have an edge, the sky's the limit as to the value placed on it. On top of that, the practice of placing, transacting, and reporting a securities trade is an arcane one that affords plenty of ways for providers to hide or disguise costs and pass them on to less savvy customers.

Estimating how high the cost would be of installing a massive system of privatized Social Security accounts was inherently problematic because nothing like it had ever existed before. In the mid-1990s, almost 150 million individual workers were paying into Social Security. Each, presumably, would receive his or her very own private account. The largest 401(k)-like structure in the country at the time, the federal employers' Thrift Savings Plan (TSP), had fewer than 3 million accounts, and all the IRAs in America only amounted to a bit less than 10 million accounts.[29]

It was possible that economies of scale would drive down costs, as the privatizers believed, but the scale of the undertaking also suggested this was a huge risk. The TSP was a closed system whose members all worked for the same employer. Private Social Security accounts would be an open system with a host of "participants," from career corporate employees to self-employed workers to the undocumented, making them infinitely more complex—and expensive—to administer, noted personal finance columnist Jane Bryant Quinn.[30]

"Adding individual accounts to Social Security could be the largest undertaking in the history of the U.S. financial market, and no system to date has the capacity to administer such a system," the Employee Benefit Research Institute concluded in a 1998 report. "The number of workers covered by Social Security ... is at least four times higher than the combined number of all tax-favored employment-based retirement accounts in the United States, which are administered by hundreds of entities."[31]

Olivia Mitchell, hardly an enemy of privatization, found in a 1996 study that the average per-year expense ratio for 401(k) plans with a high concentration in stocks was 1.44%. Another estimate made about the same time found the transaction cost for a mutual fund that turned over 50% of its holdings in a year would be 0.5% of the fund's value.* Adding up the two, Dean Baker noted, produced total administrative expenses of 1.94% a year.[32]

In stark contrast, total administrative expenses for the Social Security program in 1994—not just those incurred by the SSA but also those added in by other government agencies that serviced the program such as the IRS and the Postal Service—represented only 0.8% of the trust fund assets.[33] OASI and DI benefits were set according to a relatively simple formula; they didn't depend on the program's ability to keep track of the fluctuating value of millions of individual investment accounts. The SSA also didn't have to tailor benefits to the individual circumstances of millions of different applicants, as needs-based welfare programs must. Despite the myriad administrative and technical problems the cash-strapped SSA had to face from the mid-1970s onward, it was still able to administer its vast OASI and DI programs at an astonishingly low cost.

As a result, the price tag for running a private account-based Social Security system could be twice as high as the cost of administering the present one. Over a forty-year working career, these additional costs could eat up some 20% of the accumulated value of the worker's account, economists Peter Orszag and Joseph Stiglitz calculated. On top of this, there was the cost to the worker of annuitizing the assets in her private account once she retired: that is, of buying an annuity contract that would supply a flow of payments to her for the rest of her life.

Annuities, too, are expensive, and the cost goes up the longer the purchaser can be expected to live—a phenomenon known as "adverse selection," which private accounts wouldn't get rid of. In the U.K., which had had a decentralized system of private accounts as part of its national old-age provisions for about a decade, the cost of administration plus annuitization consumed some 40% to 45% of the value of the typical worker's account, Stiglitz and Orszag found.[34]

The AFL-CIO letter encouraged some Democratic defenders of Social Security to take a less defensive posture in the months ahead. While they still had to give lip service to the assertion that Social Security was in crisis, the federation's cost analysis tempered their instinct to respond to the Republicans' doomsday scenarios with their own rescue plan. If the crisis wasn't necessarily real, or at least not sufficiently well understood, then the best course might not be to stick their necks out with an alternative to either Clinton's or the numerous Republican proposals.

* * *

Seemingly, however, the stage was now set for the party leadership and the White House to negotiate a restructuring of Social Security. Both sides had

---

*   This figure could be higher or lower depending upon the amount of buying and selling the investor did, or that was done in the investor's name, in a particular year.

produced budget proposals that earmarked most of the ten-year surplus for Social Security, while staying within the limits set by the Balanced Budget Act—although each questioned the other's accounting. Sperling was encouraging the Republican leaders to discuss the matter with him whenever possible. Archer had engaged Ken Kies to draft a Republican proposal, expected to center on a tax break for workers who invested part of their payroll tax contribution in stocks or bonds.

"As counterintuitive as it seems, since no sword is hanging over their heads, the President and Congressional leaders seem committed to try to pass the most sweeping legislation in terms of the number of people affected since the Tax Reform Act of 1986 and possibly since the Great Society era of the 1960s," David E. Rosenbaum of the *New York Times* commented.

It didn't happen, in part because Clinton had maneuvered the Republicans into a cul de sac. They had effectively agreed with him that the surplus wasn't to be touched before Social Security "reform" had been achieved. So any legislation they wanted to pass that included a tax cut, or private Social Security accounts, or both, was by definition unacceptable, and would be spun that way by the White House.

On March 19, a group of local activists with the AFL-CIO, Citizen Action, and other groups bird-dogged a weekend "civility retreat" attended by 200 House members in Hershey, Pennsylvania. When the legislators arrived in Harrisburg to board VIP buses for the Capital of Chocolate, 300 activists greeted them with signs reading, "Be kind Congress, Don't cut Medicare," "Don't Squander the Surplus on Tax Breaks for the Rich," and "Don't Throw Mama From the Train." Some fifteen to twenty lawmakers left the gathering briefly to talk with AFL-CIO Secretary-Treasurer Richard Trumka, who was present.[35]

Republicans found themselves split two ways: on the one side, Archer and his dwindling group of allies who thought a compromise with Clinton was still possible; and on the other, those like Kasich who wanted a tax cut even if it would end any hope of crafting a Social Security bill before the next election. A third split was over what kind of partial privatization plan Republicans would support. Feldstein's plan was now bumping up against the Kolbe-Stenholm-Gregg-Breaux packages.[36] Some lawmakers liked the fact that the Feldstein plan seemed to tie the individual accounts more tightly to the traditional Social Security benefits system, making it appear less of a radical departure. In April, in his typically blustery manner, Phil Gramm unveiled another reform proposal, based on the Feldstein plan but even more complex.

Finally, in April, Republicans in both chambers served notice that a Social Security deal was taking second place on their list of priorities. For the first time in six years, Congress met the statutory deadline for passing a budget, although by narrow, close-to-party-line margins of 55-44 in the Senate and 220-208 in the House.

Although it walled off the $1.8 trillion Social Security surplus, the $1.7 trillion budget bill featured a big, $777.8 billion tax cut over the next ten years. Because it also included a stiff boost to military spending while committing Congress to stay within the spending limits set by the 1997 balanced-budget accord, the final bill promised to slash domestic discretionary spending by 12% in fiscal 2000 and 28% over the next five years. The tax cut would have been the largest since Reagan's first term. So intent were they on pursuing their program, despite the inevitability of a Clinton veto, that they rejected a proposal by conservative Democratic House members to block any tax cuts or new spending until Congress approved a plan for ensuring Social Security's long-term solvency.

The tension between the White House and Congress was now over tax cuts, not Social Security. In late April, Archer and Shaw unveiled a bill based on the Guarantee Plan that Kies had hammered out with White House aides the year before. It gained little traction with Republicans, some of whom viewed it as a strange amalgam of Clinton's USA accounts and Feldstein's "claw-back" scheme, to which they had already reacted negatively.

Clinton, perhaps still hoping to put his name on a bipartisan masterstroke, expressed a measure of support—even though Archer-Shaw was quite different from his proposal to preserve the Social Security surplus. "I think you've got an excellent plan, and I don't know why the Democrats don't embrace it," Archer recalls the president telling him at an Oval Office meeting. "I'll try to help you with the leadership, but you need to go to Dick Gephardt and Charlie Rangel, and that'll free me up." But "I have to question whether the president ever contacted either one," Archer adds.[37]

The House Republican leadership refused to bring Archer-Shaw to the floor. In the Senate, Lott opposed making Social Security an issue in 1999. On April 21, a "lock-box" bill to legally restrict use of Social Security taxes to paying down the national debt or overhauling the program failed when Republicans couldn't get the sixty votes needed to cut off debate. Nor was a new version of the Kolbe-Stenholm bill any more successful in the House.

Electoral politics, meanwhile, was encroaching, making a deal on Social Security even less likely. Gore himself stated categorically, when he announced his candidacy for president in June, that "I will never privatize Social Security or destroy it by diverting funds intended for Social Security. I will strengthen Social Security, not undermine Social Security."

On the other side, economist Lawrence Lindsey, a former Federal Reserve governor and aide to Texas Gov. George W. Bush, now a presidential aspirant, said on May 1 that Bush's three core campaign issues would be overhauling Social Security and Medicare, and boosting defense.[38] While Bush hadn't yet declared his candidacy, he was the favorite of the Republican leadership: a fact that no doubt bore some weight when the party's congressional leaders decided not to pursue a Social Security plan with Clinton.

In May, by a vote of 416 to 12, the House passed the Social Security and Medicare Safe Deposit Box Act, creating a procedural point of order in both chambers against any budget resolution or bill that would put the non-Social

Security portion of the budget in deficit. Any surpluses in the Social Security and Medicare portions would be used only to pay down the federal debt until a "reform" measure could be agreed upon. The Senate had already established a sixty-vote point of order in its budget resolution, and so the House bill established an in-principle agreement for Congress not to touch the trust funds.* With this, the Republicans hoped to insulate themselves from any charges during the upcoming campaign that they were contemplating a "raid," but without binding Congress legally.

The other consequence, however, was to accept the straitjacket Clinton had placed them in. Leaving Social Security and Medicare surpluses alone not only precluded any proposal to restructure those programs; it meant a tax cut would be nearly impossible to achieve either.

Amidst increasingly tense budget talks, on October 26, Clinton finally sent his Social Security/Medicare legislation to Congress. The bill was a stripped-down version of the package he had outlined in his State of the Union speech: a first step on the road to long-run health for the programs, Sperling told reporters, leaving out the more controversial elements of the original in the interest of bipartisanship. Dropped was the plan to invest a portion of the Social Security trust fund assets in stocks, as was the proposal for separately funded individual accounts.

What was left was Rubinomics, pure and simple. The entire payroll tax surplus would be devoted to reducing the federal debt, and the interest savings earmarked to build up the system's reserves in advance of the baby boomers' retirement. In addition, one-third of the non-Social Security surplus through 2009 would be used to establish a "Medicare surplus reserve," shoring up the health care program's solvency.

Clinton's bill was dead on arrival. Its purpose at this point was merely to highlight what he considered to be an excessive House military appropriations bill, to pay for which the government would conceivably need to dip into the Social Security surplus. And by removing his earlier proposals to invest trust fund assets and create new investment accounts, Clinton could claim to be doing exactly what the Republican leadership had been demanding of him for months: submitting a bill that met them halfway. The Republican leadership rejected it.

---

* Social Security Administration, *Social Security Legislative Bulletin*, May 28, 1999. The measures had little practical effect. The House Rules Committee could easily waive procedural points of order. And unlike the Senate bill that the Democrats had successfully filibustered earlier, the House bill and the Senate budget resolution didn't modify statutory debt ceilings (Coalition on Human Needs, *Human Needs Bulletin*, May 14, 1999).

CHAPTER 27

WASHINGTON POLITICS AND PUBLIC OPINION

The two years following the release of the Advisory Council report and passage of the 1997 Balanced Budget Act had witnessed an extraordinary effort by the White House and congressional Republicans to forge Social Security legislation that could serve both their purposes. Politically, neither side got exactly what it wanted. As a result, none of the major players in the drama have been especially eager to talk about the bipartisan attempt to restructure Social Security. Even though it was the main domestic policy initiative of his second administration, Clinton, for example, gives it barely more than two pages in his nearly 1,000-page autobiography.

But the attempt by both congressional Republicans and a Democratic White House to reshape Social Security had an enormous impact, forcing both parties to define their views on the subject more clearly and lastingly than at any time since the New Deal.

What created an opportunity for the privatizers was Clinton's strategic decision to acknowledge the existence of a Social Security "crisis" that needed to be "solved" at once. No Democratic president had ever done so before, and Clinton's decision effectively provided political cover for politicians of both parties to advance schemes for restructuring the program.

But the device of Rubinomics placed a big roadblock in the way of Republican efforts to pass a major tax cut by insisting that the Social Security surplus be saved and the national debt be paid down. Time and again in the late 1990s, the Republican-controlled Congress tried to push through a tax cut and each time it failed, principally because its command of the Senate remained too narrow to accomplish the job without Democratic cooperation—of which there was never enough. Perhaps a Republican tax-cut package could have gone through had Clinton not made "Save Social Security first" such a powerful mantra and tied it firmly to deficit reduction. But Republican control of the lawmaking process was never as absolute as it appeared.

Despite making Social Security reform the signature domestic issue of his second administration, the only major Social Security legislation President Clinton signed was the Senior Citizens' Freedom to Work Act, April 7, 2000, which eliminated earnings restrictions for beneficiaries. The much-praised law affected 800,000 seniors aged 65 to 69—about 6% of that age group.

Clinton and Rubin achieved their victory at a cost, however. The 1997 Balanced Budget Act alone anticipated reducing the total level of public debt—federal, state, local—to under 25% of GDP, its lowest level in almost eighty years—before any "entitlement" programs even existed. This made it nearly impossible for the Democratic Party to propose any new social welfare programs or even upgrades to existing ones. It prevented the party from offering anything calculated to address the social problems that the chugging late-1990s economy masked: decaying infrastructure, homelessness, declining medical coverage, erosion of the country's manufacturing base, and a working population living in increasingly precarious, debt-ridden circumstances.[1]

So even as the White House tactically disengaged itself from the New Democrat position that Social Security must embrace individual accounts and personal responsibility, it stopped short of reinvesting the Democratic Party with its traditional mission to address the conditions that held working people back.

While the White House had spared the country—temporarily, as it turned out—another dose of supply-side economics, it hadn't given the public sector much additional flexibility. Other than to repeat the "Save Social Security first" call, Clinton seemed to have no grand plans for what to do with the extra revenues except pay down the debt. All he could promise American voters was a possibly easier time funding benefits they had already been promised in a hypothetically more expensive future still many years away. The Republicans, by contrast, were offering tax cuts and new individual investment accounts now, all in pursuit of the same Social Security "reform" effort the president was calling for.

When it came to domestic policy, Social Security had become the most dramatic dividing line between Republicans and Democrats. Privatization—or Social Security "choice," as they increasingly referred to it—would appear regularly in Republican candidates' platforms from then on. And Democrats' position statements would just as regularly denounce it. But the most crucial shift coming out of the Clinton-congressional courtship was the acceptance by both sides of the "crisis" scenario.

"We won the crucial debate," says Michael Tanner, "and I give President Clinton enormous credit for this. The 1998 National Dialogue convinced Americans that Social Security needed to be saved. The public internalized the idea that Social Security is in trouble and we have to do something. The Baker-Weisbrot position, that it's not in trouble, may get attention in scholarly circles, but it has no weight in public policy calculations anymore."[2]

Many Democratic activists had misgivings about buying into the crisis discourse, but they covered them up or downplayed them in the interest of unity. The consensus among the groups tied together in the New Century Alliance was to focus instead on the drastic measures embodied in privatization plans like the NCRP's as being easier for the public to grasp.

Other considerations entered into this decision as well. One was not alienating prominent figures like Henry Aaron and Robert Reischauer, who had added their names to the anti-privatization ranks, not because they didn't see a crisis brewing, but because they objected to most of the restructuring plans on the table. This wasn't an idle worry. The most powerful seniors' organization, AARP, had declined privately to join the New Century Alliance even though its legislative director, John Rother, reluctantly agreed to sign its Statement of Principles.

While he didn't disagree that the Social Security crisis was phony, Tom Matzzie felt that this "was a losing argument to make to the public." Because "you can't convince the people that government can do anything right anymore," it was foolish to make the point, for example, that the Social Security trustees' projections may have been overly pessimistic.[3] Yet ultimately, to go along with the trustees' projections was to accept as given that, at some point in the future, benefits would have to be cut and taxes raised to "save" the program.

Despite the vast amount of time Clinton devoted to Social Security during his second term, the only improvement he and Congress actually made to the program was to completely abolish the earnings limit for Social Security recipients who had reached full retirement age. The House proudly passed this measure in February 2000 without a single No vote, and the president signed it into law the next month, neutralizing an issue the Republicans had found useful whenever they wanted to pose as populist friends of Social Security.

About 800,000 seniors in 1999 had lost some or all of their benefits because they earned too much on their own, according to the SSA. Alan Greenspan, among others, saw encouraging the elderly to keep working as a way to meet what he feared was a looming labor shortage that could drive up wages as the baby boomers retired. The problem, though, was that almost all the people affected were relatively affluent individuals in management or comparable positions. And 800,000 beneficiaries sounded like more than it was. In reality, less than 6% of people aged sixty-five to sixty-nine—the ages for which the earnings limit applied—earned enough to incur the penalty.[4] Some experts doubted that repeal of the earnings limit would have much impact at all on employment among the elderly.

But even such a modest improvement encountered righteous indignation from the staunchest exponents of the movement against Social Security. After the House approved it, Bob Kerrey ostentatiously held up the Senate vote in an attempt to force a fundamental debate on the future of the program. "We should not be doing this until we figure out what we will be doing with Social Security reform," he declared.[5]

If privatization was now a Republican Party orthodoxy, opposing privatization was now becoming a central point of identity for Democrats. And so both parties would take competing positions on Social Security into the campaign to choose Bill Clinton's successor.

* * *

But the question remains, why did it turn out this way? Why did a two-year effort—at the highest levels of government—to forge a bipartisan deal on Social Security end with the two sides more sharply defined and divided than before?

Why, if Congress and the White House were able to reach an eleventh-hour deal to "save" Social Security in 1983, could they not make a bargain in 1998 or 1999? The president wanted badly enough to do so that he committed some of his top aides to a behind-the-scenes, high-stakes series of negotiations that resulted in the Guarantee Plan—a scheme that would have undermined Social Security and, as a result, almost certainly split the Democratic Party. Two powerful Republicans, Gingrich and Archer, were prepared to work with him, even if it meant a fight with much of their own party's right wing. It's true, of course, that neither Clinton nor Gingrich ever publicly endorsed the Guarantee Plan, only making vaguely supportive statements while the proposal was being developed. But the White House abandoned the idea only when impeachment made it clear that the president could no longer afford to alienate the labor movement and the progressive wing of his party.

It had always been a long shot, however. The Social Security "crisis" wouldn't hit—if it ever did—for decades. Much else had changed as well. The Democratic leadership recognized that preserving Social Security had value as a fundamental differentiating point between themselves and the Republicans. Meanwhile, the Gingrich revolution was still doing its work of shifting control into the hands of younger, more ideological conservatives.

Oddly, the players on both sides came to more or less the same conclusions as to why the effort failed. Will Marshall, president of the New Democrats' Progressive Policy Institute, notes that after a year of intense effort, other issues were pulling Clinton away, notably the U.S. military engagement in Kosovo and a new round of attempts to broker a peace agreement in the Middle East— perhaps, in the president's mind, a more likely way to seal his tenure with a great stroke of statecraft. But Reischauer notes that the Republicans had become more difficult negotiating partners as the months wore on. Gingrich, wary of political backlash and hounded by a sex scandal of his own, decided against supporting the Guarantee Plan.[6] The congressional delegation's split between the Pain Caucus and the Free Lunch Caucus made it hard for Clinton and Gene Sperling to know which group they ought to be negotiating with.

As for the president, Archer says that more than once in private conversation, he expressed support for Archer-Shaw. As late as fall 2000, at a White House event, Clinton commended the bill to Rep. Tim Roemer, an Indiana Democrat, Archer recalls. It's possible that Clinton did so because he knew the bill had little chance of passage, and he seems never to have pressed it on Democratic congressional leaders.

Republicans uniformly decried Clinton's refusal to lead the way publicly, yet Reischauer points out that the president "showed quite a bit of ankle" with his lockbox proposal. While Clinton wanted to fund the USA accounts separately from payroll tax revenues, the pro-privatization lawmakers could have worked out a compromise with him, Reischauer suggests: for instance, to deduct, at retirement, the balances in those accounts from the "traditional" Social Security benefit a worker would receive.

Presidential leadership, so far as it extended, may actually have proved an obstacle to a deal. Clinton-hatred was practically a part of Republican DNA at this point, and with Gore preparing his own presidential campaign, the GOP Congress was rife with "partisan opposition to any legislation that would bring President Clinton or Vice President Gore any glory," Sperling later wrote.

Clinton himself was perhaps too close to being a lame duck to have put across something as ambitious as Social Security restructuring, even had he given it full-throated support. "To many in Congress, our push for Social Security reform in the late 1990s was about the desire of two retiring politicians—Bill Clinton and Bill Archer—to capture a legacy before they left office," Sperling recalled. Following a Capitol Hill briefing at the height of the negotiations, Sperling recalls that a congressional staffer told him that one House member had said, "I don't need to support the Bills' Legacy project. I'm not going anywhere."[7]

As for the main cause of the collapse, the obvious answer was simple: impeachment. Although it's difficult from his public statements to know how seriously Clinton considered partial privatization, "it might've been more likely" that he would have agreed to such a plan if the impeachment trial hadn't poisoned the atmosphere between the White House and the Republican leadership, the CAF's Tom Matzzie recalled later. Michael Tanner notes that, until less than a month before the December 1998 conference at the White House, he was convinced a deal was going to happen.[8]

To the true believers, this was a tragedy. "My view was one of great sadness" that Clinton "was encumbered with the Monica Lewinsky thing" right at the time that a Social Security deal seemed possible, Archer says. "It was a blown opportunity. The timing was right." Says Pete Peterson, "One of the biggest prices of Monica Lewinsky was the opportunity to pursue Social Security reform in a bipartisan setting."[9]

Activists on the other side of the debate find some humor in the notion that a simple blue dress from The Gap saved the nation's greatest anti-poverty program from being fatally compromised by a Clinton triangulation, as AFDC had been in 1996.[10] Gridlock, perpetuated in part by the Lewinsky scandal and the impeachment crisis, also helped prevent a president, who was anxious for one more big policy victory, from making a fateful deal with lawmakers locked into a narrow-minded belief in their own fiscal virtue.

All this may be a bit too simple. While insisting that the White House was sincere about seeking a grand compromise, Sperling contends that congressional Republicans and the Clinton administration were too far apart on matters that turned out to be articles of faith—free-standing private accounts versus carve-outs, benefits preservation versus devices to effectively reduce payouts, for example. "Both sides like the Lewinsky argument, because it allows the Republicans to blame Clinton's personal behavior and the Democrats to blame Ken Starr," Sperling says. "It lets both sides off the hook."[11]

Robert Rubin had a similar view. "My instinct is that Clinton could not have gotten more done even if the scandal had never stuck," he said later. Rubin believed, according to historian Steven Gillon, that "the Democratic interest groups would never have given the president the political wiggle room he needed to pass a reform that included private accounts, and congressional Republicans would not have passed any initiative that failed to include" them.[12] Simply because Clinton and Gingrich were ambitious enough to think they could bring it off doesn't mean they had the best reading of their parties' congressional delegations.

One aspect of the Social Security problem that might have prevented a deal under any circumstances was transition costs. None of the proposals to restructure the program that surfaced during Clinton's second term dealt with the cost of changing over to a private-account program in a politically palatable way. Each one entailed either drastic benefit cuts, immediately or over time, or else outrageous amounts of new long-term borrowing. These burdens would be "certain and directly traceable to legislators' actions," noted Princeton political scientist R. Douglas Arnold,[13] which is why, and not for the last time, enthusiasm among the congressional rank and file just wasn't there.

A great deal of credit for defeating privatization, however, goes to organized labor and other groups that joined together through the New Century Alliance, put their argument into the public discourse at last, and made clear that the coalition forged by the New Deal was still united around its flagship achievement. They pressed their point just when the president needed them for his political survival. At one meeting in the Oval Office, at which he tried to persuade the president to support Archer-Shaw, Archer recalls, "He told me, 'That's a problem for me. We stiffed [labor] on NAFTA, we can't stiff them again.'"[14]

Perhaps the most important product of the Clinton administration's flirtation with Social Security restructuring was the coalescing of this loose progressive alliance—a more or less permanent coalition representing roughly the same range of groups that had bolstered the New Deal and the Great Society agendas decades earlier, including organized labor, women advocates and people of color, retirees, and public employees. This alliance was able to work together consistently only on a few issues, Social Security being the principal one. It had to share its home in the Democratic Party with a powerful center-right wing that often joined with Republicans in caricaturing it as a collection of "interest groups" if not an evil cabal bent on bilking the taxpayer. But it couldn't be entirely ignored.

* * *

"Opinion, Queen of the World, is not subject to the power of kings; they are themselves its first slaves."
    —Jean-Jacques Rousseau[15]

Another party to the discussion arguably can claim some credit for thwarting Washington's effort to strike a grand bargain on Social Security: public opinion.

Americans are probably the most exhaustively surveyed society in human history, and during the Clinton era, Social Security was quite possibly the most heavily polled, surveyed, and focus-grouped political issue. According to the Roper Center for Public Opinion Research, national polls included 1,053 questions specifically about Social Security from 1993 through 1999, nearly quadruple the number during the previous six-year period.

One conclusion comes through clearly from an examination of a large sample of these queries. In the years leading up to Clinton's attempt to orchestrate a restructuring of the program, Americans had received and thoroughly absorbed the message that Social Security was in financial trouble. A major study conducted in 1995 for AARP by DYG, Inc., pollster Daniel Yankelovich's firm, found that 55% of respondents "doubt that we can afford Social Security anymore" and 31% supported cuts in the program, up from 11% ten years earlier. The people who answered these surveys understood that they had something to lose. More than 80% believed the strains on Social Security would pose a problem for them once they retired, according to another study by The Public Agenda, this one funded by Fidelity Investments, in 1997.

Confidence in the program had been trending down for some time, in fact. A series of surveys for the American Council of Life Insurers, dating from the mid-1970s and conducted by Yankelovich and other pollsters, found that, while 63% of respondents in 1975 were "very confident" or "somewhat confident" in Social Security, by 1994 the figure was down to 40%, although the results fluctuated considerably along the way.[16]

In 1995, Lawrence Jacobs and Robert Shapiro, with Jennifer Baggette, examined a large number of surveys on Social Security by major newspapers, magazines, television networks, and wire services, Gallup, and other organizations, some of them part of a series that went back decades.

Their conclusion from this mass of opinion: "Americans think they will receive less in benefits than they have contributed to Social Security and are split as to whether the system will be able to pay them benefits at all. There is also noticeable (split and unsteady) support for the proposal of making the system voluntary."[17]

Even within the party of the New Deal, confidence in—and loyalty to—Social Security was on the decline, according to a 1997 survey by the Democratic Leadership Council. According to its poll of 1,000 registered voters, 68% of Democrats—compared with 73% of all voters—believed Social Security faced a crisis "requiring significant reform. The poll shows strong public understanding about the need for serious entitlement reform, even though many politicians in both parties still believe talking about entitlements is a 'third rail' that they dare not touch."

Conservative Democrats used such conclusions to hammer their party's "left." Meanwhile, the financial services industry touted Social Security pessimism as a way to leverage workers to rely more on its products for retirement security. The 1997 Public Agenda survey "provides clear direction on how

Americans can be motivated to save and better prepare for their retirement years," said Paul J. Hondros, president of Fidelity Investments Retail Group, whose parent sponsored the report.

Most troubling for supporters of existing Social Security—and most encouraging to its critics—was the finding, in poll after poll, that younger people had less confidence in the program than older workers and retirees, and were more interested in the idea of individual accounts. In a pair of 1998 surveys, 39% of respondents aged thirty-five to forty-nine believed Social Security was in crisis, compared with only 16% of those over sixty-five; 45% thought the program was "not fair to people our age," versus just 15% of seniors; and 71% of the younger age group said people should be able to invest part of their Social Security payments, versus 40% of retirees.[18]

Other polls going back several years turned up similar findings. The over-sixty-five set had always been the program's biggest supporters, but if younger workers were in such a pessimistic mood and so eager for change, how much longer could the current arrangement hold?

The people answering these surveys had good reason to be concerned about Social Security. Americans were worried about getting by in their old age, some of the same polls also tended to show. "Seven out of ten working adults report that they are worried about not having enough money in their private savings when they stop working," a group of scholars noted in a report sponsored by the Henry J. Kaiser Family Foundation and the National Press Foundation, which reviewed eleven national surveys conducted in 1997–98. Nine in ten of those making less than $20,000 a year said they were not saving at all or were saving inadequately; two thirds of these said they had no money left over to do so.

Persuading Americans that Social Security was in trouble was the easy part, however. Selling them on a particular solution, especially one that dispensed with the guarantees built into the current program, was much harder. How people responded to questions about individual accounts, for example, depended on the phrasing of those questions. A Cato-sponsored survey in March 1996, for instance, found that 72% agreed that "people should be allowed to keep and invest the amounts they now pay in Social Security taxes to save for their own retirement."

But the response was drastically different when a warning was added. The Kaiser/National Press Foundation study looked at one poll in which 80% of respondents said workers should be able to shift some of their payroll tax into personal accounts. In another, which specified that benefits could be "higher or lower than expected depending on stock market's performance," the favorable response dropped to 48%.

More specific questions about individual accounts often prompted anxious responses. In a 1997 poll by The Public Agenda, 92% of respondents agreed with the statement, "People who were poor in their working years would barely survive in retirement without Social Security." The Kaiser Foundation and National Press Foundation study noted one survey in which more than half of those with opinions either way on individual accounts said they could easily change their minds.

None of which should have been surprising. "Polls that emphasize benefits and ignore costs tell us nothing more profound than that everyone likes a free lunch," R. Douglas Arnold noted.[19] But the really remarkable thing to many Social Security critics was how popular the program itself was. Whatever fiscal problems it may or may not have, polls always registered the high value the public placed on the program, not to mention a high degree of satisfaction with the way it operated.

Virtually everyone—96%—who participated in the 1995 AARP survey "views Social Security as essential retirement income," the study reported. Nor did most Americans resent paying payroll taxes to support it; 71% of AARP's respondents said they felt Social Security taxes were "very fair" or "moderately fair" in 1995—again, exactly the same percentage as ten years earlier. Asked if they would quit Social Security if they had the option to do so, 73% of respondents in 1995 said no—the same proportion that answered the same question negatively ten years earlier.

Polls also revealed how reluctant most Americans were for Social Security to change. Making the program voluntary was a bad idea, according to 56% of respondents to a 1992 CBS News/New York Times survey: slightly more had agreed in 1981. Social Security spending should actually be increased, said 46% of those who answered a Gallup survey in December 1994, while 45% preferred keeping it the same—and only 7% thought it should be reduced. Few Americans were interested in cutting the Social Security tax, either. Asked which federal tax they would most like to see cut, a Roper Organization/CBS/ New York Times poll in 1990 showed an overwhelming 78% chose the income tax against only 14% for payroll taxes.

This despite the fact that the payroll tax fell more heavily on lower-income workers. Indeed, 55% of non-retirees said they would be willing to pay more in payroll taxes if it would ensure that Social Security and Medicare would still be there for them. Significantly, almost exactly the same percentage of the youngest workers—those aged eighteen to twenty-nine—said the same thing.

Earlier data suggested that Social Security was more important to Americans than national defense. In five separate polls by Louis Harris and Associates conducted between 1982 and 1989, respondents were asked, if cuts in federal spending had to be made, should they come from defense or Social Security? Respondents favored defense cuts by percentages ranging from 72% to 89%.

Even young workers' pessimism about Social Security—and interest in individual accounts—offered less than a complete picture of their attitudes about the program. According to a NBC News/Wall Street Journal poll in 1996, 69% of workers in their forties disagreed with the statement, "The older person gets a fair break in benefits from our society." Asked whether the U.S. spends the right amount on elderly assistance, an overwhelming 78% of those in their forties said "too little."

Poring over the results of years of Social Security polling, many researchers—whatever their opinion of the program—were baffled, and reduced to blaming the messengers. "What we've found is a nation tied up in knots," warned the Brookings Institution, "whose fears could lead to a paralysis on Social Security reform."[20] Some were reduced to scolding. "Americans Need to Wake Up to the Reality About Retirement Dreams, Aetna Survey Reveals," was the headline of a press release by the big insurance company on November 8, 1995.

Americans' fears about Social Security had less to do with the programs' specific problems than with something more general, some observers suggested. Noting in a 1998 article that public confidence had already started slipping in the 1970s, Jacobs and Shapiro argued that "the real cause is the public's general loss of faith in government after Watergate and Vietnam, not any focused critique of Social Security." The 1983 Amendments, they pointed out, "produced no change in confidence in 1984 or 1985."[21]

None of this means the public were completely unwilling for Social Security to change. In one poll, for example, two-thirds said they would consider means testing the program for more affluent recipients, although the response depended a great deal on how the term "affluent" was defined. A 1999 study by Peter D. Hart Research Associates for the National Committee to Preserve Social Security and Medicare found that 71% of respondents would support a hypothetical plan to strengthen Social Security by raising payroll taxes and lowering benefits slightly—more or less the same kind of fix Washington had consensed on in 1977 and 1983.

Was the public really as "tied up in knots" about Social Security as many expert observers thought? Another way to ask this question might be: Was there really a contradiction between agreeing, on one hand, that Social Security wouldn't be there for one's retirement, and on the other, that only incremental nips and tucks to the program were acceptable—but not any fundamental changes? A couple of other findings in the Hart poll help answer this question. Two-thirds of adults said that Congress "should fix Social Security by strengthening its financial condition, so that future retirees will be guaranteed a reasonable level of benefits." More than half of voters, meanwhile, told the pollster they would be "less likely to support their member of Congress if she or he voted for … partial privatization."

One source of the experts' mystification may have been the fact that so many lawmakers, policy wonks, advocates, and upper-tier journalists—even traditional defenders of Social Security—had come to see the program primarily as an economic problem or puzzle. The main issue, for these members of the Washington elite, was no longer how well it served a very large political constituency but how to make the numbers work in a game where the goal was to get a set of figures to balance out, hypothetically, over seventy-five years, if not some longer period of time.

Democratic administrations of the New Deal and Great Society eras had failed to forge a sense of public ownership of Social Security, instead molding it into a government program administered by technocrats. Understanding of the program itself was low, and what most people knew about it was unsexy to say the least. That didn't mean working households defined it as Washington did, however: as an economic puzzle.

Instead, they saw Social Security as politics—a problem, but one they expected their elected officials to solve without upsetting an arrangement they had come to rely on. If the numbers were difficult to reconcile, that didn't mean the public didn't expect Washington to find a solution—only that they would punish politicians who tried to do it the wrong way, regardless of what the latter regarded as "politically doable." In practice, this meant the public were willing to entertain modest changes to restore the program's finances, as had been done in 1977 and 1983.

But they weren't likely to favor a restructuring that would seriously erode their benefits, and—other things being equal—were likely to punish politicians who attempted them. The guarantees that came with their Social Security benefits were especially important to them, even if demographic estimates suggested these guarantees were threatened. All this meant that the time would be right for change—significant change—only when a crisis was about to hit, not ten or twenty or thirty years before.

Poll numbers are the most postmodern of data, open to an infinite variety of textual readings. And even some conservative pundits weren't so sure that in attacking Social Security, a few of their leaders weren't perhaps taking a dangerous risk. One of these was none other than neocon godfather Irving Kristol, who had helped train Washington's attention on entitlements when he published David Stockman, Arthur Laffer, and Jude Wanniski in *The Public Interest* in the 1970s.

"I am well aware that, down the road, some reform of Social Security and Medicare will be required," wrote Kristol, now with the American Enterprise Institute, in an April 1996 *Wall Street Journal* op-ed. "But I am convinced that, for instance, Americans would not mind a new progressive payroll tax.... Contrary to some silly journalistic chatter, there is no conflict of the generations going on. What people do resent is paying taxes for public policies that seem not to work. Social Security and Medicare do work, and there is no visible resentment among their children or grandchildren for whatever comforts the elderly might enjoy—or, rather, whatever discomforts they might escape."

This perceptive observation from a person who had come of age in the era that gave birth to Social Security was ignored. A significant divide was growing up between the policy-making elite and the public, which the former seemed not to understand. "Such divergence between the general public and the policy elite is a danger signal in a democracy," warned John Mueller, a former Jack Kemp aide who had been writing on Social Security for some years. "It usually means either that the public is impervious to information freely available to the policymakers; or that the policymakers are deviating from values broadly accepted by the community."[22]

One of the few people in Washington who clearly understood Social Security's singular role and the public's complicated feelings about it, Mueller was a religious Catholic and family-values conservative who also liked to call himself a "member of the small subset of balanced-budget supply-siders." As an aide to Kemp, he worked on the 1986 tax reform bill and became something of an authority on tax and monetary policy. At the time, his views were wholly against Social Security. "I thought Social Security should be privatized not only as an economic issue but as a moral issue," he later recalled. "But Jack [Kemp] wanted to fix Social Security, not phase it out."[23]

Intending to convince Kemp that he was right, Mueller began exploring the subject more carefully, but concluded that "the privatizers have done their homework—mostly by ignoring so-called 'human capital.'" In the fall of 1987, while still working for Kemp, he published an article in *Policy Review*, the Heritage Foundation's magazine, entitled "A Subsidy for Motherhood: Why I Now Support Social Security." Mueller offered a practical objection to abolishing or drastically lowering the payroll tax and carving private accounts out of Social Security. The cost of doing so, while continuing to pay benefits to current retirees, would be enormous. "After paying Social Security taxes to support their parents, the baby-boomers would lose any benefits in return from their children," he wrote. "This amounts to a lifetime tax increase of several trillion dollars." Families, which social conservatives were supposed to want to protect and nurture, would be the two-time losers: directly, "by giving up their Social Security benefits, or indirectly, by paying higher taxes to fund a credit they do not receive."

But Mueller had a more fundamental, philosophic question for Social Security's critics. While they professed to believe the program was fatally flawed, it somehow remained tremendously popular. Why?

Mueller analogized Social Security to Roman Catholicism, of which G.K. Chesterton said, "Perhaps this extraordinary thing is really the ordinary thing; at least the normal thing, the center. Perhaps, after all, it is Christianity that is sane and all its critics that are mad—in various ways." "The American people seem to regard Social Security more like an ordinary suit of clothes," Mueller concluded. "They may agree it is an aesthetic absurdity; but that won't stop them from wearing it." Social Security and the payroll tax, coupled with the Earned Income Tax Credit and the personal exemption, constituted the main pillars of the family within the U.S. tax system, and as such, were clearly quite satisfactory to the vast majority of Americans who didn't occupy themselves with building and critiquing economic models. "It is by nature a political balancing act," Mueller conceded.

If you believed the program wasn't really in a long-term crisis—or at least, that the problem could be solved simply by some combination of reducing benefits and raising taxes—then your objective wasn't to fix it but to reduce the political tension around it. Any program that depends on each succeeding generation's ability to pay the previous generation's benefits would always be a bit out of whack fiscally. Kicking the can down the road by making incremental changes such as scheduling modest tax increases in the future or bringing state and local government employees into the system, wasn't irresponsible.

It was only appropriate for a program that was a compact between generations. Current workers, or their representatives, shouldn't unilaterally shrink a vital program for those coming after, those who could face very different challenges and opportunities—higher or lower immigration and birth rates, and productivity growth, for example.

Incremental change, therefore, was a kind of strategic evasion of what Social Security's defenders considered a phony issue, or at least an unresolvable one. The conclusion, on a slightly more cosmic level, was simple if inelegant. Sometimes politics can, and should, refuse to confine itself to a rigorous economic straitjacket. In that sense, Social Security would always be one of humanity's typically imperfect but somehow workable creations. As Mueller put it, "a constant balancing act."

After leaving Kemp's staff in 1989, Mueller joined a new economic forecasting firm, Lehman Bell Mueller Cannon. In 1995, he served on Kemp's tax reform commission, running into intense criticism from the right when he opposed replacing the income tax with a flat consumption tax that would effectively hit only labor but not property income. Meanwhile, his views on Social Security circulated. In 1996, the National Committee to Preserve Social Security and Medicare invited him to lead a research project it was cosponsoring on the consequences of privatization. This resulted in the first econometric model of Social Security that took spousal, dependent, and survivors' benefits as well as individual workers' benefits into account, yielding three important papers that made Mueller a well-known voice against private accounts.

But for many in the Washington think-tank set, in the upper echelons of the national press, and even in Congress, Social Security was no longer an issue on which the public's view mattered, for all the polling, but one on which the people needed instruction from their leaders. If only those leaders could make up their mind on the details of the lesson!

PART V

The Social Security Election

(1999–2000)

CHAPTER 28

THE POLITICS OF PROSPERITY

Early in 2000, at a presidential signing ceremony for a piece of legislation sponsored by Bill Archer, the Ways and Means chair had to walk past the president to get to his seat on the dais outside the White House. Clinton tugged at Archer's sleeve and said, "You know, if they had only left us alone, we could have solved the Social Security problem."[1]

Just what Clinton was thinking is hard to fathom, since Archer had joined the rest of his party in voting yes on all four articles of impeachment against the president little more than a year earlier. But on January 18, in a personal letter to Douglas Eakeley, a college friend, the president was a bit more specific, blaming "the leadership of both parties" and the Republican leadership in particular for "intransigence and excessive partisanship."[2]

Political circumstances as much as ideology had kept the White House and congressional Republicans from finding a middle ground for restructuring Social Security. But with another presidential election beginning and the Clinton era closing, the ideological side of the debate began to dominate Washington again.

The 2000 race was the first since the 1936 Roosevelt-Landon contest in which Social Security was the central issue. But even that doesn't adequately describe the role it played.

"Saving" Social Security, however they defined it, was the one position on which all the candidates agreed, because voters had been taught to regard it as the moral high ground for any serious candidate. Yet the sums of money required by any proposal to set the program's books straight long-term were far larger than what was needed for any other initiative any of the presidential candidates was championing—so much larger that they helped define those initiatives, as well as the election itself. Time and again, candidates for House, Senate, and White House would lock up in an unresolvable rhetorical clinch over whose proposals would guarantee the program's health for the next seventy-five years and whose would undermine it.

The elderly and near-retirees, among others, were still very sensitive to suggestions that Social Security might have to change. But the Democrats' advantage with them had been blunted by the Clinton scandals. And Republican strategists were exploring whether some other groups of voters, especially younger ones, might be attracted to a new-look campaign that framed Social Security privatization as a matter of increasing personal "choice."

Few expected the election to introduce any new wrinkles into the Social Security debate. But Democrats would have to show they weren't just going to preserve the basic shape of the program, rather that they would do something about a "crisis" many of them knew fundamentally didn't exist. Republicans would need to couch their ideas for restructuring Social Security as modernization, not privatization, and emphasize that they weren't out to cut benefits for anyone nearing retirement.

* * *

In the weeks before the Iowa caucuses and the New Hampshire primary kicked off the presidential race, those states filled up with teams from the major Social Security advocacy groups.[3]

Republicans, including advisors to Texas Gov. Bush, believed an avenue was opening to challenge the Democrats on what had once been their home turf. First, there was the validation that a Democratic president had conferred on Social Security restructuring by declaring "saving" the program a national priority. Second, many advocates of privatization believed the cultural and economic changes of the 1990s had spawned a new "investor class" who felt more confident in their ability to provide for their own retirement.

Much of the mass media echoed this scenario, even though it stood in stark contrast to the economic jitters they were reporting elsewhere in their pages or broadcasts. "They're better educated and richer than previous generations," Newsweek assured in a special section about the baby boomers as the 2000 presidential campaign heated up, "and, as their parents die, expect to benefit from the largest transfer of inherited wealth in history.... Unlike their parents, they don't have to rely on Social Security or limited pensions. A healthy economy and a strong stock market give them new options as they phase out of full-time employment. They may decide to freelance, work part time or start their own companies."[4] The voting subset of the public was even more committed to the markets, according to a *USA Today*/CC/Gallup poll conducted in April 2000, which found that 76% of likely voters owned stock, with Democrats and independents only slightly less likely to be shareholders than Republicans.

The investor class theory had its flaws. A large chunk of the rise in stock ownership was due to the fact that company pensions were being replaced by savings plans like 401(k)s, whether workers wanted the change or not. Meanwhile, Wall Street and retail bankers were aggressively pushing their customers to shift their liquid assets from personal savings accounts into annuities, mutual funds, and other vehicles whose returns depended on stock market investments. Were these people investors because they wanted to be? Or just by dint of heavy marketing and a change in their employers' benefits strategy?

There was also the irony that the role of Social Security, which had just had a close brush with privatization, was becoming ever more important. Retirement wealth—the assets workers were building up to see them through old age—actually improved for just about every demographic group in the 1980s and 1990s, a study by the Economic Policy Institute later revealed: older and younger, middle class and low income, women and minorities. But wealth from employer-based pension plans, 401(k)s, and private saving was heavily skewed toward the affluent. The only reason less well-off workers had more to look forward to was Social Security: the value of their benefits was building up fast, thanks to the healthy job market of the late 1990s and the fact that future benefits were indexed to the cost of living. Yet 27% of households between the ages of fifty-six and sixty-four could still expect to retire with incomes less than twice the poverty level.

Overall prosperity accompanied by such disturbing trends was creating a profound sense of anxiety among working people. A startling finding by pollster John Zogby in February showed that almost every population group was equally worried about becoming poor. Old and young, city dwellers and suburbanites, churchgoers and non-churchgoers, those who shopped at Wal-Mart often and those who bought at Saks—the percentage who said they could imagine themselves becoming poor wavered between 54% and 61% for all of them. The only exceptions were those age sixty-five and older. Most Social Security recipients "don't sweat their credit card balances at all," Zogby found.

Nevertheless, the Bush campaign, and particularly its top strategist, Karl Rove, enthusiastically bought the investor class argument. An internal Republican poll, taken as early as April 1999, found that 79% of voters favored letting people invest a portion of their Social Security contributions on their own, with 55% "strongly" favoring the idea. "People do have a sense that they want to be more in control of their lives," Rove said a year later, when the

Bush campaign was in full swing. As for the riskiness of the idea, Rove added, "Throw out the old paradigm. The way you win now is to take risks."[5]

The investor class theory dovetailed with Rove's desire to cast his candidate as a fresh kind of Republican, at once a "compassionate conservative" and a reformer who would offer the nation a new start, restoring moral rectitude and high purpose to squalid, Clintonian Washington. Taking on the third rail would make the Texas governor appear to be a bold leader and put him in step with Americans' confidence and optimism after a half-decade of extraordinary prosperity.[6]

This preoccupation expressed itself from the campaign's very first TV ads, which were designed to frame Bush as a Social Security reformer as well as a tax and education innovator and the putative restorer of the U.S. military—a candidate who was looking forward, not backward. Accordingly, Bush's June 12, 1999 announcement of his candidacy included an explicit endorsement of partial privatization: "We should trust Americans by giving them the option of investing part of their Social Security contributions in private accounts."

Bush himself was mildly messianic on the subject. He "felt a calling to run" for president, he later wrote, and he had "a clear vision" that he must cut taxes and "reform Social Security."[7] Message and advertising pros who went to work for Bush in the months ahead learned that Social Security "choice" was a fundamental point of his candidacy, subject to no revision or finessing. Bush's presidential appeal would have to be made to fit this position, not the other way around.[8] Within a few months he would be even more emphatic, promising to "spend political capital" to "bring Democrats and Republicans together to solve this problem" of people having the money they needed to retire.[9]

Bush's website soon featured five basic principles on Social Security reform, which the candidate reiterated like a mantra in his public appearances:

- Fulfilling the solemn commitment of Social Security, with no reduction in benefits for retirees or near retirees;

- Dedicating all Social Security money to Social Security (the "lockbox");

- Opposing any tax increase for Social Security;

- Supporting voluntary personal retirement accounts as part of Social Security reform; and

- Opposing government investment in private stocks or bonds.

But if the accounts were to be voluntary, how much money would remain to cover transition costs? Just how much of their payroll taxes would workers be allowed to keep in their private accounts? Instead of addressing these issues, Bush said he would appoint a commission to look into them once in office.

Sticking to generalities served two purposes. With the wider voting public, it allowed him to concentrate on what was most attractive about his plan: the idea of giving workers "choice" as to where their payroll taxes went. It also enabled him to fudge the differences within his own party between the Free-Lunch Caucus and the Pain Caucus.

The centerpiece of Bush's economic program, announced in early December 1999, would make his Social Security ideas more problematic, however. He proposed a tax-cut package that would reduce rates for all income brackets, phase out the estate tax, double the $500 child tax credit, reduce the marriage penalty, and expand the charitable deduction benefit. All told, this would erase more than $1.7 trillion in federal revenue over ten years, according to Citizens for Tax Justice,* eating up the entire projected non-Social Security revenue surplus over that period. Should the economy slump and tax revenues fall, the tax cut would quickly make Bush's Social Security project vastly more difficult.

* * *

Bush's probable opponent constructed his Social Security and tax positions around a very different reading of the voters' mood and of public policy realities. Gore policy advisor Elaine Kamarck, a Kennedy School of Government lecturer who was a founder of the DLC and had worked with the vice president on his reinventing government initiative, wasn't philosophically opposed to private-sector solutions. But when she put together a series of public policy seminars for the vice president while he was developing his campaign's key themes, "we were both horrified by the transition costs" of partially privatizing Social Security, she says, "and in the end we didn't think a feasible privatization scheme existed."[10]

Shifting the program into private accounts also threatened to create major market distortions, they concluded. If participants' investments suffered a bad year, they might pressure Congress into making good their losses, which over time could create an expectation that the federal government would bail out a certain group of investors whenever something bad happened. "Every step of the way with private accounts, there was the certainty that something would go wrong," Kamarck says. "Whether people are screwed by unscrupulous brokers, or have a bad year in the stock market, who would they go to?"

Instead, Gore's plan to save Social Security was the same one he had helped Clinton to formulate a year earlier—and that had already failed to win much support in Congress. He would use the Social Security surpluses to pay down the federal debt, invest a portion of the trust fund assets in the stock market,

---

*   "Analysis of Presidential Candidate George W. Bush's Tax Plan," Citizens for Tax Justice, December 1, 1999. That included $1.3 trillion of actual tax cuts, estimated by the Congressional Budget Office, plus higher interest payments generated by the corresponding reduction in funds available to pay down the federal debt.

and hope that lower interest payments on the debt would free up general revenues that could be used to help sustain Social Security—and Medicare—as the baby boomers retired. Rubinomics slightly repackaged, in other words.

But Gore was also trying to stake out a position that showed sensitivity to working- and middle-class voters—"America's forgotten majority," living in an era of economic unease. A DLC founder who had championed smaller government as a senator and in his early years as vice president, Gore set out to remake himself as a populist.

And so he unveiled a series of tax deductions targeted specifically at middle- and lower-income families, unlike the across-the-board cuts Bush was proposing. The vice president's smaller, $575 billion proposal included expanding the existing child-care tax credit to make it refundable to families that didn't earn enough to pay income taxes, a refundable tax credit for after-school programs, tax credits for health care insurance costs, and a $10,000 tuition tax deduction for families with children in college. Gore also proposed partially offsetting his cuts with $180 billion in higher business and tobacco taxes.

Gore and Bush would further flesh out their proposals, but the essentials were already in place by the beginning of 2000, and so were the criticisms that would follow them through their campaigns: of Bush, that the combination of his tax cuts and private accounts would make Social Security less financially secure, not shore it up; and of Gore, that his plan—the lockbox that was supposed to protect Social Security's revenues but that would really be used to pay down the debt—really amounted to a continuation of the status quo and thus was no plan at all.

CHAPTER 29

BUSH VS. GORE

In retrospect, the 2000 Democratic and Republican presidential nominees sorted themselves out rather quickly. Steve Forbes, back for a second try, ran second to Bush in Iowa but was out by mid-February, and John McCain, the favorite of the Washington press corps, was gone by mid-March. Gore's only opponent, former Sen. Bill Bradley, had folded his tent by then as well.

Not surprisingly, Bush and Gore had both far surpassed their rivals' contribution totals. The results indicated strongly in which direction the largest donors—the investment industry in particular—felt their interests lay. By January 3, Bush had raised $193 million—more than the combined totals of all of his eventual competitors in the November election: Gore, Green Party candidate Ralph Nader, Libertarian Harry Browne, and Independent Pat Buchanan. His take from the securities and investment industry, including both organizations and individuals employed by them, came to over $3 million, according to the Center for Responsive Politics.

Gore was far behind, and by October had still only raised $1.4 million from the industry. Insurance companies, anticipating a boost to annuities sales should Social Security be privatized, went even more solidly for Bush, contributing over $1.6 million versus $324,000 for Gore by the end of the cycle. The pattern was the same at the big bond trading houses. Bush pulled in just short of $114,000 from Goldman Sachs, compared to $95,750 for

Gore. Citigroup and Merrill Lynch, retail financial services powerhouses that could expect to loom large in a new era of privatized social insurance—but that also had large bond desks—contributed $114,300 and $132,425, respectively, to the Bush campaign, while Gore received only $111,750 from Citigroup, and Merrill didn't even make the vice president's top-twenty donors list.[1]

As their primary challengers faded and they began putting their fall campaign organizations in order, Bush and Gore filled a few gaps in their Social Security proposals. In April 2000, just a few weeks after Bradley withdrew from the Democratic race, Gore announced that he supported two changes. One would boost lower-income widows' benefits to 75% of what the deceased spouse had received; the other would create a "family-service credit" for parents who leave the workforce to care for small children. The credit would assume they had paid taxes on $16,500 of wages per year, boosting their eventual Social Security benefits.

Gore's proposals would sop up no more than 5% of the Social Security surplus over ten years, he said, and in fact they weren't overgenerous. They included no improvements for elderly divorcées, yet they created a "means test" for lower-income widows to receive the higher benefit—a violation of Social Security's universal character that might make affluent individuals less supportive of the program. Gore offered nothing for the growing number of women who provided care for aging relatives, a gender-specific role that hadn't changed as women's participation in the workforce rose. And his proposals did

Republican presidential candidate George W. Bush unveils his plan to partially privatize Social Security in a speech at a senior center in Rancho Cucamonga, California, May 15, 2000.

nothing either to boost benefits for lower-wage workers, even though women were disproportionately represented in this group.

But the fact that Gore was offering any improvements at all was significant. The last time Washington had expanded Social Security benefits for anyone, other than through its annual inflation indexing, had been in 1983. The Gore campaign seemed to be signaling that the elderly too deserved to benefit from the expanding economy and the federal government's growing tax revenues. It was also making a play for women voters, 72% of whom had recently said in a survey by New York-based EDK Associates that guaranteeing Social Security to future generations should be a higher public priority than tax cuts.

* * *

By the end of April, Bush aides were telling reporters that their candidate would soon make a major speech about his plans for Social Security. It was eventually scheduled for May 15 at the Leisure World retirement community in Rancho Cucamonga, California. That day, the Republican candidate didn't soft-pedal his promises. "I am here with a message for America," Bush said, "and to put my opponent on notice. The days of spreading fear and panic are over. When I am elected, this generation and this President will save Social Security and Medicare."

To his original five principles for Social Security reform, Bush added a sixth: preserving the existing disability and survivors' benefit systems. But most of his remarks were given over to selling the idea of personal accounts—especially to "young people," a term he used repeatedly. In addressing them, his pitch sounded as much like a wealth-building scheme as a plan for secure retirement.

"The real return people get from what they put into Social Security is a dismal 2% a year," Bush said. "Over the long term, sound investments yield about a 6% return. Investing that 4% difference, over a lifetime, can show dramatic results. A worker who invests even a limited portion of his or her paycheck could, over a career, end up with hundreds of thousands of dollars for retirement."

All this could be accomplished without raising taxes or cutting benefits, at least not for current retirees and workers nearing retirement, thanks to the $2 trillion surplus the trust funds were projected to accumulate over the next decade. And because the new accounts would offset part of Social Security's benefit obligations, a press briefing handed out by the Bush campaign the day of his speech said that the cost of the system would start to go down after the first burst of baby boomer retirements.

Neither Bush nor his aides explained how their "offset" arrangement would work without actually reducing the current benefits. Instead, Bush devoted the rest of his remarks to an attack on his opponent. The "Gore plan" amounted to no plan at all, he said, because Social Security would still be collecting IOUs from the federal government to help conceal the budget deficit. The government would issue $34 trillion in additional bonds beginning in 2011—at least three years after the next president left office, Bush estimated. "The Gore plan will eventually require either a 25% increase in income taxes, the largest in our history, or a substantial reduction in benefits."

Bush's speech helped catapult Social Security to the top of the list of issues animating the 2000 presidential race. "Suddenly, Social Security, the biggest and most popular program of big government, is the great issue in this campaign," declared conservative columnist George F. Will.[2]

Would the public buy Bush's pitch? The anti-privatization camp was already trying to sow doubts during his speech, hiring an airplane to circle overhead towing a banner sponsored by 2030 Action reading, "Don't privatize Social Security, www.2030.org." Afterward, members of the California chapter of the Coalition to Save Social Security—the renamed New Century Alliance—were on hand to criticize Bush's plan and to call upon local Republican Rep. James Rogan, then engaged in the most expensive House race in history, to make him clarify his view on privatization.

As for retired Americans, the group most wedded to the current program, Bush campaign manager Karl Rove admitted, "We've got a problem in that we have to do a lot to reassure seniors" that their own benefits wouldn't be affected. "But once you do that, you take them out of the debate."[3] The same day Bush delivered his Leisure World speech, a *New York Times*/CBS News poll showed that while 47% of respondents said Gore would "do a better job with Social Security" versus 39% naming Bush, their favorability ratings were exactly the opposite: 47% for Bush, 39% for Gore. And 63% felt Bush had strong leadership and reformist credentials, compared with 53% for Gore.[4]

* * *

The Gore forces, the Coalition to Save Social Security, and other pro-Social Security groups were nevertheless prepared with a response to Bush's Leisure World speech before he left the podium, and afterward launched a fusillade that would go on for weeks. For starters, they had an ill-considered admission that Bush himself had made to a reporter with the *Dallas Morning News* a few days before. Asked whether poor investments or a market crash could leave workers receiving less than they did under the current Social Security structure, Bush answered, "Maybe, maybe not." That statement was repeated more than thirty times in major print news outlets before the end of the month, and anti-privatization speakers and opinionizers would invoke it endlessly in the months ahead.

Bush's own advisors occasionally fed the perception that his plan would produce losers as well as winners. Sounding a bit like a Las Vegas odds maker, Feldstein noted in a *New York Times* op-ed that a twenty-one-year-old with average earnings, who invested 2% of earnings every year until retirement would have a 50% chance that his combined benefits would exceed his Social Security benefits and a 10% chance of doubling them.

The downside? "Not very risky," Feldstein wrote. "There is less than a 10 percent chance that his combined benefits will be less than 90% of his projected Social Security benefits."[5] With 148 million American workers participating in the program, that meant that something less than 14.8 million could expect lower benefits under the Bush plan: acceptable losses, presumably, to the candidate and his advisor.

Since early fall, the Coalition to Save Social Security had been demanding that House and Senate members and candidates for office state their positions on Social Security and Medicare and sign a pledge to oppose privatizing Social Security. Gore promised to fax the pledge to every Democratic candidate for House and Senate.[6] Nearly all Democratic representatives and senators from Massachusetts, Michigan, and Pennsylvania quickly signed it.

Gore also sought to turn on its head Bush's claim that his Social Security plan showed he was more of a leader than his opponent, tagging it as "irresponsible." He challenged Bush to a debate on Social Security reform in May, playing off the lack of detail in the Republican's plan. "Governor Bush can explain why he has left the door open to raising the retirement age," Gore said, "and I can explain why I think that is bad public policy and a disservice to those who work hard, physical jobs." The Bush campaign didn't respond to the suggestion.

Speaking the day after the Leisure World address, however, Bush seemed to leave open the possibility that his private account-based plan was just a stop on the road to a fully privatized system. The program couldn't go "from one regime to another overnight," he said. "It's going to take a long time to transition to a system where personal savings accounts are the predominant part of the investment vehicle. And so, this is a step toward a completely different world and an important step."

That admission wasn't an isolated one: indeed, it seemed to reveal a lot about the Bush economic team's basic thinking. In a *Washington Times* op-ed a few days before, John Goodman, one of Bush's economic policy advisors, noted, "We want invested savings to gradually replace the government obligations."

The biggest problem Gore and many analysts in the mainstream press found with the Bush plan was the sheer size of the promises he was making. His tax cut was estimated to chop federal revenues by $1.7 trillion over ten years, and transitioning to the new Social Security structure would cost another $900 billion—covering benefits to current retirees while draining an estimated 16% of the amount currently paid by employers and employees in payroll taxes. By Bush's own estimate, that would leave perhaps $512 billion of the overall ten-year surplus for all other government initiatives—and as a cushion should his economic assumptions fail to pan out. That was less than many economists were comfortable with, given that Medicare and Medicaid costs were again rising rapidly.

It would all work out, Bush said, because the surplus would grow quickly, both in the coming year and in the second half of the new decade. In early May, Bush's chief economic advisor, Larry Lindsey, announced that the candidate was predicting a roaring 4.9% growth rate for the current fiscal year versus 2.7% forecast by OMB, whose numbers Gore relied on.* Bush's longer-term estimates were equally optimistic. The budget surplus over ten years, excluding Social Security revenues, would be $1.8 trillion, his advisors said—more than double both the $893 billion CBO estimate that most economists accepted, and the more cautious $764 billion that the Gore campaign used. "It will all fit within the revenues," said Bush, who relied for his numbers on Lindsey, Feldstein, and his father's OMB director, Michael Boskin.[7]

No it wouldn't, the Gore camp replied, because Bush's economic plan would balloon the national debt again with its tax cuts and spending increases. In just the first five years, they pointed out, only $19 billion would be left over to cover those interest payments, which could total $56 billion.[8]

The Gore campaign argued ultimately that Bush's big surpluses would fail to materialize and the government would be forced to inject general revenues into Social Security to cover the benefits it could no longer pay after the new personal accounts system was running. What would that mean? A report by the Center on Budget and Policy Priorities projected that if workers shifted 2% of their Social Security payroll taxes into private accounts, the lost revenue would keep the program from being able to cover all benefits by 2023—fourteen years earlier than the trustees estimated. In effect, Bush's proposed tax cuts and personal investment accounts would be enacted at the expense of Social Security itself. Only a true believer in supply-side economics could consider it possible to have both and still protect Social Security's benefit promises.

* * *

Especially in its attack on Bush's Social Security proposals, the Gore campaign benefited from the organizing, coordination, and research that progressive groups had managed since the New Century Alliance was set up in 1998. Think tanks, including the Century Foundation, the Center on Budget and Policy Priorities, and the Economic Policy Institute had sharpened their analysis of Social Security privatization proposals and were able to respond quickly to new variations on the theme. The CAF, USAction, and the National Committee to Preserve Social Security and Medicare had developed a formidable ability to get the message out through volunteers around the nation, often community activists and retired union members and their spouses. This network pressured congressional candidates and incumbents to sign the Social Security pledge and held an endless series of meetings in

---

* Bush, as it turned out, was closer to the mark than Gore's conservative economic advisors. GDP actually grew 6.4% in fiscal 2000, according to OMB figures (Historical Tables, Budget of the United States Government, Fiscal Year 2004).

volunteers' homes and community centers to discuss the issue and put more pressure on candidates.

In 2000, the AFL-CIO mounted its biggest election-year issue-based campaign ever. While union membership had continued its long-term decline in the 1990s, union households still went to the polls more heavily than almost any other demographic, and the federation saw Social Security as key to getting the labor vote out. Unlike most other advocacy groups, the AFL-CIO had activists and a strong organization in all fifty states. Early in the 2000 race, it convened more than 100 labor activists in Washington to brief them on the threat to Social Security from privatization.

Attendees returned home to launch federation-financed efforts to educate union members and retirees about the Social Security debate.[9] These groups worked with the AFL-CIO's Washington office and the CAF to fuel the pledge campaign, setting up a website that allowed visitors to see which congressional candidates and incumbents from their state had signed the pledge.[10]

Activists from AFL-CIO unions also bird-dogged Republican candidates, especially at forums where they spoke on Social Security. After it was reported in late July that Bush's largest block of campaign contributions—$7.3 million—came from financial services firms and insurers,[11] the federation's literature began mentioning Bush's ties to Wall Street as well, relieving Gore of the need to "go negative."

The National Committee to Preserve Social Security and Medicare, meanwhile, launched a "Legacy 2000" campaign aimed at getting out the vote among groups of voters most likely to care about Social Security. It also tried to find ways to bring older voters and young workers together by cosponsoring a series of "intergenerational educational events" in California, Massachusetts, New Hampshire, Washington, and Florida.[12]

Women's organizations, too, began mobilizing around Social Security. In early March, more than a month before Gore unveiled his proposals to improve benefits for widows and caregivers, three groups held an all-day workshop at the Brookings Institution in Washington, entitled "Campaign 2000: Protecting and Strengthening Social Security for Women: A Training for Leaders and Activists." By mid-summer, the National Council of Women's Organizations had launched a website, www.women4socialsecurity.org, to alert women to the dangers of privatization.

Progressives had seldom focused on a single issue to the same degree in a presidential campaign, although the 1998 congressional races had hinted at what they could do. Increasingly, they were realizing that Social Security was their strongest election-year card now that the Republican Party was ideologically committed to privatization, and this understanding helped focus their efforts.

In Gore, they had a candidate they felt confident was firmly against partial privatization. He confirmed the view in June, when he announced his own proposal for a retirement savings account system that would be financed separately from Social Security—a scheme the AFL-CIO quickly endorsed.

The Retirement Savings Plus program would cost $200 billion over ten years and would cover only families with incomes up to $100,000 annually. In other words, it was designed to help mainly workers who didn't have the opportunity or wherewithal to contribute to IRAs or 401(k)s. The federal government would encourage them to save by matching their own contributions as follows: $3 for every $1 saved for couples earning less than $30,000 a year, up to $1,000; 1-to-1 for couples earning between $30,000 and $60,000; and 33% for couples earning between $60,000 and $100,000. The menu of investments would be limited to basic categories like corporate stock and broad-based mutual funds and could be used not just for retirement but to fund a college education, buy a first home, or cover major health expenses.

Gore advisor Elaine Kamarck saw Retirement Savings Plus as a way for Gore to address the problem of declining pension coverage in the U.S. Less than 50% of the working population were covered by any kind of pension or retirement savings plan and the bottom third was almost entirely left out of the employer-based system. These people were dependent on Social Security, which wasn't intended to provide them with all or most of their retirement income.[13]

But Gore's other big campaign promise, to pay down the debt and preserve the Social Security trust-fund surplus, complicated matters.

"Saving the surplus was a great policy, but I'm not sure it was great politics," says former Fed governor Alan Blinder, who developed the Retirement Savings Plus proposal. Forced to fit it within the $500 billion limit the Gore campaign had set for its package of tax cuts and new programs, "the details of the [RSP] proposal were dictated by hitting numbers, rather than sticking with sensible policy and then pricing it out."[14]

The plan was less generous than Clinton's USA accounts, which would have given poor families $600 a year, along with matching grants. Gore and his advisors reportedly were concerned the grants would look like welfare. But this also left the candidate open to criticism from Bush that poorer families wouldn't have the means to make contributions that would earn them the matching funds.[15] If Bush suffered from promising too much, Gore suffered from promising too little.

The Bush camp had plenty of other criticisms. They recycled the argument used against Clinton's plan for paying down the federal debt, that it "double counted" the Social Security trust fund assets. They noted that Gore would inject IOUs from general revenues into the trust funds—even though Bush's plan would require the same if his tax revenue growth projections didn't pan out. And they accused Gore of scheming to "raise taxes on our children" to the tune of 25% higher income taxes. This was nowhere in Gore's actual proposals, but was an estimate of what would be needed if Gore's own projections for lowering Social Security costs through debt reduction faltered.

Bush aides applied some of their sharpest words to Retirement Savings Plus—and aimed them squarely at more affluent, conservative voters. Since the accounts were intended to help lower income workers, they amounted to a "tax-redistribution scheme," not a tax cut—in other words, "another open-ended add-on entitlement," a further expansion of the welfare state. "Taxpayers who now pay about two-thirds of the income tax are not eligible to receive any match at all under the Gore proposal," wrote Lindsey. So why, he implied, should they support a plan aimed at creating wealth for the poor?[16]

The Republicans' attempts to fan the flames of class war posed little worry to their Democratic and progressive rivals. But Retirement Savings Plus suffered heavily from Gore's having announced it far into the presidential race, when Bush's offer of private-account carve-outs was already well established in voters' minds. Inevitably, it seemed like a half-hearted attempt to cobble together a response.

* * *

The Gore campaign was still fine-tuning other parts of its positions, even on Social Security. In late May, the vice president suddenly said that he no longer supported investing a portion of the trust funds. This came several months after Clinton had withdrawn the proposal from his own Social Security package, strengthening the impression that the president's thinking and the vice president's weren't well coordinated. In explaining his switch, Gore cited Greenspan's objections that investing the trust fund assets would politicize the stock market, although why this hadn't occurred to him over a year earlier when the Fed chairperson had first made these statements wasn't clear.

"There is a growing sense that Al Gore has never had a conviction which he could not easily change," Bush spokesperson Ari Fleischer said.[17] And Lindsey could legitimately argue that Bush wasn't the only candidate in the race who had shown indications that he might be prepared to cut Social Security benefits. Gore the New Democrat had himself voted to do so, first as a House member and then a senator, in 1977, 1983, and 1993.

In late April, Gore had still not explained how his own $250 billion tax cut would be apportioned nor had he offered details on the $432 billion he had designated to create a Medicare prescription drug benefit—his most attractive initiative and one the Bush campaign was doing very little to match. As the campaign wore on, too, progressives became less enamored of the debt paydown scheme. Some who were firmly in Gore's camp weren't afraid to challenge him on it.

Bob Kuttner went so far as to attack the "needlessly stringent cuts in public outlays that were the excessive part of the 1997 budget deal" that helped create the surplus, and questioned whether the surplus itself was good economics as opposed to just clever politics. In a *Newsweek* article, he noted that the Gore plan would result in total public debt falling to less than 25% of GDP—its lowest level since the Depression. "The Gore camp contends that when the proverbial rainy day comes it will be easier to resort to new public borrowing if we pay the debt down now, while times are good," Kuttner wrote.

But how would Democrats and Republicans agree on what constituted a genuine rainy day?

Realistically, Gore's debt paydown had no greater chance of playing out than Bush's plan to fund private Social Security accounts. Both candidates depended on the ten-year surplus to bring their proposals to life, and just like the Social Security trustees' seventy-five-year fiscal estimates, that surplus was a matter of conjecture. If the economy were to turn sour, tax revenues could shrink. The U.S. could go to war, boosting defense spending. Or a natural disaster could make huge infrastructure repairs or improvements necessary. If any of these things happened, putting the Social Security surplus in a "lockbox" would once again become politically impossible—and both private accounts and debt paydown would once again be mere academic arguments.

Dean Baker and Mark Weisbrot, now heading up their own think tank, the Center for Economic and Policy Research, lamented Gore's decision not to challenge Bush on the assumption that Social Security really was in "crisis." The basic "dishonesty" of the discussion, shared by Gore and other Democrats, they wrote in the *San Francisco Chronicle* in May, is "that Social Security needs to be 'saved.'" Whether he knew it or not, Baker and Weisbrot predicted, "by pretending that the program needs to be 'fixed,' [Gore] undermines confidence in the system and makes it more vulnerable to benefit cuts, or even partial privatization if Bush should win the election."

The Gore campaign made it known that it wasn't happy with Baker and Weisbrot's criticisms.[18] But other mainstream Democrats worried that by yoking his Social Security plan to debt paydown, Gore was making it harder for them to draw a firm distinction for voters between his position and Bush's. The AFL-CIO, in the extensive materials it supplied to its local-level activists and organizers on Social Security, omitted any mention of how Gore's economic plans would help the program. Instead, it emphasized how important Social Security was to workers and their families and how much private accounts would cut into their guaranteed benefits.

At times, Gore seemed downright reluctant to draw the same sharp line in the sand against privatization that his opponent drew in favor of it, suggesting his "populist" conversion was still incomplete. After the candidate promised to sign the Coalition to Save Social Security's anti-privatization pledge at a high-profile appearance before the Service Employees International Union in Pittsburgh in May, Gore's team suddenly told Roger Hickey that the timing and venue weren't right. And this after Hickey had published an op-ed in the *Pittsburgh Post-Gazette* announcing that Gore would do so. The vice president never did sign the pledge—despite the fact that Bush had refused to sign, offering the Democrat another perfect opportunity to attack him on the issue.[19]

Bush, meanwhile, seldom elaborated on his plans for Social Security other than to reiterate his six principles, stress his offer to allow workers more "choice" over their retirement nest eggs, reassure current retirees that their benefits wouldn't be touched, and emphasize his eagerness to lead America in a new start. One commercial, aired in June in southern and southwestern states including retiree-heavy Florida and New Mexico, blended the messages of choice and security of benefits as if they couldn't possibly conflict with each other.

"The Bush plan guarantees everyone at or near retirement every dollar of their benefits," the narrator intoned. "No cuts in Social Security. You paid into it, it's your money, and it will be there for you. And the Bush plan gives younger workers a choice to invest a small part of their Social Security in sound investments they control for higher returns." The visuals juxtaposed a rising sun and Bush shaking seniors' hands with shots of workers, symbolizing the baby boomers, running out of subway cars and up and down escalators.

Bush frustrated his opponent's aides at every turn with his refusal to offer more detail. When Gore accused Bush in June of proposing a plan that would certainly require benefits cuts because it would create fiscal problems for the program years earlier than under its current structure, Bush's response was to brush off the challenge and stay on message.

"My job," he replied, "is to be a leader who says, 'I campaigned on this issue. Here's my framework. Now let us come together to fill out the blanks and the details.' I understand what my opponent is trying to do. He's trying to force me to think like a legislator, but I'm running for president." Of course, Bush took every opportunity to attack the specifics of Gore's proposals: just as a legislator would.[20]

"It's harder to have a real debate on the issues when he refuses to say what he really intends to do," Gore spokesperson Douglas Hattaway complained in May.[21] "We used Social Security to attack them as often as possible," says Kamarck, "but we were disappointed that Bush didn't talk about it more than he did."[22]

* * *

Bush got points from Washington pundits and national editorial writers for his boldness in addressing Social Security. Gore received no such credit, because the central pillar of his economic agenda, debt paydown, was an idea Clinton had been putting into practice for some time. Meanwhile, Gore reinforced his reputation as an impenetrable policy wonk with stump speeches that lingered aggravatingly on the sometimes mystifying mechanics of debt paydown and the lockbox. "I got letters from people asking if the lockbox really has a lock on it," remembers Dana Marie Kennedy, then the Democratic National Committee's director of seniors outreach.[23]

Some Gore aides such as Kamarck argue that the lockbox was an effective metaphor for segregating the Social Security trust funds so that they couldn't be used for anything except paying benefits, and that it only became a liability when some elements of the media began using it as an example of Gore's infatuation with technical detail. And in fact, Gore's scheme to pay down the debt today as a means to bolster Social Security was distinctly less speculative than Bush's proposal to rely on a "temporary" loan of general revenues that wouldn't even be solicited for another twenty-five to thirty years.

But some local-level campaign workers found the lockbox, and Gore's style of presenting his proposals in general, frustratingly disconnected from anything that might appeal to voters' personal interests or desires. Tony Fransetta, who worked on the Gore campaign as head of the Florida chapter of the National Council of Senior Citizens, attended a rally in Orlando late in the campaign that attracted 10,000 people. Gore went over well, he says, "until he started hitting on Social Security. Then the emotion drained out of them. He was not articulating clearly and simply the issues. When he tried to explain the details about the lockbox, he lost them. It made me feel, 'Shit, we're in trouble!' That was probably during the last two or three weeks of the campaign, and I saw it on a couple of other occasions too."[24]

By early October, Gore's relentless efforts to make the lockbox a popular rallying cry were attracting the attention of comedians. A well-executed sketch on NBC's *Saturday Night Live* parodied his fixation on the arcane term, providing easy laughs for TV commentators and print columnists for the rest of the campaign. What they had forgotten was that strictly speaking, the lockbox was actually a point of agreement between Bush and Gore. One of the Republican candidate's five basic principles on Social Security was that all money paid into the trust funds should be dedicated to strengthening the program—exactly the definition of the lockbox.

Vice President Al Gore offers a lesson in Social Security's finances, July 1, 1998. Gore's tendency to wax pedantic and his evident love of the term "lockbox" during his 2000 presidential campaign inspired a popular Saturday Night Live *parody and relieved some of the pressure on Bush to explain his support of privatization.*

CHAPTER 30

THE ROAD TO
FLORIDA

Democratic congressional candidates—those who chose to attack their opponents over Social Security—were more skillful and ruthless at devising their own populist position on the issue. The CAF's pledge drive, aimed at forcing every candidate to declare his or her position on Social Security and Medicare, made no mention of the lockbox, debt paydown, or any other long-term economic goal: just a promise not to privatize the programs.

Candidates in many states jumped at the opportunity to sign the pledge and then to attack their opponents as threatening old-age benefits. Taking a page from the Republicans' book, they ignored the fact that few if any GOP candidates were suggesting a reduction in benefits for current or near retirees and instead happily implied that their opponents were bent on robbing the present-day elderly.

The strategy made sense in part because, over the past three years of intense discussion about privatization, plenty of Republicans had gone public with their support for the idea. In October, the Cato Institute surveyed all House and Senate candidates on the question, "Do you favor or oppose Social Security reform that would allow workers to save a portion of their payroll taxes in a personal retirement account?" While Democrats were overwhelmingly and expectedly negative, Republicans strongly supported partial privatization, underscoring the degree to which this had become party orthodoxy: 259 Republican candidates said they favored payroll tax carve-outs and only 7 were opposed.*

One Republican who seemed especially vulnerable was Clay Shaw, co-author of the previous year's ill-fated Archer-Shaw partial privatization bill. Shaw chaired the House Social Security Subcommittee and represented Florida's 22nd District, which had a larger over-sixty-five population than any other in the U.S. It also took in the state's super-affluent Gold Coast. But the Democrats thought the preponderance of elderly gave them a chance against the ten-termer, and Shaw's race for reelection against Democratic State Rep. Elaine Bloom quickly passed Jim Rogan's as the most expensive House contest in the country. Shaw spent $3 million to Bloom's $2.4 million and Social Security was the focus of their bitterest exchanges. When Bloom ran a television spot denouncing Shaw for voting in favor of privatizing the program, Shaw angrily complained that there had never been any such vote, and Bloom pulled the ad.[1]

Social Security was also the central issue in the year's high-profile Senate races. X-PAC: The Political Action Committee for Generation X, sprung up in June with a website, www.DUMPSANTORUM.COM, targeting Pennsylvania's Rick Santorum, one of the most conservative senators and a strong supporter of partial privatization. "The Senate race in Pennsylvania is going to be one of the closest in this political cycle," said Michael Panetta, X-PAC's executive director, "and this web site will help tilt the scale against Santorum." The senator's Democratic opponent, Ron Klink, reminded voters constantly that he had signed the no-privatization pledge while Santorum hadn't.

* * *

The presidential candidates' speeches at the Democratic and Republican conventions in July and August reinforced the impression Bush had been striving to create—that his "compassionate conservatism" blurred the lines between the two parties. Both speeches stated the candidates' intentions toward Social Security in virtually the same language. "We will strengthen Social Security and Medicare for the greatest generation, and for generations to come," Bush declared. "We will save and strengthen Social Security and Medicare, not only for this generation, but for generations to come," Gore announced. Both leaned heavily on education and prescription drug coverage for the elderly as part of their platforms.

Some pundits nevertheless found Gore's address to be the best, most confident he had given yet, right down to tweaking his own image as a wooden

---

*   Another 154 Republicans either refused to answer the question or were unavailable to give their views.

policy wonk. By the time he delivered it, however, Social Security had already become a bit of a sore point for Gore. His running mate, Connecticut Sen. Joe Lieberman, like Gore a longtime DLC member, had until very recently identified himself as a supporter of partially privatizing Social Security. "I think in the end that individual control of part of the retirement–Social Security funds has to happen," he told a reporter in May 1998, at the height of the Clinton White House's efforts to engage the public on the issue.

Lieberman had never voted on any matter related to privatization and had never said specifically what kind of private investment scheme he would support, and after accepting the vice presidential nomination, he quickly disavowed his previous point of view. But this only spawned a host of derisive comments from the right about the "flip-flops" the Democratic leadership was forcing him to execute in order to become the socially conservative, pro-business counterbalance to Gore, the reborn populist.

"Take Social Security, where Gore has been claiming the world will end if, as Bush proposes, younger voters can invest some of their own funds. Oops. Lieberman agrees with Bush," columnist Deborah Orin commented in the *New York Post*.

In response, Lieberman's office released an unpublished op-ed it said the senator had written in June at the Gore campaign's request, entitled "My Private Journey Away From Privatization." In it, he wrote that he "turned away from privatization because the promises and the numbers supporting them don't add up." Elaine Kamarck says Lieberman had indeed made his own mind up that he opposed privatization months before Gore asked him to join the ticket, and for the same reason the vice president had: the transition costs, topping $1 trillion, were overwhelming.[2] On CNN's *Larry King Live*, Lieberman complained that "the Bush campaign has taken some comments a couple of years ago and made them into holy writ. It is not true. I was intrigued with the idea of privatization of part of Social Security."

Gore nevertheless got a bounce from the convention, just as Bush had after the Republican gathering. A *New York Times*/CBS News survey held before the Los Angeles convention showed him supported by 75% of respondents who identified as Democrats, versus 86% support for Bush from Republicans. After the Democratic convention, however, Gore's Democratic backing was 84% and he was pulling even with Bush in some polls.

He quickly moved to exploit his jump in popularity in the states his advisors anticipated would be decisive in November, especially Florida. Gore visited Florida three times in the ten days up to Labor Day and his aides said Lieberman would campaign there at least once a week from then until the election. By Labor Day Gore was already buying television time in Tampa, Orlando, and West Palm Beach. Within the following week he began hitting Miami and Tallahassee as well.

By then, the Bush campaign was already announcing plans to spend some $5 million to $7 million on TV ads in twenty-one states, including Florida and others where Social Security would be important, such as Michigan, Ohio, Pennsylvania, Wisconsin, Arkansas, Delaware, Washington, Louisiana, and Missouri. The latest of these featured Bush at the convention making his pledge to "strengthen Social Security and Medicare for the greatest generation and for generations to come," intermingled with shots of retirees.

Meanwhile, the Coalition to Save Social Security was busy rallying local groups that opposed privatization, to push candidates to sign the pledge. Through September and into October, new names continued to appear, generating a steady stream of press events that showcased local organizers. And by mid-September, Gore's approach to pressing his modestly progressive platform seemed to be working, as a Pew Research Center survey of 1,495 likely voters found him running ahead of Bush, 48% to 43%. He was showing strength especially among the groups his aides most hoped he would appeal to: "people with family incomes under $50,000, and among people without college degrees," according to Democratic pollster Guy Molyneux.[3]

Seniors were still crucial to the anti-privatization coalition, which spent the weeks leading up to the first Bush-Gore debate on October 3 fashioning events that would attract retirees living on Social Security to hear what Gore's supporters expected would be his trouncing of Bush on the issue. The National Committee to Preserve Social Security and Medicare, for example, announced that "Boston-area seniors" were invited to gather at Marina Place, "a senior living residence," to watch and discuss the debate, which was being held at the nearby University of Massachusetts campus.

"With only weeks left until the election," the National Committee said in a press advisory, "this debate will be a clear opportunity for seniors to hear where the two candidates stand. Seniors made up 20% of the vote in the 1996 presidential election and will be a heavy force again this year," it reminded reporters.

* * *

Media coverage of preparations for the three October debates focused more on how the candidates' personalities came across than on the substance of their proposals. Would Gore appear too wooden and wonkish? Would Bush demonstrate the necessary gravity? Bush ultimately gained the most from the debates by staying on message throughout, while Gore veered from a mild approach in the first round to attacking his opponent unrelentingly in the second, to finally finding the middle ground in the third.

Bush used Social Security and the proposed Medicare prescription drug benefit to accuse Gore and Clinton of not having acted to resolve the country's problems over the past eight years. Bush also echoed op-eds by his advisors Lindsey and Feldstein, attacking Gore's proposals for using the surplus for debt paydown as, in fact, a dangerous expansion of the national debt. "What he's doing is loading up IOUs for future generations. He puts no real assets in the Social Security system."

But Bush hammered hardest on his twin promises: to seniors, that he wouldn't reduce their benefits; to younger workers, that they would have choice and clear ownership of their payroll taxes. And it was on choice and ownership that he drew the firmest distinction between his plan and Gore's.

"That's a difference of opinion," he said. "The vice president thinks it's the government's money. The payroll taxes are your money. You ought to put it in prudent, safe investments so that $1 trillion, over the next ten years, grows to be $3 trillion." Bush condemned the current system as a bad investment and urged voters to think not of what it did for them but of what they could do with the money instead.

In responding, Gore did what many of his supporters were hoping he wouldn't. He stressed the lockbox, and tried to explain how entitlements and the trust funds work, while assuming they understood the benefits of debt pay-down. Gore, the policy nerd, was explaining to voters why his Social Security plan was good for the national bookkeeping, not why it was good for them. And he broke all the rules of success in a presidential debate in a disastrous attempt to paint Bush into a corner on the budget.

"I know we're not supposed to answer—ask each other questions, but I'd be interested in knowing, does that trillion dollars [to pay for Bush's private accounts] come from the trust fund or does it come from the rest of the budget?" Gore asked.

"No," Bush neatly responded. "There's enough money to pay seniors and the current affairs of Social Security. The trillion comes from the surplus. Surplus is more—is money, more money than needed." This wasn't true, of course. When Bush's tax-cut proposal was added to his private-account plan, his plan would use up nearly the entire surplus, and perhaps all of it if the economy turned sour. But the larger point was made. Bush saw the surplus as an opportunity to change the role of government. Gore saw it as an accounting exercise.

Gore succeeded on Social Security, some of his advisors felt, when he stuck closest to how the system impacted people's lives. "I think it's very important to understand that cutting benefits under Social Security means that people like Winifred Skinner from Des Moines, Iowa, who's here, would really have a much harder time," he said. "Because there are millions of seniors who are living hand to mouth. And you talk about cutting benefits, I don't go along with that." Bush's proposal, he said, would "divert one out of every six dollars off into the stock market, which means that he would drain a trillion dollars out of the Social Security trust fund over the, in this generation, over the next ten years, and Social Security under that approach would go bankrupt within this generation."

Lost in the shuffle, seemingly, were Gore's Retirement Savings Accounts. And completely unmentioned in the first debate were Gore's proposals to improve Social Security for women and caregivers. Concern about the surplus, just as surely as concern over the deficit, had once again ruled out any opportunity for the Democrat to discuss improving the program, it seemed.

The irony was that both candidates were trying, not all that convincingly, to frame themselves as political mavericks—Gore as a reborn "populist," Bush as a Texas individualist unconnected to Washington. Yet their fundamental analyses of Social Security's problems placed them both firmly in line with establishment public policy thinking. Both viewed the surplus in basically the same way: as a means to overcome a future spending crunch brought about by the retirement needs of the baby boomers. Gore would pay down the debt; Bush would "pay" the boomers' successors to make their own investment decisions by giving them back some of their payroll taxes.

The only candidate who questioned the assumptions behind their proposals wasn't allowed to take part in the debates by the Democratic-Republican junta that controlled them. Ralph Nader was grabbing attention as the Green Party standard bearer, much of it from the younger voters Bush coveted. Nader had brought Dean Baker aboard his campaign to advise him on Social Security and other economic issues. Baker, fed up with the Democrats' willingness to accept the assumption that the program faced a major crisis, helped Nader put together a position that was dramatically different from either the Republican or Democratic candidates.'

"The idea that Social Security is going to run out of money is simply nonsense," Nader told any reporter who would listen. The program's base was "extremely solid" and could continue to pay full benefits until 2037 even if the trustees' forecast of an anemic 1.7% average annual growth rate came true.[4] Nader attacked Bush's plan to partially privatize the system as "unsound policy," although he didn't directly comment on Gore's debt-paydown alternative.

The urgent need, he said, was rather to improve Social Security for widows and widowers, pointing to the continuing 20% poverty rate among older women living alone. "If a small amount of additional revenue is in fact needed," he said, "this can be provided by raising the income cap on Social Security or expanding the tax to cover executive bonuses and stock options."

But the night Bush and Gore dug into the issue in their first debate, Nader wasn't there to present his argument. He had been thrown out of the auditorium at the University of Massachusetts, despite having acquired a ticket from a student. Reporters and TV and radio news crews rarely asked him about Social Security as the campaign wore down. And his opponents showed no signs of noticing any of his positions, other than to speculate obsessively on whether Nader might take votes away from Gore. In August, when Nader held a press conference specifically to discuss Social Security, none of the major U.S. media except the *New York Times* and Associated Press showed up—not even the *Washington Post*, despite the fact that the press conference took place only two blocks from the *Post*'s headquarters building.[5]

* * *

The candidates didn't mention Social Security often in the second and third debates. Both focused increasingly on Medicare and Social Security in the final weeks of the campaign, however, especially as Florida became a battleground state. A *New York Times*/CBS poll in late October showed Gore slightly ahead of Bush with all age groups and most clearly with respondents aged sixty-five and older. The elderly, who made up a third of the state's electorate and 94% of whom said they would definitely vote, also opposed partial privatization of Social Security by a wide margin.

Gore pressed his advantage by focusing the majority of his television ads on the issue. His campaign placed thousands of phone calls to Florida voters in which actor Edward Asner told them the Bush Social Security scheme "would undermine" the program. By Election Day, Gore's commercials airing in Florida were overwhelmingly aimed at seniors, hammering home the point that Bush's plan would strip nearly $1 trillion from the Social Security trust funds over ten years.[6]

Bush, who was campaigning in Florida with his brother, Gov. Jeb Bush, at about the same time the *Times*/CBS poll came out, accused Gore of using "scare tactics" on the elderly. "Let's tell Ed Asner to go back to Hollywood where he belongs!" Jeb exhorted the crowd at one rally. The Bush campaign launched a telephone counterattack featuring his mother, former First Lady Barbara Bush, and Gulf War commander Gen. Norman Schwarzkopf reassuring voters that the candidate wasn't threatening their benefits. For younger voters, Bush plucked out a scary number of his own: $40 trillion, the debt he estimated Social Security would have accumulated by mid-century under the Gore plan.

The National Committee to Preserve Social Security and Medicare meanwhile launched the largest "get out the vote" campaign in its history, concentrating on Florida. It mailed close to 35,000 postcards to seniors in October while its field staff distributed 20,000 one-page "slim jims" explaining why the election would be vital to Social Security. In at least one rural area, the National Committee teamed with the NAACP and with elder activist groups including the National Association of Area Agencies on Aging, Meals on Wheels, and the Coalition of Black Trade Unionists, to pay for buses to pick up elderly people and take them to the polls.

Nationwide, both campaigns were fully focused on Social Security by the final week. The Democratic Party's ads "obsessively attack Bush over Social Security as if it were the only issue in the campaign," observed *Washington Post* reporter Dana Milbank.[7] The Gore camp started a new website, www.bushin-security.com, to attack the Republican's Social Security and Medicare plans. The candidate devoted his final, $15 million weekend television ad blitz to two new Social Security spots, while the Republican National Committee vowed to outspend him by $18 million, including a sum for an ad that raised doubts about Gore's credibility on the issue.[8]

The RNC said that nearly half of its $6 million TV ad budget for the last week of the campaign would go for Social Security ads in Florida. The Alliance for Worker Retirement Security, the National Association of Manufacturers' Astroturf group, took out additional ads in Florida and Pennsylvania—another battleground state for the senior vote—defending private accounts. And the Bush campaign, as part of an effort to reach African-American voters with their candidate's stand on education, began running a commercial on the issue that showed Bush speaking in front of a backdrop that featured a Social Security card and a black man.

Both candidates harnessed a piece of the FDR legacy for the final push. Gore had FDR's grandson, James Roosevelt, Jr., speak to retirees in Pennsylvania, while Bush tapped another grandson, Elliott Roosevelt, to promote his plan to seniors in Ohio. But by the final week, the "scare tactics" that the Republicans complained about were beginning to work for Gore and the Democrats.

More than eighty of the party's House and Senate candidates had signed the no-privatization pledge by the end of October and grassroots groups opposed to privatization were fully mobilized against Bush. The National Council of Senior Citizens mailed 90,000 fliers to its Florida members warning them that trust fund money would be "diverted" into younger workers' private accounts. Labor-funded retiree groups in Pennsylvania, meanwhile, said they were planning to make at least two calls to all 1.25 million current and retired union members in the state before the election.

One problem, some Bush supporters worried, was that their candidate was failing to effectively counter Gore's ceaselessly repeated warning about the $1 trillion Bush would drain out of Social Security. One Bush commercial called that charge "nonsense" without elaborating, and tried instead to change the subject to Gore's history of dubious statements on other topics. Most fundamentally, as some of Bush's advisors admitted after the election, Gore seemed to have a game plan for closing the campaign while their candidate didn't. The Democrat concentrated on the swing states of Florida, Wisconsin, and Michigan, and especially on tying up crucial seniors' votes, while Bush, perhaps overconfident, made whirlwind visits to such states as California and New Jersey, where his chances of winning were small.

Bush made perhaps the worst gaffe of his campaign just five days before the election. Speaking in St. Charles, Missouri, he returned to his pledge to let younger workers invest part of their payroll tax contribution. "This frightens some in Washington," he said. "Because they want the federal government controlling the Social Security like it's some kind of federal program. We understand differently though. You see, it's your money, not the government's money." Bush's staff complained loudly to the press that the remark was just a slip of the tongue, but it was too late. "Do you want to entrust the Oval Office to somebody who doesn't even know that Social Security is a federal program?" Gore queried a rally of students in Iowa the next day.[9]

Such slips hurt Bush as Election Day neared, Scott Reed, who ran Dole's 1996 campaign, told the *New York Times*. "Gore closed very strong, picking up on the Bush mistake of Social Security not being a government program," said Reed. "He used it in his free media and paid media to clobber us. Clearly, Gore picked up a bunch of senior votes near the end." Days before the election, Gore was pressing home this advantage with email exhortations to his campaign activists to "call Seniors in your neighborhood and offer to take them to the polls on Tuesday!"

Some Bush supporters believe he lost confidence in his own rhetoric about Social Security in the final weeks as Gore appeared to be gaining elder votes in the swing states, softening his message to appeal more to seniors. Voters heard far less of Bush's visionary talk about the investor class and choice for younger workers and more blanket denials that he would touch seniors' benefits. And so the aura of leadership and optimistic vision that had helped propel Bush in the early polling wore off as he attempted to defend himself against Gore's attacks.[10]

* * *

Picking apart Social Security's impact on the 2000 election, and the election's impact on the Social Security debate, is easier than deciding who actually won the race for president. Officially, Gore took the popular vote and Bush the electoral vote, although many Democrats will heatedly disagree with the latter for many years to come. Whichever way one chose to view it, however, Gore's late surge, with its tight focus on Bush's position on Social Security, wasn't enough to give him a clear-cut victory in the Electoral College.

The Republicans found themselves with a Senate majority of just one vote compared with the four-vote advantage they had enjoyed before. But their House majority held comparatively steady at 220 to 211, down two seats. And while Congress shifted somewhat against Social Security privatization, the degree of movement wasn't that great. Of the seventy-six House incumbents and first-time candidates who signed the pledge against privatizing Social Security, fifty-seven won. But only two of these were first-timers. And anti-privatization candidates for the House and Senate won only ten of eighteen races that the National Committee to Preserve Social Security and Medicare had targeted, leaving open to question just how successful the group's get-out-the-vote effort had been.

Eight of ten Senate incumbents and first-time candidates who signed the pledge won, but the Democrats' performance in ousting incumbents who supported privatization wasn't as bright as they had expected. In Michigan, Debbie Stabenow defeated Spencer Abraham; in Florida, Bill Nelson beat Rep. Bill McCollum to replace Republican Sen. Connie Mack; and New York voters replaced the pro-privatization Pat Moynihan, who was retiring, with Hillary Rodham Clinton, who had signed the pledge. Moynihan's legislative partner on Social Security, Bob Kerrey, retired too and was replaced in the Senate by Ben Nelson, who was against privatization.

But in Pennsylvania, a state with a large elderly population, the big push to replace Santorum with Klink failed, although Klink's supporters blamed the loss on a fractured state Democratic organization far more than voter affinity for the incumbent's ideas on Social Security.[11] Still, the anti-privatization forces made major progress in 2000. They had replaced two of privatization's key champions in the Senate with opponents and had achieved their goal—set two years before when the New Century Alliance was created—of "repoliticizing" Social Security: making opposition to privatization an article of faith for Democratic candidates and lawmakers.

"There would be no more Concord Coalition–style debates on the issue," says Hans Riemer, who gives Gore a great deal of credit for disarming center-right deficit hawks like Moynihan and Kerrey by making Social Security the center of his campaign. "We got a Senate that would never vote for privatization because Gore brought the whole party along."[12]

The most striking thing about the exit polls on November 7, however, was how far down Social Security appeared on most voters' priority lists, given the nearly obsessive campaigning around it, especially during the last weeks.

CNN's poll revealed 18% of voters said the economy and jobs were the issues that mattered most to them, followed by 15% for education and 14% each for taxes and Social Security. Thirty percent said education should be the new president's top priority, followed by 26% for a tax cut and 23% for Social Security—high, but clearly not their biggest concern. Bush voters appeared to have been motivated far more by the prospect of a tax cut than by any other issue, including Social Security. Fully 80% called taxes the issue that mattered most, and 71% said taxes should be the new president's top priority.

Most disappointing for Bush strategists, their candidate failed to win the youth vote, making it difficult for him to back up his claim that a new generation of risk-taking Americans was turning out in support of his Social Security proposal. First-time voters and those aged eighteen to twenty-nine, who had supported Clinton four years before, also supported Gore this time, although by smaller margins, according to *Washington Post* exit polls. The 2000 election also handed back to the Democrats the older and retired voters they had lost in 1996 and 1998. Polls of voters sixty and older, by the nonpartisan Voter News Service, showed that they picked Gore over Bush, 51% to 47%, while those over sixty-five backed Gore by 50% to 47%.

That Social Security remained a more effective tool for bringing out Democratic voters than Republicans isn't surprising. One out of four voters in 2000 came from union households that overwhelmingly supported the program as it was, and union organizers and other voter-activist organizations that had rallied around Social Security during Clinton's flirtation with privatization continued to work hard to get out voters in swing states.[13] The privatization movement had no "grassroots" voter organizing initiatives focused on the issue. Cato's Michael Tanner later wondered if it had been a strategic mistake to leave the job of articulating the free-market position on Social Security largely to Bush and the other Republican candidates.[14]

Some experts suggested the Democrats might have relied too heavily on Social Security.[15] Gore split the senior vote with Bush almost evenly in Florida, despite his relentless campaigning there.[16] The one Florida House race in which Social Security played a major role, Shaw's race for reelection against Elaine Bloom, was also one of the closest in the country, the Republican incumbent edging out his opponent by just 599 votes on the first ballot count. But that outcome guaranteed two more years of high-seniority service in the House for one of privatization's biggest champions.

PART VI

The Ownership Society

(2001–05)

CHAPTER 31

THE VANISHING SURPLUS

A raucous crowd of protesters filled a good part of Pennsylvania Avenue on a gray January 20, 2001: Inauguration Day. Disappointed Democrats, outraged at what they regarded as a stolen election, chanted "Not Our President!" as a motorcade bearing the new Republican officeholders cruised down the boulevard. The limousines were tightly sealed; when new Vice President Dick Cheney stretched his arm out to wave to the crowd, some not-so-fresh fruit and vegetables came flying and he quickly rolled his window back up.

Presidential inaugurals generally favor high-flown rhetoric about American values rather than details of public policy, but George W. Bush included one explicit policy pledge in his inaugural address—one he must have known wouldn't please the protesters lining Pennsylvania Avenue, Gore voters and anarchists alike. "We will reform Social Security and Medicare," the new president promised, "sparing our children from struggles we have the power to prevent."

The new president was making history. "Reforming" Social Security and Medicare had never before been mentioned in a presidential inaugural. The 20,000-some protesters facing the new president out of a crowd estimated at

300,000[1] on Inauguration Day 2001 represented, in part, the remains of the Democratic coalition. Bush was not speaking to them. Instead, he was addressing a group of younger voters, nurtured in the new economic landscape of the past two decades and accustomed to believing that investing in the private sector, not any government program, was the key to their prosperity.

How large the number of people in this new "investor class," and how firmly attached to the belief that their parents had become a threat to their economic well being, wasn't yet known. But already at a luncheon in his honor during the Republican convention the previous summer, Larry Lindsey had told an audience "top-heavy with CEOs" that his boss would make Social Security his top priority, overhauling the program within six months of assuming office.

* * *

When the new administration occupied the White House, however, its first priority was taxes. Clinton had frustrated the Republican leadership's desire for a big tax cut to the last, and they were determined to get one through right away. Social Security would come next, despite exit polls on Election Day showing that more voters preferred to use the surplus to help Social Security than to give it away in a tax cut.[2] The Congressional Budget Office was estimating the federal revenue surplus over the next ten years at nearly $4.6 trillion, a bit more than half of which would come from excess Social Security revenues. Rumor had it that the CBO would add another trillion over the next few months, none of it from payroll taxes.[3] Even if the program was left completely alone, there was enormous room for tax breaks—if the Republicans took advantage.

So it seemed. By the end of 2000, however, the economy was clearly slowing, the stock market was slumping as well, and those CBO forecasts were in jeopardy. Under the circumstances, it might be easier to muscle a big tax cut package through the evenly divided Senate than to knit together a bipartisan coalition to restructure Social Security, with all the compromises that would inevitably entail. And far more inspiring to the Republican "base."

Yet Bush wasn't taking Social Security off the table. Securities and financial firms, which stood to gain the most from privatization, had topped his list of campaign donors.[4] They were pushing first and foremost for $400 billion in tax breaks to encourage employers to offer more IRAs and 401(k)s. "That's our one, blinding-sun issue," said Steve Bartlett, president of the Financial Services Roundtable. But they were also urging action on Social Security.[5]

Bush's choice as Treasury secretary, announced December 21, was Paul O'Neill, retiring CEO of aluminum giant Alcoa, who had served at OMB in the Ford administration and was a friend of Vice President-elect Dick Cheney. When then-Treasury Secretary George Shultz testified before Congress in 1973 about Social Security's fiscal straits, O'Neill briefed him for the task. O'Neill also served on the 1991 Social Security Advisory Council.

At his confirmation hearing, he said the prospect of fixing Social Security was what "convinced me that it was appropriate for me to accept the challenge to return to public service." But Cheney's main motivation for picking O'Neill was his long friendship with Greenspan, who would have to be on board for the new administration to sell a new round of tax cuts to Congress.[6]

By mid-January, the idea of a Social Security commission, which Moynihan and Kerrey had pushed the previous year, was taking hold. In the Senate, John McCain was drawing up legislation to create such a panel, while Rep. Rob Portman of Ohio, a close Bush advisor, was writing a similar bill in the House. But Bush himself said he didn't want a commission to be another way of shelving the issue. "I want the commission, if there is a commission, [to be] one that is action-oriented," he said.[7]

But the tax cut would come first. The day after the president's inauguration, Sens. Phil Gramm and Zell Miller, the conservative Georgia Democrat, introduced the president's $1.6 trillion package in the Senate under the title, Economic Growth and Tax Relief Reconciliation Act of 2001. While the details were likely to change considerably, the idea was to focus Congress's agenda on tax cuts before anything distracted it.

The CBO quickly revealed what this meant. The bureau's new projections showed the surplus hitting $5.6 trillion over the next decade. But $2.49 trillion of that was the surplus in the Social Security trust funds, which Congress had agreed to keep off the table. There was a $400 billion Medicare surplus, also covered by that agreement, plus $300 billion to $400 billion in additional interest costs on the federal debt. All of that, plus the tax cut, would leave only a few hundred billion for other new initiatives.

Some of these were bound to be funded, perhaps generously so. The bottom line: Bush was planning to burn through the surplus. The obvious question: how much longer could the Social Security portion stay locked away?

Some people who had worked for a bipartisan restructuring of Social Security under Clinton wondered whether Bush wasn't cutting the legs out from under his Social Security commission before it had a chance to meet. Gene Sperling, now with the Brookings Institution, noted that the surplus was the one thing that made consideration of any change to the program possible, from private accounts to investing the trust fund assets directly, because it would be key to covering the transition costs.

As Bush's tax cut "depletes the general revenue surpluses, it depletes the chances for any president or Congress in the near future to pass long-lasting reform," Sperling wrote in the *New York Times*[8]—especially, he might have added, if Congress again got used to relying on the Social Security surpluses to pay for its tax cuts and other giveaways.

The administration's preliminary 2002 budget blueprint, released on February 28, revealed more about the Bush priorities. While his tax cut package included more incentives for IRAs and 401(k)s, which would benefit mainly better-off workers, the budget blueprint eliminated First Accounts, a modest program to help underprivileged people get access to bank accounts and other financial services. The military and education would see generous increases in spending, but environmental and agricultural projects would be cut. And in a sign of what was in store for Social Security, the Medicare surplus wouldn't be walled off, but placed in a "contingency reserve" that could be used to fund additional defense spending. Senate Republicans were of the same mind. In February they rejected two proposals to place the Medicare surplus in a lockbox.

The ten-year tax cut that finally passed the House and Senate was a virtual kaleidoscope, changing shape depending on which of those years one was looking at. Several of the tax breaks were to phase in gradually; one such was for the estate tax, which would only be fully repealed in 2010. And in an extraordinary sleight of hand, which one Capitol Hill insider reportedly called "the miracle of the loaves and fishes,"[9] the whole package would be repealed in 2011 to stay within the ten-year surplus projection without cutting into the Social Security and Medicare surpluses. This launched a new drama that would play itself out in Washington for the remainder of the Bush administration, with Republicans pressing for permanent extension of the tax cuts, and Democrats—those who followed their leaders, anyway—urging that they be allowed to die.

The Republicans had what they had sought since they took over Congress in 1994: a signature tax cut comparable in size to the one Reagan had pushed through in 1981. This victory was one more step along the road to, perhaps, eliminating the income and capital gains taxes completely, shrinking the non-defense portions of government, and in so doing, rewarding the well-heeled individuals who bankrolled their continuing "revolution." Along the way, they would again have the chance to prove that sweeping tax cuts could revive a sagging economy and spur growth.

Much of the criticism the Bush tax cut received in succeeding months centered on its effect on Social Security and Medicare. "Extending the fully implemented tax bill through the following decade," wrote Robert Reischauer, "would require digging deeply into the Medicare and Social Security trust funds or dramatically reducing basic government services."[10] Economist and *New York Times* columnist Paul Krugman estimated that it would reduce revenues by $4 trillion over the next decade—"especially damaging," he wrote, when the baby boomers would start collecting Social Security and Medicare benefits at just about the end of that time period.[11] Yet when push came to shove, and money from the trust funds was needed to fund more tax cuts or new spending initiatives, Krugman predicted, "we'll be told that this doesn't matter, that the trust fund is a mere accounting fiction."[12]

Sure enough, by mid-July, White House budget director Mitchell Daniels was forecasting a surplus 20% lower than the CBO had projected two months earlier. A little over a month later, the situation had grown drastically worse. CBO was now estimating the non-Social Security surplus at a mere $600 million for the current fiscal year, down from $122 billion projected in April. Daniels shifted to emphasizing the total surplus, including the Social Security trust funds, which, he said, would still be the second largest on record. The days of the lockbox were over.

Congressional Republicans said the deterioration would just make it easier for them to push their other objective: spending cuts. "The budget is tight, and that's exactly what we designed and exactly what we wanted," said House Budget Committee chair Jim Nussle of Iowa.[13] Bush himself opened the door a crack to the possibility of dipping into Social Security. "I've said the only reasons we should use Social Security funds is in the case of an economic recession or war," he said.[14] By the end of August, the CBO was predicting that the downturn would force him to do so, probably before the end of the year, with the tax cuts responsible for two-thirds of surplus shrinkage.

But the vanishing surplus was also giving Democrats a useful line of attack; the Republicans had endangered Social Security and destroyed any opportunity of addressing a host of other issues, from preschool construction to defense. "It is now clear that the president will be raiding Social Security and Medicare even when he is forecasting strong economic growth," said North Dakota Democrat Sen. Kent Conrad. The Republican National Committee retaliated by taking out a series of TV ads accusing the Democrats of misleading the public, coupled with a new website, www.PROTECTSOCIALSECURITY. COM. The campaign would focus particularly on Missouri and South Dakota, the home states of the party leaders Gephardt and Daschle.

CHAPTER 32

A ZERO-TO-ONE SHOT

Passage of the landmark Bush tax cut was still a month away when the administration unveiled its 2002 budget proposal, finalized from the draft that had appeared in February. Democrats immediately jumped on it for underestimating the cost of some of the new president's initiatives. Adding a prescription drug benefit for Medicare recipients, for example, over ten years, would cost nearly twice the $153 billion Bush budgeted for it. The opposition also noted a vaguely worded $600 billion earmark for changes to Social Security over the same period.

That was a comedown from statements the White House had made in February, when it proposed to set aside $1 trillion over ten years to "rescue" Social Security. Three days after the final budget proposal was unveiled, however, O'Neill told reporters that the president would soon name a blue-ribbon commission to explore the options for restructuring the program. "As soon as we're done with this round of tax initiatives, we need to turn our attention to Social Security," the Treasury secretary said, adding that it would be "not responsible" to postpone action for another four or eight years.[1]

More details emerged in the weeks following. The commission would be split evenly, seven Republicans and seven Democrats, and would aim to give its report to the president by fall so that legislation could be drafted in 2002. But congressional Democrats were already concerned about the instructions Bush was planning to give to the panel.

"The commission should be able to consider all options without being constrained by any preconditions," Gephardt wrote in a letter to the president. "For example, it should not be charged with recommending how to privatize Social Security." It should "be truly bipartisan in its membership," meaning not just with equal numbers from both parties but with a separately appointed chair who "should be a consensus candidate selected by both Republicans and Democrats." Gephardt also asked that the commission staff, who would play a key role in shaping the panel's recommendations, be appointed half by the Democratic congressional leadership and half by the Republican. Above all, the Democrats wanted the commission not to be ideologically one-sided.

When the president named his panel in early May, it did indeed have two co-chairs, a Democrat and a Republican. Neither was chosen with any input from congressional Democrats, however. Half the membership were Republicans, half Democrats, as were the commission staff, but it wasn't ideologically mixed. In fact, there was an explicit litmus test as to who could serve and who couldn't.

"The White House did not hide that the commission ... had been screened to ensure that its members would overwhelmingly or perhaps

President Bush introduces his Commission to Strengthen Social Security, May 2, 2001. Directly behind Bush and to the right are the co-chairs, former Sen. Daniel Patrick Moynihan (D-NY) and Richard D. Parsons, co-chief operating officer of AOL Time Warner.

unanimously endorse private accounts," the *New York Times* reported. In fact, the executive order creating it explicitly stated that any plan it developed "must include individually controlled, voluntary personal retirement accounts, which will augment the Social Security safety net." That left ambiguous whether the accounts would be carved out of payroll taxes or add-ons to the existing program, but suggested strongly that younger workers' needs would be its centerpiece.

At a Rose Garden ceremony on May 2, Bush introduced the sixteen-member President's Commission to Strengthen Social Security. "We can postpone action no longer," he said. "Social Security is a challenge now. If we fail to act, it will become a crisis." His press secretary, Ari Fleischer, confidently declared, "America increasingly has a new class of people, the investor class," who would support the president's framework for change.

The co-chairs, both on record supporting private accounts, were the newly retired senator Pat Moynihan, and a representative of corporate America, Richard Parsons, co-chief operating officer of media behemoth AOL Time Warner. Moynihan was now a fixture as the leading Democratic sponsor of legislation to partially privatize Social Security. Parsons, a Republican and the personal choice of Bush advisor Karl Rove,[2] had known Moynihan for years and served in the Nixon administration with him before moving into the private sector. He hadn't previously been active in the Social Security debate, but was on record favoring private accounts.

The other members were similarly on record, some prominently so. They included: Carolyn Weaver, still at the American Enterprise Institute; John Cogan of the Hoover Institution at Stanford, a longtime Social Security critic who had advised the Bush campaign on budget and tax matters; Thomas Saving, a conservative economist at Texas A&M University and the ultra-right, Dallas-based National Center for Policy Analysis, who had recently been appointed a public trustee of Social Security by Clinton;* former Rep. Bill Frenzel of Minnesota, co-chair of a deficit reduction advocacy group called the Committee for a Responsible Federal Budget; Sam Beard, still running his privatization advocacy group, Economic Security 2000; Estelle James, the former World Bank economist, who was the principal author of its landmark study on pension privatization; former Rep. Tim Penny of Minnesota, Frenzel's co-chair of the Committee for a Responsible Federal Budget; Olivia Mitchell, executive director of the Wharton School's Pension Research Council; Robert Pozen, vice chairman of Fidelity Investments, who had served on the National Commission on Retirement Policy with James; and Robert

---

* Saving coined one of the privatization movement's most dubious clichés in a 1995 article, declaring, in a doubtless unintentional evocation of the moral squalor of Vietnam, "Strange as it sounds, we must destroy the Social Security system, as we know it, to save it" (quoted in press release, "Bush Social Security Commission Members: Who Are They?" Campaign for America's Future, May 2001).

Johnson, CEO of Black Entertainment Television, who had been helpful to the Bush White House during the tax-cut fight by defending repeal of the estate tax as being good for minorities.

The Bush Social Security commission presented a semblance of diversity, but with the emphasis on ideological correctness. Compared with the fifteen-member Greenspan commission of nearly two decades earlier, five of its members were minorities versus none and it included four women as opposed to just two. But the White House seated no representatives from the labor movement. The Bush commission instead was top-heavy with financial and investment industry executives.

Bush's choices for the commission staff were ideologically slanted as well. Andrew Biggs, a staff economist, was assistant director of Cato's Project on Social Security Privatization. Cato's media spokesperson, Randy Clerihue, joined the commission in the same role. Other staffers came from the Alliance for Worker Retirement Security.[3] One of these was the chief of staff, Chuck Blahous, formerly Judd Gregg's staff analyst on Social Security and Medicare and now a member of the White House's National Economic Council (NEC). Before his appointment to the NEC, Blahous had been executive director of the alliance. He also enjoyed a close relationship with Moynihan and had written extensively in favor of privatization. He had no strong connections to anyone on the anti-privatization side.

The commission labored under a clear weakness from the start: it included no prominent members of Congress—indeed, not a single lawmaker. Rove claims that Moynihan and Parsons reached out to Democratic leaders on the Hill, who "blew them off."[4] But no Republican lawmaker agreed to participate either. Daschle quickly labeled the Bush panel "a completely orchestrated effort to come to a desired result."[5] Blahous's and Biggs's presence, like that of virtually every other commission member, suggested just that.

Serious doubts about the prospects and even the political wisdom of launching the commission were surfacing even before it was formally announced. Republican leaders privately worried that it could cause them problems in the 2002 elections. "This will be our plan, and Democrats will hang it around our necks," one Bush aide told the *Wall Street Journal*.

Another concern was the stock market. The downturn that had begun in 2000 was continuing, and with it fears that the tech-stock bubble was collapsing. In the first three months of 2001, the NASDAQ 100 index, which tracked the highest-flying stocks of the Internet era, lost 32.8% of its value, while the more staid Standard & Poor's 500 dropped more than 12%.[6]

Throughout the second half of the 1990s, the great selling point of private Social Security accounts had been the opportunity to get rich off equities. With stocks trending distinctly down, that argument was a lot more problematic, some Republican lawmakers worried. "It doesn't look like we're going to get to it before the market goes up," said a worried Clay Shaw. The Democrats were happy to encourage this kind of thinking. "After the last six months in the stock market I am shocked that the president would really be trying to move forward with this proposal," Gephardt said.[7]

Economic jitters were indeed affecting public support for privatization. Approval of the changes Bush had outlined dropped from 64% in May 2000 to 52% in March, according to a *Washington Post*/ABC News poll.

* * *

As the Bush commission got to work, the debate quickly centered around two related matters, transition costs and benefits cuts. Moynihan and Parsons said on the day of the panel's first, four-hour meeting on June 11 that it would probably have to recommend benefit cutbacks to make the numbers add up after carving out personal accounts.

White House aides, meanwhile, were looking for support for the commission on Wall Street. Lindsey had been meeting with D. Don Ezra, an executive at Frank Russell Company, a leading pension advisory firm, about assembling a business alliance to push privatization. Ezra quickly cobbled together a well-heeled contingent including Frank Russell, State Street Corporation, and Mellon Institutional Asset Management. They called themselves the Coalition for American Financial Security and they planned an advertising campaign to support the commission's restructuring proposal when it came out in the fall.[8]

Aiming to build a $20 million war chest, the coalition organized a luncheon with O'Neill for June 18 at the posh Windows on the World restaurant, atop New York's World Trade Center. The lunch was attended by at least fifty top executives from such companies as insurers American International Group and American Skandia, Caterpillar Inc., Citigroup, Deutsche Bank, and Morgan Stanley.

While labor unions had forced the Street to back off its support of privatization initiatives during the last couple of years of the Clinton administration, the prospect of a president using his political capital to push through such a plan once again had financial services firms counting their prospective fees. A recent report by consultants McKinsey & Company calculated that a restructuring that fit the parameters Bush had set would create between 50 million and 100 million private accounts with as much as $100 billion in new funds flowing into them each year. That was "quite substantial when compared with the average new long-term equity inflow of $225 billion into retail mutual funds since 1997," the report said. The new accounts could swiftly equal 25% to 50% of existing mutual fund accounts.

Many would be money losers or only marginally profitable. But this could be alleviated depending on the details of the plan Congress decided to adopt. For example, matching contributions based on income level would fatten the accounts, thereby boosting the fees providers could charge. Providers also might be allowed to require workers to only invest in their own mutual funds and not those of rivals, limit switching between accounts, and require or offer incentives to workers to make a steady stream of contributions.

But the key would be the firms' ability to cater to the "sweet spot" amongst the new Social Security account holders: "young, middle-income, first-time savers," of whom there would be more than 20 million. "Private accounts may be these institutions' introduction to the assets of the next generation," McKinsey said, mouth-wateringly. "Can a company afford to stay out of a market that might include every worker in the country?" The opportunities for cross-selling other products and services to workers who would be their clients for decades was too good to pass up.

Accordingly, the new Coalition for American Financial Security wasn't the only pressure group helping the Bush commission to sell its message. There was also the Alliance for Worker Retirement Security as well as the Universal Savers Alliance, formed by conservative activists who had labored in the term-limits movement. Lindsey met several times during the summer with the Alliance for American Financial Security, while the *Wall Street Journal* reported that the audience sign-in sheet for the commission's first meeting "reads like a who's who of Washington lobbying firms."[9]

But O'Neill, who was expected to be the administration's chief salesperson for Social Security reform, was turning out to be a bit of a loose cannon. In a May interview with the *Financial Times*, the Treasury secretary called the current tax system an "abomination," and advocated abolishing corporate taxes and shifting the burden onto individuals. He also called for the outright abolition of Social Security and Medicare, saying, "able-bodied adults should save enough on a regular basis so that they can provide for their own retirement, and, for that matter, health and medical needs."[10]

This, from a retired Fortune 500 CEO, making some reporters skeptical that they had heard right. A *Newsday* columnist called O'Neill's spokesperson and asked, "The secretary didn't really mean to say that no matter how old, no person who has paid into the Social Security system all his or her life would be entitled to benefits until he or she is physically no longer able to work?" The spokesperson replied, "Yes, that is our position. The quotes were all accurate."[11]

At its July meeting, the commission was scheduled to release an interim report that would focus on the challenges facing Social Security. In advance of that session, conservative anti-tax pressure groups including the National Taxpayers Union and Citizens for a Sound Economy met with aides to Republican congressional leaders to plan strategy. Already their opponents on the Democratic side were organizing to counter their efforts.

Groups including the CAF, the National Committee to Preserve Social Security and Medicare, and the National Urban League had staked out Washington's Willard Inter-Continental Hotel, where the commission's first meeting was held in June. Afterward, they held a counter-press conference down the hall. This would become standard practice at each of the commission's succeeding meetings, accompanied by energetic anti-privatization picketing outside the venue. Meanwhile, the AFL-CIO reorganized the National Council of Senior Citizens, its decades-old group for retired union members, into the

Alliance for Retired Americans, which it hoped to expand into a broader alliance more specifically aimed against privatization.

Recognizing that they faced tough opposition, the anti-tax groups were pushing hard for the commission not to join the Pain Caucus, which they argued would only alienate potential supporters. Stephen Moore, now president of the tax-cut-touting Washington pressure group the Club for Growth, opposed "any type of benefit reduction as part of personal accounts," saying this would "torpedo" any plan the commission put forward. Citizens for a Sound Economy, which claimed a grassroots presence in twelve states, was planning to launch a "Make It Personal" tour of town-hall meetings around the country that it hoped would include Dick Armey and Rep. J.C. Watts of Oklahoma.

The Republican leadership were determined to connect with the people. In a speech in January to AARP, Bill Thomas threatened to instigate generational warfare by conducting field hearings on Social Security—less melodramatically, an attempt to take the argument for restructuring the program to the public. The first hearing took place at the University of Missouri campus in Columbia on June 18: the same day O'Neill held his New York luncheon with Wall Street supporters of privatization. Both ran into noisy demonstrations organized by the same coalition that had rallied in Washington the week before.

The commission issued a draft of its interim report on July 19. Five days later it held its second meeting, at which the members were scheduled to hear no public testimony but instead to discuss the report and its implications. The CAF decided on a show of strength, holding press conferences, rallies, and forums with Democratic lawmakers and community leaders in more than fifty cities around the country, as well as a press conference at the Capitol Hilton in Washington, where the commission met.

Criticisms of the report were already appearing in the press by the day of the meeting, and Republican lawmakers who had endorsed its work could barely contain their tempers at the way it was being portrayed by its opponents. Judd Gregg, who had emerged as the Senate Republican Conference's point person on Social Security restructuring, accused the Democrats of "aggressively misrepresenting the facts" and of "politicizing" and "demagoguing" the issue, which he said they were using "as a ramming device for the purpose of electing their members."

Outside the Capitol Hilton on the typically humid and unbearable afternoon of the 24th, more than 100 protesters greeted the commission members, chanting, "Hey, hey, ho, ho, Bush and Wall Street have got to go!"[12] The demonstration was organized by the AFL-CIO and the American Federation of State, County and Municipal Employees. Bill Frenzel complained that, as he was trying to get inside, he was nearly hit by a taxicab when protesters with bullhorns forced him into the street, a story he later had to tone down.[13]

Inside, Moynihan read a letter from his friend Bob Kerrey. Now ensconced as president of New School University in New York, the ex-senator urged the commissioners to throw back at the Democrats the "do-nothing alternative"—leaving the program alone—which Moynihan predicted would leave seniors in "increased poverty."[14]

The meeting at times felt like a gathering under siege, with the besieged not quite able to grasp just who these barbarians at the gates were. "The intensity of the vitriol has been surprising," remarked Tim Penny.[15] Bill Frenzel fulminated against the "know-nothing, Luddite" views of the "herd of critics … parading in front of the hotel."[16] Estelle James, who was reported to have worked closely with the commission staff preparing the interim report, expressed mystification as to what was so controversial. Holding up a copy of the report, she acknowledged that some people might have different ideas about how to resolve the issues facing Social Security, but characterized the report itself as merely a statement of the obvious about a troubled program.

Much of the report itself read more like an indictment or a list of charges than a systematic analysis, consistent with the White House's objective of using it as an educational piece to build support for the changes the commission would propose later. The Kerrey-Danforth commission, under Bill Clinton, had followed the same strategy with its intermediate report.

Moynihan and Parsons, in a prologue, said the existing program "does nothing to promote individual savings or investment…. Workers have little sense of proprietorship or a sense of what they are entitled to." Concluding, they wrote, "The system is broken. Unless we move boldly and quickly, the promise of Social Security to future retirees cannot be met without eventual resort to benefit cuts, tax increases or massive borrowing. The time to act is now."

The most striking feature of the report was that it attempted to move the point of concern from 2038, the year the trust funds were projected to run out of assets, to 2016, the first year when payroll tax receipts were expected not to cover all benefits paid out. That's when the government would have to start redeeming some of the Treasury bonds in the trust funds. Social Security would then no longer be self-supporting from year to year. And so Washington would have to either sell new bonds to the public or raise taxes to cover the cost of those redemptions.

Of course, that was no different from what the federal government did routinely when it redeemed or rolled over the Treasuries it sold to the public. But as propaganda, the shift made sense, because 2016 was a much closer and therefore more alarming date than 2038. "The year 2016 may seem a long way off, but it is not," said the report. "For a person who is 50 years old today, Social Security will begin experiencing financial difficulties just when he or she reaches retirement age."

"The debate over whether there's a problem with Social Security ends with this report," a Bush spokesperson announced. "In the coming months, we can begin to discuss the solution the president advocates."

However, cumulative media coverage of the July 24 meeting, as well as of the rallies and other events that day in Washington and elsewhere, reinforced the picture of a commission meeting under fire and failing to generate much respect for its work.[17] The *New York Times* editors dismissed the Bush commission paper as "A Biased Social Security Report" that exaggerated the problems facing the program.[18]

Some press was supportive. The *San Francisco Chronicle* praised the commissioners for "taking a hard-eyed view of the problems facing the 66-year-old program" and came down in favor of letting Americans control "at least a portion of their Social Security account." But the paper also noted that private accounts weren't what was going to set the program's finances right, and took Bush to task for "squandering" the budget surplus that could have been used to do so.[19]

That last would become another much-repeated point as the commission continued with its work. Social Security's seventy-five-year deficit amounted to some 37% of payroll tax receipts over that period, according to the commission, or about 2% of GDP. Yet, columnist Paul Krugman pointed out, the just-passed Bush tax cut "will eventually reduce revenue by about 1.7% of G.D.P." The commission, "including Mr. Moynihan," had "disqualified themselves" from any honest discussion of how to reform Social Security, Krugman concluded.[20]

Perhaps the most entertaining response to the interim report came from Rep. Bob Filner of California, who introduced an amendment to a Treasury appropriations bill that would have prohibited OMB from spending any money to implement the commission's final report. While the amendment didn't stand a chance, Filner's maneuver meant that the entire chamber had to vote on it, forcing every member to tacitly endorse—or not—the commission's project. The House voted the amendment down, 238 to 188. All Republicans voted against it, joined by twenty Democrats. The Campaign for America's Future duly reported those Democrats' names to the members of its coalition.

Whatever else its effect, Filner's action underscored the fears of some Republican leaders—even some of those most enthusiastic about private accounts—that the president's commission was electoral dead weight for them. What was happening behind the scenes to make this possible was a further metamorphosis in the anti-privatization contingent.

The coalition of labor and progressive groups that the CAF had pulled together during Clinton's second term was now, if anything, larger, more agile, and better funded. AARP, which after years of attacks from conservatives resentful of its political might had been keeping a low profile, now offered to join the battle against the Bush initiative, even to the extent of participating in local rallies. "We're usually pretty pragmatic, and we usually try to be bipartisan," said chief lobbyist John Rother. "But neither of these adjectives applies to the commission."

The Democratic National Committee, too, which had previously kept above the fray, was now eager to cooperate with these non-party groups. Gerry Kavanaugh, its new policy director, worked through the office of Rep. Bob Matsui, the Californian who was the ranking Democratic member of the House Social Security Subcommittee, to bring out as many elected officials as possible for the around-the-country events held on July 24. "We probably contacted 40 to 50 members [of Congress], and we ended up with 20 to 25 participating," a Matsui aide told the *American Prospect*. Kavanaugh was so enormously pleased with the results on the 24th—for once, voices opposed to radically restructuring Social Security seemed to have the upper hand in the media—that he looked forward to more in the future. "This is the first of many," he predicted.[21]

* * *

The commissioners had some grounds for resenting the accusation that their panel was a mere rubber stamp. The detailed work of squaring reality with the guidelines Bush had laid out for them wasn't easy. Additionally, they were growing frustrated with the spotlight they worked under and the negative attention directed at them.

Legally, the commission meetings were required to be open to the public. Wanting to keep their more sensitive discussions private, the members hit upon the gambit of dividing themselves into "subcommittees," under the rationale that these didn't have to meet publicly because they didn't form a quorum of the whole. At the August 22 meeting, for example, the morning session was closed as the panel divided into two groups: one to look at the financial estimates on private accounts that the Clinton administration had developed, the other to look at ways to administer such a program, according to Parsons.

That upset the commission's critics. "The public has a right to know what information is being presented to the commission and how its proposals to privatize Social Security are being developed," Matsui and Rep. Henry Waxman, another California Democrat, complained in a letter to the panel. Parsons told the *New York Times* that, in effect, the public had no such right. Its legal counsel had told the commission that "these were information-gathering and comprehension-enhancing meetings. There was no deliberation. There was no decision-making."[22]

But critics saw the closed-door meetings as part of a developing pattern of secretiveness within the Bush administration. Vice President Dick Cheney was already embroiled with Congress for refusing to turn over to the GAO documents relating to his energy policy panel, and the White House rejected a request from a Senate committee for access to documents concerning its roll-back of some environmental regulations.

Moynihan, as a Democrat, came under attack for allowing his commission to adopt such practices. In a *Washington Post* op-ed, Bob Ball noted that the former senator had been aware as far back as 1983, when they served together on the Greenspan commission, of all the fiscal arguments now being aimed at the program—but hadn't endorsed them. "I don't know what to make of my erstwhile ally," Ball lamented. "I have written to him, but there has been no response. His commission has taken to meeting behind closed doors. So I feel obliged to make my perplexity public: Pat? Is that you?"

As if in response to the commission's new secretiveness, the critics were ratcheting up their presence both outside and inside the commission's meeting places. Multiple press conferences opposed to its work took place in the same hotel where the August meeting was held, and the labor and other groups rallying against privatization brought even more people into the streets outside. The whole affair took on a circus aspect when Citizens for a Sound Economy sent out a small group of placard-toting counter-protesters. One, dressed in an Uncle Sam outfit, carried a sign reading, "I Want You to Support P.R.A.'s [personal retirement accounts]."

Some reporters expressed battle fatigue. The same arguments and appeals to data were cropping up again and again, with little in the way of fresh perspectives. It didn't help that, as summer turned to fall, the economic and tax revenue numbers coming out of the White House were worsening. Budget director Mitch Daniels told reporters in August that the administration planned to use most of the Social Security surplus to pay down federal debt over the next ten years, much as the Clinton administration had planned to do.[23]

It was bound to get worse. A week earlier, the CBO had announced that its latest numbers would show the federal government using up the entire non-Social Security surplus for the current fiscal year. Out of an originally projected $125 billion, $74 billion had been wiped out by the tax cut, some $40 billion more by the economic downturn, and the rest by new federal spending. The only reason Washington wouldn't be breaking open the lockbox and tapping into the Social Security trust funds was that the White House had rejiggered its payroll tax receipt calculations covering the past three years, effectively reassigning $4.3 billion as other revenues.

A week later, the CBO raised to $9 billion its estimate of the amount the administration would have to pull out of Social Security to balance its books. Overnight, White House rhetoric about the trust fund surpluses changed. Daniels referred to the lockbox, which it had previously treated as a solemn undertaking, as "symbolic," adding that it shouldn't be used to "shortchange" basic needs like defense.[24]

Democratic leaders, of course, lashed out at the administration for squandering the Clinton surplus and eroding the opportunity for bipartisan Social Security reform. "We do not want to see the fiscal policy of the last ten years unravel further," Gephardt, Daschle, John Spratt of South Carolina, and Kent Conrad told the president on August 15.

CHAPTER 33

THE BUSH
COMMISSION
PUNTS

The shrinking surplus and the Democrats' aggressive tactics were leaving the president and his commission more and more exposed on Social Security, but the White House wasn't suggesting it had lost faith in its privatization initiative. In a sense, the administration had painted itself into a corner, facing damage if the commission came out with a politically unpalatable recommendation—as seemed likely—and damage if it backed down on a major initiative so early in Bush's term. Then, five days after the commission's San Diego meeting, two Boeing jets crashed into the World Trade Center in New York, while a third damaged the Pentagon and another, intended for the White House, crashed near Shanksville, Pennsylvania. Almost 3,000 people died and the nation was in shock.

Early on, one of the heroes of the humanitarian efforts following 9/11 was the SSA. Social Security benefits swiftly emerged as a lifeline for survivors of individuals killed in the attacks and for workers disabled as a result. Less than three weeks later, the number of 9/11-related claims was already over 3,150. SSA staff were present at family assistance centers near the Pentagon and World Trade Center sites and were reaching out to hospitals and employers to find potential benefits recipients. All told, 2,357 children who lost parents during the attacks and 853 surviving spouses would become Social Security beneficiaries, along with 642 persons who were disabled on September 11, and 99 of their survivors. Social Security would pay $175 million in 9/11-related benefits in just the first five years following the terrorist acts.[1]

The agency was forced to do some rebuilding of its own. In mid-October, the New York State disability determination director was still awaiting permission to recover some 15,000 folders from an office a quarter block from the Trade Center site, but elected officials of both parties praised the SSA for its emergency work. Clay Shaw said, "SSA employees are to be commended for their responsiveness to the victims of the terrorist attacks of September 11th and for their ongoing assistance in the resulting Federal investigations of these heinous crimes."

Bush's presidency, of course, completely redefined itself. Projects that had seemed likely to keep the administration busy, or bogged down, for months or years could now easily be pushed into the background. Less than a month later the U.S. invaded Afghanistan and won an easy but superficial military victory over the Taliban regime. The new "War on Terror" was the most yawningly open-ended conflict the U.S. had ever plunged into. It provided the excuse for an enormous American power thrust into the Middle East and the growth of a wide-reaching new Homeland Security bureaucracy at home that demanded—and according to the political rules of Washington, couldn't be denied—nearly unlimited resources to carry out its work.

The president, whose administration only days earlier seemed to be losing momentum fast, seized the role of commander-in-chief with enthusiasm, promising that "America has stood down enemies before, and we will do so this time." He also attempted to tie the attacks to foreign hatred of the American way of life, implicitly bundling together political freedom and the opportunity economy his policies were designed to promote. "America was targeted for attack because we're the brightest beacon for freedom and opportunity in the world," he declared.

What Bush had achieved, or perhaps simply been handed by both parties in Congress, was the opportunity to revise his policy goals in midstream, jettisoning some and applying new rationales to those he was determined to push through. The Bush commission's final report "has been put off from this autumn until next spring," the *Washington Post* reported. Moynihan spoke as if he was entirely in agreement with any delay. "We're not trying to push it too fast," he said. "The plan is entirely doable, but there is no need to have any arguments at this point about anything so disputed."

Rumors were already rife that the commission would be shelved or rendered irrelevant. Word was also leaking out that Moynihan himself felt marginalized and was unhappy. A memo to O'Neill, which later surfaced in journalist Ron Suskind's book *The Price of Loyalty*, reported that the co-chair "has expressed a considerable amount of frustration that he is not being allowed to control the agenda and, in particular, that the White House and commission staff are controlling the agenda to a large extent."[2] One rumor asserted that Moynihan had resigned. His office had to spend several days refuting that report.[3]

The commission's next meeting, scheduled for September 21 in Cincinnati, was quickly canceled, but the following session, October 18 in Washington, was held on schedule and was relatively uneventful. On October 30, Bush met with Moynihan and Parsons. Word seeped out within days that the objective wasn't just to push off action on Social Security, but to fudge the issue. Rather than producing a single restructuring plan, the commission was to compile a menu of options for changing the program. The commissioners don't want to "tie the hands of Congress," Blahous said in confirming the reports. The result would be no single proposal that could be hung around the necks of congressional Republicans.

Their attack thus blunted even before the report came out, the Democrats were disappointed. In a letter to Parsons and Moynihan, Matsui complained that they had skirted their obligation to produce a plan they could stand behind. "The commission would do a disservice to the debate on privatization," he wrote, "if it failed to recommend a specific and comprehensive plan—one that would let us directly debate the merits of the president's policies and see the costs and tradeoffs. The American public deserves no less." The Republican commissioners, of course, asked why the Democrats didn't put their necks on the line with a restructuring plan of their own.

What was remarkable, given that the congressional Democratic leadership had accepted Bush's terms on issue after issue relating to the war and domestic security in the first two months following September 11, was the tenaciousness of the Democrats' assault on his Social Security initiative. Even if the final report of the presidential commission was likely to be a formality, the coalition in defense of the program was determined to keep the privatization forces off balance. The Democratic National Committee, for example, continued through the fall to use in its fundraising letters the threat that Bush's plans for Social Security would expose workers to the fortunes of the increasingly wobbly stock market.[4]

At its November 9 meeting in Washington, the commission confirmed that it would release its final draft report, featuring several alternatives for restructuring the program, by the time of its last session on December 11. "There are real options," Moynihan told reporters afterward. "Different members have different approaches to some of the issues raised by private accounts."[5] Perhaps. But some of the biggest supporters of privatization in Congress were now expressing disappointment that the commission wasn't following through on its original mandate.

Echoing Matsui from the other side of the ideological divide, Kolbe, Stenholm, Breaux, and Gregg urged the co-chairs to submit a single plan, its numbers fully vetted by the Social Security actuaries. "Now is the time for action," they wrote, "and the commission's plan will provide the impetus for the debate to proceed in Congress. The importance of a recommendation by the commission cannot be overstated."

Much of the commission's work was still being done in closed-door "subcommittees" as well as over email and in private telephone conversations.[6] Democrats were getting nervous that this was allowing the members to cover their tracks as they prepared to commit pen to paper with their final recommendations. Since the panel had found a way around one federal statute, Waxman and Matsui decided to create another one to plug the loophole. On November 28, the day before the commission's next meeting, at which it planned to discuss for the first time some of the options that would go into its final report, the two representatives submitted the Federal Advisory Committee Transparency (FACT) Act of 2001. The bill would require presidential advisory commissions to keep their meetings open to the public, explicitly extending the rule to subgroupings of such panels.

That legislation had little chance of passing, of course. And the November 29 meeting rendered the issue more or less academic, because it witnessed the unveiling of three fully developed alternatives for injecting private accounts into Social Security and balancing the program's books.

The first option—Reform Model 1, as it became known—would allow workers to invest 2% of their wages in personal accounts, with benefits offset by 3.5% annually. The commission said upfront that this plan wouldn't balance Social Security's books over the next seventy-five years, although the offset could result in a 30% cut in lifetime benefits. Under Reform Model 2, workers could deploy up to 4% of wages in their private accounts up to a maximum $1,000 a year, with an offsetting 2% benefit cut. This alternative would cut costs further by tying the calculation of initial benefits to prices rather than wages.

Reform Model 3 would let workers place 1% of total wages in private accounts each year with a 2.5% match from their Social Security payroll tax contributions, again up to a maximum $1,000, with a 2.5% offsetting benefits reduction. This plan would further limit the growth of benefits starting in 2009 by indexing them to life expectancy. Workers who retired early would take a larger cut in benefits while those who worked beyond retirement age would enjoy an increase.

Private accounts would be voluntary in all three models and all three were predicated on leaving alone the benefits of current or soon-to-be retirees. Model 2 would restore Social Security to long-term solvency, commission members claimed, but Model 3 would require the government to inject additional revenues into the program—from where, the commission didn't say—to make the books balance. One other idea the commission members were considering was to increase the amount of wages subject to Social Security taxes. They were seeking the president's advice whether this would be acceptable to him, Parsons said.

None of the three models succeeded in reconciling the Bush administration's dual mandates: to balance the books without cutting benefits for current retirees. "There is no pain-free way of 'saving' Social Security," Parsons conceded at the November 29 meeting. "We're slowing down the rate of growth of benefits so, over time, things can get back into balance."[7] The commission had gone ahead and submitted a report that the Free Lunch Caucus was guaranteed to hate.

For workers who would have to endure it, however, there wasn't much difference between slowing down the rate of growth of benefits and actually cutting them. "Abandoning wage-indexing for price-indexing, current and future retirees could be looking at a reduction of up to 48% in their benefits," said Matsui. "What [the commission members] have come up with is three proposals that are basically worthless."[8]

Nobody, it seemed, had any expectation that the commission's work would yield legislation any time soon. "We think it will take a good year or so—or maybe more," said Parsons.[9] At the press conference the same day, Ari Fleischer pointedly didn't name Social Security as an administration priority for the following year either. Trent Lott, the Senate minority leader, even turned down requests to meet with the commission members, citing an over-filled schedule.[10]

* * *

Going into the December 11 commission meeting, its opponents were determined to grab a good part of the media's attention with another round of events across the country. Twenty-two cities would host anti-privatization meetings and rallies, with at least eighteen House members pledging to participate along with other prominent figures such as Democratic National Committee chair Terry McAuliffe. On top of this was a press conference with Matsui at the Park Hyatt Washington Hotel, where the commission meeting was to be held.

Pro-privatization groups held their own press events afterward. Reporters who attempted to cover it all were buried in an avalanche of memos, briefing papers, press releases, and point-by-point analyses and critiques of the three models contained in the commission's final draft report, which had been released the day before. At the three-hour meeting itself, Moynihan sought to assign the commission a place in history despite its indecisive ending. "This is the first time a national panel appointed by a president has proposed that Americans acquire wealth as part of social insurance," he declared.

But the final draft report suggested Congress put the matter aside for the time being—specifically, for "a period of discussion, lasting for at least one year, before legislative action is taken to strengthen and restore sustainability to Social Security." Only a few things had changed or were fleshed out significantly from the draft that circulated at the November 26 meeting.

The commission pleased the insurance industry by deciding that personal-account holders should "be required to take at least some of their money as an annuity or as graduated withdrawals." Workers at first would be required to invest in the narrow group of funds currently offered by the federal employees' Thrift Savings Plan. Later, after the size of their accounts reached a certain "threshold amount," the funds could be shifted to "private-sector providers." The commission's definition of firms that would qualify suggested that virtually any major mutual fund provider would be acceptable, however. Finally, workers wouldn't be allowed access to any of their personal-account funds before retirement.[11]

One of the additional analytic items in the final draft report was the finding that even with the benefits "restraints" called for in the three restructuring proposals, creating private accounts would absorb more than $1 trillion in payroll tax revenue over ten years, and almost $3 trillion over twenty.[12] Over and over, the members repeated what the anti-privatization forces knew to be true: that private accounts wouldn't solve Social Security's supposed fiscal problems, but would actually create another hurdle on the road to doing so.

"That shortfall of revenue versus cost of the system needs to be fixed and that's quite independent of personal accounts," said Olivia Mitchell, fairly typically. "That is really an important lesson that we hope gets brought forward—that personal accounts really are not necessarily a silver bullet that can answer all the problems."[13]

Cato's Michael Tanner tried to put the best face on it by emphasizing that all three of the commission proposals had private accounts as their centerpiece. But other privatization supporters expressed disappointment at an opportunity they accused the commission of punting, and dismay that it had accepted the

need for painful benefit reductions rather than simply emphasizing the bounty of private accounts. The *Wall Street Journal* editors declared that the three reform models "have the aroma of political evasion" and suggested that Bush had "squandered" his mandate to change Social Security.

What even the commission's conservative critics missed, however, was that the movement against Social Security had been hoisted by its own petard. After years of condemning Social Security as fiscally unsound, any attempt the members made to fudge the numbers, selling private accounts as a panacea without subjecting the restructured program to a rigorous actuarial review, would be swiftly attacked by the coalition lined up against them.

The very first point that Peter Orszag of Brookings raised at the opposition press conference following the December 11 meeting was, "Where does the money come from?" The White House had recently conceded that, given the tax cut, slumping tax revenues, and new military and domestic security outlays, the budget wasn't likely to balance again until 2005. That meant Congress would have to somehow come up with $1 trillion over ten years to make up for the money carved out of payroll taxes.

"This is the mother of all magic asterisks," Orszag said sarcastically.[14] The commission suggested one way around this was, in effect, for the program to loan itself money to cover the shortfall—a proposal that was widely scoffed at.[15] The only real solution, then, would be to get the money from the Social Security trust funds, accelerating their fiscal deterioration. That would put at risk current retirees and workers close to retirement, despite the commission's pledge not to alter their benefits.

The commission had punted in the sense that it didn't recommend anything specific to cover that $1 trillion shortfall, its members instead declaring that they ought not to make up Congress's mind for it on such a politically sensitive matter. Yet several members had earlier promised that any plan they came up with would eliminate Social Security's long-term deficit. "The apparent failure of the commission to present even a single plan that eliminates the 75-year deficit in Social Security is remarkable," Orszag said.

This despite the fact that the benefit cutbacks it called for, over time, were severe. Under Model 2, which would switch from a wage- to a price-based COLA formula, benefits for a single average earner could fall from about $21,500 annually in 2001 dollars to roughly $12,500 by 2060.[16] The way Model 1 worked, some retirees could face an even worse plight. The model assumed a 3.5% rate of return on private accounts to determine how much less the retiree would receive in benefits to offset her investment earnings. But if she actually earned less than 3.5%, the offset wouldn't change; the same amount would be deducted from her benefits as if her return hadn't dropped.[17]

The commission had promised to leave Disability Insurance alone, but in the final draft report, this turned out not to be the case. "This commission has applied changes in defined benefits to DI recipients as well as OASI recipients in the [three] reform plans," it acknowledged—but not until the second to last page of the report. This despite the fact that "DI beneficiaries with abbreviated work histories might have relatively low account balances."

Survivors' benefits were another area where the commission was less forbearing than it had promised. On one hand, it added its voice to a chorus that for years had been calling for a boost in Social Security benefits for surviving spouses. But it neglected to mention that the change from wage- to price-based COLAs meant the spousal benefit would still be significantly lower in future decades than under current law.[18]

If the commission report met with some criticism from the right, it encountered strong disapproval even in the broad political center. Initiating a line of thought that Democrats would rehearse more and more frequently, the *New York Times* editors suggested that Bush might "find the revenues to pay for privatization by repealing part of the tax cut enacted earlier in the year." Otherwise, "instead of building a consensus for reform," the report "makes it even less likely that Congress will act on Social Security any time soon."

The anti-privatization forces were predictably more severe, gloating at the albatross their enemies had hung around their own necks. "The Commission was a stacked deck from the beginning," Gephardt said in a prepared statement. It "should have offered an opportunity for a bipartisan effort leading to a consensus and broad support from the American people. Instead, we had a biased Commission and a predetermined outcome."

Over the next several months, as Bush seemed to ride Congress to victory on any issue even remotely related to the War on Terror, the commission became one of Democrats' few easy sources of mirth. In February, Hans Riemer attended a Cato forum where he presented the panelists with a list of "Top Ten Reasons to Do Another Social Security Commission." Reason Number Ten: "Three privatization plans are not enough—Congress needs 532 more." Reason Number One: "Speaker Gephardt."

"After more than six months, a $700,000 budget, and far too many secret meetings, the commission has died a quiet death," Matsui concluded after its last session. What's striking about the commission project, however, is the lack of enthusiasm it bucked right from the start from even very conservative members of Congress—and the fact that Bush and his aides chose to go ahead with it despite clear signals from party leaders like Rep. Tom Davis of Virginia.

In 2001, the Republicans controlled the White House and both chambers of Congress for the first time in a half-century—although the Senate slipped from their hands when Vermont's Jim Jeffords declared himself an Independent after the tax-cut vote. But the party leadership wasn't sufficiently unified on any domestic issue except tax cuts, or sufficiently secure yet in its hold on Congress, to tackle such a loaded issue as Social Security. Being a few steps closer to the grassroots—to reality, perhaps—Republican lawmakers were more keenly aware than their cohorts in the White House of economic realities.

Americans with stock portfolios and mutual fund accounts were looking at flat if not lower earnings in 2001—a rare occurrence over the past two decades. For the first time in years, the Dow ended the year below the psychologically charged level of 10,000. Companies from the old line, like Polaroid, to new-economy icons like Enron were declaring bankruptcy. The stock market downturn was educating people on the risks of relying on private investments for their retirement income. Even privatization's deepest-pocketed supporters seemed to realize fairly early that the time wasn't ripe to funnel workers' payroll taxes into a sort of national 401(k), sanctioned if not run by the Social Security Administration.

How had a costly, prestigious, well-publicized presidential commission come up with a set of proposals so out of touch with current economic reality and so difficult for lawmakers—even those most sympathetic to its project— to work with? One reason was that, unlike other panels appointed at times of real emergency, like Greenspan's in 1982, the Bush commission included no sitting members of Congress. If it had, they might have made clear to their colleagues that the commission couldn't tell the House and Senate they had found a "solution" to Social Security's long-term bookkeeping issues—and then throw in Congress's lap the task of devising a way to cover trillions of dollars in transition costs.

Timing, of course, played a large part too. In a terribly grim way, the 9/11 attacks had helped convince Bush to abandon a path that was probably doomed to fail and might have cost the Republicans their House majority in 2002. Ordering up a menu of proposals that threw the difficult decision making on Social Security in the lap of Congress—but only if Congress chose to take it up—plus kicking the issue at least into 2003, enabled Bush to deflect any direct political damage.

His opponents recognized this. "If Bush gains ground in Congress, he can push the idea in 2003," Riemer predicted. But if the Republicans were to suffer setbacks, "it's dead for 10 years, for 15 years, for the foreseeable future." The AARP's John Rother took a slightly more charitable position. The real threshold, he said, would be the 2004 presidential election: "Traditionally, Social Security is a second-term presidential issue."[19]

CHAPTER 34

GUNS AND
BUTTER

The Democrats faced enormous hurdles as the 2002 election approached. Bush benefited directly from the post-9/11 national mood, and after the rapid military occupation of Afghanistan, questioning the president's foreign policy—which the vast majority of congressional Democrats had more than gone along with—would be nearly impossible. The logical course was to emphasize domestic issues. The embarrassment that the president's Social Security commission had caused was a ready-made talking point for a party looking for ways to tear down a wartime administration without appearing unpatriotic.

Bush seemed to be begging the Democrats to make an issue of Social Security again when his latest budget, submitted in February, proposed to tap $259 billion from the trust funds in the coming fiscal year to cover non-Social Security expenses and $1.4 trillion over the next decade. "You'd be headed for a federal correctional facility," Sen. Kent Conrad, the North Dakota Democrat, lectured Mitch Daniels at a Budget Committee hearing, if the White House budget director had attempted to do the same thing to a pension plan in the private sector.

A few weeks later, Bush used the opportunity of an address to a retirement savings conference, sponsored by the Labor Department, to champion private Social Security accounts. "What's fair on the top floor should be fair on the shop floor," he declared, striking an artfully populist note. "At a time when older Americans have longer lives and more options than ever before, we need to assure they have access not just to a monthly check but to personal wealth."

Democratic leaders couldn't have been happier at the president's failure to learn his lesson. "I'm pleased that Republicans are now openly discussing their plans to privatize Social Security," Daschle said. "The president is very popular in the Republican Party," a Gephardt spokesperson noted. "I assume they would want to defend his proposal."

One Republican congressional leader worried that the Democrats might give seniors the wrong idea. To reassure those who felt threatened by privatization, Dick Armey said he would bring a bill before the House proposing that every current Social Security recipient be mailed a certificate guaranteeing their future benefits payments wouldn't be cut. "Mailing out meaningless certificates to seniors is a blatant attempt to provide political cover in an election year," Matsui retorted. And even Bush's new Social Security commissioner, Jo Anne Barnhart, spoke negatively about the idea, since it might create "undo alarm" among people nearing retirement age, who wouldn't receive a certificate.[1]

Meanwhile, Stephen Schmidt, the National Republican Congressional Committee's communications director, blasted an email to GOP candidates and party leaders warning them to avoid using the term "privatization." It "carries connotations of dismantling the publicly run Social Security system, or sending participants to fend for themselves," warned the email, which swiftly leaked into the press. "It is extremely important that Democrats not be allowed to characterize GOP support for personal savings accounts as privatization. It is an imprecise and misleading description.... Do not be complicit in Democratic demagoguery."

The Democrats were scrutinizing the record of every GOP candidate for indications that he or she supported cutting or partially privatizing Social Security, and when they found such signs, they pounced. The Democratic Congressional Committee in June launched a website, BreakingTheTrust. com, compiling votes by Republican lawmakers that in any way dovetailed with the idea. The CAF also revived its "Sign the Pledge" drive to pressure all candidates and members of Congress to disavow support for any degree of privatization.

For all their ability to make their opponents squirm over Social Security, however, the Democrats couldn't put together a comprehensive attack on the Bush White House. Indeed, many Democratic lawmakers, including Daschle, went along with a second Bush tax cut in the spring—a three-year, 30% corporate writeoff for new investments including many types of equipment and technology—because it was attached to a measure extending unemployment benefits. And the Democrats permitted the administration another victory in

June when they joined in passing a bill making permanent the pension-related provisions of the 2001 tax act, a measure benefiting mainly the affluent.

The Republican Party regained control of the Senate in November, adding 2 seats to secure a narrow, 51-seat majority, and added 8 seats in the House, padding out their lead over the Democrats to 229 to 204. The Republicans' command of the House still wasn't comfortable, and they still were far from achieving the sixty seats that would render the Democrats ineffective in the Senate.

But Bush was adamant that restructuring Social Security remained on his agenda. "I still strongly believe that the best way to achieve security in Social Security for younger workers is to give them the option of managing their own money through a personal savings account," he said in a post-election press conference. He was bolstered by the victories of some Republican incumbents and candidates who had been open about their support of private accounts, including Rep. Pat Toomey in Pennsylvania; Elizabeth Dole, running for a Senate seat in North Carolina; John Sununu, running for Senate from New Hampshire; and Clay Shaw. Shaw, who had been reelected by just 599 votes in 2000, this time took 60% of the vote in his Gold Coast Florida district.

But, pointed out Roger Hickey, Republicans won largely by hewing to the RNC playbook, which meant denouncing privatization while continuing to advocate private accounts. "You don't get a mandate if you didn't run on your real position," the CAF contended in a TomPaine.com ad in the *New York Times*. "The privatizers got no mandate from this election." A *New York Times/CBS News* poll after the election found two-thirds of respondents still saying they would prefer the surplus be used to shore up Social Security and Medicare rather than pay for the president's $1.35 trillion tax cut.

Needing strong salespeople for his next round of cuts, in December Bush abruptly reshuffled his stable of economic advisors, starting with the dramatic ouster of O'Neill as Treasury secretary and Larry Lindsey as National Economic Council chief.

While he enthusiastically supported Social Security privatization, O'Neill had gotten himself in trouble making off-the-cuff comments to the press that created the impression that he was detached and unconcerned as the economy weakened. He was also too convinced a deficit hawk to have any place in a religiously supply-side administration. Lindsey was firmly on-message in this respect, but had embarrassed the administration in September when he made a pessimistic guesstimate of the cost of the Iraq invasion.

In their place, Bush named John Snow, CEO of railroad giant CSX Corporation, as Treasury secretary and Stephen Friedman, a former Goldman Sachs co-chair, as NEC director. The net effect of these changes was to move the administration's economic policy away from the faith of the deficit hawks, with which O'Neill was closely identified, and nearer to the supply-side catechism. This done, the White House was ready to aggressively promote its next round of tax cuts.

* * *

O'Neill may have departed, but he continued to haunt Washington by way of a mini-scandal that blew up in early June. Joe Lieberman, in the early stages of launching a presidential bid, wrote a letter to Secretary Snow in which he accused the administration of "stripping out" from its 2004 budget the findings of an internal Treasury paper that Snow's predecessor had ordered up the previous fall. Attempting to stake out a position as the toughest of the deficit hawks, Lieberman suggested that "this administration is trying to hide the true nature of our financial obligations from the American people in order to advance its agenda of cutting taxes indiscriminately."

The paper was written by Kent Smetters, then deputy assistant secretary for economic policy, and Jagadeesh Gokhale, the Cleveland Fed economist who had earlier lent his expertise to Larry Kotlikoff's generational accounting analyses, and was now a consultant to Treasury. Their paper for O'Neill could be considered a further application of generational accounting. Smetters claimed it had been "for internal discussion only," to try to help O'Neill "think about [the deficit] from an economic perspective." There was no conspiracy to suppress it, he said; the administration considered including it in the budget but then decided against it.[2] Smetters testified about the findings in March to the House Judiciary Committee in a hearing about, once again, a balanced budget amendment to the Constitution. Gokhale and Smetters then revised their paper and presented it four times in Washington in May, including to the American Enterprise Institute (AEI) and to an SSA conference on retirement policy. They then published it as an AEI monograph.[3]

What made the report such a hot item was the outsized estimates it produced for the long-term federal deficit and the method it used to arrive at the portion that derived from Social Security and Medicare. The CBO's most recent estimate had the entire federal debt growing to $3.8 trillion by 2008. Gokhale and Smetters brushed this aside, calculating that the federal budget's 2004 "fiscal imbalance" came to $44.2 trillion in 2003 dollars, and that this would rise to $54 trillion by 2008 if steps weren't taken immediately to correct it. Of that, Medicare would account for $36.6 trillion and Social Security for $7 trillion. The rest of the federal budget would account for "only" $500 billion.

The $7 trillion they projected for Social Security was twice the $3.5 trillion deficit the trustees had calculated the program would generate over the next seventy-five years.[4] But Gokhale and Smetters dismissed Social Security's traditional seventy-five-year projection, saying it was "arbitrary" and significantly understated the fiscal hole the program was digging.

They proposed replacing it with a "present value" measure in which "all future spending and revenue are not only reduced for inflation but additionally discounted by the government's (inflation-adjusted) long-term borrowing rate. This calculation enables us to determine how much money the government must come up with immediately to put fiscal policy on a sustainable course"—or, what it must generate in spending cuts or tax increases to do so. The advantage of their method, according to Smetters and Gokhale, was that it stretched out into "perpetuity," covering all the—many, many—future years that the seventy-five-year projections missed. The result would be "forward looking," not "backward looking," they argued, and thus would make it harder for Congress to enact new programs that hit future generations with most of the long-term costs.

Hard-line critics were delighted by this new and more dire way of viewing Social Security and Medicare. Gokhale and Smetters had performed a "great service," Olivia Mitchell declared, by making it possible for lawmakers to look beyond the seventy-five-year cutoff and, perhaps, helping to educate the public about the reality behind the federal government's promises. Robert Inman, an economist at the Wharton School, called the paper "absolutely essential information for effective budgeting."

Lieberman was anxious to put across the Smetters-Gokhale analysis as big news because he could use it to denounce the Bush tax cuts and push for a return to the Clinton-era policy of deficit reduction and debt paydown. The following year, while attempting to kick-start a presidential run, Lieberman introduced, unsuccessfully, a bill that would have forced the federal government to follow "present value" accounting rules, nailing Gokhale and Smetters's "more accurate" numbers into its official budget. "It is the necessary first step on the road back to fiscal balance," he said.[5]

Others made the obvious point, however, that an open-ended cost projection into infinity wasn't very useful to lawmakers trying to create a series of annual budgets in the real world. "We really have no idea what Medicare and Medicaid costs are going to look like in 30 to 40 years, let alone 75 or further out," said Richard Kogan, senior fellow at the Center on Budget and Policy Priorities (CBPP). "Things could be much better or they could be much worse."[6] A projection into an infinite future was also infinitely susceptible to change in any of its components. The CBPP's Jason Furman and Robert Greenstein pointed out that more than two-thirds of the "infinite" deficit was situated past the seventy-five-year point.[7]

The White House and its allies were actually of two minds. While they were happy to spin extravagant projections of the destructiveness of Social Security and Medicare, they didn't want their tax-cutting agenda undermined. On one hand, an infinite projection of Social Security's revenues and outlays made private accounts look more attractive, because, as conservative columnist Bruce Bartlett explained, "much of the saving will fall more than 75 years in the future."

On the other hand, the total picture was deceptively alarming. Using the same assumptions as Smetters and Gokhale, Bartlett calculated that the size of the future economy, which would correspond to their $44.2 trillion "present value" deficit figure, was $682 trillion. In other words, the "fiscal imbalance" would be only 6.5% of GDP: "something to be concerned about, but hardly a crisis in the making."[8]

Smetters, too, in his Judiciary Committee testimony, argued that the Bush tax cuts had relatively little impact on the long-term fiscal equation, although he declined to quantify this. But his numbers on Social Security and Medicare were scary enough that they might be of great help in selling a drastic restructuring of Social Security, if and when the administration was ready to take up that project again.

In fact, Smetters and Gokhale noted, in a *Wall Street Journal* op-ed in July, that the Social Security trustees—largely Bush political appointees—had decided to include an "infinite" solvency projection alongside the three standard seventy-five-year projections for OASI and DI in their latest annual report, which was issued in March. The new analysis arrived at the same numbers Gokhale and Smetters had: $3.5 trillion in unfunded obligations over the next seventy-five years, and $7 trillion more after that.[9]

That didn't go over well with the accredited experts. The American Academy of Actuaries, the principal professional group representing pension actuaries, objected publicly to the administration's attempt to institutionalize the infinite projection. In a letter to the Social Security trustees dated December 19, 2003, the Academy came close to accusing the Bush administration of trying to deceive the public. "The new measures," it said, "provide little if any useful information about the program's long-range finances and indeed are likely to mislead anyone lacking technical expertise in the demographic, economic and actuarial aspects of the program's finances into believing the program is in far worse financial condition than is actually indicated."

* * *

The actuaries' attack elicited no response from the administration, who were focused firmly on another tax cut. Calling it the Jobs and Growth Tax Act of 2003, the president sent his package to Congress in late February. What finally passed three months later satisfied conservatives by combining a reduction of the dividend tax with an equivalent reduction in capital gains rates to 15% for the next five years. Those were major cuts. The current capital gains rate was 20%, while the existing dividend tax rate was 38.6%. The package also accelerated the 2001 income tax cuts across the board, increased the per-child tax deduction from $500 to $1,000 and enlarged the tax break for business spending, as corporations had urged. To pull some Democrats along, $20 billion in aid to the states was folded in, to relieve the pressure of sharply lower state tax revenues.

Congressional Republican leaders played the tax cut as a way to stimulate the economy: "the perfect boost during wartime," as Arthur Laffer and Stephen Moore described it in a *Wall Street Journal* op-ed. The president and his aides went farther, selling it to the public as another step along the road to the "ownership society," a complement to his plan for private Social Security accounts. Eliminating taxes on stock dividends gave small investors a chance to get rich too, Rove said during a January press conference, embroidering the statement with the placard-worthy slogan, "Wealth is too important to be left to the wealthy." Since none of the reporters at the press event asked why eliminating a tax that few of the non-affluent would ever pay would be of much help to them, Rove could go on to say of the president, "Give him a choice between Wall Street and Main Street and he'll choose Main Street every time."

Bush hadn't stopped sounding the alarm that Social Security and Medicare were out of control, either, despite the $810 billion his tax cut would cost in lost revenues over ten years. His budget, released in February, declared that the two programs "are in deep trouble financially" because "the benefits promised ... will soon outstrip their dedicated revenues.... They must not be left hanging over the heads of our children and grandchildren."

Bush and his aides argued that their tax cuts would stimulate the economy, producing greater growth in the future, which would help lessen the impact of the "reforms" needed to stabilize Social Security. Rather than carping about a measure that was necessary to kick-start the economy, then, the administration's critics should be facing up to the "nuclear time bomb" represented by Social Security, Medicare, and the retirement of the baby boomers. The "sunsets" built into the Bush tax cuts might be a good thing, according to conservative columnist Alan Murray, since they would force Congress and the White House to face these more serious issues.[10]

Liberals were getting used to applying the exact same argument as a means of bludgeoning the Republicans. "If these tax cuts go through," *Washington Post* columnist E.J. Dionne, Jr. prophesied, "the choices just a few years from now will be sharp cutbacks in Medicare and Social Security, big tax increases or unheard-of deficits."[11]

This was pure argumentation, others responded. Dean Baker, in his weekly commentary on economic coverage in the media, reminded readers that Social Security and Medicare had their own separate revenue streams from payroll taxes and their own dedicated trust funds. Social Security's was solvent for almost forty years and Medicare's for twenty-five, according to the trustees' rather pessimistic assumptions. The Bush tax cuts could, of course, create problems down the road if the two programs needed additional funding to keep paying promised benefits—and if the tax cuts were still in place. But those decisions would be made by future presidents and Congresses.

Baker was pointing out a fundamental truth about fiscal policy that often got lost in the self-aggrandizing world of Washington. No policy choice is permanent, and each succeeding cohort of lawmakers—acting, presumably, in the interests of their constituents—is free to revise them to fit the needs of the time. Social Security was more secure than most government programs, because of its dedicated payroll tax revenues and the generational compact backing it up. The same couldn't be said of the Bush tax cuts or the fiscal constraints they might or might not create in later years.

Or could it? Tax cutting had been a way of life in Washington since the Reagan years. Even the Democrats principally used tax breaks, if in a more targeted way, to achieve their economic and social objectives. An economic package that the Democratic congressional leadership introduced in January to counter the Bush tax cuts, and which died a quick death in both houses, was built primarily around tax rebates for working families, tax relief for small businesses, and tax incentives for all businesses to invest in new plants and equipment.

While Washington lawmakers couldn't make binding promises for the future no matter how hard they tried, it would be wrong to think they couldn't alter the political culture to give some promises more force than others. Roosevelt had done this by making his Social Security scheme a blending of welfare and retirement saving elements, locked in place by a generational compact. Bush and Rove aimed to do the same thing with a series of tax cuts and, ultimately, a radical reform of the entire tax system. If they succeeded, Social Security could find itself competing directly with these other promises.

* * *

In December 2003, Bush signed one of the most important bills of his presidency, the Medicare Prescription Drug, Improvement, and Modernization Act. The new law, the most sweeping overhaul in Medicare's history, was the fruit of months of prodigious arm-twisting on Capitol Hill involving nearly 1,000 lobbyists from the pharmaceutical and managed care industries spending a combined $141 million.[12] Its most discussed feature was a new, voluntary prescription drug coverage for seniors, to be provided through outside insurers and HMOs.

This, however, was only one element of the Medicare overhaul, which also aimed to lure retirees to opt out of the traditional program and instead enroll with one of a group of HMOs. These HMOs would receive huge taxpayer subsidies to manage their care in a new program called Medicare Advantage.

Two important provisions weren't aimed at Medicare recipients at all, but at current workers.

One allowed them to set up Health Savings Accounts (HSAs), a new, tax-free vehicle through which they could save to cover medical expenses. To win Democratic voters, and lest the HSAs encourage more private employers to drop health insurance coverage for their workers, the bill also included $90 billion in subsidies for companies that continued to offer it. The new drug benefit, dubbed Medicare Part D, would go into operation in January 2006; Medicare Advantage and the new HSAs would be available immediately.

Whatever else they accomplished, HSAs and Medicare Advantage represented another step in the direction of Bush's ownership society and a further test of the concept behind privatized Social Security. The HSAs offered workers—those who could afford to do so—a way to build up assets they could use to pay for the high-deductible insurance plans that the Bush administration claimed were the consumer-driven answer to escalating health insurance costs.

Something like 401(k)s for health care, HSAs would acclimatize workers to covering their fastest growing set of expenses themselves rather than through employer- or government-subsidized plans.

The Club for Growth's Stephen Moore quickly picked up on HSAs' potential, arguing that the concept should be expanded into a whole range of accounts targeted at workers' specific needs. "I'm in favor of dramatically broadening tax-free savings accounts," he said, as a way "of short-circuiting the left's ability to create new government programs, because if people have enough money in these accounts, they don't need new government programs."[13]

Medicare Part D got off to a rocky start, however. The cost of implementing the new benefit turned out, embarrassingly, to be much higher than advertised. As for Medicare Advantage, the government was paying the private plans that participated in it an average 107% of traditional Medicare's cost, with the ratio running as high as 116% in some cities and 123% in rural counties.[14] A mini-scandal blew up over alleged misuse of federal money to promote the Medicare Modernization Act.[15] When Democrats introduced a bill that would have enabled HHS to use Medicare's purchasing power to negotiate lower drug prices with pharmaceutical companies, the White House and Republican leaders shot it down. Even many conservative members of the president's party continued to criticize the new law, fearing Part D would evolve into another expensive entitlement, despite its free-market elements.

* * *

By the time the Medicare bill was signed, talk in Washington had refocused on how to restructure Social Security. The president was doing everything he could to encourage this, proselytizing constantly about the benefits of the ownership society.

"We want more citizens owning their own home," he told a fundraiser audience in St. Paul in August. "We want people to own and manage their own retirement accounts. We want people to have control of their own medical accounts.... We understand that when America and Americans own something, he or she has a vital stake in the future of our country." While the administration had gone back and forth on prioritizing either Social Security restructuring or a sweeping tax overhaul, by now "analysts and people with ties to the White House" were telling the *New York Times* that Bush's signature second-term initiative would be his "proposal to remake the Social Security system to add private investment accounts."[16]

Diminishing one of the stumbling blocks such a project would encounter, the economy was improving, and with it, federal tax receipts. In October, the Treasury Department estimated that the federal deficit for the fiscal year just ended would be between $370 billion and $380 billion—a big improvement over the $455 billion shortfall the administration had predicted a few months earlier. Not only was this encouraging news for Bush cheerleaders seeking evidence that his tax cuts had "worked," but it offered hope that Congress could be weaned off its need for payroll tax surpluses to keep the books a little closer to being balanced. That being the case, more of the surplus might be available to cover the transition costs of revamping Social Security.

One of the goals Bush urged Congress to take on in his January 21, 2004 State of the Union address was privatization. After calling upon lawmakers to make his tax cuts permanent—"for the sake of job growth"—the president again connected private Social Security accounts with his quest to create an ownership society. "Younger workers should have the opportunity to build a nest egg by saving part of their Social Security taxes in a personal retirement account," he said. "We should make the Social Security system a source of ownership for the American people."

In his testimony before the House Budget Committee the next month, Alan Greenspan stressed the urgency of restructuring Social Security. His political antennae aquiver, the Fed chair endorsed the Bush tax cuts, even though they were now projected to increase the federal debt by $1.5 trillion over the next ten years. Making the cuts permanent, as the president desired, was a fine idea, Greenspan said, as long as Congress accompanied it with offset rules to cut spending or increase tax revenue.

The real threat to the nation's fiscal balance, according to Greenspan, was the future cost of Social Security and Medicare benefits. For the former, he suggested two changes: replacing the current COLA formula with one based on an inflation measure—the "chained CPI," which was intended to better reflect the savings consumers enjoy when they switch to less costly items—and indexing the retirement age to increases in life expectancy. Both would result in big benefit reductions for retirees, but Greenspan considered that far preferable to raising taxes.

"The crucial issue out here is the rate of growth of productivity and the rate of growth of the economy," he told the House panel. "What history does tell us is that keeping tax rates down will tend to maximize that."[17]

Greenspan's remarks ignited fury from the more progressive wing of the congressional Democrats. Sen. John Edwards of North Carolina, a presidential candidate, called it "an outrage" that Greenspan should suggest making tax cuts permanent on "unearned wealth while cutting Social Security benefits that working people earn." Sen. John Kerry of Massachusetts, another aspiring Democratic nominee, declared, "The wrong way to cut the deficit is to cut Social Security benefits. If I'm president, we're simply not going to do it."[18]

Even Bush felt the need to distance himself somewhat from the Fed guru's comments, reiterating that he wouldn't cut benefits for those nearing retirement. Yet his latest "Economic Report of the President," sent to Congress earlier that month, had also recommended Social Security benefit reductions. "Reform should include moderation of the growth of benefits that are unfunded and can therefore be paid only by assessing taxes in the future," it said, implying the same trade-off Greenspan had bluntly called for.[19]

Fear of an aging society, and the cost of supporting it, was again on the rise within the mainstream press. A few days before the Greenspan storm blew up, the *New York Times Sunday Magazine* published "Life in the Age of Old, Old Age," a feature warning of the traumas households and society as a whole would suffer if the trend toward increased longevity continued.[20] Replete with human interest tales of the lonely and aged, the article asked a series of unanswerable questions about the disreputable behavior longer life might be encouraging—which read like backstory script discussions for a remake of *Soylent Green*.

"What if the increased life expectancy we see in developed nations like France is somehow causing their lower birthrates, robbing people of the urgency to reproduce?" speculated the author, Susan Dominus. Or, citing a doomsday report by the President's Council on Bioethics, "In a world populated by able-bodied and able-minded centenarians, their aging children might remain 'functionally immature "young adults" for decades, neither willing nor able to step into the shoes of their mothers and fathers.'"

The article cited few real experts on the subject of aging, and certainly none who disagreed with its basic thesis, but it gave considerable space to Larry Kotlikoff, whose latest jeremiad, *The Coming Generational Storm*, was about to hit the press. As usual, he predicted an America crippled by skyrocketing taxes needed to support outrageous retiree benefits and social tensions that would rip the country apart, the relatively wealthy elderly on one side and on the other, "the young—mostly poor blacks and Hispanics, heavily burdened with the financial cost of caring for a class of people to whom they have little allegiance." And it could all get worse, Dominus suggested, if scientists kept searching for new ways to help people live longer.

Reading her piece, it was difficult not to conclude that cutting Social Security benefits, perhaps as Greenspan had suggested, was essential to avoiding a societal train wreck. Contrary to the impression Dominus created, the economics profession wasn't agreed upon this. Paul Krugman, also in the *New York Times*, pointed out that, according to the Gokhale-Smetters study, still being widely cited, Social Security and Medicare were a combined $44 trillion in the red. But 62% of that huge figure was projected to come after 2077: an absurd forecast on which to base drastic benefits cuts affecting workers who would retire in less than ten years.

"Why should fiscal decisions today reflect the possible cost of providing generations not yet born with medical treatments not yet invented?" Krugman asked.[21]

Dean Baker suggested a look at where the supposedly enormous costs of caring for the future elderly would come from. The vast majority, he pointed out, were due to the once-again skyrocketing cost of health care: "If U.S. health care costs, adjusted for demographic change, only grew in step with per capita GDP growth, then paying for Medicare over the next forty years would present no greater problem than it did over the last forty years."[22]

Reforming the convoluted and wasteful U.S. health care system, then, was the key to avoiding enormous Medicare expenses in the future. And to preserving the value of Social Security. A report by the SSA in October, laying out the COLAs that beneficiaries would receive over the next year, noted that almost half of the increase in payments would be swallowed up by higher Medicare premiums the Bush administration had announced some weeks earlier.*

Bob Ball again suggested legislating payroll tax increases that would automatically kick in at some point during future decades if the trust fund assets fell below a certain level. "That should avoid periodic false cries about Social Security's finances," he told Jane Bryant Quinn.[23] Of course, future Congresses could repeal Ball's "trigger." But beyond a certain point, it wasn't up to the current generation of lawmakers to tell their distant successors what to do. Economic and fiscal conditions could change in ways that the lawmakers of 2004 couldn't conceive.

Most of the mainstream media, however, continued to accept the inevitability of drastic changes in Social Security. In a Q&A on the issue, "How Sick Is Social Security?" the *Wall Street Journal* told its readers that "the anticipated strains on the system mean that some type of fix—increased taxes, smaller payouts, private accounts—will soon be adopted."[24] This assertion was presented as self-evident fact.

---

*   Medicare premiums were automatically deducted from monthly Social Security checks for the elderly and disabled (Robert Pear, "Social Security Payment Will Increase, as Will Medicare Bite," *New York Times*, October 20, 2004).

CHAPTER 35

REACHING FOR A MANDATE

The 2004 Democratic race for president started off very differently from the last one, with an unusually wide field of candidates. These included progressives bearing populist messages that left their centrist competitors distinctly uncomfortable. Some party leaders, like Iowa Sen. Tom Harkin, argued that under Clinton, the party had successfully shed its anti-business, pro-welfare image. Now, it must energize its core liberal supporters and work harder at differentiating itself from the Republicans.

In the early stages of the presidential contest, John Edwards made a name for himself by attacking Bush's "voodoo economics," his civil rights record, and of course, his promise to privatize Social Security. Another candidate, Ohio Rep. Dennis Kucinich, wanted to expand Medicare into a universal health care system and return the retirement age for full Social Security benefits to sixty-five.

Kucinich and another presidential contender, Sen. Bob Graham of Florida, were among the few congressional Democrats who had opposed the Iraq war outright in the spring of 2003, when Edwards, Kerry, and Lieberman, the most prominent names in the nomination race, had gone along with the president's plans to invade another country. And while the mainstream media dismissed Kucinich's chances, often injecting a patronizing tone into their coverage, they had a tougher time dismissing Howard Dean. The former Vermont governor was promising to swiftly end the American presence in Iraq while standing to the left of the party's more prominent names on most domestic issues as well. As did Dick Gephardt, Dean promised to repeal all the Bush tax cuts.

On the surface, a populist stand on the economy made sense. Because productivity had continued to grow since the beginning of the recession, employers could meet increases in demand while still eliminating jobs or hiring only a few workers: hence the frequently heard term, a "jobless recovery." Job opportunities were growing sluggishly even for college graduates. Unemployment numbers would have looked even uglier if many people hadn't simply stopped looking. In May 2003, it was reported that 2.8 million people had exhausted their unemployment benefits over the past year.[1]

But Bush's status as a wartime president, and anxiety over the wide margin by which donors from business and finance favored the Republicans, had the Democratic Party elders more frantic than hopeful over the prospect of a "populist revolt." Given the division in the party, the leadership had trouble assembling a program to run on that looked in any way inspiring, let alone visionary. One major element was "tax reform"—a more positive way to spin their support for repealing some of the Bush tax cuts and restructuring others to favor middle-income workers.

Another was opposition to privatizing Social Security. The legacy of the Gore campaign and the final two years of the Clinton administration was the near disappearance of the bloc of Democratic lawmakers who publicly supported private-account carve-outs. Three years later, the public seemed so emphatically opposed to the idea that passing up the opportunity to use it against Bush made no sense. None of the nine candidates running for the nomination, from Joe Lieberman, on the right, to preacher and civil rights activist Al Sharpton, on the left, supported private accounts.

"'Privatization' has become the top Democratic bogeyman," lamented *Wall Street Journal* columnist Alan Murray.[2]

A succession of polls revealed it as a clear area of vulnerability for Bush. The president's popularity had been declining during the summer of 2003, and no more so than with the elderly. A Gallup poll in October showed only 49% of all respondents agreed that they approved of the job he was doing, versus 60% of those aged thirty to forty-nine. Another survey by EMILY'S List, the Democratic women's fundraising group, found that older voters' reservations about Bush were driven by concerns about his stands on Social Security and Medicare in particular.

Polls were one thing, but the supermarket tabloids agreed as well. *Sun*, a rival in the sensation business to the *National Enquirer* and other fine titles, in January ran a front page with the screaming headline, "Social Security:

Truth They Don't Want *You* to Know." The story inside contained a simplified but fairly garden-variety discussion of the dangers of swapping a guaranteed benefit for a plunge into the stock market. But the headlines told a more alarming story: "Politicians Target Social Security: Raid will leave millions of Americans out in the cold." Brightening up the text was an illustration of a man in a suit and tie—presumably, a Wall Street type—peering greedily into a cracked-open nest egg.*

All of this encouraged the Democratic presidential candidates, both the progressives and the moderate-to-conservative faction, to hammer home the folly of Bush's proposals. The moderates were careful, however, to frame their opposition as a matter of fiscal prudence, of concern that carving out private accounts would balloon the deficit. Gene Sperling calculated for reporters that private accounts would add $2 trillion to the deficit over ten years. John Kerry, the eventual nominee, while promising that he would "never privatize [or] try to extend the retirement age for Social Security," also signaled his fiscal prudence by trumpeting the fact that during the 2000 electoral campaign he had signed a DLC manifesto called "A New Agenda for the New Decade."

Otherwise known as the Hyde Park Declaration, this document pledged the signatories to work for ways to reduce the cost of entitlements. "We can't just spend our way out of the problem," the declaration read. "We must find a way to contain future costs. The federal government already spends seven times as much on the elderly as it does on children. To allow that ratio to grow even more imbalanced would be grossly unfair to today's workers and future generations."

The signatories promised to pursue three "goals for 2010": ensuring the future solvency of Social Security and Medicare, making "structural reforms" that would "slow their future cost growth," and "create Retirement Savings Accounts to enable low-income Americans to save for their own retirement."

Nothing here suggested that Kerry would carve private accounts out of Social Security. Indeed, the only concrete idea he raised during the campaign for how to balance Social Security's books—it didn't approach the level of a formal proposal—was to explore boosting the ceiling on income against which workers paid payroll tax. But the Hyde Park Declaration did hang a question mark over Kerry's campaign pledge to keep the retirement age where it was. There was an inherent tension between promising to maintain the existing Social Security program, "with very minor changes," and a pledge to curtail entitlements. And when the first draft of the Democratic electoral platform was released in July, it too showed that the party was having a hard time drawing a clear line between the policies it favored and those of the Bush administration.

---

* Brennan Geoghan, "Politicians Target Social Security," *Sun*, January 6, 2004. The back cover of the issue contained a story on a "Biblical scholar" who claimed Jesus had foretold that "the Twin Towers of the World Trade Center will proudly rise again."

The platform promised to guard Social Security and Medicare against privatization while at the same time calling for a return to "fiscal discipline." But it also promised to rescind the Bush tax cuts only for those with incomes above $200,000 a year and didn't pledge a return to balanced budgets and surpluses. Treading a fine line between the deficit hawks and the progressives, the party leadership ran the risk of pleasing neither side.

The Republicans saw the 2004 presidential race in very different terms: as another step on the road to long-term political dominance. By the middle of 2003 they had already built up a huge lead in contributions, which only widened as the campaign got fully under way. The party also launched an ambitious voter registration drive aimed at pulling in nonvoters in Republican neighborhoods and appealing to groups such as Hispanics who the leadership felt were moving in a conservative direction.[3]

The party's strategy as regards the Democrats was to paint them as angry and out of touch with the mood of average Americans, and to contrast this with the sense of national hope that the Republicans had offered beginning with Reagan.[4] That sense of hope extended from the apparent success of U.S. military intervention in the Middle East to the return of domestic economic expansion to a vision of a new, less class-ridden society exemplified by rising rates of home ownership and the proliferation of personal retirement and health savings accounts—all of which the Bush administration claimed credit for.

Some commentators outside Republican circles were beginning to take seriously the arguments for an ownership society and an investor class that would change American politics. John Zogby, an influential pollster, wrote in April 2003 that the rise of the investor class would finally break the tie that had kept Washington divided and bickering, practically since Reagan entered office. Two out of three voters were now stock market investors at least indirectly, Zogby found, up from 45% in 1997, while "just about one-half of likely voters consider themselves to be 'a member of the investor class.'"

"This is not your grandfather's investor class," he added. They "include a substantial number of racial minorities, union members and individuals living in homes that earn modest incomes." IRAs and 401(k)s had fueled a "democratization" of the investor community that was beginning to spill over into politics. In 2002, for example, low-income investors were more likely to vote for a Republican senator, Zogby found.

The ownership society theme could be traced all through the Bush reelection campaign. It expressed itself in two ways: first, in the president's advocacy of privatizing Social Security and replacing employer-sponsored health insurance with Health Savings Accounts, and second, in his support for moving the country toward a tax system that penalized consumption rather than capital investment. Deciding which of these two, if not three, initiatives to tackle first would be a tricky task for the second Bush administration. But for now, the president's reelection campaign was free to discuss them as if each was equally doable.

To stifle the clambering of the deficit hawks, the February Economic Report of the President unveiled an astonishingly optimistic scenario for the achievement of a privatized Social Security system, based on the 2001 presidential commission's Reform Model 2, which would have allowed workers to shift 4% of their wages into private accounts, offset by a 2% benefit cut. Borrowing to cover transition costs would raise total government debt held by the public to an amount equal to 23.6% of GDP by 2036, the report estimated, by piling on as much as $4.7 trillion of new Treasury bonds over a period of forty years.

Not to worry, though. "Is this temporary increase in government borrowing a problem? Not from an economic perspective," the report blandly asserted. "The deficit initially increases, but then falls as the reform is fully phased in."

The new bonds would be repaid within twenty years, through a combination of government cost-cutting; reduced benefits from the remaining Social Security program, perhaps taking the form of CPI adjustments; and the economic effects of reducing tax burdens. The entire exercise would save the American taxpayer from the far higher cost, later on, of leaving the program as it was.[5] This was supply-side economics with a vengeance—and a massive societal investment in the nurturing of a pro-Republican investor class.

Bush's advisors weren't united on how forcefully to push privatization once the electoral campaign came down to the president and the Democratic nominee, however. One faction, including economic advisor Stephen Friedman and N. Gregory Mankiw, chair of the Council of Economic Advisers, believed the president had accomplished a great deal in his first administration and should just run on his record. Opposing them was the "big idea" faction including Treasury Secretary John Snow, Rove and his aide Ken Mehlman, and OMB director Josh Bolten.[6]

Aside from ideology, these three argued, the administration had practical reasons for touting radical initiatives such as tax restructuring and Social Security privatization. One was disgruntlement on the right. The Club for Growth and the big corporate donors who bankrolled it were contemplating a revolt against what they regarded as the White House's inclination to tolerate "RINOs" in Congress: Republicans in Name Only, who apparently didn't do enough to promote the Club's small-government, low-tax agenda.

The Club for Growth was founded in 1999 as a vehicle for bundling contributions to candidates who supported those basic positions. In 2002, it raised more than $10 million from 9,000 members, making it one of the most powerful political fundraising machines on the right, according to the Center for Responsive Politics, which tracked campaign giving. In 2004, The Club was already upset at the White House for endorsing Arlen Specter for reelection to his Pennsylvania Senate seat when they had been promoting the much more conservative Rep. Pat Toomey in a primary challenge. One way Bush could win back his support, said Tucker Anderson, an investment manager and prominent figure in the Club, was by championing Social Security privatization.[7]

The Bush camp made it known that the president would be bringing up Social Security as his campaign moved beyond the primary stage. In a campaign stop at Northern Virginia Community College in early August, the president made an explicit pledge: "I support the idea of creating a personal saving account for younger workers."[8]

In his acceptance speech on September 2, at the Republican National Convention in New York, the president proposed both Social Security privatization and a tax overhaul, essentially claiming a mandate to do both if reelected. The first he tied directly to the goal of building an ownership society.

"In an ownership society, more people will own their health care plans and have the confidence of owning a piece of their retirement," Bush told the faithful gathered in Madison Square Garden. "We'll always keep the promise of Social Security for our older workers. With the huge baby boom generation approaching retirement, many of our children and grandchildren understandably worry whether Social Security will be there when they need it. We must strengthen Social Security by allowing younger workers to save some of their taxes in a personal account, a nest egg you can call your own, and government can never take away."

* * *

While the Republicans could still out-fundraise them in a heartbeat, one of the stories of the 2004 campaign season was the Democrats' discovery of some important new sources of cash. The Dean campaign, before it flamed out, had successfully tapped the online community of progressives to collect a formidable donation total. A coalition of wealthy liberal backers, notably hedge fund mogul George Soros, were using 527s, a fundraising vehicle that the McCain-Feingold campaign finance reform law had overlooked, to direct money toward influencing the party in—often—more progressive directions.

But party leaders saw the progressive forces as tantamount to a "Democratic Party outside the Democratic Party," and it made them nervous. Still dominated by DLC thinking, they were determined to be cautious, so as not to alienate what they believed was a fundamentally conservative electorate. The Kerry campaign, in the aftermath of the Democratic National Convention in Los Angeles, was slow getting off the ground and intent on adopting a prudent, responsible profile on domestic policy. Kerry had himself become ensnared in a powerful, personality-driven onslaught by the Swift Boat Veterans for Truth, which questioned his war record, and quickly had him dancing in self-defensive circles.

Social Security offered one way out. In September, Kerry was telling reporters only that he favored a "bipartisan process" to make the program secure in coming decades. "That appeals to those who find the middle of the road the safest place to be," commented *Wall Street Journal* columnist John Harwood.

But as Bush took to including private accounts in his campaign speeches, the Democratic candidate grew more inclined to use the issue against him.

Campaigning in Florida, Kerry brandished a paper by University of Chicago economist Austan Goolsbee showing that private accounts would hand financial services firms $940 billion in profits over seventy-five years.[9] That was more than a quarter of the $3.7 trillion deficit the program was expected to run over that period. A Bush spokesperson called the paper "a Kerry campaign pseudo-study." But Cato's Michael Tanner allowed that Goolsbee's estimate, while just slightly higher than Cato's, was "not unrealistic."[10]

Like Gore before him, Kerry continued to heat up his rhetoric as the campaign progressed. "What's happening," he told a Florida audience, "is [Bush is] driving seniors right out of the middle class, squeezing them, pushing them into places they don't deserve to be and don't want to be." This came off a trifle disingenuous. The Bush campaign was quite right to respond that Kerry should explain what kind of solution he had in mind.[11]

When the two candidates met for a televised debate in Tempe, Arizona on October 14, they rehearsed their by-now familiar arguments. Bush warned Americans of "the cost of doing nothing. The cost of saying the current system is O.K. far exceeds the cost of trying to make sure we save the system for our children." And Kerry assailed Bush's privatization proposal as "an invitation to disaster," which would necessitate benefits cuts amounting to 25%–40%. It was the president who needed to spell out his plan—specifically, where he would get the money to cover the transition costs to a private-account system.

If Social Security was in trouble, Kerry said, he would "pull together the top experts in the country" to find a solution in a bipartisan effort similar to the budgets under Bush's father and under Clinton, which had helped produce a surplus in the 1990s. Bush would have none of it. "I didn't hear any plan to fix Social Security," he said. What's more, "He forgot to tell you he voted to tax Social Security benefits more than one time."

The exchange ended inconclusively and the candidates moved on to discuss the impact of Bush's tax cuts. But on the campaign trail, the larger debate was turning into a bitter back-and-forth over Bush's alleged use of the word "privatization."

The incident in question was a speech by the president to a closed-door meeting of top Republican donors, known as the Regents, in September. "I'm going to come out strong after my swearing in," an October 17 *New York Times Sunday Magazine* story by Ron Suskind reported him saying, "with fundamental tax reform, tort reform, privatizing Social Security. We have to move quickly, because after that I'll be quacking like a duck." Kerry pounced, accusing Bush of planning a "January surprise" that would "blow a $2 trillion hole in Social Security" and cost retirees "up to $500 a month." Kerry staff economist Jason Furman said the campaign derived those numbers from a CBO evaluation of the three proposals that came out of the president's 2001 Social Security commission.[12]

Bob Shrum, one of Kerry's top consultants, told reporters on a conference call that when he asked Ken Mehlman, Bush's campaign manager, about the quote on *Meet the Press*, Mehlman didn't dispute it. But a Bush spokesperson, Steve Schmidt, in an email message to the *Times*, said the president had never used the word "privatizing," accused Suskind of being an "avowed Bush antagonist," and accused Kerry's camp of using "third-hand, made-up quotes" to "scare seniors." *Times Magazine* editor Gerald Marzorati stood by his reporter: "Ron Suskind's reporting was accurate, and it was based on Republican sources."[13]

As the race approached its end, however, Bush's other priority, a revamped tax system, began to receive more attention,[14] but he still declined to reveal any details of what he had in mind. Would Bush's "fair" tax system be built around a flat tax? A value added tax? Or a straight national sales tax?[15] Given the enormous impact that any of these changes could have on consumer spending, which was propping up the economy and in turn was being propped up by a feverish housing boom, it was hard to know how serious Bush was about tax overhaul.

The combination of Bush's vagueness, or perhaps the essentially unappealing quality of his domestic agenda for working people, and the stolid Kerry's failure to overcome the image problem the president's allies had so skillfully woven about him, left the race close to deadlocked with Election Day less than two weeks away. Florida, again, was the battleground state with the most electoral votes, followed by Pennsylvania—coincidentally or not, the two states with the largest numbers of retirees. Ohio was also a toss up, making 2004 something of a replay of the 2000 race.[16]

Close elections generally aren't decided on the attractiveness of one or the other candidate's ideas, but by each campaign's effectiveness at getting out the vote. In this, Bush and the Republicans had the edge, sending Kerry to defeat by a 3.5 million-vote margin. Bush's share of the vote—50.7% compared with Kerry's 48.3%—was the smallest reelection margin any president had enjoyed since almost the beginning of the republic.[17] But for the first time in many decades, equal numbers of Democrats and Republicans went to the polls, seemingly confirming Karl Rove's prediction two years earlier that "things are moving in a new direction."

In his victory speech, Bush reiterated the two main causes with which he had identified himself during his campaign, and linked them together. "We will continue our economic progress," he declared. "We'll reform our outdated tax code. We'll strengthen the [*sic*] Social Security for the next generation."

Republican leaders in Congress were ecstatic, believing they had finally achieve the degree of control over government they had sought since 1994. "The Republican Party is a permanent majority for the future of this country," Tom DeLay said on election night. "We are going to be able to lead this country in the direction we've been dreaming of for years."[18]

* * *

Presidential elections have always been different from others, reflecting voters' affinities and aspirations at least as much as their response to the candidates' stated policies. Americans who vote—when they vote—tend to cast their ballots for the candidate with whom they personally like to identify. They made their choice in 2004 not between two sets of policies, but between the stolid, cautious Kerry and the cocky, self-confident, riding-high Bush. What role, then, did Social Security play in Bush's reelection, and what would be the consequences?

Social Security privatization scored too poorly in the polls to have contributed seriously to Bush's win. It certainly didn't defeat him, either, although he provided plenty of opportunity for it to do so. Bush talked up private accounts every chance he got starting months before his campaign was in full swing. And while he played down the potentially painful aspects of privatization—the benefits cuts, the huge new long-term federal debt burden—he didn't disavow them either, no doubt to avoid painting himself into a corner once he had the opportunity to pursue the project.

But was he taking on too much? Albert Hunt, the *Wall Street Journal*'s op-ed page's designated centrist, noted that Bush's major goals were collectively almost impossible to achieve over the next four years. Social Security privatization, revamping the tax system, more tax cuts—one would have to take precedence over the others. Whether he picked a winner to begin with would determine whether the rest had any chance at all.

CHAPTER 36

KARL ROVE'S DREAM

*"Democrats long ago wore out the effectiveness of their old
attack that Republicans want to abolish Medicare and
Social Security."*

—*Karl Rove*[1]

Nothing underscored the strangeness of the Bush-era Social Security debate quite like the controversy over global warming, which was achieving high public visibility at about the same time. The environmental consequences of allowing large amounts of carbon dioxide to remain trapped in Earth's atmosphere weren't universally accepted, any more than were the doomsday scenarios peddled by the movement against Social Security. Yet these were informed by hard scientific research and observation, not just actuaries' mathematical projections into an unknowable future.

Popular concern about global warming peaked in 2005, when Al Gore's documentary *An Inconvenient Truth* became a surprise hit. Thanks to the film, millions of people knew that scientists had been tracking global carbon emissions and that these had risen about 1.7% each year between 1990 and 2004.

If the trend continued, the results could include melting of permafrost and heating of the oceans, in turn releasing more carbon and killing plankton that absorb CO2. That could lead to, among other things, a massive meltdown in Greenland and the Arctic before 2040.[2]

The Bush administration adamantly resisted the urging of hundreds of well-credentialed scientists who regarded global warming as a more or less settled fact, to ratify the Kyoto Protocols and initiate policies to seriously address the consequences. Bush was skeptical about the facts, given that a few scientists disagreed even that global warming was real. Yet the arguments these skeptics advanced sounded curiously similar to the cautions that defenders of Social Security voiced about popular disaster scenarios for the program.

"Climate change, like most political issues, isn't simple," wrote John Tierney, the *New York Times*'s resident libertarian conservative. "While most scientists agree that anthropogenic global warming is a threat, they're not certain about its scale or its timing or its precise consequences (like the condition of California's water supply in 2090). And while most members of the public want to avoid future harm from climate change, they have conflicting values about which sacrifices are worthwhile today."[3]

With just a few changes, the same passage could describe the objections that defenders of Social Security typically cited against the predictions of "insolvency" for the program. Social Security's future wasn't just an arcane economic matter or a puzzle for actuaries. It was a political issue that very much concerned people living in the present, their values and priorities, not all of which were frivolous.

Despite the actuarial projections, no one knew what would happen to the trust funds seventy-five years in the future, any more than they could quantify the state of California's water supply in 2090. And it was an open question what sacrifices were worth making today in the name of future generations. Some of these—cuts to education and health care, for example—could inadvertently undermine our grandchildren's ability to face the challenges of later decades.

Just a few months after *An Inconvenient Truth* premiered, however, George W. Bush attempted to kick off his second administration with a drastic restructuring of Social Security, centered on private accounts. It was the biggest and most concerted effort to overturn the program since its birth seventy years earlier and the only one directed from the White House itself. Its intent was to continue and complete the project the president had begun with his 2001 Social Security commission but then shelved following 9/11.

Social Security privatization was the centerpiece of the most ambitious domestic agenda by a Republican president since Reagan's first year in office. That agenda also included another tax cut, the permanent extension of Bush's earlier rounds of tax cuts, and a massive, unprecedented downsizing of spending on social programs and government health care. It ended as the worst domestic policy disaster for the White House since Bill Clinton's universal health care initiative a dozen years before.

The centerpiece of the ownership society that Bush and his political *consigliere*, Karl Rove, expected would cement a permanent Republican majority in power, Social Security privatization instead enabled a Democratic resurgence and precipitated the Republicans' loss of control of Congress a year later. Two years after that, the Republican machine was in a shambles, a Democrat was on the verge of winning the presidency, and the long-term prospects for a privatized Social Security system looked worse than ever.

* * *

Karl Rove was the chief visionary of the ownership society. And he was convinced that, after winning two elections while identifying himself with Social Security privatization, the issue was less politically dangerous to this president than to his predecessors. After successfully engineering the president's return to office, Bush showered Rove with a set of new titles—assistant to the president, deputy chief of staff, and senior adviser—and an office a few steps from the Oval Office. The import was that Bush's chief political operative, who he referred to simply as "the architect" in his victory speech, would now have far more direct influence over policy.

Another crucial factor was the administration's astonishingly successful track record. By the time he was reelected, Bush had pushed through Congress four major tax cuts, which were projected to total trillions of dollars over the next decade. Whatever misgivings they may have had about the matter, most congressional Democrats had also sanctioned and funded Bush's wars in the Middle East, the USA PATRIOT Act, and his construction of a vast new Homeland Security apparatus. As of early 2005, he had yet to be denied anything he wanted to carry on the occupation and pacification of Afghanistan and Iraq. Likewise in the UN and the rest of the international community, however much resentment he inspired, Bush had got his way.

The day following his reelection, the president and his staff were reportedly assembling names of possible appointees to a tax reform commission that would work closely with the Treasury Department to produce a plan within the first year of his new term. There was talk that this plan would be combined with a scheme to restructure Social Security. The rationale was that both would have to move through the same congressional committees and that, together, they could be sold as a package to encourage personal saving.[4]

In his first post-election press conference, however, Bush suggested that Social Security would come first, with the White House reaching out immediately to Congress rather than appointing another commission and waiting for its proposals. "We'll start on Social Security now," he told reporters. "We'll start bringing together those members of Congress who agree with my assessment that we need to work together." Bush cited as a "good blueprint" the ideas coming out of his 2001 commission. "Reforming Social Security will be a priority of my administration.... I talked to members of my staff today as we're beginning to plan the strategy to move agendas forward about how to do this and do it effectively."

The president had his reasons for thinking the time was ripe. The economic recovery was strengthening, a development that always encouraged faith in markets. Job growth was more robust, according to data published shortly after the election. Businesses added 337,000 new jobs in October, leaving another 135,000 in order for the workforce to get back to the level it had achieved when Bush took office in 2001. Average hourly wages, too, were finally growing just about rapidly enough to keep up with inflation. While the economy had still not reclaimed the vigor of the late Clinton years, it was moving faster to get there.

Wall Street and the corporate community were showing signs that they would back the White House strongly in a push for privatization. Following the election, Derrick Max, executive director of the Alliance for Worker Retirement Security, met with both Republican and Democratic lawmakers on the issue. "We have a lot of interest in making sure we're ahead of this and producing sensible reform," he said.[5]

Max also met with Chuck Blahous, the president's new special assistant on Social Security. The meeting included representatives from the Securities Industry Association, the powerful U.S. Chamber of Commerce, and Charles Schwab & Company, the discount brokerage whose founder was a vocal supporter of privatization. The Alliance was also meeting with members of Congress in hopes of building a voting block to back change.

The Club for Growth was circulating a memo to backers, which called for a $15 million public relations campaign on behalf of private accounts and Social Security restructuring. The Investment Company Institute, the mutual fund industry's Washington lobbyist, signaled it would be active by hiring as its communications director F. Gregory Ahern, who had run State Street Bank's pro-privatization campaign several years earlier.

Why was Wall Street so eager to get back into the Social Security privatization cause, so soon after it had decided the issue was too much of a hot potato? One reason was that, in the intervening years, fees from retirement-related businesses had only become more important to the financial services barons. In 2003, according to the Fed, private and public retirement accounts in the U.S. held $10 trillion of assets—nearly half of it in stocks. That represented more than one-third of all the stocks listed on the major U.S. exchanges. Yet the bursting of the dot-com bubble in 2000 and 2001 had shown how volatile this business could be. The prospect of bolstering it with private Social Security accounts was too attractive to ignore.

For the most part, individual firms and their top executives were still reluctant to go public with their support, fearing the kind of backlash State Street had endured a few years earlier. "There has been no lobbying because the industry knows it will be accused of making windfall profits," said Robert Pozen, who had served on the Bush Social Security commission and was now chair of the mutual fund giant MFS Investment Management. But already before the election, there were signs that Wall Street backed Bush. Ten major firms, among them Morgan Stanley, Merrill Lynch, Goldman Sachs, and Citigroup, were among his biggest donors, giving anywhere from $314,000 to $605,000 to his campaign.*

Transition costs, as always, were the big stumbling block to a Social Security deal, but the White House and some congressional Republican leaders reportedly were working on ways to neutralize this. Privatization advocates had long argued that transition costs shouldn't be treated the same way on the federal balance sheet as other expenses, because issuing new Treasury bonds to cover them would merely "securitize" the implicit promises that Social Security was already making to its beneficiaries.

Besides, this really amounted to a net saving, since it would be cheaper in the long run than continuing to operate under the existing program. Under one proposed budget "reform," therefore, any new borrowing associated with restructuring Social Security—anywhere from $1 trillion to $5.3 trillion over ten years, depending on whose estimates one believed—would be omitted from the budget, meaning it wouldn't count toward any increase in the federal deficit.

"It is merely bringing forward liabilities that the United States already has," OMB director Joshua Bolten said of the ploy.[6] But even Sen. Judd Gregg, the famously deficit-hawkish New Hampshire Republican, said he was willing to go along. "You cannot look at Social Security in the context of a five-year budget," he rationalized. "To do so is naive and foolish."

On the other side, Rep. John Spratt of South Carolina, ranking Democratic member of the House Budget Committee, took issue, calling the proposed accounting change "the fiscal equivalent of having your cake and eating it too."[7]

The Center on Budget and Policy Priorities, catching wind of this contemplated end-run, issued a paper in December attacking what it considered to be "a dangerous precedent for future budget gimmickry." Turning "implicit debt" into explicit, securitized obligations is a serious matter, the center pointed out, because it meant vastly expanding Washington's outstanding public debt, locking in interest rates that otherwise could go up or down quite a bit over many decades. Social Security's promises do "not have to be financed in financial markets in coming decades—and might not have to be financed after that, because the implicit debt could, and likely would, be reduced through future policy changes."

There was a good deal of irony here. Free-lunch privatizers were happy to argue that possible future developments, such as greater economic growth and

---

* Landon Thomas, Jr., "Wall St. Lobby Quietly Tackles Social Security," *New York Times*, December 21, 2004. The rest of Bush's top ten donors were also financial services and accounting giants: PriceWaterhouseCoopers, UBS America, MBNA Corp., Credit Suisse First Boston, Lehman Brothers, and Bear Stearns (cited in Lee Drutman, "Investor Class Warfare," TomPaine.com, July 7, 2005).

productivity, higher immigration numbers, and higher birth rates shouldn't be counted on to rebalance Social Security's books in the long run. But they were equally happy to justify their proposal to blow up the long-term federal debt load, in part, on the assumption that private accounts would spark enormous economic growth, reducing the cost of servicing that debt over time.

Even for more cautious segments of the anti-Social Security movement, the idea of converting trust fund obligations into public debt held some appeal. It was the ultimate expression of faith in what Syl Schieber and John Shoven had called the "iron law" of pension mathematics—an enormous long-run bet that today's actuarial numbers weren't just projections, but were in fact the inescapable truth. Investors would consider the new bonds a good wager, presumably, because they expected Social Security benefits to be reduced in future decades. But what if benefits decreased so much, thanks to adjustments in the COLA formula, for example, that cash-strapped retirees brought pressure to bear on their elected officials to boost them back up? Those implicit promises couldn't be exorcised so easily, perhaps.[8]

Of course, the calculations behind any attempt to neutralize the deficit effect of transition costs were more political than fiscal, part of an effort by the White House to persuade some Democrats to support its efforts. In December, House minority leader Nancy Pelosi of California said she was willing to discuss Social Security changes with no preconditions. "Meanwhile," conservative *New York Times* columnist David Brooks wrote, perhaps a bit too hopefully, "a Democratic underground is forming, made up of members of Congress willing to consider a grand compromise with Bush to make the system solvent."[9]

To many of the conservative Republican hard core, Social Security privatization had an additional aura of urgency. Some of the administration's most powerful supporters were bothered that the Congress they had controlled for a decade hadn't yet had the nerve to enact anything so sweeping. History beckoned, yet sometimes it seemed that the party couldn't, or wouldn't, follow. Bush's second inauguration was the pretext for a remarkably frank exchange between House majority leader Tom DeLay and Paul Gigot, conservative ideologue and the *Wall Street Journal*'s editorial page editor, which brought some of the conservative movement's deeper neuroses to the fore.

Was this "the Republican moment," or wasn't it? Gigot asked. "When liberalism was ascendant, from the 1930s through the 1970s, Democrats permanently altered the face of government." Poverty for the elderly was "ended," or at least vastly reduced; Jim Crow was vanquished; business regulation became far more real and institutionalized; the courts became influential players in social transformation; and "the seeds" of government-run health care were planted.

As for the present Republican Congress, however, "if the GOP majorities vanished tomorrow, what couldn't the Democrats easily repeal? I've asked the latter question of numerous Republicans in recent days, and the only confident answer I get is 'welfare reform.'" HSAs had become a reality the previous year, but at the cost of creating a major new Medicare prescription drug benefit. Republicans had once hoped to impose a cost-benefit analytic test on all new federal regulations. That effort had faded away. The trillions of dollars of tax cuts all could be repealed or left to expire, said Gigot.[10]

This was too harsh, DeLay replied in a letter to the *Journal*. "After only 10 years American politics has changed forever," he wrote. The partial-birth abortion ban had broken "decades of leftist-enforced stalemate. HSAs had shifted health care insurance significantly closer to a pure for-profit model. "Congress once raised taxes as a matter of course," the House majority leader noted. "Now we only lower them, and that represents a 180-degree shift in American economic policy."

And there was more to come. "The current congressional agenda, which includes legislation to reform retirement security, reform the tax code, stream-line federal regulations, and end lawsuit abuse and judicial activism, would have been laughed across the Potomac 10 years ago, and is possible today only because of the political groundwork laid out by the first decade of Republican congressional control."[11]

If these new initiatives were the culmination of the GOP Congress's first ten years, then DeLay and Gigot were actually in complete agreement. Doing even two or three of the items DeLay ticked off "would be a major achieve-ment," Gigot wrote. Social Security privatization, especially, "is well worth any political risk," he argued, "because, among other things, it would rewrite the social compact across generations.... Over time this will reduce the demand for government, which ought to be a major Republican goal." The biggest dan-ger, according to Gigot, was that party leaders on Capitol Hill might lose their nerve and let "Democratic fence-sitters believe they can safely oppose the idea."

Not to worry, DeLay replied: "we're just getting warmed up."

* * *

Bush also had reason to expect more support this time from the "pure" deficit hawks—the Pain Caucus, who wanted Social Security scaled back and remade as essentially a welfare system, but who were leery of the cost of private accounts. The war in the Middle East was the catalyst.

America's elite foreign policy thinkers had gone into a frenzy of specula-tive idea-spinning after 9/11, attempting to rationalize the new, interven-tionist direction they felt the War on Terror required of Washington. Both conservative and even some putative liberal voices hailed the Afghan and Iraq invasions as the beginning of a new, relatively benign imperial project, a higher calling for America to defend the emerging global economic order by remaking the Middle East.

Strangely, cutting back Social Security and Medicare was being folded into a new "national greatness" agenda being propagated by pundits from the con-servative to the quasi-liberal ends of the spectrum. The year after 9/11, Philip

Bobbitt, an influential legal scholar and political scientist who had served in both Republican and Democratic administrations, published a widely praised book titled *The Shield of Achilles: War, Peace, and the Course of History*. In it, he argued that the wars of the 20th century, ending with the fall of the Berlin Wall, had been followed by the emergence of "a new constitutional order," which he called the "market-state."

This new form was something different from the "nation-state, with its mass free public education, universal franchise, and social security policies." The nation-state "promised to guarantee the welfare of the nation.... The market-state promises instead to maximize the opportunity of the people and thus tends to privatize many state activities and to make voting and representative government less influential and more responsive to the market."

The U.S. is "a principal innovator in the development of the market-state," Bobbitt wrote, and "must fashion its strategic policies with this fundamental constitutional change in mind."[12] Leaving aside the small matter that the American people hadn't been consulted in any way about this "constitutional change," the "strategic policies" the U.S. followed in the 21st century, Bobbitt argued, must be built around its responsibility to extend and protect this brave new world founded on privatization, reduced government, and vouchers for many public services. People would make what political choices remained to them, not so much by voting or active group participation, but by their consumption decisions. As for state functions that fit the description of "welfare," the answer, in a word, was outsourcing.[13]

American military intervention in the Middle East was essential if this new social model wasn't to be strangled at birth by the culturally reactionary forces of Islamic terrorism, so the argument went. Bobbitt was just one of a host of deep thinkers—including such familiar names as Christopher Hitchens, Michael Ignatieff, and George Packer—who, with their rationalizations for the Afghan and then the Iraq wars, commanded great attention in the mainstream media after 9/11. Perhaps the most widely read and admired of these was Niall Ferguson, a British scholar now at Harvard, who specialized in rehabilitating the idea of empire.

In a book titled *Colossus: The Price of American Empire*, published in December 2004, Ferguson argued that mega-states like Imperial Rome and 19th century Great Britain were the pacemakers of human progress. The present world of terrorism, pandemics, and genocidal tyrants needed a similar enlightened imperium to restore economic and military order and impose democracy on rogue states.

The U.S. was the obvious candidate, except that Americans themselves—as opposed to their leaders—didn't seem to want the role. Americans, Ferguson complained, were "consuming on credit, reluctant to go to the front line, inclined to lose interest in protracted undertakings." Impressed by the dire numbers that Smetters and Gokhale had incorporated in their report on the deficit for Paul O'Neill's Treasury Department, Ferguson worried that Americans might be reluctant to make the changes at home necessary before the U.S. could be relied on to do its imperial duty.

These would include putting Washington's fiscal house in order, cutting the deficit so that it could make the necessary long-term investment in obtaining a large number of overseas protectorates. This could best be accomplished by cutting Social Security and Medicare, which in turn would help achieve another important goal: ending the cushy lifestyles of the American working class so they could form a new mass of the jobless, ex-convicts, undocumented immigrants, and others with no alternative but to fill the overseas imperial armies needed to maintain the new Pax Americana. Just as landless, impoverished Scots and Irish filled the ranks of the British army and navy in the 19th century, so African-Americans could be "the Celts of the American empire,"[14] Ferguson suggested.

Less than a year after *Colossus* became a topic of elite conversation, another book defending U.S. imperial extension in the post-9/11 years appeared, this one by Michael Mandelbaum, director of the American Foreign Policy program at Johns Hopkins University Institute for Advanced International Studies. In his bluntly titled *The Case for Goliath*, Mandelbaum argued that the rising cost of entitlements could indirectly bring about a new nuclear arms race. "The greatest threat to the American international position in the twenty-first century," he wrote, "seems more likely to come from the competing costs of social welfare programs within the United States, which threaten to reduce support for any and every other social purpose."

Mandelbaum was doubtful the U.S. could summon the discipline needed to play its assigned role. "The entitlements explosion, especially in conjunction with rising energy costs but even without these, will create a new political climate in the United States, and in this new climate the international services that the country came to provide during and after the Cold War are not necessarily destined to flourish. Democracies favor butter over guns." A decline in the U.S. security umbrella would encourage rising superpowers like Russia and China to expand their spheres of influence—with nuclear weapons as leverage. Thanks to American workers' insistence on receiving their Social Security and Medicare, the world would become "a less secure and less prosperous place," Mandelbaum concluded.[15]

Pundits took with utmost seriousness the melodramatic scenarios that Bobbitt, Ferguson, and Mandelbaum laid out. Pete Peterson, too, took up the theme in a 2004 article for the establishment bible *Foreign Affairs*, in which he argued that, for the U.S. to fulfill its international obligations, it must have a domestic public sector that was "unburdened by excessive political promises."

The same line of thinking seeped into the administration's rhetoric, if somewhat indirectly. In his second inaugural address, Bush tied his foreign policy objective of spreading free-market democracy around the world to his domestic goals, such as delivering Social Security into that same free market. "America has need of idealism and courage, because we have essential work at home—the unfinished business of American freedom," he said.[16]

Cheney, shortly after 9/11, had stated that the U.S. found itself in a war that probably "will not end in our lifetimes." Whether the vice president had precisely the same war in mind as the one Americans found themselves in four years later, he clearly saw it as the country's major national project for the foreseeable future. But perhaps he and Bush were responding to something more atavistic and instinctual. The economic expansion of the late 1990s had vastly increased GDP. In the time-honored manner of so many states, not just the world-class empires, the U.S. was going to use the new capacity this afforded to extend its military reach. It would be necessary to damp down Americans' other expectations so as to impose on the political process the discipline needed to carry that project forward.

* * *

The Republican congressional leadership had been busily creating that discipline ever since it took over on Capitol Hill. This was another reason the White House thought it could succeed at privatizing Social Security. With Tom DeLay as majority leader, the Republicans had tightened their control of the House to an unprecedented degree. All committee chairs, as well as the memberships of key committees, were now chosen by a handful of party leaders, jettisoning the old seniority system. And they could be just as easily revoked if the incumbents showed insufficient loyalty to their leaders' agenda. Similar moves were afoot in the Senate. After the 2004 election, new majority leader Bill Frist took control of selecting committee chairs in an effort to elevate ideological loyalty over seniority in filling these powerful posts.

Meanwhile, through the K Street Project, DeLay's initiative to cement Republican dominance of the lobbyist community, the party was pressing lobby shops to hire its ex-lawmakers and ex-staffers exclusively. This promised to widen a network of Republican loyalists who had become virtual bill-writing partners with GOP lawmakers.

These changes paralleled moves the White House had already made to establish tighter discipline over Cabinet members. "I think we have used the legislative and executive branch as well as anybody to achieve our policy goals," Republican Rep. Tom Cole of Oklahoma said in May 2005. "It is a remarkable governing instrument."[17] Two of the three branches of government were no longer to provide checks and balances against each other. They were now, or soon would be, a single "governing instrument."

Removing the roadblocks to difficult legislative initiatives, such as privatizing Social Security, was what the Republican reorganization of power in Congress was designed to accomplish. Under the system DeLay and Senate majority leader Frist put in place, it would be harder to keep a bill bottled up in committee if the leadership wanted it moved through, harder for a few determined lawmakers to stall it in the Senate, and next to impossible for Democrats to influence the outcome once it went to conference. For conservatives who wanted to push through sweeping governmental changes, the levers all seemed to be in place.

But despite their improved control of the legislative process, and even after the president made clear that Social Security was the issue he wanted to tackle first, some Republican leaders were uneasy. At a private retreat prior to the White House economic conference in December, some warned that privatization would be a hard sell, given solid Democratic opposition and an AARP campaign against it.

Both DeLay and Finance Committee chair Charles Grassley of Iowa, who would be the key player in the Senate, would have preferred to do the tax code overhaul first. Grassley went so far as to suggest the administration have a tax bill ready by March. As for Social Security, one person who attended the retreat observed afterward that "unless there's a buy-in on the part of Democrats—a good number of Democrats and high-profile Democrats—there's a real reluctance to go down this road."[18]

It wasn't just a matter of which project should take priority. Pursuing Social Security privatization first could directly undermine the case for more tax cuts. One "well-connected Republican" told Gene Sperling in January that a live Social Security debate would make it impossible for the congressional leadership to call for making the previous rounds of Bush tax cuts permanent, because, said Sperling, Democrats could then "highlight the trade-off between tax cuts for the richest Americans and potential benefit cuts to Social Security."[19]

Given that the president had made his priorities known, his allies in Congress were now concerned that he shoulder the burden of building public support for privatization. "You can't just go, 'Hocus pocus, here's a package we're going to pass on Social Security,'" said Dennis Hastert. The speaker, too, believed that for any bill on this controversial topic to pass, "it has to be on a bipartisan basis."[20]

One reason the president's congressional allies were fretting was that polls showed no sizable support for Bush's initiative. A *Wall Street Journal*/NBC News survey, published the month after the election, was firmly negative. A majority of respondents said his re-election didn't give Bush a mandate to create private Social Security accounts, while 50% said it was a "bad idea" to allow private accounts versus 38% who liked the idea. Worse, in some respects, only a quarter of respondents agreed with the president that the program was in crisis, according to an ABC News/*Washington Post* poll.

The public had plenty of reasons not to be enthusiastic about further reduction of the income-support system. One was the increased volatility of working Americans' incomes. Over the past thirty years, workers' pay had come to fluctuate much more widely from year to year than in the past. According to a model constructed by Yale economist Jacob Hacker, the five-year moving average of family income volatility nearly doubled, rising 88% between 1978 and 2000. Another way to look at this was that in the 1970s, 17% of families reported that their incomes fell by at least half when they suffered a bout of unemployment; in the 2000s, that figure climbed to nearly 26%.[21] The result was that households during the Bush era often found themselves cash-poor, even if they posted respectable incomes over a stretch of years. That being the case, it was no wonder personal savings levels had plummeted.

Some conservative economists were openly pleased by the fact that the astounding corporate profits of recent years were built on a foundation of economic precarity for workers. Greenspan spoke of "growing worker insecurity" leading to "atypical restraint on compensation increases," and warned that agitation to reverse these trends would endanger profits and rates of return for investors.[22]

But stagnant wages meant that workers were relying more on debt to attain the middle-class lifestyles to which they overwhelmingly aspired. For October 2004, the Commerce Department reported that the U.S. personal savings rate had fallen to nearly an all-time low of 0.2%, down from 0.3% a month earlier, even as consumer spending rose faster than income. Credit card debt had taken the place, effectively, of the raises that workers hadn't been getting for the greater part of the past thirty years. And the economy offered little prospect that this situation would change. Not until fall 2004 did U.S. employment return to the level it had achieved prior to January 2001. Many of those new jobs, moreover, were part-time positions, meaning that millions of workers who needed to work full-time could no longer do so.[23]

Precarity had become a fact of life in America and the quickening economic recovery wasn't helping much. Rising housing, health care, and other basic costs were forcing workers as never before to choose between saving and keeping their place on the ladder of upward mobility. Saving for retirement was harder than ever, and workers' 401(k) accounts were mostly too modest to attract high-quality investment advice—the kind traditional, defined benefit plans could afford.

Seniors especially were feeling squeezed; their traditional pensions disappearing, their Social Security benefits narrowing, thanks to the changes made with the 1983 Amendments, and their personal savings no longer stretching as far as they once did. Between 1991 and 2007, an AARP study later found, the rate of personal bankruptcy among those sixty-five and older jumped 150%, while for those aged seventy-five to eighty-four, the leap was 433%. A more volatile economy translated into scarily volatile incomes.

Experts identified two principal culprits: rising health care costs—seniors were far less likely than in decades past to have employer-sponsored retiree health insurance plans to supplement their Medicare coverage—and debt loads carried over from their working years.[24]

Nor was this all. If critics of Social Security had once worried that the program would dissolve family ties and create generations of uncaring children, they needn't have. Multi-generation families, by the end of the century, found themselves swapping assistance back and forth to cope with competing financial pressures. Grandparents were stepping in to underwrite college and other big expenses. Rising health costs for the elderly were putting a squeeze on working children of the elderly, who often had to chip in to pay for nursing attendants, prescription drugs, and other needs. A study sponsored by MetLife in 2003 found the average loss of total wealth for families who had to take care of an aging relative was $659,139, including lost wages.[25]

About 21% of the U.S. adult population provided unpaid care to an adult family member in 2005, according to a study by AARP and the National Alliance for Caregiving. More and more this was impinging on their working lives—making them chronically late for work, prompting them to take leaves of absence, or forcing them to give up work entirely.[26] That, of course, would affect their Social Security benefits later on, since workers—usually women—generally found themselves taking this step during their peak earning years.

All the more reason why working people were unlikely to cotton to Republican arguments that Social Security should be only a safety net for the unfortunate few, rather than a broad-based guaranteed income for retirees, survivors, and the disabled. More than ever, they felt the precariousness of their economic position. If anything, they needed more Social Security, not less.

Which created a ready audience for the anti-privatization coalition gearing up to fight Bush. On December 14, the day before the White House economic summit began, the CAF held a press conference launching a new anti-privatization alliance, as yet unnamed. Its members included the AFL-CIO, the NAACP, the National Organization of Women, the Alliance for Retired Americans, and the Consortium for Citizens with Disabilities.

Standing apart from the new coalition, but pushing hard in the same direction, was AARP. Bush aides had hoped to extend the partnership that helped push the legislation creating HSAs and the Medicare drug benefit through Congress in 2003. They even held post-election White House meetings with AARP Chief Executive William Novelli in hopes of finding common ground. But the group was now anxious to patch up relations with members it had alienated by backing the Bush Medicare plan. "Just to switch to this new system [of private accounts] could require as much as $2 trillion or more in benefit cuts, new taxes or more debt," Novelli said in a statement issued just before the economic summit.

Later in December, AARP announced it was launching a $5 million, two-week advertising campaign opposing private accounts. "This is our signature issue," a spokesperson for the group said. "We will do whatever it takes," he added, signaling that the ad campaign was just the beginning.

Having been politically cautious at least since the frontal attacks it had sustained during the first years of the Gingrich Congress, AARP was assuming its most aggressive political stand in a long time. The ads themselves left no room for misinterpretation. In one, a middle-aged couple stared out from the page above a caption reading, "If we feel like gambling, we'll play the slots." In another, showing traders on a commodities exchange, the text read, "Winners and losers are stock market terms. Do you really want them to become retirement terms?" Yet another showed a house being bulldozed to repair a broken sink, as a voiceover asked, "Why dismantle Social Security when it can be fixed with just a few moderate changes?"

CHAPTER 37

BUSH ROLLS THE DICE

The administration defined its political strategy at the first meeting of its leadership group on Social Security, on December 16 at the White House. Bush's legislative liaison, David Hobbs, explained the scenario simply: "Seventy percent of the battle is defining the problem and putting congressional leaders on the spot. We need public pressure."[1]

Bush would shortly begin a barnstorming tour to educate the public on the crisis facing Social Security and publicize his ideas for solving it. He would use his State of the Union address to spotlight what was in effect an extension of his reelection campaign. Meanwhile, he had focused on the Senate as the key to getting any kind of plan through Congress. Bush and his aides had identified six Democrats they felt could be persuaded to vote his way—not because they had shown support, but because their states had voted heavily to reelect him. These were Ben Nelson of Nebraska, Blanche Lincoln and Mark Pryor of Arkansas, Kent Conrad and Byron Dorgan of North Dakota, and Max Baucus of Montana. Nelson had said he wouldn't take a position until he saw an actual plan. The first weeks of Bush's tour would include stops in these states.

There were two serious problems with this strategy. First, the president was using his presence to light a fire under these lawmakers before he made the attempt to win them over. Coming straight after the bitter 2004 elections, this just aggravated Senate Democrats' hard feelings.

Second, as long as the president failed to provide details of his plan, hostile Democrats could fill in those details any way they liked, painting a picture Bush would then have to work to reshape. Yet all the president would say was that he would propose more than a "Band-Aid" solution and that his plan would include private accounts for younger workers while curbing the growth of guaranteed benefits.

To the lawmakers who would have to put their careers on the line in support of his incomplete proposal, the Bush plan looked like it would give Social Security an enormous new role—providing each and every worker with a wealth-building personal account—without explaining how this would work or how to pay for it. That part of the initiative, the riskiest of all, he was leaving up to Congress. The *Wall Street Journal* editors and other armchair observers who had the luxury of preaching to the supply-side converted could dismiss these so-called transition costs as a nonissue. But for a group of elected lawmakers, however much they agreed with Bush's aims, nothing was more real.

"They're getting a thousand cuts here," said Rep. Rahm Emanuel of Illinois, who chaired the Democratic Congressional Campaign Committee.[2] Some of those came from none other than the DLC, which had consistently supported private accounts in the past but was now rethinking that stand.

"There is absolutely no trust among Democrats that you could cooperate with Republicans, and not be taken to the cleaners," said Will Marshall, president of the DLC-linked Progressive Policy Institute. Marshall had once been on record supporting private accounts. Also in early January, DLC President Bruce Reed said, "On private accounts carved out from payroll taxes, we should draw a line in the sand and say, 'No. Over my dead body. This is what we Democrats believe, and we will not compromise.'" Admittedly, this was a bit too carefully formulated. There were other ways to cut back Social Security, and Reed wasn't ruling them out.[3]

The privatization initiative ran into early trouble from the friendlier side of the aisle as well. One Republican legislator, Rep. Jack Kingson of Georgia, said fifteen to twenty House Republicans were against it, while others who didn't want to be identified said there might be forty. Some "influential Republicans" told the *Washington Post* they were already afraid of the effect Bush's Social Security push could have on the 2006 elections.

Social Security restructuring and private accounts were, nevertheless, the centerpiece of Bush's February 2 State of the Union address. As would be the case in the coming months, his principal theme was that the program was in trouble and he was trying to save it. "Social Security was a great moral success of the 20th century, and we must honor its great purpose in this new century," he declared. "The system, however, on its current path, is headed toward bankruptcy. And so we must join together to strengthen and save Social Security."

Bush offered some new details of how his private accounts would work. They would be voluntary. They would be phased in, eventually allowing workers fifty-five or younger in 2005 to place up to 4% of their wages subject to Social Security payroll tax in private accounts. Withdrawals would be permitted only after retirement. Retirees would be allowed to pass their balances along to their children or grandchildren when they died. While the assets were accumulating, they could only be invested in a conservative mix of bonds and stock funds.

"We'll make sure that your earnings are not eaten up by hidden Wall Street fees," Bush promised—without elaborating—and current retirees' benefits wouldn't be altered. "I have a message for every American who is 55 or older," he said. "Do not let anyone mislead you. For you, the Social Security system will not change in any way."

A few more details came out shortly after the speech. Most importantly, under the administration's plan, workers who opted to set up private accounts would lose a proportionate share of their guaranteed benefits, plus interest on what they would have earned if the money had instead been invested in Treasury bonds. That meant their accounts would have to earn at least 3%—the yield on Treasuries—for workers to recoup what they would have received if they had stayed in the "old" program. Bush declined to say how he would achieve that part of the project.

The Democrats didn't close the door to working with the president, but assailed the private accounts idea. The House and Senate minority leaders, Nancy Pelosi and Harry Reid, delivered their party's televised response. Reid said Bush's plan "isn't Social Security reform. It's more like Social Security roulette." While giving Americans "more choices when it comes to their retirement savings" is fine, "that doesn't mean taking Social Security's guarantee and gambling with it. And that's coming from a senator who represents Las Vegas."

Barely two weeks after the president's speech, however, he received a powerful endorsement. Alan Greenspan, appearing before the Senate Banking Committee, delivered a cheerful assessment of the U.S. economy but admonished Congress to cut the federal deficit. The shortfall had reached a record $413 billion in the past year and it was "imperative to restore fiscal discipline," the Fed guru said.

That would include cutting back Social Security. Greenspan agreed with Alabama's Richard Shelby, the Banking Committee chair, that Congress should consider reducing the growth of future benefits by substituting price for wage growth as the benchmark for benefits increases, which would gradually reduce the replacement rate for future retirees.

"If you are going to move to private accounts, which I approve of, you have to do it in a cautious, gradual way," Greenspan added, given that such a transformation could require as much as $2 trillion in new federal borrowing. But the takeaway for lawmakers was that the Fed chair, the country's most powerful economic policymaker, endorsed the president's push for private accounts. "I'm glad we're moving in that direction," he said.[4]

Greenspan's political instincts, as ever, were more impressive than his consistency in policy matters. In 2001, he had supplied vital support to Bush's efforts to push a massive tax cut through Congress, arguing that otherwise the government would pay off its debt too quickly. He had even suggested that Social Security was in less trouble than some critics thought, because rising productivity would raise payroll tax revenues and therefore improve the program's funding. Now he was warning that Social Security was on an unsustainable course. Yet he was willing to tolerate borrowing that would vastly increase the national debt, as long as it was done cautiously and gradually—a condition about which he didn't elaborate and wasn't asked to.

More surprising than Greenspan's latest policy massage was the force with which the Democratic caucus responded. Reid, during an interview on CNN's *Inside Politics*, called the supposedly untouchable Fed head "one of the biggest political hacks we have here in Washington." Greenspan's endorsement of private accounts amounted to "shilling for the president with proposals that would put us deeper in debt," a Reid spokesperson said.

Eighteen years into Greenspan's tenure, this was nearly unheard-of language on Capitol Hill. It underscored the Democratic leadership's growing conviction that anyone who supported the president's proposal had dangerously let their guard down and that there was no longer any political price to be paid for attacking them—no matter who they were. But Greenspan's support

Presidential advisor Karl Rove coordinated the White House push for Social Security privatization, which was structured like a national election campaign, out of a "war room" in the Teasury Department Building. During a special Radio Day to promote Bush's plan, April 6, 2005, he chats with talk-show host G. Gordon Liddy. Thirty radio stations across the U.S. participated.

encouraged the White House that it was racking up endorsements in powerful places, partially insulating its proposals from political attack.

The president was intent on pressing the point that he was exercising leadership on a tough subject, even if that meant pain for workers. By late January, Progress for America, an independent group set up by former Bush campaign officials and donors, was promoting his positions in the media, including by sponsoring traffic reports around the country. Initially formed in 2002, the group had raised almost $45 million to support Bush's reelection and now had more than $9 million in the bank to promote privatization. In March alone, it spent $5 million of that on TV and radio spots, phone banks, and ads.

One TV spot featured an image of an iceberg and the voiceover, "Some people say Social Security is not in trouble, just like some thought the *Titanic* was unsinkable." Another voice then asked, "Can you think of any ideas that national Democrats have offered?" Neither was the Internet forgotten. As the NCAA basketball finals approached, Mehlman launched a contest called the "National March Madness: Preserve Social Security Champion," in which college students competed to collect the most signatures on a Republican Social Security petition.

* * *

Karl Rove, the mastermind of the privatization drive, was just getting started. In particular, he was counting on the president's supreme self-confidence to make it work. With his new titles and higher rank in the White House hierarchy, Rove was now uniquely positioned to guide both the technical, policy-setting aspects of developing a fully formed Social Security proposal and the day to day politics of putting it across with lawmakers and the public.

Bill Clinton had famously turned his presidency into a perpetual campaign, which meant constantly appealing to the public and building his policies relentlessly around polling numbers. Rove, in Bush's second term, was building the ongoing equivalent of an electoral campaign in a much more literal sense, all to get the president's Social Security ideas turned into law.

Bush himself, by the end of January, had embarked on a twenty-nine-state "60 Stops in 60 Days" road trip, designed to build an irresistible groundswell of support for Social Security overhaul and private accounts. Other officials, including the vice president and Cabinet secretaries, were slated to participate as well. All this was managed by Rove, who scheduled time on the president's calendar for policy discussions, helped set his travel itinerary, and kept track of the position of every single Republican member of Congress on Social Security.

That last task was run out of a "war room" in the Treasury Department called the Social Security Information Center. Rove himself held two regular sets of meetings related to Social Security—two a week on legislative strategy and two more, usually, on the substantive issues of the debate. At the latter, much of the content was supplied by Blahous in his capacity as White House expert on Social Security. At the former, Rove made sure that key lawmakers got phone calls about their positions and were kept close to the campaign with invitations to ride on *Air Force One* and other expressions of approval or concern.

Technically, much of the work was done outside of government by the Republican National Committee, which was now run by close Rove associate Ken Mehlman. The RNC had assembled a databank on Bush supporters during the election, which Mehlman could use to solicit contributions and mobilize individuals to make phone calls or otherwise apply pressure. The RNC held regular Friday meetings on Social Security that often included Barry Jackson, a Rove deputy.

Two other closely linked groups attended the Friday meetings as well: Progress for America and the Coalition for the Modernization and Protection of America's Social Security (COMPASS), a business-funded organization that was attempting to build grassroots support for privatization. Terry Nelson, director of COMPASS, had worked for Rove as political director of the Bush reelection campaign. The organization itself was an offshoot of the Business Roundtable and the Alliance for Worker Retirement Security, which Blahous had previously run, and had some $20 million to spend by early April. Its active members kept busy staging rallies, lobbying lawmakers, and attending Bush's roadshow stops around the country, a campaign it called "Generations Together." The Alliance itself had a $500,000 budget and focused on lobbying.[5]

"I don't think there is any question that Karl Rove is masterminding the whole Social Security strategy," said Stephen Moore, who had left the Club for Growth and now headed up a new Washington advocacy group called the Free Enterprise Fund, which was pushing for private accounts under Peter Ferrara's direction. "The White House feels it can't afford to lose on this."[6]

But Rove was having trouble enforcing discipline within the White House ranks, or even keeping the message straight. In early January, the *Wall Street Journal* obtained a copy of a memo from Peter Wehner, Bush's director of strategic initiatives, that revealed just how much agonizing was going on behind the scenes about transition costs to private accounts. "You may know," it said, "that there is a small number of conservatives who prefer to push only for investment accounts and make no effort to adjust benefits.... [But] we cannot simply solve the Social Security problem with Personal Retirement Accounts alone. If the goal is permanent solvency and sustainability—as we believe it should be," private accounts "are insufficient to that task."

While Cheney, for example, was once happy to assert that deficits don't matter, the Wehner memo painted a grim picture of what might happen if private accounts were carved out of Social Security without any offsetting benefits cuts. "If we borrow $1–2 trillion to cover transition costs and make no changes to wage indexing, we will have borrowed trillions and will still confront more than $10 trillion in unfunded liabilities. This could easily cause an economic chain reaction: the markets will go south, interest rates go up, and the economy stalls out."

The memo confirmed Democrats in their assertion that private accounts would inevitably be accompanied by severe benefits cuts, and Republican congressional leaders in their fear that Bush was trying to hand them a terrifically hot potato. "I can't imagine how you can sell benefit cuts in a partisan environment," said former Speaker Gingrich.[7] Economic advisor Greg Mankiw tried to spin the story by explaining that the president just wanted to slow the growth of benefits, since those scheduled for future generations "are not sustainable … they're empty promises." But that didn't mean workers wouldn't experience the slowdown as cuts, as AARP noted in its newspaper ads.[8]

It was to avoid letting him get dragged publicly into such messy matters that the White House had decided the president shouldn't be more specific about his prescriptions during his roadshow appearances. Internally, however, the administration had more or less aligned itself with the Pain Caucus. Blahous, in particular, understood that if Social Security was restructured to include private accounts, the cost would have to be covered either by benefit cuts, by tax increases, or by borrowing—which could also necessitate tax increases down the road.

Blahous reportedly helped persuade the president that this view was correct;[9] the Wehner memo and other scuttlebutt leaking out of the White House reflected this unpleasant analysis. Yet Bush couldn't afford, at least during the early stages of the game, to alienate the Free Lunch faction, represented by Cato and the Gingrichite lawmakers who bought its argument that private accounts by themselves were the solution, or the Republican leadership who worried about convincing their members to support a bill containing painful tradeoffs.

While Rove worked at getting his team on message, Snow spent three days in January in New York cementing support from Wall Street for the privatization campaign. On the 11th he held a closed-door meeting with major bond dealers, including execs from Citigroup, Lehman Brothers, and Bear Stearns, at which he broached the prospect of Treasury issuing an additional $100 billion of bonds each year over the next decade to cover the cost of privatization.

The reaction was positive, according to attendees. "It's a big market," said John Vogt, executive vice president of the Bond Market Association, which hosted the meeting. "Clearly the consensus in the room" was that Wall Street could sustain the additional volume without demanding a "significant" increase in interest rates.[10]

Later that month, COMPASS announced a promise that its corporate sponsors, including Pfizer, Boeing, American International Group, Goldman Sachs, Merrill Lynch, and Fidelity Investments, would spend "significantly more" than $5 million to promote Bush's proposals. Derrick Max, now serving as coordinator of COMPASS, said these big employers were concerned that if Social Security wasn't "reformed," Congress might raise the payroll tax.

Other parts of the White House's Social Security coalition had their own agendas, which sometimes conflicted with the administration's. One such was the religious right. Supply-side economics and religious fundamentalism had been closely linked causes ever since the late 1970s, when Richard Viguerie helped found the Moral Majority.[11] Christian conservatives like Rev. Louis P. Shelton of the Traditional Values Coalition had long denounced Social Security as an attack on Americans' freedom. The alliance deepened during the 2004 election, when Bush made Social Security privatization the domestic centerpiece of his campaign and some conservative pastors listed the issue in voters' guides they handed out to parishioners.

But the evangelicals were hoping above all for movement on a passel of projects that were more directly relevant to them, and were impatient that the second Bush administration's legislative priorities seemed to assign these lower priority. Action came through the Arlington Group, a new coalition of some sixty religious-right organizations and individuals, including Shelton's group, Rev. James C. Dobson's powerful Focus on the Family, the American Family Association, and the Moral Majority's Jerry Falwell. In a confidential, January 18th letter to Rove, the group threatened not to support the president on Social Security if he didn't push for a constitutional amendment banning gay marriage.

"We couldn't help but notice the contrast between how the president is approaching the difficult issue of Social Security privatization where the public is deeply divided and the marriage issue where public opinion is overwhelmingly on his side," the letter said. "Is he prepared to spend significant political capital on privatization but reluctant to devote the same energy to preserving traditional marriage? If so it would create outrage with countless voters who stood with him just a few weeks ago."

Then came the threat: "When the administration adopts a defeatist attitude on an issue that is at the top of our agenda, it becomes impossible for us to unite our movement on an issue such as Social Security privatization where there are already deep misgivings."

The letter put Bush and Rove in a bind. Republican Senate leaders said that if a vote were held right away, they wouldn't have the numbers to push through a marriage amendment.[12] Doing so would require a major exercise in presidential persuasion—just when Bush had decided to use his political capital on another initiative. Nevertheless, less than a week after the letter arrived, Senate majority leader Frist said that the marriage amendment might not reach the Senate floor for another two years.[13]

* * *

Even if core constituencies like the supply-siders and the religious right ultimately fell into line, the hardest part of getting a privatization bill through Congress would be to convince a few center-right Democrats to go along—particularly in the Senate, where the Republican majority wasn't filibuster-proof. Following the election, several Democratic senators, including Diane Feinstein of California, Indiana's Evan Bayh, Delaware's Tom Carper, and ex-presidential candidate Joe Lieberman, had made noises suggesting they would like to work with their counterparts to "rescue" Social Security.[14]

But most signs suggested the liberal wing of the party had grown a bit of spine. Actually, this change had been percolating for some while. Learning from the dominating tactics that DeLay and other top Republicans had followed since 1994, the Democratic congressional leadership was tightening control of its caucus in both houses.[15] This very much extended to Social Security. After Charlie Stenholm lost his latest bid for reelection to his Texas House seat in 2004, for example, his legislative partner on the Kolbe-Stenholm Social Security bill, which they had been submitting regularly for nearly a decade, had a tough time finding a new Democratic cosponsor to keep up the bipartisan front. Finally, Allen Boyd of Florida joined him.[16]

Pelosi and Reid knew the Democrats were still deeply divided about many issues and that some would gladly work with Republicans on matters that were important to them. In the early months of Bush's second term, for example, the Republican Senate leadership had substantial support from Democrats in passing a bill restricting consumer lawsuits. Still, fewer center-right lawmakers remained in the Senate in 2005, making it easier to keep Democrats united around a few issues fundamental to the party's identity. The party leadership settled on Social Security and taxes.

One important reason for this was Reid and Pelosi themselves. The Senate and House minority leaders were older than most other Democratic members of Congress, even at the time. More to the point, they had far stronger personal connections to the New Deal and the Roosevelt legacy than almost any of their Democratic colleagues, and these ties figured in how they decided to position the party. Pelosi's father was a Roosevelt-era House member

The Senate and House minority leaders, Nancy Pelosi and Harry Reid, held off their party's center-right by firmly refusing to negotiate with Bush on Social Security on the president's terms. This set the stage for the Democrats' return to power in 2006 and 2008.

from Baltimore—later mayor—and her mother a local political organizer who supported the president's domestic policies enthusiastically. "What I got from them was about economic fairness," Pelosi later said. "That was the difference between Democrats and Republican all those years ago."[17] Reid was the product of a poor Nevada mining family. According to a later profile, "his parents' religion was Franklin D. Roosevelt; practically the only good thing that ever happened in the life of his father was joining a union.... Social Security is 'the greatest social program since the fishes and loaves,'" Reid would say.[18]

This feeling of personal connection with the party of the New Deal was far less common in the Democratic Party of the post-Reagan era—as was any consistent set of beliefs at all. The appearance of two forceful leaders who embraced it meant that the Democrats could finally start to work as an effective opposition with roughly consistent ideological underpinnings, rather than as a majority party in waiting, or a collaborator with the current majority.

Reid and Pelosi said often that they would happily work with the president—if he would publicly repudiate private-account carve-outs and work for a Social Security stabilization scheme that didn't include that feature. But they were organizing to defeat Bush on this issue, not compromise with him. Reid set up a "war room" in the Capitol, paralleling Rove's at Treasury, to coordinate the Democrats' strategy with the coalition of unions and grassroots progressive groups mobilizing against privatization. He put in charge of the Democratic response an aide to Sen. Max Baucus, a Finance Committee member who had worked closely with the Republicans on the Medicare prescription drug bill, thus denying the Republicans a potentially valuable ally on Social Security.

Just in case the White House should come around, however, opponents of privatization were busy developing alternative proposals for shoring up the program, ones that didn't involve private-account carve-outs. Bob Ball was one of them.

Ninety-one years old now, living in a retirement community, and requiring daily two-hour naps to get his work done, Ball was still deeply involved in the Social Security discussion. He kept his extensive Rolodex of Washington influentials up to date—he hadn't converted to either a BlackBerry or a computer—and worked off a small drop-leaf table in his living room.[19] But he was following the progress of Bush's plans closely and still fielded a steady flow of calls from reporters. Of course, he had his own Chinese menu of proposed tweaks ready to hand.

His list included five elements: gradually raising the cap on wages subject to payroll tax, adjusting the COLA for beneficiaries slightly downward, bringing all state and local government employees into the program, dedicating a reduced estate tax to Social Security, and slightly increasing the overall payroll tax rate over a number of years. Unlike the AARP, Ball would raise the cap gradually over forty years, giving Congress the flexibility to change course if appropriate.[20]

While the Republican Congress wasn't about to take any of these ideas seriously, they enabled the Democrats to toss the accusation of obstructionism back in the faces of the president and his allies. Not that there seemed to be much wrong with being labeled "obstructionist" on this particular issue. Venturing into the bastion of the East Coast elite in January to speak on "The Meaning of the 2004 Election" at the Kennedy School of Government, William Kristol, the neoconservative pundit and editor of *The Weekly Standard*, was asked afterward for his advice on how the Democrats could emerge from their current political trough. The Republicans had been in a similar spot before the health care battle of the first Clinton administration galvanized their partisan base. "If I were a Democrat today," Kristol observed, "I'd be looking at Social Security."[21]

Grassroots organizers who worked within the party saw the president's privatization crusade as a new chance to rebuild the Democratic coalition. "For progressives, the battle for Social Security represents a crucial opportunity to stop the newly reelected president dead in his tracks, to demonstrate the bankruptcy of his extreme conservative agenda, and to point to a new politics of 'shared security' around which we can build a new majority for change," declared Roger Hickey.

By February, the coalition that Hickey and his colleagues had announced two months before had a name—Americans United to Protect Social Security—and a list of more than 200 member groups that included the AFL-CIO (its key financial backer); USAction; the Consortium of Citizens with Disabilities; and the American Federation of State, County and Municipal Employees (AFSCME). MoveOn.org was focusing on Social Security. The day of the State of the Union speech, it ran a print ad in which Social Security cards formed the letters "WMD" and the text, "Make sure you are not misled again," tying Bush's privatization pitch to his deceptive campaign to build support for the Iraq invasion.

The Bush Social Security roadshow looked to be a watershed moment for Democratic progressives. Previous efforts to stop privatization or major cutbacks in the program had been ad hoc, shoestring affairs, despite their success. This time, the sheer size of the Bush effort had the various groups thinking differently. "Many of our allies realized we needed not just a letterhead coalition," Hickey recalls. "We needed a massive organizing campaign to take Bush on and assemble a majority in Congress against this idea."[22]

The AFL-CIO, AFSCME, and other allies in the labor movement this time were more generous with funds to support a major grassroots campaign. AFSCME contributed $1 million to the effort. USAction, finding it had a surplus of a like amount in its national coffers, decided to "go all-out on Social Security," program director Alan Charney recalls. "We put that money out on the table for our affiliates and turned Social Security into the top priority for the entire organization."[23]

Americans United retained Hildebrand Tewes Consulting, a top Washington consulting firm, to direct the effort; Paul Tewes served as campaign manager and a steering committee representing all the principal allies met regularly. Local groups that agreed to bird-dog Bush's appearances on his speaking tour received funds to make them more elaborate and attention-getting. Americans United also launched a lively blog that, among other things, kept track of lawmakers' positions on privatization.[24]

Hildebrand and Tewes had worked together previously on the Democratic Senate Campaign Committee and maintained close ties with the party leadership in Congress. This enabled Americans United to coordinate the message sent by the grassroots groups with the one progressive lawmakers were delivering. The message was coming through more loudly as well. More funding meant Americans United could afford to hire six full-time communications staff, each of whom worked directly with a half-dozen USAction affiliates.

"Bush gave us a remarkable organizing opportunity," says Charney. In a speech to USAction field organizers in Washington in March, he said that the campaign against Bush's Social Security initiative was creating a new model for progressive issue organizing. "We were very conscious that this was what we were doing," he recalls. "This was an approach that combined community organizing with the electoral model, giving us the best of grassroots campaigning along with a more concentrated media capability."

By getting its affiliates to throw in with a concentrated effort on Social Security and using the resources of AFSCME and the CAF, USAction was able to maintain a consistent message across all the events it held on the issue. When the message was picked up by local media, that got it noticed by the national press, which then broadcast it further, which in turn helped it filter back to local media. "That way we created more of an echo chamber," says Charney.[25]

CHAPTER 38

"WE NEED PUBLIC PRESSURE"

Congressional Republicans began cautiously exploring possible Social Security legislation in early January 2005, before Bush had even begun his road trip. The emphasis was on finding ways to work across the aisle. The first meeting, organized by Finance Committee chair Charles Grassley, included Lindsey Graham and Judd Gregg from the Republican side, plus the center-right Democrats Blanche Lincoln, Joe Lieberman, Ben Nelson, and Max Baucus. Baucus had been the sole member of his party admitted to the deliberations on the 2003 Medicare bill.

Meanwhile, a few ideologically motivated Republicans—including Jim Kolbe and Democratic Rep. Allen Boyd of Florida; Sen. Chuck Hagel and Rep. Clay Shaw, the longtime Social Security critic; and Reps. Jeff Flake of Arizona and Sam Johnson of Texas—were trying to drive the discussion by introducing their own proposals for private-account carve-outs.

But the Republicans disagreed on how best to package privatization. A rift was forming between Senate and House leaders' approaches. Bill Thomas, the Ways and Means chair, while announcing his goal was to pass a bill within five months, added that the Social Security initiative would be "a dead horse" unless it was combined with a revamping of the tax code, perhaps by replacing the payroll tax with a new funding source—he didn't volunteer what this should be—and creating additional savings accounts for long-term or chronic care.

Rank-and-file Republican lawmakers, meanwhile, were getting a bad case of cold feet. In January, a study commissioned by House Republicans showed that a majority of fifty-five-and-older voters believed Republican policies had hurt seniors. "Both President Bush and Republicans in Congress are deficient on messenger credibility and issue handling confidence on reforming Social Security," concluded the thirty-five-page report by the Tarrance Group and Public Opinion Strategies.[1]

Two days before delivering his State of the Union speech, an impassioned Bush had assured Senate and House Republicans at a retreat in West Virginia that he wouldn't back down. The objective was to let his party in Congress know they could put together a bill with the assurance that he would sell it as forcefully as possible. "The president said, 'I want and I expect a signing ceremony this year,'" said Rep. Paul Ryan of Wisconsin, who was sponsoring a bill out of the Cato playbook.[2]

Shortly afterward, however, Senate Democrats announced they had enough votes committed to block a bill to carve private accounts out of Social Security. "President Bush should forget about privatizing Social Security," said Reid. "It will not happen." All forty-four Democratic senators would vote no, he said, although he acknowledged that he hadn't spoken with every single one.[3]

Lawmakers' first real chance to test public response to privatization was the congressional recess the week of Presidents' Day. The results were not encouraging.

Rick Santorum hit the road with a slideshow laying out the "perfect storm" of rising benefits and declining payroll tax contributions that he said Social Security faced. At one of his ten events, at Widener University in Chester, Santorum hoped to attract an audience of young people sympathetic to the idea of private accounts. Instead, half the attendees were over fifty, and many had questions and comments with a negative edge. The age bias was in part the work of USAction, which had adopted a "mobilize, not organize" strategy that concentrated on turning out seniors and older workers. They had more intense feelings about Social Security and were easier to reach out to than younger voters, so the reasoning went.[4]

"I'm seeing a lot of older hands. I'm not seeing any younger hands," Santorum encouraged. But the tenor of the conversation remained the same.[5] At other events, the senator complained of being dogged by anti-privatization hecklers. "Clearly the other side is better organized," he said. "They had seniors lined up to ask questions, they had staff people running up passing them notes."[6]

By contrast, the Democrats who fanned out into their districts tended to attract larger crowds who welcomed the message they heard. The Democrats also launched a series of attack ads against their opponents. One such spot targeted the receipt of some $200,000 in campaign contributions in the previous few years from banks and securities firms by Rep. Jim McCrery of Louisiana, who chaired the Ways and Means Subcommittee on Social Security.

When the lawmakers returned to Washington, Grassley said that public opinion would have to swing in the opposite direction soon or the president's plan would be in trouble.[7] Still, the Republican leadership soldiered on. Thomas held his first, preliminary Ways and Means hearing on restructuring Social Security on March 9. Democratic committee members who might have expected a carefully scripted cheerleading session got something they no doubt found more gratifying. The day's star witness, Comptroller General David Walker, gave testimony heavily larded with Pain Caucus positions. While private accounts could be part of an overall restructuring, he said, by themselves they would only "exacerbate" Social Security's solvency problems. He cautioned against the transition costs Congress was liable to bring on if it tried to privatize Social Security without paying for it prudently.

Hardcore Free Lunchers were irate. Stephen Moore and his cofounder of the Free Enterprise Fund, Larry Hunter, complained in print that Bush and congressional leaders "have been suckered into a debate about shoring up the finances of Social Security, and have put on the table a series of unattractive options that voters will ultimately reject." The problem, Graham countered, was that the administration was placing too much emphasis on the private accounts rather than on first getting the program in long-term fiscal balance.[8] The rift within Republican ranks was growing deeper.

The Democrats, meanwhile, were digging in their heels even more firmly. Two centrist senators the White House was courting, Mary Landrieu and Tom Carper, both said for the first time they wouldn't support private accounts at all. Three others—Kent Conrad, Joe Lieberman, and Mark Pryor—said they wouldn't support private accounts if it involved heavy borrowing. And forty-one Democratic senators, including all of the above except Conrad, signed a letter calling the Bush plan—what was known of it—"unacceptable."

That gave the Democrats more than enough votes, including Independent Jim Jeffords of Vermont, to filibuster a privatization bill.

One Democrat, Kent Conrad, was still being heavily wooed, after a curious fashion, by the president. When Bush kicked off his Social Security roadtrip in early February, for example, Conrad accompanied him on an *Air Force One* flight to North Dakota and received prominent, camera-accessible seating at some of the town hall meetings.

But in late March, the Club for Growth, no doubt trying to be helpful, let loose a barrage of TV ads in Nebraska, urging voters to demand that Nelson, who would be up for reelection in 2006, support private accounts. After he met privately with Bush for the first time in early April, Nelson told reporters that his views hadn't changed—trillions of dollars in additional borrowing to pay for private accounts was unacceptable at a time of burgeoning deficits.[9]

Grassley hoped that by working just with his Republican members once Senate Finance began its hearings, he could get a bill out by June and at least have it debated on the Senate floor. That would encourage the House Republicans to move along with their own bill, a process they didn't want to begin until they knew how far the Senate was willing to go.

Besides the command of their leadership, the Finance Committee's Democrats had their own reasons for staying aloof, however. In past negotiations, Bush and the Republicans had agreed to changes the Democrats asked for in committee, then reversed themselves when the Senate bill was merged with the—always more conservative—measure the House produced. This had happened one too many times, and Democratic leaders weren't going to risk it on something as crucial as Social Security. Baucus, the ranking Democrat on the committee, who was typically quite willing to work with the Republicans, stated the case plainly: "We're not going to join in a bait-and-switch strategy."[10]

* * *

One thing missing, from the Republicans' point of view, was the extra spark the president had promised to provide: a groundswell of public support for privatization. Bush had been trying to supply this since immediately after his State of the Union address, when he plunged into his "60 Stops in 60 Days" tour.

"I've heard all of the complaints—and you'll hear a lot more—how this is going to ruin Social Security," he assured his first audience, in Fargo, North Dakota. "Forget it, it's going to make it stronger."[11]

The series of town hall meetings had Bush acting as emcee, pitchman, and one-on-one interviewer. Each event was planned almost precisely like the campaign stops on his reelection route the previous year, during which he had relied on his self-confident manner and penchant for putting down sophisticates to get his message across to carefully selected audiences. Along with Bush on some stops in 2005 was Andrew Biggs, the former Cato analyst and now associate commissioner for retirement policy at the SSA, who would provide some explanation of the technical issues facing Social Security before the president launched into his more upbeat message about private accounts.

Biggs also acted, occasionally, as comic foil. "Andrew has a Ph.D., and I got a C. And look who's working for who," Bush would say with a twinkle.[12]

The presentation was slick and relentlessly on-message, initially winning praise from those who could best appreciate the execution: big-time salespeople. "You can tell he has God in him!" Zig Ziglar, the legendary sales guru and motivational speaker, told the *Washington Post*. "The president walks with his shoulders erect! He makes great eye contact!" enthused Tom Hopkins, author of *How to Master the Art of Selling* and *Selling for Dummies*. "He is buoyant! He walks at a fast pace! You can tell he's a great listener!"[13]

But reporters quickly caught on to the highly stage-managed nature of the town hall meetings—"Conversations on Social Security," they were called—and began drawing attention to it. The states chosen were generally ones that had elected a senator or representative the White House felt needed a prod to vote its way. Rove and his team then worked with local Republican officials and party leaders to make lists of individuals who would receive invitations to the events. While meeting announcements went out in advance to local media, including information on how to get tickets, somehow the vast majority always ended up in Republican hands.

From the start, MoveOn.org was in touch with members in every state to which the president traveled, urging them to organize rallies. When they did, which was at almost every stop Bush made, police typically cooperated with Secret Service to keep them well away from the entrance to the chosen venue and well beyond where they could interact with the president or provide a convenient photo opportunity for the media.

Each "conversation" typically featured four to six "panelists" who the president would ask, Oprah-style, about their lives, and then would discuss with their host how private Social Security accounts would affect them. The panelists received little scripting from the president's aides because they were chosen based on reasonably sure knowledge about their views and then were questioned closely about those views prior to the meeting itself.

Erma Fingers Hendrix, a seventy-four-year-old retired nurse, told the *Washington Post* she believed she was chosen for a panel in Little Rock because she had been active for years in Republican women's clubs. She had campaigned for Bush in 2000 and 2004 and had once introduced him at a campaign rally. "The ones who contacted me in 2000 probably said, 'Erma's easy to work with,'" she said.

Hendrix said Bush aides educated her and her fellow panelists on aspects of the president's privatization plan at a rehearsal the night before the event, with an aide playing the president and asking questions. "It was just a matter of learning," she said. "We just really talked about what was going on, what the president was proposing and what did we think about it.... They didn't prompt me what to say or how to say it."[14]

The pro-privatization groups working closely with Rove and his team often played a key role in organizing the meetings. But all this artfulness presented a golden opportunity for Bush's opponents in Americans United to Protect Social Security. No president had embarked on such an extensive roadshow in a nonelection year since Woodrow Wilson toured America to proselytize for the League of Nations in 1919. At each whistle stop, the coalition parlayed the occasion into three days of press coverage for itself—press conference the day before, rallies and speeches the day of, and another press conference the day after. The more people his critics would get into the meetings, or just outside, the larger the president's opposition appeared to be, since the national media were covering each and every event.[15]

Democrats labeled the Bush "conversations" phony and manipulative. Erosion of benefits, payroll tax hikes, huge new federal borrowing, the perils of the stock market—these topics, on the rare occasions when they did come up, were brushed aside. It's difficult to imagine any president of either party organizing a series of forums on such a sensitive issue without exercising total control of the outcome, given the intense media scrutiny. But in Bush's case, stage management was even more critical given his notorious difficulty putting complicated matters into words. The following, from a February 4 "conversation" in Tampa, was the president's attempt at an answer to an audience member's question as to how his plan would fix Social Security's fiscal problems:

"Because the—all which is on the table begins to address the big cost drivers. For example, how the benefits are calculated, for example, is on the table. Whether or not benefits rise based upon wage increases or price increases. There's a series of parts of the formula that are being considered. And when you couple that, those different cost drivers, affecting those—changing those with personal accounts, the idea is to get what has been promised more likely to be—or closer delivered to what has been promised. Does that make any sense to you? It's kind of muddled. Look, there's a series of things that cause the— like, for example, benefits are calculated based upon the increase in wages, as opposed to the increase of prices. Some have suggested that we calculate—the benefits will rise based upon inflation, as opposed to wage increases. There is a reform that would help solve the red if that were put into effect. In other words, how fast benefits grow, how fast the promised benefits grow, if those—if that growth is affected, it will help on the red."[16]

What was more remarkable than the Rove team's micromanagement of the Bush forums was the speed, assurance, and thoroughness with which the Democrats responded to or even preempted the president at each step along his tour. More than 4,000 people went to hear him in Great Falls, Montana, on February 3. They cheered his remarks lustily, in particular when he brought up national security and the War on Terror, but on the issue at hand, he was laboring at a disadvantage. A statewide poll headlining the *Great Falls Tribune* the day of the town hall meeting found that Montanans disapproved of personal Social Security accounts by two to one.

MoveOn.org, meanwhile, was running ads in the state warning that the Bush plan would mean slashing benefits, resulting in a new "working retirement." The next day, Sen. Max Baucus, Montana Democrat, held his own town hall meeting in Billings. The audience were mostly retirees and they were worried about the impact of privatization on their benefits. "All this talk you hear about private accounts," Baucus said, "it really has nothing to do with the solvency of the Social Security trust fund. In fact, it makes the solvency of the Social Security trust fund much worse. Much worse."

The *New York Times* noted that Baucus "seems comfortable in his opposition to the Bush plan, even in a state that Mr. Bush carried by 20 percentage points last fall."[17]

One purpose of the town hall meetings was to capture the support of audiences Rove felt had been left out of the Social Security debate but who might be induced to support privatization, such as African and Hispanic Americans.

The argument presented was the familiar one about lifespan. "African-American men on average get two to four years of retirement benefits, while white Americans get 10 to 12 years," said a RNC spokesperson. "The odds are stacked against African-Americans."[18]

Polls early in the year indicated that as many as 40% of blacks were open to the idea of private accounts. "Let's put it this way," Cato's Michael Tanner said hopefully, "Social Security reform is more popular than [Bush] is with black voters."[19] The potential political gains were obvious. "The Democratic Party is so dependent on huge margins in the black community that if even 25 or 30 percent of blacks back personal accounts it would be a big gain for Republicans," Tanner observed bluntly.[20]

Accordingly, just before the State of the Union, Bush held a White House meeting with a carefully selected group of African-American leaders to discuss his plan. Some had supported him earlier on funding of religious organizations to provide social services and on his opposition to same-sex marriage. The idea was to navigate around the Congressional Black Caucus, which was dominated by Democrats and firmly opposed to private accounts.

Keeping the caucus out of the discussion was proving difficult, however. The same week the White House meeting was held, Bill Thomas appeared on TV discussing his view that Social Security benefits were tilted unfairly in favor of women because of their longer lives. Two Democratic members of Ways and Means, Stephanie Tubbs of Ohio and Xavier Becerra of California, promptly wrote Thomas that they were troubled that he would consider benefits cuts "which would disproportionately affect women, African-American and Hispanic workers."[21]

Appealing to minorities was one thing—and for Rove not to have tried to broaden the appeal of private accounts would have made no sense politically. The problem was that the president was failing to make much of an impression with his sales pitch.

For one thing, he was preaching to the converted. During the election he had just won, Bush had faced an opponent unable to articulate a clear message and a group of voters unsure what they wanted and so inclined to go with what they knew. That was no longer the case. Understanding this, perhaps, his staff tended to place him in front of audiences of believers rather than sending him to places where he might win converts. In the first week of the "60 Stops in 60 Days" tour, he visited fifteen states, only one of which had gone for Kerry in 2004.[22]

When the opposition managed to pierce the closely guarded bubble that surrounded Bush as he traveled from town hall to town hall, the result was often dangerously embarrassing. In Fargo, North Dakota, one of the first stops on the tour, forty residents complained that they had been barred from the event.[23] A protester was arrested outside Bush's forum in Westfield, NJ, on March 4.[24] Hecklers were showing up in the audience at some events and the authorities retaliated by tightening their grip on attendance. At the convention center in Tucson, the Tucson Metropolitan Chamber of Commerce, which hosted that event, "was able to dictate where the tickets went," the president of the chamber said. "This wasn't an open event. It was invitation only. We controlled the guest list and that's a good thing."[25]

Equally annoying, the press weren't ignoring the protesters gathered outside the venues, but in many cases were using them to garner quick responses to the president's remarks. Bush and his perspective on Social Security weren't controlling the story. A week after the Tucson event, three Denver residents were ejected from Bush's town hall meeting there when security noticed they had come in a car with a bumper sticker that said "No Blood for Oil."

An "unidentified official" grabbed them and asked them to leave the auditorium, their attorney told the *Washington Post*. Bush press secretary Scott McClellan said a volunteer had asked the three to leave "out of concern they might try to disrupt the event." None of three—Alex Young, twenty-five; Karen Bauer, thirty-eight; and Leslie Weise, thirty-nine—were doing anything disruptive and none were carrying signs or exposing T-shirts critical of Bush or his policies. According to the Associated Press, Young said the three wore T-shirts under their clothes saying "Stop the Lies," but had decided not to show them.

All three had received tickets from Rep. Bob Beauprez, whose office, along with that of fellow Republican Rep. Marilyn Musgrove, was charged by the White House with distributing the tickets. "They believe their constitutional rights were violated, as do I and that's the stuff lawsuits are made of," their attorney said.[26]

The two House members, instead of defending what was done, distanced themselves, saying the incident was handled poorly and "the Denver three," as they inevitably came to be known, should have been allowed to attend. The White House, on the other hand, stood staunchly by its tactics. "There is an active campaign underway to try and disrupt and disturb [the president's] events in hopes of undermining his objective of fixing Social Security," said Bush spokesperson Trent Duffy. "If there is evidence there are people planning to disrupt the president at an event, then they have the right to exclude those people from those events."

"They," in this case, was a "volunteer," the White House said, while declining to identify the person any more precisely.[27] A year later, after two of the three ejectees filed a lawsuit alleging violation of their First Amendment rights, the *Denver Post* obtained a copy of a Secret Service report revealing that the persons who had given them the boot were not volunteers but White House staffers.

By April, the Bush Social Security blitz was past its stated sixty-day limit but was still chugging along. So much time and money were being expended that some in Congress wanted to know the price tag. Not only the president but the vice president, four Cabinet secretaries, and seventeen lower-level officials had been traveling the country, and unofficial estimates already put the cost in the millions of dollars. Henry Waxman of California, ranking Democrat on the House Government Reform Committee, asked the GAO to ascertain the cost as well as "whether the Bush Administration has crossed the line from education to propaganda." Democrats weren't the only ones growing uneasy. Republicans on the House Appropriations Committee, less publicly, were asking the administration for an accounting as well.

The infrastructure of the White House Social Security campaign was growing. The Treasury Department War Room had four full-time employees hired specifically to staff it, according to the *Washington Post*. Not only the White House but the Small Business Administration, HHS, the Labor and Commerce departments, and the SSA itself were tapping their travel budgets to subsidize the privatization pitch meetings. The White House itself estimated that Bush's town-hall tour alone could range from $352,000 to $944,000 in cost.

One of the president's out-of-town trips took him not to an Oprah-style forum but to Parkersburg, West Virginia, home of the U.S. Bureau of the Public Debt, for a press conference and photo-op. There, he displayed to reporters a four-drawer filing cabinet containing $1.7 trillion in government bonds: the assets of the OASI and DI trust funds.

"There is no trust fund," Bush later told an audience of several hundred at West Virginia University. "Just IOUs that I saw first-hand, that future

Bush exposes the truth behind the Social Security trust funds, Bureau of Public Debt, Parkersburg, West Virginia, April 5, 2005. The stunt, alleging to demonstrate that the U.S. Treasury bonds backing the program were really a bundle of "IOUs," brought down a hail of criticism on the president.

generations will pay ... either in higher taxes or reduced benefits or cuts to other critical government programs." Driving home the point, he added, "Imagine, the retirement security for future generations is sitting in a filing cabinet."

This intellectually reckless and dishonest stunt provoked an immediate reaction from the Democrats and even from sections of the media. Reid and Pelosi fired off a letter to Bush, saying, "For a president to even suggest that the federal government might, for the first time, default on a security backed by the full faith and credit of the United States unnecessarily misleads American workers about the health of the Social Security program." A *New York Times* editorial headlined "Shameless Photo-Op" asked readers to imagine the president visiting the vault of the Bank of Japan on his next trip to that country, standing next to the cabinet where the bank's portfolio of U.S. Treasury bonds was kept, and announcing that these pieces of paper were just IOUs. "If the trust fund is a joke, so is the full faith and credit of the United States."

Bush's rhetorical overreaching only helped convince some Democratic lawmakers that the president was desperate. "Frankly, my personal view [is], privatization is dead," Baucus said. An aide to Ben Nelson, whose vote the White House was still courting, said the senator had repeatedly asked the administration for details of its Social Security proposal and received none. The public, too, was souring. A Pew Research Center poll released in mid-May found support for private accounts as a general concept had slipped from 58% the previous September, to 44% in March before inching back up to 47%. Bush himself was suffering from his association with the issue, as only 29% of Pew respondents approved his handling of Social Security.

By April 2, administration officials had participated in 108 events in 32 states, and the Republican National Committee was calculating its House members had held over 500 town meetings.[28] Rove explained—or rationalized—the White House's strategy by saying the president had completed "Phase 1" of the privatization campaign, in which he educated the public about the issues and opportunities facing Social Security. Now he was moving on to Phase 2, in which he would work with members of Congress to lay out possible solutions.[29]

In that spirit, one of Bush's favorite topics of discussion as the tour wore on was Galveston, Texas, which, along with two neighboring counties, had opted out of Social Security in 1981. He pointed to the Galveston experience as proof that private accounts work better for people than Social Security, and the Gulf Coast city as a model for the rest of the country.

But he didn't get far with the comparison. The Galveston plan had now been in effect for a generation and the real consequences of the changeover were becoming clearer. When researchers in the SSA's Office of Retirement Policy, and then the GAO in 1999, studied the Galveston story, they found it contained a number of holes.[30] The Alternate Plan, as it was known, provided no inflation indexing to retirees—and that would make all the difference, especially for low-income workers, both studies found.

Galveston provided a higher initial retirement benefit to the 10% of workers with the highest salaries, assuming they logged thirty-five to forty-five years of employment by the county, the SSA study found. It even afforded higher initial benefits to low-earning unmarried workers and to married workers at all levels. Over time, however, benefits for all but the highest earners would erode. Worst off would be lower paid county workers who lived a long time in retirement. With only a modest 3% inflation rate, the value of their benefits would drop 46% over twenty years. Even for county employees with average incomes, the GAO study showed that, after as little as four years, the value of their benefits would be less than if they had stayed in Social Security.

CHAPTER 39

PROPAGANDA AND POLITICIZATION

"The problem isn't that Americans have gotten intrinsically lazier. They're just responding to a wonderfully intentioned system that in practice promotes greed and sloth."
—*John Tierney*[1]

By mid-May, what had started as a sixty-day road tour was nearing its eightieth day and threatened to become never-ending. "I'm just beginning this debate," Bush said. "I'm going to spend whatever time it takes to continue traveling this country and make it absolutely clear to people, we've got a problem." Clearly, Rove's Phase 1—the education phase—was still not over.

The media, however, was losing interest. By the time the roadshow rolled into the Milwaukee Museum of Art on May 19, none of the TV networks were sending their regular White House correspondents to cover the presentation, which Bush repeated almost word for word at each stop. Some newspapers, such as *USA Today* and the *Washington Times*, which generally covered all presidential travels, were no longer doing so. The *Washington Post* reported that the Milwaukee town hall meeting "has the feel of a past-its-prime Broadway production that has been held over while other, newer shows steal the spotlight."

The press had other issues to cover. Bush and the Republican Senate leadership were deeply embroiled in another fight over judicial appointments, with Democrats threatening a filibuster that would grind the chamber's business to a halt.[2] That could make it even harder to get a Social Security bill out before lawmakers started to worry about the 2006 elections. More immediately, it pulled Washington's attention away from what seemed like a lost cause.

The Democrats, however, were eager to keep attention focused on the White House's sputtering privatization juggernaut, because what they regarded as another Republican scandal had materialized. It was one thing for Cabinet secretaries and lesser political appointees to be drafted into the service of Bush's Social Security roadshow, but pulling in the SSA itself was going too far, perhaps. As early as December, the agency's website and toll-free phone lines were being enlisted to "educate" the public about Social Security's alleged problems.

"Did you know that the 76 million-strong baby boom generation will begin to retire in about 10 years?" the 800 number's on-hold message asked the caller, who most likely wanted some more mundane piece of information, such as the location of the nearest Social Security office. "When that happens, changes will need to be made to Social Security—changes to make sure there's enough money to continue paying full benefits. And most experts agree, the sooner those changes are made, the less they are going to cost."

The SSA's website, in its Q&A section, used even more dire language, saying the program's fiscal problems were "very large and serious" and calling the projected long-term deficit "massive and growing." It cited private accounts as one way to "modernize and reform" the program.

Some provocative new language was appearing in workers' Social Security statements as well. Lest they assume their guaranteed benefits truly were guaranteed, it warned them, "Congress has made changes to the law in the past and can do so at any time. The law governing benefit amounts may change because, by 2042, the payroll taxes collected will be enough to pay only about 73% of benefits."[3]

But the website, the recorded messages, and the benefits statements were just the start. By January, political appointees at the SSA had created a "tactical plan" to use the agency to communicate and market the administration's point of view on Social Security. The plan document called for agency personnel to get out to "all audiences" the message that "Social Security's long-term financing problems are serious and need to be addressed soon," or it may not "be there for future generations." The agency was to use all media to propagate this line.

To make sure its employees at every level were working for the cause, SSA managers were instructed to "discuss solvency at staff meetings," "insert solvency messages in all Social Security publications," and get creative at find-ing new channels for spreading the word, such as farmers' markets and "big box retail stores." Managers were also to observe and measure how much employees knew about the solvency issue.

The White House had used taxpayers' money to promote its Medicare drug benefit legislation just two years earlier. But this time, the administration seemed to want the agency's top-to-bottom commitment to what was essentially a pro-paganda effort. Leaders of the SSA's unionized workforce were alarmed and complained to Commissioner Barnhart's deputies about the campaign. "Some of the information being imparted by agency officials is not factual, not accurate," Witold Skwierczynski, president of the Social Security Council of the American Federation of Government Employees (AFGE), told the *New York Times*.

Barnhart's deputy and associate commissioners were, in fact, the creators and chief propagators of the SSA "education" effort. The tactical plan was written by Associate Commissioner Andrew Biggs. James B. Lockhart III, the principal deputy commissioner, was a former investment banker and corporate executive who had headed the Pension Benefit Guaranty Corporation under the first President Bush and a longtime Social Security critic. He was also an old friend of the current President Bush from prep school days. Lockhart had already embarked on a speaking tour that included a slide show about the con-sequences of inaction on the trust fund shortfall.

There was irony in Bush's decision to mobilize the agency on behalf of a political message. Conservatives had complained for years that the SSA, like other segments of the liberal "permanent government," was a mechanism for developing and implementing new programs that perpetuated the welfare state. The Reagan administration had tried to eliminate the SSA's role in policy evaluation or development. Now, a Republican administration was recruiting the SSA to inculcate a controversial political message. Only the message itself was different.

A 1988 law against communications masquerading as official SSA docu-ments had been aimed specifically at the liberal National Committee to Pre-serve Social Security and Medicare. The privatization coalition received some unwelcome blowback from that law in August 2005 when the U.S. Court of Appeals for the 4th Circuit confirmed an earlier ruling against United Seniors Association. One of the astroturf seniors' groups that Richard Viguerie had godfathered during the previous decade, the group had been slapped with a $554,196 fine in 2001 for sending out mass mailings aimed at deceiving recipi-ents into thinking they were official SSA communications. Specifically, it had used nineteen phrases including "Social Security Alert" and "Social Security Information Enclosed" on its envelopes.

The SSA's fine against United Seniors, now known as USA Next, was the largest it had ever levied. The circuit court concluded, "The repeated references to 'Social Security,' the 'Social Security Alert' border, the phony handling in-structions, and the envelopes' resemblance to special shipping methods could reasonably lead recipients to believe that the envelopes contain official information relating to their Social Security benefits that must be dealt with at the earliest moment."

By this time, however, USA Next had burrowed itself into the administration. Mike Korbey, its former public affairs director, was serving as senior advisor to Lockhart. Meanwhile, Charlie Jarvis, chief executive of United Seniors, was emboldened by Bush's recent appointment of a very conservative chief justice and associate justice to the Supreme Court, and said he intended to appeal the case all the way. "I'm hopeful that a Roberts court with a Judge [Samuel] Alito on it will value basic First Amendment rights in the Social Security debate," said Jarvis, a former deputy undersecretary of the Interior under Reagan.[4]

The Bush administration didn't need USA Next to disguise its pro-privatization mailings as official SSA matter if it could create propaganda with the same ideological message within the SSA itself. None of this was too overt. Biggs's tactical plan document didn't explicitly call for SSA employees to advocate for private accounts and none of the literature the agency began churning out on the Social Security "crisis" did so either. White House counselor Dan Bartlett appeared on NBC's *Meet the Press* to defend the "education" effort. Agency employees weren't being asked "to advocate on behalf of any specific prescription for Social Security," he said. "But one thing they can do, and what anybody can do, is to look at the numbers, and they're undeniable."[5]

"The numbers" were projections, not hard facts. But the SSA was also rewriting much of the informational literature it made available to the public to reflect the administration's views. House Democrats complained about a booklet entitled "The Future of Social Security." The 2000 version of the text had included a chart showing the trust fund running out of money in 2037 and warned, "Social Security will be able to pay only 72 percent of benefits [from then on], unless changes are made," but in 2004, the booklet was revised to include the statement, "The current Social Security system is unsustainable in the long run."

This was "simply false," columnist Paul Krugman noted, since there was nothing to stop Congress from raising taxes, reducing benefits, or somehow combining the two if it wanted to keep the program solvent. And it ignored the fact that Social Security's numbers were improving, with the date the trust fund would run out of money now projected at 2042.[6]

A bit of exaggeration was in keeping with the campaign within the SSA, however, which aimed to make the shortfall appear as dire as possible. This was consistent with statements the president was making as part of his own propaganda. For instance, Bush habitually used the far more pessimistic "infinite projection" the Social Security trustees had begun including in their annual report the year before, rather than the traditional seventy-five-year projection, to describe the program's long-term financial situation. "Just one year adds $600 billion to the cost of fixing Social Security," he said, using a number based on the infinite projection.[7]

But the president never provided any context that would show how that number related to other government expenses. For example, the Center on Budget and Policy Priorities pointed out that using the same infinite projection, the cost of continuing the president's 2001 and 2003 tax cuts would be almost 110 times the cost of filling Social Security's projected funding gap.[8]

The president was free to use any set of numbers he chose in arguing for his Social Security plan. But it became more than a matter of debate for experts when SSA employees were required to assert his numbers publicly. "It's fine for the agency to answer factual questions," Bob Ball commented, "but it's unusual to use the Civil Service organization to push a political agenda, especially because what they're saying is not true. The program is not going bankrupt."[9]

The White House's reassurances weren't enough to stop the AFGE from filing a grievance in early February. Union members complained that around January 20, they were instructed to read a statement from Barnhart to whoever called in response to the president's public utterances about Social Security or about the SSA's role in the debate—a message they said was "propaganda." They were told that if they didn't comply, they would be disciplined. The commissioner denied the charge.[10]

Not long after, eight Democratic senators, including Hillary Rodham Clinton, wrote to the Government Accountability Office (GAO) contending that the SSA was improperly lobbying for the administration. A letter sent to 140 million payroll taxpayers about Social Security's funding problems was intended to prompt recipients to contact their representatives in Congress in support of Bush's plan, the senators alleged. For an agency to spend government money on lobbying would be a violation of the just-passed Consolidated Appropriations Resolution of 2005.

GAO General Counsel Anthony Gamboa wrote back in May, refusing to change the watchdog agency's standard for illegal lobbying. "We have no reason to think that Congress meant to preclude government officials from saying anything that might possibly cause the public to think about or take positions on the issues of the day and, as a result, contact their elected representatives," he wrote. The senators had criticized this as a "magic words" standard that ignored the context of the material the SSA was sending out and that gave the White House too much room to abuse its authority over the agency.[11]

Later that month, Senate Democrats obtained an electronic copy of testimony delivered before a recent Democratic Policy Committee meeting on Social Security by COMPASS Executive Director Derrick Max. The document included editing and annotation by Biggs, who had by now transferred from the SSA to the White House as deputy director of the National Economic Council. Biggs and Max had known each other since working together at Cato during the 1990s. Sen. Byron Dorgan, a North Dakota Democrat, wrote to Barnhart, warning that the incident "relates directly to whether SSA is discharging its mandate to administer the Social Security programs in a non-political, non-partisan manner."

An administration spokesperson acknowledged that Biggs had provided "minor" editorial assistance, as had Max himself. Dorgan and other Democratic senators said they were investigating.

Just as Democrats revolted at the politicization of the SSA, Republicans blew a gasket at AARP's aggressive role in fighting the Bush privatization offensive. The *Wall Street Journal* editors accused the group of spreading what it knew to be lies about the risks of privatization to low-income workers. Any "serious" privatization proposal would include a minimum guaranteed benefit and wouldn't allow workers to "gamble" their retirement assets on just anything, the *Journal* said.

"We know AARP knows all this because we had a nice conversation a year ago with President William Novelli in which he told us as much," the editors wrote acidly in early January. "He was also lamenting the political heat he was taking from Democrats and AARP activists for having endorsed the GOP's Medicare bill. The latter, we suspect, is the key to understanding this new AARP demagoguery: It's about returning the favor to Democrats, and maintaining the AARP as a left-wing outfit dedicated to preserving the current entitlement state, damn the consequences for future generations."

Despite their slightly spluttering tone, the *Journal* editors were probably right that the flack the "left-wing outfit" took over its support for Medicare drug benefits had influenced its decision to plunge into the Social Security debate. But AARP knew its audience better than the *Journal* did. Within the first five months of launching its $5 million national advertising campaign against privatization, the group had picked up almost 400,000 new members—20% more than it had anticipated.[12]

* * *

The right, meanwhile, was turning to sharper tactics. USA Next had waded aggressively into the Social Security fight partly in hopes of dealing a mortal blow to AARP. "They are the boulder in the middle of the highway to personal savings accounts," declared Charlie Jarvis. "We will be the dynamite that removes them." The group's goal was to snatch 1 million AARP members for its own rolls.[13]

USA Next allocated $10 million for a pro-privatization public relations and advertising campaign—a healthy hunk of a $28 million annual budget subsidized by wealthy donors and corporate sponsors including pharmaceutical, nutrition, and other companies that marketed to seniors. To run the new offensive, USA Next hired the same group of strategists who had orchestrated the Swift Boat veterans' attack on John Kerry's war record the year before: former Marine Chris LaCivita, PR advisor Rick Reed, Regnery Publishing, and Creative Concepts, a Virginia PR firm. Reed's firm was paid $276,000 for his work, and Creative Concepts more than $165,000.

That USA Next would turn to such hardballers was no surprise. Accordingly, the administration kept its distance. "It doesn't take a rocket scientist to see that the White House doesn't want anything to do with a group that is attacking the AARP," a Bush aide told the *New York Times*. "We are not going to drag them into this mess."

But the Swift Boat approach revealed itself quickly. On February 21, USA Next ran an ad on the website of the conservative magazine *The American Spectator* linking AARP to gay marriage. The ad showed an image of an American soldier juxtaposed with one of two men in tuxedos, kissing. An X was drawn through the soldier, while the image of the two men sported a check mark. The ad was headlined, "The real AARP agenda." AARP said it had no position on the issue, although it had opposed an amendment to the Ohio state constitution banning gay marriage, and Cato criticized USA Next for introducing homophobia into the discussion.[14] Jarvis warned that this was just the start.

"We are going to be revealing areas where the AARP is out of touch with a large number of their members, including the issue of marriage," he told the *New York Times*. "We will engage AARP with an aggressive campaign to educate the people about where they really stand on the issues."

Whether the White House really was keeping USA Next at arm's length or using the group as a surrogate, its message was generally in line with the administration's recurring theme that opponents of private accounts were "obstructionists" out of touch with the public. In his town hall meetings, Bush warned politicians over and over about "not being part of the solution."

The president's opponents ignored his advice and instead directly attacked some of the people and forces behind the push for private accounts. The AFL-CIO set up websites blasting brokerages Charles Schwab & Company and Edward D. Jones & Company for supporting private accounts. After union members picketed two Jones offices in February, the firm pulled out of the pro-privatization Alliance for Worker Retirement Security. Unions also began writing letters of concern to a list of financial services firms that were lobbying for private accounts, including J.P. Morgan Chase, Merrill Lynch, Morgan Stanley, Barclays Global Investors, T. Rowe Price Group, State Street, and Wachovia Corporation.

A letter to J.P. Morgan Chase from AFSCME said the union members were "concerned about your firm's apparent ties to efforts that are potentially injurious to the retirement security of our plans' beneficiaries." This "may be at odds with the duty to represent the best interests of our plan and its beneficiaries."

The letters stopped short of threatening to take union pension management business away from the firms, as the AFL-CIO had done during the late 1990s,[15] but within the next month another investment firm, Waddell & Reed, had quit the Alliance for Worker Retirement Security. The Financial Services Forum, a group of CEOs of financial services companies, announced it was leaving COMPASS, although it denied the union campaign affected its decision. "We're seeking to pull Wall Street money out of the [Social Security] debate," Bill Patterson, director of the AFL-CIO's Office of Investment, said forthrightly.

Union leaders also saw a huge political opportunity. "If we are able to stop George Bush in terms of this privatization effort," AFSCME President Gerald McIntee said, "it probably means the day after it is voted down or withdrawn, that's the day he becomes a lame duck president for the rest of his time in the White House."[16]

By late March, labor delegations had met about Social Security with ninety members of Congress and were distributing tens of thousands of antiprivatization fliers to workers through union shop stewards. On March 31, the AFL-CIO held a day of action in over seventy cities, including Washington, New York, and San Francisco, featuring demonstrations and town hall meetings against Social Security privatization. By this time, the federation's biggest target was Schwab. One of the protests was outside the Ritz-Carlton Hotel in New York, where the company's chairman and founder was speaking. A Schwab spokesperson complained that the unions' antagonism was "misdirected," because the firm hadn't endorsed one particular approach to privatization—skipping the matter of its founder's long-standing support for the concept.

The union campaign was at least attracting media attention, and the industry groups and Republican leaders backing private accounts were starting to get annoyed. On the AFL-CIO's day of action, RNC press secretary Tracey Schmitt told the *New York Times*, "Today's theatrics once again reveal that many labor unions are more concerned with partisan politics than the interests of their own members. Recent activities to intimidate organizations that support the president's Social Security efforts amount to thuggery and do nothing to encourage public debate."

More broadly, the *Wall Street Journal* editors accused labor of attempting "to turn entire corporations into lobbyists for their social and political goals" and "muzzle the free-speech of corporations." The paper suggested that the Labor Department and the SEC look into whether union leaders were violating their fiduciary obligations as pension sponsors by pushing companies like Schwab to take actions, like opposing private accounts, that might make them less competitive and thus less profitable to their shareholders. Two House Republicans, John Boehner of Ohio and Sam Johnson of Texas, had already done just that, asking Labor Secretary Elaine Chao to probe whether union leaders were violating federal labor and pension laws by pressuring companies to "base investment decisions on politics" by not supporting the Bush plan.

At COMPASS and the Alliance for Worker Retirement Security, Derrick Max was busy looking for other ways to extend the retaliation against labor. Marie Cocco, a columnist for *Newsday*, overheard him on a train ride to Washington discussing the possibility of finding some union members who would file a complaint against their unions for breach of fiduciary duty. When she asked him about this several days later, Max said, "I've been arguing to anyone who would listen" about the idea, including some administration officials he declined to name.

AFL-CIO officials, for their part, rejected the charge that they were violating their fiduciary duty for the simple reason that the federation didn't run any pension funds of its own. The other unions that had written letters to financial services firms, including AFSCME, didn't run pension funds either. "The only thing that's illegal is the effort to coerce the Labor Department to bring Wall Street to suppress labor's First Amendment rights," said the federation's general counsel.[17]

The Labor Department responded in early May with a letter to the AFL-CIO saying it was "very concerned" that pension plans might be using their participants' money to "advocate a particular result in the current Social Security debate." If they were, the letter said, they might be violating their fiduciary obligations. But the letter didn't mention any actual instances of this and the department made no formal accusations.

* * *

Not surprisingly, opponents and proponents of the president's plan also fought fiercely over the use of the word "privatize."

A couple of years earlier, Bush hadn't been afraid of the word. In October 2002, he had told ABC News, "What privatization does is allow the individual worker—his or her choice—to set aside money in a managed account with parameters in the marketplace." But during his reelection campaign in 2004, the president's spokespeople claimed repeatedly that he had never used the word, ever.

By the time he launched his town hall tour the following January, the administration had crafted a more neutral piece of language. A 104-page playbook that congressional Republicans began using at the end of January, titled "Saving Social Security," counseled that they should promote "personalization" rather than "privatization," since the latter "connotes the corporate takeover of Social Security."[18]

Democrats, of course, insisted on the word "private" when they heard reporters use the Republicans' preferred term. Frank Luntz, the GOP pollster, explained his side's concern. "'Private' is exclusive," he said. "'Private' is limiting. 'Private' is something that's not available to all." On the other hand, "'personal' is encompassing. It's individual. It's ownership."

A fine distinction, perhaps, but it made a difference. When Glen Bolger, another Republican pollster, asked respondents to an NPR survey whether they favored or opposed "voluntary personal accounts" as part of Social Security, 41% said they favored the idea and 49% opposed it. When asked if they supported the president's effort to "privatize Social Security and divert part of the Social Security system into private accounts," only 34% said yes while 58% said no.

The young, who Bush and Rove fervently hoped would turn out enthusiastically in favor of private accounts, were still less enamored than their supposed self-interest suggested they should be. A poll by Rock the Vote, AARP, and the Joint Center for Political and Economic Studies, released in February, found that 65% of respondents eighteen to thirty-nine would oppose private accounts if it meant "changes in the way Social Security benefits are calculated would result in cuts in guaranteed benefits for everyone, not just people who choose to participate in [the] private accounts program." ABC News and the *Washington Post* found that only 40% of eighteen- to twenty-nine-year-olds supported the president's plan.

CHAPTER 40

A TIPPING POINT

While the drift in opinion polls seemed to be moving in their direction rather than the president's, the Democratic leadership didn't have an easy job maintaining party unity against Bush's Social Security offensive. A steady stream of voices throughout the winter and spring of 2005 were demanding the Democrats come up with a Social Security rescue plan of their own. "Liberals are making a historic mistake by lining up so adamantly against Social Security reform," worried Nicholas Kristof in the *New York Times* in February.

Bob Kerrey, from his academic perch in New York, opined that Democrats shouldn't be fighting against private accounts, but rather negotiating hard with the majority party to make sure a private-accounts system was fairly structured—for instance, by keeping administrative costs low and giving lower-income workers more incentives and subsidies to invest than the affluent. Otherwise, "the disinvestment in public infrastructure caused by the growth in Medicare and Medicaid will become even worse than it is today."[1]

In a memo in early March, Stan Greenberg and James Carville warned, "To say there is no problem simply puts Democrats out of the conversation for the great majority of the country that want political leaders to secure this very important government retirement program."[2]

Just a couple of years earlier, the Democratic leadership might have agreed and gone along. But in 2005, just saying no was an immensely attractive strategy, in part because the polls—and the visible jitters among members of his own party—were making it so clear that the president had stepped in something foul. "The key question is, are you in a climate where the public is demanding action on Topic X?" argued Democratic pollster Guy Molyneux. "If you can convince the public that a particular solution is bad enough, they'll settle for the status quo." In other words, the "conversation" that Carville and Greenberg believed was taking place on Social Security was an illusion.

Bush seemed only to underscore the point in his infrequent meetings with Democratic lawmakers. When Charlie Rangel sat down with him in April and suggested the two parties could work together if he took private accounts off the table, he reported that Bush replied, "Congressman, I am the president. And private accounts are not coming off the table even if it's the last day I spend in the presidency."[3]

The Democratic leadership did introduce its own version of a private account plan in July. Needless to say, the AmeriSave program wouldn't be funded out of payroll taxes. Instead, the government would match $1 for every $1 invested by a middle- or working-class household in an IRA or 401(k) account. To help them make better decisions on how to invest their nest eggs, AmeriSave would also provide a tax credit to employers to "encourage access" for their workers to independent financial advisors.

Nearly 100 million workers would be eligible for the match, the bill's sponsors estimated. The legislation had nothing directly to do with Social Security, so it sent a message that the Democrats didn't believe the goal of encouraging retirement saving needed to be linked with stabilizing an existing government program. It implied as well that government should focus its efforts to encourage saving on less affluent workers. "Democrats will strengthen retirement security without adding to the deficit," they said. "The AmeriSave Plan will increase national savings and grow our economy while helping middle-class families prepare for a brighter future."

* * *

By the time the Democrats delivered that riposte, Bush was already buckling under the pressure to deliver a plan of his own for dealing with the transition costs his privatization scheme would generate. In late April, he thought he'd found the answer. In a prime-time news conference on April 28, he backed a solvency proposal known as "progressive indexing." Under this scheme, OASI benefits would gradually be cut for succeeding generations of workers. But the cuts would be means-tested. Those at the upper-income levels would see their benefits reduced the most, those in the middle less so. Lower-income workers would suffer no cuts at all.

Politically, the idea was to give conservative Democrats an escape hatch to justify endorsing the president's project. But Bush himself badly needed a boost. Gasoline prices were rising alarmingly, stocks were sinking, and public support for the Iraq war was disintegrating.

"Social Security has tied him down and hurt him," a "top White House strategist" admitted to the *New York Daily News*. "Somehow he has to reverse the negative trends and get some of his clout back." A *Washington Post*/ABC News poll had just showed public disapproval of Bush's Social Security efforts running two to one. The Republican leadership in Congress were stymied on how to craft legislation that wouldn't blow up in their faces.

The president even had trouble getting the major TV networks to schedule a speech on Social Security. The press conference was the first such prime-time event Bush had held in over a year. April 28th was the first night of the sweeps, the period when advertisers closely track TV ratings to set their ad rates for the coming season. A presidential press conference could well be a ratings killjoy. Initially only one network, ABC, said it would carry the president live. NBC would only do so when the White House agreed to move the press conference from 8:30 p.m. to 8 p.m., because that would allow it to start one of its more popular shows, real estate developer Donald Trump's employment contest *The Apprentice*, on time at 9. But after NBC came on board, the other two majors, CBS and Fox, agreed to carry the press conference as well.

Once he was on the air, the president admonished Congress that it "needs to address the challenges facing Social Security.... There's a hole in the safety net because Congresses have made promises it can't keep for a younger generation," he said. For them, there should be "voluntary personal accounts." But the program should also "protect those who depend on Social Security the most."

"So I propose a Social Security system in the future where benefits for low-income workers will grow faster than benefits for people who are better off." The president promised to work with Congress, listening "to any good idea from either party." Then he went on answer questions about Iraq, his energy policy, and Democratic opposition to his nominee as UN ambassador, John Bolton.

True to his deal with NBC, Bush cut off questioning a couple of minutes before 9 p.m., pleading, "I don't want to cut into any of those TV shows that are getting ready to air, for the sake of the economy." By then, however, the network, as well as rival CBS, had already pulled the plug on the president.

Having to fight for attention with Trump was an inauspicious way to begin the revival of his failing privatization effort. A scheme to index benefits by income level would have to be constructed very carefully, yet Bush offered no details about how this would be done. He was still determined, it seemed, to leave the dirty work up to his allies in Congress.

That was unwise, because progressive indexing wasn't a new idea. It was the brainchild of Robert Pozen, the Fidelity Investments executive who had been one of the Democratic members of Bush's 2001 presidential commission on Social Security. Pozen said he got the idea in 2003, when he was a visiting professor at Harvard, then developed it with help from SSA Chief Actuary

Stephen Goss, who ran computer simulations for him.[4] Pozen, by now chairman of another mutual fund giant, MFS Investment Management, first introduced the concept to the public in a March 15 op-ed in the *Wall Street Journal* and it quickly became a hot topic in Washington.

Progressive indexing got its first direct exposure to the astringent air of Capitol Hill on April 26, when the Senate Finance Committee opened hearings on Social Security. The hearing was held on a bright spring day in the largest hearing room in the Capitol, which was filled to capacity. To greet lawmakers, an antiprivatization rally pulled together by Americans United to Protect Social Security boasted appearances by more than half the Democratic Senate delegation and dozens more House members. Together, they signed a "Declaration of Unity to Protect Social Security and Stop Privatization." Chuck Grassley dismissed the rally as "political theater."

The Finance Committee heard testimony on four separate proposals to restructure the program. The one that attracted the most attention was Pozen's. Several committee Republicans made favorable comments about it, but Peter Ferrara, now Social Security director of the Free Enterprise Fund, was alarmed.

Benefits under the program would erode even more quickly for many beneficiaries under progressive indexing, he warned Grassley afterward. This could be politically disastrous for Republicans once the magnitude of the reductions was known. Ferrara, of course, advocated going ahead with private accounts, trusting that faster economic growth and federal spending cuts would fill the gap.[5] Pozen didn't captivate his fellow Democrats, either.

By the time Bush officially endorsed it, then, progressive indexing had been heavily discussed for more than a month—long enough for both friends and enemies to run numbers and pick apart its weaknesses. Although a few lawmakers who already supported benefits cuts, such as Jim Kolbe and Charlie Stenholm in the House, found something hopeful in what the president suggested, not a single Senate Democrat—the audience that most needed convincing—shifted position.

The reason was simple: While progressive indexing would cut benefits more heavily for high-income than for middle-income individuals, the latter would still sustain a significant loss of retirement benefits. Lower-income workers would continue to build up benefits according to the current formula based on the rise in wages; others' would be based on a mix of wage and price indexes, a formula that grew stingier the more they earned.

Calculations by the SSA actuaries showed that a seventeen-year-old in 2005 who then spent a lifetime earning average wages would receive 20% less from Social Security than she could expect under the current rules. Those who earned a larger but still middle-level income—say, $59,000 a year—would see a punishing 30% cut. A $90,000 earner would lose almost 40% of benefits. Cuts like these would pose a big challenge to millions of households and shift a major burden onto private accounts. Only workers making less than $25,000 on average would be unaffected.

On top of that, the only detailed plan that had yet been put forward to implement progressive indexing would only eliminate about 70% of the seventy-five-year trust fund shortfall, to say nothing of the deficit under the "infinite" calculation the White House preferred.[6] The rest would have to be made up through other measures such as raising the retirement age.

"Progressive indexing would transform Social Security over time from a retirement program to more of a welfare system that provides a modest retirement benefit largely unrelated to income," concluded Jason Furman, the former Kerry economic advisor now at the Center on Budget and Policy Priorities. Benefits for the top 70% of workers would level off. By 2100, anyone making over $25,000 would get about the same amount of money each month from OASI, which would equal roughly 9% of their average wages: far less than the current average of about one-third.

That would undermine support for Social Security amongst high earners, Furman contended, because they would then be getting the vast majority of their retirement income from their private accounts, rather than from benefits payments. The affluent would see no reason to keep on paying payroll tax, since it would largely be subsidizing low-income households.[7] As if to underscore the point, when Congress in 2005 reauthorized Temporary Aid for Needy Families (TANF), the much narrower program that had replaced welfare under Clinton, it kept funding flat through 2010. Effectively, that was a cut in benefits for TANF's nearly 4.5 million recipients and confirmed the fears of those who had argued against welfare reform at the time.

A paper the White House gave reporters a few days after the president's April 28 press conference confirmed that middle- and upper-income individuals would face major benefits cuts under progressive indexing. A closer look showed that the losers would also include survivors such as elderly widows with low incomes, divorced spouses, and children of deceased low-income workers. Many of these individuals would ordinarily be classified as low-income persons, but their benefits would be cut anyway because they qualified for them through deceased workers who had earned wages in the higher brackets.[8]

Endorsing Pozen's scheme forced the White House to make other admissions it had so far been able to sidestep. Bush had long said Social Security restructuring wouldn't involve any changes to Disability Insurance or to survivors' benefits. Social Security critics for years had tried to draw a hard line between retiree benefits and these other categories—never very convincingly. Survivors' benefits come from the same pool as old-age benefits, and the DI trust fund, theoretically, faced the same long-run funding problems as OASI. But progressive indexing, which proposed cutting benefits to eliminate the trust fund deficits, forced the issue.

"Any plan that maintains current disability benefits will need to address the transition to retirement, and those details will be worked out through the legislative process," presidential spokesperson Trent Duffy said in May. That meant that while the administration wasn't taking a particular position, it was admitting that lawmakers would have to consider cutting disability benefits to balance the books. Meanwhile, White House economic aide Allan Hubbard conceded that progressive indexing would require cutting into benefits for widows and children as well.[9]

The problems that progressive indexing would create for most workers received extensive coverage in the press. The president's allies tried to put the best face on it. *New York Times* columnist John Tierney, for example, noted that, while Democrats liked to portray Bush as "King George or Marie Antoinette," his support for progressive indexing made him sound "more like Robin Hood." By making Social Security a more progressive system, he "has finally called their bluff."

Other, more general press commentary was once again playing into the notion that "greedy geezers" needed to have their benefits trimmed. *New York Times* columnist Nicholas Kristof published a piece in May titled "The Greediest Generation," a play on the current media infatuation with "the Greatest Generation," the self-sacrificing cohort who had lived through the Depression and fought in the Second World War. Kristof invoked the now familiar argument that more elder benefits meant less for the young, castigating the boomers for "preying on children" in an "insidious way" by running up the national debt with Social Security and new programs like drug benefits for Medicare recipients. "Fiscal child abuse," he called it, quoting Larry Kotlikoff's latest book, *The Coming Generational Storm*. Ironically, the American soldiers and sailors who fought in the war against fascism were also the first to spend virtually their entire working lives paying into Social Security*—and, according to the program's critics, overburdening their children and grandchildren as a result.

Pozen himself, who cut a rumpled, professorial figure despite his powerful position in the financial services industry, was also an excellent spokesperson for his indexing idea. A Democrat who had voted for Kerry and a law school classmate of Hillary Rodham Clinton, he came off in hearings and press calls as very much the child of New Deal–era parents who wouldn't dream of violating their legacy. He also liked to speak of how solvency for Social Security came before private accounts,[10] distinguishing himself from privatization's true believers.

What mattered, though, was whether progressive indexing could break the impasse in Congress. It didn't. Instead, it armed the Democrats against the administration. "President Bush struck another blow to Americans' wallets last night when he proposed the single biggest cut in Social Security benefits for the middle class in history," Nancy Pelosi declared the day after the president's press conference.[11]

Progressive indexing also ignited a public brawl between the White House and the Free Lunch Caucus. "That's an idea that comes from the left typically—means testing," sniffed Rep. Paul Ryan of Wisconsin, who together with

---

*   Not to mention benefiting from GI loans for education, federal homeownership subsidies, a vast expansion of tuition-free public schools and university systems, and a multitude of other programs designed to nurture a large middle class.

New Hampshire Republican John Sununu in the Senate had authored a bill that would assign 4% of wages subject to payroll tax to private accounts instead of the mere 2% Pozen proposed. Ryan and Sununu said their plan would pay for itself and require no benefits cuts—the *sine qua non* of the free lunch—because their private accounts would boost federal revenues, which could then be used to pay currently promised benefits. When the SSA actuaries analyzed it, they found the Ryan-Sununu scheme would require $2.4 trillion of new borrowing over just the first ten years.[12]

To these criticisms the Free Lunchers responded that the White House had embraced a politically poisonous and unsellable plan that would pull Republican control of Washington down with it. In the Senate, Trent Lott, sounding like a Democrat, complained that progressive indexing would turn Social Security into "a welfare system."[13] Stephen Moore warned of a "nightmare" in which benefit cuts "cost the Republicans the Senate in 2006."[14] Elsewhere, he speculated that "Nancy Pelosi and Harry Reid are probably opening up Champagne bottles celebrating that they've put Republicans in this trap."[15]

Bush did receive some more promising signals. Bill Thomas partially embraced progressive indexing when he opened his Ways and Means hearings on Social Security in early May, although he proposed somewhat smaller benefits reductions than Pozen. At about the same time in the Senate, Lincoln Chaffee announced that he would support progressive indexing: but only if private accounts weren't included. But the White House needed a bit more enthusiasm. Less than a week after the president made public his support for progressive indexing, Pozen was defending his brainchild against critics in a *Wall Street Journal* op-ed.

He didn't attempt to argue that his formula wouldn't cut benefits for middle- and higher-income workers. Instead, he asserted, as so many Social Security critics had before, that something was better than nothing. Since the program was surely going broke in the next few decades, "payable benefits" under his plan could only be an improvement. He also argued that future workers would have higher retirement incomes than the current crop if their Social Security benefits under the Pozen plan were combined with the nest eggs they were building up in 401(k) account's and IRAs.

Pozen ignored the fact that not everyone agreed that the program was going broke. And he failed to explain why 401(k)s and IRAs should suddenly be regarded as a component of the Social Security system. But he did make a strong argument against raising the cap on income subject to payroll tax.

"Critics of progressive indexing have alleged that it will erode political support for the system among high-wage earners because their benefits would grow more slowly than under the current schedule," he wrote. "Yet these same critics are the ones urging substantial increases in payroll taxes for high earners. Will the political support of high earners be more likely to erode if they face a large hike in their payroll taxes for the rest of their working careers?"[16]

Probably not, Brookings economist Peter Orszag pointed out, because the payroll tax that affluent individuals had to pay had been going down, percentage-wise, for a long time. The reason for this was growing income inequality. High earners were now bringing home vastly more than they ever had, which meant that more of their income was above the cap. Additionally, the value of fringe benefits such as health insurance was rising. From 1980 to 2000, taxable payroll fell from 90% of wages to 83%, Social Security Chief Actuary Stephen Goss noted. Raising the cap wouldn't gouge the rich, proponents said, but simply remove a windfall and restore their share of payroll taxes to something like its previous level.[17] The same couldn't be said of the benefit cuts Pozen proposed.

Bush kept talking about progressive indexing for several more months. But the attempt to relaunch his privatization campaign with more of an emphasis on fiscal balance capsized only three weeks after his press conference when Pozen himself urged the president to drop private accounts from the White House proposal. "The accounts are just too large," he said at a Treasury Department forum on May 19, diverting too much revenue away from benefits, which as a result would have to be cut too drastically. He urged the president instead to back a payroll tax surcharge on all workers making more than $90,000 a year, the proceeds possibly to be used to fund private accounts.

Pozen's statements violated the preconditions Bush had set for Social Security restructuring in two ways: taxes would be raised, and the private accounts would be separately funded rather than carved out of current payroll taxes. Essentially, Pozen was telling Bush the same thing that Steve Moore and the rest of the Free Lunch Caucus had been saying for months, but from the other side of an ideological divide—a rigorous approach to fiscal balance wasn't compatible with a plan to create large private accounts. Once again, Bush found himself stuck between the Pain Caucus and the Free Lunch Caucus—two conservative philosophies that could coexist only uneasily.

* * *

A further problem was the explosion of a series of influence-peddling scandals that reached the top of the Republican leadership—the very people the president was counting on to pass a Social Security bill. At the center was Jack Abramoff, a powerful Washington lobbyist who had risen to prominence in the Republican Party along with Grover Norquist and Ralph Reed when all three were still in college. Abramoff was a board member of USA Next. He was also a close informal advisor to Tom DeLay, with innumerable connections to the Bush White House. He resigned from his law firm in 2004 after a scandal broke relating to payments made for his work on behalf of Native American nations in the casino business. By the following year, investigations into his doings touched a host of prominent Republicans, including many close DeLay associates.

The Abramoff scandals led to the jailing of Ohio Republican Rep. Bob Ney and Deputy Interior Secretary William Heaton and to disgrace and criminal charges for a dozen other prominent lobbyists, congressional staffers, and White House aides. The House majority leader himself faced calls for his resignation in March from the CAF and other Democratic groups. DeLay was indicted for campaign finance law violations. Although he hung onto his House seat and leadership post until June 2006, he was a badly damaged figure, unable to play his former strong role pushing the president's agenda.

"We may be reaching a tipping point," a White House aide told the *Wall Street Journal*, concerned that the scandals would threaten the Republican majority in Congress in 2006. Summer was approaching, when the House and Senate would have to produce bills if Social Security legislation was to stand a chance of passing before election season began. Yet it was becoming harder for the party's embattled lawmakers to justify time spent on an issue that seemed to be dragging them down them politically.

All summer, as Congress struggled to assemble a workable Social Security bill, the scandals were joined by more practical realities that combined to dampen the public's enthusiasm—such as it ever was—for private accounts. For a variety of reasons that included continuing wage stagnation, personal savings, a stock market downturn, and the increasingly evident fact that the modest economic expansion his administration was overseeing had left many workers behind, selling privatization had become even more difficult.

While payrolls rose by 207,000 jobs in July, the workforce had been declining until early in the year and America's recovery from the 2001 recession was one of the slowest on record. A poll by Harris Interactive released in August found that only 45% of workers reported receiving a raise in the past six months while 43% were working more hours and 68% had their workload boosted.

The fraction of Americans living below the poverty line rose in 2005 for the fourth consecutive year, to 12.7%. More than 15% of Americans were without health insurance, the same proportion as a year earlier, but fewer workers were insured through their employers and more were participating in government health plans, especially Medicaid. It somehow didn't help for conservative analysts like Devon Herrick of the National Center for Policy Analysis to assert that "being uninsured in America is largely a matter of choice."[18]

OASI, DI, Medicare and Medicaid—the entitlements that Bush wanted to replace with free-market alternatives—were becoming lifelines, as millions of workers struggled to keep afloat financially. Housing and health care costs were marching relentlessly upward.

Amidst these worries, Bush's town hall road show pushed on, enveloped in its own hyperreality. By early June, the president was admitting that "60 Cities in 60 Days" had evolved into a tour without end. Asked why he was still taking his roadshow from city to city, he replied cryptically, "Because it's my job."[19] Increasingly, he lashed out at "the other party" who "stand for nothing but obstruction, … the philosophy of the stop sign, the agenda of the roadblock."[20]

Other than that, the events rolled out according to the same formula they had followed for months, featuring the same mini-panels of citizens, the same charts and graphs, the same rhetoric and laugh lines from the president, now honed into vaudevillian routines. The preselected audiences contained no one who might object to Bush's assertions or rattle his delivery—not even the undecided the president was presumably trying to woo.

Nor even, necessarily, residents of the localities he was visiting. Asked if the attendees at a presidential town hall held in June at a Montgomery County, Maryland high school actually came from the town where the event took place, White House spokesperson Trent Duffy said he didn't know. Blocks of tickets were farmed out to the conservative Young America's Foundation, which then decided who to give them to. "Once we give the tickets to the organizations, the White House doesn't ask for residency information," said Duffy.[21]

The president's ideological allies were becoming more than nervous. Shortly after Bush announced his support for progressive indexing, Fred Barnes in the *Weekly Standard* warned that unless Bush devised an exit strategy from his failing initiative, the Republicans would have to defend their congressional majorities in 2006 in an election dominated by Social Security. The best bet for the president, Barnes said, would be to take up the recommendations of his tax reform panel and try to make them the centerpiece of the Republicans' election sales pitch.

In early June, in a *Washington Post*/ABC News poll, 62% of respondents said they disapproved of the way the president was handling Social Security. Support for private accounts themselves slipped to a dismal 27% when respondents were told they would be coupled with a reduction in the growth of Social Security benefits for retirees. Bush's embrace of the Pozen plan appeared to have produced as bad a result for the president as he could have feared. Adding another dimension to the picture, a *New York Times*/CBS News poll showed Bush's overall approval rating had dropped from 51% to 42% over the period he had been campaigning on Social Security—an issue that didn't even make the top six problems respondents considered the country to be facing.

CHAPTER 41

THE REPUBLICAN
DEBACLE

*"It can be said of Social Security's future, as was once memo-
rably said of the nation's, that the only thing we have to fear
is fear itself. Social Security does not face bankruptcy. It is
not going broke. The system faces only a long-term shortfall
and requires only a few sensible changes."*
—Robert M. Ball[1]

*"Let a word to the wise be sufficient. If the joker (Bush) …
had gotten his way in privatizing Social Security benefits,
then, much like the diminishing 401Ks, we would all be
sucking pond water right about now!"*
—Bill Paul[2]

After progressive indexing struck out, Republican congressional leaders were
still trying to find the formula for a viable Social Security restructuring bill. But
they had less and less room to maneuver. At the Senate Finance Committee,

one of Grassley's Republican members, Maine's Olympia Snowe, said she was opposed to both private accounts and anything that would slow the growth of benefits. "I think we'd better be very careful if we want to tinker with the essence of this guaranteed benefit," the Maine senator said. "It's been a remarkable approach to ensuring that people are prevented from falling into poverty."

But the White House still wanted Grassley to go first with a restructuring package, to be followed by the House Ways and Means Committee, on the theory that the Senate would be the harder place to push a bill through. With time running short, a proposal by Sen. Jim DeMint of South Carolina suddenly began to look like the best of a bad lot. It included no benefit cuts, it promised private accounts, and because it would snatch the trust fund surplus to fund those accounts, it could be presented as a way to "protect" the surplus from being used to fund other government expenses—a Republican counterpart, sort of, to Al Gore's "lockbox."

Of course, using the surplus to create private accounts could be portrayed by Democrats as a raid on future benefits payments. But the game now wasn't so much to pass legislation as to offer something Republican lawmakers would feel comfortable voting for. If it passed, fine. If not, the Democrats could be labeled spendthrifts and obstructionists—unwilling to protect the surplus and unwilling to "reform" Social Security even if benefits were left alone. The Free-Lunch Caucus's politics, it seemed, were more appetizing in a pinch than the Pain Caucus's.

Word leaked to the press in mid-June, via Senate aides, that Rick Santorum and Lindsey Graham were about to join DeMint in offering his proposal. It wouldn't preclude other initiatives aimed at keeping Social Security solvent. Instead, DeMint portrayed it as a first step necessary to break the logjam. In the House, Bill Thomas and Jim McCrery were said to be considering supporting his bill too while continuing to work on their own, broader measure.

The president also saw it that way. At a White House luncheon with Republican senators on June 21, Bush said once again that he preferred his plan to restructure Social Security, but he tacitly encouraged the senators to pursue two separate tracks—private accounts and solvency measures—in hopes they could be united later on. That meant the president was asking them to go forward with DeMint's proposal as well as a new proposal that Bob Bennett was floating. That one, based partly on the progressive indexing concept, wouldn't include private accounts at all but would reduce the growth of benefits for all but the bottom 30% of earners.

Supporters of privatization were, at first, delighted by the new two-track approach, especially DeMint's contribution. The Club for Growth endorsed the plan, calling it "a first step toward ownership of Social Security benefits." As DeMint fleshed it out, workers would be able to create private accounts initially invested in marketable Treasury bonds. After three years, they could trade these for mutual funds investing in stocks and corporate bonds. The account holder's Social Security benefits would be reduced by an amount reflecting the earnings on that account. The accounts would be comparatively small—about 2% of wages—so as not to create an immediate crisis once the program started to draw down trust fund assets to pay some benefits. But whatever remained in them when the beneficiary died could be passed on to his or her heirs.

"Combining good policy with good politics," DeMint's proposal "has finally broken the logjam and put Social Security reformers back on the offensive," the Club's Pat Toomey proclaimed.[3]

At the least, Republicans now had something to talk up to their constituents during the July 4 recess. But the plan had flaws. Given that the accounts would initially be invested in Treasury bonds, it was hard to argue that they were completely "private"—a potential stumbling block for some hard-core privatization advocates. And of course, by stripping the trust funds of some $1 trillion in assets to create the accounts, DeMint's plan would hasten Social Security's insolvency. When SSA actuaries evaluated the proposal, they found it would increase the federal budget deficit by about $90 billion in the next year and some $680 billion over ten years.[4] The only way to avert that would be through massive new borrowing.

Reid called Bennett's bill a "bait and switch strategy." As for DeMint's plan, Sen. Charles Schumer of New York said, "Nothing, absolutely nothing, will get us to budge until the president takes privatization off the table."[5]

Speaker Hastert, nevertheless, felt safe enough to promise for the first time at the end of June that the House would hold a vote on Social Security legislation that year. The idea now was that the House would concentrate on McCrery's bill while Grassley and his allies cobbled together something similar to the Bennett plan in the Senate. If the effort failed, they believed the McCrery-DeMint scenario would be politically popular enough to do them some good in the election.[6]

But two weeks later, with the July 4 recess past, Grassley and Thomas both said they would put off considering any Social Security legislation until September. Other priorities were getting in the way. Justice Sandra Day O'Connor had announced her retirement from the Supreme Court. The nomination and confirmation of a new justice would consume much of Grassley's time in the coming months. Senate Finance had highway and energy legislation to push through. In the House, Thomas said Ways and Means would be occupied with the Central America Free Trade Agreement for the rest of the month.

The president was still barnstorming, continuing to look for new ways to try to ignite a groundswell for his legacy builder. But nothing was happening as Washington entered its August limbo. Some reporters, checking their calendars, noted that August 14 was an important milestone: the seventieth anniversary of Roosevelt's signing of the Social Security Act. Ten years earlier, for the program's sixtieth birthday, the SSA had deployed a new slogan to mark the event: "Social Security: We're Here for Your Benefit." It had created a special postage cancellation stamp to be used on that day, placed messages on scoreboards at baseball stadiums, and otherwise used the media to mark the date.

This time, not a word.

* * *

The most effective period of George W. Bush's presidency was bracketed by two physical disasters. The September 11 terrorist attacks he exploited successfully, for a time becoming arguably the most powerful U.S. president since Franklin Roosevelt. The response to Hurricane Katrina he mishandled in a way that permanently stained his administration. Both, however, gave him the excuse to disengage from an unsuccessful Social Security restructuring effort that threatened to drag him down with it. The first time, he succeeded. The second time, the damage was already too severe.

After first hitting Florida, Hurricane Katrina made its second and most devastating landfall on the Gulf Coast on August 29, laying waste to large swaths of Mississippi, Alabama, and Louisiana while leaving 1,836 people dead and more than $80 billion of damage from the storm and subsequent flooding. Hardest hit was New Orleans, where levees failed in more than fifty places, leaving 80% of the city under water along with much of the neighboring parishes. Experts had been warning of just such a disaster for years, and Washington's failure to do anything to shore up the flood protection system reflected shamefully on both Congress and the U.S. Army Corps of Engineers.

The Bush administration bore the brunt of criticism for the lackadaisical response to the disaster, which besides the deaths, left hundreds of thousands of evacuees scattered across twenty-eight states and sparked an unseemly rush by developers and their political allies to remake New Orleans—without, it appeared, any regard for its poor and nonwhite residents. Much of the initial blame, deservedly, was heaped on the shoulders of the Federal Emergency Management Agency (FEMA), a once well-regarded operation that had been underfunded and allowed to decay under the supervision of an unqualified political crony.

While FEMA made the headlines, the SSA was one of the first agencies to respond to the Katrina disaster. Over 1.2 million Social Security beneficiaries lived in the counties affected by the hurricane, along with nearly 400,000 SSI recipients.[7] Commissioner Jo Anne Barnhart quickly activated procedures that allowed beneficiaries to receive direct, on-the-spot payments if they were no longer in a place where they could receive their benefit checks. Evacuees received their first payments within three days of Katrina's landfall, and by September 9, 30,000 emergency payments had been made. That number rose to 73,600, totaling $38 million in payments.[8] By early September, the SSA had representatives stationed in the evacuation centers across the country to which Katrina victims had been dispersed, including a temporary office in the Houston Astrodome, the largest evacuation center.

The SSA's performance was a sharp contrast to that of FEMA, which less than a year later was calculated to have lost to fraud some $1 billion in benefit payments meant for hurricane victims. Some of the scams involved use of fake Social Security numbers. One of the most audacious perpetrators made twenty-six claims to FEMA using thirteen different numbers and addresses; only one of the Social Security numbers turned out to be valid. Most improper payments occurred because FEMA didn't verify the identities of the claimants or check their addresses, audit investigators concluded.[9]

One reason for the SSA's quick response was that many of its top regional officials had experience with sudden disasters. Raymond Brammer, the area director for Louisiana, who led the post-Katrina assistance, had been one of the key personnel directing the agency's response after the bombing of the Murrah Federal Building, which had housed a large Social Security office, in Oklahoma City in 1995. But the SSA also had better leadership than FEMA under Bush. The latter was headed by Michael D. Brown, a Texan friend of Bush's 2000 campaign manager Joe Allbaugh who had no experience either in disaster relief or any other aspect of government. He resigned less than three weeks after Katrina hit. Commissioner Barnhart, too, was a political appointee, but she had held posts at both the SSA and HHS going back to the Reagan and George H.W. Bush administrations and was generally respected by agency employees as a competent administrator.

Congress quickly passed and the president signed a bill providing $62.3 billion in Katrina-related emergency appropriations, followed by a $6.1 billion package of tax breaks to individuals and corporations. One provision of the second bill waived penalties for early withdrawals from IRAs and 401(k) plans, up to $100,000 per taxpayer: a favor mainly to individuals who had that level of assets in their accounts to withdraw. For the majority of Katrina survivors, especially in the poorer sections of New Orleans, the emergency retirement, disability, and survivors' benefit payments that Social Security provided were a far more effective form of relief.

Katrina turned out the lights on Bush's campaign to restructure the program. The DeMint and Bennett bills, which together had been the most serious attempt to push privatization through Congress, vanished from sight. At a luncheon of Republican Ways and Means members in mid-September, Thomas said that he was pushing ahead with a comprehensive retirement bill that would include adding private accounts to Social Security. Rep. Tom Reynolds of New York, who also chaired the Republican Congressional Committee, then reportedly got up to say that he would recommend to the House leadership that it drop the matter.

The leadership were now preoccupied with the 2006 election and acutely worried about the difficult battles many Republican lawmakers would face. "It's more than just Katrina," a House Republican aide explained to the *Washington Post*, citing high gasoline prices, anger over the war in Iraq, and the president's dismal poll numbers.

To that list could have been added the scandals surrounding Tom DeLay and other party leaders and the public's consistently negative response to the Social Security privatization effort. In early October, Bush acknowledged as much during a Rose Garden press conference. While vowing that he would keep up pressure on Congress to "show political courage" and act, he noted that there "seems to be a diminished appetite in the short term" for transforming Social Security.

Of course, Bush never officially called a halt to the privatization campaign. But the town hall roadshow ended after Katrina, and the House and Senate quietly dropped anything from their agenda related to slowing the growth of Social Security or introducing private accounts into the program. In December, Andrew Biggs left his White House post with the National Economic Council and returned to the SSA as an associate commissioner, leaving the president without a staffer fully focused on Social Security.

* * *

It would be wrong to assert that 2005 was an uninterrupted string of legislative defeats for the White House. While the Democrats showed impressive unity and discipline on Social Security, they played into the president's hands on many other issues. In February, Congress had passed "tort reform" legislation designed to discourage class-action lawsuits. Two months later, Bush snagged one of the most important victories of his presidency when Congress passed a bill overhauling the bankruptcy laws to require more debtors to file for bankruptcy under federal law, which would make it harder for households to write off some of their debts. Critics said the new law would create a "sharecroppers' society" or a "debt peonage society," but ample Democratic support made it a winner on Capitol Hill.[10]

But the administration's momentum was running low. Permanent repeal of the estate tax, by early fall, was again out of reach. One reason was that eliminating the levy would have scratched one possible scenario for shoring up Social Security if the program ran into fiscal distress in coming decades. Bush's initiative to restructure the tax system was dead, too.

By October, with the costs from Katrina still mounting, the Republican leadership had also waited too long to pass legislation extending Bush's earlier rounds of tax cuts. After struggling into December, Grassley couldn't muster a single Democratic vote even for a partial extension. The Republican Congress, which had begun the year hoping to implement the most radical downsizing of U.S. social programs in at least a generation, not to mention further tax cuts, had to settle in November for sending its president a stopgap funding bill, just as it had had to do so embarrassingly under Bill Clinton. That would keep the government running for another month, when Congress could reassemble and try again to pass the needed spending measures.

But even before Katrina it was clear that the core of Bush's agenda was in big trouble. Social Security was the twofold reason.

First, by throwing his political energy into a cause that most everyone in Washington outside his inner circle seemed to realize was a long shot, the president wasted the opportunity to win relatively easy victories on taxes and spending.

Second, the Social Security campaign handed the Democrats a priceless opportunity to unite against an unpopular cause and restore their political relevance.

The Republicans were having trouble grasping what it was about Social Security that had tripped them up. "Personally, I've never quite understood the bed wetters' fears when it comes to Personal Retirement Accounts," commented Dick Armey. "How could you possibly lose by saving future retirees—our children and grandchildren—from another broken government promise?" Before the 2006 election, the former House majority leader wrote, he expected "able legislative entrepreneurs like Sen. Jim DeMint to drag his colleagues, kicking and screaming, into a serious, adult debate about the most important policy challenge facing our generation."

For Armey, evidently, the entire spring and summer of Bush's blundering roadshow and the accompanying disastrous polls seemed not to have occurred. Far from failing to be "adult" about Social Security, the "bed wetters" had merely realized that any attempt to push private accounts would run straight into damaging Democratic accusations that they intended to cut benefits. This was now an inescapable fact of political life, proved abundantly in the polls. The Republicans found themselves in danger of being so closely identified as enemies of Social Security that each individual lawmaker would have to distance him- or herself from the party, as Olympia Snowe had done, to prove it wasn't the case.

"I can't—we can't really identify where we went wrong in the approach, other than that we misjudged the Democrats, and particularly the leadership, and the AARP," Allan Hubbard, director of the National Economic Council, said in October.[11]

This, however, was coming from a White House that had misplayed the critical task it assigned itself in the privatization campaign: winning over enough lawmakers to pass a bill. First, it misjudged the need to work closely with congressional Republicans. The president "jumped in with a very big idea that he ran on," Lindsey Graham later said, "but he didn't lay the political groundwork in the Senate or the House. He ran on it. We didn't. He's not up for reelection. We are."

Ironically, Bush and Rove committed the same mistake the Clintons had made in their push for national health care in 1993 and 1994—formulating a plan without any input from Congress, then expecting their party's leadership to pass it. Bush compounded the error by leaving the trickiest details to the leadership to work out.

Rove later admitted as much in his political memoirs. Republican leaders were more divided about Social Security than he had expected. "We miscalculated: we took the initial reticence we encountered … as skepticism that Bush would stay engaged on the issue. But in truth, too many Republicans had lost their nerve."[12]

With a solid majority in the House, the president had just needed to convince a few Democratic senators, of whom Rove had identified six. But Bush alienated several of them by campaigning for private accounts in their states before even speaking to them about Social Security. And when Ben Nelson and Kent Conrad, two of the most likely converts, met with some of their Republican colleagues in January, suggesting a meeting with the president, Hubbard told them it couldn't be arranged.

In April, when Bush finally met in person with Conrad, private accounts were already in deep trouble, and he pitched his proposal in such a lackadaisical fashion that the senator reportedly said afterward, "It was almost as if someone told him to do it, and he was just going through the motions." Nelson also met once with the president—who preferred to talk about University of Nebraska football. When Hubbard visited with him several times, the extreme soft-sell approach remained in effect. "If I was being negotiated with, I didn't know it," Nelson later said.[13]

Intent on marginalizing all but a few Democrats of distinctly conservative views, the White House had failed to build and maintain the network of relationships within the opposition that presidents had always considered part of their job to cultivate. To create a modicum of friendship with Nelson, Conrad, and four other Democratic swing votes, and then persuade them to support the president on a highly controversial proposal involving a Democratic legacy program, was a job that required more than a few short months. Given that another congressional election was coming up in 2006, Bush hadn't the time.

Instead, Bush had done his opponents the priceless favor of centering the Social Security debate on such an extreme position—privatization—that he enabled the Democratic leadership to heal, at least temporarily, the split between progressives and center-right deficit hawks, making the party once again a more or less unified political force. Undoubtedly, a major share of blame for this fell to Rove, who seemed to have waded into the issue without any thought to the trouble it always made for Republicans, or to the advantages it consistently offered to Democrats.

The Bush White House's domestic policy staff was already widely regarded as weak,* leaving Rove with no one to counterbalance his views when he assumed his new domestic policy advisory role in the second Bush administration. "When Karl became the deputy chief of staff, in charge of policy and everything else, and he laid out Social Security as a major second-term agenda, it was a disaster," longtime Republican strategist Ed Rollins said later. "It was almost like Karl had no history and certainly he didn't have any real history relative to Washington, or what had gone on before."[14]

His approach to Social Security followed a pattern, however, observes Scott McClellan, who was White House press secretary throughout the Social Security campaign. "We were spending excessive effort on selling our sketchily

---

*   Paul O'Neill famously likened them to "kids rolling around on a lawn" in conversation with journalist Ron Suskind (Suskind, *The Price of Loyalty: George W. Bush, the White House, and the Education of Paul O'Neill*, New York: Simon & Schuster, 2004).

designed plan while skimping on other elements of the process that probably should have been at least as important," McClellan wrote in his 2008 memoir of the Bush years, *What Happened*. It all reminded McClellan of "the way we short-circuited debate over the necessity for war in Iraq and chose instead to turn it into the subject of a massive marketing blitz. We used a similar approach as we planned the Social Security campaign."[15]

What about the president himself? Arguably, Bush's greatest strengths as a politician, his preternatural self-confidence and deep conviction about whatever he came to stand for, were his downfall in the spring and summer of 2005, when he couldn't grasp the folly of his privatization campaign. Later, in his autobiography, Bush acknowledges that he "may have misread the electoral mandate by pushing for an issue on which there had been little bipartisan agreement in the first place." He notes the many warnings Republican congressional leaders had given him about taking on Social Security, but offers no real explanation why he decided to ignore them. His defeat on Social Security was "one of the greatest disappointments of my presidency," he writes, then goes on to regret that he didn't push instead for immigration reform as the first major initiative of his second term.[16]

What the White House had done, nevertheless, was spend $2.8 million of taxpayers' money transporting the president and members of his administration to various roadshow events in a fruitless effort to build public pressure for privatization. Two years later, the GAO finally completed the report Waxman had asked for on the White House's Social Security campaign. It identified 228 public speaking events, 40 of which featured the president, and reported that most of the expenses had been charged to HHS and the Treasury and Labor departments.

However, "we could not test the validity of some of those costs," the GAO reported, "because EOP [Executive Office of the President] withheld certain key information and Treasury did not have supporting documentation for amounts it reimbursed EOP under the interagency agreements." The GAO decided not to demand that its right to these documents be honored "because of the disproportionate amount of time and resources needed to pursue this matter and the limited amount of the funds involved."

But the fact remained that the White House had spent an embarrassing amount of public funds on a fruitless propaganda effort that left the administration and the Republican leadership in a worse position politically than when it began. The biggest—and the only—beneficiaries of the Bush Social Security roadshow were lobbyists. U.S. corporations and interest groups spent a total $1.16 billion lobbying Washington in the first half of 2005, 8% more than the corresponding period the year before and setting a new record, according to PoliticalMoneyLine, a nonpartisan group. The Social Security campaign drove the increased spending—$27.8 million by AARP, $6.3 million by the National Committee to Preserve Social Security and Medicare, and a total $146 million by financial services firms.[17]

The biggest winners from the Bush privatization drive were the Democratic leaders, Nancy Pelosi and Harry Reid. They had struggled to keep together a fractious delegation and show stubbornness when the party's center-right urged them to put forward a Democratic Social Security plan. But any doubts about their strategy of refusing to negotiate on Social Security unless Bush dumped private accounts dissipated as the public's displeasure grew and his own party failed to pull together a viable piece of legislation. The unexpected vigor of what conservatives had regarded as two hopelessly out-of-date and out-of-touch forces—labor and the Democratic congressional leadership—was the wild card in the Social Security debate. As early as mid-April, the Free Enterprise Fund's Stephen Moore said, "I don't think anyone anticipated the fervent opposition of the Democrats."[18]

No one should have been surprised. Essentially the same coalition had helped discourage or defeat attacks on Social Security under Carter, Reagan, Clinton, and twice now under Bush. Defending the program had helped Al Gore win the popular vote for president in 2000 and kept John Kerry's candidacy afloat four years later. Pelosi and Reid had staked out a powerful position and stuck to it, but in doing so they were following a reliable tradition within their party.

What had changed was the way the public greeted the president's attempt to sell privatization. Glenn Hubbard, who chaired the Council of Economic Advisors in Bush's first administration, later suggested that the president could have achieved essentially all his goals on Social Security if he had been willing to decouple cost containment from private accounts—creating new incentives for private saving for low-income households while slowing the growth rate of benefits for those with middle and upper incomes. Rove, in his memoirs, agreed in hindsight.[19]

Rove doesn't appear to have considered that his cherished vision of the ownership society may have been mistaken—although the fact that he barely mentions the concept in his memoirs suggests some misgivings. But the administration's relentless touting of a utopia in which everyone's a capitalist made it seem oblivious to the economic uncertainty that had made workers fearful of jeopardizing elements of the social safety net. The 1990s—the prime years of the movement against Social Security—had coincided with a period when wages were growing strongly. In those days, for lawmakers to propose privatizing the program wasn't political suicide, even if their constituents didn't necessarily buy the idea. In 2005, that era was over. Privatization was now anathema and the headlines were full of nasty fallout from the years when high-risk investing was sold as the ticket to wealth for working people.

In May, Bernard Ebbers, former CEO of former telecommunications giant WorldCom, was convicted of participating in the biggest accounting fraud in U.S. history. Among the victims were employees who had invested in WorldCom stock through its 401(k) plan. In August, David Stockman was back in the news; the former Reagan budget director who had done so much to introduce supply-side economics to Washington was now the head of a buyout firm faced with a lawsuit involving the bankruptcy of an auto parts company in which it had invested. Stockman was accused of inducing an investor to buy debt in the company by providing "materially false and misleading documents and information."

A third case didn't involve pensions or the securities markets, but it too cast a shadow over Bush's quest to turn America into an ownership society. In July, Ameriquest, a big mortgage lender owned by Roland Arnall, a top Republican donor, agreed to settle for $325 million a thirty-state lawsuit over charges of predatory lending practices, including making inflated appraisals and failing to disclose loan terms. The president had just named Arnall his ambassador to the Netherlands; Senate approval of the nomination soon followed. Some administration officials took the opportunity to push for stricter oversight of the exploding and increasingly crooked market for subprime mortgages, but Bush and Rove couldn't be persuaded.

The timing of the three cases was a coincidence. But they seemed to underscore the fears of millions of people who still felt their financial condition was precarious and their future uncertain, while the current economic expansion seemed to benefit only those at the top. The administration's campaign to privatize Social Security was completely out of step with such concerns.

PART VII

Back to Austerity

(2006–11)

CHAPTER 42

"NO ONE IS TALKING ANYMORE ABOUT A 'PERMANENT REPUBLICAN MAJORITY'"

Although some pundits and many Democrats had warned that the second Bush administration was in danger of overreaching, no one predicted 2005 would be such an *anno horribilis*. But the demise of the Social Security privatization campaign dovetailed with the beginning of the midterm election campaigns, signaling that these were going to be difficult for Republicans.

Aside from the embarrassment of coming away empty-handed on its signature domestic policy issue, the administration was pouring treasure into wars in Iraq and Afghanistan that it appeared unable to win. Health care costs were once again spiraling upward, alarming debt-ridden working families. The botched response to Hurricane Katrina—at least in parts of the Gulf Coast that didn't vote Republican—had eliminated any reputation for competence the administration might have had. Thanks to the two Middle Eastern conflicts and the earlier Bush tax cuts, the federal deficit was surging. All this was bound to hobble the Republicans as they attempted to keep control of Congress.

Understanding that their day hadn't arrived after all, the conservative advocacy groups that had supported Bush's privatization campaign most prominently pulled in their horns. COMPASS, with its Wall Street backing, faded from view. Cato, Heritage, and the American Enterprise Institute deemphasized privatization in favor of other issues, although their positions on the subject remained the same.

Instead of silencing the movement against Social Security, however, the demise of the president's privatization offensive shifted its center of gravity. Because the president's initiative had centered around private accounts, an important group of participants in the movement against Social Security—the deficit hawks—seemed to become nearly invisible in the media during those months. Fiscally conservative Republicans and center-right Democrats were divided over the notion of carving out accounts, which they knew would only move up the date when the program would face real fiscal problems. The Concord Coalition, for instance, came out against them.

But once private accounts stopped dominating the debate—for the first time in a decade—the balance shifted. As the Free-Lunch Caucus faded from view, the Pain Caucus began to stage a comeback. "Entitlement reform," not the "ownership society," once again became the watchword most closely associated with Social Security in Washington.

* * *

Shortly after the Bush privatization campaign gave up the ghost, the New America Foundation, a new, studiously bipartisan think tank with a fiscally conservative bent, unveiled a Social Security reform plan designed to prevent the program from costing more than it currently did. The authors were Jeffrey Liebman, a former Clinton economic aide and now a public policy professor at Harvard's Kennedy School of Government; Maya MacGuineas, a New America official and Social Security advisor to the 2000 McCain presidential campaign; and Andrew Samwick, a former Bush economic advisor and now a Dartmouth economics professor.

They proposed creating private accounts by carving out 1.5% of each worker's payroll taxes and requiring the worker to contribute another 1.5% from her earnings. The retirement age would go up gradually to sixty-eight and benefits would be rejiggered to keep OASI and DI from ever needing more than the current 12.4% of payroll to stay solvent. While that would amount to a 35% reduction in spending on Social Security, the proposal's architects would reduce the burden on low-income retirees by means-testing the most affluent. Additionally, they would raise the cap on earnings subject to payroll tax to 90%—the only part of the proposal that traditional defenders of Social Security would have agreed with.

The proposal's big selling point was that Social Security would never have to tap general revenues in order to keep paying full benefits. That made it an instant topic of conversation as an array of influential Washington figures fanned out in the early months of 2006 to talk up the need to control the deficit. Former CBO head Robert Reischauer, one of the most respected budget authorities in the District, who used to liken the baby boomer retiree onslaught to a tsunami, now doubled down, comparing it to global warming.[1] Comptroller General David Walker was making every speaking engagement he could muster to spread the message that "Demographics is destiny." The nation had rashly promised the elderly $33 trillion in today's money over the next seventy-five years, the impassioned Walker charged.

"We're on an imprudent and unsustainable course," declared the man the *National Journal* dubbed "Washington's new Paul Revere" in a December 2005 cover story.[2] The cover illustration, underneath the headline "Oh, Baby!" showed a man in a lab coat shoveling dollars into the gaping mouth of an enormous, doughy figure evidently representing the insatiable boomers.

The Brookings Institution, which had taken a turn to the right, chimed in with *Restoring Fiscal Sanity 2005*, a report edited by Alice Rivlin and Isabel Sawhill, both of whom had served at OMB under Clinton. "The nation faces a budget deficit of epic proportion," the report concluded. With the baby boomers retiring, "the resulting explosion of Social Security and especially Medicare spending, combined with inadequate revenues to support current commitments, will create a torrent of red ink."

Sawhill had a short-term solution: "asking" the public to "temporarily" forgo the inflation adjustment on Social Security payments as well as other programs. Once the budget was back in balance, the suspension would end. In the meantime, it would provide "elected officials with an incentive to take the additional painful actions needed to restore longer-term balance."[3]

Further fueling Washington's deficit obsession was the May 1 release of the Social Security trustees' annual report, which found that the trust funds would run out of money to pay benefits in 2040—one year earlier than previously projected. The report also estimated that payroll taxes would fall below program costs for the first time in 2017, the same as in the previous year's estimate. The trustees reported the program's seventy-five-year actuarial deficit at 2.02% of taxable income, just 0.09% higher than a year earlier.

On balance, the report showed the program only modestly worse off over a long period of time, noted Harry Reid, who denounced White House "scare tactics" on Social Security. But the numbers had moved down rather than up, and a "deterioration" was how the result was described in the *New York Times*, for example.[4]

The ominous talk spread further during the summer of 2006, when the International Monetary Fund issued a staff report declaring that the U.S. "long-term fiscal outlook" was "unsustainable and that entitlement reform was needed." Shortly thereafter, Standard & Poor's warned that, unless the U.S. did something to alter its fiscal path, by 2020 its Treasury bonds could be downgraded to BBB, or slightly above junk status.

The IMF advised the U.S. to raise payroll taxes and even suggested "withdrawing" the Bush tax cuts. New Fed chair Ben Bernanke, in a speech to the Economic Club of Washington in October, called Medicare and Social Security "unsustainable." "We can mitigate the adverse effect of the aging population on future generations," he added, "but only by forgoing consumption on leisure today." Once again, the assumption was that today's workers were squandering tomorrow's future—even though the notion that a country could save its way out of a demographic shift was highly dubious economics.

The talk of deficit-fueled disaster building up in Washington throughout this election year exuded a certain air of disconnectedness. While the federal budget went from a $200 billion surplus in 2000 to a deficit approaching twice that much, ten-year Treasury note yields dropped from more than 6% to some 4.5%. One reason might have been that the current deficit only amounted to 2.7% of GDP. Even adding in the money borrowed by Treasury from the Social Security and Medicare trust funds, the deficit only hit 4.6%—still substantially below its apex during the Reagan years.

The Social Security shortfall, too, didn't look so bad when placed in relation to GDP. The Congressional Budget Office's projected seventy-five-year deficit, pointed out Dean Baker, would only equate to 0.4% of GDP over that period—less than half the size of the defense spending splurge that followed September 11.[5] By contrast, the cost of making the Bush tax cuts permanent would be three times as much over seventy-five years, the Center on Budget and Policy Priorities estimated.[6]

The president, nevertheless, joined in the calls for austerity. In his 2006 State of the Union address, he asserted, "The rising cost of entitlements is a problem that won't go away," then called for Congress to set up a bipartisan commission to examine Social Security and Medicare. "If the president sees a political opportunity" for restructuring Social Security, a White House aide told Fred Barnes, "he'll seize it in an instant."[7]

Prior to his speech, the president even approached Alan Greenspan, about to relinquish his Fed chair, to head the effort. But Greenspan turned him down, citing a busy schedule. The *Wall Street Journal* reported, however, that people "familiar with his plans" said Greenspan felt that the kind of compromise that his earlier Social Security commission had helped Ronald Reagan and Tip O'Neill achieve wasn't possible in the present polarized atmosphere.[8] Bush mentioned the idea of a commission only a couple more times before letting it die.

That still made ending entitlements more of an administration priority than the housing market. By this time in 2006, some voices in Washington, including a few close to the president, were warning that real estate values were inflated and that Bush's own policies were encouraging a dangerous expansion of dubious subprime mortgage lending. During his first term, he had pushed the big government-sponsored institutions, Fannie Mae and Freddie Mac, to expand their lending to low-income borrowers. He pressed for new rules allowing first-time buyers to qualify for mortgages with no money down.

"No one wanted to stop that bubble," his former economic advisor, Larry Lindsey, later said. "It would have conflicted with the president's own policies."

Instead of putting the mortgage market on a tighter leash, Bush appointed as head of the Office of Federal Housing Enterprise Oversight (OFHEO)— the agency that supervised Fannie and Freddie—Jim Lockhart, who was until recently the top official at SSA charged with coordinating the agency's activities with the president's Social Security privatization campaign. After Lockhart took over in June 2006, OFHEO began pushing the two big lenders to buy up some of the riskiest subprime mortgages in an effort to remove their toxic influence from the market. That put Fannie and Freddie themselves on much shakier financial footing, but for the moment, it seemed to relieve some of the mortgage market's anxieties.

Much closer to the top of the White House's agenda was the next year's federal budget, which the president submitted to Congress on February 6. As usual, the $2.77 trillion package left the vast majority of projected spending on the Iraq and Afghanistan wars for "emergency" bills to be submitted later in the year—proven to be the most effective way to strong-arm a yes vote out of skeptical Democrats. There was no more talk of tax reform. The president wanted his tax cuts extended and the Republicans, worried that they might lose control of Congress in November, were anxious to load up legislation with as many gifts as possible to their favored constituencies.

To bolster the effort intellectually, the administration announced in February that it was creating a new office within the Treasury Department to perform "dynamic analysis" of tax legislation. The president's budget package requested $513,000 to fund the new office, which would enable the administration to present analyses projecting the effect of tax cuts on economic growth. Tax experts saw this as a step toward government adoption of dynamic scoring as a formal part of its budgeting. It could then claim to show, for accounting purposes, that tax cuts had no negative effects on federal revenues.

Treasury said it hoped to have a dynamic analysis of the president's budget ready by mid-year. Already, however, Bush was claiming his budget would lower the deficit from the equivalent of 3.2% of GDP to 1.3% by the end of his term. But he also proposed big increases in military and homeland security spending. To balance the books, he would cut discretionary domestic spending, aside from homeland security, and reduce payments to Medicare providers—mostly hospitals—by $35.9 billion over five years. Exempted, of course, would be the insurers and HMOs peddling heavily subsidized private-sector alternatives to traditional Medicare.

Perhaps the boldest element of the budget appeared with the least advance publicity and had the least chance to pass Congress: partial privatization of Social Security. Never during his 2005 Social Security barnstorming tour had the president spelled out details of his own plan to restructure the program. But his new budget submission did. Bush called for letting individuals divert up to 4% of their annual wages into "voluntary private accounts" starting in 2010, up to a maximum $1,100 in the first year and with an additional $100 added each year thereafter until 2016. OMB projected the accounts would drain $712.14 billion from payroll tax receipts in the first seven years.

The White House didn't bother to guess how large an actual cut in benefits this would translate into. But to make up the shortfall, at least partially, Bush resurrected his call for progressive indexing—tying the benefits formula for the more affluent to a less generous COLA formula. He proposed saving another $6.3 billion over ten years by eliminating the death benefit for spouses and children of deceased workers or beneficiaries of Social Security, as well as any benefits for children over sixteen who were not attending school. While the amount was comparatively small over ten years of federal spending, it hit directly at one of the most valuable benefits Social Security provided for many vulnerable families.[9]

The president's proposed budget had no chance of passing; House and Senate leaders stripped out both the Social Security and Medicare cuts as soon as it reached them. But by including a full-dress plan to carve up Social Security, Bush signaled to his party's ideological base that he was still serious about shrinking government.

"The Democrats were laughing all the way to the funeral of Social Security modernization," White House spokesperson Trent Duffy said, betraying a hint of ruefulness as he explained why the president was bothering to replay an episode his party's leaders in Congress would probably rather forget. "The president still cares deeply about this."

Bush had hoped Congress would have a budget package on his desk before April 15 so he could claim it as a just-in-time present to taxpayers. But House and Senate negotiators took until early May to reach agreement on the final $70 billion package. Rather than choose between the president's tax cuts and relief for middle-class households that were feeling pressure from the Alternative Minimum Tax (AMT), they pushed off the decision another two years, until January 1, 2011. On that date the capital gains and dividend tax cuts would expire along with a temporary patch keeping the AMT from hitting another 15.3 million taxpayers. Estate tax repeal was left for later action. However, the bill also extended a host of smaller tax breaks for business.

Bush signed the measure on May 17. That pushed the decision of what to do about the tax cuts—and the vast sums of money diverted away from the Treasury because of them—on to the next president.

Estate tax repeal died in the Senate, once again. Also dead was an ambitious effort by Judd Gregg to change federal budgeting rules. Gregg's proposal aimed to force Congress to make drastic cuts in Social Security, Medicare, and Medicaid, as well as domestic discretionary programs in advance of the baby boomers' retirement. Along with caps on discretionary spending, Gregg wanted to end the long-standing rule that required a sixty-vote Senate majority to pass legislation altering Social Security and Medicare.

Gregg's bill would set up a commission to recommend restructuring of all entitlement programs. A bare majority would be sufficient to pass the panel's recommendations on to Congress, which would then have to consider them under fast-track procedures—straight up-and-down majority votes with no committee amendments in either the House or Senate. The tradition of keeping Social Security restructuring efforts bipartisan would be over.

Gregg was proposing, essentially, the creation of a set of procedures that would force a tradeoff between raising payroll taxes, to support future Social Security and Medicare benefits, and drastically slashing those benefits. Because he defined Medicare's solvency according to how much of its total budget was funded by general revenues, using additional general revenues to maintain solvency would effectively be ruled out. And Medicaid, which was entirely funded by general revenues, would be on the way to losing half its funding by 2042.[10]

Gregg got the proposal voted out of his Budget Committee in June—perhaps the biggest victory the deficit hawks achieved all year. But before his bill could be considered by the full Congress, it ran into resistance from progressives. "They have walked off the playing field of responsible public policy, waving the bloody shirt of Social Security for the purposes of political gain," Gregg thundered in a floor speech in late June, but the Senate leadership was reluctant to press the issue, and by September had decided not to pursue it further.

The idea of an all-or-nothing deficit commission would build support in Washington over the next few years. At the moment, however, Republican leaders were concerned that draconian budget-cutting measures wouldn't go over well with the broader voting public with an election year looming. In truth, the party leadership were divided about how to address the threat to their twelve-year Capitol Hill dominance. Many were disappointed that the effort to impose serious budget cuts hadn't gone farther. Some blamed the president for not more forcefully selling the cuts he had proposed, although it was Congress that had stripped them out almost without discussion. Either way, the leadership worried that its conservative base were disillusioned and wouldn't turn out to support their candidates in the fall.

In March, to get the tax cut extension bill through the Senate, Republicans were forced to vote to raise the national debt ceiling to $9.97 trillion. "Republican voters are very discouraged," said Pat Toomey. Republican lawmakers have "abandoned their commitment to fiscal discipline. To the extent the debt limit reminds voters of that, it's not a good thing."[11]

That made the collapse of Bush's Social Security privatization drive, the previous year, doubly damaging. "A lot of folks in Washington don't want to do anything about it," Bush complained in January. "It's too hard politically."[12] He had a point, but that's not what righteous Republican conservatives wanted to hear from a president who ostensibly still controlled both houses of Congress.

* * *

Their opponents, meanwhile, were highly optimistic; as the midterm elections approached, dissatisfaction with Congress grew and voters' preference for Democrats on a range of issues expanded. By mid-October, Congress's approval rating was down to 16%, matching the low point the last Democratic majority had reached in April 1992, just before the Republican revolution. Democrats also held a 13-percentage-point lead over the Republicans on handling the economy, 10 points on ethics in government, and 28 points on which party could best handle Social Security's future.[13]

The Social Security fight had helped the Democrats achieve a remarkable (for them) degree of top-down discipline that looked like it might last. It had also cemented a close working partnership between the party leadership and grassroots progressive organizers in Americans United to Protect Social Security.[14] That effort had carried over into the 2006 elections, when Americans United worked to expose Republicans' positions on Social Security as a way to leverage more votes for progressive Democrats. After years of taking second place to the conservative DLC and the deficit hawks in the Clinton White House, progressives were starting to assert greater influence within the party.

In Congress, the result was a slightly uneasy re-creation of the old Democratic coalition. On one side were powerful lawmakers such as Sen. Chuck Schumer of New York and Rep. Rahm Emanuel of Illinois—prolific fundraisers with close ties to many of the same industries and financial backers that had mostly favored Republicans—and on the other, were rising progressives like Rep. Jan Schakowsky of Illinois; Rep. Sherrod Brown of Ohio, who was running for the Senate against Republican incumbent Mike DeWine; and Democratic National Committee chair Howard Dean. This group were pro-union, skeptical of the benefits of trades treaties like NAFTA, and not nearly as friendly to the financial services industry as Schumer or Emanuel.

None of these Democratic leaders favored Social Security privatization. But the center-rightists, imbued with the Rubinomics of the Clinton years, were intent on burnishing the party's hard-won reputation for fiscal responsibility. They were also more accepting of the corporate-friendly economy—the "new supply-side reality," one of their number, former Clinton advisor Gene Sperling, called it—that the Republicans had shepherded into being. Accordingly, the Democrats' domestic initiatives showed a bit of a split personality. Topping the list, for example, was changing the rules on Medicare Part D so that the government could negotiate lower drug prices for retirees. Another goal, however, was to convene a bipartisan budget summit. Such a panel would immediately run up against the question of how to balance the budget long-term if Social Security and Medicare weren't on the table.

Cleverly, the party negotiated around the potential schism by calling for rolling back some, if not all, of the Bush tax cuts in order to address the deficit and restore some domestic spending. That angle played well with potential voters, who were concerned about their sluggish paychecks and upset about the skewing of wealth in America toward the most affluent. It ensured that the unions and union-backed groups that had worked to stop Bush from privatizing Social Security would stay in the fight, this time to elect a Democratic Congress.

In late June, a local affiliate of Americans United organized a rally outside Jim McCrery's district office in Shreveport, Louisiana to "remind him we're still here." The rally pulled over a dozen area seniors, the president of the UAW local, and a twenty-eight-foot inflatable gorilla, which organizers said representsed the "overarching component of the Bush/McCrery privatization proposal."[15]

By then, Democrats were seeing Social Security as an issue that could create inroads with some core Republican audiences. In May, the Democratic Congressional Campaign Committee bought $100,000 worth of airtime on a number of radio stations with Christian and conservative listeners to remind them that Republicans supported privatization. Emanuel said the House committee undertook the campaign because polls showed that churchgoers and fundamentalist Christians were less certain that they agreed with their party leaders—and many of their pastors—about restructuring Social Security than they did on most other leading conservative issues.

"Retirement has become a very uncertain time for many of us," asserted a radio announcement running in Kentucky, Indiana, Ohio, and Virginia, which suggested that the president and many Republican lawmakers had supported proposals that would undermine workers' one guaranteed pension benefit. Five Republican incumbents specifically targeted—Reps. Geoff Davis of Kentucky, John Hostettler and Michael Sodrel of Indiana, Steve Chabot of Ohio, and Thelma Drake of Virginia—had all endorsed the president's call for private accounts in 2005.

In July, Americans United had launched a new anti-privatization pledge drive, similar to the one the New Century Alliance had run during the 2000 presidential race but more carefully targeted. It opened shortly after a speech by the president to the conservative Manhattan Institute, in which he said, "If we can't get [private accounts enacted] this year, I'm going to try next year. And if we can't get it done next year, I'm going to try the year after that because it is the right thing to do." The statement showed how "hopelessly out of touch he really is," said Brad Woodhouse, a spokesperson for Americans United. The group would "hound members of Congress" in twenty states to sign its anti-privatization pledge, he said.[16] As for first-time candidates, "We will be demanding to know … whether they would vote to privatize the Social Security system if their voters send them to Congress," said Roger Hickey. "We will be actively publicizing their answers."[17]

Leading Democratic lawmakers were talking up the issue aggressively, often linking it to other Republican initiatives. Max Baucus, responding to Judd Gregg's attempt to "reform" the federal budget process, called it a "backdoor" attempt to push through a Republican restructuring of Social Security.[18] Hickey encouraged party leaders to use Social Security as well against Joe Lieberman, who had just lost his Democratic Senate primary in Connecticut and was forced to run for reelection as an independent. Lieberman "was the leader of the group constantly meeting with Senate privatizers" in 2005, Hickey noted.[19]

"As for short-term politics," the *Wall Street Journal* editors added despairingly, "no one is talking anymore about a 'permanent Republican majority.' The question on everyone's lips is whether Republicans will even have a Congressional majority next year."

* * *

Unfortunately for beleaguered Republican lawmakers, the president couldn't resist bringing up Social Security even late in the 2006 midterm election campaign. October saw him traveling around the country in support of his party's candidates, noting over and over that one of the "big items" he intended to pursue in the following year was restructuring the program. He continued to "believe that a worker, at his or her option, ought to be allowed to put some of their money … in a private savings account, an account that they call their own."

"I couldn't believe it," Democratic pollster Celinda Lake said in reaction to Bush's statement. "What an opening. I think he had an out-of-body experience." Elated congressional Democrats must have felt something similar. "Just when you thought your Social Security was safe from privatization," said a Democratic Senatorial Campaign Committee statement, "George Bush is bringing back his plan to privatize Social Security and cut guaranteed benefits."[20]

As the campaign season wore on, the Democrats sharpened their focus on the positions that Republicans had taken on Social Security, attacking them at every available turn. One prominent target was Clay Shaw, the Floridian who had been pushing for one private account plan or another for more than a decade and now suddenly found himself in a dangerously competitive race for his House seat with Democratic State Sen. Ron Klein.

As longtime chair of the Ways and Means Subcommittee on Social Security, Shaw had built a strong reputation in the Washington community as a statesmanesque figure in the Pete Peterson mold, ready to make tough choices for a populace not sufficiently informed to fully understand the need. That did him little good on his home turf in 2006, however, so Shaw tried to wriggle free by highlighting whatever differences he could with the president. "I don't think you can reform Social Security by dismantling the system," he said. "I have disagreed with the president on this particular matter."

Klein would have none of it. "Shaw has a privatization plan. There's no way to get around it," the Democrat's campaign manager told *Congressional Quarterly*. "To think this is the issue he's choosing to distance himself from the president on pushes the boundaries of common sense and credibility."[21]

Few Republicans endured as relentless a hammering for their Social Security position as Rick Santorum. The Pennsylvania senator had been one of the most vocal supporters of the president's privatization campaign in 2005. Now, he had volunteers from Americans United trailing him to reelection campaign events wearing gorilla suits and carrying signs that read, "Don't monkey with our SS."[22] An ad run by Santorum's opponent, State Treasurer Bob Casey, used a photo of the senator seated next to a grinning Bush to illustrate the narration, "And he votes 98 percent of the time with George Bush. Even to privatize Social Security." Earlier, the narration noted that Santorum "voted three times to give himself a pay raise."[23]

The implication, of course, was that Santorum was happy to pay himself more money even while preaching austerity and self-reliance to workers concerned about their retirement. Just as distressingly, part of the motivation for Congress and the president to slash domestic discretionary spending and to restructure and reduce Social Security seemed to be that this would help them to keep spending money in Iraq and Afghanistan.

Conservative columnist Sebastian Mallaby, in the *Washington Post*, announced that the Democrats were plumbing "new depths of cynicism" by opposing a cut-the-deficit pledge campaign by a group of Social Security critics calling themselves For Our Grandchildren. Where were the Democrats of the 1990s, he asked, who "combined attractively progressive social policies with sensible pro-market fiscal responsibility?" Instead of "centrists" like Bob Kerrey, Mallaby complained, the party was led by people like Harry Reid who "clearly want power, but ... have no principles to guide their use of it."[24]

For Republicans, only a couple of pieces of good news brightened the months leading up to the 2006 elections. The first was an unexpected jump in tax revenues that enabled the White House to lower its deficit projections to a point that OMB could label "sustainable." The improvement was relative, of course—revenues had still only returned to their level of five years prior. And dyed-in-the-wool deficit hawks, who always had the ear of the press, still weren't happy with the direction of the numbers. "The long-term outlook is such a deep well of sorrow that I can't get much happiness out of this year," said Douglas Holtz-Eakin, who had recently stepped down as CBO head.[25]

The president's poll numbers for economic performance improved in the days leading up to the election, however, in part due to a drop in the unemployment rate from 4.6% to 4.4%, which enabled Bush to boast that Democratic criticisms of his economic policies had proved wrong. "If the Democrats' election predictions are as good as their economic predictions, we're going to have a good day on November the seventh," he told a crowd of supporters in Joplin, Missouri, where he was campaigning for Sen. Jim Talent.[26]

* * *

Jim Talent lost to Democrat Claire McCaskill, one of five seats McCaskill's party picked up to place them in a 49-49 tie with the Republicans. Given that two Independents, Bernie Sanders of Vermont and Joe Lieberman, continued to caucus with the Democrats, the election gave the party a tenuous control of the Senate. In the House, the Democrats gained 31 seats, giving them a majority of 233 to 203, but the public's preference was more emphatic than this suggested. Not a single Democratic incumbent lost in November 2006, and in almost every race where a Democrat stood for an open seat, he or she won. Two of the five Republican incumbents the Democratic Congressional Campaign Committee had targeted in May for endorsing Bush's 2005 privatization campaign, Reps. John Hostettler and Michael Sodrel of Indiana, lost their seats.

The turnaround came just two years after the Republicans had won their most comfortable election since taking over Congress in 1994. Why did it happen? The long string of scandals involving Republican politicians and power brokers no doubt contributed. So did the fading of terrorism as an issue and the administration's failure to convince the nation that it was defeating the Iraqi insurgents. On a practical level, candidates from the progressive wing of the Democratic Party were able to tap into a rich new vein of campaign cash from an alliance of comparatively progressive donors, the most conspicuous of whom were hedge fund manager George Soros and auto insurance tycoon Peter Lewis.[27] Many pundits also credited MoveOn.org and the community of progressive bloggers with helping mobilize new Democratic voters.

The election was also, in part, a testament to the success of Reid and Pelosi, the latter about to become the first female speaker of the House, at disciplining and creating unity among their members in 2005. Social Security was the issue they seized on to do so. Next year, "the campaign-style apparatus that defeated Social Security reform was ready to go on behalf of Democratic candidates," commented the *Boston Globe*'s Rick Klein.

The key, Democratic leaders said, had been getting their lawmakers to resist the urge to collaborate with Republicans or put forth a plan of their own that the Republicans could then attack. When colleagues asked Pelosi when the party would release its own Social Security reform proposal, an aide recalled, she replied simply, "Never. Does never work for you?"[28]

Conservative Republicans agreed that Social Security was the beginning of their party's downfall, but they blamed the congressional Republican leadership, not the Democrats. Armey complained that his party "missed the opportunity of a lifetime by failing to embrace retirement security based on personal ownership."[29] Fred Barnes castigated them for leaving their president in the lurch in 2005. Had they not, "voters would now be perusing the stock tables to decide how to invest their payroll taxes."[30]

It was also possible, of course, that the Democrats simply read the public's preferences better than their rivals on this key issue. Republicans had been especially proud of their party's success with the senior vote in recent elections. These were the generations that had benefited most from the so-called Era of Big Government. For a long time, they were dependably Democratic votes. Reagan had appealed strongly to seniors, however, and they had thrown their support to Bush after September 11. But the Republican debacle over Social Security appeared to have changed their minds.

Two days before the election, a Pew Research Center survey showed 48% of those sixty-five and older leaning Democratic, versus 42% tending Republican. Attacking Social Security and proselytizing for private accounts wasn't the best way to woo voters grown increasingly worried about their ability to make ends meet and their prospects for a secure retirement.

CHAPTER 43

THE REBIRTH OF
THE PAIN CAUCUS

The president betrayed no discomfort at the prospect of working with a Democratic Congress his last two years in office. Unlike his predecessor, who had greeted a change of party control with an admission of ideological defeat, Bush reaffirmed his devotion to "balancing the budget through pro-growth economic policies and spending restraint."[1] In other words, he would defend his tax cuts to the last while opposing any domestic spending measures the new Congress might try to float past him.

Despite the president's tough talk, in the months after the Republicans lost Congress, the administration was actually working on two tracks. While Bush assumed a firmly ideological stance, his Treasury secretary—starting even before the election, in fact—was quietly pursuing a new, bipartisan Social Security initiative.

Henry Paulson, former head of Goldman Sachs, took over from John Snow in July 2006 only after the president assured him that economic policy would be made at Treasury again and that he wouldn't be used merely as a salesperson for decisions made in the White House. In his Senate confirmation hearings

Paulson said he wanted to make progress toward overhauling Social Security and Medicare. He talked up the issue in the following months.[2] "The biggest economic issue facing our country is the growth in spending on the major entitlement programs," he said in a speech outlining his economic vision at Columbia University.[3]

But Paulson was careful not to include any reference to private accounts, instead emphasizing flexibility and the need to build a bipartisan consensus. The biggest mistake of the 2005 Bush privatization campaign, which Paulson didn't intend to repeat, had been to go over the heads of key Democrats while insisting that congressional Republican leaders expose themselves on the issue.

The new Big Idea dawning on Washington, in fact, was that with private accounts off the table, the way might be clear for a deal between the Bush administration and center-right Democrats to shrink Social Security while creating private accounts on the side, rather than as carve-outs. Accordingly, the Pain Caucus, with its characteristic fondness for the ideal of bipartisanship, went all atwitter over its new standard bearer. When Pelosi, in an email, opined that Paulson's efforts would amount to privatization, which she said had been "soundly rejected by the American people," the *Washington Post*—always ready to champion entitlement cuts—accused her of obstructionism. "We hope other Democrats will be less cynical," the *Post* editors sniffed.

Republican members of the Free Lunch Caucus, who were more interested in carving out private accounts than anything else that might be done with Social Security, didn't hold out much more hope for Paulson's effort than did Pelosi, however. "The Democrats cannot be bribed, cajoled or threatened into voting for Social Security reform—it can't happen," Grover Norquist said flatly.

Not much was going to happen until after the November election in any case. In the meantime, Paulson and OMB director Rob Portman, a Bush confidant and formerly a high-ranking House leader, began holding meetings with key figures on either side of the aisle. The president was supportive, White House counselor Dan Bartlett told the *Washington Post*. He wants to "openly engage at the appropriate time Republicans and Democrats on Capitol Hill. Those conversations are quietly under way."

The success of such a plan would require full commitment from the president. Potential Democratic partners were skeptical. After Paulson and Portman had met with Kent Conrad—the North Dakota Democrat whom Bush had courted so clumsily the year before—Conrad remained unconvinced that the White House would really work with leaders of both parties. "I think he's a very sincere fellow," Conrad said of Paulson. "I don't think he's in charge."

Conrad advised Paulson to pull together a working group of lawmakers and White House officials who could develop a sweeping plan covering both Social Security and Medicare, and push it onto Congress's agenda in 2007.[4] Two Republicans, Rep. Frank Wolf of Virginia and Sen. George Voinovich of Ohio, were thinking along the same lines. In August they proposed creating a bipartisan entitlement commission similar to the one Gregg had been advocating.

The membership split they proposed, however, would be 9-6 in favor of the Republicans, reflecting their position in Congress—a standing few expected them to enjoy come January.

The day after the election, the president said that he had "instructed Secretary Paulson to reach out to folks on the Hill to see if we can't at least get a dialogue started." Later that month Senate minority leader-elect Mitch McConnell challenged Reid and Pelosi, the incoming Senate majority leader and House speaker, respectively, to work with Republicans on two key issues: immigration reform and long-term financing of Social Security. "This would be the perfect time to tackle Social Security," McConnell said hopefully.

Paulson, meanwhile, told the *Washington Post* that the White House was prepared to negotiate a Social Security package with "no preconditions." That meant Bush was ready to drop his long-standing insistence that private accounts be part of any restructuring. Administration officials told the *Post* that the president was willing to listen to ideas such as creating personal accounts outside of Social Security and even raising payroll taxes as a partial means of sorting out its fiscal future.[5]

Speculation on what the president might be thinking about taxes quickly congealed around the idea that the White House would accept a raising of the cap on the income level used to calculate Social Security payroll taxes and benefits, in return for large reductions in benefits and private accounts funded outside the payroll tax system. The result: a sort of backdoor privatization, with deniability for Democratic lawmakers since the private accounts wouldn't technically be part of the program.

Former Bush economic advisor Glenn Hubbard proposed a version of this scenario on NPR's *Marketplace Radio* in early January. At the same time, Conrad and Gregg reportedly were pursuing their idea of creating a "bipartisan panel of lawmakers and administration officials" with the goal of bringing an entitlement restructuring bill before Congress some time in 2007. Asked about the project, Conrad declined to offer details, saying he didn't want to "kill this baby in the crib."[6]

A deal that included boosting payroll taxes for the affluent would have difficulty winning conservatives' support, however. "Doing so would raise the marginal rate on the entrepreneurs that Mr. Bush credits for having led the economic recovery by more than 10 percentage points," his former economic advisor, Larry Lindsey, wrote in the *Wall Street Journal*. Besides, other tax loopholes would allow many to deduct their higher payroll taxes, leaving the Treasury with not much additional revenue to show for the exercise.

Bush, however, continued the overtures in his State of the Union address in January. "We must take up the challenge of entitlements," he told Congress. "Yet we've failed in our duty. And this failure will one day leave our children with three bad options: huge tax increases, huge deficits, or huge and immediate cuts in benefits. Everyone in this chamber knows this to be true, yet somehow we have not found it in ourselves to act."

Even if "everyone" accepted the train-wreck scenario, that didn't make it true. It was, however, conventional wisdom in Washington, and by leaving out any reference to private accounts, the president signaled he was still interested in making a deal on Social Security. Little more than a week after his speech, however, the White House released a $2.9 trillion budget it said would eliminate the deficit within five years without raising taxes—although critics noted the shortfall would then shoot up again for many years because the previous rounds of tax cuts would be locked in.

For the second year in a row, the budget included a proposal for privatizing Social Security. This time, it went into somewhat more detail. The plan was to divert $712 billion from the trust funds over ten years to create voluntary private accounts. Beginning in 2012, workers could use 4% of their Social Security taxable earnings, up to $1,300 a year, to fund their personal accounts. That amount would grow by $100 a year through 2017. The rate of growth of benefits would be cut for all recipients, but most deeply for those who opted to set up private accounts. Bush was still using progressive indexing to structure his benefits formula. Anyone who earned more than $22,000 a year before retirement would feel the pain, and high earners could expect a 40% drop in lifetime benefits.

Both Congress and the president were reluctant to do anything about the Alternative Minimum Tax (AMT) right away. Bush needed the money to subsidize his tax cuts, the new congressional leadership to restore some hard-hit domestic programs. They didn't agree on much else, however. Democratic leaders were especially taken aback by the inclusion of Social Security privatization in Bush's budget.

"The $712 billion price tag and $3.2 billion in benefit cuts Bush proposes are just the tip of the iceberg," said Charles Rangel the day the president's budget was released. "To be honest, this isn't what I expected from a president who, just last week, suggested that Democrats and Republicans should hold hands and work this thing out. How can we take the president's offer at face value when his budget clearly tells us that, at the end of the day, he wants to privatize Social Security?"

But the White House was serious, at least to the extent it was willing to follow a two-track strategy: the president reassuring the supply-side true believers, while Paulson continued to pursue his back-door approach, minus the ownership society rhetoric. Rove, the chief ideologue of the ownership society, resigned in August after his name turned up a few too many times in reports about dirty tricks campaigns against White House enemies.

Paulson's strategy made some progress the following month when Conrad and Gregg introduced Senate legislation to create an entitlements commission. The panel's composition would give the edge slightly to the majority party in the House and Senate but would also include two presidential appointees, one of them the Treasury secretary, who would chair. Its recommendations would go before Congress immediately for an up-or-down vote—the same practice the Senate followed with foreign trade treaties under presidential fast-track authority. This would stifle debate on details of the plan and make it easier for lawmakers to "jump off the cliff together."

At the same time, Paulson published a series of Treasury issue briefs on entitlements, hoping to spark a discussion by establishing points of general agreement, such as the magnitude of the problem. That was the approach the Greenspan commission had begun with, successfully, in 1982.

* * *

At this point, the anti-deficit groundswell still only consisted of Paulson, with some careful White House encouragement, and a few prominent Republican and Democratic deficit hawks. How much support they enjoyed with their own party caucuses was debatable, but that was hard to notice, given the enthusiastic support they received from the corporate media in Washington. In March, *60 Minutes* ran a report featuring U.S. Comptroller General David Walker, who had launched a "Fiscal Wake-Up Tour" in 2005 to call attention to what he predicted was the nation's coming bankruptcy. More than twenty years after the show first aired a segment attacking entitlements, featuring Pete Peterson and hosted by an admiring Leslie Stahl, Walker's appearance proved that CBS News was still in thrall to the deficit hawks.

"David Walker thinks the biggest economic peril facing the nation is being ignored," said correspondent Steve Kroft, "and for nearly two years now he has been traveling the country like an Old Testament prophet, urging people to wake up before it's too late." Walker had "totaled up our government's income, liabilities, and future obligations and concluded that our current standard of living is unsustainable unless some drastic action is taken.... It's been called the 'dirty little secret everyone in Washington knows'—a set of financial truths so inconvenient that most elected officials don't even want to talk about them, which is exactly why David Walker does."[7]

Kroft didn't say who was calling the numbers behind Social Security and Medicare a "dirty little secret" or explain how this could be so when the anti-entitlement movement was so prominently placed and widely heard. Walker went on to make all the usual points about the unsustainability of Social Security and Medicare, capped by the familiar charge that spendthrift Americans "promise way more than we can afford to keep."

Walker's was the only voice heard on the segment except for that of Kent Conrad, who praised the crusading comptroller for "providing an enormous public service." *60 Minutes* dismissed any dissenters—coming close, in fact, to questioning their existence. "You're probably expecting to hear from someone who disagrees with the comptroller general's numbers, projections, and analysis," Kroft said, "but hardly anyone does. He is accompanied on the wake-up tour by economists from the conservative Heritage Foundation, the left-leaning Brookings Institution, and the nonpartisan Concord Coalition. The only dissenters seem to be a small minority of economists who believe either that the U.S. can grow its way out of the problem, or that Walker is overstating it."

"Seem to" were the operative words, since *60 Minutes* viewers heard nothing more of this "small minority" and their apparently irresponsible views. And the perspective Walker championed was more distinctly partisan than the segment implied. Brookings had never been a "left-leaning" outfit and had moved to the right in recent years. Concord was officially nonpartisan but had consistently targeted New Deal and Great Society institutions as the sacrificial lambs in its anti-deficit crusade.

Days after the segment aired, Walker was also featured in a long *Washington Post* story on the out-of-control deficit. The government's total "unfunded commitments," he declared, came to a staggering $50 trillion. "If you take that $50 trillion, that's $440,000 per household," he added helpfully. The article's author, Joel Achenbach, offered no corroboration of the figure or any breakdown of what precisely it represented. Walker and his frequent speaking companion, Pete Peterson, would repeat it often in the coming months, at one point raising it to $53 trillion.[8]

The figure was next to meaningless, however. Dean Baker, in an analysis posted on his blog some months later, found that the bulk of it was a conglomeration of the worst-case long-term scenarios for Social Security and Medicare, assuming no change in either revenues or the rapid growth of health care costs. The ballooning deficit was "almost entirely a health care story," Baker wrote, and could only be tackled by an overhaul of the entire U.S. health care financing system, not by cutting one or two particular programs.[9] Program cuts, however, were about the only thing Walker and other prominent deficit hawks seemed willing to consider.

Rhetorically, however, the deficit hawks were soon having fun at one of their favorite pastimes: boomer bashing. The occasion was the semiofficial First Baby Boomer's receipt of her first Social Security benefit check in October.

"When it comes to the nation's finances, Kathleen Casey-Kirschling is Public Enemy No. 1. Her offense: Being born," wrote the *Washington Post*'s resident national affairs wit, Dana Milbank. Although the threshold had shifted many times, the dawn of the baby boom was now spoken of as 1946, and Casey-Kirschling happened to have been the first baby born in the U.S. on January 1. *Money* magazine initially wrote her up as the First Boomer when she was about to turn forty in 1985, and the title had stuck. On October 15, the SSA held a press conference as the retired schoolteacher signed up for benefits, hoping to make the point that Social Security was keeping its promises to the first generation who had contributed to the program their entire working lives.

Milbank was there to hose down any such attempts at spin. Social Security Commissioner Michael Astrue "spent much of the news conference whistling past the graveyard of entitlement insolvency," the reporter lamented. But Casey-Kirschling wasn't the culprit. "If anything, the ones to blame are the Boomer presidents Bill Clinton and George W. Bush, and all the Boomers in Congress who have put off the painful changes everybody knows will be needed." A few paragraphs later, Milbank cited, inevitably, the UFO factoid.

Queering the argument slightly was the April release of the Social Security trustees' annual report, which showed the program running out of money in 2041, one year later than the previous year's estimate. The trustees projected the Social Security deficit over the next seventy-five years at $4.7 trillion. Yet the CBO estimated the total cost of the administration's wars in the Middle East would come to more than half that figure—$2.4 trillion—by 2017 alone. Future war spending, and not Social Security, was what prompted the CBO to declare that the country was on an "unsustainable fiscal path and something has to give." Another report, by the congressional Joint Economic Committee, looked further out and put the total cost of the Bush wars at $3.5 trillion.

Nevertheless, Paulson took the opportunity to play up the need to restructure entitlements. "Without change," he said, "rising costs will drive government spending to unprecedented levels, consume nearly all projected federal revenues and threaten America's future prosperity."

* * *

Working Americans appeared to have quite different concerns. Indeed, signs were popping up that middle-class Americans had become disenchanted with the philosophy of individual effort that was supposed to be replacing reliance on government as the answer to their problems. Which underscored the fact that Social Security, rather than shrinking in significance as free-market ideologues predicted, was likely to play a more vital role in workers' lives in the future.

A GAO study requested by Democratic Rep. George Miller of California estimated that 63% of low-income workers born in 1990 would retire with virtually no savings. According to a poll by COUNTRY Insurance & Financial Services, 34% of Americans said the biggest barrier to saving for retirement was that they didn't have the money to do so, while 17% cited the need to pay off debt.

But what was the alternative? Since more and more companies were terminating their defined benefit pension plans, freezing them, or converting them into something more 401(k)-like, one alternative was to improve Social Security.

The program was still "the best leg" of a three-legged stool," said David Langer, pension actuary and gadfly to the doomsayers. But it was deteriorating. Langer estimated that Social Security benefits had already fallen 25% in value owing to changes legislated in the 1983 Amendments, including gradual raising of the retirement age to sixty-seven, reduction of benefits for surviving children, and higher taxes levied on upper-income beneficiaries.[10] Escalating health care and energy costs were eroding benefits even further, since Social Security COLAs were now based on a price formula that rose more slowly than prices on those two commodities. Medicare premiums were pushing down Social Security benefits as well because these steadily rising charges were deducted straight from retirees' OASI benefit checks.[11]

One helpful reform, the Senior Citizens League suggested, would be to change the COLA. Since 1983, it had been based on the Consumer Price Index for Urban Wage Earners and Clerical Workers, or CPI-W. But the CPI-W tracked mainly the spending of younger workers. Another index, the CPI-E or CPI for Elderly Consumers, had existed since 1983. It measured a basket of goods that closely tracked what retirees actually spent their money on. But it was used only as an experiment—not to calculate benefits. Replacing the CPI-W with the CPI-E would have increased by several thousand dollars the payments even for retirees who qualified for relatively low levels of benefits, the league estimated. Two bills introduced in the House in 2007 would have made the switch.

Another measure, introduced by Democratic Rep. Carolyn Maloney of New York, would reduce the period of marriage required for a divorced woman to claim Social Security benefits based on her ex-spouse's earnings during those years. Meanwhile, the National Council of Women's Organizations was calling for creation of a caregiver's credit that would prevent women from losing benefits because they took time out from work to raise children or care for ailing relatives.

If not this, some women's rights activists suggested, why not create a comprehensive child care system that would reduce the amount of time women had to take off to provide these services? The gaps in wage history that cut into their Social Security benefits would be largely eliminated. Democratic Sen. Christopher Dodd of Connecticut was sponsoring a bill to provide paid leave for workers caring for sick family members, while Sen. Pat Roberts, Kansas Republican, introduced the Small Business Child Care Act, which would encourage employers to offer child care to their workers.

The fact that these ideas couldn't break through in Washington in 2007 testified to the continued ideological dominance of the movement against Social Security. Few of them would have raised the program's long-term cost significantly, while the child-care proposals would affect its balance sheet not at all. Some would have helped hard-up working families, which should have recommended them to conservative lawmakers. As long as the dominant story line about Social Security-as-looming-trainweck persisted, however, they were dismissed as counterproductive to the goal of "saving" the program.

* * *

"Not only have individual financial actors become less vulnerable to shocks from underlying risk factors, but also the financial system as a whole has become more resilient."
—*Alan Greenspan (2004)[12]*

"Bubble trouble? Not likely."
　　　　　—Chris Mayer and Todd Sinai (2005)[13]

*"Though [derivatives contracts] have famously been called
financial weapons of mass destruction by more traditional
investors like Warren Buffett (who has, nonetheless, made
use of them), the view in Chicago is that the world's
economic system has never been better protected against the
unexpected."*
　　　　　—Niall Ferguson (2008)[14]

In February 2007, just after the White House released its plan to eliminate the federal deficit within five years, HSBC, the world's largest bank, became the first major institution to write down its mortgage-backed securities containing subprime loans, to the tune of $10.5 billion. The burgeoning market for securitized assets like mortgage-backed securities was the major enabler behind the mortgage boom of the past decade, which in turn had kept the U.S. economy afloat after the dot-com collapse of 2000. By spring 2007, however, that market was shrinking almost into nonexistence.

Thus began what was perhaps the most predictable financial catastrophe in U.S. history—one that the nation's most prominent economists and economic policymakers, bankers, financial journalists, and investors all had a hand in engineering through years of folly and denial. For some months the administration either didn't realize or didn't want to acknowledge the disaster. Paulson confidently stated that "the housing market is at or near bottom" and the systemic problems, which he asserted only involved the subprime mortgage sector, were "largely contained."

Instead of addressing this, for the third year in a row, the president's budget included a proposal for private Social Security accounts offset by progressive indexing of benefits, although it only sketched out these points. The record $3 trillion request also called for close to $100 billion of cuts in Medicare over the next five years, along with more than $15 billion of Medicaid reductions. Payments to private health care providers under Medicare Advantage, of course, wouldn't be touched. Other programs would be cut too, including child care and low-income rental and energy assistance. Overall, the president proposed to hold increased spending on domestic discretionary programs to less than 1%, while making his 2001 and 2003 tax cuts permanent.

Republican leaders hailed the president's decision to take on Medicare growth. "We cannot delay action on entitlement reform any longer," declared the crusading Judd Gregg. House minority leader John Boehner of Ohio hoped Democrats would "work with Republicans to begin making these important reforms."

Their timing couldn't have been worse. The Democrats were completely uninterested in cutting holes in the safety net. Instead, they were already hammering out an economic stimulus package. When Congress voted on it, a few days after the president sent down his budget, it amounted to $168 billion of tax rebates for households and businesses. These included payments for some 20 million Social Security beneficiaries and 250,000 disabled veterans who normally wouldn't have qualified because they didn't have any earned income. The bill passed the Senate 81 to 16—a sure sign that lawmakers were worried, since "unearned" tax rebates were heresy to conservatives. The president eagerly signed the measure.

The modest measure took some of the immediate pressure off households, but did little to revive the economy. By fall, the number of workers living paycheck-to-paycheck was expanding, up from 43% the previous year to 47%, according to one survey, and including one out of five workers with incomes of $100,000 or more.[15] In such times, preaching the virtues of balanced budgets and personal thrift seemed almost cruelly irrelevant.

The housing market drop was expected to continue through 2009 and foreclosure rates were rising faster than the economy was declining. Consumers, not surprisingly, were pulling back and even starting to save a little once again. Many had no choice, however, since lenders had written off some $21 billion of bad credit card debt in the first half of the year. In response, they were cutting credit lines and raising requirements for accepting new cardholders. Just at the most inopportune time, it seemed that the new era of thrift that many of Social Security's critics had long called for might finally have begun.

Investors large and small, including big public and corporate pension funds as well as individual holders of 401(k) and IRA accounts, which had been touted for so long as the eventual replacement for Social Security, were taking a beating. According to an analyst at Credit Suisse, by late September, the market selloff had turned a collective $60 billion long-term surplus for the pension funds of companies in the Standard & Poor's 500 into a $75 billion *deficit*. Factoring in October's disastrous performance, that deficit may have ballooned to as much as $186 billion.

The staggering loss of retirement assets, coupled with the evaporation of some $4 trillion to $5 trillion in homeowners' equity, had wiped out a great deal of what working families thought was their financial security. Yet the White House, apparently, wasn't interested. The administration's entire strategy for dealing with the crisis seemed wrapped up in its fumbling effort to recapitalize the banks, even though they clearly wouldn't be willing or able to help re-stimulate the economy for a long time. When Sheila Bair, chairperson of the Federal Deposit Insurance Corporation, began arguing publicly in October that the administration should push lenders to restructure at-risk mortgages in order to reduce foreclosures and perhaps use some of the Troubled Assets Recovery Program (TARP) money for mortgage relief as well, she was essentially ignored.

Seniors and workers nearing retirement felt themselves especially at risk. "Unlike Wall Street executives, American families don't have a golden parachute to fall back on," said Rep. George Miller, chair of the House Committee on Education and Labor. "It's clear that Americans' retirement security may be one of the greatest casualties of this financial crisis."[16]

Workers in their twenties, who already saved for retirement at lower rates than other cohorts, suddenly were expressing worries that even if they saved more, their contributions might be swallowed up by the plunging markets.[17] But then, they were planning on working longer as well. For the past decade, statistics had shown that the decades-long trend toward earlier retirement was reversing itself as the percentage of retirement-age individuals in the workforce grew.[18] Between 2000 and 2006 alone, the U.S. Census Bureau reported, employment among people over sixty-five rose from 23.1% of the group to 28.1%.

This shift had many causes, including the higher retirement age and reduced benefits legislated in the 1983 Social Security amendments. More than four out of five respondents in a survey of workers with less than $100,000 in assets cited the need to earn enough to maintain an adequate standard of living.[19] Management consultants advised companies to embrace the trend because retirement age workers could be paid less—and their employers no longer had to make payroll tax contributions for them.[20] Meanwhile, a survey of financial planners found that nearly 35% of their clients were postponing retirement because of current economic conditions.[21]

The one-third of retirees living only on Social Security were feeling the pinch from the economic slump most acutely, but those with uneven or dwindling incomes outside their benefits were also hurting. "I have Social Security, but it is not enough to pay for my apartment, to buy my food and medicine," a retired doctor told the *Washington Post*. "Even the nonprescription kinds are going up. I look in the papers, but it is difficult."

Privatization—either explicitly by carving out private accounts or implicitly by slashing benefits and creating private accounts on the side—seemed far from any sensible person's mind. "The economic situation has put paid to the idea of privatizing Social Security," Jane Bryant Quinn, a longtime defender of the program, said shortly after President Obama's stimulus package passed. "There are people who hate Social Security and Medicare for ideological reasons, and they'll always be there. But they had their best shot when we had a huge bull market in the 1990s, and then under Bush. If you can't sell it during a bull market, with all the indices positive, then how can you sell it at a time like this?"

Ironically, the young, who Social Security opponents had always regarded as their prime audience, would quickly become their biggest stumbling block if the downturn continued, Quinn pointed out. "How are teenagers and people in their twenties going to look at their jobs and at what's happening to their parents?" she asked. "If these people grow up with a depression, losing their jobs, losing their bank accounts, they'll learn to be much more conservative with their money. Will this generation be the constituency for the privatizers? I think not. They'll look at their parents, and what are they living on? Social Security."[22]

The plight of the elderly, and of workers within a decade of retirement, was assuming a pattern similar to the early Depression years, when older workers were the first to be thrown out of jobs and into the arms of their families or of whatever local relief was available to them. Seventy-five years later, these people found themselves competing for relatively low-level jobs with younger workers who wouldn't have sought these positions a couple of years earlier. They were also discovering they suffered from a competitive disadvantage: employers were reluctant to hire people who might not want a job or be able to keep doing it at some point in the fairly near future. Tales cropped up in the media of people in their eighties or even nineties searching for jobs waiting tables or providing services to other seniors who couldn't leave their homes.

In January, the number of unemployed people seventy-five or older increased by 73,000—up 46% from a year before. Unemployment among this cohort was nearly 5%—58% higher than the year before.[23] If this continued, more of them would have to continue working past retirement age, making the competition for jobs even fiercer.

The safety net, it turned out, didn't offer much to these workers. There was only one federal program for them: Senior Community Services, which was geared to match up community organizations with elderly people who wanted low-key jobs. It provided twenty-four to thirty-six months of paid training, but that was all. If they hadn't found a permanent job by that point, there was no more money for them.[24] As yet, the situation for seniors wasn't anything like what it had been in the early 1930s, with higher than 50% unemployment for workers over sixty. This time, the quartet of Social Security—OASI and DI, SSI, Medicare, and Medicaid—were catching their fall.

* * *

Could it be, then, that the movement against Social Security had outlived its time? Hardly. The catastrophe that hit the housing market in 2007–08 and rapidly spread to the rest of economy seemed to revitalize the deficit hawks. In February 2008, the administration announced that the deficit would be a record $412 billion in fiscal 2009. Five months later, the figure was $482 billion. Moody's made headlines in February as well with a warning to the federal government that it could lose its AAA debt rating within a decade unless it took action to rein in health care and retirement benefits spending. "The combination of the medical programs and Social Security is the most important threat to the triple-A rating over the long term," it said.

Moody's judgment would soon come under a cloud because it had maintained high ratings for Bear Stearns and other big-name investment firms even as they loaded up on risky, mortgage-related paper. But others were striving to divert the public's attention from the disaster in the mortgage market to what they claimed was a far bigger problem.

Presidential candidate John McCain grabbed onto the fiscal 2009 deficit figure as an opportunity to display the soundness of his position on the budget. The deficit estimate made clear "the dire fiscal condition of the federal government," he said. Others noted that the projected deficit would still amount to only 3.3% of GDP, far lower than in 1983, when the Reagan administration had tolerated a gap representing 6% of the economy. But the alarm had been raised.[25]

In February, when that first record deficit number was released, the New America Foundation and the Heritage Foundation collaborated on the release of a paper entitled "Rethinking Social Insurance," co-authored by Maya MacGuineas, New America's fiscal policy director, and Stuart Butler, Heritage's vice president of domestic and economic policy. Entitlement growth was "the single greatest threat to the fiscal health of the United States," they declared. Their proposed solutions were mostly familiar: means-testing of benefits, for instance, and triggers that would force Congress to review and reauthorize all entitlement spending every five years if it was projected to pass a certain long-range threshold.

Following the lines of the kind of deal Paulson appeared to be working toward in his talks with members of Congress, MacGuineas and Butler also called for creation of mandatory savings accounts outside of Social Security, possibly with a government match for those below the poverty line. The authors dealt with the more serious problem of how to get higher-income Americans to keep supporting a means-tested system by avoiding it.

"The obligation to help those in need is an ingrained American value," they insisted. Indeed, "the spending control and fiscal improvements resulting from the reforms would likely win their strong and lasting support by improving the long-term economic climate and by reducing the huge unfunded obligations facing their children and grandchildren. Thus, a broad-based coalition of support would be maintained."[26] Depending on one's point of view, this was either colossally naive or a cynical rationalization for destroying the concept of social insurance. Other centrist think tanks were feeding the pipeline as well, however.

Isabel Sawhill, who had worked at OMB under Clinton and was now at Brookings, coauthored a paper a few months later arguing that smaller increases in Medicare benefits, plus higher premiums, should be "traded" for more subsidized child care. "We have a budget out of control and dominated by spending on the elderly," she complained. Sawhill's recommendations were similar to the ones Butler and MacGuineas had put forward, including means testing, mandatory savings, and enforceable rules requiring Congress to cut entitlements. This reflected the old zero-sum argument that liberals must cannibalize some social programs to pay for others.[27]

A month after releasing its report with New America, Heritage published another joint document, this one with the much higher profile Brookings Institution, entitled "Taking Back Our Fiscal Future." Along with Sawhill and Butler, the signatories included MacGuineas, Will Marshall of the DLC and the Progressive Policy Institute, Bob Bixby of Concord, Joe Antos of the American Enterprise Institute, and Robert Reischauer and Rudolph Penner of the Urban Institute.

These think-tank eminences had been meeting for over a year. But while they claimed to represent points of view covering "the ideological spectrum," their recommendations were almost identical to those in "Rethinking Social Insurance": means testing entitlement benefits, creating budgetary rules that would force cuts in the programs down the line, and mandatory individual savings. But if the proposals had been around and were familiar, the group's rhetoric was newly self-important and bombastic.

"We're the sons and daughters of the American fiscal revolution," Sawhill declared at the report's launch.[28] Marshall labeled entitlements a "doomsday machine."[29]

Aimed mainly at lawmakers, the bigfoot media, and other influentials, none of these wonkish efforts achieved the same degree of visibility as *I.O.U.S.A.*, a documentary bankrolled by Pete Peterson's foundation, which premiered at the Sundance Film Festival in January 2008. Directed by Patrick Creadon, who had earlier made the successful crossword puzzle documentary *Wordplay*, the new film was warmly greeted but bore its political strategy very much on its sleeve.

"Creadon's film," said *Variety*, "could just as easily have been titled *An Inconvenient Truth* and indeed has a number of things in common with Al Gore's cautionary global-warming doc: It's essentially a glorified PowerPoint presentation, and it calls for a nonpartisan response to an issue—in this case, our 'fiscal cancer'—with significantly further-reaching implications for the average American than the war on terror."

David Walker, the former U.S. comptroller general, was now president and CEO of the Peterson Foundation. He played more or less the same role in *I.O.U.S.A.* that Gore had assumed in *An Inconvenient Truth*: the educator-cum-rock star bucking the establishment by revealing the unpleasant facts to the public. When the movie premiered theatrically in June, the foundation arranged for a "town hall on economic issues" to be broadcast to 350 theaters around the country after the first screening. The event featured Walker, Peterson, and Warren Buffett answering questions submitted over the movie's website.

This was just the beginning of an effort to create a groundswell that could be termed austerity populism. Eight weeks later, the Peterson Foundation reported it had gathered more than 100,000 signatures to an online "Wake Up America" statement calling for greater national fiscal responsibility. Visitors to the site could also email their senators and representatives asking how they were going to overcome "the leadership deficit" that had allowed entitlements to spiral out of control.

"Cynics doubted our ability to build a movement around fiscal responsibility," Walker said in a press release. "Judging by the outpouring thus far, it seems that we're off to a fine start in turning such a movement into reality."

While it presented a good deal of factual information, the context created in *I.O.U.S.A.* was deeply slanted. Rattling off such dubious claims as the $53 trillion long-term deficit, it never bothered to mention what percentage of future GDP that might represent. Without that information, the viewer would have no way of knowing whether it represented a serious problem or something manageable.

The film broke into the lower reaches of the list of top-grossing documentaries, but it never threatened Michael Moore's standing as the giant of the advo-doc genre, and failed to build the mass movement Peterson and Walker had hoped for. The united front that the deficit hawks had been trying to build in support of Social Security and Medicare cutbacks was turning out to have been a bit of sleight-of-hand as well.

Some experts who had initially participated in the Heritage/Brookings project in the spring felt they had been hoodwinked because the conservative members of the panel refused to consider tax increases, or even rolling back some of the Bush tax cuts, as part of the solution to balancing Social Security's books and lowering the deficit. At Brookings, two leading economists who opposed cutting Social Security—Henry Aaron and Jason Furman—were angry at having not been informed that the institution was participating in the project.

Robert Greenstein, one of the disgruntled panelists, pulled together another group of experts, including Aaron and Nobel Prize-winning economist Robert Solow, to endorse a new paper called "A Balanced Approach to Restoring Fiscal Responsibility." Released in July, it called the Heritage/Brookings paper "misguided," pointing out that the cost over seventy-five years of not repealing or scaling back the Bush tax cuts would be three-and-a-half times the entire Social Security shortfall. It recommended that Congress focus, among other things, on reforming the health care system, while eliminating tax breaks for the rich, as a way to start bringing down the deficit.[30]

* * *

Deficit reduction had long been a "proxy for public virtue" in Washington, as Robert Kuttner of *The American Prospect* put it.[31] But why, as the worst recession since the 1930s took hold, was the deficit assuming such a high profile in Washington, and, increasingly, in the mainstream corporate media—this at a time when unemployment, mass evictions, and financial panic were perhaps more urgent concerns than long-term deficits?

Working in favor of the deficit hawks was the fact that even as the economic situation across the U.S. worsened, the political power dynamic changed curiously little. The economic stimulus package Bush signed early in 2008 was too small to have much effect, and despite the overwhelming numbers it captured in the Senate, it encountered heavy criticism from the far right. As the year wore on, and increasingly after a new administration took office in 2009, opponents of fiscal stimulus began to dig in, arguing that the failure of the Bush measure showed, once again, that government only "gets in the way" of economic recovery. The deficit hawks weren't altogether convinced that some stimulus wasn't a good thing, but the rumblings on the right enlarged the audience for much of their agenda.

Another factor was the political revival of Wall Street. The financial collapse hit its nadir in fall 2008, when the investment firm Lehman Brothers collapsed, and the insurance giant AIG and the government-sponsored mortgage packagers Fannie Mae and Freddie Mac had to be taken over by the federal government. But in responding to the crisis, the president essentially deferred to three key policymakers, all of whom had strong roots in the Wall Street culture: Fed chair Ben Bernanke, Treasury Secretary Henry Paulson, and Tim Geithner, president of the New York Fed. All three were committed to interfering as little as possible with the present structure of the financial services industry, even if it meant a massive taxpayer-funded bailout in the form of both direct capital injections and effectively limitless, cost-free loans from the Fed.

Leading institutions like Goldman Sachs, J.P. Morgan Chase, and Citigroup, despite being on life support from Washington, thus lost little of their political clout during and after the crisis. Wall Street still exercised tremendous influence over economic policy-making in general, and it directed that influence not at supporting measures to insulate the U.S. financial system from future shocks—it had no reason to want to—but at its traditional targets, very much including the deficit and the national debt.

Along with the efforts of Judd Gregg, Kent Conrad, and others to push a drastic deficit-cutting agenda in Congress, and the flurry of papers and reports coming out of Brookings, Heritage, New America, and other influential groups, this focus on debt and deficit helped turn Washington into a veritable echo chamber in which a relatively narrow cadre of budget experts, connected with a small group of think tanks and pressure groups, dominated the economic conversation. Increasingly, these groups seemed to be speaking with a single voice, right down to a common set of metaphors and turns-of-phrase, to describe the crisis that the deficit and entitlements were about to bring down.

The same names, many of which we've just encountered, appeared over and over in the *Washington Post*, the *New York Times*, the *Wall Street Journal*, *The Hill*, on CNN and other cable news sources, and on websites with growing readerships like Bloomberg.com and Politico.com, whenever data or a quote was needed from a recognized budget expert. Rivlin, Reischauer, MacGuineas, Steuerle, Walker, Sawhill, former Bush advisor and CBO head Douglas Holtz-Eakin, former Clinton domestic policy advisor William Galston, former Summers aide Douglas Elmendorf, and a few other names appeared again and again, always with the same message: deficits were out of control, America's creditors were rapidly running out of patience, and Social Security was the logical, "confidence-building" place to start cutting.

The message reflected the experts' common political origins, either in Republican administrations or the center-right Carter and Clinton teams. While they had their differences, these were of emphasis more than substance. On Social Security, they always pointed to the same narrow set of solutions: means testing benefits, raising the retirement age, and adjusting COLAs downward. Raising the cap on income subject to payroll tax sometimes merited a mention, but aside from that, the deficit hawks never mentioned raising taxes.

One reason this viewpoint became so ubiquitous was that a determined group of Wall Street grandees took an active role in spreading it. Third Way, for example, was a center-right, combination think tank and advocacy group formed in 2004. Initially operating in the shadow of the DLC, it started to acquire more stature as the DLC's influence began to fade in the latter half of the decade. Its board of trustees came to include the head of equity trading at Goldman Sachs, the co-head of the Global Financial Institutions Group at Morgan Stanley, executives at a passel of private equity and venture capital firms, and even Joe Flom, the legendary Wall Street corporate takeover lawyer.

One of the three founders of Third Way, and its president, was Jonathan Cowan, who first entered our story as the splashy co-head of Lead…or Leave in the mid-1990s. His agenda, and even his rhetoric, hadn't changed much in the intervening years. In an op-ed for Politico.com in December 2008, Cowan and Third Way's vice president for policy, Jim Kessler, argued that the American "middle … wants government to redefine the social contract from one based almost entirely on economic security to one focused more on economic success. Indeed, for today's middle class, success is the new security." As the group defined its policy position on Social Security, it included raising the retirement age, means-testing the program, cutting COLAs, and funding private retirement accounts for younger workers.[32]

Not long after Third Way opened its doors, former Treasury Secretary Bob Rubin, now a vice chairman of Citigroup, and Roger Altman, who also served at Treasury under Clinton and was now head of a private equity firm, funded a new initiative at Brookings called the Hamilton Project, to promote "sustainable" economic policies combined with deficit-cutting. The Hamilton Project gave a platform to Rubin, Altman, and Larry Summers, and other Clinton administration veterans for views that included reining in the cost of Social Security but stopped short of partial privatization.

But it was the redoubtable Pete Peterson, now eighty-one years old, who made Wall Street's greatest contribution to pulling the deficit hawks together into a more effective political force. In 2008, he announced he was sinking $1 billion of the $1.9 billion he raked in from the initial public offering of stock in the Blackstone Group into the Peter G. Peterson Foundation, which would fund projects calling attention to what he called threats to America's "economic security," such as the growing cost of Social Security and Medicare. At a stroke, the gift made Peterson one of the largest donors ever to think tank and policy-advocate organizations, a field that included the brothers David and Charles

Koch, the industrial titans who had seeded the Cato Institute, Citizens for a Sound Economy, and a host of other right-wing groups. Certainly one of the greatest beneficiaries of the financial boom that had accompanied the housing bubble, Peterson was determined to use his gains to promote national austerity during the bust that followed.

The foundation's first grant was to fund another iteration of Walker's Fiscal Wake-up Tour, in collaboration with Brookings and the American Enterprise Institute. For the rest of 2008, the Peterson Foundation dispensed grants to a host of center-right think tanks and advocacy groups with a voice in the deficit and Social Security debates. Some of the more prominent included the America's Promise Alliance, which helped launch a fiscal literacy program based on *I.O.U.S.A.* ($1 million); AmericaSpeaks, which was planning a "national discussion" on the economic crisis, including the deficit ($50,000); Brookings ($50,000); the Committee for a Responsible Federal Budget (CFRB) ($594,000); Peterson's own Concord Coalition ($500,000); and Public Agenda, a group engaged in "fiscal awareness and education programming" for college students ($250,000).[33]

"Everyone I know in the 'budget community' is trying to get Peterson money," Stan Collender, a budget consultant with Qorvis Communications, told the *New York Times* in 2011.

Indeed, almost every budget expert who could be described as a deficit hawk in the latter part of the decade was affiliated with a group that received at least some of its funding from Pete Peterson, if not with the man himself. Walker was the first president of the Peterson Foundation, and its advisory board included Bob Rubin, forging a link with Rubin's Hamilton Project. Sawhill, Galston, Reischauer, and Rivlin were all affiliated with Brookings, as was Dan Crippen, former CBO director and Reagan domestic policy advisor and Peter Orszag, a Rubin protege at the Clinton Treasury Department.

The CFRB was the closest thing to a common denominator for the deficit hawks, and even groups that didn't receive any reported Peterson money were linked with his projects through some personal association. One of these was the Urban Institute. C. Eugene Steuerle, a leading budget economist and longtime critic of Social Security, was a fellow at the Institute as well as vice president of the Peterson Foundation, while another fellow, Rudolph Penner, former CBO director, was also a director of the Committee for a Responsible Federal Budget. The American Enterprise Institute was probably a bit far to the right for Peterson's tastes, but June O'Neill, another former CBO director who was a director of the Peterson-Pew Commission on Budget Reform, was also an adjunct scholar at AEI.

It would, of course, be too much to suggest that these people who Peterson's money loosely brought together were somehow bought and paid for. All had solid credentials as budget economists, many at the highest levels of government, before they were affiliated with Brookings, the CFRB, or other of these organizations, some of which only received a modest amount of their funding from Peterson. But his money was carefully targeted at projects aimed to increase the visibility of deficit-hawk positions, in part by fostering collaboration between the various organizations and individuals.

The result was that the groups making up what could be called the deficit hawk coalition assumed something of the appearance of an interlocking mechanism, with the Peterson Foundation as the wheel's hub and the various think tanks, educational and advocacy groups as the spokes. The same names popped up again and again, and as the Peterson-funded projects multiplied, the views these individuals expressed in papers, panels, and in the press seemed to blend together. They even seemed possessed of a common style, urgent if not slightly hysterical and given to preening over their own "seriousness." By the time the 2008 presidential election was well under way, the public, and the politicians who wanted their votes, were hearing a story as tightly packaged and compelling as Bush and Rove's tale of the ownership society.

An op-ed by two members of the Committee for a Responsible Federal Budget (CRFB) put that story in a nutshell in February 2008. The end of the dot-com and housing bubbles were as nothing compared to "the most dangerous type of bubble yet: the deficit bubble," the CFRB warned. Left unattended, that problem would metastasize when foreign creditors stop buying U.S. Treasury bonds. Besides, large deficits "impose large taxes on future generations that have no say in the matter of the debt that is being racked up for them to pay. Try looking your kids in the eye and explaining how that is fair." But we had a chance to "avert disaster." Lawmakers must "turn their attention to the spiraling costs of the nation's largest entitlement programs—Medicare, Medicaid, and Social Security. Perhaps it will take a commission; perhaps we should have another summit as we did in 1990; but most importantly, we should stop delaying."[34]

CHAPTER 44

OBAMA VS. MCCAIN

Crumbling along with the housing and real estate markets and the banking system, it seemed, was the social-economic vision that conservatives had been attempting to turn into reality for nearly thirty years. Home ownership and personal saving for retirement and health care were supposed to lay the foundation of an ownership society in which everyone would be a capitalist—at least a little—and where workers would embrace risk and call it opportunity, instead of gravitating toward safety in all things.

This had been the premise underpinning the Social Security privatization movement for the better part of two decades, not to mention the push for "market solutions" to rising Medicare and health costs in general. At fever pitch in the mid-1990s, the ownership society had almost literally promised to make everyone a millionaire, to end class conflict, and to knit the globe together in a self-perpetuating "virtuous cycle" of wealth creation.

"Meet your new commissioners of Social Security," *Wall Street Journal* columnist Holman Jenkins had declared in 1998, introducing his readers to Citigroup, the giant new banking-brokerage-insurance supermarket. Ten years later, that headline was grimly humorous. Citigroup was cutting staff by the tens of thousands. Its stock slid when it was revealed the bank had turned a blind eye to a portfolio of toxic collateralized debt obligations on its books. It would soon be pleading for a massive rescue from Washington.

* * *

The politics of Social Security was changing. To argue for private accounts or for "fiscally responsible" cuts to the program at such a time would be political suicide, any serious presidential candidate must have understood. Apparently.

As an election issue, however, Social Security played out almost as if the previous two years hadn't happened. The eventual Republican nominee, John McCain, had been on record championing private accounts since before his 2000 presidential run. This didn't change in 2008, although, casting himself as the candidate of fiscal responsibility, the Arizona senator put the accent more on his commitment to making "tough decisions" on entitlements.

In this, McCain's campaign was an extension of the tactical moves the president had made since his Social Security debacle, which emphasized balancing the budget through cuts in domestic spending. McCain's 2008 program made much of his opposition to "pork barrel" projects aimed at creating jobs for lawmakers' constituents, even though these made up a minuscule share of the budget. But he undermined his fiscally virtuous position by defending the Bush tax cuts and vowing to make them permanent—even proposing to add another $300 billion a year in new tax reductions for businesses.

In July, during an appearance on ABC's *This Week with George Stephanopoulos*, McCain said he was "a supporter of sitting down together and putting everything on the table" when it came to addressing Social Security's future. The Republican right, which hadn't been completely comfortable with him to begin with, quickly protested the opening he seemed to have made for payroll tax hikes, forcing McCain to explicitly rule them out.

The Arizona senator's natural inclination was to run as a centrist, distancing himself sufficiently from the president's foreign policy—the execution, if not the general direction—and emphasizing his willingness to fight the good fight for a balanced budget with lawmakers from both parties. At a campaign stop in Independence, Missouri early in the primaries, he pledged to freeze all federal spending except military for one year and make "millions in spending reductions that will balance the budget." He then framed these as the promises of a "uniter" around whom everyone who valued the public good would want to rally.

Reviving his "maverick," centrist image after eight years supporting the Bush administration from his seat in the Senate was difficult, however, especially given the need to shore up his standing with the conservative Republican "Base." McCain had to mollify them by repeatedly pledging allegiance to the Bush tax hikes and by naming as his running mate Alaska's Gov. Sarah Palin, a comparative political novice who nevertheless had strong ties with the cultural and religious right. The result was a confused package of positions that seemed to please few people very much.

The Democrats hadn't nearly as treacherous a path to walk. Opposition to private-account carve-outs couldn't have been more fundamental to the party's identity by this time, especially since standing fast against Bush's campaign for private accounts three years earlier had reaped such rich rewards. The Bush administration's attacks on Social Security were clearly going to be part of Democratic candidates' indictment of their opponents in 2008, and none of the party's presidential contenders showed any interest in taking a different approach.

Even after reclaiming Congress in 2006, however, the Democrats remained divided between a strengthened progressive wing, who wanted to accentuate their policy differences with the Republicans and centrists who preferred to cast themselves as the party of the reasonable middle. The latter, as was becoming the norm in Washington terms, were those willing to consider tough choices—choices that usually involved some sort of budget-tightening sacrifice for the less well-off.

The split wasn't always easy to define because some Democratic candidates, who identified as deficit hawks, took more liberal positions on other matters. The two front-runners epitomized this divide.

Hillary Clinton, the former First Lady and now junior senator from New York, had been planning her run for the White House seemingly since her husband left office. Emerging as her principal opponent was Barack Obama, an Illinois senator for less than four years, who had quickly grabbed public attention with his youthful image, well-delivered speeches, and a bestselling memoir. *Advertising Age* would name him "Marketer of the Year" in October. He also had a knack for stirring a belief in progressives that he, and they, didn't have to settle for the cautiousness and limited goals of the Clinton years, while simultaneously holding himself aloof from the traditional power brokers of the Democratic left, including unions and older African-American politicians.

A major issue among the Democrats, as it had been during the Vietnam era, was who had opposed the war first and who had merely climbed aboard the antiwar wagon when doing so became politically expedient. Clinton had supported war powers when Bush requested them and failed to question the president's rationalizations for attacking Iraq. Obama had still been an Illinois state senator at the time, but had vocally opposed the invasion. Later, he appeared to take a stronger stand on ending the war more quickly than did Clinton. In this respect, Obama was a more "progressive" candidate.

On Social Security, the case was harder to settle. Clinton embraced Gene Sperling and Rahm Emanuel's idea for a Universal Savings Account to supplement OASI benefits; Obama offered nothing comparable. Obama proposed early in his campaign to raise the cap on income subject to payroll tax, prompting Clinton to attack him for planning a middle-class tax hike. He then shifted, instead proposing to slap a special 2%–4% Social Security surcharge on incomes over $250,000 starting in ten years—effectively, taxing the rich more to increase Social Security's future solvency. Obama also proposed what he called the Making Work Pay Credit, a refundable tax credit for workers making up to $75,000 per year, equal to 6.2% of their first $8,100 in earnings. Effectively, those workers would receive back their entire payroll tax contribution, prompting McCain and other Republicans to complain, "That's not a tax cut, that's welfare."[1]

Clinton refused to make any specific proposal, saying instead that as president she would concentrate on rebalancing the budget—essentially, returning to the fiscally conservative Rubinomics of her husband's administrations—and appoint a bipartisan commission to explore longer-term issues like Social Security. During their long and often bitter battle for the nomination, Obama frequently exhorted Clinton to offer further details, but she never acquiesced.

On the surface, Obama's position was the more progressive, combining an effective payroll tax cut for lower-income workers with higher taxes for the more affluent. But charging the well-off more to support Social Security while charging less—in some cases, nothing—to those with lower incomes would also give it more the profile of a welfare program. One long-standing idea for balancing the program's books had been to raise the cap on income subject to payroll tax, which currently stood at a little over $97,000. But Obama wasn't proposing this—rather, he wanted to levy a tax on wages over a certain amount. Social Security's supporters had always feared what might happen if upper middle-class and higher-income households no longer felt they had anything to gain from the program economically. If Obama's proposals were adopted, arguably the country might find out.[2]

All of this put Clinton's deliberate vagueness more in synch with progressive politics. Providing details of a plan to "save" Social Security during a presidential campaign, as Obama had done, was to fall into a Republican trap, she said: "I am not going to be repeating Republican talking points. So, when someone asks me would something like [raising the cap] be considered, well, anything could be considered when we get to a bipartisan commission. But personally I am not going to be advocating any specific fix until I am seriously approaching fiscal responsibility."[3]

Placing an issue like Social Security in the lap of a commission was one way of kicking it down the road. Given the Republicans' hostility to any reform that didn't include private accounts and deep benefit cuts, this may have been the best possible strategy for a Democratic presidential candidate.

Not long after the nominating conventions were over, the Democrats' disagreements about the best way to defend Social Security receded into the background. These were the weeks leading up to the spectacular Wall Street meltdown of late September. Suddenly, the media and, to some extent, the public were more inclined to scrutinize the Republican candidate and his support for exposing workers' Social Security benefits to the stock market. The same weekend that Paulson unveiled his $700 billion bank bailout proposal,

Obama, now the Democratic standard bearer, hit McCain hard—in Florida, appropriately enough.

Ann Widger, retiree coordinator with AFSCME, had joined the Obama campaign in Chicago to supervise its Social Security and Medicare messaging. Steve Hildebrand and Paul Tewes, the political consultants who had helped direct the campaign against Bush's push to privatize Social Security in 2005, were now Obama's deputy campaign manager and chief general election strategist, respectively, and were concentrating much of their attention on Florida.[4]

At a rally in Daytona Beach, Obama accused McCain of wanting to "gamble with your life savings" by extending the "casino culture" of Wall Street to the guaranteed benefit system. "If my opponent had his way, the millions of Floridians who rely on it would've had their Social Security tied up in the stock market this week," Obama said. "How do you think that would have made folks feel? Millions would've watched as the market tumbled and their nest eggs disappeared before their eyes."

A McCain aide called Obama's statement "a desperate attempt to gain political advantage using scare tactics and deceit." Just the day before, however, McCain had reiterated his belief that "young Americans ought to ... be able to, in a voluntary fashion ... put some of their money into accounts with their name on it." Most proposals to create private accounts would leave current and near-retirees' benefits alone, the aide pointed out.[5] But that ignored findings that any plan exempting them would require much deeper benefit cuts from younger workers to accommodate the private accounts.

Florida was again a pivotal state in the election, and Social Security a central issue for many of its residents. "If we win in Florida it is almost impossible for John McCain to win," Obama bluntly told attendees at a fundraiser in Miami.

Making matters worse for McCain, Palin was stumbling as she attempted to address some of the more complicated aspects of her running mate's platform. Social Security was one of these. Asked about her position on entitlements during a televised interview with ABC reporter Charles Gibson, Palin seemed to mistake the question as being about the program's administrative budget, not OASI or Disability Insurance themselves.

"Do you talk about entitlement reform?" Gibson asked. "Is there money you can save in Social Security, Medicare and Medicaid?"

"I am sure there are efficiencies that are going to be found in all of those agencies," Palin replied.

When Gibson tried to help her by focusing his question on the benefit programs themselves, not the agencies that administered them, she failed to take the hint and instead muddled the two topics in a rambling reply. "We have certainly seen excess in agencies, though," she said, "and in—when bureaucrats, when bureaucracy just gets kind of comfortable, going with the status-quo and not being challenged to find efficiencies and spend other people's money wisely, then that's where we get into the situation that we are into today, and that is a tremendous growth of government, a huge debt, trillions of dollars of debt that we're passing on to my kids and your kids and your grandkids. It's not acceptable."[6]

Even before the economic crisis accelerated, some Republican strategists were worried about their party's failure to address middle-class Americans' financial worries.[7] Yet the McCain campaign's efforts to respond seemed tone-deaf, especially as the anxieties of the past few years had given way to a full-scale economic crisis. McCain's persistence in supporting partial privatization of Social Security was one example. Another related problem was tax policy. While Obama called for a restructuring of the tax system that would cut levies on middle- and lower-income households and raise them for the more affluent, McCain wanted to make permanent the Bush tax cuts, which benefited largely the wealthy. By late October, one poll showed voters preferring Obama and his running mate, Delaware Sen. Joe Biden, to McCain and Palin on taxes by a 14 percentage-point margin—a striking reversal of the usual pattern.[8]

By the time Obama launched his attack on McCain's Social Security position, the difference in the candidates' economic approaches was already working to his advantage. A *Washington Post*/ABC News poll released September 24 gave the Democrat his first clear lead of the campaign, 52% to 43% for McCain. Obama was already running better than Al Gore or John Kerry in the previous two presidential races; neither of them had recorded more than 50% support in a *Post* or ABC poll at any point in their campaigns.

The economy was obviously uppermost on people's minds. Over half of respondents to the poll said they believed it was in a serious long-term decline. They also gave Obama higher marks than McCain on managing the economy, 53% to 39%. Personally, Obama was emerging as the more inspiring candidate as well. Over 60% of his supporters said they were "very enthusiastic," while only 34% of McCain supporters said so.

Both candidates' campaign war chests were loaded with Wall Street money. In September, the Center for Responsive Politics reported that Obama had actually received more from the financial services industry than his opponent: $9.8 million, versus $6.8 million for McCain. Both campaigns, too, were staffed generously with Wall Street insiders. McCain was being advised by former lobbyists for some of the chief culprits in the current debacle: AIG, Lehman, Merrill Lynch, and Bank of America.

Obama's camp included several protégés of Bob Rubin, former Clinton Treasury secretary and currently a director of embattled Citigroup.[9] One of his principal advisors was Rahm Emanuel, the former Clinton aide, who, between service in the Clinton White House and his election to Congress in 2002, had made a fast fortune as a managing director with the investment bank Wasserstein Perella. Emanuel was already emerging as one of the biggest recipients during the current election cycle of contributions from hedge funds, private equity firms, and the Wall Street powerhouses.

Both candidates essentially endorsed Paulson's $700 billion bailout plan as well, merely calling for more oversight to be built in. Often when the candidates discussed the economy, however, they seemed to be speaking of two different realities.

During the summer, McCain was forced to fire his chief economic advisor, former senator Phil Gramm, now a top official at UBS. Like so many other institutions, the Swiss bank had been hammered by writedowns on its U.S. subprime and mortgage-related holdings. It wasn't the bank's mismanagement, however, but a not-so-off-the-cuff comment by Gramm himself that created a public relations disaster for McCain.

In an interview with the Republican-friendly *Washington Times* in July, Gramm called the economic downturn "a mental depression," which he blamed largely on the press's predilection for gloominess. "Misery sells news-papers," he said. But he had a larger complaint about the American people, one that became one of the most notorious soundbites of the campaign. "We have sort of become a nation of whiners," Gramm declared in his typically exagger-ated shoot-from-the-hip manner. "You just hear this constant whining, com-plaining about a loss of competitiveness, America in decline.... Thank God the economy is not as bad as you read in the newspaper every day."

Gramm went on to say a McCain presidency would pursue a "bipartisan deal" on Social Security that could involve raising the retirement age to seventy, indexing the benefits of upper-income recipients to inflation instead of wages, and creating private accounts for younger workers. Gramm, who had been tout-ed as a possible Treasury secretary, was soon dismissed from the campaign—but for his "whiner" gaffe, not his statements about Social Security—and McCain was still offering essentially the same economic analysis months later.

In a speech on September 15, McCain insisted that the economy's funda-mentals were sound. The next day he backpedaled, calling the situation a "total crisis." Even so, he blamed the situation not on any systemic flaws but, vaguely, as being caused by "the greed by some based in Wall Street."

Obama never sounded that disconnected, although he sometimes came across as disingenuous. "It's hard to understand how Senator McCain is going to get us out of this crisis by doing the same things with the same old players," he said. He seemed to have forgotten that his own advisors in-cluded such retreads as Bob Rubin and Larry Summers, who had ruthlessly quashed efforts to more closely regulate Wall Street and derivatives trading in the 1990s.

Indeed, as his campaign steamed ahead, Obama took pains to sound more prudent and statespersonlike. "Does that mean I can do everything that I've called for in this campaign right away? Probably not," he told NBC a few days after his attack on McCain's Social Security position. "I think we're going to have to phase it in. And a lot of it's going to depend on what our tax revenues look like." That was in keeping with the deficit-phobic Rubin-Summers policy. It also sounded a lot better than McCain's defense of the Bush tax cuts to the centrist deficit hawks, who were trying energetically to have an impact on the election.

* * *

David Walker's Fiscal Wake-Up Tour, which had been continuing off and on for three years now, was also making itself heard in the election. The tour was sponsored by Pete Peterson together with the Concord Coalition, the Heritage Foundation, and the Brookings Institution. Participants included Walker, Stuart Butler from Heritage, Bob Bixby from Concord, and former Clinton OMB head Alice Rivlin. In 2008, the organizers of this "joint public engagement initiative" were directing their road show to electoral battleground states—Iowa before the Iowa caucuses and New Hampshire before the New Hampshire primary.

In September, the Wake-Up Tour hit Philadelphia, dropping in at the Wharton School's Business and Political Policy Department. "We're trying to elevate the issue in front of key constituencies in key states," said Bixby. That would include Pennsylvania, with its large retiree population. As ever, the deficit hawks wanted to mobilize younger voters around the threat entitlements posed to their economic future. "If young people get involved, and we can view the situation as a leadership problem, we'll get a long way toward getting it solved," Bixby said hopefully.

The Peterson Foundation was also underwriting a series of two-page ads touting its position in major newspapers. The presentation was a little different each time, but the message was the same. Decrying "America's $53 trillion hole," the ad that ran September 7 in the *New York Times* went on to blast "unsustainable entitlement spending," "out-of-control health care costs," and "unprecedented trade and savings deficits" that were even larger than the nation's current economic and financial difficulties.

Sensing, perhaps, that the present crisis was weighing heavily on most people's minds, the next Peterson ad, on October 5, was headlined, "THINK THE CURRENT FINANCIAL CRISIS IS BAD? YOU AIN'T SEEN NOTHING YET." In the upcoming presidential debates, the ad demanded that the candidates be asked, "How will you make fiscal responsibility and intergenerational equity a priority?" Peterson's signatories, who included Mario Cuomo, Paul Volcker, Sam Nunn, and Bob Kerrey, called once again for a "bipartisan 'fiscal responsibility commission' to recommend meaningful reforms of the government's budget processes and entitlement, health care, and tax systems."

"We owe our country, our children, grandchildren, and future generations of Americans no less," the September 7 ad concluded.

The spectacle the deficit hawks presented, urging austerity at a time of economic implosion and distress for millions, was politically out of step to the point of being insulting. But both presidential candidates took care to include the Pain Caucus in their counsels. McCain's principal economic guru after Gramm's departure was Douglas Holtz-Eakin, the former Bush economic advisor. Later, at the CBO, Holtz-Eakin had initiated a study of tax rates that flouted supply-side wisdom in finding that the cost of new tax cuts was far greater than any new revenue they brought in. Obama, meanwhile, enjoyed the endorsement and advice of former Fed chief Volcker, now on record endorsing Peterson's call to rein in "unsustainable entitlement spending."

Volcker stubbornly refused to support a proposal by the candidate in October for a modest $60 billion economic stimulus bill, arguing, according to the *Wall Street Journal*, that Americans were already spending beyond their means. Earlier, he eagerly advised Obama to endorse Paulson's $700 billion bank bailout, believing that recapitalizing the banks was the key to ending the economic crisis. However dubious his thinking might be, "Volcker whispering in Obama's ear will make even Republicans comfortable, because he's a hero of the right and a supporter of a strong dollar," said one conservative Republican economist.[10]

Perhaps believing the presence of Volcker, Rubin, and Summers on his team insulated him from the charge of fiscal recklessness, Obama didn't strain as hard as McCain to sound like a deficit hawk during their second presidential debate, televised October 7 from Nashville. Peterson's plea that the candidates be forced to address how they would make "intergenerational equity" a priority didn't go unheeded. A question called in from Ballston Spa, New York asked, "Would you give Congress a date certain to reform Social Security and Medicare within two years after you take office?" Because, host Tom Brokaw added erroneously, "in a bipartisan way, everyone agrees, that's a big ticking time bomb that will eat us up maybe even more than the mortgage crisis."

Obama agreed the problem was serious, but refused to validate the sense of panic in Brokaw's comments. "We're going to have to take on entitlements and I think we've got to do it quickly," he said. "I can't guarantee that we're going to do it in the next two years, but I'd like to do in my first term as president." His immediate priorities, he stressed, would be to make the tax system fairer for moderate- to low-income households and to reform health care. These changes, he said, would put the country "in a position to deal with Social Security and deal with Medicare," since the financial pressures on workers would then not be as great.

McCain was grimmer. "My friends, we are not going to be able to provide the same benefit for present-day workers that we are going—that present-day retirees have today," he said. "We're going to have to sit down across the table, Republican and Democrat, as we did in 1983 between Ronald Reagan and Tip O'Neill." McCain, with his commitment to end partisan "rancor," would be the ideal person to preside over such a compromise, because "I have a clear record of reaching across the aisle, whether it be Joe Lieberman or Russ Feingold or Ted Kennedy or others. That's my clear record." Obama, he implied, had no such record.

Both candidates were reaching for the center, however. McCain didn't mention private accounts and neither did Obama attack him for supporting them during the debate. Obama didn't call into question whether Social Security actually needed reform and McCain declined to accuse him of not taking the issue seriously.

* * *

Barack Obama's victory on November 4, 2008, was a milestone for several reasons. He was the first African-American to be elected president and the first president-elect who hadn't been of age during the Civil Rights movement and Vietnam War years. He was also, arguably, the first Democrat presidential candidate to run with the more or less wholehearted support of the party's progressive wing since George McGovern in 1972. Additionally, the election gave the Democrats control of both Congress and the White House for the first time in fourteen years.

Obama won convincingly, with 52.9% of the vote compared with 45.7% for McCain. In the House, the Democrats gained 21 seats and increased their majority to 257-178. In the Senate, when the last disputed race was resolved nine months later, they gained 9 seats, giving them a 60-40 majority if two Independents were counted as Democrats—just the number needed to defeat a filibuster and thus fully control the legislative agenda. That aside, the election clearly constituted a rejection of something. Whether it represented a mandate for something else was less certain.

The voters most definitely rejected the Bush administration's response to the economic crisis. A Reuters/C-Span/Zogby poll in late October found that McCain still held a significant lead among those who identified themselves as "investors," 50.4% to 43.8%. But that was down from a 15 percentage-point lead a month earlier. McCain lost badly among voters earning more than $75,000 a year—the "investor class" of 401(k) and IRA holders that Republicans had allegedly been nurturing the past eight years.[11] In this sense, the election represented a verdict on the Republicans' efforts to persuade the public to support an extension of the private-account approach to retirement provision to Social Security.

As the new face of the rebuilding Republicans, the *Wall Street Journal* recommended Rep. Paul Ryan, the thirty-eight-year-old Wisconsin Free Luncher who had been indefatigably promoting Social Security privatization since entering Congress ten years earlier. "I want to be the Paul Revere of fiscal policy," Ryan liked to say, and in the summer he released a "Road Map for America's Future," which prominently featured private accounts. This part of the basic Republican platform clearly wasn't going away.

To accuse the Republicans of being *the* party of Wall Street in 2008 would be a distortion, however. Although his campaign painted itself as something of an insurgency, Obama was a fundraising dynamo, pulling in $750 million, triple the record Bush had set four years earlier. He couldn't have done it without the generosity of big donors, who had forked over more than $200 million in gifts of $1,000 or more by mid-October.[12] Much of that money came from the financial services industry. Obama advisors such as Volcker, Bob Rubin, and Morgan Stanley executive Stephen Roach bore not the slightest stain of economic populism.

But Obama also owed his election to strong efforts by the progressive coalition that had formed to defeat Bush's Social Security privatization campaign in 2005 and helped elect a Democratic and more liberal Congress the following year. Many of the same groups that had led Americans United to Protect Social Security, created a new group, Health Care for America NOW!, reflecting a strategic choice to emphasize a positive vision after its negative-toned Social Security campaign.

"We weren't doing attacks so much," says Alan Charney of USAction. "Instead, this was about what we needed to do to turn the economy around."[13] But the coalition rebuilt the well-coordinated infrastructure, message machine, and some of the funding pipeline it had created when it took on Bush's privatization push in 2005, which in turn made it a valuable asset to Obama.[14]

The coalition helped galvanize grassroots support for the charismatic candidate, despite the vagueness of many of his positions. The progressives' priority issues—health care reform, a sustainable energy policy, and an environmentally sustainable economy—were among the major elements of his campaign. During the last month of the race, some 80% of the candidate's advertising budget was devoted to his health care initiative.[15] Obama himself had drawn on his experience as a community organizer to create a more horizontal campaign organization that blanketed the country rather than targeting only the districts considered necessary to win.

The result was an army of Obama supporters, many of whom expected to continue having a voice with their candidate after he entered the White House and a role in pushing progressive policies through. Some Democratic lawmakers were eager to address their concerns—especially health care, which topped the list. One-third of respondents in a Harris Interactive poll during summer 2008 agreed that the health care system "has so much wrong with it that we need to completely rebuild it."

Solving the health care crisis was necessary to keeping Social Security viable as well, because so much of the rise in costs anticipated for the program was related to health expenses. It could also be an important contributor to the nation's economic recovery, some argued, given the relief many households would enjoy if medical costs stopped accelerating. But clearly the new administration's first job was going to be devising a plan to resuscitate the economy, which continued to sink into what some economists predicted would be the longest and deepest recession since World War II.[16]

Financial-sector disasters were still piling up, driving more institutions to seek taxpayer help. Less than a week after the election, Treasury scrapped its original $123 billion bailout of AIG and replaced it with a $150 billion agreement with easier terms for the insurer's shareholders. Two weeks later, the government bailed out Citigroup, guaranteeing $250 billion of risky assets and injecting another $50 billion directly into the listing bank.

One collapsing financial enterprise that wouldn't be getting any government assistance was Bernard L. Madoff Investment Securities. The firm's founder and chairman was arrested on December 11 and charged with securities fraud. Madoff had admitted to his sons the day before that the firm was essentially a Ponzi scheme; returns to investors came not from the returns on its investment strategies but from successive waves of new investors. Losses came to $65 billion.

These included some of the country's—not to mention the world's—largest foundations and endowments, public and private pension funds, banks and individual investors. It would take months to sort out how Madoff had done it and who had helped him. It took much less time for the Social-Security-as-Ponzi-scheme jokes to start flowing. "Put Madoff in charge of Social Security," the *Wall Street Journal*'s Holman Jenkins jeered. Syndicated cartoonist Chip Bok ran a panel showing a glum Madoff being led before the SEC by a guard who tells the commissioners, "He ran out of new investors to pay off his old investors." One of the latter responds, "Madoff ran Social Security too?"

It was an empty comparison. Short of a nuclear disaster, Social Security wasn't going to run out of "new investors," and whereas Madoff had no real investments to support the uncannily high returns he had reported for so many years, Social Security was funded by payroll tax revenues that represented a return on the growth and prosperity of the U.S. economy. Unfortunately, American households whose assets included personal retirement accounts had something more to worry about than the proper definition of a Ponzi scheme.

* * *

What was to be done about the alarming deterioration in the private-sector retirement system? Social Security's problems, decades in the future at worst, looked minor to millions of workers contemplating retirement in a few short years. Older workers, those aged fifty-five to sixty-four, who had held 401(k)s for at least twenty years suffered an average 20% drop in their investments due to the financial market crash, according to an Employee Benefit Research Institute study. Making up the losses before they retired and in the current bleak economic climate would be quite difficult.

There was nothing intrinsically bad about 401(k)s as investment vehicles. But the economic crisis made clear that personal investment accounts were unsuited to serve as the primary pillar of retirement support for American workers. Working households, watching helplessly as their privately accumulated wealth evaporated, didn't want more new savings vehicles, it seemed. They wanted a societal guarantee of a dignified standard of living in old age, updated to meet their needs.

Many people who had followed the deterioration of workers' savings for a long time reflected, in 2008 and 2009, on the consequences if private Social Security accounts had become a reality. The impact would have been two-fold: on individuals' personal resources for retirement, and on federal and state budgets. Collapsing Social Security accounts would have left retirees and near-retirees turning to other means of support against poverty: SSI, Medicaid, food stamps, and Temporary Assistance for Needy Families (TANF). Funds for these benefits came directly from government's general revenues, not the dedicated payroll tax.

"If everybody had been investing their private Social Security accounts in 2007 and 2008, future welfare costs in the U.S. would have exploded," noted financial columnist Jane Bryant Quinn.[17]

As for workers themselves, not only would they have sustained major losses that would take years to recoup, but there was also the tradeoff—the quid pro quo for getting those personal accounts most likely would have been a cut in their remaining guaranteed benefit under the program.

"What a nightmare it would have been if the risks in individual accounts had been amplified in the Social Security system!" said Thomas Jones, former president of TIAA-CREF, who had served on the 1994–96 Social Security Advisory Council. "Instead, and although the general public may not understand it, Social Security was the one asset they have that gained in value last year."[18] Just as it had with 401(k)s, the crisis called into question the nature and purpose, hypothetically, of private Social Security accounts. If the worker really "owned" the assets in her account, what justification was there to stop her from using them in an emergency?

* * *

In December, while Obama was still putting his team together, the lame-duck Bush administration proceeded with its stumbling efforts to manage the crisis in the financial services industry. By mid-December, the federal government had committed a total of $8.7 trillion to its various rescue operations, Politico.com reported. Some of that was through direct cash investments, tax breaks, and loans, but the vast majority consisted of loan guarantees from the Fed, the FDIC, Treasury, and other bodies. Much of it the taxpayers might later recoup or even, in some cases, earn a profit on. But the financial sector was much larger than it had been in the 1930s, and so the size of the commitment was remarkable—more than seventeen times the cost of the New Deal, in present-day dollars.

Also striking was how little of it was geared to help homeowners, whose plight was at the root of the economic crisis—only some $300 billion in back-up assistance from the Federal Housing Authority.[19] In fact, in November the Treasury decided not to go ahead with a plan it had been considering to refinance subprime mortgages.

The composition of the new Obama administration team didn't promise much of a departure. A Harvard Law School alumnus, the incoming president preferred much the same people Bill Clinton had—thoroughly mainstream economic thinkers and administrators, often connected with the nexus of deficit-hawkish groups that had been closing ranks for the past couple of years.

More than a dozen were in fact former Clinton-era advisors, all boasting close ties to Bob Rubin.[20]

Larry Summers, the former Treasury secretary and a director of the entitlement-phobic Committee for a Responsible Federal Budget, would head the National Economic Council (NEC). He had lately been a part-time managing director of D.E. Shaw & Co., a $25 billion hedge fund. He earned nearly $2.5 million during his last two years with the firm, according to the White House.[21] One of his first hires at the NEC was a former Citigroup executive.[22] Peter Orszag, the new OMB director, and Jason Furman, working under Summers at the NEC, were both associated with Bob Rubin's Hamilton Project, as was Summers. Volcker, a member of the Committee for a Responsible Federal Budget, would head a new Economic Recovery Advisory Board.

Tim Geithner, the new Treasury secretary and a Summers protégé, had been president of the New York Fed for over five years. As such, he had been one of those responsible for the lax regulation that allowed Wall Street—including Citigroup, where his former boss, Bob Rubin, was a top executive—to make reckless use of derivatives like credit-default swaps. Geithner was also one of the architects of TARP and the other rescue efforts of the past year. As such, his appointment was hailed by Wall Street as a confidence-builder for the powerful Treasury bond market. As his chief of staff, Geithner appointed a former lobbyist for Rubin's previous firm, Goldman Sachs. As a senior counselor he retained former Clinton economic advisor Gene Sperling, who had been a deputy to Rubin and had argued passionately for the former Treasury secretary's antideficit approach in his 2005 book, *The Pro-Growth Progressive*.

Summers and Geithner were clearly the economic team's leading members. They wasted no time making clear that their approach to the credit crisis would be substantially the same as Paulson's. Summers, testifying before the House Budget Committee two months before the election, had said that any further stimulus should be "timely, targeted and temporary." To avoid "undermining confidence" among "investors," Congress shouldn't tolerate a rise in projected budget deficits "beyond a short horizon of a year or two at most." Nor did the new administration have anything drastic in store for Wall Street. "We have a financial system that is run by private shareholders, managed by private institutions, and we'd like to do our best to preserve that system," Geithner stated soon after he was confirmed in January.

That meant the people in charge of the financial services sector would suffer as little pain as possible and would thus feel little inclination to behave differently once back on their feet. Instead of nationalizing and cleaning up the banks, which many economists advocated as the cheaper and better solution, the new administration was prepared to spend a great deal more money to prop them up.

When the Obama team's $800 billion-plus stimulus package was unveiled a few days before the new president was to be inaugurated and hours before the Senate approved release of the second half of the TARP bailout funds, liberals worried it wasn't big enough. The package equaled slightly less than 3% of annual GDP[23]—by comparison, the $600 billion stimulus plan that China had announced in November represented fully 14% of that country's 2008 GDP.[24]

"Economic recovery in an existential crisis like this means actually building a new economy," suggested James Galbraith, who was an informal advisor to Obama's campaign, perhaps by creating a National Infrastructure Fund that could borrow on its own, exempt from federal budget rules. Meanwhile, one way to shore up the consumer economy without reinflating it would be to help the elderly, whose purchasing power had been depleted by the drop in the stock market.

"The best way is to increase Social Security benefits," Galbraith wrote in December. "Useful steps would include boosting the formula for widowed spouses, ensuring a minimum benefit for retirees who worked their whole lives in low-wage jobs, and allowing college students to receive survivors' benefits up until the age of 22."

Galbraith also advocated raising benefits across the board, which hadn't been done since the Nixon administration. "I'd say raise them 30 percent, and let the federal government make the contributions for five years. This would be good for the elderly, who could retire; good for working-age people, who would replace the retiring; and good for the economy, since people who need money spend it when they get it."[25]

Liberals like Galbraith weren't the only ones thinking of ways to make Social Security an economic recovery tool. Another proposal came in December from Rep. Louie Gohmert, a conservative Texas Republican. Instead of spending the remaining $350 billion of TARP money to bail out more banks, he suggested, why not use it to fund a two-month holiday from both the personal income tax and the payroll tax? Gohmert's thinking was elegantly simple. "Why try to decide how to prevent foreclosures?" he asked. "Just give the taxpayers their own money to catch up on their payments."

Gohmert said he was preparing a bill embodying his tax holiday idea. Neither this measure nor Galbraith's ideas for expanding Social Security went anywhere at the time, despite strong support for Gohmert, behind the scenes, from Republican elder statesperson Newt Gingrich ("Think of no personal or corporate income tax and no fica tax for a year as a stimulus package," he wrote to his aides. "Am I nuts in rome or is the contrast startling.").[26] Instead, both the president-elect and Congress were encouraging the view that they hadn't abandoned the goal of a balanced budget and planned to "pivot" as quickly as possible from stimulating the economy to addressing the "entitlement crisis."

At a Washington news conference on January 7, Obama said he and his advisors "are working currently on our budget plans. We are beginning consultations with members of Congress around how we expect to approach the deficit. We expect that discussion around entitlements will be part, a central part, of those plans. And I would expect that by February, in line with the announcement of at least a rough budget outline, that we will have more to say about how we're going to approach entitlement spending."

Initially, journalists leapt at the idea that the new Democratic president might be planning to propose long-term cuts or spending constraints for Social Security and Medicare as a tradeoff for concessions of some sort from Republicans. The *New York Times* noted that Obama "provided no details of his approach to rein in Social Security and Medicare" and warned that he was "opening up a potentially risky battle that neither party has shown much stomach for." A news analysis in the same publication the same day made the customary, if inaccurate, statement that the two programs "are the fastest-growing parts of the federal budget and the biggest long-run threats to fiscal stability."

Dean Baker, on his blog, noted that Obama hadn't said anything about cutting either program, only about addressing entitlement spending. That could mean a number of other things, including that he planned to cut Medicare costs by reforming the entire health care system.

Deficit hawks, however, were getting excited by the possibility that the two programs were being set up for direct cuts in a "Grand Bargain" to solve all of the nation's long-term budget problems. "While it is understandable that [the economic stimulus] package will worsen our near-term budget picture," said Conrad, "we should not enact provisions that will exacerbate our long-term deficits and debt."[27]

As they had regularly since their discussions with Paulson two-and-a-half years earlier, Conrad and Judd Gregg called for Congress to authorize a "bipartisan fiscal task force" to create a package of antideficit legislation. "Everything, including spending and revenue," would be on the table. The resulting bill "would be given fast-track consideration in Congress." Since the stimulus package would certainly be passed first, Gregg and Conrad called for it to be "linked" to their budget-balancing initiative, although they didn't explain how this could be done.

What would be the components of a Grand Bargain? Certainly they would include a restructuring of Social Security, Alice Rivlin said in testimony before the House Committee on the Budget. "The [economic] crisis may have made Social Security less of a political 'third rail,'" she said hopefully. Besides, "fixing" the program "is a relatively easy technical problem. It will take some combination of several much-discussed marginal changes: raising the retirement age gradually in the future (and then indexing it to longevity), raising the cap on the payroll tax, fixing the COLA, and modifying the indexing of initial benefits so they grow more slowly for affluent people."

Rivlin didn't bother to address the pain her "marginal changes" would surely cause. Over time, however, workers currently in their twenties and thirties would see their Social Security benefits slashed or even reduced to insignificance. Nowhere in her testimony did Rivlin mention any of this; the chances for a bipartisan deal were too alluring.

"In view of the collapse of market values, no one is likely to argue seriously for diverting existing revenues to private accounts," she predicted, "so the opportunity to craft a compromise is much greater than it was a few years ago."

Cutting Social Security would be "a confidence-building achievement," she urged, "and would enhance our reputation for fiscal prudence."

Obama himself "was not supportive" of the idea of creating a powerful fiscal task force when he met with Senate Republicans in late January, according to Judd Gregg.[28] It wasn't unreasonable to believe Obama had something big in mind when he spoke of addressing entitlements, however. Perhaps the most repeated soundbite from any of the president-elect's team was something Rahm Emanuel, the new White House chief of staff, said days after the election: "Rule one: Never allow a crisis to go to waste." Whether that dictum pointed to action on Social Security and Medicare, health care, refundable tax credits for low-income families, or something else wasn't clear.

So it remained after the new president was inaugurated on January 20. As had become almost expected in the more than two months since his election, Obama had given everyone something to feel hopeful about, including Republicans and earnest centrists who dearly desired a "bipartisan" White House. He spoke of "our collective failure to make hard choices and prepare the nation for a new age." The turn of phrase could only hearten veterans of the movement against Social Security, who had been arguing for years that the program was unaffordable and perhaps, in the entrepreneurial ownership society they had been struggling to nurture for thirty years, unnecessary.

But when Obama went on to describe what would be the building blocks of the "new age," he seemed to lay out an agenda for government investment, not for removing it further from workers' lives. He also seemed to dismiss the issue of whether a program like Social Security was affordable or not. "The question we ask today is not whether our government is too big or too small," he said, "but whether it works, whether it helps families find jobs at a decent wage, care they can afford, a retirement that is dignified."

This was far removed from the words of Obama's predecessor, who eight years before had spoken of Social Security "reform" as a matter of "sparing our children from struggles we have the power to prevent." Instead, it seemed to promise that the new administration would invest in resources that make a people more productive and their economy richer over time—better able to support a larger population of Social Security recipients. What the elderly deserved from society, Obama said, wasn't just a benefit barely sufficient to survive, but the means to live out their lives in "dignity": the standard Eleanor Roosevelt and her colleagues had set in the Universal Declaration of Human Rights sixty years earlier.

Over one-and-a-half million people came to see the new president sworn in. Two weeks later, he announced the name of his new Secretary of Commerce. A Republican, the new cabinet member would be part of the president's extended economic team. It was Sen. Judd Gregg of New Hampshire.

CHAPTER 45

OBAMA STUMBLES

"If we consistently act on the optimistic hypothesis, this hypothesis will tend to be realised; whilst by acting on the pessimistic hypothesis we can keep ourselves forever in the pit of want."

—John Maynard Keynes[1]

"Clearly, Judd and I don't agree on every issue," President Obama hastened to say after naming the New Hampshire senator to his Cabinet, and none of the Beltway buzz indicated he would be a major voice on Social Security. In fact, Gregg withdrew his acceptance a few days afterward, as Republicans elected to close ranks against the president's stimulus bill.

But his brief membership on the Obama team was a warning to progressives who were wont to think that America's political trajectory was at last returning to the track it had occupied before the economic upheavals of the 1970s—before Nixon, Reagan, Clinton, the Bush tax cuts, and 9/11. That had been the hope cherished by Bob Ball, who died in January 2008, too soon to see the Democrats retake the White House. He had looked forward to a time when tax legislation didn't automatically skew to benefit the wealthy; deficit fetishism coupled with an impregnable Pentagon budget didn't rule Washington; and Social Security, Medicare, and other necessary programs could again evolve to meet the needs of working families.

In fact, as Obama took office, the balance of power in Washington was only a little more favorable to the Democrats than it had been after the 1992 election that brought Bill Clinton to the White House: a Democratic majority of 258 seats in the House, 1 more than the party's contingent 18 years earlier; and a majority of 58 seats—plus 2 Independents caucusing with the Democrats— in the Senate, versus 56 after the 1992 election. Once again, the Democrats had fairly comfortable control of the House but were short of being filibuster-proof in the Senate.

Bill Clinton, working with such a Congress, had pushed through a deficit-cutting economic package and the NAFTA treaty. He failed to create a national health insurance system. A bipartisan group of deficit hawks represented the swing votes between the two parties and these outcomes reflected their priorities.

So they would again, it seemed, fifteen years later. In fact, it wasn't just the Democratic Party that had made a remarkable comeback in 2008, but the party's center-right as well. While Pelosi and Reid's insistence on standing by New Deal principles during Bush's 2005 push for Social Security privatization had put the Democrats in a position to win in 2008, many of the beneficiaries were less devoted to the Roosevelt legacy. This was partly thanks to an effort to recruit more centrist candidates who could win in conservative states that suddenly seemed up for grabs.

Another reason, however, was the influence of money—especially coming from the financial services industry—on Democratic politics. Wall Street was one of the last business sectors where some well-heeled donors still gave more generously to Democrats than Republicans. The candidates they had chosen to support in recent years tended to be from the center-right, which defined itself as anti-tax, anti-debt, and deficit-hawkish. They were often younger, their personal backgrounds reflecting little contact with the working people for whom Social Security was so important, and they had more natural affinity with the likes of Larry Summers and Tim Geithner.

One of the highest profile members of the Class of '08, for example, was Mark Warner, the new senator from Virginia. Warner had made a fortune investing in telecommunications and served as governor from 2002 to 2006, in which role he cut income taxes, raised sales taxes, and balanced the budget. Entering the Senate, he quickly emerged as a leading deficit hawk eager to build a deficit-cutting alliance with Republican lawmakers.

A bipartisan core of center-right senators helped dictate the final shape of the economic stimulus bill, which passed less than a month after Obama's inauguration. Three Republican members of this group—Arlen Specter of Pennsylvania, soon to switch labels; and Olympia Snowe and Susan Collins of Maine—provided the margin of victory for the final bill, enabling others of their party to retain their ideological purity by voting against it.

What emerged closely reflected the center-right's inclinations. The final American Recovery and Reinvestment Act was trimmed from the $820 billion Obama had asked for, to $787 billion. By keeping the stimulus as small as possible,* this at a time when economic indicators from housing to employment to the stock market continued to plunge, the centrists served notice that they expected the White House to change direction as quickly as possible. The administration did manage to push through three measures that directly helped two key groups: low-income households and Social Security recipients. First, it expanded the Earned Income Tax Credit, and second, it passed Obama's "Making Work Pay" tax credit, which would provide $400 payments—$800 for couples—to low- and middle-income working households, gradually decreasing for individuals making more than $75,000 and couples earning $150,000-plus. The credits would take the form of lower tax withholding and would be parceled out in stages starting April 1.

Finally, the bill included a one-time $250 stimulus payment to anyone eligible for old-age, survivor's, or disability benefits through Social Security. Later, the SSA announced that year's COLA: 5.8%, the largest in twenty-seven years, mainly due to a spike in energy prices. The combination amounted to a major boost for people struggling not only with high oil and gas prices but, in many cases, the collapse of their retirement savings and rising health care costs. From a traditional Democratic perspective, this—and the Making Work Pay credit—was precisely the kind of action the government should be taking at such a time.

The deficit hawks, on the other hand, were disturbed. Evan Bayh complained that the $410 billion appropriations bill his fellow Democrats were trying to pass in early March "lacks the slightest hint of austerity." To reduce the deficit, he insisted that "spending should be held in check before taxes are raised, even on the wealthy."[2]

Progressive groups still felt encouraged, but guardedly so. "There's more respect for progressives" in the upper reaches of the Democratic Party than there was before the 2006 and 2008 elections, Hickey noted in February, "but we can still be taken for granted." They had drawn a few lessons from their experience of the Clinton years, when they had to fight for the White House's attention. "We've learned that we've got to have a movement even when we've got the presidency."[3]

On Social Security, at least, the progressives seemed to be holding their own. On February 23, just days after Obama signed the stimulus bill, the administration held a high-profile Fiscal Responsibility Summit, inaugurating a national conversation on how to improve the nation's medium- to long-term

---

* Of that total, $70 billion couldn't actually be classified as "stimulus," since it was merely the latest allocation to stop the Alternative Minimum Tax from hitting middle-class taxpayers.

budgetary health. The participants—more than a hundred attended—were a mix of Democrats and Republicans, lawmakers, economists, think tankers, and interest-group advocates. The three-hour event included breakouts on taxes, health care, budget reform, contracting and procurement—and Social Security, the latter conducted by Summers and Sperling.

Before the summit, some administration sources had been putting out the word that the president would use it to announce formation of a high-level task force to recommend ideas for "reforming" Social Security. It didn't happen. In fact, Pete Peterson was denied a spot as a featured speaker at the summit. Afterward, it was clear that restructuring Social Security was low on the administration's priority list.[4] Washington insiders attributed this reversal to heavy, united opposition from congressional Democratic leaders and groups like the Campaign for America's Future, which loomed larger in the capital after the election.

Summers and Sperling made clear that the administration wasn't going to take on Social Security—at least not during its first year in office. Instead, the administration's major reform effort would be to reform the health care system, which Summers said had "overwhelming importance" to the effort to achieve "long-term budget control."[5]

Pete Peterson was disappointed. In the early weeks of the new administration, he pulled out all the stops to press the need for a "responsible budget," which for him meant, above all, reining in entitlements. In late January, he stirred up an ethical hornet's nest when his foundation awarded a $1 million, one-year grant to WNET, New York City's PBS affiliate. In exchange, the station's news and public affairs program, *Worldfocus*, would produce reports looking at how other countries had dealt with problems funding health care and retirement benefits.

Worldfocus would have "total control over the content," assured Peterson Foundation CEO David Walker,[6] but, as the media watchdog group Fairness and Accuracy in Reporting pointed out, the program's producers—and possibly other WNET programmers—might think twice about running a segment that gave airtime to critics of Peterson's point of view. "There are huge financial pressures facing this place," the station's chief executive admitted in a *New York Times* article.

About the same time, the foundation announced the launch of a new, $1 million campaign "aimed at raising awareness of America's fiscal challenges." The announcement took place on Capitol Hill and featured Walker, along with a typically bipartisan assortment of leading deficit hawks, Sen. Kent Conrad and Rep. Jim Cooper on the Democratic side and Sen. George Voinovich and Rep. Frank Wolf from the Republican. The campaign included a national TV ad to begin airing during the morning public affairs shows on Sunday, February 22—the day before the Fiscal Responsibility Summit and two days before the president's scheduled first address to Congress.

The situation around the country in the following months suggested that it would take much more than $1 million to properly focus people's "awareness."

Job losses accelerated in the first half of the year, pushing the unemployment rate to 9.5% in July. By that time, sixteen states had exhausted their unemployment benefit funds; the jobless benefit program was in the worst financial condition since the early 1980s. Unemployment crossed the 10% mark in November, and when the Bureau of Labor Statistics threw in part-time workers who wanted full-time jobs and workers who dropped out of the official number because they'd been jobless more than a year, the figure rose to 17.5%. Many of those with jobs weren't doing well, either. Almost half of large and mid-sized American companies froze wages in 2009, while 10% cut salaries, according to a Hewitt Associates survey.

Social Security, bolstered by the $250 bonus in the stimulus working its way through the economy, was keeping many households propped up. Thanks to rising unemployment and stagnating or declining wages, payroll tax receipts fell slightly in 2009, to $667.3 billion from $672.1 billion, while applications for retirement benefits rose 23% and Disability Insurance claims 20%. As a result, the SSA expected payroll taxes to fall $10 billion short of benefit payouts in 2010, and $9 billion short in 2011[7]—the first shortfalls in nearly thirty years. This was far less of an emergency than it seemed. Treasury's interest payments on the bonds in the trust funds, added to those payroll tax revenues, would keep Social Security's books comfortably balanced both years—and, indeed, through 2037, according to the trustees' estimates.

But news reports that Social Security was "tapping out" its "IOUs" contributed to the deficit panic that was again engulfing Washington. The deficit for fiscal 2009—ending September 30—hit $1.4 trillion, the largest figure since World War II, representing about 10% of GDP.[8] The news encouraged opposition to White House efforts to extend some elements of its stimulus package. In the second quarter, the only part of the original stimulus bill that had any impact on GDP was the $250 Social Security bonus,[9] yet when the president proposed another round of the payments in 2010, both Republicans and some key Democrats, including House Majority Leader Steny Hoyer of Maryland, spoke against it.

Obama wanted to continue the payments because consumer prices stagnated in 2009 after jumping on higher fuel costs the previous year. That would make 2010 the first year seniors wouldn't receive a COLA since the adjustments became automatic almost four decades earlier. But while some lawmakers called upon Congress not to forget the aged, they quickly attracted accusations of pandering to seniors. "This is an issue where groups on all ends of the political spectrum all happen to agree," said Maya MacGuineas, who was becoming the go-to voice of the deficit hawks in her capacity as president of the Committee for a Responsible Budget.[10]

In this, she was incorrect. The Senior Citizens League (SCL), a retired veterans group, called attention to the fact that COLAs had for years underrepresented health care costs, which were growing more rapidly for the elderly. That, along with the disturbing fact that unemployment among seniors was hitting a seventy-year high even though more of them were looking for work, argued that seniors needed assistance—not a benefits freeze. Instead of the $250 bonus, the SCL proposed an emergency 3% COLA boost to keep more elderly from falling into poverty.

That idea went nowhere, although both parties in the House rallied in December to easily approve $626 billion in new spending requested by the Pentagon for continuing operations in Afghanistan and Iraq—almost forty-five times the cost of Obama's COLA bonus. The irony was apparently lost on Washington, even though defense spending was growing far more rapidly than Social Security: more than doubling the Pentagon's take over the past decade, compared with a 50% rise in benefits payments for the elderly, survivors, and the disabled.[11]

All year long, nevertheless, Republican leaders and Democratic deficit hawks had been looking for some way to force a showdown on the deficit. By December, they thought they had found it. On the 9th, Gregg and Conrad once again reintroduced their bill calling for a "fiscal task force" to recommend a sweeping deficit reduction plan that Congress would then be bound to put to an up-or-down vote. They had twenty-two cosponsors in the Senate—ten Democrats and fourteen Republicans—and said they wouldn't support an increase in the national debt limit, due to be voted on in February, unless their proposal was included in the measure. Conrad and Gregg wanted their commission to have eighteen members—eight Democrats, eight Republicans, and two appointed by the administration. These last they hoped would include a high-ranking official such as the Treasury secretary.

The foot-in-the-door tactic worked, at least initially. On the 16th, the House approved a short-term rise in the debt ceiling, which would carry over until February—enough time, presumably, for the leadership of both chambers to put together a package that could be combined with a further boost in the debt limit, which would get the government through to the following November. The Senate passed a companion measure shortly thereafter.

All eyes then turned to the White House. Would the president throw his weight behind the Conrad-Gregg commission? Already in November, OMB head Peter Orszag had met with Conrad to discuss the idea. "Two officials" told the *Wall Street Journal*, however, that the administration was inclined to support a panel that didn't have the power to force an up-or-down vote in Congress.

Republican leaders, already feeling hopeful about the 2010 elections, weren't inclined to side with the deficit hawks either, suspecting the commission would become a vehicle for the Democrats to raise taxes. "Why should Republicans sign up as tax collectors for this agenda?" a *Journal* editorial asked. A coalition of fifty progressive groups, including the AFL-CIO, assumed differently—that the commission would be rigged to produce a plan to gut domestic programs—including Social Security and Medicare. This, at a time when the economy was still bleeding jobs. They warned especially against a panel "focused on illegitimate targets like Social Security," as Roger Hickey put it, stressing that Social Security didn't cause the deficit and shouldn't be cut as a way to reduce the overhang.[12]

By the end of the month, Gregg and Conrad had thirty-five senators backing their commission. But two weeks later, their campaign appeared to have stalled, as Gregg conceded that he didn't have the sixty votes needed to pass the bill. More serious, perhaps, Max Baucus was completely opposed. As chair of the powerful Finance Committee, he had the most to lose if a commission that could bypass the usual committee process in the Senate was set up. As the deadline to increase the debt ceiling approached, Baucus insisted on a full Senate vote to amend the Conrad-Gregg proposal, requiring that any changes to Social Security be voted on separately and by the usual procedure. No one wanted to be tagged as setting the program up to be butchered, so the amendment passed overwhelmingly, whereupon the commission proposal lost all Republican support. When the full Senate voted on the amended Conrad-Gregg plan, it got only fifty-three votes—not the sixty votes needed to pass. The same day, January 28, the Senate voted to raise the debt ceiling anyway.

But the commission lived on. A week earlier, Vice President Biden, Peter Orszag, and Democratic leaders struck a deal whereby the president would create the body by executive order. By the end of the year, it would submit recommendations to lower the deficit over the next decade and also—more vaguely—improve the country's long-term fiscal position. According to a letter from Biden, the House and Senate leaders agreed to put the commission's report to a vote. The Senate would go first, and the House would follow if the senators could reach a sixty-vote supermajority.

Gregg and Conrad were less than impressed. "It's a fraud among anyone interested in fiscal responsibility to claim an executive order could structure something that would actually lead to action," Gregg complained.[13] But this was all the fiscal austerity the deficit hawks were going to get from the administration in 2010.

In his State of the Union speech on the 28th, Obama put off until the following year an earlier proposal to freeze domestic spending—after his commission had submitted its report. But he stressed that he took that project seriously. "This can't be one of those Washington gimmicks that lets us pretend we've solved a problem," he said. When Obama submitted his budget to Congress in early February, it included new spending on jobs and, as he had promised during his campaign, let the Bush tax cuts expire for families making more than $250,000 a year. It also proposed extending the Making Work Pay tax credit and giving Social Security recipients another $250 bonus.

* * *

Republican leaders flirted with the idea of boycotting the "National Commission on Fiscal Responsibility and Reform," as it was named in the executive order the president signed on February 18. By then, however, they were as deeply engaged, as were the Democratic deficit hawks, in efforts to pull the process in their direction.

The majority and minority leaders of both houses of Congress each named three members of the commission, while the president got four picks, including the co-chairs. House minority leader John Boehner, in naming his commissioners, said the Republicans would participate only if the panel rejected any tax increases. Two of his three picks—Reps. Jeb Hensarling of Texas and Paul Ryan of Wisconsin—were firmly identified with the extreme free-market wing of the party, while the third—David Camp of Michigan—was only slightly less so. Ryan was still touting his "Road Map" to a balanced budget, with its plan for Social Security privatization.

Mitch McConnell, the Senate minority leader, named Sens. Judd Gregg, Tom Coburn of Oklahoma, and Mike Crapo of Idaho. Gregg was the closest thing to an automatic pick for such a project, and Coburn, a freshman, was making a name for himself with his constant attacks on, seemingly, any and all federal spending. All three subscribed to the orthodox Republican position on Social Security—namely, that it should be "reformed," which they defined as shrinking it.

Nancy Pelosi's picks—Reps. Jan Schakowsky of Illinois, John M. Spratt, Jr. of South Carolina, and Xavier Becerra of California—were, as expected, the most liberal members of the commission and the most firmly on the record against Social Security cuts.

Even after the 2008 election, the Senate Democratic caucus still veered more toward the middle of the road than their counterparts in the House, and this was reflected in Harry Reid's choices. Sen. Dick Durbin of Illinois, one of the president's political mentors, was thought to be a safe vote against any attack on Social Security. Kent Conrad, like Gregg, was a more or less automatic appointment, given that the commission was their idea. Max Baucus, who had scuttled the Gregg-Conrad amendment weeks earlier, had a history of consistently defending Social Security, accusing the deficit hawks at the time of having "painted a big red bull's eye" on the program. But many Democrats were uncertain how he would respond to overtures from the Republican side, given that he had voted for the Bush tax cuts in 2001 and then helped pass the Bush prescription drug plan for Medicare three years later.

The president's picks were a mixed bag. None were members of Congress. They included no high-ranking member of Obama's administration who could speak for the president, as Gregg had hoped. To all appearances, they were chosen to represent as many major interest groups as possible and not tip the administration's hand about its own views, while collectively reassuring the deficit hawks that the White House was "serious" about deficit reduction. The most notable in this respect was Alice Rivlin, the former Clinton head of OMB who, from her perch at Brookings, was now a tireless crusader for "fiscal responsibility."

David Cote, CEO of the big defense contractor Honeywell, and Ann Fudge, former head of the advertising agency Young & Rubicam Brands, were among the major business leaders who had supported Obama for president. Cote's appointment to a commission whose mandate included Social Security and Medicare would prove embarrassing in the coming months, as Honeywell in June locked out its union workers when they refused to accept a contract that would eliminate health care and pension plans for new hires. Fudge had worked on the Obama campaign's messaging effort. Andy Stern, president of the Service Employees International Union, was the only labor leader on the commission. But Stern, who would soon resign from his post, was rumored to have political ambitions and had lately been urging labor, in general terms, to adopt deficit reduction as a goal.

Obama's co-chairs were Alan Simpson and Erskine Bowles. Simpson's record as a critic of Social Security was long and colorful, and he would add further color in the months ahead. But he wasn't automatically against raising taxes, which made him something of an outsider to the hard right despite the fact that he was the second-ranking Republican in the Senate at the time he retired in 1997.

Bowles, an investment banker before and after his service in the Clinton administration, had recently retired as president of the University of North Carolina and was now a member of the board of Morgan Stanley, one of the larger recipients of bailout money from the Treasury and Federal Reserve during the 2008 crisis. Bowles's board seat earned him over $300,000 a year. Like Rivlin, he was a longtime, passionate deficit hawk, although he had expressed few explicit opinions about specific topics such as Social Security. That changed shortly after he was appointed, when he gave a speech in which he said, "We're going to mess with Medicare, Medicaid, and Social Security because if you take those off the table, you can't get" significant deficit reduction.

That comment had some observers wondering what the commission's objectives really were, since nothing of the sort was explicitly stated in its charter. Its mission was to "propose recommendations to balance the budget, excluding interest payment on the debt, by 2015. This result is projected to stabilize the debt-to-GDP ratio at an acceptable level once the economy recovers." At the same time, the commission "shall propose recommendations to the President that meaningfully improve the long-run fiscal outlook, including changes to address the growth of entitlement spending." "Changes" didn't necessarily mean the commission was supposed to balance the overall budget at the expense of Social Security and the other programs, rather than simply put them on a more sustainable footing. But Bowles was more than implying that that was what he and Simpson intended.

Reinforcing that impression was Bruce Reed, Bowles's and Simpson's choice to be executive director of the commission. A friend of Rahm Emanuel,[14] Reed was taking a leave from his post as head of the DLC, which had been pushing to shrink Social Security—and, sometimes, privatize it—for decades. But the DLC wasn't the only outside voice that seemed to have a pipeline to the commission: another was Pete Peterson and his patronage network. Rivlin, with her Brookings affiliation, was the only member directly tied to the deficit-hawk godfather, but two of its staffers, Marc Goldwein and Ed Lorenzen, had day jobs with Peterson-funded groups—Goldwein with the Committee for a Responsible Federal Budget and Lorenzen with the Peterson Foundation itself.

When this came out in the press later in the year, Reed retorted that the commission had six staff members from outside organizations, including one from the liberal Economic Policy Institute. The panel had a small budget for such projects—$500,000—and Reed said that "we begged everyone we could find in both parties across the spectrum to sign up and help. Part of our job is not to add to the problem ourselves."[15]

But the commission revealed a closer connection with Peterson in April, when it was still fresh from its first official meeting. A story by Lori Montgomery in the *Washington Post* noted that the commission "will partner with other groups to get the word out, including the Peter G. Peterson Foundation, which will hold a fiscal summit Wednesday featuring former president Bill Clinton. And in June, commission members plan to participate in a 20-city electronic town hall meeting on the budget organized by the nonprofit America Speaks."

America Speaks was another Peterson-funded group. The meeting that Montgomery referred to was titled "2010 Fiscal Summit: America's Challenge and a Way Forward." Held the day after the deficit commission's first meeting, its participants also included two commission members, Alice Rivlin and Judd Gregg.

Like the Kerrey-Danforth commission sixteen years earlier, the leaders of Obama's deficit commission understood that their job wasn't just to put together a unified proposal—hard enough, given that they would have to corral fourteen of eighteen members to vote for it—but to sell the urgency of the project itself to the public and members of Congress. Appearing on CNBC in June, Rivlin was asked why Social Security was such a ripe target. She replied, "Because I think that would send a message to our creditors around the world that we're serious about making long-term change."

This line of reasoning dovetailed perfectly with the advice the commission was getting in op-eds by prominent deficit hawks. "They could begin with Social Security, which oddly enough has gone from being the 'third rail of American politics' to the low-hanging fruit," Bob Bixby of the Concord Coalition wrote, encouragingly, without explaining why or how this supposed shift had taken place.[16] Burton Malkiel, the Princeton economist and investment guru, said almost precisely the same thing. "While [Social Security] is not the biggest part of our long-run budgetary shortfall, it is the easiest to fix," he suggested in a *Wall Street Journal* op-ed.

The deficit hawks'—and the deficit commission's—staunchest supporter within the corporate media was the *Washington Post*, which was losing circulation and in the Internet age was by no means as influential as it once had been. But it was still the preeminent newspaper in the nation's capital, and, as such, helped set the tone for other outlets' coverage of news in and around Pennsylvania Avenue. It had been championing the deficit-hawk position for so long, both in its editorials and its daily coverage, that it had by now thrown off any semblance of impartiality. It took an extra step in this direction, though, in late December, shortly before the deal that created the deficit commission was struck, when it announced that it was partnering with the *Fiscal Times*, an Internet news service that Peterson was funding to cover matters related to the deficit debate.

Stories by *Fiscal Times* reporters, some of whom were former longtime *Post* reporters, would be appearing in the paper as well in a content-sharing agreement. Not surprisingly, the first stories to appear in the *Post* under the deal were larded with viewpoints from prominent deficit hawks like Kent Conrad, Bob Bixby, David John of Heritage, and little, if any, from opponents of Social Security cutbacks. Criticized for publishing such material, the *Post*'s executive editor, Marcus Brauchli, responded that when the paper used "material from outside sources, we always disclose the source of such journalism and ensure it meets the *Post*'s standards for independence and authority."

But the *Fiscal Times* pieces that appeared in the paper didn't disclose that they were subsidized by Peterson. The *Post*'s ombudsman, Andrew Alexander, denied there was any "scandal" in all this, noting that Peterson had assured him in a letter that he was funding *Fiscal Times* "with no strings attached" and that he "will not influence nor in any way be involved in decisions about editorial content." Given the status that deficit hawk viewpoints had attained in the Beltway echo chamber, and Peterson's reputation there as an honest broker taking a seemingly middle-of-the-road position, Brauchli's and Alexander's protestations may have been quite genuine. They simply didn't see it as problematic that Peterson was funding *Fiscal Times* until the *Columbia Journalism Review* and a few other sources complained. Afterward, they continued to publish pieces from *Fiscal Times*, but noted in a tag line where its funding came from.*

But even with the firm support of the capital media, Simpson, Bowles, and their supporters felt besieged. One reason was that they knew it would be tough assembling fourteen votes for a deficit reduction plan. They knew the members from the center-right would be with them, but should they attempt to bring this group together with the progressives on a plan that would probably emphasize tax hikes for the affluent? Or with Republican conservatives who would insist on spending cuts and not much else? That would be tricky, but Bowles's and Simpson's comments suggested it as the course they had chosen. That meant they would face at least five votes solidly

---

* Interestingly, the *CJR* was now receiving Peterson money as well. According to reporter Trudy Lieberman, the Peterson Foundation was funding a "part-time fellow" to "encourage the business media to look at the consequences of the government bailout and the larger financial crisis, which is occurring in the context of two wars, potential expansive and expensive reforms such as health care, and amid rising entitlement spending." The fellow's stories would appear on the magazine's website.

opposed—Schakowsky, Becerra, Spratt, Baucus, and—one or the other or both—Stern and Durbin.

Any sign that forces outside the commission were encouraging this crew to stick together, the co-chairs found annoying. But there it was. Marginalized by the mainstream media, and understanding that Simpson and Bowles understood the need to outreach, the commission's critics had launched a communications effort, which aimed at rallying traditional supporters of Social Security and getting their point of view out to the public. They gained only limited access to the mainstream outlets—mostly as the obligatory contrary view in articles and video segments built around the deficit hawks' arguments, although websites like HuffingtonPost.com and FireDogLake.com afforded them better exposure. Accordingly, they turned to less orthodox tactics.

Early in the year, Eric Kingson and Nancy Altman, both leading Social Security scholars, founded Social Security Works, which started issuing a series of reports on how the program benefited specific groups including women, people of color, veterans, and children. As their principal full-time operative they hired Alex Lawson, a young staffer with the Campaign for America's Future.

The commission's general meetings were open to the public and press, but substantive discussions were reserved for its subcommittee meetings, which were closed—just as they had been when Bush's Social Security commission were discussing cutting the program in 2001. Lawson was soon haunting the hallways during the closed meetings, armed with a video camera in case he got the chance to ask a few questions of one of the commissioners. At a June meeting, Simpson stopped briefly to talk with him. When Simpson said the commission's objective was to ensure Social Security's "solvency," Lawson asked him if they were looking to preserve the adequacy of benefits as well.

"Where do you come up with all the crap you come up with?" the seventy-eight-year-old ex-senator snapped back.

"We're trying to take care of the lesser people in society," Simpson continued, "and do that in a way without getting into all the flash words you love to dig up, like cutting Social Security, which is bullshit. We're not cutting anything, we're trying to make it solvent."

Simpson's rant, which received exposure across the country, prompted *Los Angeles Times* columnist Michael Hiltzik to dub him "the embodiment of cocksure ignorance." Bowles and Simpson had given every indication that their notion of making Social Security "solvent" would mean slowing the growth of benefits in a way that was tantamount to steep benefit cuts for younger workers. Simpson's reference to "lesser people" at best made clear how vague a role lower-income workers played in his calculations, and at worst, the arrogant obliviousness that three terms in the Senate could instill in a person who was himself elderly.

It's doubtful that Obama named Simpson a co-chair in order to embarrass the deficit hawks. But one could wonder. On April 27, the first day the commission met, Ashley Carson, executive director of the Older Women's League, wrote a piece for HuffingtonPost.com questioning Simpson's presence on the panel, given his "constant bashing of seniors." Getting wind of the article some time later, Simpson shot an email to Carson in which he defiantly acknowledged that "yes, I've made some plenty smart cracks about people on Social security who milk it to the last degree. You know 'em too. It's the same with any system in America. We've reached a point now where it's like a milk cow with 310 million tits!"

While "people like you babble into the vapors about 'disgusting attempts at ageism and sexism' and all the rest of that crap," Simpson wrote, he himself had "spent many years in public life trying to stabilize" Social Security. He signed off with the suggestion that Carson, whose organization was well established as an advocate for middle-aged to older women, "call when you get honest work."

This outburst resulted in a brief groundswell from progressive groups and some labor unions demanding that Simpson be removed. The White House, anxious to not appear to be interfering with the commission's work, looked the other way. As for *le tout* Washington, the ex-senator was what passed for a charming curmudgeon in the capitol, and while he made a partial apology for his comments, he also received plenty of bucking up from insiders.

Mainstream media quickly picked up and assimilated even the most incendiary claims by Bowles and Simpson about the danger of not attacking the deficit, but seemed to ignore progressives when they attempted something similar, for instance when they began referring derisively to the deficit panel as the "Catfood Commission."

Within the commission itself, discussion was turning increasingly away from short-term deficit reduction and toward Bowles's and Simpson's more ambitious designs to shrink Social Security and Medicare and remake the tax code in a more "investment-friendly" direction. There was no clear need to do so. Social Security was actually less of a concern than it had been thirteen years earlier, when the trustees put the projected cost of immediately zeroing out the program's seventy-five-year deficit at 2.23% of payroll. By 2010, the trustees were projecting just 2.01%. Nevertheless, the more progressive members had a hard time directing any of the commission's attention to their views and concerns—for instance, the economic impact of Social Security cuts on current workers and those who would depend on it in the future.

"I asked a gazillion times for a distributional analysis of this and every other proposal," remembers Jan Schakowsky, "but we never got that from the commission. This wasn't a green-eyeshade exercise, either. It could have been done in an afternoon."[17]

* * *

This should have been no surprise. Despite the presence of a dozen sitting members of Congress amongst its members, the deficit commission was evolving into something like the Kerrey-Danforth: a vehicle for two very forceful deficit hawks to frame the deficit debate. Its meetings saw plenty of discussion, but the real work of developing a set of proposals went on behind the scenes, directed by Bowles and Simpson and carried out by executive director Bruce Reed.

Meanwhile, the commission was serving the Obama administration's purposes by allowing it to focus on matters other than the deficit for the remainder of the year. The economy was supposed to be healing itself, gently nudged along by Washington's stimulus money. The White House was determined especially to pass two major pieces of legislation: a financial-sector reform bill and a bill to restructure the national health care system. Shortly thereafter, it would have to wade into a bruising midterm election.

The Patient Protection and Affordable Care Act and the Health Care and Education Reconciliation Act went months over schedule and took all of Pelosi's and Reid's considerable parliamentary skills to push through. The bruising battle over "ObamaCare" also exposed serious rifts between the progressive wing of the party and the center-right, which had been papered over during Bush's Social Security privatization campaign in 2005 and then during the 2006 and 2008 elections. This was probably inevitable, but some of the trouble was the president's own fault.

First, he had done nothing to mobilize the 13 million-strong grassroots following that came together during his election. Organizing for America, as this organization was known, had been folded into the more conservative Democratic National Committee after the 2008 election, and there it had atrophied.[18]

Most disappointing to progressives who had provided some of Obama's most dedicated supporters was the decision by the White House and the congressional Democratic leadership to drop their support for a single-payer, public option for health insurance. While this may have been necessary to get any kind of bill passed, it left many progressives wondering why they had supported this administration. Passage of the most sweeping health care legislation since the Johnson era somehow felt like a defeat.

Conservatives felt much the opposite. Just as had ClintonCare in 1993, the health care bill gave Republican leaders the target they needed to galvanize their most passionate constituents against the latest symptom of "big government" overreach. Cleverly, they extrapolated from proposed cuts in Medicare Advantage to assent that seniors would lose their benefits. Sarah Palin, now a standard-bearer for ideological conservatives, made her first contribution to a substantive national political debate by charging that the Democrats' proposals to improve the process for approving new treatments amounted to creating "death panels."

Perhaps no one will ever firmly establish whether the right-wing Tea Party movement that grew up with the health care debate was a genuine grassroots phenomenon or a Frankenstein brought to life by right-wing advocacy shops. But, for a long time, the right had been seeking to develop a ground-level organization capable of mobilizing activists in the same way that MoveOn.org, USAction, the National Alliance of Senior Citizens, and the various progressive groups backed by organized labor had done so effectively in recent years. Dick Armey's FreedomWorks, which grew out of Citizens for a Sound Economy, a group funded by right-wing industrialists David and Charles Koch (whose father, a powerful Texas newspaper baron, had opposed Social Security during the time of its creation), had been part of Bush's anti-Social Security coalition in 2005.[19] FreedomWorks was focused on creating a grassroots organization on the right and quickly became one of the main engines of the Tea Party.

In any case, the Tea Party had its national debut in summer 2009, when activists bird-dogged Democratic members of Congress holding town hall meetings to build support for the health care legislation. The tactic, which progressives had been honing for years in successive campaigns to defend Social Security, worked for the right as well, garnering enormous attention in the press. FreedomWorks played the role of the Campaign for America's Future, helping out with a "Healthcare Freedom Action Kit" that schooled Tea Partiers on how to "keep socialized medicine out of the budget."

By the time the package of health care bills passed, Tea Party organizers—many of them long-time Republican Party hands—were scrambling to raise funds, build a permanent organization, and field a slate of candidates in the 2010 election, sometimes in opposition to those the GOP elders had picked. What they weren't trying to do—not yet—was to more sharply define the movement ideologically, since a certain fuzziness beyond the oft-repeated message to end government "waste" and stop giving handouts to the unworthy was serving the cause well. Meanwhile, Congress and the administration inflicted another deep disappointment on progressives—and even some Tea Partiers—with passage in July of the Dodd-Frank Wall Street Reform and Consumer Protection Act, the much-watered down bill intended to reform Wall Street practices following the 2007–08 mortgage market meltdown.

As the summer rolled on, however, the administration may have inflicted the most damage on itself by its lukewarm response to the still-sluggish economy.

Much of the 2009 stimulus had been offset by drastic workforce cuts by state and local governments. These had hit seniors especially hard, underscoring the need for the $250 bonus to Social Security recipients in lieu of a COLA. In July, the Center on Budget and Policy Priorities reported that at least twenty-five states, plus the District of Columbia, had reduced programs such as meal deliveries, housekeeping, and aid to family members providing care. When these were services the elderly couldn't do without, they were forced to pay out of their own pockets—that is, out of their Social Security checks. Not surprisingly, more people—2.74 million—filed for Social Security than in any previous year; the number filing for early retirement benefits was up especially sharply.[20]

Social Security was proving to be the one steadily effective part of the safety net. While states were cutting Medicaid, the big 2009 COLA bump-up, along with Obama's $250-per-person bonus payment, boosted income for seniors more than in any year since 1973, according to the Census Bureau. In fact, seniors for the first time out-earned fifteen- to twenty-four-year-olds.[21] Congress, however, seemed deaf to the need to do something to assist the flagging economic recovery. In July, it had no problem approving $59 billion of additional funding for the war in Afghanistan, but the Senate quickly stripped out $20 billion in additional domestic spending, which the House had added to the bill.

* * *

The 2010 elections echoed, strongly, the 1980 campaign that inaugurated the war against Social Security. A Democratic Party that was blamed, rightly or wrongly, for failing to end an economic recession faced a rejuvenated Republican Party that pledged to cut taxes, or at least hold the line against tax increases, while balancing the federal budget by cutting supposedly massive waste and fraud. Already in the spring, polls were starting to show voters leaning toward the Republicans, and by summer, many pundits were predicting a blow-out, turning over one or perhaps both houses of Congress to the GOP. The numbers just kept getting better for the right clear up through the election. But whether the shift meant voters had suddenly fallen in love with Republican ideology or simply wanted to punish the Democrats—and if so, for what—wasn't clear.

"That's a conundrum, isn't it?" Jodine White, a Tea Party supporter in Rickin, California, told Kate Zernike, a *New York Times* reporter who was writing a book on the movement. "I guess I want smaller government and my Social Security." This despite the fact that Social Security was just the sort of "redistributive" program that conservatives had always most loathed. "Tea Partiers

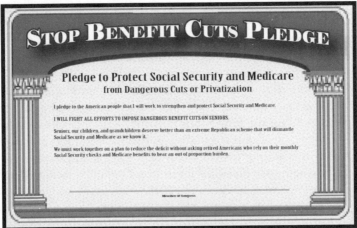

Democrats, fighting the Tea Party backlash against their health care legislation, once again leaned heavily on Social Security to hold off Republican challengers in the 2010 elections.

tended to believe that they had done all the right things," Zernike concluded. "They had earned their place in the middle class, and they were out to protect what they saw as theirs."[22]

While the media routinely described the Tea Partiers as "antigovernment," this was far from the truth, as their enthusiastic support for a quasi-Orwellian crackdown on undocumented immigrants and "voter fraud" makes clear. What they didn't want was for groups that they felt hadn't done "all the right things" to be rewarded undeservedly. The movement itself can be said to have started in February 2009, when a conservative CNBC financial commentator blew a fuse about the administration's program to help homeowners whose mortgages were underwater. "How many of you people want to pay for your neighbor's mortgage that has an extra bathroom and can't pay their bills?" His rant quickly went viral.

That didn't mean the most enthusiastic group of Republican voters in 2010 opposed Social Security or wanted it abolished. But their leaders—or at least the people who claimed to speak for them—were another story. At Freedom-Works' Pennsylvania Avenue headquarters, staff members liked to display symbols of the things they opposed. "We're like the Japanese," the group's press secretary told Zernike. "We seize our enemies' flags." One of these "flags" was the oft-reproduced photo of Franklin Delano Roosevelt signing the Social Security Act.

Fox radio and TV personality Glenn Beck beat the drum steadily against Social Security all year, in his relentlessly hyperbolic manner. "Do you think programs like Social Security and Medicare represent socialism and should have never been created in the first place?" he asked during his January 27 broadcast. "Oh, gosh, Democrats, this is a scary question. Another trap. You know what? It's only scary if you don't know who you are or what you believe in.

"I'm an American. I read. I believe in the Constitution. And, of course, Social Security and Medicare represent socialism and should have never been created. Since FDR and his progressive buddies started Social Security, not our Founding Fathers, that should be fairly obvious to people."

When Beck needed to bolster his views, however, he had available not a fringe conspiracy theorist but a well-ensconced Washington figure: David Walker. As early as 2007, before he moved from CNN Headline News to Fox News Channel, and when the Fiscal Wake Up tour was still in its early stages, Beck recommended Walker to his listeners as "a Cassandra." At the end of a lengthy on-air interview with the former comptroller general on January 18, 2010, as the midterm election year was heating up, he enthused, "David Walker, I can't tell you, sir. You are going to go down in the history books as a patriot. I appreciate you speaking out, and don't stop. And anything we can do, you please let us know, sir." On April 15, Beck largely gave over another broadcast to Chris Edwards, tax policy director at Cato, explaining the need to swap Social Security for "a system of private ... accounts like two dozen other countries around the world have."

This had long been the mainstream Republican viewpoint. The major change the party had undergone since 2008 was an intense focus on cutting domestic spending. Gone were the days, seemingly, when a national Republican leader could opine that "deficits don't matter." Instead, the party—and especially the Tea Party candidates—promised to cut $100 billion from the budget for domestic discretionary programs and take the overall budget back to its level in 2008—the last year of the Bush presidency.

The party took care not to explicitly advocate cuts to Social Security, but its candidates and incumbents—many of them—were more forthright, sometimes outrageously so. The most quotable Tea Partier was Sharron Angle, a former Nevada state legislator who was running for the Senate. One of the purest of the pure, Angle beat a more conventional Republican in the primary, but then lost some of her outsider status when the Republican elders decided she had a chance to defeat one of the chief thorns in their side, Harry Reid, whereupon the Angle campaign became one of the most expensive of the year. "My grandfather wouldn't even take his Social Security check because he was not up for welfare," Angle said. Later, she embraced private accounts, telling the *Las Vegas Sun*, euphemistically, "What we need to do is personalize Social Security so the government can no longer raid it."*

Rep. Michelle Bachmann of Minnesota, who liked to say that she was "Tea Party before there was Tea Party," was similarly blunt. In February, she said that while it was important to "keep faith with the people that are already in the system, … what we have to do is wean everybody else off. And wean everybody off because we have to take those unfunded net liabilities off our bank sheet."[23] Rand Paul, who defeated the party leadership's hand-picked candidate for Senate from Kentucky and whose father, Rep. Ron Paul of Texas, was a longtime advocate of privatization, spoke freely about means-testing Social Security and raising the retirement age. Sen. Richard Shelby of Alabama, who once, as a Democrat, fended off a challenge for his House seat by attacking his opponent as an enemy of the program, now spoke of the need to raise the Social Security retirement age "every several years."[24]

Members of the Republican congressional leadership were out front with their criticisms of Social Security itself. Minority leader John Boehner said in interviews that he supported raising Social Security's full-benefits retirement age to seventy for people with at least twenty years to go before retirement, ratcheting COLAs down, and means-testing the program—the standard prescriptions supported by deficit hawks like Bowles, Simpson, and Rivlin. In all,

---

*   The only time the Social Security trust funds can be said to have been raided, in point of fact, was under a Republican president: Ronald Reagan. In August 1985, facing a temporary but severe cash flow problem, Treasury Secretary James Baker began cashing in Treasury bonds in the OASI and DI trust funds to make interest payments to other federal-government creditors. After complaints by AARP and members of Congress and a threatened lawsuit, Treasury repaid the sums.

a review of public statements and voting records by ThinkProgress.org, a blog run by the liberal-leaning Center for American Progress, found that almost half of congressional Republicans had gone on record supporting some version of private-account carve-outs.

The Republicans were clearly moving to the right on Social Security as well as on other topics. Democrats and some Independents, naturally, worked hard to exploit the opportunity this created. When the seventy-fifth anniversary of the Social Security Act's signing came up on August 13, the Alliance for Retired Americans held a series of "birthday parties" for the program at SSA offices around the country. Obama raised the temperature during his weekly radio address, charging that "some Republican leaders in Congress" want to privatize Social Security. "I'll fight with everything I've got to stop those who would gamble your Social Security on Wall Street," he vowed. "Because you shouldn't be worried that a sudden downturn in the stock market will put all you've worked so hard for—all you've earned—at risk."[25]

Shortly thereafter, a coalition of sixty progressives groups including MoveOn.org and the Campaign for America's Future began circulating a "Hands Off Social Security" pledge. Members of Congress who signed, pledged to oppose any cuts to the program, including raising the retirement age. Pelosi and Reps. Raul Grijalva and Lynn Woolsey, co-chairs of the House Progressive Caucus, were among thirteen members who added their names immediately. A handful of Democratic candidates and incumbents, including Rep. Joe Baca of California and Rep. Sander Levin of Michigan, chair of the Ways and Means Subcommittee on Social Security, published op-eds accusing Republicans of wanting to "dismantle" Social Security and repeat the Bush administration's attempt at privatization.

The fiercest fight over Social Security was taking place in Nevada, however, where Angle ran TV ads pledging to "save" the program and accusing Reid of "raiding" the trust funds. Reid, fighting for his political life, countered with an ad that caught Angle saying, "We need to phase Medicare and Social Security out." That was in August. Two months later, in perhaps the most bizarre exchange of the midterm elections, Angle responded to the Senate majority leader during a televised debate by admonishing, "Man up, Harry Reid. You need to understand that we have a problem with Social Security."[26]

Angle's incongruous attack on her opponent's masculinity added to the increasingly eccentric image Nevadans were forming of her, but probably didn't shift anyone's position, either way, on Social Security. Indeed, one of the many problems the Democrats faced in the 2010 election was that Social Security wasn't the killer issue it had been for them in recent elections, even though the public generally agreed with their position.

In contrast to previous years, Republicans had a counterspin strategy. They could point out that as a group they weren't promoting privatization, which was unmentioned in official position papers, and express puzzlement that the Democrats kept bringing this up. Privatization wasn't exactly a non sequitur; Paul Ryan, widely touted as a rising intellectual leader of the GOP, was obviously being groomed for a top leadership role. His "Road Map for America's Future" explicitly called for privatizing Social Security. Besides, the distinction between privatizer and deficit hawk was less meaningful than met the eye, since the degree of cuts needed to significantly reduce Social Security spending would be so great that most people would be forced to depend more on personal savings and investments, whether private accounts were part of the package or not.

But instead of responding directly when the subject came up, Republican candidates could simply turn the conversation around. Over and over, they accused Democrats of ignoring problems with "entitlements" and called instead for bipartisan cooperation to develop a solution. And if push came to shove, they could always accuse their opponents of using Social Security to paper over the failure of Congress and the White House to orchestrate a strong economic recovery.

That formed a natural segue into their favorite topic, especially in the year of the Tea Party. "By embracing an agenda of runaway government spending," Ken Spain, the National Republican Congressional Committee's communications director said, "Democrats have pushed Social Security further into the red and made it even less likely that Americans will see the benefits of a system they continue to fund through their hard-earned tax dollars."[27]

Another problem was that the Democrats themselves were divided. They had won the 2008 election, in part, by recruiting more center-right candidates. These new lawmakers now faced formidable challenges from a more ideologically severe set of Republican candidates, and were doing everything they could to tack further right. First-term Rep. Jim Hines of Connecticut, for example, a Goldman Sachs banker before he went into politics, spoke of Social Security's "massive unfunded liabilities." Even Sen. Dick Durbin, a two-termer running for reelection, was complaining from his perch on the deficit commission that "the bleeding heart liberals … have to … make real sacrifices to strengthen our nation."[28]

* * *

The November 2 election, as expected, was a victory for the Republicans, although not as big a one as they had hoped. In the House, sixty-three seats changed hands, giving the GOP a comfortable forty-nine-seat majority. The Democrats held onto the Senate, their majority dropping from fifty-nine seats—including two Independents—to fifty-three. Ironically, the biggest losers were the deficit-hawkish Blue Dogs, whose House caucus shrank to twenty-six members from fifty-four. That, and the fact that four Tea Party candidates—Rand Paul, Dan Coats in Indiana, Kelly Ayotte in new Hampshire, and Marco Rubio in Florida—won Senate seats, while some seventy candidates, backed by one or another Tea Party organization, won seats in the House, meant that the new Congress would be even more ideologically divided.

Congress would also be richer than ever. According to a study by the Center for Responsive Politics, 69% of the new senators were millionaires, as were more than 40% of new House members. Median estimated wealth for the new senators was $3.96 million; in the House, $570,418. The wealthiest was Sen. Richard Blumenthal, Connecticut Democrat, with an estimated net worth of $94.87 million. Following him were seven new House members worth between $22.1 million and $49.4 million each. For perspective, only about 1% of Americans could claim membership in households with $1 million or more in assets. The distance between American lawmakers and the population that depended on Social Security continued to widen.

Social Security did affect the outcome at least in one state—Nevada—where Reid out-fundraised and defeated Angle to win his fifth term, and retain his post as Senate majority leader. Indeed, one of the biggest disappointments for Republicans was certainly the fact that the Democratic disaster failed to shake Reid and Pelosi's control of the congressional Democratic organization. Republican backers had poured money into Angle's marginal campaign hoping to dislodge Reid, and spent $65 million on election ads targeting Pelosi.[29] But Pelosi easily survived a palace revolt by center-right House members who wanted to knock her out of the minority leader's post in favor of one of their own. Rather than the headless body that the GOP had hoped to face for the next two years, the Democrats would continue to have strong leaders holding their various factions in line.

The disturbing truth for the Democrats, however, was that they had again been outplayed for what used to be one of their most reliable constituencies: the elderly. Seniors voted Republican by a 59% to 38% margin. Yet a survey of voters who cast ballots on November 2 commissioned by the Progressive Change Campaign Committee, found that when respondents were given the choice between cutting the defense budget, raising taxes on the rich, and cutting Social Security, 43% said raise taxes on the rich, 22% said cut

Ironically, the "Catfood Commission" that supplied Democratic candidates with one of their more potent metaphors in 2010 was created by a Democratic president.

the Pentagon, and only 12% said take it out of Social Security. So what had happened?

Republicans' keynote claim was that the administration was going to cut Medicare by $500 billion followed by a warning to seniors that their benefits would disappear and their very lives would be threatened by bureaucratic "death panels." Of course, the new law proposed to find cost reductions mostly by reducing subsidies to Medicare Advantage. And even the 25% of seniors who received coverage through Medicare Advantage would gain from other parts of the legislation, such as elimination of the "donut hole" in Medicare prescription drug coverage. But the Republican campaign worked and, in June, 60% of seniors in a Gallup poll said passage of the new health care law was a "bad thing."

Democrats would wrangle for months over what they had done wrong. The center-right, with Third Way its most audible voice, argued that the Obama administration had veered too far to the left and enraged independent voters. Progressives disagreed. If Democrats had better articulated a set of core values, they argued—for example, by supporting and pushing through a single-payer option that would have made ObamaCare a true social insurance program rather than an unsatisfactory simulacrum—perhaps they would have reenergized the supporters who had flocked to Obama in 2008, and won.

Whoever was more correct, the debate itself was a symptom of the Democrats' troubles. It's hard for a party to express core values when it's being pulled in two very different directions at once—one way by the left and the other by the center-right. Voters, a distinct minority of the American public with their own quirky habits, can smell weakness, and the Democratic leadership's struggles to push even watered-down versions of its 2008 campaign promises into law surely persuaded many undecided voters to support what appeared to be the more dynamic, self-assured party.

CHAPTER 46

THE DEFICIT COMMISSION

ALAN SIMPSON: We're really working on solvency… the key is solvency.

ALEX LAWSON: What about adequacy? Are you focusing on adequacy as well?

ALAN SIMPSON: Where do you come up with all the crap you come up with?[1]

The Republican leaders—Mitch McConnell in the Senate and John Boehner, the new House speaker—quickly laid out an ambitious program for the next two years. The party would do all it could to kill ObamaCare piecemeal— through court challenges, symbolic repeal votes in Congress, and denial of funding. Around the country, where they picked up control of twenty state governments, they would slash spending, including for Medicaid and programs that assisted seniors. In Washington, impelled by the new Tea Party members, McConnell and Boehner promised not just to slash discretionary spending and root out "waste," but to force a confrontation with the White House that would lead to a more sweeping downsizing of government, including entitlements.

They would do this, in part, through a series of rule changes in the House. One of these would switch from the "pay-as-you-go" rule the Democrats had previously adopted—any new spending would have to be paid for through spending cuts elsewhere or revenue increases—to "cut-go"—eliminating tax increases from the equation. Republican leaders also suggested that they would hold up a vote to boost the national debt limit, which would be needed some time in the spring. Otherwise, the government wouldn't be able to roll over its existing obligations and a credit crisis could result. But Republicans saw the debt limit vote as a good opportunity to force the administration into a grand bargain on taxes, entitlements, and future government spending.

Initially, it seemed that such a deal would include Social Security. Paul Ryan, the incoming Budget Committee chair, boasted that dozens of Republican candidates had endorsed his Road Map during the campaign, producing what amounted to a mandate for change. "People are ready for an adult conversation, they're ready for the truth, they're ready for solutions no matter whether they agree on every detail or not," Ryan told *USA Today*. "This is no longer the third rail it was once thought to be."

* * *

Ryan was already attracting considerable attention as a member of the Bowles-Simson deficit commission. As Budget Committee chair, House leaders gave him unprecedented new authority, geared to push Republican budget cuts through the chamber with little opportunity for the other party to interfere. The new rules authorized the chair to submit total spending and revenue limits and spending allocations to the House committees, in place of the traditional budget resolution if the Senate and House couldn't reach one together. That gave Ryan the power to set binding limits on spending and revenues even if no one else had ever seen his numbers or had a chance to amend or even comment on them.[2]

More than this, the lanky, forty-year-old House member from rural Wisconsin, who traced his ideological leanings to a close study of "anti-collectivist" godparent Ayn Rand, had become one of the pivotal figures in the deficit debate.

What turned Ryan into something of a matinee idol in the mainstream media, during the summer and fall, was his claim that the Road Map would not only slash taxes and hobble, if not eliminate, the welfare state, but zero out the deficit in fifty years. Ryan was a dyed-in-the-wool supply-sider, but he also gave out that he was willing to accept less than the ideal in order to make progress toward hobbling Social Security, Medicare, and Medicaid. That he seemed sincere about accomplishing both goals made him a kind of one-person harmonic convergence—the lawmaker who could bring the Free Lunch Caucus and the Pain Caucus, the deficit hawks and the free-marketeers of both parties together on a deficit-slashing Grand Bargain. With his rising influence in the Republican leadership and his seat on the deficit commission, he seemed to be in exactly the right spot to help broker a deal.

"Mr. Ryan appears to be the rare kind of guy who actually dreams of making Social Security solvent, rather than of using the issue to bludgeon opponents or get himself on television," enthused Matt Bai, the *New York Times*'s chief Washington correspondent and a close friend of Third Way's Jonathan Cowan. *Washington Post* reporter Perry Bacon, Jr., tagged Ryan as "the GOP's leading intellectual in Congress," who "occasionally seems to forget that he is a politician himself." No less a free-market ideologue than Phil Gramm, from his lucrative perch at Swiss bank UBS, praised Ryan for his "vision and energy."[3]

Aside from his somewhat Boy Scoutish demeanor, why did so many supposedly well-informed people think Ryan could be both deficit hawk and Free Luncher at the same time? Not the Road Map itself—a collection of standard Cato-Heritage prescriptions of tax cuts and entitlement reductions, which relied on optimistic projections of tax revenue growth to eliminate the deficit. Rather, it was his willingness to talk the language of fiscal austerity and to huddle with the deficit hawks on the president's commission that made him such a popular figure with the Washington press corps. The commission's critics, a small number of whom were invited to testify, struggled for attention.

Economist James K. Galbraith excoriated the commission for conflicts of interest, for keeping its most crucial deliberations out of the public eye, and for basing its work on what he considered to be flawed economic estimates by the CBO. "If cuts are proposed and enacted in Social Security and Medicare, they will hurt millions, weaken the economy and the deficits will not decline," he told the commissioners. "The Republic would be better served by advancing no proposals at all."

Janice M. Gregory, president of the National Academy of Social Insurance, was less angry, but pointed out that seniors were more dependent on Social Security than ever and that the cost of the program itself was projected to rise by only 0.7% of GDP over the next forty years—hardly enough to make it a grave danger to government finances.

Yung-Ping Chen, a renowned gerontologist and public policy scholar at the University of Massachusetts, Boston, objected to the entire focus of the commission when it came to Social Security. "Solvency is not the issue," he wrote in a paper for the Roosevelt Institute. "Updating the program's rules on family benefits should be the first priority" because otherwise "it will continue to leave many vulnerable people unprotected." Divorced persons, widowed spouses, surviving children—Social Security's rules were outdated for all of these groups and no longer served them well, Chen wrote.[4]

None of this seemed to make much impression on the co-chairs or their supporters. When Schakowsky questioned the CBO's estimates—which, among other things, assumed away any budget savings from ObamaCare in its second decade—Simpson and Kent Conrad responded sharply. Letting the Bush tax cuts lapse was estimated to roughly cover the cost of any Social Security shortfall over the next seventy-five years, but, the *Wall Street Journal* blandly reported a week before the November election, "the panel isn't expected to weigh in on this issue."

As the commission's December deadline drew closer, it became clear that Bowles and Simpson were aiming to woo their right-wing colleagues while essentially ignoring the progressives. In July, eager to reassure Republicans that spending cuts would outweigh tax increases in the final report, Bowles floated the long-term goal of reducing all future federal spending as a percentage of GDP to 21%. The Center for Budget and Policy Priorities estimated that that would lead to drastic cuts in everything other than interest payments on the national debt—and was unrealistic in any case, given rising costs for homeland security, the Middle East wars, health care, and other government responsibilities. The 21% proposal was, however, calculated to appeal to Republicans eager for budget-cutting trophies in an election year.

Outside the commission, prominent Democrats complained vociferously about the direction it was obviously taking. Well before the election, Pelosi said flatly that Social Security would not be a target for budget cutting during the lame-duck session, emphasizing that Social Security was a completely separate issue from the deficit. Some of this talk was aimed directly at the White House, which could determine the fate of the commission's work by embracing or rejecting it in December.[5]

The commission's supporters waxed indignant. A *Washington Post* editorial blasted the "denialists" and their "maddening strategy of minimizing the existence of any problem." These people should cease "preemptively bashing the commission," the *Post* editors urged, while the commissioners themselves should "ignore the denialists and tackle" the issue. The day after the election, Peter Orszag, who had just left the administration—and would soon announce he was taking a senior post at Citigroup—urged the commission to take on Social Security on the now-familiar grounds that it would restore "credibility" in the bond market. And he denounced "the left's strident opposition to any serious discussion of Social Security reform."[6]

A week later, friends and foes of the commission alike had something tangible to talk about. On November 10, Bowles and Simpson abruptly called a press conference at which they laid out their own long-range deficit reduction proposal, which they called a "starting point" for members to discuss as they tried to agree on a final plan. Inadvertently, the phrase had the tone of a punch line. The commission had existed for seven months and its deadline was only three weeks away. No word coming out of the panel's closed-door meetings suggested fourteen members were near agreement on anything. The co-chairs' action looked like a last-ditch attempt to bring the larger community of Washington deficit hawks into the discussion, applying pressure to members who might be wavering.

The plan itself made headlines with its enormous numbers: $3.8 trillion in deficit reduction over the next decade; military and domestic spending cuts amounting to $200 billion a year; more savings from Medicare; cuts in "entitlements" such as farm subsidies, federal and military pensions, and student loan subsidies. As a down payment on the long-term, confidence-building deficit reduction measures that Congress would surely have to make, the co-chairs also proposed a package of cuts in Social Security spending. All told, the co-chairs claimed they had found a way to reduce deficits to "sustainable levels" by 2015 and to balance the budget by 2037, while reducing both spending and revenues to 21% of GDP.

"We have harpooned every whale in the ocean—and some minnows," Simpson chuckled with satisfaction, adding that he expected he and Bowles would "be on the witness protection list when this is over."

Other commission members—especially the progressive Democrats—felt blindsided. "It was, like, 'Here it is, take or leave it,'" says Schakowsky, whose understanding had been that "there would be a meeting of the commission, a plan would be presented and we would have a conversation about it. But toward the end they just decided to call the press and announce it."[7]

The Bowles-Simpson blueprint wasn't just a deficit reduction proposal. In reality, it was an ambitious plan to reset the direction of the country's economic growth and development for at least the next generation. The real centerpiece was the tax overhaul, which was actually split into three separate options. The basic design of all three was the same, and quite similar to the 1986 tax reform law: lower marginal income tax rates, in exchange for elimination of all or most "tax expenditures" or deductions.

These would include everything from the Earned Income Tax Credit and the child tax credit—vital supports for low- and moderate-income households—to 401(k)s, IRAs, and the mortgage interest deduction. In addition, capital gains would be taxed at the income-tax rate, meaning that the more income one derived from capital gains, the more taxes one would pay. That was the most—and almost the only—progressive part of the plan. Corporate taxes would get the same treatment: lower rates overall, in exchange for elimination of a host of special incentives and deductions.

The purpose, Bowles would say over and over in coming months, was not just to reduce the deficit but "to make America the best place to start and grow a business and create jobs."

The Bowles-Simpson proposals for "reforming Social Security" were familiar, merely combining the standard prescriptions that deficit hawks had been offering for the past five years. The retirement age would be indexed to increases in longevity, which Bowles-Simpson projected would raise it to sixty-nine by 2075 and perhaps higher thereafter. Brookings budget expert Henry Aaron calculated this would produce a 6.7% across-the-board benefits cut for every additional year before retirement, for a total 13.3% cut.[8] That was on top of the 13% cut that everyone born after 1960 would suffer due to raising of the full retirement age from sixty-five to sixty-seven legislated in the 1983 Amendments.[9]

That was on average. In fact, raising the retirement age would hurt lower income workers much more than those at the higher end. Since the mid-1970s, despite the common assumption that life expectancy was rising for all Americans, it had increased by only one year for lower-income men aged sixty-five, versus five years for upper-income males. The same pattern held for women, with those at the lower end of the income scale actually suffering a decline in life expectancy. Result: workers with lower incomes and lower life expectancy at retirement would see lower benefits than their better-compensated counterparts, because they would have fewer years to collect them. In effect, more of their payroll taxes would go to subsidize retirement for people who lived longer—usually, the more affluent.[10]

Also under Bowles-Simpson, COLAs would immediately be reduced by replacing the current CPI formula with a stingier one, the "chained CPI." That meant the cuts wouldn't only affect future retirees. The elderly would find their benefits decreasing perceptibly within a few years—going against a pledge that many Social Security critics had been repeating for years, to hold seniors "harmless."

Bowles-Simpson would apply a means test to benefits for most workers, resulting in lower benefits for all but those with very low incomes starting in 2050. Benefits for the poorest 20% of retirees would be improved with the creation of a new special minimum benefit, indexed to the more generous CPI. But for many of the rest, the changes could be devastating.

Under current projections, the cap on income subject to payroll tax was expected to fall from 86% to 82.5% over the next decade. In a nod to progressives on the commission, Bowles-Simpson would restore the cap to its original 90% coverage. But it would not go back up until 2050. They also proposed including all new state and local government workers in Social Security starting in 2020.

Altogether, most analysts found that spending cuts would make up 70% of the deficit cutting in Bowles-Simpson, and tax increases only 30%—in part because the lower marginal rates mostly canceled out the elimination of deductions and other tax breaks. For the Social Security segment of the proposal, the ratio was about the same. Raising the cap would account for 35% of the cost reductions, the co-chairs calculated; the rest would be from benefit cuts.

Politically, this was designed to win Republican votes on the commission. "But relying on spending cuts," while at the same time holding revenues to 21% of GDP, would mean setting "targets for overall spending and taxation so low that it will be impossible to sustain even basic promises to provide pension and health benefits to the elderly, disabled, and poor," Aaron found in his analysis of the plan.

Making matters worse, Bowles-Simpson proposed to start cutting spending in fiscal-year 2012, which would begin in October 2011—barely eleven months away. How would an economy still riddled with high unemployment, sluggish tax revenues, and overburdened social services, sustain the blow? At the same time, except for a few relatively modest changes, Bowles and Simpson left health care alone. But they called upon Congress to "set [a] global target for total federal health expenditures after 2020 (Medicare, Medicaid, CHIP, exchange subsidies, employer health exclusion), and review costs every 2 years. Keep growth to GDP+1%."

This, and the overall 21%-of-GDP goal for spending and revenues, amounted to an enormous magic asterisk—a mandate that Congress would be unable to stick to in coming decades without eviscerating public services.

Despite repeated urging from Schakowsky and other progressives on the commission, the co-chairs' proposal said nothing about its impact on the people who would be most affected by all this. Would it lower consumer spending? Would it overburden families? Would it lead more people without means to turn to crime or drop out of the above-ground economy?

The co-chairs' few efforts to acknowledge the potential ill effects of their plan seemed like afterthoughts. What about Social Security for people who spent their careers in physically demanding jobs and couldn't keep working until age sixty-nine? Bowles-Simpson would "direct SSA to design a way to provide for the early retirement needs of workers in physical labor jobs," and to "have accommodation in place before longevity indexation begins and set aside funds to pay for new policy."

This was bound to be an enormously complex task, requiring the agency to write a multitude of new rules and procedures to determine if an individual qualified for this special treatment. The SSA was already struggling with a backlog of eligibility cases for disability benefits that extended for years—and the incoming Congress was likely to cut its budget substantially. Social Security employees had coped with many, often unreasonable demands from presidents and Congress over the past three decades,[11] but Bowles and Simpson were expecting a lot from their "can do" spirit.

As Obama's fiscal commission continues to meet in Washington, people rally outside San Francisco's Commonwealth Club, where Pete Peterson and the Concord Coalition were presenting the case for major cuts to Social Security and Medicare, September 23, 2010.

Finally, what about the co-chairs' pledge not to use Social Security as a tool to reduce the overall deficit? In a table summarizing their deficit-reduction figures through 2020, Bowles and Simpson included the following footnote: "Projections based off of constructed plausible baseline (see last slide). *Including off-budget savings from Social Security*, the plan would reduce deficits to 2.0% of GDP in 2015 and 1.4% of GDP in 2020."[12]

The net effect of Bowles-Simpson on Social Security would certainly be to "mess with" it, as Bowles had once promised, and more specifically to shrink it—ultimately, into insignificance. Along the way, Social Security would take on more of the contours of a welfare program, rendering it more vulnerable to further cuts.

The reaction from Democrats of the more progressive persuasion was predictable. Pelosi called Bowles-Simpson "simply unacceptable."[13] Schakowsky responded, "I think every member of the commission would agree that this is not the plan."[14] When it came to specifics, the public seemed to agree. In a *Wall Street Journal*/NBC News poll, 57% of respondents said they weren't comfortable with the higher retirement age for Social Security and 70% said they weren't comfortable with cutting the program to cut the deficit.

Los Angeles Times columnist Michael Hiltzik, who had been writing about Social Security for years, flagged the use of the chained CPI in Bowles-Simpson. The chained CPI was supposedly a more accurate measure of price inflation because it took into account the "substitution effect"—consumers' propensity to substitute chicken for beef, say, when beef prices rose. But Hiltzik pointed out that health care, which is the biggest cost for seniors, didn't provide many opportunities for substitution, making the chained CPI an inappropriate measure for them. "It looks like a back-door benefit cut," Hiltzik concluded.

The mere fact that the chained CPI had come to be so popular in center-right circles—described, always, as a "technical correction" rather than a benefit-cutting device—suggested something more disturbing about how the Washington political elite viewed the future of America and its economy. "It's a death spiral," Richard (RJ) Eskow, a consultant with the Campaign for America's Future, wrote some months later.

> Soon we'll be calculating the cost of *survival*, not the cost of *living*. It's a process that leads nowhere but down, until even survival is factored out of the equation.… What are we saying about ourselves if we calculate our cost of living by subtracting out all the things we can no longer afford? The chained CPI is institutionalized pessimism. It's a way to prefabricate our own shrinking future, to accelerate an ever-diminishing way of life while hiding the truth from ourselves.[15]

Bowles-Simpson's proposals to make the tax system simpler and fairer by lowering rates and eliminating tax breaks and loopholes, sounded to some like an attempt to revive another failed strategy. Robert Borosage, also of the Campaign for America's Future, noted this had been tried before—in the Tax Reform Act of 1986. Lobbyists and tax lawyers responded by pushing through another slew of loopholes over the succeeding decades, or else scrounging them up out of a fresh look at the tax code, while standard rates stayed low.[16] The same thing was bound to happen again.

The co-chairs expressed little more than annoyance at such criticisms, because progressive Democrats weren't the crowd they were playing to. With their audience of choice, their proposal was a big hit. "It is truly a remarkable plan," Maya MacGuineas, president of the Committee for a Responsible Federal Budget, enthused. "This plan does it all—allows time for the economy to strengthen, brings down future deficits and debt, protects the most disadvantaged, makes government more effective and efficient, and promotes economic growth and competitiveness."

MacGuineas represented the center-right, deficit-hawk viewpoint. Even more important to Bowles and Simpson was to win over the hard right. They seemed to have made progress. Some Republicans complained that the 21%-of-GDP barrier for federal revenue was too high. One leading ideologue, Grover Norquist, president of Americans for Tax Reform, outright rejected Bowles-Simpson. The co-chairs "propose 'giving our children a better life' by spending, taxing more," he said, and urged conservatives in Congress to renew their vows never to raise taxes.[17]

But conservative members of Congress, including some on the commission itself, were more enthusiastic. Judd Gregg praised it as "an aggressive and comprehensive plan." Paul Ryan called it "a serious and impressive effort.... It's a good start."[18] Asked whether fourteen commission members might reach agreement given Bowles-Simpson to work with, Tom Coburn, perhaps the most conservative member—and one of the most conservative lawmakers in Congress—said "I think it's possible."[19]

Hanging over the capital as it digested Bowles-Simpson, however, was the question of what the president would do. Deficit hawks like Jon Cowan at Third Way urged him to embrace the ideas Bowles and Simpson had laid out, even before the commission had voted and even if it meant picking a fight with progressive Democrats—or perhaps because of that. "If you're looking at reelection, your No. 1 imperative has got to be winning back the center of the electorate," Cowan said.[20]

Obama wasn't there, at least not yet. "The President will wait until the bipartisan fiscal commission finishes its work before commenting," the White House said in a statement. But at a press conference soon after, Obama also resisted entreaties from the liberal side to condemn the proposal.

Coverage in the mainstream press of Bowles-Simpson was mostly complimentary, praising the co-chairs for tackling a difficult issue, yet seldom exploring their proposal in detail. With the exception of only a few left-of-center columnists like Paul Krugman, none of the major media outlets tried to analyze who would be hit hardest by the spending cuts, now or in the future. Instead, they seemed satisfied with Bowles's and Simpson's assurances that "everyone's ox gets gored."[21]

"Words found nowhere in the deficit commission's draft include 'fairness,' 'the wealthiest,' and 'the top 1%,'" noted *Wall Street Journal* columnist Daniel Henninger. "Even in our current political universe of smirking cynics, this is progress."

* * *

Bowles and Simpson never developed the same companionable relationship with progressives on their commission that they did with right-wing members like Coburn. From the first meeting, Schakowsky complained, the co-chairs had made it clear they were going to focus on Social Security, even though restructuring the program wasn't something the commission had an explicit mandate to do. Neither did she ever have "any clarity on process."[22] The co-chairs' proposal evidently arose out of closed-door meetings and staff work from which members who didn't come from the hard right or center-right were excluded.

Progressives, in general, felt that they had been waiting for months for a process in which they had little or no voice to play out, but that meanwhile exposed them to repeated attacks in the mainstream Washington media as "denialists" and peevish "do-nothings."

In fact, progressives generally acknowledged that if nothing was done and current projections proved accurate, the trust funds would be exhausted and Social Security would only be able to pay about 79% of benefits after 2037—although payroll tax receipts would be sufficient to keep benefits at that level for many decades to come.[23] Progressives also had plenty of ideas for improving that outcome. Above all, they argued that the commission's attention was misdirected. If the commission—or Congress—wanted to "save" Social Security, it should be looking to strategies to raise American workers' wages, not cut benefits.

A study by the Economic Policy Institute found that if wage growth had kept up with productivity growth plus inflation between 1983 and 2007, as Congress had expected when it passed the 1983 Amendments, 8% of the currently projected Social Security shortfall would be eliminated. If wage growth kept up over the next quarter-century, another 43% of the gap would be erased, for a total of 51%. Income inequality was also a problem, the EPI found, because, thanks to the cap on income subject to payroll tax, the share that was untouched had grown from 10% to 16% from 1983 to 2008 and would account for 47% of Social Security's projected long-term deficit.

That didn't mean giving workers a raise and narrowing the income gap would bring the program's books into balance all by themselves. Since taxable earnings are indexed to average wages, it's difficult to tell what part of the Social Security shortfall is related to one rather than the other. "It is safe to say, however, that the two trends together account for the bulk of the projected shortfall," the EPI concluded.[24]

The answer, progressives argued, was more economic stimulus—and not just temporary, make-work projects, but ones that would provide good-paying jobs for long periods, such as rebuilding the nation's infrastructure. Some also called for revisiting the trade treaties that had forced American workers to compete with those in low-wage countries, or for measures that would directly boost income for workers and retirees. Galbraith called for lowering, not raising, the retirement age for full Social Security benefits—"say, to 62 for the next three years." Many if not most of the good jobs that were wiped out by the economic crash would never return, he noted. By eliminating the early retirement penalty, Congress could remove from the jobs market some of the people least likely to be rehired, giving a break to younger workers and assuring more people an easier transition to retirement.[25]

Perhaps engineering wage growth was a bit outside the commission's mandate. If so, it could consider the oldest and most reliable way to improve Social Security's fiscal position: raise payroll taxes. Every time the program's finances had threatened to go out of whack in the past, up through and including the 1983 Amendments, this was what Congress had done. Since then, a payroll tax hike had become politically impossible in Washington—supposedly, because taxpayers wouldn't tolerate the strain on their paychecks. But in poll after poll, the public indicated it was willing to pay more to preserve benefits.

Some pro-Social Security scholars and researchers had shown that, even without a major boost in wages to cushion the effect, Congress could raise payroll taxes without causing working people any pain. Larry Thompson, former principal deputy commissioner of Social Security, demonstrated this in a 2005 research paper.

Using estimates made by the Urban Institute,[26] Thompson found that even with a 6.5-percentage-point hike in payroll taxes for employers and employees—the amount needed to close the projected funding gap for both Social Security and Medicare by 2035—workers would still see their average income after spending rise by 21%. Why? One major factor would be Social Security benefits, the annuity value of which Thompson projected would go up by 18%. In other words, even in the low-wage-growth environment that most experts projected over the next few decades, the average income would grow fast enough—thanks in large part to Social Security—that payroll taxes could be raised without putting unreasonable pressure on future workers' pocketbooks.

A few people were willing to talk about how to implement a payroll tax hike—although they tended to be a long way from the Washington political hothouse. Two amateur researchers, Dale Coberly, a retired Oregon construction surveyor, and Bruce Webb, a Seattle-based property development specialist for private real estate developers, began tinkering with the numbers a couple of years prior to the appointment of Obama's deficit commission. They developed what they called the "Northwest Plan" to supply "a permanent fix for Social Security that requires no change in retirement age or scheduled benefit."

Coberly and Webb noted that the Social Security trustees measured the health of the OASI and DI trust funds in two ways: Short Term Actuarial Balance, extending through the next ten years; and Long Term Actuarial Balance, extending over seventy-five. The two researchers proposed to start phasing in tax increases for each of the trust funds as soon as it failed the short-term benchmark. For instance, in 2009 the DI trust funds, which had been hit hard by the increase in disability benefit claims that accompanied the recession, was already out of short-term balance. So Coberly and Webb would start raising the portion of payroll tax that went to DI by .20%—split by employer and employee—in 2010, .10% in 2011, and then another .10% in 2039. That would work out to an extra $1 per worker household per week in the first year, and less thereafter. OASI was still in short-term balance, but to keep it there for the long term would require a .20% boost for ten years starting in 2026, with further increases only every four to ten years starting in 2036.

Coberly and Webb proposed making their payroll tax hikes subject to change every year, depending on the latest calculations from Social Security's actuaries. "The Northwest Plan is designed to be a flexible planning tool that can respond to new data in real time," they wrote. "Or we could lock ourselves into policy based on assumptions about economic performance after the dawn of the 22nd century and on to the Infinite Future. A better choice for those people would be to relax and watch *Star Trek*."[27]

The CBO, in an analysis it prepared for the deficit commission, created two scenarios that would close the projected Social Security and Medicare funding gap entirely through payroll tax increases. One, which would increase the combined payroll tax rate by 3-percentage-points over sixty years, was similar in some respects to the Northwest Plan. The question remained: was it fair to balance the books entirely through payroll tax hikes, even if it could be done without pain?

If the deficit commission just couldn't bring itself to answer yes, progressives had other ideas to offer. Bob Ball had been busy until the end turning out variations on the menu of adjustments he had been proposing ever since the 1994–96 Social Security Advisory Council. His latest package, embodied in an article he drafted a month before his death in January 2008, included four principal elements:

- Raise the cap on income subject to Social Security payroll tax back to 90% of earnings—the figure had fallen to 83% due to a glitch in the adjustment formula;

- Shift revenues from the estate tax to Social Security, giving the program an additional source of revenue besides payrolls;

- Gradually invest up to 20% of the trust fund assets in publicly traded stocks; and

- Extend Social Security coverage to all newly hired state and local government employees.

All told, the program's oldest and smartest defender calculated, these changes would eliminate the trust funds' seventy-five-year deficit and replace it with a 0.1% surplus. Ball had an idea what to do as well if a deficit reappeared beyond the seventy-five-year horizon. He recommended setting a "contingency contribution-rate increase"—a deferred payroll tax raise that would only kick in if it was needed.

Henry Aaron, the Brookings Institution's longtime resident Social Security and Medicare expert, thought the government couldn't avoid some measures to induce older workers to keep working longer. But he opposed raising the normal retirement age—only the early retirement age of sixty-two. Instead, he suggested paying a direct subsidy to employers to cover the cost of health insurance for older workers. He also advocated steepening the increase in Social Security benefits that workers would enjoy if they waited longer to begin collecting. Raising the wage base, as Ball suggested, would keep this change from hurting lower-wage workers.[28]

Other ideas focused on the revenue side. By the time Bowles and Simpson unveiled their proposal, Dean Baker had been calling for at least two years for Congress to enact a financial transactions tax that would discourage pure speculation of the kind that fueled the housing market bubble. This wasn't a marginal or purely left-wing idea—even the International Monetary Fund was pushing for much heavier taxation of the financial sector. Based on the experience of the U.K., which had levied such a tax for decades, Baker calculated a 0.5% tax on stock trades could easily raise $150 billion a year.[29] This could be applied either to deficit reduction or to directly supplement payroll tax revenue to help Social Security.

Progressives disagreed among themselves about some of these options. Coberly and Webb, for instance, felt it would be dangerous for Social Security to rely on funding other than from payroll taxes, despite the fact that it wasn't a progressive tax, because this would erode the system's independence. Others, such as Galbraith, argued that the program's dependence on payroll taxes had become a straitjacket and a source of "scare numbers" that its enemies could use to make a case that it had become unaffordable.

Which is only to say that by the time Bowles and Simpson released their blueprint, progressives had a broad portfolio of alternatives to offer. The difference was that they proposed to address future problems with Social Security carefully and incrementally. By comparison, the co-chairs' favorite solutions—higher retirement age, chained CPI, means testing—amounted to a sledgehammer approach that would cut benefits almost immediately, and reduce the program to insignificance over time.

A couple of days after Bowles and Simpson unveiled their blueprint, Schakowsky called her staff and had them pull together a full-dress counterproposal.

"There were a number of studies already done, for instance by Economic Policy Institute and Demos and by Barney Frank, so I thought we had all the data we needed. My staff worked literally night and day over the weekend so we were ready with an alternative by the next Tuesday."[30]

Schakowsky introduced her plan at a "modestly attended" press conference. The mainstream Washington press barely noted the event, in contrast to the media frenzy that greeted Bowles and Simpson, although coverage picked up in the following days and weeks. Schakowsky said it would reduce the deficit over the next five years, the primary requirement Obama had set in his executive order, by $441 billion—far beyond the $250 billion target the president had set, while still finding room for $200 billion of extra economic stimulus. Like Bowles-Simpson, it included both spending cuts and tax increases. But unlike the co-chairs' plan, it relied mostly on tax hikes, not spending cuts.

Some of the savings would come from health care, by allowing the government to use its bargaining power to negotiate better drug prices—something ObamaCare didn't do. It would also create a public option, which Schakowsky calculated would force private providers to lower their prices. But most of the cuts—amounting to $110.7 billion—would come from slashing military spending, including canceling unneeded weapons systems.

Schakowsky's version of tax reform differed starkly from Bowles and Simpson's. She would let the Bush tax cuts expire for the richest households, tax capital gains as ordinary income, restore the estate tax to its 2009 level, and install a cap-and-trade regime for polluters. She also proposed to raise taxes on corporations, not lower them, by limiting the deductibility of corporate debt and closing tax subsidies to companies that earn substantial revenues overseas.

As for Social Security, Schakowsky proposed to ensure its "long-term solvency" by not just raising the cap on income subject to payroll tax, but by eliminating the cap completely for employers and raising it back to 90% of income for employees. She also proposed a "modest legacy tax on wealthier Americans."

While few challenged the numbers Schakowsky put together, her plan had no chance of being accepted by the deficit commission—a telling point all by itself. A "staggering wealth transfer to the super-rich" had been the essence of U.S. tax policy for some thirty years, she observed—so much so that "if you propose a plan that actually raised taxes on people who would afford it, it's not viewed as a viable plan."[31]

Bowles-Simpson spurred the release of a series of alternative deficit-reduction plans, of which Schakowsky's was just the first. At the end of the month, a new blueprint called "Investing in America's Future" came out from Our Fiscal Security (OFS), a joint project of Demos, the Economic Policy Institute, and the Century Foundation. It proposed to balance the budget by 2018, again by cutting defense spending and raising taxes on the affluent. Like Schakowsky's, the OFS plan proposed eliminating the cap for employer contributions to Social Security and raising the employee cap back to 90% in the employee side.

To make up any remaining gap, it recommended either contributing some income tax revenues to the trust funds or "modestly increasing the payroll tax."

Another group, the Citizens' Commission on Jobs, Deficits and America's Economic Future, released a set of recommendations a day later, on November 30. Assembled by the Campaign for America's Future, it was made up of leading progressive economists and policy experts including Robert Reich, Jeff Madrick, Dean Baker, Teresa Ghilarducci, and Heidi Hartmann. The Citizens' Commission didn't propose to eliminate the deficit by 2015, but to reduce it from 4% of GDP to 3% through spending cuts and tax revenues, leaving more room for public investment. The payroll tax cap would be completely removed for both employers and employees, eliminating 95% of Social Security's projected long-term deficit. To fill the rest of the gap, the commission recommended adding in revenues from the estate tax and from a financial transactions tax, and "giving the Trust Fund more investment flexibility."

The Washington media and policy community largely chose to ignore the blueprints coming from the progressive side, but they took others coming from the center-right very seriously. Already unveiled by the time Bowles and Simpson went public with their proposal were "Red Ink Rising," a plan created by the Peterson-Pew Commission on Budget Reform; "The Future Is Now," from Maya MacGuineas and Bill Galston of the Committee for a Responsible Federal Budget; and even a proposal from a group of ex-senators sitting as the bizarrely named *Esquire* (magazine) Commission to Balance the Federal Budget.

The Peterson-Pew report actually appeared in December 2009, but was still being widely discussed eleven months later. Its most talked-about feature was a "debt trigger" mechanism that would mandate cuts if the legislative process became stuck. The goal was to put the debt on a declining trajectory as a share of GDP from 2018 on. "Programs that are growing faster than the economy—notably Medicare, Medicaid, Social Security, and certain tax policies"—would be included under the trigger mechanism.

Other than Bowles-Simpson itself, however, no deficit-reduction plan garnered more attention during fall 2010 than the report unveiled on November 17 by the Debt Reduction Task Force of the Bipartisan Policy Centrist, a center-right think tank founded by a group of former senators. The authors were Pete Domenici and, still serving on the Bowles-Simpson panel, the ubiquitous Alice Rivlin. Titled "Restoring America's Future," this one proposed far more deficit cutting than even Bowles-Simpson: $5.9 trillion over eight years. It was somewhat more evenly balanced between tax increases and spending cuts, and didn't include the 21%-of-GDP required limit for federal revenues and spending.

But the changes Rivlin and Domenici proposed for Social Security were largely the same ones Bowles and Simpson recommended: means-testing benefits; indexing the retirement age to life expectancy; reducing the COLA; increasing the minimum benefit for long-term, low-wage workers and "the most vulnerable elderly"; and adding all new state and local government employees to the program. Like Bowles-Simpson, Rivlin-Domenici also proposed to raise the payroll tax cap to 90% of wages by 2050.

Rivlin-Domenici encouraged deficit hawks to believe that a "surprisingly broad consensus is forming" around the actions needed to tame the deficit, according to a *Washington Post* report. That, and the fact that Tom Coburn was keeping an open mind about Bowles-Simpson on the deficit commission, kept Washington buzzing with talk of a grand bargain in the weeks after the co-chairs' proposal was unveiled.

This was deceptive. Many of the parties involved overlapped from one center-right deficit-reduction project to another. Rivlin seemed to be everywhere, for instance. And Barry Anderson, a former OMB official who served on the Pew-Peterson commission was also the numbers-cruncher for the *Esquire* senators. None of the panels, or Bowles and Simpson, considered much of anything beyond a narrow band of ideas, especially concerning Social Security, making it clear that they had shut progressive Democrats—the "hard left," as Bowles called them—out of the conversation.

As the date neared for the deficit commission to take a final vote, however, it was becoming clear that the co-chairs wouldn't snag fourteen votes for their proposal. Accordingly, Bowles and Simpson and their supporters inside and outside of the commission worked to change the definition of victory. If their plan got a bare majority of commission members to support it, they said, with good representation from both parties, that could be enough to force Congress to act.

Looking ahead a few months, David Walker suggested that Obama could "lead by incorporating some of these ideas in his budget."[32] A reply came from the Strengthen Social Security Campaign, a new progressive coalition that was pounding home, as best it could, the message that Social Security hadn't caused the rising deficit numbers and shouldn't be drafted to provide a solution. Now, Nancy Altman, a co-director of the group, issued a direct threat: "If Washington politicians choose to cut Social Security benefits against the will of the overwhelming majority of Americans the 2010 midterm will seem like a walk in the park for incumbents compared to what will await them in 2012."

To which the deficit hawks had a quick answer. Introducing the panel of ex-senators who would be putting together the magazine's austerity proposal, the editors of *Esquire* in July suggested to Americans who didn't want to take up the cause of deficit reduction, "Just ask Greece if deficits don't matter. Just ask our Chinese bankers."

One of the ideological drivers of the Social Security privatization movement in the mid-1990s was the seeming success of Chile, Argentina, and other Latin American nations that partially privatized their pension systems. That, and the World Bank's aggressive program to persuade other countries in the region, as well as in formerly Communist Eastern Europe to undertake similar "reforms," helped convince Washington lawmakers and policy entrepreneurs that such a change was inevitable in the U.S. A similar dynamic seemed to be at work following the 2008 recession. Mounting budgetary and debt crises in Europe were propelling center-right and traditionally social-democratic governments to drastically slash public spending, including for pensions.

The most severe debt crisis erupted in Greece in February 2010, almost at the same time Obama's deficit commission was announced. The U.K., which was in far more robust fiscal condition, elected a new coalition government in May, led by the Conservatives, that promised a new "age of austerity." That same month, Spain announced severe budget cuts, including a freeze on public-sector pensions, and the French government announced a plan to raise the retirement age. The French plan ignited massive protests, but passed at the end of October. Greece passed a new pension-cutting law in July.

Some observers hastened to point out that Europe's situation was quite different from America's. Hard-hit peripheral countries like Greece, Spain, Portugal, and Ireland lacked an essential tool to deal with a deep recession: their own currency. Since they were all part of the Euro zone, they were at the mercy of the European Central Bank, which was reluctant to devalue the E.U. currency. On top of that, governments across the continent, fearing banks would dump their bonds, couldn't bring themselves to take the other obvious course: a partial default that would force the banks to take a loss on those bonds. And the U.S. debt burden, while larger than at any time since World War II—the country was undergoing its worst recession since the war, after all—was still not overburdening the taxpayer, thanks to the comparatively low interest rates borrowers were demanding from the Treasury.

None of which seemed to matter to a wide range of elite opinion in the U.S. In May, Moody's issued a report concluding that the U.S. had moved "substantially" closer to losing its ultra-safe bond rating. In October, the other major ratings agency, Standard & Poor's, warned that retirement expenditures in most industrialized countries were "on an explosive path," and that, while pension costs in the U.S. were lower than in some other places, it too faced a budgetary crisis if it didn't take action.

Accordingly, Princeton economist Alan Blinder announced the return of the "bond market vigilantes," the bankers who in the early 1990s supposedly forced the Clinton administration to shift from a policy of economic stimulus to one of austerity before it had been even six months in office. The vigilantes were already roaming Europe, Blinder wrote in the *Wall Street Journal* in May, and would soon cross the Atlantic if America couldn't convince them that it had "got religion on fiscal responsibility." The best way to placate the mob, Blinder recommended, was for Washington to take on Social Security—once the third rail of American politics, but "now the low-hanging fruit of deficit reduction."

Less orthodox economists warned that there wasn't much evidence to support the notion that either short-term budget cutting or long-term program reductions would change investors' minds. Investors were still flocking to U.S. Treasury bonds as the ultimate safe asset. But that wasn't the point, said economists like Blinder. The U.S. had a window of opportunity to avoid becoming the next Greece. Cutting Social Security, whose spending gap over the next seventy-five years was expected to represent only .7% of GDP,[33] wasn't the key to restoring fiscal virtue, or even the most serious problem. That was the exploding cost of health care. But restructuring Social Security was a necessary sign of good faith, a down payment on the other painful choices still to be made.

Such thoughts no doubt buoyed Bowles and Simpson as they struggled to find something approaching fourteen votes for their fiscal plan. At the end of November, they introduced a revised version that included more and deeper cuts in discretionary spending, a faster timeline for revenues to drop to 21% of GDP, and cuts in the Tricare health plan for military personnel and their families. The new version would also scrap one of ObamaCare's most important features: its long-term care insurance plan.

For friends of Social Security, the co-chairs offered some reassurances. They fleshed out their promise to help workers in physically demanding jobs, saying they would direct the SSA to develop a "hardship exemption" for the 20% or so who fell into that category. They would send any savings from phasing out the income tax exclusion for employer-provided health care to the Social Security trust funds. And, in answer to criticisms that their spending cuts didn't take the still-wobbly economy into account, they offered a payroll tax holiday for 2011—an idea borrowed from the Rivlin-Domenici proposal.

The document still contained no analysis of its impact on workers or on current and future retirees, and therefore offered an incomplete picture of what the commissioners would be voting for. Mainstream press coverage almost never mentioned this fact, however.

The revised version of what was now called "The Moment of Truth: Report of the National Commission on Fiscal Responsibility and Reform" was unveiled on December 1, the same day the president had mandated that they submit their report. The timetable was quite sensitive. If they couldn't find fourteen votes by December 1, the House and Senate leaders would no longer be bound by their commitment to put the panel's plan to a vote, and it probably wouldn't play a part in the tax negotiations between the White House and Congress, which would be concluded during the lame-duck session.

On Tuesday, November 31, however, Bowles and Simpson had already announced they would put off the final vote on their proposal until Friday the 3rd, to give the other members more time to study the plan—a decision the president reportedly approved of.[34] The co-chairs were still looking to secure conservative Republican votes, and in this, the generally more drastic nature of their final blueprint helped. The day after they unveiled the revision, Tom Coburn and Mike Crapo, possibly the two most conservative members of the commission, announced their support. Despite some increases in tax revenue, Coburn declared "The Moment of Truth" was consistent with the "Pledge for America," a tax-slashing plan the Club for Growth had created. "This tax plan," he said enthusiastically at a press conference, "is Reagan on steroids."[35]

No formal vote took place at the commission's last meeting on the 3rd. By this time, however, it was known that eleven members would have voted for the final report against seven opposed. Supporters virtually ignored the fact that it had missed its deadline and failed to garner fourteen votes, insisting that the important thing was that a majority of the commission had endorsed the plan, including three Republican and three Democratic lawmakers. At the Committee for a Responsible Budget, MacGuineas called the commission members "real fiscal heroes" and praised "The Moment of Truth" as "a truly historic accomplishment." The *Washington Post* described a "groundswell of support" and a "significant victory" for the co-chairs in the face of "strident" calls for "short-term spending to boost the economy," a "powerful signal" to Congress and the White House that they could no longer "ignore" the deficit problem."[36]

The reality was a bit less storybook. At least a couple of the eleven yes votes arrived only late in the game, when it was clear Bowles and Simpson wouldn't get fourteen. Most crucially, Dick Durbin, a close Obama ally and the Senate majority whip, indicated he would vote yes, calling the result "a breakthrough." But Durbin made clear he mainly intended to send a message that the deficit discussion should continue in Congress and that he would vote against the proposal if it actually came up on the Senate floor. Ryan and David Camp voted no, Ryan indicating that for all the verbal support he had offered the co-chairs, he wouldn't be bound to sacrifice tax cuts for long-term fiscal goals come January. Max Baucus, who would continue as Senate Finance Committee chair, also voted no.

Progressives, of course, denounced the "commission plan"—as the media quickly came to refer to "The Moment of Truth," despite the fact that it had failed to gather the fourteen votes by December 1 that would have legitimated the title. "Retirees temporarily dodged a bullet," the Alliance for Retired Americans declared in a press release after the commission's final meeting. Ways and Means Committee chair Sander Levin called the recommendations "imbalanced and unworkable" and a "disproportionate burden" on "seniors and middle- and lower-income families."

Most revealing from the point of view of the program's defenders was language in the final report calling for consideration of private Social Security accounts. These "should encourage Americans to build wealth through savings and investment that will generate a return sufficient to allay fears that retirees will outlive their savings, and should permit Americans to have the option to transmit the remainder of their accumulated savings to their heirs."

This fit in perfectly with the approach that deficit hawks had been recommending ever since the Bush privatization debacle in 2005: cut benefits, and create supplemental private accounts to help workers make up the difference. The intention clearly wasn't to "preserve" Social Security, as Bowles and Simpson maintained was their intention, but to gradually wean American workers away from the program as benefits dwindled into insignificance.

The president, however, disappointed Bowles and Simpson's supporters by not embracing the co-chairs' plan. "The commission's majority report," he said in a press release, "includes a number of specific proposals that I—along with my economic team—will study closely in the coming weeks as we develop our budget and our priorities for the coming year."

Obama appears to have consistently pursued two objectives ever since he announced the commission in February: first, to reassure a Washington elite that had whipped itself into a near-panic about the deficit and the national debt that he too was serious about these issues; and second, not to commit himself to any action that might enrage progressives—or, as the *Washington Post* characterized them, "interest groups that have already vowed to bury the plan in Congress if it begins to gain traction." A third objective may have been to maintain amity amongst his own advisors. Geithner, Sperling, and Sperling's deputy, Jason Furman—the Rubinites on his team—were known to favor action on the deficit, including some cuts in Social Security benefits. Obama's political advisors, especially his former campaign manager, David Axelrod, were opposed.[37]

But even though the deficit commission failed to force action in Congress, it achieved the important incremental step of bringing the Republican right and the Democratic deficit hawks closer to a working alliance and moving the "reasonable" middle ground in the deficit debate further rightward. The co-chairs' final report laid out a menu of spending cuts, program reductions, and tax system rejiggerings that could form the basis for the fiscal Grand Bargain that Judd Gregg, Kent Conrad, and Henry Paulson had first discussed four years earlier. The next year in Washington would be consumed with efforts to achieve this.

CHAPTER 47

THE RETURN TO AUSTERITY

"The way to do it is similar to the way Ronald Reagan and Tip O'Neill fixed Social Security back in 1983. They said, Okay, we'll make some modest adjustments that are phased in over a very long period of time. Most folks don't notice 'em."
    —Barack Obama[1]

GWEN IFFIL: Why is there so much focus on reducing entitlement programs as opposed to the military or other forms of spending?

BILL CLINTON: For the same reason Willie Sutton robbed banks. That's where the money is.[2]

The Republican Congress, now preparing to take its seats, assumed it was elected to cut spending, eliminate Washington "waste," and repeal or at least defund ObamaCare. And that's what its leaders set out to do. Helping or hindering them, depending on one's perspective, was a calendar of fiscal deadlines, all falling within nine months after the November election that brought them to power.

First, there was the statutory expiration of the Bush tax cuts at the end of the year—before the new Congress even took over. In mid-December, the White House and the Republican leadership agreed on a nearly $900 billion tax and spending package—larger than the stimulus bill Obama signed at the beginning of his presidency—that included extension of the tax cuts for two more years along with protection for people whose unemployment benefits were expiring.

Next came a series of stopgap spending measures to fund the federal government through the end of the current fiscal year. Because the Democrats hadn't passed a budget resolution in 2010, Congress was making do by approving a series of continuing resolutions—the alternative being a government shutdown of the sort that had occurred fifteen years earlier, when the Clinton administration refused to go along with the Gingrich Congress's Medicare cuts. The last continuing resolution before the new Congress took charge was passed on December 21 and extended funding through March 4. Since spending measures have to originate in the House, in January the Republicans assumed control of that process. Two more resolutions extended the deadline to March 18, and then, after agonizing negotiations, until April 8.

On that day, after an even more painful ordeal, Boehner, Reid, and Vice President Joe Biden concluded a spending deal for the rest of the fiscal year that brought the cuts to a total of $38 billion—reductions the Democrats hadn't dreamed at the beginning of the year that they would find themselves agreeing to. At about the same time, the House Republicans were due to release their budget blueprint for fiscal 2012. But Congress faced an additional deadline: to raise the federal debt limit. Lawmakers would have to do so by July at the latest or figure out some other way to fund the government's day-to-day activities.

How would the Bowles-Simpson fiscal blueprint—and especially, its Social Security proposals—fit into all this? Initially, it seemed, not very well. Soon after the commission's final vote, Bowles and Simpson, supported by Conrad, called for the White House to convene a bipartisan summit that would agree on "a serious fiscal responsibility plan to strengthen our economy for the long term." They were politely turned down.

The deal to extend the Bush tax cuts, announced less than a week after the deficit commission's final meeting, didn't move the deficit hawks any closer to their goals, although the White House argued that the medium- to long-term deficit outlook wouldn't be any worse. Negotiated behind the scenes principally by Biden and McConnell, the agreement also revived the estate tax for two years, but at a lower rate than it would have hit if current law had remained in force. In exchange, the administration won extension of unemployment insurance for thirteen more months, a two-year extension of the child tax credit, and the customary "patch" on the Alternative Minimum Tax to keep it at or near current levels for all taxpayers it affected.

Obama touted the deal as not just a compromise but a victory for the middle class, "an essential step on the road to recovery." On the surface, this made no sense. Over half the dollar value of the deal consisted of the Bush tax-cut extension, and at least one dollar in every four would go to the wealthiest 1% of taxpayers.[3] The president's aides responded that, while he had killed the Making Work Pay tax credit, which had been a major item in his 2008 campaign platform, the Republicans had agreed to a one-year payroll tax "holiday" that the administration calculated would inject $120 billion into the economy.

The payroll tax holiday was an idea that had been kicking around Washington for some time. Within the Obama administration, Sperling had been pushing it for at least a year, and he had latched on to the tax-cut negotiations as an opportunity to revive it.[4] Al Gore supported it. So did some leading progressives, including, most prominently, economist James Galbraith, who worried that Social Security's "political credibility" had become too closely tied to economically dubious arguments about the trust funds' "actuarial balance." That helped give the holiday genuine bipartisan appeal.

Indeed, Congress had already tinkered with the payroll tax the previous June, when it passed the Hiring Incentives to Restore Employment Act. The HIRE Act offered employers a credit on their entire payroll tax contribution for the balance of 2010 when they hired workers who had been unemployed for at least sixty days prior to their hire or had worked less than forty hours for another firm during the previous sixty days.

The measure that Biden and McConnell shook hands on would extend the idea to employees, but in a less generous form. The worker's payroll tax contribution for the coming year would be cut 2%, to 4.2% of wages. The Treasury would make transfers to the OASI and DI trust funds to staunch the loss of revenues to Social Security, and earnings would be credited to workers' records. So SSA Chief Actuary Steve Goss calculated that the effect on the OASI and DI trust funds would be "negligible," while workers' future benefits would be "unaffected."[5]

Still, the payroll tax holiday was unprecedented, and the biggest change in practice for Social Security since the 1983 Amendments, even if it was temporary. Friends of Social Security, who claimed they had no advance warning that the payroll tax holiday would be part of the tax-cut deal,[6] found it both unconvincing as stimulus and a very bad omen for the program itself. The Making Work Pay tax credit, which was being sacrificed in favor of the temporary payroll tax cut, was closely targeted at low- to middle-income households, and was more generous to the former than the latter. The tax credit would be much more generous to relatively high earners, putting an extra $1,397 in the pockets of individuals earning $70,000, for example, versus only $400 under Making Work Pay. Someone earning $106,000 would receive no tax credit under Making Work Pay, but with the payroll tax holiday, would pocket more than $2,100 extra. In other words, households less likely to spend the money right away would receive more money through the payroll tax holiday.[7]

Within days of the deal's announcement, in fact, financial advisors were counseling their clients to save the extra money rather than spend it. "Think before you spend," wrote *New York Times* household budget columnist Ron Lieber—appropriately, on Christmas Day. "This is too much of a potential win for you to be anything but deliberate in your effort to put every dollar to good use." Sound advice, certainly, but not the sort of wisdom likely to precipitate another $120 billion into the consumer economy.

What really bothered many of Social Security's defenders, however, was the precedent the tax holiday could set. "This 2% payroll tax cut is the beginning of the end of Social Security as we know it," warned Barbara Kennelly, president and CEO of the National Committee to Preserve Social Security and Medicare. By substituting Treasury contributions for workers' contributions, even temporarily, the holiday violated the principle that Social Security should be a self-funding program. The federal government would effectively be borrowing twice to pay the same benefits, with the result that for the first time in its history, the program would technically be adding to the deficit. Besides, said Kennelly, "there's no such thing as a 'temporary' tax cut." When the expiration of the tax holiday loomed less than a year later, Republicans would surely have great fun accusing their opponents of acquiescing in a major "tax hike."

Republicans couldn't have agreed more. "A key to reforming Social Security is making people realize it's an unsustainable entitlement program rather than the pay-as-you-go Old-Age and Survivors Insurance it was intended to be," wrote columnist Kyle Wingfield in the *Atlanta Journal-Constitution*. "As crazy as it may sound, reducing the tax without enforcing a corresponding drop in benefits might help do that."

When ABC News/*Washington Post* pollsters tried to dissect public response to elements of the tax-cut deal, they found that extension of unemployment benefits was overwhelmingly popular—more than half of Republicans supported it, not to mention 88% of Democrats—but that the payroll tax holiday wasn't. Only 18% strongly supported the move, while 39% strongly opposed it and another 18% opposed it "somewhat."

Not surprisingly, then, several Democratic lawmakers launched last-ditch efforts to replace it with either refund checks drawn on general revenues or a temporary extension of Making Work Pay. But no one at the White House would listen.[8] Obama was trying to sell the tax-cut deal as a boon to the middle class. The payroll tax holiday offered him a better mechanism to appeal to this group.

It was clear to everyone, however, that this was just the first act in a tortuous drama that might or might not conclude with a sweeping debt-and-deficit reduction deal, possibly including Social Security. Because it created a potential issue as to what would happen to the payroll tax in a year, the tax-cut deal "puts Social Security squarely in the middle of the debate over Bush tax rates for higher and middle incomes, business expensing tax deductions, and the Alternative Minimum Tax," Rep. Rush Holt, a New Jersey Democrat, warned in an article for HuffingtonPost.com.

* * *

The 1983 Social Security amendments and the 1986 tax reform had both been concluded during periods of divided government. Looked at this way, the next year or so—at least until the 2012 election season got under way—seemed to the deficit hawks a perfect opportunity to achieve their goals. The tax-cut deal, along with "the report issued by the bipartisan deficit-reduction commission"—as he incorrectly described it—was "helping set the table for a fundamental reform of the tax system," declared Gerald Seib of the *Wall Street Journal*.

The center-right faced three problems, however. First, the progressive caucus in Congress, including the Democratic leaders in both houses, opposed any changes to Social Security or Medicare. Bolstering them was the same large activist network that had opposed Bush's privatization offensive in 2005, now shorn of any illusion that it could count on the Obama administration to do the right thing. Second, the Republican House majority and the enlarged Senate Republican minority had slid to the right. Many didn't feel they needed to accept even token tax hikes in exchange for spending cuts. Some were fiercely opposed to such a deal, even if it called itself tax reform and promised lower rates overall.

Third, and most importantly, the deficit hawks would need the support of an embattled president who was worried about reelection. In the weeks leading up to his State of the Union address on January 25 and the unveiling of his fiscal 2012 budget, White House officials actually weighed two changes to Social Security—raising the cap and changing the COLA formula. The first would bring more payroll tax revenue into the program, the second would cut benefits, jointly splitting the difference between progressive and center-right approaches. A third idea, supported by elements on both sides, was to require all new state and local government employees to join Social Security. These proposals would serve as the starting point for a bipartisan "conversation" leading, presumably, to a deal in Congress.

But the administration decided against coming out in support of any Social Security changes. The protests by progressive groups helped change the minds of the president's aides. These groups had provided crucial support during the fight over the new health care law and would again be indispensable if Obama-Care was to be preserved from Republican attacks. They had an important political argument as well. The Democrats had lost the seniors' vote in 2010, in large part because enough elderly voters had believed Republican stories that the health care law would create "death panels" empowered to decide which patients would be kept alive. Obama himself hadn't won seniors in 2008. If he wanted their support in 2012, he couldn't afford to gamble with Social Security. Meanwhile, some Senate Democrats who faced tough reelection campaigns in 2012 feared that anything other than full White House defense of Social Security would create problems for them.

A meeting between Obama and AFL-CIO president Richard Trumka in early January reportedly helped drive the message home.[9]

In his speech on January 25, Obama worked strenuously both to assure the center-right he was serious about fixing the deficit and to calm progressives' fears that he would cut Social Security. He agreed with his deficit commission, that "the only way to tackle our deficit is to cut excessive spending wherever we find it.... To put us on solid ground, we should also find a bipartisan solution to strengthen Social Security for future generations."

However, "we must do it without putting at risk current retirees, the most vulnerable, or people with disabilities; without slashing benefits for future generations; and without subjecting Americans' guaranteed retirement income to the whims of the stock market." Obama also vowed to make sure the portion of the Bush tax cuts that benefited the top 2% of Americans wouldn't be permanently extended.

Progressives were relieved that Obama seemed to be drawing a line against some of the proposals Republicans had been making for Social Security. But some weren't sure how firm that line was. Barry Rand, CEO of AARP, noted in a press release that the president seemed to be framing Social Security as part of the deficit issue—an association progressives preferred not to make. Others noted that the president only said he wouldn't agree to "slash" benefits—suggesting that some benefit reduction might not be off the table. Over the next several weeks, White House officials continued to use words like "slash" when stating the president's position, offering little solid reassurance to progressives.

Bob Bixby of the Concord Coalition pronounced himself disappointed with both parties for not attacking the deficit head on. "Very depressing," he said.[10] Yet a remarkable change in the policy discourse had taken place on Capitol Hill. Fiscal retrenchment was now the dominant domestic issue—perhaps the only one, it seemed—thanks to a new, more conservative Congress, a president unable or disinclined to refocus attention on the nation's economic distress, and the deficit hawks' campaign to build on the Bowles-Simpson proposal's high media profile.

The result was one concession after another by the Democrats, as Republican House leaders aggressively pushed to cut spending. Obama's budget for fiscal 2012, unveiled soon after the State of the Union, proposed to freeze non-security discretionary spending for three years and cut the deficit by over $1 trillion, reducing it to 3.2% of GDP by 2015. That opening bid was rejected. As Washington waited for Ryan's Budget Committee to essentially dictate the shape of the House budget resolution—due in early April—the Republicans won victory after victory in the continuing resolutions that kept the federal government from shutting down.

Everyone involved knew that cutting discretionary spending for the current fiscal year was only a sign of good faith by the Republican leadership to their more ideological members. Making a serious, long-term dent in the deficit would require cutting the Pentagon budget, agricultural subsidies, tax incentives and loopholes, Social Security and Medicare, or some combination of the above. This was what Ryan's committee would be deciding upon shortly.

Social Security wasn't actually that high on the Republicans' agenda, given their focus on health care—and particularly on chipping away at ObamaCare. An additional full-frontal assault on Social Security would violate longstanding Washington wisdom that addressing both health care and Social Security in the same year was politically self-destructive. Boehner made clear in early March that his party wouldn't offer its own detailed Social Security plan.

Some Republican lawmakers couldn't stop talking about it, however. Eric Cantor, the new House majority leader, raised alarms when he suggested on *Meet the Press* in January, regarding the Ryan Road Map, that Republican lawmakers stood behind his colleague's proposals to cut and partially privatize Social Security. "We put a chapter in our book about it because the direction in which the Road Map goes is something we need—we need to embrace."

Despite the dangers Social Security had always held for them, many Republicans seemed to believe they had less to fear—that the issue actually played in their favor now. According to Mike Allen, Politico.com's widely read inside-Washington reporter, "House Republican leaders say that by taking on entitlements, they hope to send an ADULTS IN CHARGE message, and hope the party's presidential candidates will support them rather than flee (see Bush, George W., 1999). Leaders believe they'll get credit for being HONEST WITH THE PEOPLE, and that their INTELLECTUAL INTEGRITY will be challenged if they shy away now after building the case that hard changes are necessary."

The Democratic leadership's more experienced members knew how to counterattack. In mid-March, Reid, in an interview on MSNBC, drew a line against changes to Social Security. Rejecting both an increase in the retirement age and means-testing benefits, Reid insisted the program wasn't in crisis and that the time wasn't right to address any future problems it might have. "Leave Social Security alone," he declared. "We have a lot of other places we can look that is in a crisis. But Social Security is not."[11]

No Labels, a center-right pressure group that David Walker had helped set up the previous year, quickly denounced the majority leader as being "out of step with the majority of the country.... Most Americans want bipartisan action." But progressive lawmakers were acting as if they expected the public would be on their side.

In March, Reid and Sen. Bernie Sanders, the Vermont Independent, co-sponsored the Sanders-Reid Social Security Protection Amendment, expressing a sense of the Senate that "benefits for current and future beneficiaries should *not* be cut" and that "Social Security should *not* be privatized." It found eleven co-sponsors and was the centerpiece of a "Call Congress Day" on March 30 in which thousands of activists asked their senators to support Sanders-Reid. Two days before, Reid, Sanders, and three other Democratic senators—Tom Harkin of Iowa, Al Franken of Minnesota, and Richard Blumenthal of Connecticut—held a rally in the Dirksen Senate Office Building, telling Republicans to "Back Off Social Security." According to Reuters, the senators were "treated like rock stars" by a "standing-room only audience" attempting—to only mild interest from the national media—to highlight the human cost of cutting the program.

The Democratic leadership's strategy of calling out the Republicans as extremists for their single-minded pursuit of budget cuts and ideological fixation on Social Security, while refusing to pick direct fights with the center-right of their own party, seemed to work with the public. In a Pew Research Center poll in mid-March, 65% of respondents opposed making changes to Social Security and Medicare. More than a third said the poor job market was their chief economic concern, considerably more than the 24% who cited the budget deficit.

Curiously enough, despite their constant complaints about the president's failure to take the lead in "saving" Social Security, Republican leaders felt the same way about the prospects for passing a bill to rein in the program. The budget resolution that Ryan unveiled on April 5, and that his Budget Committee quickly approved, focused on Medicare and Medicaid—although it by no means ignored Social Security.

Titled "The Path to Prosperity: Restoring America's Promise," the resolution wasn't so much a budget outline as a Republican wish list fleshed out into a kind of utopian vision: the ownership society made manifest. It was also, intentionally or not, their 2012 economic campaign platform. The resolution was packaged like a slickly produced think tank report—which, in a sense, it was, because, in its current form, it was guaranteed to die in the Senate. Yet it was the most audacious budget proposal any Republican administration or

House Budget Committee Chairman Paul Ryan (R-WI) unveils the House Republican budget blueprint, April 5, 2011. The "Ryan resolution" called for effectively dismantling Medicare and transforming Medicaid into block grants to the states. A public relations disaster, it also included recommendations to means-test Social Security and raise the age for full retirement benefits.

Congress had submitted since Reagan's first year in office. It promised to cut $6.2 trillion more than the president's budget would over the next ten years, reduce the deficit by $4.4 trillion, and put the U.S. on a path to paying off its national debt, although it left out many of the steps needed to get there. A "binding cap" would keep federal spending from rising to more than 20% of the economy.

As for health care, Medicaid and food stamps would be turned into block grants to the states, which would have wide latitude to structure the programs as they wished. Medicare for new enrollees starting in 2021 would be transformed into what Ryan called "premium support" in which the government subsidized individuals to purchase private insurance. Lower-income individuals would receive a larger subsidy than higher earners. The result would be to repeal ObamaCare and turn all of Medicare into a system like Medicare Advantage—effectively, privatizing it.

Federal spending on health care would drop so drastically in later decades that government spending as a whole would plummet as a percentage of GDP, according to a Congressional Budget Office analysis. But unless one believed the private insurance market could perform miracles, there would be no real reduction in health care spending. It would simply be shifted to the elderly, who would see their costs rise even faster than under the current system.[12]

What about Social Security? "This budget heads off a crisis by forcing action from the President and both chambers of Congress to ensure the solvency of this critical program," the resolution said, "creating the space for bipartisan solutions." How it would do this was vague. If and when "the Social Security program is not sustainable," the president and the trustees would have to submit a plan "for restoring balance." Congressional leaders in both houses would then be required "to put forward their best ideas as well." Unstated was how the authorities would know the program was "not sustainable," what the president and congressional leaders would then do with their "best ideas," and whether there would be some kind of enforcement mechanism, such as including Social Security under that 20% binding cap.

But Ryan had some detailed suggestions, derived from the Bowles-Simpson report: means-testing of higher-income workers' benefits and raising the retirement age—or, as he put it, "reforms to take account of increases in longevity." He also called for "more targeted assistance" for "lower-income seniors." Other of the "commission's proposals"—as he incorrectly labeled them—"particularly on the tax side, are of debatable merit." This would be a reference to raising the cap on income subject to payroll tax.

Progressives were especially suspicious of the following wording: "Any value in the balances in the Social Security trust fund is derived from dubious government accounting. The trust fund is not a real savings account." The government borrowed all the money and spent it, the resolution asserted. "The ability to redeem these securities is completely dependent on the Treasury's ability to raise money through taxes or borrowing."

That wasn't news: Washington also spent all the money it raised by selling Treasury bonds to the Bank of China and other investors, and would have to redeem them in the same way. What made the statement disturbing, noted Nancy Altman, was that it suggested the Republicans didn't view the bonds in the Social Security trust funds as having equal standing with other U.S. government debt. "Ryan has clearly signaled the intention of his Party to raid the reserves," Altman concluded.[13]

Whatever the case, the general intention of the budget resolution—aside from the overall goal of taking tax increases completely off the table in deficit-cutting negotiations—was to put Social Security on track to being transformed from a social insurance program into welfare. By stopping short of concrete steps, Ryan was attempting to avoid the political blunder of tackling both health care and Social Security directly in the same year, while ensuring that action would happen soon on the latter, moving in the direction he desired.

The administration's initial response to the budget resolution was negative, and zeroed in on its human impact. It "cuts taxes for millionaires and special interests while placing a greater burden on seniors who depend on Medicare or live in nursing homes, families struggling with a child who has serious disabilities, workers who have lost their health care coverage, and students and their families who rely on Pell grants," said the White House press secretary.[14]

Progressives, of course, were outraged if not surprised. The Center on Budget and Policy Priorities estimated that two-thirds of the resolution's deficit reductions would be at the expense of "people of limited means."[15] "Mr. Ryan is declaring war on entitlements—and war on the elderly and the poor," said his former colleague on the deficit commission, Jan Schakowsky.[16]

Conservatives, especially longtime critics of Social Security, hailed the resolution as a visionary document charting a bold new direction for America. Ryan, it seemed, was now Moses leading them to the promised land. David Brooks, in the *New York Times*, praised the Budget Committee chair for having the courage to "leap into the vacuum left by the president's passivity." The resolution embodied a "new vision of the social contract" and would "set the standard of seriousness for anyone who wants to play in this discussion." Most importantly, Ryan had written what would "become the 2012 Republican platform, no matter who is the nominee."

Nobody on the Republican side—at first—seemed to be running from Ryan's handiwork. "There is hope! Serious & necessary leadership rolls out serious & necessary reform proposal Good start," Sarah Palin tweeted her followers. The Ryan plan "is what a real conservative budget should look like," declared Grover Norquist's Americans for Tax Reform.[17] The *Wall Street Journal* editors called it "the most serious attempt to reform government in at least a generation."

Perhaps most significantly, however, the center-right kept a measured distance. The Committee for a Responsible Federal Budget praised Ryan for producing a "bold budget" that would lead to a larger discussion. The scheme to force action on Social Security was a positive. But MacGuineas also criticized the budget resolution as polarizing and worried that it might derail progress toward a bipartisan deal. Bowles and Simpson were "pleased" by the Social Security action scheme, but also criticized Ryan for going easy on the Pentagon and not applying any of his savings from spending cuts to deficit reduction.

Kent Conrad went further. Ryan's proposal was "partisan and ideological," he wrote in a press statement—the cardinal sins in the eyes of deficit hawks. Conrad didn't mention the Social Security proposal, but rejected the Medicare and Medicaid schemes, which he said "would simply shift costs and increase the number of uninsured."

Still flush with their successes at the polls and in negotiating extension of the Bush tax cuts, the House Republican leadership went ahead and put the Ryan resolution to a vote, winning passage, 235 to 193, not a single Democrat stepping across the aisle. Opponents quickly noted that the House was now aiming to eliminate all the elements of ObamaCare that would save money for Medicare recipients.

The fallout came a month later, in a House special election. On May 24, Democrat Kathy Hochul won the House seat from New York's 26th District, representing the Buffalo suburbs, after running a campaign that hammered the GOP for attempting to slash Medicare. The irony couldn't have been lost on Republicans, who owed a good part of their success in the 2010 elections to their adeptness at pinning the same charge on Democrats who had voted for ObamaCare.

Undeterred, Ryan accused Democrats of "shamelessly demagoguing and distorting" his budget. Republican leaders vowed to keep pressing their position, arguing that it simply hadn't been "framed right."[18]

Democrats were delighted, suspecting that their opponents were further isolating themselves from the American public's real concerns. In an April poll by the Democratic firm Greenberg Quinlan Rosner, 70% said they opposed changes to Medicare as described in the Ryan resolution; 65% in a Pew Research poll a month earlier were against changing Social Security as a way to reduce the deficit. The Obama White House, however, seemed to be moving in another direction. Influenced by Tim Geithner and his political advisor David Plouffe, the president appeared to have concluded that he needed to shore up his support among independent voters, and that the best way to do that was to make a grand bargain with congressional Republicans to cut the deficit and reduce the national debt.

Before the House budget resolution had even passed, Obama floated a twelve-year deficit reduction plan that would leave Social Security alone but would cut Medicare spending automatically if the program's costs grew more than 0.5% faster than GDP—a threshold that would be nearly impossible to avoid, at least in the short run. The president followed Bowles-Simpson in laying out a deficit-cutting blueprint consisting of two-thirds spending cuts and one-third tax increases. Predictably, the president's offering pleased no one, from center-rightists who complained that he didn't tackle Social Security to progressives who disliked the arbitrary target for Medicare growth.

Soon afterward, the administration opened talks with Boehner, McConnell, and other congressional Republican leaders—senior Democrats occupied a secondary place in the discussions—on another hike in the debt ceiling. The tone of the talks became clear early, when Boehner demanded a dollar of spending cuts for every dollar increase in the ceiling, and no revenue increases, and Obama, rather than push back at this unprecedented move, warned Democrats to be flexible. The White House's basic bargaining position was also clear from the start: major cuts in programs, possibly including entitlements, in exchange for tax hikes. The administration also wanted some economic stimulus measures, including another year added on to its partial payroll tax holiday.

A hint of just how far Obama was willing to bend peeked through on June 20, when a White House spokesperson, on C-SPAN, refused to rule out raising the eligibility age for Medicare. Two days later, the *Wall Street Journal* reported that the chained CPI had come up in talks led by Biden with congressional leaders. Members of the House Progressive Caucus quickly denounced the idea.

That made little impression on the White House. Obama secretly met with Boehner on Sunday, July 3. Two days later, he told reporters, "We've got a unique opportunity to do something big, to tackle our deficit in a way that forces our government to live within its means. This will require both parties to get out of our comfort zones, and both parties to agree on real compromises." He then pledged to take on "entitlement programs" as part of the deal he contemplated. Next day, according to the *Washington Post*, "people in both parties" said that Obama was pressing for a long-term debt reduction package "that would force Democrats to accept major changes to Social Security and Medicare in exchange for Republican support for fresh tax revenue."[19]

Democratic leaders, members of Congress of a progressive bent, and pro-Social Security groups were surprised and incensed. In April, Obama had said publicly that he supported raising the cap to bring the program into better long-term balance, but had reiterated that Social Security wasn't the cause of the deficit. Now, it appeared, he was prepared to make a major restructuring part of his deal with the Republicans.

"We didn't understand their strategy—if there was a strategy," Max Richtman of the National Committee to Preserve Social Security and Medicare, said later. "Was it a ploy? Were they just trying to draw the Republicans out—offer them something and see if they take the bait? But what if the Republicans say yes?"[20] The National Committee announced that it was ready to deliver 700,000 petitions to the White House opposing any changes in COLAs for seniors. Pelosi held a news conference at which she promised that House Democrats "would not reduce the deficit or subsidize tax cuts for the rich on the backs of America's seniors."

White House spokesperson Jay Carney hastened to declare that the *Post* story "overshoots the runway" and repeated the by-now familiar formula that the president wanted only to "strengthen Social Security in a balanced way that preserves the promise of the program and doesn't slash benefits." The program's defenders were not reassured. "Shorter Carney: 'You betcha Social Security's on the table,'" Eric Kingson of Social Security Works said in an email to supporters.

The deficit talks lurched from crisis to crisis over the next several weeks as Obama continued to pursue a grand bargain with Boehner, and Republicans persisted in rejecting any suggestion of additional tax revenues. Those weeks included much high drama, impolite behavior, and posturing by the principal negotiators as well as persistent media speculation that uncertainty over the U.S. debt ceiling was contributing to wild swings in the global financial markets. Obama continued to play up his role as the last reasonable statesperson in Washington, promoting his payroll tax holiday to Republicans while admonishing Democrats to accept entitlement cuts.

Despite the White House's efforts to downplay them, those cuts went beyond anything a Democratic president had ever before offered. Among the ideas he advanced in his talks with Republican leaders was to phase in an increase in the eligibility age for Medicare from sixty-five to sixty-seven by 2036 and means-test benefits for more affluent retirees. Although he stopped short of offering further increases in the Social Security eligibility age, Obama also said he would support switching the Social Security benefits formula to the chained CPI.

On July 19, Obama nevertheless went further, praising a just-released, $3.75 trillion deficit reduction plan from the Gang of Six, a bipartisan group of senators organized by Virginia Democrat Mark Warner and Georgia Republican Saxby Chambliss who had become the great hope of the center-right since they began meeting in December. Like Obama, the Gang of Six endorsed the chained CPI. They also would have required the Senate Finance Committee to develop a plan to balance Social Security's books over the next seventy-five years. If it couldn't do so, a group of ten senators—five from each party—could bring a reform bill directly to the floor. The Gang of Six also proposed drastic cuts in Medicare benefits.

The spectacle was close to surreal: the most popular options for balancing Social Security's books and narrowing the federal budget deficit, according to years of polling—raising the income cap on payroll contributions and raising taxes on Social Security benefits for the wealthy—weren't even under discussion. Meanwhile, a Democratic White House was offering major reductions in Social Security and Medicare that Republicans didn't seem to want. As the presidential concessions piled up, so did the anger of the programs' supporters. The Medicare eligibility change could actually raise government's health care spending, not lower it, some argued, because many younger seniors would be forced into the more expensive, less efficient Medicaid program. Politically, the chained CPI would expose Democrats—correctly—to the charge that they were using Social Security to cut the deficit, since the new measure would start to erode current seniors' benefits right away.

Obama's repeated concessions sparked a near-revolt among his own party and progressives generally. House Democrats introduced a resolution on July 12 against "further increasing the retirement age or otherwise decreasing benefits." The AFL-CIO and MoveOn.org initiated days of action, urging their followers to call their senators and demand rejection of any cuts to Social Security. AARP, which recently had seemed ready to consider benefit cuts, now firmed up against any attempt to tie Social Security changes to deficit reduction. Many Democratic lawmakers denounced extension of the payroll tax holiday as well, arguing that if it became permanent, it could undermine Social Security's finances down the road. Consumers hadn't been helped much by the December payroll tax cut, the Democrats noted, due to rising food prices and the need to pay down household debt. Lawmakers also worried openly that the president's Medicare proposals would neutralize the political advantage they had gained from the Ryan budget resolution's attempt to restructure the program out of existence.

Neither did Obama's move away from his "comfort zone" buy him much favor with Republicans. They quickly denounced his Social Security proposals as not "serious": not the kind of fundamental restructuring that they would be willing to swap for tax increases. Just how much farther the administration would have to go became clear in late July, when Boehner released his own deficit reduction plan, which called for $1.2 trillion of discretionary spending cuts over ten years, and then $1.8 trillion more to be decided by the end of the year. The Center on Budget and Policy Priorities called the Boehner plan "class warfare," since it would require "draconian policy changes." In a virtually unprecedented move, Boehner didn't protect Social Security and Medicare from the knife. No deficit-reduction legislation in the past quarter-century, including Gramm-Rudman-Hollings, had gone so far.

The White House appeared to have made a big political miscalculation in the debt-ceiling talks. The other side, goaded by its Tea Party faction, wasn't interested in trading revenue increases for anything, and was determined to extract as much as possible in spending cuts.

In the deal that finally emerged at the end of July, Obama got the thing he most needed politically: a boost in the debt ceiling that would probably be sufficient to carry him through the 2012 election without the need for another torturous round of negotiations. It wasn't the grand bargain he had sought; it contained no new revenues. In fact, it mandated total deficit cuts amounting to even more than the increase in the debt ceiling—just as Boehner had demanded in May.

The deal came in three parts. First, it ordered nearly $1 trillion in spending cuts over ten years—a little more than was needed to pay for extension of the Bush tax cuts in the December deal. Second, it set up a "bipartisan commission process" charged with identifying another $1.5 trillion in deficit reduction, including from entitlements and changes to the tax system. The Joint Select Committee on Deficit Reduction—or the Super Committee, as it quickly became known—would have until November 23 to make its recommendations, which Congress must then vote on, up or down with no amendments, by December 23. If the commission failed to make any recommendations, that would trigger

$1.2 trillion of across-the-board cuts in both domestic and defense spending—with Social Security, Medicare, and poverty programs excluded. These cuts would go into effect January 2013. Third, Congress was required to vote on—but not necessarily pass—a Balanced Budget Amendment by year-end.

Two-thirds of the first round of spending cuts would come from domestic rather than military spending, reducing domestic spending to its lowest level since the Eisenhower administration. "A Tea Party triumph," the *Wall Street Journal* editors proclaimed. "The deal is a victory for the cause of smaller government, arguably the biggest since welfare reform in 1996." Deficit hawks were less pleased. The ten-year deficit reduction, at best, wouldn't approach the $4 trillion that had become their magic number. Over and over in the next few months, figureheads of the center right like Maya MacGuineas of the Committee for a Responsible Federal Budget would express their disappointment that Obama and the Republican leaders hadn't gone after "the 'big ticket' items"—namely, Social Security and Medicare—and urge the Super Committee to "go big," targeting the $4 trillion in savings over ten years that Bowles-Simpson had turned into a mantra of the deficit hawks.

Democratic lawmakers outside the center-right were furious. "Today we, and everyone we have worked to speak for and fight for, were thrown under the bus," said Rep. Raul Grijalva of Arizona, co-chair of the Congressional Progressive Caucus. "This deal is a cure as bad as the disease."

The White House quickly declared victory, claiming it had "saved Medicare, Medicaid and Social Security" with the deal. But this was disingenuous. The Super Committee would be free to include entitlement cuts in its recommendations. Only if it couldn't reach agreement would Social Security and Medicare be removed from harm's way. And most observers expected the panel to at least try to submit a plan including entitlement cuts, since failure would trigger deep reductions in military as well as domestic spending—unthinkable to members of Congress who represented districts with a heavy military or military-industrial presence. Less than a week after the deal was made, Leon Panetta, Obama's new Secretary of Defense, urged that defense cuts be kept to a minimum. Joe Lieberman offered a slightly hysterical plea, declaring from the Senate floor, "We can't protect these entitlements and also have the national defense … to protect us … with Islamist extremists."

The structure of the Super Committee, with its promise of an up-or-down, no-amendments vote by Congress on the committee's handiwork, was a descendant of the entitlement commission Judd Gregg and Kent Conrad had pushed for following the collapse of Bush's Social Security privatization campaign. It seemed to deliver just what Social Security's center-right critics had always wanted: a way to short-circuit the democratic process, providing cover for lawmakers to cut Social Security and Medicare without leaving anyone's fingerprints too prominently displayed on the remains.

That would set up the scenario that Social Security's defenders had feared since Reagan first proposed slashing the program to pay for his tax cuts in

1981. The program, even with its independent source of financing through payroll taxes, would no longer be looked upon as existing outside the normal budget process. It would be just another piece in the game of making the federal government's long-term balance sheet come out in the black.

Some analysts worried about something else as well. In part because Obama hadn't taken the threat seriously when he negotiated the extension of the Bush tax cuts in December, the Republicans had added a new weapon to Congress's parliamentary arsenal—the debt-ceiling hold-up. "In the future," Mitch McConnell said as the Senate prepared to vote on the Budget Control Act of 2011—as the deal was titled—"any president, this one or another one, when they request us to raise the debt ceiling, it will not be clean anymore." Every increase in the Treasury's borrowing limit, as long as the Republicans held the upper hand, would come at the price of dollar-for-dollar spending cuts. This "ultimately would require the dismantling of much of the Great Society and even the New Deal, thereby paving the way for vast increases in poverty and deprivation," concluded Robert Greenstein of the Center on Budget and Policy Priorities.

* * *

The Social Security wars have never been fought entirely, or even primarily, in Washington. They play themselves out whenever candidates for office raise the issue in their campaigns—and, of course, when working households and their communities become fearful that one of the foundations of middle-income American life is about to the taken from them.

"The U.S. is engaged in an epic debate over the size and scope of government that will play out over several years, and the most important battle comes in the election of 2012," the *Wall Street Journal* editors wrote after the debt ceiling deal was concluded. Republican leaders were perhaps less confident about that election than they sometimes appeared. After their 2010 victory, they had two goals: to tear down as much of ObamaCare as they could, and to deny Obama a second term. Social Security could wait until they had a firmer grip on power.

By the time the Budget Control Act was enacted in August, however, Obama-Care, while threatened, was still largely on course. By then, too, more than 1.2 million persons previously without health coverage were expected to become insured in 2011, many of them young adults benefiting from a provision of the new law that allowed them to stay on their parents' policies.[21] Such developments threatened to immunize many key elements of the law from repeal.

Meanwhile, Social Security was becoming an issue again—largely because Republican lawmakers and presidential candidates insisted on making it one. Almost as soon as the 2010 election was over, conservative members of Congress had begun spitting out bills to "reform" Social Security. Rep. Cynthia Lummis, a Wyoming Republican, in early March introduced a bill to phase in a higher retirement age beginning in 2024. Soon afterward, a group of twenty-two Republican senators, led by Indiana's Dan Coats, threatened to vote against raising the debt ceiling unless the president agreed to Social Security and Medicare cuts. In April, Sens. Lindsey Graham, Rand Paul, and Mike Lee of Utah previewed their Social Security plan on Fox News. Their idea was two-fold: to gradually raise the eligibility age to seventy, then index it for longevity, and to means-test benefits for higher earners.

Next up, in June, was Rep. Pete Sessions of Texas, who wanted to divert 6.2% of every worker's wages from Social Security into a private account. Later that month, Sen. Kay Bailey Hutchison of Texas dropped another bill to raise the retirement age for Social Security, this time to sixty-nine, and cut CO-LAs by 1-percentage-point. August saw Tom Coburn join the parade, with a measure that would begin indexing the eligibility age to life expectancy and severely cut benefits for those taking early retirement.

None of these proposals represented anything but orthodox Republican thinking, but they compounded the trouble for potential Republican candidates, whose economic platform had already been written in the form of the Ryan resolution, with its blueprint for phasing out the existing Medicare system. Not that some of those candidates were being careful to avoid inflicting damage on themselves. In August, Texas Gov. Rick Perry declared his candidacy and almost immediately set off a media mini-frenzy by calling Social Security a Ponzi scheme and questioning the constitutionality of Washington—as opposed to the states—setting up "a federally operated program of pensions."

Former Massachusetts Gov. Mitt Romney, widely considered to be preferred candidate of the party leadership, was trying to position himself as the "electable" Republican in a field of rivals made up largely of Tea Party favorites like Perry and Michelle Bachmann. The "Ponzi scheme" charge was "a monstrous lie," he said, adding, with some truth, "If we nominate someone who the Democrats can correctly characterize as being opposed to Social Security, we would be obliterated as a party."

The comic side of this was all too apparent. Romney himself was firmly on the record favoring means-testing Social Security benefits and raising the retirement age, and supported adding on private accounts as the best way to help workers replace the lost benefits. Moreover, in his 2010 book, *No Apology: The Case for American Greatness*, Romney had compared Social Security to a criminal fraud, asserting that a banker who managed a trust fund the way Congress managed Social Security, would go to jail. Other presidential aspirants, too, were eager to fudge their established positions. Bachmann, like Perry and Newt Gingrich—also running for president—supported allowing younger workers to move their payroll tax contributions into private accounts. She had previously spoken of her desire to "wean" Americans away from Social Security. Now, she sensed an opening, and began emphasizing that "we have to keep our promises to our senior citizens."

Beyond this, of course, the Ponzi scheme charge had been a staple of right-wing rhetoric for decades. Yet Perry's opponents were eager to obscure this record—as were Karl Rove and Dick Cheney, who had worked hard to privatize the program as members of the Bush administration but now denounced Perry for his reckless language.

If Republicans had anything to gain from Obama's recent, clumsy attempts to sell Social Security cuts to congressional negotiators, they most likely lost it in the Romney-Perry fracas. Other GOP presidential candidates, too, were doing their best to compound the problem. Former Pennsylvania Sen. Rick Santorum was advocating tying benefits calculations to prices instead of wages, which would drastically reduce the real value of payments over time. Former restaurant executive Herman Cain pushed a tax-restructuring plan that would eliminate the payroll tax, robbing Social Security of its independent source of funding—and participants of their claim to ownership of benefits. Ultimately, he wanted to replace Social Security with a "Chilean model" private-accounts system, as did another candidate, Newt Gingrich.

Arguably, most Americans were less interested in fanciful ideas for remolding the tax code—or the super committee's deficit reduction talks, for that matter—than in the disturbing economic news that seemed to greet them nearly every day. The economic recovery, never very vigorous, was losing momentum. Unemployment remained locked above 9.1%, and in early September, the administration acknowledged that the number might stay that high at least through 2012. GDP growth for the year thus far, which the Congressional Budget Office had projected at 3.1%, was running more like 1%.[22] The Census Bureau reported that 46.2 million people were living in poverty, the highest number in the more than fifty years the bureau had kept records.[23]

Social Security, including Disability Insurance and SSI, were, as usual, part of working people's first line of defense, and the SSA itself was feeling the anxiety level rise. In early September, the agency announced that threats against its employees had jumped to 2,800 in 2010—43% more than the previous year—and that it was banning anyone from visiting its field offices who had made a threat against agency workers or buildings.[24]

Economists and pundits were talking about what had once been unthinkable—the long-term decline of the American middle class, the vast center of the population that Social Security had helped to create and that anchored the nation's political and social stability, and the rise of a new, two-tier economy of haves and have-nots. Especially disturbing was the decline in American manufacturing—the economic home of the urban industrial workers for whom Social Security had originally been designed and which for decades had provided the most stable, high-paying, private-sector jobs to American workers.[25] The middle class not only benefited most from Social Security, but their payroll tax contributions were critical to keeping it financially viable. If nothing was done to keep millions of middle-class households from sliding into a more precarious economic state, the program's existence could truly be threatened.

The outpouring of studies and proposals from the deficit hawks rarely touched on such concerns. Out in the everyday world, however, signs were emerging that people threatened by the worsening conditions were prepared to do something about it. One such was the unexpectedly strong opposition by public employees when the newly elected Republican governors of New Jersey, Wisconsin, Ohio, and Michigan moved to restrict their collective bargaining rights. Just as significant was the high degree of support they enjoyed in public opinion polls, despite strong efforts to vilify them in the media as overpaid and overprotected.

Another sign was the strong grassroots labor response earlier in the year when Obama reportedly was considering including Social Security cuts in his State of the Union speech. A new Emergency Labor Network, initiated by 100 local union activists in Cleveland, quickly developed into a national effort that included the launch of a campaign to defend and expand Social Security and Medicare.[26] The Strengthen Social Security Campaign, meanwhile, employing heavy support from progressive bloggers, generated a quarter of a million comments submitted to the White House before the speech, urging the president to keep his promises and not cut Social Security.[27] Following Obama's offer to introduce the chained CPI in the debt ceiling talks, AARP and MoveOn.org launched new campaigns to defend the program. Meanwhile, Democratic Sens. Bernard Sanders of Vermont and Sheldon Whitehouse of Rhode Island introduced a new "Scrap the Cap" bill that would make all income over $250,000 a year subject to payroll tax, but exempt income between the current $106,800 limit and $250,000.

The most dramatic evidence that a revolt was brewing against Washington's austerity economics and its seeming failure to give ordinary working households the same degree of consideration it had shown to mismanaged financial institutions was more generalized, however. On September 17, several hundred activists took control of Zuccotti Park, a small square near Wall Street, and began an occupation that was quickly emulated in cities across the country.

The new movement seemed to combine the directly democratic, anarchist-inspired organizing of the movement against corporate-backed trade treaties almost a decade earlier with the new economic discontent of the post-crash era. Conservatives quickly condemned "class warfare" by a "growing mob" (Eric Cantor) and the "noise, filth and stink" inflicted on the financial district by an "aggressive, often drugged-out crew" of "kids" (*Wall Street Journal* columnist L. Gordon Crovitz).

Progressive Democrats, however, noted the activists' rage at the lopsided economic "recovery" that seemed to benefit the perpetrators of the 2007–08 crash but not its victims. Occupy Wall Street could turn out to be something like a left version of the Tea Party, and, despite the initially scornful coverage it received from the mainstream media, just as significant politically. Labor unions, MoveOn.org, and even the Campaign for America's Future hastened to throw verbal support, and even some funds, behind the protests. In several locations, such as Ft. Lauderdale, Occupy camps helped support protests by seniors' groups against the threat of Social Security cuts by the super committee.

Obama, as it happened, was already making efforts to move in a more populist direction. In early September, he made his latest stab at selling an economic recovery strategy with the American Jobs Act, a $447 billion package of tax cuts and new government spending. More than half the dollar value of the proposal was taken up by the president's now very familiar payroll tax holiday. This time, he proposed reducing the tax even further for workers, from 4.2% to 3.1% of pay—and throwing in a generous cut for their employers as well. Companies that added a new worker or increased wages would have their payroll tax contributions completely forgiven for the coming year, up to the first $50 million in payroll increases. As for the rest of the employer contribution, it would be cut in half, to 3.1%, for the first $5 million of wages that companies paid. All told, 98% of businesses would receive at least some payroll tax relief, the White House claimed.

Republicans called it a "sugar high" and instead urged, once again, "fundamental reform" of Social Security. Progressive Democrats complained that it was the economy, not high payroll taxes, that kept companies from hiring, and doubted the tax holiday would result in more. They noted, too, that the administration was still offering nothing very substantial to help homeowners facing foreclosure, despite the fact that rising numbers of people were again losing their homes. But Obama's proposal enabled him to offer a degree of relief to the middle class and, in so doing, upend the usual political dynamic in Washington by making the Democrats the champions of a tax cut that the Republicans opposed.

This being deficit-obsessed Washington, however, the White House couldn't offer stimulus without an accompanying proposal to offset the cost. Less than two weeks after making his jobs bill public, Obama offered a slew of tax increases and spending cuts that he projected would shrink the deficit by $3.1 trillion over ten years. About half the savings would come from raising taxes, for instance by limiting itemized deductions for households making $250,000 or more a year, and ending tax breaks for oil companies and hedge fund managers. This had obvious appeal to progressives and even the activists in Zuccotti Park, since thirty years of tax cuts for the "investor class" had succeeded in lowering federal tax revenues from a postwar high of 18.2% of GDP in 1988 to 14.4%—explaining a great deal of the current deficit at a stroke. The president's plan included cuts in Medicare and Medicaid, although these would mostly affect payments to doctors and drug companies.

Pointedly, it contained no cuts to Social Security. Obama had taken back, it seemed, the chained CPI offer he had made to Republican leaders in the debt-ceiling talks.

Why the shift? One reason was that progressive groups like MoveOn.org and the AFL-CIO threw themselves into pressuring the White House to leave the program alone. Another, reportedly,[28] was that the administration had been impressed by polls that suggested it had gained no advantage from its effort to appeal to independent voters by casting the president as a moderate, and indeed had only succeeded in making him appear weak in relation to Republican leaders. Recent polls, in fact, showed that independent voters were no more inclined to make Social Security part of a plan to cut the deficit than were Democrats—or Republicans, most of whom disliked the idea as well.[29]

Were Obama and "the left," as Politico.com concluded, "back in synch"? This was hard to accept at face value, given the administration's closeness to the financial services industry and many Democrats' dependence on contributions from hedge funds.

But perhaps Obama found himself in a situation similar to the one the last Democratic president had encountered when the Republicans with whom he had hoped to make a deal on Social Security instead impeached him. Obama's attempts to work with Republican leaders had been a political disaster. His jobs bill quickly died on a GOP filibuster in the Senate and he was reduced to traveling the country, trying to drum up support for bits and pieces of the package—including the expanded payroll tax holiday. For once, he couldn't afford to take his party's progressive wing for granted.

* * *

The collapse of the congressional Super Committee came on Sunday, November 20, following a week of frantic, last-minute efforts to strike a deal. The committee failed either to "go big" or even to do what much of Washington had minimally expected of it: to extend the payroll tax holiday and the time limit for unemployment insurance coverage and find a formula for offsetting the cost that would be acceptable to both parties. That meant Congress would have to spend much of 2012 managing the impact of $1.2 trillion of automatic spending cuts, the lion's share coming from the normally off-limits Pentagon budget. More immediately, it left two of the chief ingredients in what passed for Washington's anti-recession program scheduled to expire at the end of the current year. Millions of people, if nothing was done, would see their payroll tax rates jump, and millions more—these quite economically vulnerable— would lose their unemployment benefits. How had it come to this?

Despite its stern tone, the Budget Control Act was, arguably, a toothless beast. Any Congress could mandate budget cuts over ten years, but these could always be canceled by a later Congress. Some suggested that the Democrats wanted to let the super committee fail, since this would protect Social Security and Medicare while setting up a new battle with the Republicans in the lame-duck session of Congress following the 2012 election, when the expiration of the Bush tax cuts would place them in a stronger bargaining position. The Republicans, for their part, didn't relish the automatic military cutbacks, but even before the super committee gave up, McCain and several other lawmakers were busy concocting plans to short-circuit them.

Neither side, as a result, felt a Grand Bargain was worthwhile unless it could obtain major concessions on one or more key issues. For the Republicans, the only concession worth bargaining for was permanent extension of the Bush tax cuts, undoing the mistake they had made in 2005, when the Bush administration postponed that goal in favor of Social Security privatization. Along with some modest revenue raisers, Democratic negotiators dangled such ideas as boosting the Medicare eligibility age and adopting the chained CPI for Medicare and Social Security. Pointedly, Reid and Pelosi, the programs' most powerful defenders on Capitol Hill, declined to rule out such ideas, despite the harm they would do to retirees and future retirees. If enacted, the Democratic proposals would have netted some $2.4 trillion to $3 trillion of savings over ten years and would have been even more heavily skewed than Bowles-Simpson in the direction of spending cuts rather than tax hikes.

Chris Van Hollen, one of the Democratic negotiators, explained the chained CPI offer, saying it "should be done in the context of strengthening Social Security for the long term, through more revenues and reforms." None of the Democratic leadership ever explained what those "revenues and reforms" might be, although they would presumably include raising the cap on income subject to the Social Security payroll tax. Progressive groups expressed alarm, and Trumka angrily threatened to withhold campaign support from any lawmaker who supported the Medicare and Social Security cuts. In any event, the Republicans turned down the Democratic offers, some arguing that they didn't go far enough in the direction of "structural changes" to the programs, which presumably would have included raising the retirement age and means-testing benefits.

Two other factors contributed to the super committee's failure. Deficit hawks had been issuing increasingly panicked warnings that unless the committee struck a Grand Bargain that would include entitlements, the bond market would lose confidence, triggering a credit crisis comparable to the one then besetting the eurozone countries. Joe Lieberman predicted a "grassroots uprising" and a downgrade of the U.S.'s credit rating. But as the committee's deadline approached, it became clear that nothing of the sort would happen. A week before the collapse, Moody's and Standard & Poor's both said no downgrade would take place as long as the already-approved spending cuts stayed on track—a position they reaffirmed after the committee disbanded.

Another reason was Occupy Wall Street, which had goaded at least some of the political class to shift the conversation from debt and the deficit to unemployment and the disadvantaged. The ongoing protests were now taking place in cities all over the country. On November 2, Occupy Oakland had organized a shutdown of the Port of Oakland, and a shutdown of all West Coast ports was planned for December 12. When the super committee died on November 20, the Strengthen Social Security Campaign hailed the event as a victory of "the 99 percent over the 1 percent," using the Occupy movement's popular articulation of the gap between the economic and political elite and the rest of the public.

Joblessness and the recession, partly as a consequence, were the focus in the weeks after the committee called it quits, when Congress had to decide what to do about the payroll tax break, unemployment benefits, and several other pieces of unfinished business before leaving town for the holidays. What followed was the third great confrontation of the year between the White House and the Senate and House leaders. The Democrats not only wanted to extend the payroll tax holiday but make the cut deeper and expand it to include a break for employers, along the lines Obama had advocated earlier in the fall. They wanted to pay for the tax break by applying a tax surcharge to incomes over $1 million.

Once again, the Republicans were divided. Fundamentally, they opposed the payroll tax holiday, preferring to focus the negotiations, again, on long-term tax breaks that would benefit their backers. But the House leaders, Boehner and Cantor, understood that their party ran the risk of being perceived as standing in the way of a middle-class tax cut. Arguably, the payroll tax holiday hadn't resulted in much economic stimulus. But not everybody agreed—and nobody could be sure it hadn't relieved some pressure on working people, who might resent it being snatched away from them. So Boehner and Cantor agreed that the holiday should be extended, but proposed to pay for it principally by freezing federal workers' pay for three years. They also encouraged their members to turn the deal into a Christmas tree, loading it up with a host of measures from the Republican wish list, from stingier time limits for unemployment benefits to abortion funding restrictions.

With time again threatening to run out, Reid and McConnell made a deal to extend the payroll tax holiday and unemployment insurance by two months, until February 2012. The payroll tax break would only be extended, however, not expanded. It would be paid for by raising the fees the government-sponsored mortgage securitizers, Fannie Mae and Freddie Mac, charged lenders. The Republican wish list was eliminated, except for one big item: Obama would be required to quickly make a decision on Keystone XL, a U.S.-Canadian oil pipeline project opposed by environmentalists but coveted by energy companies. A further extension of the payroll tax holiday, for the balance of 2012, could be worked out in the new year.

Less than a week before Christmas, however, House Tea Party members revolted, voting down the bipartisan deal after their Senate Republican counterparts had overwhelmingly supported it. A sort of panic erupted in Washington. Reid declared that "the clock ticks towards a middle class tax hike." A senior Senate GOP aide told Politico.com, "This is a colossal fumble by the House Republicans. Their inability to recognize a win is costing our party our long-held advantage on the key issue of tax relief." As many as 2.2 million people stood to lose their unemployment benefits by mid-February, according to the Labor Department, and 3.6 million by the end of March.

Despite having made the Obama administration look foolish repeatedly over the past eleven months, the *Wall Street Journal* editors called 2011 "a year of political disappointment" for Tea-Party-fueled Republicans who had ridden into town with an exceedingly ambitious agenda. Yet they had failed to end ObamaCare. They couldn't muster two-thirds of the House to pass their Balanced Budget Amendment, which they had structured to facilitate cuts in

Social Security benefits, when they brought it to a vote two days earlier. They had forced "no major policy concessions beyond extending the Bush tax cuts for two years." The Republican leadership needed a face-saving victory badly, and were letting it slip through their fingers.

Facing enormous pressure, Boehner called back his members and more or less ordered them to vote to accept the Reid-McConnell deal—which they did, with only slight changes, on Christmas Eve.

In an eerie replay of the first Clinton administration, the Republicans' brinkmanship had rescued the president in the polls, in spite of the fact that he had done little more than insist that Congress not leave town without extending the payroll tax holiday. The confrontation also ensured that in the tax and spending battles that were sure to follow in 2012, the Democrats would be fighting from a much stronger position. At a December 8 press conference, Reid suggested that even the expiration of the payroll tax holiday after the 2012 election wasn't a big concern for him, since the Bush tax cuts would expire then as well. The Democrats could use that confluence as leverage to negotiate a broader tax reform that would shift the advantage from more affluent taxpayers to the middle class while returning the Social Security payroll tax to its previous level.

Whether or not it would come to that, Republican lawmakers could have been forgiven for marveling at the power of Social Security, and the uncanny political power it gave the Democrats. The battle over the payroll tax holiday proved, apparently, that the public would always accept the Democrats as defenders of Social Security, even as they pushed through Congress a temporary tax cut that threatened to shake the program's untouchable status in the tax and spending wars. If Republicans objected to the holiday—as some did—on the grounds that it would destabilize Social Security, they were accused of gouging the middle class. The attack hit the party of FDR with about as much impact as a wet sponge on a thick coating of Teflon.

But for the union leaders, working households, and activists who had been organizing repeatedly for decades to keep Social Security from being adulterated or destroyed, the payroll tax fight suggested more ominous lessons. Over and over in 2011, Democratic congressional leaders had indicated a new willingness to bargain away key elements of the program—principally the CPI's pivotal role in the benefit formula—in exchange for tax increases or other revenue raisers that could easily be canceled by a later, more conservative Congress. Would that be the kind of deal congressional Democrats envisioned negotiating after the November 2012 election? Did they expect the goodwill their party had accumulated as defenders of Social Security would enable them to do so without paying a price?

"What worries me most," Eric Kingson of the Strengthen Social Security Campaign wrote in an email as the payroll tax fight gathered steam, "is the silence of some Democrats who should know better and a sneaking suspicion that some Democratic leaders may not think that Social Security is worth fighting for."

CHAPTER 48

THE RETIREMENT CRISIS

"The lifespan of any civilization can be measured by the respect and care that is given to its elderly citizens, and those societies which treat their elderly with contempt have the seeds of their own destruction within them."
—Arnold J. Toynbee[1]

"An entitlement society ... is a fundamental corruption of the American spirit."
—Mitt Romney[2]

Lindsey Graham was the epitome—from the Republican side—of the center-right deficit hawk: eternally concerned about the deficit, almost religious in his devotion to bipartisanship, always optimistic that the system, in the end, would work. In early March 2011 he expressed his strong hopes for a deal to restructure Social Security.

"I've never seen a better moment to deal with Social Security in a bipartisan fashion than right now," he told reporters. To back this up, he noted that employer-based pensions "are going by the wayside" and that "a lot of Americans are going to outlive their 401(k) plans."[3]

The convoluted course of the Social Security debate snarled itself hopelessly with this statement. Certainly, if private-sector pensions and retirement savings plans were evaporating, on top of which working Americans were drowning in debt, preserving Social Security was an important goal. Yet the ways Graham proposed to "deal with" it—means-testing benefits and raising the retirement age—would shrink the program, forcing people to rely more on disappearing pensions and their own dwindling savings. This being Washington, the Reuters story reporting Graham's remarks didn't raise any question about his logic.

The astounding, and potentially tragic, aspect of the Social Security debate was that it carried on with practically no reference to the challenges facing the program's participants. Politicians on the right and center-right felt free to decry the resistance to even "modest cuts" in Social Security benefits with no reference to the vulnerability of seniors who were living the effects of the reductions already mandated in the 1983 Amendments. But the situation of those seniors was becoming alarming. A new, supplemental poverty measure introduced by the Census Bureau in November 2011 nearly doubled the official estimate of Americans over sixty-five living in poverty, to 15.9%, mainly due to medical costs not counted in the official numbers. More than 34% were either poor or near-poor—defined as having family income less than twice the poverty line. Half of all retirement-age persons who were no longer working— that is, who were receiving Social Security—had total yearly income of less than $16,140—only a fraction more than the federal minimum wage.

Even small reductions in benefits, or slower growth over a period of years, could tip many of these people over that line. Countless others, who once believed their personal savings, 401(k)s, or employer-sponsored pensions made their retirements secure, were finding out that this wasn't the case either. Meanwhile, Congress and state and local governments were scrounging for ways to cut back the rest of the safety net for seniors—targeting Medicaid funds for nursing homes and home health care, housing subsidies, and other benefits.[4] A true retirement crisis was looming in the U.S., but politicians, obsessed with Social Security projections decades into the future, were disinclined to address it. Current retirees were already affected; those who came after, beginning with financially vulnerable workers in their late fifties and early sixties, would be hit much harder.

The Social Security "deficit"—the amount by which payouts under OASI and Disability Insurance were expected to exceed revenues—was projected in 2011 to total about $6.5 trillion over the next seventy-five years. But for all the political attention focused on it, the economic impact of that shortfall would be quite moderate, equaling just .7% of GDP. Even the baby boom retirement wave wouldn't make a very big dent in the economy, according to the Social Security trustees, whose 2011 Annual Report estimated that the annual cost of benefits would rise gradually to 6.2% of GDP by 2035, decline to about 6% by 2050, and then remain at about that level.

This was the most relevant way to measure Social Security's impact, since the program depended on payroll tax receipts to pay benefits, and payroll tax receipts only rise appreciably in an expanding economy where wages are growing at a healthy pace. Even after decades of wage stagnation, Social Security still faced no emergency that a rise in wages couldn't significantly alleviate. While Social Security benefits would be a bigger burden relative to other parts of the federal government, then, they wouldn't be a major problem.

By contrast, the U.S. faced a "retirement income deficit" of $6.6 trillion—larger than Social Security's projected seventy-five-year shortfall and five times the size of the current-year federal deficit.[5] The Retirement Income Deficit was a new measure unveiled in fall 2010 by the Center for Retirement Research at Boston College. It lumped together all the resources that Americans in the peak earning years between thirty-two and sixty-four years of age would have to retire on: Social Security and pension benefits, retirement savings, home equity, and other assets. It calculated the income people would need in retirement, based on tax scenarios as well as the income replacement targets that Americans at different income levels would likely need to meet.[6]

Social Security and Medicare were perhaps the only ingredients in the Retirement Income Deficit calculation that provided benefits the elderly could really rely upon. Nearly two-thirds of all retirees depended on Social Security for more than half their income, and roughly one in five for all of it. Without Social Security, nearly half of Americans over sixty-five would be living in poverty.[7] If anything, dependence on Social Security was increasing during the latest economic slump, thanks to the collapsed housing market, the recession, decades of stagnating wages, and the disintegration of other elements of the social safety net, among other factors.

Not that it was a lot to lean on. In 2010, Social Security still only replaced 37% of the average worker's pre-retirement income at sixty-five. More than 95% of recipients got less than $2,000 a month from the program. Women averaged less than $12,000 a year in benefits, compared to $14,000 for retirees overall, thanks to the gender pay gap—partially explaining why 75% of old people living in poverty in the U.S. were women. Little of this seemed to merit discussion in deficit-obsessed Washington or on Wall Street, but it created an alarming picture for anyone familiar with what was happening in the rest of the country, where a Gallup poll found that 90% of people aged forty-four to seventy-five agreed that the country faced a retirement crisis.

Even before the economic slump, however, there were reasons to worry about the erosion of Social Security and to ask how it might be improved. First was the age at which retirees could begin to collect full benefits—which, under the 1983 Amendments, was scheduled to rise gradually from sixty-five to sixty-seven for those born in 1938 or later. Second were the premiums for Medicare Parts B and D, which the government deducts straight from recipients' Social Security checks, and were expected to go up sharply. Third, seniors with moderate incomes could expect the tax rate on their Social

Security payments to rise because the ceilings built into the tax code weren't inflation-indexed.[8]

The fourth, and perhaps largest problem, was wage stagnation. Rising wages alone don't ensure Social Security's solvency. While higher wages boost payroll taxes, they also raise benefits. But the fact remained that Social Security can't pay benefits without an adequate revenue stream to cover the payments over time. That income stream is made up of interest on trust fund assets, taxes on benefits, and—much the largest component—payroll tax contributions.

Wage stagnation had been depressing payroll taxes for many years—real hourly wages in 2010 were at about 1974 levels[9]—and the economic crisis was exacerbating the problem. Payroll tax revenues declined by 1.13-percentage-points of payroll in 2010—more than $60 billion—from what the Trustees had projected in 2009, "due to a deeper recession and slower recovery than had been expected."

How did the recession translate into lower payroll tax receipts? The proportion of Americans living in poverty rose sharply to 14.3% in 2010, according to the Census Bureau, up from 13.2% in 2009—the highest proportion since 1994.[10] A larger percent of people of working age—between eighteen and sixty-four—lived in poverty than in any year since 1959.[11] Unemployment was hovering in the 9% range and wasn't expected to fall to pre-recession levels until 2016, according to the CBO.[12]

Median family income was falling too, according to the Census Bureau. And this was a decline not from a period of wage expansion, but from the 2003–07 period of already-stagnating incomes. The result was that the first decade of the new millennium was a "lost decade" for American wage earners, leaving them about where they had been in the late 1990s. "This is the first time in memory that an entire decade has produced essentially no economic growth for the average American family," observed Harvard economist Lawrence Katz.[13] And it was likely to get worse: companies were cutting wages to an extent not seen since the 1981–82 recession—frequently by 20% or more. That suggested workers who accepted lower wages might be stuck at those levels for many years, leaving their children exposed to economic hardship and threatening prospects for upward mobility.

Unless Americans got a raise, their prospects—and Social Security's—would only worsen, because other resources that working people once thought would carry them through retirement—and thus relieve the pressure on Social Security—were disappearing.

Home equity had always been one of the chief sources of household wealth for working families, but the value of homes had been devastated by the housing bubble's collapse—a deflation that was still proceeding three years after the crash. The administration's programs to help households facing foreclosure were ill-conceived failures, and congressional Republicans were determined to cancel them without putting anything better in their place. Home equity was unlikely to reassume its role once the economy recovered either, because the government—this was one area where the Obama administration and Republicans saw eye to eye—was getting out of the business of guaranteeing home mortgages. What would take over the role of home ownership as a wealth-builder for working people was unknown.

As for personal savings, the mounting pressures on working households made it harder for them to put anything away for retirement. Baby boomers and Gen Xers were becoming known collectively as the "Sandwich Generation": households whose working members were bringing up children and caring for aging relatives. According to a 2006 poll by John Hancock Life Insurance, 15% of those polled said they were using money intended for their retirement to cover care-giving expenses. Nearly two-thirds of respondents, or their spouses, were helping provide long-term care.[14]

The crisis was approaching especially fast for older workers. A poll of Americans aged forty-seven to sixty-five, by the Associated Press and LifeGoesStrong. com, found that almost three-quarters expected to work after reaching retirement age. Getting work wouldn't be easy, however. Labor Department statistics showed that 17.4% of Americans nearing retirement—those between fifty-five and sixty-five—either were unemployed or had been looking for work so long that they had given up. More than 60% of those over fifty, in a Rutgers University survey, said they didn't expect to hold another full-time position in their field. Employers showed a distinct preference for younger workers, who could be paid less and were considered—rightly or wrongly—more adaptable.

One reason many older workers wanted to postpone retirement was that their 401(k) balances had dropped precipitously, or just weren't enough to support an adequate standard of living. According to the Center for Retirement Research, only 8% of households had enough in their 401(k) accounts to generate $39,465 a year of income. The median 401(k) held $149,400—enough to generate only $9,073 a year.[15] The accounts themselves were becoming less generous. After the 2001–02 recession, some 5% of companies reduced or eliminated their matching contributions to 401(k)s; many never restored them. After 2008, 9–10% reduced or eliminated theirs.[16]

Some workers' retirement assets, meanwhile, were disappearing through more nefarious channels. In 2011, state-level investigators reported that a nationwide surge in scams and dubious investment deals was making prey of older workers and retirees. Some financial advisors, for example, were offering to pay lump sums to older workers in return for signing over their pension checks to the advisor. The catch, in many cases, was exorbitantly high interest charged on the lump-sum payments.

Roughly 50% of workers weren't affected by these troubles—because, of course, they had no pension or employer-sponsored retirement savings account at all.

Elements of Social Security itself were being dangerously overloaded. From 6.6 million beneficiaries in 2000, Disability Insurance was paying out to 10.2 million people in 2010. That resulted in a huge imbalance in the OASI and DI trust funds. While the OASI fund by itself was projected to run out of money in 2040, the Social Security trustees expected the DI fund to tap out in just four years.[17]

By itself that didn't constitute an emergency: funds could be shifted from OASI if Congress approved, and the trust funds together would still be solvent until 2036. But it demonstrated, again, that the price the country paid for having created an economy with a low-wage, "flexible" labor force was far greater worker dependence on programs like Social Security.

The nature of those programs, as a result, was changing. Far from easing into retirement, nearly half of all American workers aged fifty-eight and older held physically demanding jobs that put them at risk of becoming disabled.[18] DI was becoming a sort of early-early retirement plan for some workers, although a stingy one—it paid an average of only $1,064 a month in 2009. The ranks of "disability retirees" were bound to grow, too, swelled by the aging baby boomers.

Medicaid, which had started out as a program to aid low-income people who couldn't afford health coverage, had meanwhile become one of the most vital supports for the elderly. Two-thirds of Medicaid dollars in 2010 went to seniors, mostly for home health care and nursing home accommodations.[19]

In the effort to reduce the backlog of applications, Congress was literally moving backward. The April 2011 spending deal between the White House and Republican leaders cut $1.7 billion from the SSA's budget, which led to the closing of dozens of local hearing offices.

As retirees were forced to spend more of their Social Security checks on medical costs, OASI was morphing into a quasi-health plan. Medicare co-pays only covered between 20% and 45% of the cost of many outpatient treatment programs and services. The average cost of a private room in a nursing home was over $75,000 a year, and government didn't provide assistance unless the patient was financially tapped out. Medigap insurance policies could help, but the premiums ran $150 to $250 a month per person, and many insurance companies were getting out of covering long-term care. It was welcome news in October 2011 when the SSA announced that seniors would be getting their first COLA in two years in 2012—a healthy boost of 3.6%. For retirees who were lower-income earners, however, Medicare Part B premiums would slice about 43% off the increase, deducted before their Social Security checks were even printed.[20]

Yet, according to the Center for Retirement Research, some two-thirds of Americans were expected to require long-term care at some point during their retirement, whether at home or in nursing facilities. One study projected that spending on long-term care for the elderly would triple by 2040.[21] Alzheimer's Disease was increasing among the very old. Medicare itself remained largely a reactive system, however, emphasizing acute in-patient care over preventive care.[22]

Obama had made a first stab at addressing the coming long-term care crisis with Community Living Assistance Services and Support (CLASS), an element of his health care legislation that would create a voluntary, government-sponsored, self-funded long-term care insurance option. To be launched in 2014, CLASS would at least partially fulfill one of the late Claude Pepper's long-time aspirations. However, CLASS was poorly designed and was unlikely to be able to pay for itself unless it was retooled. Republicans preferred to cancel it. They got their way, essentially, in October 2011, when Health and Human Services announced that CLASS wouldn't be implemented since HHS couldn't figure out a viable long-term funding mechanism.

Even if CLASS, or something like it, could be made to work, what kind of medical care were seniors likely to receive in coming decades, when they couldn't take care of themselves anymore? Probably not the kind that's informed by the special needs of the elderly. Geriatric medicine, which concentrates on conditions related to aging, is a relatively neglected field in the U.S. In 2008, geriatric departments were still rare in American medical schools, and less than a third of all the medical and surgical specialties taught in those schools included specific geriatric training. By 2011, geriatric psychiatry, in particular, was in a near-crisis situation. Even in Florida, the state with the highest proportion of people over sixty-five, there were only seventeen specialists with board certification in mental health for the aged.[23]

Washington hadn't been especially helpful in establishing a positive trend. In 2005, the Bush administration and Congress actually eliminated all federal funding for geriatric training. The money was restored the next year, but the unpredictability of government commitment to geriatrics "further weakened the ability to attract doctors to enter the field," noted Robert N. Butler, the gerontologist and advocate for the elderly, in a book published just before his death.[24] ObamaCare included money for some promising projects that focused care on the small number of patients—including many of the elderly—who drove the rise in health care spending. But the House, in 2011, was determined to wipe these out along with the rest of the law.[25]

The need for geriatric care wasn't yet at crisis levels in 2011. But the fiscal pinch in state capitals continued, and senior services that were less expensive but also vital were targeted for cutbacks. Governors and legislators of both parties vowed not to raise taxes—and in some cases even lowered them, in what they described as an effort to encourage investment. Instead, they cut services for seniors. In New York City, Mayor Michael Bloomberg closed twenty-nine senior centers in 2010; in Albany, Democratic Gov. Andrew Cuomo, the following year, proposed redirecting $25 million from the centers to fund child welfare—a shift the state legislature rejected. In California, Democratic Gov. Jerry Brown proposed shutting all of the state's 310 adult day health centers and cutting funding for home and community care programs.[26] In some states, home-care workers, a vital element in the support system for seniors, were losing their unionized status and suffering cuts in their already-low wages and benefits, with elimination of many of these jobs a possible next step.

* * *

While politicians beavered away at plans to cut supports for seniors and their families, a few voices were doing what they could to raise awareness of the retirement crisis—not just in the U.S. but in other countries that were attempting to balance budgets on the backs of the elderly. Michael Hodin, a fellow at the Council on Foreign Relations who worked on aging issues, urged governments, the United Nations, and the private sector to launch initiatives akin to the Manhattan Project to find ways for the U.S. and other societies to prepare for much older populations.

The Commission to Modernize Social Security, a coalition that included labor-funded groups as well as ethnic advocates like the National Council of La Raza and the National Asian Pacific Center on Aging, was trying to bring attention to the need to make the program serve its participants better. In October 2011, it released a report calling on Congress to update Social Security to fit the profile of what would soon be a "majority-minority" U.S. population, much of it low-income. The commission's "Plan for a New Future" included eliminating the cap on income subject to payroll tax and making the Social Security benefit formula less generous for high earners. With the savings, the commission proposed four ideas for benefits improvement:

- Updating the special minimum benefit to 12% of the poverty level, to help people who had worked largely in low paying jobs;

- Reversing the Reagan-era cancellation of survivors' benefits for students through age twenty-two;

- Increasing benefits for low-income widowed spouses; and

- Providing benefits for unpaid caregivers.

In the Senate, meanwhile, Bernie Sanders was collecting sponsors for an amendment to the Older Americans Act that would increase funding for programs that directly benefited the elderly, including meals programs, senior centers, and services to help them find employment. Significantly, Sanders's bill would change the stated objective of the original, 1965 legislation from providing the elderly with "an adequate income in retirement in accordance with the American standard of living," to "economic security in later life in accordance with...." Another Senate bill, introduced by Democrats Sherrod Brown of Ohio and Barbara Mikulski of Maryland, would replace the CPI in the Social Security benefits formula—not with the stingier chained CPI, but with the CPI-E.

What made all of these proposals so starkly different was that they accepted the reality that the industrialized economies were aging. No magic-bullet solution—shifting the responsibility for old-age income support to working households in the form of personal investment accounts, for instance—was going to allow society as a whole to avoid addressing this change collectively—unless, of course, the elites preferred to let a much larger percentage of elderly working people sink into poverty. Instead, society would have to figure out collectively how best to adjust its policies on housing, health care, and many other vital needs to the fact of an aging society. Arguably, more money could be saved by finding better ways to prevent and treat Alzheimer's than by shoehorning seniors and their families into a consumer-empowered system of health-care buying. But that would require investing in old age—for instance, by increasing funding for research at the National Institute on Aging.

The preference in Washington was simply to cut spending on the aged and to rely on the market to somehow take up the slack. The four ideas that the Commission to Modernize Social Security was advancing had all been circulating for well over a decade; several had even been in Al Gore's 2000 presidential platform. None had ever enjoyed serious consideration on Capitol Hill.

Yet the need for Social Security and other social protections kept growing. In 1980, according to the Census Bureau, 30% of American households received Social Security, subsidized housing, unemployment insurance, or other government benefits. In third-quarter 2008, the figure was 44%. In 2010, a record 18.3% of total personal income in the U.S. consisted of payments from these programs—up from a fairly stable 12.5% from 1980 to 2000.[27] The title of an article in the *Wall Street Journal*, which covered this trend, indicates the attitude of most members of the policymaking elite: "Obstacle to Deficit Cutting: A Nation on Entitlements." But one reason the public remained loyal to Social Security was their quite realistic assessment that they couldn't get its modest—but essential—benefits anywhere else.

It would cost a sixty-six-year-old male $128,000 to purchase an annuity providing $10,000 a year for life, according to one estimate; a woman of the same age would have to pay some $138,000.[28] An annuity paying out $40,000 a year—a more realistic income requirement for most people—would cost about $550,000. A survey by the Employee Benefit Research Institute found that less than half of workers had $25,000 in savings, while only one-third had saved $50,000 or more. Most life insurance companies didn't offer inflation-protected annuities—essential for retirees expecting to live a long time—and those that did, charged more.

"During the financial crisis," *Wall Street Journal* personal-finance writer Brett Arends reported, "I got a lot of anxious emails from readers who held annuities from stricken insurance giant AIG. If the company went bankrupt, they asked, would their checks stop? For a 75-year-old widow, this was no joke. So an annuity backed by the federal government provides a lot of peace of mind."

What would happen if a proposal similar to Bowles-Simpson—the gold standard of the center-right—were enacted? Contrary to its sponsors' assertions, current retirees would be affected very quickly by the stingier COLAs built into the plan. But most of the impact would be felt by workers who would retire beginning in the 2020s. The share of income replaced by Social Security was expected to drop from about 41.8% in 2002 to 36.2% in 2030, thanks largely to rising medical costs and higher taxes on benefits.[29] Gradually eroding benefits would force retirees to rely more on SSI and Disability Insurance and other forms of relief from state and local governments. Costs would go up for those governments. They, in turn, would move to cut costs. The end result: a growing burden on retirees, their families and communities, and on non-profit relief organizations.

Not that the math would be simple. In New York State, where some 600,000 residents received disability, activists in 2009 were distressed about proposed SSI cutbacks of as little as $24 a month in the governor's proposed 2009–10 budget. "When you have unpaid bills," said Leah Farrell of the Center for Disability Rights, "that leads to evictions and when you have an evicted person who is in need of medical care, they're going to be funneled through hospitals and into institutions, which is more costly to the state."[30] The front line, however, would be workers and their families.

The plight of the elderly, the ways in which the system of public support that had done so much to lift them out of poverty in the pre-Reagan decades was now failing them, and the refusal of Washington and the private sector to prepare for their needs in coming years, weren't ignored in the media, exactly. Articles and features appeared fairly often in major publications, TV, radio, and on the Internet. But every feature that spotlighted the threats to the well-being of the aged, was counterbalanced, it seemed, by coverage like a perky entry that *Investors' Business Daily* published in April, by columnist Michelle Malkin.

"It's time for a 21st-century retirement age," Malkin announced. "If 40 is the new 20 and 50 is the new 30, why shouldn't 70 be the new 65? ... We're living longer, working longer and, in general, holding down jobs that are far less physically taxing than those of previous generations." In fact, the numbers showed that this was true only for relatively affluent people. But Malkin thought she could see the future—on TV. "Some senior citizens' lobbying groups fret that today's workforce wouldn't be able to handle longer careers. Tell that to Betty White or Joan Rivers or Helen Mirren."

It was easy to counter Malkin's narrative. A few months earlier, the Frances Perkins Center embarked on the Social Security Stories Project, which collected and posted online stories about the role the program played in the lives of some of its beneficiaries. Many were spouses and children of workers who died young, leaving their families to depend on Social Security Survivor's Insurance. Many of the others, too, highlighted the insurance aspect of the program—the role it played for people who often had never thought they'd have need of it and at some point in their lives might have been ridiculed as "greedy geezers." One, in particular, epitomized the struggles that many elderly people faced:

But for Social Security, I would be living on the street out of a grocery cart. I am a 70 year old able bodied vet with 26 years experience in law enforcement. Apparently, I'm "over qualified" for any work as no one will hire me … or give me an interview. Obvious age discrimination, but how do you prove that? Due to an incompetent retirement program and an expensive divorce, I've lost everything. Not qualified for unemployment. Not eligible for food stamps (I make too much money, SS only!) As such, I'm NOT EVEN COUNT-ED among the unemployed. I didn't even get counted by the census. No mail, no knock, nothing. I'm sick and tired of the way my country is being run. Congress votes themselves a raise but denies cost of living for Social Security recipients. How is that fair?

Still, the mainstream media almost never linked the mounting problems facing the aged to the ongoing effort to slash Social Security, Medicare, and Medicaid. Even coverage of the 2011 Republican budget resolution focused almost entirely on how deeply it would cut spending and the deficit, largely ignoring its

January 26, 1939

impact on seniors and other at-risk groups. Since the mainstream media tended to reflect the thinking of center-right Washington, this wasn't unexpected.

This obliviousness explains why the Washington press corps for years had given Alan Simpson a free pass for his rantings against the retirees he imagined were getting fat off Social Security. More seriously, it meant that one of the fundamental concepts behind Social Security seldom made it into the public discourse, and when it did, only to be dismissed. When mutual aid was translated into State-administered social insurance programs in the decades after Bismarck, it passed on the understanding that each generation owed a debt to the ones that came before—a debt it paid through, among other things, old-age pensions.

In place of this idea, Social Security's critics were attempting to implant the notion that each generation should begin and end with a clean balance sheet—that virtually any intergenerational debt was somehow unfair. This was an impossibility—or at least, a utopian vision that had never existed on earth. To journalists whose public-policy school was Capitol Hill and the think-tank community, however, it sounded at least plausible—and more hard-headed than the idea of mutual aid. That's why pundits like David Brooks could reflexively describe "entitlements" as "fundamentally diseased" and dismiss politicians who balked at cutting them as "too ideologically rigid."[31]

This tone-deafness has a long history—one that extends the length of the story we've just related. The tragedy of the unresolvable, speculative, three-decade debate over Social Security's future solvency wasn't just that it froze the program in place, rendering any effort to update and improve benefits nearly impossible, but that it desensitized the business and policy-making elite, as well as the punditocracy, to the needs of the very people Social Security was created to serve. Washington, both knowingly and unknowingly, was running away from the real retirement crisis, preferring to focus on a fiscal future that might be an illusion.

EPILOGUE

I. Making It Work

"We are not a nation of accountants, however much our government tries to turn us into one."

—Peggy Noonan[1]

In January 2011, with Washington shifting its attention from the wrap-up of the president's deficit commission to the upcoming release of the House budget resolution, conservative columnist David Brooks waxed prophetic. "We're in the middle of a global race to see who can most intelligently reform the welfare state," he wrote.[2] Replacing "intelligently reform" with more straightforward wording—for instance, "phase out"—this pretty fairly summed up the situation.

Commenting in April on the budget-resolution's proposals for Medicare and Medicaid, *Washington Post* blogger Ezra Klein noted, "What saves money is not the reform. It's the cut."[3] There was no reform, in fact—merely an exhortation that working households trust the market and, implicitly, the hope that Washington wouldn't cut the program even more in the future. The same could be said of the Bowles-Simpson Social Security proposals that Ryan recommended to his colleagues.

Like most everything in politics, what drove the pushback against State-based social programs—including the war against Social Security—was a combination of self-interest and ideology. The right and the center-right in the U.S. represented, in varying degrees, the interests of the affluent and the corporate establishment—and especially, in recent years, the financial services sector. The overriding concern of these groups was to maintain and, they hoped, expand the low-tax regime that their representatives had been putting in place since the Carter administration.

Their fundamental opposition to programs for the aged stemmed from their fear that these people would absorb a bigger share of government spending in coming decades as the population aged—necessitating, at some point, higher taxes. It was the same apprehension that had led them to caricature the Townsend movement as quasi-fascist during the 1930s and 1940s. Their response was twofold: first, to relocate more of their operations in countries with young populations and that spent less on "welfare"; second, to lobby for reduction of government spending on the aged in the U.S. This meant, in practice, persuading the public to accept a transfer of the responsibility for supporting income in old age back to the individual and the family.

Social Security wasn't just the biggest program for the elderly; it was also symbolic of the nation's commitment to them. As a form of social insurance, it assumed a position above politics. It was always understood, then, that the first step in protecting wealth from the threat represented by an aging population was to eliminate the features that made Social Security and Medicare "social insurance"—to turn them into welfare or "social assistance" programs that could then be more easily cut back. The many, many plans, proposals, and legislative schemes that Washington produced in the decades we've explored in this book—whether they focused on private investment accounts, means-testing, raising the retirement age, or some other gambit—were all concocted with this goal in mind.

It was easy to demonstrate, as we've seen, that Social Security wasn't necessarily destined to be a huge drain on either the taxpayer or the economy, while if costs did rise substantially, they couldn't be wished away by shifting them to households or injecting payroll tax receipts into private accounts. But this wasn't the point. The elite who directed American politics and policymaking didn't want to live with the prospect that they would have to bear some portion of those costs—the expense of maintaining elderly people they didn't know and who represented no direct economic value to them.

As more and more of the economically powerful became used to the low-tax policies of the past thirty-plus years, this impulse spread from Republicans, with their traditional dislike of anything resembling a "progressive" shifting of burdens, to the Democratic center-right. The result was the tacit alliance we have watched come together: an alliance that made it possible for the center-right to largely support the Bush tax cuts but also hyperventilate about the dangers of entitlements.

Why was Social Security not phased out or privatized in the years begin-ning with Reagan? Above all, the public's loyalty to the program, demonstrated over and over, prevented it from being gutted. Another factor, ironically, was the right and center-right's failure to agree on one way to do it. They repeatedly bogged down on the question of how deeply to cut, how to integrate private accounts into the scheme—or not—and how to cover the transition costs.

If there are heroes in our story, they are the labor and grassroots political organizers, progressive advocates, agitators, and lawmakers who resisted this trend and time and again rallied to keep Washington from restructuring Social Security out of existence. The traditional Democratic coalition disarmed itself and bargained away a great deal of its achievements during the years we've covered, but stood firm, generally with success, on this one issue—and that in the face of enormous pressure from the political and economic elite. Credit for Social Security's survival also goes to Franklin Delano Roosevelt and his New Deal advisors. Long dead, they continued to exert a powerful influence because of the ingeniousness of their creation, which combined personal savings, social insurance, and public assistance in a way that booby-trapped it for anyone hoping to dismantle it.

But it was a Sisyphean struggle, since the political environment never im-proved sufficiently for the New Dealers' heirs to be able to act creatively rather than defensively. Compounding the problem, Democratic presidents—Carter, Clinton, and Obama—increasingly positioned themselves not as party leaders but as "post-partisan" policy arbitrators. One intriguing piece of advice for ending this cycle came from a most unfriendly source: William McGurn, a longtime conservative journalist and former speechwriter for George W. Bush. Now a *Wall Street Journal* columnist, McGurn wrote in April 2011,

> American liberals continue to overlook their greatest strength: their ability to set goals for our society. Whether it be increasing access to good housing, a dignified retirement, or a decent education for every child, liberals have won most of the arguments. In fact, even if our unpopular health-care law is repealed, it's a good bet that Republicans will still have to find a way to meet another goal set by liberals, that of en-suring that Americans with pre-existing medical conditions can get coverage.[4]

Sooner or later, if they wanted to "win" in any lasting way, progressives would have to look past the fiscal arguments that conservatives used to un-dermine Social Security and refocus on its purpose as a collective means of providing income security. They would have to think again about how to im-prove, expand, and update the program. Otherwise, the movement against So-cial Security would continue to frame the issue as one of taxpayer affordability rather than social need and obligation. Over the past thirty years, the former argument had acquired a far more powerful grip than the latter on Washington decision makers. As long as that continued to be the case, the right and center-right would keep searching for the political gambit that would at last enable them to begin winding down Social Security. One day, they might succeed.

Opposing this was the reality that every industrial and post-industrial society continued to need social insurance to provide an adequate life for people in their old age, to take care of their survivors, and to otherwise keep over-burdened, underpaid working households from sliding into poverty. If any-thing, the need was growing, because working people—even those who fancied themselves "knowledge workers"—had so few other resources to fall back on.

A surprisingly wide range of economists, policy wonks, and even private-sector consultants understood that American workers faced a retirement crisis. The more progressive agitated, to little avail, for improvements to Social Se-curity: a more generous benefits formula for divorcees and widows, a higher minimum benefit for low-wage workers.

Health care reform offered one possible way to revitalize social insurance. Jack Rasmus, an economist and independent journalist, proposed recapturing the Social Security trust fund surplus, including the interest earned on its as-sets, and using it to finance a universal, single-payer health care system.[5] That way, the new system would be part of the same, self-funded social insurance structure as Social Security and Medicare—not just another government pro-gram that Congress could cut at will. At the same time, he advocated investing part of Washington's economic stimulus package in sectors for which there was a growing need, such as health care for seniors.

In the 19th century, the government had subsidized the development of ag-ricultural and mining expertise through the funding of land-grant colleges. "It could just as well be done for healthcare and other essential services industries in the 21st," Rasmus wrote in *Z Magazine*.[6]

Most creative thinking about retirement, however, focused on ways to supplement the program—but not replace it—with personal savings vehicles. Employer-based pension plans had never reached more than about 50% of the workforce in the private sector. Rather than expand Social Security to fill the gap, the idea was to create, with government support, a more universal version of the employer-based system.

An odd convergence of conservative and liberal advocates were pushing variations on the supplemental account idea. Paul O'Neill, Bush's former Trea-sury secretary, proposed creating American Birthright Grants for every child born in the U.S. Each child, regardless of income, would start out life with $5,000 in the bank, to be administered by the federal Thrift Savings Plan, which would form "a second tier of federal retirement security."[7] Gene Sperling and Rahm Emanuel proposed a "Universal 401(k)" funded in part by a gen-erous matching contribution from the government to low-income workers.[8] Obama endorsed this plan in principle in *The Audacity of Hope*—although not Sperling's additional call for cuts in Social Security.[9] Teresa Ghilarducci was promoting a Guaranteed Retirement Account with a matching contribution by the government and, as well, a guaranteed minimum return.

Robert Fogel, a Nobel-Prize-winning economist from the University of Chicago, proposed setting up a second national pension system alongside Social Security. Structured like the national wealth funds in which Norway and Alaska, for example, captured some profits from their oil industries, it would consist of individual mandatory savings accounts, all invested in a single, broadly diversified portfolio. To make sure low-income, as well as high-income, workers reaped significant benefits, accounts belonging to the former would be augmented with revenues from higher taxes on the affluent.[10]

Rasmus proposed something similar: a "single national 401(k) pool" made up of contributions from individuals and partially matching amounts from the government. The latter would be funded by a national value-added tax on sales between businesses, making them, in effect, a contribution from employers. But instead of being allocated to the standard mix of stocks and bonds of big, established companies in the U.S. and elsewhere, the assets would be invested in public works projects or loans to public-private joint ventures in such areas as alternative energy and green technology.[11]

In 2009, an initiative called Retirement USA was launched to work for a national retirement system, alongside Social Security, that was "universal, secure, and adequate." The principal sponsors included the Pension Rights Center, an advocacy group for retirees and workers preparing for retirement; the AFL-CIO; and the National Committee to Preserve Social Security and Medicare. But when it solicited proposals for a conference on "Re-envisioning Retirement Security" in October 2009, it attracted submissions from a much wider range of sources, extending from Ghilarducci and Dean Baker, at the progressive end, to academics, financial and private pension consultants.

Most of the Retirement USA proposals involved portable private accounts, and most would require the worker to convert her account into a stream of lifetime payments such as an annuity. Most would be funded by contributions from both employer and employee, some including a further contribution by the government for low-income workers. Some included cost-of-living formulas or other mechanisms to make sure the worker received a minimum benefit at retirement, whatever investment return her account achieved. One, from the Economic Opportunity Institute in Washington State, would allow workers without employer-based pensions to set up separate accounts that were managed as part of the public-employee retirement systems of their states, taking advantage of the low administrative costs of those plans. This idea actually had legislative backers in several states, including California, Connecticut, Maryland, and Massachusetts.

A few proposals went farther. Nancy Altman offered a scheme to create a national defined-benefit plan: a traditional pension plan, administered by the federal government. The goal was to make sure all workers, regardless of whether their employer offered one, had a guaranteed pension—not just a retirement savings account. Everyone covered by Social Security would participate; funding would come from employers, employees, income on the plan's investments, and, in one version, the estate tax, although low-income workers would receive a counterbalancing tax credit. This new national pension plan would provide an additional 20% on top of Social Security benefits through a joint and survivor annuity.

How to make sure workers didn't have to tap out their pension savings when they were out of a job? Another intriguing idea that surfaced during the Bush years—wage insurance—addressed this issue.

Originally promoted by economists Robert Litan and Lori Kletzer, the idea was to create a federally run system similar to unemployment insurance that would partially make up the difference in wages when a worker moved from a higher to a lower paying job. Litan and Kletzer were aiming to help workers who had been displaced as a result of competition from low-wage overseas labor. Sperling, in 2005, proposed expanding the structure to include anyone over fifty, and possibly younger, who lost a job or could only find part-time work. More workers would stay longer in the job force, Sperling predicted, easing the burden on Social Security.[12]

Behind all of these ideas were three common understandings: one, that a retirement crisis was looming and that the current system—Social Security plus private pensions plus personal saving—no longer worked; two, that there were still ways to make it work using existing structures; and three, that Social Security itself was essentially a finished product, its role in the retirement system not to be changed. But there were problems with each of these assumptions.

Other countries had simpler, more comprehensive, and more generous national pension systems. Was Social Security's basic structure really unimprovable? For instance, people who spent their lives in activities that didn't fit the program's definition of "work," such as family caregivers, could only participate as survivors or, in some cases, as qualified disabled persons. Couldn't these definitions be broadened?

As for the other major part of the U.S. retirement system, employer-sponsored pensions: perhaps it could be reformed in ways that raised participation and made it more generous and secure. But the experience of the past three decades, at least, made it clear that most employers wanted out. They were unwilling to provide pensions worthy of the name to any but their top executives. Perhaps they could be forced to do so. But was channeling pensions through employers really the best model?

It was also troubling that most of the ideas under discussion still centered on helping workers save more for themselves for retirement—perhaps with a government contribution and a minimum guaranteed benefit at retirement. However it was structured, such a system could play into the hands of lawmakers who wanted to use the returns from those accounts as a pretext to cut Social Security benefits. It begged another question as well: given that the country's transportation network, schools, non-commercial research and development facilities, and other infrastructure were falling apart from neglect, was the best use of the money that these accounts would generate to give it to private portfolio managers?

Certainly the overall retirement system wasn't working for most Americans. Social Security, as a result, was becoming more and more of a lifeline. For at least thirty years, the government had been failing to reform the structure of laws and regulations that the retirement system was built upon, in part because of the persistent anxiety about Social Security's "solvency." By spring 2011, Republicans and center-right Democrats had again pushed Washington to the brink of destroying Medicare and placing Social Security on a fast track to phase-out. A strong case could be made that the State, too, wanted out of the business, not just of welfare but of maintaining social insurance systems of any sort. If so, what to do?

II. Returning to the Source

"The older I get, the more convinced I am that to really work programs have to be owned by the people they're serving. That isn't just rhetoric, it's real. There's got to be ownership."

—George Latimer, former mayor of St. Paul,
Minnesota[13]

The great achievement of social insurance, the French philosopher and social thinker Michel Foucault said in an interview shortly before his death in 1984, was to increase people's income security, thus imparting greater autonomy to their lives.[14] Thanks to programs like Social Security, workers were no longer worried—as worried—about who would care for their parents, their families, or themselves in old age. Therefore they had far greater choice in how they decided to live. This created "a growing aspiration on the part of individuals and groups for autonomy." But how was this desire for personal autonomy to be integrated into a system based, fundamentally, on mutual aid—that is, on mutual dependence?

Foucault's answer wasn't to privatize social insurance schemes like Social Security, but to democratize them. "We certainly need to undertake a process of decentralization," he said, "for example, to bring the decision-making centers and those who depend on them closer ... thus avoiding the kind of grand totalizing integration that leaves people in complete ignorance of what is involved in this or that regulation."

Unfortunately, policymaking for Social Security suffered from what Foucault called "decisional distance." "Social security, in its present form, is perceived as a distant institution, having a state character—even if it isn't so—because it is a huge centralized machine."* But social insurance wasn't just a politically effective way to construct a set of government programs. It was a way of "posing the question of what life is worth and the way in which one can confront death." When the individuals who made up society were distanced from this central question, the result was "a sort of sterilization" that froze social insurance schemes in place, keeping them from evolving to serve the new needs of their participants, many of whom would be encouraged to hunker down and protect what they had rather than advocating to enhance and extend it to other, less advantaged groups.

This couldn't continue. Populations aged and the demand for health care grew. But if decisions about who got what in the way of health services and what standard of living the aged should expect were left to the market, it would allocate resources based on affluence. If a state bureaucracy did the job, it would receive no direct input from the people it supposedly served and might make decisions contrary to their interests.

There was a third alternative: "for people to assume responsibility for what affects them fundamentally, namely, their life and well being." Instead of abandoning these decisions to individuals, however, Foucault believed they "ought to be the effect of a kind of ethical consensus so that the individual may recognize himself in the decisions made and in the values that inspired them. Only then would such decisions be acceptable."

Foucault didn't prescribe how to achieve that "ethical consensus," but clearly it would mean placing decisions about the future of programs like Social Security, and the knowledge to make such decisions, more directly into the hands of participants. At one time, that had been the case. The mutual aid societies, tongs, and friendly or fraternal orders that supplied unemployment, health care, survivors', and old-age insurance to millions of American households before the Great Depression represented an incomplete, patchwork solution to the needs of an uprooted, post-agricultural society. However, they had the advantage that their members directly controlled the programs, understood them, and could modify them as needed.

Social Security, as an institution, was very far from this decentralized, self-governing model. It hadn't completely replaced welfare. Instead of acting as a moderating influence, it was being dragged back into the zero-sum battle for scarce resources that fueled class and racial warfare.

The trajectory that Harry Truman had once seen for social programs in the U.S., from welfare to social insurance, was reversing itself. By the turn of the century, Social Security's development had become blocked, retarded by the dead-end tax policy wrangles of the last three decades and by a muddled and unresolvable solvency debate that threatened to kill the program slowly by preventing it from evolving to meet its participants' changing needs. While

---

* Foucault was referring to the more comprehensive French national pension system. But his remarks fit the U.S. Social Security program as well.

advocates for the elderly fought fiercely to preserve it, the program was also a great frustration to them.

Some of Social Security's deficiencies were closely tied to other political issues. More and more non-heterosexuals, for instance, were forming joint households, having children, and developing patterns of living that differed from the so-called traditional family. Almost a third of households were headed by a single parent in 2004, compared with a little over 12% in 1960, according to U.S. Census figures. Unmarried couples—gay and straight—made up more than 5% of households, compared with virtually none in 1960.[15] Still others, especially in low-income communities, were headed by grandparents, stretching the traditional definition of caregiver. These people were demanding access for their family members to Social Security and Medicare as well as unemployment insurance and pension benefits, despite lacking the traditional marriage contract.[16] Whether Social Security could evolve to better serve nontraditional households was up to Congress, where a powerful bloc of conservative lawmakers would oppose any such change.

Politicians and the mainstream media tend to explain such developments as "failures of leadership," underscoring their nostalgia for larger-than-life statespeople in the FDR, or at least the Reagan, mold. But maybe the trouble wasn't who was making the decisions so much as how they were being made. Certainly, behind the rise in popular suspicion of government in the last decades of the 20th century were such specifics as Vietnam, the economic upheavals of the 1970s, and right-wing loathing of liberal social agendas. But the "decisional distance" that had grown up between the people and the policy-making process, starting with the institutions put in place under Roosevelt and his successors, were also to blame. One reason some politicians and some of their constituents fell in love with the idea of personal choice and private accounts was that they had fallen out of love with the technocratic philosophy of the New Deal.

"The welfare state has produced and been produced by national experts in 'social administration' ... who then explained it to further professionals ... who try to distribute its effects to consumers or clients," British social services scholar Stephen Yeo quipped. That didn't leave much of a role for those "consumers" and "clients." Welfare in general "is framed as something given to those it was designed to benefit, not something that its users could themselves take a predominant role in producing and organizing," argues Patrick Reedy, another British scholar.[17]

Bob Ball, during his decades directing the Social Security system, exemplified this approach to social insurance. He worked to create a sort of priesthood within the SSA, versed in the philosophical principles of the program and dedicated to making sure it evolved to meet the changing needs of the public. Ball's cadre of technocrats were taught to work within the framework of representative democracy, but their role was to supply what democracy couldn't. They were wise, far-sighted stewards of the public interest who saw farther and more clearly than the people's representatives could. They enabled the agency to respond admirably to participants' needs even after the 1970s, when budgets grew stingy and new, politically fraught responsibilities like SSI were heaped on it.

At least in principle, the career staff at SSA accepted the need for Social Security participants to understand the program and feel a sense of ownership in it. But did the public really need to understand the arcana of the benefits formula, the relationship between Treasury and the OASI and DI trust funds, and the minutiae of the trustees' long-term solvency projections? Were they entitled—so to speak—to a role in running it? No one in Washington seemed to think so. For instance, one reason mainstream journalists could routinely dismiss the Treasury bonds in the Social Security trust funds as "IOUs," with very few challenging the notion, was that most people had no clear sense that those bonds belonged to them, not the government.

Increasingly, government looked upon workers, survivors, retirees, and the disabled as clients of the agency, not as participants in a cooperative lifetime security arrangement that belonged to them rather than to the government. It was comparatively liberal administrations like Clinton-Gore, in fact, that were most enamored of the idea of government-as-enterprise and citizen-as-client.

For many members of the American political elite, keeping complex issues like Social Security away from the masses—or at least from the congressional committee structure, where they would be exposed to public testimony from at least a few experts who questioned the conventional wisdom—came to seem like a good thing. The Super Committee that Congress charged at the end of July 2011 with finding $1.5 trillion of deficit reduction measures—from virtually any source—was just the latest evidence of this deep-seated yearning to bypass democracy.

Phasing out Social Security and replacing it with personal retirement saving was one way to get the people out of politics.

Bob Ball, and the many coalitions he aided and helped to create, were able to keep the program from being gutted and transformed into a conduit for payroll tax contributions to fee-earning portfolios on Wall Street. But they couldn't get Social Security moving again—shepherding creative responses to the needs of women and low-income workers, for example, through the legislative process.

One problem was that the liberal political class that had traditionally defended and nurtured Social Security was aging if not dying out. The program was unlikely to suffer much tampering as long as Reid and Pelosi commanded the Senate and House Democratic caucuses, but their successors would probably be younger, from more affluent backgrounds, with less intimate understanding of the important role that the program played and less sympathy generally for the social insurance concept. They would almost certainly have more in common personally and intellectually with people like Bill Clinton, Larry Summers, Mark Warner, and Pete Peterson than with Tip O'Neill, Claude Pepper, or Bob Ball.

Even if that weren't the case, Reid and Pelosi couldn't recreate the sense of collective ownership that Social Security was supposed to inspire in working people. In January 1935, when the Roosevelt administration was fighting to get the Social Security Act through Congress, Labor Secretary Frances Perkins wrote in the *New York Times* that the concept of social insurance was no less than "a fundamental part of another great forward step in that liberation of humanity which began with the Renaissance." Yet for almost its whole existence, Social Security had been running away from its own radicalism in the hope that technocratic professionalism could keep it above politics. It hadn't worked. While the notion that Social Security was on the verge of a fiscal crisis was debatable, certainly the program faced an ongoing political crisis that already extended back three decades.

The root of that crisis was the fact that, while the public was still intensely loyal to Social Security, their understanding of how the program worked and the nature of the threats against it was low. In a NBC/*Wall Street Journal* poll in March 2011, less than one in four respondents supported making significant cuts in Social Security as part of a deficit-reduction package. But, asked another way, 62% supported reducing benefits for wealthier retirees and 56% favored raising the retirement age to sixty-nine.

"Most voters do not consider these changes to be 'significant' cuts because the ideas strike them as common sense," John Sununu, the former Republican senator, noted with some satisfaction in a *Boston Globe* column the same month.[18] Yet, as the debate over progressive indexing revealed, to make much of a dent in the program's future payouts, means-testing would have to extend far below the income level most people would consider "wealthy." Raising the retirement age would result in major cuts that would hit low- and middle-income workers especially hard.

Because the solvency debate made it politically unfeasible to do so, however, Congress wasn't stepping in to make sure Social Security responded to new needs as they came along. The cost of private-sector services was rising rapidly, just like all other health care expenses. It was eating up seniors' Social Security checks and even cutting into their children's retirement savings. Working households needed a solution. But Washington's perpetual anxiety about the long-term cost of entitlements stood in the way.

Counterbalancing these problems was the fact that Social Security had been around for over seventy years and had earned the people's devotion by consistently keeping its promises. It opponents "have waged a very effective campaign," says Jane Bryant Quinn, "and yet people want it. It has political support despite the fact that people don't think it will be there."[19]

But if the traditional defenders of Social Security couldn't find a way politically to address people's evolving needs through the program, the logic of the financialization of society—the logic governing the movement against Social Security—stood ready to assert itself.

* * *

"A common purpose of the tongs was to collect & invest membership dues & initiation fees in insurance funds for the indigent, unemployed, widows & orphans of deceased members, funeral expenses, etc. In an era like ours when the poor are caught between the cancerous Scylla of the insurance industry & the fast-evaporating Charybdis of welfare & public health services, this purpose of the Secret Society might well regain its appeal."

—*Hakim Bey*[20]

If Social Security's supporters wanted to re-cement the social conditions that made it possible in the first place, they would have to democratize it. In other words, they would have to reduce the "decisional distance" that Foucault identified as its Achilles' heel. Even some hardcore administrators and policy wonks were concocting schemes to bring this about.

Social insurance schemes work best when they cover as close to the entire population as possible, argued Colin Gillion, director of the Social Security Department of the International Labour Organization, the UN agency dealing with working conditions.[21] That means they need a high degree of social consensus to thrive. Any social benefit system that's financed through workers' contributions "becomes acceptable only when workers have, through their representatives, the right to influence the use of what, at the end of the day, remains their money," Gillion wrote in a paper published in 2000. That includes both influencing the decision-making process and monitoring the administration of the programs themselves.

Gillion laid out two ways to achieve this. The first was a "tripartite" management board to run the program itself, including representatives of workers, employers, and the government. The second was through "lobbying, voting, and ... otherwise being involved in the political process."

One of the fundamental arguments for Social Security privatization had always been that private accounts were necessary to put old-age benefits out of reach of politicians who were all too likely to overpromise and underdeliver. The management board Gillion was advocating implied that Social Security was a common possession, not the property of individuals, that should be jointly managed by each group having an interest in it. Keeping the political process involved also implied that society as a whole had a legitimate stake in how older persons were provided for—that this shouldn't be considered just an individual or family matter.

Industrialized nations like the U.S. faced wage stagnation, a declining industrial base, and a lack of well-paying jobs that would enable the people to share in future economic growth—or support an adequate social insurance system. Perhaps Social Security itself could be part of the solution. Because the federal government borrowed the payroll tax receipts in the Social Security trust funds and replaced them with Treasury bonds, it was widely believed that the trust funds had been ripped off. Why not instead invest Social Security's assets in targeted investments?

This wasn't a new idea. Arthur Altmeyer, the first commissioner of Social Security, had talked of investing the funds in "social undertakings such as ... low-cost housing, schools, hospitals," and even in manufacturing "that could be justified from the point of view of social welfare."[22]

These "undertakings" would be run from Washington in the same top-down manner as the existing Social Security system. Some of the most intriguing ideas about the future of social insurance, however, involved decentralizing and democratizing it: taking the concept back to its roots in mutual aid, as Foucault had suggested.

In another book on pensions, *Banking on Death*, published in 2002, the British social historian Robin Blackburn spotlighted a fascinating scheme that nearly came to be in Sweden in the early 1980s. It was the brainchild of Rudolf Meidner, the German refugee who thirty years earlier had been one of the architects of Sweden's postwar welfare state. Meidner's plan would have required Swedish companies to issue shares equaling up to 20% of their equity to their own workers. The assets would be grouped into "wage-earner funds" controlled by unions, which could bankroll socially useful activities such as pensions. After some twenty years, Meidner calculated that his plan would give workers, collectively, majority control of all the companies they worked for.

The ruling Social Democratic Party endorsed the idea and ran on it in the 1982 elections, to the consternation of Swedish business leaders, who campaigned hard in opposition. The Social Democrats won, but afterward got cold feet as the devil appeared in some of the details. How would unemployed or self-employed persons benefit, for example? And how to decide which socially useful purposes the funds would back? While some wage-earner funds were set up, they never became the force Meidner had hoped; the last ones were wound down in the mid-1990s.[23]

In his book, Blackburn recast the Meidner plan as a pension scheme with a more decentralized architecture. Rather than big national unions or the State, the wage-earner funds would be controlled by a wide assortment of affinity groups centered around workplaces, local communities or even neighborhoods, collectives, credit unions, and consumer groups. These would gradually gain control of capital and business and steer them in directions that fit the needs and desires of the communities that controlled the funds—such as programs to develop alternatives to fossil fuels.[24] The objective, Blackburn wrote, was to "reconnect the mass of citizens and employees with the processes whereby strategic economic decisions are made."[25]

Blackburn wasn't proposing top-down socialism, as might be expected from a longtime social democrat and editor of the *New Left Review*. Instead, he was advocating a decentralized economic model that put decision making back in the hands of small communities, variously defined. "The institutions which I have been sketching," he wrote, "would encourage those bound together by a sense of place, of profession, or a common past or future, to help them devise their own solution."[26]

Even in a time of desperation, such a model could hardly attract the support of business or capital—and it contained some major landmines. Shareholders, even majority shareholders, didn't control corporations. Management did, by manipulating classes of stock and appointing directors who made sure the incumbents stayed in office. Transferring shares to workers wouldn't necessarily change this. And while the community funds that held the shares might initially want to use them for sound social purposes, they would quickly find themselves conflicted. Since the value of their capital would depend on the profitability of the companies they owned, they might gear their decisions more to the demands of their portfolio than those of their members. The result, ironically, might be something more closely resembling Bush's ownership society than a libertarian Marxist ideal.

The direction rather than the details were perhaps what mattered most, however. Gillion and Blackburn, in their different ways, were both suggesting it was no longer politically advantageous for institutions like Social Security to run away from their radical origins. If these programs were to have a future, working people must re-embrace the populism that had forced the political class to accept them in the first place.

Instead of being run as one big pool and collectively invested in the activities of government through their Treasury bond portfolios, the Social Security trust funds could form a network of social investment trusts. These could be run by a latticework of cooperative groups including credit unions, autonomous collectives, labor unions, and consumer groups. The cooperatives could use the funds to develop sustainable agricultural and industrial economies on a regional, local, or even neighborhood level, the proceeds going to support health care, housing, and a guaranteed adequate income for the elderly.

Besides orienting the U.S. economy away from its present wasteful, resource-intensive, and environmentally destructive direction, this decentralized, directly democratic structure could impart to workers the sense of ownership of Social Security that the New Deal program had never given them. The connection between the benefits the program paid out and the health of the economy would become clearer and more direct. The appeal of private accounts would be neutralized. And Social Security would be freed from its problematic relationship with government and the State, to which working people both left and right, it seemed, had lost any strong emotional attachment.

With control of the program moving closer to the grassroots, Social Security could respond better to people's evolving needs. It could even, perhaps, help bring about a long-overdue redefinition of the relationship between work and reward, production and individual and community desires. Social Security—in fact, all State-run social insurance programs—was built on the premise that workers must earn their benefits by contributing to the program with their payroll tax or else by being part of such a person's household. Occupations that didn't fit the traditional definition of "work"—a category that stretched from homemakers to many artists to urban nomads to the growing number of people rendered permanently unemployed by the economic shifts of recent decades—never had a comfortable place in the social insurance model.

Tying the wealth accumulated in Social Security more closely to direct community development, and putting control more directly in the hands of the people who would not only enjoy the benefits but implement that development, could create the opportunity to redefine not only what society regards as productive work, but work itself. This possibility—for a healthier, more unified human community—has always existed within the concept of mutual aid.

"All production is social," writes one contemporary anarchist. "We enrich each other—not only spiritually, but materially as well—as we work, think and play together; and without the efforts of society as a whole no one prospers."[27] Other, more mainstream economists have looked in the same direction, not altogether unknowingly. A few years before the Social Security Act was passed, Keynes wrote that, despite the Great Depression, he "still hopes that the day is not far off when the Economic Problem will take a back seat where it belongs, and that the arena of the heart and head will be occupied, or re-occupied, by our real problems—the problems of life and of human relations, of creation and behaviour and religion."[28]

By the time Obama was beginning his third year in office, the "Economic Problem"—the alleged unaffordability of any social promise of a fulfilling life to every human being—was being painted as intractable, just as it often had been during the 1930s. The answer then, Keynes strongly implied, was to return to the basic principle of mutual aid. "Our task must be to decentralise and devolve wherever we can, and in particular to establish semi-independent corporations and organs of administration to which duties of government, new and old, will be entrusted."[29] Startling words from the economist often taken to be the major intellectual stimulus behind the technocratic, centralizing New Deal.

Almost eighty years later, writes anthropologist and anarchist David Graeber, with Social Security and the other achievements of the New Deal under siege, "we ... find ourselves attempting to save the very global work machine that's threatening to destroy the planet"[30] due to global warming and the fossil-fuel industry. That overlapped, partially, with Galbraith's call for lowering the retirement age: letting the people at last enjoy some of the dividends of decades of rising worker productivity. "We can and do enjoy far more farm and factory goods than our forebears, with much less effort," he wrote in January 2011. "Only a small fraction of today's workers make things. Our problem is finding worthwhile work for people to do, not finding workers to produce the goods we consume."[31]

Reactivating something like the original conception of mutual aid could make it possible once again for communities to address such fundamental issues. In fact, the years leading up to the mortgage and credit crises revealed a pattern of households and communities searching for collective ways to cope with needs that government no longer prioritized and the private sector only wanted to approach when it could make the largest possible profit.

In 2011, some 130 million Americans participated in co-ops, worker-owned companies, credit unions, and other collective enterprises—a movement that the latest "jobless recovery" from recession was speeding up, noted political economist Gar Alperovitz. Earlier, in 2007, it was reported that elderly people in more than 100 communities in the U.S. were banding together to supply services to each other or buy them collectively, enabling individuals to live the rest of their lives at home rather than moving into expensive assisted-living or nursing-home establishments. Members of these communities were sharing information and advice online and organizing local and national conferences. Residents even of relatively affluent neighborhoods, like Beacon Hill in Boston, were forming these mutual aid groups in part because many types of elder care were becoming so expensive that they ate away the assets of upper middle-class households as well as poorer ones.[32] Even some city governments, concerned about neighborhoods with large elderly populations, were starting to allocate funds to projects geared to make those areas more livable for the old.[33]

Some communities went further. Take Back the Land, a group of homeless people and local activists in Miami, in 2007 began identifying vacant government-owned homes and moving homeless families into them.

Take Back the Land published a set of three principles that could apply roughly as well to the social movements sprouting up or entrenching themselves in Argentina, Brazil, India, and Peru.

- The movement is fundamentally about land. Black people have the right to control land in their own community and use it for the public good.

- The government is an integral part of the problem. Therefore, it cannot be depended upon to shape the solution.

- Development is not about buildings, paved streets or technology. True development is about the lives and potential of actual people.

One of the technocratic arguments in favor of Social Security was the parochialism of the decentralized web of fraternal societies that had supplied social services to a large chunk of working families in the century before the Social Security Act.[34] Built around points of affinity—local communities or neighborhoods, workplaces, professions, skill sets, religious sects—these groups never covered anything close to the entire workforce. Many were too inward-looking to see their efforts in a broader context. Because they charged dues, they automatically shut out the poorest workers, and they never attempted to set up a federated structure capable of addressing the problem of how to include these individuals.

But the late 20th century had produced new means of seeking and establishing affinity, such as the Internet. This, in turn, could make it easier for people living at great geographic distances from each other to form cooperative communities, and even facilitate the creation of larger federations that could extend resources to groups that needed help organizing their own services.

Mutual aid societies maintained loyalty because their democratic, decentralized structures kept them directly answerable to an informed, involved membership. Washington at the beginning of the 21st century, by contrast, still seemed politically incapable of enhancing Social Security to meet its participants' changing needs, even though the financial services industry that was supposed to take the program's place was distrusted and surviving on Washington largesse. Solutions built on mutual aid tended to nurture trust amongst their members, partly through directly democratic processes and partly because members believed their individual concerns wouldn't be ignored or shelved for some later date that would never arrive.

That being the case, there was reason to think that mutual aid might once again be a source of practical solutions for millions of people seeking ways to restore their lives and reduce precarity through collective efforts.

In Washington's most influential circles, the Social Security debate was about how to scale back the program and devolve more of the responsibility for income in old age onto households. The unspoken assumption within Obama's deficit commission was that Social Security and Medicare would continue to operate in the familiar technocratic, top-down manner. But what if Washington were instead to incorporate decentralized elements, along the lines of the wage-earner funds that Meidner and Blackburn had proposed?

There were reasons why traditional progressives who believed in using government for social good might want to support a revamped Social Security. For better than sixty years, the program had been a vital tool for legitimizing the capitalist state itself, reassuring Americans that The System understood and would alleviate the extremes of economic precariousness. Updating and democratizing Social Security would reinvigorate this function and give progressives a fresh structural framework for creating new programs, all as part of the process of economic recovery.

Along the way, the Democratic Party would find itself in possession of the new "big idea" it had been seeking ever since the 1960s, something that could checkmate the enticing free-market rhetoric of the Republicans and launch a new era in American politics. That would be the Democrats' reward for, effectively, midwifing a new social contract into existence.

More likely, however, Washington progressives would reject any proposal to democratize Social Security. Like their conservative counterparts, they were accustomed to seeking and securing power, not giving it up. They could always justify this by appealing to the threat that whatever they surrendered, the right-wing enemy would retrieve and put to use.

The Democratic Party and even many on its left flank remained suspicious of deep democratization. In part this was because Republicans, since the days of the Silent Majority, had learned so much better how to use a populist style to build support even for initiatives that directly harmed working people. It also stemmed from uncomfortable memories of the racism, xenophobia, religious fundamentalism, and antisemitism that populist leaders had sometimes indulged in even during the New Deal era.

Most of all, though, it sprang from the technocratic, professionalized conception of government that was the heritage of the Roosevelt era. Many progressives still regarded their larger task as being to restore Americans' affection for this model of government and society, detaching them from the free-market populism of Reagan. But curiously, many of the same Democratic leaders who seemed to accept the Republican argument about the need to scale back, if not phase out New Deal hold-overs like Social Security, remained committed to a vision of change driven by a highly educated technocracy—the heirs of the New Deal brain trust.

Conservatives often seemed to grasp the irony better than most progressives. "Barack Obama, with rhetoric alone, conveyed in 2008 that he was enlisting the whole nation to participate in his sweeping vision," *Wall Street Journal* columnist Daniel Henninger wrote three years later. "He has not sustained the sweep or the vision. Instead, he withdrew into a truly wonky world of Beltway-driven policy."[35]

* * *

"Real generosity toward the future consists in giving all to what is present."

—Albert Camus[36]

Social Security wasn't, in the strictest sense, the property of the "government." A myth accepted for many decades by both sides in the debate was that Franklin Delano Roosevelt created the program. In this telling, Social Security was FDR's grand conception, given form and substance by the New Deal brain trust. According to many of Social Security's defenders, the result was a distinctively Democratic creation and America's most successful social program, despite the constant attacks of Republicans and, later, the privatization movement. According to some of its critics, Social Security was a modest program that Roosevelt never intended to become the nation's primary form of old-age support but that opportunistic liberal Democrats later transformed into a vast, unsustainable machine for keeping workers dependent on government.

In reality, Social Security was the product of a popular movement with no political party allegiance, which demanded that Washington create a system guaranteeing a decent standard of living for the elderly. It was an audacious demand that perhaps could never have been accepted at any other time in American history. It mobilized millions of people across the country through grassroots organizations like the Townsend Clubs. It grew out of economic desperation, social unrest, the sudden collapse of much social hierarchy during the dismal Hoover years, as well as a deep desire for social renewal, not the optimistic atmosphere of the New Deal.

In the decades following Reagan's election, as we've seen, mass support for Social Security mobilized itself again and again—successfully—when the program was under threat. From whence might a similar upsurge appear in the Obama years? Perhaps from some of the same places where the new president had drawn his support. "The authentic hope of the Obama campaign," wrote Noam Chomsky, "is that the 'grass-roots army' organized to take instructions from the leader might 'break free' and return to the old ways of doing politics, by direct participation in action."[37]

Deliberately or not, Obama's advisors had done everything possible since the election to demobilize the activists who had rallied around him during his campaign. But some of these people were still searching for ways to reactivate the "old ways of doing politics."

When newly elected Republican governors in New Jersey, Wisconsin, Ohio, Michigan, and elsewhere aimed to address their states' budget shortfalls by abolishing or restricting state employees' right to collective bargaining, labor, surprisingly, woke up.

Wisconsin public employees occupied the rotunda of the state capital and were joined by thousands more in the streets of Madison. Over 100,000 took to the streets in support on the last weekend of February 2011, while public-sector unions held solidarity rallies in all the other forty-nine state capitals. Counterprotests by Tea Party supporters more or less fizzled. Obama and other Democratic leaders denounced the legislation as an "assault on unions."

Fourteen Democrats in the Wisconsin State Senate left the state to prevent their colleagues from assembling to pass the bill. Their Republican colleagues ended the stalemate on March 9 by stripping some appropriations items out of the bill, allowing them to vote on it without the Democrats.

But the showdown had a powerful effect. The new Republican governors of Florida and Pennsylvania, for example, hastened to reassure public-sector workers that they wouldn't employ similar tactics and weren't going to attack collective bargaining. An even more severe bill in Indiana was allowed to die, although a similar one in Ohio passed. Public-sector unions and the AFL-CIO worked to keep the momentum from flagging. On April 4, they held an even more impressive day of action called "We Are One," which brought out more than 1 million people around the country for marches, rallies, and teach-ins designed to encourage lobbying against the anti-union agenda.

What made the Wisconsin fight especially surprising was what it revealed about opinion among the wider public. Several polls, including one by the

Democratic-leaning firm Public Policy Voting, revealed that a majority of Wisconsinites supported the unions against Walker and backed public employees' right to collectively bargain.[38] That in turn cast a shadow over one of the most dramatic results of the 2010 election: the Republican takeover of five of the seven Upper Midwestern states. Traditionally Democratic strongholds, Minnesota, Wisconsin, Iowa, Illinois, Indiana, Michigan, and Ohio now all had Republican governors and legislatures. Clearly, voters in those states had wanted change. But had they really wanted the kind that the new Republican governors and legislators set out to impose?

Scapegoating public employees had seemed like smart politics right after the election. But much of the public seemed to draw a close connection between the attacks on collective bargaining in the public realm and the erosion of workers' status in the private sector. Quickly following the final vote in the Wisconsin Senate, labor-backed groups announced recall campaigns against fourteen Republican state lawmakers, attracting $360,000 in contributions in just twenty-four hours.[39]

For a time, there was even talk of a general strike. The South Central Federation of Labor, the AFL-CIO's regional affiliate in Wisconsin, overwhelmingly passed a resolution setting up a mechanism to train and educate members about what a general strike would entail. The purpose of the resolution was largely to draw "a political line in the sand," warning the governor of what the consequences of his action might be.[40] But it was significant that unionists had revived the idea of the general strike, at least rhetorically, for the first time since the Great Depression. The last time such actions took place in the U.S.—in San Francisco and Minneapolis in 1934—was during the depths of the Depression, when the Townsend movement was attracting millions of members and the elements of the Social Security Act were being cobbled together.

Holman Jenkins, Jr., in the *Wall Street Journal*, called the Wisconsin battle over public-sector unions "a perfect microcosm of the battle that every sentient American knows, and has known for a generation, awaits Social Security and Medicare."[41] Ending public pension promises in Wisconsin and elsewhere, while neutralizing organized labor's ability to defend them, corresponded closely with the effort in Washington, by the right and center-right, to broker a political deal—excluding the voices of progressive lawmakers, labor, the Gray Lobby, and grassroots activists—that would begin phasing out Social Security.

At the height of the Madison standoff, Paul Ryan drew a parallel he doubtless quickly regretted, between the situation in Wisconsin and the current street-level resistance to Egypt's Mubarek regime, saying, "It looks like Cairo moved to Madison." A few months later, so did the Lower Manhattan financial district, where hundreds of activists initiated the Occupy Wall Street action. Initially given little chance of success, that insurgency quickly spread to cities across the country and then around the world. In a *Time* magazine poll a few weeks after the initial action, a majority of respondents said they had a favorable impression of the movement. Significantly, that included a majority of independent voters and even a third of Republicans.

The Occupy movement was in synch with the public's priorities as well. A poll taken at Zuccotti Park by the center-right political consultancy Penn, Schoen & Berland—not a sympathetic source—found that 65% of the activists agreed that government had a moral responsibility to guarantee all citizens a secure retirement, while 77% supported raising taxes on the wealthy. Yet the activists resisted associating themselves too closely with the Democratic party, as the Tea Party had done the year before with the Republicans, and maintained a directly democratic decision-making process that kept authority from concentrating in the hands of a politically ambitious "leadership."

If Occupy Wall Street and a newly aroused labor movement contained the seeds of a new populist leftism opposed to the elite consensus, counterbalancing forty years of right-wing populism, what would be its objectives? One might be to pressure Washington to update Social Security and recommit itself to the basic principles of social insurance: not just protection against the extremes of poverty but the guarantee of a dignified standard of living for every worker who was no longer able to work. Drawing from the lessons provided by Wisconsin public employees and the Take Back the Land campaign, perhaps the labor and community organizers could revive the grassroots insurgency that enabled the success of the New Deal, reviving the Rooseveltian model of the State as incubator and administrator of vital social services.

Doing so would require these groups to adopt a very different approach to politics—one of confrontation, not cooperation with Washington. They would have to do better at creating a diverse movement that cut across ethnic groups, income groups, gender, and other dividing lines—something that progressives and the left had a poor track record of accomplishing. They would also have to answer for themselves some basic questions about what kind of society the U.S. should be with a much older population—what kinds of communities and support networks it would require, how the elderly could be integrated back into the larger society rather than segregated as patients and dependents or exploited as cheap labor. The answers would most likely rely more on mutual aid.

While that might seem ambitious, it wasn't unreasonable to expect people who wanted to preserve the improvements that social insurance had brought about to develop a broader social vision to go along with it—a vision that Washington had failed to provide even at the height of the New Deal era. The right had produced its own vision: the ownership society. Working people, the elderly, people of color, immigrants, and other groups increasingly left to their own devices by a State focused on the needs of the propertied and powerful would need something at least as compelling.

What if such an effort failed or never coalesced in the first place, the Washington policy consensus held, and the New Market State, shorn of any social role other than to facilitate market-driven "opportunity," came into existence as planned?

With benefits slashed and older workers subsiding into poverty, the next step, paradoxically, might be a return to mutual aid. The ownership society, based on the profit-maximizing activities of millions of fragmented households, was a utopian impossibility. Inevitably, working households would have to work together, whether the State wanted a role in the effort or not. Unless they wanted to return to the Victorian era of haves and have-nots, they must set about creating a new, universal system of old-age support, with a durable, dependable benefits structure; that addressed the needs of divorced women, lifetime low-wage workers, queer folk, and others marginalized by the existing Social Security structure; and that was closely connected to the real economy through a network of social investments. Perhaps private and even public employers' abandonment of traditional pension plans and Washington's failure to shed its aversion to "welfare" and deficit spending were signals that it was time for this project to begin.

"Effective mutual aid arises in particular social conditions," writes Patrick Reedy, "often in ones where trust and confidence in government is very low. The history of [fraternal] societies demonstrates that much of the glue that binds such groups together is opposition to authority."[42]

An indispensable condition for successful direct action is an active culture of mutual aid. This is true of any social insurance system, including Social Security. If people's needs and desires in the battered, deindustrializing society of the early-21st century were pushing them beyond the framework of the New Deal, perhaps their activism would move in the same direction. If Social Security itself—indeed, the entire idea of social insurance—couldn't change, then perhaps the people would return to the source and create it anew. The project would continue, with or without the institution that arose out of the New Deal.

BIBLIOGRAPHIC NOTE

I wrote this book in part because no comprehensive history existed of what I believed to be one of the most important public policy debates in the U.S. in my adult life. However, the books listed below tell parts of the story behind the Social Security struggle and explicate the various positions in the debate. They were invaluable to me in piecing together the story of *The People's Pension*. Other books that yielded important information are identified in the Notes.

My point of view should be clear in these pages, but I've gleaned important information and insights from books on all sides of the issue. With the help of many different sources from all sides of the Social Security question, I've tried to write a fair account that doesn't ignore facts that don't obviously bolster my own position.

Achenbaum, W. Andrew, *Social Security: Visions and Revisions* (New York: Cambridge University Press, 1986)

Altman, Nancy J., *The Battle for Social Security: From FDR's Vision to Bush's Gamble* (New York: John Wiley & Sons, Inc., 2005)

Averting the Old Age Crisis: Policies to Protect the Old and Promote Growth (Washington DC/New York: The World Bank/Oxford University Press, 1994)

Baker, Dean, ed., *Getting Prices Right: The Debate over the Consumer Price Index* (Armonk, NY: M.E. Sharpe, Inc., 1998)

Baker, Dean, and Mark Weisbrot, *Social Security: The Phony Crisis* (Chicago: The University of Chicago Press, 1999)

Ball, Robert M., *The Greenspan Commission: What Really Happened* (New York: The Century Foundation Press, 2010)

Barr, Nicholas, *Economics of the Welfare State* (Palo Alto, CA: Stanford University Press, 1987)

Beito, David T., *From Mutual Aid to the Welfare State: Fraternal Societies and Social Services, 1890 1967* (Chapel Hill: University of North Carolina Press, 1999)

Béland, Daniel, *Social Security: History and Politics from the New Deal to the Privatization Debate*, Lawrence: University Press of Kansas, 2005)

Berkowitz, Edward D., *Robert Ball and the Politics of Social Security* (Madison: University of Wisconsin Press, 2003)

Bernstein, Merton C., and Joan Brodshaug Bernstein, *Social Security: The System That Works* (New York, Basic Books, 1988)

Blackburn, Robin, *Banking on Death: Or, Investing in Life: The History and Future of Pensions* (New York: Verso, 2002)

Blahous, Charles, *Social Security: The Unfinished Work* (Stanford: Hoover Institution Press, 2010)

Bush, George W., *Decision Points* (New York: Crown Publishers, 2010)

Butler, Robert N., *The Longevity Revolution: The Benefits and Challenges of Living a Long Life* (New York: PublicAffairs, 2008)

Campbell, Andrea Louise, *How Policies Make Citizens: Senior Political Activism and the American Welfare State* (Princeton: Princeton University Press, 2003)

Collins, Joseph, and John Lear, *Chile's Free-Market Miracle: A Second Look* (Oakland CA: The Institute for Food and Development, 1995)

Derthick, Martha, *Policymaking for Social Security* (Washington, DC: The Brookings Institution, 1979)

Derthick, Martha, *Agency Under Stress: The Social Security Administration in American Government* (Washington, DC: The Brookings Institution, 1990)

Edwards III, George C. *Governing by Campaigning: The Politics of the Bush Presidency* (New York: Pearson Longman, 2007)

Ferrara, Peter J., *Social Security: The Inherent Contradiction* (San Francisco: Cato Institute, 1980)

Galbraith, James K., *Created Unequal: The Crisis in American Pay* (New York: The Free Press, 1998)

Graebner, William, *The Engineering of Consent: Democracy and Authority in Twentieth-Century America* (Madison: University of Wisconsin Press, 1987)

Greider, William, *The Education of David Stockman and Other Americans* (New York: E.P. Dutton, Inc., 1981, 1982)

Haber, Carole, and Brian Grattan, *Old Age and the Search for Security: An American Social History* (Bloomington and Indianapolis: Indiana University Press, 1994)

Hiltzik, Michael A., *The Plot Against Social Security: How the Bush Plan Is Endangering Our Financial Future* (New York: HarperCollins, 2005)

Hodgson, Godfrey, *The Gentleman from New York: Daniel Patrick Moynihan: A Biography* (Boston: Houghton Mifflin, 2000)

Jacoby, Susan, *Never Say Die: The Myth and Marketing of the New Old Age* (New York: Pantheon Books, 2011)

Kirk, Russell, *The Conservative Mind: From Burke to Santayana* (Chicago: Henry Regnery Company, 1953)

Kotlikoff, Laurence J., *Generational Accounting: Knowing Who Pays, and When, for What We Spend* (New York: The Free Press, 1992)

Light, Paul, *Artful Work: The Politics of Social Security Reform* (New York: Random House, 1983)

Longman, Phillip, *Born to Pay: The New Politics of Aging in America* (Boston: Houghton Mifflin, 1987)

Myers, Robert J., with Richard L. Vernaci, *Within the System: My Half Century in Social Security* (Winsted, Conn.: ACTEX Publications, 1992)

Orloff, Ann Shola, *The Politics of Pensions* (Madison, University of Wisconsin Press, 1993)

Peterson, Peter G., and Neil Howe, *On Borrowed Time: How the Growth in Entitlement Spending Threatens America's Future* (San Francisco: Institute for Contemporary Studies, 1988)

Rove, Karl, Courage and Consequence: *My Life as a Conservative in the Fight* (New York: Threshold Editions, 2010)

Schieber, Sylvester J., and John B. Shoven, *The Real Deal: The History and Future of Social Security* (New Haven: Yale University Press, 1999)

Seligman, Joel, *The Transformation of Wall Street: A History of the Securities and Exchange Commission and Modern Corporate Finance, 3rd Edition* (New York: Aspen Publishers, 2003)

Sperling, Gene, *The Pro-Growth Progressive: An Economic Strategy for Shared Prosperity* (New York: Simon & Schuster, 2005)

Stockman, David A., *The Triumph of Politics: How the Reagan Revolution Failed* (New York: Harper & Row, 1986)

Thurow, Lester C., *The Zero-Sum Society: Distribution and the Possibilities for Economic Growth* (New York: Penguin Books, 1980)

White, Joseph, and Aaron Wildavsky, *The Deficit and the Public Interest* (Berkeley: University of California Press; New York, Russell Sage Foundation, 1989)

Woodward, Bob, *The Agenda: Inside the Clinton White House* (New York: Simon and Schuster, 1994)

NOTES

Prologue

1   Thomas Paine, "Agrarian Justice," in Eric Foner, ed., *Thomas Paine: Collected Writings* (New York: The Library of America, 1995), p. 397.

2   Jeanne Sahadi, "Fixing Social Security: The 'low-hanging fruit,'" CNNMoney.com, May 11, 2010.

3   *The 2010 Annual Report of the Board of Trustees of the Federal Old-Age and Survivors Insurance and Federal Disability Insurance Trust Funds*, p. 2.

4   "The Budget and Fiscal Outlook: Fiscal Years 2010 to 2020," Congress of the United States, Congressional Budget Office, January 2010.

5   Rep. Barbara Lee, "Black History and Social Security," Politico.com, February 25, 2011.

6   Lee Price and William E. Spriggs, "Productivity Growth and Social Security's Future," Economic Policy Institute report, May 10, 2005.

7   Monique Morrissey, "Beyond 'Normal': Raising the Retirement Age is the Wrong Approach for Social Security," Briefing Paper #287, Economic Policy Institute, Washington, D.C., January 26, 2011.

8   Eric Laursen, "Social Security: It's All in the Adjectives," HTTP://PEOPLESPEN-SION.INFOSHOP.ORG/BLOGS-MU/2011/02/14/SOCIAL-SECURITY-ITS-ALL-IN-THE-ADJECTIVES/#MORE-264, February 14, 2011.

9   Virginia P. Reno and Elizabeth Lamme, "Social Security Finances: Findings of the 2010 Trustees Report," Social Security Brief No. 34, National Academy of Social Insurance, August 2010.

10 Frederick Douglass, West India Emancipation Day speech, Canandaigua, New York, August 3, 1857.

11　A. Haeworth Robertson, "Social Security Reform: Let's Just Do It," *Contingencies*, May/June 2001.

12　Paine, "Agrarian Justice," Eric Foner, pp. 404–06.

13　Roy Lubove, *The Struggle for Social Security: 1900–1935* (Cambridge: Harvard University Press, 1968), p. 139.

14　David T. Beito, *From Mutual Aid to Welfare State: Fraternal Societies and Social Services, 1890–1967* (Chapel Hill: University of North Carolina Press, 2000) provides a history of fraternal orders and mutual aid societies in the U.S.

15　Arthur Delancy and Ryan Grim, "The Poorhouse: Aunt Winnie, Glenn Beck, and the Politics of the New Deal," HuffingtonPost.com, December 29, 2010.

16　Ann Shola Orloff, *The Politics of Pensions* (Madison, University of Wisconsin Press, 1993), pp.147–48; Report To The President of the Committee on Economic Security, January, 1935.

17　Mary Poole, *The Segregated Origins of Social Security* (Chapel Hill: University of North Carolina Press, 2006), p. 23.

18　Ibid., pp. 285–87.

19　Some of these were instituted earlier. Orloff, *The Politics of Pensions*, pp. 269–70.

20　Patricia P. Martin and David A. Weaver, "Social Security: A Program and Policy History," *Social Security Bulletin*, Vol. 66, Issue 1, 2005/2006.

21　"Poverty Rate Increase," Hearings before the Subcommittee on Oversight and Subcommittee on Public Assistance and Unemployment Compensation of the Committee on Ways and Means of the House of Representatives, 98th Congress, 1st session, 1983, table 5, p. 239, cited in Merton C. and Joan Brodshaug Bernstein, *Social Security: The System That Works* (New York, Basic Books, 1988), p. 208.

22　The Social Security Network, "Who's at Risk?" Issue Brief #7, November 5, 1998; Kathryn H. Porter, Kathy Larin, and Wendell Primus, "Social Security and Poverty Among the Elderly," Center on Budget and Policy Priorities, April 1999.

23　Social Security Online, "Beneficiary Data," HTTP://WWW.SOCIALSECURITY.GOV/CGI-BIN/CURRENTPAY.CGI; Arloc Sherman, "Social Security Lifts 1 Million Children Above the Poverty Line," Center for Budget and Policy Priorities, May 2, 2005.

24　Budget of the United States Government, FY 2002: Historical Tables, table 3.1 (1940–2006).

25　Excerpted in Larry DeWitt, Daniel Béland, and Edward D. Berkowitz, eds., *Social Security: A Documentary History* (Washington DC: CQ Press, 2008), p. 34.

26　Braithwaite and Beveridge both cited in Patrick Reedy, "From Collective Struggle to Customer Service: The story of how self-help and mutual aid led to the welfare state and became co-opted in market managerialism," paper presented at Nottingham Trent University HRM Seminar Series, February 4, 2009.

27　I.M. Rubinow, "Social Security and Intergroup Relations," address to the National Conference of Christians and Jews, August 28, 1935, Rubinow Papers, Box 25, The Institute of Human Relations, Williams College, Williamstown, Massachusetts; quoted in J. Lee Kreader, "Isaac Max Rubinow: Pioneering Specialist in Social Insurance," unpublished undated doctoral dissertation, University of Chicago, p. 597.

28　Rubinow, quoted in Kreader, p. 597.

29　Quoted in David Brody, *In Labor's Cause: Main Themes on the History of the American Worker* (New York: Oxford University Press, 1993), pp. 210–11.

30　Nancy J. Altman, *The Battle for Social Security: From FDR's Vision to Bush's Gamble* (New York: John Wiley & Sons, 2005), p. 160.

31   Mary Ann Glendon, *A World Made New: Eleanor Roosevelt and the Universal Declaration of Human Rights* (New York: Random House, 2001), pp. 205, 213.

32   Richard Hofstadter, *The Age of Reform: From Bryan to F.D.R.* (New York: Alfred A. Knopf, 1955), p. 11. Schlesinger makes essentially the same argument in his three-volume *The Age of Roosevelt* (Boston: Houghton Mifflin Company, 1957–60).

33   Ibid., p. 326. Hofstadter's book is primarily a critique of what he regarded as the excessively "individualistic" politics of the Populist and Progressive eras. He either didn't know that the mutual aid movement that was a major component of Populism or, perhaps, didn't consider it important.

34   Ibid., p. 326.

35   Quoted in Sam Tanenhaus, "In Kennedy, the Last Roar of the New Deal Liberal," *New York Times*, August 28, 2009.

36   Paul Goodman, "The Great Society," *New York Review of Books*, October 1965.

37   Christopher Lasch, *The Culture of Narcissism: American Life in an Era of Diminished Expectations* (New York: W.W. Norton & Company, 1978), p. 224.

38   Wilbur J. Cohen, "Urgent Needs in Retirement Planning," remarks to the University of Michigan's 12th Annual Conference on Aging, June 23, 1959.

39   Michael J. Sandel, "America's Search for a New Public Philosophy," *The Atlantic Monthly*, March 1996.

40   Max J. Skidmore, *Social Security and Its Enemies* (Boulder, CO: Westview Press, 1999). Skidmore traces Reagan's evolving position on Social Security and the role it played in his pre-presidential political career.

41   "Ford Derides Reagan's Idea of Investing Social Security Funds in the Stock Market," *Wall Street Journal*, February 11, 1976, quoted in Roger Lowenstein, *Origins of the Crash: The Great Bubble and Its Undoing* (New York: The Penguin Press, 2004), p. 1.

Chapter 1

1   Richard Viguerie, the Republican direct-mail magnate, quoted in John S. Saloma III, *Ominous Politics: The New Conservative Labyrinth* (New York: Hill and Wang, 1984), pp. 149–50.

2   David A. Stockman, *The Triumph of Politics: How the Reagan Revolution Failed* (New York: Harper & Row, 1986), p. 53.

3   Ibid., p. 11.

4   Ibid., p. 73.

5   David Stockman, "Avoiding a GOP Economic Dunkirk," appendix to William Greider, *The Education of David Stockman and Other Americans* (New York: E.P. Dutton, Inc., 1981, 1982), p. 140.

6   Ibid., pp. 153–55.

7   John A. Farrell, *Tip O'Neill and the Democratic Century* (Boston : Little, Brown, 2001), p. 545.

8   Greider, *The Education of David Stockman*, pp. 20–21.

9   Joseph White and Aaron Wildavsky, *The Deficit and the Public Interest* (Berkeley: University of California Press; New York, Russell Sage Foundation, 1989), p. 78.

10   John M. Berry and Lee Lescaze, "Reagan Sends Budget to Hill as 'Mandate for Change,'" *Washington Post*, March 11, 1981.

11 Lee Lescaze, "Reagan Uses Talk Show to Tout Economic Program," *Washington Post*, April 22, 1981.

12 Paul Light, *Artful Work: The Politics of Social Security Reform* (New York: Random House, 1983), p. 36.

13 W. Andrew Achenbaum, *Social Security: Visions and Revisions* (New York: Cambridge University Press, 1986), pp. 64–65.

14 1972 and 1978 Annual Report of the Board of Trustees of the Federal Old-Age and Survivors Insurance and Disability Insurance Trust Funds, Table 2.

15 Martha Derthick, *Agency Under Stress: The Social Security Administration in American Government* (Washington: The Brookings Institution, 1990), p. 33.

16 Paul Light, *Artful Work*, p. 49.

17 Ibid., p. 41.

18 Caspar Weinberger to the president, December 9, 1974, Box 5, Needham Papers.

19 Achenbaum, *Social Security: Visions and Revisions*, p. 69.

20 Richard W. Stevenson, "For Bush, a Long Embrace of Social Security Plan," *New York Times*, February 27, 2005.

21 Geoffrey Kollmann, "Social Security: Summary of Major Changes in the Cash Benefits Program," Social Security Administration, Domestic Social Policy Division, May 18, 2000.

22 Sylvester J. Schieber and John B. Shoven, op. cit., p. 177.

23 Robert J. Myers with Richard L. Vernaci, *Within the System: My Half Century in Social Security* (Winsted, Conn.: ACTEX Publications, 1992), p. 8.

24 Jane Bryant Quinn, "Clarifying the Notch Baby Distortion," *Washington Post*, March 2, 1999.

25 White and Wildavsky, *The Deficit and the Public Interest*, p. 313.

26 1983 Annual Report of the Board of Trustees of the Federal Old-Age and Survivors Insurance and Disability Insurance Trust Funds, Table 2.

27 David Shribman, "The Social Security Crisis: Legacy of Hopeful Guesses," *New York Times*, January 5, 1983.

28 Interview with John Trout, September 14, 2006.

29 Edward D. Berkowitz, *Mr. Social Security: The Life of Wilbur J. Cohen* (Lawrence, KS: University Press of Kansas, 1995), p. 302.

30 Cohen interviewed in Edward D. Berkowitz, *Mr. Social Security*, p. 301.

31 Achenbaum, *Social Security: Visions and Revisions*, p. 69.

32 Andrea Louise Campbell, *How Policies Make Citizens: Senior Political Activism and the American Welfare State* (Princeton: Princeton University Press, 2003), pp. 75–76.

33 National Election Studies time series, cited in Campbell, *How Policies Make Citizens*, pp. 28, 30.

34 Campbell, *How Policies Make Citizens*, pp. 75–76.

35 Roger Sanjek, *Gray Panthers*, (Philadelphia: University of Pennsylvania Press, 2009), p. 152.

36 Interview with Bill Arnone, March 11, 2009.

37 Henry J. Pratt, *Gray Agendas: Interest Groups and Public Pensions in Canada, Britain, and the United States* (Ann Arbor: The University of Michigan Press, 1993), pp. 183–85, 198.

38 Sanjek, *Gray Panthers*, p. 234.

39 Campbell, *How Policies Make Citizens*, p. 90.

40 Achenbaum, *Social Security: Visions and Revisions*, p. 68.

41 Martha Derthick, *Agency Under Stress*, pp. 36, 128.

Chapter 2

1   Letter to Edgar Newton Eisenhower, Nov. 8, 1954, Document #1147, *The Papers of Dwight David Eisenhower, Volume XV—The Presidency: The Middle Way* (Baltimore: Johns Hopkins University Press, 1996).

2   Derthick, *Agency Under Stress*, p. 36.

3   Stockman, *The Triumph of Politics*, p. 161.

4   Ibid., p. 162.

5   Hedrick Smith, *The Power Game: How Washington Works* (New York: Random House, 1988), pp. 357–58.

6   Spencer Rich and Caroline Atkinson, "Proposed Cuts in Benefits Easily Pass First Tests," *Washington Post*, March 17, 1981.

7   Light, *Artful Work*, p. 89.

8   Spencer Rich, "Subcommittee Approves Social Security Shift," *Washington Post*, April 1, 1981.

9   Stockman, *The Triumph of Politics*, pp. 181–83.

10 David A. Stockman, "The Social Pork Barrel," *The Public Interest*, No. 39, Spring 1975.

11 Luther Gulick, "Memorandum on Conference with FDR Concerning Social Security Taxation, Summer, 1941," FDR Presidential Library, Hyde Park, New York.

12 Stockman, "The Social Pork Barrel."

13 Myers with Vernaci, *Within the System*, p. 20.

14 Stockman, *The Triumph of Politics*, p. 189.

15 Myers with Vernaci, *Within the System*, p. 10.

16 Laurence I. Barrett, *Gambling with History: Reagan in the White House* (New York: Doubleday, 1983), p. 157.

17 C. Eugene Steuerle, *The Tax Decade: How Taxes Came to Dominate the Public Agenda* (Washington, DC: The Urban Institute, 1992), p. 62.

18 Art Pine, "Regan: Higher Rates, Business Slowdown Possible," *Washington Post*, May 7, 1981.

19 Farrell, *Tip O'Neill and the Democratic Century*, p. 158.

20 Achenbaum, *Social Security: Visions and Revisions*, p. 78.

21 Stockman, *The Triumph of Politics*, p. 190.

22 Caroline Atkinson, "Social Security Trims Seen Reflection of Pact To Lower 'Safety Net,'" *Washington Post*, May 14, 1981.

23 Stockman, *The Triumph of Politics*, pp. 191–2. Stockman's emphasis.

24 Quoted in Myers with Vernaci, *Within the System*, p. 24.

25 Light, *Artful Work*, p. 130.

26 Spencer Rich, "90 Organizations Join Up To Guard Social Security," *Washington Post*, May 28, 1981.

27 Edward D. Berkowitz, *Robert Ball and the Politics of Social Security* (Madison: The University of Wisconsin Press, 2003), pp. 25–27.

28 Email from Edward D. Berkowitz, December 1, 2008.

29 Robert M. Ball, letter to Robert J. Myers, August 21, 1993.

30 Interview with Thomas N. Bethell, February 2, 2009.

31 Robert Ball, "Possible Approaches to Social Security Financing Problem," February 2, 1981, Ball Papers, quoted in Berkowitz, *Robert Ball and the Politics of Social Security*, p. 282.

32 Helen Dewar, "Politicians Spar on Social Security," *Washington Post*, July 22, 1981.

33 Lee Lescaze and Spencer Rich, "Reagan Favors Voting Rights Act Extension," *Washington Post*, August 6, 1981.
34 Spencer Rich, "House Democrats Start New Battle Over Cuts in Social Security," *Washington Post*, September 11, 1981.
35 Stockman, *The Triumph of Politics*, pp. 276, 306–7.
36 Farrell, *Tip O'Neill and the Democratic Century*, p. 581.

Chapter 3

1   Greider, *The Education of David Stockman*, p. 50.
2   Warren Weaver, Jr., "Arguing Against Social Security Cuts," *New York Times*, October 17, 1981.
3   Greider, *The Education of David Stockman*, p. 59.
4   Mike Causey, "Federal Diary: Social Security," *Washington Post*, December 26, 1981.
5   Myers with Vernaci, *Within the System*, p. 24; Robert J. Myers, letter to Robert H. Finch, Secretary of Health, Education, and Welfare, April 14, 1970.
6   Letter dated December 14, 1981; quoted in Myers with Vernaci, *Within the System*, p. 27.
7   Spencer Rich, "Republican Social Security Expert Quits in Anger," *Washington Post*, December 19, 1981.
8   Herbert H. Denton, "Aides Acknowledge Reagan Made Mistakes in News Conference," *Washington Post*, April 2, 1982.
9   Stockman, *The Triumph of Politics*, p. 353.
10 Helen Dewar, "Democrats Push Their Alternative," *Washington Post*, February 11, 1982.
11 Helen Dewar and Thomas B. Edsall, "Governors Agree to Begin Talks on 'Federalism,'" *Washington Post*, February 24, 1982.
12 Helen Dewar, "No Suggestion Made on Social Security," *Washington Post*, February 27, 1982.
13 Helen Dewar, "O'Neill, Mocking Reagan Vow, Says President Must 'Go First,'" *Washington Post*, April 22, 1982.
14 Spencer Rich, "Cap on Living Cost Raise Seen as Costing Elderly In Benefits, Buying Power," *Washington Post*, April 24, 1982.
15 Helen Dewar and William Chapman, "Senate Republicans Abandon Social Security Savings," *Washington Post*, May 19, 1982.
16 Cited in William Safire, "Third Rail," *New York Times Sunday Magazine*, February 18, 2007.
17 Will Sentell, "Social Security crackdown stirs ill will," *Kansas City Times*, December 8, 1982.
18 Margot Hornblower, "O'Neill Fought Back, Feels Like a Winner," *Washington Post*, October 10, 1982.
19 Bill Peterson, "Parties Reckon With 'Angry Seniors'," *Washington Post*, October 28, 1982.
20 Spencer Rich, "GOP Fund-Raising Letter Mentions 3 Possible Social Security Revisions," *Washington Post*, October 28, 1982.
21 John M. Berry, "Gains by Democrats Seen Precluding Cuts In Domestic Programs," *Washington Post*, November 4, 1982.

22 David S. Broder, "Duck-and-Run Politics," *Washington Post*, August 4, 1982.
23 David S. Broder, "Are the Democrats Ready to Govern?" *Washington Post*, December 8, 1982.

Chapter 4

1 Stanford G. Ross, "Doctrine and practice in social security pension reforms," *International Social Security Review*, Vol. 53, No. 2, Spring 2000.
2 1983 Annual Report—Federal Old-Age and Survivors Insurance and Disability Insurance Trust Fund, p. 2.
3 Berkowitz, *Robert Ball and the Politics of Social Security*, p. 287.
4 Ibid., p. 291.
5 Ibid., p. 302.
6 1983 Annual Report—Federal Old-Age and Survivors Insurance and Disability Insurance Trust Fund, pp. 22,25.
7 Ibid., pp. 30, 25.
8 U.S. Department of Health and Human Services, Indicators of Welfare Dependence: Annual Report to the Congress, 2002, Appendix A: Program Data.
9 See Martha Derthick, *Agency Under Stress*, pp. 22–33, for an account of the establishment of SSI.
10 1983 Annual Report—Federal Old-Age and Survivors Insurance and Disability Insurance Trust Funds, p. 5; 1983 Annual Report of the Federal Hospital Insurance Trust Fund, p. 23.
11 Internal Revenue Service, letter to the Hon. Sue Kelly, U.S. House of Representatives, September 29, 2000 (Info. 2000-0275).
12 1983 Annual Report—Federal Old-Age and Survivors Insurance and Disability Insurance Trust Fund, pp. 20, 29. Includes interest in amounts obtained from interfund transfers.
13 Interview with Robert J. Myers, June 21, 2000.
14 Interview with Stephen C. Goss, June 4, 2009.
15 Congressional Budget Office, "Financing Social Security: Issues and Options for the Long Run," a CBO Study, November 1982.
16 Merton C. Bernstein and Joan Brodshaug Bernstein, *Social Security: The System That Works* (New York: Basic Books, 1988), p. 55.
17 Kelly A. Olsen and Don Hoffmeyer, "Social Security's Special Minimum Benefit," *Social Security Bulletin*, Vol. 64, No. 2, 2001/2002, p. 11.
18 National Commission on Social Security reform, "Transcript of Commission Meeting," August 20, 1982, quoted in Edward D. Berkowitz, *Robert Ball and the Politics of Social Security* (Madison: University of Wisconsin Press, 2003), p. 303.
19 Interview with Stephen J. Entin, January 29, 2009.
20 Interview with Aldona Robbins, January 23, 2009.
21 U.S. Bureau of Economic Analysis figures, cited in Robert B. Firiedland and Laura Summer, "Demographics Is Not Destiny, Revisited," Center on an Aging Society, Georgetown University, March 20065.
22 Interview with Stephen J. Entin, January 29, 2009.
23 Edward D. Berkowitz, "Robert Ball's Legacy," Notes for remarks to Gerontological Society of America meeting, session on Ball, November 22–23, 2008.
24 Interview with Thomas N. Bethell, February 2, 2009.

25   David Lindeman, email to author, November 12, 2008.

26   Interview with David Lindeman, December 5, 2006.

27   Robert M. Ball, *The Greenspan Commission: What Really Happened* (New York: The Century Foundation Press, 2010), p. 48.

28   Bernstein and Bernstein, *Social Security: The System That Works*, p. 43.

29   Thomas B. Edsall, "Social Security Plan Seen Up to Reagan, O'Neill," *Washington Post*, December 13, 1982.

30   Lou Cannon and David Hoffman, "Reagan Discusses the Soviets, Nuclear Arms," *Washington Post*, December 19, 1982.

Chapter 5

1   David Hoffman, "Congressional Rejection Of Reagan's '84 Budget Appears Likely," *Washington Post*, December 12, 1982.

2   Light, *Artful Work*, p. 179.

3   Edward D. Berkowitz, *Robert Ball and the Politics of Social Security* (Madison: University of Wisconsin Press, 2003), pp. 307–8.

4   Myers with Vernaci, *Within the System*, p. 47.

5   Source for this account of the talks, unless otherwise noted, is Light, *Artful Work*.

6   Quoted in Berkowitz, *Robert Ball and the Politics of Social Security*, p. 321.

7   Eric R. Kingson, "Financing Social Security: Agenda-Setting and the Enactment of the 1983 Amendments to the Social Security Act," *Policy Studies Journal*, Vol. 13, No. 1, September 1984.

8   Tom Morganthau and Mary Hager, "Legions of the Old," *Newsweek*, January 24, 1983.

9   Harry Anderson with Gloria Borger, Mary Hager and Howard Fineman, "The Social Security Crisis," *Time*, January 24, 1983.

10   Ball, *The Greenspan Commission*, pp. 63–4.

11   Ball, *The Greenspan Commission*, p. 64.

12   1983 Annual Report—Federal Old-Age and Survivors Insurance and Disability Insurance Trust Fund, p. 10.

13   Steuerle, *The Tax Decade*, p. 63.

14   David Shribman, "Reagan hails plan to Social Security," *New York Times*, March 26, 1983.

15   See, for example, Richard E. Neustadt and Ernest R. May, *Thinking in Time: The Uses of History for Decision Makers* (New York: The Free Press, 1986), Chapter 2: "A Second Success."

16   Light, *Artful Work*, p. 3.

17   Ibid., p. 188.

18   Bernstein and Bernstein, *Social Security: The System That Works*, p. 56.

19   This analysis from David Cay Johnston, *Perfectly Legal: The Covert Campaign to Rig Our Tax System to Benefit the Super Rich—and Cheat Everybody Else* (New York: Portfolio, 2003), pp. 118–23.

20   Charles P. Blahous, "The 1983 Social Security Reforms: Real and Misremembered Lessons for Today's Leaders," The Hudson Institute, 2009.

21   Email from Nancy J. Altman, assistant to Alan Greenspan, 1982, to the author, March 11, 2009.

22   Daniel Patrick Moynihan, "More Than Social Security Was at Stake," *Washington Post*, January 18, 2009.

Chapter 6

1 Interview with Peter Ferrara, September 27, 2004.
2 Report of the National Commission on Social Security Reform, January 1983, Chapter 2, p. 2.
3 A. Haeworth Robertson, "The National Commission's Failure to Achieve Real reform," *Cato Journal*, Vol. 3, No. 2 (Fall 1983), an edited version of the author's testimony before the Senate Finance Committee.
4 Peter G. Peterson, "A Reply to Critics," *New York Review of Books*, March 17, 1983.
5 Edgar K. Browning, "Why the Social Insurance Budget Is Too Large in a Democracy," *Economic Inquiry*, Vol. XIII, Sept. 1975.
6 Carolyn L. Weaver, "Social Security: Has the Crisis Passed?" Cato Policy Report, January, 1979.
7 Robert B. Hudson, "The 'Graying' of the Federal Budget and its Consequences for Old-age Policy," *The Gerontologist*, Vol. 18, No. 5, 1978, p. 431.
8 Quoted in Phillip Longman, "Justice Between Generations," *The Atlantic Monthly*, June 1985, p. 79.
9 Interview with John Snee, September 26, 1977, quoted in Martha Derthick, *Policymaking for Social Security* (Washington, DC: The Brookings Institution, 1979), p. 388.
10 For a review of the rise of right-wing think tanks, see Sally Covington, "Moving a Public Policy Agenda: The Strategic Philanthropy of Conservative Foundations," National Committee for Responsive Philanthropy report, July, 1997.
11 Figures compiled by Media Transparency.
12 John Gray, *Black Mass: Apocalyptic Religion and the Death of Utopia* (New York: Farrar, Straus and Giroux, 2007), p. 122.
13 Leonard Schapiro, *The Communist Party of the Soviet Union* (New York: Vintage Books, 1960), pp. 342–44, 469–70.
14 Susan George, "How to Win the War of Ideas: Lessons from the Gramscian Right," *Dissent*, Summer 1997, Vol. 44, No. 3.
15 Stuart Butler and Peter Germanis, "Achieving a 'Leninist' Strategy," *Cato Journal*, Vol. 3, No. 2 (Fall 1983).
16 Larry DeWitt, "The 1937 Supreme Court Rulings on the Social Security Act," 1999. Many conservatives were never satisfied with this decision. But some found that it bolstered their views in a curious way, contending that the Supreme Court had "admitted" that Social Security isn't a system of social insurance but a welfare program in disguise, since it depends upon a tax, not voluntary contributions.
17 Carolyn L. Weaver, "Social Security: Has the Crisis Passed?" Cato Policy Report, January 1979.
18 Peter J. Ferrara, *Social Security: The Inherent Contradiction* (San Francisco: Cato Institute, 1980), p. 314.
19 James Buchanan, "Social Insurance in a Growing Economy: A Proposal for Radical Reform," *National Tax Journal* 386, December 21, 1968.
20 Wilbur J. Cohen and Milton Friedman, "Social Security: Universal or Selective?" (Washington, DC: American Enterprise Institute, 1972).
21 Martin Feldstein, "Social Security, Induced Retirement, and Aggregate Capital Accumulation," *Journal of Political Economy*, Vol. 82, No. 5, Sept.–Oct. 1974.
22 Selig D. Lesnoy and Dean R. Leimer, "Social Security and Private Saving: Theory and Historical Evidence," *Social Security Bulletin*, January 1985, Vol. 48, No. 1.

23   Alicia H. Munnell, *The Effect of Social Security on Personal Savings* (Cambridge: Ballinger Publishing Co., 1974).

24   George Katona, "Private Pensions and Individual Saving," Survey Research Center, Institute for Social Insurance, University of Michigan, 1965; Phillip Cagan, "The Effect of Pension Plans on Aggregate Saving," National Bureau of Economic Research. New York, 1965.

25   Cited in Teresa Ghilarducci, "How Unions and Social Security Create Savings," undated memo, 1996.

26   Dean R. Leimer and Selig D. Lesnoy, "Social Security and Private Saving: A Reexamination of the Time-Series Evidence Using Alternative Social Security Wealth Variables," Working Paper No. 19, Office of Research and Statistics, Office of Policy, Social Security Administration, 1980.

27   Martin S. Feldstein, "Social Security, Induced Retirement and Aggregate Capital Accumulation: A Correction and Updating," Working Paper No. 579, National Bureau of Economic Research, New York, 1980.

28   Irwin Friend and Stanley Schor, "Who Saves?" *The Review of Economics and Statistics*, Vol. XLI. No. 2, Part 2, May 1959, cited in John Kenneth Galbraith, *The New Industrial Society*, Boston: Houghton Mifflin Company, 1967, p. 37).

29   Martin Feldstein, "Toward a Reform of Social Security," *The Public Interest*, No. 40, Summer 1975; Martin Feldstein, "Facing the Social Security Crisis," Discussion Paper No. 492, Harvard Institute of Economic Research, July 1976.

30   Peter F. Drucker, *The Pension Fund Revolution* (New York: Harper & Row, 1976); republished with new material (New Brunswick, NJ: Transaction Publishers, 1996), p.102–03.

31   Arthur B. Laffer and David Ranson, "A Proposal for Reforming Social Security," H.C. Wainwright and Co., May 19, 1977.

32   Carolyn L. Weaver, "Social Security: Has the Crisis Passed?" Cato Policy Report, January, 1979.

33   Ferrara, *Social Security*, pp. 384–85.

34   Ibid., p. 394.

Chapter 7

1   Philip Jenkins, *Decade of Nightmares: The End of the Sixties and the Making of the Eighties* (New York: Oxford University Press, 2006), pg. 167.

2   Cited in Sperling, *The Pro-Growth Progressive*, p. 37.

3   Figures from U.S. Census Bureau, Current Population Reports, ser. P-60, cited in Sheldon Danziger and Peter Gottschalk, *America Unequal* (New York: Russell Sage Foundation, Cambridge, Massachusetts: Harvard University Press, 1995), pp. 49–51.

4   Figures here quoted from Peter G. Peterson, "The Salvation of Social Security," *New York Review of Books*, December 16, 1982, and "A Reply to Critics," *New York Review of Books*, March 17, 1983.

5   Interview with Aldona Robbins, January 23, 2009.

6   Ibid.

7   For comparison, see 1980 and 1984 Annual Report of the Board of Trustees of the Federal Old-Age and Survivors Insurance Trust Fund and the Federal Disability Insurance Trust Fund.

8   Interview with Stephen C. Goss, June 4, 2009.

9   1984 Annual Report of the Board of Trustees of the Federal Old-Age and Survivors Insurance Trust Fund and the Federal Disability Insurance Trust Fund, p. 5.

10   Interview with Barbara Boyle Torrey, October 6, 2005.

11   Robert B. Hudson, "The 'Graying' of the Federal Budget and its Consequences for Old-age Policy," *The Gerontologist*, Vol. 18, No. 5, 1978.

12   Joseph A. Califano, Jr., "The aging of America: Questions for the four-generation society," address to the American Academy of Political and Social Science, Philadelphia, April 1978,

13   Robert J. Samuelson, "The Withering Freedom to Govern," *Washington Post*, March 5, 1978.

14   Lester C. Thurow, *The Zero-Sum Society: Distribution and the Possibilities for Economic Growth* (New York: Penguin Books, 1980), p. 12.

15   Ibid., p. 194.

16   Ibid., p. 208.

17   Lester C. Thurow, "Undamming the American economy," *New York Times Sunday Magazine*, May 3, 1981.

18   Fred C. Pampel, "Population Aging, Class Context, and Age Inequality in Public Spending," *American Journal of Sociology*, Vol. 100, No. 1 (July 1994).

19   Peter G. Peterson, "Social Security: The Coming Crash," *New York Review of Books*, December 2, 1982; "The Salvation of Social Security," *New York Review of Books*, December 16, 1982.

20   James R. Capra, Peter D. Skaperdas, and Roger M. Kubarych, "Social Security: An Analysis of Its Problems," *Federal Reserve Bank of New York Quarterly Review*, Autumn 1982.

21   U.S. Census figures cited in Peterson, "The Salvation of Social Security."

22   Phillip Longman, "Justice Between Generations," *The Atlantic Monthly*, June 1985.

23   Peter G. Peterson, "A Reply to Critics," *New York Review of Books*, March 17, 1983.

24   Hillary Mills, "Pete and Joan."

25   Interview with Peter G. Peterson, February 16, 2006.

26   Interview with Peter Ferrara, September 27, 2005.

27   Alicia H. Munnell, "A Calmer Look at Social Security," *The New York Review of Books*, March 17, 1983.

28   Peter G. Peterson, "A Reply to Critics."

29   Rosemary Rinder, "We Can Afford to Support the Elderly," *The New York Review of Books*, March 17, 1983.

30   Robert Kuttner, "The Social Security Hysteria," *The New Republic*, December 27, 1982.

31   Robert H. Binstock, "The Aged as Scapegoat," *The Gerontologist*, Vol. 23, No. 2, 1983.

32   Robert Kuttner, "Flawed Fixes," *The New Republic*, January 6 & 13, 1986.

33   Robert Kuttner, "The Social Security Hysteria," *The New Republic*, December 27, 1982.

34   Peter G. Peterson, "A Reply to Critics."

35   Robert Kuttner, "The Social Security Hysteria," *The New Republic*, December 27, 1982.

36   Richard D. Lamm, *Megatraumas: America at the Year 2000* (Boston: Houghton Mifflin, 1985), p. 19.

37 Michael J. Boskin, Laurence J. Kotlikoff, Douglas J. Puffert, John B. Shoven, "Social Security: A Financial Appraisal Across and Within Generations," *National Tax Journal*, Vol. XL, March 1987, pp. 32.

Chapter 8

1   Robert H. Binstock, "The Aged as Scapegoat."
2   Interview with Phillip Longman, October 4, 2005.
3   Phillip Longman, "Taking America to the Cleaners," *Washington Monthly*, November 1982.
4   James Fallows, "Entitlements," *The Atlantic Monthly*, November 1982.
5   Robert Kuttner, "The Social Security Hysteria."
6   Phillip Longman, Letter, *The New Republic*, February 7, 1982.
7   Interview with Barbara Boyle Torrey, October 6, 2005.
8   Norman Ornstein, "Roots of 'Entitlements,' and Budget Woes," *Wall Street Journal*, December 14, 1993.
9   Cited in Saloma, *Ominous Politics*, p. 73.
10 George Gilder, *Wealth and Poverty* (New York: Basic Books, Inc., 1981), p. 111.
11 Howard Fineman, "Can Social Security Be Cut?" *Newsweek*, May 13, 1985.
12 Interview with Phillip Longman, October 4, 2005.
13 Phillip Longman, *Born to Pay: The New Politics of Aging in America* (Boston: Houghton Mifflin, 1987), p. 85.
14 Peter G. Peterson, "The Morning After," *The Atlantic Monthly*, October 1987.
15 Peter G. Peterson and Neil Howe, *On Borrowed Time: How the Growth in Entitlement Spending Threatens America's Future* (San Francisco: Institute for Contemporary Studies, 1988).
16 Werner Sollors, *Beyond Ethnicity: Consent and Descent in American Culture* (New York: Oxford University Press, 1986), pp. 212, 209–10.
17 William Graebner, *The Engineering of Consent: Democracy and Authority in Twentieth-Century America* (Madison: University of Wisconsin Press, 1987), pp. 118–24.
18 Harry Anderson with Gloria Borger, Mary Hager and Howard Fineman, "The Social Security Crisis," *Time*, January 24, 1983.
19 Lee Smith, "Does an Economic War Between the Generations Loom?" *Fortune*, July 20, 1987.
20 Daniel Callahan, *Setting Limits: Medical Goals in an Aging Society* (New York: Simon & Schuster, 1987).
21 Robert H. Binstock, "Scapegoating the Old: Intergenerational Equity and Age-Based Health Care Rationing," Chapter Nine of *The Generational Equity Debate*, John B. Williamson, Diane M. Watts-Roy, and Eric R. Kingson, eds. (New York: Columbia University Press, 1999), p. 166.
22 Edward Ross Dickinson, "Welfare, Democracy, and Fascism: The Political Crises in German Child Welfare, 1922–1933," *German Studies Review*, Vol. 22, No. 1, February 1999.
23 Robert H. Binstock, "The Aged as Scapegoat."
24 Subrata N. Chakravarty and Katherine Weisman, "Consuming Our Children," *Forbes*, November 14, 1988.
25 A.F. Ehrbar, "Heading for the Wrong Solution," *Fortune*, December 13, 1982.
26 Lee Smith, "The War Between the Generations," *Fortune*, July 20, 1987.

27   David Croteau, "Challenging the 'Liberal Media' Claim," *Extra!* July/August 1998.

28   This and the next paragraph draw on Hillary Mills, "Pete and Joan."

29   Doug Henwood, *Wall Street: How It Works and for Whom* (New York: Verso, 1997), p. 294–97.

30   Interview with Phillip Longman, October 4, 2005.

31   Interview with Paul Hewitt, September 27, 2005.

32   David Durenberger, letter to AGE director and members, December 1, 1986.

33   Interview with Phillip Longman, October 4, 2005.

34   Interview with Dallas Salisbury, June 19, 2000.

35   Lee Smith, "The War Between the Generations," *Fortune*, July 20, 1987.

36   Jim Jones, Letter from the President, *Of Age* (AGE newsletter), Fall 1987.

37   Richard D. Lamm, "A Debate: Medicare in 2020," in *Medicare Reform and the Baby Boom Generation*, edited proceedings of the second annual conference of Americans for Generational Equity, April 30–May 1, 1987 (Washington, DC: Americans for Generational Equity), p. 77.

38   "Senator pessimistic on health care," *Kansas City Star*, May 3, 1987.

39   Anthony Beilenson, "Let's put Social Security back on deficit-negotiations table," *Tallahassee Democrat*, November 11, 1988.

40   Christopher Cuomo, "The Generation Gambit: The Right's Imaginary Rift Between Old and Young," *Extra!* March/April 1997.

Chapter 9

1   Lester C. Thurow, *The Future of Capitalism: How Today's Economic Forces Shape Tomorrow's World* (New York: William Morrow and Co., 1996), p. 277.

2   George F. Will, "The COLA Question," *Washington Post*, August 7, 1983.

3   Helen Dewar, "Senate Presses On in Quest to Cut Deficit," *Washington Post*, November 5, 1983.

4   Henry Kaufman, *Interest Rates, the Markets, and the New Financial World* (New York: Times Books, 1986), p. 19.

5   A fine discussion of the NAIRU debate is contained in James K. Galbraith, *Created Unequal: The Crisis in American Pay* (New York: The Free Press, 1998), Chapter 10, "The NAIRU Trap." See also Robert Eisner, *The Misunderstood Economy: What Counts and How to Count It* (Boston: Harvard Business School Press, 1994).

6   James K. Galbraith, *Created Unequal: The Crisis in American Pay* (New York: The Free Press, 1998), pp. 191–93.

7   Budget of the U.S. Government for Fiscal Year 1995.

8   Peter L. Bernstein, "All the Things Deficits Really Don't Do," *Wall Street Journal*, November 10, 1988.

9   Galbraith, *Created Unequal*, p. 188.

10   Robert Eisner, "Don't Privatize Social Security," Letter to the Editor, *New York Times*, October 1, 1988.

11   Robert Eisner, *The Misunderstood Economy*, p. 83.

12   E.J. Dionne, Jr., "Spending, Politics And Darman's Slap at The Profligate American," *New York Times*, July 30, 1989.

13   John Maynard Keynes, *A Tract on Monetary Reform* (London: Macmillan, 1924).

14   Karl Marx, *Grundrisse*, Martin Nicolaus, trans. (New York: Penguin, 1973), pp. 511–12.

15 Henwood, *Wall Street*, p. 293.

16 John Maynard Keynes, *The General Theory of Employment, Interest, and Money*, Vol. VII of *The Collected Writings of John Maynard Keynes*, Donald Moggridge, ed. (New York: Harcourt Brace Jovanovich, 1973), pp. 104–5.

17 George Bernard Shaw, *The Intelligent Woman's Guide to Socialism and Capitalism* (New York: Brentano's, 1928), p. 6.

18 Raoul Vaneigem, *The Revolution of Everyday Life*, Donald Nicholson-Smith, trans. (London: Rebel Press, 2006), pp. 234, 116.

19 Christopher J. Niggle, "Globalization, Neoliberalism and the Attack on Social Security," *Review of Social Economy*, March 1, 2003.

20 Thurow, *The Zero-Sum Society*, p. 197.

21 Moshe Adler, "Saving Social Security with Snake Oil," *Plan Sponsor*, May 1997.

22 John Maynard Keynes, "Economic Possibilities for Our Grandchildren," in *Essays in Persuasion* (New York: W.W. Norton & Company, 1963), p. 370.

23 Robert Eisner, "Don't Privatize Social Security," *New York Times*, October 1, 1988.

24 Atul Gawande, "The Way We Age Now," *New Yorker*, April 30, 2007.

25 Moshe Adler, "Saving Social Security with Snake Oil," *Plan Sponsor*, May 1997.

26 Shaw, *The Intelligent Woman's Guide*, p. 6.

27 Colin Gillion, "The development and reform of social security pensions: The approach f the International Labour Office," *International Social Security Review*, Vol. 53, No. 1, Winter 2000, p. 49.

28 Nicholas Barr, *Economics of the Welfare State* (Palo Alto, CA: Stanford University Press, 1987).

29 Interview with David Lindeman, November 30, 2006.

30 Richard A. Posner, *Aging and Old Age* (Chicago: University of Chicago Press, 1995), pp. 289, 296.

Chapter 10

1 Rudolf Goldscheid, *Staatssozialismus oder Staatskapitalismus: Ein finanzsoziolo-gischer Beitrag zur Lösung des Staatsschulden-Problems* [State Socialism or State Capitalism: A Financial-Sociological Contribution to the Solution of the Problem of Public Debts], (Vienna: 1917).

2 Alan Murray, "Revamping Tax Battles Won and Lost," *Wall Street Journal*, August 18, 1986.

3 Steuerle, *The Tax Decade*, p. 164.

4 Gerald F. Seib and Jeffrey H. Birnbaum, "Democrats Set To Unveil Plan To Cut Deficit," *Wall Street Journal*, November 10, 1987.

5 Charles Krauthammer, "Is the retrospective horse race hiding missiles in the caves?" *Washington Post*, February 19, 1988.

6 Kenneth S. Baer, *Reinventing Democrats: The Politics of Liberalism from Reagan to Clinton* (Lawrence, KS: University Press of Kansas, 2000), pp. 268–71.

7 Robert Dreyfuss, "How the DLC Does It," *American Prospect*, April 23, 2001.

8 Baer, *Reinventing Democrats*, pp. 136–37.

9 Clyde H. Farnsworth, "Strauss's Deficit Remarks Stirring Angry Reactions," *New York Times*, September 22, 1988.

10 John Schwartz with Eleanor Clift and Rich Thomas, "War Over the 'Hidden Tax'," *Newsweek*, January 22, 1990.

11 Rep. Andrew Jacobs Jr., Letter to the Editor: "Social Security Lotto: Win Without a Ticket," *Wall Street Journal*, June 28, 1990.

12 Dan Morgan and Walter Pincus, "You Think the Budget's Solved? Maybe So, Maybe No," *Washington Post*, November 18, 1990.

13 Robert J. Samuelson, "Pampering the Elderly," *Newsweek*, October 24, 1990.

14 Rep. Mary Rose Oakar, "'Pampering the Elderly,'" *Washington Post*, November 6, 1990.

15 E.J. Dionne Jr., "Buchanan Challenges Bush With 'America First' Call," *Washington Post*, December 11, 1991.

16 Daniel Goodgame, "Who'll Feel the Pain?" *Time*, August 16, 1993.

17 Editorial: "Austerity Paul," *Wall Street Journal*, March 12, 1992.

18 Steven Mufson, "Can Anyone Here Govern America?" *Washington Post*, October 18, 1992.

19 Bob Woodward, *The Agenda: Inside the Clinton White House* (New York: Simon and Schuster, 1994), pp. 82–93.

20 Moynihan, memo to Robert Rubin, February 5, 1993, in Steve R. Weisman, ed., *Daniel Patrick Moynihan: A Portrait in Letters of an American Visionary* (New York: PublicAffairs, 2010), p. 603.

21 Georgette Jasen, "How Clinton's Tax Plan Will Hit the Elderly," *Wall Street Journal*, March 11, 1993.

22 Woodward, *The Agenda*, pp. 303–09.

23 Paul Starr, "The Hillarycare Mythology," *The American Prospect*, October 2007.

24 Richard L. Kaplan, "Top Ten Myths of Social Security," *Elder Law Journal*, Vol. 3, No. 2, 1995, p. 210.

Chapter 11

1 Robert Pear, "Cuts and Tax Rises Urged to Bolster Social Security," *New York Times*, April 19, 1994; Nancy J. Perry, "Why Social Security cuts are coming—but not this year," *Money*, June 1994.

2 Eric Pianin, "New GAO Report Faults Rigid Entitlement Caps," *Washington Post*, July 20, 1994.

3 Patrice Hill, "House members reject caps on benefit programs Social Security to stay untouched," *Washington Times*, July 22, 1994.

4 Patrice Hill, "House kills bill to debate on entitlement spending," *Washington Times*, October, 1994.

5 Interview with Bob Kerrey, June 7, 2006.

6 Jill Quadagno, "Creating a Capital Investment Welfare State: The New American Exceptionalism," *American Sociological Review*, 1999, Vol. 64 (February), p. 5.

7 Peter G. Peterson, *Facing Up: How to Rescue the Economy from Crushing Debt and Restore the American Dream* (New York: Simon & Schuster, 1993).

8 Interview with a commission staffer.

9 Mark Weinberger, "Social Security: Facing the Facts," SSP No. 3, Cato Institute, April 10, 1996.

10 George Melloan, "A GOP Challenge: How to De-Invent Government," *Wall Street Journal*, November 14, 1994.

11 Christopher Georges, "Clinton Now Faces a Race With GOP Congress To Cut Taxes, Budget While Protecting His Base," *Wall Street Journal*, November 14, 1994.

12 Eric Kingson, "Social Security and Aging Baby Boomers," in In E.W. Markson & L. Hollis-Sawyer, editors, *Aging in the Twenty First Century: Issues and Inequalities in Social Gerontology* (Los Angeles: Roxbury Publishing Company, 2000).

13 S.K. Chand & A. Jaeger, "Aging Populations and Public Pension Schemes," International Monetary Fund, Occasional Paper No. 147, December 1996.

14 Norma Cohen, "A Bloody Mess,' *The American Prospect*, November 1, 2005.

15 Eric Kingson, "A National Conversation on Social Security: Can It Bring Order to a Policy Mess?" draft presentation for the University of Pennsylvania, February 23, 1998.

Chapter 12

1   "The Budget: Unbalanced," *The Economist*, February 11–17, 1995.

2   Jackie Calmes, "Budget Plan Fails in Senate, Setting Back GOP Agenda," *Wall Street Journal*, March 3, 1995.

3   Karen Tumulty, "Getting the Edge," *Time*, June 5, 1995.

4   Bill Clinton, *My Life* (New York: Alfred A. Knopf, 2004), pp. 680–84.

5   Clinton T. Bass, "Shutdown of the Federal Government: Causes, Processes, and Effects," Congressional Research Service, February 18, 2011.

6   Peter A. Schulkin, "Upward bias in the CPI; consumer price index," *Challenge*, September, 1993.

7   Michael F. Bryan and Jagadeesh Gokhale, "The Consumer Price Index and national saving," *Federal Reserve Bank of Cleveland Economic Commentary*, October 15, 1995.

8   Schieber and Shoven, *The Real Deal*, pp. 304–5.

9   Peter A. Schulkin, "Upward bias in the CPI; consumer price index," *Challenge*, September, 1993.

10 Howard Gleckman, "Uncle Sam's Stats: Call Them Unreliable," *Business Week*, July 18, 1994.

11 Reform Proposal of Senators J. Robert Kerrey and John C. Danforth, Final Report of Bipartisan Commission on Entitlement an Tax Reform, pp. 7–34.

12 Richard E. Cohen, "Tinkering with a Political Explosive," *National Journal*, March 11, 1995.

13 Ibid.

14 Michael K. Frisby and Rick Wartzman, "Clinton Downgrades Idea of a Balanced Budget By 2002 if It Were to Hurt Medicare, Education," *Wall Street Journal*, February 7, 1995.

15 Dean Baker, "Does the CPI Overstate Inflation? An Analysis of the Boskin Commission Report," in Dean Baker, ed., *Getting Prices Right: The Debate over the Consumer Price Index* (Armonk, NY: M.E. Sharpe, Inc., 1998), p. 8.

16 Katharine G. Abraham, "The consumer price index: what does it measure?" *Challenge*, May, 1995

17 Both cited in Jeff Madrick, "The Cost of Living: A New Myth," *New York Review of Books*, March, 1997.

18 Aaron Bernstein, "The CPI: Why Politicians Should Butt Out," *Business Week*, May 22, 1995.

19 Teresa Tritch, "How the Inflation Debate Affects You," *Money*, September 1996.

20 Jonathan Chait, "More Moynihan Malarkey," Slate.com, June 1, 2000.

21 Leon Jaroff, "The Quickest Fix of All," *Time*, October 9, 1995.

22 Christopher Georges, "Senators Back Adjusting CPI To Cut Deficit," *Wall Street Journal*, September 27, 1995.

23 David Wessel, "Why the CPI Fix Looks So Likely," *Wall Street Journal*, December 11, 1995.

24 Cited in Jeff A. Schnepper, "Adjusting the Consumer Price Index," *USA Today* (Magazine), January, 1996.

25 Kate O'Beirne, "Bread & Circuses," *National Review*, December 31, 1996.

26 Godfrey Hodgson, *The Gentleman from New York: Daniel Patrick Moynihan: A Biography* (Boston: Houghton Mifflin, 2000), p. 382.

27 Advisory Commission to Study the Consumer Price Index, "Toward a More Accurate Measure of the Cost of Living: Final Report to the Senate Finance Committee," December 4, 1996, in Dean Baker, ed., *Getting Prices Right: The Debate over the Consumer Price Index* (Armonk, NY: M.E. Sharpe, Inc., 1998), p. 59–65.

28 See, for instance, Brad Edmondson, "Inflation Infatuation, or Is the Price Right?" *American Demographics*, December, 1996; and Irwin M. Stelzer, "'Lies, Damned Lies, and Statistics' Revisited," *The Weekly Standard*, December 23, 1996.

29 Teresa Tritch, "How the Inflation Debate Affects You," *Money*, September 1996.

30 Jim Klumpner, "Fact and fancy: CPI biases and the federal budget; Consumer Price Index," *Business Economics*, April, 1996.

31 Jeff Madrick, "The Cost of Living: A New Myth," *New York Review of Books*, March 6, 1997.

32 Leonard I. Nakamura, "Measuring inflation in a high-tech age," *Business Review* (Federal Reserve Bank of Philadelphia), November/December 1995.

33 Dean Baker, "The overstated CPI—can it really be true?" *Challenge*, September, 1996.

34 Herbert Stein, "The Consumer Price Index: Servant or Master?" *Wall Street Journal*, November 1, 1995.

Chapter 13

1 Frank Luntz, "Communication Strategy for the Upcoming Budget Battle," memo to the Republican Conference, January 9, 1995, cited in "Attention! All Sales Reps For the Contract With America," *New York Times*, February 5, 1995.

2 Christopher Georges, "Bid to Overhaul Social Security Picks Up Support in Congress as System's Guardians Soften Stance," *Wall Street Journal*, May 5, 1995.

3 Julie Kosterlitz, "Touching the Rail," *National Journal*, December 23, 1995.

4 Ron Chernow, "The Bull Market to Come," *Wall Street Journal*, August 30, 1993.

5 Bob Kerrey and Alan K. Simpson, "How to Save Social Security," *New York Times*, May 23, 1995.

6 Christopher Georges, "Bid to Overhaul Social Security Picks Up Support in Congress as System's Guardians Soften Stance," *Wall Street Journal*, May 5, 1995.

7 Lindsay Wyatt, "The Social Security Debate," *Pension Management*, September 1995.

8 Ibid.

9 Julie Kosterlitz, "Touching the Rail," *National Journal*, December 23, 1995; Robert Dreyfuss, "The end of Social Security as we know it?" *Mother Jones*, November/December 1996.

Chapter 14

1   David Hage, "Privatizing Social Security," *U.S. News & World Report*, April 3, 1995.

2   Stan Luxenberg, "Get your share of the shrinking social security pie," *Medical Economics*, June 13, 1994

3   Alex Beam, "Doom and Boomers: The End of Social Security As We Know It," reprinted in *Pittsburgh Post-Gazette*, March 26, 1993.

4   Lynn Garrett, "Investment dollars & sense," *Publishers Weekly*, October 2, 1995.

5   Sylvester J. Schieber and John B. Shoven, "Population Aging and Saving for Retirement," paper prepared for the Center for Economic Policy Research conference on Growth and Development: The Economics of the 21st Century, Stanford University, June 3–4, 1994, pp. 25–26.

6   Bernard Wysocki, Jr., "Many Baby Boomers Save Little, May Run Into Trouble Later," *Wall Street Journal*, June 5, 1995.

7   I.M. Rubinow, *Social Insurance: With Special Reference to American Conditions* (New York: Henry Holt, 1913), pp. 3–12.

8   Analysis of US Bureau of the Census, Current Population Reports, in Danziger and Gottschalk, *America Unequal*, pp. 49–50, 59.

9   Data cited in Louis Uchitelle, "Job Extinction Evolving Into a Fact of Life in U.S.," *New York Times*, March 22, 1994.

10   United States General Accounting Office, "Private Pensions: Changes Can Produce a Modest Increase in Use of Simplified Pension Plans, Report to the Honorable Nancy Landon Kassebaum, U.S. Senate," July 1992. Within ten years, the figure would balloon to some $150 billion (Gene Sperling, *The Pro-Growth Progressive: An Economic Strategy for Shared Prosperity*, New York: Simon & Schuster, 2005, p. 185).

11   Ellen E. Shultz, "Retirement Planners Try to Scare Up Business," *Wall Street Journal*, June 22, 1992.

12   Paula Mergenhagen, "Rethinking Retirement," *American Demographics*, June, 1994.

13   Charles Gasparino, "Mutual-Fund Aide Eyes Social Security," *Wall Street Journal*, April 29, 1996.

14   Ellen E. Shultz and Charles Gasparino, "Privatizing a Portion of Social Security Could Shower Billions on Mutual Funds," *Wall Street Journal*, February 20, 1996.

Chapter 15

1   Saloma, *Ominous Politics*, pp. 68–72.

2   Joel Seligman, *The Transformation of Wall Street: A History of the Securities and Exchange Commission and Modern Corporate Finance*, 3rd Edition (New York: Aspen Publishers, 2003), p. 70.

3   "Only perform," *The Economist*, November 27, 1993.

4   William M. O'Barr and John M. Conley, "Managing Relationships: The Culture of Institutional Investing," *Financial Analysts Journal*, September–October 1982.

5   "Only perform."

6   William G. Poortvliet and Thomas P. Laine, "A global trend: Privatization and reform of social security pension plans," *Benefits Quarterly*, Third Quarter 1995.

7   Interview with Michael Tanner, May 14, 2003.

8   Julie Kosterlitz, "Touching the Rail," *National Journal*, December 23, 1995.

9   Rose Darby and Michelle Celarier, "Where's the Payoff?" *Investment Dealers Digest*, August 9, 1999.

10 John J. Fialka, "Cato Institute's Influence Grows in Washington As Republican-Dominated Congress Sets Up Shop," *Wall Street Journal*, December 14, 1994.

11 Kosterlitz, "Touching the Rail."

12 Robert Dreyfuss, "The end of Social Security as we know it?" *Mother Jones*, November/December 1996.

13 Trudy Lieberman, "Social Insecurity," *The Nation*, January 27, 1997.

14 Ibid.

15 Ibid.

16 See, for example, John A. Brittain, *The Payroll Tax for Social Security* (Washington, DC: Brookings Institution, 1972), p. 79.

17 Robert Dreyfuss, "The Biggest Deal," *The American Prospect*, May–June 1996.

Chapter 16

1   Galbraith, *The New Industrial State*, p. 262.

2   William E. Beach and Gareth E. Davis, "Social Security's Rate of Return," Heritage Foundation Center for Data Analysis Report #98-01, January 15, 1998.

3   Steve Goss, "Problems with 'Social Security's Rate of Return,' A Report of the Heritage Center for Data Analysis," January 27, 1998.

4   "Social Security: The Real Deal," Issue Brief #1, The Century Foundation, April 7, 1998.

5   The argument is repeated in, for example, Michael Tanner, "Disparate Impact: Social Security and African Americans," Cato Institute Briefing Paper No. 61, February 5, 2001.

6   John Williamson, "Should women support the privatization of Social Security," *Challenge*, July 17, 1997.

7   Patricia Murphy, "Target: Generation X," *Bank Investment Marketing Ultimate Sales Guide*, July 1998.

8   Nancy Opiela, "The impact of emerging demographic trends on financial planning," *Journal of Financial Planning*, December 1997.

9   Andrew Cohen, "Me and my Zeitgeist," *The Nation*, July 19, 1993.

10 Interview with Richard Thau, November 26, 2006.

11 Christopher John Farley, "Taking Shots at the Baby Boomers," *Time*, July 19, 1993.

12 Neil Howe and William Strauss, *Generations: The History of America's Future*, 1584 to 2069 (New York: William Morrow, 1991), p. 403.

13 Neil Howe and William Strauss, *13th Gen: Abort, Retry, Ignore, Fail?* (New York: Vintage, 1993), p. 97.

14 Newsday, July 14, 1993.

15 Christopher John Farley, "Taking Shots at the Baby Boomers," *Time*, July 19, 1993.

16 Interview with Richard Thau, November 22, 2006.

17 Annys Shin, "Gen-X Rift Over Social Security," *National Journal*, February 15, 1997.

18   Deroy Murdock, "Social Security, the Tooth Fairy and Other Myths," *Washington Times*, September 26, 1994.

19   Lawrence R. Jacobs and Robert Y. Shapiro, "UFO Stories," *The New Republic*, August 10, 1998.

20   Employee Benefit Research Institute, "Public Attitudes on Social Security: The UFO Fallacy," *EBRI Notes*, Vol. 19, No. 3 (March 1998).

21   Eric B. Schnurer and Linda Colvin Rhodes, "Listening to Generation X," *Washington Monthly*, November, 1998.

22   Christopher John Farley, "Taking Shots at the Baby Boomers," *Time*, July 19, 1993; Paul Magnusson, "Young America's Rallying Cry: 'Dis the Deficit,'" *Business Week*, August 9, 1993.

23   Andrea Petersen, "All the Hot Gen X Pundits, Like, Vanished," *Wall Street Journal*, August 31, 1999.

24   "Third Millennium: Organizational History & Accomplishments," internal document, 2001.

25   Gayle Lee and Laura Raposa, "Tears for Di," *Boston Herald*, September 3, 1997.

26   Shin, "Gen-X Rift Over Social Security."

Chapter 17

1   Speech to the World Health Care Congress Europe, April 2008, quoted in Maggie Mahar, "The Mythology of Boomers Bankrupting Our Healthcare System," Alternet, April 10, 2008.

2   Laurence J. Kotlikoff, *Generational Accounting: Knowing Who Pays, and When, for What We Spend* (New York: The Free Press, 1992), pp. 120–21.

3   Ibid., p. 115.

4   Ibid., p. 127.

5   Ibid., p. xii.

6   Ibid., p. xvi.

7   The methodology is explained in Kotlikoff, *Generational Accounting*, pp. 125–26.

8   Interview with Laurence J. Kotlikoff, June 25, 2007.

9   Kotlikoff, *Generational Accounting*, p. 21.

10   Interview with Barry Anderson, July 3, 2007

11   Sylvia Nasar, "The Spend-Now, Tax-Later Orgy," *New York Times*, January 23, 1993.

12   Alex Beam, "Doom and Boomers: The End of Social Security As We Know It," reprinted in *Pittsburgh Post-Gazette*, March 26, 1993.

13   David Lightman, "Lawmakers struggle with how to reduce the deficit," *Hartford Courant*, February 21, 1993.

14   Joseph White and Aaron Wildavsky, *The Deficit and the Public Interest* (Berkeley: University of California Press, 1991), p. 340.

15   See, for example, Andre Masson, "Accounting-based approach to equity: achievements and arguments," *La Lettere de l'Observatoire des Retraits*, February 2000.

16   Interview with June Ellenoff O'Neill, July 19, 2007.

17   Congressional Budget Office, "Who Pays and When? An Assessment of Generational Accounting: A CBO Study," November 1995.

18   Alan J. Auerbach, Jagadeesh Gokhale, Laurence J. Kotlikoff, "Generational Accounting: A Meaningful Way to Evaluate Fiscal Policy," *Journal of Economic Perspectives*, Vol. 8, No. 1, Winter 1994.

19 Congressional Budget Office, "Who Pays and When?"

20 Baker, "Robbing the Cradle? A Critical Assessment of Generational Accounting" (Washington: Economic Policy Institute, 1995), p. 17.

21 Congressional Budget Office, "Who Pays and When?"

22 Baker, "Robbing the Cradle?"

23 Kotlikoff, *Generational Accounting*, pp. 168–69.

24 Congressional Budget Office, "Who Pays and When?"

25 Robert Eisner, "A Legacy Worth Paying For," *Wall Street Journal*, December 14, 1994.

26 Congressional Budget Office, "Who Pays and When?"

27 Joseph Spiers, "Bankrupting Future Generations," *Fortune*, May 30, 1994.

Chapter 18

1   Howard Gleckman, "Assume a Can Opener," TaxVox: The Tax Policy Center blog, February 4, 2010.

2   Laurence J. Kotlikoff and Scott Burns, *The Coming Generational Storm: What You Need to Know about America's Economic Future* (Cambridge, MA: The MIT Press, 2004), p. 143.

3   Interview with Laurence J. Kotlikoff, August 22, 2011.

4   Cited in Shirley P. Burggraf, *The Feminine Economy and Economic Man* (Reading, MA: Addison-Wesley Publishing Co., Inc., 1997), p. 89.

5   Quoted in Trudy Lieberman, "Social Insecurity," *The Nation*, January 27, 1997.

6   Lawrence R. Jacobs and Robert Y. Shapiro, "The News Media's Coverage of Social Security," March 1995, National Academy of Social Insurance.

7   Lieberman, "Social Insecurity."

8   Don Bauder, "Chain letter, Ponzi scheme—that's Social Security," *San Diego Union-Tribune*, June 7, 1996.

9   Schieber and Shoven, *The Real Deal*, p. 289.

10 Lawrence H. Thompson, "Principles of Financing Social Security Pensions," *International Social Security Review*, Vol. 49, March 1996, p. 57.

11 Charles E. Rounds, Jr., "Property Rights: The Hidden Issue of Social Security Reform," Cato Project on Social Security Privatization, SSP No. 19, April 19, 2000.

12 David Langer, "Social fund isn't really a Ponzi scheme of IOUs," *Pensions & Investments*, June 24, 1996.

13 Vincent J. Truglia, "Can Industrialized Countries Afford Their Pension Systems?" *The Washington Quarterly*, Summer 2000.

14 Dean Baker, "Nine Misconceptions About Social Security," *The Atlantic Monthly*, July 1998.

15 Laura D'Andrea Tyson, "Social Security Is Working Just Fine, Thank You," *Business Week*, June 26, 2000.

16 See, for example, Andrew G. Biggs, "Social Security: Is It 'A Crisis That Doesn't Exist'?" Cato Project on Social Security Privatization, SSP No. 1, October 5, 2000.

17 Hilary Waldron, "Literature Review of Long-Term Mortality Projections," *Social Security Bulletin*, Vol. 66, No. 1, 2005.

18 David C. Langer, "Social Security's Finances Are in Fine Shape," *Contingencies*, May/June 1999.

19   Cited in Merton C. Bernstein, "Social Security: The Battle of the Millennium," speech to Milwaukee Investment Analysts Society, October 29, 1997.

20   Cited in David Langer, "Social Security Finances Are in Fine Shape," *Contingencies*, May/June 1999.

21   David R. Francis, "Save Social Security? It's already solvent," *Christian Science Monitor*, September 20, 1999.

22   Ronald Lee and Timothy Miller, "Immigration, Social Security, and Broader Fiscal Impacts," *The American Economic Review*, Vol. 90, No. 2, May 2000, p. 353.

23   Dean Baker, "Nine Misconceptions About Social Security," *The Atlantic Monthly*, July 1998.

24   Langer, "Social Security Finances Are in Fine Shape."

25   Biggs, "Social Security: Is It 'A Crisis That Doesn't Exist'?"

26   Interview with Stephen C. Goss, June 4, 2009.

27   David Langer, "Re: The GAO's $0.5 million study fails to dispel disturbing doubts about Social Security's shaky actuarial foundations," letter to correspondents, May 3, 2000.

28   Dean Baker and Mark Weisbrot, "Social Security Scaremongering," *Washington Post*, December 13, 1999.

29   Robertson cited in Michael A. Hiltzik, *The Plot Against Social Security: How the Bush Plan Is Endangering Our Financial Future* (New York: HarperCollins, 2005), p. 64.

Chapter 19

1   Richard Hofstadter, "The Pseudo-Conservative Revolt," *The American Scholar*, Winter 1954–55.

2   Harry Turtledove, "Elder Skelter," *George*, February 1, 1997.

3   Alexei Bayer, "Let's Give Parents an Extra Right to Vote," *New York Times*, May 4, 1997.

4   Sam Beard, *Restoring Hope in America: The Social Security Solution* (San Francisco: ICS Press, 1996).

5   Robert Dreyfuss, "The Real Threat to Social Security," *The Nation*, February 8, 1999; Trudy Lieberman, "Social Insecurity," *The Nation*, January 27, 1997.

6   Schieber and Shoven, *The Real Deal*, p. 253.

7   Susan George, "How to Win the War of Ideas: Lessons from the Gramscian Right," *Dissent*, Summer 1997, Vol. 44, No. 3.

8   Robert M. Ball, unpublished memoir, pp. 274–75, cited in Berkowitz, *Robert Ball and the Politics of Social Security*, p. 333.

9   Eric R. Kingson and John B. Williamson, "Understanding the Debate Over the Privatization of Social Security," *Journal of Sociology and Social Welfare*, September 1998, Vol. XXV, No. 3.

10   Jeff Nygaard, "Social Security Reform," *Z Magazine*, April 1999.

11   David Brock, *Blinded by the Right: The Conscience of an Ex-Conservative* (New York: Crown, 2002).

12   Charles R. Morris, *The AARP: America's Most Powerful Lobby and the Clash of Generations* (New York: Times Books, 1996), pp. xi–xiii, 4, 240–42.

13   Interview with John Rother, July 11, 2007.

14   Marilyn Werber Serafini, "Senior Schism," *National Journal*, May 6, 1995.

Chapter 20

1   Jose Pinera, "Empowering Workers: The Privatization of Social Security in Chile," *Cato Journal*, Vol. 15, Nos. 2–3 (Fall/Winter 1995/96).

2   Jean de Fougerolles, "Pension privatization in Latin America," *Russian & East European Finance & Trade*, May/June 1996.

3   Speech cited on www.josepinera.com.

4   Letter cited on www.josepinera.com.

5   Jose Pinera, "Empowering Workers."

6   Peter Diamond and Salvador Valdes-Prieto, "Social Security Reforms," in Barry P. Bosworth, Rudiger Dornbusch, Raul Laban, eds., *The Chilean Economy: Policy Lessons and Challenges* (Washington DC: The Brookings Institution, 1994), p. 261.

7   Greg Palast, "Tinker Bell, Pinochet and the Fairy Tale Miracle of Chile," *Baltimore Chronicle & Sentinel*, December 10, 2006.

8   Joseph Collins and John Lear, *Chile's Free-Market Miracle: A Second Look* (Oakland CA: The Institute for Food and Development, 1995), p. 33.

9   Roger Charlton and Roddy McKinnon, *Pensions in Development* (Aldershot, U.K.: Ashgate, 2001), pp. 238, 250.

10   Diamond and Valdes-Prieto, "Social Security Reforms," p. 303.

11   Robert J. Myers, "Privatization of Social Security: A Good Idea?" *Journal of the American Society of Chartered Life Underwriters and Chartered Financial Consultants*, July 1996.

12   CB Capitales, Comentario macroeconómico: primera quincena de abril de 1999 (Santiago: CB Capitales, 1999), cited in Stephen J. Kay, "Privatizing Pensions: Prospects for the Latin American Reforms," *Journal of Interamerican Studies and World Affairs*, Vol. 42, No. 1, Spring 2000.

13   Diamond and Valdes-Prieto, "Social Security Reforms," p. 283.

14   Alberto Arenas de Mesa and Veronica Montesinos, "The Privatization of Social Security and Welfare: Gender Effects of the Chilean Reform," *Latin American Research Journal*, Vol. 34, No. 3, 1999. This article was based on a 1995 presentation to the Latin American Studies Association.

15   Ibid.

16   Joe Klein, "If Chile can do it ... couldn't (North) America privatize its social-security system?" *Newsweek*, December 12, 1994.

17   Matt Moffett, "Latin American Model For Financial Reform," *Wall Street Journal*, August 22, 1994.

18   *Averting the Old Age Crisis: Policies to Protect the Old and Promote Growth* (Washington DC/New York: The World Bank/Oxford University Press, 1994).

19   Monika Queisser, "Pension reform and international organizations: From conflict to convergence," *International Social Security Review*, Vol. 53, No. 2, Spring 2000, p. 39.

Chapter 21

1   Peter J. Ferrara, "The New Politics of Social Security," *Wall Street Journal*, February 14 1996.

2   Quoted in Mark A. Hofmann, "Advisory Panel to Issue Proposals," *Business Insurance*, May 20, 1996.

3   Interview with David Lindeman, December 5, 2006.

4   Robert M. Ball, unpublished memoir, pp. 344–45, cited in Berkowitz, *Robert Ball and the Politics of Social Security*, p. 346.

5   Interview with Robert M. Ball, July 25, 2001.

6   Ball biographer Edward D. Berkowitz to author, December 1, 2008; interview with Thomas Bethell, February 2, 2009.

7   Interview with Edward M. Gramlich in James Edward Gibson III, "The Last Council: Social Security Policymaking as Coalitional Consensus and the 1994–1996 Advisory Council as Institutional Turning Point," unpublished dissertation, Virginia Polytechnic Institute and State University, submitted July 5, 2007, p. 347.

8   Ibid.

9   Interview with David Lindeman, November 20, 2007.

10   Interview with Sylvester J. Schieber, May 21, 2009.

11   David Lindeman to author, August 24, 2009.

12   Edith M. Fierst, "Proposals Affecting Equity and Adequacy," memo to 1994–1996 Advisory Council on Social Security, November, 1994.

13   Quoted in David C. Beeder, "Council Starts to Tackle Social Security Changes," *Omaha World-Herald*, April 22, 1995.

14   Memorandum from S.J. Schieber to David Lindeman, April 19, 1995; Schieber and Shoven, *The Real Deal*, p. 273.

15   Ball and Fierst, transcript of April 11 meeting of the 1994–1996 Advisory Council on Social Security, Washington DC, pp. 79–81, 88.

16   Bob Davis, "A Consensus Emerges: Social Security Faces Substantive Makeover," *Wall Street Journal*, July 9, 1996.

17   Interview with David Lindeman, November 20, 2007.

18   Report of the 1994–1996 Advisory Council on Social Security, Vol. I: Findings and Recommendations, p. 28; R. Douglas Arnold, "The Politics of Reforming Social Security," *Political Science Quarterly*, Vol. 113, No. 2, 1998.

19   Interview with Gerald M. Shea, cited in Gibson, "The Last Council," p. 401.

20   Ibid.

21   Judith Burns, "Clinton Cautious on Social Security Privatization," Dow Jones News Service, July 16, 1996.

22   Brett D. Fromson, "A Safety Net Whets Wall St. Appetites; Social Security Proposals Could Mean Billions in Fees," *Washington Post*, January 7, 1997.

23   Henry J Aaron, "The Myths of the Social Security Crisis," *Washington Post*, July 21, 1996.

24   Judith Burns, "Social Security Report May Not Be Out Until After Election," Dow Jones News Service, August 15, 1996.

25   Steve Forbes, "How to Replace Social Security," *Wall Street Journal*, December 18, 1996.

26   Christopher Georges, "Forbes's Proposal to Restructure Social Security Suggests System Is No Longer Political Third Rail," *Wall Street Journal*, February 9, 1996.

27   "Bill Would Allow Private Investment of Some Social Security Tax," Associated Press, July 9, 1996.

28   Vineeta Anand, "Election Could Clog Social Security fix," *Pensions & Investments*, September 2, 1996.

29   Bob Davis, "A Consensus Emerges: Social Security Faces Substantive Makeover," *Wall Street Journal*, July 9, 1996.

30 Report of the 1994–1996 Advisory Council on Social Security, Vol. I: Findings and Recommendations, pp. 17, 25–27.

31 Interview with Stephen C. Goss, June 4, 2009.

32 Interview with Sylvester J. Schieber, June 1, 2007.

33 Interview with Edward M. Gramlich, November 8, 2006.

34 Cited in Gibson, "The Last Council," p. 198.

35 Interview with Gerald M. Shea, in Gibson, "The Last Council, p. 412.

36 David C. Breedon, "Low Election Profile Of Social Security Seen Aiding Action," *Omaha World-Herald*, November 3, 1996.

37 Paul J. Samuelson, "Can Clinton Do a Nixon" *Newsweek*, December 9, 1996.

38 "Council Members Vow Social Security Privatization Fight," *Congress Daily*, January 6, 1997.

39 Michael Tanner, "How to reform Social Security: True privatization is the way to go," *Greensboro News & Record*, January 12, 1997.

40 Judie Lynn Shivula, "Policy and Politics of Reform: Social Security in the United States," PhD. thesis in social welfare, University of California, Berkeley, Spring 2005.

41 Interview with Sylvester J. Schieber, May 22, 2007.

42 Interview with Sylvester J. Schieber, in Gibson, "The Last Council," p. 383.

43 Rob Wells, "Wall Street expects minimal boost if Social Security reforms adopted," Associated Press, January 6, 1997.

44 Brett D. Fromson, "Wall St.'s Quiet Message: Privatize Social Security," *Washington Post*, September 20, 1996.

45 Brett D. Fromson, "A Safety Net Whets Wall St. Appetites; Social Security Proposals Could Mean Billions in Fees," *Washington Post*, January 7, 1997.

46 Brett D. Fromson, "Labor Leader Attacks Wall Street Plan; Trumka Says Move to Privatize Social Security Reflects 'Greed,'" *Washington Post*, October 18, 1996.

Chapter 22

1 Interview with Gene Sperling, June 24, 2004.

2 Laura Tyson, Gene Sperling, Memorandum to the President on Social Security Responses, The White House, March 21, 1996.

3 Bill Clinton, note to Laura Tyson, May 21, 1996.

4 Interviews with Bill Archer, May 13, 2003 and September 1, 2011.

5 Steve M. Gillon, *The Pact: Bill Clinton, Newt Gingrich, and the Rivalry that Defined a Generation* (New York: Oxford University Press, 2008), p. 213–14.

6 Quoted in Sally Bedell Smith, *For Love of Politics: Bill and Hillary Clinton: The White House Years* (New York: Random House, 2007), p. 269.

7 Jonathan M. Orszag, Peter R. Orszag, and Laura D. Tyson, "The Process of Economic Policy-Making During the Clinton Administration," in Jeffrey Frankel and Peter Orszag, eds., *American Economic Policy in the 1990s* (MIT Press, Cambridge MA, 2002); interview with Peter Orszag, Oct. 17, 2002.

8 Clinton, *My Life*, page 143.

9 Gene Sperling, Memorandum to the President, August 5, 1997.

10 Gillon, *The Pact*, pp. 214–19; interview with Kenneth J. Kies, November 2, 2011.

11 Ibid, pp. 220–21.

12 Richard W. Stevenson, "U.S. Leaders Plan to Grapple A Hot Potato: Social Security," *New York Times*, January 8, 1998.

13   Gillon, *The Pact*, p. 224.

14   Richard W. Stevenson, "Fixing Social Security Should Come Before Any Surplus Free-For-All, President Says," *New York Times*, January 28, 1998.

15   Michael Waldman, *POTUS Speaks: Finding the Words that Defined the Clinton Presidency* (Simon & Schuster: New York, 2000).

16   Smith, *For Love of Politics*, p. 320.

17   Interview with Peter G. Peterson, February 16, 2006.

18   Cited in Daniel Gross, "What Makes a Nation More Productive? It's Not Technology," *New York Times*, December 25, 2005.

19   Interview with Gene Sperling, June 24, 2004.

20   Robert B. Reich, "The Sham of Saving Social Security First," *Harper's*, June 1998.

21   Gene Sperling, memorandum for the president, "Background on Social Security for April 7 conference," April 5, 1998.

22   Daniel Patrick Moynihan, "Social Security, As We Knew It," *New York Times*, January 5, 1997.

23   Interview with David Podoff, December, 2000.

24   Ibid.

25   Cited in James K. Glassman, "Moynihan's Social Security Plan," *Washington Post*, March 24, 1998.

26   Christopher Georges, "Social-Security 'Privatization' Effort Makes Headway," *Wall Street Journal*, June 22, 1998.

Chapter 23

1   Interview with Brad Belt, CSIS, April 28, 2003.

2   Robert Dreyfuss, "Wall Street Is Putting Money Into Privatization Efforts, But Doing It Quietly," *The Nation*, February 8, 1999.

3   Interview with Mark Schoeff Jr., CSIS director of external affairs, May 13, 2003.

4   Ibid.

5   Richard W. Stevenson, "Bipartisan Plan for Rescue of Social Security Involves Markets and Retirement at 70," *New York Times*, May 19, 1998; Christopher Georges, "Overhaul of Social Security Is Endorsed by Panel," *Wall Street Journal*, May 18, 1998.

6   "The 21st Century Plan: Final Report of the National Commission on Retirement Policy," Center for Strategic and International Studies, March 1999. The final report was substantially the same as the initial report, issued May 1998.

7   Christopher Georges, "Social-Security 'Privatization' Effort Makes Headway," *Wall Street Journal*, June 22, 1998.

8   Dreyfuss, "Wall Street Is Putting Money Into Privatization Efforts," February 8, 1999.

9   Oppenheimer Funds Newswire, January 21, 1999.

10   Interview with Roger Hickey, June 19, 2003.

11   Interview with Tom Matzzie, May 7, 2003.

12   Interview with Hans Riemer, June 26, 2003.

13   Interview with Lisa Witter, July 21, 2003.

14   Interview with Roger Hickey, June 19, 2003.

15   Interview with Tim Fuller, May 13, 2003.

16   Interview with Pat Conover, May 12, 2003.

17 Interview with Tom Matzzie, May 7, 2003.

18 Interview with Tom Matzzie, May 7, 1998.

19 Gene Sperling and Lawrence Summers, draft memorandum for the president, "Social Security and the Unified Surplus, Version 2," December 4, 1997.

20 Interview with Pat Conover, May 12, 2003.

21 Dean Baker, "Saving Social Security in Three Steps," Economic Policy Institute, Briefing Paper #77, Nov. 1998.

22 Interview with Roger Hickey, June 19, 2003.

Chapter 24

1 John Harwood and Michael K. Frisby, "Democrats, Searching For Election Theme, Question Who Should Fix Social Security," *Wall Street Journal*, July 8, 1998.

2 Quoted in Robert A. Rosenblatt, "GAO Warns About Raising Age for Retirees," *Los Angeles Times*, July 15, 1998.

3 Glenn Burkins, "Labor Gears Up Now for '99 Debate on Social Security," *Wall Street Journal*, September 28, 1998.

4 Greg Hitt, "House GOP Unveils Plan for $80 Billion in Tax Cuts to Be Financed by Surplus," *Wall Street Journal*, September 14, 1998.

5 Jackie Calmes and Greg Hitt, "Clinton Warns That GOP's Tax-Cut Bill Will Hurt Social Security, U.S. Image," *Wall Street Journal*, September 19, 1998.

6 Clinton, *My Life*, p. 822.

7 Howard Kurtz, "Democrats Chase Votes With a Safety Net; Candidates Nationwide Hammer Republicans on Ensuring Social Security's Future," *Washington Post*, October 28, 1998.

8 Thomas Frank, *What's the Matter with Kansas? How Conservatives Won the Heart of America* (New York: Metropolitan Books, 2004), pp. 75–6.

9 Interview with Tom Matzzie, May 7, 2003.

10 Howard Kurtz, "Democrats Chase Votes With a Safety Net," *Washington Post*, October 28, 1998.

11 Interview with Gerald Shea, Sean O'Brien, and Ken Grossinger, July 11, 2003.

Chapter 25

1 Grover Norquist, "The Republican Stumble," *The American Enterprise*, January/February 1999.

2 Jeanne Cummings, "Democrats Ready Quick Legislative Initiatives As GOP Aims to Recover From Election Results," *Wall Street Journal*, November 18, 1998.

3 "While Social Security Helped Democrats in '98 Election, Poll Shows Americans Dissatisfied with Debate About 'Saving' Social Security," Institute for America's Future press release, November 18, 1998.

4 Agenda, Social Security Reform Meeting with Economic Advisors, Wednesday November 4, 1998, Cabinet Room.

5 Cited in Gillon, *The Pact*, p. 263.

6 Interview with Tom Matzzie, May 7, 2003.

7   "Group to fight Social Security privatization," Reuters, Dec. 3, 1998.

8   Interview with Tom Matzzie, May 7, 2003.

9   Interview with Heidi Hartmann, February 13, 2004.

10   Interviews with Reischauer, Archer, Matzzie, Peter Orszag.

11   Interviews with Bill Archer, May 12, 2003 and September 1, 2011.

12   Richard W. Stevenson, "Clinton Meets 48 in Congress On Future of Social Security," *New York Times*, December 10, 1998.

13   Quoted in Will Marshall, "The New Democrat," January 1, 1999.

14   Dreyfuss, "Wall Street Is Putting Money Into Social Security Privatization."

15   David Rogers and Jeffrey Taylor, "A President Impeached And a Congress Torn— The Show Must Go On," *Wall Street Journal*, December 21, 1998.

Chapter 26

1   Interview with Gene Sperling, June 24, 2004.

2   Interview with Sylvester J. Schieber, May 12, 2003.

3   Berkowitz, *Robert Ball and the Politics of Social Security*, pp. 351–54.

4   Interview with Michael Tanner, May 14, 2003.

5   Interview with Hans Riemer, June 26, 2003.

6   Interview with Gene Sperling, June 24, 2004.

7   Interview with Michael Tanner, May 14, 2003.

8   "More Social Or Less? Clinton Plan Faces Lots of Questions," *Wall Street Journal*, January 20, 1999.

9   David Broder, "Off Target on Schools—Bull's-Eye on Social Security," *Washington Post*, January 21, 1999.

10   James Ridgway, "The Next Battle in Washington," *Village Voice*, January 26, 1999.

11   Robert Kuttner, "The Politics Of Good Economics," *Boston Globe*, February 28, 1999; Paul Davidson and James K. Galbraith, "The Dangers of Debt Reduction," *Wall Street Journal*, March 3, 1999.

12   Interview with Gene Sperling, June 24, 2004.

13   Roger Hickey, director, New Century Alliance for Social Security, memo re: "New Grassroots Plan for Action on Social Security," January 11, 1998.

14   Alice Ann Love, "Social Security Campaign Under Way," Associated Press, March 10, 1999.

15   Sara Hansard, "Wall Street, mutual funds get reminder of labor's pension clout," *Investment News*, February 1, 1999.

16   Standard & Poor's, 1999 Money Market Directory of Pension Funds and their Investment Managers.

17   Hansard, "Wall Street, mutual funds get reminder of labor's pension clout."

18   Beth Healy, "On State Street; Carter praises the Clinton plan," *Boston Herald*, February 3, 1999.

19   Gene Sperling, "NEC Weekly Report," memorandum to the president, February 12, 1999.

20   Interview with Bill Archer, May 13, 2003.

21   Interview with Gene Sperling, June 24, 2004.

22   Martin Feldstein, "Clinton's Social Security Sham," *Wall Street Journal*, February 1, 1999.

23   Michael M. Weinstein, "In the Red. No, Black," *New York Times*, Jan. 30, 1999.

24 Bob Davis, "Clinton Aide Blends Issues With 'Permanent Campaign,'" *Wall Street Journal*, March 9, 1999.

25 Michael Weinstein, "News Analaysis: The Debate Over Social Security Proposal Misfires in Focus on Double Counting," *New York Times*, January 30, 1999.

26 Transcript, "Fox News Sunday," February 21, 1999.

27 James Bennet, "President, in West, Is Mixing Politics, Rest and Fund-Raising," *New York Times*, February 26, 1999.

28 Greg Hitt and Jeanne Cummings, "Clinton, GOP Chiefs Vow to Work Jointly As Social-Security Issue Leads Agenda," *Wall Street Journal*, February 26, 1999.

29 Peter Diamond, "Administrative Costs and Equilibrium Charges with individual Accounts," in John B. Shoven, ed., *Administrative Aspects of Investment-Based Social Security Reform*, (Chicago: The University of Chicago Press, 2000), p. 139.

30 Interview with Jane Bryant Quinn, February 19, 2009.

31 Kelly A. Olsen and Dallas L. Salisbury, "Individual Social Security Accounts: Issues in Assessing Administrative Feasibility and Costs," Employee Benefit Research Institute, Issue Brief #203, November 1998.

32 Olivia Mitchell, "Administrative Costs in Public and Private Pension Systems," National Bureau of Economic Research, Working Paper No. 5734, 1996; Pat A. White, Paul Kupiec, and Gregory Duffee, "A Securities Transaction Tax: Beyond the Rhetoric, What Can We Say?" Finance and Economics Discussion Series (Washington, DC: Division of Research and Statistics, Division of Monetary Affairs, Federal Reserve Board, August 1990), p. 17; cited in Dean Baker, "Saving Social Security with Stocks: The Promise Doesn't Add Up," a Twentieth Century Fund/Economic Policy Institute Report, 1997, pp. 27–9.

33 Annual Report of the Board of Trustees of the Old-Age and Survivors and Disability Insurance Trust Funds (Washington, DC: U.S, Government Printing Office, 1995), cited in Robert J. Myers, "Privatization of Social Security: A Good Idea?" *Journal of the American Society of Chartered Life Underwriters*, July 1996.

34 Peter R. Orszag and Joseph E. Stiglitz, "Rethinking Pension Reform: Ten Myths about Social Security Systems, in *New Ideas about Old Age Security* (Washington, DC: The World Bank, 2001), pp. 35–6

35 Memo from Laura Townsend, Committee for the Future (Citizen Action).

36 Interview with Michael Tanner, May 14, 2003.

37 Interviews with Bill Archer, August 22 and October 3, 2011.

38 Caren Bohan, "Social Security A Top Issue For Bush, Adviser Says," Reuters, May 1, 1999.

Chapter 27

1 Current population Survey data, cited in Colleen Barry and Julie Donohue, The Uninsured in the U.S.: An Issue Brief, *Harvard Health Policy Review*, Fall 2000, Vol. 1, No. 1.

2 Interview with Michael Tanner, May 14, 2003.

3 Interview with Tom Matzzie, May 7, 2003.

4 Dean Baker, *Economic Reporting Review*, June 5, 2000.

5 Jim VanderHei, "Kerrey to Delay Bill To Repeal Limit On Retirees' Work," *Wall Street Journal*, March 6, 2000; Jim VanderHei and John D. McKinnon, "Senate

Votes to Repeal Earnings Limit For Social Security Recipients 65 to 69," *Wall Street Journal*, March 23, 2000.

6   Interview with Bill Archer, May 12, 2003; interview with Robert Reischauer, May 29, 2003.

7   Sperling, *The Pro-Growth Progressive*, pp. 259, 260, 294.

8   Interview with Tom Matzzie, May 7, 2003; interview with Michael Tanner, May 14, 2003.

9   Interview with Peter G. Peterson, February 15, 2006.

10   Interview with Tom Mazzie, May 7, 2003.

11   Interview with Gene Sperling, June 24, 2004.

12   Gillon, *The Pact*, p. 267.

13   R. Douglas Arnold, "The Politics of Reforming Social Security," *Political Science Quarterly*, Vol. 113, No. 2, 1998.

14   Interview with Bill Archer, January 11, 2011.

15   Quoted in C. Wright Mills, "Mass Education and Liberal Society," in *Power, Politics and People: The Collected Essays of C. Wright Mills*, Irving Louis Horowitz, ed. (New York: Ballantine Books, 1963), p. 356.

16   Cited in Jennifer Baggette, Robert Y. Shapiro, Lawrence R. Jacobs, "Social Security—An Update," *Public Opinion Quarterly*, Vol. 59, 1995, pp. 426–27.

17   Ibid., p. 421.

18   Time, CNN, Yankelovich Partners poll, April 18, 1998, and Harvard University/Chilton poll, May 6, 1998. Cited in Robert J. Blendon, John M. Benson, Mollyann Brodie, and Flint Wainess, "America in Denial: The Public's View of the Future of Social Security," *The Brookings Review*, Summer 1998.

19   Arnold, "The Politics of Reforming Social Security."

20   Blendon, Benson, Brodie, and Wainess, "America in Denial."

21   Lawrence R. Jacobs and Robert Y. Shapiro, "UFO Stories," *The New Republic*, August 10, 1998.

22   John Mueller, "A Subsidy for Motherhood," *Policy Review*, Fall 1987.

23   Interview with John Mueller, December 18, 2000.

Chapter 28

1   Interview with Bill Archer, May 12, 2003.

2   Quoted in Smith, *For Love of Politics*, p. 445. Emphasis in source.

3   Interviews with Michael Tanner, Hans Riemer.

4   Barbara Kantrowitz, "The Road Ahead: A Boomer's Guide to Happiness: The New Middle Age," *Newsweek*, April 3, 2000.

5   Paul A. Gigot, "Why Bush Thinks He Can Win On Social Security," *Wall Street Journal*, April 28, 2000.

6   Stuart Stevens, *The Big Enchilada: Campaign Adventures with the Cockeyed Optimists from Texas Who Won the Biggest Prize in Politics* (New York: The Free Press, 2001), pp. 63, 153.

7   George W. Bush, *Decision Points* (New York: Crown Publishers, 2010), p. 36.

8   Stevens, *The Big Enchilada*, p. 62.

9   Jackie Calmes, "Bush Vows to Spend Political Capital If Elected, for Social Security Overhaul," *Wall Street Journal*, November 22, 1999.

10   Interview with Elaine Kamarck, March 3, 2004.

Chapter 29

1   "2000 Presidential Race: Contributions from Selected Industries," Center for Responsive Politics, www.opensecrets.org.

2   George F. Will, "Bush's Solution for Social Security," *Washington Post*, May 28, 2000.

3   Paul A. Gigot, "Gore Waves White Flag In Class War," *Wall Street Journal*, June 19, 2000.

4   Richard L. Berke and Janet Elder, "Poll Showed Bush Ahead of Gore, With Leadership a Crucial Issue," *New York Times*, May 16, 2000.

5   Martin Feldstein, "Bush's Low-Risk Pension Reforms," *New York Times*, May 22, 2004.

6   Press alert, "Al Gore to Sign Our Pledge to Protect Social Security and Medicare," Campaign for America's Future, May 5, 2000.

7   Jackie Calmes, "Bush Boost Economic-Growth Forecast, Maintains Plan Protects Social Security," *Wall Street Journal*, May 3, 2000.

8   Adam Clymer, "Surplus a Gulf Between Candidates," *New York Times*, April 30, 2000.

9   Monica Richardson, "Group Seeking Pledges to Save Social Security," *Lexington Herald-Leader*, August 9, 2000.

10 Interview with Tom Mattzie, April 8, 2004.

11 Greg Hitt, "Bush's major donors have a long wish list," *Arkansas Democrat-Gazette*, August 6, 2000.

12 "Legacy 2000 Campaign: Final Report, June 1, 2000–November 7, 2000."

13 Interview with Elaine Kamarck, March 3, 2004.

14 Interview with Alan Blinder, March 23, 2004.

15 Bob Davis, "Gore Proposes a New Retirement-Savings Account," *Wall Street Journal*, June 19, 2000.

16 Lawrence B. Lindsey, "Would Al Gore's Social Security Reform Be Good for Taxpayers?" InsightMag.com, August 28, 2000.

17 Richard W. Stevenson and James Dao, "Gore Defends Stock Investment Switch," *New York Times*, May 25, 2000.

18 Interview with Dean Baker, March 24, 2004.

19 Interview with Roger Hickey, March 5, 2004.

20 Jackie Calmes and John Harwood, "Bush Brushes Off Gore Attack, Places His Focus on Leadership," *Wall Street Journal*, June 23, 2000.

21 Alison Mitchell, "Bush's Strategy: Offer Big Ideas First, Work Out Details Later," *New York Times*, May 24, 2000.

22 Interview with Elaine Kamarck, March 3, 2004.

23 Interview with Dana Marie Kennedy, February 17, 2004.

24 Interview with Tony Fransetta, February 10, 2004.

Chapter 30

1   Michael Barone and Richard E. Cohen, *The Almanac of American Politics 2004* (Washington: National Journal Group, 2003), p. 441.

2   Interview with Elaine Kamarck, March 3, 2004.

3   Thomas B. Edsall, "Populism 'Working' For Gore," *Washington Post*, September 15, 2000.
4   "Campaign Notebook," *Boston Globe*, September 20, 2000.
5   Interview with Dean Baker, Feb. 27, 2004.
6   Interview with Michael Tanner, March 19, 2004.
7   Dana Milbank, *Smashmouth* (New York: Basic Books, 2001), p. 360.
8   John Harwood and Bob Davis, "Gore Campaign Puts Social Security in Spotlight During 11ᵗʰ Hour," *Wall Street Journal*, October 30, 2000.
9   Katharine Q. Seelye, "Attacks Grow Sharp as Time Dwindles," *New York Times*, November 4, 2000.
10   Interview with Michael Tanner, March 19, 2004.
11   Interview with Tom Mattzie, April 8, 2004.
12   Interview with Hans Riemer, April 2, 2004.
13   Steven Greenhouse, "Labor Is Feeling Embattled As Union Leaders Convene," *New York Times*, March 9, 2004.
14   Interview with Michael Tanner, March 19, 2004.
15   Thomas B. Edsall, "Fissures Widening Among Democrats After Gore's Loss," *Washington Post*, December 16, 2000.
16   Poll cited in Michael Tanner, "Election Lessons for Social Security," The Cato Institute, November 17, 2000.

Chapter 31

1   Karlyn Barker and Serge F. Kovaleski, "Day Is Filled With Drama And Defiance," *Washington Post*, January 21, 2001; "Protesters line inaugural parade route," CNN. com allpolitics.com, January 20, 2001; author's eyewitness observation.
2   Alan Murray, "2001 Prediction: Support for Tax Cut," *Wall Street Journal*, December 18, 2000.
3   Richard W. Stevenson, "The Politics of Surplus Cut Across Partisanship," *New York Times*, November 19, 2000.
4   Tom Hamburger, "Big GOP Contributors Look for Return on Their Money," *Wall Street Journal*, December 28, 2000.
5   Jacob M. Schlesinger and John D. McKinnon, "Bush Tax Cuts Send Corporate Lobbyists Into a Feeding Frenzy," *Wall Street Journal*, February 2, 2001.
6   Ron Suskind, *The Price of Loyalty: George W. Bush, the White House, and the E ducation of Paul O'Neill* (New York: Simon & Schuster, 2001), p. 49.
7   Jackie Calmes, "Social Security May Get Lost in Priority Shuffle," *Wall Street Journal*, January 15, 2001.
8   Gene Sperling, "The Reforms a Tax Cut Ruins," *New York Times*, March 21, 2001.
9   Paul Krugman, "The Big Lie," *New York Times*, May 27, 2001.
10   Robert D. Reischauer, "Don't Count on That Tax Cut," *New York Times*, June 7, 2001.
11   Paul Krugman, "The Big Lie," *New York Times*, May 27, 2001.
12   Paul Krugman, "Red Tide Rising," *New York Times*, July 6, 2001.
13   Richard W. Stevenson, "Bush Projections Show Sharp Drop in Budget Surplus," *New York Times*, August 23, 2001.
14   David E. Sanger, "President Asserts Shrunken Surplus May Curb Congress," *New York Times*, August 25, 2001.

Chapter 32

1 Andrew Cassel, "Social Security makes fix-it list," *Philadelphia Inquirer*, April 13, 2001.

2 Karl Rove, *Courage and Consequence: My Life as a Conservative in the Fight* (New York: Threshold Editions, 2010), p. 406.

3 John D. McKinnon and John Harwood, "Wall Strreet Ponies Up to Back Bush's Social Security Plan," *Wall Street Journal*, June 12, 2001.

4 Rove, *Courage and Consequence*, p. 406.

5 Jim VandeHei and John D. McKinnon, "Bush Picks His Panel, but Social Security May Ba a Long Way From an Overhaul," *Wall Street Journal*, May 2, 2001.

6 Spencer Rich, "Stoking Social Security Fears," *National Journal*, April 14, 2001.

7 "Moynihan To Head Commission," Associated Press, May 2, 2001.

8 Hiltzik, *The Plot Against Social Security*, pp. 139–40.

9 John D. McKinnon and John Harwood, "Wall Strreet Ponies Up to Back Bush's Social Security Plan," *Wall Street Journal*, June 12, 2001.

10 Amity Shlaes, "US Treasury chief mulls tax reform," *Financial Times*, May 19 and 22, 2001.

11 Newsday, May 24, 2001; cited in "Action Alert: 'Political Dynamite' Fails to Explode," Fairness & Accuracy in Reporting, June 13, 2001.

12 Donna Smith, "Bush Social Security Panel Meets Under Fire," *New York Daily News*, July 24, 2001.

13 John D. McKinnon, "For Panel, Social-Security Overhaul Is Much More Difficult Than Expected," *Wall Street Journal*, August 22, 2001.

14 Stephen Norton, John Bennett, and Lisa Caruso, "Congress Daily," *National Journal*, July 24, 2001.

15 John D. McKinnon, "For Panel, Social-Security Overhaul Is Much More Difficult Than Expected," *Wall Street Journal*, August 22, 2001.

16 Robert Dreyfuss, "Bush's House of Cards," *The American Prospect*, September 20, 2001.

17 Roger Hickey and Hans Riemer, press summary memo, Social Security Information Project, July 31, 2001.

18 Editorial, "A Biased Social Security Report," *New York Times*, July 27, 2001.

19 Editorial, "Social Security crunch," *San Francisco Chronicle*, July 26, 2001.

20 Paul Krugman, "2016 and All That," *New York Times*, July 22, 2001.

21 Robert Dreyfuss, "Bush's House of Cards," *The American Prospect*, September 10, 2001.

22 Adam Clymer, "Social Security Panel Says Cuts in Benefits Are an Option," *New York Times*, August 23, 2001.

23 Dana Milbank, "New Social Security Indexing Mulled," *Washington Post*, August 23, 2001.

24 Jonathan Weisman and Richard Benedetto, "Bush backs off pledge for Social Security Vow to protect reserves is called a 'symbolic goal,'" *USA Today*, August 28, 2001.

Chapter 33

1 Nancy Altman, "Reflections on the Importance of Social Security: Social Security on the Tenth Anniversary of 9/11," HuffingtonPost,com, September 11, 2011.

2   Richard W. Stevenson, "Bush Finds a Backer in Moynihan, Who's Not Talking," *New York Times*, January 26, 2005.

3   Leigh Strope, "Social Security commission leaders say they will press forward with overhaul report," Associated Press, October 18, 2001.

4   Leigh Strope, "Options Likely on Soc. Sec. Overhaul," Associated Press, November 6, 2001.

5   Donna Smith, "Social Security Panel to Suggest Alternatives," Reuters, November 9, 2001.

6   Kurt Ritterpusch, Tax, Budget & Accounting, No. 227, Bureau of National Affairs, November 28, 2001.

7   Sue Kirchhoff, "Panel outlines Social Security plan," *Boston Globe*, November 30, 2001.

8   John D. McKinnon, "Bush Panel Proposes Specific Benefits Cuts To Make Social Security More Progressive," *Wall Street Journal*, November 30, 2001

9   Amy Goldstein, "Panel Agrees on Options for Social Security," *Washington Post*, November 30, 2001.

10   Tony Pugh and James Kuhnhenn, "Commission to issue recommendations on Social Security," Knight Ridder/Tribune News Service, December 11, 2001.

11   "Strengthening Social Security and Creating Personal Wealth for All Americans," Report of the President's Commission on Strengthening Social Security, December 11, 2001, pp. 46–48.

12   Henry Aaron, Alicia Munnell, and Peter Orszag, "The Social Security Reform: The Questions Raised by the Plans Endorsed by President Bush's Social Security Commission," The Century Foundation/Center on Budget and Policy Priorities, November 30, 2001.

13   Donna Smith, "Private Social Security Accounts Seen as No Panacea," *New York Daily News*, November 26, 2001.

14   Richard W. Stevenson, "A Finale in Three-Part Harmony," *New York Times*, December 12, 2001.

15   Hans Riemer, "Bush Social Security Commission Proposes Benefits Cuts to Pay for Privatization," Institute for America's Future, December 6, 2001.

16   Aaron, Munnell, and Orszag, "The Social Security Reform."

17   Riemer, "Bush Social Security Commission Proposes Benefits Cuts to Pay for Privatization."

18   Press release, "Women's Advocate Warns Women to Watch Bottom Line of Social Security Commission Report," National Women's Law Center, December 7, 2001.

19   Susan Page, "Why Social Security reform is dead, for now," *USA Today*, December 4, 2001.

Chapter 34

1   Robert Schlesinger, "Bush backs pension privatization," *Washington Post*, March 1, 2002; Elizabeth Bumiller, "Bush Renews Push to Partly Privatize Social Security," *New York Times*, March 1, 2002.

2   Wharton Policy and Management, "Fate Worse Than Debt: Can the U.S. Deficit Rise to $45.47 Trillion?" KNOWLEDGE@WHARTON, August 13, 2003.

3   Jagadeesh Gokhale and Kent Smetters, "Fiscal and Generational Imbalances: New Budget Measures For New Budget Priorities," American Enterprise Institute, AEI

Monograph, June 4, 2003.

4   *The 2003 Annual Report of the Board of Trustees of the Federal Old-Age and Survivors and Disability Insurance Trust Funds* (Washington, DC: U.S. Government Printing Office 2003), p. 3.

5   Joe Lieberman, "America Needs Honest Fiscal Accounting," *Financial Times*, May 25, 2004.

6   Wharton Policy and Management, "Fate Worse Than Debt: Can the U.S. Deficit Rise to $45.47 Trillion?" Knowledge@Wharton, August 13, 2003.

7   Jason Furman and Robert Greenstein, "What the New Trustees' Report Shows About Social Security," Center on Budget and Policy Priorities, March 23, 2005.

8   Bruce Bartlett, "Our 'Astronomical' Debt—Not really, at closer look," *National Review*, June 9, 2003.

9   *The 2003 Annual Report of the Board of Trustees of the Federal Old-Age and Survivors and Disability Insurance Trust Funds* (Washington, DC: U.S. Government Printing Office 2003), pp. 69–70.

10 Alan Murray, "Tax Break's 'Sunset' May Set the Stage For Fiscal Reckoning," *Wall Street Journal*, May 20, 2003.

11 E.J. Dionne, Jr., "No Excuse for Tax Cuts," *Washington Post*, March 25, 2003.

12 "The Medicare Drug War," Public Citizen Congress Watch, June 2004.

13 Mary Dalrymple, "Medicare Bill Has New Tax-Free Accounts," Associated Press, November 23, 2003.

14 Robert Pear, "Private Plans Costing More For Medicare," *New York Times*, September 17, 2004.

15 Robert Pear, "Ruling Says White House's Medicare Videos Were Illegal," *New York Times*, May 20, 2004.

16 Richard W. Stevenson, "As '04 Nears, Bush Campaign Works on a Theme," *New York Times*, August 29, 2003.

17 Edmund L. Andrews, "To Trim Deficit, Greenspan Urges Social Security and Medicare Cuts, *New York Times*, February 26, 2004; Greg Ip, "Greenspan Favors Entitlement Cuts," *Wall Street Journal*, February 26, 2004.

18 Greg Ip, "Greenspan Favors Entitlement Cuts," *Wall Street Journal*, February 26, 2004

19 Cited in Richard W. Stevenson, "The Hot Potato of Issues Is Dropped Anew," *New York Times*, February 27, 2004.

20 Susan Dominus, "Life in the Age of Old, Old Age," *New York Times Sunday Magazine*, February 22, 2004.

21 Paul Krugman, "Social Security Scares," *New York Times*, March 5, 2004.

22 Dean Baker, Economic Reporting Review, March 1, 2004

23 Jane Bryant Quinn, "Social Security Isn't Doomed," *Newsweek*, March 29, 2004.

24 Kelly Greene, "How Sick Is Social Security?" *Wall Street Journal*, June 28, 2004.

Chapter 35

1   Joe E. Hilsenrath, "Why for Many This Recovery Feels More Like a Recession," *Wall Street Journal*, May 29, 2003.

2   Alan Murray, "Democrats Need Clear Ideas to Win Debate on Economy," *Wall Street Journal*, August 12, 2003.

3 Adam Clymer, "Buoyed by Resurgence, G.O.P. Strives for an Era of Dominance," *New York Times*, May 25, 2003.

4 Elisabeth Bumiller and Richard W. Stevenson, "Aides Say Bush Is Already Absorbed in 2004 Race," *New York Times*, January 11, 2004.

5 U.S. Council of Economic Advisers, 2004 Economic Report of the President, cited in Fred Schneyer, "Bush Panel: Privatizing Social Security Could Mushroom Debt," Plansponsor.com, February 9, 2004; Greg Ip, "Social Security Option Is Reviewed," *Wall Street Journal*, February 9, 2004.

6 Jackie Calmes, "Ambitions to Fix Social Security Present Big Hurdles for Bush," *Wall Street Journal*, September 2, 2004.

7 David D. Kirkpatrick, "Some Big Conservative Donors, Unhappy With Bush, Say They Won't Back His Campaign," *New York Times*, June 4, 2004.

8 Jacob M. Schlesinger and Jackie Calmes, "Bush Unveils Economic Priorities," *Wall Street Journal*, August 10, 2004.

9 Austan Goolsbee, "The Fees of Private Accounts and the Impact of Social Security Privatization on Financial Managers," University of Chicago, September 2004.

10 Jonathan Weisman, "The Politics of Social Security," *Washington Post*, September 22, 2004.

11 Richard W. Stevenson, "Kerry Maintains Domestic Focus, Turning to Social Security and Medicare," *New York Times*, September 23, 2004.

12 David E. Rosenbaum and David M. Halbfingber, "Kerry Goes Beyond Some of Bush Positions," *New York Times*, October 19, 2004.

13 David M. Halbfinger, "Campaigning Furiously, With Social Security in Tow," *New York Times*, October 18, 2004.

14 Greg Hitt, "Bush on Stump Revives His Call for Tax Overhaul," *Wall Street Journal*, October 27, 2004.

15 Daniel Altman, "What Is a Sales Tax Were the Only Tax?" *New York Times*, October 17, 2004.

16 Adam Nagourney and Katharine Q. Seelye, "Bush and Kerry Focus Campaigns on 11 Key States," *New York Times*, October 24, 2004.

17 Terry M. Neal, "Bush's Poll Position Is Worst on Record," *Washington Post*, April 11, 2005.

18 John F. Harris and Jim VandeHei, "Doubts About Mandate for Bush, GOP," *Washington Post*, May 2, 2005.

Chapter 36

1 Rove, *Courage and Consequence*, p. 75.

2 Jon Berg, "Global Warming: Looking at the Numbers," *Z Magazine*, October 2007.

3 John Tierney, "Politics in the Guise of Pure Science," *New York Times*, February 24, 2009.

4 Greg Hitt and Jacob M. Schlesinger, "Social Security, Tax Code Are Part Of the New Plan," *Wall Street Journal*, November 4, 2004.

5 Adam Luna, "Corporate Lobbyists Set to Push SS Privatization," memo, Institute for America's Future, November 17, 2004.

6 Edmund L. Andrews, "Bush Says He Won't Raise Taxes for Social Security Overhaul," *New York Times*, December 10, 2004.

7   Jonathan Weisman, "Republicans Finding Ways To Account For Overhaul," *Washington Post*, November 23, 2004.

8   Jason Furman, William G. Gale, and Peter R. Orszag, "Should the Budget Rules Be Changed So That Large-Scale Borrowing to Fund Individual Accounts Is Left Out of the Budget?" Center on Budget and Policy Priorities, December 13, 2004.

9   David Brooks, "Real Reform for Social Security," *New York Times*, December 11, 2004.

10   Paul A. Gigot, "The Republican Moment," *Wall Street Journal*, January 20, 2005.

11   Tom DeLay, "'American Politics Has Changed Forever,'" *Wall Street Journal*, February 3, 2005.

12   Philip Bobbitt, *The Shield of Achilles: War, Peace, and the Course of History* (New York: Alfred A. Knopf, 2002), p. 211.

13   Philip Bobbitt, *Terror and Consent: The Wars of the Twenty-first Century* (New York: Alfred A. Knopf, 2008), p. 519.

14   Niall Ferguson, *Colossus: The Price of America's Empire* (New York: Penguin, 2004), pp. 210, 269–74.

15   Michael Mandelbaum, *The Case for Goliath: How America Acts as the World's Government* (New York: PublicAffairs, 2005), pp 185–86, 188.

16   John D. McKinnon and Christopher Cooper, "To Enact Second-Term Agenda, Bush Keeps On Campaigning," *Wall Street Journal*, January 20, 2005.

17   Jim VandeHei, "GOP Tilting Balance of Power to the Right," *Washington Post*, May 26, 2005.

18   John D. McKinnon and Jackie Calmes, "Administration Sets Meeting To Push Its Economic Agenda," *Wall Street Journal*, December 3, 2004.

19   Gene Sperling, *The Pro-Growth Progressive: An Economic Strategy for Shared Prosperity* (New York: Simon & Schuster, 2005), p. 256.

20   David Rogers, "Hastert Performs Delicate Balancing Act," *Wall Street Journal*, December 10, 2004.

21   Peter Gosselin, *High Wire: The Precarious Financial Lives of American Families* (New York: Basic Books, 2008), p. 87.

22   Alan Greenspan, remarks before the Boston College Conference on the New Technology, March 6, 2000; statement before the Joint Economic Committee of the United States Congress, March 20, 1997.

23   Jack Rasmus, "Bush's Ten Toxic Economic Legacies," *Z Magazine*, November 2008.

24   Christine Dugas, "Bankruptcy rising among seniors," *USA Today*, June 18, 2008.

25   Michelle Huggins, "How to Protect Yourself From Your Parents," *Wall Street Journal*, April 23, 2003.

26   Janet Aschkenasy, "Eldercare Grows Up," Financial-Planning.com, September 1, 2005.

Chapter 37

1   Scott McClellan, *What Happened: Inside the Bush White House and Washington's Culture of Deception* (New York: PublicAffairs, 2008), p. 248.

2   Robin Toner, "Bush on Social Security and Clinton on Heath Care: Oh, Those Devilish Details," *New York Times*, February 1, 2005.

3   John Heilemann, "The Last Battle," *New York*, January 24, 2005.

4   Nell Henderson and Jim VandeHei, "Borrow Cautiously, Greenspan Advises," *Washington Post*, February 17, 2005.

5   Glen Justice, "Groups That Clashed in the Campaign Are Facing Off Again," *New York Times*, April 12, 2005.

6   Brendan Murray, "Rove Uses Campaign Playbook to Mastermind Social Security Fight," Bloomberg.com, March 2, 2005; Mike Allen, "For GOP, Urgency On Social Security," *Washington Post*, March 1, 2005; Richard W. Stevenson, "With Bush Safely Re-elected, Rove Turns Intensity to Policy," *New York Times*, March 28, 2005.

7   Jackie Calmes, "White House Memo Argues for Social Security Cuts," *Wall Street Journal*, January 6, 2005.

8   Joseph Rebello, "Bush Economic Adviser Defends Social Security Plans," *Wall Street Journal*, January 10, 2005.

9   Jackie Calmes, "Architect of Social Security Plan Perseveres," *Wall Street Journal*, April 22, 2005.

10   Aaron Lucchetti, "Snow Tests Social Security Waters," *Wall Street Journal*, January 12, 2005.

11   Bill Berkowitz, "Falwell Builds His Legacy," *Z Magazine*, December 2006.

12   David D. Kirkpatrick and Sherl Gay Stolberg, "Backers of Gay Marriage Ban Use Social Security as Cudgel," *New York Times*, January 25, 2005.

13   Charles Babington, "Social Security Changes, Tax Cuts Among GOP Senators' 10 Priorities," *Washington Post*, January 25, 2005.

14   Joshua Micah Marshall, "Talking Points Memo," January 5, 2005.

15   Jeffrey H. Birnbaum and Jim VandeHei, "DeLay's Influence Transcends His Title," *Washington Post*, October 3, 2005.

16   Jackie Calmes, "Bush Loses Key Group on Social Security," *Wall Street Journal*, March 14, 2005.

17   Michael Barone and Richard E. Cohen, *The Almanac of American Politics 2008* (Washington, D.C.: National Journal Group, 2007), p. 184.

18   Nicholas Lemann, "Desert Storm," *The New Yorker*, October 25, 2011.

19   Thomas N. Bethell, "Roosevelt Redux: Robert M. Ball and the Battle for Social Security," *The American Scholar*, Spring 2005.

20   Thomas N. Bethell, "What's the Big Idea?" *AARP Bulletin*, April 2005.

21   John Heilemann, "The Last Battle," *New York*, January 2005.

22   Interview with Roger Hickey, February 27, 2009.

23   Interview with Alan Charney, December 16, 2008.

24   Interview with Roger Hickey, February 27, 2009.

25   Interview with Alan Charney, December 16, 2008.

Chapter 38

1   Mike Allen, "Bush Seeks to Allay GOP Doubts," *Washington Post*, January 26, 2005.

2   Jackie Calmes, "Bush Rallies Lawmakers on Social Security," *Wall Street Journal*, January 31, 2005.

3   Charles Babington and Mike Allen, "Democrats Claim Votes to Halt Social Security Plan," *Washington Post*, February 2, 2005.

4   Interview with Alan Charney, December 16, 2008.

5   Robin Toner, "On Social Security, a Political Appeal to the Young Draws the Attention of Their Elders," *New York Times*, February 23, 2005.

6   Sheryl Gay Stolberg and Robin Toner, "Republicans Are Chastened About Social Security Plan," *New York Times*, February 27, 2005.

7   David E. Rosenbaum, "Public View on Social Security Need to Swing Soon, Senator Says," *New York Times*, March 1, 2005.

8   Jackie Calmes, "In Congress, Republicans Are Split on Social Security," *Wall Street Journal*, March 10, 2005.

9   Christopher Cooper and Shailagh Murray, "Bush Begins to Woo Democrats To Back His Social Security Plan," *Wall Street Journal*, February 4, 2005.

10 Robin Toner and David E. Rosenbaum, "Senate Takes Up Bid to Overhaul Social Security," *New York Times*, April 25, 2005.

11 Richard W. Stevenson, "Bush, On Road, Pushes Warning on Retirement," *New York Times*, February 4, 2005.

12 David E. Sanger, "Bush Takes Social Security to 2 'Town Halls,'" *New York Times*, February 11, 2005.

13 Mark Leibovich, "Birth of a Salesman: Pitching Social Security," *Washington Post*, February 6, 2005.

14 Jim VandeHei and Peter Baker, "Social Security: On With the Show," *Washington Post*, March 12, 2005.

15 Interview with Alan Charney, December 16, 2008.

16 Quoted in Daniel Kurtzman, "Social Security reform for Dummies," About.com February 10, 2005.

17 Robin Toner, "In Montana, Bush Faces a Tough Sell on Social Security," *New York Times*, February 6, 2005.

18 Edmund L. Andrews, "G.O.P. Courts Blacks and Hispanics on Social Security," *New York Times*, March 20, 2005.

19 Peter Wallstein and Richard Simon, "Bush Shifts Focus to Race in Debate on Social Security," *Los Angeles Times*, January 26, 2005.

20 Edmund L. Andrews, "G.O.P. Courts Blacks and Hispanics on Social Security," *New York Times*, March 20, 2005.

21 Wallstein and Simon, "Bush Shifts Focus to Race in Debate on Social Security."

22 George C. Edwards III, *Governing by Campaigning: The Politics of the Bush Presidency* (New York: Pearson Longman, 2007), p. 266.

23 Jim VandeHei, "Three Were Told to Leave Bush Town Meeting," *Washington Post*, March 30, 2005.

24 Anne E. Kornblut and Sam Roberts, "Pro and Con Line Up as Bush Presses Social Security Effort," *New York Times*, March 5, 2005.

25 C.J. Karamargin, "Crowd rallies for Bush," *Arizona Daily Star*, March 22, 2005.

26 VandeHei, "Three Were Told to Leave Bush Town Meeting."

27 Colorado Pols Webblog, "White House Admission, Denver Three, Beauprez," April 2005.

28 David E. Rosenbaum, "Few See Gains From Social Security Tour," *New York Times*, April 3, 2005.

29 Richard W. Stevenson and Robin Toner, "Bush to Shift His Social Security Focus to Solutions," *New York Times*, April 10, 2005.

30 Theresa M. Wilson, "Opting Out: The Galveston Plan and Social Security," Pension Research Council, Working Paper 9922, 1999; Government Accounting Office study, February 1999, cited in Eric Kingson and Jack Cornman, "Memo to Bush: Galveston plan not answer for Social Security," *Houston Chronicle*, May 9, 1999.

Chapter 39

1 John Tierney, "The Old and the Rested," *New York Times*, June 14, 2005.
2 Richard W. Stevenson, "Fight on Judges Obscures Social Security," *New York Times*, May 20, 2005.
3 Jonathan Tasini, "The Birthday Bush Wants To Ignore," TomPaine.com, August 11, 2005.
4 Cindy Skrzycki, "Agency Stamps Out Use of 'Social Security,'" *Washington Post*, November 8, 2005.
5 Robert Pear, "No Call for Agency to Sell Fix For Social Security, Aide Says," *New York Times*, January 17, 2005.
6 Paul Krugman, "Slanting Social Security," *New York Times*, March 11, 2005.
7 Thomas R. Saving, "$74 Trillion = Crisis," *Wall Street Journal*, March 9, 2005.
8 David Kamin and Richard Kogan, "The Administration's Misleading $600 Billion Estimate of the Cost of Waiting to Act on Social Security," Center on Budget and Policy Priorities, February 2, 2005.
9 Robert Pear, "Social Security Enlisted to Push Its Own Revision," *New York Times*, January 16, 2005.
10 "News Dash," Plansponsor.com, February 7, 2005.
11 Fred Schneyer, "GAO Rejects Dems Challenge of Social Security Ruling," Plansponsor.com, May 3, 2005.
12 Jonathan Weisman, "GOP Lawmakers Acknowledge Uphill Fight on Social Security," *Washington Post*, May 2005.
13 Glen Justice, "A New Battle For Advisers To Swift Vets," *New York Times,* February 21, 2005.
14 Sheryl Gay Stolberg and Richard W. Stevenson, "Flare-Ups in Battle to Push or Bury Bush Social Security Plan," *New York Times*, February 24, 2005.
15 Jeffrey H. Birnbaum and Ben White, "Social Security Tactics Escalate," *Washington Post*, February 23, 2005.
16 Richard W. Stevenson, "White House May Accept Benefits Shift," *New York Times*, March 3, 2005.
17 Marie Cocco, "Dirty battle in the Social Security war," *Newsday*, March 29, 2005.
18 Mike Allen, "Congressional Republicans Agree to Launch Social Security Campaign," *Washington Post*, January 31, 2005.

Chapter 40

1 Bob Kerrey, "Pride and Prejudice," *Wall Street Journal*, February 1, 2005.
2 Dan Balz, "Social Security Stance Risky, Democrats Told," *Washington Post*, March 8, 2005.
3 David Rosenbaum, "At Social Security Hearing, Bush's Fight Largely Uphill," *New York Times*, April 27 2005.
4 Judy Keen, Bush: Rein in Social Security: Plan slows benefits for higher earners," *USA Today*, April 29, 2005.
5 Jonathan Weisman and Michael A. Fletcher, "GOP May Be Splintering on Social Security," *Washington Post*, April 27, 2005.

6　Richard W. Stevenson, "President's Big Social Security Gamble," *New York Times*, April 30, 2005.

7　Jason Furman, "An Analysis of Using 'Progressive Indexing' to Set Social Security Benefits," Center on Budget and Policy Priorities, March 21, 2005.

8　Jason Furman, "New White House Document Shows Many Low-Income Beneficiaries Would Face Social Security Benefit Cuts Under President's Plan," Center on Budget and Policy Priorities, May 10, 2005.

9　David Espo, "White House Leaves Disabled Benefits Open," Associated Press, May 13, 2005.

10　David E. Rosenbaum and Robin Toner, "Bush's Plan: Investing Part of the Nest Egg and Slowing the Growth of Benefits," *New York Times*, April 29, 2005.

11　Jonathan Weisman, "Bush Plan Greeted With Caution," *Washington Post*, April 30, 2005.

12　Robert Greenstein and Richard Kogan, "The Ryan-Sununu Social Security plan," Center on Budget and Policy Priorities, April 26, 2005.

13　Jackie Calmes, John D. McKinnon and Brody Mullins, "Bush's Embrace of New Initiatives Gains House Social-Security ally," *Wall Street Journal*, May 4, 2005.

14　Dana Milbank and Jim VanDeHei, "A Gambler Decides to Raise the Stakes," *Washington Post*, April 29, 2005.

15　Richard W. Stevenson, "President's Big Social Security Gamble," *New York Times*, April 30, 2005.

16　Robert C. Pozen, "A Win-Win Proposition," *Wall Street Journal*, May 3, 2005.

17　Greg Ip, "Wage Gap Figures in Social Security's Ills," *Wall Street Journal*, April 11, 2005.

18　Robert Guy Matthews, "Recovery Bypasses Many Americans," *Wall Street Journal*, August 31, 2005.

19　David E. Sanger, "Bush's Road Tour Rolls On in Push to Sell Social Security Changes," *New York Times*, June 3, 2005.

20　Mike Allen and Michael A. Fletcher, "Bush, at GOP Fundraiser, Cites Democrats' 'Obstruction,'" *Washington Post*, June 15, 2005.

21　Nancy Trejos, "Bush's Invitation-Only Speech Riles Crowd in Montgomery," *Washington Post*, June 24, 2005.

Chapter 41

1　Robert M. Ball, "Strengthening Social Security for the Long Run," draft of unpublished article, December 2007.

2　Bill Paul, Chicopee, Massachusetts, letter to *The [Greenfield MA] Recorder*, January 31, 2009.

3　Pat Toomey, "Good Policy, Good Politics," *Wall Street Journal*, June 28, 2005.

4　Robin Toner and David E. Rosenbaum, "The '06 Vote Is Echoing In the Social Security War," *New York Times*, June 24, 2005.

5　Robin Toner and David E. Rosenbaum, "The '06 Vote Is Echoing In the Social Security War," *New York Times*, June 24, 2005.

6　David E. Rosenbaum, "House G.O.P. Promises Vote on Social Security," *New York Times*, June 30, 2005.

7　Scott Szymendera, "Hurricane Katrina: Activities of the Social Security Administration," Congressional Research Service Report for Congress, September 9, 2005.

8 "The First Year After Katrina: What the Federal Government Did," U.S. Department of Homeland Security, HTTP://WWW.DHS.GOV/XPREPRESP/PROGRAMS/GC_I157649340I00.SHTM, last modified June 9, 2008.

9 Suzanne Goldenberg, "Fraudsters stole $1bn of Hurricane Katrina relief cash, Congress told," *The Guardian*, June 15, 2006.

10 Paul Krugman, "The Debt-Peonage Society," *New York Times*, March 8, 2005; Michael Schroeder, "Senate Approves Bill to Overhaul Bankruptcy System," *Wall Street Journal*, March 11, 2005; "Bush Signs Into Law Bankruptcy Overhaul," *Wall Street Journal*, April 21, 2005.

11 Jackie Calmes, "How a Victorious Bush Fumbled Plan to Revamp Social Security," *Wall Street Journal*, October 20, 2005.

12 Rove, *Courage and Consequence*, p. 407.

13 Jackie Calmes, "How a Victorious Bush Fumbled Plan to Revamp Social Security," *Wall Street Journal*, October 20, 2005.

14 Paul Alexander, *Machiavelli's Shadow: The Rise and Fall of Karl Rove* (New York: Modern Times, 2008), p. 180.

15 McClellan, *What Happened*, pp. 248–49.

16 Bush, *Decision Points*, pp. 299–306.

17 Brody Mullins, "U.S. Lobbying Tab Hits Record," *Wall Street Journal*, February 14, 2006.

18 Jackie Calmes, "Social Security Becomes Bipartisan Enigma," *Wall Street Journal*, April 15, 2005.

19 R. Glenn Hubbard, "Obama's Mixed Messages," *New York Times*, August 30, 2009; Rove, *Courage and Consequence*, p. 409.

Chapter 42

1 Jackie Calmes, "Budget Wish Lists Come and Go, But 'Entitlements' Outweigh All," *Wall Street Journal*, February 3, 2006.

2 Julie Kosterlitz and Marilyn Werber Serafini, "Must It Be Gloom and Doom For the Baby Boomers?" *National Journal*, December 3, 2005.

3 Isabel V. Sawhill, "Severe Need for Fiscal Courage, *Baltimore Sun*, January 27, 2006.

4 Robert Pear, "Finances of Social Security And Medicare Deteriorate," *New York Times*, May 2, 2006.

5 Dean Baker, "Reporting on Social Security and Medicare: Better, but not Good," Beat the Press (blog), My 2, 2006.

6 Jason Furman and Robert Greenstein, "What the New Trustees' Report Shows about Social Security," Center on Budget and Policy Priorities, May 1, 2006.

7 Fred Barnes, "We Are What We Own," *Wall Street Journal*, January 31, 2006.

8 Brody Mullins and Jackie Calmes, "Transforming Bipartisan Rhetoric Into Reality May Be a Tall Order," *Wall Street Journal*, February 2, 2006.

9 "Women and Children Last—Again: An Analysis of the President's FY 2007 Budget," National Women's Law Center, February 2006.

10 Robert Greenstein, Richard Kogan, and Edwin Park, "Elements of Forthcoming Medicare Trustees' Report Could Spell Trouble for Beneficiaries in Future Years," Center on Budget and Policy Priorities, March 22, 2005.

11 Jackie Calmes, "Ahead of Elections, as Painful Reminder," *Wall Street Journal*, March 17, 2006.

12 Jackie Calmes, "Expanding Bush budget Irks Conservatives," *Wall Street Journal*, January 24, 2006.

13 Jackie Calmes and John Hardwood, "Poll Signals More Republican Woes As Disapproval of Congress Grows," *Wall Street Journal*, October 18, 2006.

14 Interview with Alan Charney, December 16, 2008.

15 Terry L. Jones, "Seniors reaffirm their fight against Social Security privatization," *The Shreveport Times*, June 21, 2006.

16 Amy Fagan, "Social Security battle reignites," *Washington Times*, July 6, 2006.

17 Roger Hickey and Jeff Cruz, "Back From The Dead: Privatization," TomPaine.com, August 10, 2006.

18 Amy Fagan, "Social Security battle reignites," *Washington Times*, July 6, 2006.

19 Roger Hickey and Jeff Cruz, "Back From The Dead: Privatization," TomPaine.com, August 10, 2006.

20 Lori Montgomery, "Social Security Enters Elections," *Washington Post*, October 25, 2006.

21 Rachel Kapochunas, "Shaw's Latest Ad in Fla. Draws Skepticism of Klein Camp," *CQ Politics*, August 10, 2006.

22 Will Lester, "Democrats Reviving Social Security Issue," Associated Press, October 2, 299\\006.

23 Drew Westen, "Gut Instincts," *The American Prospect*, December 2006.

24 Sebastian Mallaby, "A Party Without Principles," *Washington Post*, October 2, 2006.

25 Edmund L. Andrews, "Surprising Jump in Tax Revenues Curbs U.S. Deficit," *New York Times*, July 9, 2006.

26 David D. Kirkpatrick and Anne E. Kornblut, "G.O.P. Candidates Turn Their Focus to the Economy," *New York Times*, November 3, 2006.

27 See Matt Bai, *The Argument: Billionaires, Bloggers, and the Battle to Remake Democratic Politics* (New York: The Penguin Press, 2007).

28 Rick Klein, "Social Security at roots of shift: Democrats set groundwork in reform fight," *Boston Globe*, November 12, 2006.

29 Dick Armey, "End of the Revolution," *Wall Street Journal*, November 9, 2006.

30 Fred Barnes, "'It Didn't Have to Be That Way,'" *Wall Street Journal*, November 6, 2006.

Chapter 43

1 George W. Bush, "What the Congress Can Do for America," *Wall Street Journal*, January 3, 2007.

2 Deborah Solomon, "Treasury Nominee Urges Pressing China on Yuan," *Wall Street Journal*, June 28, 2006.

3 "Paulson to press for entitlement reforms," *Baltimore Sun*, August 2, 2006.

4 Michael Abramowitz, "President Remains Eager to Cut Entitlement Spending," *Washington Post*, August 11, 2006.

5 Michael A. Fletcher, "Bush Sees 'Opportunities' on Social Security, Immigration," *Washington Post*, December 20, 2006.

6 "Panel Sought to Tackle Social Security Costs," *Washington Post*, January 12, 2007.

7 "U.S. Heading for Financial Trouble," "60 Minutes," CBS News, March 4, 2007.

8 David M. Walker, "America's $53 trillion debt problem," CNN Commentary, October 7, 2008.

9   Dean Baker, "Post Gives Rave Review to Anti-Social Security Propaganda Flick," Beat the Press (blog), August 7, 2008.

10 David R. Francis, "Social Security: a contrarian view," *Christian Science Monitor*, February 26, 2007.

11 Robert M. Ball, "A Social Security Fix For 2008," *Washington Post*, October 29, 2007.

12 Quoted in Edward S. Herman, "Neoliberalism and Bottom-Line Morality," *Z Magazine*, December 2008.

13 Mayer, Paul Milstein Professor of Real Estate, Columbia Business School; and Sinai, Associate Professor of Real Estate, The Wharton School, "Bubble Trouble? Not Likely," *Wall Street Journal*, September 19, 2005.

14 Ferguson, *The Ascent of Money: A Financial History of the World* (New York: The Penguin Press, 2008), p. 228.

15 Rebecca Moore, "Worker Finances Stretched too Thin to Save," PlanSponsor.com, September 4, 2008.

16 Nancy Trejos, "Retirement Savings Lose $2 Trillion in 15 Months," *Washington Post*, October 8, 2008.

17 Mary Pilon, "Market Turmoil Frightens Off Young Investors," *Wall Street Journal*, September 25, 2008.

18 Murray Gendell, "Older Workers: Increasing their labor force participation and hours of work," *Monthly Labor Review*, January 2008; Fred Schneyer, "New Data Confirms Americans Working Through Retirement," PlanSponsor.com, September 16, 2008; Nevin E. Adams, "Study Says Social Security Shifts Influencing Retirement Patterns," PlanSponsor.com, December 29, 2008.

19 Nevin Adams, "Younger Workers Expect to Work Longer," PlanSponsor.com, October 2, 2008.

20 "Talkin 'Bout My Generation: The Economic Impact of Aging US Baby Boomers," McKinsey & Co., June 2008.

21 Survey by the American Institute of Certified Public Accountants, cited in Rebecca Moore, "Would-Be Retirees Plan to Work Longer in Down Economy," PlanSponsor,com, February 5, 2009.

22 Interview with Jane Bryant Quinn, February 19, 2009.

23 Kelly Greene, "There Goes Retirement," *Wall Street Journal*, February 14–15, 2009.

24 Clare Ansberry, "Elderly Emerge as a New Class Of Workers—and the Jobless," *Wall Street Journal*, February 23, 2009.

25 Dean Baker, "The Post Misreports the Budget Deficit (Again)," Beat the Press (blog), February 3, 2008; Robert Pear and David M. Herszenhorn, "White House Predicts Bush Will Leave $482 Billion Deficit," *New York Times*, July 29, 2008.

26 Stuart M. Butler and Maya MacGuineas, "Rethinking Social Security," The Heritage Foundation and the New America Foundation, February 2008.

27 Isabel Sawhill and Emily Monea, "Old News," *Democracy: A Journal of Ideas*, Summer 2008.

28 David Wessel, "Deficit Hawks Try, Try Again," *Wall Street Journal*, April 3, 2008.

29 Will Marshall, "Let's Pop the Deficit Bubble," *Wall Street Journal*, May 3, 2008.

30 Henry Aaron et al, "A Balanced Approach to Restoring Fiscal Responsibility," Center on Budget and Policy Priorities, July 9, 2008.

31 Robert Kuttner, *Obama's Challenge: America's Economic Crisis and the Power of a Transformational Presidency* (White River Junction, VT: Chelsea Green Publishing, 2008), p. 77.

32 Heidi Przybyla, "Democratic Policy Group Would Cut Social Security for Top Earners in U.S.," Bloomberg.com, November 30, 2010.

33 Sourced from Peter G. Peterson Foundation's 2009 Form 990 filing, and cited in Jane Hamsher, "Where Pete Peterson Spends His Money: 2008 Grants," FireDogLake.com, May 25, 2010.

34 Bill Frenzel and Leon Panetta, "Deficit Bubble Boiling, Trouble is Close Behind," *Roll Call*, February 28, 2008.

Chapter 44

1 Steven Greenhouse, "For Incomes Below $100,000, a Better Tax Break in Obama's Plan," *New York Times*, October 30, 2008.

2 Andrew G. Biggs, "Obama Wants Social Security to Be a Welfare Plan," *Wall Street Journal*, October 24, 2008.

3 John Ydstie, "Where Do the Candidates Stand on Social Security?" All Things Considered, National Public Radio, October 31, 2007.

4 Interview with Roger Hickey, February 27, 2009; "Obama's Top Generals Dispatched to Florida," Marc Ambinder: A Reported Blog on Politics, October 8, 2008.

5 Jeff Zeleny, "Obama Criticizes McCain on Social Security," *New York Times*, September 21, 2008; Laura Meckler and Nick Timiraos, "Crisis Draws Attention ton McCain Social Security Plan," *Wall Street Journal*, September 22, 2008.

6 Anne E. Kornblut, "Palin Leaves Entitlement Reform Position Unclear," *Washington Post*, September 13, 2008.

7 See David Frum, "The Vanishing Republican Voter," *New York Times Sunday Magazine*, September 7, 2008.

8 Jonathan Weisman, "Republican Party No Longer Owns the Tax Issue," *Wall Street Journal*, October 29, 2008.

9 "McCain, Obama & Wall Street 'Reform': The Good, Bad & Ugly," CAF Blog for Our Future, Campaign for America's Future, September 15, 2008.

10 Monica Langley, "Volcker Makes a Comeback As Part of Obama Brain Trust," *Wall Street Journal*, October 21, 2008.

11 Editorial, "President-Elect Obama," *Wall Street Journal*, November 5, 2008.

12 Alex MacGillis and Sarah Cohen, "Final Fundraising Tally for Obama Exceeded $750 Million," *Washington Post*, December 6, 2008.

13 Interview with Alan Charney, December 16, 2008.

14 Interview with Roger Hickey, February 27, 2009.

15 Ibid.

16 Chad Stone, chief economist, Center on Budget and Policy Priorities, December 5, 2008.

17 Interview with Jane Bryant Quinn, February 19, 2009.

18 Interview with Thomas Jones, January 13, 2008.

19 Jeanne Cummings, "Bailout payout tops $8 trillion," Politico.com, December 16, 2008.

20 Jonathan Alter, *The Promise: President Obama, Year One* (New York: Simon & Schuster, 2010), p. 29.

21 Louise Story, "A Rich Education for Summers (After Harvard)," *New York Times*, April 6, 2009.

22 Yalman Onaran and Michael McKee, "In Geithner We Trust Eludes Treasury as Market Fails to Recover," Bloomberg.com, February 25, 2009.

23 Mark Weisbrot, "Stimulus Time: The Fierce Urgency of Now," Center for Economic and Policy Research, January 5, 2009.

24 Albert Keidel, "China's Stimulus Lesson for America," *Washington Times*, November 10, 2008.

25 James K. Galbraith, "Stimulus Is for Suckers," *Mother Jones*, December 8, 2008.

26 Matt Bai, "Newt. Again," *New York Times Sunday Magazine*, March 1, 2009.

27 Edmund L. Andrews, "A Crisis Trumps Constraint," *New York Times*, January 8, 2009.

28 Lori Montgomery, "Obama, Democrats seek 'grand bargain' on budget," *Washington Post*, February 1, 2009.

Chapter 45

1 John Maynard Keynes, *Essays in Persuasion* (New York: W.W. Norton & Company Inc., 1963) pp. vii–viii.

2 Evan Bayh, "Deficits and Fiscal Credibility," *Wall Street Journal*, March 4, 2009.

3 Interview with Roger Hickey, February 27, 2009.

4 Robert Kuttner, "The Deficit Hawks' Attack on Our Entitlements," *Washington Post*, February 23, 2009; interview with Roger Hickey, February 27, 2009.

5 Amy Goldstein, "The Summit Breakouts: Social Security," WashingtonPost.com, February 23, 2009.

6 Elizabeth Jensen, "WNET News Program Gains a Foothold but Draws Internal Complaints," *New York Times*, February 3, 2009.

7 Stephen Ohlemacher, "Job losses, early retirements hurt Social Security," Associated Press, September 27, 2009.

8 John D. McKinnon, "Deficit of $1.4 Trillion Limits Democrats," *Wall Street Journal*, October 16, 2009.

9 Jack Rasmus, "Economic Crisis in 2010 and Beyond," *Z Magazine*, January 2010.

10 Elizabeth Williamson and Henry J. Pulizzi, "Checks for Seniors Face Opposition," *Wall Street Journal*, October 22, 2009.

11 Dean Baker, "Defense Spending Has Been Growing More Rapidly Than Social Security," Beat the Press, February 7, 2010.

12 Bill Scher, "Progressives Issue 'Warning' On Debt Commission," OurFuture.org, January 20, 2010.

13 Lori Montgomery, "White House, Democratic lawmakers cut deal on deficit commission," *Washington Post*, January 20, 2010.

14 Mathew Skomarovsky, "Obama Packs Debt Commission with Social Security Looters," AlterNet, March 28, 2010.

15 Dan Eggen, "Many deficit commission staffers paid by outside groups," *Washington Post*, November 10, 2010.

16 Jeanne Sahadi, "Fixing Social Security: The 'low-hanging fruit,'" CNNMoney.com, May 11, 2010

17 Interview with Rep. Jan Schakowsky, February 22, 2011.

18 Tom Dickinson, "No We Can't," RollingStone.com, February 2, 2010.

19 Conason, *The Raw Deal*, pp. 71–2.

20 Matt Sedensky, "In weak economy, more people are filing early for Social Security," *Washington Post*, August 9, 2010.

21 Dennis Cauchon and Richard Wolf, "Despite recession, seniors see income gains," *USA Today*, September 18–19, 2010.

22 Kate Zernike, *Boiling Mad: Inside Tea Party America* (New York: Times Books/ Henry Holt and Company, 2010), p. 9.

23 Kevin Diaz, "Ouch! Bachmann touches 'third rail' of American politics," StarTribune.com (Minneapolis), February 10, 2010.

24 Dan Froomkin, "GOP Senator Proposes Increasing Social Security Retirement Age 'Every Several Years,'" HuffingtonPost.com, February 8, 2011.

25 Jackie Calmes, "Obama Warns of Privatizing Social Security," *New York Times*, August 15, 2010.

26 Jessica Yellin, "Who won Reid-Angle debate?" CNN.com, October 15, 2010.

27 Richard E. Cohen, "Jittery Dems turn to Social Security," Politico.com, September 21, 2010.

28 Jane Hamsher, "Alice Rivlin wants to Cut Social Security So John Boehner Can Spend It On Wars," FireDogLake.com, June 29, 2010.

29 Christopher Weber, *Politics Daily*, November 10, 2010.

Chapter 46

1 June 17, 2010. Quoted in Jane Hamsher, "Alan Simpson: Cutting Social Security Benefits to "Take Care of the Lesser People in Society," FireDogLake.com, June 17, 2010.

2 Robert Greenstein and James R. Horney, "House Republican Rule Changes Pave the Way For Major Deficit-Increasing Tax Cuts, Despite Anti-Deficit Rhetoric," Center on Budget and Policy Priorities, January 5, 2011.

3 Phil Gramm, "Echoes of the Great Depression," *Wall Street Journal*, October 2, 2010.

4 Yung-Ping Chen, "Social Security's Family Benefits and the Fiscal Commission," Newdeal 2.0, Roosevelt Institute, June 24, 2010.

5 John Maggs, "Dems feud over plan to fix deficits," Politico.com, October 9, 2010.

6 Peter Orszag, "Saving Social Security," *New York Times*, November 3, 2010.

7 Interview with Rep. Jan Schakowsky, February 22, 2011.

8 Michael Hiltzik, "Using ideology to cut the deficit," *Los Angeles Times*, November 14, 2010.

9 "Raising the Social Security retirement Age," Strengthen Social Security Campaign, April 2011.

10 Hilary Waldron, "Trends in Mortality Differentials and Life Expectancy for Male Social Security-Covered Workers, by Socio-economic Status," *Social Security Bulletin*, Vol. 67, No. 3, 2007, and Julian Cristia, "Rising Mortality and Life Expectancy Differentials by Lifetime Earnings in the United States," IDB Working Paper, International Development Bank, 2009. Both cited in Harry C. Ballantyne, Lawrence Mishel, and Monique Morrissey, "Social Security and the Federal Deficit: Not Cause and Effect," Economic Policy Institute Briefing Paper #273, August 6, 2010; Maya Rockeymoore, "Don't save Social Security by raising the retirement age," *Houston Chronicle*, October 21, 2008

11 Mark Miller, "What deficit cutting would mean for Social Security," Reuters.com, November 10, 2010.

12   Italics added. This footnote was spotted—quickly—by masaccio, "Catfood Co-Chairs Explicitly Use Social Security To Cut Deficit," FireDogLake.com, November 10, 2010.

13   Alexander Bolton, "Pelosi, political left rip proposal from debt commission chairmen," *The Hill*, November 10, 2010.

14   Jackie Calmes, "Panel Seeks Cuts in Social Security and Higher Taxes," *New York Times*, November 11, 2010.

15   Richard (RJ) Eskow, "The 'Social Security Chained-CPI Massacre': Underhanded, Unnecessary, Unfair, Un-American," HuffingtonPost.com, June 30, 2011.

16   Robert Borosage, "Bipartisan Blight: The Great Tax Reform Mirage," HuffingtonPost.com, December 3, 2010.

17   James P. Pinkerton, "The Deficit Commission Is a Big, Fat Dud," FoxNews.com, November 11, 2010.

18   Stephen Spruiell, "What's the Ratio, Kenneth?" NationalReview.com, November 10, 2010.

19   Jackie Calmes, "Panel Seeks Cuts in Social Security and Higher Taxes," *New York Times*, November 11, 2010.

20   John D. McKinnon and Laura Meckler, "Deficit Directive Tracks GOP Aims," *Wall Street Journal*, November 13, 2010.

21   David Wessel, "Two Tests of a Gridlock Mentality," *Wall Street Journal*, November 18, 2010.

22   David Moberg, "The Progressive Deficit Hawk," *In These Times*, November 29, 2010.

23   Dean Baker, "Who Can Fight Off the Social Security Pillagers?" CommonDreams.org, January 21, 2011.

24   Monique Morrissey, "Beyond 'Normal,'" EPI Briefing Paper #287, Economic Policy Institute, January 26, 2011.

25   James K. Galbraith, "James K. Galbraith Champions The Beast Manifesto," DailyBeast.com, August 2, 2010.

26   Lawrence H. Thompson, "Paying for Retirement: Sharing the Gain," in Tereas Ghilarducci, Van Doorn Ooms, John L. Palmer, and Catherine Hill, eds., *In Search of Retirement Security: The Changing Mix of Social Insurance, Employee Benefits, and Individual Responsibility* (New York: The Century Foundation, 2005), pp. 115–25.

27   Bruce Webb, data by Dale Coberly, "NW Plan for a real Social Security Fix Ver. 2.0: 2009 Trigger," AngryBearBlog.com, May 21, 2009.

28   Henry J. Aaron, "A Vision for the U.S. Pension System at 100,"Brookings Institution, January 29, 2009.

29   Dean Baker, "Attack Wall Street, Not Social Security," *The Guardian*, April 12, 2010.

30   Interview with Rep. Jan Schakowsky, February 22, 2011.

31   Ibid.

32   John Maggs, "Deficit panel doomed from start?" Politico.com. November 29, 2010.

33   "Social Security and the Budget," Committee for a Responsible Federal Budget, March 24, 2011.

34   Damian Paletta and John D. McKinnon, "Mortgage Tax Break Is in Crosshairs," *Wall Street Journal*, December 1, 2010.

35   Richard Eskow, "A President At The Crossroads (Who Needs A Little Help From His Friends), HuffingtonPost.com, December 2, 2010.

36   Dan Baltz, "Bipartisan deficit commission puts politicians on notice," *Washington Post*, December 3, 2010; Lori Montgomery and Shailagh Murray, "Rival lawmakers join to rally for deficit plan," *Washington Post*, December 4, 2010.

37   Alexander Bolton, "Social Security reform splits White House political, economic teams," *The Hill*, March 15, 2010.

Chapter 47

1   Quoted in Richard (RJ) Eskow, "Higher Retirement Age? Lower Benefits? The President Says You Won't 'Notice,'" AmericasFuture.org, August 17, 2011.

2   Clinton, speaking at Peterson Foundation 2011 Fiscal Summit, May 25, 2011.

3   David Kocieniewski, "Tax Package Will Aid Nearly All, With the Highest Earners Benefiting Most," *New York Times*, December 8, 2010.

4   Jonathan Weisman and Damian Paletta, "Obama Turns to Old Clinton Hand," *Wall Street Journal*, January 8–9, 2011.

5   Stephen C. Goss, letter to the Hon. Timothy F. Geithner, Secretary of the Treasury, December 10, 2010.

6   Sean Higgins, "Social Security Reform Possible? Payroll Tax Cut May Be a Step," *Investor's Business Daily*, December 17, 2010.

7   Stephen Ohlemacher, "Tax Cut Worries Social Security Advocates," Associated Press, December 12, 2010; "Tax Cuts for Illustrative Earners Under 'Making Work Pay' and the Proposed Payroll Tax Cut," Social Security Works, December 13, 2010.

8   Brian Beutler, "Top Democrat Identifies Another Threat To Social Security In Obama Tax Plan," TalkingPointsMemo.com, December 15, 2010.

9   Laura Meckler, "White House Retreats on Social Security Offer," *Wall Street Journal*, February 11, 2011.

10   Lori Montgomery, "Obama won't endorse raising retirement age or reducing Social Security benefits," *Washington Post*, January 24, 2010.

11   Michael O'Brien, "Reid: 'Leave Social Security alone,'" *The Hill*, March 16, 2011.

12   Janet Adamy, "Medicare Cost Would Rise for Many Under Ryan Plan," *Wall Street Journal*, April 6, 2011; Alan S. Blinder, "Paul Ryan's Reverse Robin Hood Budget," *Wall Street Journal*, April 19, 2011.

13   Email from Nancy Altman, April 6, 2011.

14   Jackie Calmes, "A Conservative Vision, With Bipartisan Risks," *New York Times*, April 6, 2011.

15   "Statement of Robert Greenstein, President, on Chairman Ryan's Budget Plan," Center on Budget and Policy Priorities, April 5, 2011.

16   Robert Pear, "G.O.P. Blueprint would Remake Health Policy," *New York Times*, April 5, 2011.

17   Jonathan Weisman, "New Proposal Inspires Political Rallying Calls," *Wall Street Journal*, April 6, 2011.

18   Naftali Bendavid and Janet Hook, "No Retreat on Medicare," *Wall Street Journal*, May 26, 2011.

19   Lori Montgomery, "In debt talks, Obama offers Social Security cuts," *Washington Post*, July 6, 2011.

20   Interview with Max Richtman, October 18, 2011.

21   Rick Ungar, "More Solid Proof That ObamaCare Works," Forbes.blogs, May 23, 2011.

22 Robert Kuttner, "Now Back to the Economy," The American Prospect Blogs, August 2, 2011.

23 Sabrina Tavernise, "Poverty Reaches a 52-Year Peak, Government Says," *New York Times*, September 14, 2011.

24 Ed O'Keefe, "Social Security offices to ban people who make threats," WashingtonPost.com, September 9, 2011.

25 See Paul Mason, "America's Poor: the end of the middle class dream," *The Guardian*, October 12, 2010; Louis Uchitelle, "Is Manufacturing Falling Off the Radar?" *New York Times*, September 11, 2011; Paul Harris, "The Decline and Fall of the American Middle Class," *The Guardian*, September 14, 2011.

26 Jack Rasmus, "Emerging Labor Responses to the Economic Crisis," *Z Magazine*, September 2011.

27 Interview with Frank Clemente, Strengthen Social Security, June 27, 2011

28 Carrie Budoff Brown and Ben Smith, "Obama and the left back in synch," Politico.com, September 19, 2011.

29 See, for example, *On the Edge: Economic Insecurity After the Great Recession,* Institute for Women's Policy Research/Rockefeller Foundation Survey of Economic Security, September 2011.

Chapter 48

1 Quoted in Robert W. Schrier, *Clinical Internal Medicine in the Aged* (London: Saunders (W.B.) Co Ltd, 1982).

2 Philip Rucker, "Romney sees choice between 'entitlement society' and 'opportunity society,'" *Washington Post*, December 20, 2011.

3 Richard Cowan, "Social Security reform debate stirs in Congress," Reuters, March 1, 2011.

4 Excellent introductions to this problem can be found in Robert N. Butler, *The Longevity Revolution: The Benefits and Challenges of Living a Long Life* (New York: PublicAffairs, 2008); and Susan Jacoby, *Never Say Die: The Myth and Marketing of the New Old Age* (New York: Pantheon Books, 2011).

5 Karen Friedman, "A retirement deficit that's only deepening," *Philadelphia Inquirer*, November 30, 2010.

6 "The Retirement Income Deficit," RetirementUSA, http://www.retirement-usa. org/retirement-income-deficit-0.

7 Analysis of Current Population Survey Annual Social and Economic Supplement, cited in Media Advisory, Institute for Women's Policy Research, January 25, 2011.

8 Alicia H. Munnell, Anthony Webb, and Alex Golub-Sass, "How Much Risk Is Acceptable?" Center for Retirement Research at Boston College, Issue Brief Number 8–20, November 2008.

9 Alan S. Blinder, "Our Dickensian Economy," *Wall Street Journal*, December 17, 2010.

10 Damien Paletta, Janet Hook, and Jonathan Weisman, "Deficit Outlook Darkens," *Wall Street Journal*, January 27, 2011.

11 Census Bureau data, cited in Charles M. Blow, "Hard-Knock (Hardly Acknowledged) Life," *New York Times*, January 29, 2011.

12 Sudeep Reddy and Sara Murray, "Jobless Rate Falls Further," *Wall Street Journal*, March 5, 2011.

13 Erik Eckholm, "Recession Raises U.S. Poverty Rate to a 15-Year High," *New York Times*, September 17, 2010.

14 Fred Schneyer, "Caregivers Tap Retirement, Other Sources, to Cover Expenses," PlanSponsor.com, November 17, 2006.

15 E.S. Browning, "Retiring Boomers Find 401(k) Plans Fall Short," *Wall Street Journal*, February 19–20, 2011.

16 Estimate by Fidelity Investments, cited in Fran Hawthorne, "A Hesitancy to restore Those 401(k) Matches," *New York Times*, September 16, 2011.

17 Damian Paletta, "Insolvency Looms as States Drain U.S. Disability Fund," *Wall Street Journal*, March 22, 2011.

18 Hye Jin Rho, "Hard Work? Patterns in Physically Demanding Labor Among Older Workers," Center for Budget and Policy Priorities, August 2010.

19. Paul Krugman, "Seniors, Guns and Money," *New York Times*, May 13, 2011

20 Mark Miller, "Medicare will cut Social Secuirty's 'raise' in 2012," Reuters, October 12, 2011.

21 Robert B. Friedland and Laura Summer, "Demographics Is Not Destiny, Revisited," Center on an Aging Society, Georgetown University, March 2005.

22 Robert N. Butler, *The Longevity Revolution*, pp. 142, 224.

23 Jane Gross, "A Doctor's Undivided Focus on the Minds of the Elderly," *New York Times*, May 1, 2011.

24 Robert N. Butler, *The Longevity Revolution*, pp. 216–22.

25 Atul Gawande, "The Hot Spotters," *The New Yorker*, January 24, 2011.

26 Paul Kleyman, "Can Budget Balancers First Do No Harm?" Generations Beat Online, NewAmericaMedia.org, March 30, 2011.

27 Dennis Cauchon, "Americans depend more on federal aid than ever," *USA Today*, April 26, 2011.

28 Estimate by ImmediateAnnuities.com, cited in Brett Arends, "Could You Retire Without Social Security?" December 17, 2010.

29 Alicia H. Munnell, Marric Buessing, Mauricio Soto, and Steven Sass, "Will We Have to Work Forever?" Issue Brief, Series 4, Center for Retirement Studies at Boston College, July 2006.

30 Paul Merrill, "Proposed SSI Cuts Anger New Yorkers," Fox23News, January 27, 2009.

31 David Brooks, "The Lost Decade?" *New York Times*, September 27, 2011.

Epilogue

1 Peggy Noonan, "Can Washington Cut Spending?" *Wall Street Journal*, February 20–21, 2010

2 David Brooks, "Mr. Hamilton and Mr. Burke," *New York Times*, January 28, 2011.

3 Ezra Klein, "What Paul Ryan's budget actually does," WashingtonPost.com, April 4, 2011.

4 William McGurn, "After the Welfare State," *Wall Street Journal*, April 5, 2011.

5 Jack Rasmus, "Who Pays?" *Z Magazine*, September 2007.

6 Jack Rasmus, "Obama's Economic Plan vs. An Alternative," *Z Magazine*, March 2009.

7 Cited in Bill Bradley, *The New American Story* (New York: Random House, 2007), p. 131.

8   Gene Sperling, "A Progressive Framework for Social Security Reform," Center for American Progress, January 10, 2005.

9   Barack Obama, *The Audacity of Hope: Thoughts on Reclaiming the American Dream, 6th Edition* (New York: Crown, 2006), p. 183.

10   Cited in William Greider, "Riding Into the Sunset," *The Nation*, June 27, 2005.

11   Jack Rasmus, "Obama's Economic Plan vs. An Alternative," *Z Magazine*, March 2009.

12   Gene Sperling, *The Pro-Growth Progressive: An Economic Strategy for Shared Prosperity* (New York: Simon & Schuster, 2005), p. 79.

13   David Osborne and Ted Gaebler, *Reinventing Government: How the Entrepreneurial Spirit Is Transforming the Public Sector* (New York: Addison-Wesley Publishing Company, Inc., 1992), p. 49.

14   Michel Foucault, "A Finite Social Security System Confronting an Infinite Demand," Chapter 10 of *Politics, Philosophy, Culture: Interviews and Other Writings, 1977–1984*, Lawrence D. Kritzman, ed. (New York: Routledge, 1990), pp. 159–177.

15   U.S. Census Bureau figures, cited in Robert B. Friedland and Laura Summer, "Demographics Is Not Destiny, Revisited," Center on an Aging Society, Georgetown University, March 2005.

16   Michael Bronski, "Beyond 'Beyond Same-Sex Marriage,'" *Z Magazine*, September 2006.

17   Patrick Reedy, "From Collective Struggle to Customer Service: The story of how self-help and mutual aid led to the welfare state and became co-opted in market managerialism," paper presented at Nottingham Trent University HRM Seminar Series, February 4, 2009.

18   John E. Sununu, "The significance of 'significant' cuts," *Boston Globe*, March 14, 2011.

19   Interview with Jane Bryant Quinn, February 19, 2009.

20   Hakim Bey, "The Tong," in *Immediatism: Essays by Hakim Bey* (San Francisco: AK Press, 1994), p. 14.

21   Colin Gillion, "The development and reform of social security pensions: The approach of the International Labour Office," *International Social Security Review*, Vol. 53, No. 1, Winter 2000.

22   Cited in Michael A. Hiltzik, *The Plot Against Social Security: How the Bush Plan Is Endangering Our Financial Future* (New York: HarperCollins, 2005), p. 102.

23   Robin Blackburn, *Banking on Death: Or, Investing in Life: The History and Future of Pensions* (New York: Verso, 2002), pp. 14–16.

24   Ibid., p. 521.

25   Ibid., p. 477.

26   Ibid., p. 511.

27   Jon Bekken, "Anarchist Economics," pamphlet (Johannesburg, South Africa: Zabalaza Books, undated).

28   John Maynard Keynes, *Essays in Persuasion* (New York: W.W. Norton & Company, 1963), p. vii.

29   John Maynard Keynes, "Am I a Liberal?" in Essays in Persuasion (New York: W.W. Norton & Company, 1963), p. 331.

30   David Graeber, "Against Kamikaze Capitalism: Oil, Climate Change and the French Refinery Blockades," *Shift Magazine*, November 2010.

31   James K. Galbraith, "Unconventional Wisdom," *Foreign Policy*, January/February 2011.

32 Jane Gross, "A Grass-Roots Effort to Grow Old at Home," *New York Times*, August 14, 2007.

33 Lauran Neergaard, "Aging America: Communities take creative steps to prepare for silver tsunami of baby boomers," Associated Press, July 11, 2011.

34 See David T. Beito, *From Mutual Aid to the Welfare State: Fraternal Societies and Social Services, 1890–1967* (Chapel Hill: University of North Carolina Press, 1999) for a history of social service provision by fraternal societies.

35 Daniel Henninger, "A Ronald Reagan Budget," *Wall Street Journal*, April 7, 2011.

36 Albert Camus, *The Rebel: An Essay on Man in Revolt*, tr. Anthony Bower (New York: Vintage Books, 1992).

37 Noam Chomsky, "Elections 2008 & Obama's 'Vision,'" *Z Magazine*, February 2009.

38 Greg Sargent, "Poll: Scott Walker losing P.R. Battle," WashingtonPost.com, March 1, 2011.

39 Monica Davids and A.G. Sulzberger, "In Wisconsin Battle on Unions, State Democrats See a Big Gift," *New York Times*, March 11, 2011.

40 Frank Emspak, executive producer, *WIN, Workers Independent News*, interviewed on *Democracy Now!* March 1, 2011.

41 Holman Jenkins, Jr., "Let's Begin Obama's 'Conversation' on Entitlements," *Wall Street Journal*, February 25, 2011.

42 Patrick Reedy, "From Collective Struggle to Customer Service: The story of how self-help and mutual aid led to the welfare state and became co-opted in market managerialism," paper presented at Nottingham Trent University HRM Seminar Series, February 4, 2009.

INDEX

B

C

H

N

O

P

S

U

Y

Z

X

Support AK Press!

AK Press is one of the world's largest and most productive  anarchist publishing houses. We're entirely worker-run and democratically managed. We operate without a corporate structure—no boss, no managers, no bullshit. We publish close to twenty books every year, and distribute thousands of other titles published by other like-minded independent presses from around the globe.

The Friends of AK program is a way that you can directly contribute to the continued existence of AK Press, and ensure that we're able to keep publishing great books just like this one! Friends pay a minimum of $25 per month, for a minimum three month period, into our publishing account. In return, Friends automatically receive (for the duration of their membership), as they appear, one free copy of every new AK Press title. They're also entitled to a 20% discount on everything featured in the AK Press Distribution catalog and on the website, on any and every order. You or your organization can even sponsor an entire book if you should so choose!

There's great stuff in the works—so sign up now to become a Friend of AK Press, and let the presses roll!

Won't you be our friend? Email friendsofak@akpress.org for more info, or visit the Friends of AK Press website: http://www.akpress.org/programs/friendsofak

Photo: Nick Romanenko

About the Author:

Eric Laursen is an independent financial and political journalist, activist, and commentator. He first began researching Social Security over fifteen years ago while serving as Managing Editor of *Plan Sponsor*, a magazine for pension fund executives that he co-founded. "It was the strangest political debate I'd ever encountered," he says. "The fate of hundreds of millions of working people is being decided by an argument over Social Security's cost projections seventy five years, or even farther, into the future. There's no way to know if those projections will even come true. Yet the Washington political establishment has been obsessed with the coming 'bankruptcy' of Social Security for more than three decades. I wanted to understand the political dynamic, and the truth behind the arguments."

Laursen is co-author (with Seth Tobocman and Jessica Wehrle) of *Understanding the Crash* (2010). His work has appeared in a wide variety of publications, including *The Nation, Institutional Investor*, the *AICPA Journal of Accounting, The Village Voice, Z Magazine, The Indypendent*, the *Huffington Post*, and *Investment Dealer's Digest*. He blogs on Social Security and related issues at http://peoplespension.infoshop.org/blogs-mu/. He lives in Buckland, Massachusetts.